Master the Past, Conquer the Future

SSC CPO SI

Delhi Police / BSF / CISF / CRPF / ITBP / SSB

Exam 2025

Authors
Sushil Singh, Sanjeev Dixit
Deepali, Pradeep Srivastava

Previous years Papers with 100% Explantions

Master the Past, Conquer the Future

SSC CPO SI

Delhi Police / BSF / CISF / CRPF / ITBP / SSB

Exam 2025

ISBN 978-93-7078-377-5

Arihant Publications (India) Limited

Published by Arihant Publications (India) Ltd.
For further information about the books published by Arihant, log on to www.arihantbooks.com or e-mail at info@arihantbooks.com

Follow us on...  

Administrative Offices

Regd. Office
'Ramchhaya' 4577/15,
Agarwal Road, Darya Ganj,
New Delhi -110002
Tele: 011- 47630600, 43518550

Head Office
Kalindi, TP Nagar, Meerut (UP)
250002, Tel: 0121-7156203, 7156204

Sales & Support Offices

Agra, Ahmedabad, Bengaluru, Bareilly, Chennai, Delhi, Guwahati, Hyderabad, Jaipur, Jhansi, Kolkata, Lucknow, Nagpur & Pune.

PO No. : TXT-59-T065477-06-25

PRICE ₹ 465.00

Contents

Solved Papers

Exam Pattern & Syllabus

PAPER I

Part	Subject	Number of Ques./ Max. Marks	Time Duration
I	General Intelligence and Reasoning	50/50	2 Hrs
II	General Knowledge and General Awareness	50/50	
III	Quantitative Aptitude	50/50	
IV	English Comprehension	50/50	

PAPER II

Subject	Number of Ques./ Max. Marks	Time Duration
English language & Comprehension	200/200	2 Hrs

- Questions in both papers will be of Objective Multiple Choice Type. Questions will be set in Hindi and English in Parts-I, II and III of Paper-I. There will be negative marking of 0.25 marks for each wrong answer in Paper-I & Paper-II. Candidates are, therefore, advised to keep this in mind while answering the questions.

Syllabus for Computer Based Mode Examination:

PAPER-I

- **General Intelligence and Reasoning** It would include questions of both verbal and non-verbal type. This component may include questions on analogies, similarities and differences, space visualization, spatial orientation, problem solving, analysis, judgment, decision making, visual memory, discrimination, observation, relationship concepts, arithmetical reasoning and figural classification, arithmetic number series, non-verbal series, coding and decoding, statement conclusion, syllogistic reasoning etc. The topics are, Semantic Analogy, Symbolic/ Number Analogy, Figural Analogy, Semantic Classification, Symbolic/ Number Classification, Figural Classification, Semantic Series, Number Series, Figural Series, Problem Solving, Word Building, Coding & de-coding, Numerical Operations, symbolic Operations, Trends, Space Orientation, Space Visualization, Venn Diagrams, Drawing inferences, Punched hole/ pattern-folding & un-folding, Figural Pattern- folding and completion, Indexing Address matching, Date & city matching Classification of centre codes/ roll numbers, Small & Capital letters/ numbers coding, decoding and classification, Embedded Figures, Critical thinking, Emotional Intelligence, Social Intelligence, etc.
- **General Knowledge and General Awareness** Questions in this component will be aimed at testing the candidates general awareness of the environment around him and its application to society. Questions will also be designed to test knowledge of current events and of such matters of every day observations and experience in their scientific aspect as may be expected of any educated person. The test will also include questions relating to India and its neighboring countries especially pertaining to History, Culture, Geography, Economic Scene, General Polity, Indian Constitution, scientific Research etc.

- **Quantitative Aptitude** The questions will be designed to test the ability of appropriate use of numbers and number sense of the candidate. The scope of the test will be computation of whole numbers, decimals, fractions and relationships between numbers, Percentage, Ratio and Proportion, Square roots, Averages, Interest, Profit & Loss, Discount, Partnership Business, Mixture and Allegation, Time and distance, Time & work, Basic algebraic identities of School Algebra and Elementary surds, Graphs of Linear Equations, Triangle and its various kinds of centres, Congruence and similarity of triangles, Circle and its chords, tangents, angles subtended by chords of a circle, common tangents to two or more circles, Triangle, Quadrilaterals, Regular Polygons, Circle, Right Prism, Right Circular Cone, Right Circular Cylinder, Sphere, Hemispheres, Rectangular Parallelepiped, Regular Right Pyramid with triangular or square base, Trigonometric ratio, Degree and Radian Measures, Standard Identities, Complementary angles, Heights and Distances, Histogram, Frequency polygon, Bar diagram & Pie chart.
- **English Comprehension** Candidates' ability to understand correct English, his/ her basic comprehension and writing ability, etc. would be tested.

PAPER-II

- **English Language and Comprehension** Questions in this components will be designed to test the candidates understanding and knowledge of English Language and will be based on error recognition, filling in the blanks (using verbs, preposition, articles etc), Vocabulary, Spellings, Grammar, Sentence Structure, Synonyms, Antonyms, Sentence Completion, Phrases and Idiomatic use of words, comprehension etc.

The Indispensable Role of PYQs *in SSC Exam Success*

The Previous Year Question Papers (PYQs) hold immense importance for candidates preparing for the Staff Selection Commission (SSC) exams. Here's a breakdown of their significance:

01

Understanding Exam Pattern and Syllabus

- **Familiarisation:** PYQs provide a clear understanding of the exam pattern, including the number of sections, types of questions asked, marking scheme and time duration.
- **Syllabus Insights:** By analysing PYQs, candidates can identify frequently asked topics and the weightage given to different sections of the syllabus. This helps in prioritising their studies.

02

Assessing Difficulty Level

- **Gauge Preparation:** Solving PYQs helps candidates assess the difficulty level of the actual exam. This allows them to understand the level of preparation required to crack the exam.
- **Identify Trends:** Regular practice with PYQs helps in identifying any changes in the difficulty level over the years.

03

Identifying Important Topics

- **Focus on Repetition:** SSC often repeats concepts and question patterns. By solving PYQs, candidates can identify frequently asked topics and focus more on them.
- **Strategic Study:** This knowledge enables candidates to channel their efforts in the right direction, maximising their chances of scoring well.

04

Improving Time Management and Accuracy

- **Simulate Exam Conditions:** Solving PYQs within the stipulated time frame helps candidates develop effective time management skills.
- **Enhance Speed and Accuracy:** Regular practice improves both speed and accuracy in solving questions, which is crucial for competitive exams like SSC.

05

Boosting Confidence and Reducing Exam Anxiety

- **Familiarity Breeds Confidence:** Solving PYQs creates a sense of familiarity with the actual exam, reducing anxiety and boosting confidence.
- **Performance Evaluation:** It allows candidates to track their progress and identify their strengths and weaknesses.

06

Understanding Question Framing

- **SSC's Perspective:** PYQs provide insights into how the SSC frames questions, the language used and the common tricks employed.
- **Effective Problem-Solving:** This understanding helps candidates approach questions more strategically and avoid common pitfalls.

In conclusion, Previous Year Question Papers are not just practice material; they are a crucial tool for strategic preparation, offering insights into the exam pattern, syllabus, difficulty level and question trends. Consistent practice with PYQs is indispensable for success in SSC exams like CGL, CHSL and CPO SI.

PAPER-1

SSC CPO SI SOLVED PAPER

29 June 2024 (Shift III)

MM : 200

Time : 2 hr

Instructions

1. This paper contains 200 questions.
2. It has 4 Parts, **Part I** General Intelligence and Reasoning, **Part II** General Knowledge and General Awareness, **Part III** Quantitative Aptitude and **Part IV** English Comprehension.
3. Each question carries **1 marks.**

Part I

General Intelligence and Reasoning

1. Which two signs should be interchanged to make the given equation correct?

$30 + 3 \times 990 - 11 \div 63 = 237$

(a) × and + (b) ÷ and −
(c) − and × (d) + and −

2. Six students P, Q, R, S, T and U are sitting around a circular table, facing the centre.
Q is sitting second to the left of U.
T is sitting third to the right of P.
P is the immediate neighbour of Q and U. S is not the neighbour of U.
Who among the following is the neighbour of both U and T?
(a) P (b) S
(c) R (d) Q

3. The sequence of folding a piece of paper and the manner in which the folded paper has been cut is shown below. Choose the figure which would most closely resemble the unfolded form of the paper.

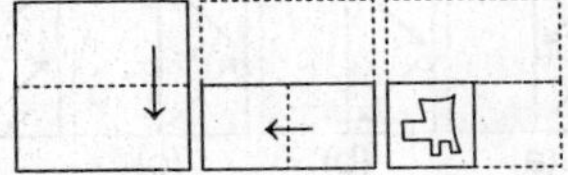

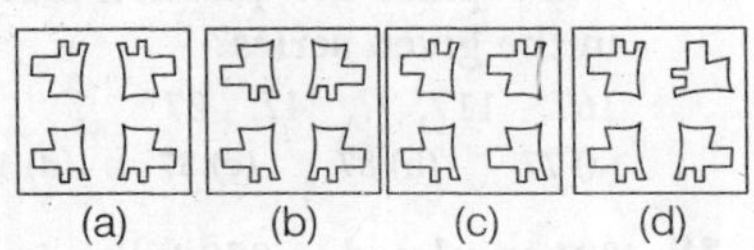

4. In a code language, 'TREE' is written as 'WSHF', and 'BALL' is written as 'EBOM'. How will 'WALL' be written in that language?
(a) ZOMB (b) ZBOM
(c) MOZB (d) OZBM

5. In a certain code language,
'A × B' means 'A is the son of B',
'A − B' means 'A is the brother of B',
'A + B' means 'A is the wife of B',
'A % B' means 'A is the father of B'.
How is M related to T if 'M × N % P − S + T'?
(a) Wife's father's mother's brother
(b) Brother's wife's mother's father
(c) Wife's brother
(d) Wife's mother's father

6. In a certain code language,
A + B means 'A is the mother of B'
A − B means 'A is the brother of B'
A × B means 'A is the wife of B'
A ÷ B means 'A is the father of B'
Based on the above, how is R related to U if 'U − P × Q ÷ R + S − T'?
(a) Daughter
(b) Sister's daughter
(c) Wife's sister
(d) Sister

7. Which of the following letter-clusters will replace the question mark (?) in the given series?
aaabcccccccc, aaabbcccc, aaabbbcc, ?
(a) aabbbbbbbbc (b) aaabbbbbbccc
(c) aaabbbbbbbbc (d) aaabbbbbbbcc

8. Kiara starts from Point A, which is 5 km towards the North of Z. From Point A, she turns towards the East and drives 8 km. She then takes a right turn and drives 9 km. Finally, she takes a right turn, drives for 15 km and stops at Point B. In which direction is Point B with respect to Point Z?
(a) North-East (b) South-West
(c) South (d) North-West

9. Two statements are given, followed by three conclusions numbered as I, II and III. Assuming the statements to be true, even if they seem to be at variance with commonly known facts, decide which of the conclusions logically follow(s) from the given statements.

Statements
All scanners are printers.
Some scanners are copiers.

Conclusions
I. Some printers are copiers.
II. No copier is a printer.
III. Some printers are scanners.

(a) All of the conclusions follow
(b) Only Conclusions I and II follow
(c) Only Conclusions I and III follow
(d) Only Conclusions II and III follow

10. A sheet of paper is folded along the dotted line successively along the directions shown and is then punched in the last. How would the paper look when unfolded?

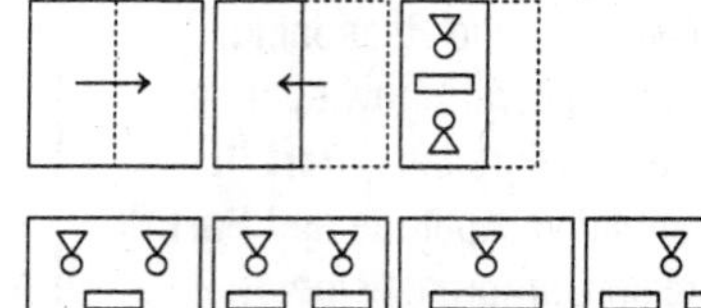

(a) (b) (c) (d)

11. In a certain code language, 'NODE' is coded as '6297' and 'BONE' is coded as '9716'. What is the code for 'D' in that language?
(a) 6 (b) 2 (c) 7 (d) 1

12. Which of the following terms will replace the question mark (?) in the given series?
DIQ, EJR, FKS,?
(a) GLT (b) DKO
(c) ETH (d) DLS

13. Select the correct mirror image of the given figure when the mirror is placed at MN as shown below

hYRawK (mirror MN)

(a) ꓘwɘᴙYɥ (b) KwɘᴙYɥ
(c) ꓘwaᴙYɥ (d) KwɘRYɥ

14. Which letter cluster will replace the question mark (?) to complete the given series?
TEKS, YLBD, ?, IZJZ, NGAK
(a) JKDO (b) DSSO
(c) DXTO (d) FGCW

15. If + means −, − means ×, × means ÷, ÷ means +, what will come in place of the question mark (?) in the given equation.
$60 + 378 \times 18 \div 23 - 2 = ?$
(a) 85 (b) 58
(c) 57 (d) 75

16. Based on the English alphabetical order, three of the following four letter-clusters are alike in a certain way and thus form a group. Which letter-cluster does not belong to that group?
(**Note** The odd letter-cluster is not based on the number of consonants/vowels or their position in the letter-cluster.)
(a) IFM (b) OLR
(c) TQX (d) GDK

17. Identify the figure given in the options which when put in place of (?) will logically complete the series.

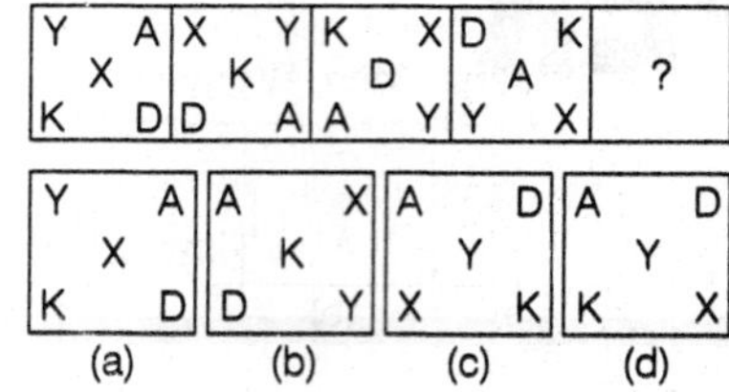

18. Which of the following numbers will replace the question mark (?) in the given series?
167, 117, ?, 47, 27
(a) 77 (b) 87 (c) 37 (d) 107

19. 824 is related to 329 following a certain logic. Following the same logic, 271 is related to 505. Which of the following numbers is related to 408 using the same logic?
(a) 612 (b) 434
(c) 822 (d) 325

20. In a code language, 'KIRAT' is coded as 50-40-85-0-95 and 'WASIM' is coded as 110-0-90-40-60. How will 'MRINAL' be coded in the same language?
(a) 85-40-50-75-0-65
(b) 55-60-45-65-0-85
(c) 75-50-60-55-0-65
(d) 60-85-40-65-0-55

21. The sequence of folding a paper and the manner in which the folded paper is cut is shown in the following figures. How would this paper look when unfolded?

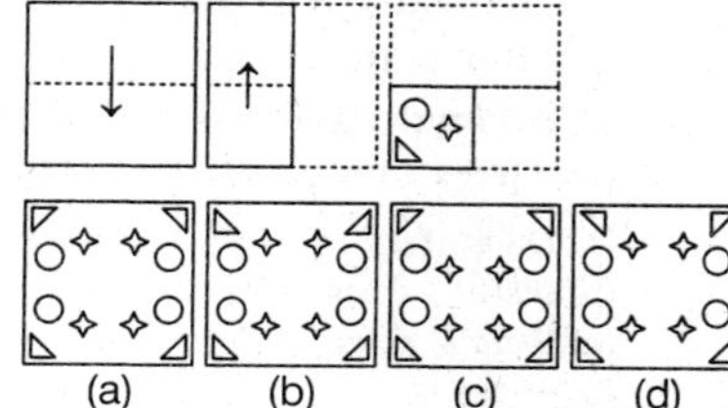

22. Ajay starts from Point A and drives 10 km towards North. He then takes a right turn, drives 3 km, turns right and drives 15 km. He then takes a right turn and drives 8 km. He takes a final right turn, drives 5 km and stops at Point P. How far (shortest distance) and towards which direction should he now drive to reach Point A again? (All turns are 90° turns only.)
(a) 5 km towards East
(b) 3 km towards West
(c) 5 km towards West
(d) 3 km towards East

23. Select the number from among the given options that can replace the question mark (?) in the following series.
53, 62, 77, 98, ?
(a) 123 (b) 121
(c) 122 (d) 125

24. In a certain code language, 'bring the bags' is written as 'nd sm pf' and 'bags of gold' is written as 'rg tx sm'. How is 'bags' written in the given language?
(a) rg (b) nd
(c) sm (d) pf

25. In a code language, 'SERIES' is coded as 87 and 'DISMAY' is coded as 91. How will 'SPRINT' be coded in the same language?
(a) 66 (b) 52 (c) 57 (d) 71

26. What will come in place of the question mark (?) when + and − are interchanged and 8 and 16 are also interchanged?
$3 \times 6 + 16 - 8 \div 2 = ?$
(a) 18 (b) 20 (c) 19 (d) 17

27. A transparent sheet with a pattern is given below. Select the option that depicts the pattern that would appear when the given transparent sheet is folded at the middle vertical line.

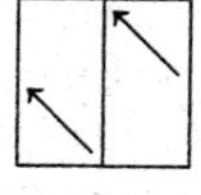

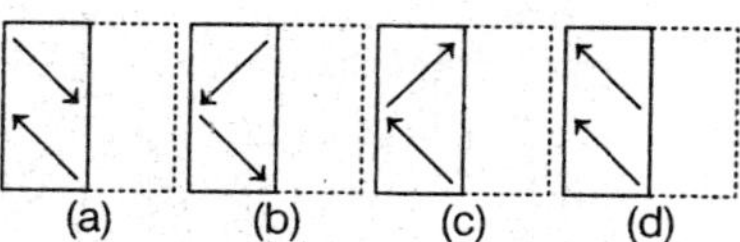

28. Select the option that indicates the correct arrangement of the given words in the order in which they appear in an English dictionary.

1. Junction 2. Jupiter
3. Jungle 4. Jump
5. Juncture

(a) 1, 5, 4, 2, 3 (b) 4, 5, 1, 3, 2
(c) 1, 5, 3, 2, 4 (d) 4, 1, 5, 3, 2

29. Select the option that represents the correct order of the given words as they would appear in an English dictionary.

1. Larkiness 2. Larcenist
3. Larceners 4. Lariated
5. Laryngal 6. Largely

(a) 3, 2, 1, 4, 6, 5 (b) 3, 2, 1, 6, 4, 5
(c) 3, 2, 4, 1, 6, 5 (d) 3, 2, 6, 4, 1, 5

30. If 'I' stands for '×', 'J' stands for '+', 'K' stands for '÷' and 'L' stands for '–', what will come in place of the question mark (?) in the following equation?

(40 J 32 K 4) I 5 L 155 J 7 I 9 = ?

(a) 126 (b) 156
(c) 134 (d) 148

31. Select the number from among the given options that can replace the question mark (?) in the following series.

22, 27, 37, 52, 72, ?

(a) 97 (b) 95
(c) 100 (d) 92

32. Select the option in which the numbers share the same relationship as that shared by the given pair of numbers.

50 : 130

(a) 35 – 120 (b) 60 – 120
(c) 30 – 80 (d) 75 – 110

33. 24 is related to 8 following a certain logic. Following the same logic, 54 is related to 20. Which of the following numbers is related to 18 using the same logic?

(a) 12 (b) 42
(c) 63 (d) 26

34. If + means –, – means ×, × means ÷, ÷ means +, what will come in place of the question mark (?) in the given equation?

$180 \times 60 - 33 \div 1 + 50 = ?$

(a) 40 (b) 55
(c) 51 (d) 50

35. Select the option that is related to the fifth letter-cluster in the same way as the second letter-cluster is related to the first letter-cluster and the fourth letter-cluster is related to the third letter-cluster.

ABIDE : GFKDC :: CHARM : OTCJE :: BLOOM : ?

(a) OQQND (b) OPQND
(c) DNQQO (d) OQQDN

36. Select the venn diagram that best illustrates the relationship between the following classes.

Painters, Men, Women

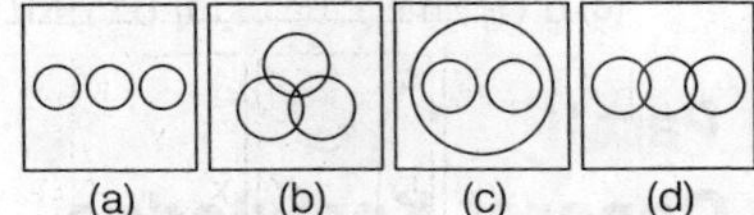

37. In a certain code language, 'BYE' is written as '32' and 'ANGER' is written as '45'. How will 'LOVE' be written in that language?

(a) 54 (b) 39
(c) 46 (d) 37

38. Select the set in which the numbers are related in the same way as are the numbers of the following sets.

(**Note** Operations should be performed on the whole numbers, without breaking down the numbers into its constituent digits. E.g. 13 – Operations on 13 such as adding /subtracting /multiplying etc. to 13 can be performed. Breaking down 13 into 1 and 3 and then performing mathematical operations on 1 and 3 is not allowed.)

(599, 236, 363)

(481, 145, 336)

(a) (641, 314, 327)
(b) (612, 278, 344)
(c) (547, 217, 310)
(d) (426, 159, 287)

39. Select the option that is related to the fifth letter-cluster in the same way as the second letter-cluster is related to the first letter-cluster and the fourth letter-cluster is related to the third letter-cluster.

DIETY : CJFSX :: GRACE : FQBBF :: GLORY : ?

(a) FKMQX (b) FKRQX
(c) FKPQX (d) FKPSX

40. Given below are two statements and two conclusions. Take the statements to be true even if they are at variance with commonly known facts and decide whether the conclusion(s) follow(s) the given statements.

Statements

All plastics are fibres.

Some fibres are leathers.

Conclusions

I. Some plastics are leathers.

II. Some fibres are plastics.

(a) Only Conclusion II follows
(b) Neither Conclusion I nor II follows
(c) Only Conclusion I follows
(d) Both the Conclusions follow

41. Identify the figure given in the options which when put in place of '?' will logically complete the series.

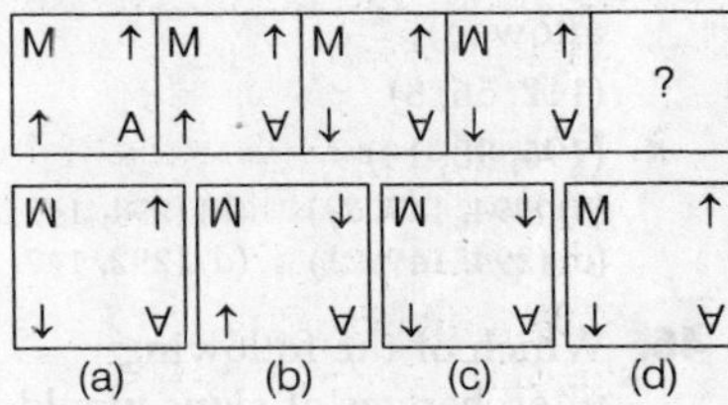

42. Two statements are given, followed by two conclusions numbered I and II. Assuming the statements to be true, even if they seem to be at variance with commonly known facts, decide which of the conclusions logically follow(s) from the given statements.

Statements

All carroms are ludos.

All ludos are scrabbles.

Conclusions

I. Some carroms are not scrabbles.

II. Some scrabbles are carroms.

(a) Only Conclusion II follows
(b) Only Conclusion I follows
(c) Both Conclusions I and II follow
(d) Neither Conclusion I nor II follows

43. Select the correct mirror image of the given figure when the mirror is placed at MN as shown below.

Gry4d7 M | N

(a) Ꞁ4dγɿG (b) ⅃bᔭγɿG
(c) ꞀbᔭγɿG (d) ⅃ᔭqʎɹG

44. If + means – , – means ×, × means ÷ , ÷ means +, what will come in place of the question mark (?) in the given equation?
99 × 33 – 70 ÷ 90 + 100 = ?
(a) 100 (b) 201
(c) 300 (d) 200

45. Select the set in which the numbers are related in the same way as are the numbers of the following sets.
(**Note** Operations should be performed on the whole numbers, without breaking down the numbers into its constituent digits. E.g. 13 – Operations on 13 such as adding /subtracting /multiplying etc. to 13 can be performed. Breaking down 13 into 1 and 3 and then performing mathematical operations on 1 and 3 is not allowed)
(112, 56, 8)
(196, 98, 14)
(a) (294, 147, 21) (b) (294, 147, 19)
(c) (294, 149, 21) (d) (292, 147, 21)

46. Which of the following interchanges of signs would make the given equation correct?
3 – 15 + 10 ÷ 2 × 7 = 43
(a) ÷ and × (b) + and ×
(c) – and × (d) – and +

47. Select the correct mirror image of the given figure when the mirror is placed at MN as shown below.

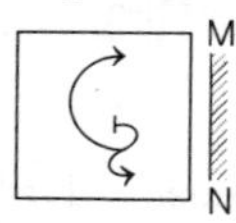

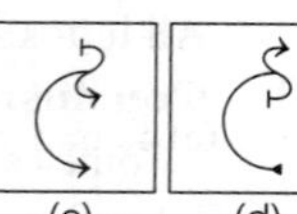

(a) (b) (c) (d)

48. Select the figure from among the given options that can logically replace the question mark (?) in the following series.

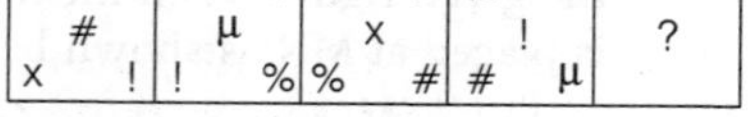

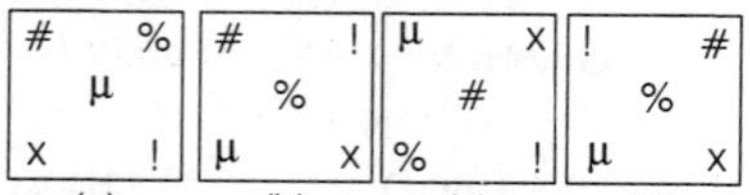

μ %	x #	! μ	% x	?
#	μ	x	!	
x !	! %	% #	# μ	

(a)	(b)	(c)	(d)
# %	# !	μ x	! #
μ	%	#	%
x !	μ x	% !	μ x

49. Which of the following numbers will replace the question mark (?) in the given series?
10, 50, 250, 1250, 6250, ?
(a) 61250 (b) 31250
(c) 21250 (d) 91250

50. Select the correct mirror image of the given figure when the mirror is placed at MN.

Yh4g7b | (mirror MN)

(a) d٢ϱ4ηY (b) d٢ϱ4hY
(c) d٢ϱ4ηY (d) d٢g4ηY

Part II

General Knowledge and General Awareness

51. Which of the following organisms can initiate ecological succession even in bare rocks?
(a) Orchids (b) Lichens
(c) Aspergillums (d) Lily

52. In which of the following parts of India are thorn forests and scrub forests found?
(a) North-Eastern India
(b) South-Western India
(c) North-Western India
(d) South-Eastern India

53. Match column A with column B.

Column A	Column B
A. Lemon	1. Tartaric acid
B. Milk	2. Citric acid
C. Vinegar	3. Lactic acid
D. Tamarind	4. Acetic acid

Codes
(a) A-2, B-1, C-3, D-4
(b) A-1, B-2, C-3, D-4
(c) A-4, B-3, C-2, D-1
(d) A-2, B-3, C-4, D-1

54. What is the chemical formula for butane?
(a) C_2H_{10} (b) C_4H_8 (c) C_2H_6 (d) C_4H_{10}

55. Choose the correct statements about the Western Ghats.
A. The height of the Western Ghats progressively increases from North to South.
B. Mahendragiri is the highest peak in the Western Ghats.
C. The Western Ghats are higher than the Eastern Ghats.
D. The height of the Western Ghats progressively decreases from North to South.

Codes
(a) C and D (b) A and C
(c) A and B (d) B, C and D

56. What are the colours of the antenna used on the volleyball net?
(a) Red and white
(b) Black and white
(c) Green and white
(d) Yellow and black

57. Of the total water content available globally, how much percentage of water is received from freshwater resources?
(a) 3.5% (b) 2.5% (c) 0.5% (d) 4.5%

58. In 2011-12, what percentage of Indian workforce was engaged in secondary sector?
(a) 15.8% (b) 60.4%
(c) 30.0% (d) 24.3%

59. Pulakeshin II belonged to which of the following dynasties?
(a) Chalukya (b) Pandya
(c) Chera (d) Rashtrakuta

60. Lakshya Sen was born in ....
(a) Uttarakhand
(b) Telangana
(c) Himachal Pradesh
(d) Uttar Pradesh

61. The Great Indian desert/Thar desert is located on the Western margin of which of the following mountain ranges?
(a) Eastern ghats (b) Aravalli range
(c) Vindhya range (d) Satpura range

62. As of December 2022, the 'Kalidas Samman' Award is given in the field of art by the Government of which Indian state?
(a) Telangana (b) Madhya Pradesh
(c) Rajasthan (d) Tamil Nadu

63. What do the words 'aus', 'aman' and 'boro' signify in the context of agricultural calendar in India?
(a) Types of seasons of sowing rice in West Bengal.
(b) Types of traditional wells in Gujarat.
(c) Types of alluvial soils in the Gangetic plains.
(d) Types of harvest festivals in Assam.

64. Directive Principles of State Policy comes under which Articles?
(a) Articles 14-35 (b) Articles 36-51
(c) Articles 34-50 (d) Articles 12-35

65. In which of the following months of the Hindu calendar is the festival of Holi celebrated?
(a) Sravana (b) Magha
(c) Asadha (d) Phalguna

66. If the value/percentage of the cash reserve ratio falls, then the value of money multiplier ....
(a) remains stable
(b) falls
(c) rises
(d) None of the above

67. How many Fundamental Duties were added by the 42nd Constitutional Amendment Act, 1976?
(a) 12 (b) 10
(c) 14 (d) 8

68. Which of the following is known as the Steel 'City of India'?
(a) Mumbai (b) Ranchi
(c) Patna (d) Jamshedpur

69. Who among the following is the author of the book 'Making India Awesome' ?
(a) Aravind Adiga
(b) Vikram Seth
(c) Chetan Bhagat
(d) Siddhartha Mukherjee

70. What distinguishes a bank from other financial institutions ?
(a) Accepting deposits
(b) Accepting loans and borrowings
(c) Lending
(d) Providing long-term loans

71. Which of the following options is not correctly matched?
(a) Chilika Lake–Odisha
(b) Wular Lake–Jammu and Kashmir
(c) Sardar Sarovar Lake–Karnataka
(d) Vembanad Lake–Kerala

72. As per Census 2011, what is the percentage of rural population in India?
(a) 65.2% (b) 68.8%
(c) 59.3% (d) 52.4%

73. Deepa Kartha represents .... dance.
(a) Odissi (b) Manipuri
(c) Kathak (d) Sattriya

74. Which of the following revolutionists was associated with the Anushilan Samiti ?
(a) Bhagat Singh
(b) Jatindra Mohan Sengupta
(c) Rajguru
(d) Sukhdev

75. The concept of limited government is a major advancement to protect the .... of the Citizens from the ruling governments.
(a) fundamental rights
(b) separation of power
(c) check and balance
(d) fundamental duties

76. Who discovered a principle that states the buoyant force on an object is equal to the weight of the fluid displaced by the object?
(a) Niels Bohr (b) Isaac Newton
(c) Galileo Galilei (d) Archimedes

77. Dharmapala is known to have founded which of the following universities near Bhagalpur in Bihar?
(a) Takshila (b) Vallabhi
(c) Nalanda (d) Vikramashila

78. 'The forty minutes raga' is an album composed by ....
(a) Amjad Ali Khan
(b) Ali Akbar Khan
(c) Hariprasad Chaurasia
(d) Bhimsen Joshi

79. According to Dalton, which of the following represents the phosphorus element?

(a)
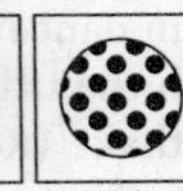
(b)

(c)
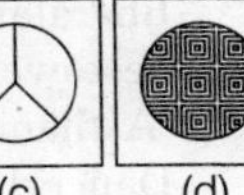
(d)

(a) c (b) b
(c) d (d) a

80. Which of the following is not true with regard to the Green Revolution?
(a) Cultivation became more intensive in nature.
(b) Cultivation became more extensive in nature.
(c) In its second phase, there was a shift from dry to wet (irrigated) cultivation in dry and semi-arid regions of India.
(d) There was change in the cropping pattern and types of crops grown in its second phase.

81. Which of the following scientists grouped the elements into triads?
(a) Henry Moseley
(b) Dmitri Mendeleev
(c) Johann Wolfgang Döbereiner
(d) John Newlands

82. Who among the following wrote the book 'Chanakya's Chant'?
(a) Amish Tripathi
(b) Samit Basu
(c) Ashwin Sanghi
(d) Novoneel Chakraborty

83. Which festival comes at the end of Navratri and Durga Pooja?
(a) Dussehra
(b) Christmas
(c) Pongal
(d) Holi

84. Special Drawing Rights are also known as ....
(a) Paper Gold
(b) Golden Papers
(c) International Reserves Money
(d) Gold Papers

85. Which instrument was used to measure economic growth during the planning era?
(a) Gross Domestic Product
(b) Per Capita Gross Domestic Product
(c) Per Capita Income
(d) National Income

86. Identify the structure that controls the size of the pupil.
(a) Vitreous humour
(b) Iris
(c) Ciliary muscles
(d) Cornea

87. What is the size of a standard table tennis ball?
(a) 42 mm (b) 39 mm
(c) 40 mm (d) 41 mm

88. Begum Akhtar a famous singer from India is known for which of the following genres?
(a) Sufi music
(b) Folk music
(c) Ghazal music
(d) Carnatic music

89. Which Article of the Indian Constitution deals with the annual financial statement of the Government of India?
(a) Article 110 (b) Article 112
(c) Article 116 (d) Article 120

90. What is the correct way to mix acid and water?
(a) The acid must be slowly added to the water.
(b) The water must be heated before mixing.
(c) The water must be added to the acid.
(d) The acid must be heated before mixing.

91. Kandariya Mahadeva temple at Khajuraho was built under which of the following dynasties?
(a) Solanki (b) Rashtrakuta
(c) Chera (d) Chandela

92. Who among the following was the co-winner of Bharat Ratna with Lata Mangeshkar in the year 2001?
(a) Bhimsen Joshi
(b) Asha Bhosle
(c) Ravi Shankar
(d) Bismillah Khan

93. Who among the following personalities was awarded the Sangeet Natak Akademi Award (for her contribution to Manipuri Dance)?
(a) Urmila Nagar
(b) Nirmala Ramachandran
(c) Mallika Sarabhai
(d) Kalavati Devi

94. Which of the following statements are correct regarding the special powers of the Governors according to the Indian Constitution?
A. The Governor of Nagaland shall have special responsibility related to law and order in the State.
B. The Governor of Manipur will submit a special annual report to the President on the administration of hilly areas in the State.
C. The Governor of Sikkim shall have special responsibility for peace and for an equitable arrangement for ensuring the social and economic advancement of different sections.
D. The Governor of Arunachal Pradesh shall have special responsibility with respect to law and order in the State of Arunachal Pradesh.

Codes
(a) A, B and C (b) A, B, C and D
(c) A, C and D (d) B, C and D

95. Identify the organism that shows bioluminescence.
(a) Tapeworm (b) Liver fluke
(c) Fasciola (d) Ctenoplana

96. International Army Games, 2021 was held in which of the following countries from 22nd August to 4th September?
(a) India (b) Uzbekistan
(c) Russia (d) Belarus

97. Which of the following was widely considered as the 'Heaven Born Service' for Indians during British rule?
(a) Military service on the Burma front
(b) The Indian Judicial Service
(c) The British Indian Army
(d) The Indian Civil Service (ICS)

98. What Article of the Indian Constitution provides that the State Governor has the authority to reserve a bill for the consideration of the President?
(a) Article 267
(b) Article 200
(c) Article 181
(d) Article 190

99. Who among the following founded the Mohammedan Anglo-Oriental College in Aligarh for the spread of Western education?
(a) Syed Ameer Ali
(b) Maulana Abul Kalam Azad
(c) Sir Syed Ahmad Khan
(d) Badrudin Tyabji

100. Who among the following Bharatanatyam dancers was bestowed with the title of 'Asthana Narthaki' (Resident Dancer) by the Tirumala Tirupati Devasthanam temple?
(a) Yamini Krishnamurthy
(b) Padma Subramanyam
(c) Rita Ganguly
(d) Indrani Rahman

Part III

Quantitative Aptitude

101. The value of
$$\frac{61+\frac{2}{5}\times 75\div 6-\left(3\times 6\div\frac{1}{3}\right)\times\frac{1}{6}}{5+\frac{2}{3}\times(58-37)}$$ is
(a) 3 (b) 11 (c) 19 (d) 57

102. An alloy contains the metals *A*, *B* and *C* in the ratio 2 : 3 : 1 and another contains the metals *B*, *C* and *D* in the ratio 5 : 4 : 3. If equal weights of both alloys are mixed together to form a third alloy, then how much part of the Metal *B* is in new alloy?
(a) $\frac{1}{8}$ (b) $\frac{1}{6}$
(c) $\frac{3}{24}$ (d) $\frac{11}{24}$

103. What is the value of $\frac{[(\sin x+\sin y)(\sin y-\sin x)]}{[(\cos x+\cos y)(\cos y-\cos x)]}$?
(a) −1 (b) 0
(c) 2 (d) 1

104. The length of a side of an equilateral triangle is 18 cm. The area (in cm^2) of the region lying between the circumcircle and the incircle of the triangle is $\left[\text{use } \pi=\frac{22}{7}\right]$
(a) $254\frac{4}{7}$ (b) $254\frac{3}{7}$
(c) $254\frac{2}{7}$ (d) $254\frac{1}{7}$

105. In a sweet, one-third is sugar. If the price of sugar now is $\frac{7}{6}$ of the previous price, what is the effective percentage increase in the cost of the sweet?
(a) $\frac{200}{9}\%$ (b) $\frac{100}{3}\%$
(c) $\frac{100}{18}\%$ (d) $\frac{100}{9}\%$

106. The following pie-chart represents the data of movies released in a city throughout a year.

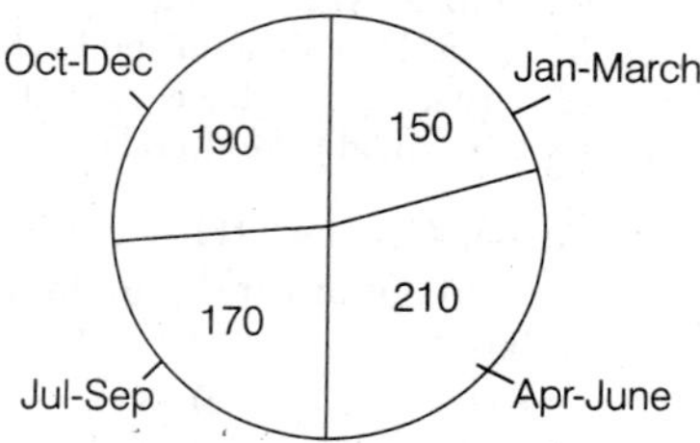

The combined angle made by Jan-Mar and Jul-Sep is .... than the combined angle made by Apr-Jun and Oct-Dec.
(a) 40° more (b) 80° more
(c) 80° less (d) 40° less

107. The following table gives information of Panchayat elections held in four villages P, Q, R and S.

Villages	Total available votes (in thousands)	Votes polled (in %)	Valid votes (in %)
P	40	80	90
Q	50	90	80
R	60	75	80
S	80	80	85

Find the ratio of invalid votes of Village P to that of Village S.

(a) 1 : 3 (b) 2 : 3
(c) 1 : 2 (d) 3 : 4

108. Simplify the given expression.

$$\frac{53 - \frac{2}{7} \text{ of } 63 - 9}{72 - \frac{2}{5} \text{ of } (96 - 31)}$$

(a) $\frac{13}{23}$ (b) $\frac{7}{23}$ (c) $\frac{11}{23}$ (d) $\frac{26}{23}$

109. A dishonest dealer claims to sell his products at 24% loss on the cost price but uses 100 g weight instead of 200g weight. His profit percentage is

(a) 55% (b) 52%
(c) 40% (d) 48%

110. If $x^2 - 6x - 1 = 0$, then find the value of $x^2 + \frac{1}{x^2} - 8$.

(a) 34 (b) 32 (c) 28 (d) 30

111. The side PR of a $\angle PQR$ is extended to S such that $QR = RS$. If $\angle PRQ = 86°$, then find the value of $\angle PSQ$.

(a) 43° (b) 86° (c) 54° (d) 94°

112. Simplify the following expression

$$\frac{3\frac{1}{7} \div 1\frac{4}{7} + 3 \text{ of}}{2\frac{2}{3} + 2.5 \times 2.4 \div 3\frac{1}{3} - 4 \text{ of } 3}$$

(a) $-\frac{4}{5}$ (b) $-\frac{3}{5}$
(c) $-\frac{1}{5}$ (d) $-\frac{2}{5}$

113. Simplify

$8.16 \times 5.35 + 17.9 - 19.5 \text{ of } \frac{1}{15} + \frac{1}{5}$

(a) 60.456 (b) 70.225
(c) 57.426 (d) 65.234

114. A shopkeeper sold 3 wrist watches for ₹ 2800 each. If he has sold the watches with 40%, 25% and 12% profit, respectively, then find his overall profit percentage (correct to 2 decimal places).

(a) 0.2455 (b) 0.2475
(c) 0.2419 (d) 0.2463

115. In a circle, the chords AB and CD intersect each other at point L (internally). If $AL = 8$ cm, $LB = 6$ cm and $LD = 5$ cm, then find the CL.

(a) 10.6 cm (b) 8.6 cm
(c) 7.6 cm (d) 9.6 cm

116. Two Trains, P and Q, are running on parallel tracks in opposite directions with lengths of 110 m and 140 m, respectively. Train P is running at a speed of 70 km/h and took 5 sec to cross Train Q. The speed of Train Q is

(a) 100 km/h (b) 120 km/h
(c) 110 km/h (d) 90 km/h

117. Simplify : $45 \div 5 \times 5 + 10 - 5$.

(a) 60 (b) 30
(c) 50 (d) 40

118. The value of

$$\frac{17}{\sec^2\theta} + 10\sin^2\theta + \frac{7}{1+\cot^2\theta} \text{ is}$$

(a) 34 (b) 19
(c) 17 (d) 20

119. Simplify

$250 + [100 - \{50 - (30 + 15)\}]$

(a) 280 (b) 255
(c) 360 (d) 345

120. A man travels some distance from his house to the exhibition ground by an auto at a speed of 30 km/h and returns by a cab at a speed of 50 km/h. What is his average speed (in km/h)?

(a) 37.5 (b) 40
(c) 28 (d) 38

121. The ratio of the speed of a boat to that of the current water is 35 : 8. The boat goes along with the current in 5 h 10 min. What will be the time taken by the boat to come back?

(a) 5 h 15 min 58 sec
(b) 9 h 30 min 49 sec
(c) 6 h 45 min 10 sec
(d) 8 h 13 min 48 sec

122. Ramesh spent ₹ 30000 on Diwali shopping and ₹ 45000 on buying a TV set and the remaining 40% of the total amount he had as cash with him. What was the total amount (in ₹)?

(a) 135000 (b) 110000
(c) 125000 (d) 122000

123. If 12 people can print 540 identical books in 10 days, then how many more people will be required to print 720 such books in 8 days?

(a) 8 (b) 6
(c) 12 (d) 4

124. A scalene triangle ABC has two sides whose measures are 3.8 cm and 6 cm,respectively. Which of the following cannot be the measure (in cm) of its third side?

(a) 3.0 (b) 2.4 (c) 2.7 (d) 2.2

125. The area of a circle is 256π cm^2. The length of its longest chord (in cm) is

(a) 32 (b) 36
(c) 34 (d) 16

126. The following pie-chart shows details of the per month expenditure of a family. Study the pie-chart carefully and answer the question that follows.

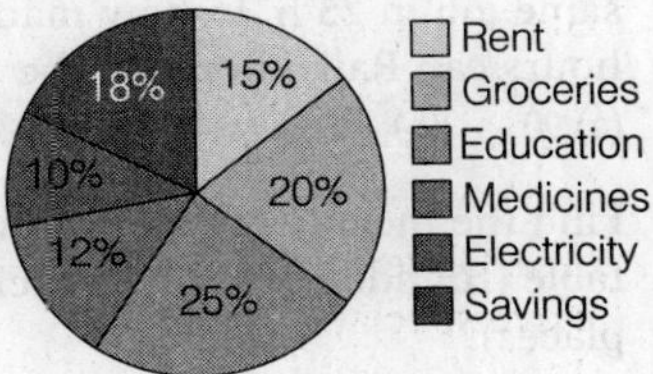

The expenditure on rent, mediciens and electricity together is what percentage of the expenditure on groceries and education together?

(a) 82.22% (b) 80.22%
(c) 70.82% (d) 76.52%

127. The quantity of a milk in a mixture of milk and water is $\frac{4}{5}$ of the volume of the mixture. After adding 1 L of milk to 5 L of the mixture, the percentage of water in the mixture is

(a) $\frac{200}{6}$% (b) 15%
(c) $\frac{100}{6}$% (d) 17.5%

128. The following bar graph shows the production of cement(in lakh tonnes) of four companies W, X, Y, and Z over the years.

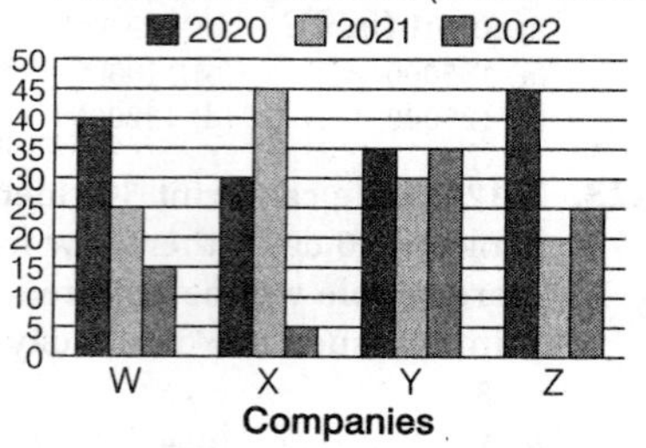

The production of cement by Company X in 2020 and production of cement by Company Z in 2022 together is what percentage of the production by Company W in 2021?

(a) 275 (b) 180 (c) 250 (d) 220

129. The value of

$\sin^2 15° + \sin^2 25° + \sin^2 35° + \sin^2 45° + \sin^2 55° + \sin^2 65° + \sin^2 75°$ is

(a) 7 (b) $\frac{7}{2}$ (c) 4 (d) $\frac{7}{3}$

130. Sumit and Rajiv, working together, can do a job in 20 h whereas Sumit alone can do the same job in 25 h. In how many hours can Rajiv alone do the job?

(a) 90 (b) 100 (c) 70 (d) 80

131. Find the mean from the following table (rounded off to two decimal places).

Score	Frequencies
15	2
18	3
21	4
22	1
19	5
23	1
24	2

(a) 17.56 (b) 20.82
(c) 18.44 (d) 19.78

132. If $\cos A = \frac{4}{5}$, then find the value of $(8 + \sin A)(3 - \tan A)$.

(a) $\frac{373}{20}$ (b) $\frac{387}{20}$
(c) $\frac{381}{20}$ (d) $\frac{367}{20}$

133. Study the given table and answer the question that follows.

The table shows the production of five different types of cars by a company from 1989 to 1994.

Year→ Type↓	1989	1990	1991	1992	1993	1994	Total
P	8	20	16	17	21	6	88
Q	16	10	14	12	12	14	78
R	21	17	16	15	13	8	90
S	4	6	10	16	20	31	87
T	25	18	19	30	14	27	133
Total	74	71	75	90	80	86	476

In which year was the production of cars of all types taken together approximately equal to the average of the total production during the period?

(a) 1993 (b) 1990
(c) 1992 (d) 1991

134. The table below shows the number of mobile phones that were sold by the showrooms in the years from 2016-2020.

Years/Show room	P	Q	R	S	T	U
2016	220	230	250	280	240	260
2017	310	300	320	340	330	350
2018	400	380	410	420	440	430
2019	450	350	380	420	410	430
2020	420	430	410	440	400	420

What will be the average number of mobile phones sold by all the showroom in the year 2020?

(a) 410 (b) 405 (c) 420 (d) 415

135. Simplify the given expression.

$$55\frac{1}{3} \div \left[3\frac{1}{5} + \left\{2\frac{1}{2} - \left(2\frac{1}{3} + \frac{3}{5}\right)\right\}\right]$$

(a) 25 (b) 15
(c) 20 (d) 35

136. If the length and breadth of a cuboid are increased by 6% and 8% respectively, then the percentage increase in its volume (correct to two decimal places) is

(a) 11.48% (b) 13.96%
(c) 12.96% (d) 14.48%

137. A shopkeeper offers a 10% discount on dairy products and still manages to make a 20% profit. What is the actual cost (in ₹) to the shopkeeper of a dairy product marked ₹ 420 ?

(a) 325 (b) 340 (c) 350 (d) 315

138. If $a = (\sqrt{2} - 1)^{\frac{1}{3}}$, then the value of $\left(a - \frac{1}{a}\right)^3 + 3\left(a - \frac{1}{a}\right)$ is

(a) $\sqrt{2}$ (b) 2 (c) -2 (d) $-\sqrt{2}$

139. A seller marks an item for ₹ 500 and sells it at a discount of 25%. He also gives a gift worth ₹ 65. If he still makes 24% profit, then the cost price of the item (in ₹) is

(a) 320 (b) 270
(c) 250 (d) 280

140. The population of a town is 15000. If the population increases by 15% in the first year, by 25% in the second year and due to pollution it decreases by 6% in the third year, what will be its population after 3 yr?

(Round off number in answer)

(a) 20269 (b) 25269
(c) 28269 (d) 15269

141. In an election, 95% of the total voters cast their votes. In this election, there were only two candidates *A* and *B*. The Winner *A*, by obtaining 75% of the total votes, defeated his Contestant *B* by 5500 votes. Find the total number of voters in the election.

(a) 12000 (b) 11000 (c) 13000 (d) 10000

142. A student goes to his school by cycle. The distance from his house to school is 5 km and he covers this distance in 1 h. While going he stops twice for 5 min each. Find his average speed (in km/h).

(a) 5.5 (b) 6 (c) 6.5 (d) 4.5

143. If $2a + 2b + c = 0$, then find the value of $\frac{4a^2 + 4b^2 + 4c^2}{5c^2 - 8ab}$.

(a) -1 (b) 1
(c) $-2\sqrt{3}$ (d) $2\sqrt{3}$

144. A man borrowed ₹ 29000 for 3 yr and ₹ 45000 for 5 yr at the same rate of simple interest. If he paid a total interest of ₹ 62400, then what was the rate of interest?

(a) 18% (b) 20%
(c) 27% (d) 25%

145. If the radius of a sphere is increased by 20%, then find the percentage increase in its volume.
(a) 68.5% (b) 72.8%
(c) 70.6% (d) 75.5%

146. The ratio of the slant height and the height of a cone is 4 : 3. If the curved surface area of the cone is $4\sqrt{7}\pi$ square units, then the radius of the cone is .... units.
(a) 7 (b) $7\sqrt{7}$
(c) $\frac{\sqrt{7}}{7}$ (d) $\sqrt{7}$

147. The value of $15 - 16 \div [4 + (5 + 7) \div 3]$ is equal to
(a) 11 (b) 18
(c) 17 (d) 13

148. Find the value of $[16 \div 2 - 7 \times 15 \div 3 + \{(1 + 4) \times 5\} + 4 \times 3 - 10]$
(a) 2 (b) 0
(c) 4 (d) −2

149. If a car runs at a speed of 60 km/h and takes 180 min to cover a certain distance,then what time will it take to cover the same distance at a speed of 40 km/h?
(a) 4 h 30 min (b) 3 h
(c) 3 h 15 min (d) 3 h 45 min

150. Two rectangular sheets of paper, each 60 cm × 36 cm are made into two right circular cylinders, one by rolling the paper along its length and the other along the breadth.The ratio of the volumes of the two cylinders, thus formed, is
(a) 5 : 6 (b) 5 : 3
(c) 8 : 3 (d) 7 : 4

Part IV
English Comprehension

151. Select the most appropriate antonym of the underlined word from the given options.
The new government allowed all the corrupt ministers to feel the sufficiency of money by banning the specific currency.
(a) indeficiency (b) plenty
(c) enough (d) dearth

152. Select the most appropriate option to substitute the underlined part of the given sentence.
All the kith and kin of my deceased landlady were present to attend her funeral.
(a) office colleagues
(b) secret enemies
(c) special students
(d) blood relatives

153. Select the option that can be used as a one-word substitute for the given group of words.
Modesty or shyness resulting from a lack of self-confidence
(a) Assurance
(b) Determination
(c) Conviction
(d) Diffidence

154. Select the option that will improve the underlined part of the given sentence. In case no improvement is needed, select 'No improvement required'.
What flavour ice-cream do you want?
(a) No improvement required
(b) flavours ice-cream
(c) flavour of ice-cream
(d) ice-cream flavoured

155. Three segments of the following sentence have been underlined and given as options.One of them may contain an error. Select the option that contains the error. If you don't find any error, mark 'No error' as your answer.
Although there is no proven data, the Centre for Policy Research estimate that India has the largest stock of iron-ore in the world.
(a) Although there is no proven data,
(b) Centre for Policy Research estimate
(c) No error
(d) India has the largest stock

156. Select the most appropriate option that can substitute the highlighted words in the given sentence.
The serenity of the river was a sight to behold.
(a) confusing for all
(b) ready to be sold
(c) inviting for boating
(d) pleasant to see

157. Select the most appropriate synonym of the word in brackets to fill in the blank.
Her million-dollar wedding was a .... display of wealth. (pompous)
(a) prestigious (b) outrageous
(c) mock (d) pretentious

158. Parts of the following sentences have been given as options. Select the option that contains a grammatical error.
Mr. Prabhakar was first man to arrive at the venue.
(a) was first man (b) Mr. Prabhakar
(c) to arrive (d) at the venue

159. Select the most appropriate option to substitute the underlined segment in the given sentence to make it a meaningful sentence. If no substitution is required, select 'No substitution'.
The quality of students of an educational institute is of great importance and a crucial starting point.
(a) The quality of students in an educational institute is in great importance and a crucial starting point.
(b) The quality of students in an educational institute is of great importance and a crucial starting point.
(c) No substitution
(d) The quality of students in an educational institute is of great importance and is a crucial start point.

160. Parts of the following sentence have been given as options. Select the option that contains a spelling error.
Grievances cannot be redresed unless they are known.
(a) Grievances cannot
(b) be redresed
(c) unless they
(d) are known

161. Parts of the following sentence have been given as options. Select the option that contains an error.
For the past / three years, / my uncle is /away from home.
(a) three years, (b) For the past
(c) my uncle is (d) away from home.

162. Choose the most appropriate meaning of the given idiom.
Back to back
(a) Present and discuss the details of something.
(b) Do something very fast or with great energy.
(c) Something follows immediately after something else.
(d) Try to get something

163. Select the most appropriate meaning of the given idiom.
Spill the beans
(a) To have an excuse
(b) To be in a state of shock
(c) To have happy period of your life
(d) To expose a secret

164. Select the option that rectifies the spelling error in the given sentence.
She is going to resiev a package in the mail today.
(a) reseive (b) receive
(c) resieve (d) recieive

165. Select the word from the sentence below, which is an antonym for the word 'dishearten'. Many of the world's greatest art pieces are encouraged by kings and are inspired by nature and society.
(a) Greatest
(b) Pieces
(c) Inspired
(d) Encouraged

166. Select the incorrectly spelt word.
(a) Interogative
(b) Auditions
(c) Interference
(d) Greengrocers

167. In the question four alternatives are given for the underlined word in the sentence. Choose the alternative which best expresses the opposite meaning of the word.
We <u>embraced</u> each other overjoyed at our success, then I took photograph of Tenzing holding aloft the flags of Great Britain, Nepal, the United Nations and India."
(a) Cradled (b) Junked
(c) Contained (d) Limited

168. Select the most appropriate synonym of the given word.
Destitute
(a) Broken (b) Corrupt
(c) Broke (d) Firm

169. Select the incorrectly spelt word.
(a) obscurity (b) schedule
(c) assasination (d) buoyant

170. The following sentence has been divided into parts. One of them contains an error. Select the part that contains the error from the given options.
Mr. Raghav / brushes his / teeth four / times the day.
(a) brushes his (b) times the day
(c) Mr. Raghav (d) teeth four

171. Select the most appropriate synonym of the given word.
Prudent
(a) Precious (b) Diffident
(c) Judicious (d) Doubtful

172. Select the most appropriate meaning of the given idiom.
Up the ante
(a) Increase demands
(b) Cost cutting
(c) Mediocre
(d) Expensive

173. Select the most appropriate antonym of the underlined word in the given sentence.
Her <u>sarcastic</u> comment earned a few chuckles from the audience, who understood the irony in her words.
(a) Unsavoury (b) Courteous
(c) Sardonic (d) Humorous

174. In the following sentence, four words are underlined, out of which one word is misspelt. Select the misspelt word.
Everyone admired her because of her <u>charesma</u>, but she was a <u>narcissist</u> full of <u>self-admiration</u> and <u>treachery</u>.
(a) treachery (b) self-admiration
(c) charesma (d) narcissist

175. Select the most appropriate option to fill in the blank and make the sentence the meaningful.
Rathna is known for .... tears.
(a) student's (b) babies'
(c) animal's (d) crocodile

176. Select the most appropriate option that can substitute the underlined segment in the given sentence. If there is no need to substitute it, select 'No substitution'.
He is feeding <u>a male dog and female dog</u>.
(a) a dog and puppy
(b) a dog and a bitch
(c) a male dog and lady dog
(d) No substitution

177. Select the most appropriate antonym of the underlined word in the following sentence.
The woman in the crowd broke down in <u>hysterics</u>.
(a) Aghast (b) Cray
(c) Calm (d) Insanity

178. Select the most appropriate option that can substitute the underlined segment in the given sentence.
She asked me where my <u>hometown is</u> and where I worked.
(a) hometown has been
(b) hometown would be
(c) hometown were
(d) hometown was

179. The following sentence has been split into four segments. Identify the segment that contains a grammatical error.
Raveena has made / up her mind to/ carried minimum / luggage with her.
(a) Raveena has made
(b) up her mind to
(c) carried minimum
(d) luggage with her.

180. Select the incorrectly spelt word.
(a) Matriculation (b) Prohibition
(c) Humorous (d) Addmission

181. Select the most appropriate meaning of the underlined segment in the following sentence.
Don't you think that the <u>cat's in the cradle</u> ? You never make time for me.
(a) Newly married life
(b) Busy in your work
(c) Complicated relationship
(d) Busy in minting money

182. Select the option that is similar in meaning to the underlined word in the following sentence.
Chameleon usually <u>disguises</u> itself to avoid predators.
(a) changes (b) camouflages
(c) transposes (d) swaps

183. Select the most appropriate option that can substitute the underlined segment in the given sentence. If there is no need to substitute it, select 'No substitution'.
Inspite mother's milk is vital to a child's health, a number of FMCG companies wrongly advertise artificially prepared infant formulas as being the best for the child.
(a) Mother's milk
(b) No substitution
(c) Though mother's milk
(d) Despite mother's milk

184. Select the most appropriate option that can substitute the underlined words in the given sentence.
My grandmother helps us in all the problems. She has a remedy for all the diseases.
(a) Service (b) Panacea
(c) Fanatic (d) Heretic

185. Select the option that can be used as a one-word substitute for the given group of words.
A person who is a lover of women.
(a) Philologist (b) Monogamist
(c) Philogynist (d) Misogynist

186. Select the option that can be used as a one-word substitute for the given group of words.
A person who is critical of the motives of others
(a) Cynic (b) Interviewer
(c) Chauffeur (d) Curator

187. Select the most appropriate idiom to fill in the blank.
The team always .... to come up with unique advertisements for all its clients.
(a) thinks outside the box
(b) throw caution to the winds
(c) take a back seat
(d) turn the tables

188. Select the most appropriate option that can substitute the underlined words in the given sentence.
Ice melts fastly, in the sun.
(a) melts fastest (b) melt fastly
(c) melt fast (d) melts fast

189. Select the most appropriate idiom that can substitute the underlined segment in the given sentence. I sometimes accept excess work to please my manager, so I take more responsibilities than one can manage.
(a) bite off more than I can chew
(b) get a taste of my own medicine
(c) burn my boats
(d) hear it straight from the horse's mouth

190. Select the most appropriate meaning of the given idiom.
Make waves
(a) To cause difficulty
(b) To give up
(c) To take it easy
(d) To have patience

Directions (Q. Nos. 191-195) *In the following passage, some words have been deleted. Read the passage carefully and select the most appropriate option to fill in each blank.*

Literature is a reflection of society and often ...(1)... insight into the human experience. Through various forms like novels, poems and plays, literature allows us to ...(2)... different emotions and perspectives. It can serve as a ...(3)... for social issues, shedding light on topics that need attention. Reading literature not only enhances our language skills but also ...(4)... empathy by helping us understand the feelings of characters. In a rapidly changing world, literature ...(5)... a timeless portal to diverse worlds and cultures.

191. Select the most appropriate option to fill in blank number 1.
(a) denies (b) suggests
(c) offers (d) garners

192. Select the most appropriate option to fill in blank number 2.
(a) explain (b) exploit
(c) explore (d) exclaim

193. Select the most appropriate option to fill in blank number 3.
(a) planking (b) plank
(c) platform (d) planks

194. Select the most appropriate option to fill in blank number 4.
(a) withers (b) avoids
(c) cultivates (d) provokes

195. Select the most appropriate option to fill in blank number 5.
(a) became (b) becomes
(c) become (d) becoming

Directions (Q. Nos. 196-200) *Read the given passage and answer the questions that follow.*

Several major airlines have pledged to reach net-zero carbon emissions by mid-century to fight climate change. It's an ambitious goal that will require an enormous ramp-up in sustainable aviation fuels, but that alone won't be enough, the latest research shows.

The idea of jetliners running solely on fuel made from used cooking oil from restaurants orcorn stalks might seem futuristic, but it's not that far away.

Airlines are already experimenting with sustainable aviation fuels, including bio fuels made from agriculture residues, trees, corn and used cooking oil and synthetic fuels made with captured carbon and green hydrogen.

United Airlines, which has been using a blend of used oil or waste fat and fossil fuels on some flights from Los Angeles and Amsterdam, recently announced plans to power 50,000 flights a year between its Chicago and Denver hubs using ethanol-based sustainable aviation fuels by 2028. The airline also launched a US$100 million fund on 21 February 2023, with Air Canada, Boeing, GE Aerospace, JP Morgan Chase and Honeywell to invest in sustainable aviation fuel start-ups to expand the industry.

196. Biofuels are not made from ....
(a) agricultural residue
(b) cooking oil
(c) coal
(d) trees

197. Why have major airline companies pledged to reach net-zero carbon emissions by mid-century?
(a) To moderate expenditure
(b) To create better revenue
(c) To reduce traffic jam
(d) To fight climate change

198. Select the most suitable word from the passage which means 'empirical'.
(a) Ambitious (b) Sustained
(c) Latest (d) Enormous

199. What is the tone of the speaker?
(a) Depressing (b) Casual
(c) Worried (d) Hopeful

200. Identify the most suitable title for the passage.
(a) Success Story of Airline Companies
(b) Threats of Climate Changes
(c) Biofuels Vs Synthetic Fuels
(d) One Good Turn from the Aviation Industry

Know Correct Answers

1. (b)	2. (c)	3. (a)	4. (b)	5. (c)	6. (b)	7. (c)	8. (b)	9. (c)	10. (b)
11. (b)	12. (a)	13. (a)	14. (b)	15. (a)	16. (b)	17. (c)	18. (a)	19. (c)	20. (d)
21. (a)	22. (a)	23. (d)	24. (c)	25. (a)	26. (a)	27. (c)	28. (d)	29. (d)	30. (d)
31. (a)	32. (b)	33. (c)	34. (d)	35. (a)	36. (d)	37. (a)	38. (a)	39. (c)	40. (a)
41. (c)	42. (a)	43. (c)	44. (d)	45. (a)	46. (c)	47. (a)	48. (b)	49. (b)	50. (a)
51. (b)	52. (c)	53. (d)	54. (d)	55. (b)	56. (a)	57. (b)	58. (d)	59. (a)	60. (a)
61. (b)	62. (b)	63. (a)	64. (b)	65. (d)	66. (c)	67. (b)	68. (d)	69. (c)	70. (a)
71. (c)	72. (b)	73. (c)	74. (b)	75. (a)	76. (d)	77. (d)	78. (b)	79. (a)	80. (b)
81. (c)	82. (c)	83. (a)	84. (a)	85. (a)	86. (b)	87. (c)	88. (c)	89. (b)	90. (a)
91. (d)	92. (d)	93. (d)	94. (b)	95. (d)	96. (c)	97. (d)	98. (b)	99. (c)	100. (a)
101. (a)	102. (d)	103. (a)	104. (a)	105. (c)	106. (d)	107. (a)	108. (a)	109. (b)	110. (d)
111. (a)	112. (c)	113. (a)	114. (d)	115. (d)	116. (c)	117. (c)	118. (c)	119. (d)	120. (a)
121. (d)	122. (c)	123. (a)	124. (d)	125. (a)	126. (a)	127 (c)	128. (d)	129. (b)	130. (b)
131. (d)	132. (b)	133. (a)	134. (c)	135. (c)	136. (d)	137 (d)	138. (c)	139. (c)	140. (a)
141. (d)	142. (b)	143. (b)	144. (b)	145. (b)	146. (d)	147. (d)	148. (b)	149. (a)	150. (b)
151. (d)	152. (d)	153. (d)	154. (c)	155. (b)	156. (d)	157. (d)	158. (a)	159. (d)	160. (b)
161. (c)	162. (c)	163. (d)	164. (b)	165. (d)	166. (a)	167. (c)	168. (c)	169. (c)	170. (b)
171. (c)	172. (a)	173. (b)	174. (c)	175. (d)	176. (b)	177. (c)	178. (d)	179. (c)	180. (d)
181. (c)	182. (b)	183. (c)	184. (b)	185. (c)	186. (a)	187. (a)	188. (d)	189. (a)	190. (a)
191. (c)	192. (c)	193. (c)	194. (c)	195. (b)	196. (c)	197. (d)	198. (d)	199. (d)	200. (d)

Answer & Solutions

1. (b) Given equation,

$$30 + 3 \times 990 - 11 \div 63 = 237$$

From option (b),

$$30 + 3 \times 990 \div 11 - 63 = 237$$
$$\Rightarrow \quad 30 + 270 - 63 = 237$$
$$\Rightarrow \quad 300 - 63 = 237$$
$$\Rightarrow \quad 237 = 237$$

2. (c) According to the question,

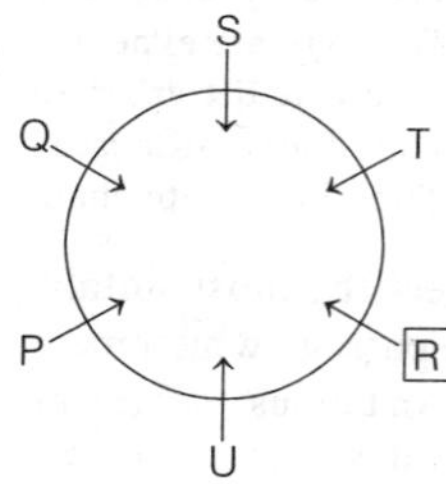

Hence, R is the neighbour of both U and T.

3. (a) When opened, the paper will appear as shown in option figure (a).

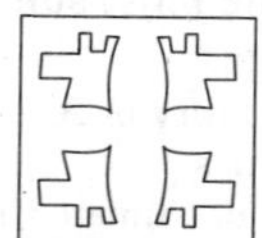

4. (b) As,

T R E E
+3 +1 +3 +1
W S H F

And

B A L L
+3 +1 +3 +1
E B O M

Similarly,

W A L L
+3 +1 +3 +1
Z B O M

5. (c) Given expression,

$$M \times N \% P - S + T$$

According to the question,

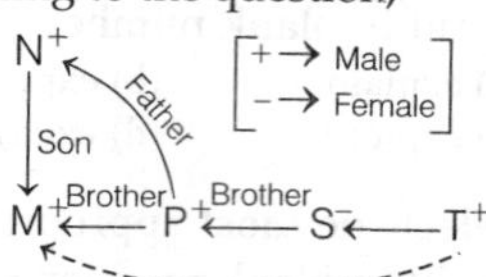

Hence, M is wife's brother of T.

6. (b) Given expression,

$$U - P \times Q \div R + S - T$$

According to the question,

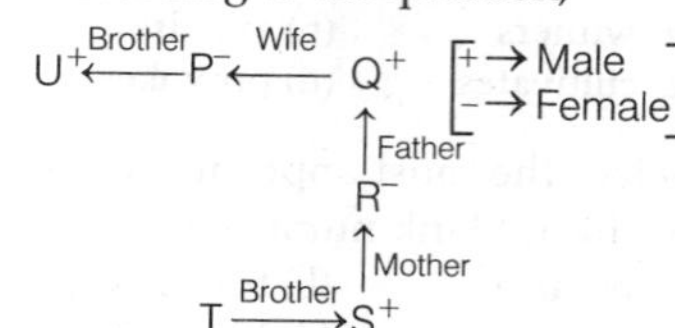

Hence, R is sisters daughter of U.

7. (c) The pattern of the series is aaabcccccccc, aaabbcccc, aaabbbbcc

aaabbbbbbbbc

8. (b) According to the question,

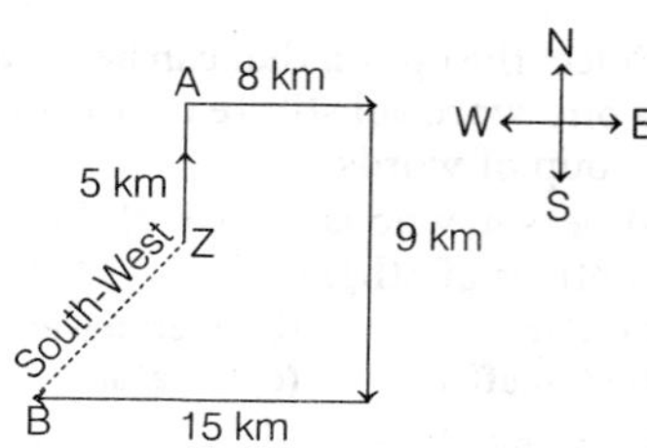

Hence, point B is in South-West direction with respect to point Z.

9. (c) According to the statements,

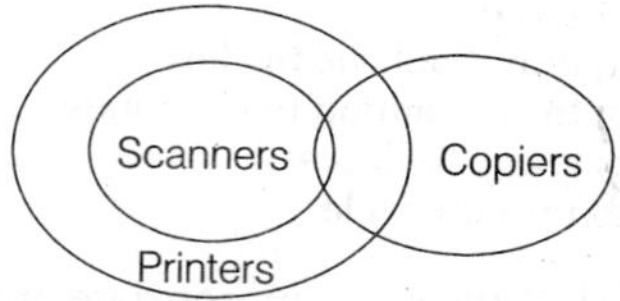

Conclusions

I. (✓) II. (✗) III. (✓)

Hence, only Conclusions I and III follow.

10. (b) When unfolded, the paper will appear as shown in option figure (b).

11. (b) According to the question,

(N)(O) D (E) ⟶ (6) 2 (9)(7)

B (O)(N)(E) ⟶ (9)(7) 1 (6)

Hence, the code for D is 2.

12. (a) The pattern of the given series is as follows,

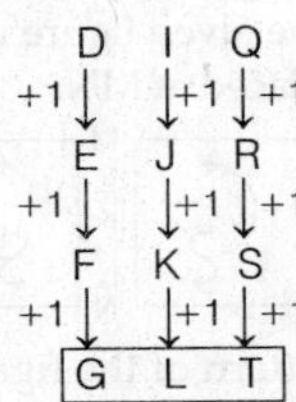

13. (a) Option figure (a) is correct mirror image of the given figure when the mirror is placed at MN.

M
hYRawK | KwaRYh
N

14. (b) The pattern of the given series is as follows,

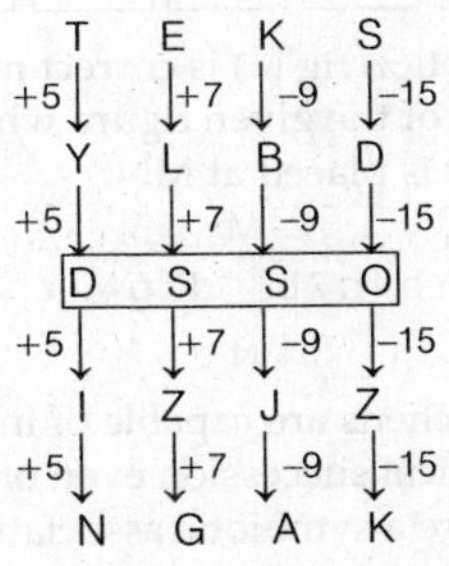

15. (a) Given equation,

$60 + 378 \times 18 \div 23 - 2 = ?$

After interchanging the signs,

+ ⟶ −	− ⟶ ×
× ⟶ ÷	÷ ⟶ +

$? = 60 - 378 \div 18 + 23 \times 2$

$? = 60 - 21 + 46 = 85$

$= 106 - 21 = 85$

16. (b) As, I $\xrightarrow{-3}$ F $\xrightarrow{+7}$ M

T $\xrightarrow{-3}$ Q $\xrightarrow{+7}$ X

G $\xrightarrow{-3}$ D $\xrightarrow{+7}$ K

But, O $\xrightarrow{-3}$ L $\xrightarrow{+6}$ R

17. (c) Here, the series follows the pattern which is as follows,

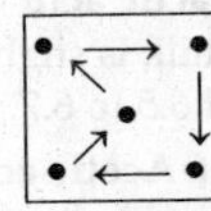

Hence, option figure (c) will replace the question mark.

18. (a) The pattern of the given series is as follows,

167 ⟶(−50) 117 ⟶(−40) 77 ⟶(−30) 47 ⟶(−20) 27

19. (c) As, 824 : 329

$\Rightarrow 8 + 2 + 4 = 14$

$\Rightarrow 3 + 2 + 9 = 14$

and 271 : 505

$\Rightarrow 2 + 7 + 1 = 10$

$\Rightarrow 5 + 0 + 5 = 10$

Similarly, 408 : 822

$\Rightarrow 4 + 0 + 8 = 12$

$\Rightarrow 8 + 2 + 2 = 12$

20. (d) As,

11	9	18	1	20
K	I	R	A	T
−1	−1	−1	−1	−1
10×5	8×5	17×5	0×5	19×5
50	40	85	0	95

and

23	1	19	9	13
W	A	S	I	M
−1	−1	−1	−1	−1
22×5	0×5	18×5	8×5	12×5
110	0	90	40	60

Similarly,

13	18	9	14	1	12
M	R	I	N	A	L
−1	−1	−1	−1	−1	−1
12×5	17×5	8×5	13×5	0×5	11×5
60	85	40	65	0	55

21. (a) When unfolded, the paper will appear as shown in option figure (a).

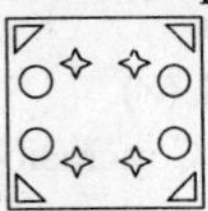

22. (a) As per the question,

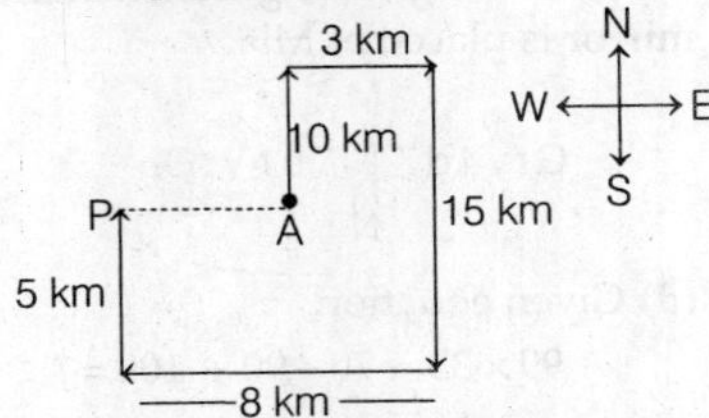

Ajay should drive 5 km in East direction to each point A again.

23. (d) The pattern of the given series is as follows,

53 ⟶(+9) 62 ⟶(+15) 77 ⟶(+21) 98 ⟶(+27) 125

+6, +6, +6

24. (c) According to the question,

bring the (bags) ⟶ nd (sm) pf

(bags) of gold ⟶ rg tx (sm)

∴ The code for bags is sm.

25. (a) Logic : Opposite letter place value.

As, S E R I E S

8 + 22 + 9 + 18 + 22 + 8 = 87

and D I S M A Y

23 + 18 + 8 + 14 + 26 + 2 = 91

Similarly,

S P R I N T

8 + 11 + 9 + 18 + 13 + 7 = 66

26. (a) Given equation,

$3 \times 6 + 16 - 8 \div 2 = ?$

After interchange the signs and numbers + and − and 8 and 16.

$3 \times 6 - 8 + 16 \div 2 = ?$

$? = 18 - 8 + 8 = 18$

27. (c) When folded, the sheet will appear as shown in option figure (c).

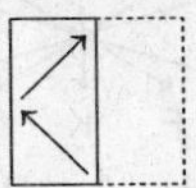

28. (d) According to the English dictionary order,

Jump (4) ⟶ Junction (1) ⟶ Juncture (5)

Jungle (3) ⟶ Jupiter (2)

$\Rightarrow$ 4, 1, 5, 3, 2.

29. (d) According to the English dictionary order

Larceners (3) ⟶ Larcenist (2) ⟶ Largely (6)

⟶ Lariated (4) ⟶ Larkiness (1)

⟶ Laryngal (5)

$\Rightarrow$ 3, 2, 6, 4, 1, 5.

30. (d) Given equation,

(40 J 32 K 4) I 5 L 155 J 7 I 9 = ?

After interchange the signs,

I ⟶ ×	J ⟶ +
K ⟶ ÷	L ⟶ −

$? = (40 + 32 \div 4) \times 5 - 155 + 7 \times 9$

$? = 48 \times 5 - 155 + 63$

$? = 240 - 155 + 63 \Rightarrow 148$

31. (a) The pattern of the given series is as follows,

22 ⟶(+5) 27 ⟶(+10) 37 ⟶(+15) 52 ⟶(+20) 72 ⟶(+25) 97

+5, +5, +5, +5

32. (b) As, 50 : 130

50 + 130 = 180

Similarly, 60 : 120

60 + 120 = 180

33. (c) As, 24 : 8
2×4=8

and 54 : 20
5×4=20

Similarly, [63] : 18
6×3=18

34. (d) Given equation,

$$180 \times 60 - 33 \div 1 + 50 = ?$$

After interchange of the signs,

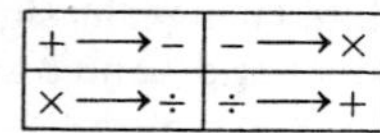

+ ⟶ −	− ⟶ ×
× ⟶ ÷	÷ ⟶ +

$? = 180 \div 60 \times 33 + 1 - 50$

$? = 99 + 1 - 50 = 50$

35. (a) As,

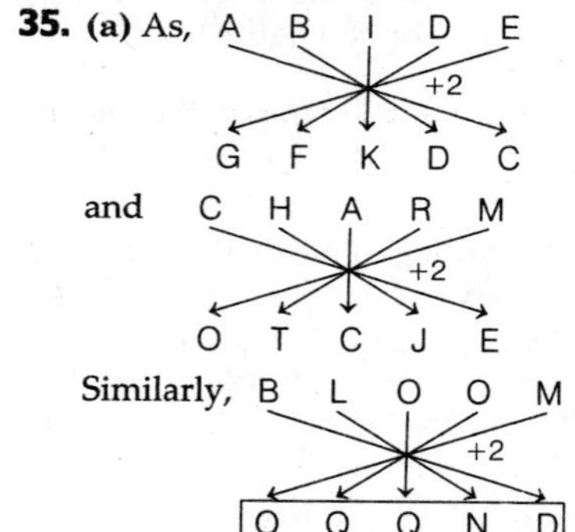

36. (d) As per the venn diagram,

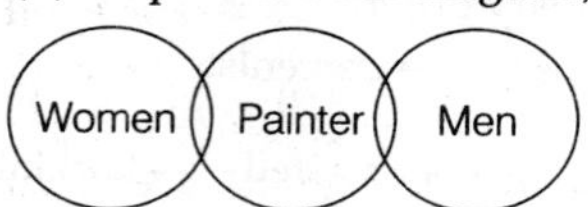

Same painter can be both men and women.

37. (a) As, B Y E
2 + 25 + 5 = 32

and A N G E R
1 + 14 + 7 + 5 + 18 = 45

Similarly, L O V E
12 + 15 + 22 + 5 = [54]

38. (a) As, (599, 236, 363)

599 − 236 = 363

and (481, 145, 336)

481 − 145 = 336

Similarly, (641, 314, 327)

641 − 314 = 327

39. (c) As, D I E T Y
−1 +1 +1 −1 −1
C J F S X

[Logic
∵ Vowels = +1
Consonants = −1]

and G R A C E
−1 −1 +1 −1 +1
F Q B B F

Similarly, G L O R Y
−1 −1 +1 −1 −1
[F K P Q X]

40. (a) According to the given statements,

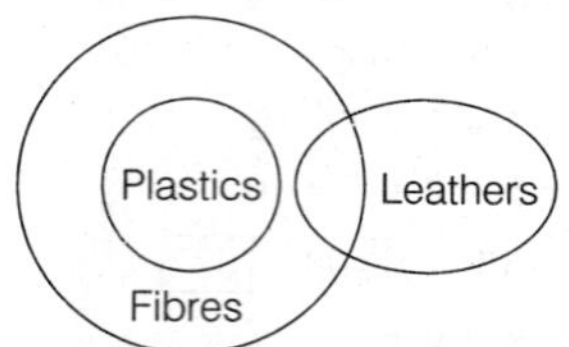

Conclusions

I. (✗) II. (✓)

Hence, only Conclusion II follows.

41. (c) In the given series the letters and arrows rotates 180° in clockwise direction starting from A. So, option figure (c) will replace the question mark.

42. (a) According to the given statements,

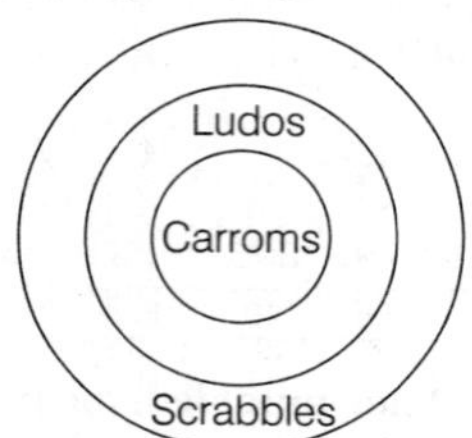

Conclusions

I. (✗) II. (✓)

Hence, only Conclusion II follows.

43. (c) Option figure (c) is correct mirror image of the given figure when the mirror is placed at MN.

M
Gry4d7 | Gry4d7 (mirrored)
N

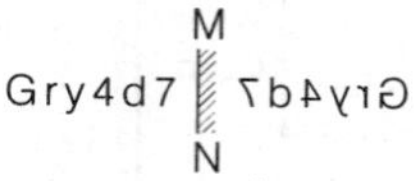

44. (d) Given equation,

$$99 \times 33 - 70 \div 90 + 100 = ?$$

After interchanging the signs,

+ ⟶ −	− ⟶ ×
× ⟶ ÷	÷ ⟶ +

$? = 99 \div 33 \times 70 + 90 - 100$

$? = 210 + 90 - 100 =$ [200]

45. (a) As, (112, 56, 8)
÷2 ÷7

and (196, 98, 14)
÷2 ÷7

Similarly, (294, 147, 21)
÷2 ÷7

46. (c) Given equation,

$$3 - 15 + 10 \div 2 \times 7 = 43$$

From option (c),

After interchanging the signs, − and ×.

$3 \times 15 + 10 \div 2 - 7 = 43$

$\Rightarrow 45 + 5 - 7 \Rightarrow 43 = 43$

47. (a) Option fig. (a) is correct mirror image of the given figure when the mirror is placed at MN.

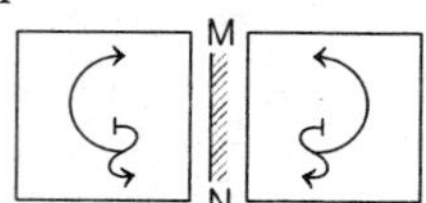

48. (b) The pattern of the figure series is as follows,

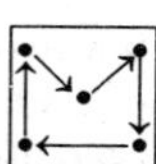

Hence, option figure (b) will replace the question mark.

49. (b) The pattern of the given series is as follows,

10 50 250 1250 6250 [31250]
×5 ×5 ×5 ×5 ×5

50. (a) Option fig (a) is correct mirror image of the given figure when the mirror is placed at MN.

M
Yh4g7b | Yh4g7b (mirrored)
N

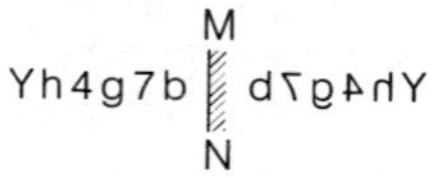

51. (b) Lichens are capable of initiating ecological succession even on a bare rock are a symbiotic association of algae and fungi.

- Ecological succession is the gradual process of change in the species composition of an ecosystem over time.

52. (c) Thorn forests and scrub forests are found in the North-Western part of India.

- It also includes semi-arid areas of Gujarat, Rajasthan, Uttar Pradesh, Chhattisgarh, Haryana and Madhya Pradesh where rainfall is less than 70 cm.

53. (d) The correct matching is A-2, B-3, C-4, D-1.

- **Lemon-Citric acid**
  - It is mostly found in Citrus fruits.
- **Milk-Lactic acid**
  - The milk is slightly acidic, with a PH of 6.5 to 6.7.
- **Vinegar-Acetic acid**
  - It is used for fermentation process.
- **Tamarind-Tartaric acid**
  - It is used as an antioxidant agent.

54. (d) C_4H_{10} is the chemical formula for butane.

- Butane is a saturated hydrocarbon containing 4 carbons, with an unbranched structure.
- It is a colourless, flammable gas and a vommon fuel source found in crude oil and natural gas.

55. (b) Statements (A) and (C) are correct about the Western Ghats.

- The height of the Western Ghats progressively increases from North to South. The Western Ghats are higher than the Eastern Ghats.
- Mahendragiri is the highest peak in the Eastern Ghats.
- Anamudi (2965m) is the highest peak of Western Ghats.

56. (a) Red and white are the colours of the antenna used on the volleyball net.

- The antenna are used to help keep track of whether or not the ball passes across the net in the crossing space.

57. (b) Of the total water content available globally, 2.5% of water is received from freshwater resources.

- About 71% of the Earth's surface is water-covered, while the other 29% consists of continents and islands.
- 96.5% of all the Earth's water is contained within the oceans as saltwater, while the remaining 3.5% is freshwater lakes and frozen water locked up in glaciers and the polar ice caps.

58. (d) In 2011-12, 24.3 percent of the Indian workforce was engaged in the secondary sector.

- The secondary sector, also known as the production sector, includes the manufacturing and industrial sectors.
- The secondary sector encompasses raw material secondary processing, food production, textile manufacture and industry.

59. (a) Pulakeshin II belonged to the Chalukya dynasty.

- Pulakeshin II reigned over the Chalukyas of Badami and Central India between the 6th and the 12th centuries.
- Pulakeshin II reigned from 610 to 642 CE.
- The famous **Aihole inscription** was issued by **King Pulakeshin II.**

60. (a) Lakshya Sen was born in Almora, Uttarakhand.

- Lakshya Sen is a badminton player. He was also a part of the Indian team which won the 2022 Thomas Cup.
- He also won the Gold medal at the 2022 Commonwealth Games.
- He has won Gold medals at the 2018 Asian Junior Championships in the Boys' Singles.

61. (b) The Great Indian desert/Thar desert is located on the Western margin of Aravalli mountain ranges.

- The Thar desert is world's 18th largest desert and the world's 9th largest hot subtropical desert.
- Aravalli is surrounded by 'The Great Boundary Fault' in the East.

62. (b) As of December 2022, the 'Kalidas Samman' Award is given in the field of art by the Government of Madhya Pradesh.

- A seven days event held in every year in Ujjain city of MP.
- It was named after the renowned classical Sanskrit writer Kalidas and was first awarded in 1980.
- It was given in four fields : classical music, classical dance, theatre and plastic arts.

63. (a) The words 'aus', 'aman' and 'boro' signify the types of seasons of sowing rice in West Bengal.

- Aman variety is sown in the rainy season (July-August) and harvested in winter.
- The quality of this rice is rough. Boro, rice sown in winter and harvested in summer. This is also called spring rice.

64. (b) Directive Principles of State Policy comes under Articles 36-51 in Part IV, the Constitution.

- Directive Principles of State Policy in India have been taken from the Constitution of Ireland.
- Directive Principles of State Policies (DPSPs) are a set of social and economic obligations imposed on the Government (Union and State) to establish a welfare society.

65. (d) The festival of Holi is celebrated in the Phalguna month of the Hindu calendar.

- Holi is popularly known as the festival of colours.
- It celebrates the eternal and divine love of the deities Radha and Krishna.
- Additionally, the day signifies the triumph of good over evil, as it commemorates the victory of Vishnu as Narasimha over Hiranyakashipu.

66. (c) If the value/percentage of the cash reserve ratio falls, then the value of money multiplier rises.

- An increase in a cash reserve ratio prevents the banks from lending more money and reduces the money multiplier.

67. (b) 10 fundamental duties were added by the 42nd Constitutional Amendment Act, 1976.

- Fundamental Duties of the Indian Constitution are mentioned in Article 51 A.
- It was added by the recommendation of Swaran Singh Committee in 1976.
- The 86th Amendment Act, 2002 later added the 11th Fundamental Duty to the list.

68. (d) Jamshedpur in Jharkhand is known as the 'Steel City of India'.

- It is because the first steel plant by TATA was established here.
- Jamshedpur was also the first industrial city in India, and almost the entire town works in the steel industry.

69. (c) Chetan Bhagat is the author of the book 'Making India Awesome'.

- 'Chetan Bhagat's other famous works are Five Point Someone, The 3 Mistakes of My Life, Half Girlfriend, 2 States, etc.

70. (a) Accepting deposits distinguishes a bank from other financial institutions.

- Demand deposits are exclusively accepted by the bank, not by any other financial institution.
- The money in the account can be withdrawn at any time by the depositor *via* cheque, ATM or online banking.

71. (c) Sardar Sarovar Lake is located in Karnataka is not correctly matched.

- It is located in Kevadia, Gujarat.
- Nearby lake, India's third highest concrete dam Sardar Sarovar dam was built on Narmada river.

72. (b) As per Census 2011, 68.8% of rural population lines in India, while the remaining 31.2% live in urban areas.

- Uttar Pradesh has the largest proportion of rural population in India.
- According to 2011 Census, Sikkim had the lowest rural population in India.

73. (c) Deepa Kartha represents Kathak dance.

- Deepa Kartha is an acclaimed Bharatanatyam and Kathak performer, trainer, choreographer from Kerala.

74. (b) The revolutionaries associated with the Anushilan Samiti were Jatindra Mohan Sengupta.

- Anushilan Samiti was formed 24th March, 1902 by Barinder Kumar Ghosh, Jatindernath Banerji and Pramathanath Mitra.
- It was headed by Barindra Kumar Ghosh, younger brother of Sri Aurobindo Ghosh.
- 'Jugantar Patrika' was the official journal of Anushilan Samiti.

75. (a) The concept of limited government is a major advancement to protect the **Fundamental Rights** of the Citizens from the ruling governments.

- A Limited Govt is restricted by a Constitution and cannot act arbitrary or override the Constitution.
- The concept of limited government holds that there should be legal constraints on the power of political authorities, especially with respect to individual rights.

76. (d) Archimedes discovered a principle that states the buoyant force on an object is equal to the weight of the fluid displaced by the object.

- When an object is immers in a fluid, the fluid exerts an upward force on the object, known as buoyant force.

77. (d) Vikramshila University was established by king Dharmapala of Pala dynasty, during the 8th to 9th century AD.

- It was one of the three most important Buddhist Mahaviharas of its time in India, along with Nalanda and Odantapuri.
- The university emerged as a leading hub for **Tantric Buddhism** and **Vajrayana Buddhism**.

78. (b) 'The forty minutes raga' is an album composed by Ali Akbar Khan.

- Ali Akbar Khan was an Indian Hindustani classical musician of the Maihar Gharana, known for playing the sarod.
- He was the first Indian musician to record the long, elaborate manifestations of Indian music performances.

79. (a) Figure (c) represents the phosphorus element.

Phosphorus is a chemical element, it has symbol, P and atomic number 15.

- Elemental phosphorus exists in two major forms, white phosphorus and red phosphorus, but because it is highly reactive, phosphorus is never found as a free element on Earth.

80. (b) Cultivation became more extensive in nature is not true regard to Green revolution.

- Green Revolution was initiated in 1960 to make India self-sufficient in Production of food grains.
- In India, the Green Revolution was mainly led by MS Swaminathan. Features of Green Revolution are as follows
  - Cultivation became more intensive in nature.
  - There was change in cropping pattern and type of crops grown in second phase.
  - In its second phase, there was a shift from dry to wet cultivation in dry and semi-arid regions of India.
  - There was excessive use of chemicals and water consumption.

81. (c) Johann Wolfgang Dőbereiners grouped the elements into triads.

- Dőbereiner's triads were groups of elements with similar properties that were identified by the German chemist Johann Wolfgang Dőbereiner.
- He observed that groups of three elements (triads) could be formed in which all the elements shared similar physical and chemical properties.

82. (c) 'Chanakya's Chant (2010)' is a novel written by Indian author Ashwin Sanghi.

- First novel written by him was 'The Rozabal Line (2008), India.

83. (a) Dussehra comes at the end of Navratri and Durga Pooja.

- Dussehra is also called as 'Vijayadashmi'.
- Dussehra is celebrated following Navratri because it is believed that Lord Rama worshipped Goddess Durga before embarking on his journey to defeat Ravana, following the guidance of Lord Vishnu.
- This festival signifies the triumph of Lord Rama over the demon king Ravana.

84. (a) Special Drawing Rights are also known as Paper Gold.

- It is because at the time of its creation, it was viewed as an asset that could act as a reserve asset that would supplement gold reserves and other currencies.
- It was created by IMF in 1969 in order to supplement the existing official reserves of member countries.

85. (a) Gross domestic product was the instrument used to measure economic growth during the planning era.

- Gross Domestic Product (GDP) is the total valuation of final goods and services produced within the geographical borders of a country during a specified period (usually a year).
- GDP signals whether the economy is expanding or contracting.

86. (b) Iris is the structure that controls the size of the pupil.

- Iris contains a group of two smooth muscles attached at the corner of the pupil.
- They stretch when there is less light and shrink when it is too bright.
- These muscles are known as sphincter pupillae.

87. (c) 40 mm is the size of a standard table tennis ball and weighs 2.7 g.

- Ping pong balls are coloured as either white or orange depending on the table surface and game style.

88. **(c)** Begum Akhtar a famous singer from India is known for Ghazal music.

- She is also known as 'Mallika-e-Ghazal' (Queen of Ghazals).
- She is regarded as one of the greatest singers of ghazal, dadra and thumri genres of Hindustani classical music.
- She received the Sangeet Natak Akademi Award for vocal music in 1972, Padma Shri (1963) and later a Padma Bhushan Award (1975) posthumously by the Government of India.

89. **(b)** Article 112 of the Indian Constitution deals with the annual financial statement of the Government of India, also called budget.

- It is a statement of estimated receipts and expenditure in respect of every financial year, from 1st April, to 31st March.
- This statement is called the annual financial statement.
- It is presented by Finance Minister.
- The term 'Budget' is not mentioned in the Constitution of India.

90. **(a)** To correctly mix acid and water the acid must be slowly added to the water.

- Adding water to a concentrated acid releases a huge amount of heat, which can cause an explosion and acid burns on the skin, clothing and other body parts.

91. **(d)** Kandariya Mahadeva temple at Khajuraho was built under Chandela dynasty.

- The temple dedicated to Shiva was constructed by king Dhandadeva of Chandela dynasty in 999 CE.
- Khajuraho was once the capital of the Chandela dynasty.

92. **(d)** Bismillah Khan was the co-winner of Bharat Ratna with Lata Mangeshkar in the year 2001.

- It was established in year 1954.
- The first recepient were C. Rajagopalachari, S./ Radhakrishnan and CV Raman in 1954.
- In 2024, five personalities have been conferred with the Bharat Ratna namely Karpoori Thakur, LK Advani, PV Narasimha Rao, Charan Singh and MS Swaminathan.

93. **(d)** Kalavati Devi was awarded the Sangeet Natak Akademi Award (for her contribution to Manipuri Dance).

- It is the highest Indian recognition given to people in the field of performing arts.

94. **(b)** All the given options are correct so the right option is (b).

- Governor of Nagaland has special responsibility related to law and order mention in Article-371A of the Constitution.
- Governor of Manipur under Article- 371C of the Constitution is responsible for submitting an annual report to President regarding the administration in hilly areas.
- Governor of Sikkim has a special responsibility for peace and for equitable arrangement for ensuring the social and economic advancement of different rections.
- Governor of Arunachal Pradesh has special responsibility with respect to law and order in the state under Article-371H.

95. **(d)** The organism that shows bioluminescence is ctenoplana.

- Ctenoplana is a small, marine animal, belonging to the genus of comb jellies.
- These organisms are transparent or sometimes colourless and belong to the phylum ctenophora.
- These organisms exhibit the property of bioluminescence which is achieved by the activation of calcium activated proteins.

96. **(c)** International Army Games, 2021 was held in Moscow Russia from 22nd August to 4th September.

- The International Army Games is an annual international military sports event organised by the Ministry of Defence (MoD) of Russia.
- The games have been referred to as the War Olympics.

97. **(d)** The Indian Civil Service (ICS) was widely considered as the 'Heaven Born Service' for Indians during British rule.

- It was started in 1855 and the first batch joined in 1856.
- The British Parliament had acknowledged in 1833 that Indians must be admitted to the higher posts of service.

98. **(b)** Article 200 of the Indian Constitution deals with the powers of the Governor with regard to assent given to bills passed by the State Legislature and other powers of the Governor such as reserving the bill for the President's consideration.

99. **(c)** Sir Syed Ahmad Khan founded the Mohammedan Anglo-Oriental College in Aligarh for the spread of Western education in 1875.

- Lord Northbook gave personal donation of ₹ 10,000 to Sir Syed Ahmad Khan to continue with reform activities with the help of these money he started Muhammadan Anglo-Oriental College.
- Later, this college grew into the famous Aligarh Muslim University.

100. **(a)** Bharatanatyam dancer Yamini Krishnamurthy was bestowed with the title of 'Asthana Narthaki' (Resident Dancer) by the Tirumala Tirupati Devasthanam temple.

- She received many awards for her work, including the Padma Shri (1968), the Sangeet Natak Akademi Award (1977) and the Padma Bhushan (2001).

101. **(a)** $$\frac{61+\frac{2}{5}\times 75\div 6-\left(3\times 6\div\frac{1}{3}\right)\times\frac{1}{6}}{5+\frac{2}{3}\times(58-37)}$$

$$=\frac{61+\frac{2}{5}\times\frac{75}{6}-(3\times 6\times 3)\times\frac{1}{6}}{5+\frac{2}{3}\times 21}$$

$$=\frac{61+5-9}{5+2\times 7}=\frac{66-9}{5+14}=\frac{57}{19}=3$$

102. **(d)** In the first alloy,

ratio of $A:B:C=2:3:1$

Let the weight of first alloy be 12 kg

$\therefore$ Weight of $A = 4$ kg,

Weight of $B = 6$ kg

Weight of $C = 2$ kg

Now, In second alloy,

ratio of $B:C:D=5:4:3$

Let the weight of second alloy be 12 kg.

$\therefore$ Weight of $B = 5$ kg

Weight of $C = 4$ k

Weight of $D = 3$ kg

Weight of new alloy $= 12 + 12 = 24$ kg

$\therefore$ Amount of Metal B in new alloy

$$=\frac{6+5}{24}=\frac{11}{24}$$

103. (a) Expression

$$=\frac{[(\sin x+\sin y)(\sin y-\sin x)]}{[(\cos x+\cos y)(\cos y-\cos x)]}$$

$$=\frac{\sin^2 y-\sin^2 x}{\cos^2 y-\cos^2 x}$$

$$=\frac{\sin^2 y-\sin^2 x}{(1-\sin^2 y)-(1-\sin^2 x)}$$

$$=\frac{(\sin^2 y-\sin^2 x)}{-(\sin^2 y-\sin^2 x)}=-1$$

104. (a) Side of equilateral triangle

$= a = 18\text{cm}$

Circumradius $(R)=\frac{a}{\sqrt{3}}=\frac{18}{\sqrt{3}}$

Inradius $(r)=\frac{a}{2\sqrt{3}}=\frac{18}{2\sqrt{3}}$

Area of region in between

$$=\pi(R)^2-\pi(r)^2$$

$$=\pi\left[\left(\frac{18}{\sqrt{3}}\right)^2-\left(\frac{18}{2\sqrt{3}}\right)^2\right]$$

$$=\pi\left[\left(\frac{18\times 18}{3}\right)-\left(\frac{18\times 18}{4\times 3}\right)\right]$$

$$=\pi(108-27)$$

$$=81\,\pi=81\times\frac{22}{7}$$

$$=\frac{1782}{7}=254\frac{4}{7}\text{ cm}^2$$

105. (c) Given, $\frac{1}{3}$ of the sweet is sugar.

Present price of sugar

$=\frac{7}{6}$ of its original price

$\therefore$ Increase in price $=\frac{7}{6}-1=\frac{1}{6}$

$=\frac{1}{6}\times 100=16.67\%$

Now, contribution of sugar to the cost

$=\frac{1}{3}$

Remaining $\frac{2}{3}$ is not affected by change in price.

$\therefore$ Effective increase $=\frac{1}{3}\times 16.67\%$

$=5.56\%=\frac{100}{18}\%$

106. (d) Total movies released

$= 190 + 150 + 170 + 210$

$= 720$

Here, 720 represents 360°.

Combined angle made by Jan - Mar and Jul-Sep $=\frac{(150+170)}{720}\times 360°$

$= 160°$

Combined angle made by Apr-Jun and Oct-Dec $=\frac{(210+190)}{720}\times 360°$

$=\frac{400}{720}\times 360°=200°$

$\therefore$Required difference $= 200° - 160°$

$= 40°$ less

107. (a) Invalid votes of Village P

$=40000\times\frac{80}{100}\times\frac{10}{100}$

$= 3200$

Invalid votes of Village

$S=80000\times\frac{80}{100}\times\frac{15}{100}=9600$

$\therefore$Required ratio $=\frac{3200}{9600}=1:3$

108. (a) $\dfrac{53-\frac{2}{7}\text{ of }63-9}{72-\frac{2}{5}\text{ of }(96-31)}$

$$=\frac{53-2\times 9-9}{72-\frac{2}{5}\times 65}=\frac{53-18-9}{72-2\times 13}$$

$$=\frac{26}{72-26}=\frac{26}{46}=\frac{13}{23}$$

109. (b) Percentage gain by using 100g weight instead of 200g

$=\frac{(200-100)}{100}\times 100=100\%$

Percentage loss = 24%

Net percentage change $=x-y-\frac{xy}{100}$

Where, x = 100% gain and y = 24% loss

$\therefore$ Net percentage change

$=100-24-\frac{24\times 100}{100}=76-24=52\%$

Hence, his profit percentage is 52 %.

110. (d) Given, $x^2-6x-1=0$

Dividing it by x, we get

$x-6-\frac{1}{x}=0\Rightarrow x-\frac{1}{x}=6$

Squaring it on both the sides, we get

$$\left(x-\frac{1}{x}\right)^2=(6)^2$$

$$\Rightarrow x^2+\frac{1}{x^2}-2\times x\times\frac{1}{x}=36$$

$$\Rightarrow\quad x^2+\frac{1}{x^2}=36+2$$

$$\Rightarrow\quad x^2+\frac{1}{x^2}=38$$

Now, the value of $x^2+\frac{1}{x^2}-8$

$\therefore\ x^2+\frac{1}{x^2}-8=38-8=30$

111. (a)

Given, $\angle PRQ = 86°$

and $QR = RS$

$\angle QRS = 180° - 86° = 94°$

Now, in triangle QRS

$QR = RS$

$\therefore\ \angle RQS=\angle RSQ=x°$ (let)

$\therefore\ 94° + x° + x° = 180°$

$\Rightarrow\ 94° + 2x° = 180°$

$\Rightarrow 2x° = 180° - 94° = 86°$

$\Rightarrow\ x = 43°$

$\therefore\ \angle PSQ = 43°$

112. (c) $\dfrac{3\frac{1}{7}\div 1\frac{4}{7}+3\text{ of}}{2\frac{2}{3}+2.5\times 2.4\div 3\frac{1}{3}-4\text{ of }3}$

$=\dfrac{\frac{22}{7}\div\frac{11}{7}+3\text{ of}}{\frac{8}{3}+2.5\times 2.4\div\frac{10}{3}-12}$

$=\frac{22}{7}\times\frac{7}{11}+8+2.5\times 2.4\times\frac{3}{10}-12$

$=2+8+2.5\times\frac{7.2}{10}-12$

$=2+8+\frac{18}{10}-12=10+1.8-12$

$=11.8-12=-0.2=-\frac{2}{10}=-\frac{1}{5}$

113. (a) $8.16\times 5.35+17.9-19.5\text{ of }\frac{1}{15}+\frac{1}{5}$

$=8.16\times 5.35+17.9-1.3+\frac{1}{5}$

$=43.656+17.9-1.3+0.2$

$=61.756-1.3=60.456$

114. (d) Total SP of 3 watches

$=3\times 2800=₹8400$

Total CP of three watches

$=\left(\frac{2800}{140}\times 100+\frac{2800}{125}\times 100+\frac{2800}{112}\times 100\right)$

$= ₹ (2000 + 2240 + 2500)$

$= ₹ 6740$

Profit percentage

$=\frac{8400-6740}{6740}\times 100\%$

$=\frac{166}{674}\times 100\%$

$= 0.2463$

115. (d) Given,

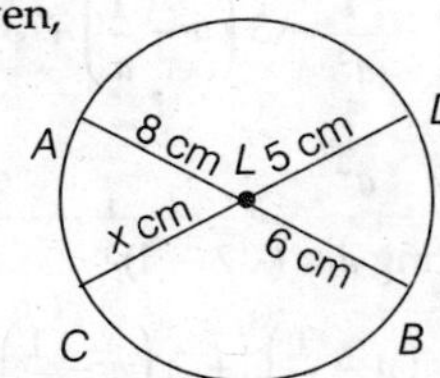

Let $CL = x$ cm

Now, we know that when two chords intersect internally,

$AL \times LB = CL \times LD$

$\Rightarrow 8 \times 6 = x \times 5$

$\Rightarrow x = \frac{8 \times 6}{5} \Rightarrow x = \frac{48}{5}$

$\Rightarrow x = 9.6$ cm

$\therefore CL = 9.6$ cm

116. (c) Length of Train $P = 110$ m

Length of Train $Q = 140$ m

Speed of Train $P = 70$ km/h

Let the speed of Train $Q = x$ km/h

Now, relative speed $= (70 + x)$ km/h

According to the given condition,

Time taken $= \frac{\text{Total length of trains}}{\text{Relative speed}}$

$\Rightarrow 5 \text{ sec} = \frac{(110 + 140)}{(70 + x) \times \frac{5}{18}}$

$\Rightarrow 5 = \frac{250 \times 18}{(70 + x) 5}$

$\Rightarrow \frac{250 \times 18}{25} = 70 + x$

$\Rightarrow 70 + x = 180$

$\Rightarrow x = 110$ km/h

$\therefore$ Speed of Train $Q = 110$ km/h

117. (c) $45 \div 5 \times 5 + 10 - 5$

$= 9 \times 5 + 10 - 5$

$= 45 + 10 - 5 = 50$

118. (c) $\frac{17}{\sec^2 \theta} + 10\sin^2 \theta + \frac{7}{1 + \cot^2 \theta}$

$= 17 \times \frac{1}{\sec^2\theta} + 10\sin^2 \theta + \frac{7}{\text{cosec}^2\theta}$

$\left[\because 1 + \cot^2 \theta = \text{cosec}^2\theta \text{ and } \frac{1}{\sec^2\theta} = \cos^2 \theta\right]$

$= 17\cos^2 \theta + 10\sin^2 \theta + 7\sin^2 \theta$

$= 17\cos^2 \theta + 17\sin^2 \theta$

$= 17 (\cos^2 \theta + \sin^2 \theta)$

$= 17 \times 1 = 17$

119. (d) $250 + [100 - \{50 - (30 + 15)\}]$

$= 250 + [100 - \{50 - 45\}]$

$= 250 + [100 - 5]$

$= 250 + 95 = 345$

120. (a) Let the distance between his house to exhibition ground = 150 km

Now,

Average speed $= \frac{\text{Total distance}}{\text{Total time taken}}$

$= \frac{150 + 150}{\frac{150}{30} + \frac{150}{50}} = \frac{300}{5 + 3}$

$= \frac{300}{8} = 37.5$ km/h

121. (d) Let the speed of boat be $35x$ and that of water current $= 8x$

Upstream speed $= 35x - 8x$

Downstream speed $= 35x + 8x$

Now, according to the question,

$\frac{\text{Distance }(D)}{(35x + 8x)} = 5 \text{ h } 10 \text{ min}$

$\Rightarrow \frac{D}{43x} = 310$ min

$\Rightarrow D = 310 \times 43x$ ...(i)

Now, let the time taken to go upstream $= T$

$\therefore \frac{D}{(35x - 8x)} = T$

$\Rightarrow D = 27x \times T$ ...(ii)

Equating (i) and (ii),

$27x \times T = 310 \times 43x$

$T = 493.7$ min

$\Rightarrow T = 8.228$ h

$\therefore T = 8$ h 13 min 48 sec

122. (c) Let the total amount be ₹x.

Amount spent = ₹30000 + ₹45000

= ₹75000

$\therefore$ Savings = ₹$(x - 75000)$

Now, according to the question,

₹$(x - 75000)$ = 40% of ₹x

$\Rightarrow x - 75000 = \frac{40}{100}x$

$\Rightarrow x - \frac{40}{100}x = 75000$

$\Rightarrow \frac{60}{100}x = 75000$

$\Rightarrow x =$ ₹125000

Hence, the total amount = ₹125000.

123. (a) We know that,

$\frac{M_1 \times D_1}{W_1} = \frac{M_2 D_2}{W_2}$

Here, $M_1 = 12, D_1 = 10$

and $W_1 = 540$

and $D_2 = 8, W_2 = 720$

Let the extra people needed be x.

$\therefore M_2 = 12 + x$

Hence, $\frac{12 \times 10}{540} = \frac{(12 + x) \times 8}{720}$

$\Rightarrow 12 + x = 20$

$\Rightarrow x = 8$

So, 8 more people will be required.

124. (d) We know that in a triangle, the measure of any one side is always less than the sum of other two sides and always greater than difference of these two sides.

Given sides = 3.8 cm and 6 cm

Now, let third side $= x$ cm

$(6 - 3.8) < x < (6 + 3.8)$

$2.2 < x < 9.8$

Hence, it cannot be equal to 2.2 cm.

125. (a) Longest chord of a circle will be diameter.

Area of a circle $= \pi r^2$

$256\pi = \pi r^2$

$\Rightarrow r^2 = 256$

$\Rightarrow r = 16$ cm

$\therefore$ Diameter $= 2r = 32$ cm

Hence, length of longest chord = 32 cm

126. (a) Expenditure on rent, medicines and electricity together

= (15 + 12 + 10)% of total expenditure

= 37% of total expenditure

Expenditure on groceries and education together = (20 + 25)% of total expenditure = 45% of total expenditure

$\therefore$ Required percentage

$= \frac{37}{45} \times 100 = 82.22\%$

127. (c) Given, Volume of mixture = 5 L

$\therefore \frac{\text{Milk}}{\text{Mixture}} = \frac{4}{5}$

$\therefore$ Ratio of milk and water in 5 L mixture i.e. Milk : Water = 4 : 1

Now, 1 L of milk is added, so total quantity of milk becomes 5 L and that of mixture becomes 6 L. Quantity of water remains same i.e. 1 L.

$\therefore$ Percentage of water in the mixture

$= \frac{1}{6} \times 100 = \frac{100}{6}\%$

128. (d) Cement produced in 2020 by Company X = 30 lakh tonnes

Cement produced in 2022 by Company Z = 25 lakh tonnes

Cement produced by Company W in 2021 = 25 lakh tonnes

$\therefore$ Required percentage

$= \frac{(30 + 25)}{25} \times 100$

$= 55 \times 4 = 220\%$

129. **(b)** We know that, $\sin^2\theta + \cos^2\theta = 1$

Also, $\sin^2(90° - \theta) = \cos^2\theta$

Now,

$\sin^2 15° + \sin^2 25° + \sin^2 35° + \sin^2 45° + \sin^2 55° + \sin^2 65° + \sin^2 75°$

$= \sin^2 15° + \sin^2 25° + \sin^2 35° + \sin^2 45° + \sin^2(90° - 35°) + \sin^2(90° - 25°) + \sin^2(90° - 15°)$

$= \sin^2 15° + \sin^2 25° + \sin^2 35° + \sin^2 45° + \cos^2 35° + \cos^2 25° + \cos^2 15°$

$= (\sin^2 15° + \cos^2 15°) + (\sin^2 25° + \cos^2 25°) + (\sin^2 35° + \cos^2 35°) + \sin^2 45°$

$= 1 + 1 + 1 + \frac{1}{2} = 3 + \frac{1}{2} = \frac{7}{2}$

130. **(b)** Work done by Sumit and Rajiv together of 1 h $= \frac{1}{20}$

Work done by Sumit alone in one h $= \frac{1}{25}$

Work done by Rajiv alone in 1 h

$= \frac{1}{20} - \frac{1}{25} = \frac{5-4}{100} = \frac{1}{100}$

Time taken by Rajiv to do the complete Job = 100 h.

131. **(d)** Mean $= \frac{\Sigma n_i f_i}{\Sigma f_i}$

(Where, $f \rightarrow$ frequency $n \rightarrow$ score)

$= \frac{(15\times 2) + (18\times 3) + (21\times 4) + (22\times 1) + (19\times 5) + (23\times 1) + (24\times 2)}{2+3+4+1+5+1+2}$

$= \frac{356}{18} = 19.78$

132. **(b)** Given, $\cos A = \frac{4}{5}$

$\because \sin^2 A = 1 - \cos^2 A = 1 - \left(\frac{4}{5}\right)^2$

$\therefore \sin A = \frac{3}{5}$

We also know,

$\tan A = \frac{\sin A}{\cos A} = \frac{3\times 5}{5\times 4} = \frac{3}{4}$

Now, $(8 + \sin A)(3 - \tan A)$

$= \left(8 + \frac{3}{5}\right)\left(3 - \frac{3}{4}\right)$

$= \frac{43}{5} \times \frac{9}{4} = \frac{387}{20}$

133. **(a)** Average of total production during 1989 to 1994

$= \frac{476}{6} = 79.33$

$\therefore$ In 1993, the production of cars of all types taken together approximately equal to the average of the total production during the period.

134. **(c)** Average number of mobile phones sold by all showrooms in 2020.

$= \frac{\text{Sum of mobile phones sold by all showroom in 2020}}{\text{Total number of showroom}}$

$= \frac{420 + 430 + 410 + 440 + 400 + 420}{6}$

$= \frac{2520}{6} = 420$

135. **(c)** $55\frac{1}{3} \div \left[3\frac{1}{5} + \left\{2\frac{1}{2} - \left(2\frac{1}{3} + \frac{3}{5}\right)\right\}\right]$

$= \frac{166}{3} \div \left[\frac{16}{5} + \left\{\frac{5}{2} - \left(\frac{7}{3} + \frac{3}{5}\right)\right\}\right]$

Using BODMAS rule,

$= \frac{166}{3} \div \left[\frac{16}{5} + \left\{\frac{5}{2} - \left(\frac{35+9}{15}\right)\right\}\right]$

$= \frac{166}{3} \div \left[\frac{16}{5} + \left\{\frac{5}{2} - \frac{44}{15}\right\}\right]$

$= \frac{166}{3} \div \left[\frac{16}{5} + \left\{\frac{75-88}{30}\right\}\right]$

$= \frac{166}{3} \div \left[\frac{16}{5} - \frac{13}{30}\right]$

$= \frac{166}{3} \div \left(\frac{96-13}{30}\right)$

$= \frac{166}{3} \times \frac{30}{83} = 20$

136. **(d)** Required percentage change

$= \left(x + y + \frac{xy}{100}\right)\%$

Here, $= \left(6 + 8 + \frac{6\times 8}{100}\right)\% = 14.48\%$

137. **(d)** Let the cost price be ₹x.

Given, marked price = ₹420

Selling price $= 420 - 420 \times \frac{10}{100} =$ ₹378

According to the question,

$378 = x + \frac{20x}{100} \Rightarrow 378 = \frac{120}{100}x$

$\Rightarrow x = \frac{378 \times 100}{120}$

$\therefore x =$ ₹315

$\therefore$ Cost price of dairy products = ₹315

138. **(c)** $\left(a - \frac{1}{a}\right)^3 + 3\left(a - \frac{1}{a}\right)$

We know that,

$(a-b)^3 = a^3 - b^3 - 3ab(a-b)$

$\therefore \left(a - \frac{1}{a}\right)^3 + 3\left(a - \frac{1}{a}\right)$

$= a^3 - \left(\frac{1}{a}\right)^3 - 3 \times a \times \frac{1}{a}\left[a - \frac{1}{a}\right] + 3\left(a - \frac{1}{a}\right)$

$= a^3 - \frac{1}{a^3} - 3\left(a - \frac{1}{a}\right) + 3\left(a - \frac{1}{a}\right)$

$= a^3 - \frac{1}{a^3}$

Putting $a = (\sqrt{2} - 1)^{\frac{1}{3}}$

$\therefore \left(a - \frac{1}{a}\right)^3 + 3\left(a - \frac{1}{a}\right)$

$= [(\sqrt{2}-1)^{\frac{1}{3}}]^3 - \left[\frac{1}{(\sqrt{2}-1)^{\frac{1}{3}}}\right]^3$

$= (\sqrt{2} - 1) - \frac{1}{\sqrt{2} - 1}$

$= \sqrt{2} - 1 - \frac{1 \times (\sqrt{2}+1)}{(\sqrt{2}-1)(\sqrt{2}+1)}$

$= \sqrt{2} - 1 - \sqrt{2} - 1 = -2$

139. **(c)** Let the cost price (CP) be ₹x.

Given, marked price (MP) of item = ₹500

According to the question,

Selling price (SP)

$= \left[500 - \left(\frac{25}{100} \times 500\right) - 65\right]$

$= (500 - 125 - 65) =$ ₹ 310

Also, cost price = SP $- \frac{24}{100}$ (CP)

$x = 310 - \frac{24}{100}x$

$x\left(1 + \frac{24}{100}\right) = 310$

$x = \frac{310 \times 100}{124} = 250$

$\therefore$ Cost price of item = ₹250

140. **(a)** Population at beginning of a town = 15000

Population after 1st yr

$= 15000 + \frac{15}{100} \times 15000 = 17250$

Population after 2nd yr

$= 17250 + \frac{25}{100} \times 17250$

$= 17250 + 4312.5 = 21562.5$

Population after 3rd yr

$= 21562.5 - \frac{6}{100} \times 21562.5$

$= 21562.5 - 1293.75 = 20268.75$

$\therefore$ Population after 3rd yr $\approx$ 20269.

141. **(d)** Let the total number of votes be $100x$.

Total votes cast = 95%

Winner got 75% of votes.

$\therefore$ Loser got (95 – 75) = 20% votes

Hence, [75% – 20%] × 100x = 5500

55% of 100x = 5500

$x = 100$

$\therefore$ Total number of voters $= 100x$

$= 100 \times 100 = 10000$

142. (b) Distance from house to school $= 5$ km

Total time taken by student from house to school = 1 h

Since, student stops twice for 5 min each.

$\therefore$ Actual time taken to cover 5 km by student $= 1\text{h} - 10\text{ min} = 50\text{ min} = \frac{50}{60}$ h

$$\text{Average speed} = \frac{\text{Total distance}}{\text{Total time taken}}$$

$$= \frac{5\text{ km}}{\left(\frac{50}{60}\right)\text{h}} = \frac{5 \times 60}{50} = 6\text{ km/h}$$

143. (b) Given, $2a + 2b + c = 0$

$\Rightarrow \quad 2a + 2b = -c$

$\Rightarrow \quad (2a + 2b)^2 = (-c)^2$

$\Rightarrow (2a)^2 + (2b)^2 + 8ab = c^2$

$\Rightarrow \quad 4a^2 + 4b^2 - c^2 = -8ab$

$\Rightarrow 4a^2 + 4b^2 - c^2 + 5c^2 = 5c^2 - 8ab$

$\therefore \quad \frac{4a^2 + 4b^2 + 4c^2}{5c^2 - 8ab} = 1$

144. (b) Let the rate of interest be $R\%$.

$\therefore$ Interest on ₹29000 for 3 yr

$= I_1 = \frac{29000 \times R \times 3}{100} = ₹870\,R$

Interest on ₹45000 for 5 yr

$= I_2 = \frac{45000 \times R \times 5}{100} = ₹2250\,R$

$\therefore$ Total interest paid $= I_1 + I_2$

$= (870 + 2250)\,R \Rightarrow 62400 = 3120\,R$

$\therefore R = \frac{62400}{3120} = 20\%$

145. (b) Radius of sphere $(r) = 20\%$

$\because$ Volume of sphere $= \frac{4}{3}\pi r^3 \Rightarrow V \propto r^3$

For two successive percentage, change in percentage

$= \left(20 + 20 + \frac{20 \times 20}{100}\right)\% = 44\%$

Again, Required change in volume

$= \left(44 + 20 + \frac{44 \times 20}{100}\right)$

$= (64 + 8.8)\,\% = 72.8\%$

146. (d) Let slant height (l) of cone be $4x$ and height of cone (h) be $3x$ then radius (r) of cone $= \sqrt{l^2 - h^2}$

$= \sqrt{(4x)^2 - (3x)^2} = \sqrt{16x^2 - 9x^2}$

$= \sqrt{7}x$ unit

Now, CS A of cone $= 4\sqrt{7}\pi$

$\Rightarrow \quad \pi rl = 4\sqrt{7}\pi$

$\Rightarrow \quad \sqrt{7}x \times 4x = 4\sqrt{7}$

$\Rightarrow \quad x^2 = 1$

$x = 1$

$\therefore$ Radius of cone

$= \sqrt{7}x = \sqrt{7} \times 1 = \sqrt{7}$ units

147. (d) Using BODMAS rule.

$15 - 16 \div [4 + (5 + 7) \div 3]$

$= 15 - 16 \div [4 + 12 \div 3]$

$= 15 - 16 \div [4 + 4]$

$= 15 - 16 \div 8$

$= 15 - 2 = 13$

148. (b) Using BODMAS rule,

$\Rightarrow [16 \div 2 - 7 \times 15 \div 3 + \{(1 + 4) \times 5\} + 4 \times 3 - 10]$

$= [16 \div 2 - 7 \times 15 \div 3 + \{5 \times 5\} + 4 \times 3 - 10]$

$= [16 \div 2 - 7 \times 15 \div 3 + 25 + 4 \times 3 - 10]$

$= [8 - 7 \times 5 + 25 + 4 \times 3 - 10]$

$= [8 - 35 + 25 + 12 - 10]$

$= [45 - 35 - 10]$

$= 45 - 45 = 0$

149. (a) Speed of car = 60 km/h

Distance cvered by car in 180 min (3 h) $= 60 \times 3 = 180$ km

Time taken $= \frac{180}{40}$ h

$= 4.5\text{ h} = 4\text{ h } 30\text{ min}$

150. (b) Let the length of 1st rectangular sheet be 60 cm and breadth of 1st rectangular sheet be 36 cm.

Volume of cylinder (made by rolling along length) $= \pi r^2 h$

$V_1 = \pi\left(\frac{60}{2\pi}\right)^2 \times 36$

$V_1 = \frac{3600}{4\pi} \times 36$

$V_1 = \frac{9 \times 3600}{\pi}\text{ cm}^3$

Similarly volume of cylinder (made by rolling along breadth) $= \pi r^2 h$

$V_2 = \pi\left(\frac{36}{2\pi}\right)^2 \times 60$

$V_2 = \frac{36 \times 36 \times 15}{\pi}\text{ cm}^3$

$\therefore$ Ratio of volumes $= \frac{V_1}{V_2}$

$= \frac{9 \times 3600}{\pi} \times \frac{\pi}{36 \times 36 \times 15}$

$\therefore \quad \frac{V_1}{V_2} = \frac{5}{3}$

$\therefore \; V_1 : V_2 = 5 : 3$

151. (d) The correct antonym for 'sufficiency' is 'dearth'. So in the given sentence, the new government allowed corrupt ministers to feel the lack of money by banning the specific currency.

152. (d) The most suitable replacement for 'kith and kin' in the sentence would be 'blood relatives'.

153. (d) The term 'diffidence' serves as a one word substitute for 'modesty or shyness resulting from a lack of self-confidence'. It describes a lack of assertiveness due to insecurity or self-doubt.

154. (c) The given option makes the sentence grammatically correct reposition 'of' connects the two words 'flavour' and 'ice-cream' showing the relationship between them.

155. (b) The error is in the phrase 'Centre for Policy Research estimate.' The subject 'Centre for Policy Research' is singular, so the verb should be in the singular form.

Therefore, it should be 'Centre for Policy Research estimates that India has the largest stock of iron-ore in the world'.

156. (d) The original sentence 'The serenity of the river was a sight to behold' is already meaningful.

However, the most appropriate option to substitute the highlighted words is option (d). This choice maintains the intended meaning and improves the sentence.

157. (d) The word 'pompous' means self-important or arrogant, which does not fit the context of a million-dollar wedding.

The most appropriate synonym for 'pompous' in this context is 'pretentious.

So, the sentence would read 'Her million-dollar wedding was a pretentious display of wealth.'

158. (a) The grammatical error is in the phrase 'was first man'. It should be 'was the first man'. Therefore, the correct answer is option (a).

159. (d) The original sentence lacks a parallel structure. The second phrase 'and a crucial starting point' is missin a verb. Option (d) fixes this error.

160. (b) The spelling error is in the word 'redresed'. The correct spelling is 'redressed'.

161. (c) The error is in the phrase 'my uncle is'. It should be 'my uncle has been' to indicate an action that started in the past and continues into the present.

162. (c) The idiom 'Back to back' means something follows immediately after something else.

163. (d) The idiom 'Spill the beans' means to expose a secret.

164. (b) The spelling error in the sentence 'She is going to resiev a package in the mail today' is the word 'resiev'. The correct spelling is 'receive'.

165. (d) The antonym for the word 'dishearten' is 'encouraged'.

166. (a) The incorrectly spelled word is 'Interogative' The correct spelling is 'Interrogative'.

167. (c) The underlined word 'embraced' means held closely or hugged warmly. 'Contained' is the best opposite as it means hold back or not showing affection openly.

168. (c) The most appropriate synonym for the word 'Destitute' is 'Broke'. The word 'destitute' means extremely poor or having no money. 'Broke' means the same as 'destitute'.

169. (c) The incorrectly spelled word is 'assasination'. The correct spelling is 'assassination'.

170. (b) The error is in the phrase 'times the day'. It should be 'four times a day' to indicate frequency.

171. (c) The word 'prudent' means showing good judgement and being cautious. The most appropriate synonym for it is 'judicious'. It means showing good judgement or being wise.

172. (a) The idiom 'Up the ante' means to increase the stakes or level of risk. It is often used in contexts related to gambling or negotiations.

173. (b) The word 'sarcastic' refers to using irony or mocking humour. The antonym for this would be 'courteous'. It means polite, respectful and showing manners.

174. (c) The misspelt word in the sentence is 'charesma'. The correct spelling is 'charisma'.

175. (d) The phrase 'crocodile tears' refers to insincere or fake display of emotion. It is often used to describe someone pretending to be upset or sympathetic.

176. (b) The sentence mentions 'a male dog and female dog' which is incorrect. Male dog is called 'dog' and its female is called 'bitch'.

177. (c) The word 'hysterics' refers to extreme emotional reactions, often involving uncontrollable laughter or crying. The antonym for this would be 'calm'.

178. (d) The most appropriate option to substitute the underlined segment is 'hometown was'. This maintains the correct tense and makes the sentence grammatically accurate.

179. (c) The segment that contains a grammatical error in the sentence is 'carried minimum'. The correct phrase should be 'carry minimum' to indicate a specific amount of luggage.

180. (d) The incorrectly spelled word is 'Addmission'. The correct spelling is 'Admission'.

181. (c) The phrase 'cat's in the cradle' is often used to refer to situations in which one person doesn't make enough time for the other. It describes a relationship where someone neglects another.

182. (b) The word 'disguises' means to change appearance or behaviour to avoid detection. The most appropriate synonym for this is 'camouflages'.

183. (c) 'Inspite mother's milk' is incorrect and it should be replaced by a subordinating conjunction 'Though'.

184. (b) The underlined phrase means a solution or cure for a problem. The most appropriate one word substitute for this is 'panacea'.

185. (c) A person who is a lover of women is called a 'philogynist'.

186. (a) A person who is critical of the motives of others is called a 'cynic'

187. (a) The idiom 'thinks outside the box' means to approach problems or tasks in an unconventional or creative way.

188. (d) The word 'fastly' is incorrect, it should be 'fast'.

189. (a) The idiom 'bite off more than I can chew' means to take on more responsibilities or tasks than one can handle.

190. (a) The idiom 'make waves' means to cause difficulty or create a disturbance.

191. (c) The correct option to fill blank no. 1 is 'offers'.

192. (c) The correct option to fill blank no. 2 is 'explore'.

193. (c) The correct option to fill blank no. 3 is 'platform'.

194. (c) The correct option to fill biank no. 4 is 'cultivates'.

195. (b) The correct option to fill blank no. 5 is 'becomes'.

196. (c) Biofuels are not made from coal. The correct answer is option (c).

197. (d) Major airline companies have pledged to reach net-zero carbon emissions by mid-century to fight climate change.

198. (d) The most suitable word from the passage that means 'empirical' is 'Enormous'.

199. (d) The tone of the speaker in the passage is hopeful.

200. (d) The most suitable title for the passage is 'One Good Turn from the Aviation Industry'.

CPO SI P-1 SP 02

PAPER-1

SSC CPO SI SOLVED PAPER

29 June 2024 (Shift II)

Instructions

1. This paper contains 200 questions.
2. It has 4 Parts, **Part I** General Intelligence and Reasoning, **Part II** General Knowledge and General Awareness, **Part III** Quantitative Aptitude and **Part IV** English Comprehension.
3. Each question carries **1 marks.**

MM : 200 **Time :** 2 hr

Part I

General Intelligence and Reasoning

1. From his office, Mukesh went 12 km straight. Then, he turned 45° right and covered 8 km. From here he turned left and travelled 7 km and finally turning left he covered 11 km. If he was going North-West at last, then in which direction did he start from his office?

(a) East (b) South
(c) West (d) North

2. Which of the following numbers will replace the question mark (?) in the given series?

46, ?, 81, 100, 120, 141

(a) 59 (b) 61
(c) 63 (d) 66

3. Identify the figure given in the options, which when put in place of '?' will logically complete the series.

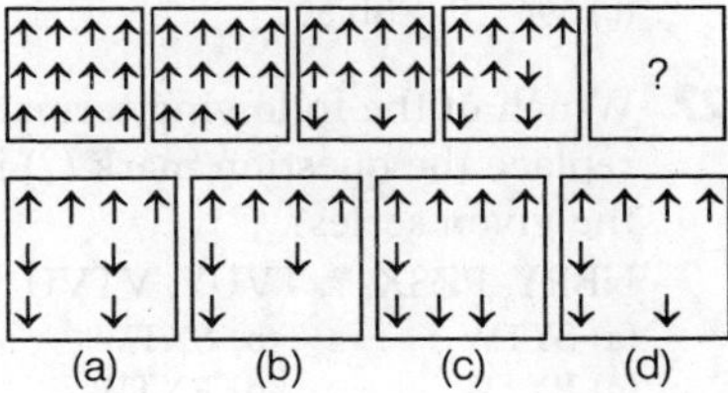

4. Which of the following terms will replace the question mark (?) in the given series?

GXMA, IVOY, KTQW, MRSU, ?

(a) OQVS (b) OQUT
(c) OPUS (d) OPVS

5. Which of the following numbers will replace the question mark (?) in the given series?

8, 9, 13, 22, ?

(a) 42 (b) 48 (c) 32 (d) 38

6. Select the option that represents the correct order of the given words as they would appear in an English dictionary.

1. Purposively 2. Pursuit
3. Purgatory 4. Purify
5. Purports 6. Purchased

(a) 6, 3, 1, 5, 4, 2 (b) 6, 3, 4, 5, 1, 2
(c) 4, 5, 3, 1, 6, 2 (d) 4, 5, 6, 3, 1, 2

7. A transparent sheet with a pattern is given below. Select the option that depicts the pattern that would appear, when the given transparent sheet is folded at the middle vertical line.

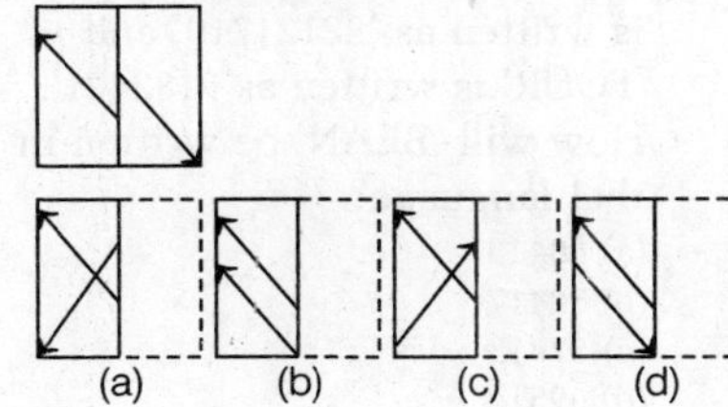

8. In a certain code language, 'FROM' is written as 'HSNK' and 'WAKE' is written as 'YBJC'. How will 'JUMP' be written in the given language?

(a) LVLN (b) LTKN
(c) MTKN (d) MULM

9. Which letter-cluster can replace the question mark (?) to complete the given series?

UBIG, PDKL, ?, FHOV, AJQA

(a) LEMR (b) JEMQ
(c) KEMR (d) KFMQ

10. A transparent sheet with a pattern is given below. Select the option that depicts the pattern that would appear, when the given transparent sheet is folded at the middle vertical line.

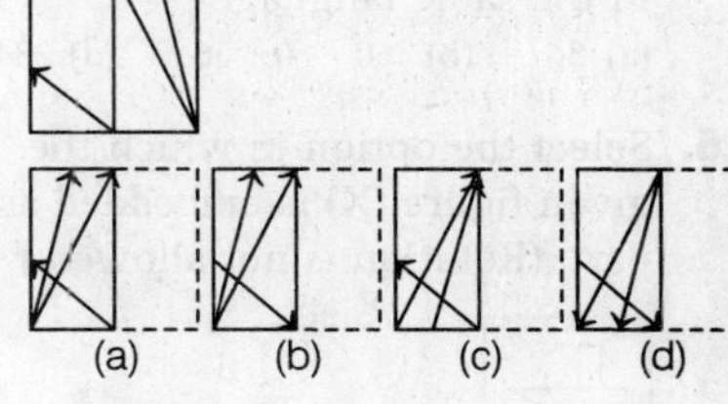

11. What will come in place of the question mark (?), when + and − are interchanged?

$8 - 3 \times 4 + 16 \div 2 = ?$

(a) 12 (b) 11
(c) 10 (d) 14

12. Select the option that is related to the fifth term in the same way as the second term is related to the first term and the fourth term is related to the third term.

DRIVE : RDEVI :: STOCK : TSKCO :: MOULD : ?

(a) OMDLU (b) MODLU
(c) OMULD (d) OMLUD

13. Select the Venn-diagram that best illustrates the relationship between the following classes.

Animals, Lions, Jackals

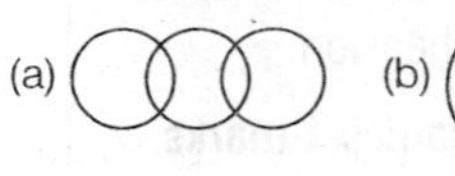

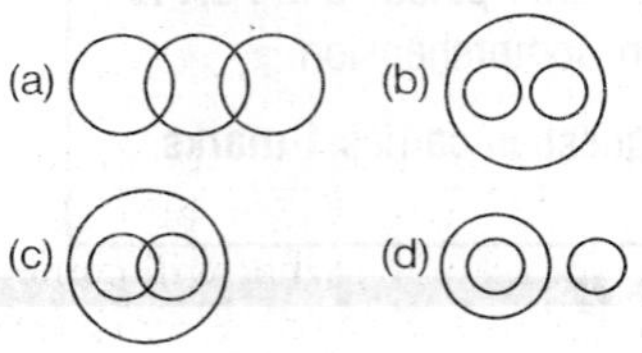

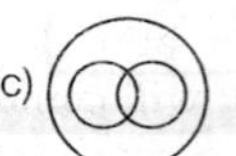

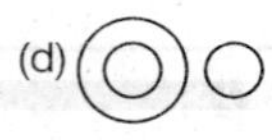

14. Select the set in which the numbers are related in the same way as are the numbers of the following sets.

(**Note** Operations should be performed on the whole numbers, without breaking down the numbers into its constituent digits. e.g. 13 – Operations on 13 such as adding /subtracting /multiplying etc. to 13 can be performed. Breaking down 13 into 1 and 3 and then performing mathematical operations on 1 and 3 is not allowed.)

(84, 28, 4)

(147, 49, 7)

(a) (231, 77, 11) (b) (231, 77, 13)
(c) (241, 77, 11) (d) (231, 67, 11)

15. In a code language, 'COOL' is coded as '180' and 'MAN' is coded as '84'. How will 'QUIET' be coded in the same language?

(a) 36 (b) 360 (c) 56 (d) 284

16. Select the option in which the given figure (X) is embedded as its part. (Rotation is not allowed.)

(X)

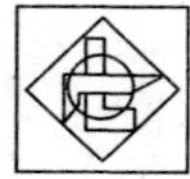

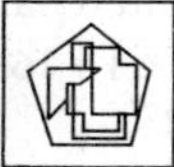

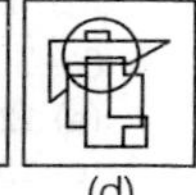

(a) (b) (c) (d)

17. If 'A' stands for '÷', 'B' stands for '×', 'C' stands for '+' and 'D' stands for '–', what will come in place of the question mark (?) in the following equation?

96 A 4 D 5 B 7 C 20 = ?

(a) 9 (b) 2
(c) 4 (d) 7

18. Select the set in which the numbers are related in the same way as are the numbers of the following sets.

(**Note** Operations should be performed on the whole numbers, without breaking down the numbers into its constituent digits. e.g. 13 – Operations on 13 such as adding /subtracting /multiplying etc. to 13 can be performed. Breaking down 13 into 1 and 3 and then performing mathematical operations on 1 and 3 is not allowed.)

(21, 63, 378)

(23, 69, 414)

(a) (26, 81, 486)
(b) (27, 81, 486)
(c) (27, 80, 486)
(d) (27, 81, 476)

19. In the given question figure, three of the following four letter-clusters are alike in a certain way and thus form a group. Which letter-cluster does not belong to that group?

(**Note** The odd letter-cluster is not based on the number of consonants/vowels or their position in the letter-cluster.)

(a) SWT (b) QUS
(c) OSP (d) UYV

20. Which of the following numbers will replace the question mark (?) in the given series?

101, 103, 107, 109, ?, 127, 131, 137

(a) 125 (b) 111
(c) 123 (d) 113

21. In a certain code language, 'SING' is written as '22121710' and 'FOUR' is written as '9182421'. How will 'BEAN' be written in that language?

(a) 68418
(b) 58417
(c) 57413
(d) 69516

22. Select the option that is related to the third word in the same way as the second word is related to the first word. (The words must be considered as meaningful English words and must not be related to each other based on the number of letters/number of consonants/vowels in the word.)

Conchology : Shells :: Paleonology :?

(a) Metals (b) Fossils
(c) Planets (d) Soil

23. Select the correct mirror image of the given figure, when the mirror is placed at MN as shown below.

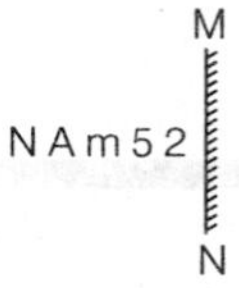

M

N A m 5 2

N

(a) Ƨ ɘ m A И (b) 5 2 m A И
(c) Ƨ ꙅ m ∀ N (d) Ƨ ɘ ɯ A И

24. 9 is related to 90 following a certain logic. Following the same logic, 12 is related to 156. Which of the following numbers is related to 72 using the same logic?

(a) 6 (b) 9
(c) 7 (d) 8

25. In a certain code language,

'A × B' means 'A is the son of B',
'A – B' means 'A is the brother of B',
'A + B' means 'A is the wife of B',
'A % B' means 'A is the father of B'.

How is M related to T if 'M + N – P × S % T' ?

(a) Mother's brother's daughter
(b) Brother's wife
(c) Father's brother's son's wife
(d) Wife's sister

26. What will come in place of the question mark (?) in the following equation, if '+' and '–' are interchanged and '×' and '÷' are interchanged?

$76 \div 6 + 18 \times 6 - 49 = ?$

(a) 524 (b) 569
(c) 596 (d) 502

27. Which of the following terms will replace the question mark (?) in the given series?

NBRY, PZSX, ?, TVUV, VTVU

(a) SYTW (b) SXTW
(c) RYTW (d) RXTW

28. Select the figure from among the given options that can logically replace the question mark (?) in the following series.

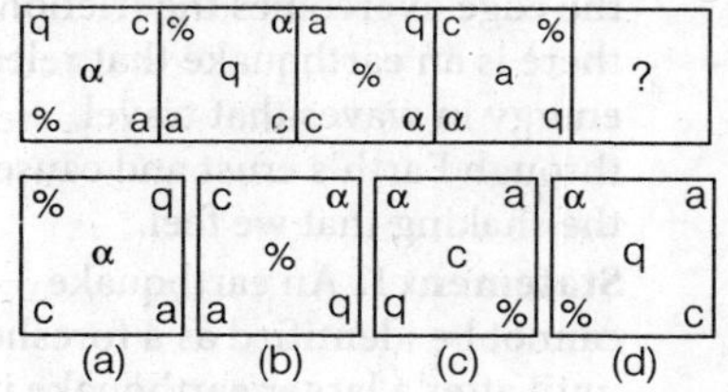

29. Select the set in which the numbers are related in the same way as are the numbers of the given sets.
(**Note** Operations should be performed on the whole numbers, without breaking down the numbers into its constituent digits. e.g. 13 – Operations on 13 such as adding/subtracting/multiplying, etc. to 13 can be performed. Breaking down 13 into 1 and 3 and then performing mathematical operations on 1 and 3 is not allowed.)
(18, 3, 9)
(36, 6, 18)
(a) (72, 13, 36) (b) (78, 13, 39)
(c) (72, 14, 39) (d) (78, 14, 39)

30. If + means –, – means ÷, × means + and ÷ means ×, what will be the value of the following expression?
$16 \times 9 + 5 \div 4 - 2 = ?$
(a) 20 (b) 15
(c) 40 (d) 35

31. In a code language, 'CRAB' is written as 'YTWD' and 'CALM' is written as 'YCHO'. How will 'ZOOM' be written in that language?
(a) VKOQ (b) KVOQ
(c) KOVQ (d) VQKO

32. Select the Venn-diagram that best illustrates the relationship between the following classes.
Furniture, Chair, Table

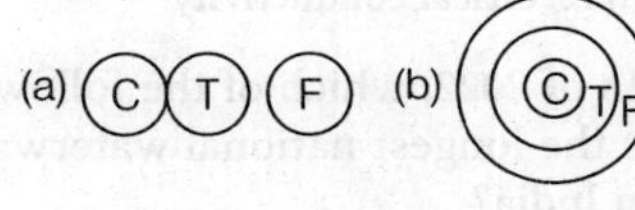

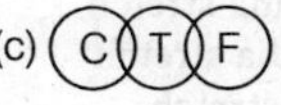

33. Select the correct mirror image of the given figure, when the mirror is placed at MN as shown below.

M
E % y 9 5 A
N

(a) ∀ ƨ ɘ ʎ % E (b) A ƨ ɘ ʎ % Ǝ
(c) ∀ ƨ ɘ ʎ % Ǝ (d) ∀ S 6 ʎ % Ǝ

34. In a code language, 'BEST' is written as 'GKXZ' and 'EDGE' is written as 'JJLK'. How will 'WIND' be written in that language?
(a) BOSJ (b) SJBO
(c) BSJO (d) JSOB

35. A, B, C, D, E and F are sitting around a circular table facing the centre. Only two people sit between A and F. Only one person sits between F and E. C sits to the immediate left of D. C is not an immediate neighbour of A. Who is sitting to the immediate left of F?
(a) E (b) A
(c) D (d) B

36. Select the number from among the given options that can replace the question mark(?) in the following series.
228, 209, 192, 179, 168, ?
(a) 162 (b) 160
(c) 165 (d) 161

37. Three different positions of the same dice are shown below. Find the number on the face opposite to the face showing '1'.

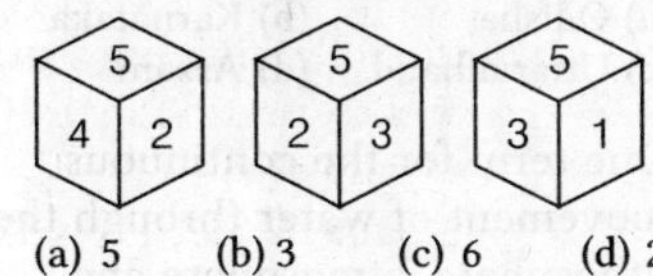

(a) 5 (b) 3 (c) 6 (d) 2

38. Point B is 35 m to the East of point A. Point C is 26 m to the North of point A. Point C is 15 m to the West of point D. Point E is 13 m to the South of point D. Point F is 20 m to the East of point E. In which direction is Point B with respect to point F?
(a) South (b) South-East
(c) West (d) North-West

39. Which two signs should be interchanged to make the given equation correct?
$7 \div 255 + 5 \times 3 - 20 = 140$
(a) – and ÷
(b) + and ÷
(c) × and +
(d) + and –

40. In a certain code language, 'BEDROOM' is written as '28' and 'MOON' is written as '16'.How will 'CHAIN' be written in that language?
(a) 20 (b) 26
(c) 24 (d) 23

41. If 'A' stands for '+', 'B' stands for '–', 'C' stands for '×' and 'D' stands for '÷', what will come in place of the question mark (?) in the following equation?
80 B 12 C 5 A 27 D 9 = ?
(a) 19 (b) 25
(c) 23 (d) 27

42. Two statements are given followed by two Conclusions numbered I and II. Assuming the statements to be true, even if they seem to be at variance with commonly known facts, decide which of the conclusions logically follow(s) from the statements?

Statements
No plate is a bowl.
All plates are tumblers.

Conclusions
I. No tumbler is a plate.
II. Some tumblers are bowls.
(a) Only Conclusion I follows
(b) Only Conclusion II follows
(c) Either Conclusion I or II follows
(d) Neither Conclusion I nor II follows

43. Select the correct mirror image of the given figure, when the mirror is placed at MN as shown below.

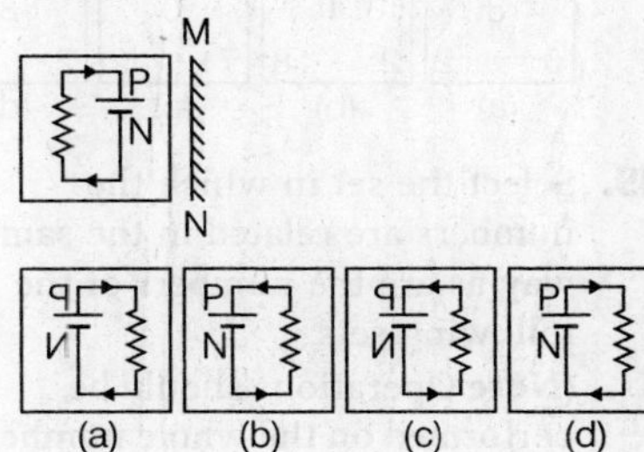

44. Select the correct mirror image of the given figure, when the mirror is placed at MN as shown below.

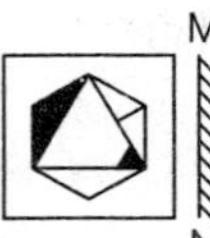

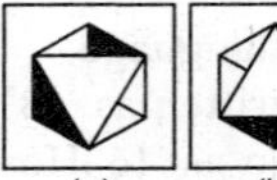
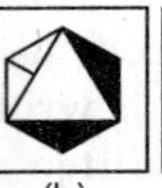
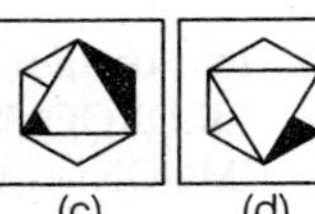

(a) (b) (c) (d)

45. What will come in the place of (?) in the following equation, if '+' and '–' are interchanged and also '×' and '÷' are interchanged?

$11 \div 12 - 78 \times 6 + 54 = ?$

(a) 104 (b) 91 (c) 86 (d) 99

46. Select the option that represents the correct order of the given words as they would appear in an English dictionary?

1. Unfaithful 2. Unfamiliar
3. Uneasiness 4. Undone
5. Understand 6. Undetermined

(a) 5, 6, 4, 3, 2, 1 (b) 5, 6, 4, 3, 1, 2
(c) 5, 6, 4, 2, 1, 3 (d) 5, 6, 1, 2, 4, 3

47. Select the Venn-diagram that represent the relation of following classes.

Mother, Actor, Women

(a) 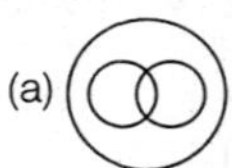 (b) 

(c) 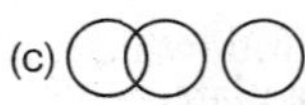 (d) 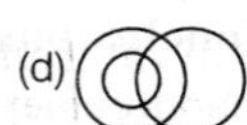

48. Identify the figure given in the options, which when put in place of the question mark(?) will logically complete the series.

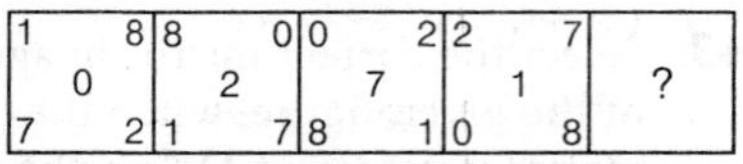

1 8 / 0 / 7 2	8 0 / 2 / 1 7	0 2 / 7 / 8 1	2 7 / 1 / 0 8	?

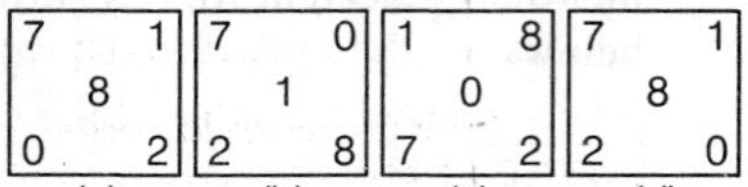

(a)	(b)	(c)	(d)
7 1 / 8 / 0 2	7 0 / 1 / 2 8	1 8 / 0 / 7 2	7 1 / 8 / 2 0

49. Select the set in which the numbers are related in the same way as are the numbers of the following sets.

(**Note** Operations should be performed on the whole numbers, without breaking down the numbers into its constituent digits. e.g. 13 – Operations on 13 such as adding /subtracting /multiplying etc. to 13 can be performed. Breaking down 13 into 1 and 3 and then performing mathematical operations on 1 and 3 is not allowed.)

(16, 20, 80)

(12, 16, 64)

(a) (20, 25, 100) (b) (18, 22, 88)
(c) (19, 23, 82) (d) (11, 15, 70)

50. In a certain code language,

A+ B means 'A is the mother of B'
A – B means 'A is the brother of B'
A × B means 'A is the wife of B'
A ÷ B means 'A is the father of B'

Based on the above, how is T related to Q, if 'P – Q + R – S ÷ T × U' ?

(a) Wife's sister
(b) Daughter's daughter
(c) Son's daughter
(d) Sister

Part II

General Knowledge and General Awareness

51. Which Union Territory has the lowest literacy rate, according to the Census of India 2011?

(a) Lakshadweep
(b) Dadra and Nagar Haveli
(c) Andaman and Nicobar Islands
(d) Delhi

52. Ugadi is celebrated primarily in which of the following states on the first day of the Chaitra month of the Hindu calendar?

(a) Odisha (b) Karnataka
(c) Uttarakhand (d) Assam

53. One term for the continuous movement of water through the lithosphere, atmosphere and hydrosphere is

(a) hydrological cycle
(b) hydro equilibrium cycle
(c) hydrostatical equilibrium
(d) water circulation

54. Which Article of the Indian Constitution mentions about the qualification for membership of the State Legislature?

(a) Article-173 (b) Article-179
(c) Article-171 (d) Article-180

55. Identify whether the given statements about an earthquake are correct or incorrect.

Statement I When the stress on the edge overcomes the friction, there is an earthquake that releases energy in waves that travel through Earth's crust and causes the shaking that we feel.

Statement II An earthquake cannot be identified as a foreshock until after a larger earthquake in the same area occurs.

(a) Both Statements I and II are incorrect
(b) Only Statement I is correct
(c) Only Statement II is correct
(d) Both Statements I and II are correct

56. Select the correct alternative on the basis of the statements given about 'Rasa'.

Statement I It is the aesthetic experience that one derives while enjoying an artistic presentation.

Statement II It deals with the creation of human sentiments in the spectator or the aesthete.

(a) Only Statement I is true.
(b) Neither Statement I nor Statement II is true.
(c) Only Statement II is true.
(d) Both Statement I and Statement II are true.

57. If tax rate decreases with increase in taxable base, then this type of taxation is called

(a) degressive (b) regressive
(c) progressive (d) increasing

58. Manyakheta or Malkhed was the capital of which of the following kingdoms?

(a) Shaka (b) Rashtrakuta
(c) Kushan (d) Satavahana

59. ...... is commonly represented by the Greek letter ρ (rho).

(a) Electrical resistivity
(b) Current
(c) Flow of charges
(d) Electrical conductivity

60. As of 2022, which of the following is the longest national waterway in India?

(a) Godavari-Krishna stretch
(b) Allahabad-Haldia stretch
(c) Sadiya-Dhubri stretch
(d) Kottapuram-Kollam stretch

61. In which district of Uttarakhand does the Ramganga river originates from the Dudhatoli ranges?
(a) Champawat (b) Chamoli
(c) Pauri Garhwal (d) Almora

62. Who among the following is not a vocalist?
(a) Pt. Kumar Gandharva
(b) Pt. Shivkumar Sharma
(c) Pt. Bhimsen Joshi
(d) Gangubai Hangal

63. Arrange the following battles fought during Mughal period in correct chronological order.
A. Battle of Khanwa
B. First Battle of Panipat
C. Battle of Ghaghra
D. Battle of Chausa
(a) A, C, B, D (b) D, A, B, C
(c) C, A, D, B (d) B, A, C, D

64. What kind of energy does a Yo-Yo have before it is released?
(a) Kinetic energy (b) Chemical energy
(c) Light energy (d) Potential energy

65. The book 'Godaan' was authored by ...... in 1936.
(a) Munshi Premchand
(b) Mulk Raj Anand
(c) Jawaharlal Nehru
(d) Mahatma Gandhi

66. ...... was the first fast bowler who was the Indian test team captain.
(a) Zaheer Khan
(b) Javagal Srinath
(c) Kapil Dev
(a) Jasprit Bumrah

67. Mohan Veena player Pandit Vishwa Mohan Bhatt won the Grammy Award in the year ....
(a) 1992 (b) 1990
(c) 1994 (d) 1996

68. 'Along The Red River: A Memoir' is a book about the life of ....
(a) Nirupama Borgohain
(b) Sabita Goswami
(c) Mitra Phukan
(d) Pushpalata Das

69. Which of the following leaders had gone to Lucknow to invite Mahatma Gandhi to see the plight of the peasants in Champaran?
(a) Raj Kumar Shukla
(b) Hasan Mohani
(c) JB Kripalani
(d) Rajendra Prasad

70. Garlic is good source of
(a) iron and copper
(b) manganese and selenium
(c) zinc and cobalt
(d) magnesium and aluminium

71. Montane forests have which of the following types of wildlife species?
(a) Sloth (b) Scorpion
(c) Yak (d) Snail

72. Which river originates South of the equator and flows North through North-Eastern Africa to drain into the Mediterranean Sea?
(a) Congo River (b) Nile River
(c) Amazon River (d) Lena River

73. Ashoka sent his son Mahendra and daughter Sanghamitta to spread the message of Dhamma to which of the following countries?
(a) Sri Lanka (b) Burma
(c) Afghanistan (d) China

74. Who has the power to make law and policies for the country, as per the Indian Constitution?
(a) Political pressure groups
(b) The Prime Minister
(c) Political parties
(d) The Parliament

75. Which article of the Indian Constitution deals with the Union Executive?
(a) Articles 38 to 50
(b) Articles 52 to 78
(c) Articles 80 to 86
(d) Articles 112 to 118

76. Name the white precipitate formed in the reaction of sodium sulphate and barium chloride.
(a) Barium hydroxide
(b) Barium sulphate
(c) Sodium chloride
(d) Sodium oxide

77. The minimum strength of the Council of Ministers in a state as per the Indian Constitution is ......
(a) 15 persons (b) 13 persons
(c) 12 persons (d) 14 persons

78. Which vitamin is involved in red blood cell formation, neurological function and DNA synthesis?
(a) Vitamin K (b) Vitamin B-7
(c) Vitamin E (d) Vitamin B-12

79. Bundu Khan was a ..... player of Delhi Gharana.
(a) sarangi (b) sarod
(c) flute (d) santoor

80. The International Olympic Committee was established in the year ....
(a) 1894 (b) 1892
(c) 1896 (d) 1890

81. What is the literacy rate in India as per the Census of 2011?
(a) 16.68% (b) 65.46%
(c) 82.14% (d) 72.98%

82. The RBI act provides for how many members in RBI Monetary Policy Committee (MPC)?
(a) 6 (b) 4
(c) 8 (d) 5

83. Growth, as envisaged in the Five-Year Plans, refers to
(a) improvement in the state of equity in the country.
(b) improvement in the level of education and primary health in the country.
(c) self-reliance in producing all goods and services it requires, within its geographical boundaries.
(d) increase in the country's capacity to produce the output of goods and services within the country.

84. What is the number of protons present in beryllium.
(a) 1 (b) 4
(c) 3 (d) 2

85. Who among the following founded the Ramakrishna Mission to carry on humanitarian and social work?
(a) Debendranath Tagore
(b) Swami Vivekananda
(c) Ishwar Chandra Vidyasagar
(d) Aurobindo Ghosh

86. Which of the following statements are correct in the context of the Indian Constitution?
1. There are three major organs of the government, namely Legislature, Executive and Judiciary.
2. A separation of functions rather than powers is followed.
3. All organs of the government are independent.
(a) 1, 2 and 3 (b) 1 and 3
(c) 1 and 2 (d) 2 and 3

87. Which festival is celebrated as the birth of Lord Krishna?
(a) Janmashtami
(b) Navratri
(c) Diwali
(d) Ganesh Chaturthi

88. Which of the following awards is not given in the field of dance and music?
(a) Kalidas Samman
(b) Sangeet Natak Akademi Award
(c) Dronacharya Award
(d) Mahari Award

89. Which wave oscillates parallel to the motion of the sound wave?
(a) Transverse wave
(b) Electromagnetic wave
(c) Mechanical wave
(d) Longitudinal wave

90. Sangeeta Majumdar was felicitated by Casa De La, Spain for her contribution to which of the following Indian Classical Dances?
(a) Kathak (b) Mohiniyattam
(c) Bharatanatyam (d) Kuchipudi

91. How many major ports are there in India for maritime transportation?
(a) 13 (b) 21 (c) 18 (d) 15

92. The ...... is/are given for outstanding performance in sports and games over a period of the previous four years and for showing qualities of leadership, sportsmanship and a sense of discipline.
(a) Arjuna Awards
(b) Rashtriya Khel Protsahan Puraskar
(c) Dronacharya Awards
(d) Maulana Abul Kalam Azad (MAKA) Trophy

93. Which of the following classical dance forms was initiated by Srimant Shankardev, a Vaishnava saint?
(a) Manipuri (b) Odissi
(c) Sattriya (d) Kathak

94. Which of the following was not one of the factors leading to the Economic Reforms in 1991?
(a) There was inflation in the economy.
(b) There was a fall in India's foreign reserves.
(c) There was a rise in the fiscal deficit of the country.
(d) There was stagflation in the economy.

95. Article 50 of the Constitution of India refers to the ....
(a) reservation of seats
(b) separation of judiciary from executive
(c) right to elementary education
(d) appointment of Governor

96. Which of the following foods generally increase blood pressure?
(a) Food with low salt and low sugar
(b) Food high in protein
(c) Food high in fibre
(d) Food high in salt, sugar and saturated or trans fats

97. How many members (elected and nominated) were there in the Council of State under the Government of India Act, 1919 passed by the Parliament of the United Kingdom to expand participation of Indians in the Government of India?
(a) 70 (b) 50
(c) 75 (d) 60

98. Who among the following was first female swimmer to win seven medals at a Single Olympics, in Tokyo Olympics, 2020?
(a) Kylie Masse (b) Mary Hanna
(c) Regan Smith (d) Emma McKeon

99. Which of the following phenomena is not related to the monsoon in India?
(a) Arabian Sea Branch
(b) Rainfall interval
(c) Cloud burst
(d) Western disturbance

100. Who among the following was awarded the Bharat Ratna for his contribution to the Green Revolution in India?
(a) APJ Abdul Kalam
(b) C. Subramaniam
(c) Govind Ballabh Pant
(d) PV Kane

Part III
Quantitative Aptitude

101. The value of

$$\frac{1}{2^2}+\frac{1}{2^3}\div\left(\frac{1}{2}+\frac{1}{2}\div 1\right)+3\frac{1}{3}\div\frac{5}{2}\times\frac{3}{4}\div 6\frac{2}{3}\times\frac{7}{6}\text{ is}$$

(a) $\frac{7}{40}$ (b) $\frac{21}{20}$ (c) $\frac{11}{20}$ (d) $\frac{11}{30}$

102. The population of a town increases annually by 20%. If the present population is 80 lakh, then what is the difference between the population 3 yr ago and 2 yr ago?
(a) 925925.93 (b) 85592.6
(c) 65592.6 (d) 75592.6

103. The height of a cylinder is 8 cm and its area of the base is 20 cm^2. Find its volume?
(a) 80 cm^3 (b) 180 cm^3
(c) 160 cm^3 (d) 100 cm^3

104. Rajan and Rajat can do a work in 64 days and 48 days, respectively. Starting with Rajat, they work on alternate days. In how many days will the work be completed?
(a) 55 (b) $54\frac{3}{4}$ (c) 54 (d) $55\frac{3}{4}$

105. The secant *CD* intersects the circle at *E* and *CF* is tangent to the circle at *F*. If the length of the secant *CD* is equal to 20 cm and the length of tangent *CF* is 15 cm, find the length of the chord *DE*.
(a) 8.75 cm (b) 11.25 cm
(c) 9.25 cm (d) 3.75 cm

106. Melting a metal ball of radius 3 units, 27 identical dice and a ball of radius 1 units are made. What is the side of dice?
(a) 1.7 units (b) 1.5 units
(c) 1.4 units (d) 1.6 units

107. Simplify the given expression.
$12.3-[7+0.8 \text{ of}(5.6-3.8\times 1.03)]$
(a) 1.2368 (b) 7.8539
(c) 5.2314 (d) 3.9512

108. If $\frac{5x+3y}{5x-3y}=\frac{7}{3}$, then find $x:y$.
(a) 2 : 3 (b) 5 : 3 (c) 3 : 2 (d) 3 : 5

109. A dishonest dealer sells an article at a 10% loss on the cost price, but uses a weight of 40 gm instead of 50 gm. What is his percentage of profit?
(a) 12.5% (b) 10.0% (c) 11.5% (d) 18.4%

110. The total percentage change in the volume of a cuboid if its length and breadth are decreased by 15% and 25%, respectively, while its height is increased by 60% is
(a) 5% decrease (b) 2% decrease
(c) 2% increase (d) 5% increase

111. If $x + \cfrac{1}{1 + \cfrac{1}{3 + \cfrac{1}{2}}} = 1$, then the value of x is equal to

(a) $\frac{2}{9}$ (b) $\frac{1}{7}$ (c) $\frac{7}{9}$ (d) $\frac{3}{7}$

112. A man rows 48 km and back in 48 h. He can row 4 km with the stream in the same time as 3 h against the stream. The speed of the stream (in km/h) is

(a) $\frac{7}{21}$ (b) $\frac{3}{29}$ (c) $\frac{5}{21}$ (d) $\frac{7}{24}$

113. The breadth of a rectangular lawn is decreased by 8% and its length is increased by 15%. Find the percentage change in the lawn area.

(a) 8.5% decrease (b) 8.5% increase
(c) 5.8%decrease (d) 5.8% increase

114. The inradius of triangle is 8 cm and the sum of the lengths of its sides is 125 cm. The area of the triangle (in cm^2) is

(a) 480 (b) 250 (c) 500 (d) 1000

115. If $\sin(x+y) = \cos\{3(x+y)\}$, then the value of $\cot\{2(x+y)\}$ is ......

(a) 2 (b) 1 (c) −1 (d) −2

116. The value of $\frac{2\cos 15° \sin 15°}{\cos^2 15° - \sin^2 15°}$ is

(a) $\frac{1}{\sqrt{3}}$ (b) $\sqrt{3}$ (c) $\frac{\sqrt{5}-1}{\sqrt{5}+1}$ (d) ∞

117. Study the given table and answer the question that follows. The table shows the production of five different types of cars by a company from 1989 to 1994.

Year → Type ↓	1989	1990	1991	1992	1993	1994	Total
P	8	20	16	17	21	6	88
Q	16	10	14	12	12	14	78
R	21	17	16	15	13	8	90
S	4	6	10	16	20	31	87
T	25	18	19	30	14	27	133
Total	74	71	75	90	80	86	476

Which type of car constituted 25% of the total production of all types of cars in 1993 ?

(a) R (b) Q (c) P (d) S

118. The value of $\frac{7 + 8 \times 8 \div 8 \text{ of } 8 + 8 \div 8 \times 5}{4 \div 4 \text{ of } 4 + 4 \times 4 \div 4 - 4 \div 4}$ is

(a) 4 (b) 3 (c) 2 (d) 1

119. The value of $\frac{(275 \times 275 \times 275 + 725 \times 725 \times 725)}{(275 \times 275 + 725 \times 725 - 725 \times 275)} \times \frac{(275 \times 275 \times 275 - 725 \times 725 \times 725)}{(275 \times 275 + 725 \times 725 + 725 \times 275)}$ is

(a) −45000 (b) 450000 (c) 45000 (d) −450000

120. If $x^2 + 4y^2 + 2x + 1 = 0$, then find the value of $x^{39} + y^{36}$.

(a) 1 (b) −1 (c) 2 (d) −2

121. The value of $(12 + 18) \div 2 - 11 + 16 \times 4 - 28 + 13(-18 + 15)$ is

(a) 3 (b) 0 (c) 1 (d) 2

122. A trader gives a 40% discount on his goods. Further, he gives 20% discount on the goods. Find the single discount equivalent to these two successive discounts.

(a) 30% (b) 60% (c) 50% (d) 52%

123. The area of a triangle is 486 cm^2 and its sides are in the ratio 3:4:5. The perimeter of the triangle is

(a) 108 cm (b) 308 cm (c) 218 cm (d) 105 cm

124. A drink is made by mixing water and juice in the ratio 9 : 7. If x L of water and $2x$ L of juice are mixed in 160 L of drink, then the new ratio becomes 13 : 15. The quantity of drink (in litres) is

(a) 240 (b) 280 (c) 300 (d) 260

125. Study the given table and answer the question that follows. The table shows the number of voters at three different centres A, B, C.

Centre	Total number of registered voters	Percentage of people who voted (Out of the total number of registered voters)
A	4600	78
B	5400	70
C	6500	85

Number of people who did not vote at centre B is what percentage more than those, who did not vote at centre C?

(a) $66\frac{3}{13}\%$ (b) $66\frac{1}{13}\%$
(c) $66\frac{2}{13}\%$ (d) $66\frac{5}{13}\%$

126. Simplify $\frac{\tan 71° + \tan 19°}{1 - \tan 71° \tan 19°}$.

(a) 0 (b) $\sqrt{3}$ (c) undefined (d) 1

127. The following table gives the number of males, females, educated males and educated females in a village over the years 2016-2020. Study the table carefully and answer the question.

Year / Number	2016	2017	2018	2019	2020
Males	1050	1200	1250	1300	1400
Females	900	1000	1020	1100	1200
Educated males	850	1000	1100	1150	1200
Educated females	600	820	950	980	1000

Find the percentage of the total number of educated females to the total number of females over all the years.

(a) 0.9233 (b) 0.8623
(c) 0.8333 (d) 0.8923

128. Simplify $63 - [15 + \{17 - (9 - 7 + 1)\}]$.

(a) 44 (b) 40 (c) 34 (d) 30

129. The distance between two stations A and B is 800 km. A train covers the journey from A to B at a speed of 90 km/h and returns to A with a uniform speed of 65 km/h. Find the average speed of train during the whole journey (in km/h)?
(a) 75.48 (b) 70.45 (c) 82.36 (d) 80.50

130. Find the value of the following expression.
$(1+\tan\theta+\sec\theta)\times(1+\cot\theta-\text{cosec }\theta)$
(a) $\cos\theta\sin\theta$ (b) 1 (c) 2 (d) $\tan\theta$

131. Study the given pie-graph and answer the question that follows. In a certain company, allocations to various sectors of the yearly budget per ₹ 7200 crores are represented by this pie-diagram.

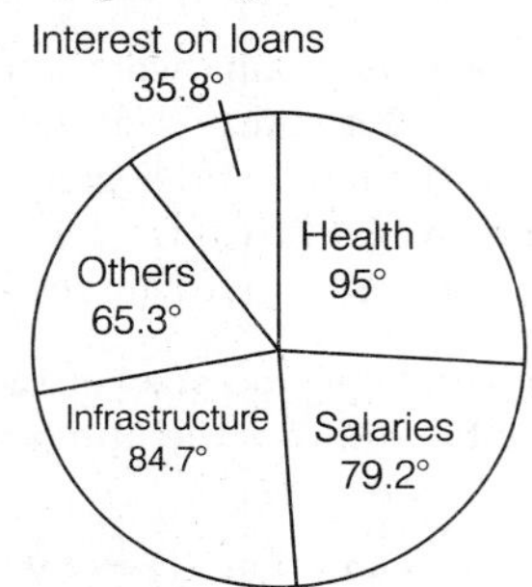

The expenditure (in ₹) on infrastructure is
(a) ₹ 6098 crores (b) ₹ 1649 crores
(c) ₹ 6089 crores (d) ₹ 1694 crores

132. The following table shows the shares traded on Mumbai, Rajasthan, Uttar Pradesh and Uttarakhand stock exchanges.

	Mumbai		Uttarakhand		Rajasthan		Uttar Pradesh	
Name of the compny	High	Low	High	Low	High	Low	High	Low
Aata Tea	540	395	450	4255	320	510	440	310
Kolgate	34	57	60	42	25	60	20	70
Jumbuja Cement	150	155	120	125	160	135	145	170

For Jumbuja cement, the ratio of the high rate of share to the low rate is maximum in the stock exchange at
(a) Rajasthan (b) Mumbai
(c) Uttar Pradesh (d) Uttarakahand

133. 18 students of a class took part in a quiz. If the number of girls is 8 more than the number of boys, find the product of the number of boys and girls.
(a) 63 (b)36 (c) 56 (d) 65

134. If $a+b+c=13$ and $ab+bc+ca=22$, then the value of $a^3+b^3+c^3-3abc$ is ....
(a) 1225 (b) 1625 (c) 1339 (d) 1911

135. A hostel had food provision for 300 students for a month. After 20 days, 50 students left the hostel. How long would the remaining food last? (1 month = 30 days)
(a) 14 days (b) 12 days (c) 10 days (d) 16 days

136. A person bought two buffaloes for ₹ 11520. One is sold at a loss of 15% and the other is sold at a gain of 19%. If the selling price of both buffaloes is equal, find the cost price of the first one.
(a) ₹ 6700 (b) ₹ 6720 (c) ₹ 6710 (d) ₹ 6715

137. If the simple interest on a certain sum of money for 20 months at the rate of 19.2% per annum exceeds the simple interest on the same sum for 15 months at the rate of 11.2% per annun by ₹ 2920, then what is the sum (in ₹ to the nearest hundreds)?
(a) 16620 (b) 12660 (c) 16660 (d) 16200

138. Find the surface area (in m^2) of a cuboid that is 11 m long, 7 m broad and 4 m high.
(a) 249 (b) 289 (c) 298 (d) 320

139. The following table shows the Gross Turnover (in crores) of a company over 5 yr.

Year	Gross Turnover
2015	13
2016	20
2017	15
2018	23
2019	25

The Gross Turnover for 2017 is what per cent of the Gross Turnover for 2019 ?
(a) 16 (b) 60 (c) 6 (d) 0.06

140. Find the volume (in cm^3) of a hemisphere of radius 18 cm. (Use, $\pi=\frac{22}{7}$) (Rounded off to two decimal places.)
(a) 12200.43 (b) 12219.43 (c) 18750.23 (d) 11250.25

141. A 234 m long train passes a person running at 9 km/h in the opposite direction, in 6 sec. In how much time (in sec) will it pass another person, who is moving at 23.4 km/h, in the same direction?
(a) 7.8 (b) 7.2 (c) 8 (d) 8.4

142. The speed of a boat, when travelling downstream is 33 km/h, whereas when travelling upstream it is 27 km/h. What is the speed of the boat in still water?
(a) 30 km/h (b) 60 km/h
(c) 12 km/h (d) 6 km/h

143. Swati earns a sum of ₹ 40000, out of which she saves 25%. She spends the remaining amount on food and education in the ratio of 3 : 2. What is the percentage of expenditure incurred on education to her total income?
(a) 30% (b) 60% (c) 40% (d) 20%

144. What is the area of the sector of a circle, whose radius is 35 cm and whose arc subtends an angle of 72° at the centre of the circle? $\left(\text{Use, } \pi=\frac{22}{7}\right)$
(a) 770 cm^2 (b) 610 cm^2 (c) 810 cm^2 (d) 970 cm^2

145. Simplify; $27 \div 4$ of $6 \times [16 \div 8 \times (12-8)] - (14 \div 7 \times 28)$
(a) 62 (b) –51
(c) –47 (d) 27

146. Taking any three of the line segments out of segments of length 2 cm, 5 cm, 7 cm and 8 cm, the number of triangles that can be formed is
(a) 1 (b) 3
(c) 4 (d) 2

147. The value of
$264 \div 8 - 1 - 32 \times 2 + 80 \div 5 \times 40 \div 20$ is
(a) 0 (b) 1
(c) 3 (d) 2

148. Study the given table and answer the question that follows.
The table shows the yearly production (in thousand) of scooters in five different factories (P, Q, R, S and T) from 1985 to 1989.
Yearly production (in thousand) of scooters in different factories.

Factory	1985	1986	1987	1988	1989
P	20	15	24	13	17
Q	16	23	41	20	15
R	14	21	30	16	12
S	25	17	15	12	22
T	40	32	39	41	35
Total	115	108	149	102	101

The ratio of the production of scooters by factory P to that by factory T in 1985 is
(a) 3 : 2 (b) 1 : 2
(c) 2 : 3 (d) 2 : 1

149. The marked price of an immersion rod in an electronic store is ₹ 900. The store offers a discount of 12% on its sale. At what price (in ₹) can a customer buy, it from the electronic store?
(a) 782 (b) 797
(c) 787 (d) 792

150. Sapna is double efficient as compared to Rakesh. If they both work together on a project and complete it in 48 days, then the number of days in which Sapna alone can complete the project is
(a) 68 (b) 72
(c) 52 (d) $69\frac{1}{2}$

Part IV

English Comprehension

151. Select the most appropriate antonym of the underlined word in the following sentence.
The teacher praised the student for his <u>diligent</u> work and consistent effort.
(a) Frazzle (b) Persistent
(c) Lazy (d) Squander

152. Select the most appropriate synonym of the underlined word.
will <u>strive</u> to win the race.
(a) trouble (b) Support
(c) Assume (d) Attempt

153. Select the most appropriate antonym of the given word.
Pitiable
(a) Eradicate (b) Pleasant
(c) Grievous (d) Aggregate

154. Identify from the given options the word which is similar in meaning to the following word.
Efface
(a) Hidden (b) Makeup
(c) Daily (d) Destroy

155. Select the most appropriate synonym of the underlined word.
I was <u>astonished</u> to know the truth.
(a) Stunned (b) Awesome
(c) Blindsided (d) Sickened

156. When our principal said she was leaving the company, <u>I played out the opportunity</u> to fill the job.
(a) glided at the opportunity
(b) jumped at the opportunity
(c) started at the opportunity
(d) ran to the opportunity

157. The following sentence has been split into four segments. Identify the segment that contains a grammatical/spelling error.
The sons of the old farmer / fell off after their father / breathed his last / in the village.
(a) in the village.
(b) breathed his last
(c) The sons of the old farmer
(d) fell off after their father

158. Select the most appropriate option with correct usage of the preposition to substitute the underlined segment in the given sentence.
<u>The core part in Artificial Intelligence (AI)</u> is knowledge engineering, machine learning, machine perception and robotics.
(a) The core part on Artificial Intelligence
(b) The core part of Artificial Intelligence
(c) The core part from Artificial Intelligence
(d) The core part with Artificial Intelligence

159. Select the most appropriate antonym of the given word.
Quaint
(a) Brisk
(b) Ridiculous
(c) Ordinary
(d) Distinct

160. Select the sentence that has the correct use of words and spellings from the options given below.
(a) The profesional athlete pushed her body to the limit, surpassing all expectations and acheiving a new personal record.
(b) The profesional athlete pushed her body to the limit, surpasing all expectasions and achieving a new personal record.
(c) The professional athlete pushed her body to the limit, surpasing all expectations and acheving a new personal record.
(d) The professional athlete pushed her body to the limit, surpassing all expectations and achieving a new personal record.

161. Select the most appropriate antonym of the given word.
Languid
(a) Exceptional
(b) Lazy
(c) Loyal
(d) Energetic

162. Select the most appropriate meaning of the idiom in the given sentence.
She's feeling <u>under the weather</u> today.
(a) She's feeling happy and energetic.
(b) She's feeling adventurous and ready for a challenge.
(c) She's feeling worried about something.
(d) She's not feeling well or is a bit sick.

163. Select the option that can be used as a one-word substitute for the given group of words.
Madness or obsession with males
(a) Polygamy (b) Loquacious
(c) Misandrist (d) Andromania

164. Select the incorrectly spelt word.
(a) Assimilation (b) Pluckiness
(c) Accumulation (d) Exestenalism

165. Select the most appropriate option that can substitute the underlined segment in the given sentence. If no substitution is required, select 'No substitution'.
Not a word didnt they speak to the others about the sad turn of events.
(a) did they speak
(b) No substitution
(c) do they speak
(d) had they speak

166. Select the most appropriate meaning of the given idiom.
A vicious cycle
(a) a situation in which one problem causes another one, making the original problem impossible to solve.
(b) a situation in which one problem causes another one, making the first one easy to solve.
(c) a situation in which one problem creates another one, making the original problem easy to forget.
(d) a situation in which several problems merge and become one extremely complex problem.

167. The following sentence has been divided into parts. One of them may contain an error.
Select the part that contains the error from the given options. If you don't find any error, mark 'No error' as your answer.
I had done/my cooking when/ Vishnu came to see me.
(a) No error
(b) I had done
(c) Vishnu came to see me
(d) my cooking when

168. Select the option that can be used as a one-word substitute for the given group of words.
A mythological animal with one horn on its forehead.
(a) Unicameral
(b) Unipod
(c) Unific
(d) Unicorn

169. Select the most appropriate segment to substitute the underlined words in the given sentence.
Mr. Patel is likely to win the elections in the sweeping majority.
(a) elections by a sweeping majority
(b) elections on a sweeping majority
(c) elections of a sweeping majority
(d) elections at a sweeping majority

170. Select the option that can be used as a one-word substitute for the given group of words.
One who does not express himself freely.
(a) Approachable (b) Immodest
(c) Introvert (d) Outgoing

171. Select the most appropriate meaning of the given idiom.
The best of both worlds
(a) Everyone gets a chance
(b) Stay strong in a difficult situation
(c) Do a perfectly good job
(d) Good in every way

172. Select the most appropriate idiom that can substitute the underlined words in the given sentence.
I have been living without a lot of money since I lost my job.
(a) receiving a kickback
(b) living hand to mouth
(c) keeping my chin up
(d) as genuine as a three-dollar bill

173. Identify the incorrect spelt word in the given sentence.
Thousands of years ago, great masters of Ayurveda, notebly Sushrut and Charaka, discussed in detail the use of spices for culinary and medical purpose.
(a) parpose (b) notably
(c) discused (d) cullinary

174. Identify the incorrectly spelt word in the given sentence and select the option that rectifies the spelling error.
The veteran footballer was expected for reach here by 10 o clock, the notice said.
(a) expected on reach here
(b) expected to reach here
(c) expected of reach here
(d) expected by reach here

175. The boys seem irresponsibly insaucient about bullying the juniors.
(a) insoucient (b) insuociant
(c) insouciant (d) insouceant

176. Underlined word in the sentence is not spelt correctly. Identify the correct spelling from the options given below.
'At the last hour'
(a) half (b) eleventh (c) sixth (d) twelfth

177. Select the most appropriate option that can substitute the underlined word in the given idiom.
The Sumo wrestler seemed to be incapable in being tired.
(a) incapable of being tired
(b) incapable from being tired
(c) incapable to being tired
(d) incapable by being tired

178. Select the most appropriate option that can substitute the underlined segment in the given sentence.
Ratul's capability of being able to speak two languages is apt for this post.
(a) bilingual (b) bicultural
(c) bidialectical (d) lingual

179. There are four tributaries / of Ganga and it / is ranked as the fifth / most polluted river of the world.
(a) is ranked as the fifth
(b) of Ganga and it
(c) There are four tributaries
(d) most polluted river of the world

180. Select the most appropriate meaning of the given idiom.
Bite the bullet
(a) To avoid a situation
(b) To help someone achieve their goals
(c) To eat something unpleasant
(d) To face a difficult situation

181. Select the incorrectly spelt word in the given sentence.
Mount Vesuvius is a volcano that erapts hot ashes which fall from the sky like a blizzard.
(a) erapts (b) blizzard
(c) ashes (d) volcano

182. Select the most appropriate antonym of the given word.
Suspend
(a) Extend (b) Terminate
(c) Project (d) Resume

183. Select the word which means the same as the group of words underlined in the given sentence.
Today, a man who betrayed his own country in exchange for money was the topic of every news report.
(a) Gangster (b) Terrorist
(c) Traitor (d) Conman

184. Select the most appropriate meaning of the given idiom.
Beat around the bush
(a) To avoid talking about what is important
(b) To await an explanation
(c) To take on a task that is way too big
(d) To do something without any hesitation

185. The artists abstract painting was enigmatic to the viewers.
(a) Mysterious (b) Instigating
(c) Clear (d) Thrilling

186. Select the most appropriate meaning of the given idiom.
Through thick and thin
(a) Always supporting someone even if there are problems or difficulties
(b) Sometimes thin, sometimes thick
(c) Never giving up a friendship
(d) Never giving up on a goal

187. The road is too busy for elderly people that they cannot cross safely.
(a) that it is difficult to cross.
(b) to cross safely.
(c) that it cannot be crossed properly.
(d) that it is impossible for them to cross.

188. Rectify the sentence by selecting the correct spelling of the underline word from the option.
The baby smiled and laughed at the pickaboo game.
(a) peakaboo (b) pikaboo
(c) peekaboo (d) pekaboo

189. The given sentence is divided into four segments. Identify the segment that contains a grammatical error.
Had you been/working regularly/ you had completed/the project yesterday.
(a) Had you been
(b) the project yesterday
(c) you had completed
(d) working regularly

190. Select the most appropriate option that can substitute the underlined segment in the given sentence.
Before she began, she asked the teacher whether she write with a pen or a pencil.
(a) she can write (b) she wrote
(c) she should write (d) she did write.

Directions (Q. Nos. 191-195) *In the following passage, some words have been deleted. Read the passage carefully and select the most appropriate option to fill in each blank.*

Childhood is an important phase in a person's life. Children are free from worries, tensions and stresses so they lead a very .....(1)..... life. This is the only reason they create golden and beautiful memories during this period which are ......(2)...... in their adulthood. It is the responsibility of parents and guardians to shape the future of a child as he is very ......(3)...... and can drift in any direction. If they have made any mistakes, we should ......(4)...... them instead of misbehaving with them. How we have behaved with them will be ......(5)...... on their minds which will reflect in later stages.

191. Select the most appropriate option to fill in blank number 1.
(a) carefree (b) careful
(c) stressful (d) cautious

192. Select the most appropriate option to fill in blank number 2.
(a) cherished (b) blocked
(c) dumped (d) neglected

193. Select the most appropriate option to fill in blank number 3.
(a) mature (b) innocent
(c) crafty (d) guilty

194. Select the most appropriate option to fill in blank number 4.
(a) damage (b) create
(c) design (d) rectify

195. Select the most appropriate option to fill in blank number 5.
(a) published (b) bleached
(c) imprinted (d) coloured

Directions (Q. Nos. 196-200) *In the following passage, some words have been deleted. Read the passage carefully and select the most appropriate option to fill in each blank.*

Have you ever taken the time to stop and consider the dirt under your feet? Leonardo da Vinci said, "We know more about the movement of celestial bodies than about the soil underfoot." Yet, our very survival as humans - and life on this planet - is intimately linked with the health of a thin layer of soil enveloping the Earth.

Soil provides society with essential food, feed, fibre and raw materials, as well as being home to a quarter of the earths biodiversity. Soils are also the largest organic carbon reservoir on Earth and although highly dynamic, are very fragile. Chop a forest down and it might grow back in 50 years, but lose 10 cm of soil and get ready to wait 1,000 years to get it back. Without soil, our planet would be unrecognisable to us, and more like the barren and inhospitable surface of the Moon or Mars.

Until recently, we did not even know how deep the soil is below our feet. Like the best mysteries, a bit of digging is required for soils to be fully understood and for their history to be laid bare.

When they are visible, a range of questions arise. What does the variation in colour with depth mean? How much carbon is stored? Is the soil dense or light, damaged or healthy? Answering these questions is important, but presents a significant challenge and may require years of training.

196. Select the most suitable word from the passage which means difficult to stay or live in.
(a) Inhospitable (b) Dense
(c) Barren (d) Essential

197. How many years are required to renew the loss of 10 cm of soil?
(a) 1,00,000 (b) 1,000
(c) 100 (d) 10,000

198. What is the tone of the speaker?
(a) Derisive (b) Dogmatic
(c) Sarcastic (d) Alarming

199. Identify the most suitable title for the given passage.
(a) Moon and Mars Expedition
(b) Necessity of Mining
(c) The Uninhabitable Universe
(d) Mysteries Under Man's Feet

200. Mankind's survival, according to the passage, solely depends on
(a) inventions
(b) celestial bodies
(c) soil
(d) reproduction

Know Correct Answers

1. (a)	2. (c)	3. (a)	4. (c)	5. (d)	6. (b)	7. (a)	8. (a)	9. (d)	10. (a)
11. (a)	12. (a)	13. (b)	14. (a)	15. (b)	16. (a)	17. (a)	18. (b)	19. (b)	20. (d)
21. (b)	22. (b)	23. (a)	24. (d)	25. (b)	26. (d)	27. (d)	28. (c)	29. (b)	30. (b)
31. (d)	32. (d)	33. (b)	34. (a)	35. (d)	36. (d)	37. (d)	38. (a)	39. (b)	40. (a)
41. (c)	42. (d)	43. (c)	44. (c)	45. (b)	46. (b)	47. (d)	48. (d)	49. (b)	50. (c)
51. (b)	52. (b)	53. (a)	54. (a)	55. (d)	56. (d)	57. (b)	58. (b)	59. (a)	60. (b)
61. (c)	62. (b)	63. (d)	64. (d)	65. (a)	66. (c)	67. (c)	68. (b)	69. (a)	70. (b)
71. (c)	72. (b)	73. (a)	74. (d)	75. (b)	76. (b)	77. (c)	78. (d)	79. (a)	80. (a)
81. (d)	82. (a)	83. (d)	84. (b)	85. (b)	86. (c)	87. (a)	88. (c)	89. (d)	90. (a)
91. (a)	92. (a)	93. (c)	94. (d)	95. (b)	96. (d)	97. (d)	98. (d)	99. (d)	100. (b)
101. (c)	102. (a)	103. (c)	104. (b)	105. (a)	106. (d)	107. (d)	108. (c)	109. (a)	110. (c)
111. (a)	112. (d)	113. (d)	114. (c)	115. (b)	116. (a)	117. (d)	118. (a)	119. (d)	120. (b)
121. (c)	122. (d)	123. (a)	124. (b)	125. (c)	126. (c)	127 (c)	128. (c)	129. (a)	130. (c)
131. (d)	132. (a)	133. (d)	134. (c)	135. (b)	136. (b)	137 (d)	138. (c)	139. (b)	140. (b)
141. (a)	142. (a)	143. (a)	144. (a)	145. (c)	146. (d)	147. (a)	148. (b)	149. (d)	150. (b)
151. (c)	152. (d)	153. (b)	154. (d)	155. (a)	156. (b)	157. (d)	158. (b)	159. (c)	160. (d)
161. (d)	162. (d)	163. (d)	164. (d)	165. (a)	166. (a)	167. (a)	168. (d)	169. (a)	170. (c)
171. (d)	172. (b)	173. (b)	174. (b)	175. (c)	176. (b)	177. (a)	178. (a)	179. (b)	180. (d)
181. (a)	182. (d)	183. (c)	184. (a)	185. (c)	186. (a)	187. (b)	188. (c)	189. (c)	190. (c)
191. (a)	192. (a)	193. (b)	194. (d)	195. (c)	196. (a)	197. (b)	198. (d)	199. (d)	200. (c)

Answer & Solutions

1. (a) According to the question,

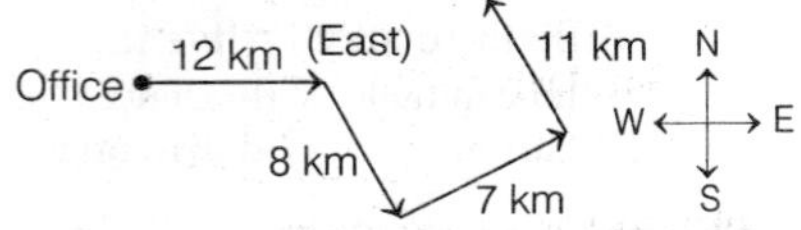

∴ He started from East direction from his office.

2. (c) Pattern of the series is as follows,

46 [63] 81 100 120 141

+17 +18 +19 +20 +21

3. (a) In the given figure series, one arrow is removed and second arrow moves 180° in the box. Hence, option (a) will replace the question mark (?) in the given series.

4. (c) Pattern of the series is as follows,

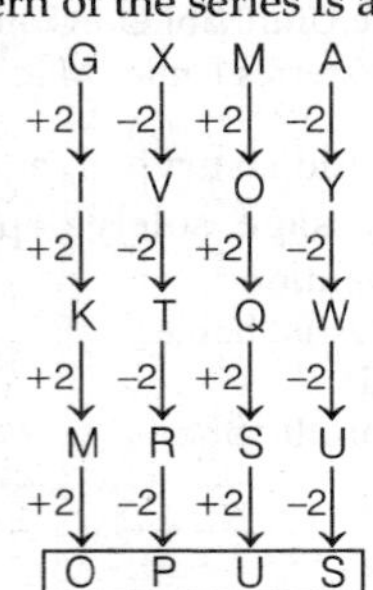

5. (d) Pattern of the series is as follows,

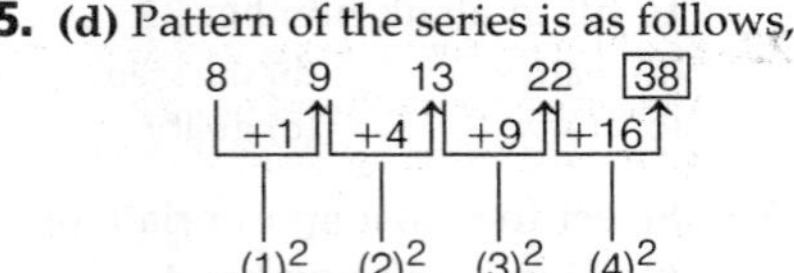

6. (b) The order of words according to dictionary is

Purchased → Purgatory → Purify
(6) (3) (4)
→ Purports → Purposively → Pursuit
(5) (1) (2)

∴ Required order ⇒ 6, 3, 4, 5, 1, 2

7. (a) When we folded the question figure along the vertical line, then it look like as option figure (a).

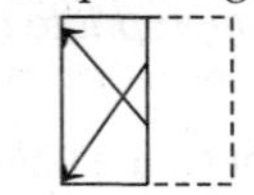

8. (a) As,

F R O M
+2 +1 −1 −2
H S N K

and

W A K E
+2 +1 −1 −2
Y B J C

Similarly,

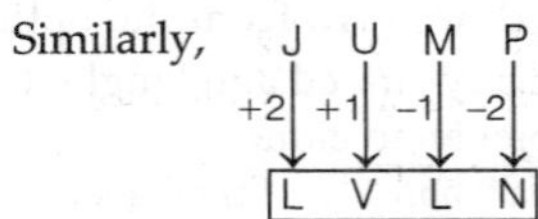

9. (d) Pattern of the series is as follows,

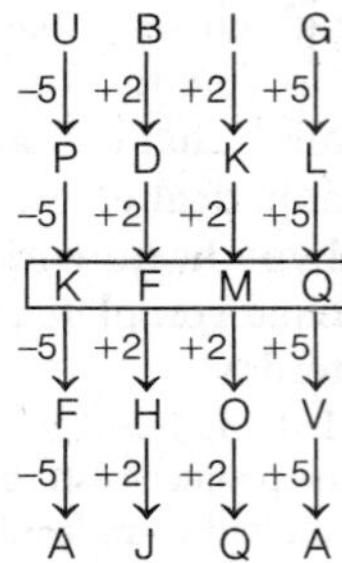

10. (a) When we folded the question figure along the vertical line, then it looks like as option figure (a).

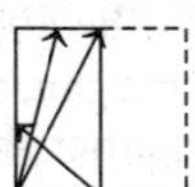

11. (a) Given equation,

$$8 - 3 \times 4 + 16 \div 2$$

After interchange the signs '+' and '−',

$? = 8 + 3 \times 4 - 16 \div 2 = 8 + 12 - 8 = \boxed{12}$

12. (a) As, D R I V E → R D E V I

and S T O C K → T S K C O

Similarly, M O U L D → O M D L U

13. (b) Venn diagram would be as follows,

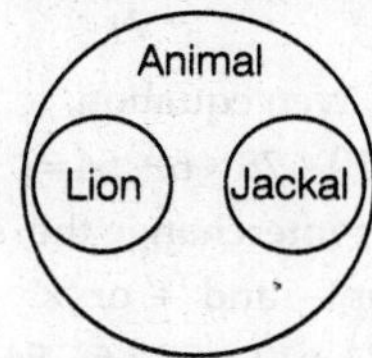

∴ Both Lion and Jackal are animal.

14. (a) As, (84, 28, 4)
×3 ×7

and (147, 49, 7)
×3 ×7

Similarly, (231, 77, 11)
×3 ×7

15. (b) As, C O O L = 180

$\Rightarrow$ $3+15+15+12=45\times4=180$

(Number of letters) = 4

and M A N = 84

$\Rightarrow$ $13+1+14=28\times3=84$

(Number of letters) = 3

Similarly,

Q U I E T

$\Rightarrow$ $17+21+9+5+20=72$

Number of letters = 5

$\therefore 72\times5=$ **360**

16. (a) The given figure (X) is embedded in option figure (a).

17. (a) Given equation, 96A4D5B7C20 = ?

After interchange the signs,

A ⇒ ÷	B ⇒ ×
C ⇒ +	D ⇒ −

$? = 96\div4-5\times7+20$

$= 24-35+20=?$

$? = 44-35=$ **9**

18. (b) As, (21, 63, 378)
×3 ×6

and (23, 69, 414)
×3 ×6

Similarly, (27, 81, 486)
×3 ×6

19. (b) As, O $\xrightarrow{+4}$ S $\xrightarrow{-3}$ P

S $\xrightarrow{+4}$ W $\xrightarrow{-3}$ T

U $\xrightarrow{+4}$ Y $\xrightarrow{-3}$ V

But, Q $\xrightarrow{+4}$ U $\xrightarrow{-2}$ S

20. (d) Pattern of the series is as follows,

101, 103, 107, 109, **113**, 127, 131, 137

All are prime numbers series.

21. (b) As,

S	I	N	G
19	9	14	7
+3	+3	+3	+3
22	12	17	10

and

F	O	U	R
6	15	21	18
+3	+3	+3	+3
9	18	24	21

Similarly,

B	E	A	N
2	5	1	14
+3	+3	+3	+3
5	8	4	17

22. (b) As, Conchology is the study of Shells.

Similarly, Paleontology is the study of Fossils.

23. (a) Option figure (a) is the correct mirror image of the given figure, when the mirror is placed at MN.

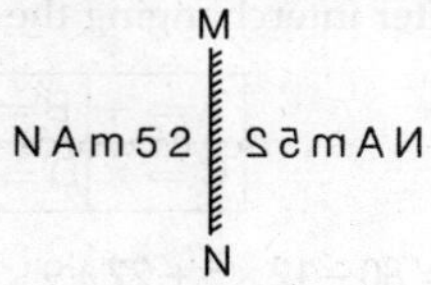

M

NAm52 | (mirror image)

N

24. (d) As, 9 : 90
$9^2+9=90$

and 12 : 156
$12^2+12=156$

Similarly, **8** : 72
$8^2+8=72$

25. (b) According to the question,

M + N − P × S % T

The family diagram is as shown below,

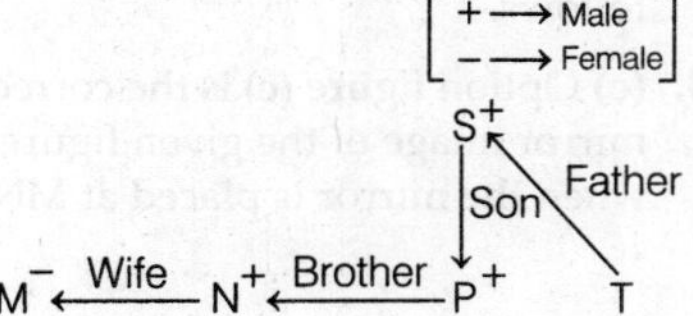

∴ M is the Brother's wife of T.

26. (d) Given equation,

$76\div6+18\times6-49=?$

After interchange the signs,

$+\leftrightarrow-$ and $\times\leftrightarrow\div$, we get

$?=76\times6-18\div6+49$

$?=456-3+49$

$?=$ **502**

27. (d) Pattern of the series is as follows,

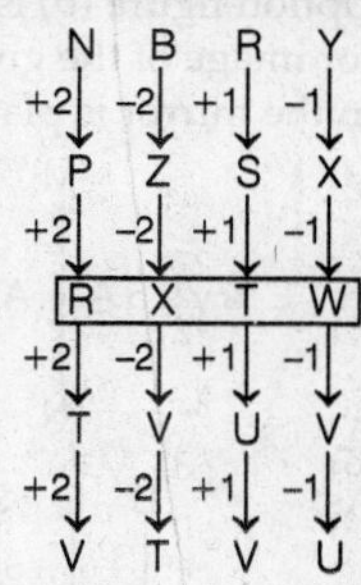

28. (c) Pattern of the series is as follows,

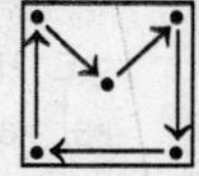

So, after following the same pattern option figure (c) will replace the question mark.

29. (b) As, (18, 3, 9)
÷6 ×3

and (36, 6, 18)
÷6 ×3

Similarly, (78, 13, 39)
÷6 ×3

30. (b) Given equation,

$16\times9+5\div4-2=?$

After interchange the signs,

+ ⇒ −	− ⇒ ÷
× ⇒ +	÷ ⇒ ×

$16+9-5\times4\div2$

$=16+9-10$

$=25-10=$ **15**

31. (d) As,

C	R	A	B
−4	+2	−4	+2
Y	T	W	D

and

C	A	L	M
−4	+2	−4	+2
Y	C	H	O

Similarly,

Z	O	O	M
−4	+2	−4	+2
V	Q	K	O

32. **(d)** According to the venn diagram,

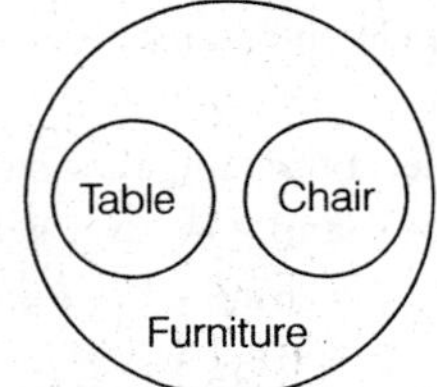

Both table and chair are furniture.

33. **(b)** Option figure (b) is the correct mirror image of the given figure, when the mirror is placed at MN.

M

E % y 9 5 A | A ट ɐ γ ℅ Ǝ

N

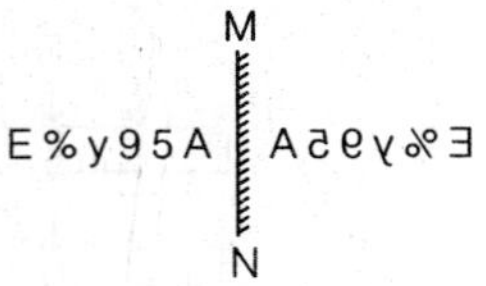

34. **(a)** As,

B E S T
+5 +6 +5 +6
G K X Z

and

E D G E
+5 +6 +5 +6
J J L K

Similarly,

W I N D
+5 +6 +5 +6
B O S J

35. **(d)** According to the question,

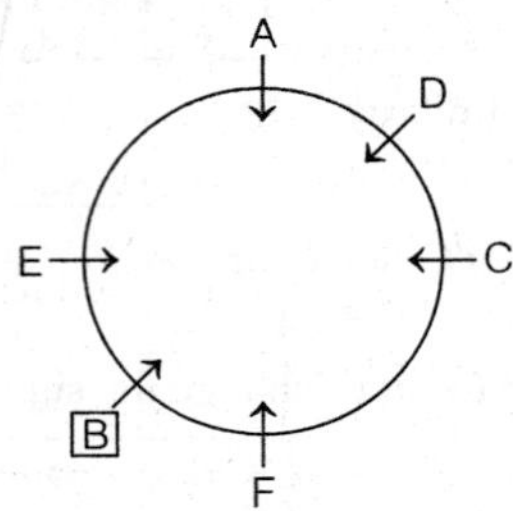

Clearly B is sitting to the immediate left of F.

36. **(d)** Pattern of the series is as follows,

228, 209, 192, 179, 168, 161

−19 −17 −13 −11 −7

37. **(d)** From the given two positions of dice 1 and 3 we find that number 5 is common. So, moving in a clockwise direction from common.

From dice (1) 5 2 4

↕ ↕ opposite

From dice (3) 5 1 3

Clearly, 2 is opposite to 1.

38. **(a)** According to the question,

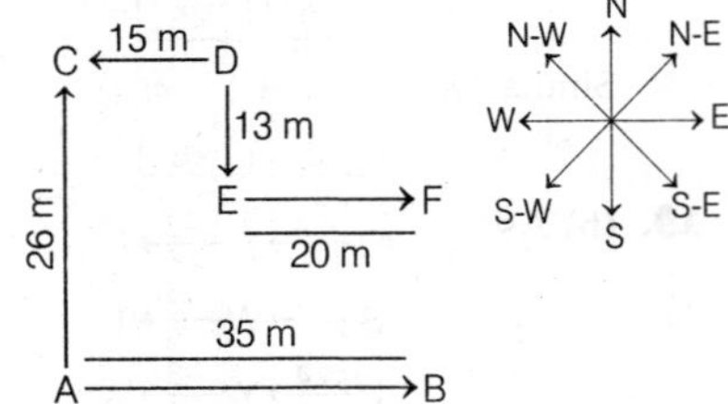

Hence, point B is in South direction to point F.

39. **(b)** Given equation,

$7 \div 255 + 5 \times 3 - 20 = 140$

From option (b), interchanging the signs, '+' and '÷'.

$7 + 255 \div 5 \times 3 - 20 = 140$

$\Rightarrow \quad 7 + 51 \times 3 - 20 = 140$

$\Rightarrow \quad 7 + 153 - 20 = 140$

$\Rightarrow \quad 160 - 20 = 140$

$\Rightarrow \quad 140 = 140$

40. **(a)** As, BEDROOM = 28

Number of letters = 7

$7 \times 4 = 28$

and MOON = 16

Number of letters = 4

$4 \times 4 = 16$

Similarly, CHAIN

Number of letters = 5

$5 \times 4 = \boxed{20}$

41. **(c)** Given equation,

80B12C5A27D9 = ?

After interchanging the signs,

A ⇒ +	B ⇒ −
C ⇒ ×	D ⇒ ÷

$? = 80 - 12 \times 5 + 27 \div 9$

$? = 80 - 60 + 3$

$? = 83 - 60 = \boxed{23}$

42. **(d)** According to the statements,

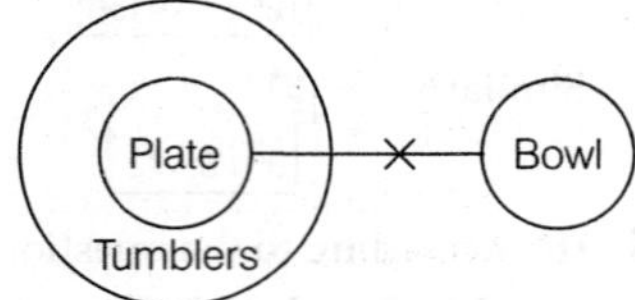

Conclusions I. (✗) II. (✗)

Hence, neither Conclusion I nor II follows.

43. **(c)** Option figure (c) is the correct mirror image of the given figure, when the mirror is placed at MN.

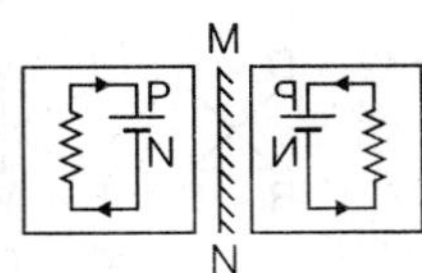

44. **(c)** Option figure (c) is the correct mirror image of the given figure, when the mirror is placed at MN.

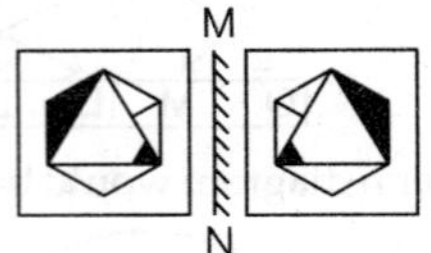

45. **(b)** Given equation,

$11 \div 12 - 78 \times 6 + 54 = ?$

After interchange the signs,

'+' or '−' and '÷' or '×'

$? = 11 \times 12 + 78 \div 6 - 54$

$= 132 + 13 - 54$

$= 145 - 54 = \boxed{91}$

46. **(b)** As per the English dictionary order,

Understand → Undertermined →
(5) (6)
Undone → Uneasiness → Unfaithful
(4) (3) (1)
→ Unfamiliar
(2)

∴ Correct order ⇒ 5, 6, 4, 3, 1, 2

47. **(d)** According to the venn diagram,

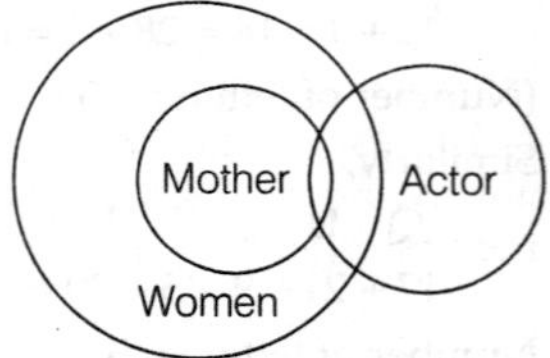

All mother are women and some mother and women may be actor.

48. **(d)** Pattern of the series is as follows,

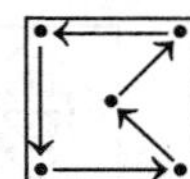

So, after following the same pattern option figure (d) will be replace the question mark (?).

49. **(b)** As, (16, 20, 80)

and (12, 16, 64)

Similarly, (18, 22, 88)

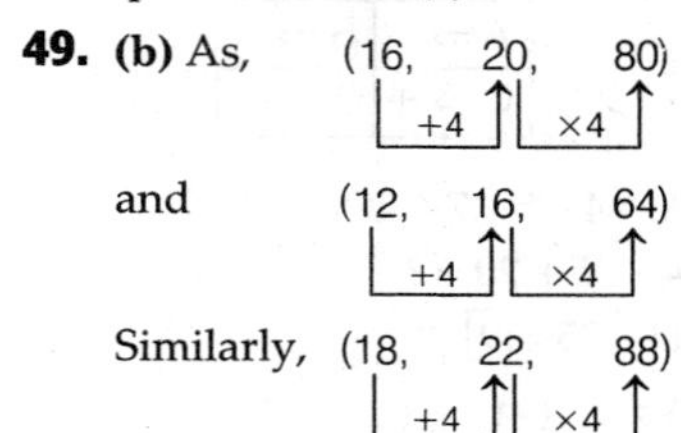

50. **(c)** Given expression,

$P - Q + R - S \div T \times U$

The family diagram is as shown below

$P^{(+)}$ Brother $Q^{(-)}$ [+ ⟶ Male; – ⟶ Female]

Mother

$R^{(+)}$ Brother $S^{(+)}$

Father

$T^{(-)}$ Wife $U^{(+)}$

Clearly, T is son's daughter of Q.

51. **(b)** According to the Census of India 2011, Dadra and Nagar Haveli, had the lowest literacy rate is 77.24 %.

- The literacy rate in India as of 2011 Census was 74.04%.
- Kerala has the highest literacy rate in India.

52. **(b)** Ugadi is celebrated primarily in Karnataka state on the first day of the Chaitra month of the Hindu calendar.

- It symbolises the beginning of the New Year.
- It is celebrated on the first day of the month of Chaitra in the Indian calendar, which falls in March or April.
- During this festival, people decorate the entrance of their homes with fresh mango leaves and create colourful rangoli designs.

53. **(a)** The continuous cyclical movement of water through the lithosphere, atmosphere and hydrosphere is called the **hydrological cycle**.

- The water cycle is a biogeochemical cycle that involves the continuous movement of water on, above and below the surface of the Earth.
- The mass of water on Earth remains fairly constant over time.

54. **(a)** Article-173 of the Indian Constitution mentions about the qualification for membership of the State Legislature.

- The candidate must be a citizen of India.
- The minimum age for membership of the Legislative Assembly is 25 years, while for the Legislative Council, it is 30 years.

55. **(d)** Both Statements (I) and (II) are correct about an earthquake.

- When the stress on the edge overcomes the friction, there is an earthquake that releases energy in waves that travel through Earth's crust and causes the shaking that we feel.
- An earthquake cannot be identified as a foreshock until after a larger earthquake in the same area occurs.

56. **(d)** Both Statements (I) and (II) are true about 'Rasa'.

- Rasa is the aesthetic experience that one derives while, enjoying an artistic presentation.
- It deals with the creation of human sentiments in the spectator or the aesthete.

57. **(b)** If tax rate decreases with increase in taxable base, then this type of taxation is called regressive tax.

- Digressive taxation is a method of collecting revenue in which the tax rates rise in proportion to the amount collected.
- A progressive tax is a tax in which the tax rate increases as the taxable amount increases.

58. **(b)** Manyakheta or Malkhed was the capital of Rashtrakutas.

- The city was founded in the 9th century by the Rashtrakuta ruler Amoghavarsha I and became the capital of the dynasty.
- Dantivarman or Dantidurga was the founder of the Rashtrakutas dynasty.

59. **(a)** Electrical resistivity is commonly represented by the Greek letter p (rho).

- It is a measure of the resistance of a specific material of a given size, to the electrical current conduction that flows through it.
- It is also referred to as the specific electrical resistance or volume resistivity

60. **(b)** As of 2022,Allahabad-Haldia stretch is the longest national waterway in India.

- The Allahabad-Haldia National Waterway connects Prayagraj or Allahabad in Uttar Pradesh and Haldia in West Bengal.
- It is 1620 km long.
- This waterway is called National Waterway Number One.

61. **(c)** Ramganga river originates from the Dudhatoli ranges in Pauri Garhwal district of Uttarakhand.

- It originates from the glaciers of the Himalayas in the district of Pauri Garhwal.
- It is a tributary of Ganga and passes through Corbett National Park.

62. **(b)** Pt. Shivkumar Sharma is not a vocalist.

- Pt. Kumar Gandharva, Pt. Bhimsen Joshi and Gangubai Hangal are all vocalists.
- Pandit Shivkumar Sharma was an Indian classical musician and santoor player.
- Pt. Shivkumar Sharma was awarded the Padma Shri in 1991 and Padma Vibhushan in 2001.

63. **(d)** The correct chronology of the battles fought during the Mughal period is First Battle of Panipat (1526), Battle of Khanwa (1527), Battle of Ghaghra (1529), Battle of Chausa (1539).

- First Battle of Panipat, Battle of Khanwa and Battle of Ghaghra associated with Babur.
- Battle of Chausa was faught between Humayun and Sher Shah Suri.

64. **(d)** Yo-Yo has a potential energy before it is released. When you hold it, it a has a potential energy.

- But when you release it, the potential energy gradually converts to kinetic energy, because it starts to move.

65. **(a)** The book 'Godaan', was authored by Munshi Premchand in 1936. His works include Godaan, Karmabhoomi, Gaban, Mansarovar, Pratigya, Nirmala and Idgah.

66. **(c)** Kapil Dev was the first fast bowler who was the Indian test team captain. Dev is the only player in the history of cricket to have taken more than 400 wickets (434 wickets) and scored more than 5,000 runs in test.

- Dev captained the Indian Cricket Team that won the 1983 Cricket World Cup, becoming the first Indian captain to win the Cricket World Cup.

67. **(c)** Mohan Veena player Pandit Vishwa Mohan Bhatt won the Grammy Award in the year 1994.

- He was conferred with Sangeet Natak Akademi Award, 1998,Padma Shri, 2002, Padma Bhushan, 2017.

68. **(b)** 'Along The Red River: A Memoir' is a book about the life of Sabita Goswami.

- Veteran journalist Sabita Goswami has written a unique, unusual and rare autobiography, documenting the extraordinary, single-handed fight of an ordinary woman in the heart of Assam, against family and social obstacles, and her attempt to establish herself emotionally and professionally.

69. **(a)** Raj Kumar Shukla had gone to Lucknow to invite Mahatma Gandhi to see the plight of the peasants in Champaran.

- His resolve to take Gandhiji to Champaran resulted in the first successful Civil Disobedience Movement, Champaran Satyagraha, in the history of India.

70. **(b)** Garlic is good source of manganese and selenium.

- Garlic is an excellent source of vitamin B6 which helps the body's metabolism and immune system.
- It is a good source of minerals like manganese and selenium, which support strong bones, "reproduction, blood clotting and a healthy immune system".

71. **(c)** Montane forests have distinct type of wildlife species called Yak. Montane ecosystems refer to any ecosystem found in mountains.

- Dense forests are common in areas of moderate elevations.
- The montane ecosystems are highly affected by the climate which gets colder as the elevation increases.

72. **(b)** The Nile River originates South of the equator and flows North through North-Eastern Africa to eventually flowing through Egypt and then drain into the Mediterranean Sea.

- The Nile is the longest river in Africa and has historically been considered the longest river in the world.

73. **(a)** Ashoka sent his son Mahendra and daughter Sanghamitta , to spread the message of Dhamma to Sri Lanka (Ceylon).

- Their names are mentioned in the Buddhist text 'Mahavamsa' written in Sri Lanka. Missionaries for spreading Buddhism were also sent to Burma and Central Asia.

74. **(d)** The Parliament has the power to make law and policies for the country, as per the Indian Constitution.

- The Schedule of the Constitution contains three lists a Union List, a State List and a Concurrent List. These lists set out the various subjects on which Parliament and State Legislatures are empowered to make laws.
- The Indian Parliament is competent to make laws on matters enumerated in the Union List.

75. **(b)** Articles 52 to 78 of the Indian Constitution deals with the Union Executive.

- The Union Executive, a vital part of the political executive, includes three significant positions:
- The President (Article 52-62), The Prime Minister and the Council of Ministers (Article 74-75 and Article- 78), The Attorney-General of India (Article-76).

76. **(b)** The white precipitate formed in the reaction of sodium sulphate and barium chloride is barium sulphate. The reaction is Barium chloride + Sodium sulphate – Barium sulphates + Sodium chloride.

77. **(c)** The minimum strength of the Council of Ministers in a state as per the Indian Constitution is 12 persons and the maximum is 15 percent of the Legislative Assembly.
Article-164 of Indian Constitution consists prouisions regarding appointment at state council of ministers.

78. **(d)** Vitamin B-12 is involved in red blood cell formation, neurological function and DNA synthesis.

- Vitamin B-12 is required for the development, myelination and function of the central nervous system.
- Organ meats, such as liver and kidneys, are very high in vitamin B12.

79. **(a)** Bundu Khan was a **sarangi** player of Delhi Gharana.

- He was trained by his grandfather Saungi Khan, father Ali Jan Khan.
- He played the Sarangi from All India Radio, Delhi station.
- He served the Princely Court of Indore for 27 years as a court musician.

80. **(a)** The International Olympic Committee was established in the year 1894.

- It is a non-governmental sports organisation based in Lausanne. Switzerland.
- It was founded by Pierre de Coubertin and Demetrius Vikelas,
- It is the authority responsible for organising the modern (Summer, Winter) Youth Olympic Games.
- As of March 2025, its President is **Thomas Bach**.

81. **(d)** As per the Census of 2011,the literacy rate in India is 72.98%

- The literacy rate for females and males are 64.63% and 80.9%, respectively.
- During the last decade (2001-2011), the highest improvement in literacy rate was observed among rural females (24%).
- Kerala was the highest literacy cate.

82. **(a)** The RBI act provides for 6 members in RBI Monetary Policy Committee (MPC).

- The Monetary Policy responsible for fixing the benchmark interest rate in India. The meetings of the Monetary Policy Committee are held atleast four times a year.
- The committee comprises six members (three officials of the Reserve Bank of India and three external members) nominated by the government of India.

83. **(d)** Growth, as envisaged in the Five-Year Plans, refers to increase in the country's capacity to produce the output of goods and services within the country.

- Five Year Planes, is a method of centralised economic planning.
- India adopted the Five Year Plan from Soviet Union.

84. **(b)** The number of protons present in beryllium is 4, 5 neutrons and 4 electrons.

- The atomic mass number of beryllium will be the sum of 4 protons and 5 neutrons and that will be equal to 9.
- Beryllium is used industrially in three forms as a pure metal, as beryllium oxide, and most commonly, as an alloy with copper, aluminium, magnesium or nickel.

85. **(b) Swami Vivekananda** founded the Ramakrishna Mission to carry on humanitarian and social work.

- Ramakrishna Math and Ramakrishna Mission (RKM) is a spiritual and philanthropic organisation headquartered in Belur Math, West Bengal.
- The mission is named after the Indian Hindu spiritual guru and mystic Ramakrishna.

86. **(c)** Statements (1) and (2) are correct in the context of the Indian Constitution.

- There are three major organs of the government, namely Legislature, Executive and Judiciary.
- Legislature is responsible for making the laws, executive is responsible for enforcing law and judiciary is responsible for implementing laws.
- A separation of functions rather than powers is followed.

87. **(a)** Janmashtami is celebrated as the birth of Lord Krishna on the eighth (Ashtami) day of the dark fortnight of the month of Bhadrapada (August-September).

88. **(c)** Dronacharya Award is given in the field of sports.

- The award is given to honour coaches for their outstanding work in sportspersons to excel in international events.
- It was established in 1985.
- Kalidas Samman, Sangeet Natak Akademi Award and Mahari Award are given in the field of dance and music.

89. **(d)** Longitudinal wave oscillates parallel to the motion of the sound wave.

- Sound waves similarly oscillate parallel to the direction of propagation, forming the compressions and rarefactions. Hence, sound waves are called longitudinal waves.

90. **(a)** Sangeeta Majumdar was felicitated by Casa De La, Spain for her contribution to **Kathak**.

- Awarded by 'Meera Award' in the year 2009 for the 'Excellence in Kathak dance' from Agra, Uttar Pradesh.

91. **(a)** There are 13 major ports in India for maritime transportation. India's 95%of trading by volume is done through maritime transport.

- It stands at 70% by value. Jawaharlal Nehru Port Trust (JNPT) is the largest container port in India.

92. **(a)** The Arjuna Award is given for outstanding performance in sports and games over a period of the previous four years and for showing qualities of leadership, sportsmanship and a sense of discipline.

- It was first given in 1961.
- It is given by the Ministry of Youth Affairs and Sports, Government of India.
- An award of 15 lakh rupees, a bronze statue of Arjuna and a citation are given. India fast bowler Mohammed Shami was bestowed with the Arjuna Award in 2024.

93. **(c) Sattriya** was initiated by Srimant Shankardev, a Vaishnava saint. Sattriya dance is prevalent in the state of Assam.

- Sattriya dance is prevalent in the Vaishnava monasteries of Assam, these mathas are known as 'Satras'.
- The Sattriya dance is basically based on the mythological stories of Lord Vishnu. 'Mati-Akhora' is associated with this classical dance.

94. **(d) Stagflation** was not at all the factors leading to the Economic Reforms in 1991.

- Some of the factors leading to the economic reforms in 1991 are inflation in the economy, fall in India's foreign reserves, rise in the fiscal deficit of the country.

95. **(b) Article-50** of the Constitution in Part IV dealing with Directive Principles of State Policy states of India refers to the separation of judiciary from executive.

- Directive Principles of State Policy in India have been taken from the Constitution of Ireland.
- Directive Principles of State Policies (DPSP) are a set of social and economic obligations imposed on the Government (Union and State) to establish a welfare society.
- They are enumerated in Part IV of the Constitution.

96. **(d)** Food high in salt, sugar and saturated or trans fats generally increase blood pressure and damage your heart health.

- The liberal use of salt, often found in excess within processed and packaged foods.

97. **(d)** 60 members (elected and nominated) were there in the Council of State under the Government of India Act, 1919.

- It was passed by the Parliament of the United Kingdom to expand participation of Indians in the Government of India.
- The act is also known as the Montague Chelmsford Reform.

98. **(d)** Australian Swimmer Emma McKeon was the first female swimmer to win seven medals at a Single Olympics, in Tokyo Olympics, 2020.

- Four of them were gold, the other three bronze.

99. **(d)** Western disturbance phenomenon is not related to the monsoon in India.

- The Western cyclonic disturbances are low pressure systems that originate over the Mediterranean Sea.
- Western disturbances, specifically the ones in winter, bring moderate to heavy rain in low-lying areas and heavy snow to mountainous areas of the Indian Sub-continent.
- They are the cause of most winter and post-monsoon season rainfall across Pakistan and north-west India.

100. **(b)** C. Subramaniam was awarded the Bharat Ratna for his contribution to the Green Revolution in India.

- As the Minister for Food and Agriculture, the ushered in the Indian Green Revolution, an era of self-sufficiency in food production along with MS.
- Swaminathan, B. Sivaraman and Norman E.Borlaug.
- He is also known as Father of Green revolution in India.
- It was started in third Five Year Plan.

101. **(c)** Using BODMAS rule for simplification,

$$\frac{1}{2^2} + \frac{1}{2^3} \div \left(\frac{1}{2} + \frac{1}{2} \div 1\right) + 3\frac{1}{3}$$

$$\div \frac{5}{2} \times \frac{3}{4} \div 6\frac{2}{3} \times \frac{7}{6}$$

$= \frac{1}{4} + \frac{1}{8} \div \left(\frac{1}{2} + \frac{1}{2} \div 1\right) + \frac{10}{3} \div \frac{5}{2} \times \frac{3}{4} \div \frac{20}{3} \times \frac{7}{6}$

$= \frac{1}{4} + \frac{1}{8} \div \left(\frac{1}{2} + \frac{1}{2}\right) + \frac{10}{3} \div \frac{5}{2} \times \frac{3}{4} \div \frac{20}{3} \times \frac{7}{6}$

$= \frac{1}{4} + \frac{1}{8} \div (1) + \frac{10}{3} \div \frac{5}{2} \times \frac{3}{4} \div \frac{20}{3} \times \frac{7}{6}$

$= \frac{1}{4} + \frac{1}{8} + \frac{10}{3} \times \frac{2}{5} \times \frac{3}{4} \times \frac{3}{20} \times \frac{7}{6}$

$= \frac{1}{4} + \frac{1}{8} + \frac{7}{40} = \frac{10+5+7}{40} = \frac{22}{40} = \frac{11}{20}$

102. (a) Present population = 80 lakh

Let the population 3 yr ago be x.

$\therefore\ x\left(1 + \frac{20}{100}\right)^3 = 80$ lakh

$\Rightarrow x\left(\frac{6}{5} \times \frac{6}{5} \times \frac{6}{5}\right) = 80$ lakh

$\Rightarrow\ x = 80 \text{ lakh} \times \frac{125}{216}$

Let the population 2 yr ago be 'y'.

$\therefore y\left(1 + \frac{20}{100}\right)^2 = 80$ lakh

$\Rightarrow\ y\left(\frac{6}{5} \times \frac{6}{5}\right) = 80$ lakh

$\Rightarrow\ y = 80 \text{ lakh} \times \frac{25}{36}$

$\therefore$ Required difference

$= x - y = 80 \text{ lakh}\left[\frac{25}{36} - \frac{125}{216}\right]$

$= 80 \text{ lakh}\left[\frac{150 - 125}{216}\right]$

$= 8000000 \times \frac{25}{216} = 925925.93$

103. (c) Area of the cylinder base,

$= \pi R^2 = 20 \text{ cm}^2$

Volume of the cylinder $= \pi R^2 \times H$

$= 20 \times 8 = 160 \text{ cm}^3$

104. (b) (Rajan + Rajat)'s 2 days work

$= \frac{1}{64} + \frac{1}{48} = \frac{7}{192}$

In 54 days, work of (Rajan + Rajat)

$= \frac{54}{2} \times \frac{7}{192} = \frac{189}{192}$

Remaining work $= 1 - \frac{189}{192} = \frac{3}{192}$

Time takan to completed remaining work by Rajat $= \frac{3}{192} \times 48 = \frac{3}{4}$ day

Hence, required time $= 54 + \frac{3}{4}$

$= 54\frac{3}{4}$ days

105. (a) Given, $CF = 15$ cm and $CD = 20$ cm

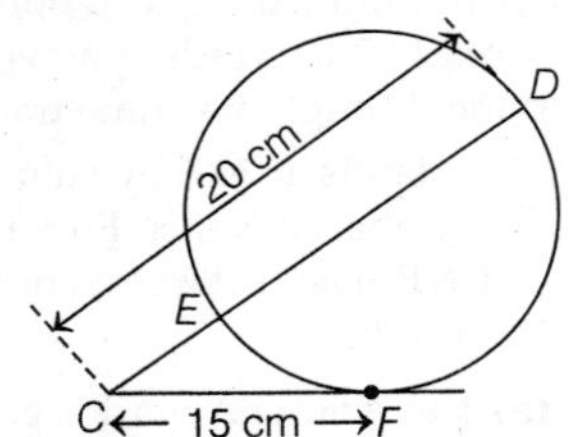

Using the tangent-secant theorem,

$CF^2 = CE \times CD$

$\Rightarrow 15 \times 15 = CE \times 20$

$\Rightarrow\ CE = \frac{225}{20}$

$\Rightarrow\ CE = 11.25$ cm

$\therefore$ length of chord $DE = CD - CE$

$= 20 - 11.25$

$= 8.75$ cm

106. (d) Let the side of the cube formed be 'a'.

Volume of the metal ball

$= \frac{4}{3}\pi r^3 = \frac{4}{3}\pi \times (3)^3$

Now, volume of metal ball = Volume of dice formed + Volume of ball formed

$\Rightarrow\ \frac{4}{3}\pi \times 3^3 = 27(a)^3 + \frac{4}{3}\pi \times 1^3$

$\Rightarrow\ \frac{4}{3}\pi(27 - 1) = 27(a)^3$

$\Rightarrow\ 27a^3 = \frac{4}{3} \times \frac{22}{7} \times 26$

$\Rightarrow a^3 = \frac{4 \times 22 \times 26}{3 \times 7 \times 27} \Rightarrow a^3 = 4.04$ units

3

$\therefore\ a = 1.6$ units

107. (d) Given expression,

$12.3 - [7 + 0.8 \text{ of } (5.6 - 3.8 \times 1.03)]$

$= 12.3 - [7 + 0.8 \text{ of } (5.6 - 3.914)]$

$= 12.3 - [7 + 0.8 \text{ of } 1.686]$

$= 12.3 - [7 + 1.3488] = 12.3 - 8.3488$

$= 3.9512$

108. (c) $\frac{5x + 3y}{5x - 3y} = \frac{7}{3}$

$\Rightarrow\ 15x + 9y = 35x - 21y$

$\Rightarrow\ 30y = 20x$

$\Rightarrow\ \frac{x}{y} = \frac{30}{20}$

$\therefore\ x : y = 3 : 2$

109. (a) Let the cost of 1 gm be ₹ 1.

$\therefore$ CP of 50 gm = ₹ 50

SP of 40 gm = ₹ 50 – (10% of 50)

= ₹ 45

$\therefore$ Profit percentage

$= \frac{\text{Error}}{\text{True weight}} \times 100$

$= \frac{5}{40} \times 100 = 12.5\%$

110. (c) Let the original length, breadth and height of the cuboid be l, b and h, respectively.

New length $= 0.85\,l$

New breadth $= 0.75\,b$

New height $= 1.6\,h$

Original volume of cuboid $= l \times b \times h$

New volume of cuboid

$= 0.85l \times 0.75b \times 1.6h$

$= 1.02\,lbh$

$\therefore$ Percentage change in volume

$= \frac{1.02\,lbh - lbh}{lbh} \times 100$

$= 0.02 \times 100$

$= 2\%$ (increase)

111. (a) $x + \cfrac{1}{1 + \cfrac{1}{3 + \cfrac{1}{2}}} = 1 \Rightarrow x + \cfrac{1}{1 + \cfrac{1}{\cfrac{7}{2}}} = 1$

$\Rightarrow\ x + \cfrac{1}{1 + \cfrac{2}{7}} = 1 \Rightarrow x + \frac{7}{9} = 1$

$\Rightarrow\ x = 1 - \frac{7}{9}$

$\therefore\ x = \frac{9 - 7}{9} = \frac{2}{9}$

112. (d) Let the speed of boat be 'a' km/h.

Let the speed of stream be 'b' km/h.

Upstream speed $= (a - b)$ km/h

Downstream speed $= (a + b)$ km/h

According to the question,

$\frac{4}{a + b} = \frac{3}{a - b}$

$\Rightarrow\ a = 7b$ ...(i)

and $\frac{48}{a + b} + \frac{48}{a - b} = 48$ h

$\Rightarrow\ \frac{1}{8b} + \frac{1}{6b} = 1$ [From Eq. (i)]

$\Rightarrow\ \frac{3 + 4}{24b} = 1 \Rightarrow b = \frac{7}{24}$

$\therefore$ Speed of the stream $= \frac{7}{24}$ km/h .

113. (d) Let the original length and breadth of rectangular lawn be 'l' and 'b', respectively.

Original area $= lb$, New length $= 1.15l$

and New breadth $= 0.92b$

$\therefore$ New area $= 1.15l \times 0.92b = 1.058\,lb$

Now, percentage change in the lawn area

$= \frac{1058\, lb - lb}{lb} \times 100$

$= 0.058 \times 100$

$= 5.8\%$ increase

114. **(c)** Let the sides of the triangle be a, b and c.

$\therefore a + b + c = 125$ cm

$\therefore$ Semi-perimeter $= \frac{a+b+c}{2} = \frac{125}{2}$ cm

We know that,

In-radius $= \frac{\text{Area of } \Delta}{\text{Semi-perimeter of } \Delta}$

$\Rightarrow \quad 8 = \frac{\text{Area of } \Delta}{\frac{125}{2}}$

$\therefore$ Area of $\Delta = \frac{125 \times 8}{2} = 500 \text{ cm}^2$

115. **(b)** $\sin(x+y) = \cos\{3(x+y)\}$

$\Rightarrow \sin(x+y) = \sin[90° - \{3(x+y)\}]$

$\Rightarrow \ (x+y) + 3(x+y) = 90°$

$\Rightarrow \quad 4(x+y) = 90°$

$\Rightarrow \quad 2(x+y) = 45°$

$\therefore \cot\{2(x+y)\} = \cot 45° = 1$

116. **(a)** Given, $\frac{2\cos 15° \cdot \sin 15°}{\cos^2 15° - \sin^2 15°}$

We know that, $\sin 2\theta = 2\sin\theta \cdot \cos\theta$

$\therefore \quad \frac{2\cos 15° \cdot \sin 15°}{\cos^2 15° - \sin^2 15°}$

and $\cos 2\theta = \cos^2\theta - \sin^2\theta$

$= \frac{\sin(2 \times 15°)}{\cos(2 \times 15°)} = \frac{\sin 30°}{\cos 30°}$

$= \tan 30° = \frac{1}{\sqrt{3}}$

117. **(d)** In 1993, total production of all cars $= 80$

Production of car type S in 1993 $= 20$

$\therefore$ Percentage of production of car type $S = \frac{20}{80} \times 100 = 25\%$

118. **(a)** $\frac{7 + 8 \times 8 \div 8 \text{ of } 8 + 8 \div 8 \times 5}{4 \div 4 \text{ of } 4 + 4 \times 4 \div 4 - 4 \div 4}$

$= \frac{7 + 8 \times 8 \div 64 + 8 \div 8 \times 5}{4 \div 4 \text{ of } 4 + 4 \times 4 \div 4 - 4 \div 4}$

$= \frac{7 + \frac{8 \times 8}{64} + 1 \times 5}{\frac{4}{16} + 4 \times 1 - 1}$

$= \frac{7 + 1 + 1 \times 5}{\frac{1}{4} + 4 - 1} = \frac{13 \times 4}{1 + 16 - 4}$

$= \frac{13 \times 4}{13} = 4$

119. **(d)** Let, $275 = a$ and $725 = b$

$\therefore$ Value of given expression

$= \frac{a^3 + b^3}{(a^2 + b^2 - ab)} \times \frac{a^3 - b^3}{(a^2 + b^2 + ab)}$

$= \frac{(a+b)(a^2 + b^2 - ab)}{(a^2 + b^2 - ab)} \times \frac{(a-b)(a^2 + b^2 + ab)}{(a^2 + b^2 + ab)}$

$= (a+b)(a-b) = a^2 - b^2$

$= (275)^2 - (725)^2$

$= 75625 - 525625 = -450000$

120. **(b)** $x^2 + 4y^2 + 2x + 1 = 0$

$\Rightarrow (x^2 + 2x + 1) + (4y^2) = 0$

$\Rightarrow \quad (x+1)^2 + (2y)^2 = 0$

Thus, $x + 1 = 0 \Rightarrow x = -1$

and $2y = 0 \Rightarrow y = 0$

$\therefore x^{39} + y^{36} = (-1)^{39} + (0)^{36}$

$= -1 \, [\because (-1)^{\text{odd}} = -1]$

121. **(c)** $(12 + 18) \div 2 - 11 + 16 \times 4 - 28 + 13(-18 + 15)$

$= 30 \div 2 - 11 + 16 \times 4 - 28 + 13(-3)$

$= 15 - 11 + 64 - 28 - 39$

$= 79 - 78 = 1$

122. **(d)** Successive discount are 40% and 20%.

Equivalent discount

$= (-40) + (-20) + \frac{(-40)(-20)}{100}$

$= -60 + \frac{800}{100}$

$= -60 + 8 = -52\%$

$\therefore$ The single equivalent discount $= 52\%$

123. **(a)** Given,

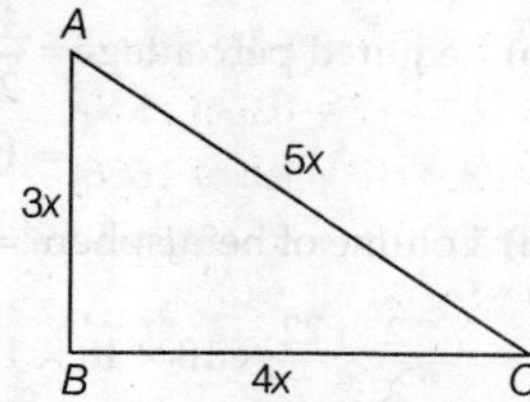

$\therefore$ Area of $\Delta ABC = \frac{1}{2} \times AB \times BC$

$\Rightarrow \quad 486 = \frac{1}{2} \times 3x \times 4x$

$\Rightarrow \quad 6x^2 = 486$

$\Rightarrow \quad x^2 = 81$

$\Rightarrow \quad x = 9$ cm

$\therefore$ Perimeter of $\Delta ABC = 3x + 4x + 5x$

$= 12x$

$= 12 \times 9$

$= 108$ cm

124. **(b)** Given,

A drink is made by mixing water and juice in the ratio 9 : 7.

In 160 L of drink, water = 90 L and juice = 70 L

According to the question,

$\frac{90 + x}{70 + 2x} = \frac{13}{15}$

$\Rightarrow 1350 + 15x = 910 + 26x$

$\Rightarrow \quad 440 = 11x \Rightarrow x = 40$

Total addition of extra water and juice in the drink

$= x + 2x = 3x = 120$ L

$\therefore$ The new quantity of drink

$= 160 + 120 = 280$ L

125. **(c)** Number of people not voted at centre $B = 30\%$ of 5400

$= \frac{30}{100} \times 5400 = 1620$

Number of people not voted at centre $C = 15\%$ of 6500

$= \frac{15}{100} \times 6500 = 975$

$\therefore$ Required percentage

$= \frac{1620 - 975}{975} \times 100$

$= \frac{645}{975} \times 100 = 66\frac{2}{13}\%$

126. **(c)** Given, $\frac{\tan 71° + \tan 19°}{1 - \tan 71° \cdot \tan 19°}$

We know that,

$\tan(A+B) = \frac{\tan A + \tan B}{1 - \tan A \cdot \tan B}$

$\Rightarrow \frac{\tan 71° + \tan 19°}{1 - \tan 71° \cdot \tan 19°} = \tan(71° + 19°)$

$= \tan 90° = \infty$ (undefined)

127. **(c)** Total number of educated females $= 600 + 820 + 950 + 980 + 1000 = 4350$

Total number of females

$= 900 + 1000 + 1020 + 1100 + 1200 = 5220$

$\therefore$ Required percentage $= \frac{4350}{5220} \approx 0.8333$

128. **(c)** $63 - [15 + \{17 - (9 - 7 + 1)\}]$

$= 63 - [15 + \{17 - 3\}]$

$= 63 - [15 + 14]$

$= 63 - 29 = 34$

129. **(a)** Average speed $= \frac{2S_1 S_2}{S_1 + S_2}$

$= \frac{2 \times 90 \times 65}{90 + 65}$

$= \frac{11700}{155} = 75.48$ km/h

130. (c) Given expression,

$(1+\tan\theta+\sec\theta)\times(1+\cot\theta-\csc\theta)$

$=\left(1+\frac{\sin\theta}{\cos\theta}+\frac{1}{\cos\theta}\right)\times\left(1+\frac{\cos\theta}{\sin\theta}-\frac{1}{\sin\theta}\right)$

$=\frac{\cos\theta+\sin\theta+1}{\cos\theta}\times\frac{\sin\theta+\cos\theta-1}{\sin\theta}$

$=\frac{(\sin\theta+\cos\theta)^2-1^2}{\sin\theta\cdot\cos\theta}$

$[\because (a+b)(a-b)=a^2-b^2]$

$=\frac{\sin^2\theta+\cos^2\theta+2\cos\theta.\sin\theta-1}{\sin\theta\cdot\cos\theta}$

$=\frac{1+2\sin\theta\cdot\cos\theta-1}{\sin\theta\cdot\cos\theta}$

$=\frac{2\sin\theta\cdot\cos\theta}{\sin\theta\cdot\cos\theta}=2$

131. (d) Expenditure (in ₹) on infrastructre

$=\frac{84.7^\circ}{360^\circ}\times$ ₹7200

= ₹ 1694 crores

132. (a) Ratio for Mumbai $=\frac{150}{155}=\frac{30}{31}$

Ratio for Uttarakhand $=\frac{120}{125}=\frac{24}{25}$

Ratio for Rajasthan $=\frac{160}{135}=\frac{32}{27}$

Ratio for Uttar Pradesh $=\frac{145}{170}=\frac{29}{34}$

Since, only for Rajasthan, the numerator > denominator.

∴ The ratio of high rate of share to low rate of share is maximum for Rajasthan.

133. (d) Let the number of boys be x.

∴ Number of girls $= x+8$

∴ $x+(x+8)=18$

$\Rightarrow 2x=18-8 \Rightarrow x=5$

Number of boys × Number of girls

$=x\times(x+8)=5\times(5+8)=65$

134. (c) Given, $a+b+c=13$ and

$ab+bc+ca=22$

$(a+b+c)^2=a^2+b^2+c^2+2(ab+bc+ca)$

$\Rightarrow (13)^2=(a^2+b^2+c^2)+2(22)$

$\Rightarrow a^2+b^2+c^2=169-44$

$\Rightarrow a^2+b^2+c^2=125$

$a^3+b^3+c^3-3abc$

$=(a+b+c)[a^2+b^2+c^2-(ab+bc+ca)]$

$=13[125-22]=13\times103=1339$

135. (b) Here, $M_1=300$, $T_1=10$ days,

$T_2=?$ and $M_2=300-50=250$

∴ $M_1\times T_1=M_2\times T_2$

$\Rightarrow 300\times10=250\times T_2$

$\Rightarrow T_2=\frac{300\times10}{250}=12$ days

136. (b) Let the CP of first buffalo be ₹ x.

∴ CP of the second buffalo

= ₹ $(11520-x)$

According to the given question,

$\Rightarrow x\times\frac{85}{100}=(11520-x)\times\frac{119}{100}$

$\Rightarrow \frac{11520-x}{x}=\frac{85}{119}$

$\Rightarrow \frac{11520-x}{x}=\frac{5}{7}$

$\Rightarrow 80640-7x=5x$

$\Rightarrow x=\frac{80640}{12}\Rightarrow x=$ ₹ 6720

∴ CP of the first buffalo is ₹ 6720.

137. (d) Let the original sum be ₹ P.

According to the given question,

$P\times\frac{20}{12}\times\frac{19.2}{100}=P\times\frac{15}{12}\times\frac{11.2}{100}+$ ₹ 2920

$\Rightarrow 0.32P=2920+0.14P$

$\Rightarrow 0.32P-0.14P=2920$

$\Rightarrow 0.18P=2920\Rightarrow P=\frac{2920}{0.18}$

$\Rightarrow P=$ ₹ 16222.22

∴ The sum (in ₹, to the nearest hundreds) is ₹ 16200.

138. (c) Surface Area of cuboid

$=2(lb+bh+hl)$

$=2[(11\times7)+(7\times4)+(4\times11)]$

$=2(77+28+44)$

$=2\times149=298\text{ m}^2$

139. (b) Required percentage $=\frac{15}{25}\times100$

$=15\times4=60\%$

140. (b) Volume of hemisphere $=\frac{2}{3}\pi r^3$

$=\frac{2}{3}\times\frac{22}{7}\times18\times18\times18$

$=12219.43\text{ cm}^3$

141. (a) Let the speed of the rain be x km/h.

∴ Relative speed of train and person running in opposite direction

$=(x+9)$ km/h $=(x+9)\times\frac{5}{18}$ m/s

According to the question,

$\frac{234}{6}=\left(x+9\times\frac{5}{18}\right)$

$\Rightarrow 39=x+2.5=36.5$ m/sec

Speed of another person = 23.4 km/h

$=23.4\times\frac{5}{18}=6.5$ m/s

Relative speed of train and person running in the same direction

$=36.5-6.5=30$ m/s

∴ Time taken $=\frac{\text{Length of train}}{\text{Relative speed}}$

$=\frac{234}{30}=7.8$ sec

142. (a) Given, upstream speed (U)

= 27 km/h

and downstream speed (D)

= 33 km/h

∴ Speed of boat in still water

$=\frac{U+D}{2}=\frac{27+33}{2}$

= 30 km/h

143. (a) Let the amount spent on food and education be $3x$ and $2x$, respectively.

Savings of Swati

$=\frac{25}{100}\times$ ₹40000 = ₹ 10000

Remaining balance

$=40000-10000=$ ₹ 30000

So, spends on food and education

$(3x+2x)=30000$

$\Rightarrow 5x=30000$

$\Rightarrow x=6000$

∴ Amount spent on education

$=2x=2\times6000=$ ₹ 12000

Hence, required % $=\frac{12000}{40000}\times100$

= 30%

144. (a) Given, Radius of the circle = 35 cm

Angle (θ) subtended by the arc = 72°

∴ Area of sector of the circle

$=\pi r^2\times\frac{\theta}{360^\circ}$

$=\frac{22}{7}\times35\times35\times\frac{72}{360}$

$=22\times35=770\text{ cm}^2$

145. (c) Given equation,

$27\div4$ of $6\times[16\div8\times(12-8)]-(14\div7\times28)$

$=27\div4$ of $6\times[16\div8\times4]-(2\times28)$

$=27\div4$ of $6\times[2\times4]-(56)$

$=27\div4$ of $6\times8-56$

$=27\div24\times8-56$

$=\frac{27}{24}\times8-56$

$=9-56=-47$

146. (d) If sides of a Δ are a, b, c, then a triangle can be formed if
$|a-b| < c < |a+b|$

Case 1 Taking 3 sides as 2cm, 5cm, 7cm.
$|2-5| < 7 < |2+5|$
$\Rightarrow 3 < 7 < 7 \rightarrow$ Not possible.

Case 2 Taking 3 sides as 2cm, 5cm, 8cm.
$|2-5| < 8 < |2+5|$
$\Rightarrow 3 < 8 < 7 \rightarrow$ Not possible

Case 3 Taking 3 sides as 5cm, 7cm, 8cm.
$|5-7| < 8 < |5+7|$
$\Rightarrow 2 < 8 < 12 \rightarrow \Delta$ is possible

Case 4 Taking 3 sides as 2cm, 7cm, 8cm
$\Rightarrow |2-7| < 8 < |2+7|$
$\Rightarrow 5 < 8 < 9 \rightarrow \Delta$ is possible

$\therefore$ 2 triangles can be formed by taking any three of the line segments out of the segments of length 2cm, 5cm, 7cm and 8cm.

147. (a) Given expression,
$264 \div 8 - 1 - 32 \times 2 + 80 \div 5 \times 40 \div 20$
$= \frac{264}{8} - 1 - 32 \times 2 + \frac{80}{5} \times \frac{40}{20}$
$= 33 - 1 - 64 + 16 \times 2$
$= 32 - 64 + 32$
$= 64 - 64 = 0$

148. (b) Required ratio $= \frac{20}{40} = 1:2$

149. (d) Selling price of the rod
$= 900 - (12\% \text{ of } 900)$
$= 900 - \left(\frac{12}{100} \times 900\right)$
$= 900 - 108 = ₹\,792$

150. (b) Ratio of efficiency of Sapna and Rakesh = 2 : 1
$\therefore$ Total work $= (2+1) \times 48$
$= 144$ unit
Hence time taken to complete the project by sapana $= \frac{144}{2} = 72$ days

151. (c) 'Diligent' means showing careful and persistent effort in doing something; hard-working. Hence, its antonym is 'Lazy'.

152. (d) The word 'strive' means to make great efforts or attempt; to struggle or work hard towards achieving something.

153. (b) 'Pitiable' means deserving or arousing pity; pathetic. Hence, its antonym is 'Pleasant'.

154. (d) The word 'Efface' means to erase or destroy completely; to make oneself inconspicuous.

155. (a) The word 'Astonished' means feeling shocked or surprised. Hence, its synonym is 'stunned.'

156. (b) The phrase/idiom that will improve the underlined part of the sentence is 'jumped at the opportunity.' This idiom means to eagerly accept or seize an opportunity. It fits well in the context of being proactive in filling a job position after the principal's departure.

157. (d) Part 'fell off after their father' contains an error. The use of 'fell off' is incorrect in the sentence. We need to use 'fell apart' which mean destroyed.

158. (b) The underlined part of the sentence contains an error. Use 'The core part of Artificial Intelligence'. Prepositions 'of' is commonly used to show possession or association.

159. (c) 'Quaint' refers to attractively unusual or old-fashioned. Hence, its nearest antonym is 'Ordinary'.

160. (d) Sentence given in option (d) has correct spellings and gramatical structure.

161. (d) 'Languid' displaying or having a disinclination for physical exertion or effort; slow and relaxed. Hence, its antonym is 'Energetic'.

162. (d) The idiom 'under the weather' means that someone is not feeling well or is slightly sick.

163. (d) 'Andromania' is madness or obsession with males.

164. (d) 'Exestenalism' is incorrectly spelt word. The correct spelling is 'existentialism'.

165. (a) The underlined part of the sentence contains an error. To correct this, we should use the affirmative form of the sentence, which is 'did they speak.'

166. (a) The idiom 'a vicious cycle' refers to a situation where one problem or negative factor exacerbates another, leading to a worsening or self-perpetuating cycle.

167. (a) The given sentence is grammatically correct and contextually meaningful.

168. (d) A 'unicorn' is a mythological animal with one horn on its forehead.

169. (a) The underlined part of the sentence contains an error. 'By a sweeping majority' correctly indicates the manner in which Mr. Patel is likely to win the elections, emphasising the magnitude or extent of the majority.

170. (c) 'Introvert' means a shy, reticent person.

171. (d) The idiom 'the best of both worlds' means to have the advantages or benefits of two different things at the same time, usually where one might expect to have to choose between them.

172. (b) The most appropriate idiom that can substitute the underlined words is 'living hand to mouth'. This idiom means living with just enough money to cover basic needs, without any surplus. It accurately describes the situation of living without a lot of money.

173. (b) The correct spelling is 'notably'.

174. (b) The underlined part of the sentence contains an error. Use 'to' in place of 'for' to correct the sentence.

175. (c) The correct spelling is 'insouciant'. It means free from concern, worry or anxiety.

176. (b) The idiom 'at the eleventh hour' typically means doing something at the very last possible moment or just before a deadline.

177. (a) The underlined part of the sentence contains an error. The phrase 'incapable of being tired' is the correct expression. It means that the Sumo wrestler does not seem to get tired.

178. (a) The correct substitution is 'bilingual', which refers to someone who can speak two languages fluently. It fits perfectly with the context of the sentence.

179. (b) Part 'of Ganga and it' contains an error. The use of 'it' is incorrect in the sentence as plural pronoun is used. Hence, use 'they are' in place of 'it is.'

180. (d) 'To face a difficult situation', The idiom 'bite the bullet' means to bravely face something painful or unpleasant that is unavoidable.

181. (a) 'Erapts' is the incorrectly spelt word. The correct spelling is 'erupts'.

182. (d) 'Suspend' means to temporarily prevent from continuing or being in force or effect. Hence, its antonym is 'Resume'.

183. (c) A person who betrays their country for personal gain is called a 'traitor', making it the correct one-word substitute.

184. (a) To avoid talking about what is important - 'Beat around the bush' means to dodge the main topic or not speak directly about something important.

185. (c) 'Enigmatic' means something that is mysterious, puzzling or difficult to understand. Hence, its antonym is 'Clear'.

186. (a) Always supporting someone even if there are problems or difficulties 'Through thick and thin' refers to unwavering loyalty or support, no matter the circumstances.

187. (b) The underlined part of the sentence contains an error.
The most appropriate option to substitute the underlined words is 'to cross safely' as the correct structure is 'too...to'.

188. (c) The correct spelling is 'peekaboo'. It is the name of a game.

189. (c) 'you had completed' The segment contains a tense error. It should be 'you would have completed' to match the conditional structure 'Had you been working...'

190. (c) The underlined part of the sentence can be substituted with option (c) 'she should write'.
The sentence is in past tense and 'should' is appropriate when asking permission or seeking guidance.

191. (a) 'Carefree' means without worries, fitting the context of children leading a carefree life.

192. (a) 'Cherished' means valued or loved, fitting the context of cherishing memories in adulthood.

193. (b) 'Innocent' means without guilt, fitting the context of a child being innocent.

194. (d) 'Rectify' means to correct, fitting the context of rectifying children's mistakes.

195. (c) 'Imprinted' means fixed in the mind, fitting the context of behaviour being imprinted on children's minds.

196. (a) The word 'Inhospitable' refers to a place or environment that is difficult or unpleasant to live in.

197. (b) The passage states that if 10 cm of soil is lost, it can take upto 1,000 years to regenerate that amount of soil naturally.

198. (d) The speakers tone is alarming as they emphasise the critical importance of soil for human survival and the fragile nature of soil resources.

199. (d) The most suitable title for the passage is 'Mysteries Under Man's Feet. 'This title reflects the theme of exploring and understanding the soil beneath our feet, which the passage discusses as an essential yet often overlooked aspect of our environment.

200. (c) The passage explicitly states that our survival as humans and life on this planet are intimately linked with the health and preservation of soil. Soil provides essential resources for human existence, including food, fiber and raw materials and supports biodiversity.

CPO SI P-1 SP 03

PAPER-1

SSC CPO SI SOLVED PAPER

29 June 2024 (Shift I)

MM : 200 **Time : 2 hr**

Instructions

1. This paper contains 200 questions.
2. It has 4 Parts, **Part I** General Intelligence and Reasoning, **Part II** General Knowledge and General Awareness, **Part III** Quantitative Aptitude and **Part IV** English Comprehension.
3. Each question carries 1 marks.

Part I

General Intelligence and Reasoning

1. If + means −, − means ×, ÷ means +, × means ÷ what will come in place of the question mark (?) in the given equation?

$1200 \times 3 - 1 \div 100 + 499 = ?$

(a) 5 (b) 3 (c) 2 (d) 1

2. The sequence of folding a paper and the manner in which the folded paper is cut is shown in the following figures. How would this paper look when unfolded?

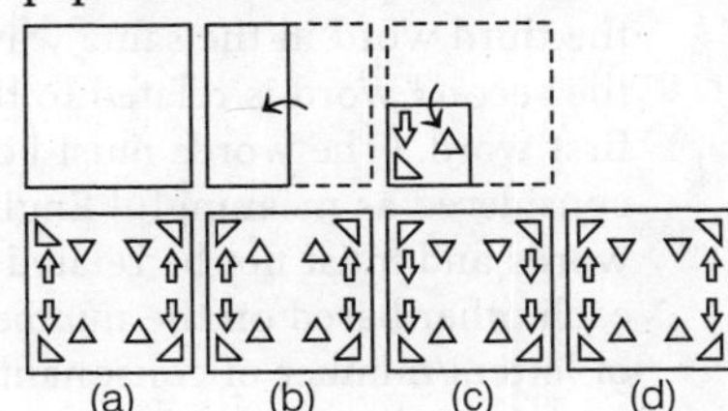

3. Select the option figure in which the given figure is embedded as its part (rotation is not allowed).

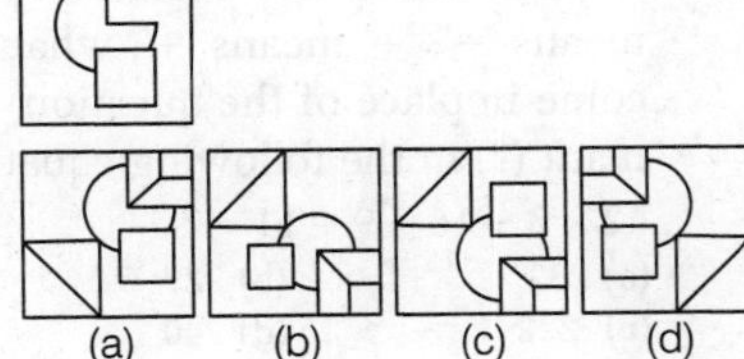

4. Two statements are given, followed by two conclusions numbered I and II. Assuming the statements to be true, even if they seem to be at variance with commonly known facts, decide which of the conclusions logically follow(s) from the statements.

Statements

All papers are trees.

Some papers are leaves.

Conclusions

I. Some trees are leaves.

II. Some trees are papers.

(a) Only Conclusion I follows

(b) Both Conclusions I and II follow

(c) Neither Conclusion I nor II follows

(d) Only Conclusion II follows

5. Six students namely Van, Luke, Jude, Tess, Ruth and Max are sitting around a circular table facing the centre. Van is sitting second to the left of Luke. Luke is an immediate neighbour of both Ruth and Max. Jude is sitting second to the left of Van. Ruth is an immediate neighbour of both Luke and Van. Who is the immediate neighbour of Jude and Luke?

(a) Ruth (b) Tess (c) Max (d) Van

6. Select the set in which the numbers are related in the same way as are the numbers of the following sets.

(**Note** Operations should be performed on the whole numbers, without breaking down the numbers into its constituent digits. e.g. 13- Operations on 13 such as adding/subtracting/ multiplying etc. to 13 can be performed. Breaking down 13 into 1 and 3 and then performing mathematical `operations on 1 and 3 is not allowed.)

(104, 26, 13)

(168, 42, 21)

(a) (216, 54, 27) (b) (216, 52, 27)

(c) (210, 54, 27) (d) (216, 54, 29)

7. Select the set in which the numbers are related in the same way as are the numbers of the following sets.

(**Note** Operations should be performed on the whole numbers, without breaking down the numbers into its constituent digits. e.g. 13-Operations on 13 such as adding/ subtracting/ multiplying etc. to 13 can be performed. Breaking down 13 into 1 and 3 and then performing mathematical operations on 1 and 3 is not allowed.)

(145, 76)

(182, 113)

(a) (163, 94)

(b) (153, 74)

(c) (149, 72)

(d) (174, 112)

8. Harini starts from a cafe and walks 4 km towards the south. She then turns right and walks 2 km, again turns right and walks 4 km, and then turns left and walks 4 km. How many kilometres will Harini need to walk to reach the cafe straight from this point?
(a) 8 km (b) 6 km
(c) 4 km (d) 2 km

9. Select the set in which the numbers are related in the same way as are the numbers of the following sets.
(**Note** Operations should be performed on the whole numbers, without breaking down the numbers into its constituent digits. E.g. 13-Operations on 13 such as adding/subtracting/ multiplying etc. to 13 can be performed. Breaking down 13 into 1 and 3 and then performing mathematical operations on 1 and 3 is not allowed.)
(15, 60, 10)
(21, 84, 14)
(a) (31, 132, 22) (b) (33, 132, 24)
(c) (33, 134, 22) (d) (33, 132, 22)

10. A dice has its faces marked by symbols α, β, θ, γ, π and δ. Two positions of the same dice are given below. Which face is opposite to face β ?

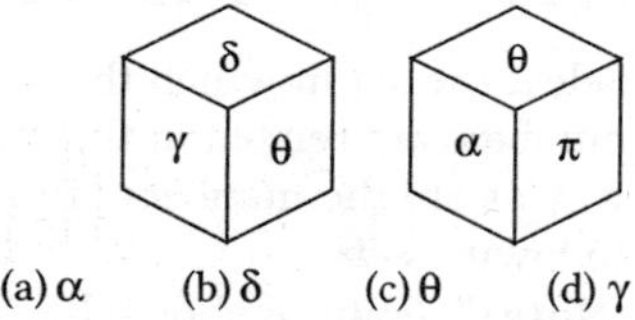

(a) α (b) δ (c) θ (d) γ

11. If '+' means, '–', '–' means '×', '×' means '÷' and '÷' means '+', what will come in place of '?' in the following equation?
59 ÷ 6 – 28 ×7 +30 = ?
(a) 49 (b) 53
(c) 67 (d) 58

12. If 'A' stands for '+', B' stands for '–', 'C' stands for '×' and 'D' stands for '÷', what will come in place of the question mark (?) in the following equation?
69 D 3 A 4 C 7 B 10 = ?
(a) 39 (b) 41
(c) 37 (d) 35

13. Select the option that is related to the third word in the same way as the second word is related to the first word.
(The words must be considered as meaningful English words and must not be related to each other based on the number of letters/number of consonants/ vowels in the word.)
Ounce : Kilogram : : Quart : ?
(a) Ounces (b) Liquid
(c) Stone (d) Litres

14. In a certain code language, 'BELT' is written as 78, and 'CASH' is written as '62'. How will 'DISC' be written in that language?
(a) 86 (b) 82
(c) 70 (d) 92

15. Which letter cluster will replace the question mark (?) to complete the given series?
PFBR, MKUA, ?, GUGS, DZZB
(a) HKPE (b) JPNJ
(c) JLEJ (d) QYGC

16. Select the figure from among the given options that can logically replace the question mark (?) in the following series.

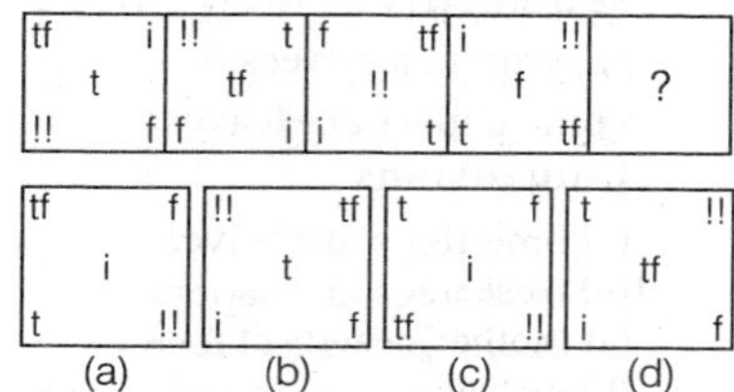

17. Identify the figure given in the options which when put in place of (?) will logically complete the series.

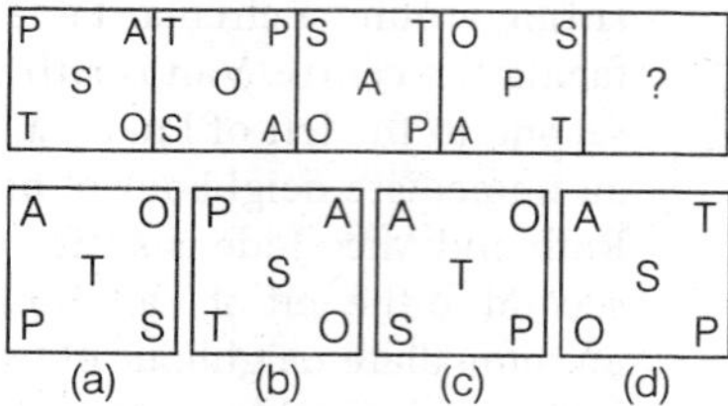

18. Which of the following terms will replace the question mark (?) in the given series?
MLV, NMW, ONX, ?
(a) FJM
(b) EFG
(c) POY
(d) GNM

19. Two statements are given followed by two conclusions numbered I and II. Assuming the statements to be true, even if they seem to be at variance with commonly known facts, decide which of the conclusions logically follow(s) from the given statements.
Statements
All networks are fibers.
Some fibers are wires.
Conclusions
I. All networks can never be wires.
II. Some networks are wires.
(a) Neither Conclusion I nor II follows
(b) Both Conclusions I and II follow
(c) Only Conclusion I follows
(d) Only Conclusion II follows

20. Select the correct mirror image of the given figure when the mirror is placed at MN as shown below.

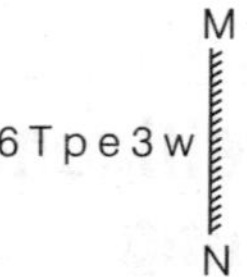

(a) we3qTə (b) ʍɛeq⊥ə
(c) wƐed⊥9 (d) wƐəqTə

21. If 'A' stands for '÷', 'B' stands for '×', 'C' stands for '+' and 'D' stands for '–', what will come in place of the question mark (?) in the following equation?
228 B 5 C 89 D 328 A 4 = ?
(a) 1774 (b) 1174
(c) 1147 (d) 1474

22. Select the option that is related to the third word in the same way as the second word is related to the first word. (The words must be considered as meaningful English words and must not be related to each other based on the number of letters/number of consonants/ vowels in the word.)
Swan : Cygnet : : Dog : ?
(a) Puppy (b) Calf
(c) Pet (d) Omnivores

23. If '+' means '–', '–' means '×', '×' means '÷', '÷' means '+', what will come in place of the question mark (?) in the following equation?
42 × 3 – 16 ÷ 9 + 11 = ?
(a) 232 (b) 227
(c) 222 (d) 240

24. Select the option that represents the correct order of the given words as they would appear in an English dictionary.
1. Winterish
2. Wingspread
3. Windblast
4. Wintertide
5. Windscreen
6. Winkling
(a) 3, 5, 2, 6, 1, 4
(b) 3, 5, 4, 2, 6, 1
(c) 3, 5, 2, 4, 6, 1
(d) 3, 5, 2, 4, 1, 6

25. In a code language, 'ROCK' is written as 'PKAG', and 'CLUB' is written as 'AHSX'. How will 'SHOP' be written in that language?
(a) MQDL (b) QMLD
(c) QDML (d) QMDL

26. In a certain code language, 'COOL' is written as '45' and 'TREE' is written as '48'. How will 'WELL' be written in that language?
(a) 46 (b) 52
(c) 36 (d) 51

27. Select the option that indicates the correct arrangement of the given words in the order in which they appear in an English dictionary.
1. Circle
2. Cinema
3. Circus
4. Circumference
5. Cipher
(a) 2, 5, 1, 4, 3 (b) 2, 1, 5, 4, 3
(c) 5, 2, 4, 1, 3 (d) 5, 4, 3, 1, 2

28. Rajesh starts from Point A and drives 17 km towards West. He then takes a left turn, drives 10 km, turns left and drives 40 km. He then takes a left turn and drives 30 km. He takes a final left turn, drives 23 km and stops at Point Q. How far (shortest distance) and towards which direction should he now drive to reach Point A again?
(All turns are 90° turns only.)
(a) 20 km towards South
(b) 20 km towards North
(c) 15 km towards North
(d) 15 km towards South

29. Two statements are given, followed by two conclusions numbered I and II. Assuming the statements to be true, even if they seem to be at variance with commonly known facts, decide which of the conclusions logically follow(s) from the statements.
Statements
Some clothes are sarees.
All sarees are silks.
Conclusions
I. Some clothes are silks.
II. Some silks are sarees.
(a) Only Conclusion II follows
(b) Only Conclusion I follows
(c) Neither Conclusion I nor II follows
(d) Both Conclusions I and II follow

30. 254 is related to 524 following a certain logic. Following the same logic, 912 is related to 642. Which of the following numbers is related to 188 using the same logic?
(a) 900 (b) 845 (c) 825 (d) 840

31. In a certain code language,
'A @ B' means 'A is the daughter of B'.
'A # B' means 'A is the brother of B'.
'A + B' means 'A is the wife of B'.
'A % B' means 'A is the father of B'.
How is M related to T if 'M # N @ P + S % T'?
(a) Brother
(b) Husband
(c) Mother's brother
(d) Father

32. Select the pair which is related to each other in the same way as the following.
72 : 25
(a) 68 : 8 (b) 54 : 30
(c) 28 : 36 (d) 46 : 14

33. In a certain code language,
'A + B' means 'A is the mother of B'.
'A – B' means 'A is the husband of B'.
'A × B' means 'B is the sister of A'
and 'A ÷ B' means 'A is the father of B'.
Based on the above information, how is R related to T if 'R ÷ S – V + Q × T'?
(a) Father
(b) Father's father
(c) Brother
(d) Son

34. Which of the following numbers will replace the question mark (?) in the given series?
67, 78, 103, 118, ?
(a) 171 (b) 184 (c) 147 (d) 241

35. Find the two signs to be interchanged for making the following equation correct.
$9 + 8 \times 4 - 8 \div 2 = 11$
(a) + and ÷ (b) ÷ and ×
(c) – and + (d) ÷ and –

36. Which letter cluster can replace the question mark (?) to complete the given series?
TCVH, RETJ, ?, NIPN, LKNP
(a) MGSK (b) MFSK
(c) PGRL (d) PFRL

37. Select the figure from among the given options that can logically replace the question mark (?) in the following series.

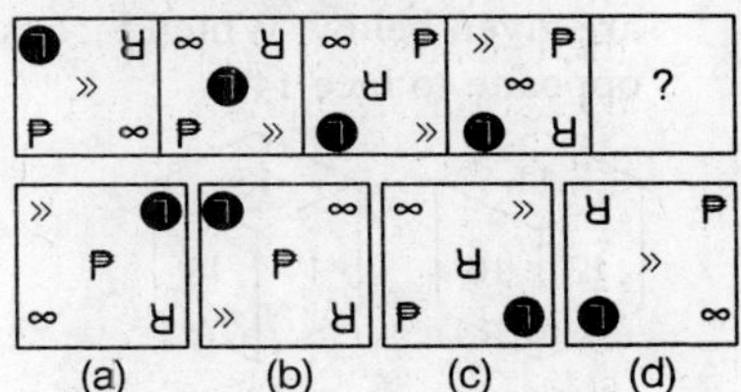

38. Select the option in which the given figure (X) is embedded as its part. (Rotation is not allowed.)

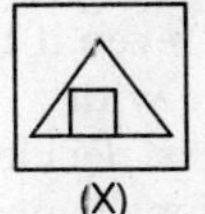

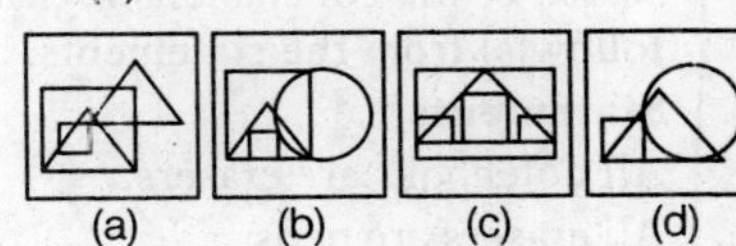

39. Which of the following numbers will replace the question mark (?) in the given series?
43, 48, 46, ?, 49, 54, 52
(a) 52 (b) 51
(c) 50 (d) 47

40. In a code language, 'DILIP' is coded as 46-36-30-36-22 and 'PRINCE' is coded as 22-18-36-26-48-44. How will 'FIROZ' be coded in the same language?
(a) 42-36-18-24-2 (b) 2-36-18-42-52
(c) 56-36-18-32-52 (d) 48-36-18-38-6

41. If +, means –, – means ×, × means ÷, ÷ means +, what will come in place of the question mark (?) in the given equation.

$300 - 12 \times 120 \div 9 + 32 = ?$

(a) 7 (b) 5 (c) 12 (d) 10

42. Which of the following numbers will replace the question marks (?) in the given series?

2, 6, 12, 20, ?, ?, 56, 72

(a) 36, 40 (b) 30, 38
(c) 30, 42 (d) 32, 44

43. Select the number from among the given options that can replace the question mark (?) in the following series.

1024, 899, 835, 808, 800,?

(a) 795 (b) 798 (c) 797 (d) 799

44. A dice has its faces marked by numbers 11, 12, 13, 14, 15 and 16. Two positions of the same dice are given below. Which face is opposite to face 14?

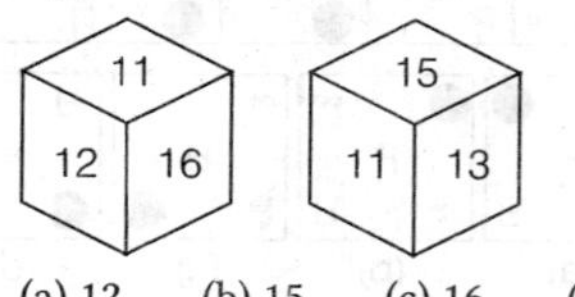

(a) 12 (b) 15 (c) 16 (d) 11

45. Two statements are given, followed by two conclusions numbered I and II. Assuming the statements to be true, even if they seem to be at variance with commonly known facts, decide which of the conclusions logically follow(s) from the statements.

Statements

All notebooks are erasers.

All erasers are pens.

Conclusions

I. All notebooks are pens.

II. Some pens are notebooks.

(a) Neither Conclusion nor II follows
(b) Only Conclusion I follows
(c) Only Conclusion II follows
(d) Both Conclusions I and II follow

46. Select the correct mirror image of the given figure when the mirror is placed at MN as shown below.

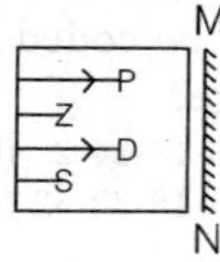

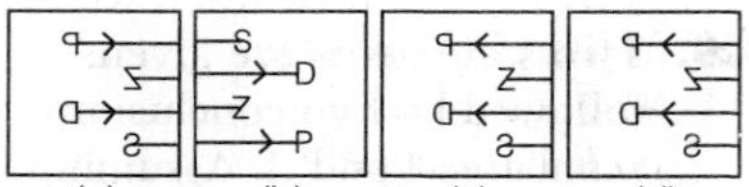

(a) (b) (c) (d)

47. In a certain code language, 'revise the lesson' is written as 'rx cd st' and 'the lesson plan' is written as 'cd nq rx'. How is 'revise' written in the given language?

(a) st (b) cd (c) rx (d) nq

48. In a certain code language, 'print the cards' is written as 'cd fm px' and 'cards for sale' is written as 'nt px ym'. How is 'cards' written in the given language?

(a) px (b) cd (c) nt (d) fm

49. Three different positions of the same die are shown below. What is the number on the face opposite to the one having 6?

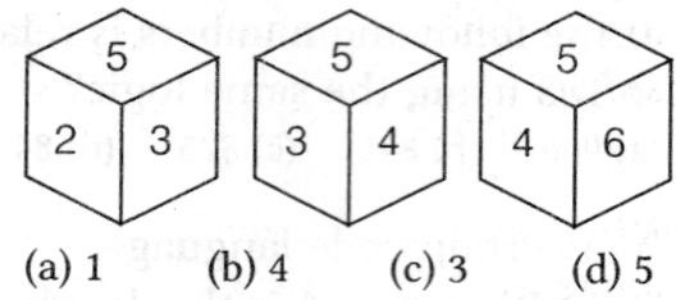

(a) 1 (b) 4 (c) 3 (d) 5

50. Based on the English alphabetical order, three of the following four letter-clusters are alike in a certain way and thus form a group. Which letter-cluster does not belong to that group?

(**Note** The odd letter-cluster is not based on the number of consonants/vowels or their position in the letter-cluster.)

(a) PUR (b) RWT (c) NSP (d) TYU

Part II

General Knowledge and General Awareness

51. Identify the reason for formation of dental plaque.

(a) When acids stick to the teeth.
(b) Masses of bacterial cells together with food particles stick to the teeth.
(c) Saliva sticks to the pulp.
(d) When bacteria acting on sugars produce acids.

52. Which of the following books is written by Rabindranath Tagore?

(a) The Essential Writings
(b) The Way to God
(c) Nationalism
(d) Non-Violent Resistance

53. Indian musician, composer and singer Shubha Mudgal was awarded with the .... in 2000.

(a) Padma Bhushan
(b) Padma Vibhushan
(c) Sangeet Natak Akademi
(d) Padma Shri

54. Which of the following statements about privatisation is false?

(a) Improved performance is one of the advantages of privatisation.
(b) There is no possibility of exploitation of monopoly power by private companies after privatisation.
(c) There was an increase in the cases of disinvestment after the economic reforms of 1991 as compared to the pre-1991 period.
(d) Maruti Udyog Limited was a public sector enterprise before the 1991 economic references.

55. As of 2022, according to the Ministry of Petroleum and Natural Gas of the Government of India, how many oil refineries are there in India in total?

(a) 35 (b) 23 (c) 21 (d) 15

56. Which of the following physiographic divisions of India has extensive alluvial soil ?

(a) The Himalayan Range
(b) The North Indian Plain
(c) The Island Group
(d) The Great Indian Desert

57. What is the shape of the eyeball?

(a) Spherical (b) Oval
(c) Cylindrical (d) Circular

58. Pipelines as a means of transport are looked after by the ...... of the Government of India.

(a) Ministry of Petroleum and Natural Gas
(b) Ministry of Home Affairs
(c) Ministry of Railways
(d) Ministry of Road Transport and Highways

59. Which of the following teams won the 12th edition of the Ice-Hockey Association of India's (IHAI) National Ice-Hockey Championship for men in 2023?

(a) Jammu and Kashmir Blue Team
(b) Ladakh Scouts
(c) Indo-Tibetan Border Police (ITBP)
(d) Rimo Club Leh

60. The Swaran Singh Committee had formulated .... point code of Fundamental Duties.
(a) 11 (b) 7 (c) 9 (d) 8

61. The author of Tarikh-i-Mubarak Shahi, Yahya Sirhindi claims that the founder of ...... dynasty of Delhi Sultanate was a descendant of Prophet Muhammad.
(a) Sayyid (b) Mamluk
(c) Lodi (d) Khilji

62. Match Column-A with Column-B.

	Column-A		Column-B
A.	Alkanes	1.	Ethane
B.	Alkenes	2.	Butyne
C.	Alkynes	3.	Propene
D.	Aldehyde	4.	Methanal

(a) A-1, B-3, C-2, D-4
(b) A-1, B-3, C-4, D-2
(c) A-4, B-3, C-2, D-1
(d) A-3, B-4, C-2, D-1

63. Prof M. Yunus won the Nobel Peace Prize in which year?
(a) 2002 (b) 2006 (c) 2004 (d) 2001

64. In which year India will organise the ICC Men's One-Day International World Cup Cricket?
(a) 2031 (b) 2027 (c) 2025 (d) 2030

65. According to Mendeleev's Periodic Table, which element's properties matched up remarkably well with eka-aluminium?
(a) Titanium (b) Germanium
(c) Gallium (d) Scandium

66. The adoption of the Industrial Policy of 1956 coincided with which Five-Year Plan?
(a) Third Five-Year Plan
(b) First Five-Year Plan
(c) Second Five-Year Plan
(d) Fourth Five-Year Plan

67. Which of the following classical dance forms is usually concluded with Tarangam?
(a) Kuchipudi (b) Sattriya
(c) Kathakali (d) Odissi

68. For which of the following sources of financial resources may financial intermediation not be required?
(a) Raising equity *via* public offering
(b) Family funds
(c) Borrowing from banks
(d) Borrowing from All India Development Financial Institutions

69. Which festival is popularly known as the festival of colours?
(a) Janmashtami (b) Holi
(c) Diwali (d) Maha Shivratri

70. Who among the following Indian Classical dancers received the National Nritya Shiromani Award 2022?
(a) Aditi Mangaldas
(b) Shovana Narayan
(c) Aparna Satheesan
(d) Sangeeta Majumdar

71. Generally, Directive Principles are ......
(a) negative directions
(b) arbitrary actions
(c) positive directions
(d) prohibitive in nature

72. Which is an advanced weather satellite of India configured with improved imaging system and atmospheric sounder?
(a) RS-D1 (b) GSAT-7A
(c) INSAT-3D (d) SROSS-2

73. Which of the following statements is not correct about River Ganga?
(a) The water level of River Ganga never depends on monsoon and climatic condition of the Himalaya.
(b) River Ganga and its river basin support lots of wonderful wildlife, particularly river dolphins, otters, freshwater turtles and gharials.
(c) River Ganga flows from the Himalayas all the way to the Bay of Bengal.
(d) River Ganga in India is more than 2500 km long and is the most populated river basin in the world.

74. In India, the International Day of Non-Violence is also celebrated as ....
(a) Swami Vivekanand Jayanti
(b) Gandhi Jayanti
(c) Guru Ravidas Jayanti
(d) Mahavir Jayanti

75. Which of the following cities of Delhi was founded by Ghiyasuddin Tughlaq?
(a) Qila-i-Rai Pithora
(b) Sin
(c) Tughlaqabad
(d) Jahanpanah

76. The number of players in baseball is
(a) 7 (b) 8 (c) 9 (d) 6

77. Who was executed as an accomplice to the murder of AMT Jackson?
(a) Matangini Hazra
(b) Khudiram Bose
(c) Hemu Kalani
(d) Krishnaji Gopal Karve

78. Which of the following are salt-water lakes?
A. Sambhar lake
B. Dal lake
C. Wular lake
D. Chilika lake
(a) A and D (b) C and D
(c) A and B (d) A and C

79. The Indian National Congress formally took up the Swadeshi call in its Benaras Session of 1905 under the presidentship of ....
(a) Gopal Krishna Gokhale
(b) Jawaharlal Nehru
(c) Rajendra Prasad
(d) Motilal Nehru

80. Which of the following Ashokan rock edicts declares prohibition of animal sacrifice?
(a) Major Rock Edict-II
(b) Major Rock Edict-I
(c) Major Rock Edict-IV
(d) Major Rock Edict-III

81. In which of the following is nicotine present in high quantity?
(a) Lime soda (b) Tea
(c) Tobacco (d) Butter milk

82. According to the Global Hunger Index 2022, which neighbouring country is only behind India with a rank of 109 out of 121 countries?
(a) Afghanistan (b) Nepal
(c) Pakistan (d) Bangladesh

83. Which of the following gases are found in coal mines and marshy places?
(a) Nitrogen dioxide
(b) Ozone
(c) Methane
(d) Steam

84. Radheshyam Barle, a recipient of Padma Shri in 2021, is an exponent of which of the following dance forms?
(a) Pal (b) Karma
(c) Diwari (d) Panthi

85. Which of the following events happened in 1950?
(a) First Five-Year Plan was started
(b) First National Agricultural Policy was adopted
(c) Industrial Policy Resolution was adopted
(d) The Planning Commission was set up

86. Identify the largest phylum in the animal kingdom.
(a) Annelida
(b) Mollusca
(c) Platyhelmenthis
(d) Arthropoda

87. Which Article of the Indian Constitution mentions that 'All the executive action of the Government of a state shall be expressed to be taken in the name of the Governor'?
(a) Article 166(1) (b) Article 163(1)
(c) Article 164(1) (d) Article 165(1)

88. Satyashodhak Samaj (truth seeker society) was established by which of the following social reformers?
(a) Bhimrao Ramji Ambedkar
(b) Jyotiba Phule
(c) Mahatma Gandhi
(d) Mahadev Govind Ranade

89. The body of the phylum .... is unsegmented and dorsoventrally flattened.
(a) Coelenterata
(b) Mollusca
(c) Arthropoda
(d) Platyhelminthes

90. Who among the following is known as Tuti-e-Hind?
(a) Tansen (b) Naubat Khan
(c) Surdas (d) Amir Khusrau

91. Which of the following is a joint sector industry in India?
(a) Dabur
(b) NALCO
(c) Oil India Limited
(d) TISCO

92. Which Article of the Indian Constitution states that 'There shall be a High Court for each state'?
(a) Article 214 (b) Article 125
(c) Article 245 (d) Article 275

93. How much will be 59°F in Celsius?
(a) 45°C (b) 59°C
(c) 15°C (d) 30°C

94. As per the National Multidimensional Poverty Index Report 2023, which of the following UTs has the lowest poverty rate?
(a) Lakshadweep
(b) Ladakh
(c) Jammu and Kashmir
(d) Puducherry

95. Who is the Chief Executive Head of the State?
(a) PM (b) Governor
(c) President (d) CM

96. In which year, for the first time, was a resolution on the National Sports Policy laid in both Houses of Parliament?
(a) 1948 (b) 2000 (c) 1984 (d) 2014

97. Which of the following committees recommended the Fundamental Duties?
(a) Ashok Mehta Committee
(b) Nehru Committee
(c) Balwinder Singh Committee
(d) Swaran Singh Committee

98. Which of the following dance forms is represented by Kelucharan Mohapatra?
(a) Bharatanatyam (b) Manipuri
(c) Odissi (d) Kathak

99. .... wins the Best Male Playback Singer at the 67th National Film Awards.
(a) B Praak (b) Sonu Nigam
(c) Shaan (d) Arijit Singh

100. Who among the following is the author of the book 'Those Pricey Thakur Girls'?
(a) Anuja Chauhan
(b) Anita Nair
(c) Pratibha Ray
(d) Preeti Shenoy

Part III

Quantitative Aptitude

101. Simplify the following
$72 \div 8 \times 4 + 40 - 35 \div 5 + 15$
(a) 24 (b) 84 (c) 9 (d) 48

102. Solve the following
$(\tan\theta + \sec\theta + 1)(\cot\theta - \operatorname{cosec}\theta + 1) = ?$
(a) 0 (b) 2
(c) – 1 (d) 1

103. The value of $(\operatorname{cosec}\theta - \sin\theta)(\sec\theta - \cos\theta)(\tan\theta + \cot\theta)$ is
(a) 1 (b) $\sec\theta \cdot \operatorname{cosec}\theta$
(c) 3 (d) – 3

104. The breadth of a room is twice its height and half its length. The volume of the room is 1728 m^3. The length of the room is
(a) 28 m (b) 20 m
(c) 34 m (d) 24 m

105. In triangle ABC, $AB = AC$ and $\angle A = 70°$. Find the value of $\angle C$.
(a) 75° (b) 65°
(c) 45° (d) 55°

106. Two successive price increases of 25% and 25% of an article are equivalent to a single price increase of
(a) 52.25% (b) 50.25%
(c) 48.50% (d) 56.25%

107. Find the curved surface area (in cm^2) of a cone of radius 3 cm and height 4 cm.
(a) 12π (b) 14π (c) 15π (d) 7π

108. A part of ₹ 48500 is invested at a simple interest of 15% per annum. The rest of the money is invested at the rate of 10% simple interest per annum after 2 years of the first investment. The ratio of interest after 5 years from the time when the first amount was invested is 5 : 3. How much is the second part that was invested (in ₹) at the rate of 10% simple interest?
(a) 29100 (b) 20940
(c) 19400 (d) 24900

109. The value of $\left(2\frac{1}{2} + 1\frac{3}{4} - \frac{1}{6}\right) \times 16 \div 49$ is
(a) $\frac{4}{7}$ (b) $\frac{3}{9}$ (c) $1\frac{1}{3}$ (d) $2\frac{3}{4}$

110. Sita takes a loan of ₹ 35000 at an interest rate of 10% compound interest, compounded annually. She agrees to pay two equal instalments in 2 years, one instalment at the end of each year. Find the value of each instalment. (Round off to the nearest integer)
(a) ₹ 10167 (b) ₹ 30167
(c) ₹ 20167 (d) ₹ 40167

111. The following table shows the marks of a student in 5 tests in the subjects Maths, Physics, and Chemistry (out of 100 for each subject). Study the table and answer the question that follows.

Tests	Maths	Physics	Chemistry
1	80	69	91
2	94	79	85
3	88	81	95
4	92	76	90
5	96	90	84

The ratio of the average marks obtained by the student in test 2 to the average marks he got in Maths in all tests, is:

(a) 21 : 25 (b) 4 : 7
(c) 4 : 3 (d) 43 : 45

112. Simplify the given expression

$$\frac{\left(2\frac{1}{7}+6\frac{1}{7}\right)\div\frac{9}{7}}{1\frac{1}{9}\div\left\{\frac{7}{9}+\left(\frac{4}{9}\div\frac{4}{3}\right)\right\}}$$

(a) $\frac{56}{9}$ (b) $\frac{55}{9}$
(c) $\frac{58}{9}$ (d) $\frac{53}{9}$

113. The following table shows the yearly production of bags (in thousands) by different companies.

Company	2012	2013	2014	2015
A	29	37	38	42
B	30	38	40	39
C	35	30	45	43
D	37	35	42	45

The total production of company A over the given years is what percentage of the total production of company D over the given years?

(a) 91.82% (b) 98.21%
(c) 82.91% (d) 89.21%

114. In a school, the total number of boys is 20% more than the total number of girls. What is the ratio of the number of boys to that of girls in the school?

(a) 6 : 5 (b) 4 : 5
(c) 5 : 3 (d) 5 : 6

115. If one angle of triangle *PQR* is greater than the sum of the other two, the triangle *PQR* will be

(a) equilateral (b) acute angle
(c) obtuse angle (d) right angle

116. If two kinds of rice which cost ₹ 25 a kg and ₹ 40 a kg are mixed in the ratio of 3 : 2, then find the cost of the mixture per kg.

(a) ₹ 31 (b) ₹ 30 (c) ₹ 32 (d) ₹ 33

117. In the following table, the achievement of 10 boys and 10 girls in Math has been given. Study the table and select the correct statement.

Boys	Girls
56	35
75	88
34	95
49	99
89	67
99	82
94	97
59	63
82	79
79	81

(a) The average achievement of the boys and girls is same.
(b) The given data is insufficient to draw any meaningful conclusion.
(c) The average achievement of the girls is more than that of the boys.
(d) The average achievement of the boys is more than that of the girls.

118. A shopkeeper wanted to sell ₹ 2000 worth of products. But he had two options, giving three successive discounts of 10% each or giving a single discount of 28%. What was the difference between the two options of discounts (in ₹)?

(a) 16 (b) 28 (c) 18 (d) 22

119. Amita can build a room in the same amount of time that Bina and Sita working together can build. If Amita and Bina together could do it in 25 days and Sita alone in 35 days, then how many days are required for Bina alone to do the same work?

(a) 180 days (b) 165 days
(c) 152 days (d) 175 days

120. The cost price of two articles is equal. One article is sold at a profit of 12% and the other article for ₹ 3600 more than the first. If the net profit is $15\frac{27}{51}$%, then what is the cost price of each article?

(a) ₹ 50990 (b) ₹ 50000
(c) ₹ 51000 (d) ₹ 52150

121. Simplify

$$\left[\left(7\frac{1}{4}\right)^2-\left(5\frac{4}{5}\right)^2\right]\div 5\frac{4}{5}\times\frac{16}{9}$$

(a) 9.3 (b) 7.4
(c) 5.8 (d) 3.1

122. $\tan^4 A + \tan^2 A$ is equal to

(a) $\sec^4 A - \sec^2 A$
(b) $\sec^2 A - \sec^4 A$
(c) $\sec^4 A + \sec^2 A$
(d) $-(\sec^2 A + \sec^4 A)$

123. A boat can travel 16.9 km downstream in 52 min. If the speed of the current is 3 km/h, then how much time (in hours) will the boat take to travel 84 km upstream?

(a) 6.22 (b) 6
(c) 13.5 (d) 7.5

124. In a 100-km journey, the average speed of *S* is 40 km/h. He covers the first 60 km in 40 min and the next 20 km in 50 min. What is his speed in the last 20 km (in km/h)?

(a) 30 (b) 40
(c) 25 (d) 20

125. If $m \times 7 + 4 - 6 \div 3 - 7 + 45 \div 5 \times 4 + 49 = 87$, then the value of *m* is

(a) 0 (b) 14
(c) 1 (d) 7

126. The following table shows the marks obtained out of 100, by four students in four different subjects.

Students	Hindi	Maths	Science	Social
Arnav	83	87	90	92
Ronak	75	89	79	82
Shivam	88	95	90	87
Sonu	92	85	90	88

The total marks scored by Ronak in all the subjects is what percentage of the total marks scored by Shivam, Sonu, Arnav together in all the subjects?

(a) 44.46% (b) 34.63%
(c) 40.63% (d) 30.46%

127. Akash and Vikash can complete a work in 40 days and 60 days, respectively. In how many days will the entire work be completed if they work on alternate days, starting with Akash?

(a) 52 (b) 50 (c) 48 (d) 42

128. Find the value of the following expression.
$2 \times 8 \div 4 - 5$ of $3 + 6 \div 3 \times 2 - 6$ of $3 + 5$
(a) – 20 (b) 20
(c) – 15 (d) 15

129. Determine the value of the product $(4a + 3b)(16a^2 - 12ab + 9b^2)$ for $a = 2$ and $b = 3$.
(a) 1141 (b) 1231
(c) 1241 (d) 1131

130. A school has two rectangular playgrounds, which are similar in shape. If the length and the breadth of the first playground are given as 224 m and 160 m, respectively, then which of the following options cannot be the dimensions of the second playground?
(a) Length = 168 m; Breadth = 120 m
(b) Length = 343 m; Breadth = 255 m
(c) Length = 273 m; Breadth = 195 m
(d) Length = 210 m; Breadth = 150 m

131. 42% of Ranita's weekly income is equal to 56% of Bhaskar's weekly income. If Bhaskar's weekly income was raised by ₹ 200, while Ranita's weekly income did not change, the ratio of the weekly incomes of Ranita and Bhaskar, respectively, would have been 5 : 4. What is Ranita's weekly income (in ₹)?
(a) 3000 (b) 4000
(c) 3600 (d) 4200

132. A trader sells an article at 16% below its cost price. Had he sold it for ₹ 192.20 more, he would have gained 15%. The new selling price (in ₹) of the article is:
(a) 724 (b) 742 (c) 731 (d) 713

133. Simplify the given expression.
$4 \times 5 \div 4$ of $5 \times 4 \div (6 + 6 \times 6 \div 6$ of $6 - 6 \div 6 \times 6)$
(a) 12 (b) 4 (c) 2 (d) 20

134. If $\sin^4 \theta + \cos^4 \theta = 2 \sin^2 \theta \cos^2 \theta$, $0° < \theta < 90°$, then find the value of $\cot \theta$.
(a) $\frac{1}{\sqrt{2}}$ (b) $\frac{1}{3}$
(c) 1 (d) $\frac{1}{2}$

135. A woman working in a company was supplied a rectangular solid (cuboid shape) of wax with dimensions 70 cm, 44 cm and 20 cm to prepare cylindrical candles, each 14 cm in diameter and 20 cm of height. Find the number of candles.
(a) 20 (b) 15
(c) 10 (d) 30

136. Two trains, 140 m and 120 m in length, are running in the same direction at the speed of 60 km/h and 78 km/h, respectively. In how much time will they completely cross each other?
(a) 58 sec (b) 65 sec
(c) 48 sec (d) 52 sec

137. The difference between the two perpendicular sides of a right-angled triangle is 2 cm and its area is 24 cm. What is the perimeter (in cm) of the triangle?
(a) 18 (b) 16
(c) 14 (d) 24

138. A 320 m long train completely crosses a 240 m long train, coming from the opposite direction, in y seconds. If the first train is travelling at the speed of 44 km/h and the second train is travelling at 56.8 km/h, then what is the value of y?
(a) 18 (b) 22 (c) 21 (d) 20

139. Study the given table and answer the question that follows.
Percentage of marks obtained by 5 students in different subjects.

Subjects /Students	History	Maths	Economics	Hindi	English
	250	200	250	150	150
Vikas	60	80	90	60	95
Shyam	90	70	80	70	40
Sohan	70	90	95	80	75
Mohan	80	60	70	95	80
Mohit	90	50	85	85	80

The marks obtained by Sohan in maths are .... than that obtained by Shyam in maths.
(a) 40 more
(b) 30 less
(c) 40 less
(d) 30 more

140. Study the given table and answer the question that follows.
The table shows the number of students studying in 6 different classes of 6 different schools.

School	V	VI	VII	VIII	IX	X
P	152	160	145	156	147	144
Q	148	166	150	155	157	143
R	161	152	140	145	143	165
S	159	142	149	140	142	168
T	147	144	158	163	154	150
U	150	160	162	160	161	140
Total	917	924	904	919	904	910

The number of students studying in class VII from school U forms approximately what percentage of the total number of students from all the classes together from that school?
(a) 19% (b) 15% (c) 21% (d) 17%

141. Simplify the given expression
$\left(7.2 \times 4.1 \div 12.3 + 22.5 \text{ of } \frac{1}{25} - \frac{1}{10}\right)$
(a) 4.9 (b) 9.6 (c) 7.4 (d) 3.2

142. If $a + b + c = 15$ and $ab + bc + ca = 35$, then find the value of $a^3 + b^3 + c^3 - 3abc$.
(a) 1200 (b) 2100
(c) 1800 (d) 1500

143. Simplify
$\left(\frac{3}{4} + \frac{5}{4}\right) \times \left(\frac{9}{5} - \frac{4}{5}\right) \div \left(\frac{3}{2} + \frac{1}{2}\right).$
(a) 1 (b) – 1 (c) 2 (d) – 2

144. A shopkeeper offers a discount of 24 % on the marked price. On a special sale day, he offers an extra 30% off coupon after the first discount. If the article was sold for ₹ 7700.70, what is the marked price left parenthesis in ₹ right parenthesis of the article?
(a) 17475 (b) 14745
(c) 14475 (d) 17745

145. The distance between the centres of the two circles, with radius 3 cm and 2 cm, respectively, is 13 cm. The length (in cm) of a transverse common tangent is:
(a) 18 cm (b) 9 cm
(c) 16 cm (d) 12 cm

146. The given bar-graph shows the strength of employees (in lakhs) of a company during four different years.

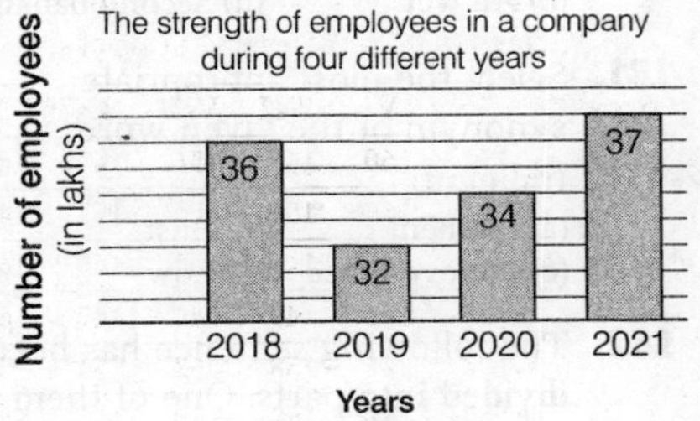

What was the percentage increase in employees in 2020 over 2019?

(a) $6\frac{1}{4}\%$ (b) $6\frac{3}{4}\%$
(c) $5\frac{1}{4}\%$ (d) $4\frac{3}{4}\%$

147. What must be added to $(x^3 - 3x^2 + 4x - 75)$ to obtain a polynomial that is exactly divisible by $(x - 5)$?

(a) 4 (b) 6
(c) 2 (d) 5

148. A is 25% more than B and B is 30% less than C. If C is 20% more than D, then by what percentage is A more than D?

(a) 5% (b) 3%
(c) 6% (d) 2%

149. The height and radius of a cone-shaped storage tank are 9 ft. and 7 ft., respectively. Find the volume of water the tank can hold? (use $\pi = \frac{22}{7}$)

(a) 1423 cubic ft. (b) 462 cubic ft.
(c) 1386 cubic ft. (d) 527 cubic ft.

150. A cone of slant height 4.2 units has a lateral surface area 13.2 units^2. The radius of the base is

(a) 2 units (b) 1.5 units
(c) 2.5 units (d) 1 unit

Part IV

English Comprehension

151. Select the most appropriate synonym of the given word.
Habitual

(a) Diverse (b) Pertinent
(c) Considerate (d) Continuous

152. Select the most appropriate synonym of the given word.
Unhappiness

(a) Willing
(b) Wicked
(c) Wilful
(d) Woe

153. Select the sentence that has a grammatical error.

(a) I could be deriving into town later on.
(b) I will be drive into town later on.
(c) I will be driving into town later on.
(d) I might drive into town later on.

154. Select the most appropriate synonym of the given word.
Insipid

(a) Obscure
(b) Tasteless
(c) Dismal
(b) Idle

155. Select the option that can be used as a one-word substitute for the given group of words.
A person who is filled with excessive enthusiasm

(a) Extrovert
(b) Horiticulturial
(c) Introvert
(d) Narcissist

156. The following sentence has been split into four segments. Identify the segment that contains a grammatical error.
Most of the committee / are here to / decide the fate of/ this ancient building.

(a) decide the fate of
(b) this ancient building
(c) are here to
(d) Most of the committee

157. Select the most appropriate meaning of the underlined segment in the given sentence.
I sent the agreement over for them to sign so <u>the ball is now in their court</u>.

(a) It is time for someone to deal with a problem or make a decision, because other people have already done as much as they can.
(b) A time when after which programmes for older audiences may be aired on TV.
(c) An approach that uses traditional ideas that have previously worked.
(d) Better to be satisfied with what you have than risk losing it by trying to get something.

158. Select the most appropriate idiom to fill in the blank.
She now has more than a year as minister ....

(a) down for the count
(b) on her thin ice
(c) under her belt
(d) in the fast lane

159. Select the option that rectifies the spelling error in the given sentence.
They brogth their dog to the park for a walk.

(a) brught
(b) brahgt
(c) brought
(d) braoght

160. Select the most appropriate meaning of the given idiom.
See eye to eye

(a) To agree with someone
(b) To do something pointless
(c) To get upset with something
(d) To ignore someone

161. Select the option that is similar in meaning to the underlined word in the following sentence.
Looking after small children is a real <u>conundrum</u> for working parents.

(a) pacification (b) peace
(c) plan (d) problem

162. Select the incorrectly spelt word.

(a) Ambigous
(b) Luminous
(c) Gregarious
(d) Nostalgia

163. Select the most appropriate option that can substitute the underlined segment in the given sentence.
Had I known that you were planning to visit me, <u>I should have done</u> all the necessary arrangements.

(a) I must have made
(b) I would have made
(c) I would have do
(d) I should have made

164. Select the most appropriate option that can substitute the highlighted words in the given sentence.
His interpretation of the facts was impressive.

(a) understood of realities
(b) understand of realities
(c) understanding of realities
(d) understands of realities

165. Select the incorrectly spelt word.
(a) Vagabond (b) Gallantry
(c) Notation (d) Witharing

166. Select the option that can be used as a one-word substitute for the underlined group of words.
The liberal leadership simply joined the ranks of the existing government by the few.
(a) Democracy (b) Oligarchy
(c) Autocracy (d) Plutocracy

167. Select the most appropriate option that can substitute the underlined segment in the given sentence. If there is no need to substitute it, select 'No substitution'.
If his father will give money, he will buy a sports bike.
(a) No substitution
(b) If his father gave money
(c) If his father gives money
(d) If his father give money

168. Select the most appropriate antonym of the given word.
Cowardice
(a) Hazard (b) Boldness
(c) Abundance (d) Vigour

169. Select the most appropriate option that can substitute the underlined segment in the given sentence.
He wanted to visiting the Golden Temple in Amritsar.
(a) wanted to visitor
(b) wanted to be visit
(c) wanted to visit
(d) wanted to visited

170. Select the most appropriate antonym of the underlined word.
Her behaviour was consistent even in challenging situations.
(a) appreciative (b) enthusiastic
(c) standard (d) unpredictable

171. Select the most appropriate meaning of the given idiom.
From cradle to grave
(a) Buying something very cheap or very expensive
(b) During the whole span of one's life
(c) Giving directions and telling someone to follow
(d) To achieve something you needed

172. Select the most appropriate meaning of the given idiom.
Chip on the shoulder
(a) Happy (b) Offended
(c) Elated (d) Emotional

173. Select the most appropriate option that can substitute the underlined segment in the given idiom.
A piece of biscuit
(a) cake (b) pastry
(c) tart (d) toast

174. In the following question a statement has been given with highlighted text. You are required to replace the text with correct phrase given in the options.
His intriguing mastery of the English language allowed him to write eloquently.
(a) master
(b) wellness known skill
(c) captivating expertise
(d) least known talent

175. Select the most appropriate antonym of the underlined word in the given sentence.
Recession fettered the company from any further investments.
(a) depended (b) valuable
(c) concealed (d) liberated

176. Select the most appropriate antonym of the underlined word.
The reports of the medical tests done are now accessible on phone.
(a) free (b) invisible
(c) restricted (d) useless

177. Select the most appropriate article to fill in the blank (ϕ-no article).
……… SDO is the head of the sub-division of …… government organisation.
(a) ϕ; a (b) a; a (c) an; a (d) an; ϕ

178. Select the option that can be used as a one-word substitute for the underlined words.
I do not like him because he always disapproves the things or opinions of others.
(a) is jealous of other people
(b) is critical of others
(c) is a hate monger
(d) is insensitive of others feelings

179. Select the option that can be used as a one-word substitute for the given group of words.
During vacations, Geeta saw a saltwater lake separated from the sea by rocks and sand where she did kayak for the first time.
(a) river (b) lagoon
(c) sea (d) ditch

180. The meaning of which of the following options is 'Good luck'?
(a) Break a leg (b) Hang in there
(c) All wet (d) Second banana

181. Select the most appropriate synonym of the given word.
Indigent
(a) Affluent (b) Bust
(c) Impoverished (d) Low

182. The following sentence has been divided into parts. One of them may contain an error.
Select the part that contains the error from the given options. If you don't find any error, mark 'No error' as your answer.
When Ramu was working / as a clerk, / he asked me money.
(a) No error
(b) as a clerk
(c) When Ramu was working
(d) he asked me money

183. Identify the proper explanation of the error in the given sentence.
Mohan insisted to go there.
(a) Error is in the sentence formation. Preposition and gerund are required. The correct sentence should read like this: Mohan insisted on going there.
(b) Error is with the verb. The correct sentence should read like this: Mohan insist to going there.
(c) Error is with the tense. The correct sentence should read like this: Mohan insisting to go there.
(d) Error is with the preposition. The correct sentence should read like this: Mohan insisted go there.

184. Select the most appropriate meaning of the given idiom.
Spill the beans
(a) Accomplish a lot
(b) Tremble at possibilities
(c) Reveal a secret
(d) Cornered by someone

185. The following sentence has been divided into parts. One of them contains an error. Select the part that contains the error from the given options.
Mrs. Rani / works for/a international / school.
(a) Mrs. Rani
(b) school
(c) a international
(d) works for

186. Select the incorrectly spelt word.
(a) Buraeucracy (b) Miscellaneous
(c) Acquaintance (d) Rhinoceros

187. Select the most appropriate meaning of the given idiom.
Nip in the bud
(a) To suppress something at an early stage
(b) To publicise a long-kept secret
(c) To complete a prolonged or unfinished work
(d) To stop something from growing beyond limit

188. Select the option that correctly rectifies the spelling error in the given sentence.
The movie is just beggining.
(a) Beginning (b) Beginnig
(c) Biginning (d) Begining

189. Select the most appropriate option that can substitute the underlined segment in the given sentence.
What exactly have the <u>teachers being doing wrong</u>?
(a) teachers being done
(b) teachers been doing
(c) teachers are doing
(d) teachers have been doing

190. Select the option that can be used as a one-word substitute for the given group of words.
A soldier who fights for the sake of money
(a) Veteran (b) Marine
(c) Mercenary (d) Admiral

Directions (Q. Nos. 191-195) *In the following passage, some words have been deleted. Read the passage carefully and select the most appropriate option to fill in each blank.*

It was an unusual dark night. In the ...(1)... of an enjoyable dream, Jim thought he heard his dog ...(2)... loudly. He groaned and glanced ...(3)... his clock sleepily. 12 O'clock the green fluorescent ...(4)... of his clock read. Suddenly, Jim ...(5)... hushed voices outside his house. He immediately became alert and jumped out of bed. As his parents had gone on a holiday, Jim was alone at home. He decided to look who was outside.

191. Select the correct option to fill in blank no. 1.
(a) end (b) between
(c) middle (d) side

192. Select the correct option to fill in blank no. 2.
(a) dancing (b) shouting
(c) barking (d) jumping

193. Select the correct option to fill in blank no. 3.
(a) on (b) in
(c) at (d) upon

194. Select the correct option to fill in blank no. 4.
(a) light (b) points
(c) hands (d) dial

195. Select the correct option to fill in blank no. 5.
(a) saw (b) heard
(c) thought (d) listened

Directions (Q. Nos. 196-200) *Read the given passage and answer the questions that follow.*

The story of Joanne Kathleen Rowling's near magical rise to fame is almost as well-known as the characters she creates.

Rowling was constantly writing and telling stories to her younger sister Dianne. " The first story I ever wrote down was about a rabbit called Rabbit." Rowling said in an interview. "He got the measles and was visited by his friends including a giant bee called Miss Bee. And ever since Rabbit and Miss Bee, I have always wanted to be a writer, though I rarely told anyone. So, however, my parents, both of whom come from impoverished backgrounds and neither of whom had been to college, took the view that my overactive imagination was an amusing personal quirk that would never pay a mortgage or secure a pension.

A writer from the age of six, with two unpublished novels in the drawer, she was stuck on a train when Harry walked into her mind fully formed. She spent the next five years constructing the plots of seven books, one for every year of his secondary school life. Rowling says, she started writing the first book, Harry Potter and the Sorcerer's Stone, in Portugal, where she was teaching English.

At first nobody wanted to publish Harry Potter. She was told that the plot was too complex. Refusing to compromise, she found a publisher.

In 1997, Rowling received her first royalty cheque. By book three, she had skyrocketed to the top of the publishing world. A row of zeros appeared on the author's bank balance and her life was turned upside down. Day and night she had journalists knocking on the unanswered door of her flat.

Rowling's quality control has become legendary, as is her obsession with accuracy. She's thrilled with Stephen Fry's taped version of the books and outraged that an Italian dust jacket showed Harry minus his glasses. "Don't they understand that the glasses are the clue to his vulnerability?"

196. Select an appropriate title for the passage.
(a) Rowling's Life
(b) The Publishing Journey
(c) The Craft of Writing
(d) Rowling's Mystery

197. What is the tone of the passage?
(a) Mystical (b) Anxious
(c) Gloomy (d) Informative

198. What quality do we get to know about JK Rowling that helps her become a successful writer?
(a) Flexibility (b) Perseverance
(c) Humility (d) Focus

199. What was Rowling doing when she started writing 'Harry Potter and the Sorcerer's Stone'?
(a) Accounting
(b) Teaching
(c) Writing full-time
(d) Designing

200. Select the word from the passage that is the antonym for 'Conformity'.
(a) Constantly (b) Secure
(c) Quirky (d) Amusing

Know Correct Answers

1. (d)	2. (d)	3. (a)	4. (b)	5. (c)	6. (a)	7. (a)	8. (b)	9. (d)	10. (c)
11. (b)	12. (b)	13. (d)	14. (c)	15. (b)	16. (c)	17. (a)	18. (c)	19. (a)	20. (d)
21. (c)	22. (a)	23. (c)	24. (a)	25. (c)	26. (b)	27. (a)	28. (a)	29. (d)	30. (b)
31. (a)	32. (c)	33. (b)	34. (c)	35. (d)	36. (c)	37. (a)	38. (b)	39. (b)	40. (a)
41. (a)	42. (c)	43. (d)	44. (d)	45. (d)	46. (d)	47. (a)	48. (a)	49. (c)	50. (d)
51. (b)	52. (c)	53. (d)	54. (b)	55. (b)	56. (b)	57. (a)	58. (a)	59. (c)	60. (d)
61. (a)	62. (a)	63. (b)	64. (a)	65. (c)	66. (c)	67. (a)	68. (b)	69. (b)	70. (c)
71. (c)	72. (c)	73. (a)	74. (b)	75. (c)	76. (c)	77. (d)	78. (a)	79. (a)	80. (b)
81. (c)	82. (a)	83. (c)	84. (d)	85. (d)	86. (d)	87. (a)	88. (b)	89. (d)	90. (d)
91. (c)	92. (a)	93. (c)	94. (d)	95. (b)	96. (c)	97. (d)	98. (c)	99. (a)	100. (a)
101. (b)	102. (b)	103. (a)	104. (d)	105. (d)	106. (d)	107. (c)	108. (a)	109. (c)	110. (c)
111. (d)	112. (c)	113. (a)	114. (a)	115. (c)	116. (a)	117. (c)	118. (c)	119. (d)	120. (c)
121. (c)	122. (a)	123. (a)	124. (d)	125. (c)	126. (d)	127 (c)	128. (a)	129. (c)	130. (b)
131. (b)	132. (d)	133. (b)	134. (c)	135. (a)	136. (d)	137 (d)	138. (d)	139. (a)	140. (d)
141. (d)	142. (c)	143. (a)	144. (c)	145. (d)	146. (a)	147. (d)	148. (a)	149. (b)	150. (d)
151. (d)	152. (d)	153. (b)	154. (b)	155. (*)	156. (c)	157. (a)	158. (c)	159. (c)	160. (a)
161. (d)	162. (a)	163. (b)	164. (c)	165. (d)	166. (b)	167. (c)	168. (b)	169. (c)	170. (d)
171. (b)	172. (b)	173. (b)	174. (c)	175. (d)	176. (c)	177. (d)	178. (b)	179. (b)	180. (a)
181. (c)	182. (d)	183. (a)	184. (c)	185. (c)	186. (a)	187. (a)	188. (a)	189. (d)	190. (c)
191. (c)	192. (c)	193. (c)	194. (d)	195. (b)	196. (b)	197. (d)	198. (b)	199. (b)	200. (c)

Answer & Solutions

1. (d) Given equation,

$1200 \times 3 - 1 \div 100 + 499 = ?$

After interchange of the signs,

$+ \Rightarrow -$	$- \Rightarrow \times$
$\times \Rightarrow \div$	$\div \Rightarrow +$

$1200 \div 3 \times 1 + 100 - 499$

$\Rightarrow 400 + 100 - 499 = 1$

2. (d) When unfolded, the paper will appear as shown in figure (d)

3. (a) The given figure is embedded, in option figure (a).

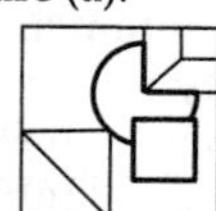

4. (b) According to the statements,

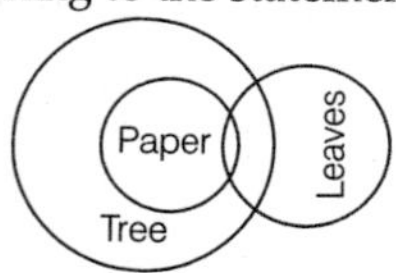

Conclusions

I. (✓) II. (✓)

Hence, both Conclusions I and II follow.

5. (c) According to the question,

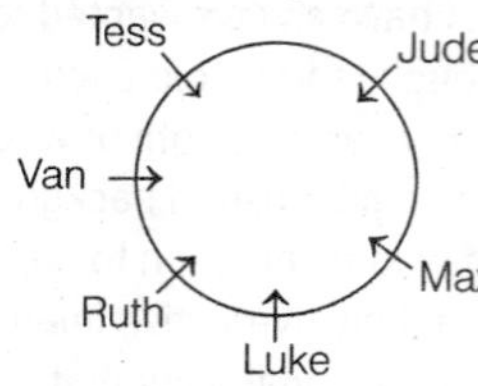

Hence, max is the immediate neighbour of Jude and Luke.

6. (a) As, (104, 26, 13) [÷4, ÷2]

and (168, 42, 21) [÷4, ÷2]

Similarly, (216, 54, 27) [÷4, ÷2]

7. (a) As, (145, 76)

$\Rightarrow 145 - 76 = 69$

and (182, 113)

$\Rightarrow 182 - 113 = 69$

Similarly, (163, 94)

$\Rightarrow 163 - 94 = 69$

8. (b) According to the question,

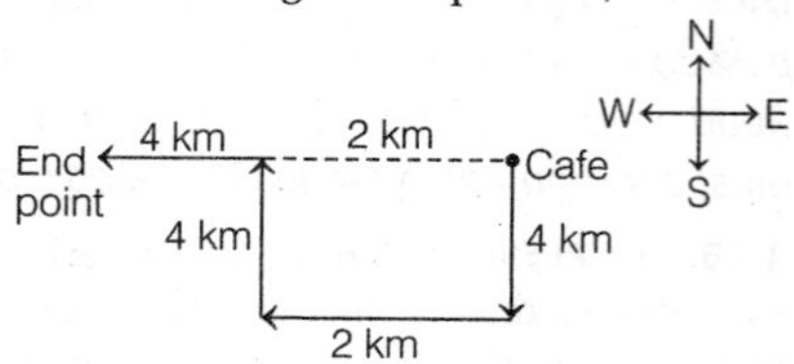

Total distance from end point to cafe

$= 4 + 2$

$= 6\text{ km}$

9. (d) As, (15, 60, 10) [×4, ÷6]

and (21, 84, 14) [×4, ÷6]

Similarly, (33, 132, 22) [×4, ÷6]

10. **(c)** In both positions of dice, θ is common, so moving in clockwise direction from common.

From position I θ γ δ
↓ Common
From position II θ π α

Hence, θ will be opposite to β.

11. **(b)** Given equation,

59 ÷ 6 – 28 × 7 + 30 = ?

After interchange of the signs,

+ ⇒ –	× ⇒ ÷
– ⇒ ×	÷ ⇒ +

59 + 6 × 28 ÷ 7 – 30

= 59 + 24 – 30

= 83 – 20 = 53

12. **(b)** Given equation, 69 D 3 A 4 C 7 B 10

After interchange of the signs,

A ⇒ +	B ⇒ –
C ⇒ ×	D ⇒ ÷

69 ÷ 3 + 4 × 7 – 10

= 23 + 28 – 10

= 51 – 10 = 41

13. **(d)** As ounce and kilogram are units of weight. Similarly quart and litre are units of volume.

14. **(c)** As,

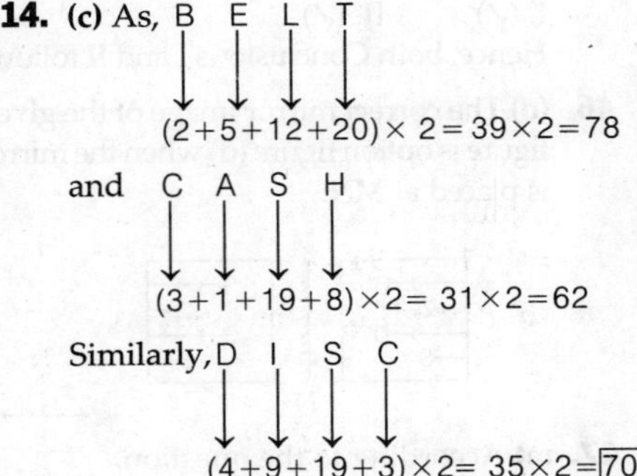

15. **(b)** The pattern of the given series as follows,

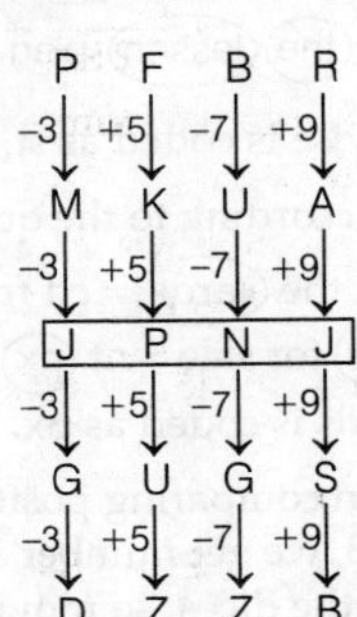

16. **(c)** The series follows the pattern, which is as follows.

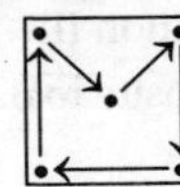

Hence, option figure (c) will replace the question mark.

17. **(a)** The series, follows the pattern which is as follows

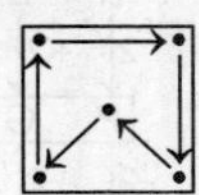

Hence, option figure (a) will replace the question mark.

18. **(c)** The pattern of the given series as follows,

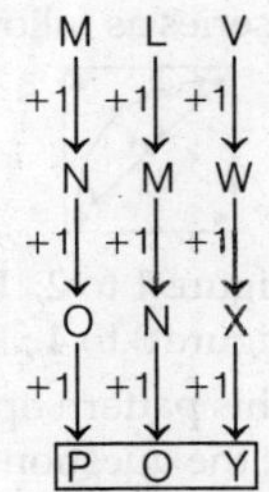

19. **(a)** According to the statements,

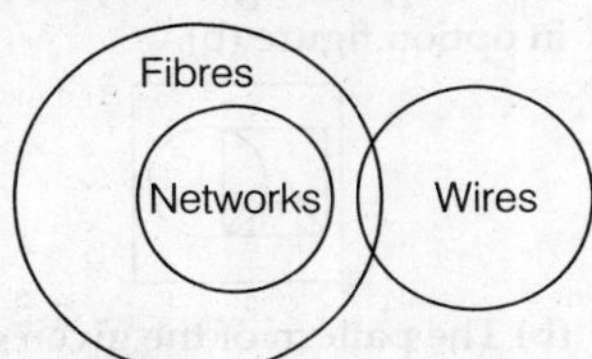

Conclusions

I. (✗) II. (✗)

Hence, neither Conclusion I nor II follows.

20. **(d)** The correct mirror image of the given figure is the option figure (d) when the mirror is placed at MN.

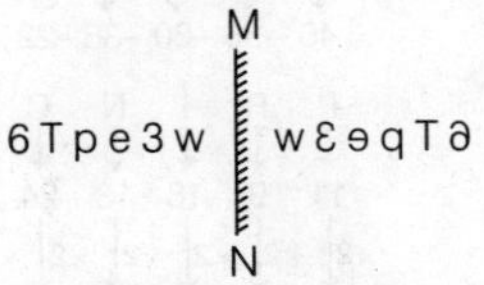

M
6Tpe3w | wƐeqTƋ
N

21. **(c)** Given equation,

228 B 5 C 89 D 328 A 4

After interchange of the signs,

A ⇒ ÷	B ⇒ ×
C ⇒ +	D ⇒ –

228× 5 + 89 – 328 ÷ 4

= 1140 + 89 – 82

= 1229 – 82

= 1147

22. **(a)** As, cygnet is the young one of swan.

Similarly, puppy is the young one of Dog.

23. **(c)** Given equation,

42 × 3 – 16 ÷ 9 + 11

After interchange of the signs,

+ ⇒ –	– ⇒ ×
× ⇒ ÷	÷ ⇒ +

42 ÷ 3 × 16 + 9 – 11

= 224 + 9 – 11

= 233 – 11 = 222

24. **(a)** The correct dictionary order of the given word,

Windblast → Windscreen →
(3) (5)
Wingspread → Winkling →
(2) (6)
Winterish → Wintertide →
(1) (4)

∴ The correct order is 3, 5, 2, 6, 1, 4.

25. **(c)** As, R O C K
–2 –4 –2 –4
P K A G

and C L U B
–2 –4 –2 –4
A H S X

Similarly, S H O P
–2 –4 –2 –4
Q D M L

26. **(b)** As, C O O L
3+15+15+12 = 45

and T R E E
20+18+5+5 = 48

Similarly, W E L L
23+5+12+12 = 52

27. **(a)** The correct dictionary order of the given word.

Cinema → Cipher → Circle →
(2) (5) (1)
Circumference → Circus
(4) (3)

⇒ 2, 5, 1, 4, 3

28. **(a)** According to the question,

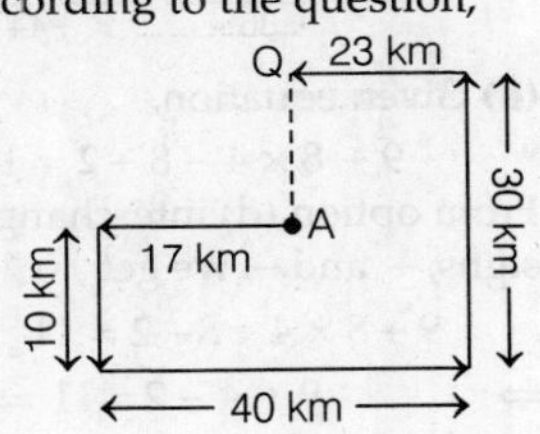

Distance from point Q to $A = (30 - 10)$ km $= 20$ km

Hence, Rajesh should drive 20 km in South direction to reach point A again.

29. **(d)** According to the statements,

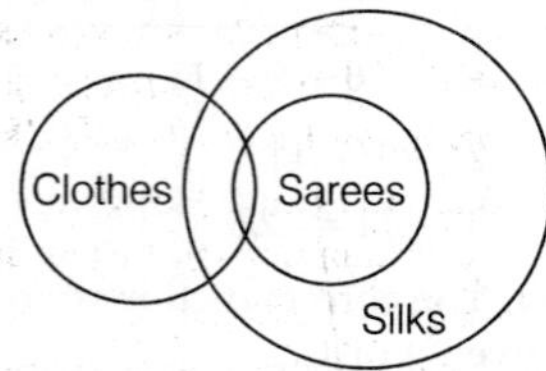

Conclusions

I. (✓) II. (✓)

Hence, both Conclusions I and II follow.

30. **(b)** As, 254 : 524

$\Rightarrow 2 + 5 + 4 = 11; 5 + 2 + 4 = 11$

and 912 : 642

$\Rightarrow 9 + 1 + 2 = 12; 6 + 4 + 2 = 12$

Similarly, 188 : $\boxed{845}$

$\Rightarrow 1 + 8 + 8 = 17; 8 + 4 + 5 = 17$

31. **(a)** According to the question,

[+ ⇒ Male, – ⇒ Female]

M # N @ P + S % T

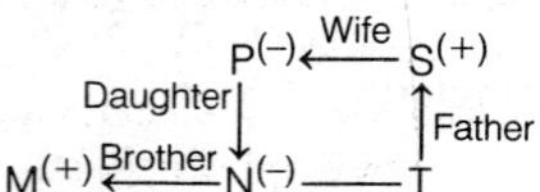

Hence, M is brother of T.

32. **(c)** As, 72 : 25

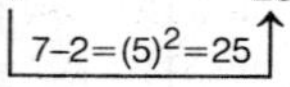

$7-2=(5)^2=25$

Similarly, 28 : 36

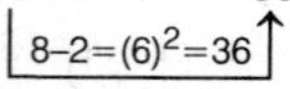

$8-2=(6)^2=36$

33. **(b)** According to the question,

R ÷ S – V + Q × T

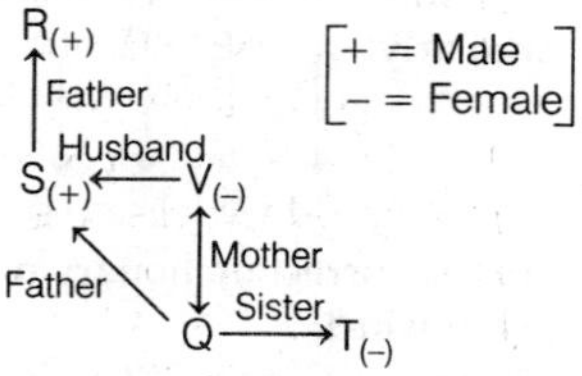

R(+), Father, S(+), Husband, V(–), Mother, Father, Q, Sister, T(–)

[+ = Male, – = Female]

∴ R is the Father's father of T.

34. **(c)** Pattern of the series is as follows,

67, 78, 103, 118, $\boxed{147}$

+36, +40, +44

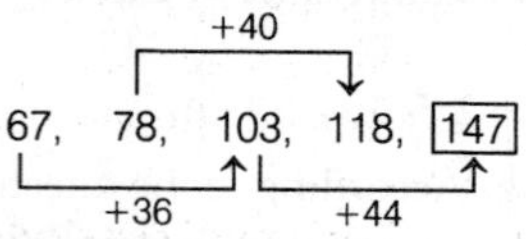

35. **(d)** Given equation,

$9 + 8 \times 4 - 8 \div 2 = 11$

From option (d) interchange of the signs, ÷ and –, we get

$9 + 8 \times 4 \div 8 - 2 = 11$

$\Rightarrow 9 + 4 - 2 = 11 \Rightarrow 11 = 11$

36. **(c)** Pattern of the series is as follows,

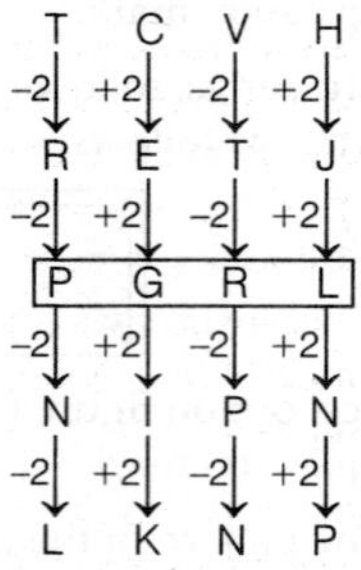

37. **(a)** The alternate pattern of the given figure series as follows,

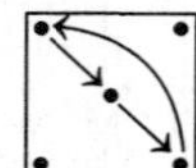 ; 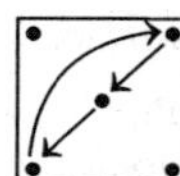

From figure 1 to 2; From figure 2 to 3

From figure 3 to 4 ; From figure 4 to 5.

From this pattern option figure (a) will replace the question mark(?) of the given series.

38. **(b)** The given figure (X) is embedded in option figure (b).

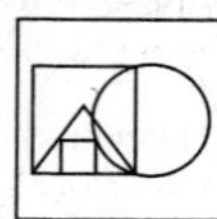

39. **(b)** The pattern of the given series is as follows,

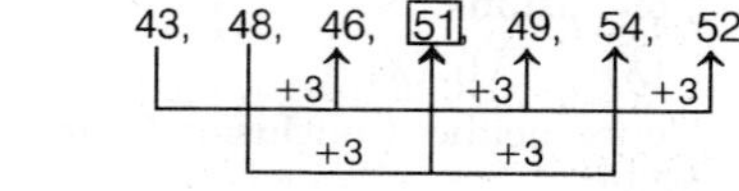

40. **(a)** As,

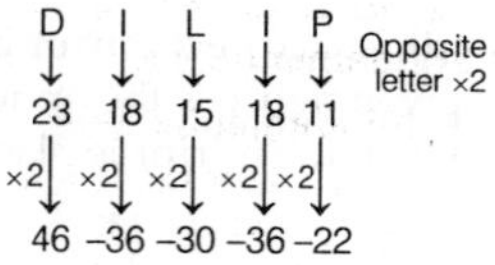

D I L I P (Opposite letter ×2)

23 18 15 18 11

×2 ×2 ×2 ×2 ×2

46 –36 –30 –36 –22

and

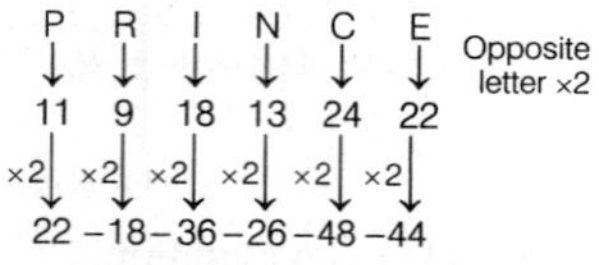

P R I N C E (Opposite letter ×2)

11 9 18 13 24 22

×2 ×2 ×2 ×2 ×2 ×2

22 –18 –36 –26 –48 –44

Similarly, F I R O Z (Opposite letter ×2)

21 18 9 12 1

×2 ×2 ×2 ×2 ×2

$\boxed{42\ -36\ -18\ -24\ -2}$

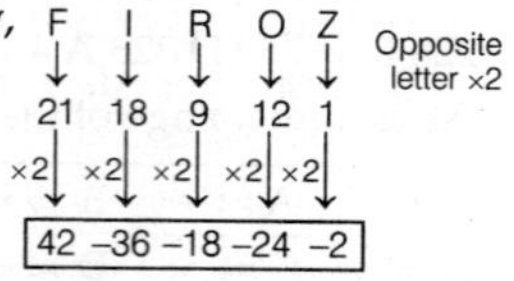

41. **(a)** Given equation,

$300 - 12 \times 120 \div 9 + 32 = ?$

After interchange of the signs,

+ ⇒ –	– ⇒ ×
× ⇒ ÷	÷ ⇒ +

$300 \times 12 \div 120 + 9 - 32$

$= 30 + 9 - 32$

$= 39 - 32 = \boxed{7}$

42. **(c)** Pattern of the series is as follows,

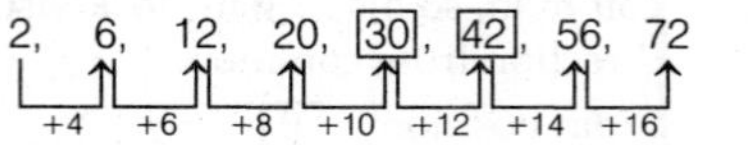

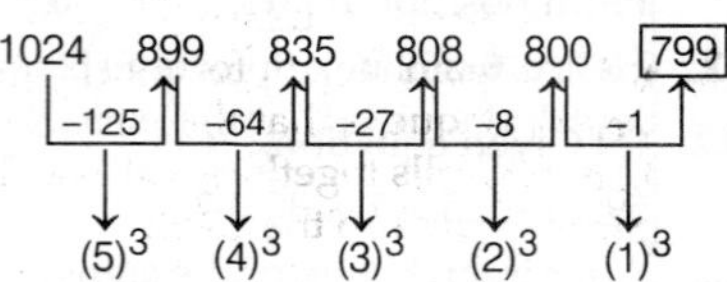

43. **(d)** Pattern of the series is as follows,

1024 899 835 808 800 $\boxed{799}$

–125 –64 –27 –8 –1

$(5)^3$ $(4)^3$ $(3)^3$ $(2)^3$ $(1)^3$

44. **(d)** Comparing both position of the dices, number 11 is common in both the dices, so moving in clockwise direction from common.

From position I 11 $\boxed{16}$ $\boxed{12}$

From position II 11 $\boxed{15}$ $\boxed{13}$

Hence, 14 is opposite to 11.

45. **(d)** According to the statements,

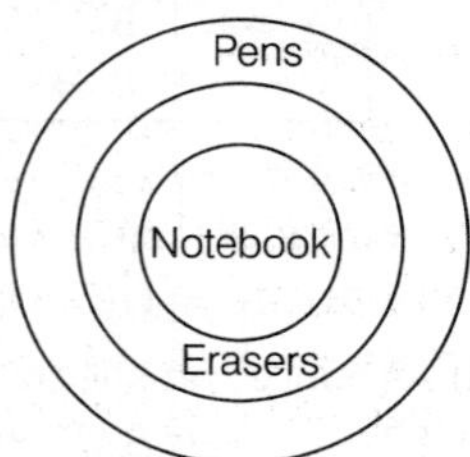

Conclusions

I. (✓) II. (✓)

Hence, both Conclusions I and II follow.

46. **(d)** The correct mirror image of the given figure is option figure (d) when the mirror is placed at MN.

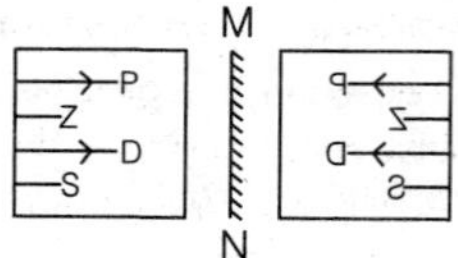

47. **(a)** According to the question,

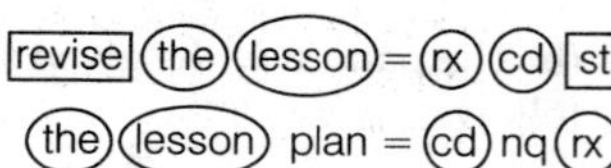

∴ revise is coded as st.

48. **(a)** According to the question,

print the (cards) = cd fm (px)

(cards) for sale = nt (px) ym

∴ cards is coded as px.

49. **(c)** On comparing position of dice 1 and 3, we get number 5 is common in both the dices, so moving in a clockwise direction from common.

From position I. 5 $\boxed{3}$ 2

From position III. 5 $\boxed{6}$ 4

∴ 3 is opposite to 6.

50. **(d)** As, $N \xrightarrow{+5} S \xrightarrow{-3} P$

$R \xrightarrow{+5} W \xrightarrow{-3} T$

$P \xrightarrow{+5} U \xrightarrow{-3} R$

But, $T \xrightarrow{+5} Y \xrightarrow{-4} U$

51. **(b)** The main reason for formation of dental plaque is that the masses of bacterial cells together with food particles stick to the teeth.

52. **(c)** 'Nationalism' book is written by Rabindranath Tagore.

- Nationalism is a comprehensive exploration of the historical, political and cultural phenonmenon of nationalism.
- Rabindranath Tagore won the Nobel Prize in Literature in 1913 for his poetry collection Gitanjali.
- He was the first Asian to receive this prize.

53. **(d)** Indian musician, composer and singer Shubha Mudgal was awarded with the Padma Shri Award in 2000.

- Shubha Mudgal is an Indian musician, composer, singer and multi-instrumentalist known for her works in Hindustani classical music, Indian pop and Tamil cinema.

54. **(b)** Statement (b) is false about privatisation. In privatisation, there is no possibility of exploitation of monopoly power by private companies after privatisation.

- Privatisation is a process of selling public sector assets to the private sector to help the economy grow.
- It can be achieved through a number of methods, including Disinvestment, Deregulation, Contracting out, Management contracts, etc.
- The privatisation process in India began in 1991-92 with the sale of minority stakes in some public sector undertakings (PSUs).

55. **(b)** As of 2022, according to the Ministry of Petroleum and Natural Gas of the Government of India, there are in total 23 oil refineries in India of which 18 were state-owned, 3 were privately owned and 2 were joint ventures.

- India is the third largest consumer of crude oil in the world, after the United States and China.

56. **(b)** The North Indian Plain of India extensive alluvial soil.

- It is said to be the highly fertile soil and it is deposited largely in the Northern plains of India out of the deposition work of Indus-Ganga-Brahmaputra rivers.
- In Peninsular India, this type of soil is mostly found in deltas and estuaries.

57. **(a)** The eyeball is spherical in shape with even a diameter of about 2.3 cm.

- Most of the refraction for the light rays happens on the outer cornea surface.

58. **(a)** Pipelines as a means of transport are looked after by the Ministry of Petroleum and Natural Gas of the Government of India.

- Natural Gas is important for the environment as the by-products are not that dangerous to the atmosphere.
- Natural gas is a mixture of hydrocarbon gases, and examples of these gases include Methane, Ethane, Propane, Butane and Pentane.

59. **(c)** The 12th edition of the Ice-Hockey Association of India's (IHAI) National Ice-Hockey Championship for men in 2023 was won by Indo-Tibetan Border Police (ITBP).

- It was held in Leh, Ladakh.

60. **(d)** The Swaran Singh Committee had formulated an 8 point code of Fundamental Duties.

- Fundamental Duties of the Indian Constitution are mentioned in Article 51 A.
- The Swaran Singh Committee in 1976 recommended Fundamental Duties.
- The 42nd Amendment Act of 1976 added 10 Fundamental Duties to the Indian Constitution.
- The 86th Amendment Act 2002 later added the 11th Fundamental Duty to the list.

61. **(a)** The author of Tarikh-i-Mubarak Shahi, Yahya Sirhindi claims that the founder of the Sayyid dynasty of Delhi Sultanate was a descendant of Prophet Muhammad.

- It also contains the history of Muhammad Ghori and his rulers upto the third ruler of the Sayyid dynasty.

62. **(a)** The correct matching is A-1, B-3, C-2, D-4.

- Ethane is an alkane because it is a straight-chain hydrocarbon comprised of only single bonds and no other substituents, C_2H_6.
- Propylene, also known as propene, is an Alkenes compound with the chemical formula $CH_3CH = CH_2$.
- Butyne is an unsaturated hydrocarbon that is classified as an alkyne, (C_4H_6)
- Formaldehyde is also known as methanal, it is a simplest aldehyde and is colourless. (CH_2O).

63. **(b)** Muhammad Yunus and Grameen Bank were awarded the Nobel Peace Prize for 2006 for their work to 'create economic and social development from below'.

- Grameen Bank's objective since its establishment in 1983 has been to grant poor people small loans on easy terms so-called micro-credit and Yunus was the bank's founder.

64. **(a)** In 2031, India will organise the ICC Men's One-Day International World Cup Cricket.

- The decision was announced by the International Cricket Council (ICC) confirming the landmark event.

65. **(c)** According to Mendeleev's Periodic Table, Gallium's properties matched up remarkably well with eka-aluminium.

66. **(c)** The adoption of the Industrial Policy of 1956 coincided with Second Five-Year Plan.

- The Second Five-Year Plan in India was from 1956-1961 and was based on the Mahalanobis model.
- The plan's main objective was to rapidly industrialise the country, with a focus on heavy and basic industries.

67. **(a)** Kuchipudi is usually concluded with Tarangam.

- Kuchipudi dance is a famous Indian classical dance, which is performed in the state of Andhra Pradesh.
- The Kuchipudi classical dance is accompanied with Carnatic Music.
- The name of Kuchipudi dance originated from 'Kuchelapuram', a village in the Krishna district of Andhra Pradesh.

68. **(b)** Financial intermediation not be required family funds.

- A financial intermediary is an institution or individual that serves as a 'middleman' among diverse parties in order to facilitate financial transactions.
- Common types include commercial banks, investment banks, stockbrokers, insurance and pension funds, pooled investment funds, leasing companies and stock exchanges.

69. **(b)** 'Holi' is popularly known as the festival of colours. It celebrates the eternal and divine love of the deities Radha and Krishna.

- Additionally, the day signifies the triumph of good over evil, as it commemorates the victory of Vishnu as Narasimha over Hiranyakashipu.
- It falls on the Hindu calendar month of Phalguna.

70. **(c)** Aparna Satheesan, the international Kuchipudi dancer received the National Nritya Shiromani Award for 2022 at the 13th Cuttack Mahotsav.

- National Nritya Shiromani Award is an annual award given to exceptional classical dancers and musicians of India for their contribution to art and culture.

71. **(c)** Generally, Directive Principles are positive directions as they aim to establish a welfare state.

- Directive Principles of State Policy in India have been taken from the Constitution of Ireland.
- Directive Principles of State Policies (DPSP) are a set of social and economic obligations imposed on the Government (Union and State) to establish a welfare society.
- They are enumerated in Part IV of the Constitution.

72. **(c)** INSAT-3D is an advanced weather satellite of India configured with improved imaging system and atmospheric sounder.

73. **(a)** The water level of River Ganga depends on the monsoon and climatic condition of the Himalaya is not correct about River Ganga.

- The Ganga River originates from the Gangotri Glacier near Gomukh in the Uttarkashi district of Uttarakhand.
- The Ganga is named at Devprayag, Uttarakhand, where the Bhagirathi meets the Alaknanda River.
- Some tributaries of the Ganga River include - Kosi, Yamuna, Ramganga, Ghaghra, Gandak, Mahananda, Sone, Chambal and Betwa.

74. **(b)** In India, the International Day of Non-Violence is also celebrated as Gandhi Jayanti.

- 2nd October is also the birth anniversary of former Indian Prime Minister and freedom fighter Lal Bahadur Shastri.
- 9th January is celebrated as Pravasi Bharatiya Divas to commemorates the return of Mahatma Gandhi from South Africa.

75. **(c)** Ghiyasuddin Tughlaq found Tughlaqabad city in Delhi.

- He was also known as Ghazi Malik. Ghiyasuddin Tughlaq was the founder of the Tughlaq dynasty.

76. **(c)** The number of players in baseball is 9.

- The game is divided into nine innings, each divided into two halves.

77. **(d)** Krishnaji Gopal Karve was executed as an accomplice to the murder of AMT Jackson.

- He was a member of the Abhinav Bharat Society in Nashik.
- On 21st December, 1909, he along with Anant Laxman Kanhere and Vinayak Narayan Deshpande shot Jackson, the Collector of Nashik.

78. **(a)** Sambhar lake and Chilika lake are salt-water lakes.

- Sambhar Lake is a salt lake located in the Jaipur district of Rajasthan, India. It is one of the largest salt lakes in India and is known for its pink colour, which is due to the presence of algae.
- Chilika lake is the largest saltwater lake in India. The lake spreads across the districts of Puri, Khurda and Ganjam in the state of Odisha in Eastern India.

79. **(a)** The Indian National Congress formally took up the Swadeshi call in its Benaras Session of 1905 under the presidentship of Gopal Krishna Gokhale.

- Its primary objective was to promote the use of **indigenous goods** and **boycott British products**a s a means of economic self-sufficiency and political resistance.
- The Swadeshi movement was started in response to the British government's decision to partition Bengal is 1905.

80. **(b)** Major Rock Edict-I of Ashoka declares prohibition of animal sacrifice especially during the festive gatherings.

- Rock Edict IV mentioned consideration and non-violence to animals and courtesy to relations.

81. **(c)** Nicotine is present in tobacco in high quantities. The amount of nicotine in each cigarette was from 6.17 to 12.65 mg in domestic cigarettes.

- Nicotine is a highly addictive chemical compound present in a tobacco plant.
- Frequent use of nicotine leads to health risk.

82. **(a)** According to the Global Hunger Index, 2022, Afghanistan is the only neighbouring country behind India with a rank of 109 out of 121 countries.

- The Global Hunger Index (GHI) is a peer-reviewed report that is published annually by Concern Worldwide and Welthungerhilfe.
- India in ranked 111th out of 125 countries included in the ranking in the 2023 GHI report.

83. **(c)** Methane gas is found in coal mines and marshy places.

- Methane is colourless, odourless gas that occurs abundantly in nature as the chief constituent of natural gas, as a product of the angerobic bacterial decomposition of vegetable matter under water.

84. **(d)** Radheshyam Barle, a recipient of Padma Shri in 2021, is an exponent of Panthi dance form.

- Panthi dance is a popular folk dance form that belongs to the state of Chhattisgarh.

85. **(d)** The Planning Commission was set up in 1950. It is formulated the Five-Year Plans of India.

- On 17th August, 2014, it was dissolved and replaced by the NITI Aayog.

- The First Five-Year Plan of India was implemented from 1951 to 1956.
- The first ever National Agriculture Policy was announced in July, 2000.
- The Industrial Policy Resolution (IPR) was adopted by teh Indian Parliament in April 1956.

86. (d) Arthropoda is the largest phylum in the animal kingdom, has more than 9,000 species.

- They occur in almost all habitats around the world. It includes species such as lobsters, crabs, spiders, mites, insects, centipedes and millipedes.
- About 84 percent of all known species or animals are members of this phylum.

87. (a) Article 166(1) of the Indian Constitution mentions that 'All the executive action of the Government of a state shall be expressed to be taken in the name of the Governor'.

- Article 163(1) ofthe Constitution of India states that there shall be a Council of Ministers headed by the Chief Minister.
- Article 165(1) of the Constitution of India states that the Governor of each state must appoint the Advocate General for the state.

88. (b) Satyashodhak Samaj (truth seeker society) was established by Jyotiba Phule.

- It aimed for the education and increased social rights and political access for under privileged groups, focusing especially on women, shudras and dalits, in Maharashtra.
- Jyotirao's wife Savitribai was the head of the women's section of society.

89. (d) The body of the phylum platyhelminthes is unsegmented and dorsoventrally flattened. Their heads are flat.

- They are devoid of the anus and circulatory system but have a mouth.
- They respire by simple diffusion through the body surface. They are also called as flatworms.

90. (d) Amir Khusrau is also known as Tuti-e-Hind.

- He was a Sufi poet, musician and scholar who served in the royal courts of various kings and sultans (from Balban to Muhammad Tughlaq).
- He was a disciple of the famous Sufi saint Sheikh Nizamuddin Auliya.
- Amir Khusrau is often considered the first poet of Urdu, Amir Khusrau is called the 'Father of the Sitar'.

91. (c) Oil India Limited is a joint sector industry in India.

- Oil India Limited (OIL) is a central public sector undertaking engaged in the business of exploration, development and production of crude oil and natural gas, transportation of crude oil and production of liquid petroleum gas.
- The central public sector undertaking is a Maharatna, with the Ministry of Petroleum and Natural Gas overseeing its operations.
- It's headquartered in Duliajan, Assam.

92. (a) Article 214 of the Indian Constitution states that 'There shall be a High Court for each state'.

- Article 125 deals with the Salaries and others of Judges.
- Article 245 of the Constitution of India deals with the distribution of legislative powers between the Union and the States.
- Article 275 of the Constitution of India provides for grants-in-aid from the Consolidated Fund of India to states in need of assistance.

93. (c) 59°F is 15° Celsius. The formula to convert Celsius to Fahrenheit is given by °F = °C × (9/5) + 32.
Given that, C = 15.

94. (d) As per the National Multidimensional Poverty Index Report 2023, Puducherry has the lowest poverty rate.

- If seeks to measure poverty across its multiple dimensions and in effect complements existing poverty statistics based on per capita consumption expenditure.
- It has three equally weighted dimensions-health, education and standard of living.

95. (b) The **Governor** is the **Chief** Executive head of the state. The President appoints the Governor for a period of 5 years.

- The Governor appoints the Chief Minister, Council of Ministers and Government Officials.
- The articles in the Constitution of India that relate to the Governor of a state are Articles 152-162.

96. (c) A resolution on the National Sports Policy was laid in both Houses of Parliament in August 1984.

- The National Sports Policy, 1984 was formulated with the objective of raising the standard of sports in the country.

97. (d) The Swaran Singh Committee was recommended the Fundamental Duties. Fundamental Duties of the Indian Constitution are mentioned in Article 51A.

- The Swaran Singh Committee in 1976 recommended Fundamental Duties.
- The 42nd Amendment Act of 1976 added 10 Fundamental Duties to the Indian Constitution.
- The 86th Amendment Act 2002 later added the 11th Fundamental Duty to the list.

98. (c) Odissi is represented by Kelucharan Mohapatra.

- He was the first Odissi dancer from Odisha to receive Padma Vibhushan in 2000.
- Odissi is one of the eight recognised classical dances of India.
- The Jagannath temple in Puri depicts the Odissi classical dance form. This dance was supported by King Kharavela of Odisha.
- Jayadeva was the first poet who composed songs to be sung in Odissi performances.

99. (a) B Praak won the Best Male Playback Singer at the 67th National Film Awards for the song 'Teri Mitti' from Hindi film 'Kesari'.

- Sikkim has bagged the award for being 'Most Film Friendly State'.

100. (a) Anuja Chauhan is the author of the book 'Those Pricey Thakur Girls'.

- She has written three novels: The Zoya Factor (2008), Battle For Bittora (October 2010) and Those Pricey Thakur Girls (January 2013).

101. (b) By using BODMAS rule,

$72 \div 8 \times 4 + 40 - 35 \div 5 + 15$
$= 9 \times 4 + 40 - 7 + 15$
$= 36 + 40 - 7 + 15$
$= 91 - 7 = 84$

102. **(b)** $(\tan\theta + \sec\theta + 1)(\cot\theta - \text{cosec}\theta + 1)$

$= \left(\frac{\sin\theta}{\cos\theta} + \frac{1}{\cos\theta} + 1\right)\left(\frac{\cos\theta}{\sin\theta} - \frac{1}{\sin\theta} + 1\right)$

$= \left(\frac{\sin\theta + \cos\theta + 1}{\cos\theta}\right)\left(\frac{\cos\theta + \sin\theta - 1}{\sin\theta}\right)$

$= \frac{(\sin\theta + \cos\theta)^2 - (1)^2}{\sin\theta \cdot \cos\theta}$

$= \frac{(\sin^2\theta + \cos^2\theta) + 2\sin\theta\cdot\cos\theta - 1}{\sin\theta\cdot\cos\theta}$

$= \frac{1 + 2\sin\theta\cdot\cos\theta - 1}{\sin\theta\cdot\cos\theta} = \frac{2\sin\theta\cdot\cos\theta}{\sin\theta\cdot\cos\theta}$

$= 2$

103. **(a)** $(\text{cosec}\,\theta - \sin\theta)(\sec\theta - \cos\theta)$ $(\tan\theta + \cot\theta)$

$= \left(\frac{1}{\sin\theta} - \sin\theta\right)\left(\frac{1}{\cos\theta} - \cos\theta\right)\left(\frac{\sin\theta}{\cos\theta} + \frac{\cos\theta}{\sin\theta}\right)$

$= \left(\frac{1 - \sin^2\theta}{\sin\theta}\right)\left(\frac{1 - \cos^2\theta}{\cos\theta}\right)\left(\frac{\sin^2\theta + \cos^2\theta}{\sin\theta\cdot\cos\theta}\right)$

$= \left(\frac{\cos^2\theta}{\sin\theta}\right)\left(\frac{\sin^2\theta}{\cos\theta}\right)\left(\frac{1}{\sin\theta\cdot\cos\theta}\right)$

$= \left(\frac{\cos\theta}{1}\right)\left(\frac{\sin\theta}{1}\right)\left(\frac{1}{\sin\theta\cdot\cos\theta}\right)$

$= 1$

104. **(d)** Let the height of the room be H m.

$\therefore$ The length of the room = $4H$ m

The breadth of the room = $2H$ m

Volume of the room = $1728\ \text{m}^3$

$\Rightarrow$ $(4H)(2H)(H) = 1728$

$\Rightarrow$ $8H^3 = 1728$

$\therefore$ $H = 6$

$\therefore$ The length of the room is (6×4) m i.e., 24 m.

105. **(d)** Given, $\angle A = 70°$

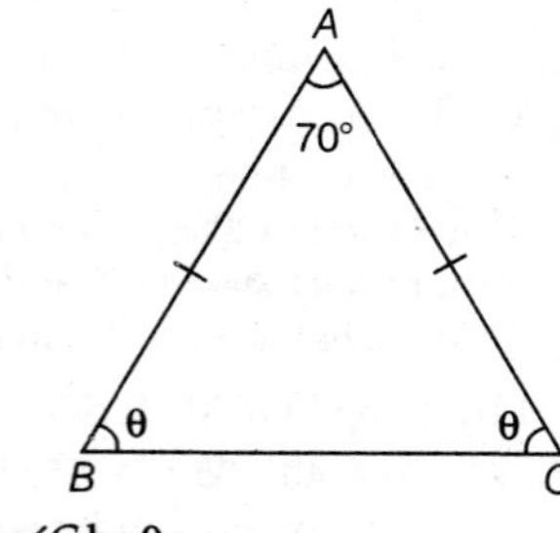

Let $\angle C$ be θ.

$\because$ $AB = AC$

$\therefore$ $\angle C = \angle B$

$\angle A + \angle B + \angle C = 180°$

$\Rightarrow$ $70 + \theta + \theta = 180°$

$\Rightarrow$ $2\theta = 110°$

$\therefore$ $\theta = 55°$

106. **(d)** Equivalent of a single price

$= 25 + 25 + \frac{25 \times 25}{100}$

$= 50 + \frac{625}{100} = 56.25\%$

107. **(c)** Given, radius of cone, $r = 3$ cm

Height of cone, $h = 4$ cm

$\therefore$ Slant height of cone,

$l = \sqrt{r^2 + h^2} = \sqrt{9 + 16}$

$= \sqrt{25} = 5$ cm

Curved surface area of cone = πrl

$= \pi \times 3 \times 5\ \text{cm}^2$

$= 15\pi\ \text{cm}^2$

108. **(a)** Let ₹ A is invested at 15% for 5 yr.

$\therefore$ Interest of ₹ A = ₹ $\frac{A \times 15 \times 5}{100}$

Let ₹ B is invested at 10% for 3 yr.

$\therefore$ Interest of ₹ B = ₹ $\frac{B \times 10 \times 3}{100}$

$\frac{\text{Interest of } A}{\text{Interest of } B} = \frac{A \times 15 \times 5 \times 100}{B \times 10 \times 3 \times 100} = \frac{5}{3}$

$\frac{A}{B} = \frac{2}{3}$

$\therefore$ $B = \frac{3}{5} \times 48500$

= ₹ 29100

109. **(c)** $\left(2\frac{1}{2} + 1\frac{3}{4} - \frac{1}{6}\right) \times 16 \div 49$

$= \left(\frac{5}{2} + \frac{7}{4} - \frac{1}{6}\right) \times 16 \div 49$

$= \left(\frac{30 + 21 - 2}{12}\right) \times \frac{16}{49}$

$= \frac{49}{12} \times \frac{16}{49} = \frac{4}{3} = 1\frac{1}{3}$

110. **(c)** Let the value of each instalment be ₹ X.

Total amount is ₹ P.

$\therefore$ $P = X(K + K^2 + K^3 + \ldots)$

Where, $K = \frac{100}{100 + R}$

In this question, there are only two years and $R = 10\%$, then,

$P = X(K + K^2)$

$\Rightarrow$ $35000 = X\left\{\left(\frac{10}{11}\right) + \left(\frac{10}{11}\right)^2\right\}$

$\Rightarrow$ $35000 = X\left\{\frac{10}{11} + \frac{100}{121}\right\}$

$\Rightarrow$ $35000 = X\left\{\frac{210}{121}\right\}$

$\therefore$ X = ₹ 20167

111. **(d)** Average marks obtained by student in test 2

$= \frac{94 + 79 + 85}{3} = 86$

Average marks obtained by student in maths in all test

$= \frac{80 + 94 + 88 + 92 + 96}{5} = 90$

$\therefore$ Required ratio $= \frac{86}{90} = \frac{43}{45}$

112. **(c)** $\frac{\left(2\frac{1}{7} + 6\frac{1}{7}\right) \div \frac{9}{7}}{1\frac{1}{9} \div \left\{\frac{7}{9} + \left(\frac{4}{9} \div \frac{4}{3}\right)\right\}}$

$= \frac{\left(\frac{15}{7} + \frac{43}{7}\right) \div \frac{9}{7}}{\frac{10}{9} \div \left\{\frac{7}{9} + \left(\frac{4}{9} \times \frac{3}{4}\right)\right\}}$

$= \frac{\frac{58}{7} \times \frac{7}{9}}{\frac{10}{9} \div \left\{\frac{7}{9} + \frac{1}{3}\right\}} = \frac{\frac{58}{9}}{\frac{10}{9} \div \frac{10}{9}}$

$= \frac{\frac{58}{9}}{\frac{10}{9} \times \frac{9}{10}} = \frac{58}{9}$

113. **(a)** Total production of company A from 2012 to 2015 is

$= 29 + 37 + 38 + 42 = 146$

Total production of company D from 2012 to 2015 is

$= 37 + 35 + 42 + 45 = 159$

$\therefore$ Required percentage

$2015 = \frac{146}{159} \times 100$

$= 91.82\%$

114. **(a)** Let the number of girls be 10.

$\therefore$ Number of boys

$= 10 + 10 \times \frac{20}{100} = 12$

$\therefore$ Ratio of boys to that of girls

$= \frac{12}{10} = \frac{6}{5}$

115. **(c)** Let ABC be a triangle.

$\angle C > \angle A + \angle B$

Adding $\angle C$ to both sides,

$2\angle C > \angle A + \angle B + \angle C$

$2\angle C > 180°$ $(\because \angle A + \angle B + \angle C = 180°)$

$\Rightarrow \angle C > 90°$

$\therefore \Delta ABC$ is an obtuse angled triangle.

Hence, PQR will be obtuse angled triangle.

116. (a) Price of rice-I = ₹ 25/kg
Price of rice-II = ₹ 40/ kg
Cost of 5 kg mixture of rice mixed (3 kg rice-I and 2 kg rice-II) is
$= 25 \times 3 + 40 \times 2$
= ₹ 155
∴ Cost of 1 kg mixture = ₹ $\frac{155}{5}$ = ₹ 31

117. (c) Average achievement of 10 girls in math
$= (35 + 88 + 95 + 99 + 67 + 82 + 97 + 63 + 79 + 81) \div 10$
$= 78.6$
Average achievement of 10 boys in math
$=(56 + 75 + 34 + 49 + 89 + 99 + 94 + 59 + 82 + 79) \div 10 = 71.6$
∴ The average achievement of girls is more than that of boys.

118. (c) Cost price of product = ₹ 2000
Selling price of product after three successive discounts of 10% each
$= 2000 \times \frac{90}{100} \times \frac{90}{100} \times \frac{90}{100}$
= ₹ 1458
Selling price of product after a single discount of 28% is
= ₹ 2000 − 2000 × $\frac{28}{100}$
= ₹ 1440
∴ Difference = ₹ 1458 − 1440
= ₹ 18

119. (d) Given, efficiency of Amita
= Efficiency of (Bina + Sita)
According to the question,

	Days	Total work	Efficiency
Amita + Bina	25	175	7
Sita	35		5

Now,
Amita = Bina + Sita
Amita − Bina = 5 ...(i)
[∵ Efficiency of Sita = 5]
and Amita + Bina = 7 ...(ii)
From Eq. (i) and (ii),
Efficiency of Bina = 1
Hence, Bina alone can complete the work = $\frac{175}{1}$ = 175 days

120. (c) Let the cost price of each article by ₹ x.
Profit on article-I = $\frac{12x}{100}$
Profit on article-II = $\frac{12x}{100} + 3600$
Total profit = $\frac{12x}{100} + \frac{12x}{100} + 3600$
$= 15\frac{27}{51} \times \frac{1}{100} \times 2x$
$\frac{24x}{100} + 3600 = \frac{1584}{5100}x$
$3600 = \left(\frac{1584 - 1224}{5100}\right)x$
x = ₹ 51000

121. (c) $\left[\left(7\frac{1}{4}\right)^2 - \left(5\frac{4}{5}\right)^2\right] \div 5\frac{4}{5} \times \frac{16}{9}$
$= \left[\left(\frac{29}{4}\right)^2 - \left(\frac{29}{5}\right)^2\right] \div \frac{29}{5} \times \frac{16}{9}$
$= \left[(29)^2\left(\frac{1}{16} - \frac{1}{25}\right)\right] \div \frac{29}{5} \times \frac{16}{9}$
$= (29)^2 \times \frac{9}{16 \times 25} \times \frac{5}{29} \times \frac{16}{9}$
$= \frac{29}{5} = 5.8$

122. (a) $\tan^4 A + \tan^2 A = \tan^2 A[\tan^2 A + 1]$
$= \tan^2 A\,[\sec^2 A]$
$= [\sec^2 A - 1]\,[\sec^2 A]$
$= \sec^4 A - \sec^2 A$

123. (a) Let the speed of boat be x km/h.
The speed of stream = y = 3 km/h
According to the question,
$x + y = \frac{16.9}{52} \times 60$
⇒ $x = 19.5 - 3$
⇒ $x = 16.5$ km/h
Let the time taken by boat to travel 84 km upstream be t h.
$x - y = \frac{84}{t}$
$16.5 - 3 = \frac{84}{t}$
$t = \frac{84}{13.5}$
$t = 6.22$ h

124. (d) Total distance = 100 km.
Average speed = $\frac{\text{Total distance}}{\text{Total time}}$
40 km/h = $\frac{100}{\text{Total time}}$
Total time = $\frac{100}{40}$ = 2.5 h = 150 min
∴ Time taken for last 20 km
= 150 − (40 + 50) = 60 min
∴ Speed in last 20 km
= $\frac{20}{60} \times 60$ km/h = 20 km/h

125. (c) $m \times 7 + 4 - 6 \div 3 - 7 + 45 \div 5 \times 4 + 49 = 87$
$\Rightarrow m \times 7 + 4 - 2 - 7 + 9 \times 4 + 49 = 87$
$\Rightarrow m \times 7 + 4 - 2 - 7 + 36 + 49 = 87$
$\Rightarrow m \times 7 + 89 - 2 - 7 = 87$
$\Rightarrow m \times 7 + 80 = 87$
$\Rightarrow m \times 7 = 7$
$\therefore m = 1$

126. (d) Total marks scored by Ronak in all subject = 75 + 89 + 79 + 82 = 325
Total marks scored by Shivam, Sonu and Arnav altogether in all subjects
= (83 + 87 + 90 + 92)
+ (88 + 95 + 90 + 87)
+ (92 + 85 + 90 + 88)
= 1067
∴ Required percentage
$= \frac{325}{1067} \times 100$
= 30.46%

127. (c) According to the question,

	Days	Total work	Efficiency
Akash	40	120	3
Vikash	60		2

2 days work of Akash and Vikash
= 3 + 2 = 5
Hence, required time = $\frac{120}{5} \times 2$
= 48 days

128. (a) $2 \times 8 \div 4 - 5$ of $3 + 6 \div 3 \times 2 - 6$ of $3 + 5$
$= 2 \times 8 \div 4 - 15 + 6 \div 3 \times 2 - 18 + 5$
$= 2 \times 2 - 15 + 2 \times 2 - 18 + 5$
$= 4 - 15 + 4 - 18 + 5 = -20$

129. (c) $(4a + 3b)(16a^2 - 12ab + 9b^2)$
$= (4a + 3b)[(4a)^2 - (4a)(3b) + (3b)^2]$
$= (4a)^3 + (3b)^3$
Put, $a = 2$ and $b = 3$
$= (4 \times 2)^2 + (3 \times 3)^3$
$= (8)^3 + (9)^3$
$= 512 + 729 = 1241$

130. (b) Length of first playground = 224 m
Breadth of first playground = 160 m
Ratio of length to breadth of first play ground = $\frac{224}{160} = \frac{7}{5}$
∴ Ratio of length to breadth of 2nd playground should also be $\frac{7}{5}$.
∴ Length = 343 m and breadth = 255 m does not follow the ratio.

131. **(b)** Let the weekly income of Ranita be ₹ R.

The weekly income of Bhaskar be ₹ B.

According to the question,

$$R \times \frac{42}{100} = B \times \frac{56}{100}$$

$$\frac{R}{B} = \frac{4}{3} \quad ...(i)$$

If Bhasker's weekly income become ₹ $(B + 200)$.

Then, ratio of income

$$= \frac{R}{B + 200} = \frac{5}{4} \quad ...(ii)$$

Solving equation (i) and (ii), we get

$R =$ ₹ 4000

∴ Weekly income of Ranita = ₹ 4000.

132. **(d)** Let the cost price of article be ₹ x.

Old selling price $= x - \frac{16}{100}x = \frac{84}{100}x$

New selling price

$$= \frac{84}{100}x + 192.20 = x + \frac{15x}{100}$$

$$192.20 = \frac{115x}{100} - \frac{84x}{100}$$

$19220 = 31x$

∴ Cost price $(x) =$ ₹ 620

∴ New selling price

$$= \frac{115}{100} \times 620 = ₹\,713$$

133. **(b)** By using BODMAS rule,

$= 4 \times 5 \div 4$ of $5 \times 4 \div (6 + 6 \times 6 \div 6$ of $6 - 6 \div 6 \times 6)$

$= 4 \times 5 \div 4$ of $5 \times 4 \div (6 + 6 \times 6 \div 36 - 6 \div 6 \times 6)$

$= 4 \times 5 \div 4$ of $5 \times 4 \div \left(6 + 6 \times \frac{1}{6} - 1 \times 6\right)$

$= 4 \times 5 \div 4$ of $5 \times 4 \div (6 + 1 - 6)$

$= 4 \times 5 \div 4$ of $5 \times 4 \div 1$

$= 4 \times 5 \div 20 \times 4 \div 1$

$= 4 \times \frac{1}{4} \times 4 = 4$

134. **(c)** $\sin^4\theta + \cos^4\theta = 2\sin^2\theta \cdot \cos^2\theta$

$\Rightarrow (\sin^2\theta)^2 + (\cos^2\theta)^2 - 2\sin^2\theta \cdot \cos^2\theta = 0$

$\Rightarrow (\sin^2\theta - \cos^2\theta)^2 = 0$

$\Rightarrow \sin^2\theta - \cos^2\theta = 0$

$\Rightarrow \cos^2\theta = \sin^2\theta$

$\Rightarrow \frac{\cos^2\theta}{\sin^2\theta} = 1 \Rightarrow \cot^2\theta = 1$

$\therefore \cot\theta = 1$

135. **(a)** Volume of cuboid = Length × Breadth × Height

Volume of wax (cuboid shape)

$= 70 \times 44 \times 20\ \text{cm}^3$

Volume of cylinder $= \pi r^2 h$

Volume of 1 cylindrical candle

$= \frac{22}{7} \times 7 \times 7 \times 20\ \text{cm}^3$

$= 22 \times 7 \times 20\ \text{cm}^3$

∴ Total number of candles

$$= \frac{70 \times 44 \times 20}{22 \times 7 \times 20} = 20$$

136. **(d)** Total distance = (140 + 120) m

= 260 m

Relative speed of train

= (78 − 60) km/h

$= \frac{18 \times 1000}{60 \times 60}$ m/sec

Time taken $= \frac{\text{Distance}}{\text{Speed}}$

∴ Time taken $= \frac{260 \times 60 \times 60}{18 \times 1000}$

= 52 sec

137. **(d)** Given, $a - b = 2$ cm ...(i)

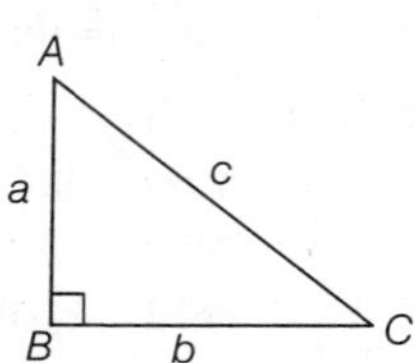

Area of triangle $= \frac{1}{2} \times \text{Base} \times \text{Height}$

$24\ \text{cm}^2 = \frac{1}{2} \times b \times a$

$ab = 48\ \text{cm}^2$

Since, $a - b = 2$

$(a - b)^2 = 4$

$\Rightarrow a^2 + b^2 - 2ab = 4$

$a^2 + b^2 = 4 + 2ab$

$\Rightarrow a^2 + b^2 + 2ab = 4 + 2ab + 2ab$

$(a + b)^2 = 4 + 4 \times 48$

$a + b = \sqrt{4(1 + 48)} = 14$ ...(ii)

From equation (i) and (ii),

$a = 8$ cm and $b = 6$ cm

Since, ΔABC is a right angled Δ.

$\therefore a^2 + b^2 = c^2$

$8^2 + 6^2 = c^2 \Rightarrow c = 10$ cm

∴ Perimeter of

$\Delta ABC = 8 + 6 + 10 = 24$ cm

138. **(d)** Total distance

= 320 + 240 = 560 m

∵ Both trains are moving in opposite direction.

∴ Relative speed of trains

= 56.8 + 44 = 100.8 km/h

Time taken to completely cross each other = y sec

$\because\ y = \frac{560 \times 18}{100.8 \times 5}$ sec

= 20 sec

139. **(a)** Marks obtained by Sohan in maths

$= \frac{90}{100} \times 200 = 180$

Marks obtained by Shyam in maths

$= \frac{70}{100} \times 200 = 140$

∴ Sohan scored 40 more marks than Shyam in maths.

140. **(d)** Number of students in class VII from school U = 162

Total number of students in school,

U = 150 + 160 + 162 + 160 + 161 + 140 = 933

∴ Percentage $= \frac{162}{933} \times 100$

≈ 17%

141. **(d)** By using BODMAS rule,

$= 7.2 \times 4.1 \div 12.3 + 22.5$ of $\frac{1}{25} - \frac{1}{10}$

$= 7.2 \times 4.1 \div 12.3 + 22.5 \times \frac{1}{25} - \frac{1}{10}$

$= 7.2 \times \frac{1}{3} + \frac{9}{10} - \frac{1}{10}$

$= \frac{24}{10} + \frac{9}{10} - \frac{1}{10}$

$= \frac{32}{10} = 3.2$

142. **(c)** Given, $a + b + c = 15$ and

$ab + bc + ac = 35$

We know, $(a + b + c)^2 = a^2 + b^2 + c^2 + 2(ab + bc + ac)$

$(15)^2 = a^2 + b^2 + c^2 + 2 \times 35$

$a^2 + b^2 + c^2 = 225 - 70 = 155$

$a^2 + b^2 + c^2 = 155$

Also we know that,

$a^3 + b^3 + c^3 - 3abc = (a + b + c)[a^2 + b^2 + c^2 - (ab + bc + ac)]$

$= 15 \times [155 - 35]$

$= 15 \times 120$

$= 1800$

143. **(a)** $\left(\frac{3}{4} + \frac{5}{4}\right) \times \left(\frac{9}{5} - \frac{4}{5}\right) \div \left(\frac{3}{2} + \frac{1}{2}\right)$

$= \left(\frac{8}{4}\right) \times \left(\frac{5}{5}\right) \div \left(\frac{4}{2}\right)$

$= \left(\frac{8}{4}\right) \times \left(\frac{5}{5}\right) \times \left(\frac{2}{4}\right)$

$= \frac{80}{80} = 1$

144. (c) Let the MP be ₹ 100.

After first discount of 24%,

$SP_1 = 100 - (24\% \text{ of } 100) = ₹ 76$

After extra 30% off coupon,

$SP_2 = 76 - (30\% \text{ of } 76) = ₹ 53.2$

When the final SP is ₹ 53.2, then MP is ₹ 100.

∴ When the final SP is ₹ 7700.7, then

$$MP = \frac{100}{53.2} \times 7700.7 = ₹ 14475$$

145. (d) Given, Distance between the centres of two circles, $d = 13$ cm.

Radius of first circle, $R_1 = 3$ cm

Radius of another circle, $R_2 = 2$ cm

Length of transverse common tangent

$$= \sqrt{d^2 - (R_1 + R_2)^2}$$

$$= \sqrt{(13)^2 - (3+2)^2}$$

$$= \sqrt{169 - 25}$$

$$= \sqrt{144} = 12 \text{ cm}$$

146. (a) Number of employees in 2020 = 34

Number of employees in 2019 = 32

∴ % Increase in employees in 2020 over 2019 $= \frac{(34-32)}{32} \times 100\%$

$$= \frac{2}{32} \times 100$$

$$= \frac{25}{4} = 6\frac{1}{4}\%$$

147. (d) Let 't' be added to the polynomial to be divisible by $(x - 5)$

For $(x^3 - 3x^2 + 4x - 75 + t)$ to be exactly divisible by $(x - 5)$.

$$x^3 - 3x^2 + 4x - 75 + t = 0$$

Put, $x = 5$ in above equation,

$$125 - 3(25) + 4(5) - 75 + t = 0$$

$$\Rightarrow 125 - 75 + 20 - 75 + t = 0$$

$$\Rightarrow 145 - 150 + t = 0$$

$$\Rightarrow -5 + t = 0$$

$$\Rightarrow t = 5$$

148. (a) Let the value of D be 100.

Then, value of C

$= 100 + (20\% \text{ of } 100) = 120$

Value of $B = 120 - (30\% \text{ of } 120)$

$= 120 - 36 = 84$

Value of $A = 84 + (25\% \text{ of } 84)$

$= 84 + 21 = 105$

A is more than D by

$$\frac{105 - 100}{100} \times 100 = 5\%$$

149. (b) Given,

Height of the cone, $h = 9$ ft.

Radius of the cone, $r = 7$ ft.

Volume of the cone-shaped storage

$$= \frac{1}{3}\pi r^2 h$$

$$= \frac{1}{3} \times \frac{22}{7} \times (7)^2 \times 9$$

$$= \frac{1}{3} \times \frac{22}{7} \times 49 \times 9$$

$$= 462 \text{ cubic ft.}$$

150. (d) Lateral surface area of cone = πrl

$$\Rightarrow \pi rl = 13.2$$

$$\Rightarrow \frac{22}{7} \times r \times 4.2 = 13.2$$

$$\Rightarrow r = \frac{13.2 \times 7}{22 \times 4.2}$$

$$r = 1 \text{ unit}$$

151. (d) The most appropriate synonym of the given word 'Habitual' is 'Continuous'. 'Habitual' refers to something done regularly or repeatedly.

152. (d) The most appropriate synonym of the given word 'Unhappiness' is 'Woe', which means a feeling of sadness or misery. 'Unhappiness' refers to a state of being unhappy or sorrowful.

153. (b) The sentence that has a grammatical error is 'I will be drive into town later on'. The correct phrase should be 'I will be driving into town later on'.

154. (b) The most appropriate synonym of the given word 'Insipid' is 'Tasteless'. 'Insipid' refers to lacking flavour or interest.

155. (*) None of the given options is a suitable one-word substitute for the given group of words.

Extrovert means someone who is outgoing and social.

Horticultural is a misspelt word.

Introvert is someone who is shy or reserved.

Narcissist is a person who is excessively self-obsessed.

156. (c) The segment that contains a grammatical error in the sentence is 'are here to'. The correct phrase should be 'is here to'.

157. (a) The most appropriate meaning of the underlined segment in the given sentence is 'It is time for someone to deal with a problem or make a decision, because other people have already done as much as they can'.

158. (c) The most appropriate idiom to fill in the blank is 'under her belt'. This idiom means having experience or achievement in a particular field.

159. (c) The option that rectifies the spelling error in the given sentence is 'brought'.

160. (a) The most appropriate meaning of the given idiom 'See eye to eye' is 'To agree with someone'.

161. (d) The option that is similar in meaning to the underlined word in the sentence is 'problem'. A conundrum refers to a difficult or confusing problem.

162. (a) The incorrectly spelt word is 'Ambigous'. The correct spelling is 'Ambiguous'.

163. (b) The most appropriate option that can substitute the underlined segment in the given sentence is 'I would have made'.

164. (c) The most appropriate option that can substitute the highlighted words in the given sentence is 'understanding of realities'.

165. (d) The incorrectly spelt word is 'Witharing'. The correct spelling is 'Withering'.

166. (b) The option that can be used as a one-word substitute for the underlined group of words is 'Oligarchy'. 'Oligarchy' refers to a system of government where power is concentrated in the hands of a small group of people.

167. (c) The most appropriate option that can substitute the underlined segment in the given sentence is 'If his father gives money'.

168. (b) The most appropriate antonym of the given word 'Cowardice' is 'Boldness'. 'Cowardice' refers to a lack of courage or fearfulness.

169. (c) The correct option to substitute the underlined segment in the sentence is 'wanted to visit'. The sentence should read. "He wanted to visit the Golden Temple in Amritsar."

170. (d) The most appropriate antonym of the underlined word 'consistent' in the sentence is 'unpredictable'. 'consistent' means unchanging or reliable, while, 'unpredictable' means not following a pattern.

171. (b) The most appropriate meaning of the given idiom 'From cradle to grave' is 'During the whole span of one's life'. It signifies the entirety of a person's life from birth to death.

172. (b) The most appropriate meaning of the given idiom 'Chip on the shoulder' is 'Offended'. It refers to someone who is easily offended or harbours resentment.

173. (b) The most appropriate option that can substitute the underlined segment in the given idiom 'A piece of biscuit' is 'cake'. 'A piece of cake' means something that is easy to do.

174. (c) The most appropriate phrase that can replace the highlighted text in the sentence is 'captivating expertise'.

175. (d) The most appropriate antonym of the underlined word 'fettered' in the sentence is 'liberated'. 'Fettered' means restricted or restrained.

176. (c) The most appropriate antonym of the underlined word 'accessible' in the sentence is 'restricted'. 'Accessible' means easily available or reachable.

177. (d) The most appropriate article to fill in the blank is 'an; ϕ'.

178. (b) The option that can be used as a one-word substitute for the underlined words is 'is critical of others'.

179. (b) The option that can be used as a one-word substitute for the given group of words is 'lagoon'.

180. (a) The meaning of the option 'Break a leg' is 'Good luck'. It is a common expression used to wish someone well before a performance or event.

181. (c) The synonym for 'Indigent' is 'Impoverished'. It refers to someone who is poor or lacking financial resources.

182. (d) The error in the sentence 'When Ramu was working as a clerk, he asked me money' lies in the phrase 'he asked me money.' The correct version should be 'he asked me for money.' The preposition 'for' is needed after the verb 'asked' to indicate what he requested.

183. (a) The correct explanation for the error in the sentence 'Mohan insisted to go there' is that the preposition 'on' should be used. The sentence should read 'Mohan insisted on going there' to express his strong recommendation or desire.

184. (c) The idiom 'spill the beans' means 'to reveal a secret'. So, 'reveal the secret' is the correct choice.

185. (c) The error in the sentence article 'a.' It should be 'an' because the word 'international' begins with a vowel sound. The corrected sentence is 'Mrs Rani works for an international school'.

186. (a) The incorrectly spelled word is 'Buraeucracy'. The correct spelling is 'Bureaucracy'.

187. (a) The idiom 'Nip in the bud' means 'to suppress something at an early stage'. So, 'to supress something at an early stage' is the correct choice.

188. (a) The correct spelling is 'beginning'. The sentence should be 'The movie is just beginning' to indicate the start of the movie.

189. (d) The most appropriate option to substitute the underlined segment in the sentence is 'teachers have been doing'. The corrected sentence reads 'What exactly have the teachers been doing wrong?'.

190. (c) The word that represents 'a soldier who fights for the sake of money' is 'mercenary'.

191. (c) The correct option to fill in blank no. 1 is 'middle'.

192. (c) The correct option to fill in blank no. 2 is 'barking'.

193. (c) The correct option to fill in blank no. 3 is 'at'.

194. (d) The correct option to fill in blank no. 4 is 'dial'.

195. (b) The correct option to fill in blank no. 5 is 'heard'.

196. (b) The most suitable title for the passage is 'The Publishing Journey'. The passage discusses Joanne Kathleen Rowling's journey to fame and her experiences as an author.

197. (d) The tone of the passage is 'Informative'. It provides factual information about Rowling's life, writing process and challenges she faced.

198. (b) The quality we learn about JK Rowling that helped her become a successful writer is 'Perseverance'. Despite initial rejections, she persisted and found a publisher for her work.

199. (b) When she started writing 'Harry Potter and the Sorcerer's Stone,' Rowling was 'Teaching' English in Portugal.

200. (c) The antonym for 'Conformity' in the passage is 'Quirky'. Rowling's overactive imagination and desire to be a writer were seen as an amusing personal quirk by her parents.

CPO SI P-1 SP 04

PAPER-1

SSC CPO SI SOLVED PAPER

28 June 2024 (Shift III)

MM : 200 **Time** : 2 hr

Instructions

1. This paper contains 200 questions.
2. It has 4 Parts, **Part I** General Intelligence and Reasoning, **Part II** General Knowledge and General Awareness, **Part III** Quantitative Aptitude and **Part IV** English Comprehension.
3. Each question carries **1 marks.**

Part I

General Intelligence and Reasoning

1. Select the figure from among the given options that can logically replace the question mark (?) in the following series.

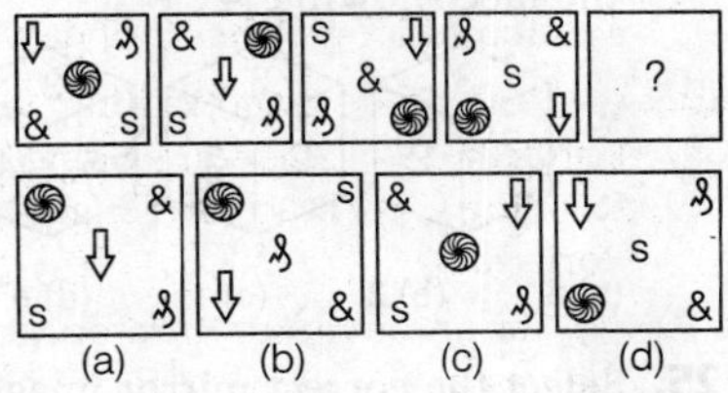

2. Select the set in which the numbers are related in the same way as are the numbers of the following sets.
(**Note** Operations should be performed on the whole numbers, without breaking down the numbers into its constituent digits. E.g. 13 – Operations on 13 such as adding /subtracting /multiplying etc to 13 can be performed. Breaking down 13 into 1 and 3 and then performing mathematical operations on 1 and 3 is not allowed)
(16, 48 , 4)
(24, 72, 6)
(a) (21, 60, 6) (b) (20, 60, 6)
(c) (21, 60, 5) (d) (20, 60, 5)

3. In a certain code language, 'God is great' is coded as 'tg so rf' and 'we love God' is coded as 'ae rf xd'. How is 'God' coded in that language?
(a) xd
(b) rf
(c) tg
(d) ae

4. Select the Venn-diagram that best illustrates the relationship between the following classes.
Teacher, Guitarist, Lawyer

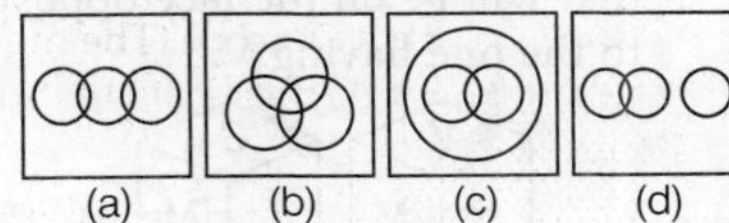

5. Anil starts from point A and drives 8 km towards North. He then takes a right turn, drives 2 km, turns right and drives 11 km. He then takes a right turn and drives 5 km. He takes a final right turn, drives 3 km and stops at point P. How far (shortest distance) and towards, which direction should he drive in order to reach point A again?
(All turns are 90 degrees turns only unless specified.)
(a) 3 km towards East
(b) 2 km towards East
(c) 2 km towards West
(d) 3 km towards North

6. Based on the English alphabetical order, three of the following four letter-clusters are alike in a certain way and thus form a group. Which letter-cluster does not belong to that group?
(**Note** The odd letter-cluster is not based on the number of consonants/vowels or their position in the letter-cluster.)
(a) QNR (b) TQV
(c) NKP (d) KHM

7. Point A is 35 m to the East of point B. point C is 48 m to the North of point A. Point D is 23 m to the East of point C. point D is 14 m to the North of point E. Point E is 48 m to the East of point F. In which direction is point F with respect to point A?
(a) North-East (b) North
(c) East (d) North-West

8. Select the option that is related to the third word in the same way as the second word is related to the first word.
(The words must be considered as meaningful English words and must not be related to each other based on the number of letters/number of consonants/vowels in the word.)
Summon : Call :: Disperse : ?
(a) Surround (b) Remove
(c) Spread (d) Disappear

9. In a code language, 'MARS' is written as 'KXPP' and 'BODY' is written as 'ZLBV'. How will 'TEST' be written in that language?
(a) RBQQ (b) RQBQ
(c) QQRB (d) QRQB

10. Select the option that represents the correct order of the given words as they would appear in an English dictionary.
1. Breathable 2. Brevetting
3. Breakfast 4. Breviaries
5. Breacher 6. Breakthrough
(a) 5, 6, 3, 1, 4, 2 (b) 6, 5, 3, 1, 4, 2
(c) 6, 3, 5, 1, 2, 4 (d) 5, 3, 6, 1, 2, 4

11. Find the two signs to be interchanged for making the following equation correct.
$6+3\times8-12\div4=4$
(a) ÷ and − (b) + and ÷
(c) − and + (d) ÷ and ×

12. Which of the following numbers will replace the question mark (?) in the given series?
192, 185, 171, ?, 122, 87
(a) 149 (b) 147 (c) 151 (d) 150

13. Two statements are given followed by two conclusions numbered I and II. Assuming the statements to be true, even if they seem to be at variance with commonly known facts, decide which of the conclusions logically follow(s) from the statements.
Statements
All cards are plastics.
Some plastics are woods.
Conclusions
I. Some cards are woods.
II. No card is a wood.
(a) Only Conclusion II follows
(b) Neither Conclusion I nor II follows
(c) Only Conclusion I follows
(d) Either Conclusion I or II follows

14. The sequence of folding a paper and the manner in which the folded paper is cut is shown in the following figures. How would this paper look when unfolded?

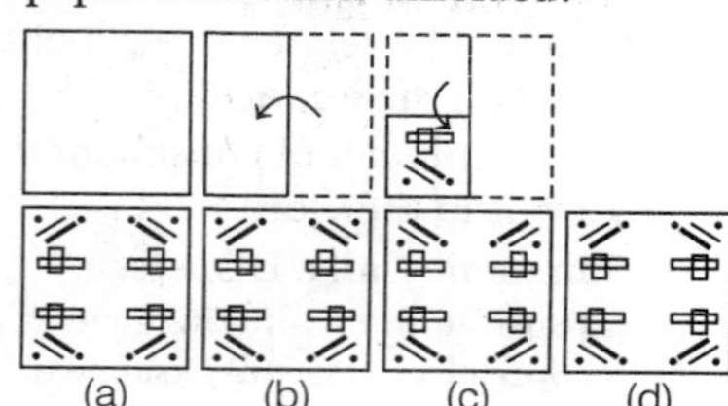

15. Which letter cluster will replace the question mark (?) to complete the given series?
YFJW, BJEC, ?, HRUO, KVPU
(a) EHSI (b) TDFI
(c) NWRF (d) ENZI

16. Which of the following letter-clusters will replace the question mark (?) in the given series?
AM, DK, GI, JG, ?
(a) NE (b) ND
(c) MD (d) ME

17. In a certain code language,
'A + B' means 'A is the father of B'
'A − B' means 'B is the sister of A'
'A × B' means 'A is the wife of B'
'A ÷ B' means 'A is the mother of B'
Based on the above, how is L related to 'K if N × M − K ÷ L + P'?
(a) Mother (b) Father
(c) Brother (d) Son

18. If 'A' stands for '÷', 'B' stands for '×', 'C' stands for '+' and 'D' stands for '−', what will come in place of the question mark (?) in the following equation?
8 B 9 C 49 A 7 D 25 = ?
(a) 25 (b) 54
(c) 57 (d) 62

19. A dice has letters M, Q, R, S, T and V on its sides. Two different positions of the same dice are shown below. Select the letter that will be on the face opposite to the one having V.

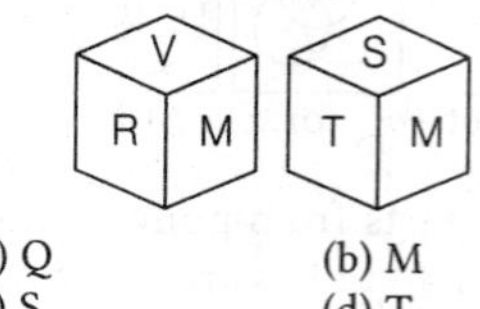

(a) Q (b) M
(c) S (d) T

20. In a code language, 'GOOD' is written as 'HMPB', and 'HALL' is written as 'IYMJ'. How will 'TOOL' be written in that language?
(a) JUMP (b) PUMJ
(c) UPJM (d) UMPJ

21. In a code language, 'HOPE' is coded as 'FRRL' and 'TAIL' is coded as 'MKDX'. How will 'STORY' be coded in the same language?
(a) ZRTXX (b) ZTRYY
(c) ZRTYY (d) ZTRXX

22. Select the set in which the numbers are related in the same way as are the numbers of the following sets.
(**Note** Operations should be performed on the whole numbers, without breaking down the numbers into its constituent digits. E.g. 13 – Operations on 13 such as adding /subtracting /multiplying etc. to 13 can be performed. Breaking down 13 into 1 and 3 and then performing mathematical operations on 1 and 3 is not allowed.)
(128, 62, 190)
(114, 86, 200)
(a) (98, 68, 146)
(b) (102, 73, 165)
(c) (95, 54, 149)
(d) (106, 69, 195)

23. Which of the following numbers will replace the question mark (?) in the given series?
6, 10, 15, 21, ?, 36, 45
(a) 30 (b) 31
(c) 28 (d) 26

24. Three different positions of the same dice are given. Find the number on the face opposite to the face showing '4'.

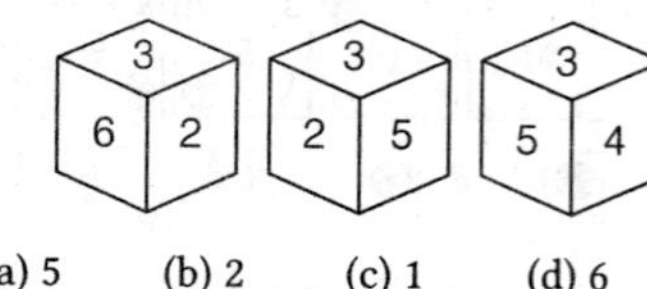

(a) 5 (b) 2 (c) 1 (d) 6

25. Select the correct mirror image of the given figure, when the mirror is placed at MN as shown below.

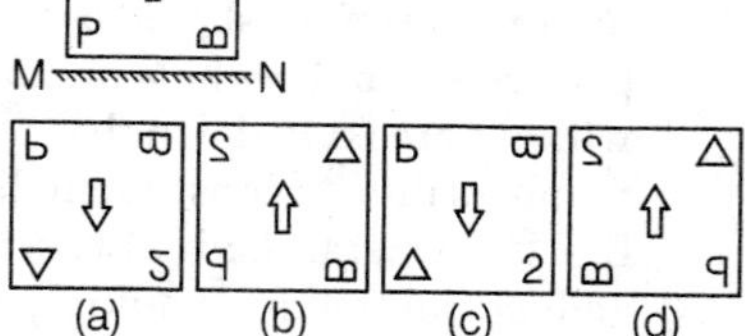

26. If 'A' stands for '+', 'B' stands for '−', 'C' stands for '×' and 'D' stands for '÷', what will come in place of the question mark (?) in the following equation?
6 C 7 C 8 B 71 A 11 B 32 C 2 = ?
(a) 198 (b) 228
(c) 212 (d) 192

27. A dice has its faces named by letters B, C, D, R, S and T. Two positions of the same dice are given below. Which face is opposite to face R?

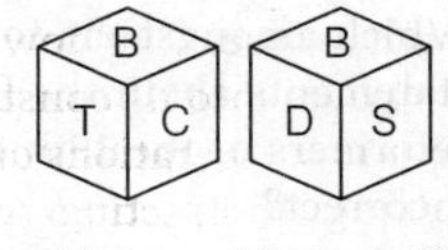

(a) D (b) B (c) T (d) S

28. Which of the following interchanges of signs would make the given equation correct?

$40 + 45 \times 5 - 12 \div 4 = 1$

(a) ÷ and × (b) – and ×
(c) + and × (d) – and +

29. In a certain code language, 'APPLE' is coded as 250 and 'BERRY' is coded as 340. How will 'LITCHI' be coded in the same language?

(a) 330 (b) 306 (c) 305 (d) 350

30. Which two signs should be interchanged to make the given equation correct?

$16 \times 121 \div 11 + 4 - 10 = 50$

(a) + and × (b) – and ÷
(c) ÷ and + (d) + and –

31. Which of the following numbers will replace the question mark (?) in the given series?

80, 101, 120, ?, 168

(a) 143 (b) 147
(c) 145 (d) 149

32. In a certain code language, 'FEED' is written as '24' and 'ACCOUNT' is written as '42'. How will 'PIZZA' be written in that language?

(a) 38 (b) 36 (c) 40 (d) 30

33. Select the correct mirror image of the given figure, when the mirror is placed at MN as shown below.

M

Merga52

N

(a) Ƨ2agɿɘM (b) 52agɿɘM
(c) ƧƧagɿɘM (d) ƧƧagɿɘM

34. Two statements are given followed by two conclusions numbered I and II. Assuming the statements to be true, even if they seem to be at variance with commonly known facts, decide which of the conclusions logically follow(s) from the statements.

Statements

Some snacks are meals.
All juices are snacks.

Conclusions

I. All juices can never be meals.
II. All meals are snacks.

(a) Only Conclusion II follows
(b) Both Conclusions I and II follow
(c) Only Conclusion I follows
(d) Neither Conclusion I nor II follows

35. Select the option that indicates the correct arrangement of the given words in the order in which they appear in an English dictionary.

1. Perplex 2. Peroration
3. Perpetrate 4. Perpetuity
5. Perpetual

(a) 2, 3, 5, 4, 1 (b) 1, 2, 4, 3, 5
(c) 3, 2, 4, 5, 1 (d) 4, 2, 5, 3, 1

36. Identify the figure given in the options, which when put in place of '?' will logically complete the series.

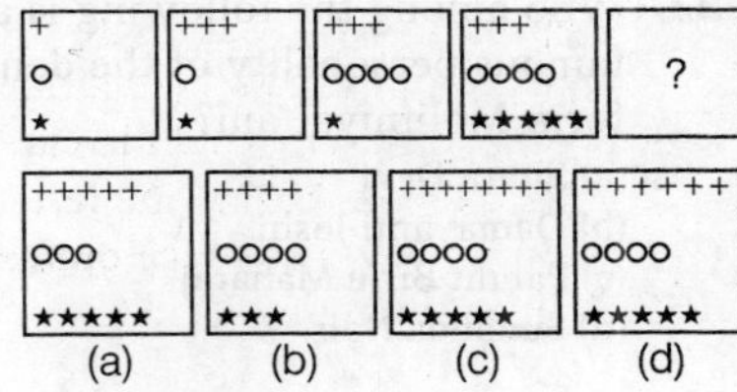

37. Select the correct mirror image of the given figure, when the mirror is placed at MN as shown below.

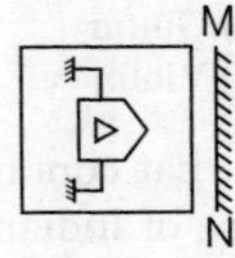

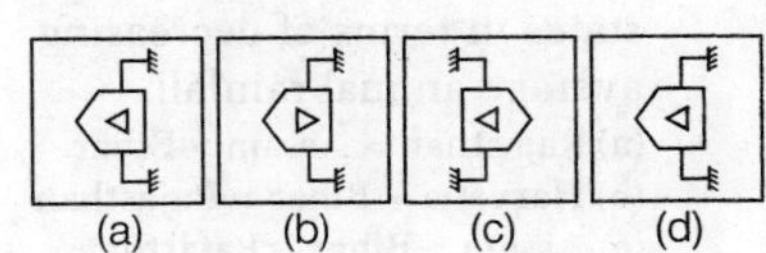

38. Two statements are given, followed by two conclusions numbered I and II. Assuming the statements to be true, even if they seem to be at variance with commonly known facts, decide which of the conclusions logically follow(s) from the statements.

Statements

Some streams are rivers.
Some rivers are oceans.

Conclusions

I. Some streams are oceans.
II. All rivers are oceans.

(a) Only Conclusion I follows
(b) Both Conclusions I and II follow
(c) Only Conclusion II follows
(d) Neither Conclusion I nor II follows

39. Select the option that is related to the fifth letter-cluster in the same way as the second letter-cluster is related to the first letter-cluster and the fourth letter-cluster is related to the third letter-cluster.

UNREAL : MCHVSA :: CREATE : FVDIWI :: AROUND : ?

(a) FPXSWF (b) FQXSWG
(c) EPXSXE (d) EPXSWG

40. Select the number from among the given options that can replace the question mark(?) in the following series.

45, 46, 50, 59, 75, ?

(a) 95 (b) 100
(c) 105 (d) 90

41. Six students A, B, C, D, E and F are sitting around a circular table, facing the centre.

A. is the immediate neighbour of both E and F.
B. is sitting second to the right of E.
C. is the immediate neighbour of both B and F.
D. is sitting third to the left of F.

Who among the following is the immediate neighbour of both A and D?

(a) E (b) B
(c) C (d) F

42. A dice has its faces marked by symbols $\theta, \delta, \omega, \varepsilon, \eta$ and %. Two positions of the same dice are given below. Which face is opposite to face %?

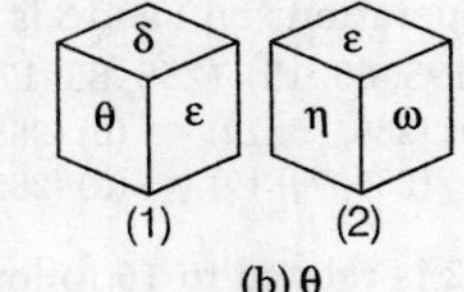

(a) η (b) θ
(c) ω (d) ε

43. In a certain code language,
'A × B' means 'A is the son of B',
'A − B' means 'A is the brother of B',
'A + B' means 'A is the wife of B',
'A % B' means 'A is the father of B'.
How is M related to T if
M× N + P− S % T '?
(a) Wife's father's brother
(b) Father's brother's son
(c) Mother's mother's brother
(d) Mother's brother

44. Identify the figure given in the options, which when put in place of (?) will logically complete the series.

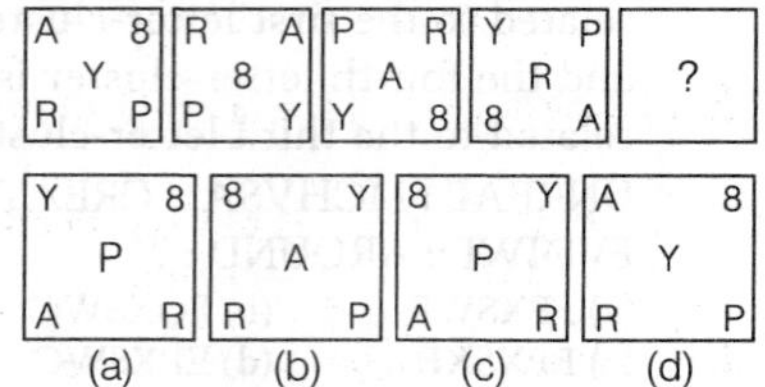

45. Which of the following terms will replace the question mark (?) in the given series?
RJO, SKP, TLQ,?
(a) GRS (b) MRW
(c) UMR (d) HKL

46. If 'A' stands for '+', 'B' stands for '−', 'C' stands for '×' and 'D' stands for '÷', what will come in place of the question mark (?) in the following equation?
74 A (17 C 2 B 24) D 2 A 16 C 3 B 8 = ?
(a) 119 (b) 134 (c) 128 (d) 109

47. Select the set in which the numbers are related in the same way as are the numbers of the following sets.
(**Note** Operations should be performed on the whole numbers, without breaking down the numbers into its constituent digits. E.g. 13 – Operations on 13 such as adding /subtracting /multiplying etc to 13 can be performed. Breaking down 13 into 1 and 3 and then performing mathematical operations on 1 and 3 is not allowed)
(195, 65, 13), (255, 85, 17)
(a) (280, 95, 19) (b) (285, 95, 19)
(c) (285, 90, 19) (d) (285, 95, 21)

48. 12 is related to 16 following a certain logic. Following the same logic, 18 is related to 24. Which of the following numbers is related to 28 using the same logic?
(a) 21 (b) 22 (c) 23 (d) 24

49. If 'A' stands for '÷', 'B' stands for '×', 'C' stands for '+' and 'D' stands for '−', what will come in place of the question mark in the following equation?
8 B 9 C 49 A 7 D 25 = ?
(a) 44 (b) 52 (c) 54 (d) 56

50. Select the pair, which is related to each other in the same way as the following
72:27
(a) 27:45 (b) 56:33 (c) 32:14 (d) 48:24

Part II

General Knowledge and General Awareness

51. Why are the intermediate goods not included in the National Income?
(a) For the prevention of double counting.
(b) Intermediate goods decrease the income.
(c) Intermediate goods are not reliable.
(d) Intermediate goods increase the income.

52. Who among the following is a famous personality of the dance form Mohiniyattam?
(a) Sitara Devi
(b) Damayanti Joshi
(c) Pandit Birju Maharaj
(d) Sunanda Nair

53. Brij Bhushan Kabra was considered an expert in which of the following instruments in the field of Indian classical music?
(a) Veena (b) Guitar
(c) Santoor (d) Violin

54. Identify the option that contains the correct sequence of Indian states in terms of decreasing average annual rainfall.
(a) Rajasthan > Assam > Bihar
(b) Haryana > Bihar > Rajasthan
(c) Assam > Bihar > Rajasthan
(d) Uttar Pradesh > Bihar > West Bengal

55. What is the national male workforce participation rate as per the Census of India 2011?
(a) 53.26% (b) 51.26%
(c) 50.26% (d) 52.26%

56. What is the name of the Northern part of the Western coastal plain between Mumbai and Goa?
(a) Konkan coast (b) Coromandel coast
(c) Malabar coast (d) Kannad plain

57. Which amongst the following statements about the Indian social reformers of the 19th century is incorrect?
(a) Ishwar Chandra Vidyasagar was the founder of the Brahmo Samaj.
(b) The Aligarh Movement was started by Sir Syed Ahmad Khan in 1875.
(c) Mahadev Govind Ranade is associated with the Poona Sarvajanik Sabha.
(d) Dayananda Saraswati founded the Arya Samaj in 1875.

58. Which of the following is an incorrectly stated social impact of the Green Revolution?
(a) Primarily, the medium and large farmers were benefitted.
(b) Worsened the condition of landless and marginal farmers.
(c) Only farmers involved in subsistence agriculture were benefitted.
(d) There was displacement of service caste group.

59. The 42nd Amendment of the Indian Constitution, 1976 states that India is a/an ...... nation.
(a) aristocratic (b) oligarchic
(c) capitalist (d) secular

60. Choose the correct statement about the peninsular rivers.
A. The Narmada river rises in the Malwa plateau.
B. The Godavari river rises from the slopes of the Western Ghats near Nashik.
C. The Mahanadi river rises in the highlands of Chhattisgarh.
D. The Krishna river rises from a spring near Mahabaleshwar.
(a) B, C and D (b) A, B and C
(c) A, B, C and D (d) A, C and D

61. Who among the following are eligible for free legal aid under the National Legal Services Authority?
A. A member of a Scheduled Caste or Scheduled Tribe.
B. A victim of trafficking in human beings or beggar as referred to in Article 23 of the Constitution.

C. An industrial workman.
D. A person under circumstances of undeserved want such as being a victim of a mass disasters.
E. To file any case in Supreme Court, if any person needs free legal aid, the person's annual income must be below ₹10 lakhs.

(a) B, C and D (b) A, B, C, D and E
(c) A, B, C and D (d) A, B and E

62. Which of the following was not an advantage of privatisation?
(a) Additional source of revenue for the government
(b) Low interference of political motives
(c) Overall improved performance
(d) Reduced competition

63. Tattwabodhini Patrika promoted the study of India's past in which language?
(a) Sanskrit (b) Bengali
(c) Hindi (d) English

64. In Andhra region, who among the following translated a few portions of Mahabharata in Telugu?
(a) Nanniah (b) Tikkana
(c) Kamban (d) Pampa

65. Who among the following was the Founding President of the Indian Olympic Association?
(a) Dadabhai Naoroji
(b) Jamsetji Tata
(c) AG Noehren
(d) Dorabji Tata

66. Pt. Shivkumar Sharma, an accomplished Santoor player, originally hails from the State/UT of ....
(a) Jammu and Kashmir
(b) Lakshadweep
(c) Assam
(d) Himachal Pradesh

67. The Carnatic classical vocalist and first ever musician to receive the Bharat Ratna Award, also known as 'Queen of Songs', is ....
(a) Shubha Mudgal
(b) Girija Devi
(c) MS Subbulakshmi
(d) Gangubai Hangal

68. 'A Flight of Pigeons' is a famous book written by...... .
(a) Ruskin Bond
(b) Salman Rushdie
(c) Khushwant Singh
(d) Vikram Seth

69. Which unit is used to measure the concentration of contaminants in soil and sediment?
(a) PPBB (b) TDS
(c) DPMO (d) PPM

70. Who among the following is the author of the book 'The Oath of the Vayuputras'?
(a) Indrapramit Das
(b) Vikram Chandra
(c) Amish Tripathi
(d) Ravi Subramanian

71. The ...... Project has been organised by the Central Government for the villagers, to conserve water for drinking, irrigation, fisheries and afforestation.
(a) Neeru-Meeru
(b) Hariyali
(c) Chipko Andolan
(d) Arvary Pani Sansad

72. Devanampiya Piyadasi is another name for whom among the following Mauryan kings?
(a) Samprati (b) Ashoka
(c) Shatadhanvan (d) Bindusara

73. To what phylum does a blood sucking leech belong?
(a) Aschelminthes
(b) Cnidarian
(c) Platyhelminthes
(d) Annelida

74. Who described the algae Spirogyra in 1674 and named the motile organisms Animalcules, meaning 'little animals'?
(a) Maurice Wilkins
(b) Anton Van Leeuwenhoek
(c) Robert Remak
(d) Barthelemy Dumortier

75. Which of the following mountains of India is famous for tea and coffee production?
(a) Aravalli (b) Vidhyanchal
(c) Himalaya (d) Nilgiri

76. Which Article of the Indian Constitution mentions that a person may be appointed as the Governor of two or more states?
(a) Article 153 (b) Article 150
(c) Article 151 (d) Article 152

77. Which of the following statements is correct about 'Loo' winds in the context of the Indian climate?
(a) They blow in the winter and rainy season.
(b) They blow in the summer season.
(c) They blow in the winter season.
(d) They blow in the rainy season

78. Which part of the bifocal lens facilitates near vision?
(a) Lower part with concave lens
(b) Upper part with convex lens
(c) Lower part with convex lens
(d) Upper part with concave lens

79. Shovana Narayan has been honoured with the Padma Shri for her contribution to which Indian dance form?
(a) Kathakali (b) Kathak
(c) Kuchipudi (d) Odissi

80. Dalkhai is a popular folk dance of ....
(a) Bihar (b) Uttar Pradesh
(c) Odisha (c) Punjab

81. Which Article specifies the procedure for amending the Indian Constitution?
(a) Article 367 (b) Article 368
(c) Article 365 (d) Article 366

82. Which Article of the Indian Constitution mentions about the salaries and allowances of members of the Legislative Assembly and the Legislative Council of a State?
(a) Article 199 (b) Article 198
(c) Article 195 (d) Article 194

83. Indian Classical Dance is an umbrella under which various performing arts whose theory and practice can be traced to the Sanskrit text, Natya Shastra, the foundational treatise by ....
(a) Bhasa (b) Panini
(c) Patanjali (d) Bharata Muni

84. Which of the following is the main active ingredient of clove oil?
(a) Eugenol
(b) Curcuma
(c) Malic acid
(d) Tartaric acid

85. As per the National Multidimensional Poverty Index Report 2023, which of the following states has the least population concentration in the Multidimensional Poverty Index?
(a) Tamil Nadu (b) Kerala
(c) Goa (d) Sikkim

86. 2-Methylpropan-2-ol is commonly known as
(a) tert-butyl alcohol (b) prim-propyl alcohol
(c) ethyl alcohol (d) methanol

87. The inaugural edition of the National Beach Soccer Championship was held at ...... in 2023.
(a) Surat (b) Daman (c) Diu (d) Goa

88. In which year was the Department of Sports transformed into the 'Department of Youth Affairs and Sports'?
(a) 1984 (b) 1985 (c) 1983 (d) 1982

89. The Tableau of which of the following states was given the title of 'Best Tableau' on Republic Day, 2023, which was themed as 'Manaskhand'?
(a) Uttarakhand (b) Bihar (c) Jharkhand (d) Assam

90. What was the main purpose of establishing the Agricultural Prices Commission in 1965?
(a) To determine the prices for various farm products purchased by the government.
(b) To determine the price of fertiliser and electricity paid by farmers.
(c) To determine the price of seeds used in agriculture.
(d) To determine the prices for various farm products for sale in the open market.

91. In which of the following years did Antoine Lavoisier discover the law of conservation of mass and state that mass is conserved in a chemical reaction?
(a) 1786 (b) 1787 (c) 1788 (d) 1789

92. Which festival is popularly known as the festival of light?
(a) Bihu (b) Navratri (c) Diwali (d) Holi

93. One mole of Aluminium Sulphate $Al_2(SO_4)_3$ contains ....
(a) 4 moles of oxygen atoms (b) 3 moles of oxygen atoms
(c) 12 moles of oxygen atoms (d) 6 moles of oxygen atoms

94. How much percentage of the capital of MUDRA is contributed by SIDBI?
(a) 75 (b) 100 (c) 50 (d) 90

95. The 35th National Games were held in the state of ....
(a) Gujarat (b) Kerala (c) Assam (d) Jharkhand

96. Which bacteria have a thick cell wall with several layers of peptidoglycan and teichoic acid?
(a) Salmonella enterica (b) Staphylococcus aureus
(c) Pseudomonas aeruginosa (d) Escherichia coli

97. Which of the following is the longest Highway Tunnel in India (as of 2022)?
(a) Atal Tunnel (b) Pir Panjal Tunnel
(c) Karbude Tunnel (d) Jawahar Tunnel

98. Who among the following stated in 1902, India was not ruled for its benefit, but rather for the benefit of its conquerors?
(a) Bal Gangadhar Tilak (b) Lala Lajpat Rai
(c) Annie Besant (d) Sarojini Naidu

99. The Battle of Kannauj was fought between Sher Shah Suri and the Mughals led by...... .
(a) Humayun (b) Jahangir (c) Aurangzeb (d) Akbar

100. According to Dr. BR Ambedkar's views, which of the following is the key feature of the Directive Principles of the Constitution?
(a) Basic law (b) Mandatory feature
(c) Novel feature (d) Basic feature

Part III

Quantitative Aptitude

101. The sum of any two sides of a triangle is
(a) less than the third side (b) greater than the third side
(c) equal to third side (d) less than or equal to third side

102. The percentage of marks obtained by six students in five different subjects in an examination and the maximum marks in each subject (in parenthesis) are given in the following table.

Student	Hindi (150)	English (100)	Geography (175)	Mathematics (120)	Physics (75)
P	85	56	65	82	90
Q	76	84	52	84	76
R	89	98	67	60	56
S	82	64	56	70	80
T	58	68	78	68	71
U	64	75	94	64	60

What was the aggregate of marks obtained by S in all the five subjects?
(a) 324 (b) 429 (c) 356 (d) 405

103. A solid metal cylinder of 12 cm height 7 cm radius is melted and recast into two cones in the proportion of 1 : 2 (volume), keeping the height 12 cm. What would be the percentage change in the flat surface area before and after? [Use, $\pi = \frac{22}{7}$]
(a) 45% (b) 20% (c) 50% (d) 35%

104. Find the perimeter of a triangle with sides equal to 13 cm, 12 cm and 5 cm.
(a) 15 cm (b) 25 cm (c) 30 cm (d) 15 cm

105. Simplify the following expression.
$(4.2 \text{ of } 2.5 \div 3.5) - (3.6 \div 2.4 + 2.5 \text{ of } 3 \div 7.5) + (6 - 3 \text{ of} 2 + 4 \text{ of} 3 \div 6)$
(a) 4.5 (b) 3.5 (c) 1.5 (d) 2.5

106. The distance between the parallel sides of a trapezium is 18 cm. If the area of the trapezium is 1188 cm^2, then what is the sum of the lengths of the parallel sides?
(a) 115 cm (b) 126 cm (c) 132 cm (d) 150 cm

107. If $\sin(x+y) = 1$ and $\cos(x-y) = \frac{\sqrt{3}}{2}$, find the value of '$y$'.
(a) 90° (b) 30° (c) 20° (d) 60°

108. A travels for 8 h at the rate of 4 km/h and for 4 h at the rate of 8 km/h. The average speed of the journey (in km/h) is

(a) $4\frac{2}{3}$ (b) $5\frac{1}{3}$ (c) $4\frac{1}{3}$ (d) $5\frac{2}{3}$

109. The table below shows employees of a company in 5 different towns over the period of 5 yr.

Year	Town				
	Hyderabad	Punjab	Pune	Kolkata	Delhi
2016	520	325	152	425	545
2017	680	475	250	765	645
2018	874	850	179	857	820
2019	745	780	375	856	765
2020	954	822	425	880	923

Note All figures are fictitious.

Employees from Pune in 2018 are what per cent of the total employees of all towns together in that yr?

(a) 3% (b) 6% (c) 4% (d) 5%

110. If the polynomial $(2x^3 + ax^2 + 3x - 5)$ and $(x^3 + x^2 - 2x + a)$ leave the same remainder, when divided by $(x - 2)$, find the remainder.

(a) 4 (b) 2 (c) 3 (d) 5

111. The simple interest on a certain sum for 4 yr at 14% per annum is ₹ 6160 less than the simple interest on the same sum at the same rate for 8 yr. Find the sum.

(a) ₹ 9000 (b) ₹ 12000 (c) ₹ 11000 (d) ₹ 10000

112. Let a be a positive number and $b = \frac{4}{a}$. What is the mean proportional of a and b?

(a) a (b) 3 (c) 2 (d) 4

113. Simplify the given expression $\frac{13 \div \{6 - 6 \div (7 - 9) \times 8 + 9\}}{5 + 5 \times 5 \div 5 \text{ of } 5}$

(a) $\frac{1}{18}$ (b) 13 (c) 39 (d) $\frac{1}{2}$

114. If $\frac{a}{b} + \frac{b}{a} = 1, a \neq 0, b \neq 0$, then find the value of $\frac{a^3 + b^3}{3ab}$.

(a) 3 (b) 2 (c) −3 (d) 0

115. Find the value of

$$[9 + 3 - 2 \times \left\{\left[\left(4 \div \frac{1}{4}\right) - 4\right\} + 81 \div 9 + 81 \div 9 + 3 - 9\right] + 9$$

(a) 3 (b) 9 (c) 6 (d) 0

116. In an election between P, R and S, $\frac{1}{10}$ of the total votes polled are invalid. Votes polled in favour of R and S are half of the total votes polled and they get equal votes. Due to a fault in the machine, half of the votes of S and half of the invalid votes are counted additionally in favour of R. What is the overall percentage of votes secured by R due to the fault ?

(a) 42.5% (b) 38.5% (c) 41.55% (d) 37.55%

117. If $x = 11$, then the value of $(x^5 - 12x^4 + 12x^3 - 12x^2 + 12x - 1)$ is

(a) 14 (b) 9 (c) 8 (d) 10

118. Three circles each of radius 5 cm touch one another. The area (in cm^2) subtended between them is

(a) $25\left(\sqrt{3} + \frac{\pi}{2}\right)$ (b) $25\left(2\sqrt{3} - \frac{\pi}{2}\right)$

(c) $50\left(\sqrt{3} - \frac{\pi}{2}\right)$ (d) $25\left(\sqrt{3} - \frac{\pi}{2}\right)$

119. The value of $\left(\frac{2\cos^3\theta - \cos\theta}{\sin\theta - 2\sin^3\theta}\right)^2 + 1, \theta \neq 45°$ is

(a) $\sec^2\theta$ (b) $\cot^2\theta$ (c) $\text{cosec}^2\theta$ (d) $\sin^2\theta$

120. The cost of Compressed Natural Gas (CNG) per litre is increased by 65%. By what percentage must Manish reduce his consumption of CNG so as not to increase his expenditure? (correct up to two decimal places)

(a) 25.39% (b) 45.13% (c) 39.39% (d) 30.13%

121. Study the following table chart carefully and answer the question that follows.

The table given below shows the number of registered voters and the percentage of the people, who voted among them in different voting centres.

Centres	Total number of Registered Voters	Percentage of People, who Voted
Centre 1	26000	70%
Centre 2	28000	60%
Centre 3	25000	80%
Centre 4	30000	76%

According to the given above, which centre has the maximum number of voting ?

(a) Centre 1 (b) Centre 3 (c) Centre 2 (d) Centre 4

122. Arrange the following ratios in ascending order.

3 : 4, 3 : 5, 2 : 11, 7 : 2

(a) 3 : 5 < 2 : 11 < 3 : 4 < 7 : 2 (b) 2:11 < 3: 5 < 3 : 4 < 7 : 2

(c) 7 : 2 < 3 : 4 < 3 : 5 < 2 : 11 (d) 3 : 4 < 3 : 5 < 2 : 11 < 7: 2

123. P can do a piece of work in 30 days and Q in 40 days. They work together for 4 days and then Q leaves. The number of days taken by P to finish the remaining work is

(a) 28 days (b) 23 days (c) 30 days (d) 7 days

124. Ashish covers 72 km at a speed of 45 km/h by bike, 28 km at a speed of 4 km/h by bicycle and another 160 km at a speed of 20 km/h by car. Find his average speed (in km/h) for the whole journey. (Rounded off to two decimal places)

(a) 15.66 (b) 28.33 (c) 25.25 (d) 27.65

125. If $56 \div 4 + p \times 3 - 24 \div 12 + 4 = 21 \div 3 + 3$, then the value of p is

(a) 2 (b) 1 (c) −1 (d) −2

126. The volume of a right circular cone is $150\pi \text{ cm}^3$ and its height is 18 cm. Find its slant height (in cm) (correct to 2 decimal places).
(a) 28.68 (b) 25.35 (c) 15.25 (d) 18.68

127. The curved surface area of a cone is 308 cm^2 and its slant height is 28 cm. Find the radius of its base.
$\left(\text{use } \pi = \frac{22}{7}\right)$
(a) 3.5 cm (b) 2.8 cm (c) 3.0 cm (d) 2.5 cm

128. A school has four section A, B, C, D of Class X students. The results of half yearly and annual examination are shown in the table given below

Result	Number of students			
	Section A	Section B	Section C	Section D
Students failed in both exams	25	22	18	20
Student failed in half yearly but passed in Annual exam	20	25	24	12
Students passed in half yearly but failed in Annual exam	12	15	8	10
Student passed in both exams	15	20	22	18

How many students are there in Class X in the school?
(a) 286 (b) 256 (c) 206 (d) 226

129. A train covers a distance of 72 km in 40 min. Travelling at the same speed, how many metres will the train cover in 6 sec?
(a) 210 (b) 174 (c) 192 (d) 180

130. If the number of school going children in a town is 64000 and it is increasing annually by 10%, then what will be the number of school going children in the town at the end of 3 yr?
(a) 85000 (b) 85100 (c) 85184 (d) 80000

131. Find the value of $\frac{3 \div 3 \times 2 - 6 \div 3 + 7}{5 \div 5 \times 6 \div 6 + 3 + 3}$.
(a) 1 (b) $\frac{6}{7}$ (c) $\frac{8}{7}$ (d) 2

132. Simplify $\frac{\sin^3 A + \cos^3 A}{\sin A + \cos A}$
(a) $1 - \cos A \cot A$ (b) $1 - \sin A \tan A$
(c) $1 - \sin A \cos A$ (d) $1 - \tan A \sec A$

133. The marked price of a table is ₹ 5980. If the shopkeeper offers a discount of 18%, what is its selling price (in ₹, to the nearest rupee)?
(a) 4940 (b) 4490 (c) 4094 (d) 4904

134. A vessel contains 18 L mixture of milk and water in the ratio 5 : 1. If 3 L of milk is added to the vessel, then how much water (in L) should be added to the vessel to have milk and water in the ratio 9 : 2 ?
(a) 2 (b) 1.5 (c) 1 (d) 0.5

135. Two trains are moving in the same direction at 60 km/h and 42 km/h. The faster train crosses a man in the slower train in 36 sec. Find the length of the faster train.
(a) 185 m (b) 195 m (c) 180 m (d) 175 m

136. Study the given table and answer the question that follows. The table shows the yearly production (in thousands) of scooters in five different factories (P, Q, R, S and T) from 1985 to 1989.

Factory	1985	1986	1987	1988	1989
P	20	15	24	13	17
Q	16	23	41	20	15
R	14	21	30	16	12
S	25	17	15	12	22
T	40	32	39	41	35
Total	115	108	149	102	101

In which year was the total production of scooters of all factories 20% of the total production of scooters from 1985 to 1989?
(a) 1985 (b) 1986 (c) 1988 (d) 1989

137. A vegetable vendor bought 100 kg of potatoes at the rate of ₹ 19 per kg and spent ₹ 100 as cartage. He sold 60 kg of potatoes with a 50% profit and half of the remaining stock with a 40% profit. He sold half of the still remaining potatoes with a 25% profit. What profit percentage should he aim for, when selling the ultimate remaining potatoes to achieve an overall profit of 42%?
(a) 0.1 (b) 0.15 (c) 0.12 (d) 0.16

138. Simplify the following

$$\frac{2\left\{3+3\left(\frac{1}{4} \div \frac{15}{20}+2\right)-18 \times \frac{1}{3}\right\}}{2(4+20 \div 4)}$$

(a) $\frac{7}{18}$ (b) $\frac{11}{18}$ (c) $\frac{4}{9}$ (d) $\frac{5}{9}$

139. A trader sells pulses at a 32% profit and uses weights 20% less than the actual measure. Find his gain percentage.
(a) 72% (b) 62% (c) 58% (d) 65%

140. Consider the data of a certain number of activities of type P, Q and R in the percentage of the total activities of the cities B, C, D and K in the table below.

Activity/City	B	C	D	K
P	45	30	25	35
Q	25	30	35	30
R	30	40	40	35

If the total activities of B and C are 500 and 400, respectively, then what is the difference in activity R of B and C ?
(a) 15 (b) 10 (c) 30 (d) 20

141. A shopkeeper kept the marked price of an item at ₹ 500. He sold it at a scheme discount of 10% and 20% and got a profit of 25%. What was the cost price of the item?
(a) ₹188 (b) ₹ 482 (c) ₹ 288 (d) ₹ 384

142. The value of $72 \div 8 - 210 \div 15 - 5 + 2 \times 5$ is
(a) 3 (b) 0 (c) 1 (d) 2

143. If A, B and C are the interior angles of ΔABC, then what is the value of $\left\{\tan\frac{A}{2} + \operatorname{cosec}\frac{B+C}{2}\right\}\left\{\tan\frac{A}{2} - \operatorname{cosec}\frac{B+C}{2}\right\}$?
(a) −1 (b) 2 (c) −2 (d) 1

144. The following table shows the number of new employees added to different categories of employees in a university and also the number of employees from these categories, who left the university every year

Year	Professor		Assistant Professor		Associate Professor		Peon	
	New	Left	New	Left	New	Left	New	Left
2018	80	-	100	-	90	-	60	-
2019	100	60	150	40	110	30	80	10
2020	150	40	160	30	140	40	70	20
2021	180	60	200	50	190	50	80	30
2022	200	80	220	60	220	60	90	40

What is the difference between the total number of professors added to the university and the total number of associate professors added to the university during the years 2019 to 2022?
(a) 30 (b) 40 (c) 50 (d) 120

145. What is the ratio between S and T if S is 75% of T?
(a) 2 : 3 (b) 4 : 3 (c) 75 : 1 (d) 3 : 4

146. Simplify $22.0625 - [15 + 0.25 \times (4.78 - 1.5 \times 3.02)]$
(a) 7.1 (b) 7.3 (c) 7.2 (d) 7.0

147. A gear 15 cm in diameter is turning a gear 21 cm in diameter. When the smaller gear has 105 revolutions, how many has the larger one made?
(a) 100 (b) 75 (c) 85 (d) 90

148. Simplify $13.5 - [5 + 0.5 \times (9 - 3 \times 2)]$
(a) 5 (b) 7 (c) 6 (d) 8

149. The area of the canvas cloth needed to erect a right conical tent of height 20 ft and circular base of circumference 30π ft is
(a) 375π sq.ft. (b) 589π sq.ft. (c) 470π sq.ft. (d) 455π sq.ft.

150. Tarun is twice as good as Tripti in doing a work. Together, they can complete the work in 16 days. In how many days can Tripti alone complete the same work?
(a) 48 (b) 24 (c) 50 (d) 25

Part IV

English Comprehension

151. Select the option that can be used as a one-word substitute for the given group of words.
Referring to something from the past of high quality
(a) Epoch (b) Vintage (c) Outdated (d) Culture

152. Select the most appropriate antonym of the given word.
Accolade
(a) Criticism (b) Tribute (c) Promotion (d) Assurance

153. Select the most appropriate synonym of the given word.
Eagerly
(a) Stringently (b) Dubiously (c) Keenly (d) Playfully

154. Select the option that can be used as a one-word substitute for the given group of words.
The approach or style of teaching
(a) Pedagogy (b) Media (c) Philology (d) Platform

155. Select the most appropriate option to fill in the blank.
She .... her painting by this time next week.
(a) will have finished (b) will finish
(c) finishes (d) finished

156. Select the most appropriate synonym of the given word.
Entail
(a) Assume (b) Necessitate (c) Eliminate (d) Flaw

157. Select the option that best explains the underlined idiom in the given sentence.
A team's captain always <u>keeps a level head</u>, even in the most challenging situations.
(a) Prefers to keep his head covered with a cap
(b) Maintains an equal number of players on the field
(c) Remains calm and composed
(d) Keeps his head protected with a helmet

158. Select the most appropriate synonym of the underlined word.
The <u>hypothesis</u> that the police believed in led to a lot of chaos.
(a) speculation (b) breakthrough (c) trepidation (d) encounter

159. Select the incorrectly spelt word.
(a) Irritate (b) Necessitate (c) Reciept (d) Hindrance

160. Select the most appropriate synonym of the given word.
Grisly
(a) Pleasant (b) Atrocious (c) Glorious (d) Dire

161. Select the most appropriate option to substitute the underlined segment in the given sentence.
Amit is also <u>a chip off the old block</u> like his brother, Tandon.
(a) getting ready for the future endeavours
(b) planning things ahead neatly
(c) talking to others tough like a stone
(d) resembling his parents in character and appearance

162. Select the option that can be used as a one-word substitute for the given group of words.
The original inhabitants of a country
(a) Primitive (b) Citizens (c) Aborigines (d) Aliens

163. The following sentence has been split into four segments. Identify the segment that contains an error.
Ramesh licked (A) / honey and (B) / said that (C) / it tasted sweetly. (D)
(a) D (b) A (c) B (d) C

164. Select the most appropriate idiom that can substitute the underlined segment in the given sentence.
Even after becoming bankrupt, Charlie is able to maintain an outward show.
(a) bring down the house
(b) keep up appearances
(c) bell the cat
(d) cut a sorry figure

165. Select the incorrectly spelt word.
(a) Dictionary (b) Reference
(c) Infurmary (d) Ordinary

166. Select the most appropriate antonym of the underlined word.
Maria thinks the animals that live in freedom have a sad look in their eyes.
(a) Carefree (b) Liberty
(c) Surrendered (d) Captivity

167. Select the most appropriate synonym of the given word.
Concordant
(a) Certain
(b) Unanimous
(c) Abnormal
(d) Harmonious

168. Select the option that can be used as a one-word substitute for the given group of words.
A news article that reports the recent death of a person.
(a) Culinary (b) Obituary
(c) Centenary (d) Mortuary

169. Select the most appropriate meaning of the given idiom.
Get itchy feet
(a) Judge something primarily on appearance
(b) Learn something by memorising it without a thought to what is being learnt
(c) To start to want to travel or do something different
(d) Join a popular trend or activity

170. The following sentence has been divided into four segments. Identify the segment that contains an adverbial usage error.
Mr. Sukesh and / his family / ate the / food greedy.
(a) ate the
(b) Mr. Sukesh and
(c) his family
(d) food greedy.

171. Choose the most appropriate meaning of the underlined phrase.
He's still keeping his chin up despite all his health problems.
(a) To keep one's chin clean and moist
(b) To stay safe during difficulty
(c) To stay cheerful during difficult times
(d) To save others during difficult times

172. Select the option that can be used as a one-word substitute for the given group of words.
Words inscribed on a tomb.
(a) Epitaph (b) Prologue
(c) Epilogue (d) Post-script

173. Select the sentence that has the correct use of words and spellings from the options given below.
(a) The scientiest meticulously analysed the complex data, uncovering ground-breaking insights that would revolutionice the field.
(b) The scientist meticulusly analysed the complex data, uncovering ground-breaking insights that would revaulutionise the field.
(c) The scientist meticulously anelysed the complex data, uncovering ground-breaking insights that would revolutionise the feild.
(d) The scientist meticulously analysed the complex data, uncovering ground-breaking insights that would revolutionise the field.

174. The following sentence has been divided into four segments. One of them contains an error. Select the segment that contains the error from the given options.
The people of / Jammu and Kashmir / has emphasised and / appreciated transparency.
(a) appreciated transparency
(b) The people of
(c) has emphasised and
(d) Jammu and Kashmir

175. Select the most appropriate option that can substitute the underlined segment in the given sentence. If there is no need to substitute it, select 'No substitution'.
The woman to who I sold my house was a criminal.
(a) No substitution (b) to whom I sold
(c) to whom I sell (d) to whom sold

176. Select the option that can be used as a one-word substitute for the given group of words.
Fertile watery place in a desert
(a) Obsolete (b) Obscure
(c) Ode (d) Oasis

177. Select the most appropriate meaning of the given idiom.
On thin ice
(a) In a risky position
(b) Communicating with friends
(c) On a summer vacation
(d) On an investigating job

178. Identify the incorrectly spelt word in the given sentence and select the option that rectifies the misspelling.
There are difficult times too, especially when the economy takes a dip and we have to lai people off.
(a) Economie (b) Dificult
(c) Lay (d) Dipe

179. Identify the most appropriate antonym of the underlined word in the given sentence.
The door was ajar and a faint wisp of smoke floated through it.
(a) Itchy (b) Lot
(c) Trickle (d) Wind

180. Select the most appropriate meaning of the given idiom.
Keep your pants on
(a) To wear the dress neatly
(b) To keep calm and quiet
(c) To make things proper
(d) To work like a tailor

181. Select the most appropriate idiom that can substitute the underlined segment in the given sentence.
Reena decided not to go to work today because she was feeling sick.
(a) under the weather
(b) fit as a fiddle
(c) sitting on the fence
(d) going down in flames

182. Select the most appropriate meaning of the given idiom.
Bread and butter
(a) Breakfast
(b) Sharing
(c) Livelihood
(d) Party

183. Underlined word in the sentence is not spelt correctly. Identify the correct spelling from the options given below.
He was a benaevolent young man who would help his colleagues.
(a) Benavolent (b) Benevolent
(c) Benevalant (d) Banevolent

184. Parts of the following sentence have been given as options. Select the option that contains an error.
Himalayas include the highest mountains in the world and feed almost 20% of the earth's population.
(a) almost 20% of the earth's population.
(b) highest mountains in
(c) the world and feed
(d) Himalayas include the

185. Select the option that can be used as a one-word substitute for the given group of words.
Someone who speaks more than one language
(a) Heretic (b) Fatalist
(c) Polyglot (d) Insolvent

186. Select the most appropriate option that can substitute the underlined segment in the given sentence. If there is no need to substitute it, select 'No substitution'.
Half of the property given to his sons by the businessman last year.
(a) No substitution
(b) Half of the property is given
(c) Half of the property was given
(d) Half of the property has been given

187. Select the most appropriate synonym of the given word.
Fabulous
(a) Remarkable (b) Resourceful
(c) Regrettable (d) Restful

188. Select the incorrectly spelt word in the given sentence.
Large-scale hunting scenes and slaugter of wild animals is a heinous crime.
(a) Slaugter (b) Heinous
(c) Scenes (d) Hunting

189. Select the most appropriate option that can substitute the underlined words in the given sentence.
We should not underestimate the signification of female education.
(a) underestimate the significance
(b) underestimate at signification
(c) underestimate on signification
(d) underestimate signification

190. Select the most appropriate option that can substitute the underlined segment in the given sentence. If no substitution is required, select 'No substitution'.
A sharp fall in the price of jute have led the poor jute farmers to the brink of starvation.
(a) have lead the poor jute farmers
(b) have led the poor farmers
(c) has led the poor jute farmers
(d) No substitution

Directions (Q. Nos. 191-195) *In the following passage, some words have been deleted. Read the passage carefully and select the most appropriate option to fill in each blank.*

It is important to ...(1)... a healthy lifestyle to maintain good physical and mental well-being. Regular ...(2)... helps improve cardiovascular health and boosts the immune system. Eating a balanced diet rich in ...(3)... vitamins and minerals is crucial for overall health. Additionally, ...(4)... stress through activities like yoga or meditation can enhance mental clarity. Getting an adequate amount of ...(5)... each night is essential for restorative activity and optimum bodily functions.

191. Select the most appropriate option to fill in blank number 1.
(a) adopt (b) adeptly
(c) adapt (d) adept

192. Select the most appropriate option to fill in blank number 2.
(a) exalt (b) exclaim
(c) exertion (d) exercise

193. Select the most appropriate option to fill in blank number 3.
(a) necessarily (b) necessity
(c) necessitate (d) essential

194. Select the most appropriate option to fill in blank number 4.
(a) managing
(b) manages
(c) management
(d) managed

195. Select the most appropriate option to fill in blank number 5.
(a) resting (b) relax
(c) slumber (d) sleep

Directions (Q. Nos. 196-200) *Read the following passage and answer the questions that follow*

Facial recognition is based on AI technology that recognises human faces. In fact, the technology considers a number of factors for face recognition: jawline length, the form of the cheekbones, eye sockets depth, and so on. A majority of these factors assist the technology "recall" who's the proprietor of the face. Other than unlocking your phone, facial identification brings different advantages to the agencies: The primary component to start with is surveillance. With the assistance of face recognition technology , it will likely be less complicated to catch any burglars, thieves, or different trespassers. On the governmental level, facial recognition can help us to find out terrorists or other criminals. Face recognition is the most effective means in today's world. The procedure of recognising a face takes a second or much less. Considering that facial recognition is almost instant, it offers a quick and successful verification of a person.

196. Based on your reading of the passage, select the most appropriate antonym of 'Excessive'.
(a) Accurate (b) Lavish
(c) Extreme (d) Moderate

197. Read the following line from the passage and select the most appropriate option that describes it :
Considering that facial recognition is almost instant, it offers a quick and successful verification of a person.
(a) Face recognition is uneasy and verifies a person successfully.
(b) Face recognition is easy and verifies a person unsuccessfully.
(c) Face recognition is not on spot and verifies a person partly.
(d) Face recognition is fast and verifies a person successfully.

198. As per the passage which facial factors are not recognized with face recognition?
(a) Jawline length
(b) Face shape
(c) Cheekbones structure
(d) Eye sockets

199. Select the most appropriate title for the given passage:
(a) Hacking and Safety
(b) AI interface
(c) Face Recognition
(d) Human Face

200. What is the primary component of face recognition?
(a) Surveillance
(b) Verification
(c) Identification
(d) Locking

Know Correct Answers

1. (b)	2. (d)	3. (b)	4. (b)	5. (a)	6. (a)	7. (d)	8. (c)	9. (a)	10. (d)
11. (a)	12. (d)	13. (d)	14. (a)	15. (d)	16. (d)	17. (d)	18. (b)	19. (c)	20. (d)
21. (d)	22. (c)	23. (c)	24. (b)	25. (a)	26. (c)	27. (b)	28. (a)	29. (c)	30. (a)
31. (c)	32. (d)	33. (d)	34. (d)	35. (a)	36. (c)	37. (a)	38. (d)	39. (d)	40. (b)
41. (a)	42. (d)	43. (b)	44. (c)	45. (c)	46. (a)	47. (b)	48. (a)	49. (c)	50. (b)
51. (a)	52. (d)	53. (b)	54. (c)	55. (a)	56. (a)	57. (a)	58. (c)	59. (d)	60. (a)
61. (c)	62. (d)	63. (b)	64. (a)	65. (d)	66. (a)	67. (c)	68. (a)	69. (d)	70. (c)
71. (b)	72. (b)	73. (d)	74. (b)	75. (d)	76. (a)	77. (b)	78. (c)	79. (b)	80. (c)
81. (b)	82. (c)	83. (d)	84. (a)	85. (b)	86. (a)	87. (a)	88. (b)	89. (a)	90. (a)
91. (d)	92. (c)	93. (c)	94. (b)	95. (b)	96. (b)	97. (a)	98. (c)	99. (a)	100. (c)
101. (b)	102. (b)	103. (c)	104. (c)	105. (d)	106. (c)	107. (b)	108. (b)	109. (d)	110. (d)
111. (c)	112. (c)	113. (a)	114. (d)	115. (b)	116. (a)	117. (d)	118. (d)	119. (c)	120. (c)
121. (d)	122. (b)	123. (b)	124. (a)	125. (d)	126. (d)	127 (a)	128. (a)	129. (d)	130. (c)
131. (a)	132. (c)	133. (d)	134. (c)	135. (c)	136. (a)	137 (b)	138. (c)	139. (d)	140. (b)
141. (c)	142. (b)	143. (a)	144. (a)	145. (d)	146. (d)	147. (b)	148. (b)	149. (a)	150. (a)
151. (b)	152. (a)	153. (c)	154. (a)	155. (a)	156. (b)	157. (c)	158. (a)	159. (c)	160. (b)
161. (d)	162. (c)	163. (a)	164. (b)	165. (c)	166. (d)	167. (d)	168. (b)	169. (c)	170. (d)
171. (c)	172. (a)	173. (d)	174. (c)	175. (a)	176. (d)	177. (a)	178. (c)	179. (b)	180. (b)
181. (a)	182. (c)	183. (b)	184. (d)	185. (c)	186. (c)	187. (a)	188. (a)	189. (a)	190. (c)
191. (a)	192. (d)	193. (d)	194. (a)	195. (d)	196. (d)	197. (d)	198. (b)	199 (c)	200. (a)

Answer & Solutions

1. **(b)** In the given figure series, pattern follows as,

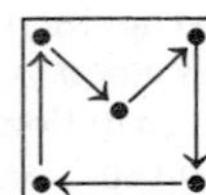

So, the option (b) will be replace the question mark (?) of the given series.

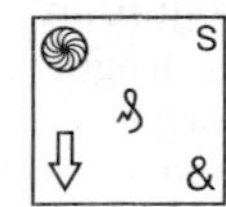

2. **(d)** As,

16, 48, 4 and 24, 72, 6
×3 ÷12 ×3 ÷12

Similarly, 20, 60, 5

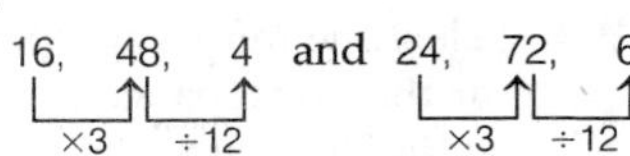

3. **(b)** According to the question,

God is great → tg so rf
we love God → ae rf xd

Thus, God is coded as rf.

4. **(b)** According to the question,

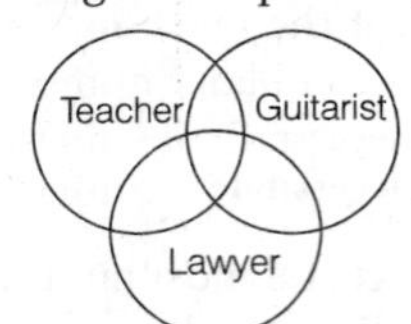

Some layers can be teachers or guitarist.

5. **(a)** According to the question,

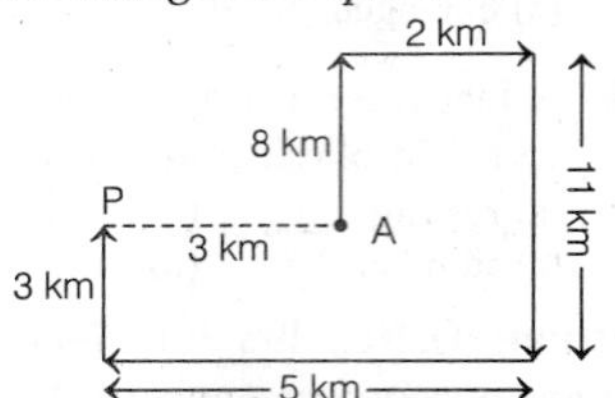

He must drives 3 km towards East direction.

6. **(a)** As,

K $\xrightarrow{-3}$ H $\xrightarrow{+5}$ M

T $\xrightarrow{-3}$ Q $\xrightarrow{+5}$ V

N $\xrightarrow{-3}$ K $\xrightarrow{+5}$ P

But, Q $\xrightarrow{-3}$ N $\xrightarrow{\boxed{+4}}$ R

7. **(d)** According to the question,

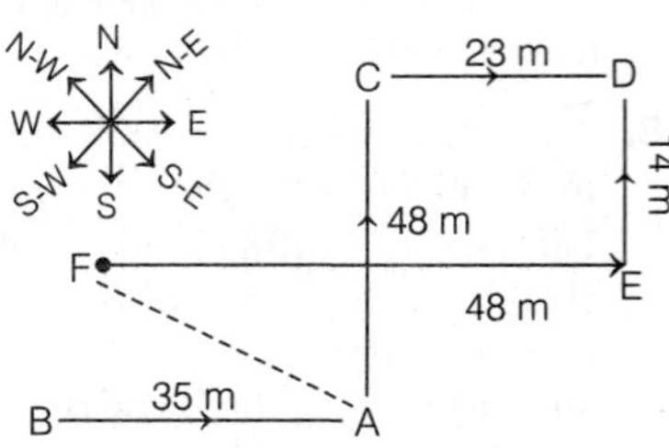

Hence, point F is North-West to point A.

8. **(c)** As, Summon and Call are synonyms of each other.

Similarly, Disperse and Spread is synonym of each other.

9. **(a)** As,

M A R S
−2 −3 −2 −3
K X P P

and B O D Y
−2 −3 −2 −3
Z L B V

Similarly, T E S T

−2 −3 −2 −3

R B Q Q

10. **(d)** The correct dictionary order of given words is given below.

Breacher → Breakfast →
(5) (3)

Breakthrough → Breathable →
(6) (1)

Brevetting → Breviaries
(2) (4)

Required order is 5, 3, 6, 1, 2, 4.

11. (a) Given equation,

$6 + 3 \times 8 - 12 \div 4 = 4$

From option (a) interchanging the signs, ÷ and −

$6 + 3 \times 8 \div 12 - 4 = 4$

$\Rightarrow \quad 6 + 2 - 4 = 4$

$\Rightarrow \quad 8 - 4 = 4$

$\Rightarrow \quad 4 = 4$

LHS = RHS

12. **(d)** Pattern of the series is as follows,

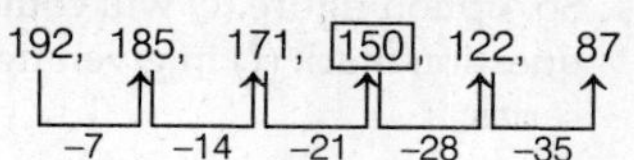

13. **(d)** According to the statements

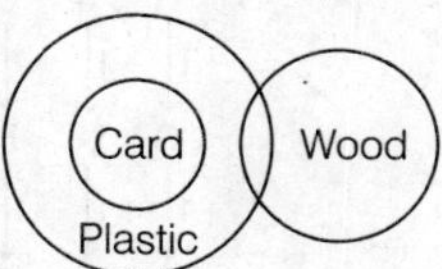

Conclusions I. (✗) II. (✗)

Both conclusions are wrong, but one is positive and other one is negative, variable are same.

So, either Conclusions I or II follow.

14. **(a)** When paper is unfolded it looks like a option figure (a).

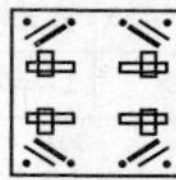

15. **(d)** Pattern of the series is as follows,

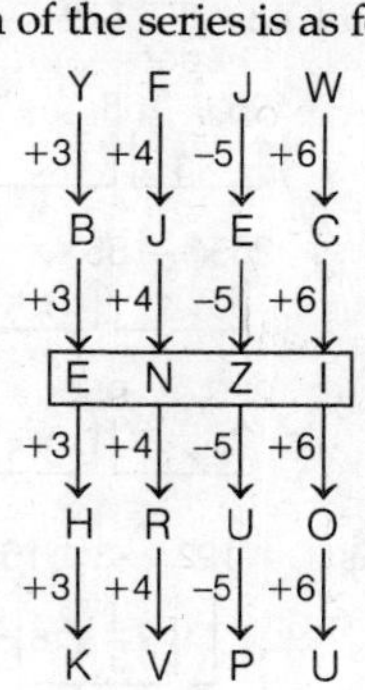

16. **(d)** Pattern of the series is as follows,

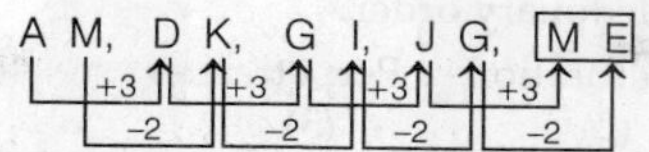

17. **(d)** According to the question,

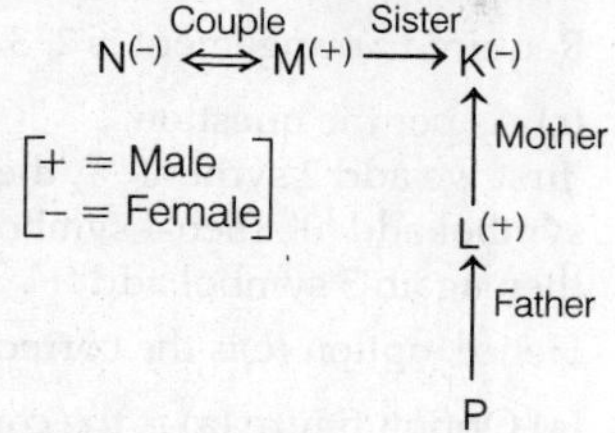

L is the son of K.

18. **(b)** Given, 8 B 9 C 49 A 7 D 25

After interchange the signs, we get

A ⇒ ÷	B ⇒ ×
C ⇒ +	D ⇒ −

$= 8 \times 9 + 49 \div 7 - 25$

$= 72 + 7 - 25$

$= 79 - 25 = 54$

19. **(c)** In both position of dice letter 'M' is common,

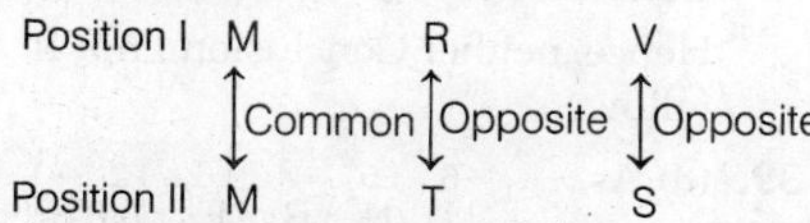

∴ The face having 'S' is opposite to the face having V.

20. **(d)** As, G O O D
+1 −2 +1 −2
H M P B

and H A L L
+1 −2 +1 −2
I Y M J

Similarly, T O O L
+1 −2 +1 −2
U M P J

21. **(d)** As, H O P E
+4 +3 +2 +1
F R R L

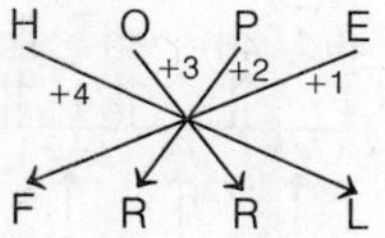

and T A I L
+4 +3 +2 +1
M K D X

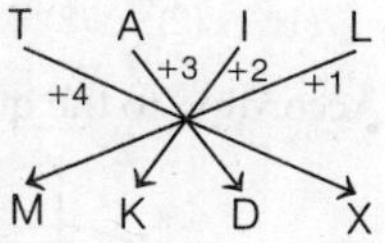

Similarly, S T O R Y
+5 +4 +3 +2 +1
Z T R X X

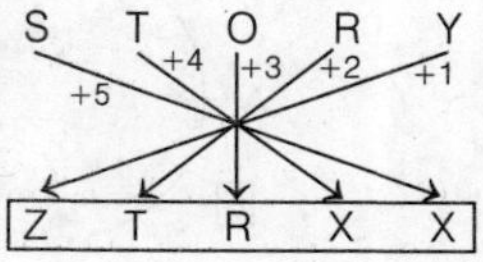

22. **(c)** As, (128,62,190)

[Logic = First term + Second term = Third term]

$\Rightarrow \quad 128 + 62 = 190$

and (114, 86, 200)

$114 + 86 = 200$

Similarly, (95, 54, 149)

$95 + 54 = 149$

23. **(c)** Pattern of the series is as follows,

6 10 15 21 28 36 45
+4 +5 +6 +7 +8 +9

24. **(b)** In dice position II and III number '3' and 5 are common.

So, the number '2' on the face opposite to the face showing '4'.

25. **(a)** As per the question,

Option (a) figure is the correct mirror image of the given figure, when the mirror is placed at MN.

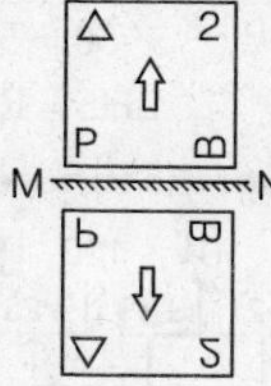

26. **(c)** Given equation,

6 C7C8B71A11B32C2

A ⇒ +	B ⇒ −
C ⇒ ×	D ⇒ ÷

After interchanging the signs,

$6 \times 7 \times 8 - 71 + 11 - 32 \times 2$

$\Rightarrow \quad 336 - 71 + 11 - 64$

$\Rightarrow \quad 347 - 135$

$\Rightarrow \quad 212$

27. **(b)** In two position of dice. letter B is common.

Position I B C T
Common Opposite Opposite
Position II B S D

Hence, face 'B' is opposite to face

28. **(a)** Given equation,

$40 + 45 \times 5 - 12 \div 4 = 1$

From option (a) interchanging the signs, ÷ and ×, we get

$40 + 45 \div 5 - 12 \times 4 = 1$

$\Rightarrow \quad 40 + 9 - 48 = 1$

$\Rightarrow \quad 1 = 1$

LHS = RHS

29. (c) As,

A P P L E (Place value)

1+16+16+12+5=50
⇒ 50×5=250

and

B E R R Y (Place value)

2+5+18+18+25=68
⇒ 68×5=340

Similarly, L I T C H I (Place value)

12+9+20+3+8+9=61
⇒ 61×5=305

30. (a) Given equation,

$16 \times 121 \div 11 + 4 - 10 = 50$

From option (a) interchanging the signs, '+' and '×'

$16 + 121 \div 11 \times 4 - 10 = 50$

$16 + 44 - 10 = 50$

$50 = 50$

LHS = RHS

31. (c) Pattern of the series is as follows,

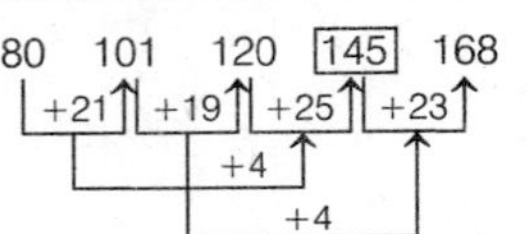

32. (d) As, FEED = 24
⇒ [Number of letter = 4
⇒ 4 × 6 = 24]
⇒ and ACCOUNT = 42
[Number of letter = 7
⇒ 7 × 6 = 42]
Similarly, PIZZA = 30
⇒ [Number of letters = 5
⇒ 5 × 6 = 30]

33. (d) Option (d) is the correct mirror image of the given figure, when the mirror is placed at MN.

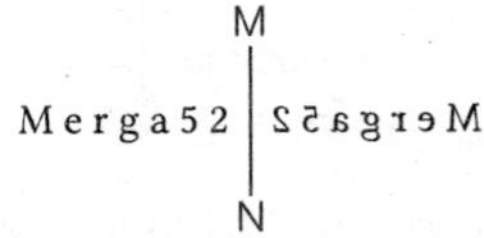

34. (d) According to the statements

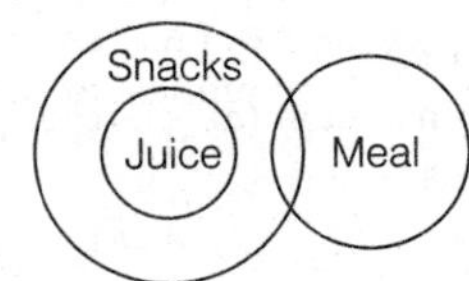

Conclusions I. (✗) II. (✗)

Hence, neither Conclusion I nor II follows.

35. (a) According to the English dictionary order,

Peroration → Perpetrate →
(2) (3)
Perpetual → Perpetuity → Perplex
(5) (4) (1)

Required arrangement is 2, 3, 5, 4, 1.

36. (c) As per the question,
first we add 2 symbol '+', then 3 symbol add '0', then 4 symbol add '*', then again 5 symbol add '+'.

Hence, option (c)is the correct answer.

37. (a) Option figure (a) is the correct mirror image of the given figure, when the mirror is placed at MN.

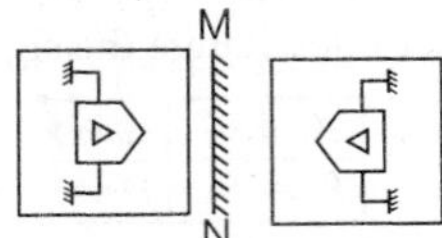

38. (d) According to the statements

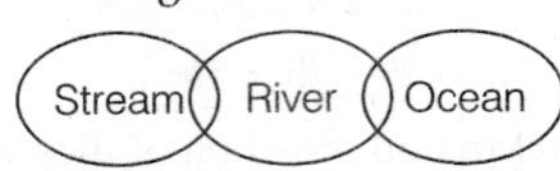

Conclusions I. (✗) II. (✗)

Hence, neither Conclusion I nor II follows.

39. (d) As,

+6 +5 +4 +3 +2 +1
U N R E A L
M C H V S A

and

C R E A T E
+6 +5 +4 +3 +2 +1
F V D I W I

Similarly,

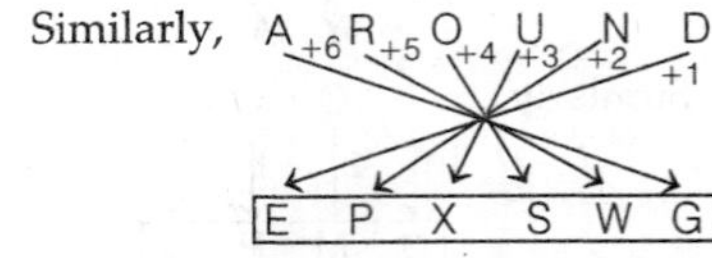

40. (b) Pattern of the series is as follows,

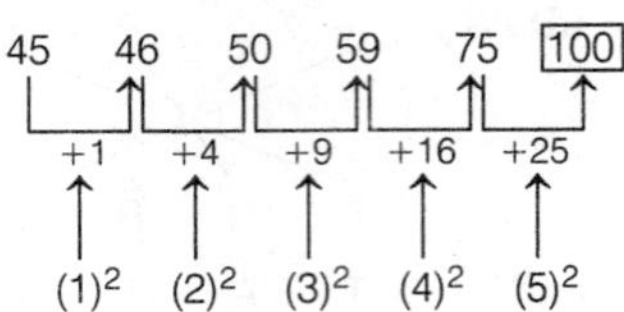

41. (a) According to the question,

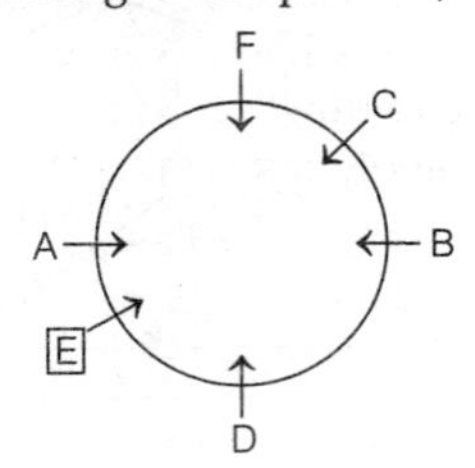

Hence, the immediate neighbour of both A and D is 'E'.

42. (d) As per the question,

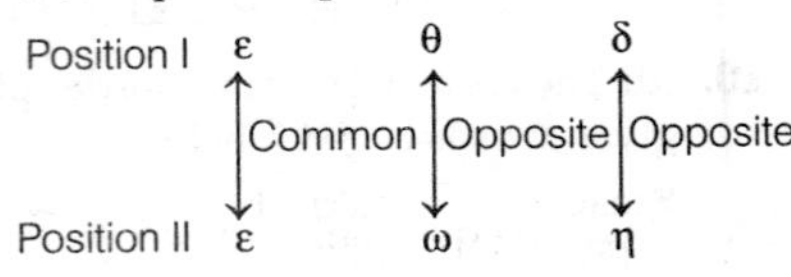

Hence, remaining symbol % will be opposite 'ε'.

43. (b) According to the question,
[+ = Male, − = Female]

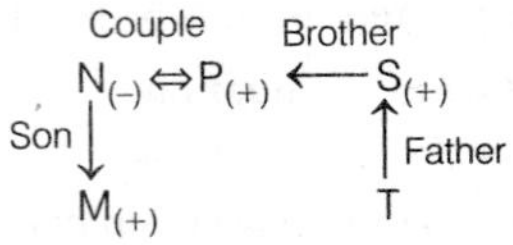

Couple Brother
$N_{(-)}$ ⇔ $P_{(+)}$ ← $S_{(+)}$
Son ↓ ↑ Father
$M_{(+)}$ T

Hence, M is father's brother son of T.

44. (c) The pattern of the given figure series as follows,

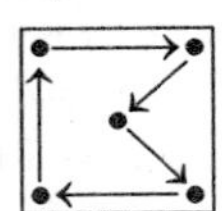

So, option figure (c) will come to the question mark (?) in given figure series.

45. (c) Pattern of the series is as follows,

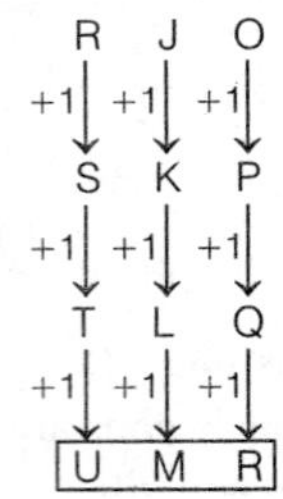

46. (a) Given equation,

74A (17C2B24)D2A16C3B8 = ?

After interchanging the signs,

A ⇒ +	B ⇒ −
C ⇒ ×	D ⇒ ÷

$74 + (17 \times 2 - 24) \div 2 + 16 \times 3 - 8$

$74 + 5 + 48 - 8 = 119$

47. (b) As, 195, 65, 13
×3 ×5

and 255, 85, 17
×3 ×5

Similarly, 285, 95, 19
×3 ×5

48. (a) As, 12 : 16

$12 \times \frac{4}{3} = 16$

and 18 : 24 ($18\times\frac{4}{3}=24$)

Similarly, 21 : 28 ($21\times\frac{4}{3}=28$)

49. (c) Given equation,

8B9C49A7D25 = ?

After interchanging the signs,

A ⇒ ÷	B ⇒ ×
C ⇒ +	D ⇒ −

$8\times9+49\div7-25$

$\Rightarrow 72+7-25$

$\Rightarrow 79-25=54$

50. (b) As, 72 : 27 ($7+2=9$, $9\times3=27$)

Similarly, 56 : 33 ($5+6=11$, $11\times3=33$)

51. (a) Intermediate goods are not included in the National Income to prevent double counting.

- Intermediate goods are products used as inputs in the production of other goods.
- Including them in National Income calculations would result in double counting because their value is already embedded in the final goods.

52. (d) Sunanda Nair is associated with the Mohiniyattam dance form.

- Mohiniyattam is an Indian classical dance form originating from the state of Kerala.
- The dance is performed by women in honour of the Hindu God Vishnu in his incarnation as the enchantress 'Mohini'.

53. (b) In the field of Indian classical music Brij Bhushan Kabra is associated with **Guitar.**

- Pandit Brij Bhushan Kabra is credited for being the only musician to introduce and include the guitar artistically to Indian classical music and he was the first artist to play raga on guitar.

54. (c) Assam > Bihar > Rajasthan is the correct sequence of Indian states in terms of decreasing average annual rainfall.

- Mawsynram in Meghalaya receives the highest rainfall in the world.
- Rainfall in India mainly occurs in the months of July, August and September.
- As a result, the regions situated on the wind ward side receives greater rainfall than the region located on the leeward side.

55. (a) According to the 2011 Census of India, the national male workforce participation rate is 53.26% and for females it is 25.51%.

- Rural sector has a better female workforce participation rate of 30:02% compared with 53.03% for males whereas for the urban sector.

56. (a) The Northern part of the Western coastal plain between Mumbai and Goa is called Konkan coast.

- It stretches from the Daman Ganga river to the terekhol river.
- The central stretch is called the Kannad Plain, while the Southern stretch is referred to as the Malabar Coast.

57. (a) **Raja Ram Mohan Roy** was an Indian reformer and the founder of Brahmo Samaj.

- He was given the title of Raja by Akbar II, the Mughal emperor.
- The Aligarh Movement was started by Sir Syed Ahmad Khan in 1875.
- Mahadev Govind Ranade is associated with the Poona Sarvajanik Sabha.
- Dayananda Saraswati founded the Arya Samaj in 1875.

58. (c) The Green Revolution had social impacts for example, the medium and large farmers were benefitted.

- It worsened the condition of landless and marginal farmers, only farmers involved in commercial agriculture benefitted, there was a large displacement of service caste groups.
- In the year 1965, the Government of India launched the Green Revolution with the help of MS **Swaminathan** is also known as the 'Father of Green Revolution'.

59. (d) The 42nd Amendment of Indian Constitution, 1976 states that India is a secular nation.

- The words Secular, Integrity and Socialist were added in the Preamble.
- This was done in the tenure of Prime Minister Indira Gandhi.
- Fundamental Duties were also added through 42nd Constitutional Amendment Act.

60. (a) Statements B, C and D are correct.

- The Narmada river rises in Amarkantak hills in Madhya Pradesh.
- The Godavari river rises from the slopes of the Western Ghats near Nashik.
- The Mahanadi river rises in the highlands of Chhattisgarh.
- The Krishna river rises from a spring near Mahabaleshwar.

61. (c) The following numbers are eligible for free legal aid under National Legal services Authority.

- A member of a Schedule Caste or Schedule Tribe.
- A victim of trafficking in human beings or beggar as referred to in Article 23 of the Indian Constitution.
- An industrial worker.
- A person under circumstances of undeserved want such as being a victim of a mass disasters.

62. (d) Reduced competition was not an advantage of privatisation.

- LPG reforms were brought into effect from the year 1991 and had many advantages such as increased competition, additional source of revenue for the government, low interference of political motives and overall improved performance.

63. (b) 'Tattwabodhini Patrika promoted the study of India's past in Bengali.

- It was established by Debendranath Tagore on 16th August, 1843, as a journal of the Tattwabodhini Sabha and continued publication until 1883.

64. (a) In Andhra region, Nanniah translated a few portions of Mahabharata in Telugu at the request of the East Chalukya king Rajaraja Narendra.

- 'Andhra Mahabharatham' is the Telugu version of Mahabharata written by Kavitrayam (Trinity of poets), consisting of Nannayya, Tikkana and Yerrapragada.

65. **(d)** Dorabji,the founder of Tata Group was the Founding President of the Indian Olympic Association.
- The Indian Olympic Association is the governing body for the Olympic Movement and the Commonwealth Games in India.
- It is an affiliated member of the International Olympic Committee (IOC).
Recently, **PT Usha** has become the first woman President of the Indian Olympic Association (IOA).

66. **(a)** Pandit Shivkumar Sharma, an accomplished Santoor player, originally hails from the Union Territory of Jammu and Kashmir.
- He is the recipient of the Sangeet Natak Akademi Award (1986), Padma Shri (1991) and Padma Vibhushan (2001).
- Pandit Bhajan Sopori was also a famous exponent of Santoor.

67. **(c)** The Carnatic classical vocalist and first ever musician to receive the Bharat Ratna Award also known as 'Queen of Songs' is **MS Subbulakshmi**.
- She was also the first Indian musician to receive the Ramon Magsaysay Award in 1974 and the first Indian to perform at the United Nations General Assembly in 1966.

68. **(a)** 'A Flight of Pigeons' is a famous book written by Ruskin Bond.
- The book is set in British-India Shahjahanpur, it is the story of Ruth Labadoor and how her English family survived the mutiny of 1857, when the Indians waged a war against the colonists Britishers.

69. **(d)** PPM is the unit which is used to measure the concentration of contaminants in soil and sediments.
- Parts Per Million (PPM) is the number of units of mass of a contaminant per million units of total mass.

70. **(c)** Amish Tripathi is the author of the book 'The Oath of the Vayuputras'.
- The Shiva Trilogy and Ram Chandra Series, 'The Immortals of Meluha' are other known works.

71. **(b)** The 'Hariyali Project' has been organised by the Central Government for the villagers, to conserve water for drinking, irrigation, fisheries and afforestation.
- The project is being executed by Gram Panchayats with people's participation.

72. **(b)** 'Devanampiya Piyadasi' is another name for 3rd Mauryan Emperor Ashoka.
- 'Devanampiya' means 'Beloved of the Gods'
- It is often used by Ashoka in conjunction with the title 'Priyadasi', which means 'who regards others with kindness', 'Humane'.
- James Prinsep was the first English Scholar to decipher the edicts of Ashoka.

73. **(d)** Blood sucking leech belongs to annelida phylum.
- It is a segmented worm which belongs to Annelida, a large phylum, with over 22,000 extant species including ragworms, earthworms and leeches.
- The Annelids are found in aquatic as well as terrestrial environments.

74. **(b)** Anton Van Leeuwenhoek described the algae Spirogyra in 1674 and named the motile organisms Animalcules meaning 'little animals'.
- While, using a microscope to examine pond water in 1674, he observed dozens of protists, which he called 'animalcules' as well as spirogyra or green algae.

75. **(d)** Nilgiri Mountains of India is famous for tea and coffee production.
- Karnataka is the largest producer of coffee in India and Assam is the largest producer of tea.
- Nilgiri Mountain is spread across the borders among the states of Tamil Nadu, Karnataka and Kerala.
- The Nilgiri Hills are part of Western Ghats.

76. **(a)** **Article 153** of the Indian Constitution mentions that a person may be oppointed as the Governor of two or more states.
- The 7th Constitutional Amendment Act of 1956 promoted the appointment of the same person as a governor for two or more states.
- The Governor in India is the head of state and appointed by the President of India.

77. **(b)** 'Loo' winds blow in the summer season.
- The Loo is a strong, dusty, gusty, hot and dry summer wind from the West which blows over the Indo-Gangetic Plain region of North India and Pakistan.
- It is especially strong in the months of May and June.

78. **(c)** Lower part with the convex lens of the bifocal lens facilitates near vision.
- In a bifocal lens, the upper portion of the lens consists of a concave lens.
- It facilitates distant vision (myopia). The lower part is a convex lens.
- It facilitates near vision (hypermetropia).

79. **(b)** Shovana Narayan has been honoured with the Padma Shri for her contribution to Kathak in the year 1992.
- She works for the Indian Audit and Accounts Service as a career officer.
- She performs both domestically and abroad and has been mentored by Pandit Birju Maharaj.

80. **(c)** Dalkhai is a popular folk dance of Odisha.
- It is performed at Bhai Jiuntia in the districts of Bargarh, Sambalpur Jharsuguda, Deogarh, Balangir, Sonepur and Boudh.
- It is a religion based traditional folk dance linked to the agrarian culture of society.

81. **(b)** **Article 368** specifies the procedure for amending the Indian Constitution.
- A bill for the amendment of the Constitution can be introduced only in either house of the Parliament, not in the State Legislatures.
- It is compulsory for a President to give his assent to a Constitutional Amendment Bill.

82. **(c)** **Article 195** of the Indian Constitution mentions about the salaries and allowances of members of the Legislative Assembly and the Legislative Council of a State.
- The Parliament of India has the sacrosanct right to decide the salary of the members of the Parliament.

83. **(d)** Indian Classical Dance is an umbrella under which various performing arts whose theory and practice can be traced to the Sanskrit text, Natya Shastra, the foundational treatise by Bharata Muni.
- Natya Shastra is a Sanskrit text on dance art and music.
- The text consists of 36 chapters with a cumulative total of 6000 poetic v/s describing performance arts.

84. **(a)** Eugenol is the main active ingredient of clove oil.
- Clove oil is a mixture of different compounds, with the three main active ingredients being eugenol, eugenyl acetate and caryophyllene.
- Eugenol is the major compound of clove oil, comprising 83%-95% of the oil.
- It is slightly water-soluble and easily soluble in organic solvent, colourless or yellowish in colour.

85. **(b)** As per the National Multidimensional Poverty Index Report 2023, Kerala has the least population concentration in the Multidimensional Poverty Index.
- Bihar has the highest Multidimensional Poverty Index.
- It has three equally weighted dimensions health, education and standard of living.

86. **(a)** 2-Methylpropan-2-ol is commonly known as tert-butyl alcohol.
- Test-butanol is a tertiory alcohol that is isobutane substituted by a hydroxy group at position 2.

87. **(a)** The inaugural edition of the National Beach Soccer Championship was held at Surat in 2023.
- Beach soccer is a game played barefoot on sand, where both teams field five players each.
- It was organised by the All India Football Federation.
- Goa is going to host 2024 Beach Soccer Championship 2024.

88. **(b)** In 1985, the Department of Sports transformed into the 'Department of Youth Affairs and Sports'.
- The Ministry of Youth Affairs and Sports was initially set up as the Department of Sports in 1982 at the time of organisation of the IX Asian Games in New Delhi.
- Subsequently, the Ministry has been bifurcated in Department of Youth Affairs and Department of Sports under two separate secretaries from 2008.

89. **(a)** The Tableau of Uttarakhand was given the title of 'Best Tableau' on Republic Day, 2023, which was themed as 'Manaskhand'.
- Recently, Odisha's colourful tableau, which showcased women empowerment and the state's rich handicraft and handloom sector during the 75th Republic Day parade, has won the first prize among the tableaux.

90. **(a)** The main purpose of establishing the Agricultural Prices Commission in 1965 is to determine the prices for various farm products purchased by the government and to motivate cultivators and farmers to adopt the latest technology in order to optimise the use of resources and increase productivity.

91. **(d)** In the year 1789, Antoine Lavoisier discovered the law of conservation of mass and state that mass is conserved in a chemical reaction.
- It observed that mass can neither be created nor destroyed in a chemical change.
- It remains conserved throughout the reaction.

92. **(c)** Diwali is popularly known as the festival of light.
- It is celebrated in the Hindu Luni solar months of Ashwin and Kartika (mid-October to mid-November).
- The ancient calendar states that Diwali is celebrated annually on Amavasya or the fifteenth day of the month of Kartika.

93. **(c)** One mole of Aluminium Sulphate $Al_2(So_4)_3$ contains 12 moles of oxygen atoms.
- Each sulphate ion in aluminium sulfate contains four oxygen atoms. Since there are three sulfate ions in aluminium sulfate, the total number of oxygen atoms is 12.

94. **(b)** 100 percent of the capital of MUDRA is contributed by SIDBI.
- MUDRA stands for Micro Units Development and Refinance Agency Ltd.
- Pradhan Mantri MUDRA Yojana (PMMY) is a scheme launched by the Prime Minister Narendra Modi on 8th April, 2015, for providing loans upto ₹ 10 lakh to the non-corporate, non-farm small/micro-enterprises.

95. **(b)** The 35th National Games were held in the state of Kerala. Kerala hosted this game for the second time.
- Former cricketer Sachin Tendulkar was selected as the goodwill ambassador for the games.
- Ammu, the Great Hornbill (the state bird of Kerala) was chosen as the Mascot.

96. **(b)** Staphylococcus aureus bacteria have a thick cell wall with several layers of peptidoglycan and teichoic acid.
- Staphylococcus aureus is a gram-positive spherically shaped bacterium, a member of the bacilleta, and is a usual member of the microbiota of the body, frequently found in the upper respiratory tract and on the skin.

97. **(a)** Atal Tunnel is the longest Highway Tunnel in India (as of 2022).
- Tunnel is the world's longest highway tunnel above 10,000 (3,048 m) feet.
- Atal Tunnel is also known as Rohtang Tunnel.
- It connect Manli and Lahaul spiti valley.

98. **(c)** Annie Besant stated in 1902 that India was not ruled for its benefit, but rather for the benefit of its conquerors.
- She encouraged a national awakening while, fighting against social evils such as caste discrimination and child marriage.
- She founded the Central Hindu College at Benaras and organised the Home Rule League.
- New India was a newspaper founded by her.
- She become the first congress women president in 1917 at Calcutta session.

99. **(a)** The Battle of Kannauj was fought between Sher Shah Suri and the Mughals led by Humayun.
- The Battle of Kannauj took place on 17th May, 1540, at Kannauj, Uttar Pradesh, India.

- This battle is also known as the Battle of Bilgram.
- The battle resulted in the defeat of Humayun by Sher Shah Suri.

100. **(c)** According to Dr. BR Ambedkar's views, Directive Principles of the Constitution is the Novel feature of the Indian Constitution.

- Directive Principles of State Policies (DPSPs) are a set of social and economic obligations imposed on the Government (Union and State) to establish a welfare society.
- They are enumerated in Part IV of the Constitution.

101. **(b)** The sum of any two sides of a triangle is always greater than its third side.

102. **(b)** Marks obtained by S in

Hindi $= 82\%$ of $150 = \frac{82}{100} \times 150 = 123$

English $= 64\%$ of $100 = \frac{64}{100} \times 100 = 64$

Geography $= 56\%$ of 175

$= \frac{56}{100} \times 175 = 98$

Mathematics $= 70\%$ of $120 = 84$

Physics $= \frac{80}{100} \times 75 = 60$

$\therefore$ Aggregate of marks obtained by S in all subjects

$= 123 + 64 + 98 + 84 + 60 = 429$

103. **(c)** Let radius of cylinder, cone 1 and cone 2 be R, r_1 and r_2, respectively.

Let their volums be V, V_1 and V_2, respectively.

$\therefore\ V = V_1 + V_2$

$V = x + 2x \quad [\because V_1 = x \text{ and } V_2 = 2x]$

$V = 3x$

Now, $\frac{22}{7} \times R^2 \times 12 : \frac{1}{3} \times \frac{22}{7} \times r_1^2 \times 12$

:

$\frac{1}{3} \times \frac{22}{7} \times r_2^2 \times 12 = 3:1:2$

$\Rightarrow R^2 : r_1^2 : r_2^2 = 3:3:6$

Let R^2 be $3K$, r_1^2 be $3K$ and r_2^2 be $6K$.

Flat surface area of cylinder

$= 2\pi R^2 = 6\pi K$

Flat surface area of two cones

$= \pi(r_1^2 + r_2^2) = 9\pi K$

Hence, required percentage change

$= \frac{9\pi K - 6\pi K}{6\pi K} \times 100$

$= \frac{3\pi K}{6\pi K} \times 100 = 50\%$

104. **(c)** Perimeter of triangle

$= (13 + 12 + 5)$ cm $= 30$ cm

105. **(d)** $(4.2 \text{ of } 2.5 \div 3.5) - (3.6 \div 2.4 + 2.5 \text{ of } 3 \div 7.5) + (6 - 3 \text{ of } 2 + 4 \text{ of } 3 \div 6)$

$= (10.5 \div 3.5) - (1.5 + 7.5 \div 7.5) + (6 - 6 + 12 \div 6)$

$= 3 - (1.5 + 1) + 2$

$= 3 - 2.5 + 2 = 2.5$

106. **(c)** Area of trapezium $= 1188 \text{ cm}^2$

$= \frac{1}{2} \times$ Sum of parallel sides $\times$ (18 cm)

$\Rightarrow \frac{1188 \times 2}{18} =$ Sum of parallel sides

$\Rightarrow\ 66 \times 2 =$ Sum of parallel sides

$\therefore$ Sum of parallel sides = 132 cm

107. **(b)** $\sin(x + y) = 1$

$\therefore\ (x + y) = 90° \quad$ ...(i)

and $\cos(x - y) = \frac{\sqrt{3}}{2}$

$\Rightarrow\ (x - y) = 30° \quad$ ...(ii)

Adding Eqs. (i) and (ii),

$2x = 120°$

$x = 60°$

$\therefore\ y = 90° - 60°$

$\Rightarrow\ y = 30°$

108. **(b)** Total distance travelled by A

$= (8 \times 4)$ km $+ (4 \times 8)$ km

$= (32 + 32) = 64$ km

Total time $= (8 + 4)$ h $= 12$ h

$\therefore$ Average speed $= \left(\frac{64}{12}\right)$ km/h

$= \left(5\frac{1}{3}\right)$ km/h

109. **(d)** Number of employees in Pune in 2018 = 179

Total number of employees in 2018

$= 874 + 850 + 179 + 857 + 820 = 3580$

$\therefore$ Required percentage $= \frac{179}{3580} \times 100$

$= 0.05 \times 100$

$= 5\%$

110. **(d)** Here,

$(x - 2) = 0 \Rightarrow x = 2$

Putting the value of x in

$2x^3 + ax^2 + 3x - 5$

$= 2(2)^3 + a(2)^2 \times 3(2) - 5$

$= 2 \times 8 + a \times 4 + 6 - 5$

$= 16 + 4a + 1$

$= 17 + 4a \quad$ ...(i)

Now, using $x = 2$ in $(x^3 + x^2 - 2x + a)$

$= (2)^3 + (2)^2 - 2(2) + a$

$= 8 + 4 - 4 + a$

$= 8 + a \quad$ ...(ii)

Now, $17 + 4a = 8 + a \Rightarrow a = -3$

Using it in Eq. (i),

$17 + 4(-3) = 17 - 12 = 5$

$\therefore$ Remainder = 5

111. **(c)** According to the given condition,

$\frac{P \times 14 \times 8}{100} - \frac{P \times 14 \times 4}{100} = 6160$

$\Rightarrow \quad \frac{14P}{100}(8 - 4) = 6160$

$\Rightarrow \quad \frac{14P}{100} \times 4 = 6160$

$\Rightarrow \quad P = \frac{6160 \times 100}{14 \times 4}$

$\therefore \quad P =$ ₹ 11000

112. **(c)** Given, $b = \frac{4}{a}$

Mean proportional of a and $b = \sqrt{ab}$

$= \sqrt{a \times \frac{4}{a}} = \sqrt{4} = 2$

113. **(a)** $\frac{13 \div \{6 - 6 \div (7 - 9) \times 8 + 9\}}{5 + 5 \times 5 \div 5 \text{ of } 5}$

$= \frac{13 \div \{6 - 6 \div (-2) \times 8 + 9\}}{5 + 5 \times 5 \div 25}$

$= \frac{13 \div \{6 - (-3) \times 8 + 9}{5 + 5 \times \frac{1}{5}}$

$= \frac{13 \div \{6 + 24 + 9\}}{5 + 1} = \frac{13 \div (39)}{6}$

$= \frac{13}{39 \times 6} = \frac{1}{3 \times 6} = \frac{1}{18}$

114. **(d)** Given, $\frac{a}{b} + \frac{b}{a} = 1$

$\Rightarrow \quad \frac{a^2 + b^2}{ab} = 1 \Rightarrow a^2 + b^2 = ab$

$\Rightarrow\ a^2 + b^2 - ab = 0 \quad$ ...(i)

Now, the value of $\frac{a^3 + b^3}{3ab}$

$= \frac{(a + b)(a^2 + b^2 - ab)}{3ab}$

$= \frac{(a + b) \times 0}{3ab} \quad$ [using Eq. (i)]

$= 0$

115. **(b)** $\left[9 + 3 - 2 \times \left\{\left(4 \div \frac{1}{4}\right) - 4\right\} + 81 \div 9 + 81 \div 9 + 3 - 9\right] + 9$

$= [9 + 3 - 2 \times \{16 - 4\} + 9 + 9 + 3 - 9] + 9]$

$= [9 + 3 - 2 \times 12 + 9 + 9 + 3 - 9] + 9$

$= [9 + 3 - 24 + 9 + 9 + 3 - 9] + 9$

$= 9$

116. (a) Let the total votes polled be $100x$.

Invalid votes $= \frac{1}{10}$ of $100x = 10x$

$\therefore$ Valid votes $= 90x$

Now, votes of $(R+S) = \frac{1}{2}(100x)$

$\Rightarrow R + S = 50x$

$\because$ They get equal voltes.

$\therefore \quad R = 25x$ votes and

$S = 25x$ votes

Now, votes received by

$R = 25x + \frac{1}{2}(25x) + \frac{1}{2}(10x)$

$= 25x + 12.5x + 5x = 42.5x$

$\therefore$ Percentage votes secured by

$R = \frac{42.5x}{100x} \times 100 = 42.5\%$

117. (d) Given, $x = 11$

$(x^5 - 12x^4 + 12x^3 - 12x^2 + 12x - 1)$

$= (x^5 - 11x^4) - x^4 + 11x^3 + x^3 - 11x^2 - x^2 + 11x + x - 1$

$= x^4(x-11) - x^3(x-11) + x^2(x-11) - x(x-11) + (x-1)$

$\Rightarrow 11 - 1 = 10$

118. (d) Area of sector $= \frac{\theta}{360°} \times \pi r^2$

and area of equilateral triangle $= \frac{\sqrt{3}}{4}a^2$

Center distance between the circle

= Side of triangle = (5 + 5) = 10 cm

$\therefore$ Area subtended between the circles.

$\therefore$ Area of equilateral triangle

$- 3 \times$ Area of sector

A B C

$= \frac{\sqrt{3}}{4}a^2 - 3 \times \frac{\theta}{360°} \times \pi r^2$

$= \frac{\sqrt{3}}{4} \times (10)^2 - 3 \times \frac{60°}{360°} \times \pi(5)^2$

$= \frac{100\sqrt{3}}{4} - \frac{25\pi}{2}$

$= 25\sqrt{3} - \frac{25\pi}{2} = 25\left(\sqrt{3} - \frac{\pi}{2}\right)$

119. (c) $\left(\frac{2\cos^3\theta - \cos\theta}{\sin\theta - 2\sin^3\theta}\right)^2 + 1$

$= \left[\frac{\cos\theta(2\cos^2\theta - 1)}{\sin\theta(1 - 2\sin^2\theta)}\right]^2 + 1$

$= \left(\frac{\cos\theta \times \cos 2\theta}{\sin\theta \times \cos 2\theta}\right)^2 + 1$

$= \frac{\cos^2\theta}{\sin^2\theta} + 1 = \frac{\cos^2\theta + \sin^2\theta}{\sin^2\theta}$

$= \frac{1}{\sin^2\theta} = \text{cosec}^2\theta$

120. (c) Required percentage

$= \frac{165 - 65}{165} \times 100$

$= \frac{6500}{165} = 39.39\%$

121. (d) Voting at center 1 = 70% of 26000

$= \frac{7}{10} \times 26000 = 18200$

Voting at center 2 = 60% of 28000

$= \frac{60}{100} \times 28000 = 16800$

Voting at center 3 = 80% of 25000

$= \frac{80}{100} \times 25000 = 20000$

Voting at center 4 = 76% of 30000

$= \frac{76}{100} \times 30000 = 22800$

$\therefore$ Maximum voting happened in center 4.

122. (b) Given, $\frac{3}{4}, \frac{3}{5}, \frac{2}{11}, \frac{7}{2}$

$= 0.75, 0.6, 0.18, 3.5$

$\therefore$ Ascending order $= 0.18 < 0.6 < 0.75 < 3.5$

$= \frac{2}{11} < \frac{3}{5} < \frac{3}{4} < \frac{7}{2}$

$= 2 : 11 < 3 : 5 < 3 : 4 < 7 : 2$

123. (b) According to the question,

$P \longrightarrow 30 \quad 4$

120

$Q \longrightarrow 40 \quad 3$

Work alone done in 4 days

$= (4 + 3) \times 4 = 28$ units

$\therefore$ Remaining work

$= 120 - 28 = 92$ units

So, time taken by P to finish the remaining work $= \frac{92}{4} = 23$ days

124. (a) Average speed $= \frac{\text{Total distance}}{\text{Total time taken}}$

$= \frac{(72 + 28 + 160)\text{ km}}{\left(\frac{72}{45} + \frac{28}{4} + \frac{160}{20}\right)\text{h}}$

$= \left(\frac{260}{16 + 7 + 8}\right)\text{km/h}$

$= \left(\frac{260}{16.6}\right) = 15.66$ km/h

125. (d) $\therefore$ $56 \div 4 + p \times 3 - 24 \div 12 + 4 = 21 \div 3 + 3$

$\Rightarrow 14 + 3p - 2 + 4 = 7 + 3$

$\Rightarrow \quad 16 + 3p = 10$

$\Rightarrow \quad 3p = -6$

$\therefore \quad p = -2$

126. (d) volume of cone $= 150\pi \text{ cm}^3$

$\frac{1}{3}\pi r^2 h = 150\pi$

$\Rightarrow \quad \frac{1}{3}\pi r^2 \times 18 = 150\pi$

$\Rightarrow \quad r^2 = \frac{150 \times 3}{18}$

$\Rightarrow r^2 = 25 \Rightarrow r = 5$ cm

Slant height, $l = \sqrt{h^2 + r^2}$

$= \sqrt{(18)^2 + (5)^2}$

$= \sqrt{324 + 25} = \sqrt{349}$

$\therefore \quad l = 18.68$ cm

127. (a) Curved surface area of cone $= \pi rl$

$\therefore \quad 308 = \pi rl$

$\Rightarrow \quad 308 = \frac{22}{7} \times r \times 28$

$\Rightarrow \quad 308 = 22 \times r \times 4$

$\Rightarrow \quad r = \frac{308}{22 \times 4}$

$\Rightarrow \quad r = 3.5$ cm

128. (a) Total number of students in Class X

= Sum total of all students of all the four Section A, B, C and D

$= (25 + 20 + 12 + 15) + (22 + 25 + 15 + 20) + (18 + 24 + 8 + 22) + (20 + 12 + 10 + 18)$

$= 72 + 82 + 72 + 60 = 286$

129. (d) Speed of the train $= \frac{72 \text{ km}}{\frac{40}{60}\text{ h}}$

$= \frac{72 \times 60}{40} = 108$ km/h

$= 108 \times \frac{5}{18} = 30$ m/s

$\therefore$ Distance covered by the train in 6 sec $= 30 \times 6 = 180$ m

130. (c) Present number of school going children = 64000

$\therefore$ Number of school going children in the town at the end of 3 yr

$= 64000 \times \frac{110}{100} \times \frac{110}{100} \times \frac{110}{100} = 85184$

131. (a) $\frac{3 \div 3 \times 2 - 6 \div 3 + 7}{5 \div 5 \times 6 \div 6 + 3 + 3}$

$= \frac{1 \times 2 - 2 + 7}{1 \times 1 + 3 + 3}$

$= \frac{2 - 2 + 7}{1 + 3 + 3} = \frac{7}{7} = 1$

132. (c) We know that,

$a^3 + b^3 = (a+b)(a^2 + b^2 - ab)$

Now, $\dfrac{\sin^3 A + \cos^3 A}{\sin A + \cos A}$

$= \dfrac{(\sin A + \cos A)(\sin^2 A + \cos^2 A - \sin A \cos A)}{\sin A + \cos A}$

$= 1 - \sin A \cos A$

133. (d) Selling price $= (100 - 18)\% \times 5980$

$= 82\% \times 5980 = \dfrac{82}{100} \times 5980$

$= ₹ 4904$

134. (c) Amount of mixture in vessel = 18 L

Let milk be $5x$ L and water be x L.

Hence, $5x + x = 18$

$\Rightarrow 6x = 18$

$\Rightarrow x = 3$

$\therefore$ Amount of milk $= 5x = 15$ L

Amount of water $= x = 3$ L

Now, let 'w' L of water be added.

$\therefore$ According to the given condition,

$\dfrac{18}{3+w} = \dfrac{9}{2}$

$\Rightarrow 3 + w = 4$

$\Rightarrow w = 1$

Hence, 1 L of water should be added to the vessel.

135. (c) Relative speed of trains

$= (60 - 42) = 18$ km/h

$= 18 \times \dfrac{5}{18} = 5$ m/s

Now, length of the faster train

$=$ Speed $\times$ Time $= 5 \times 36 = 180$ m

136. (a) Total production of scooters from 1985 to 1989

$= 115 + 108 + 149 + 102 + 101$

$= 575$ (in thousand)

Now, 20% of 575 $= \dfrac{20}{100} \times 575 = 115$

Which is equal to the total production of scooters of all factories in 1985.

137. (b) Let profit percentage incurred on remaining 10 kg potatoes be $x\%$.

Now, according to the question,

60 kg $\times$ 50% + 20 kg $\times$ 40% + 10 kg $\times$ 25% + 10 kg $\times$ $x\%$

$= 100$ kg $\times 42\%$

$\Rightarrow 3000\% + 800\% + 250\% + 10x\%$

$= 4200\%$

$\Rightarrow 4050\% + 10x\% = 4200\%$

$\Rightarrow 10x\% = 4200\% - 4050\%$

$\Rightarrow 10x\% = 150\% \Rightarrow x\% = 15\%$

$\therefore$ 15% profit incurred on remaining 10 kg potatoes.

$\therefore$ Required answer $= \dfrac{15}{100} = 0.15$

138. (c) $\dfrac{2\left\{3 + 3\left(\dfrac{1}{4} \div \dfrac{15}{20} + 2\right) - 18 \times \dfrac{1}{3}\right\}}{2(4 + 20 \div 4)}$

$= \dfrac{2\left\{3 + 3\left(\dfrac{1}{4} \times \dfrac{20}{15} + 2\right) - 6\right\}}{2(4+5)}$

$= \dfrac{2\left\{3 + 3\left(\dfrac{1}{3} + 2\right) - 6\right\}}{2 \times 9}$

$= \dfrac{2\left\{3 + 3 \times \dfrac{7}{3} - 6\right\}}{18}$

$= \dfrac{2\{3 + 7 - 6\}}{18} = \dfrac{2 \times 4}{18} = \dfrac{4}{9}$

139. (d) $\therefore$ Let the cost price (CP) of pulses be ₹ x.

$\therefore$ Selling price = 132% of ₹ x

$= \dfrac{132}{100} \times x = ₹\, 1.32x$

Faulty weights are 20% less than the actual measure.

$\therefore$ Faulty weight = 1 kg − 20% of 1 kg

$= (1000 - 200)$ gm $= 800$ gm

Now, SP of 800 gm pulses = ₹ $1.32x$

So, SP of 1000 gm pulse

$= \dfrac{1.32x \times 1000}{800} = ₹\, 1.65x$

$\therefore$ Profit percentage

$= \dfrac{(1.65x - x)}{x} \times 100$

$= 0.65 \times 100 = 65\%$

140. (b) Let the total activities of B be 'x' and that of C be 'y'.

Now, according to the question,

$(45 + 25 + 30)x = 500$

$\Rightarrow 100x = 500 \Rightarrow x = 5$

$\therefore$ Activity R of $B = 30x = 30 \times 5 = 150$

Now, For C,

$(30 + 30 + 40)x = 400$

$\Rightarrow 100x = 400$

$\Rightarrow x = 4$

$\therefore$ Activity R of $C = 40x = 40 \times 4 = 160$

Hence, required difference

$= 160 - 150 = 10$

141. (c) According to the question,

Cost price of the item

$= 500 \times \dfrac{90}{100} \times \dfrac{80}{100} \times \dfrac{100}{125} = ₹\, 288$

142. (b) $72 \div 8 - 210 \div 15 - 5 + 2 \times 5$

$= 9 - 14 - 5 + 10$

$= 19 - 19 = 0$

143. (a) $\angle A + \angle B + \angle C = 180°$

$\Rightarrow \dfrac{\angle(A + B + C)}{2} = 90°$

Now, $\left\{\tan\dfrac{A}{2} + \text{cosec}\dfrac{B+C}{2}\right\}\left\{\tan\dfrac{A}{2} - \text{cosec}\dfrac{B+C}{2}\right\}$

$= \left\{\tan\dfrac{A}{2} + \text{cosec}\left(90° - \dfrac{A}{2}\right)\right\}\left\{\tan\dfrac{A}{2} - \text{cosec}\left(90 - \dfrac{A}{2}\right)\right\}$

$= \left\{\tan\dfrac{A}{2} + \sec\dfrac{A}{2}\right\}\left\{\tan\dfrac{A}{2} - \sec\dfrac{A}{2}\right\}$

So, $\tan^2\dfrac{A}{2} - \sec^2\dfrac{A}{2} = -1$

$[\because \sec^2\theta - \tan^2\theta = 1]$

144. (a) Number of professors added to the university during 2019 to 2022

$= 100 + 150 + 180 + 200 = 630$

Number of associate professors added to the university during 2019 to 2022

$= 110 + 140 + 190 + 220 = 660$

Hence, difference between them

$= 660 - 630 = 30$

145. (d) Given, $S = \dfrac{75}{100} \times T \Rightarrow S = \dfrac{3}{4} \times T$

$\Rightarrow \dfrac{S}{T} = \dfrac{3}{4}$ or $S : T = 3 : 4$

146. (d)

$22.0625 + [15 + 0.25 \times (4.78 + 1.5 \times 3.02)]$

$= 22.0625 - [15 + 0.25 \times (4.78 - 4.53)]$

$= 22.0625 - [15 + 0.25 \times 0.25]$

$= 22.0625 - [15 + 0.0625]$

$= 22.0625 - 15.0625 = 7$

147. (b) $(\text{Circumference})_1 \times (\text{Number of revolutions})_1 = (\text{Circumference})_2 \times (\text{Number of revolutions})_2$

$\Rightarrow 2\pi \times r_1 \times N_1 = 2\pi r_2 \times N_2$

$\Rightarrow r_1 \times N_1 = r_2 \times N_2$

$\Rightarrow \dfrac{15}{2} \times 105 = \dfrac{21}{2} \times N_2$

$\Rightarrow N_2 = 75$

Hence, Number of revolutions of larger gear = 75

148. (b) $13.5 - [5 + 0.5(9 - 3 \times 2)]$

$= 13.5 - [5 + 0.5(9 - 6)]$

$= 13.5 - [5 + 0.5 \times 3]$

$= 13.5 - [5 + 1.5]$

$= 13.5 - 6.5 = 7$

149. (a) Height of cone = 20 ft.

Circumference $= 2\pi r = 30\pi$

$\Rightarrow \quad r = 15$ ft.

$\therefore$ Area of cloth needed $= \pi rl$

Where, l is the slant height

$= \sqrt{h^2 + r^2}$

$l = \sqrt{(20)^2 + (15)^2}$

$= \sqrt{400 + 225}$

$= \sqrt{625} = 25$ ft.

Thus, Area of canvas used for it $= \pi rl$

$= \pi \times 15 \times 25$

$= 375\,\pi$ sq. ft.

150. (a) Let the efficiency of Tripti be x.

$\therefore$ Efficiency of Tarun $= 2x$

Total work = Time × Efficiency

$= 16 \times (x + 2x)$

$= 16 \times 3x$

$= 48x$

$\therefore$ Time taken by Tripti alone to do the work $= \frac{48x}{x} = 48$ days

151. (b) 'Vintage' means belonging to the past but having very high quality and value.

152. (a) 'Accolade' refers to an award or honour given as a mark of recognition or approval. Hence, its antonym is 'Criticism' which is the expression of disapproval of someone or something based on perceived faults or mistakes

153. (c) The word 'Eagerly' in a manner showing keen interest or enthusiasm; eagerly implies a strong desire or enthusiasm for something.

154. (a) Pedagogy is the method of how teachers teach, in theory and in practice.

155. (a) 'will have finished' is the correct future perfect tense used to indicate that the action (painting) will be completed before a specific time in the future.

156. (b) The word 'Entail' means to involve something as a necessary part or consequence.

157. (c) The idiom 'keeps a level head' means to remain calm and composed, especially during difficult or stressful situations.

158. (a) The word 'Hypothesis' refers to a supposition or proposed explanation made on the basis of limited evidence as a starting point for further investigation. Hence, its synonym is 'speculation' which refers to Ideas or guesses about something without firm evidence.

159. (c) The incorrectly spelt, word is 'reciept' correct spelling is 'receipt'.

160. (b) The word 'grisly' means something that is extremely unpleasant or shocking, often involving death or injury. Hence, its synonym is 'atrocious' which means extremely wicked, brutal or cruel; appalling.

161. (d) 'resembling his parents in character and appearance' is the substitution of 'A chip off the old block' means someone who is very similar to their parent in character or appearance.

162. (c) 'Aborigines' word refers to the original or earliest known inhabitants of a country or region.

163. (a) The segment that contains the error is answer (D). The correct adverbial form should be 'sweet', not 'sweetly.' Therefore, the corrected segment should be 'it tasted sweet.'

164. (b) The idiom 'keep up appearances' means 'to maintain an outward show.' It refers to maintaining a facade of normalcy despite underlying difficulties.

165. (c) The incorrectly spelt word is 'Infurmary'. The correct spelling is 'infirmary'. It refers to a hospital.

166. (d) 'Captivity' means the condition of being imprisoned or confined. Hence, it is the correct antonym of 'Freedom'.

167. (d) The word 'Concordant' refers to something that is in agreement or harmony, especially in music or opinions.

168. (b) An 'obituary' is a news article that reports the recent death of a person.

169. (c) The idiom 'get itchy feet' means to start to want to travel or do something different, often due to a desire for change or adventure.

170. (d) Part 'Food greedy' contains an error. The correct adverbial form should be 'greedily.' Therefore, the corrected segment should be 'ate the food greedily.'

171. (c) The underlined phrase 'keeping his chin up' means to stay cheerful and optimistic during difficult times or adversity.

172. (a) An 'epitaph' are the words that are inscribed on a tomb.

173. (d) The sentence with correct spelling is : 'The scientist meticulously analysed the complex data, uncovering ground-breaking insights that would revolutionise the field.' 'Revolutionise' is correctly spelled, meaning change something radically or fundamentally.

174. (c) Part 'has emphasised and' contains an error. The correct verb form should agree with the plural subject 'people,' so it should be 'have emphasised and.' Therefore, the corrected sentence would be 'The people of Jammu and Kashmir have emphasised and appreciated transparency'.

175. (a) The underlined part is grammatically and contextually correct.

176. (d) An 'oasis' is a small area in a desert where water and plants are found.

177. (a) 'On thin ice' describes being in a situation where one is at risk of causing trouble or facing consequences.

178. (c) The correct spelling is 'lay'.

179. (b) A wisp refers to a thin, delicate strand or fragment, often used to describe a faint trace of something, like smoke in this case. Hence, its antonym is 'Lot' which refers to a large quantity or amount.

180. (b) The idiom 'keep your pants on' means to remain patient and composed.

181. (a) The idiom 'under the weather' means 'feeling sick.' It describes someone who is not feeling well.

182. (c) 'Livelihood' is meaning of the idiom 'bread and butter' refers to a person's main source of income or means of living.

183. (b) The correct spelling of the given word is 'benevolent'. It means kind.

184. (d) Part 'himalayas include the' contains an error. The correct form should be 'The Himalayas include,' as 'Himalayas' is a plural noun and requires a plural verb form. Therefore, the corrected sentence would be 'The Himalayas include the highest mountains in the world and feed almost 20% of the earths population.'

185. (c) A 'polyglot' is someone who can speak more than one language.

186. (c) The underlined part of the sentence contains an error. As the sentence refers to past, the past tense form 'was given,' making the sentence grammatically correct and meaningful.

187. **(a)** The word 'Fabulous' means something that is extremely good or impressive; often used to describe something wonderful or amazing. Hence, its synonym is 'remarkable.'

188. **(a)** The correct spelling is 'slaughter'. It means to kill.

189. **(a)** The correct word is 'significance', not signification. The sentence means we should not undervalue the importance of female education.

190. **(c)** The underlined part of the sentence contains an error.
The subject 'a sharp fall' is singular, so the verb should agree with it in singular form. 'Has led' is the correct form of the verb to match with a singular subject.

191. **(a)** 'Adopt' means to take up or start, fitting the context of adopting a healthy lifestyle.

192. **(d)** 'Exercise' means physical activity, fitting the context of improving cardiovascular health.

193. **(d)** 'Essential' means necessary, fitting the context of a balanced diet rich in essential vitamins and minerals.

194. **(a)** 'Managing' means to control or handle, fitting the context of managing stress through activities.

195. **(d)** 'Sleep' means rest, fitting the context of getting an adequate amount of sleep each night.

196. **(d)** The word 'excessive' implies something beyond what is necessary or normal.
Hence, its antonym is 'moderate' which means within reasonable limits or not extreme.

197. **(d)** The passage states that facial recognition is almost instant and provides quick and successful verification of a person's identity.

198. **(b)** The passage mentions factors like jawline length, the form of cheekbones and eye sockets depth as considerations for facial recognition.
However, it does not explicitly mention 'face shape' as a factor that the technology considers.

199. **(c)** The passage primarily discusses facial recognition technology, its workings, and its benefits.

200. **(a)** According to the passage, the primary component of facial recognition is surveillance.
Facial recognition technology aids in surveillance by helping to identify individuals for various purposes, including catching criminals and enhancing security measures.

CPO SI P-1 SP 05

PAPER-1

SSC CPO SI SOLVED PAPER

28 June 2024 (Shift II)

Instructions

1. This paper contains 200 questions.
2. It has 4 Parts, **Part I** General Intelligence and Reasoning, **Part II** General Knowledge and General Awareness, **Part III** Quantitative Aptitude and **Part IV** English Comprehension.
3. Each question carries **1 marks.**

MM : 200 **Time : 2 hr**

Part I

General Intelligence and Reasoning

1. Given, below are two statements and two conclusions. Take the statements to be true even if they are at variance with commonly known facts, and decide whether the conclusion(s) follow(s) the given statements.

Statements

All trains are buses.

Some buses are cars.

Conclusions

I. All cars are buses.

II. Some buses are trains.

(a) Neither Conclusion I nor II follows
(b) Only Conclusion II follows
(c) Both the Conclusions follow
(d) Only Conclusion I follows

2. Select the option that is related to the fifth number in the same way as the fourth number is related to the third number and the second number is related to the first number.

76 : 69 :: 49 : 45 :: 69 : ?

(a) 62 (b) 63 (c) 67 (d) 85

3. In a certain code language, 'HEMANT' is coded as 24-15-39-3-42-60 and 'VINAY' is coded as 66-27-42-3-75. How will 'MOHAN' be coded in the same language?

(a) 36-3-41-24-39 (b) 43-24-3-56-7
(c) 39-45-24-3-42 (d) 24-39-4-42-27

4. In a certain code language, 'MARCH' is written as 'LBQDG' and 'TAXAS' is written as 'SBWBR'. How will 'PIECE' be written in the given language?

(a) OJDDD (b) QHCED
(c) QJDDF (d) OJDED

5. Select the Venn diagram that best illustrates the relationship between the following classes.

Tigers, Snakes, Elephants

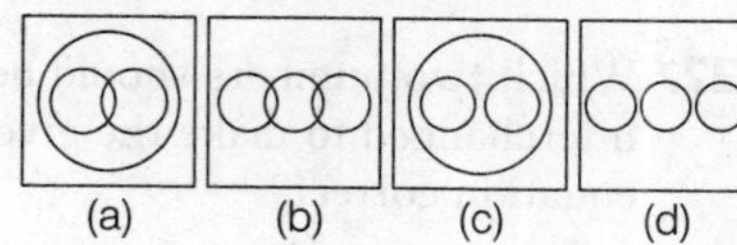

6. Select the correct mirror image of the given figure when the mirror is placed at MN as shown below.

MaGe4

(a) (b) (c) (d)

7. Select the option that is related to the fifth letter-cluster in the same way as the second letter cluster is related to the first letter-cluster and the fourth letter-cluster is related to the third letter-cluster.

NAPE : MZOD :: DULL : CTKK :: KIND : ?

(a) IFLB (b) LJOE
(c) LHOC (d) JHMC

8. Which of the following numbers will replace the question mark (?) in the given series?

$-32, -8, -2, ?, -\frac{1}{8}$

(a) -4 (b) $-\frac{1}{2}$
(c) -1 (d) $-\frac{1}{4}$

9. What will come in the place of '?' in the following equation, if '+' and '–' are interchanged and also '×' and '÷' are interchanged?

$47 \div 3 - 126 \times 6 + 18 = ?$

(a) 138 (b) 156
(c) 144 (d) 149

10. A dice has numbers 2, 3, 4, 5, 8 and 9 on its sides. Two different positions of the same dice are shown below. Select the number that will be on the face opposite to the one having (3).

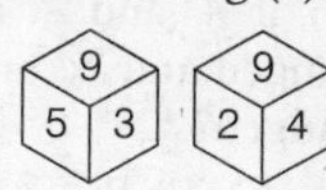

(a) 4 (b) 8
(c) 2 (d) 5

11. Which of the following numbers will replace the question mark (?) in the given series?

78, 86, 258, 322, ?

(a) 1288 (b) 1360
(c) 1610 (d) 1420

12. Select the figure from among the given options that can logically replace the question mark (?) in the following series.

(a) (b) (c) (d)

13. In a certain code language,
'A × B' means 'A is the son of B',
'A – B' means 'A is the brother of B',
'A + B' means 'A is the wife of B',
'A % B' means 'A is the father of B'.
How is M related to T if 'M + N × P % S – T'?

(a) Mother's mother
(b) Brother's wife's father's mother
(c) Wife's father's mother
(d) Brother's wife

14. Select the option figure in which the given figure (X) is embedded as its part (rotation is not allowed).

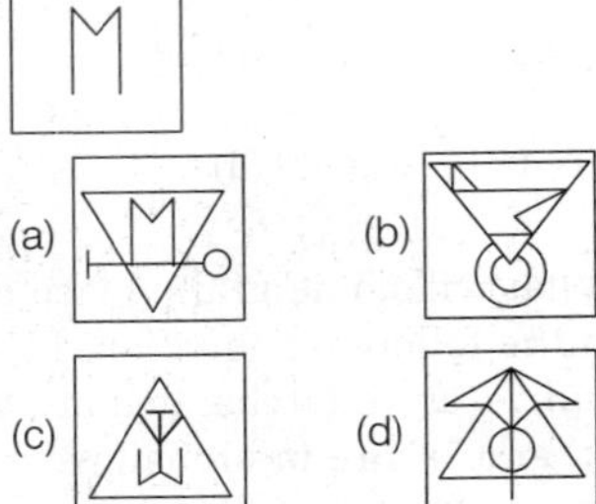

15. Which of the following terms will replace the question mark (?) in the given series?

ADO, DGR, GJU,?

(a) LON (b) JMX (c) JCB (d) RCB

16. What will come in place of the question mark (?) in the following equation, if '+' and '–' are interchanged and '×' and '÷' are interchanged?

$712 \div 6 - 15 \times 3 + 15 = ?$

(a) 4263 (b) 4262
(c) 4256 (d) 4265

17. In a certain code language, 'HEN' is coded as '9' and 'AFTER' is coded as '25'. How will 'SMALLEST' be coded in that language?

(a) 31 (b) 64 (c) 81 (d) 56

18. J, K, L, M, O and P are sitting around a circular table facing the centre. Both L and M are immediate neighbours of J. Only one person sits between M and P. O sits second to the right of J. O is not an immediate neighbour of L. Who is sitting to the immediate right of K?

(a) L (b) J
(c) P (d) O

19. Which of the following numbers will replace the question mark (?) in the given series?

324, 361, 400, 441, 484, ?

(a) 592 (b) 567
(c) 529 (d) 586

20. If '+' means '–', '–' means '×', '×' means '÷', and ÷ means '+', what will be the value of the following expression?

$20 \times 5 - 7 \div 4 + 3 = ?$

(a) 25 (b) 18
(c) 35 (d) 29

21. Select the Venn diagram that best illustrates the relationship between the following classes.

Grapes, Apples, Fruits

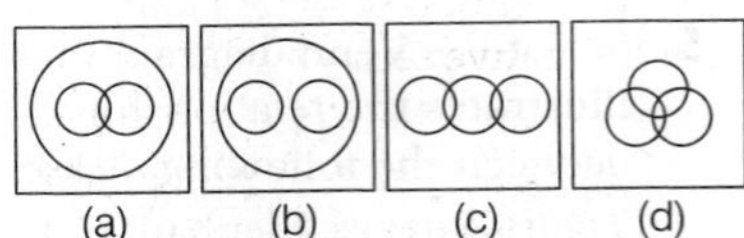

22. Which two numbers should be interchanged to make the given equation correct?

$$71 + 32 \times 2 - 63 \div 7 + \left[(81)^{\frac{1}{4}}\right] \times 3 - 22 = 113$$

(a) 2 and 3 (b) 32 and 22
(c) 3 and 7 (d) 71 and 22

23. Select the option in which the numbers share the same relationship as that shared by the given pair of numbers.

23 – 27

(a) 15 – 25 (b) 11 – 33
(c) 15 – 45 (d) 11 – 55

24. Select the number from among the given options that can replace the question mark(?) in the following series.

125, 150, 177, 207, 242, ?

(a) 290 (b) 282
(c) 280 (d) 284

25. Select the option that indicates the correct arrangement of the given words in the order in which they appear in an English dictionary.

1. Incest 2. Inception
3. Incense 4. Incapacity
5. Incentive

(a) 5, 3, 2, 1, 4 (b) 4, 3, 5, 2, 1
(c) 5, 4, 3, 2, 1 (d) 4, 5, 3, 2, 1

26. In a certain code language, M & N means 'M is the husband of N', M @ N means 'M is the brother of N', M $ N means 'M is the father of N', M # N means 'M is the mother of N'. Based on the above, how is F related to J if 'F & G # H @ I $ J'?

(a) Mother's father (b) Mother
(c) Sister (d) Father's father

27. In a code language, 'BEAM' is written as 'AFZN', and 'BILL' is written as 'AJKM'. How will 'WELL' be written in that language?

(a) VFKM (b) MVKF
(c) KMVF (d) VKMF

28. 20 is related to 30 following a certain logic. Following the same logic, 30 is related to 45. Which of the following numbers is related to 120 using the same logic?

(a) 80 (b) 75 (c) 70 (d) 60

29. Which letter cluster will replace the question mark (?) to complete the given series?

RDLS, VKBF, ?, DYHF, HFXS

(a) ZRRS (b) KBET
(c) FHWR (d) ZTTS

30. A dice has letters A, B, C, R, S and T on its sides. Two different positions of the same dice are shown below. Select the letter that will be on the face opposite to the one having A.

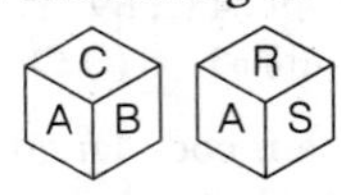

(a) C (b) R
(c) S (d) T

31. Select the correct mirror image of the given figure when the mirror is placed at MN as shown below.

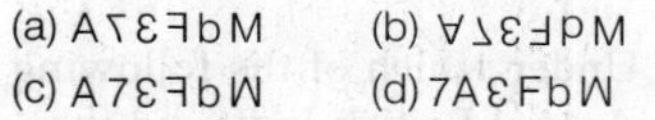

M
MdF37A
N

(a) AϒƐꟻbM (b) ∀ㄥƐℲpM
(c) A7ƐꟻbW (d) 7AƐFbW

32. Select the option that represents the correct order of the given words as they would appear in an English dictionary.

1. Dinnerware 2. Dingiest
3. Dinosaurs 4. Dinucleotide
5. Dinkier 6. Dingling

(a) 5, 2, 3, 6, 1, 4 (b) 2, 6, 3, 5, 1, 4
(c) 5, 2, 6, 3, 1, 4 (d) 2, 6, 5, 1, 3, 4

33. 15 is related to 20 following a certain logic. Following the same logic, 6 is related to 8.Which of the following numbers is related to 12 using the same logic?

(a) 9 (b) 10
(c) 8 (d) 7

34. Priya starts from point A and drives 9 km towards North. She then takes a right turn, drives 4 km to reach point B. She then turns right, drives 10 km and stops at point C. In which direction is point C with respect to point A?

(a) North-West (b) North-East
(c) South-East (d) South

35. Identify the option figure that when put in place of the question mark (?) will logically complete the series.

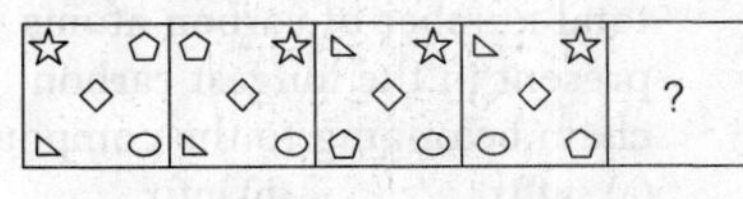

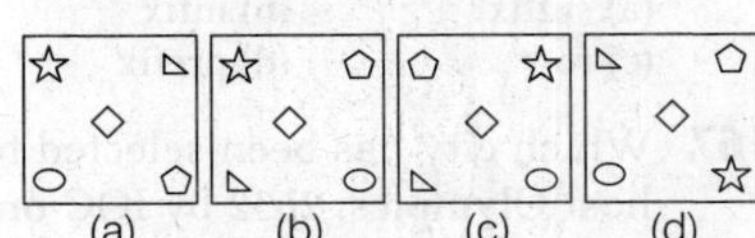

(a) (b) (c) (d)

36. Select the set in which the numbers are related in the same way as are the numbers of the following sets.
(Operations should be performed on the whole numbers, without breaking down the numbers into its constituent digits. E.g. 13 – Operations on 13 such as adding /deleting /multiplying etc. to 13 can be performed. Breaking down 13 into 1 and 3 and then performing mathematical operations on 1 and 3 is not allowed.)

(54, 51, 48)
(46, 40, 34)

(a) (58, 47, 36) (b) (42, 45, 32)
(c) (50, 42, 28) (d) (48, 53, 38)

37. Which of the following letter-clusters will replace the question mark (?) in the given series?

ICE, LGJ, OKO, ?

(a) RPT (b) ROT
(c) QPT (d) SPT

38. A transparent sheet with a pattern is given below. Select the option that depicts the pattern that would appear when the given transparent sheet is folded at the middle vertical line.

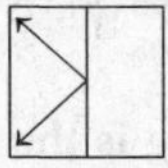

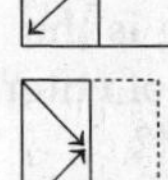
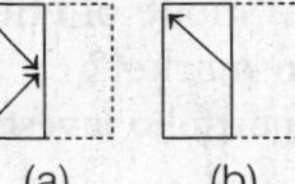
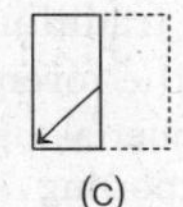
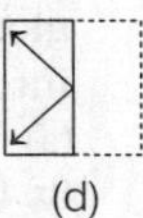

(a) (b) (c) (d)

39. What will come in the place of '?' in the following equation, if '+' and '–' are interchanged and also '×' and '÷' are interchanged?

$53 - 48 \times 6 \div 9 + 11 = ?$

(a) 114 (b) 107 (c) 129 (d) 101

40. If 'I' stands for '×', 'J' stands for '+', 'K' stands for '÷' and 'L' stands for '–', what will come in place of the question mark (?) in the following equation?

17 I (11 L 8 J 4) L 148 K 4 J 22 = ?

(a) 114 (b) 128 (c) 104 (d) 98

41. Select the option that is related to the fifth letter-cluster in the same way as the second letter-cluster is related to the first letter-cluster and the fourth letter-cluster is related to the third letter-cluster.

TRUTH : IVXVY :: SIMPLE : FNSQNY :: AROUND : ?

(a) EPXSRA (b) DNUORA
(c) EPXSWG (d) EOVPSB

42. Two statements are given, followed by two conclusions numbered I and II. Assuming the statements to be true, even if they seem to be at variance with commonly known facts, decide which of the conclusions logically follow(s) from the statements.

Statements

All pebbles are stones.

No stones are shells.

Conclusions

I. Some pebbles are shells.

II. No shells are stones.

(a) Neither Conclusion I nor II follows
(b) Both Conclusions I and II follow
(c) Only Conclusion I follows
(d) Only Conclusion II follows

43. In a certain code language, 'PANDA' is coded as 33-78-39-69-78 and 'SNAKE' is coded as 24-39-78-48-66. How will 'ZEBRA' be coded in the same language?

(a) 3 – 66 – 75 – 27 – 78
(b) 6 – 46 – 63 – 38 – 78
(c) 7 – 46 – 65 – 13 – 78
(d) 5 – 66 – 71 – 29 – 78

44. In a code language, 'ACID' is written as 'XDFE', and 'HAND' is written as 'EBKE'. How will 'ZEST' be written in that language?

(a) PUWF (b) WFPU
(c) WPUF (d) UWPF

45. The sequence of folding a paper and the manner in which the folded paper is cut is shown in the following figures. How would this paper look when unfolded?

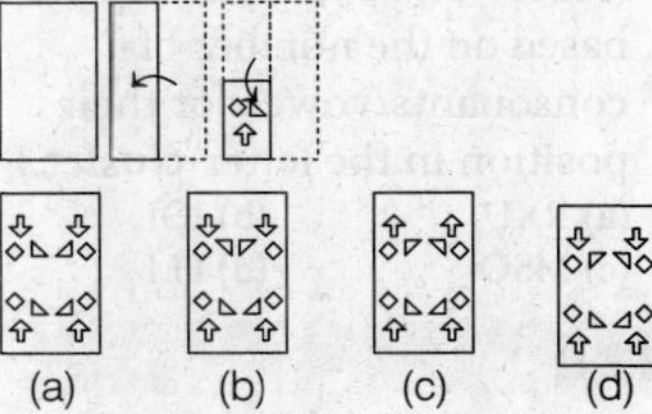

(a) (b) (c) (d)

46. If 'A' stands for '÷', 'B' stands for '×', 'C' stands for '+' and 'D' stands for '–', what will come in place of the question mark (?) in the following equation?

342 A 2 C 125 B 1 D 43 = ?

(a) 253 (b) 251
(c) 250 (d) 252

47. Select the figure from among the given options that can logically replace the question mark (?) in the following series.

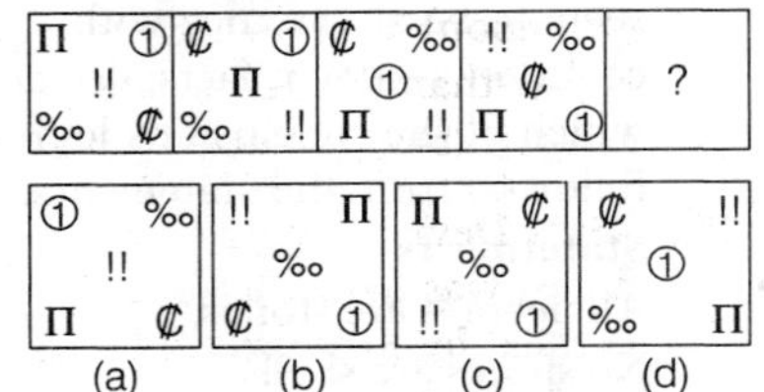

48. Select the correct mirror image of the given figure when the mirror is placed at MN as shown below.

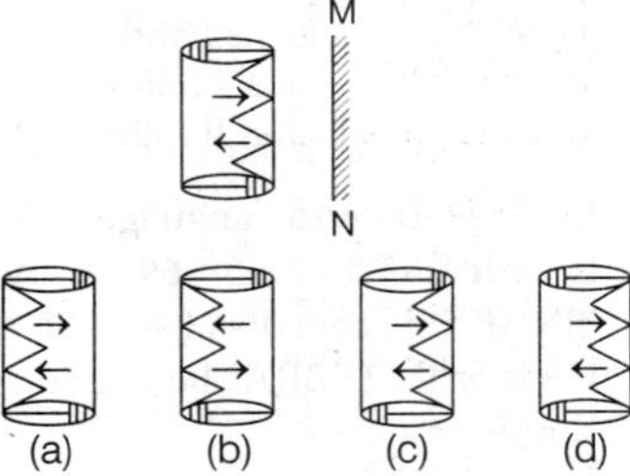

49. Shivani drives 17 km to the North, then drives 9 km East, and then drives 17 km South. How far is Shivani from the starting point when considered in a straight line?
(a) 9 km (b) 17 km
(c) 12 km (d) 26 km

50. Based on the English alphabetical order, three of the following four letter-clusters are alike in a certain way and thus form a group. Which letter-cluster does not belong to that group?
(**Note** The odd letter-cluster is not based on the number of consonants/vowels or their position in the letter-cluster.)
(a) RXU (b) IOL
(c) MSO (d) FLI

Part II

General Knowledge and General Awareness

51. Which hairpin-like structure serves to anchor and stabilise the tick's mouthparts to its host's skin and to channel the exchange of fluids?
(a) Substratum (b) Hypostome
(c) Peduncle (d) Trunk

52. Where is the Atal Bihari Vajpayee Institute of Mountaineering and Allied Sports situated?
(a) Uttar Kashi, Uttarakhand
(b) Pahalgam, Jammu and Kashmir
(c) Darjeeling, West Bengal
(d) Manali, Himachal Pradesh

53. What was the winning throw of Neeraj Chopra in Tokyo Olympics, 2020?
(a) 87.58 m (b) 90.58 m
(c) 80.00 m (d) 90.00 m

54. Article 21 is related to which of the following Fundamental Rights?
(a) Protection of Language, Culture of Minorities
(b) Freedom of Speech
(c) Freedom to Manage Religious Affairs
(d) Protection of Life and Personal Liberty

55. In which year was the Mahatma Gandhi National Rural Employment Guarantee Act passed?
(a) 2003 (b) 2005
(c) 2004 (d) 2006

56. Which of the following is the most traditional mode of entering into the foreign market?
(a) Undertaking portfolio investment
(b) Exporting
(c) Setting up fully owned manufacturing facilities
(d) Mergers and acquisitions

57. Who won the Bronze medal in women's boxing in Tokyo Olympics, 2020?
(a) Mirabai Chanu
(b) MC Mary Kom
(c) Lovlina Borgohain
(d) Aditi Ashok

58. Pandit Acchan Maharaj was a Kathak legend of which of the following gharanas?
(a) Raigarh (b) Banaras
(c) Lucknow (d) Jaipur

59. The Supreme Court of India consists of .... Judges and Chief Judges of India.
(a) 35 (b) 33 (c) 30 (d) 28

60. Who received the 67th National Film Award for Best Music Direction?
(a) M. Jayachandran
(b) AR Rahman
(c) Jyeshthoputro
(d) Gopi Sundar

61. Which of the following compounds is an alicyclic compound?
(a) Cyclopropane
(b) Isobutane
(c) Acetic acid
(d) Ethane

62. Under which of the following Acts of British India did the British Government take direct control of the administration of India in its own hands?
(a) Bengal Regulation Act of 1818
(b) Indian Contract Act of 1872
(c) Charter Act of 1813
(d) Government of India Act, 1858

63. The Sadir dancer R. Muthukannammal is the recipient of which of the following awards in the year 2022?
(a) Padma Bhushan Award
(b) Padma Shri Award
(c) Bharat Ratna Award
(d) Padma Vibhushan Award

64. Identify a conventional source of energy from the following options.
(a) Cattle dung
(b) Solar power
(c) Atomic energy
(d) Geothermal energy

65. Who among the following is the pioneer and founder of Kirana Gharana of Hindustani music?
(a) Firoz Dastur
(b) Abdul Karim Khan
(c) Sawai Gandharva
(d) Bhimsen Joshi

66. In the IUPAC name of a compound, the .... indicates the total number of carbon atoms present in the longest carbon chain belonging to the compound.
(a) suffix (b) infix
(c) root (d) prefix

67. Which city has been selected to host Olympics, 2032 by IOC on 21st July, 2021?
(a) Moscow (b) Sydney
(c) Brisbane (d) New York

68. What is a population (or sub-species or race) that is adapted to local environmental conditions called?
(a) Biome (b) Prototype
(c) Ecotype (d) Niche

69. When was the Prime Minister's Employment Generation Programme (PMEGP) launched ?
(a) 2012 (b) 2006 (c) 2009 (d) 2008

70. Which Five-Year Plan period saw the initiation of the Hill Area Development Programme?
(a) Eighth Five-Year Plan
(b) Fourth Five-Year Plan
(c) Fifth Five-Year Plan
(d) Sixth Five-Year Plan

71. Which of the following acts gave the British Indian Government the authority to arrest anyone without a trial?
(a) The Indian Press Act
(b) Pitt's India Act
(c) The Indian Slavery Act
(d) The Rowlatt Act

72. Which of the following statements are correct regarding State Legislatures?
A. Notwithstanding anything in Part XVII, but subject to the provisions of Article 348,business in the Legislature of a State shall be transacted in the official language or languages of the State or in Hindi or in English.
B. The Speaker of the Legislative Assembly or Chairman of the Legislative Council can permit any member to speak in his mother tongue.
C. Only the Supreme Court is entitled to inquire into the proceeding of the State Legislature.
(a) B and C (b) A and C
(c) A and B (d) A, B and C

73. How much percentage of Earth's water make up the oceans?
(a) 97% (b) 7% (c) 57% (d) 37%

74. The Himalayas have uplifted from which of the following geosynclines?
(a) Appalachian geosynclines
(b) Aravalli geosynclines
(c) Caledonian geosynclines
(d) Tethys geosynclines

75. Which of the following kings of Vijayanagara took the title of 'Establisher of the Yavana Kingdom'?
(a) Krishnadeva Raya
(b) Viranarasimha Raya
(c) Achyuta Deva Raya
(d) Sadasiva Raya

76. Which of the following is a tributary of river Indus?
(a) Lohit (b) Shyok
(c) Betwa (d) Dibang

77. Identify an organelle found both in eukaryotic as well as prokaryotic.
(a) Ribosomes (b) Mitochondria
(c) Lysosomes (d) Endosomes

78. Which physicist is known to establish the relationship between mechanical work and heat transfer?
(a) William Henry
(b) James Prescott Joule
(c) Hermann Helmholtz
(d) John Dalton

79. Who among the following wrote the novel 'Grimus'?
(a) Amitav Ghosh (b) Vikram Seth
(c) Arvind Adiga (d) Salman Rushdie

80. Which Article of the Indian Constitution mentions that 'The Council of Ministers shall be collectively responsible to the Legislative Assembly of the State'?
(a) Article 164(3) (b) Article 164(4)
(c) Article 164(2) (d) Article 164(1)

81. Which of the following is a term for the common local wind that blows in North and North-Western parts of India during summers?
(a) Loo (b) Bora
(c) Foehn (d) Chinook

82. The tendency of an atom or a functional group to attract a shared pair of electrons toward itself, is known as
(a) electropositivity
(b) electron affinity
(c) electro attraction
(d) electronegativity

83. In which of the following years, were separate electorates introduced in the Imperial Legislative Assembly elections in the name of Morley-Minto Reforms?
(a) Government of India Act, 1919
(b) Government of India Act, 1935
(c) Indian Councils Act, 1909
(d) Indian Councils Act, 1861

84. Mallika Sarabhai is famous for which of the following dances?
(a) Kathak (b) Odissi
(c) Sattriya (d) Kuchipudi

85. As per the decision by the Cabinet Committee on Economic Affairs (CCEA) of the Government of India in 2023, the MSP for Paddy (Common) has been fixed at .... higher than the last season.
(a) 8% (b) 9% (c) 7% (d) 5%

86. Sitara Devi, a doyen of .... dance, was hailed as 'The Queen of Kathak' by Rabindranath Tagore.
(a) Manipuri (b) Odissi
(c) Sattriya (d) Kathak

87. Which of the following is not an agro-based industry?
(a) Sugar (b) Fertiliser
(c) Edible oil (d) Jute

88. Which of the following books was written by Chitra Banerjee Divakaruni?
(a) The Feast of Roses
(b) Malgudi Days
(c) The Palace of Illusions
(d) A Fine Balance

89. Which of the following is an open chain organic compound?
(a) Benzene (b) Tetrahydrofuran
(c) Toluene (d) Acetaldehyde

90. Which festival is celebrated by Christi as the birth of Jesus Christ?
(a) Christmas (b) Easter
(c) Good Friday (d) Eid-al-Fitr

91. Taxes like gift tax, wealth tax, etc., are also referred to as which type of taxes?
(a) Paperless taxes (b) Rich taxes
(c) Direct taxes (d) Paper taxes

92. 'Harshacharita' book was written by which of the following writers?
(a) Harisena (b) Amarasimha
(c) Vararuchi (d) Banabhatta

93. Krishna III of Rashtrakuta dynasty established a victory pillar and a temple at which of the following cities of South India after defeating the Chola ruler Parantaka I?
(a) Thakkolam (b) Udaiyalur
(c) Poompuhar (d) Rameswaram

94. If a person who is arrested, is not produced before the Magistrate within 24 hours from the time of arrest, he will be entitled to be released on the writ of ....
(a) Prohibition (b) Quo-Warranto
(c) Mandamus (d) Habeas Corpus

95. The advisory board under provisions of Article 22 of the Constitution is to be consisted of persons who are, have been or are qualified to be appointed as ....
(a) Judges of Lower Court (b) Judges of Supreme Court
(c) Judges of High Court (d) Judges of District Court

96. In 2023, the President of which of the following countries was invited as the Chief Guest at India's Republic Day celebration?
(a) Egypt (b) Japan
(c) Russia (d) United States of America

97. According to Agricultural Statistics at a Glance 2022, Government of India, which state recorded the highest production of Bajra?
(a) Maharashtra (b) Haryana
(c) Madhya Pradesh (d) Rajasthan

98. Identify a muscle responsible for exit of waste material from the body.
(a) Pectoralis (b) Sphincter (c) Rectus (d) Gastrocnemius

99. Assume that the value of the Cash Reserve Ratio is 25%. What will be the value of money multiplier?
(a) 4 (b) 3 (c) 2 (d) 5

100. Who among the following belongs to Patiala Gharana?
(a) Nathu Khan (b) Chhajju Khan
(c) Abdul Wahid Khan (d) Ali Baksh Khan

Part III
Quantitative Aptitude

101. If $855 \div 15 - K + 32 \times 5 = 1152 \div 16 \times 111 \div 37$, then the value of K is
(a) 0 (b) 3 (c) 2 (d) 1

102. In an election between *A* and *B*, every fifth vote polled was marked as invalid by the machine. In the remaining votes, *A* wins the election with a margin of 2500 votes or 10% of the total votes polled, over *B*. If 90% of the invalid votes would have been in favour of *B*, then which of the following would have been the result of the election?
(a) *A* would have won by 3% (b) *A* would have won by 8%
(c) *B* would have won by 8% (d) *B* would have won by 3%

103. Find the simplified value of $5055 - (1002 \div 20.04)$.
(a) 50.05 (b) 4050 (c) 5050 (d) 5005

104. The population of a city increases every year at the rate of 5%. If the population of the city is 16000, what will be the population after 2 years?
(a) 17700 (b) 17600 (c) 17000 (d) 17640

105. Study the given table and answer the question that follows.
The table shows the number of students in various courses in various cities A, B, C, D and E in India during the academic year 2022-2023.

City	MBA	Science	Engineering	Medicine	MCA	Total
A	1200	2560	4520	1100	960	10340
B	1350	2650	5100	1050	850	11000
C	1250	2640	4580	1120	750	10340
D	1960	1250	3500	1850	1600	10160
E	1200	2100	3500	1960	1540	10300
Total	6960	11200	21200	7080	5700	

In city A, the number of students in Medicine is nearly what percentage of MBA?
(a) 87% (b) 85% (c) 92% (d) 89%

106. A dishonest dealer professes to sell his goods at cost price but uses a false weight of 950 gm instead of 1 kg. His gain percentage is
(a) $6\frac{5}{19}\%$ (b) $7\frac{5}{19}\%$ (c) $4\frac{5}{19}\%$ (d) $5\frac{5}{19}\%$

107. Find the value of 15% of $1.5 + 0.15 \div 0.1 + 0.01$ of $1.1 \times 0.5 + 2.5 \times 25$.
(a) 6.42305 (b) 62.2305 (c) 77.2305 (d) 64.2305

108. If $\sin x + \cos x = \sqrt{2} \sin x$, then the value of $\sin x - \cos x$ is
(a) $\sqrt{2} \sin x$ (b) $2 \sin x$ (c) $-\sqrt{2} \cos x$ (d) $\sqrt{2} \cos x$

109. If the radius of a sphere is increased by 125%, then by what percentage will its surface area increase (correct to two decimal places)?
(a) 509.54% (b) 409.76% (c) 406.25% (d) 506.25%

110. Simplify $\left[3\frac{2}{5} \times \left\{2\frac{3}{4} + 3.3\left(5\frac{1}{3} + 3\frac{1}{3} - 2\frac{1}{3}\right)\right\}\right]$
(a) 46.29 (b) 80.41 (c) 70.25 (d) 53.25

111. If the three sides of a triangle are 12, 22 and *m* units, then which of the following is correct?
(a) $10 \le m < 34$ (b) $10 \le m \le 34$ (c) $10 < m < 34$ (d) $10 < m \le 34$

112. A cylinder of radius 7 cm has a curved surface area of 2200 cm^2. Find its total surface area. $\left(\text{Use } \pi = \frac{22}{7}\right)$
(a) 2508 cm^2 (b) 2260 cm^2 (c) 2550 cm^2 (d) 1580 cm^2

113. The value of $66 \div [34 - (32 \text{ of } 2 - 4) \div (4 \times 15)]$ is equal to
(a) 3 (b) 2 (c) 0 (d) 1

114. The following table shows the total number of employees in 4 different colleges and the percentage of female employees and that of male employees. Study the table carefully and answer the question that follows.

College	Total Number of Employees	Percentage of Female Employees	Percentage of Male Employees
A	700	35%	65%
B	550	30%	70%
C	600	40%	60%
D	800	55%	45%

The number of females in colleges A and D together is what percentage of the number of males in colleges B and C together (rounded off to two decimal places)?
(a) 80.84% (b) 80.95% (c) 91.95% (d) 90.86%

115. The following table shows the population (in hundreds) of five different cities (A, B, C, D and E) categorised by gender

City	Population	Men : Women
A	2340	1 : 2
B	900	3 : 1
C	1510	3 : 2
D	2010	2 : 3
E	1750	4 : 3

What is the total number of women (in hundreds) in City A and City B?

(a) 1998 (b) 1898 (c) 1658 (d) 1785

116. A shopkeeper gives a discount of 12% on the purchase of 10 kg of sugar. The cost price of the sugar is ₹ 30/kg, and the marked price is ₹ 38/kg. The weighing machine of the shopkeeper is faulty, and it shows weight of 1 kg when the actual weight is 900 grams. Find the percentage profit of the shopkeeper (rounded off to two decimal places).

(a) 23.85% (b) 22.25% (c) 12.5% (d) 30.18%

117. The distance (d) a moving body travels, varies directly with the time (t) when it moves. A train travels 72 km in 2 hours. Find the equation that relates d and t.

(a) $d = \frac{t}{36}$ (b) $d = t - 36$ (c) $d = t + 36$ (d) $d = 36t$

118. A hollow sphere of external and internal diameters of 10 cm and 6 cm, respectively, is melted and made into another solid in the shape of a right circular cone of base diameter 10 cm. Find the height of the cone.

(a) 13.68 cm (b) 16.68 cm (c) 14.68 cm (d) 15.68 cm

119. The area of a sector of a circle having radius 14 cm is 231 cm^2. Find the degree measure of the corresponding central angle. $\left(\text{Use } \pi = \frac{22}{7}\right)$

(a) 140° (b) 135° (c) 150° (d) 125°

120. If $(a-18)^2 + (b-12)^2 + (c-6)^2 = 0$, then find the value of $(a+b+c)^{\frac{1}{2}}$.

(a) ± 3 (b) ± 2 (c) ± 4 (d) ± 6

121. The below table shows the number of trees of 3 different fruits, planted during 2018-2022 Study the table carefully and answer the question based on it.

Year	Jackfruit	Mango	Butter Fruit
2018	35000	40000	55000
2019	38000	48000	58000
2020	42000	52000	62000
2021	45000	55000	65000
2022	48000	58000	68000

What was the percentage increase in the number of mango trees planted in 2020 compared to the number of mango trees planted in 2018?

(a) 30% (b) 17.5% (c) 23.08% (d) 15%

122. Study the given table and answer the question that follows.

Category	2019	2020
Raw material	5000	6000
Power and fuel	10000	12000
Salary and wages	8000	12000
Advertising	10000	20000

Find the difference between the least percentage increase and the highest percentage increase in year 2019-2020.

(a) 50% (b) 60% (c) 70% (d) 80%

123. Simplify: $(4+4)\times(4 \div 4)\times(4\times 4)$.

(a) 124 (b) 130 (c) 144 (d) 128

124. The sum of two numbers is 28 and the sum of their squares is 528. Find the square root of the product of both the numbers.

(a) $4\sqrt{2}$ (b) $6\sqrt{2}$ (c) $2\sqrt{2}$ (d) $8\sqrt{2}$

125. A train covers a distance of 850 m in 45 sec. Travelling at the same speed, how many kilometres will the train cover in an hour?

(a) 69 (b) 67.2 (c) 67.5 (d) 68

126. Applied to a bill for ₹ 1000, what is the difference between a discount of 40% and two successive discounts of 36% and 4%?

(a) ₹ 154 (b) ₹ 144 (c) ₹ 14.40 (d) ₹ 15.40

127. Ronak and Riya can do a work in 12 and 18 days, respectively. They worked together for six days and then Ronak left. Find the time taken by Riya to complete the work.

(a) 3 days (b) 5 days (c) 6 days (d) 7 days

128. Simplify the following expression.

$(6+6 \text{ of } 5 \div 5) \div 6 \text{ of } 5 + (24 \div 2 \text{ of } 3 - 6 \text{ of } 5 + 4)$

(a) $-26\frac{2}{5}$ (b) $-21\frac{3}{5}$ (c) $-17\frac{2}{5}$ (d) $-23\frac{1}{5}$

129. A certain sum of money is given at a certain rate of simple interest for 4 years. Had it been given at 11% higher rate for the same time, it would have fetched ₹ 1320 more. Find the sum (in ₹).

(a) 4580 (b) 3000 (c) 2500 (d) 3240

130. A person covers 11 km with a speed of 7 km/h, 25 km with a speed of 10 km/h and 30 km with a speed of 20 km/h. What is the average speed of the person?

(a) $11\frac{9}{13}$ km/h (b) $11\frac{7}{13}$ km/h (c) $11\frac{11}{13}$ km/h (d) $11\frac{10}{13}$ km/h

131. If four distinct positive numbers, a, b, c and d, in the order given are in proportion, then which of the following options is not correct?

(a) b, a, d and c, in the order given are in proportion.
(b) c, d, b and a, in the order given are in proportion.
(c) a, c, b and d, in the order given are in proportion.
(d) d, c, b and a, in the order given are in proportion.

132. $(1-\cos^2 A)\sec^2 A$ is equal to

(a) $\text{cosec}^2 A$ (b) $\tan^2 A$
(c) $\cos^2 A \cdot \cot^2 A$ (d) $\cot^2 A$

133. Shiya invests ₹ 153000, which is 30% of her annual income, in mutual funds. What is her monthly income (in ₹)?

(a) 45800 (b) 42500
(c) 55600 (d) 52300

134. In a class, there are 60 students. The average weight of the entire class is 42 kg. If there are 36 boys in the class and the average weight of all the boys is 50 kg, then what is the average weight (in kg) of all the girls?

(a) 32 (b) 30 (c) 36 (d) 34

135. Simplify the given expression.

$1000 \times 100 - 1000 + 4000 \div 200$

(a) 99235 (b) 99980
(c) 99020 (d) 99999

136. If $x - y = 25$ and $xy = 444$, compute the value of $x^3 - y^3$.

(a) 28495 (b) 48925
(c) 42985 (d) 26725

137. A cylinder has a radius of 7 cm and the area of its curved surface is 396 cm^2. The volume of the cylinder is

(a) 1381 cm^3 (b) 1391 cm^3
(c) 1386 cm^3 (d) 1396 cm^3

138. Two towns *P* and *Q* are 275 km apart. A motorcycle rider starts from *P* towards *Q* at 10:00 am at the speed of 25 km/h. Another rider starts from *Q* towards *P* at 12 noon on the same day at the speed of 20 km/h. At what time will they cross each other?

(a) 1:15 pm (b) 3:00 pm
(c) 4:30 pm (d) 5:00 pm

139. If $4\sin^2\theta = 3(1+\cos\theta), 0° < \theta < 90°$, then what is the value of

$\sqrt{15}\tan\theta + \frac{4}{\sqrt{15}}\sin\theta + 2\sec\theta$?

(a) 8 (b) 24 (c) $4\sqrt{15}$ (d) $\frac{8}{\sqrt{15}}$

140. Study the given table and answer the question that follows. The Table shows the number of eggs produced in five farms.

Year	Farm				
	P	Q	R	S	T
2010	1020	1418	1630	1740	1580
2011	1260	1390	1460	1530	1620
2012	1120	1765	1480	1515	1640
2013	1465	1555	1746	1418	1545

What is the respective ratio of the dozens of eggs produced by farm P to farm T in the year 2011?

(a) 7 : 5 (b) 5 : 7 (c) 9 : 7 (d) 7 : 9

141. A spherical box has surface area 528 cm^2. Find the radius of the spherical box.

(a) $\sqrt{35}$ cm (b) $\sqrt{42}$ cm
(c) $\sqrt{29}$ cm (d) $\sqrt{37}$ cm

142. What is the length (in cm) of chord *PQ* in a circle with a radius of 7 cm, where a diameter *AB* and non-diameter chord *PQ* intersect perpendicularly at point C, and the ratio of *AC* to *BC* is 4 : 3?

(a) $6\sqrt{3}$ (b) $2\sqrt{3}$ (c) $4\sqrt{3}$ (d) $8\sqrt{3}$

143. A man travels 1200 km by train at 80 km/h, 1600 km by ship at 40 km/h, 1000 km by plane at 400 km/h, and 200 km by car at 50 km/h. What is the average speed for the entire distance? (rounded off to 2 decimal places)

(a) 65.04 km/h (b) 72.40 km/h
(c) 68.14 km/h (d) 75.40 km/h

144. Simplify the given expression.

$[\{9 \times 81 + (142 \div 2)\} + 350 - 155 + 5] \div [(25 \times 25) - 125]$

(a) 1 (b) −1 (c) −2 (d) 2

145. Study the given table and answer the question that follows. The table below shows the number of people who responded to a survey about their favourite style of music

Age	25 – 30	31 – 50	51 +
Classical	2	9	16
Pop	10	16	8
Hip-Hop	4	7	6
Rock	14	17	14
Ambient	7	13	20
Total	37	62	64

What percentage of respondents aged (31 – 50) indicated a favourite style other than Pop music (rounded off to 2 decimal places)?

(a) 82.39% (b) 76.25%
(c) 74.19% (d) 78.20%

146. Manish, Nakul and Pintoo alone can complete a certain work in 21days, 28 days and 15 days, respectively. Manish and Pintoo started the work together while Nakul joined them after 5 days and worked with them till the completion of the work. For how many days did Nakul work?

(a) $5\frac{1}{2}$ (b) $2\frac{6}{7}$ (c) $2\frac{1}{2}$ (d) $3\frac{1}{2}$

147. If $\tan\theta + \cot\theta = 6$, then the value of $\tan^2\theta + \cot^2\theta$ is

(a) 20 (b) 24
(c) 34 (d) 22

148. If the sides of a triangle are 7, 12 and *x*, and *x* is an integer, then find the number of possible values of *x*.

(a) 13 (b) 14 (c) 12 (d) 15

149. Ramnarayan's salary was reduced by $3\frac{1}{8}$% and then the reduced Salary was increased by $7\frac{2}{5}$%. By what percentage (rounded off to two decimal places) is his new salary more/ less as compared to his original salary?

(a) 4.04% less (b) 4.04% more
(c) 3.03% less (d) 3.03% more

150. On the tag price, a seller offers a 10% discount and a cashback of ₹ 250. He still earns 10% profit. If the cost price is ₹ 1200, then the tag price (rounded off to 2 decimal places) is ₹ ....

(a) 1774.44 (b) 1777.44
(c) 1744.44 (d) 1447.44

Part IV

English Comprehension

151. Select the option that can be used as a one-word substitute for the the given group of words.

A place for storage of arms and ammunition

(a) Monastery (b) Scullery
(c) Arsenal (d) Mint

152. Identify the incorrectly spelt word in the given sentence.

Generousity is a godly feature among many individuals on the Earth.

(a) Generousity (b) feature
(c) individuals (d) godly

153. Select the most appropriate option with correct usage of the preposition to substitute the underlined segment in the given sentence.
The Centre of Excellence for Data Analytics (CEDA) provides quality data analytic services to <u>various government departments on all levels</u> as well as to public sector units at the Centre and in States.
(a) various government departments through all levels
(b) various government departments from all levels
(c) various government departments in all levels
(d) various government departments at all levels

154. Select the most appropriate idiom from the options to replace the underlined segment in the given sentence.
After his business failed, he <u>had to reduce spending</u> and adjust to a frugal lifestyle.
(a) tighten his belt
(b) hit the nail on the head
(c) kick the bucket
(d) let the cat out of the bag

155. Select the most appropriate meaning of the given idiom.
Sacred cow
(a) Harmful
(b) Hateful
(c) Unquestionable
(d) Interrogate

156. Select the option that can be used as a one-word substitute for the given group of words.
One who does not believe in God
(a) Atheist (b) Reverent
(c) Catholic (d) Priest

157. Select the incorrect form of the verb.
(a) Struck (b) Stricken
(c) Strike (d) Strucken

158. Select the most appropriate option that can substitute the underlined segment in the given sentence. If there is no need to substitute it, select 'No substitution'.
In yesterday's fire accident, <u>her feets are</u> burnt badly.
(a) No substitution
(b) her feet was
(c) her feet were
(d) her foots were

159. Select the most appropriate meaning of the given idiom.
Black sheep
(a) Intelligent (b) Disreputable
(c) Miscreant (d) Naive

160. Select the sentence that uses the given idiom correctly.
Have your head in the clouds
(a) He had his head in the clouds during an important meeting.
(b) She had her head in the clouds by wearing a cloud-shaped hat.
(c) The pilot had his head in the clouds while flying a plane.
(d) They had their heads in the clouds by looking up at the sky during a meteor shower.

161. Select the most appropriate antonym of the given word.
Upright
(a) Immoral (b) Brave
(c) Ethical (d) Stout

162. Select the most appropriate synonym for the word in brackets to fill in the blank.
Emotional stimulation provides the necessary ... for creative imagination. (fecundity)
(a) force (b) freedom
(c) fulcrum (d) fertility

163. Parts of the following sentence have been given as options. Select the option that contains a spelling error.
My strength is as the strenght of ten because my heart is pure.
(a) as the strenght
(b) of ten because
(c) My strength is
(d) my heart is pure

164. Select the word segment that can substitute the bracketed word segment correctly and complete the sentence meaningfully.
The Minister promised to provide free laptops to the public if his (party came in power).
(a) he comes to a party
(b) he loses the election
(c) party forms the government
(d) party loses the election

165. Select the most appropriate option that can substitute the underlined word in the given idiom.
A <u>goose's</u> eye view
(a) hornet's (b) bird's
(c) fool's (d) dog's

166. Select the sentence that has the correct use of words and spellings from the options given below.
(a) The delicious arauma of freshly baked cookies waftad through the kitchen, making mouths water.
(b) The delicious arauma of freshely baked cookes wafted through the kitchen, making mouths water.
(c) The delicius aroma of freshely baked cookies wafted through the kitchen, making mouths water.
(d) The delicious aroma of freshly baked cookies wafted through the kitchen, making mouths water.

167. Select the most appropriate option that can substitute the underlined segment in the given sentence. If there is no need to substitute it, select 'No substitution'.
This is the group of leaders <u>in whom the ruling government</u> has placed its trust.
(a) No substitution
(b) in who the ruling government
(c) with who the ruling government
(d) on who the ruling government

168. Select the most appropriate idiom for the underlined part in the given sentence.
Amar was left <u>in a difficult situation</u> by his business partners.
(a) head and shoulders above
(b) heart and soul
(c) hard and fast
(d) high and dry

169. Select the option that can be used as a one-word substitute for the given group of words.
The patronage bestowed in consideration of family relationships and not of merit.
(a) Egotism (b) Neologism
(c) Mannerism (d) Nepotism

170. Select the incorrectly spelt word.
(a) Passage (b) Supremecy
(c) Reconsidered (d) Prevention

171. Based on the situation in the sentence, select the most appropriate idiom for the underlined segment.
He always takes up <u>difficult tasks-those which are beyond his capabilities.</u>
(a) Pull someone's leg
(b) Miss the boat
(c) No pain no gain
(d) Bite off more than you can chew

172. Select the most appropriate antonym of the underlined word.
The arrival of spring brings an ebullient feeling as flowers bloom and the weather warms.
(a) clamant (b) deciduous
(c) rude (d) weary

173. Select the correctly spelt word.
(a) Refridgerator (b) Registration
(c) Litrature (d) Allegater

174. Select the most appropriate segment to substitute the underlined words in the given sentence.
You have tears, prepare to shed them now.
(a) If you have tears
(b) Unless you have tears
(c) Until you have tears
(d) Yet you have tears

175. Select the most appropriate synonym of the given word.
Bind
(a) Disengage (b) Amuse
(c) Secure (d) Flourish

176. Select the most appropriate meaning of the given idiom.
When pigs fly
(a) Something that will get completed
(b) Something that will never happen
(c) Something that will never last-long
(d) Something that will never deviate

177. Identify the error in the verb form in the following sentence and choose the correct sentence from the given options (Present Tense).
The committee work diligently to ensure fair and unbiased decision.
(a) The committee has work diligently to ensure fair and unbiased decision.
(b) The committee is work diligently to ensure fair and unbiased decision.
(c) The committee works diligently to ensure fair and unbiased decision.
(d) The committee worked diligently to ensure fair and unbiased decision.

178. The following sentence has been divided into four segments. Identify the segment that has a grammatical error.
Soldiers in the Indian Armed Forces are / trained never to / fight cowardly.
(a) fight cowardly
(b) Soldiers in
(c) the Indian Armed Forces are
(d) trained never to

179. Three segments of the following sentence have been underlined and given as options. One of them may contain an error. Select the option that contains the error. If you don't find any error, mark 'No error' as your answer.
When my father will come, I will make sure that I discuss the possibilities of a new business venture with him.
(a) When my father will come
(b) I discuss the possibilities
(c) No error
(d) I will make sure

180. Select the most appropriate antonym of the given word.
Aggravate
(a) Humiliate (b) Ignorant
(c) Exasperate (d) Alleviate

181. Select the most appropriate antonym of the given word.
Tight
(a) Slack (b) Comfortable
(c) Resilient (d) Cordial

182. Select the option that can be used as a one-word substitute for the given group of words.
A doubtful look or examination of one's motives.
(a) Introspect (b) Suspect
(c) Retrospect (d) Circumspect

183. Select the most appropriate antonym of the underlined word in the following sentence.
The government is proposing to incinerate cattle carcasses at many sites, some of which are in populated areas.
(a) oxidise (b) extinguish
(c) blaze (d) combust

184. Select the option that can be used as a one-word substitute for the given group of words.
Dwarfed varieties of trees and shrubs in pots.
(a) Botanical (b) Bonsai
(c) Orchard (d) Bonafide

185. Select the option that can be used as a one-word substitute for the given group of words.
Vivacious and enthusiastic
(a) Effervescent
(b) Introverted
(c) Brazen
(d) Rowdy

186. Select the most appropriate antonym of the underlined word.
The brave knight set out to vanquish the fearsome dragon and protect the kingdom from its menace.
(a) measure (b) instill
(c) engage (d) liberate

187. Select the option that can be used as a one-word substitute for the given group of words.
Consonance of sounds
(a) Woodwinds (b) Troupe
(c) Orchestration (d) Symphony

188. Select the incorrectly spelt word.
(a) Dissapear (b) Vicinity
(c) Entrepreneur (d) Supersede

189. Select the option that expresses the meaning of the underlined segment.
Partly, it may be a desire to stop emotions in front of strangers.
(a) smash (b) quiet
(c) quell (d) put out

190. Select the most appropriate option that can substitute the underlined segment in the given sentence.
During the preparation for competitive exams, Meena avoided going to parties.
(a) whispered a secret
(b) fired a cracker
(c) cracked a joke
(d) steered clear of

Directions (Q. Nos. 191-195) *In the following passage, some words have been deleted. Read the passage carefully and select the most appropriate option to fill in each blank.*

Mowgli is a ...(1)... haracter from Rudyard Kipling's classic 'The Jungle Book' raised by wolves in the Indian jungle, Mowgli ...(2)... thrilling adventures and forms friendships with various animals, like Bagheera (the panther) and Baloo (the bear). Throughout the story, he ...(3)... the challenges of living among both humans and jungle creatures, all while learning essential life lessons. The Jungle Book continues to ...(4)... readers of all ages with its ...(5)... portrayal of Mowgli's remarkable journey of self-discovery and the beauty of the natural world.

191. Select the most appropriate option to fill in blank number 1.
(a) scorned (b) beloved
(c) despised (d) overlooked

192. Select the most appropriate option to fill in blank number 2.
(a) experiences (b) enunciates
(c) excavates (d) exaggerates

193. Select the most appropriate option to fill in blank number 3.
(a) coordinates (b) navigates
(c) customises (d) procures

194. Select the most appropriate option to fill in blank number 4.
(a) captivate (b) register
(c) magnify (d) manipulate

195. Select the most appropriate option to fill in blank number 5.
(a) surprising (b) ordinary
(c) enchanting (d) abnormal

Directions (Q. Nos. 196-200) *Read the given passage and answer the questions that follow.*

On 3rd September, 2016, a magnitude 5.8 earthquake struck just North-West of Pawnee, Oklahoma, causing moderate to severe damages in buildings near the epicentre. It was the largest ever recorded in the state.

The Pawnee earthquake followed the dramatic increase of seismic events in the Central United States beginning in 2009, associated with the increase of underground wastewater disposal by oil and gas operators. This and other events in the area raised public concerns and led governmental agencies to shut-down injection wells and establish new regulations regarding wastewater injections.

While, human-caused earthquakes have been documented for more than a century, their increasing number reported worldwide has drawn much scientific, social and political attention. Such earthquakes are related to industrial activities such as mining, construction of water dams, injection of liquids such as wastewater and carbon dioxide and extractions associated with oil and gas exploitation.

With the ever-increasing demand for energy and mineral supplies worldwide, the number of Human-caused earthquakes is expected to rise in the upcoming years. Some of the largest and more destructive earthquakes of the past few years have been related to man-made activities, such as the 2008 magnitude 7.9 Wenchuan (China) earthquake and the 2015 magnitude 7.8 Nepal earthquake.

In most of the cases, industrial activities do not induce earthquakes. But this becomes problematic when such activities are close to active faults. In this case, even small stresses underground caused by man-made activities can destabilise faults, inducing earthquakes.

196. Human-caused earthquakes are related to ....
(a) space expedition
(b) artificial intelligence
(c) population explosion
(d) industrial activities

197. What is the tone of the speaker?
(a) Cynical (b) Dogmatic
(c) Apologetic (d) Contemptuous

198. Select the most suitable word from the passage which means 'create'.
(a) increase (b) deplete
(c) destabilise (d) seismic

199. Why does the passage observe that more human-caused earthquakes are expected?
(a) It is due to the fragility of the Earth.
(b) It is due to the Greenhouse Effect.
(c) It is due to the over soil erosion.
(d) It is due to the demand for energy and minerals.

200. Identify the most suitable title for the passage.
(a) Man vs Man
(b) Industrial Threats
(c) How Safe Are We on This Earth
(d) Seismic Depression

Know Correct Answers

1. (b)	2. (b)	3. (c)	4. (a)	5. (d)	6. (b)	7. (d)	8. (b)	9. (c)	10. (a)
11. (c)	12. (a)	13. (d)	14. (a)	15. (b)	16. (b)	17. (b)	18. (a)	19. (c)	20. (d)
21. (b)	22. (c)	23. (c)	24. (d)	25. (b)	26. (d)	27. (a)	28. (a)	29. (a)	30. (d)
31. (a)	32. (d)	33. (a)	34. (c)	35. (d)	36. (a)	37. (b)	38. (d)	39. (a)	40. (c)
41. (c)	42. (d)	43. (a)	44. (b)	45. (d)	46. (a)	47. (b)	48. (b)	49. (a)	50. (c)
51. (b)	52. (d)	53. (a)	54. (d)	55. (b)	56. (b)	57. (c)	58. (c)	59. (b)	60. (c)
61. (a)	62. (d)	63. (b)	64. (a)	65. (b)	66. (c)	67. (c)	68. (c)	69. (d)	70. (c)
71. (d)	72. (c)	73. (a)	74. (d)	75. (a)	76. (b)	77. (a)	78. (b)	79. (d)	80. (c)
81. (a)	82. (d)	83. (c)	84. (d)	85. (c)	86. (d)	87. (b)	88. (c)	89. (d)	90. (a)
91. (d)	92. (d)	93. (d)	94. (d)	95. (c)	96. (a)	97. (d)	98. (b)	99. (a)	100. (d)
101. (d)	102. (c)	103. (d)	104. (d)	105. (c)	106. (d)	107. (d)	108. (d)	109. (c)	110. (b)
111. (c)	112. (a)	113. (b)	114. (c)	115. (d)	116. (a)	117. (d)	118. (d)	119. (b)	120. (d)
121. (a)	122. (d)	123. (d)	124. (d)	125. (d)	126. (c)	127 (a)	128. (b)	129. (b)	130. (c)
131. (b)	132. (b)	133. (b)	134. (b)	135. (c)	136. (b)	137 (c)	138. (d)	139. (b)	140. (d)
141. (b)	142. (d)	143. (a)	144. (d)	145. (c)	146. (b)	147. (c)	148. (a)	149. (b)	150. (c)
151. (c)	152. (a)	153. (d)	154. (a)	155. (c)	156. (a)	157. (d)	158. (c)	159. (b)	160. (a)
161. (a)	162. (d)	163. (a)	164. (c)	165. (b)	166. (d)	167. (a)	168. (d)	169. (d)	170. (b)
171. (d)	172. (d)	173. (b)	174. (a)	175. (c)	176. (b)	177. (c)	178. (a)	179. (a)	180. (d)
181. (a)	182. (d)	183. (b)	184. (b)	185. (a)	186. (d)	187. (d)	188. (a)	189. (c)	190. (d)
191. (b)	192. (a)	193. (b)	194. (a)	195. (c)	196. (d)	197. (a)	198. (c)	199. (d)	200. (b)

Answer & Solutions

1. (b) According to the statements,

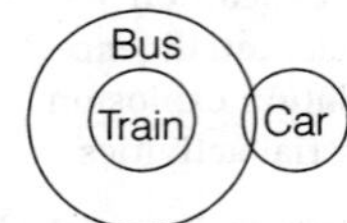

Conclusions I. (✗) II. (✓)

Hence, only Conclusion II follows.

2. (b) Logic : First number − First digit = Third number

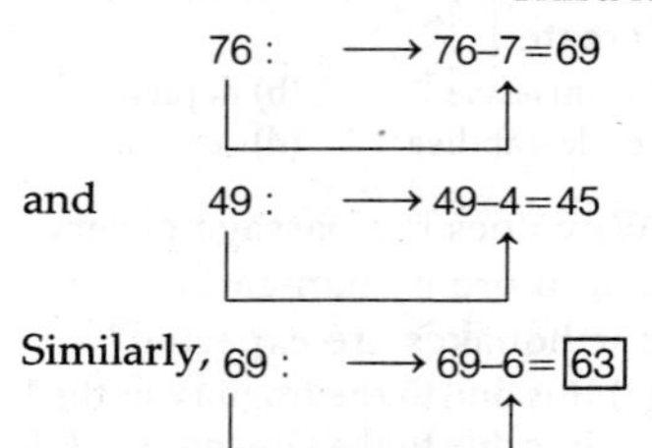

3. (c) As,

H E M A N T
8 5 13 1 14 20
× × × × × ×
3 3 3 3 3 3
24 −15 −39 −3 −42 −60

and

V I N A Y
22 9 14 1 25
× × × × ×
3 3 3 3 3
66 − 27− 42 − 3 −75

Similarly,

M O H A N
13 15 8 1 14
× × × × ×
3 3 3 3 3
39 − 45− 24 − 3 − 42

4. (a) As,

M A R C H
−1 +1 −1 +1 −1
L B Q D G

and

T A X A S
−1 +1 −1 +1 −1
S B W B R

Similarly,

P I E C E
−1 +1 −1 +1 −1
O J D D D

5. (d) As per the Venn diagram,

As, Tiger, Snake and Elephant all are different from one another.

6. (b) Option (b) is the correct mirror image of the given figure, when the mirror is placed at MN.

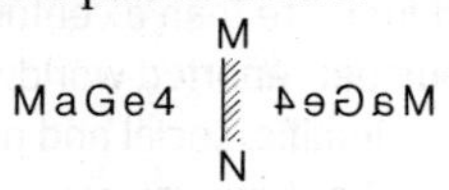

M
MaGe4 | ⅎeƏaM
N

7. (d) As,

N A P E
−1 −1 −1 −1
M Z O D

and

D U L L
−1 −1 −1 −1
C T K K

Similarly,

K I N D
−1 −1 −1 −1
J H M C

8. (b) The pattern in the given series as follows,

−32, −8, −2, **−1/2**, −1/8
÷4 ÷4 ÷4 ÷4

9. (c) Given equation,

$$47 \div 3 - 126 \times 6 + 18 = ?$$

After interchanging the signs, '+' and '−' and '×' and '÷', we get

$$47 \times 3 + 126 \div 6 - 18 = ?$$
$$? = 141 + 21 - 18$$
$$? = 162 - 18 = 144$$

10. (a) According to the question,

Position I ⟶	9	3	5
	Common	Opposite	Opposite
Position II ⟶	9	④	②

∴ 4 is opposite to 3.

11. (c) The pattern of the series is as follows,

78 86 258 322 **1610**
+8 ×3 +64 ×5

12. (a) According to the question, pattern follow as,

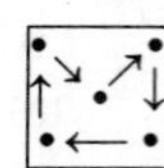

Hence, option (a) is the answer.

13. (d) According to the question,

[+ = Male, − = Female]

P^+ ←Father— ; Son ↓
M^- ⟷(Couple) N^+ ⟵(Brother) S^+ ⟵(Brother) T

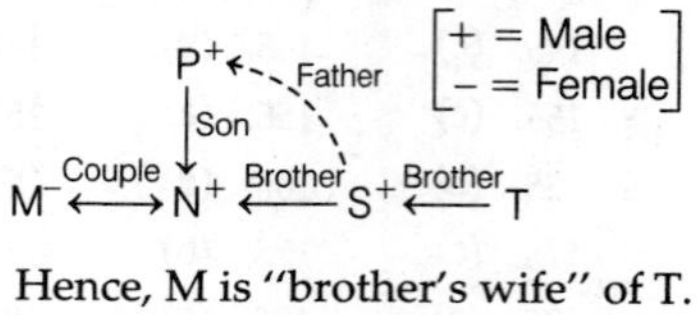

Hence, M is "brother's wife" of T.

14. (a) Option (a) figure in which the given figure is embedded.

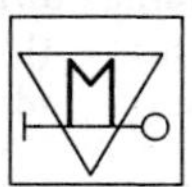

15. (b) The pattern of the series is as follows,

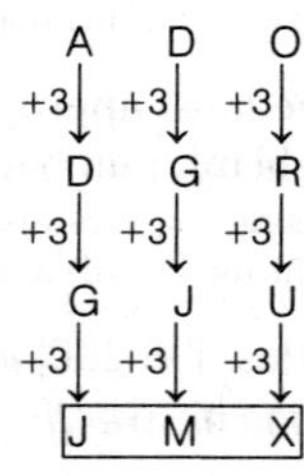

16. (b) Given equation,

$$712 \div 6 - 15 \times 3 + 15 = ?$$

After interchanging the signs, '+' and '−', '×' and '÷', we get

$$? = 712 \times 6 + 15 \div 3 - 15$$
$$? = 4272 + 5 - 15 = 4262$$

17. (b) As, H E N = 9

Number of letters = 3

$\Rightarrow$ $(3)^2 = 9$

and A F T E R = 25

Number of letters = 5

$\Rightarrow$ $(5)^2 = 25$

Similarly,

SMALLEST = 64

Number of letters = 8

$\Rightarrow$ $(8)^2 = \boxed{64}$

18. (a) As,

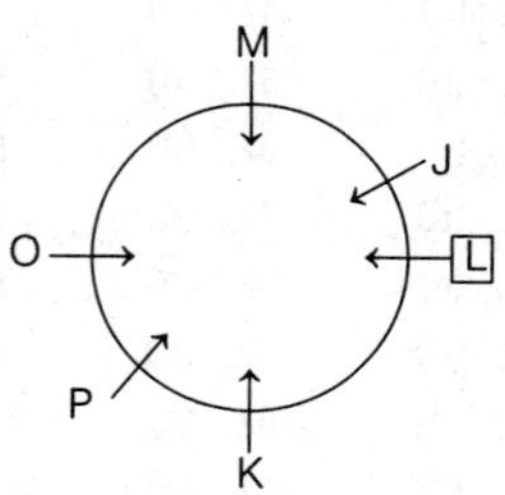

Hence, L is sitting immediate right of K.

19. (c) The pattern of the series is as follows,

324	361	400	441	484	**529**
↓	↓	↓	↓	↓	↓
$(18)^2$	$(19)^2$	$(20)^2$	$(21)^2$	$(22)^2$	$(23)^2$

20. (d) According to the question,

$20\times5-7\div4+3=?$

After interchanging the signs,

$+\Rightarrow-$	$-\Rightarrow\times$
$\times\Rightarrow\div$	$\div\Rightarrow+$

$? = 20\div5\times7+4-3$

$\Rightarrow \quad ? = 28+4-3=29$

21. (b) According to the question,

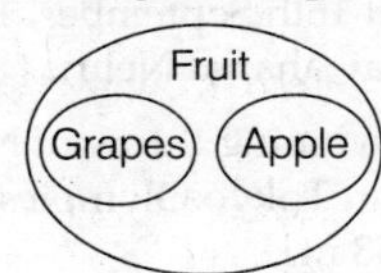

Both Grapes and Apple are different type of fruits.

22. (c) Given equation,

$$71+32\times2-63\div7+\left[(81)^{\frac{1}{4}}\right]\times3-22=113$$

After interchange the numbers 3 and 7.

$$71+32\times2-63\div3+\left[(81)^{\frac{1}{4}}\right]\times7-22$$

$$=71+64-21+3\times7-22$$

$$=135-21+21-22=113$$

LHS = RHS

23. (c) As, (23 – 27)

$$23+27=\frac{50}{2+3}=\frac{50}{5}=10$$

Similarly, (15 – 45)

$$15+45=\frac{60}{1+5}=\frac{60}{6}=10$$

24. (d) The pattern in the given series is as follows,

125 → 150 → 177 → 207 → 242 → [284]

+25, +27, +30, +35, +42

+2, +3, +5, +7

25. (b) As per the English dictionary order,

Incapacity → Incense → Incentive → Inception → Incest
(4) (3) (5) (2) (1)

$\Rightarrow$ 4, 3, 5, 2, 1

26. (d) According to the question,

F⁺ ←Couple→ G⁻
G⁻ —Mother→ H⁺
H⁺ ←Brother→ I⁺
I⁺ —Father→ J

[+ = Male, – = Female]

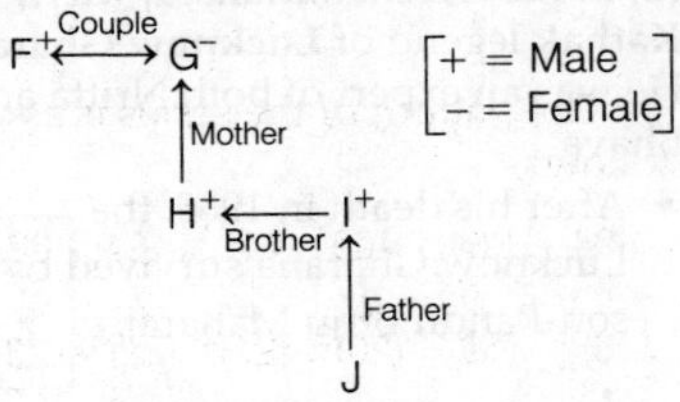

Hence, F is father's father of J.

27. (a) As,

B E A M
–1 +1 –1 +1
A F Z N

and

B I L L
–1 +1 –1 +1
A J K M

Similarly,

W E L L
–1 +1 –1 +1
[V F K M]

28. (a) As, 20 : 30 ($20\times\frac{3}{2}=30$)

and 30 : 45 ($30\times\frac{3}{2}=45$)

Similarly, [80] : 120 ($80\times\frac{3}{2}=120$)

29. (a) Pattern of the series as follows,

R D L S
+4 +7 –10 –13
V K B F
+4 +7 –10 –13
[Z R R S]
+4 +7 –10 –13
D Y H F
+4 +7 –10 –13
H F X S

30. (d) As per the question,

Position I A [C] [B]

Position II A [R] [S]

$\therefore$ A is opposite to opposite remaining face T.

31. (a) Option (a) is the correct mirror image of the given figure when the mirror is placed at MN.

M
MdF37A ‖ A\ƐꟻbM
N

32. (d) As per the English dictionary order.

Dingiest → Dingling → Dinkier → Dinnerware → Dinosaurs → Dinucleotide
(2) (6) (5) (1) (3) (4)

$\Rightarrow$ 2, 6, 5, 1, 3, 4.

33. (a) As, 15 : 20 ($15\times\frac{4}{3}=20$)

and 6 : 8 ($6\times\frac{4}{3}=8$)

Similarly, [9] : 12 ($9\times\frac{4}{3}=12$)

34. (c) According to the question,

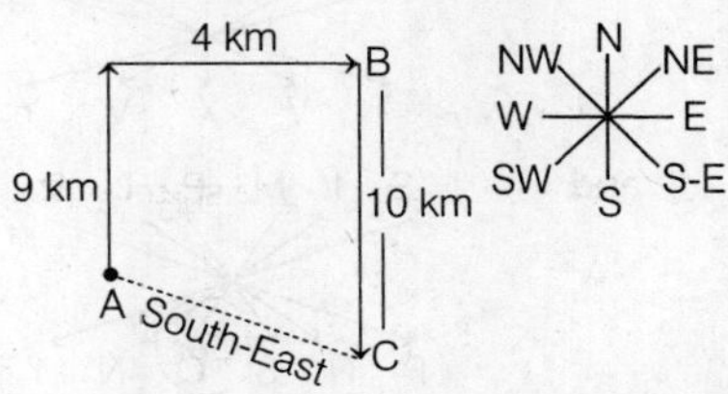

Hence, direction of C with respect to A is South-East.

35. (d) In the given series,

Pattern follow as,

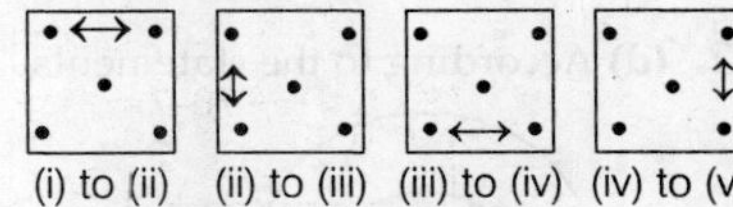

Hence, option (d) is the correct answer.

36. (a) As, (54, 51, 48)

$54+48=102\div2=51$

and (46, 40, 34)

$46+34=80\div2=40$

Similarly, (58, 47, 36)

$58+36=94\div2=47$

37. (b) The pattern of the given series is as follows,

I —+3→ L —+3→ O —+3→ [R]

C —+4→ G —+4→ K —+4→ [O]

E —+5→ J —+5→ O —+5→ [T]

38. (d) According to the question, the sequence of folding a paper and the manner in which the folding paper is cut is shown in the figures, option (d) would the paper look when unfolded.

39. (a) As per the question,

$53-48\times6\div9+11$

After interchange the signs, '+' and '–', '×' and '÷', we get

$? = 53+48\div6\times9-11$

$\Rightarrow \quad ? = 53+72-11$

$\Rightarrow \quad ? = 125-11=114$

40. (c) As per the question,

17I(11L8J4) L148K4J22=?

After interchange the signs,

$I\Rightarrow\times$	$K\Rightarrow\div$
$J\Rightarrow+$	$L\Rightarrow-$

$? = 17\times(11-8+4)-148\div4+22$

$? = 17\times7-37+22$

$? = 119-37+22=104$

41. **(c)** As, T R U T H (+5, +4, +3, +2, +1) → I V X V Y

and S I M P L E (+6, +5, +4, +3, +2, +1) → F N S Q N Y

Similarly, A R O U N D (+6, +5, +4, +3, +2, +1) → E P X S W G

42. **(d)** According to the statements,

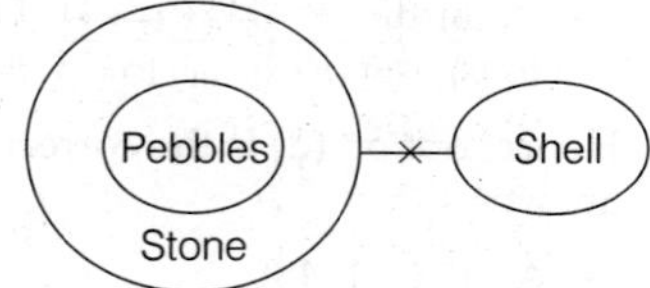

Conclusions

I. (✗) II. (✓)

Hence, only Conclusion II follows.

43. **(a)** As,

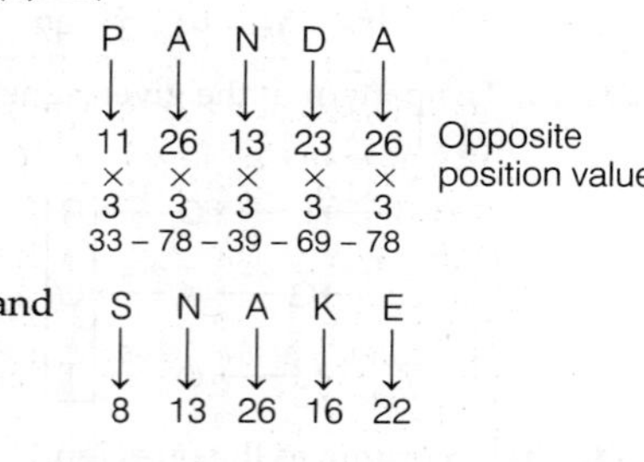

Similarly,

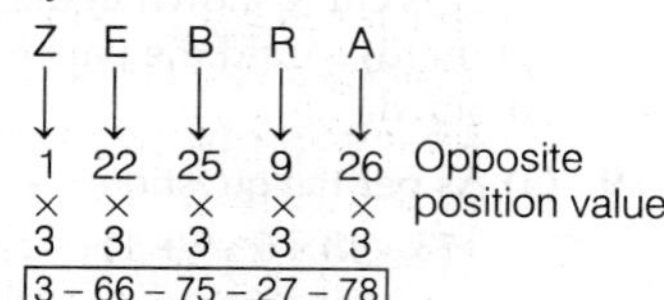

44. **(b)** As, A C I D (–3, +1, –3, +1) → X D F E

and H A N D (–3, +1, –3, +1) → E B K E

Similarly, Z E S T (–3, +1, –3, +1) → W F P U

45. **(d)** According to the question, the sequence of folding a paper and the manner in which the folded paper is cut is shown in the figures. option (d) would the paper look when unfolded.

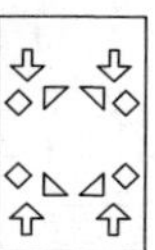

46. **(a)** Given equation,

342A2C125B1D43 = ?

After interchange the signs,

A ⇒ ÷	B ⇒ ×
C ⇒ +	D ⇒ –

$? = 342 \div 2 + 125 \times 1 - 43$

$? = 171 + 125 - 43$

$? = 296 - 43 = 253$

47. **(b)** The pattern of the figure series is as follows,

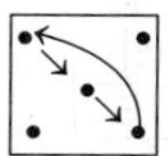

In fig. (i) to (ii) and fig. (iii) to (iv)

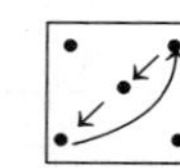

In fig. (ii) to (iii) and fig. (iv) to (v)

Hence, option (b) is the answer.

48. **(b)** Option (b) is the correct mirror image of the given figure when the mirror is placed at MN.

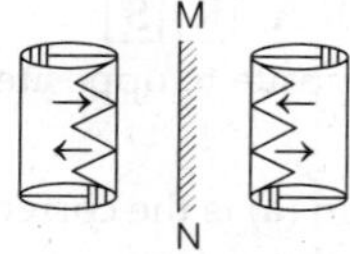

49. **(a)** According to the question,

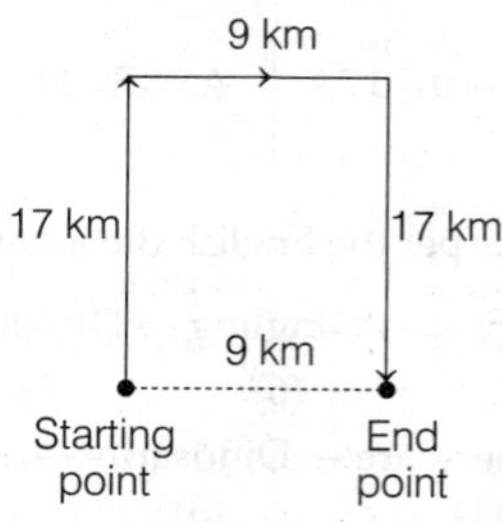

Hence, she is 9 km far from the starting point.

50. **(c)** As per the question,

Option (a), $F \xrightarrow{+6} L \xrightarrow{-3} I$

Option (b), $R \xrightarrow{+6} X \xrightarrow{-3} U$;

And option (d), $I \xrightarrow{+6} O \xrightarrow{-3} L$

But, option (c), $M \xrightarrow{+6} S \xrightarrow{\boxed{-4}} O$

51. **(b)** **Hypostome** is a hairpin-like structure that serves to anchor and stabilise the tick's mouthparts to its host's skin and to channel the exchange of fluids is also called the maxilla, radula or labium.

52. **(d)** Atal Bihari Vajpayee Institute of Mountaineering and Allied Sports situated in **Manali**, Himachal Pradesh. Founded 16th September, 1961 by Pandit Jawaharlal Nehru.

53. **(a)** The winning throw of Neeraj Chopra in Tokyo Olympics, 2020 was 87.58 m.

- Neeraj Chopra is First Indian Olympian to win a Gold medal in athletics and the first post-independence Indian Olympic medalist in athletics.
- Neeraj Chopra won silver medal at Paris Olympic 2024.

54. **(d)** Article 21 of Fundamental Rights is related to Protection of Life and Personal Liberty.

- No person shall be deprived of his life or personal liberty except according to procedure established by law.

55. **(b)** Mahatma Gandhi National Rural Employment Guarantee Act was passed in 2005.

- The Act gives legal guarantee of a hundred days of wage employment in a financial year to adult members of a rural household who demand employment and are willing to do unskilled manual work.

56. **(b)** Exporting is the most traditional mode of entering into the foreign market.

- It is the direct sale of goods and/or services in another country.

57. **(c)** Lovlina Borgohain won the Bronze medal in women's boxing in Tokyo Olympics, 2020.

- She is the third Indian boxer after Mary Kom and Vijender Singh to bag an Olympic medal.

58. **(c)** Pandit Acchan Maharaj was a **Kathak** legend of **Lucknow Gharana**. He was an expert of both Nritta and Bhava.

- After his death in 1960, the Lucknow Gharana survived by his son-Pandit Birju Maharaj.

- Pandit Birju Maharaj was an Indian dancer, composer, singer and exponent of the Banaras 'Kalka-Bindadin' Gharana of Kathak dance in India.
- He was the recipient of numerous awards for his contributions to the performing arts, including the Padma Vibhushan in 1986.

59. **(b)** The Supreme Court of India consists of 33 Judges and Chief Judges of India appointed by the President of India.

- As of March 2025, the Chief Justice of India is Sanjiv Khanna.
- He is the 51st CJI of India.

60. **(c)** Jyeshthoputro received the 67th National Film Award for Best Music Direction.

- More Awards : Best Lyrics has been given to kolaambi (Malayalam).

61. **(a)** Cyclopropane is an alicyclic compound. (C_3H_6)

- Alicyclic compounds may have one or more aliphatic side chains attached.
- Cyclopropane is the smallest alicyclic compound.

62. **(d)** Under the Government of India Act, 1858, the British Government took direct control of the administration of India in its own hands.

- Following the 1857 Mutiny, the British Parliament passed this act to liquidate the East India Company.
- The Colonial Rule of India came directly under the control of the British Government.
- This act marks the beginning of the British Raj.

63. **(b)** Sadir dancer R. Muthukannammal is the recipient of Padma Shri Award in the year 2022.

- She is the only surviving person among the 32 Devadasis who served the deity at the Viralimalai Murugan temple.
- She is the last woman to have the ceremony pottukkattutal of dedicating oneself to God performed at the Viralimalai Temple.

64. **(a)** **Cattle dung** is a conventional source of energy.

- Energy resources can be classified as conventional and non-conventional sources.
- Conventional sources include firewood, cattle dung cake, coal, petroleum, natural gas and electricity (both hydel and thermal).
- Non-conventional sources include solar, wind, tidal, geothermal, biogas and atomic energy.

65. **(b)** Abdul Karim Khan is the pioneer and founder of **Kirana Gharana** of Hindustani music.

- Kirana Gharana is one of the most prominent Indian Classical Khayal Gharanas and is associated mostly with the perfect intonation of notes.
- Famous vocalists of Kirana Gharana are Saraswati Rane, Sureshbabu Mane and Hirabai.

66. **(c)** In the IUPAC name of a compound, the root indicates the total number of carbon atoms present in the longest carbon chain belonging to the compound.

- For example, 'Meth' refers to a chain with 1 carbon atom and 'Pent' refers to a chain with 5 carbon atoms.

67. **(c)** Brisbane (Australia) has been selected to host the Olympics, 2032 by the IOC on 21st July, 2021.

- It is an upcoming international multi-sport event.

68. **(c)** Population (or sub-species or race) that is adapted to local environmental conditions called **ecotype**.

- An Ecotype is a population of species that differs genetically from other populations of the same species.
- An Ecotype is broader than a biotype and narrower then a species.
- Ecotypes are also known as **ecospecies**.

69. **(d)** The Prime Minister's Employment Generation Programme (PMEGP) was launched in 2008.

- The main objectives of this schemes are to generate employment opportunities in rural as well as urban areas of the country through setting up of new self-employment ventures.
- PMEGP is a credit-linked subsidy scheme, launched by the Ministry of MSME.
- Individual applicants above 18 years to set up small businesses by inviting project proposals *via* portal.

70. **(c)** The Fifth Five-Year Plan (1974-1979) period saw the initiation of the Hill Area Development Programme.

- It covers 15 districts comprising all the hilly districts of Uttar Pradesh (present Uttarakhand), Mikir Hill and North Cachar Hills of Assam, Darjeeling district of West Bengal and Nilgiri district of Tamil Nadu.

71. **(d)** The Rowlatt Act (1919) gave the British Indian Government the authority to arrest anyone without a trial.

- The acts allowed certain political cases to be tried without juries and permitted internment of suspects without trial.
- The official name of the Rowlatt Act was Anarchical and Revolutionary Crimes Act, 1919.

72. **(c)** Statements (A) and (B) are correct regarding State Legislatures.

- Notwithstanding anything in part XVII, but subject to the provisions of Article 348, business in the Legislature of a State shall be transacted in the official language or languages of the State or in Hindi or in English.
- The Speaker of the Legislative Assembly or Chairman of the Legislative Council can permit any member to speak in his mother tongue.

73. **(a)** 97% of Earth's water makes up the oceans.

- The remaining 3% is found in many other places, including glaciers and ice.
- Below the ground, in soil moisture and aquifers, in rivers and lakes, in the atmosphere as water vapour.

74. **(d)** The Himalayas have uplifted from **Tethys geosynclines**.

- The Tethys Sea lies between the Eurasian and the Indo-Australian plate.
- **Leopold Kober**, an Austrian geologist formulated the **Geosyncline** Theory.
- This theory explains the formation of the Himalayas.

75. **(a)** Krishnadeva Raya was the king of Vijayanagara empire who took the title of 'Establisher of the Yavana Kingdom' or 'Yavanarajya Pratistapanacharya'.

- Krishnadevaraya was an emperor of the Vijayanagara empire who reigned from 1509-1529.
- He was the third ruler of the Tuluva dynasty and is considered to be its greatest ruler.
- Amuktamalyada' an epic poem in Telegu was composed by Krishnadevaraya.
- He was also known as 'Andhra Bhoj'.

76. **(b) Shyok** is a tributary of river **Indus** that flows through Northern Ladakh and enters Gilgit-Baltistan, in Pakistan, spanning some 550 km.

- Other tributaries of the Indus are Jhelum, Chenab, Ravi, Beas and Sutlej.
- The Zanskar river is also the first major tributary of the Indus river.

77. **(a) Ribosome** is an organelle found both in eukaryotic as well as prokaryotic.

- Ribosomes are composed of Ribonucleic Acid (RNA).
- Ribosomes are the site of protein synthesis in the cell.

78. **(b)** James Prescott Joule is a physicist is known to establish the relationship between mechanical work and heat transfer.

- James Prescott Joule experimented with engines, electricity and heat throughout his life.
- Joule's findings resulted in his development of the mechanical theory of heat and Joule's law, which quantitatively describes the rate at which heat energy is produced from electric energy by the resistance in a circuit.

79. **(d) Salman Rushdie** wrote the novel 'Grimus'.

- Grimus is a 1975 fantasy and science fiction novel.
- It was his literary debut and Salman Rushdie is an Indian-born British-American novelist.
- He has written **Midnight's Children** (for which he won the Booker Prize in 1981, the Booker of Bookers in 1993 and, in 2008, the Best of the Booker), Shame, **The Satanic Verses**, Haroun and the Sea of Stories,

80. **(c)** Article 164(2) of the Indian Constitution mentions that 'The Council of Ministers shall be collectively responsible to the Legislative Assembly of the State.

81. **(a)** 'Loo' is a term for the common local wind that blows in North and North-Western parts of India during summers.

- Chinook winds are warm dry winds that blow down the Eastern slopes of rockey mountains, they are also known as **Fohn**.

82. **(d)** The tendency of an atom or a functional group to attract a shared pair of electrons toward itself, is known as electronegativity.

- **Electroposetivity** is the ability to donate electrons and form positive ions.

83. **(c)** Through Indian Councils Act, 1909 separate electorates were introduced in the Imperial Legislative Assembly elections in the name of **Morley-Minto Reforms**.

- The members could discuss the budget and move resolutions. Morley-Minto Reforms were named after the names of the then Secretary of State (Lord Morley) and the then Viceroy (Lord Minto).

84. **(d) Mallika Sarabhai** is famous for Kuchipudi classical dance.

- Sarabhai was a leading exponent of the Bharatanatyam and Kuchipudi dance forms.
- She is the daughter of a classical dancer Mrinalini Sarabhai and space scientist Vikram Sarabhai, Mallika is an accomplished Kuchipudi and Bharatanatyam dancer.

85. **(c)** As per the decision by the Cabinet Committee on Economic Affairs (CCEA) of the Government of India in 2023, the MSP for Paddy (Common) has been fixed at **7%** higher than the last season.

- Minimum Support Price (MSP) is a form of market intervention by Government to insure farmer for prices.

86. **(d)** Sitara Devi, a doyen of **Kathak dance**, was hailed as the 'Queen of Kathak' by Rabindranath Tagore. At a young age Devi met Rabindranath Tagore.

- He out of affection described her as 'Nritya Samragni'.
- She recieved a number of awards, including Sangeet Natak Akademi Award (1969), the Padma Shree (1973) and the Kalidas Samman (1995).

87. **(b)** Fertiliser is not an agro-based industry. In India, major agro-based industries are sugar industry, cotton textile industry, oil industry, jute industry, food processing industries, paper industry, etc.

88. **(c)** The **Palace of Illusions** was written by Chitra Banerjee Divakaruni. In order to bring the issues of women into the limelight she wrote the book.

89. **(d)** Acetaldehyde is an open chain organic compound.

- Acetaldehyde (IUPAC systematic name ethanol) is an organic chemical compound with the formula CH_3 CHO, sometimes abbreviated as MeCHO.
- It is a colourless liquid or gas, boiling near room temperature.

90. **(a)** Christmas is an annual festival commemorating the birth of Jesus Christ, observed primarily on 25th December.

91. **(d)** Taxes like gift tax, wealth tax, etc., are also referred to as paper taxes.

- Both wealth tax and gift tax are referred to as paper taxes because they are not widely enforced and are often evaded by taxpayers.

92. **(d)** 'Harshacharita' book was written by **Banabhatta**.

- Banabhatta was a writer in Harsha's court.
- It was written in the Sanskrit language.
- He additionally composed a show called **Kadambari**.

93. **(d)** Krishna III of Rashtrakuta dynasty established a victory pillar and a temple at **Rameswaram** cities of South India after defeating the Chola ruler Parantaka I.

- Krishna III also known as 'Kannara', ruled from Manyakheta (939-967 CE).

94. **(d)** If a person who is arrested, is not produced before the Magistrate within 24 hours from the time of arrest, he will be entitled to be released on the writ of Habeas Corpus.

- Mandamus means 'we command', directive issues by a court to public officials.
- Prohibition - 'To Forbid' -Preventing acting beyond its legal authority.

- Quo-warranto - 'By what authority or warrant', to inquire the legality of person's claim to hold a public office.

95. **(c)** The advisory board under provisions of Article 22 of the Constitution is to be consist of persons who are, have been or are qualified to be appointed as **Judges of High Court.**

96. **(a)** In 2023, the President of Egypt was invited as the Chief Guest at India's Republic Day celebration.

- In 2024, the President of France, Emmanuel Macron.
- 2025 Republic Day chief guest was the President of Indonesia Prabowo Subianto.

97. **(d)** According to Agricultural Statistics at a Glance 2022, Government of India, Rajasthan recorded the highest production of Bajra.

- Uttar Pradesh, Haryana, Maharashtra and Gujarat are the next major producers contributing 15% in Indian economy.
- Bajra is the main coarse cereal crop grown mainly in Africa and Asia.
- It is cultivated in the dry and warm climatic regions.
- In 2025, Rajasthan ranks as the top producer of bajra in India.

98. **(b)** Sphincter is a muscle responsible for the exit of waste material from the body.

- Sphincters are circular muscles that open and close passages in the body to regulate the flow of substances, such as bile, urine and faeces, through the body.

99. **(a)** If the value of the Cash Reserve Ratio is 25%. The value of money multiplier will be 4.

- Cash Reserve Ratio (CRR) is the percentage of money, which a bank has to keep with RBI in the form of cash.
- Money Multiplier is a relationship butween money supply and the reserves in the banking system. Money multiplier

$$= \frac{1}{\text{Cash reserve ratio}}$$

100. **(d)** **Ali Baksh Khan** belongs to Patiala Gharana.

- Ustad Ali Baksh Jarnail Khan (1850-1920) was an Indian classical singer.
- Together with his friend Fateh Ali Khan, he founded the Patiala Gharana in the 19th century.
- They used to sing together as a team back then and were called Ali-a-Fattu duo.

101. **(d)** $855 \div 15 - K + 32 \times 5 = 1152 \div 16 \times 111 \div 37$

$$\Rightarrow \quad 57 - K + 160 = 72 \times 3$$
$$\Rightarrow \quad 217 - K = 216$$
$$\therefore \quad K = 1$$

102. **(c)** Given, $A - B = 2500$ or 10% of total votes polled.

i.e., 2500 = 10% of total votes polled.

$\therefore$ Total votes polled = 25000

Now, $\frac{1}{5}$th vote polled is invalid

$$\therefore \text{ Invalid votes} = \frac{1}{5} \times 25000 = 5000$$

Hence, total valid votes
$$= 25000 - 5000 = 20000$$

$$\therefore \quad A + B = 20000 \quad \ldots(i)$$
$$A - B = 2500 \quad \ldots(ii)$$

On solving Eqs. (i) and (ii), we get
$$A = 11250$$
and
$$B = 8750$$

Now, 90% of invalid votes
$$= \frac{9}{10} \times 5000 = 4500$$

According to the question, votes that B would have got
$$8750 + 4500 = 13250$$

$\therefore$ B would have won by
$$\frac{(13250 - 11250) \times 100}{25000} = 8\%$$

103. **(d)** $5055 - (1002 \div 20.04)$
$$= 5055 - 50 = 5005$$

104. **(d)** Population of a city after 2 yr
$$= 16000\left(1 + \frac{5}{100}\right)^2 = 16000\left(\frac{105}{100}\right)^2$$
$$= 16000\left(\frac{21}{20}\right)^2 = 16000 \times \frac{21}{20} \times \frac{21}{20}$$
$$= \frac{70560}{4} = 17640$$

105. **(c)** Number of students in medicine in city $A = 1100$

Number of students in MBA in city $A = 1200$

$$\therefore \text{Required percentage} = \frac{1100}{1200} \times 100 = 91.66\% \approx 92\%$$

106. **(d)** Gain in weight
$$= 1000 \text{ g} - 950 \text{ g} = 50 \text{ g}$$
$$\therefore \text{ Profit \%} = \frac{50}{950} \times 100 = \frac{100}{19} = 5\frac{5}{19}\%$$

107. **(d)** $15\% \text{ of } 1.5 + 0.15 \div 0.1 + 0.01 \text{ of } 1.1 \times 0.5 + 2.5 \times 25$
$$= 0.225 + 1.5 + 0.011 \times 0.5 + 62.5$$
$$= 0.225 + 1.5 + 0.0055 + 62.5$$
$$= 64.2305$$

108. **(d)** $\sin x + \cos x = \sqrt{2} \sin x$
$$\Rightarrow \quad \cos x = \sqrt{2} \sin x - \sin x$$
$$\Rightarrow \quad \cos x = (\sqrt{2} - 1) \sin x.$$

Multiplying both the sides by $(\sqrt{2} + 1)$

$$(\sqrt{2} + 1) \cos x = (\sqrt{2} + 1)(\sqrt{2} - 1) \sin x$$
$$[\because a^2 - b^2 = (a + b)(a - b)]$$
$$\Rightarrow \quad \sqrt{2} \cos x + \cos x = (2 - 1) \sin x$$
$$\Rightarrow \quad \sqrt{2} \cos x = \sin x - \cos x$$
$$\therefore \quad \sin x - \cos x = \sqrt{2} \cos x$$

109. **(c)** Required change in surface area
$$= \left(x + y + \frac{xy}{100}\right)\%$$
$$= \left(125 + 125 + \frac{125 \times 125}{100}\right)\%$$
$$= (250 + 156.25) = 406.25\%$$

110. **(b)** $\left[3\frac{2}{5} \times \left\{2\frac{3}{4} + 3.3\left(5\frac{1}{3} + 3\frac{1}{3} - 2\frac{1}{3}\right)\right\}\right]$
$$= \left[\frac{17}{5} \times \left\{\frac{11}{4} + 3.3\left(\frac{16}{3} + \frac{10}{3} - \frac{7}{3}\right)\right\}\right]$$
$$= \left[\frac{17}{5} \times \left\{\frac{11}{4} + 3.3 \times \frac{19}{3}\right\}\right]$$
$$= \left[\frac{17}{5} \times \left\{\frac{11}{4} + 1.1 \times 19\right\}\right]$$
$$= [3.4 \times \{2.75 + 20.9\}]$$
$$= 3.4 \times 23.65 = 80.41$$

111. **(c)** In a triangle, if the lengths of three sides are a,b and c, then the length of any one side is greater than the difference of other two sides and less than the sum of other two sides.

$\therefore$ If three sides of the triangle are 12,22 and m units,

$$(22 - 12) < m < (12 + 22) \Rightarrow 10 < m < 34$$

112. **(a)** Radius (r) of cylinder = 7 cm

Curved surface area of cylinder
$$= 2200 \text{ cm}^2$$
$$\Rightarrow \quad 2\pi rh = 2200$$
$$\Rightarrow \quad 2 \times \frac{22}{7} \times 7 \times h = 2200$$

$\Rightarrow$ height of cylinder (h) = 50 cm

Now, total surface area of cylinder
$$= 2\pi r(h + r)$$
$$= 2 \times \frac{22}{7} \times 7(50 + 7)$$
$$= 2 \times 22 \times 57$$
$$= 44 \times 57 = 2508 \text{ cm}^2$$

113. (b) $66 \div [34-(32 \text{ of } 2-4)\div(4\times 15)]$
$= 66\div[34-(64-4)\div(60)]$
$= 66\div[34-60\div 60]$
$= 66\div(34-1)$
$= 66\div 33 = 2$

114. (c) Number of females in college A
$= 35\%$ of $700 = 245$
Number of females in college D
$= 55\%$ of $800 = 440$
Number of males in college B
$= 70\%$ of $550 = 385$
Number of males in college C
$= 60\%$ of $600 = 360$
∴ Required percentage
$= \frac{(245+440)}{(385+360)}\times 100$
$= \frac{685}{745}\times 100 = 91.95\%$

115. (d) Number of women in city A
$= \frac{2}{3}\times 2340 = 1560$
Number of women in city B
$= \frac{1}{4}\times 900 = 225$
∴ Total number of women in city A and B
$= 1560 + 225 = 1785$

116. (a) Marked price = ₹ 38/kg
Discount = 12% on 10 kg sugar
∴ Selling price of 1 kg
$= \frac{\frac{MP\times 88\%}{900}}{1000} = \frac{38\times\frac{88}{100}}{0.9}$
$= \frac{38\times\frac{22}{25}}{0.9} =$ ₹ 37.15
Now, cost price = ₹ 30/kg
∴ Profit per cent
$= \frac{(37.15-30)}{30}\times 100$
$= \frac{7.15\times 100}{30} = 23.85\%$

117. (d) We know that, distance (d) is directly proportional to time (t)
i.e., $d \alpha t$
or $d = kt$ where 'k' is a proportionality constant
Now, given $d = 72$ km
and $t = 2$ h
∴ $k = \frac{d}{t} = \frac{72}{2} = 36$
Hence, $d = 36t$ will be correct equation.

118. (d) External radius (R) of sphere
$= \frac{10}{2}$ cm $= 5$ cm
Internal radius (n) of sphere
$= \frac{6}{2}$ cm $= 3$ cm
Now, according to the question,
Volume of hollow sphere
= Volume of cone
$\Rightarrow \frac{4}{3}\pi[R^3 - r^3] = \frac{1}{3}\pi r_1^2 h$
$\Rightarrow \frac{4}{3}\times[(5)^3-(3)^3] = \frac{1}{3}\times(5)^2\times h$
$\Rightarrow 4[125-27] = 25\times h$
$\Rightarrow 4\times 98 = 25h$
$\Rightarrow h = 15.68$ cm

119. (b) Area of a sector of a circle
$= \frac{\theta}{360}\times\pi r^2$
Given, Radius (r) of circle = 14 cm
Area of sector = 231 cm^2
∴ $231 = \frac{\theta}{360}\times\pi r^2$
$\Rightarrow 231 = \frac{\theta}{360}\times\frac{22}{7}\times 14\times 14$
$\Rightarrow 231\times 360 = \theta\times 22\times 2\times 14$
∴ $\theta = 135°$

120. (d) Given,
$(a-18)^2 + (b-12)^2 + (c-6)^2 = 0$
$\Rightarrow (a-18)^2 = 0$ [∴ $a = 18$]
$\Rightarrow (b-12)^2 = 0$ [∴ $b = 12$]
$\Rightarrow (c-6)^2 = 0$ [∴ $c = 6$]
Now, $(a+b+c)^{\frac{1}{2}} = \sqrt{(a+b+c)}$
$= \sqrt{(18+12+6)}$
$= \sqrt{36} = \pm 6$

121. (a) Number of mango trees planted in 2018 = 40000
Number of mango trees planted in 2020 = 52000
∴ Required percentage increase
$= \frac{(52000-40000)}{40000}\times 100$
$= \frac{12000}{40000}\times 100$
$= \frac{12}{40}\times 100 = 30\%$

122. (d) Highest percentage increase in the year 2019-2020 is of advertising
$= \frac{(20000-10000)}{10000}\times 100$
$= 100\%$
Least percentage increase in the year 2019-2020 is of Raw material
$= \frac{(6000-5000)}{5000}\times 100$
$= \frac{1000}{5000}\times 100 = 20\%$
Hence, required difference
$= 100\% - 20\% = 80\%$

123. (d) $(4+4)\times(4\div 4)\times(4\times 4)$
$= 8\times 1\times 16 = 128$

124. (d) Let the two number be x and y.
Now, $x + y = 28$ ...(i)
$x^2 + y^2 = 528$ ...(ii)
On squaring Eq. (i), we get
$(x+y)^2 = (28)^2$
$\Rightarrow x^2 + y^2 + 2xy = 784$
$\Rightarrow 528 + 2xy = 784$ [from Eq. (ii)]
$\Rightarrow 2xy = 256$
$xy = 128$
Now, $\sqrt{xy} = \sqrt{128} = 8\sqrt{2}$

125. (d) Speed of the train
$= \frac{\text{Distance covered}}{\text{Time taken}} = \frac{850}{45}$ m/s
$= \frac{850}{45}\times\frac{18}{5} = 68$ km/h
Hence, the train will cover 68 km in one hour.

126. (c) Discount of 40% on ₹ 1000
= 1000 – 40% of ₹ 1000
= 1000 – 400
= ₹ 600 will be the selling price.
Now, net discount after two successive discounts of 36% and 4%
$= \left(x + y - \frac{xy}{100}\right) = \left(36 + 4 - \frac{36\times 4}{100}\right)\%$
$= 40 - 144 = 38.56\%$
∴ Selling price = 6144% of ₹ 1000
= ₹ 614.4
Hence, the required difference
= (614.4 – 600) = ₹ 14.40

127. (a) 1 day's work of Ronak $= \frac{1}{12}$
1 day's work of Riya $= \frac{1}{18}$
1 day's work by both $= \frac{1}{12} + \frac{1}{18}$
$= \frac{3+2}{36} = \frac{5}{36}$
6 days work by both $= \frac{6\times 5}{36} = \frac{30}{36}$
Remaining work $= 1 - \frac{30}{36} = \frac{6}{36} = \frac{1}{6}$
∴ This remaining work done by Riya in
$= \frac{1}{6}\times 18 = 3$ days

128. (b) $(6+6 \text{ of } 5 \div 5) \div 6 \text{ of } 5 + (24 \div 2 \text{ of } 3 - 6 \text{ of } 5 + 4)$

$= (6+30 \div 5) \div 30 + (24 \div 6 - 30 + 4)$

$= (6+6) \div 30 + (4 - 30 + 4)$

$= \frac{12}{30} + (-30+8) = \frac{12}{30} - 22 = \frac{2}{5} - 22$

$= \frac{2-110}{5} = \frac{108}{5} = -21\frac{3}{5}$

129. (b) $SI = \frac{PRT}{100}$

Here, $T = 4$ yr

$\therefore \quad SI = \frac{4PR}{100}$

According to the question,

$\frac{4P(R+11)}{100} - \frac{4PR}{100} = 1320$

$\Rightarrow \frac{4P}{100}(R+11-R) = 1320$

$\Rightarrow P \times 11 = \frac{1320 \times 100}{4}$

$\therefore \quad P = ₹3000$

130. (c) Average speed

$= \frac{\text{Total distance}}{\text{Total time taken}} = \frac{(11+25+30)}{\frac{11}{7}+\frac{25}{10}+\frac{30}{20}}$

$= \frac{66 \times 140}{780} = \frac{154}{13} = 11\frac{11}{13}$ km/h

131. (b) If a, b, c and d in the given order are in proportion, then

$\frac{a}{b} = \frac{c}{d}$ or $\frac{a}{c} = \frac{b}{d}$ or $\frac{d}{c} = \frac{b}{a}$

Hence, option (b) is incorrect.

132. (b) $(1-\cos^2 A)\sec^2 A$

$= \sin^2 A \cdot \sec^2 A = \sin^2 A \cdot \frac{1}{\cos^2 A}$

$= \frac{\sin^2 A}{\cos^2 A} = \tan^2 A$

133. (b) Let the annual income of shiya be ₹ $100x$.

According to the question,

30% of ₹ $100x$ = ₹153000

$\Rightarrow \quad 100x = \frac{153000 \times 100}{30}$

$\Rightarrow \quad 100x = ₹510000$

$\therefore$ Monthly income $= \frac{510000}{12} = ₹42500$

134. (b) Total number of students = 60

Average weight of the class = 42 kg

Number of boys = 36

Average weight of boys = 50 kg

$\therefore$ Number of girls = 60 − 36 = 24

Let the average weight of girls be 'x' kg.

Now, $60 \times 42 = 36 \times 50 + 24 \times x$

$\Rightarrow \quad 2520 - 1800 = 24x$

$\Rightarrow \quad 720 = 24x$

$\Rightarrow \quad x = 30$ kg

$\therefore$ Average weight of girls = 30 kg.

135. (c) $1000 \times 100 - 1000 + 4000 \div 200$

$= 100000 - 1000 + 20 = 99020$

136. (b) We know that,

$(x-y)^3 = x^3 - y^3 - 3xy(x-y)$

Given, $x - y = 25$ and $xy = 444$

Using it in the above identity, we have

$(25)^3 = x^3 - y^3 - 3 \times 444 \times 25$

$\Rightarrow \quad 15625 = x^3 - y^3 - 33300$

$\Rightarrow \quad x^3 - y^3 = 15625 + 33300$

$\therefore \quad x^3 - y^3 = 48925$

137. (c) Radius (r) of cylinder = 7 cm

Curved surface area of cylinder

$= 2\pi rh$

$\Rightarrow \quad 396 = 2 \times \frac{22}{7} \times 7 \times h$

$\Rightarrow \quad h = \frac{396}{44} = 9$

Now, Volume of cylinder $= \pi r^2 h$

$= \frac{22}{7} \times 7 \times 7 \times 9 = 1386 \text{cm}^3$

138. (d)

P ⟶ 275 km ⟵ Q
10 am 12 pm

In 2 h distance covered by first rider

$= 25 \times 2 = 50$ km

Remaining distance = 275 − 50 = 225 km

Relative speed = (25 + 20) = 45 km/h

(opposite direction)

Time after they will meet each other

$= \frac{225}{45} = 5$ h

$\therefore$ Required time of meeting each other

= 12 pm + 5 h = 5.00 pm

139. (b) Given, $4\sin^2\theta = 3(1+\cos\theta)$

$\Rightarrow \quad 4(1-\cos^2\theta) = 3 + 3\cos\theta$

$\Rightarrow \quad 4 - 4\cos^2\theta = 3 + 3\cos\theta$

$\Rightarrow \quad 4\cos^2\theta + 3\cos\theta - 1 = 0$

$\Rightarrow \quad 4\cos^2\theta + 4\cos\theta - \cos\theta - 1 = 0$

$\Rightarrow \quad 4\cos\theta(\cos\theta+1) - 1(\cos\theta+1) = 0$

$\Rightarrow \quad (4\cos\theta - 1)(\cos\theta + 1) = 0$

$\Rightarrow \quad \cos\theta = \frac{1}{4}$

$\sin\theta = \sqrt{1 - \frac{1}{16}}$

$\sin\theta = \frac{\sqrt{15}}{4}$

$\therefore \quad \tan\theta = \sqrt{15}$

$\therefore \quad \sqrt{15}\tan\theta + \frac{4}{\sqrt{15}}\sin\theta + 2\sec\theta$

$= \sqrt{15} \times \sqrt{15} + \frac{4}{\sqrt{15}} \times \frac{\sqrt{15}}{4} + 2 \times 4$

$= 15 + 1 + 8 = 24$

140. (d) Eggs produced in farm P in 2011

= 1260

Eggs produced in farm T in 2011

= 1620

$\therefore$ Required ratio $= \frac{1260}{1620} = 7:9$

141. (b) Surface area of spherical box $= 4\pi r^2$

$528 = 4 \times \frac{22}{7} \times r^2$

$\Rightarrow \quad r^2 = \frac{528 \times 7}{4 \times 22}$

$\Rightarrow \quad r^2 = 42$

$\Rightarrow \quad r = \sqrt{42}$

$\therefore$ Radius of the spherical box

$= \sqrt{42}$ cm

142. (d) AB = diameter = 14 cm

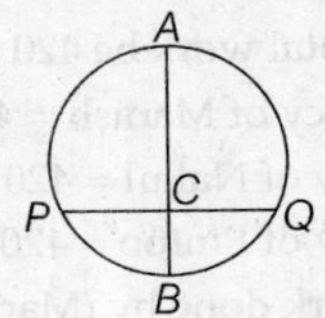

$AC : BC : 4 : 3$

$\therefore \quad AC = \frac{4}{7} \times 14 = 8$ cm

and $\quad BC = \frac{3}{7} \times 14 = 6$ cm

Now, OC will be perpendicular to chord PQ and divide it into two equal parts i.e., a each

We know that here,

$AC \times CB = PC \times CQ$

$\Rightarrow \quad 8 \times 6 = a \times a$

$\Rightarrow \quad 48 = a^2$

$a = 4\sqrt{3}$ cm

$\therefore \quad PQ = 2 \times 4\sqrt{3}$

$= 8\sqrt{3}$ cm

143. (a) Average speed

$= \frac{\text{Total distance}}{\text{Total time taken}}$

$= \frac{1200+1600+1000+200}{\frac{1200}{80}+\frac{1600}{40}+\frac{1000}{400}+\frac{200}{50}}$

$= \left(\frac{4000}{15+40+2.5+4}\right)$

$= \left(\frac{4000}{61.5}\right) = 65.04$ km/h

144. **(d)** $[\{9\times 81+(142\div 2)\}+350-155+5]\div[(25\times 25)-125)]$

$=[\{729+71\}+200]\div[625-125]$

$=1000\div 500=2$

145. **(c)** Total number of respondents aged 31-50 = 62

Now, percentage of them who like

$$\text{Pop music} = \frac{16}{62}\times 100 = 25.806\%$$

Hence, Percentage of respondents aged 31-50, who like other music than Pop music

$=(100-25.806)$

$=74.19\%$

146. **(b)** Time taken by Manish to complete a work = 21 days

Time taken by Nakul to complete the work = 28 days.

Time taken by Pintoo to complete the work = 15 days

Let the total work be 420 units.

$\therefore$ Efficiency of Manish = 420 / 21 = 20

Efficiency of Nakul = 420 / 28 = 15

Efficiency of Pintoo = 420 / 15 = 28

Now, work done by (Manish + Pintoo) in 5 days

$=(20+28)\times 5=240$

$\therefore$ Remaining work = 420 − 240 = 180 units

$\therefore$ Time taken to finish the remaining work by all

$$=\frac{180}{20+15+28}=\frac{180}{63}=\frac{20}{7}\text{ days}=2\frac{6}{7}\text{ days}$$

So, Nakul worked for $2\frac{6}{7}$ days.

147. **(c)** $\tan\theta+\cot\theta=6$

Squaring both the sides,

$(\tan\theta+\cot\theta)^2=6^2$

$\Rightarrow \tan^2\theta+\cot^2\theta+2\tan\theta\cdot\cot\theta=36$

$\Rightarrow \tan^2\theta+\cot^2\theta+2=36$

$\therefore \tan^2\theta+\cot^2\theta=34$

148. **(a)** We know that, the third side of any triangle is always greater than the difference of the other two sides and less than the sum of the other sides.

So, $(12-7)<x<(12+7)$

$\Rightarrow 5<x<19$

$\therefore$ The value of x can be any value from 6 to 18.

Hence, number of possible value of $x=13$.

149. **(b)** Let the original salary of Ramnarayan be ₹ x.

Now, according to the question,

$$x-3\frac{1}{8}\%\text{of } x = x-\frac{25}{8\times 100}x = x-\frac{1}{32}x=\frac{31}{32}x$$

Now, this salary is increased by $7\frac{2}{5}\%$.

$$\text{New salary, }\left(\frac{31}{32}x+7\frac{2}{5}\%\text{of}\frac{31}{32}x\right)=\frac{31}{32}x+\frac{37}{500}\times\frac{31}{32}x$$

$=₹\,(0.968x+0.0716x)=₹\,1.04x$

$\therefore$ Percentage increase in salary

$$=\frac{₹\,(1.04x-x)}{x}\times 100=4.04\%$$

150. **(c)** Given, cost price = ₹ 1200

Profit earned = 10%

$\therefore$ Selling price = 110% of ₹ 1200

$$=\frac{110}{100}\times 1200=₹\,1320$$

Now,

Marked price × 90% = Selling price + Cashback

$\Rightarrow$ Marked price $\times\frac{90}{100}=1320+250$

$\Rightarrow$ Marked price (tag price)

$$=₹\,1570\times\frac{100}{90}=₹\,1744.44$$

151. **(c)** The option that can be used as a one-word substitute for the given group of words 'A place for storage of arms and ammunition' is 'Arsenal'.

152. **(a)** The incorrectly spelt word in the given sentence is 'Generousity'. The correct spelling is 'Generosity'.

153. **(d)** The most appropriate option with correct usage of the preposition to substitute the underlined segment in the given sentence is 'various government departments at all levels'.

154. **(a)** The most appropriate idiom from the options to replace the underlined segment in the given sentence is 'tighten his belt'. This idiom conveys the idea of cutting down expenses.

155. **(c)** The most appropriate meaning of the given idiom 'Sacred cow' is 'Unquestionable'. A 'sacred cow' refers to an idea, custom or institution that is considered immune from criticism or questioning.

156. **(a)** The option that can be used as a one-word substitute for the given group of words 'One who does not believe in God' is 'Atheist'.

157. **(d)** The incorrect form of the verb is 'strucken'. The correct form is 'struck'.

158. **(c)** The most appropriate option to substitute the underlined segment in the given sentence is 'her feet were'.

159. **(b)** The most appropriate meaning of the given idiom 'Black sheep' is 'Disreputable'. A 'black sheep' refers to a person who is considered disreputable or behaves differently from the rest of a group.

160. **(a)** The sentence that uses the given idiom correctly is 'He had his head in the clouds during an important meeting'. The idiom 'have your head in the clouds' means to be 'daydreaming or not paying attention'.

161. **(a)** The most appropriate antonym of the given word 'Upright' is 'Immoral'. 'Upright' means honest and morally correct.

162. **(d)** The most appropriate synonym for the word in brackets is 'fertility'. 'Fecundity' refers to the ability to produce offspring or creative ideas.

163. **(a)** The part that contains a spelling error in the sentence is 'as the strenght'. It should be 'as the strength'.

164. **(c)** The word segment that can substitute the bracketed word segment correctly and complete the sentence meaningfully is 'party forms the government'.

165. **(b)** The most appropriate option that can substitute the underlined word in the given idiom is 'bird's'. The idiom refers to a high vantage point or perspective.

166. **(d)** The sentence that has the correct use of words and spellings is 'The delicious aroma of freshly baked cookies wafted through the kitchen, making mouths water'.

167. **(a)** There is no need to substitute the sentence.

168. **(d)** The most appropriate idiom for the underlined part in the given sentence is 'High and dry'.

Being 'left high and dry' means being abandoned or left in a difficult situation without help.

169. **(d)** The word 'Nepotism' means the practice among those with power or influence of favouring relatives or friends, especially by giving them jobs.

170. (b) The incorrectly spelt word is 'Supremecy'. The correct spelling is 'Supremacy'.

171. (d) Based on the situation in the sentence, the most appropriate idiom for the underlined segment is 'Bite off more than you can chew'. This idiom means attempting something that is too difficult or ambitious.

172. (d) The most appropriate antonym of the underlined word 'ebullient' in the sentence is 'Weary'. While, 'ebullient' means enthusiastic and lively, 'weary' means tired or lacking energy.

173. (b) The correctly spelt word is 'registration'.

174. (a) The most appropriate segment to substitute the underlined words in the given sentence is 'If you have tears'.

175. (c) The most appropriate synonym for the given word 'Bind' is 'Secure'. Both words imply holding something together or making it firm.

176. (b) The most appropriate meaning of the given idiom 'When pigs fly' is 'Something that will never happen'. It refers to an event or situation that is highly unlikely.

177. (c) The error in the verb form in the sentence is that it should be 'The committee works diligently to ensure fair and unbiased decision' in the present tense.

178. (a) In the given sentence 'cowardly' has been used as an adjective but here we need an adverb to qualify the verb 'fight'. Hence, 'in a cowardly manner' will be used here.

179. (a) The option that contains an error in the sentence is 'When my father will come'. It should be 'When my father comes' to correct the verb tense.

180. (d) The most appropriate antonym of the given word 'Aggravate' is 'Alleviate'. While 'aggravate' means to make something worse, 'alleviate' means to make it better or relieve it.

181. (a) The antonym of 'Tight' is 'Slack'. When something is tight, it lacks looseness or room for movement, while 'slackness' implies a relaxed or loose state.

182. (d) The one-word substitute for 'A doubtful look or examination of one's motives' is 'Circumspect'. It refers to being cautious, considering all aspects before making a decision.

183. (b) The antonym of 'incinerate' in the sentence is 'extinguish'. While, incineration involves burning something completely, extinguishing means putting out a fire or stopping it.

184. (b) The one-word substitute for 'Dwarfed varieties of trees and shrubs in pots' is 'Bonsai'. 'Bonsai' refers to the art of growing miniature trees in containers.

185. (a) The one-word substitute for 'Vivacious and enthusiastic' is 'Effervescent'. It describes someone who is lively, bubbly and full of energy.

186. (d) The antonym of 'Vanquish' in the sentence is 'Liberate'. 'Vanquishing' means defeating or conquering, while liberating means setting free.

187. (d) The one-word substitute for 'Consonance of sounds' is 'Symphony'. It refers to a harmonious combination of musical sounds.

188. (a) The incorrectly spelled word is 'Dissapear'. The correct spelling is 'Disappear'.

189. (c) The option that expresses the meaning of the underlined segment is 'quell'. It means to suppress or calm down emotions.

190. (d) The most appropriate option that can substitute the underlined segment in the given sentence is 'steered clear of'.
It means avoiding something or staying away from it.

191. (b) The correct option to fill in blank number 1 is 'beloved'.

192. (a) The correct option to fill in blank number 2 is 'experiences'.

193. (b) The correct option to fill in blank number 3 is 'navigates'.

194. (a) The correct option to fill in blank number 4 is 'captivate'.

195. (c) The correct option to fill blank number 5 is 'enchanting'.

196. (d) Human-caused earthquakes are related to industrial activities such as mining, construction of water dams, injection of liquids like wastewater and carbon dioxide and extractions associated with oil and gas exploitation.

197. (a) The tone reflects concern and skepticism about the increasing human-induced earthquakes and the consequences of industrial activity. It warns about future risks and presents a some what critical viewpoint.

198. (c) The most suitable word from the passage that means 'create' is 'destabilise'.

199. (d) The passage observes that more human-caused earthquakes are expected due to the demand for energy and minerals worldwide.

200. (b) The most suitable title for the passage could be 'Industrial Threats'.

CPO SI P-1 SP 06

PAPER-1

SSC CPO SI SOLVED PAPER

28 June 2024 (Shift I)

MM : 200 **Time : 2 hr**

Instructions

1. This paper contains 200 questions.
2. It has 4 Parts, **Part I** General Intelligence and Reasoning, **Part II** General Knowledge and General Awareness, **Part III** Quantitative Aptitude and **Part IV** English Comprehension.
3. Each question carries **1 marks.**

Part I
General Intelligence and Reasoning

1. Two statements are given followed by two conclusions numbered I and II. Assuming the statements to be true, even if they seem to be at variance with commonly known facts, decide which of the conclusions logically follow(s) from the statements.

Statements

All games are tournaments.

Some tournaments are matches.

Conclusions

I. All games are matches.

II. No game is a tournament.

(a) Only Conclusion I follows
(b) Neither Conclusion I nor II follows
(c) Both Conclusions I and II follow
(d) Only Conclusion II follows

2. Select the correct mirror image of the given figure when the mirror is placed at MN.

hj52dR | M N

(a) Яb2ꙅįԋ (b) Яbƨꙅįԋ
(c) Яpƨꙅįԋ (d) Яbƨ5įԋ

3. If + means –, – means ×, × means ÷, ÷ means +, then what will be the value of the following expression?

$145 \div 96 \times 12 + 13 = ?$

(a) 170 (b) 120
(c) 140 (d) 185

4. In a code language, 'GAME' is written as 'KCQG' and 'FARM' is written as 'JCVO'. How will 'TOWN' be written in that language?

(a) XQAP (b) PAXQ
(c) XAPQ (d) AXQP

5. Select the option that is related to the third term in the same way as the second term is related to the first term and the sixth term is related to the fifth term.

29 : 61 :: 47 : ? :: 15 : 33

(a) 108 (b) 89 (c) 76 (d) 97

6. Select the option that is related to the fifth letter-cluster in the same way as the second letter-cluster is related to the first letter-cluster and the fourth letter-cluster is related to the third letter-cluster.

MAILED : DELMAI :: FABRIC : CIRFAB :: JACKET : ?

(a) JKTACE (b) JEKCAT
(c) TEKCAJ (d) TEKJAC

7. A transparent sheet with a pattern is given below. Select the option that depicts the pattern that would appear when the given transparent sheet is folded at the middle horizontal line.

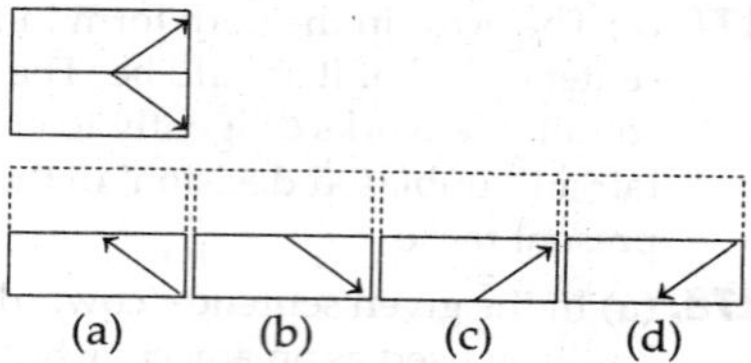

8. Two statements are given followed by Three conclusions numbered I, II and III.Assuming the statements to be true, even if they seem to be at variance with commonly known facts, decide which of the conclusions logically follow(s) from the statements.

Statements

All blues are reds.

All greens are blues.

Conclusions

I. No red is a blue.

II. No blue is a green.

III. No green is a red.

(a) Both Conclusions I and III follow
(b) None of the conclusions follow
(c) Both Conclusions I and II follow
(d) Both Conclusions II and III follow

9. Select the number from among the given options that can replace the question mark(?) in the following series.

38, 40, 42, 42, 46, 44, ?

(a) 52 (b) 50
(c) 48 (d) 54

10. Which of the following numbers will replace the question mark (?) in the given series?

55, 62, ?, 72, 75, 82

(a) 65 (b) 69
(c) 71 (d) 68

11. In the given number-pairs, the second number is obtained by applying certain mathematical operations to the first number. Select the number-pair in which the numbers are related in the same way as are the numbers of the given number-pairs.

(Note Operations should be performed on the whole numbers, without breaking down the numbers into its constituent digits. E.g., 13 – Operations on 13 such as adding/subtracting/multiplying etc. to 13 can be performed. Breaking down 13 into 1and 3 and then performing mathematical operations on 1 and 3 is not allowed.)

(19, 200)
(15, 160)

(a) (23, 300) (b) (22, 230)
(c) (25, 250) (d) (18, 200)

12. In a certain code language, 'FLY' is written as '38' and 'NUT' is written as '26'. How will 'GOD' be written in that language?

(a) 55 (b) 34
(c) 28 (d) 46

13. In a code language, 'PEN' is coded as '70' and 'NEST' is coded as '116'. How will 'PEON' be coded in the same language?

(a) 162 (b) 46
(c) 100 (d) 99

14. If 'P' stands for '÷', 'Q' stands for '×', 'R' stands for '+' and 'S' stands for '–', what will come in place of the question mark (?) in the following equation?

174 P 2 S 45 R (16 P 4) Q 5 S 26 = ?

(a) 32 (b) 48
(c) 36 (d) 44

15. Find the two signs to be interchanged for making the following equation correct.

$9 + 6 \times 3 - 9 \div 1 = 10$

(a) × and ÷ (b) + and –
(c) – and + (d) ÷ and +

16. Based on the English alphabetical order, three of the following four letter-clusters are alike in a certain way and thus form a group. Which letter-cluster does not belong to that group?

(Note The odd letter-cluster is not based on the number of consonants/vowels or their position in the letter-cluster.)

(a) OVS (b) LSP (c) JQM (d) NUR

17. Six friends – A,B, C, D, E and F are sitting around a circular table, facing towards the centre of the table. D and C are immediate neighbours of A. B is second to the right of A. F is an immediate neighbour of E , and fourth to the left of D. What is the position of E?

(a) Third to the left of A
(b) Immediate left of C
(c) Second to the right of A
(d) Immediate neighbour of D and F

18. Select the set in which the numbers are related in the same way as are the numbers of the following sets.

(Note Operations should be performed on the whole numbers, without breaking down the numbers into its constituent digits. E.g., 13 – Operations on 13 such as adding /deleting /multiplying etc. to 13 can be performed. Breaking down 13 into 1 and 3 and then performing mathematical operations on 1 and 3 is not allowed.)

(21, 105, 35)
(27, 135, 45)

(a) (39, 195, 65) (b) (39, 195, 55)
(c) (39, 185, 65) (d) (37, 195, 65)

19. If 'A' stands for '÷', 'B' stands for '×', 'C' stands for '+' and 'D' stands for '–', what will come in place of the question mark (?) in the following equation?

455 A 5 D 17 C 36 B 4 = ?

(a) 214 (b) 216
(c) 220 (d) 218

20. If 'A' stands for '+', 'B' stands for '–', 'C' stands for '×' and 'D' stands for '÷', what will come in place of the question mark (?) in the following equation?

29 A 37 B 14 C 3 A (84 D 4) A 46 = ?

(a) 78 (b) 91
(c) 83 (d) 97

21. Three different positions of the same dice are given. Find the number on the face opposite to the face showing '6'.

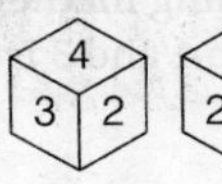

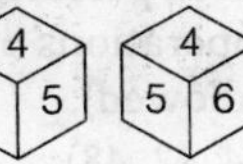

(a) 3 (b) 4 (c) 2 (d) 1

22. Vani starts from point A and drives 6 km towards West. She then takes a left turn,drives 8 km. She then turns left and drives 6 km to reach point B. In which direction is point B with respect to point A?

(a) North (b) South
(c) South-West (d) South-East

23. 3 is related to 2 following a certain logic. Following the same logic, 9 is related to 6.Which of the following numbers is related to 12 using the same logic?

(a) 16 (b) 18
(c) 20 (d) 14

24. Identify the figure given in the options which when put in place of '?' will logically complete the series ?

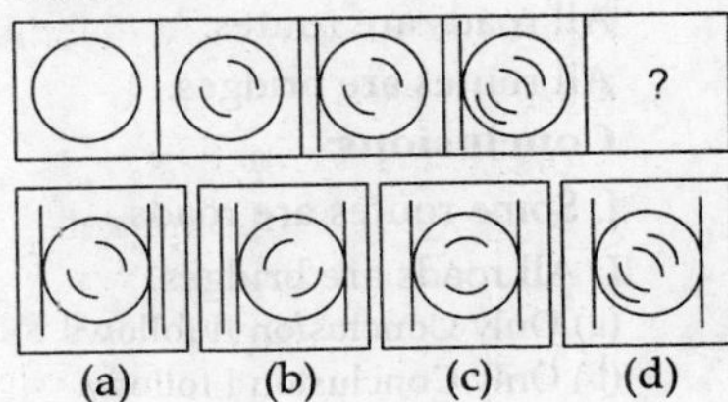

25. Which of the following terms will replace the question mark (?) in the given series?

HMW, INX, JOY,?

(a) KPZ (b) EHM
(c) DHM (d) DJB

26. In a certain code language, 'JAM' is written as '24' and 'GEL' is written as '24'. How will'LAW' be written in that language?

(a) 32 (b) 24 (c) 36 (d) 28

27. Select the set in which the numbers are related in the same way as are the numbers of the given sets.
(**Note** Operations should be performed on the whole numbers, without breaking down the numbers into its constituent digits. E.g. 13 – Operations on 13 such as adding/subtracting/multiplying, etc. to 13 can be performed. Breaking down 13 into 1 and 3 and then performing mathematical operations on 1 and 3 is not allowed).
(4, 12, 48)
(9, 27, 108)
(a) (13, 39, 146) (b) (13, 36, 146)
(c) (13, 39, 156) (d) (13, 36, 156)

28. Select the Venn diagram that best illustrates the relationship between the following classes.
Mother, Women, Husband

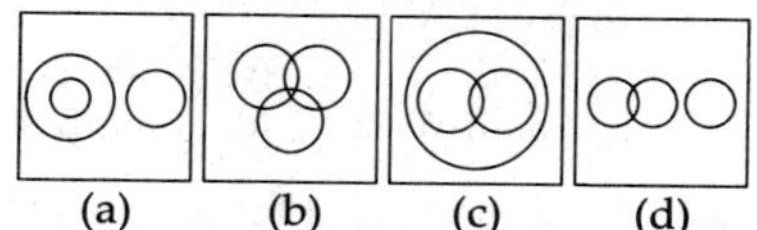

29. Two statements are given, followed by two conclusions numbered I and II. Assuming the statements to be true, even if they seem to be at variance with commonly known facts, decide which of the conclusions logically follow(s) from the statements.
Statements
All roads are routes.
All routes are bridges.
Conclusions
I. Some routes are roads.
II. All roads are bridges.
(a) Only Conclusion II follows
(b) Only Conclusion I follows
(c) Both Conclusions I and II follow
(d) Neither Conclusion I nor II follows

30. In a certain code language, 'CITY' is written as '241872', and 'DRUG' is written as'239620'. How will 'GOLF' be written in that language?
(a) 7121521
(b) 20121521
(c) 7151212
(d) 18151215

31. In a certain code language,
'A × B' means 'A is the son of B',
'A – B' means 'A is the brother of B',
'A + B' means 'A is the wife of B',
'A % B' means 'A is the father of B'.
How is M related to T if 'M × N + P % S – T'?
(a) Mother's brother
(b) Brother
(c) Husband
(d) Father

32. Which letter-cluster will replace the question mark (?) to complete the given series?
WTNM, SYHT, ? , KIVH, GNPO
(a) OFHA (b) ODBA
(c) UIDS (d) HREK

33. Select the figure from among the given options that can logically replace the question mark (?) in the following series.

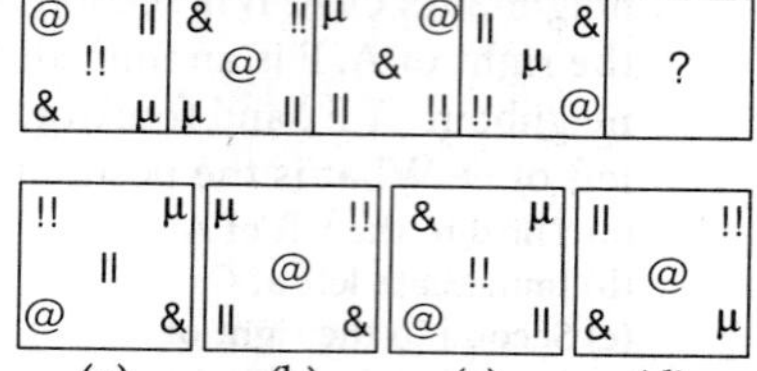

34. Which of the following numbers will replace the question mark (?) in the given series?
9, 20, 42, 86, 174, ?
(a) 350 (b) 370
(c) 360 (d) 380

35. If + means – , – means × , × means ÷ , ÷ means +, what will come in place of the question mark (?) in the given equation?
$180 \times 60 - 30 \div 30 + 20 = ?$
(a) 199 (b) 200 (c) 100 (d) 160

36. In a certain code language, 'stay for dinner' is written as 'px rn tf' and 'dinner is ready'is written as 'sq mv rn'. How is 'dinner' written in the given language?
(a) px (b) rn
(c) tf (d) sq

37. Which of the following interchanges of signs would make the given equation correct?
$10 + 23 - 3 \times 63 \div 7 = 70$
(a) + and × (b) – and ×
(c) ÷ and × (d) – and +

38. Sunil drives 5 km from point A towards the West. He then takes a left turn and drives 6km. He again takes a left turn and drives 11 km. He then takes a left turn and drives 6km. He finally takes a right turn and drives 6 km to arrive at point B. How much and in which direction does he have to drive to return to point A?
(All the turns are 90° turns only.)
(a) 12 km towards the West
(b) 10 km towards the East
(c) 10 km towards the West
(d) 14 km towards the East

39. Select the option that indicates the correct arrangement of the given words in the order in which they appear in an English dictionary.
1. Kibble 2. Kennel
3. Kettle4. Kicker 5. Kernel
(a) 5, 2, 3, 1, 4 (b) 2, 5, 3, 1, 4
(c) 5, 3, 2, 1, 4 (d) 2, 3, 5, 4, 1

40. Select the option that is related to the third word in the same way as the second word is related to the first word.
(The words must be considered as meaningful English words and must not be related to each other based on the number of letters/number of consonants/ vowels in the word.)
Episode : Series :: Chapter : ?
(a) Author (b) Book (c) Drama (d) Page

41. A sheet of paper is folded along the dotted line successively along the directions shown and is then punched in the last. How would the paper look when unfolded?

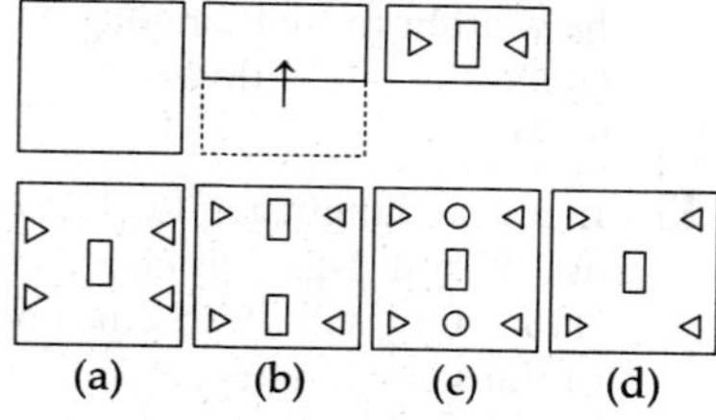

42. Select the option that represents the correct order of the given words as they would appear in an English dictionary.
1. Infant 2. Indolent
3. Inert 4. Infamous
5. Inefficient 6. Ineffable
(a) 2, 6, 5, 3, 4, 1 (b) 5, 4, 3, 2, 1, 6
(c) 5, 3, 4, 6, 2, 1 (d) 2, 5, 6, 1, 4, 3

43. Identify the figure given in the options, which when put in place of the question mark(?) will logically complete the series.

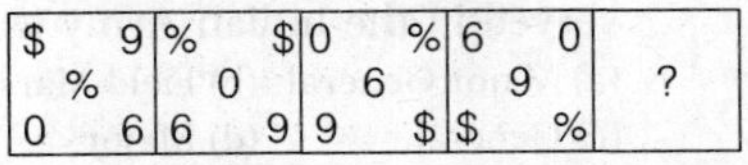

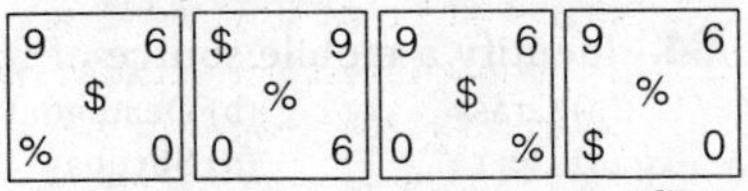

(a) (b) (c) (d)

44. Select the correct mirror image of the given figure when the mirror is placed at MN as shown below.

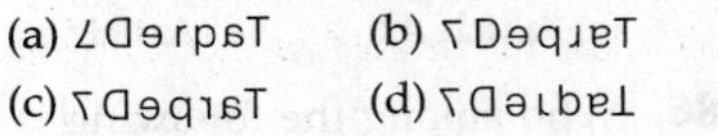

(a) ⅃ᗡerpaT (b) ⅂ᗡeqraT
(c) ⅂ᗡeqraT (d) ⅂ᗡerabɅ

45. Which of the following numbers will replace the question mark (?) in the given series?
5, 8, 13, ?, 29, 40
(a) 30 (b) 25 (c) 18 (d) 20

46. Select the option figure in which the given figure is embedded as its part. (Rotation is not allowed.)

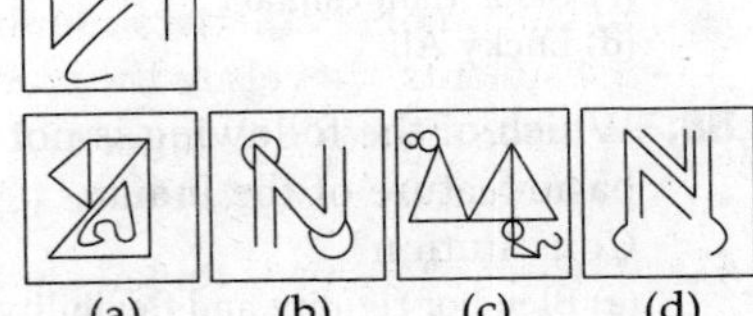

(a) (b) (c) (d)

47. Which letter-cluster will complete the given series?
DHMX, GJKU, ..., MNGO
(a) IMIR (b) JLIS
(c) JLIR (d) IMIS

48. In a certain code language,
A + B means 'A is the mother of B'
A − B means 'A is the brother of B'
A × B means 'A is the wife of B'
A ÷ B means ' A is the father of B'
Based on the above, how is A related to E if 'A ÷ B − C + D − E × F'?
(a) Brother (b) Father's father
(c) Father (d) Mother's father

49. A dice has its faces named by alphabets H, I, J, X, Y and Z. Two positions of the same dice are given below. Which face is opposite to face Y?

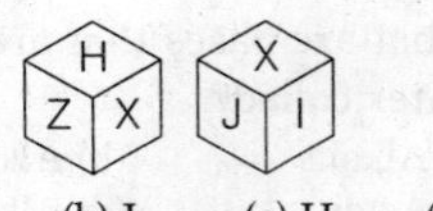

(a) X (b) J (c) H (d) Z

50. A dice has its faces named by letters L, M, N, V, W and X. Two positions of the same dice are given below. Which face is opposite to face X?

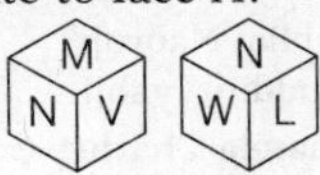

(a) N (b) L (c) M (d) W

Part II

General Knowledge and General Awareness

51. Kalidas Samman 2022 for Classical Music was given to
(a) KG Subramanyan
(b) Pandit Venkatesh Kumar
(c) Mallikarjun Mansur
(d) Semmangudi Srinivasa Iyer

52. The book 'A Suitable Boy' was authored by .... in 1993.
(a) Vikram Seth (b) Arundhati Roy
(c) Kiran Desai (d) David Davidar

53. The signs of charges of electron, proton and neutron are ...., respectively.
(a) negative, positive and neutral
(b) positive, negative and neutral
(c) neutral, positive and negative
(d) negative, neutral and positive

54. Kojagiri Poornima is a festival celebrated primarily in ...... on the full moon day of Ashwin month.
(a) Bihar (b) Maharashtra
(c) Andhra Pradesh (d) Kerala

55. Which of the following States/ Union Territories of India receives the highest average annual rainfall?
(a) Delhi (b) Meghalaya
(c) Ladakh (d) Rajasthan

56. In case, the President is satisfied with the Governor's report, he may declare President's Rule under Article 356 but such proclamation is initially for a period of ....
(a) three months (b) six months
(c) one month (d) two months

57. In which year did women take part in Modern Olympics for the first time?
(a) 1900 (b) 1916
(c) 1896 (d) 1904

58. In which of the following schedules of the Wildlife (Protection) Act, 1972 is the most common wild cat in India 'Felis Chaus' listed?
(a) Schedule IV (b) Schedule II
(c) Schedule I (d) Schedule III

59. When was 'The Objective Resolution' moved by Pt.Jawaharlal Nehru?
(a) 15th August, 1947
(b) 13th December, 1946
(c) 16th November, 1948
(d) 17th November, 1946

60. Who among the following was primarily an exponent of Bharatanatyam dance?
(a) Kelucharan Mohapatra
(b) Rukmini Devi Arundale
(c) Pandit Birju Maharaj
(d) Guru Bipin Singh

61. Eutrophication can be defined as
(a) the gradual increase in the concentration of phosphorus, nitrogen and other plant nutrients in an grassland ecosystem
(b) the gradual decrease in the concentration of phosphorus, nitrogen and other plant nutrients in an ageing aquatic ecosystem such as a lake
(c) the gradual increase in the concentration of phosphorus nitrogen and other plant nutrients in desert areas
(d) the gradual increase in the concentration of phosphorus nitrogen and other plant nutrients in an ageing aquatic ecosystem such as a lake

62. Which of the following is the IUPAC name of m-Dichlorobenzene?
(a) 3,4-Dichlorobenzene
(b) 1,2-Dichlorobenzene
(c) 1,3-Dichlorobenzene
(d) 2,3-Dichlorobenzene

63. World Athletics Under-20 Championship, 2021 was held from 18th to 22nd August, 2021 at ....
(a) South Africa (b) Brazil
(c) Argentina (d) Kenya

64. Who among the following wrote 'Gulamgiri' ?
(a) Bal Gangadhar Tilak
(b) Mahatma Gandhi
(c) BR Ambedkar
(d) Jyotiba Phule

65. Which of the following pairs of physicists and their contributions/ discoveries is incorrect?
(a) Heinrich Rudolf Hertz – Generation of electromagnetic waves
(b) Albert Einstein – Explanation of photoelectric effect
(c) Michael Faraday – Laws of electromagnetic induction
(d) Galileo Galilei – Wave theory of light

66. Dantivarman or Dantidurga was the founder of which of the following dynasties?
(a) Chera (b) Pala
(c) Pratihara (d) Rashtrakuta

67. In which year was the Foreign Investment Board established?
(a) 1991 (b) 1968 (c) 1960 (d) 1965

68. The Salal Hydroelectric Power Station is located in which Union Territory of India?
(a) Ladakh (b) Lakshadweep
(c) Chandigarh (d) Jammu and Kashmir

69. Selling of bonds by the RBI will cause money supply to ....
(a) decrease
(b) fluctuate
(c) increase
(d) No relationship exists between selling bonds and money supply

70. Which of the following banks is incharge of India's banking and monetary system?
(a) RBI (b) Union Bank
(c) BOB (d) SBI

71. Among the following, which is not a qualification for membership in the Vidhan Sabha?
(a) Not hold any office of profit
(b) Citizen of India
(c) Knowledge of politics
(d) Have attained the age of 25 years

72. Which Article of the Indian Constitution mentions about the right of the Advocate-General of a State to speak in the State Legislature ?
(a) Article-181 (b) Article-177
(c) Article-179 (d) Article-183

73. What are bases that are soluble in water called?
(a) Alkalis (b) Alkanes
(c) Acids (d) Alkenes

74. Who amongst the following became the President of the second session of the Indian National Congress held in Calcutta in December 1886?
(a) Dadabhai Naoroji
(b) Badruddin Tyabji
(c) P. Ananda Charlu
(d) William Wedderburn

75. In which year was Dattopant Thengadi National Board for Workers Education and Development established?
(a) 1978 (b) 1968
(c) 1958 (d) 1948

76. When did the second urbanisation in Ganga Valley take place?
(a) 3rd century BCE
(b) 5th century BCE
(c) 6th century BCE
(d) 2nd century BCE

77. Which festival is celebrated after the month of Ramzan?
(a) Milad-un-nabi (b) Jammat-ul-vida
(c) Eid-al-Fitr (d) Muharram

78. Veteran Kathak Dancer Aditi Mangaldas bagged the ....
(a) Mahari Award 2022
(b) Padma Vibhushan Award 2022
(c) Bharat Ratna Award 2022
(d) Padma Bhushan Award 2022

79. In which year did Lord Dalhousie introduce the railway line in British India?
(a) 1849 (b) 1870
(c) 1853 (d) 1861

80. Which river flows into the Wular lake in the North and then into Baramulla?
(a) Beas (b) Sutlej
(c) Jhelum (d) Ravi

81. A long, winding ridge of stratified sand and gravel is known as
(a) esker (b) moraine
(c) erratic (d) aquifer

82. Identify a substance that is not an allotrope of carbon.
(a) Graphite
(b) Buckminsterfullerene
(c) Diamond
(d) Phosphorus

83. The Government of India recently changed the name of Rajiv Gandhi Khel Ratna Award to Dhyan Chand Khel Ratna Award, Dhyan Chand served in the Indian Army as a
(a) Major General (b) Field Marshal
(c) General (d) Major

84. Identify a mobile source of food.
(a) Grass (b) Dead goat
(c) Deer (d) Shrubs

85. Which Article of the Indian Constitution mentions that 'The state shall endeavour to organise agriculture and animal husbandry on modern and scientific lines'?
(a) Article 43 (b) Article 48
(c) Article 42 (d) Article 46

86. Who among the following is not an Odissi dancer?
(a) Kumkum Mohanty
(b) Sonal Mansingh
(c) Protima Bedi
(d) Anita Ratnam

87. Which Assamese playback singer was conferred with the Bharat Ratna in 2019?
(a) Kishore Kumar
(b) Bhupen Hazarika
(c) Usha Mangeshkar
(d) Lucky Ali

88. Which of the following is not a basic feature of the Indian Constitution?
(a) Blend of rigidity and flexibility
(b) Lengthiest Written Constitution
(c) Parliamentary system
(d) Drawn from one source

89. Siyaram Tewari belongs to which of the following music Gharanas?
(a) Bettiah (b) Dagari
(c) Kirana (d) Darbhanga

90. In a basketball, when a referee throws the ball up into the centre circle to determine who receives the ball it is called ....
(a) Dunk ball (b) Jump ball
(c) Hook ball (d) High ball

91. At higher levels of development, which sector of the economy contributes less to the GDP?
(a) Service secto
(b) Both service and agriculture sector
(c) Industrial sector
(d) Agriculture sector

92. Which of the following depicts the Modern Periodic Table?

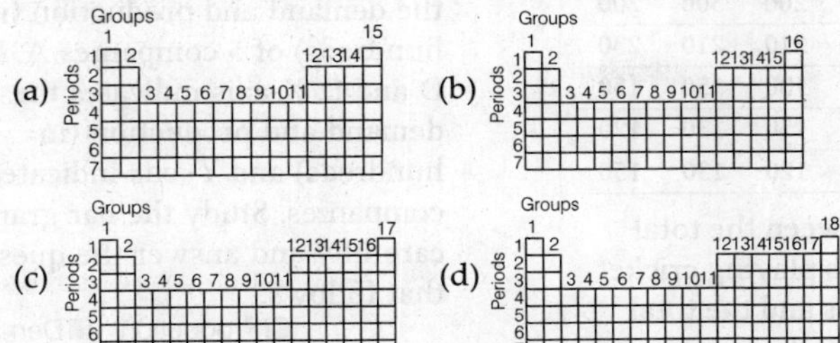

93. Diwan-i Kohi was the Department of .... introduced by Muhammad bin Tughlaq.
(a) Military (b) Market (c) Charity (d) Agriculture

94. In which of the following districts is Baira Siul Dam located?
(a) Kinnaur (b) Mandi (c) Bilaspur (d) Chamba

95. According to Census 2011, which of the following languages is spoken by the least population in India?
(a) Assamese (b) Dogri (c) Sanskrit (d) Konkani

96. 'Unladylike' is a memoir by ....
(a) Aishwarya Mohanraj (b) Supriya Joshi
(c) Aditi Mittal (d) Radhika Vaz

97. In which of the following ways were farmers encouraged to begin to use high yielding variety seeds?
(a) Agricultural labourers were paid wages directly by the government.
(b) Farmers' children were given free education in government colleges and universities.
(c) Farmers were given monetary support in cash to cultivate food grains.
(d) The government provided seeds and other inputs at prices lower than those prevailing in the market.

98. What is the name of the physical feature that is the longitudinal valley lying between the lesser Himalayas and the Siwalik in India?
(a) Terai (b) Doab (c) Duns (d) Bhabhar

99. Ram Sahay Panday, a 'Rai' dancer from Madhya Pradesh was conferred with which of the following awards in 2022?
(a) Arjuna Award (b) Saraswati Samman
(c) Padma Shri (d) Dronacharya Award

100. Which river originates from 'Rakshastal North-Western tip' near Mansarovar?
(a) Sutlej river (b) Ravi river
(c) Narmada river (d) Tapti river

Part III

Quantitative Aptitude

101. Find the natural number obtained when the number 13 is subtracted from the mean proportional of 75 and 12.
(a) 14 (b) 27 (c) 17 (d) 30

102. The value of $64 \div [44 - (8 \text{ of } 3 - 16) \div 4 \times 20]$ is equal to
(a) 15 (b) 16 (c) 18 (d) 12

103. The value of $5\frac{1}{4} - \left[3\frac{1}{2}\left\{\frac{5}{6} - \left(\frac{3}{5} \times \frac{1}{10} \div \frac{4}{15}\right)\right\}\right]$ is
(a) $2\frac{43}{120}$ (b) $1\frac{18}{120}$ (c) $1\frac{97}{120}$ (d) $2\frac{47}{120}$

104. The following table shows the classification of 100 students based on the marks obtained by them in Maths and Science in an examination.

Subjects	Marks out of 100				
	80 and above	60 and above	40 and above	20 and above	0 and above
Maths	12	35	80	94	100
Science	16	43	76	88	100
Average (Aggregate)	14	39	78	91	100

Find the number of students scoring less than 40% marks in aggregates.
(a) 28 (b) 26 (c) 24 (d) 22

105. *S* drives his car and covers 37 km and 500 m in 90 minutes. What is his average speed (in km/h)?
(a) 25 (b) 20 (c) 40 (d) 22.5

106. Which of the following statements is/are correct?
A. A triangle can have all angles less than 60°.
B. A triangle can have one obtuse angle.
C. A triangle can have two right angles.
D. A triangle can have two acute angles.
(a) A (b) B and D (c) B (d) A and C

107. If $x[-5\{-4(-a)\}] + 6[-3\{-3(-a)\}] = 6a$, then the value of x is
(a) −3 (b) −1 (c) 2 (d) 0

108. If $a + 2b + 3c = 0$, then what is the value of $(a^3 + 8b^3 + 27c^3)$?
(a) $18abc$ (b) $12abc$ (c) $6abc$ (d) 0

109. The following bar graph shows the sales (in thousands) of magazines from six branches (A, B, C, D, E and F) of a publishing company during two constructive years 2021 and 2022.

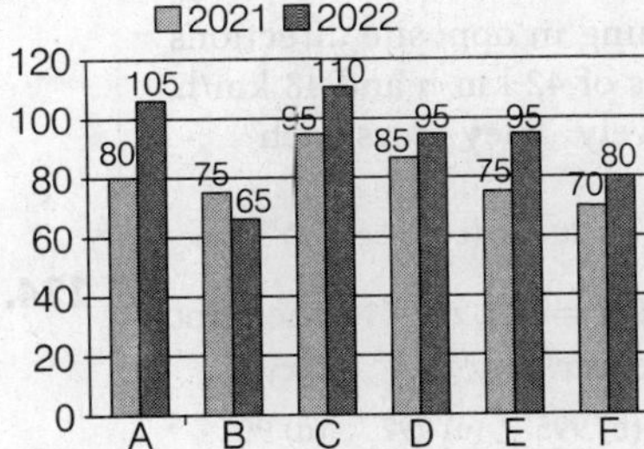

What percentage of the total sales of branch C for both years is the total sales of branch F for both years ? (around your answer up to two decimal places)
(a) 53.25% (b) 85.25% (c) 73.17% (d) 65.21%

110. *A* and *B* together can complete a piece of work in 25 days, *B* and *C* together can complete the same piece of work in 36 days, while *C* and *A* together can complete it in 30 days. If *A*, *B*, *C*, and *D* together can complete this piece of work in 18 days, then in how many days can *D* alone complete this piece of work?
(a) 210 (b) 180 (c) 200 (d) 225

111. Anwesha's marks in a class text of Sanskrit were incorrectly entered as 99 instead of 66. If there are 55 students in the class, then what is the increment in the average marks of the class in Sanskrit because of this typing error?
(a) 0.4 (b) 0.8 (c) 0.6 (d) 0.2

112. Bhavani spends 68% of her income. Her income increases by 15% and her expenditure increases by 10%. How much is the increase in the percentage of saving? (Use decimal up to 2 digits)
(a) 24.80% (b) 20.57%
(c) 28.42% (d) 25.62%

113. One laddoo with a radius of 5 cm belongs to a shopkeeper. How many laddoos of radius 2.5 cm may be created from the same one laddoo?
(a) 8 (b) 4 (c) 6 (d) 2

114. Of the three angles of a triangle, one is twice the smallest and another one is thrice the smallest. Find the value of the smallest angle.
(a) 65° (b) 60° (c) 30° (d) 45°

115. The cost of painting a spherical vessel of diameter 14 cm is ₹ 21560. What is the cost of painting (in ₹) per square centimeter? $\left(\text{Use, } \pi = \frac{22}{7}\right)$
(a) 32 (b) 35 (c) 28 (d) 30

116. Two trains 230 m and 270 m long are running in opposite directions at speeds of 42 km/h and 48 km/h, respectively. They cross each other in
(a) 22 sec (b) 20 sec (c) 25 sec (d) 30 sec

117. If $x = 110, y = 111, z = 112$, then find the value of $x^3 + y^3 + z^3 - 3xyz$.
(a) 999 (b) 995 (c) 997 (d) 991

118. A retailer marks up his goods by 130% and offers 25% discount. What will be the selling price (in ₹) if the cost price is ₹ 1600 ?
(a) 2760 (b) 1980 (c) 3680 (d) 1765

119. The following table gives the information of number of students from various schools playing various games (one student play one game only)

Game/School	A	B	C	D	E
Cricket	100	150	200	300	200
Tennis	200	220	210	210	230
Football	150	170	130	150	150
Basket ball	180	170	150	130	120
Badminton	100	150	120	130	150

The difference between the total number of students playing cricket from all the schools and the total number of students playing Tennis from all the schools is
(a) 120 (b) 80 (c) 100 (d) 150

120. A boatman rows 2 km in 10 mins, along the stream and 12 km in 2 h against the stream. What is the speed of the stream?
(a) 4 km/h (b) 35 km/h
(c) 3 km/h (d) 2.5 km/h

121. In an election between two candidates, the candidate who gets 35% of the votes polled is defeated by 15900 votes. What is the total number of votes polled?
(a) 45000 (b) 35000 (c) 43000 (d) 53000

122. The value of $1 - \cfrac{1}{1 + \cfrac{1}{2 - \cfrac{1}{2 + \cfrac{1}{3}}}}$ is
(a) $\frac{7}{18}$ (b) $\frac{3}{11}$ (c) $\frac{7}{15}$ (d) $\frac{3}{16}$

123. A boat covers 24 km upstream and 36 km downstream in 10 h, and 36 km upstream and 24 km downstream in 12 h. The speed of the current is
(a) $\frac{33}{13}$ km/h (b) $\frac{26}{9}$ km/h
(c) $\frac{24}{7}$ km/h (d) $\frac{25}{8}$ km/h

124. A certain amount of money becomes thrice in 5 yr at compound interest. How many years it will take to become 9 times ?
(a) 15 yr (b) 10 yr (c) 8 yr (d) 25 yr

125. Simplify $[25-(-4)\{9-(6-2)\}] \div [3 \times \{6+(-3)\times(-3)\}]$
(a) 1 (b) 6 (c) 4 (d) 2

126. Simplify

$$1898 \div \left[\frac{13}{4} \times (35+45) - \frac{91}{4}\right]$$

(a) 4 (b) 8 (c) 12 (d) 16

127. The following bar graph indicates the demand and production (in hundreds) of 5 companies A, B, C, D and E. X-axis indicates the demand and production (in hundreds) and Y-axis indicates the companies. Study the bar graph carefully and answer the question that follows.

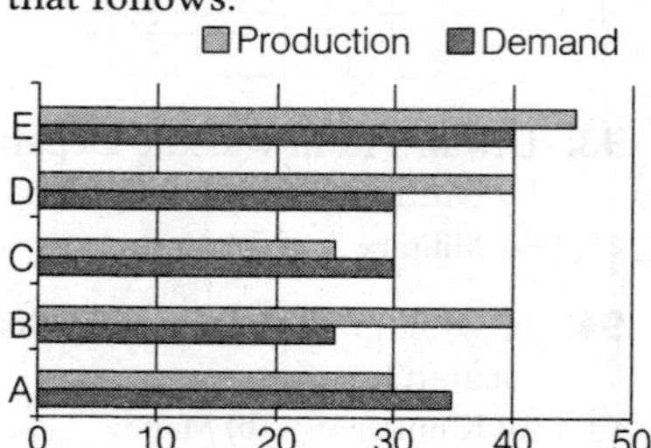

Find the difference between the average demand and average production of the five companies taken together.
(a) 500 (b) 2000 (c) 1000 (d) 400

128. In how many years will ₹ 2500 be invested at the rate of 12% per annum simple interest, which amounts to ₹ 4900 ?
(a) 4 (b) 6 (c) 8 (d) 2

129. The radius of the base and height of a cone are 5 cm and 6 cm, respectively, whereas the radius of the base and height of a cylinder and 2.5 cm and 3 cm, respectively. The ratio of the volume of the cone to that of the cylinder is $\left(\text{Where, } p = \frac{22}{7}\right)$
(a) 8 : 5 (b) 3 : 5 (c) 9 : 4 (d) 8 : 3

130. Simplify the following expression

$$\frac{3.2 \times 3.2 - 0.2 \times 0.2}{0.2 \times 0.2 - 2 \times 0.2 \times 3.2 + 3.2 \times 3.2}$$

(a) $\frac{13}{15}$ (b) $\frac{19}{15}$ (c) $\frac{17}{15}$ (d) $\frac{11}{15}$

131. A shopkeeper buys oranges at the rate of 10 oranges for ₹ 50 and sells them at the rate of 12 oranges for ₹ 74. Find his gain or loss percentage.
(a) $23\frac{1}{3}$% gain (b) $25\frac{1}{3}$% loss
(c) 25% gain (d) 30% loss

132. The angles of a triangle are in the ratio 1 : 2 : 3, then find the ratio of the corresponding sides.
(a) $1 : \sqrt{3} : 2$ (b) $1 : 2 : \sqrt{3}$
(c) $1 : \sqrt{2} : 3$ (d) 1 : 2 : 3

133. Find the value of
$[\{(82+48 \div 8 \times 3)+5 \times 6\}-7.5 \times 2]$
(a) 115 (b) 125 (c) 121 (d) 130

134. A number is first decreased by 10%, then increased by 30% and then further it is decreased by 20%. What is the net decrease percentage in the number?
(a) $4\frac{1}{5}\%$ (b) $3\frac{4}{5}\%$
(c) $6\frac{2}{5}\%$ (d) $5\frac{3}{5}\%$

135. Find the value of $\frac{1-\cot^2\theta}{\tan^2\theta-1}$
(a) $\tan^2\theta$ (b) $\tan\theta$ (c) $\cot^2\theta$ (d) $\cot\theta$

136. Ravi and Sanju together can do a job in 2 days, Sanju and Mahesh can do it in 4 days,while Ravi and Mahesh can do it in 2 days. What is the number of days required for Ravi to do the same job alone?
(a) 4 days (b) $\frac{8}{3}$ days
(c) $\frac{5}{3}$ days (d) 9 days

137. A seller offers a discount of 12% if the total sale price of different products purchased by a single customer is below ₹ 3000, and discount of 15% if the total sale value of all the products exceeds ₹ 3000. A shirt costing ₹ 900 was sold to Anand after earning a margin of 9% and also a jacket costing ₹ 1900 was sold to him after a margin of 6%.How much does Anand have to pay (in ₹) for the final settlement of the bill?
(a) 2645.60 (b) 2953.60
(c) 3005.40 (d) 2635.60

138. The radius of a hemispherical bowl is 9 cm. The capacity of the bowl is $\left(\text{Use, } \pi=\frac{22}{7}\right)$
(a) 1625.37 cm^3 (b) 1821.47 cm^3
(c) 1428.78 cm^3 (d) 1527.43 cm^3

139. If $\frac{(\sec A+\tan A)}{(\sec A-\tan A)}=2\frac{51}{79}$, then the value of $\sin A$ is equal to
(a) $\frac{87}{169}$ (b) $\frac{65}{144}$ (c) $\frac{77}{144}$ (d) $\frac{61}{169}$

140. Simplify : $20 \div 5$ of $4 \times 8+6 \div 24$ of $3 \times 48-6 \div 18 \times 9$.
(a) 6 (b) 4 (c) 9 (d) 1.125

141. The length of the side of a cube is 8 cm. Find the volume of the cube?
(a) 664 cm^3 (b) 612 cm^3
(c) 512 cm^3 (d) 564 cm^3

142. A reduction of 7.5% in the cost price of a commodity enables a shopkeeper to purchase 15 kg more than what he previously purchased for a sum of ₹ 7400. In order to make a profit of 32.5% on the prereduction cost price of the commodity, at what price (in ₹) per kg should the commodity be sold?
(a) 54 (b) 52 (c) 51 (d) 53

143. A sum of ₹ 17600 was divided between Jeevan, Praveen and Kanan, such that the ratio of the sums received by Jeevan and Praveen was 5 : 8, while the ratio of the sums received by Praveen and Kanan was 3 : 2. How much money did Jeevan receive as his share?
(a) ₹ 4850 (b) ₹ 4750 (c) ₹ 4800 (d) ₹ 4900

144. The following table shows the gross turnover (in crores) of a company over 5 yr.

Year	Gross Turnover
2016	12
2017	18
2018	25
2019	25
2020	30

By what percentage is the gross turnover of 2020 higher than the gross turnover of 2018?
(a) 20% (b) 5% (c) 25% (d) 13%

145. The given pie-chart shows the budget estimated by a family for their monthly expenses. Monthly expenses = ₹ 58000.

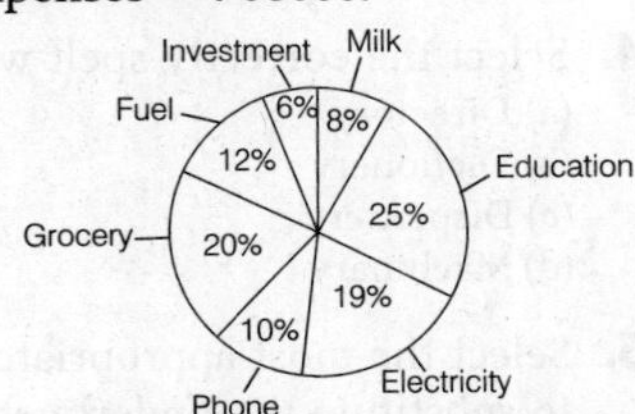

Find the difference between the amount budget amount for grocery and electricity to the amount spent on grocery and electricity, if the family actually spent ₹ 18875 on both grocery and electricity.
(a) ₹ 4573 (b) ₹ 4375
(c) ₹ 3745 (d) ₹ 3547

146. Study the given tables and answer the question that follows.
The tables show the number of candidates (in lakh) appearing in an entrance exam from four different cities and the ratio of candidates passing and failing in the same.

City	P	Q	R	S
Number of Candidates	1.10	2.26	2.12	1.46

Ratio of candidates passing and failing within the city

City	Passing	Failing
P	6	5
Q	3	7
R	5	7
S	3	5

The number of candidates passing the exam from City Q is what percentage of the total number of candidates appearing from all the cities together (rounded off to 2 decimal places)?
(a) 11.25% (b) 10.70%
(c) 12.93% (d) 9.77%

147. The value of
$29-[(48 \div 12)+2 \times(8 \div 4+4)]$ is equal to
(a) 15 (b) 21 (c) 19 (d) 13

148. Solve the equation for A (in degrees).
$2\cos^2 A+3\cos A-2=0,\ 0<A<90°$
(a) 45° (b) 60° (c) 80° (d) 30°

149. Find the area (in cm^2) of the sector of a circle of radius 21 cm with a central angle of 60°. [Use p = $\frac{22}{7}$]
(a) 302 (b) 289
(c) 231 (d) 245

150. Simplify $\frac{\cos 13°+\sin 13°}{\cos 13°-\sin 13°}$
(a) $\cot 58°$ (b) $\cos 26°$
(c) $\tan 32°$ (d) $\tan 58°$

Part IV
English Comprehension

151. Select the option that can be used as a one-word substitute for the given group of words.
The period of time in a person's life when they are developing into an adult.
(a) Adolescence (b) Adultery
(c) Teenage (d) Childhood

152. The following sentence has been divided into parts. One of them contains an error. Select the part that contains the error from the given options.
Mr. Thomas / is going / to buy / horse.
(a) is going (b) Mr. Thomas
(c) to buy (d) horse

153. The following sentence has been divided into parts. One of them may contain an error. Select the part that contains the error form the given option. If you don't find any error, mark ' No error' as your answer.
By the time I reaching / the metro station, / the train had departed.
(a) No error
(b) the metro station
(c) the train had departed
(d) By the time I reaching

154. Select the most appropriate option to substitute the underlined segment in the given sentence.
Rajans caused extremely painful headaches.
(a) excruciating (b) horrible
(c) extreme (d) devastating

155. Select the most appropriate synonym of the given word.
Pacify
(a) Rebuke (b) Blame
(c) Strengthen (d) Soothe

156. Select the most appropriate option that can substitute the underlined segment in the given sentence.
The company plans to expand its business to the international market.
(a) to reduce (b) to contract
(c) to increase (d) to limit

157. Select the most appropriate antonym of the underlined word in the given sentence.
The beauty of cherry blossoms is ephemeral, as the delicate pink petals bloom for only a short period.
(a) uniform (b) unwavering
(c) permanent (d) transient

158. Select the most appropriate antonym of the underlined word.
Indians tend to be quite conservative in most aspects of life, particularly in rural areas.
(a) liberal (b) fantastic
(c) determined (d) authentic

159. Select the most appropriate meaning of the underlined idiom.
Despite multiple obstacles, she continued with her endeavour, demonstrating that she has nerves of steel.
(a) Extraordinary beauty
(b) An absence of fear or anxiety
(c) Relentless determination
(d) The capacity to maintain composure when stressed

160. Select the option that can be used as a one-word substitute for the italicised segment in the given sentence.
Tin is easy to shape in any desired form
(a) Malleable (b) Rigid
(c) Immutable (d) Gullible

161. Select the most appropriate synonym of the given word.
Dainty
(a) Vulgar (b) Fine
(c) Elegant (d) Sable

162. Select the most appropriate synonym of the given word.
Filthy
(a) Tidy (b) Visual
(c) Shiny (d) Dirty

163. Select the most appropriate idiom that can substitute the underlined word in the given sentence.
Its Christmas and everything looks so beautiful. It makes me believe that life is wonderful and pleasant.
(a) I'm up in the air
(b) I'm facing the music
(c) I'm changing my tune
(d) life is a bowl of cherries

164. Select the correctly spelt word.
(a) Directory
(b) Dictionery
(c) Dispensery
(d) Machinary

165. Select the most appropriate option to substitute the underlined part of the following sentence.
Mathew decided to complete the marathon to prove that he is still fit as a fiddle in his eighties.
(a) an owner of a fit horse
(b) a man of great qualities
(c) proud and unreliable
(d) a fit and energetic person

166. Select the most appropriate option to substitute the underlined segment in the given sentence.
The manager, decided at last to bring the stenographer to book for her illegal money transactions after trying to ignore it several times.
(a) bring her for a detailed investigation
(b) take her into great confidence
(c) place her in a safe supportive position
(d) make her accountable for her conduct

167. Identify the incorrectly spelt word in the given sentence and select the option that rectifies the spelling error.
The idea is to encourage tourism and allow visitors to enjoy the spectacular Rockies, but to ensure that it is done in hermony with the environment.
(a) Enssure (b) Harmony
(c) Encaurage (d) Touresm

168. Select the most appropriate option to fill in the blank.
Mihir's ability to think outside....... always gives our team the upper hand when tackling complex problems.
(a) the room (b) the cupboard
(c) the box (d) the bowl

169. Select the most appropriate option that can substitute the underlined words in the given sentence.
My son will carry out my business in my absence.
(a) carry at (b) carry on
(c) carry for (d) carry in

170. Select the option that can be used as a one-word substitute for the given group of words.
The study of Man
(a) Autobiography (b) Anthropology
(c) Biography (d) Biology

171. The following sentence has been divided into four segments. One of them contains an error. Select the segment that contains the error from the given options.
Last night I dreamed that / I am looking for the/ abominable snowman high / up in the Himalayas.
(a) abominable snowman high
(b) up in the Himalayas
(c) I am looking for the
(d) Last night I dreamed that

172. Select the most appropriate idioms that can substitude the underlined segment in the given sentence.
We need to make sure that criminals like these get more from the authorities than a very mild punishment.
(a) a slap on the wrist
(b) an axe to grind
(c) a blessing in disguise
(d) a taste of their own medicine

173. Select the option that can be used as a one-word substitute for the underlined group of words.
There was a huge fire for celebration on the occasion of Diwali.
(a) Lohri (b) Flash
(c) Bonfire (d) Firecracker

174. Select the incorrectly spelt word.
(a) Granary (b) Dictionary
(c) Directory (d) Chancellary

175. In question four alternative are given for the underlined Idiom / Phrases in the sentence. Choose the alternative which best expresses the meaning of the Idiom / Phrases.
In life, there will be many situations where you have to choose between the devil and the deep blue sea.
(a) To be in dilemma to choose
(b) To be in the deep sea
(c) To be in a good condition
(d) To choose wisely

176. Select the option that can be used as a one-word substitute for the given group of word.
A film shown during the day, especially in the afternoon.
(a) Dramatics (b) Matinee
(c) Cinema (d) Theatre

177. Select the option that expresses the meaing of the underlined segment.
The regulation bans any direct or indirect promotion through radio or television of supernatural practices.
(a) questionable (b) obtuse
(c) occult (d) evident

178. Select the most appropriate option to substitute the underlined segment in the given sentence.
It is a fact that the same judgement can often be taken by more than one way.
(a) be taken on more than
(b) be taken in more than
(c) be taken for more than
(d) be taken of more than

179. Parts of the following sentence have been given as options. Select the option that contains an error.
My father / is / comparatively better / today.
(a) comparatively better (b) is
(c) My father (d) today

180. Select the sentence that has the correct use of words and spellings from the options given below.
(a) The skilled surgeon delicately performed the intricate procedure, saving the patient's life with his stedy hands and unwavering focus.
(b) The skilled surgeon delicately performed the intrecate procedure, saving the patient's life with his steady hands and unwavering focus.
(c) The skiled surgeon delicately performed the intricate procedure, saving the patient's life with his stedy hands and unwavering focus.
(d) The skilled surgeon delicately performed the intricate procedure, saving the patient's life with his steady hands and unwavering focus.

181. Select the option that can be used as a one-word substitute for the given group of word.
A list of books
(a) Lexicon (b) Manuscript
(c) Bibliography (d) Catalogue

182. Select the most appropriate segment to substitute the underlined words in the given sentence.
He always used to say that he was not a beggar by choice and if someone could employ him, he would like to eat.
(a) love to work (b) listen to me
(c) linger at work (d) live to work

183. Select the most appropriate meaning of the given idiom.
Beat around the bush.
(a) To go around the bush.
(b) To live around the bush.
(c) To avoid talking about what is important.
(d) To talk about something important.

184. Select the most appropriate idiom that can substitute the underlined segment in the given sentence.
I don't know which career he will choose. He delays making strong decisions.
(a) Sits on the fence
(b) Is as clean as a whistle
(c) Turns a blind eye
(d) Spills the beans

185. The following sentence has been split into four segments. Identify the segment that contains a grammatical error.
If I have recovered from fever, / I will start going / for swimming classes / from tomorrow.
(a) I will start going
(b) for swimming classes
(c) from tomorrow
(d) If I have recovered from fever

186. Which of the following words has a similar meaning to the underlined word?
Numerous tremors without any tectonic plate movement have baffled geologists.
(a) Angered (b) Irritated
(c) Perplexed (d) Amused

187. Which is the right set of antonyms from the options for 'Confidential'?
(a) Familiar, Revealed
(b) Offstage, Sneaking
(c) Public, Concealed
(d) Hushed, Common

188. Select the most appropriate synonym of the given word.
Voracious
(a) Quenched (b) Appreciate
(c) Compensated (d) Greedy

189. Choose the incorrectly spelt word in the given sentence.
It may seem pretintious to say so but I cannot live without my essential articles.
(a) essential (b) cannot
(c) articles (d) pretintious

190. Select the incorrectly spelt word.
(a) Programe (b) Unexpected
(c) Pilgrimage (d) Campaign

Directions (Q. Nos. 191-195) *In the following passage, some words have been deleted. Read the passage carefully and select the most appropriate option to fill in each blank.*

"Can I come along with you on your fishing trip, please?" asked Millie. Her two elder brothers ......(1)...... at her scornfully. "Fishing is a mans ......(2)....... ," said her older brother, Derek. "Girls are not ......(3)...... at fishing." ......(4)...... a while, however, Millie managed to persuade her brothers to take her ......(5)...... . When they reached the fishing pond, the two brothers wandered off by themselves.

191. Select the most appropriate option to fill in blank no. 1.
(a) looked (b) observed
(c) saw (d) watched

192. Select the most appropriate option to fill in blank no. 2.
(a) matches (b) gaming
(c) competition (d) sport

193. Select the most appropriate option to fill in blank no. 3.
(a) good (b) sound
(c) likeable (d) acceptable

194. Select the most appropriate option to fill in blank no. 4.
(a) Nearly (b) After
(c) Then (d) Before

195. Select the most appropriate option to fill in blank no. 5.
(a) among them (b) within
(c) along (d) with them

Directions (Q. Nos. 196-200) *Read the given passage and answer the questions that follow.*

New media is a catch-all term used for various kinds of electronic communications that are conceivable due to innovation in computer technology. In contrast to old media, which includes newspapers, magazines, books, television and other such non-interactive media, new media comprises websites, online video/audio streams, emails, online social platforms, online communities, online forums, blogs, internet telephony, web advertisements, online education and much more. It is not very easy to draw a line between the new and old media because the so-called old media has found new ways of representation in digital forms, leaving behind its conventional methods of representation.

New media is considered to be the multimedia and digital form of communication happening *via* desktop and laptop computers as well as phones, tablets and other devices. New media has introduced user interaction, rather than simply consuming media. New media can be customised to user's preferences and it can be selectively linked from one form of content to another.

196. Select the most appropriate synonym of the word 'Customise'.
(a) Personalise (b) Realise
(c) Generalise (d) Ritualised

197. Why is it not easy to draw a line between old media and new media?
(a) Because new media can be customised to user's preferences.
(b) Because new media is considered to be the multimedia and digital form of communication.
(c) Because both include various kinds of medium.
(d) Because old media has found new ways of representation in digital forms.

198. How does the passage distinguish new media from old media?
(a) New media includes user interaction, whereas, through old media, we only consume information.
(b) New media increases screen time and could be addictive and unhealthy, unlike old media.
(c) New media is fast and digitally based, whereas old media has never been beyond the conventional methods of representation.
(d) New media caters to a larger audience and is more popular than old media.

199. Which of the following is not a type/kind of new media?
(a) Web advertisements
(b) Television
(c) E-mails
(d) Online video streams

200. What does the term Catch-all mean?
(a) A category which includes all the types of media.
(b) A category that includes all the sources of information.
(c) A category that includes all the sources of entertainment.
(d) A category which includes many different things.

Know Correct Answers

1. (b)	2. (b)	3. (c)	4. (a)	5. (d)	6. (d)	7. (b)	8. (b)	9. (b)	10. (a)
11. (b)	12. (a)	13. (c)	14. (c)	15. (b)	16. (c)	17. (b)	18. (a)	19. (d)	20. (b)
21. (c)	22. (b)	23. (b)	24. (d)	25. (a)	26. (c)	27. (c)	28. (a)	29. (c)	30. (b)
31. (b)	32. (b)	33. (a)	34. (a)	35. (c)	36. (b)	37. (b)	38. (a)	39. (b)	40. (b)
41. (b)	42. (a)	43. (a)	44. (c)	45. (d)	46. (a)	47. (c)	48. (d)	49. (a)	50. (a)
51. (b)	52. (a)	53. (a)	54. (b)	55. (b)	56. (b)	57. (a)	58. (b)	59. (b)	60. (b)
61. (d)	62. (c)	63. (d)	64. (d)	65. (d)	66. (d)	67. (b)	68. (d)	69. (a)	70. (a)
71. (c)	72. (b)	73. (a)	74. (a)	75. (c)	76. (c)	77. (c)	78. (a)	79. (c)	80. (c)
81. (a)	82. (d)	83. (d)	84. (c)	85. (b)	86. (d)	87. (b)	88. (d)	89. (d)	90. (b)
91. (d)	92. (d)	93. (d)	94. (d)	95. (c)	96. (d)	97. (d)	98. (c)	99. (c)	100. (a)
101. (c)	102. (b)	103. (a)	104. (d)	105. (a)	106. (b)	107. (a)	108. (a)	109. (c)	110. (c)
111. (c)	112. (d)	113. (a)	114. (c)	115. (b)	116. (b)	117. (a)	118. (a)	119. (a)	120. (c)
121. (d)	122. (a)	123. (d)	124. (b)	125. (a)	126. (b)	127 (d)	128. (c)	129. (d)	130. (c)
131. (a)	132. (a)	133. (a)	134. (c)	135. (c)	136. (b)	137 (d)	138. (d)	139. (b)	140. (c)
141. (c)	142. (d)	143. (c)	144. (a)	145. (c)	146. (d)	147. (d)	148. (b)	149. (c)	150. (d)
151. (a)	152. (d)	153. (d)	154. (a)	155. (d)	156. (c)	157. (c)	158. (a)	159. (b)	160. (a)
161. (c)	162. (d)	163. (d)	164. (a)	165. (d)	166. (d)	167. (b)	168. (c)	169. (b)	170. (b)
171. (c)	172. (a)	173. (c)	174. (d)	175. (a)	176. (b)	177. (c)	178. (b)	179. (a)	180. (d)
181. (d)	182. (a)	183. (c)	184. (a)	185. (d)	186. (c)	187. (a)	188. (d)	189. (d)	190. (a)
191. (a)	192. (d)	193. (a)	194. (b)	195. (d)	196. (a)	197. (d)	198. (a)	199. (b)	200. (d)

Answer & Solutions

1. (b) According to the statements,

Conclusions

I. (✗) II. (✗)

Hence, neither Conclusion I nor II follows.

2. (b) As per the question, option (b) is the correct mirror image of the figure, when the mirror is placed at MN.

M

hj52dR | (mirror image of hj52dR)

N

3. (c) Given equation,

$145 \div 96 \times 12 + 13$

After interchange the signs, we get;

$+ \Rightarrow -$	$- \Rightarrow \times$
$\times \Rightarrow \div$	$\div \Rightarrow +$

$\Rightarrow 145 + 96 \div 12 - 13$

$\Rightarrow 145 + 8 - 13$

$\Rightarrow 153 - 13 = 140$

4. (a) As, G A M E → (+4, +2, +4, +2) → K C Q G

and F A R M → (+4, +2, +4, +2) → J C V O

Similarly, T O W N → (+4, +2, +4, +2) → X Q A P

5. (d) As, 29 : 61 [29×2+3=61]

and 15 : 33 [15×2+3=33]

Similarly, 47 : 97 [47×2+3=97]

6. (d) As, M A I L E D → D E L M A I

and F A B R I C → C I R F A B

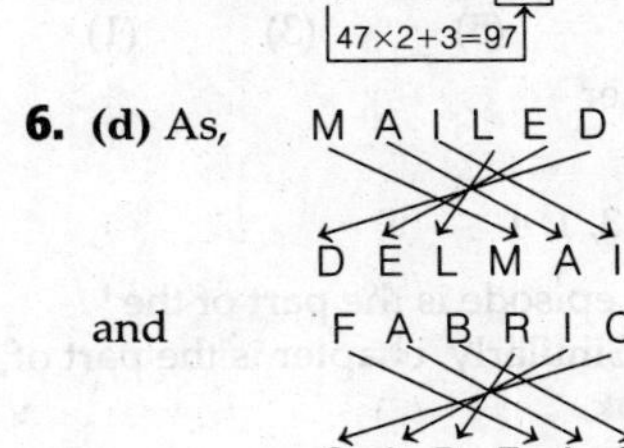

Similarly, J A C K E T → T E K J A C

7. (b) As per the question, option (b) depicts the pattern that would appear when the given transparent sheet is folded at the horizontal line.

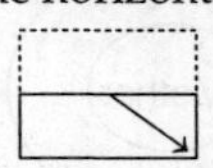

8. (b) According to the statements,

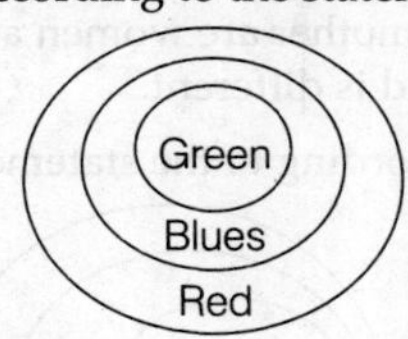

Conclusions

I. (✗) II. (✗) III. (✗)

Hence, none of the conclusions follow.

9. (b) Pattern of the series is as follows,

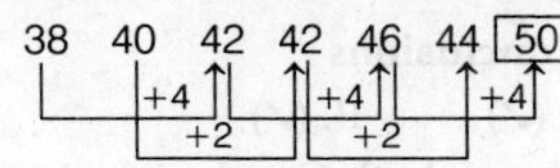

10. (a) Pattern of the series is as follows,

55 62 65 72 75 82

+7 +3 +7 +3 +7

11. (b) As,

$(19, 200) \Rightarrow 19 + 1 = 20 \times 10 = 200$

and $(15, 160) \Rightarrow 15 + 1 = 16 \times 10 = 160$

Similarly,

$\Rightarrow (22, 230) \Rightarrow 22 + 1 = 23 \times 10 = 230$

12. (a) As, F L Y → Opposite place value → $(21+15+2) = 38$

and N U T → Opposite place value → $(13+6+7) = 26$

Similarly, G O D → Opposite place value → $(20+12+23) = 55$

13. (c) As, P E N = 70

Place value →

$(16 + 5 + 14) = 35 \times 2 = 70$

and N E S T = 116

Place value →

$(14 + 5 + 19 + 20) = 58 \times 2 = 116$

Similarly, P E O N = ?

Place value →

$(16 + 5 + 15 + 14) = 50 \times 2 = 100$

14. (c) Given equation,

174 P 2 S 45 R (16 P 4) Q 5 S26

After replacing the signs, we get

$P \Rightarrow \div$	$Q \Rightarrow \times$
$R \Rightarrow +$	$S \Rightarrow -$

$= 174 \div 2 - 45 + (16 \div 4) \times 5 - 26$

$= 87 - 45 + 4 \times 5 - 26$

$= 87 - 45 + 20 - 26$

$= 107 - 71 = 36$

15. (b) Given equation,

$9 + 6 \times 3 - 9 \div 1 = 10$

From option (b), interchanges the signs '÷' and '−', we get

$\Rightarrow 9 + 6 \times 3 \div 9 - 1 = 10$

$\Rightarrow 9 + 2 - 1 = 10$

$\Rightarrow 11 - 1 = 10$

$\therefore \quad 10 = 10$

16. (c) As, O →(+7)→ V →(−3)→ S

L →(+7)→ S →(−3)→ P

N →(+7)→ U →(−3)→ R

But, J →(+7)→ Q →(−4)→ M

17. (b) According to the question,

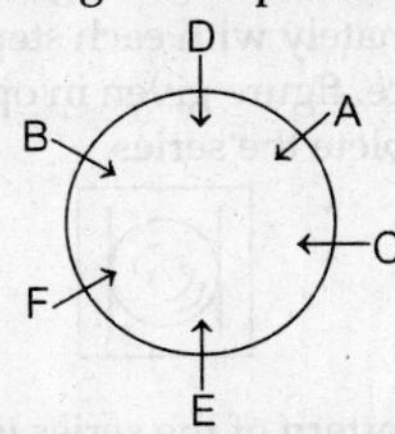

Hence, E is the immediate left of C.

18. (a) As, (21, 105, 35) → 7×3, 7×15, 7×5

and (27, 135, 45) → 9×3, 9×15, 9×5

Similarly, (39, 195, 65) → 13×3, 13×15, 13×5

19. (d) Given equation,

455 A 5 D 17 C 36 B 4 = ?

After replacing the signs, we get

$A \Rightarrow \div$	$B \Rightarrow \times$
$C \Rightarrow +$	$D \Rightarrow -$

$\Rightarrow \quad 455 \div 5 - 17 + 36 \times 4$

$\Rightarrow \quad 91 - 17 + 144$

$\Rightarrow \quad 235 - 17 = \boxed{218}$

20. (b) Given equation,

29 A 37 B 14 C 3 A (84 D 4) A 46

After replacing the signs, we get

A ⇒ +	C ⇒ ×
B ⇒ −	D ⇒ ÷

$= 29 + 37 - 14 \times 3 + (84 \div 4) + 46$

$= 29 + 37 - 42 + 21 + 46$

$= 133 - 42 = \boxed{91}$

21. (c) As per the question, from dice (2) and (3), 4 and 5 numbers are common in dice. So, 2 is opposite to 6.

22. (b) According to the question,

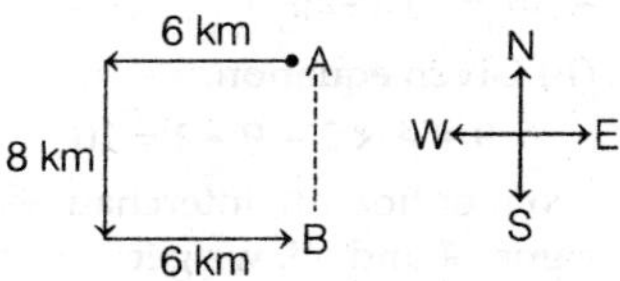

∴ Point B is in South direction of point A.

23. (b) As, 3 : 2

$2 \times 1.5 = 3$

and 9 : 6

$6 \times 1.5 = 9$

Similarly, 12 : ?

$12 \times 1.5 = \boxed{18}$

24. (d) In the given series two arcs [()] and one line is getting added alternately with each step.
Hence, figure given in option (d) will complete the series.

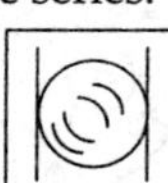

25. (a) Pattern of the series is as follows,

$H \xrightarrow{+1} I \xrightarrow{+1} J \xrightarrow{+1} \boxed{K}$

$M \xrightarrow{+1} N \xrightarrow{+1} O \xrightarrow{+1} \boxed{P}$

$W \xrightarrow{+1} X \xrightarrow{+1} Y \xrightarrow{+1} \boxed{Z}$

26. (c) As, J A M = 24

Place value → 10 + 1 + 13 = 24

and G E L = 24

Place value → 7 + 5 + 12 = 24

Similarly, L A W

Place value → 12 + 1 + 23 = $\boxed{36}$

27. (c) As, (4 12 48)

↓ 4×1 4×3 4×12

and (9 27 108)

↓ 9×1 9×3 9×12

Similarly, (13 39 156)

↓ 13×1 13×3 13×12

28. (a) According to the venn diagram,

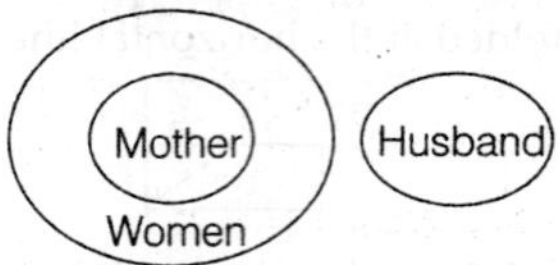

As, all mother are women and husband is different.

29. (c) According to the statement,

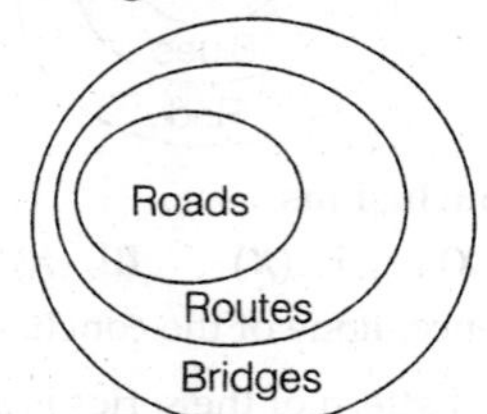

Conclusions

I. (✓) II. (✓)

Hence, both Conclusions I and II follow.

30. (b) As,

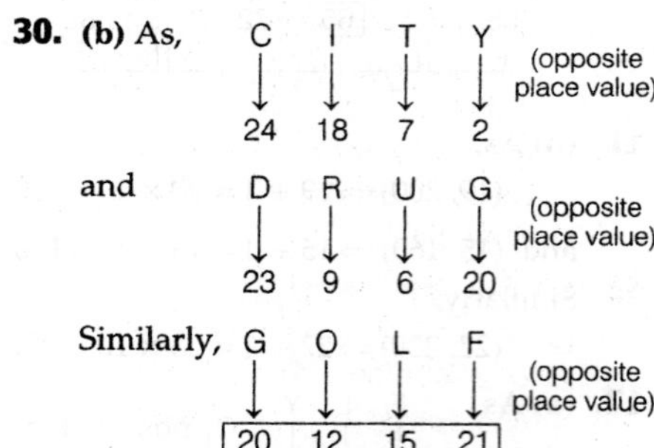

31. (b) According to the question,

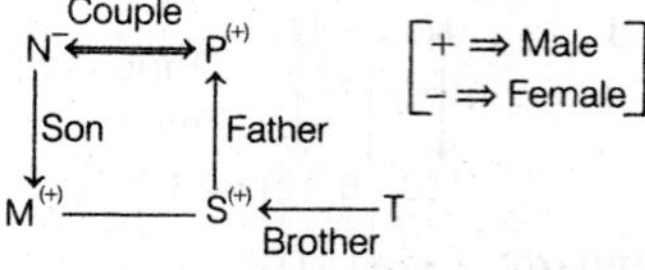

Hence, M is brother of T.

32. (b) The pattern of the series as follows,

$W \xrightarrow{-4} S \xrightarrow{-4} \boxed{O} \xrightarrow{-4} K \xrightarrow{-4} G$

$T \xrightarrow{+5} Y \xrightarrow{+5} \boxed{D} \xrightarrow{+5} I \xrightarrow{+5} N$

$N \xrightarrow{-6} H \xrightarrow{-6} \boxed{B} \xrightarrow{-6} V \xrightarrow{-6} P$

$M \xrightarrow{+7} T \xrightarrow{+7} \boxed{A} \xrightarrow{+7} H \xrightarrow{+7} O$

33. (a) In the figure series, pattern is as follows,

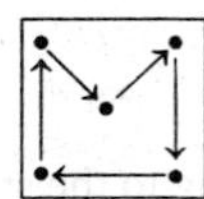

Hence, option figure (a) will replace the question mark.

34. (a) Pattern of the series is as follows,

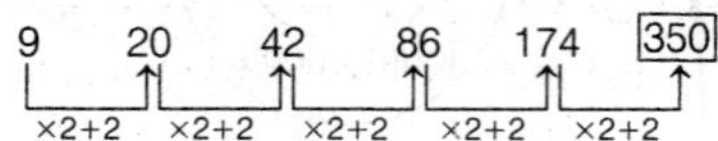

35. (c) Given equation,

$180 \times 60 - 30 \div 30 + 20$

After interchanging the signs, we get

+ ⇒ −	− ⇒ ×
× ⇒ ÷	÷ ⇒ +

$= 180 \div 60 \times 30 + 30 - 20$

$= 3 \times 30 + 30 - 20$

$= 90 + 30 - 20$

$= 120 - 20 = \boxed{100}$

36. (b) According to the question,

stay for (dinner) ⟶ px (rn) tf

(dinner) is ready ⟶ sq mv (rn)

Hence, the code of dinner is rn.

37. (b) Given equation,

$10 + 23 - 3 \times 63 \div 7 = 70$

From option (b) after interchanging the signs, − and ×, we get

$\Rightarrow \quad 10 + 23 \times 3 - 63 \div 7 = 70$

$\Rightarrow \quad 10 + 69 - 9 = 70$

$\Rightarrow \quad 79 - 9 = 70$

$\therefore \quad 70 = 70$

38. (a) According to the question,

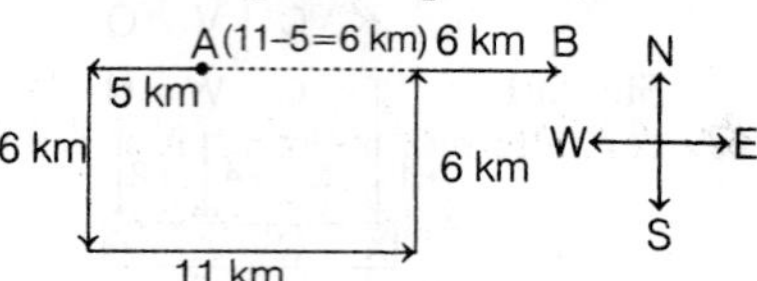

Hence, he must drive 12 km towards the West direction to return at point A.

39. (b) As per the English dictionary,

Kennel → Kernel → Kettle → Kibble
(2) (5) (3) (1)

→ Kicker
(4)

⇒ 2, 5, 3, 1, 4

40. (b) As, episode is the part of the series. Similarly, chapter is the part of the book.

41. (b) A sheet of paper is folded along the dotted line successively along the direction shown and is then punched in the last. The paper book when unfolded like option (b).

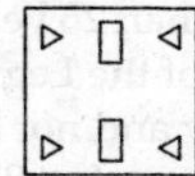

42. (a) As per the English dictionary,

Indolent → Ineffable → Inefficient →
(2) (6) (5)
Inert → Infamous → Infant
(3) (4) (1)

⇒ 2, 6, 5, 3, 4, 1

43. (a) In the figure series, pattern is as follow,

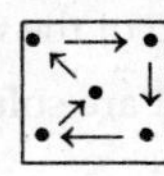

Hence, option figure (a) will replace the question mark.

44. (c) According to the question, Option (c) is the correct mirror image of the given figure when the mirror is placed at MN.

M
TarpeD7 | TarpeD7 (mirrored)
N

45. (d) Pattern of the series is as follows,

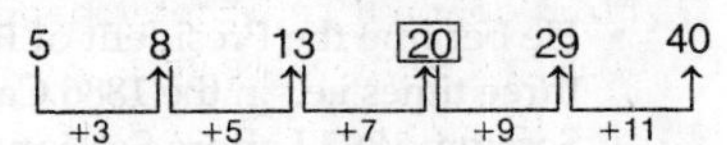

46. (a) The given figure is embedded in option figure (a).

47. (c) Pattern of the series is as follows,

D $\xrightarrow{+3}$ G $\xrightarrow{+3}$ J $\xrightarrow{+3}$ M
H $\xrightarrow{+2}$ J $\xrightarrow{+2}$ L $\xrightarrow{+2}$ N
M $\xrightarrow{-2}$ K $\xrightarrow{-2}$ I $\xrightarrow{-2}$ G
X $\xrightarrow{-3}$ U $\xrightarrow{-3}$ R $\xrightarrow{-3}$ O

48. (d) According to the question,

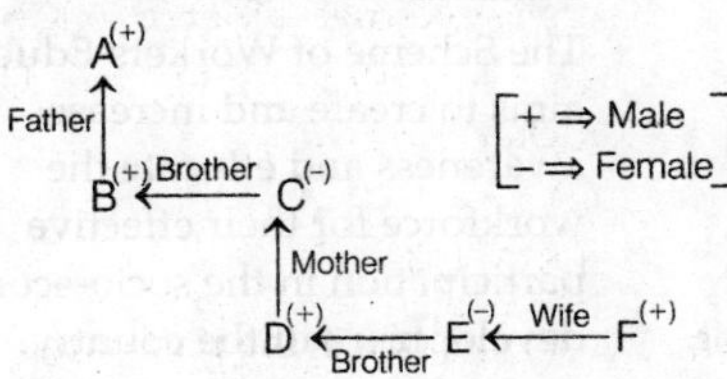

∴ A is mother's father to E.

49. (a) From the given two positions of dice (a) and (b) we find letter X is common. So, moving in a clockwise direction from common.

Figure (a) ⟶ X Z H
Figure (b) ⟶ X I J
opposite

∴ X is opposite to face Y.

50. (a) From the given two positions of dice (a) and (b) we find letter N is common. So, moving in a clockwise direction from common.

Figure (a) ⟶ N M V
Figure (b) ⟶ N L W
opposite

∴ N is opposite to X.

51. (b) Kalidas Samman 2022 for Classical Music was given to Pandit Venkatesh Kumar. Pandit M. Venkatesh Kumar is an Indian Hindustani vocalist.

- He is best known for his rendition of devotional songs composed by Swami Haridas.
- Kalidas Samman is an annual Award given by the Madhya Pradesh Government for outstanding contributions in the field of art and culture.

52. (a) The book 'A Suitable Boy' was authored by Vikram Seth in 1993.

- It is one of the longest novels published in a single volume.
- 'A Suitable Boy' is set in a newly post-independence, post-partition India.
- In 2022, a drama-series is made, based on this book directed by Mira Nair.

53. (a) The signs of charges of electron, proton and neutron are negative, positive and neutral, respectively.

- The charge on the proton and electron are exactly the same size but opposite.
- The same number of protons and electrons exactly cancel one another in a neutral atom.

54. (b) Kojagiri Poornima is a festival celebrated primarily in Maharashtra on the full moon day of Ashwin month.

- This festival is also known as Kojagiri Purnima and is celebrated on the full moon day of the Hindu lunar month of Ashwin.
- On this day, people worship Goddess Lakshmi, who is believed to bless them with wealth, prosperity and happiness.

55. (b) India receives the highest average annual rainfall in Meghalaya.

- Mawsynram is a town in the East Khasi Hills district of Meghalaya State in North-Eastern India, 69 kilometres from Shillong, the state capital.
- It is reportedly the wettest place on Earth, with an average annual rainfall of 11,872 millimetre.

56. (b) In case, the President is satisfied with the Governor's report, he may declare President's Rule under Article 356 but such proclamation is initially for a period of six months.

- It can be extended for a period of three years with parliamentary approval, every six months.
- The proclamation of Presidents' rule should be approved in both houses of parliament with two months of its issue.

57. (a) Women took part in the Modern Olympics for the first time in the year 1900 Games in Paris.

- Of a total of 997 athletes, 22 women competed in five sports: tennis, sailing, croquet, equestrianism and golf.
- Countess Helene de Pourtalls became the first women to win an olympic gold medal in their 1900 Paris Summer Olympics.

58. (b) The most common wild cat in India 'Felis Chaus' listed in Schedule II of the Wildlife (Protection) Act, 1972.

- One of the most common wild cats in India, the jungle cat, also called reed cat and swamp cat is often mistaken for leopards due to physical similarities.

59. (b) 'The Objective Resolution' was moved by Pt. Jawaharlal Nehru on 13th December, 1946.

- It established the concept and guiding principles for building the Constitution and eventually took the shape of the Preamble to the Indian Constitution.
- It was adopted by Constituent Assembly on 22nd January, 1947.

60. (b) Rukmini Devi Arundale was primarily an exponent of Bharatanatyam dance.

- She was an Indian theosophist, dancer and choreographer of the Indian classical dance form of

Bharatanatyam and an activist for animal welfare.

- She was the first woman to be nominated for election to India's upper body of Parliament, the Rajya Sabha.

61. **(d)** Eutrophication can be defined as the gradual increase in the concentration of phosphorus, nitrogen and other plant nutrients in an ageing aquatic ecosystem such as a lake.

- It increased nutrient levels lead to rapid growth of algae and aquatic plant, forming blooms that can block sunlight and reduce water clarity.

62. **(c)** IUPAC name of *m*-Dichlorobenzene is 1,3-Dichlorobenzene.

- It is an aryl chloride and isomer of dichlorobenzene with the formula $C_6H_4Cl_2$.
- It is the least common of the three isomers of dichlorobenzene and is a colourless liquid that is insoluble in water.

63. **(d)** World Athletics Under-20 Championship, 2021 was held from 18th to 22nd August, 2021 at Kenya.

- The 2021 Word Athletics U-20 Championships, also known as the World Junior Championships, was an International Athletics Competition for Athletes qualifying as juniors (born no earlier than 1st January, 2002).
- India stood 21st in medal table.

64. **(d)** 'Gulamgiri' is written by Jyotiba Phule to establish a link between lower-caste Indians and enslaved Americans treated as lower castes in America.

- In 1873, he founded the Satyashodhak Samaj to advocate for the rights of oppressed communities, including women, dalits and shudras.

65. **(d)** The 'wave theory of light' proposed by Christian Huygens whereas.

- Heinrich Rudolf Hertz gave theory on Generation of electromagnetic waves.
- Albert Einstein gave explanation of photoelectric effect.
- Michael Faraday gave laws of electromagnetic induction.

66. **(d)** Dantivarman or Dantidurga was the founder of Rashtrakuta.

- Dantidurga occupied all territories between the Godavari and Vima. He is said to have conquered Kalinga, Kosala, Kanchi, Srisril, Malava, Lata, etc.
- Rashtrakuta dynasty was famous for 'forts'.

67. **(b)** Foreign Investment Board was established in 1968.

- The Foreign Investment Promotion Board (FIPB) was a national agency under the Government of India that offered a single-window clearance for FDI applications which did not come under the automatic route.
- It was under the Ministry of Finance and the Finance Minister was incharge of the FIPB.

68. **(d)** The Salal Hydroelectric Power Station is located in Jammu and Kashmir.

- Also known as Salal Hydroelectric Power Station, is a run-of-the-river hydropower project on the Chenab River in the Reasi district of Jammu and Kashmir.
- It was the first hydropower project built by India in Jammu and Kashmir under the Indus Water Treaty regime.

69. **(a)** Selling of bonds by the RBI will cause money supply to decrease.

- When the Central Bank wants interest rates to be higher, it sells off bonds, pulling money out of the money market and decreasing the money supply.
- If the Central Bank wants interest rates to be lower, it buys bonds. Buying bonds injects money into the money market, increasing the money supply.

70. **(a)** RBI is incharge of India's banking and monetary system.

- RBI, is India's Central Bank and regulatory body responsible for regulation of the Indian Banking System.
- Owned by the Ministry of Finance, Government of India, it is responsible for the control, issue and maintaining supply of the Indian rupee.

71. **(c)** Knowledge of politics is not a qualification for membership in the Vidhan Sabha.

- The person should be a citizen of India.
- Not less than 25 years of age to be a member of the Legislative Assembly and not less than 30 years (as per Article 173 of Indian Constitution) to be a member of the Legislative Council.

72. **(b)** Article 177 of the Indian Constitution mentions about the right of the Advocate.

- Advocate General of state is the highest-law-officer of the state.
- It is appointed by Governor under Article-165 of the Constitution.

73. **(a)** Bases that are soluble in water are called alkalis.

- They completely dissociate into hydroxide ions in aqueous medium. Not all bases dissolve in water.
- Those that dissolve in water are called alkalis. Examples of alkalis are: sodium hydroxide (NaOH), potassium hydroxide (KOH), etc.

74. **(a)** Dadabhai Naoroji became the President of the second session of the Indian National Congress held in Calcutta in December 1886.

- He became the President of INC three times i.e., in the 1886 Calcutta Session, 1893 Lahore Session and 1906 Calcutta Session.
- He was the first Indian Member of Parliament elected to the UK House of Commons.
- He established the (London) Indian Society in the year 1865 and the East India Association in the year 1866.

75. **(c)** Dattopant Thengadi National Board for Workers Education and Development was established in 1958.

- Development is an autonomous body under the Ministry of Labour and Employment, Government of India.
- The Scheme of Workers Education aims to create and increase awareness and educate the workforce for their effective participation in the socio-economic development of the country.

76. **(c)** The second urbanisation in Ganga Valley took place in 6th century BCE.
- The period of second urbanisation noticed large-scale beginning of town life in the middle Gangetic basin.
- The widespread use of iron tools and weapons helped the formation large of territorial states.
- The cities of second urbanisation are mainly located in the Ganga valley which did not see urbanism during the days of Harappan urbanism.

77. **(c)** Eid-al-Fitr is celebrated after the month of Ramzan.
- Eid al-Fitr marks the end of Ramadan, the Muslim holy month of fasting and is celebrated during the first three days of Shawwal, the 10th month of the Islamic calendar (though the Muslim use of a lunar calendar means that it may fall in any season of the year).

78. **(a)** Veteran Kathak Dancer Aditi Mangaldas bagged the Mahari Award 2022.
- She is renowned for her repertoire in both classical Kathak and 'contemporary dance based on Kathak'.
- Mangaldas is regarded as one of the best Kathak dancers in the world, both in India and outside.

79. **(c)** Lod Dalhousie introduced the railway line in British India in 1853.
- India's first train journey began at Mumbai to Thane.
- He was famous for his Doctrine of Lapse Policy.
- He also implemented Wood's Dispatch in 1854, which laid to the foundation for modern education system in India.

80. **(c)** Jhelum river flows into the Wular lake in the North and then into Baramulla.
- At Baramulla, the river enters a Gorge in the hills. It originates at Verinag and flows through the Indian Union Territory of Jammu and Kashmir, into Pakistan-administered Azad Kashmir, then the Pakistani province of Punjab.
- It is the Westernmost of the five rivers of the Punjab region and flows through the Kashmir valley.
- It is a tributary of the Chenab river.

81. **(a)** An esker is a long, winding ridge of stratified sand and gravel deposited by a sub-glacial or englacial meltwater stream.
- They are formed inside the ice, in tunnels in which meltwater streams flowed.

82. **(d)** Phosphorus is not an allotrope of carbon.
- The definition of an allotrope is one or more forms of a chemical element that can exist in the same physical state.
- Well-known forms of carbon include diamond and graphite, buckminsterfullerene and sheets such as graphene.

83. **(d)** The Government of India recently changed the name of Rajiv Gandhi Khel Ratna Award to Dhyan Chand Khel Ratna Award, Dhyan Chand served in the Indian Army as a Major.
- In 2025, D Gukesh (Chess), Harmanpreet Singh (Hockey), Manu Bhaker (Shooting) and Praveen Kumar (Para-Athletics) receive the award.

84. **(c)** Deer is a mobile source of food.
- A deer is a primary consumer.
- In a food chain, the primary consumers are the ones that eat the producers.
- Deer are herbivores, which means they eat plants.

85. **(b)** Article 48 of the Indian Constitution mentions that 'The state shall endeavour to organise agriculture and animal husbandry on modern and scientific lines'.
- It is mention in Directive Principles of State Policy (DPSP) in Part-IV of the Constitution.
- DPSPs are not justiciable, taken from Irish Constitution.

86. **(d)** Anita Ratnam is not an Odissi dancer.
- Kumkum Mohanty, Sonal Mansingh and Protima Bedi are prominent exponents of Odissi.
- Odissi is a classical Indian dance form associated with Odisha state.
- It is known for its sensvous and lyrical movements, expressive gestures and in-tricate footwork.

87. **(b)** Bhupen Hazarika is an Assamese playback singer who was conferred with the Bharat Ratna in 2019.
- He was an Indian playback singer, lyricist, musician, poet from Assam.
- The Bhupen-Hazarika Setu, also known as Dhola-Sadiya Bridge is named after Bhupen Hazarika.

88. **(d)** Drawn from one source is not a basic feature of the Indian Constitution.
- Some basic features of the Indian Constitution are the lengthiest Written Constitution, Drawn from Various Sources, Blend of Rigidity and Flexibility, Federal System with Unitary Bias and Synthesis of Parliamentary Sovereignty.
- Judicial Supremacy, Rule of Law, Integrated and Independent Judiciary are also the features of Constitution.

89. **(d)** Siyaram Tewari belongs to Darbhanga music Gharanas.
- Siyaram Tiwari was an Indian classical singer and leading exponent of Dhrupad- genre of Hindustani classical music.
- He belonged to the Darbhanga gharana and was based in Patna.

90. **(b)** In basketball, when a referee throws the ball up into the center circle to determine which team receives the ball it is called a jump ball.

91. **(d)** At higher levels of development, the agriculture sector of the economy contributes less to the GDP. The current contribution of agriculture to India's GDP is around 18-19%.

92. **(d)** Figure (d) depicts the Modern Periodic Table.
- The periodic table is an ordered arrangement of the chemical elements into rows and columns. Mendeleev had proposed a periodic table based on the mass number and properties of elements.
- Elements with similar properties were placed in the same group and arranged to increase atomic masses.

93. **(d)** Diwan-i Kohi was the Department of Agriculture introduced by Muhammad bin Tughlaq.
- The main object of the department was to increase the land under cultivation.
- The department provided loans to farmers, introduced new agricultural techniques and improve irrigation systems.

94. **(d)** Baira Siul Dam is located in Chamba district.

- It is constructed on the Baira Siul river, a tributary of Rani river.
- It has an installed capacity of 198 MW operated by National Hydro-electric Power Corporation (NHPC).

95. **(c)** According to Census 2011, Sanskrit is spoken by the least population in India.

- The ancient language speaking population is just 0.00198 percent of India's total population of 121 crore.
- According to 2011 Census, Hindi is the most spoken language in India, with 43.63% of the population followed by Bengali with 8.03%.

96. **(d)** 'Unladylike' is a memoir by Radhika Vaz.

- It is a memoir that spans four decades of the author's life.

97. **(d)** The government provided seeds and other inputs at prices lower than those prevailing in the market to encourage farmers to use high yielding variety seeds.

- Subsidy in agriculture means providing some important inputs to farmers at a concession rate i.e. much lower than their market price.
- During the 1960s, in order to ensure the Green Revolution, HYV seeds, fertilisers and insecticides were provided at a subsidised rate to the farmers.

98. **(c)** The longitudinal valley lying between the Lesser Himalayas and the Siwalik in India is called Duns.

- They are formed due to deposits of the rivers which once accumulated in the region.
- The water drains out leaving behind deposits which are known as Duns in the West and Duars on the Eastern side.

99. **(c)** Ram Sahay Panday, a 'Rai' dancer from Madhya Pradesh was conferred with Padma Shri in 2022.

- Rai was traditionally associated with the Bedia tribe.
- The dance form Raai (or Rai) is basically a folk dance of the Bundelkhand region.

100. **(a)** Sutlej river originates from 'Rakshastal North-Western tip' near Mansarovar.

- Rakshastal lake is a freshwater lake and it is believed to be connected underground to the Mansarovar lake.
- The Sutlej river i.e., the longest of the five rivers that flow through the historic crossroads region of Punjab in Northern India and Pakistan.
- It enters India through Shipki-La pass.

101. **(c)** Mean proportion of 'a' and 'b' $=\sqrt{ab}$

$\therefore$ Mean proportion of 75 and 12 $=\sqrt{75\times 12}=30$

Hence, required number $= 30 - 13 = 17$

102. **(b)** $64 \div [44 - (8 \text{ of } 3 - 16) \div 4 \times 20]$

$= 64 \div [44 - (24 - 16) \div 4 \times 20]$
$= 64 \div [44 - (8 \div 4) \times 20]$
$= 64 \div [44 - 2 \times 20]$
$= 64 \div [44 - 40]$
$= 64 \div 4$
$= 16$

103. **(a)** $5\frac{1}{4} - \left[3\frac{1}{2} - \left\{\frac{5}{6} - \left(\frac{3}{5} \times \frac{1}{10} \div \frac{4}{15}\right)\right\}\right]$

$= \frac{21}{4} - \left[\frac{7}{2} - \left\{\frac{5}{6} - \left(\frac{3}{5} \times \frac{1}{10} \times \frac{15}{4}\right)\right\}\right]$

$= \frac{21}{4} - \left[\frac{7}{2} - \left\{\frac{5}{6} - \left(\frac{9}{40}\right)\right\}\right]$

$= \frac{21}{4} - \left[\frac{7}{2} - \frac{73}{120}\right] = \frac{21}{4} - \left[\frac{420 - 73}{120}\right]$

$= \frac{21}{4} - \frac{347}{120} = \frac{630 - 347}{120}$

$= \frac{283}{120} = 2\frac{43}{120}$

104. **(d)** From the given table we can infer that, students scoring an aggregate of more than zero = 100

Students scoring more than 40% marks in aggregate = 78

$\therefore$ Students scoring less than 40% marks in aggregate

$= 100 - 78 = 22$

105. **(a)** Average speed

$= \dfrac{37.5 \text{ km}}{\frac{90}{60} \text{ h}} = \left(\dfrac{37.5 \times 60}{90}\right) \text{km/h}$

$= 25$ km/h

106. **(b)** The sum of all the angles of a triangle is 180°.

Hence, all the angles cannot be less than 60°.

A triangle can have one obtuse angle i.e., more than 90°.

A triangle cannot have two right angles, because then the third angle will be zero which is not possible.

A triangle can have two acute angles.

107. **(a)** $x[-5\{-4(-a)\}] + 6[-3\{-3(-a)\}] = 6a$

$\Rightarrow \quad x[-5\{4a\}] + 6[-3\{3a\}] = 6a$

$\Rightarrow \quad x[-20a] + 6[-9a] = 6a$

$\Rightarrow \quad -20ax - 54a = 6a$

Dividing it by a,

$\Rightarrow \quad -20x - 54 = 6$

$\Rightarrow \quad -20x = 60$

$\Rightarrow \quad x = -3$

108. **(a)** We know that,

$a^3 + b^3 + c^3 - 3abc = (a + b + c)(a^2 + b^2 + c^2 - ac - bc - ab)$

If $a + b + c = 0$

Then, $a^3 + b^3 + c^3 = 3abc$

Now, $a + 2b + 3c = 0$

$\therefore \quad a^3 + 8b^3 + 27c^3 = 3a \times 2b \times 3c$

$= 18abc$

109. **(c)** Total sales of branch C for 2021 and 2022 = 95 + 110 = 205

Total sales of branch F for 2021 and 2022 = 70 + 80 = 150

$\therefore$ Required percentage

$= \frac{150}{205} \times 100 = 73.17\%$

110. **(c)** According to the question,

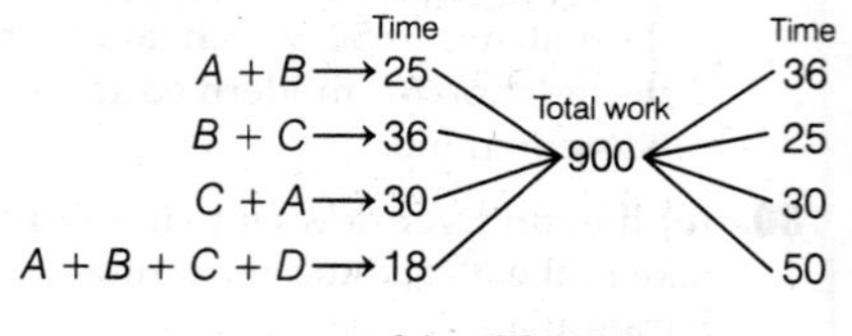

$\therefore (A + B + C) = \dfrac{36 + 25 + 30}{2}$

$= \frac{91}{2} = 45.5$

and $A + B + C + D = 50$

Efficiency of $D = 50 - 45.5 = 4.5$

Hence, D can do the entire work alone in $= \frac{900}{4.5} = 200$ days

111. (c) Correct marks of Anwesha = 66

Incorrect entry = 99

$\therefore$ Difference or error in marks

$= 99 - 66 = 33$

Total number of students = 55

Hence, Increasing in the average marks of the class because of typing error $= \frac{33}{55} = \frac{3}{5} = 0.6$

112. (d) Let Bhavani's income be ₹ $100x$.

$\therefore$ Expenditure = 68% of $100x$ = ₹ $68x$

Hence, savings = $100x - 68x$ = ₹ $32x$

Now, Increased income = 115% of $100x$ = ₹ $115x$

and increased expenditure = 110% of $68x$ = ₹ $74.8x$

$\therefore$ New savings = ₹ $115x$ − ₹ $74.8x$

= ₹ $40.2x$

Hence, Percentage increase in savings

$= \frac{(40.2x - 32x)}{32x} \times 100$

$= \frac{8.2}{32} \times 100 = 25.62\%$

113. (a) Let 'N' number of small laddoo be created from big laddoo.

$\therefore$ Volume of big laddoo = 'N' $\times$ Volume of small laddoo

$\Rightarrow \quad \frac{4}{3}\pi R^3 = N \times \frac{4}{3}\pi r^3$

$\Rightarrow \quad R^3 = N \times r^3$

$\Rightarrow \quad (5)^3 = N \times (2.5)^3$

$\Rightarrow \quad N = \frac{5 \times 5 \times 5}{2.5 \times 2.5 \times 2.5}$

$\therefore \quad N = 8$

114. (c) Let the smallest angle be $x°$.

Second angle = $2x°$

And third angle = $3x°$

Now,

$x° + 2x° + 3x° = 180°$

$6x° = 180°$

$x = 30°$ (smallest angle)

115. (b) Let the cost of painting per square centimeter = ₹ x

Now, according to the question,

$4\pi r^2 \times x = 21560$

$\Rightarrow \quad 4 \times \frac{22}{7} \times \left(\frac{14}{2}\right)^2 \times x = 21560$

$\Rightarrow \quad 4 \times \frac{22}{7} \times \frac{14}{2} \times \frac{14}{2} \times x = 21560$

$\Rightarrow \quad x = \frac{21560}{616} \Rightarrow x =$ ₹ 35

116. (b) Total distance to be covered

$= (230 + 270)$ m $= 500$ m

Relative speed $= (42 + 48) = 90$ km/h

$= \left(90 \times \frac{5}{18}\right)$ m/s $= 25$ m/s

$\therefore$ Time taken by the trains to cross each other $= \frac{500 \text{ m}}{25 \text{ m/s}} = 20$ sec

117. (a) Given, $x = 110,\ y = 111,\ z = 112$

We know that,

$x^3 + y^3 + z^3 - 3xyz = \frac{1}{2}(x + y + z)$
$[(x - y)^2 + (y - z)^2 + (z - x)^2]$

$= \frac{1}{2}(110 + 111 + 112)$
$[(110 - 111)^2 + (111 - 112)^2 + (112 - 110)^2]$

$= \frac{1}{2} \times 333 \times [(-1)^2 + (-1)^2 + (2)^2]$

$= \frac{1}{2} \times 333 \times [1 + 1 + 4]$

$= \frac{1}{2} \times 333 \times 6 = 999$

118. (a) Cost price of the article = ₹ 1600

$\therefore$ Marked price = 1600 + 130% of 1600

= 1600 + 2080 = ₹ 3680

Discount percentage = 25%

$\therefore$ Selling price = 75% of 3680

$= \frac{75}{100} \times 3680 = \frac{3}{4} \times 3680 =$ ₹ 2760

119. (a) Total number of students playing cricket from all the schools

$= 100 + 150 + 200 + 300 + 200 = 950$

Total number of students playing tennis from all the schools

$= 200 + 220 + 210 + 210 + 230 = 1070$

$\therefore$ Required difference

$= 1070 - 950 = 120$

120. (c) Let the speed of boat be 'B' km/h. and that of stream be 'S' km/h.

Now, according to the question,

$\frac{10}{\frac{2}{60}} = B + S \Rightarrow \frac{2 \times 60}{10} = B + S$

$\Rightarrow \quad B + S = 12$ km/h ...(i)

And $\frac{12}{2} = B - S$

$\Rightarrow \quad B - S = 6$ km/h ...(ii)

Adding Eqs. (i) and (ii), we get

$B = 9$ km/h

$\therefore$ Speed of stream $= S = 12 - B$

$= 12 - 9 = 3$ km/h

121. (d) Let the total number to votes polled $= 100x$

Loser gets 35% of votes

$\therefore$ Winner gets 65% of votes

So, according to the question,

$(65 - 35)\%$ of $100x = 15,900$

$\Rightarrow \quad 30\%$ of $100x = 15900$

$\Rightarrow \quad \frac{30}{100} \times 100x = 15900$

$\Rightarrow \quad 3x = 1590$

$\Rightarrow \quad x = 530$

$\therefore$ Total votes $= 100x = 100 \times 530$

$= 53000$

122. (a) $1 - \cfrac{1}{1 + \cfrac{1}{2 - \cfrac{1}{2 + \cfrac{1}{3}}}}$

$= 1 - \cfrac{1}{1 + \cfrac{1}{2 - \cfrac{1}{\frac{7}{3}}}} = 1 - \cfrac{1}{1 + \cfrac{1}{2 - \frac{3}{7}}}$

$= 1 - \cfrac{1}{1 + \cfrac{1}{\frac{11}{7}}} = 1 - \cfrac{1}{1 + \frac{7}{11}}$

$= 1 - \cfrac{1}{\frac{18}{11}} = 1 - \frac{11}{18} = \frac{7}{18}$

123. (d) Let the speed of boat $= B$ km/h and speed of current/stream $= S$ km/h

According to the question,

$\frac{24}{B - S} + \frac{36}{B + S} = 10$

Let $\frac{1}{B - S} = a$ and $\frac{1}{B + S} = b$

So, $\quad 24a + 36b = 10$

$\Rightarrow \quad 12a + 18b = 5$ ...(i)

Now, $\frac{36}{B - S} + \frac{24}{B + S} = 12$

$\Rightarrow \quad 36a + 24b = 12$

$\Rightarrow \quad 9a + 6b = 3$ ...(ii)

On solving Eqs. (i) and (ii), we get

$a = \frac{4}{15}$ and $b = \frac{1}{10}$

$\Rightarrow \quad B - S = \frac{15}{4}$ ...(iii)

And $B + S = 10$ ...(iv)

On solving Eqs. (iii) and (iv)

$2B = \frac{15}{4} + 10 \Rightarrow 2B = \frac{55}{4} \Rightarrow B = \frac{55}{8}$ km/h

$\therefore S = 10 - \frac{55}{8} = \frac{80 - 55}{8} = \frac{25}{8}$ km/h

(speed of current)

124. (b) Let the sum be P.

It becomes $3P$ in 5 yr.

i.e., $P\left(1+\frac{r}{100}\right)^5 = 3P$ [$t = 5$ yr]

$\Rightarrow \left(1+\frac{r}{100}\right)^5 = 3$

Now, when it becomes 9 times i.e. $(3)^2$,

$\Rightarrow \left[\left(1+\frac{r}{100}\right)^5\right]^2 = (3)^2$

$\Rightarrow \left(1+\frac{r}{100}\right)^{10} = 9$

$\therefore t = 10$ yr

125. (a) $[25-(-4)\{9-(6-2)\}] \div [3\times\{6+(-3)\times(-3)\}]$

$= [25-(-4)\{9-4\}] \div [3\times\{6+9\}]$

$= [25-(-4)(5)] \div [3\times 15]$

$= [25+20] \div [3\times 15]$

$= 45 \div 45 = 1$

126. (b) $1898 \div \left[\frac{13}{4}\times(35+45)-\frac{91}{4}\right]$

$= 1898 \div \left[\frac{13}{4}\times 80-\frac{91}{4}\right]$

$= 1898 \div \left[13\times 20-\frac{91}{4}\right]$

$= 1898 \div \left[260-\frac{91}{4}\right] = 1898 \div \frac{949}{4}$

$= 1898 \times \frac{4}{949} = 2\times 4 = 8$

127. (d) Total production in hundred

$= 30+40+25+40+45 = 180$

Average production $= \frac{180}{5} = 36$ (in hundred)

Total demand

$= 35+25+30+30+40 = 160$ (in hundred)

Average demand $= \frac{160}{5} = 32$ (in hundred)

$\therefore$ Required difference $= (36-32)$ (in hundred)

$= 4$ (in hundred) $= 400$

128. (c) Given, Principal (P) = ₹ 2500

and Amount (A) = ₹ 4900

$\therefore$ SI = ₹ 4900 − ₹ 2500 = ₹ 2400

Now,

$SI = \frac{P\times R\times T}{100}$ [Rate $= R = 12\%$ p.a.]

$\Rightarrow 2400 = \frac{2500\times 12\times T}{100}$

$\Rightarrow T = \frac{2400\times 100}{2500\times 12} \Rightarrow T = 8$ yr

129. (d) Volume of cone $= \frac{1}{3}\pi r^2 h$

$= \frac{1}{3}\times\frac{22}{7}\times(5)^2\times 6$

Volume of cylinder $= \pi r^2 h$

$= \frac{22}{7}\times(2.5)^2\times 3$

$\therefore$ Required ratio $= \frac{\frac{1}{3}\times\frac{22}{7}\times 5\times 5\times 6}{\frac{22}{7}\times 2.5\times 2.5\times 3}$

$= \frac{2\times 2\times 2}{3}$

$= \frac{8}{3}$ or $8:3$

130. (c) $\frac{3.2\times 3.2-0.2\times 0.2}{0.2\times 0.2-2\times 0.2\times 3.2+3.2\times 3.2}$

$= \frac{(3.2)^2-(0.2)^2}{(0.2)^2-2\times 0.2\times 3.2+(3.2)^2}$

Let $a = 3.2$ and $b = 0.2$

$\therefore \frac{a^2-b^2}{b^2-2\times b\times a+a^2} = \frac{a^2-b^2}{(a-b)^2}$

$= \frac{(a-b)(a+b)}{(a-b)^2} = \frac{a+b}{a-b}$

$= \frac{3.2+0.2}{3.2-0.2} = \frac{3.4}{3} = \frac{34}{30} = \frac{17}{15}$

131. (a) Cost price of 1 orange $= \frac{50}{10}$ = ₹ 5

Selling price of one orange

$= \frac{74}{12}$ = ₹ $\frac{37}{6}$

Gain percentage $= \frac{SP-CP}{CP}\times 100$

$= \frac{\left(\frac{37}{6}-5\right)}{5}\times 100 = \left(\frac{37-30}{6\times 5}\right)\times 100$

$= \frac{7}{6}\times 20 = \frac{70}{3} = 23\frac{1}{3}\%$ gain

132. (a) For a triangle ABC,

$A:B:C = 1:2:3$

Now, $\angle A+\angle B+\angle C = 180°$

$x+2x+3x = 180°$

$\Rightarrow 6x = 180°$

$\Rightarrow x = 30°$

$\therefore \angle A = 30°, \angle B = 60°, \angle C = 90°$

Using sine rule,

[where a, b and c are the corresponding sides of $\angle A$, $\angle B$ and $\angle C$, respectively.]

$\frac{a}{\sin A} = \frac{b}{\sin B} = \frac{c}{\sin C}$

$\Rightarrow \frac{a}{\sin 30°} = \frac{b}{\sin 60°} = \frac{c}{\sin 90°}$

$\Rightarrow \frac{a}{1/2} = \frac{b}{\frac{\sqrt{3}}{2}} = \frac{c}{1}$

$\Rightarrow \frac{a}{1} = \frac{b}{\sqrt{3}} = \frac{c}{2}$

$\therefore$ Ratio of corresponding sides

$= a:b:c = 1:\sqrt{3}:2$

133. (a) $[\{(82+48\div 8\times 3)+5\times 6\}-7.5\times 2]$

$= [\{(82+6\times 3)+30\}-15]$

$= [\{(82+18)+30\}-15]$

$= [\{100+30\}-15]$

$= [130-15] = 115$

134. (c) According to the question,

$\therefore$ Required net % decrease

$= 100-100\times\frac{90}{100}\times\frac{130}{100}\times\frac{80}{100}$

$= 100-93.6 = 6.4\% = 6\frac{2}{5}\%$

135. (c) $\frac{1-\cot^2\theta}{\tan^2\theta-1}$

$\frac{1-\frac{\cos^2\theta}{\sin^2\theta}}{\frac{\sin^2\theta}{\cos^2\theta}-1} = \frac{\frac{\sin^2\theta-\cos^2\theta}{\sin^2\theta}}{\frac{\sin^2\theta-\cos^2\theta}{\cos^2\theta}} = \frac{\cos^2\theta}{\sin^2\theta}$

$= \cot^2\theta$

136. (b) According to the question,

Ravi + Sanju ⟶ 2 — 2

Sanju + Mahesh ⟶ 4 — 4 — 1

Ravi + Mahesh ⟶ 2 — 2

Efficiency of (Ravi + Sanju + Mahesh)

$= \frac{2+1+2}{2} = \frac{5}{2}$

$\therefore$ Efficiency of Ravi $= \frac{5}{2}-1 = \frac{3}{2}$

Hence, total tine taken by Ravi to do

work done $= \frac{4}{\frac{3}{2}} = \frac{8}{3}$ days

137. (d) Total bill = Cost of shirt + Cost of jacket

= (₹ 900 + 9% of 900) + (₹ 1900 + 6% of ₹ 1900)

= ₹ 981 + ₹ 2014

= ₹ 2995 i.e., below ₹ 3000

Hence, a discount of 12% will be given.

$\therefore$ Amount that Anand had to pay

= 88% of ₹ 2995

$= \frac{88}{100}\times 2995$

= ₹ 2635.60

138. (d) Capacity/volume of the bowl

$$= \frac{2}{3}\pi r^3 = \frac{2}{3}\times\frac{22}{7}\times(9)^3 = 1527.43\text{ cm}^3$$

139. (b) $\frac{(\sec A + \tan A)}{(\sec A - \tan A)} = 2\frac{51}{79}$

$$\Rightarrow \frac{\left(\frac{1}{\cos A} + \frac{\sin A}{\cos A}\right)}{\left(\frac{1}{\cos A} - \frac{\sin A}{\cos A}\right)} = \frac{209}{79}$$

$$\Rightarrow \frac{1+\sin A}{1-\sin A} = \frac{209}{79}$$

$$\Rightarrow \frac{(1+\sin A)+(1-\sin A)}{(1+\sin A)-(1-\sin A)} = \frac{209+79}{209-79}$$

$$\Rightarrow \frac{2}{2\sin A} = \frac{288}{130}$$

$$\therefore \quad \sin A = \frac{65}{144}$$

140. (c) $20 \div 5 \text{ of } 4 \times 8 + 6 \div 24 \text{ of } 3 \times 48 - 6 \div 18 \times 9$

$$= 20 \div 20 \times 8 + 6 \div 72 \times 48 - \frac{1}{3}\times 9$$

$$= 1\times 8 + \frac{1}{12}\times 48 - 3 = 8 + 4 - 3 = 9$$

141. (c) Volume of cube $= a^3 = (8)^3$

$$= 512\text{ cm}^3$$

142. (d) Owing to reduction in cost price of the commodity, there is a saving of 7.5% on ₹ 7400.

i.e., $\frac{7.5}{100}\times 7400 =$ ₹ 555

with ₹ 555, he can purchase 15 kg more.

∴ Reduced price of 15 kg = ₹ 555

So, reduced price of 1 kg $= \frac{555}{15} =$ ₹ 37

Hence, original price $= \frac{100}{92.5}\times 37 =$ ₹ 40

Now, to make a profit of 32.5%

Selling price of the commodity

= 132.5% of ₹ 40

$$= \frac{132.5}{100}\times 40 = ₹\ 53$$

143. (c) Given, Jeevan's amount : Praveen's amount = 5 : 8

And Praveen's amount : Kanan's amount = 3 : 2

∴ Jeevan : Praveen : Kanan

= 15 : 24 : 16

Now, $15x + 24x + 16x = 17600$

$$55x = 17600$$

$$x = \frac{17600}{55} = 320$$

∴ Jeevan's share $= 15x = 15\times 320$

= ₹ 4800

144. (a) Required percentage

$$= \frac{(30-25)}{25}\times 100$$

$$= \frac{5}{25}\times 100 = 20\%$$

145. (c) Total estimated budget for grocery and electricity

= (20% + 19%) of ₹ 58000

= 39% of 58000

= 39 × 580 = ₹ 22620

Actual money spent on grocery and electricity = ₹ 18875

∴ Required difference

= ₹ 22620 − ₹18875 = ₹ 3745

146. (d) Number of candidates passing the exam from City Q $= \frac{3}{10}\times 2.26 = 0.678$ L

Number of candidates appearing from all cities together

= (1.10 + 2.26 + 2.12 + 1.46) = 6.94 L

∴ Required percentage

$$= \frac{0.678}{6.94}\times 100 = 9.77\%$$

147. (d) $29 - [(48 \div 12) + 2\times(8 \div 4 + 4)]$

$= 29 - [4 + 2\times(2+4)]$

$= 29 - [4 + 2\times 6]$

$= 29 - [4 + 12] = 29 - 16 = 13$

148. (b) Let $\cos A = x$

So, $2\cos^2 A + 3\cos A - 2 = 0$

$\Rightarrow \quad 2x^2 + 3x - 2 = 0$

$\Rightarrow \quad 2x^2 + 4x - x - 2 = 0$

$\Rightarrow \quad 2x(x+2) - 1(x+2) = 0$

$\Rightarrow \quad (2x-1)(x+2) = 0$

$\Rightarrow \quad x = -2;\ x = \frac{1}{2}$

Now, $x = -2 = \cos A$, which is not possible.

$\therefore \quad \cos A = x = \frac{1}{2}$

$\therefore \quad A = 60°$

149. (c) Area of sector $= \frac{\theta}{360°}\times \pi r^2$

$$= \frac{60°}{360°}\times\frac{22}{7}\times 21\times 21$$

$$= 231\text{ cm}^2$$

150. (d) $\frac{\cos 13° + \sin 13°}{\cos 13° - \sin 13°}$

Dividing the numerator and denominator by cos 13°, we get

$$\frac{1+\tan 13°}{1-\tan 13°} = \frac{1+\tan 13°}{1 - 1\cdot\tan 13°}$$

$$\left[\because \tan(x+y) = \frac{\tan x + \tan y}{1 - \tan x\cdot\tan y}\right]$$

$$= \frac{\tan 45° + \tan 13°}{1 - \tan 45° \cdot \tan 13°}$$

$$= \tan(45° + 13°) = \tan 58°$$

151. (a) Adolescence is the period of time in a person's life when they are developing into an adult.

152. (d) Part (d) 'horse' contains the error. The error lies in the omission of the article 'a' before the word 'horse.'

153. (d) Part (d) 'By the time I reaching' contains the error. The error lies in the incorrect verb form 'reaching.' It should be changed to 'reached' to match the past tense structure of the sentence.

154. (a) The word 'excruciating' means extremely painful.

155. (d) The word 'Pacify' means to calm or soothe someone who is angry, upset or agitated.

156. (c) 'To expand' means to increase.

157. (c) 'Ephemeral' means lasting for a very short time, fleeting or transient. Hence, its antonym is 'permanent'.

158. (a) Conservative refers to a tendency to preserve existing traditions and resist change.

Hence, its antonym is 'liberal' which means open to new behaviour or opinions and willing to discard traditional values.

159. (b) The idiom 'nerves of steel' is used for someone who can face situations without fear or anxiety, remaining calm and composed.

160. (a) 'Malleable' means (of a metal or other material) able to be hammered or pressed into shape without breaking or cracking.

161. (c) The word 'Dainty' is used for something delicate, elegant, fine and often small, especially in relation to food or objects.

162. (d) The word 'Filthy' means covered or smeared with dirt; disgustingly dirty.

163. (d) The idiom 'life is a bowl of cherries' means 'life is wonderful and pleasant.' It suggests that life is full of enjoyable moments and is often used to express contentment and happines.

164. (a) The correctly spelled word is 'directory'. The correct spelling of other words are dictionary, dispensary and machinery.

165. **(d)** The idiom 'fit as a fiddle' means a healthy, fit and energetic person.
It describes someone who is healthy and in excellent physical condition.

166. **(d)** The phrase 'bring to book' means to hold someone accountable for their actions.

167. **(b)** The correct spelling is 'harmony'.

168. **(c)** The correct phrase is 'think outside the box,' which means to think creatively or differently.

169. **(b)** The underlined part of the sentence contains an error.
Use the phrasal verb 'carry on' which means to continue doing something. It fits the context as it implies that the son will continue to manage or operate the business while the speaker is absent.

170. **(b)** Anthropology is the scientific study of humans, their behaviour, societies and cultures.

171. **(c)** Part (c) 'I am looking for the' contains the error. In reported speech or narrative past tense, the verb form 'am looking' should be changed to 'was looking' to maintain consistency with the past tense structure of the sentence.

172. **(a)** The idiom 'a slap on the wrist' means 'a very mild punishment.' It suggests that the punishment is not severe enough for the offence committed.

173. **(c)** A bonfire is a huge fire made during festivals or celebrations.

174. **(d)** The correct spelling is 'chancellery'. It refers to the position, court or department of a chancellor.

175. **(a)** The idiom 'between the devil and the deep blue sea' means to be faced with two equally difficult choices or options, often in a dilemma where neither choice is desirable.

176. **(b)** A Matinee is a film shown during the day, especially in the afternoon

177. **(c)** The word 'Occult' refers to supernatural practices, magic or mystical beliefs that are beyond ordinary understanding, often involving hidden or secret knowledge.

178. **(b)** The correct phrase is 'taken in more than one way, meaning something can have multiple interpretations.

179. **(a)** Part (a) 'comparatively better' contains an error. The word 'comparatively' is redundant here because the word 'better' already implies a comparison.

180. **(d)** The sentence with correct spelling is 'The skilled surgeon delicately performed the intricate procedure, saving the patient's life with his steady hands and unwavering focus.'

181. **(d)** A catalogue is a systematic list of items, especially books, often found in libraries or stores.

182. **(a)** The corrected sentence should read: 'if someone could employ him, he would love to work. It fits the context better than 'like to eat, which is awkward.

183. **(c)** The idiom 'beat around the bush' means to avoid getting to the main point or delaying the topic.

184. **(a)** The idiom 'sits on the fence' means 'delays making strong decisions.' It describes someone who is indecisive or avoids committing to a side.

185. **(d)** Part (d) 'If I have recovered from fever' contains an error.
The use of 'have recovered' is incorrect here because the sentence is in the future tense, indicating a condition that will happen in the future ('will start going'). Therefore, it should use the simple present tense ('If I recover from fever').

186. **(c)** 'Baffled' means confused or puzzled and 'perplexed' is the closest in meaning among the options.

187. **(a)** Confidential' means secretive. Hence, its antonyms are 'Familiar' which means well-known or easily recognised by someone and 'Revealed' which means made known or disclosed, especially after having been kept secret.

188. **(d)** The word 'Voracious' describes someone who has a very eager approach to an activity, often in an insatiable or greedy manner, especially related to consuming food or knowledge.

189. **(d)** The correct spelling is 'pretentious'.

190. **(a)** The correct spelling is 'programme'.

191. **(a)** 'Looked' means directed their eyes, fitting the context of her brothers looking at her scornfully.

192. **(d)** 'Sport' means an activity involving physical exertion, fitting the context of fishing being a man's sport.

193. **(a)** 'Good' means skilled, fitting the context of girls not being good at fishing.

194. **(b)** 'After' means following in time, fitting the context of Millie persuading her brothers after a while.

195. **(d)** The phrase 'take her with them' is grammatically and contextually correct, meaning she joined them on the trip.

196. **(a)** The word 'customise' means to modify or tailor something to meet individual preferences.
Hence, its synonym is 'personalise' as it also refers to making something specific to an individual's needs or preferences.

197. **(d)** The passage states that old media has adapted and found new ways of representation in digital forms, blurring the distinction between old and new media. This makes the differentiation between the two categories challenging.

198. **(a)** The passage highlights that new media involves user interaction, such as customisation and linking of content, whereas old media is characterised as non-interactive, where consumers primarily receive information without active participation.

199. **(b)** The passage categorises television under old media, contrasting it with new media that includes websites, online streams, e-mails and various digital platforms.

200. **(d)** In a broader sense, 'Catch-all' can refer to a category that includes a wide variety of different things or items. This interpretation aligns with the idea that new media encompasses diverse forms of electronic communications, covering everything from websites and social platforms to online video/audio streams and more.

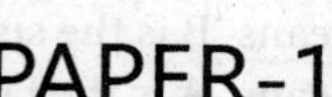

PAPER-1

SSC CPO SI SOLVED PAPER

27 June 2024 (Shift III)

CPO SI P-1 SP 07

MM : 200 **Time : 2 hr**

Instructions

1. This paper contains 200 questions.
2. It has 4 Parts, **Part I** General Intelligence and Reasoning, **Part II** General Knowledge and General Awareness, **Part III** Quantitative Aptitude and **Part IV** English Comprehension.
3. Each question carries 1 **marks.**

Part I

General Intelligence and Reasoning

1. Select the figure from among the given options that can logically replace the question mark (?) in the following series.

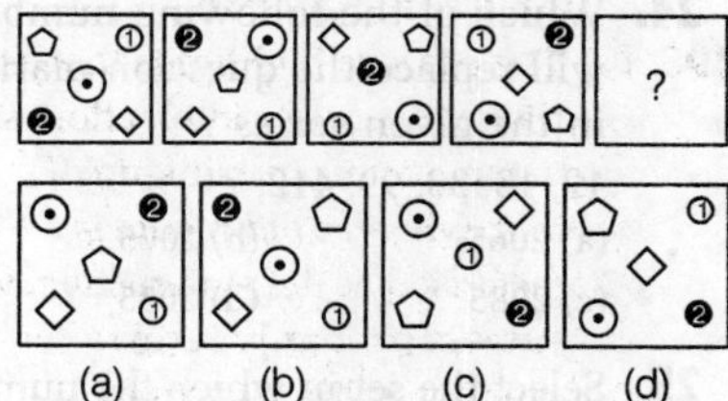

2. Select the correct mirror image of the given figure when the mirror is placed at MN as shown below.

G w B 7 4 A | M N

(a) ∀ ᔭ B ⅃ w ⅁ (b) A ᔭ Ɩ ᗺ w ⅁
(c) ∀ ᔭ ⅃ ᗺ ʍ ⅁ (d) ∀ ᔭ Ɩ ᗺ w ⅁

3. Select the set in which the numbers are related in the same way as are the numbers of the following sets.
(**Note** Operations should be performed on the whole numbers, without breaking down the numbers into its constituent digits. e.g. 13 – Operations on 13 such as adding /subtracting /multiplying etc. to 13 can be performed. Breaking down 13 into 1 and 3 and then performing mathematical operations on 1 and 3 is not allowed)
(288, 144, 24)
(432, 216, 36)
(a) (504, 252, 42) (b) (506, 252, 42)
(c) (504, 252, 44) (d) (504, 250, 42)

4. Based on the English alphabetical order, three of the following four letter-clusters are alike in a certain way and thus form a group. Which letter-cluster does not belong to that group?
(**Note** The odd letter-cluster is not based on the number of consonants/vowels or their position in the letter-cluster.)
(a) FIK (b) JMP
(c) ORT (d) DGI

5. In a code language, 'BASIC' is coded as 101 and 'MAGIC' is coded as 102. How will 'LIGHT' be coded in the same language?
(a) 85 (b) 79
(c) 8 (d) 86

6. Select the set in which the numbers are related in the same way as are the numbers of the given sets.
(**Note** Operations should be performed on the whole numbers, without breaking down the numbers into its constituent digits. E.g. 13 – Operations on 13 such as adding/subtracting/multiplying, etc. to 13 can be performed. Breaking down 13 into 1 and 3 then performing mathematical operations on 1 and 3 is not allowed.
(16, 4, 20)
(28, 7, 35)
(a) (52, 13, 65) (b) (52, 13, 60)
(c) (50, 13, 65) (d) (50, 13, 60)

7. What will come in place of the question mark (?) when + and – are interchanged and 8 and 6 are also interchanged?
8 – 6 + 10 = ?
(a) 7 (b) 4 (c) 6 (d) 5

8. The sequence of folding a paper and the manner in which the folded paper is cut is shown in the following figures. How would this paper look when unfolded?

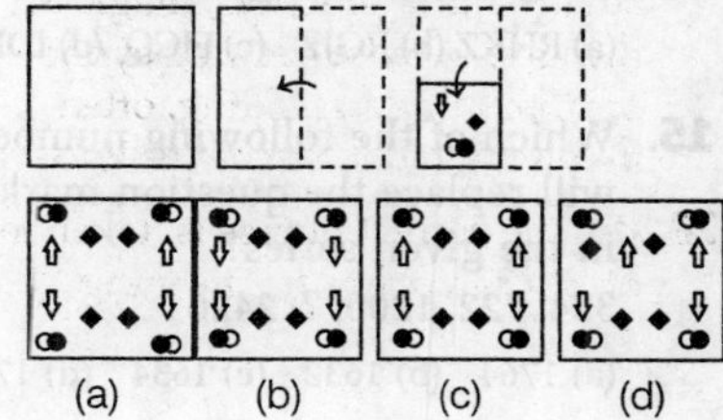

9. Select the option that is related to the fifth letter-cluster in the same way as the second letter-cluster is related to the first letter-cluster and the fourth letter-cluster is related to the third letter-cluster.
ISLAND : ANDISL :: EITHER : HEREIT :: IMPACT : ?
(a) ICAPMT (b) TCAPMI
(c) IPMCTA (d) ACTIMP

10. If 'P' stands for '÷', 'Q' stands for '×', 'R' stands for '+' and 'S' stands for '–', what will come in place of the question mark (?) in the following equation?
[(18 S 5) Q 4] P 2 R 22 Q 3 S 24 R 9 = ?
(a) 89 (b) 77 (c) 82 (d) 63

11. Select the Venn diagram that best illustrates the relationship between the following classes.
Mechanic, Peon, Lawyer
(a) (b)
(c) (d)

12. What will come in the place of '?' in the following equation, if '+' and '–' are interchanged and also '×' and '÷' are interchanged?
154 × 11 – 24 ÷ 3 + 19 = ?
(a) 62 (b) 67 (c) 71 (d) 54

13. Select the figure from among the given options that can logically replace the question mark (?) in the following series.
(a) (b) (c) (d)

14. Which letter cluster will replace the question mark (?) to complete the given series?
TDQR, SFNV, ?, QJHD, PLEH
(a) RHKZ (b) RGJZ (c) FJCQ (d) IDBZ

15. Which of the following numbers will replace the question mark (?) in the given series?
324, 722, 1200, ?, 2420
(a) 1764 (b) 1632 (c) 1634 (d) 1736

16. Two statements are given, followed by two conclusions numbered I and II. Assuming the statements to be true, even if they seem to be at variance with commonly known facts, decide which of the conclusions logically follow(s) from the statements.
Statements
All wings are whites.
No whites are wands.
Conclusions
I. Some wings are wands.
II. No wand is a white.
(a) Only Conclusion II follows
(b) Both Conclusions I and II follow
(c) Neither Conclusion I nor II follows
(d) Only Conclusion I follows

17. If 'P' stands for '÷', 'Q' stands for '×', 'R' stands for '+' and 'S' stands for '–', what will come in place of the question mark (?) in the following equation?
45 R (26 Q 2) P 4 R 19 S 32 = ?
(a) 50 (b) 35
(c) 45 (d) 40

18. Select the set in which the numbers are related in the same way as are the numbers of the following sets.
(**Note** Operations should be performed on the whole numbers, without breaking down the numbers into its constituent digits. E.g. 13 – Operations on 13 such as adding /subtracting /multiplying etc. to 13 can be performed. Breaking down 13 into 1 and 3 then performing mathematical operations on 1 and 3 is not allowed)
(21, 3 , 15)
(49, 7, 35)
(a) (84, 12, 60) (b) (85, 12, 60)
(c) (84, 12, 62) (d) (85, 13, 60)

19. Select the Venn diagram that best illustrates the relationship between the following classes.
Humans, Painters, Men

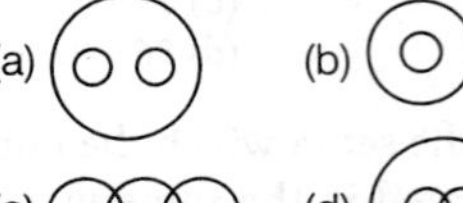

(a) (b)
(c) (d)

20. In a certain code language,
'A + B' means 'A is the mother of B'
'A – B' means 'A is the husband of B'
'A × B' means 'B is the sister of A'
'A ÷ B' means 'A is the father of B'
Based on the above, how is B related to E if D ÷ E – C + A × B?
(a) Wife (b) Son
(c) Mother (d) Daughter

21. Which of the following terms will replace the question mark (?) in the given series?
CJS, DKT, ELU,?
(a) DLO (b) DHB
(c) DRT (d) FMV

22. Select the option figure in which the given figure is embedded as its part (rotation is Not allowed).

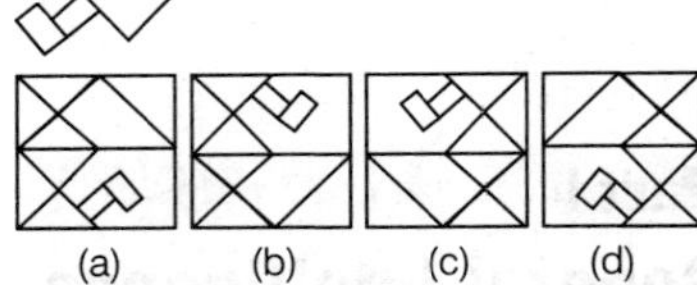

(a) (b) (c) (d)

23. Which of the following numbers will replace the question mark (?) in the given series?
29, 30, 26, 35, 19, ?
(a) 41 (b) 42
(c) 44 (d) 43

24. Which of the following numbers will replace the question mark (?) in the given series ?
12, 13, 30, 99, 412, ?
(a) 2065 (b) 2075
(c) 2085 (d) 2055

25. Select the set in which the numbers are related in the same way as are the numbers of the following sets.
(**Note** Operations should be performed on the whole numbers, without breaking down the numbers into its constituent digits. E.g. 13 – Operations on 13 such as adding /subtracting /multiplying etc. to 13 can be performed. Breaking down 13 into 1 and 3 then performing mathematical operations on 1 and 3 is not allowed).
(14, 28 , 84)
(17, 34, 102)
(a) (21, 42, 126) (b) (20, 41, 126)
(c) (20, 41, 136) (d) (21, 42, 136)

26. In a certain code language, 'FOX' is coded as '14' and 'GOAT' is coded as '21'. How will'TOMMY' be coded in that language?

(a) 45 (b) 35
(c) 30 (d) 25

27. Select the number from among the given options that can replace the question mark(?) in the following series.

115, 140, 160, 175, 185, ?

(a) 193 (b) 195
(c) 192 (d) 190

28. If 'P' stands for '÷', 'Q' stands for '×', 'R' stands for '+' and 'S' stands for '–', what will come in place of the question mark '?' in the following equation?

(121 S 46) R 19 Q 5 R 126 P 6 S 38 = ?

(a) 139 (b) 144
(c) 153 (d) 159

29. In a certain code language, 'MAP' is written as '102' and 'ROT' is written as '56'. How will 'SEC' be written in that language ?

(a) 108 (b) 112
(c) 98 (d) 84

30. In a code language, 'ROAD' is written as 'QKZZ' and 'BAND' is written as 'AWMZ'. How will 'TASK' be written in that language?

(a) SWRG (b) RSWG
(c) SRGW (d) GRSW

31. Select the option that is related to the fifth letter-cluster in the same way as the second letter-cluster is related to the first letter- cluster and the fourth letter-cluster is related to the third letter-cluster.

JOCK : GLZH :: HURT : EROQ :: SPIN : ?

(a) QNFK (b) PNEL
(c) PMFK (d) QMEK

32. Select the option in which the given figure (X) is embedded as its part. (rotation is not allowed.)

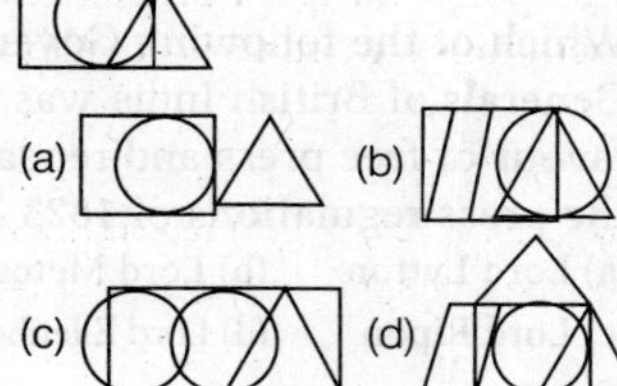

(a) (b) (c) (d)

33. In a code language, 'POET' is coded as '14-13-3-18' and 'SOON' is coded as '17-13-13-12'. How will 'WRITE' be coded in the same language?

(a) 19-16-5-18-3 (b) 21-16-7-18-3
(c) 21-16-7-9-3 (d) 19-16-7-18-5

34. P, Q, R, S, T and U are sitting around a circular table facing the centre. Only one person sits between T and R. Only one person sits between R and U. Only two peoples sit between U and Q. S sits to the immediate left of T. Who sits second to the left of P?

(a) S (b) Q (c) R (d) U

35. Which letter-cluster will complete the given series ?

FPW, FFPPPWW, FFFFPPPPWWW, ...

(a) FFFFFFPPPPPPWWWWW
(b) FFFFFFFFPPPPPPWWWW
(c) FFFFFFFPPPPPPPPPPWWWWW
(d) FFFFFFPPPPPWWWW

36. If 'A' stands for '÷', 'B' stands for '×', 'C' stands for '+' and 'D' stands for '–', what will come in place of the question mark (?) in the following equation?

905 B 2 C 47 D 903 A 3 = ?

(a) 1556 (b) 1155
(c) 1165 (d) 1655

37. In the given number-pairs, the second number is obtained by applying certain mathematical operations to the first number. Select the number-pair in which the numbers are related in the same way as are the numbers of the given number-pairs.

(**Note** Operations should be performed on the whole numbers, without breaking down the numbers into its constituent digits. E.g., 13 – Operations on 13 such as adding/subtracting/multiplying etc. to 13 can be performed. Breaking down 13 into 1and 3 and then performing mathematical operations on 1 and 3 is not allowed).

(45, 88)
(26, 50)

(a) (15, 32) (b) (21, 41)
(c) (22, 42) (d) (18, 36)

38. Identify the option figure that when put in place of the question mark (?) will logically complete the series.

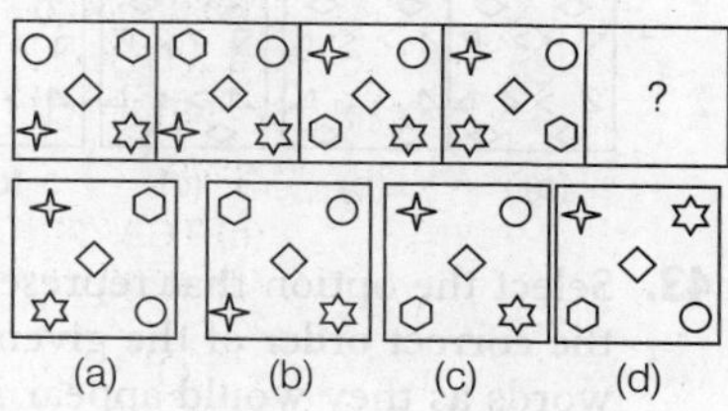

(a) (b) (c) (d)

39. Aditi departs from her home and walks 38m towards West and then turns right and walks 19m. Now she turns right and walks 25m. She then takes a left turn and walks 21 m. She then takes a left turn again and walks 38m. She takes a final left turn and walks 25 m to stop at Point X. How far is she from a pole which is 15 m North of her house? (assume that all turns are 90° turns only.)

(a) 38 m (b) 49 m (c) 57 m (d) 51 m

40. Select the correct mirror image of the given figure when the mirror is placed at MN as shown below.

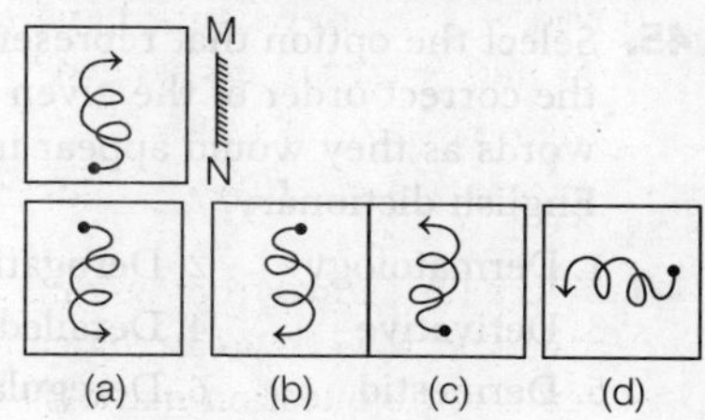

(a) (b) (c) (d)

41. Ajay starts from Point *A* and drives 20 km towards South. He then takes a left turn, drives 5 km, turns left and drives 30 km. He then takes a right turn and drives 8 km. He takes a final right turn, drives 10 km and stops at Point Q. How far (shortest distance) and towards which direction should he now drive to reach Point A again? (all turns are 90° turns only).

(a) 13 km towards East
(b) 5 km towards West
(c) 13 km towards West
(d) 8 km towards West

42. The sequence of folding a paper and the manner in which the folded paper is cut is shown in the following figures. How would this paper look when unfolded?

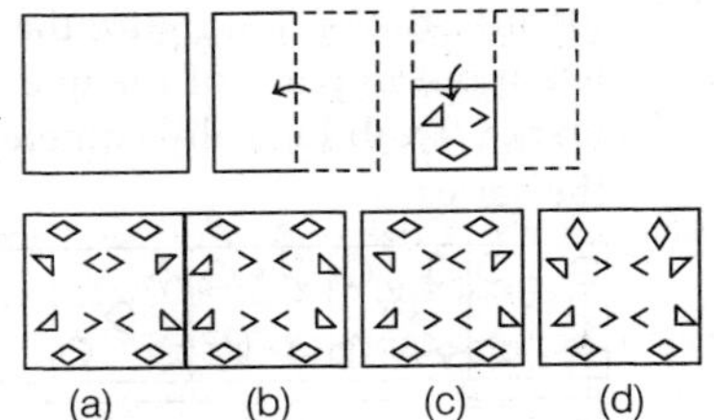
(a) (b) (c) (d)

43. Select the option that represents the correct order of the given words as they would appear in an English dictionary.

1. Temperament 2. Tenure
3. Tenant 4. Tender
5. Temptation 6. Temperature

(a) 1, 6, 5, 2, 4, 3 (b) 1, 6, 5, 3, 2, 4
(c) 1, 6, 5, 3, 4, 2 (d) 1, 6, 5, 2, 3, 4

44. Three different positions of the same dice are shown. Find the number on the face opposite the face showing '2'.

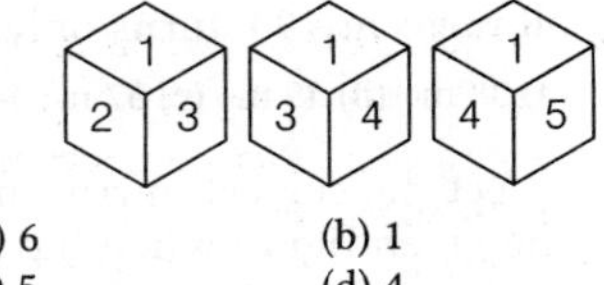

(a) 6 (b) 1
(c) 5 (d) 4

45. Select the option that represents the correct order of the given words as they would appear in an English dictionary.

1. Dermatology 2. Derogation
3. Derivative 4. Derailed
5. Dermestid 6. Deregulation

(a) 4, 3, 2, 1, 5, 6 (b) 4, 6, 3, 2, 1, 5
(c) 4, 6, 3, 1, 5, 2 (d) 4, 6, 1, 5, 3, 2

46. Which of the following interchanges of signs would make the given equation correct?

$56 \div 8 - 14 \times 2 + 12 = 23$

(a) + and × (b) – and ×
(c) ÷ and × (d) – and +

47. A, B, C, D, E and F are six members of a family. There are parents, their children and grandchildren in the family. A is the son of C and E is the daughter of A. D is the daughter of F who is the mother of E. Which of the following pairs is the grandchildren of the parents?

(a) C, E (b) D, E
(c) A, E (d) A, D

48. Select the venn diagram that best illustrates the relationship between the following classes.
India, Tamil Nadu, Chennai

(a) 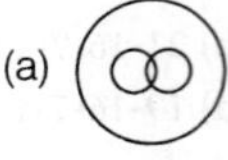 (b) 

(c) (d)

49. A dice has its faces marked by numbers 2, 4, 6, 8, 10 and 12. Two positions of the same dice are given below. Which face is opposite to face 4?

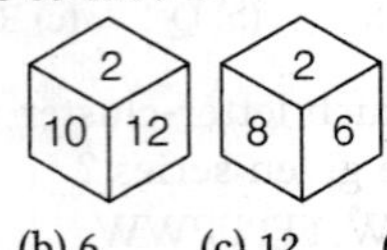

(a) 10 (b) 6 (c) 12 (d) 2

50. In a code language, 'PIG' is coded as 29 and 'COW' is coded as 38. How will 'CAMEL'be coded in the same language?

(a) 27 (b) 29 (c) 22 (d) 34

Part II

General Knowledge and General Awareness

51. In 1596, who suggested in his work 'Thesaurus Geographicus' that the continents of the earth were not always located in their present positions?

(a) Dan Peter McKenzie
(b) Georges Cuvier
(c) Louis Agassiz
(d) Abraham Ortelius

52. Gobinda Chandra Pal is an awardee of the Sangeet Natak Akademi Amrit Award for the year 2022. He contributed to the field of

(a) Odissi Dance (Gotipua)
(b) Dance (Kathak)
(c) Puppetry
(d) Theatre (Acting)

53. In how many categories are loans provided under the MUDRA loan scheme?

(a) 4 (b) 3 (c) 1 (d) 2

54. Which of the following is a selective credit instrument?

(a) Variable reserve ratio
(b) Bank rate
(c) CRR
(d) Credit rationing

55. Which of the following forces can only be applied when in contact with an object?

(a) Frictional force
(b) Gravitational force
(c) Electrostatic force
(d) Magnetic force

56. In which year were four new Directive Principles added to the original list?

(a) 1976 (b) 1980 (c) 1977 (d) 1975

57. With progressive delicensing of industries as part of liberalisation, which of the following is the industry that is removed from the requirement of license?

(a) Cigars and cigarettes of tobacco and manufactured tobacco substitutes
(b) Coal and lignite
(c) Industrial explosives
(d) Hazardous chemicals

58. Who among the following is a distinguished and experienced scion of the famous Kavungal family associated with 'Kathakali' for six generations?

(a) Meenakshi Sundaram Pillai
(b) Ammannur Madhava Chakyar
(c) Chathunni Panicker
(d) Padma Subramanyam

59. Kamalini Asthana and Nalini Asthana, veteran dancers who represent Banaras Gharana of Kathak, were conferred with which of the following awards in the year 2022?

(a) Sangeet Natak Akademi
(b) Padma Bhushan
(c) Padma Vibhushan
(d) Padma Shri

60. Which country won the 15th Men's Hockey World Cup-2023 title?

(a) Belgium (b) India
(c) Germany (d) Pakistan

61. Which of the following Governor-Generals of British India was in favour of free press and repealed the press regulations of 1823 ?

(a) Lord Lytton (b) Lord Metcalfe
(c) Lord Ripon (d) Lord Ellenborough

62. How many types of makeup (vesham) are used for the performers of Kathakali dance?
(a) 7 (b) 11
(c) 5 (d) 9

63. Epilimnetic, Metalimnetic and Hypolimnetic water strata are example of
(a) typical thermal stratification of a lake
(b) typical layers of hard rock
(c) various ecological phases
(d) different layers of underground water

64. Which of the following is correctly matched?
(a) Hariprasad Chaurasia – Sarod
(a) Zakir Husain – Sitar
(c) Bismillah Khan – Tabla
(d) Sultan Khan – Sarangi

65. Anup Rag Vilas' is a book written by which of the following musicians?
(a) Pandit Jasraj
(c) Pandit Birju Maharaj
(c) Pandit Kumar Gandharva
(d) Pandit Dinkar Kaikini

66. Which is an integral membrane protein that forms the tetramer and facilitates the diffusion of water and some small, unmodified solutes across cellular membranes?
(a) Immunoglobulins
(b) Aquaporins
(c) Mucins
(d) Transferrin

67. Identify the organelle present in plant cell that is not there in an animal cell.
(a) Plastids (b) Nucleus
(c) Neuron (d) Cytoplasm

68. Who among the following physicists invented the voltaic pile, the forerunner of the modern battery, in 1800?
(a) Andre-Marie Ampere
(b) Hans Christian Oersted
(c) George Simon
(d) Alessandro Volta

69. Pandit Ravi Shankar, founder of National Orchestra of India, was a ...... player.
(a) Sitar (b) Sarangi
(c) Sarod (d) Flute

70. According to Airports Authority of India, what is the total number of International airports in India as on 2022?
(a) 13 (b) 14 (c) 16 (d) 17

71. Whose memoir is titled 'Once Upon a Life: Burnt Curry and Bloody Rags'?
(a) Easterine Kire (b) Patricia Mukim
(c) Janice Pariat (d) Temsula Ao

72. Which of the following statements are correct regarding the jurisdiction of the Supreme Court of India?
A. Original Jurisdiction extends to any dispute between the Government of India and one or more states or between the Government of India and any State or states on one side and one or more states on the other or between two or more states.
B. Appellate Jurisdiction extends when the Union plus some states are one side and some other states on the other side of the dispute.
C. Under Articles 129 and 142 of the Constitution, the Supreme Court has been vested with the power to punish for contempt of court.
D. As of now, the International Commercial Arbitration cannot be initiated in the Supreme Court.
(a) A and B (b) B and D
(c) A and C (d) A, B, C and D

73. Directive Principles of State Policy in India have been taken from the Constitution of which country?
(a) Britain (b) USSR
(c) Ireland (d) The US

74. What is the fourth step in mitosis where non-kinetochore spindle fibres lengthen and elongate the cell?
(a) Metaphase (b) Prophase
(c) Telophase (d) Anaphase

75. Which of the following organic compounds is a benzenoid ?
(a) Acetaldehyde (b) Propane
(c) Hexane (d) Aniline

76. According to the Census of India 2011, 'Other Religions and Persuasions' formed what percentage of the country's population?
(a) 1.7% (b) 0.7% (c) 2.3% (d) 0.4%

77. Which of the following countries will host the World Badminton Championship event 2026?
(a) Japan (b) Indonesia
(c) India (d) China

78. Choose the coasts that are running along the Arabian sea.
1. Northern Circars
2. Malabar
3. Konkan
4. Coromandel
(a) 2 and 3 (b) 1 and 3
(c) 2, 3 and 4 (d) 1, 2 and 3

79. Which of the following statement/statements is/are true regarding the light year?
1. Light year is a unit of distance.
2. Light is a unit of time.
3. A light year is the distance that light travels in one Earth year.
4. Light year is the measurement of light intensity.
(a) Only 1 (b) 1 and 2
(c) 1 and 3 (d) Only 2

80. According to Agricultural Statistics at a Glance 2022, Government of India, which state recorded the highest production of sugarcane?
(a) Karnataka (b) Gujarat
(c) Uttar Pradesh (d) Maharashtra

81. Which of the following states of India receives initial rainfall by the Arabian Sea branch of monsoon?
(a) Mizoram (b) Tamil Nadu
(c) Kerala (d) Assam

82. Abolition of titles is mentioned in which Article of the Indian Constitution?
(a) Article 23 (b) Article 13
(c) Article 18 (d) Article 24

83. In which amongst the following acts was Delhi declared the capital of British India in place of Calcutta?
(a) Government of India Act, 1858
(b) Government of India Act, 1935
(c) Morley - Minto Act, 1909
(d) Montagu Chelmsford Act, 1919

84. Which Article of the Indian Constitution mentions about the salaries and allowances of the Chairman and Deputy Chairman of the Rajya Sabha and the Speaker and Deputy Speaker of the Lok Sabha ?
(a) Article-92 (b) Article-97
(c) Article-94 (d) Article-95

85. Which of the following Articles of the Indian Constitution mentions that the Vice-President of India shall be the Ex-Officio Chairman of the Council of States?
(a) Article-89 (b) Article-92
(c) Article-91 (d) Article-90

86. Under whose rule did the Mughal empire achieve its largest territorial limits?
(a) Bahadur Shah II (b) Shah Jahan
(c) Akbar (d) Aurangzeb

87. Under the Bahmani kingdom, the provinces were administered by ....
(a) Afaqis (b) Tarafdars
(c) Khalisa (d) Amirs

88. Who among the following has been elected as the 36th President of BCCI?
(a) Anil Kumble
(b) Roger Binny
(c) Sourav Ganguly
(d) Chetan Sharma

89. Goga Navami, which is primarily celebrated in the Indian state of ...... is dedicated to the snake God, Gogaji.
(a) Andhra Pradesh (b) Odisha
(c) Rajasthan (d) Karnataka

90. Which State was founded by Nizam-ul-Mulk in 1724?
(a) Awadh (b) Hyderabad
(c) Mysore (d) Bengal

91. The 2026 Winter Olympics will be held in ....
(a) The US (b) Japan
(c) The UK (d) Italy

92. Select the correct statements from the following.
i. In the Tenth Plan period, the Indian economy grew at 7.7% per year.
ii. The targeted growth for the Eleventh Five-Year Plan was 9% per year.
iii. In the Ninth Plan period, India realised a growth of 7.5% per year.
(a) i and iii (b) ii and iii
(c) Only iii (d) i and ii

93. Damodar Mauzo, who received the 57th Jnanpith Award, is primarily a/an ...... writer.
(a) Bengali (b) Konkani
(c) Odia (d) Maithili

94. Which of the following was the port-city of the Pandyan Kingdom?
(a) Tenkasi
(b) Korkai
(c) Dindigul
(d) Virudhunagar

95. In the context of local storms of hot weather season, Nor Westers are
(a) the dreaded evening thunderstorms in Bengal and Assam.
(b) a nearby wind that blows coffee flowers in Kerala.
(c) the hot, dry and oppressing winds blowing in the Northern plains from Punjab to Bihar with higher intensity between Delhi and Patna.
(d) the pre-monsoon showers that are a common phenomenon in Kerala and coastal areas of Karnataka.

96. Identify the device used to change the resistance in an electric circuit.
(a) Ammeter (b) Conductor
(c) Rheostat (d) Voltmeter

97. A choice of goals has been made in each plan due to
(a) unlimited manpower
(b) limitation of resources
(c) unlimited resources
(d) limitation of choice

98. Which of the following rivers is joined by river Chambal from the South?
(a) Teesta (b) Ganga
(c) Yamuna (d) Kosi

99. According to the Global Hunger Index 2022, what is the rank of the neighbouring country, Bangladesh out of 121 countries?
(a) 99th (b) 109th
(c) 107th (d) 84th

100. Good Friday is related to
(a) Hindus (b) Sikhs
(c) Jains (d) Christians

Part III

Quantitative Aptitude

101. Two similar triangles of ΔXYZ and ΔLMN. If area of $(\Delta XYZ) = 16 \text{ cm}^2$, area of $(\Delta LMN) = 25 \text{ cm}^2$ and $YZ = 2.4$ cm, then the measure of MN is.
(a) 3 cm (b) 1 cm (c) 4 cm (d) 2 cm

102. A train covers a distance of 56 km in 35 minutes. Travelling at the same speed, in how many seconds will the train cover a distance of 720 m ?
(a) 32 (b) 27 (c) 30 (d) 24

103. Simplify : $\dfrac{92736}{(274+830) \text{ of } \dfrac{7}{4}} + 513$
(a) 574 (b) 546 (c) 561 (d) 526

104. If $\tan\theta = \dfrac{3}{10}$, then find the value of $\dfrac{(1+\sin\theta)(1-\sin\theta)}{(1+\cos\theta)(1-\cos\theta)}$
(a) $\dfrac{50}{3}$ (b) $\dfrac{100}{7}$ (c) $\dfrac{100}{9}$ (d) $\dfrac{100}{3}$

105. Study the given table and answer the question that follows.
The table shows the number of students in various courses in various cities A, B, C, D and E in India during the academic year 2022-2023.

City	MBA	Science	Engineering	Medicine	MCA	Total
A	1200	2560	4520	1100	960	10340
B	1350	2650	5100	1050	850	11000
C	1250	2640	4580	1120	750	10340
D	1960	1250	3500	1850	1600	10160
E	1200	2100	3500	1960	1540	10300
Total	6960	11200	21200	7080	5700	

What was the average number of students in Science course in the all the cities altogether during the academic year 2022-2023?
(a) 2220 (b) 2200 (c) 2250 (d) 2240

106. A man travels some distance at a speed of 12 km/h and returns at a speed of 8 km/h. If the total time taken by him is 3 h and 45 min, then the total distance (in km) travelled is
(a) 42 (b) 24 (c) 32 (d) 36

107. If $\tan\theta = \dfrac{7}{24}$, then find the value of $(\cos^2\theta - \sin^2\theta)$
(a) 1 (b) $\dfrac{520}{625}$ (c) $\dfrac{576}{550}$ (d) $\dfrac{527}{625}$

108. A rectangular sheet of metal is 60 cm by 25 cm. Equal squares of side 5 cm are cut off at the corners and the remainder is folded up to form an open rectangular box. Find the volume of the box.

(a) 3750 cm^3 (b) 5750 cm^3
(c) 4750 cm^3 (d) 2750 cm^3

109. If 40 % of $A = 60\%$ of $B = \frac{1}{6}$ of C, then find the ratio of $A: B: C$.

(a) 15 : 10 : 36 (b) 36 : 10 : 15
(c) 15 : 10 : 18 (d) 10 : 15 : 36

110. The following bar graph shows the recruitment of employees in different year of a particular department.

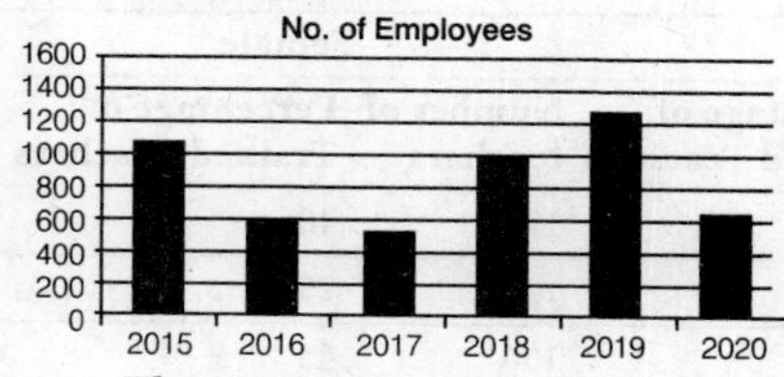

The percentage increase in the recruitment of employees from 2017 to 2018 is

(a) 150% (b) 130% (c) 100% (d) 120%

111. Simplify

$35 - [30 + \{10 + (12 - 10 - 4)\}]$

(a) –3 (b) 2 (c) –2 (d) 3

112. A grocer purchased 10 kg rice for ₹ 700. He spends some amount on transportation and then sells it for ₹ 1400. If the percentage of profit made by the grocer is 30%, then what is the amount (in ₹) he spends on transportation? (round off to the nearest integer)

(a) 300 (b) 380 (c) 377 (d) 350

113. If two circles of radii 35 cm and 25 cm touch each other externally, then the length (in cm) of a common tangent is (rounded off to 2 decimal places)

(a) 60.00 (b) 59.16
(c) 45.29 (d) 52.25

114. If $16x^4 + \frac{1}{16x^4} = 14159$, then find the value of $2x + \frac{1}{2x}$.

(a) 12 (b) 11
(c) 15 (d) 9

115. A man's speed in still water is 4 km/h more than the speed of the current. If the man takes a total of 10 h to cover 45 km downstream and 35 km upstream, then the speed of the man in still water is

(a) 15 km/h (b) 22 km/h
(c) 18 km/h (d) 20 km/h

116. In a store, an item with marked price of ₹ 82500 is available at a discounted price of ₹ 79200. What is the percentage of discount given on that item?

(a) 1% (b) 4% (c) 2% (d) 3%

117. If 24 people can build 90 identical walls in 25 days, then how many more days will 27 people require to build 162 such walls?

(a) 14 (b) 13 (c) 15 (d) 16

118. Find the surface area (in cm^2) of a sphere of diameter 28 cm. (use $\pi = \frac{22}{7}$)

(a) 1731 (b) 2856 (c) 1724 (d) 2464

119. Simplify the following expression.

$$\frac{(525 + 175)^2 - (525 - 175)^2}{(525 \times 175)}$$

(a) 700 (b) 4
(c) 2 (d) 350

120. The population of a town increases 8% annually. If its present population is 142560,what was the population one year ago?

(a) 133000 (b) 134000
(c) 131000 (d) 132000

121. The value of $5 + [6 + (3 + 5) \div 2] \div 2$ is equal to

(a) 8 (b) 12 (c) 10 (d) 14

122. The following table shows the number of delivery partners (in thousands) who joined five different companies during six different years.

Year	Companies				
	Emazon	Clipkart	Twiggy	Tomato	Pyntra
2016	2.4	4.5	1.2	0.9	4.2
2017	1.8	5.4	1.5	1.2	5.6
2018	3.2	7.2	2.4	2.1	6.3
2019	3.9	5.6	2.8	2.7	6.5
2020	4.2	6.4	3.2	3.3	7.0
2021	5.0	7.2	3.6	3.6	7.2

If Emazon decides to give an averages salary of a ₹ 21000 to the delivery partners and allocates ₹ 13.44 crore for the same in 2022, find the percentage increase in the number of delivery partners from 2021 to 2022.

(a) 20% (b) 25%
(c) 28% (d) 22.5%

123. If $x + \frac{1}{x} = 2$, then find the value of $(x^4 + \frac{4}{x^4})(x^3 - \frac{4}{x^3})$

(a) –10 (b) 10 (c) –15 (d) 15

124. In a ΔABC, angle $BAC = 30°$ and angle $BCA = 60°$. If $AC = 13$ cm and $AB = 12$ cm, then BC is equal to

(a) 7 cm (b) 5 cm (c) 4 cm (d) 6 cm

125. 18 workers can complete a piece of work in 96 days. They start working together and after 26 days 10 more workers join them. In how many days in all will the work be completed?

(a) 72 (b) 69 (c) 71 (d) 70

126. Study the given table and answer the question that follows.

The table shows the number of students in various courses in various cities A, B, C, D and E in India during the academic year 2022-2023.

City	MBA	Science	Engineering	Medicine	MCA	Total
A	1200	2560	4520	1100	960	10340
B	1350	2650	5100	1050	850	11000
C	1250	2640	4580	1120	750	10340
D	1960	1250	3500	1850	1600	10160
E	1200	2100	3500	1960	1540	10300
Total	6960	11200	21200	7080	5700	

In all the cities altogether, what is the difference between the students of science and those of MBA ?

(a) 4240 (b) 4440
(c) 4540 (c) 4340

127. A person deposited some amount of money in the bank at simple interest. After 20 yr, the amount became nine times the amount deposited. In how many years will the amount become 13 times the amount if the interest rate remains the same?

(a) 28 (b) 30 (c) 25 (d) 23

128. In alloys *A* and *B*, the ratio of lead to tin is 5 : 3 and 3 : 1, respectively. 80 kg of alloy *A* and 100 kg of alloy *B* are mixed together to form a new alloy. What is the amount of tin(in kg) in the new alloy?
(a) 90 (b) 55 (c) 81.3 (d) 68

129. In an election between two candidates, 10% of the voters did not cast their votes and 75 votes were found invalid. The winner got 50% of the total votes expected and won by 170 votes. How many voters were enrolled in the voters' list?
(a) 800 (b) 850 (c) 950 (d) 855

130. If the radius of a sphere is increased by 40%, then find the percentage increase in its surface area.
(a) 85% (b) 88% (c) 96% (d) 92%

131. The value of $(4^2)^2 + 4 \times 4 \div 4 - 4$ is
(a) 4^0 (b) 4^2 (c) 4^3 (d) 4^4

132. A product was offered at a 10% trade discount on the marked price. After a cash discount of 10%, the product was sold for 7290. The marked price (in ₹) is
(a) 8510 (b) 9000 (c) 8900 (d) 8720

133. *R* reaches office from home in 30 min and comes back in 20 min. The distance to his office from home is 12.5 km. What is his average speed (in km/h) from home to office and then back home?
(a) 30 (b) 60 (c) 25 (d) 20

134. The value of $1 + \cfrac{1}{1 + \cfrac{1}{5 + \cfrac{1}{2 + \cfrac{1}{3}}}}$ is
(a) $2\frac{11}{45}$ (b) $1\frac{38}{45}$ (c) $2\frac{17}{45}$ (d) $1\frac{13}{45}$

135. A dishonest dealer sells his goods at 20% loss on the cost price, but uses a faulty weight that weighs 25% less. His profit or loss percentage (rounded off to 2 decimal places) is
(a) 6.67%, profit (b) 3.33%, profit (c) 3.33%, loss (d) 6.67%, loss

136. Which of the following is true when $x = \sin A + \cos A : y = \sec A + \operatorname{cosec} A$?
(a) $y + 2x = x^2y$ (b) $y(1 + x^2) = 2x$
(c) $y(1 - 2x^2) = x$ (d) $y - 2x = x^2y$

137. In an election, *A* received 27% of the votes and *B* received 125,982 votes. 19% did not cast their votes. Find the number of votes received by *A*.
(a) 188973 (b) 62991 (c) 57827 (d) 44327

138. Simplify : $[\{38 - (-6)\} \times \{9 - (8 - 1)\}] \div [4 \times \{6 + (-4)\}]$
(a) 14 (b) 18 (c) 11 (d) 22

139. Mitu can do a piece of work in 12 h, Titu and Situ together in 2 h, and Mitu and Situ together in 3 hours. How long will Titu alone take to do it?
(a) 6 h (b) 4 h (c) 7 h (d) 8 h

140. Triangle *DEF* is an equilateral triangle with a side length of 12 cm. If Point G is the mid-point of side *DE*, what is the length (in cm) of side *FG*?
(a) 12 (b) $6\sqrt{3}$ (c) 6 (d) $3\sqrt{6}$

141. The ratio of marks of *A* and *B* is 3 : 4 and the ratio of marks of *B* and *C* is 4 : 5. If the difference in the marks of *C* and *A* is 30, then how much marks does *B* get?
(a) 52 (b) 60 (c) 56 (d) 64

142. The value of $\frac{1}{4} + \frac{2}{5} \div \left[\left\{2\frac{1}{5} - 2\right\} \times 5\right] - \frac{2}{3}$ of $\frac{3}{5}$ is
(a) $\frac{2}{3}$ (b) $\frac{1}{4}$ (c) $\frac{3}{5}$ (d) $\frac{5}{6}$

143. The following table shows the number of teachers in four colleges (male and female) and the percentage of trained teachers among them.

Colleges	Male		Female	
	Number of teachers	Percentage of Trained Teachers	Number of teachers	Percentage of Trained Teachers
A	225	44	175	40
B	250	30	128	25
C	290	55	100	45
D	350	60	150	30

What is the total number of non-trained male teachers in College A and non-trained female teachers in College B?
(a) 222 (b) 230 (c) 224 (d) 228

144. Find the maximum value of $(19\sin\theta + 6\cot\theta\sin\theta)$.
(a) $\sqrt{197}$ (b) $\sqrt{397}$ (c) $\sqrt{497}$ (d) $\sqrt{297}$

145. A drainage tile is a cylindrical shell 42 cm long. The inside and outside diameters are 8 cm and 14 cm, respectively. What is the volume (in cm^3) of clay required for the tile ? (Use $\pi = \frac{22}{7}$)
(a) 4125 (b) 4881 (c) 4356 (d) 5241

146. Simplify : $22 \times 10 \div 5 \times 2 + 12$.
(a) 101 (b) 103 (c) 100 (d) 102

147. Study the given table and answer the question that follows. The table shows the production of five types of cars P, Q, R, S and T by a company from the year 1989 to 1994.

Type of Car	1989	1990	1991	1992	1993	1994	Total
P	8	20	16	17	21	6	88
Q	16	10	14	12	12	14	78
R	21	17	16	15	13	8	90
S	4	6	10	16	20	31	87
T	25	18	19	30	14	27	133
Total	74	71	75	90	80	86	476

In which year was the total production of cars of types P and Q together equal to the total production of cars of types R and S together?

(a) 1992 (b) 1991
(c) 1993 (d) 1989

148. The savings and expenditure of a family in a month on different heads is shown in the given pie-chart. The family saves ₹ 8000 per month.

Monthly Expenditure of a family

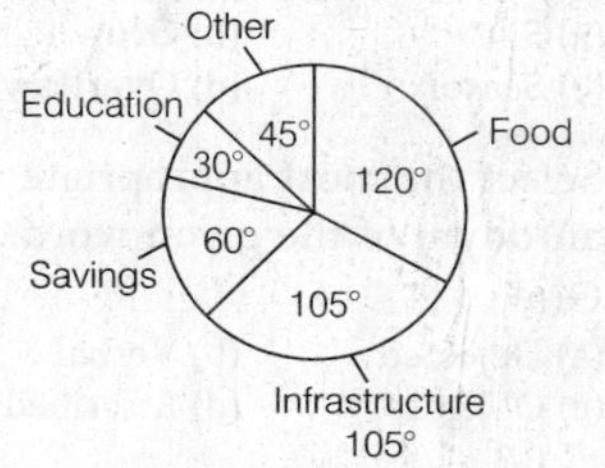

Find the total monthly expenditure (in ₹) of the family.

(a) 30000 (b) 40000
(c) 35000 (d) 25000

149. If the surface areas of two spheres are in the ratio of 9 :49, then the ratio of their volumes is (where, $\pi = \frac{22}{7}$)

(a) 27 : 343 (b) 16 : 216
(c) 25 : 512 (d) 49 : 363

150. The value of $9 \times 9 + 9 \div 9 - 9 \times 9 + 9 + 9 \times 9 - 9 - 9 \times 9$ is

(a) 9 (b) 81
(c) 1 (d) 0

Part IV
English Comprehension

151. Select the most appropriate idiom for the given situation focusing on the underlined words.

I invited them to my anniversary dinner but they had other plans, so they decided <u>to politely decline with the implication that they may come at a later date</u>.

(a) took it with a grain of salt
(b) to take a rain check
(c) to spoil a moment
(d) call it a day

152. Select the option that can be used as a one-word substitute for the underlined words.

He was promoted to a higher position in the first year due to his <u>careful nature and hard-working efforts</u>.

(a) diligence
(b) business mindedness
(c) extraordinary
(d) elegance

153. Select the option that can be used as a one-word substitute for the given group of words.

A lively, cheerful outgoing person

(a) Ambivert (b) Introvert
(c) Orator (d) Extrovert

154. Select the option that can be used as a one-word substitute for the given group of words.

Weak and cowardly

(a) Meek
(b) Pusillanimous
(c) Anxious
(d) Timid

155. Select the most appropriate idiom that can substitute the underlined segment in the given sentence.

The players like the coach because he is honest, <u>realistic and practical</u> in dealing with them.

(a) by and large (b) sick and tired
(c) far and wide (d) down to earth

156. Select the most appropriate idiom that can substitute the underlined segment in the given sentence and complete the sentence correctly.

It is important to take this opportunity to make a name for yourself- <u>beat around the bush</u>.

(a) bare the foot
(b) strike while the iron is hot
(c) pass with flying colours
(d) fight tooth and claw

157. The following sentence has been divided into parts. One of them contains an error. Select the part that contains the error from the given options.

Mr. Vinu / has never / slept in / a Igloo.

(a) a Igloo (b) slept in
(c) has never (d) Mr. Vinu

158. Select the most appropriate option that can substitute the underlined segment in the given sentence.

No sooner had she finished her breakfast <u>that she had received</u> a phone call from her boss, informing her that she needed to come to work immediately.

(a) than she received
(b) that she receives
(c) that she received
(d) than she receives

159. Select the word from the sentence below, which is an antonym for the word 'advance'.

Clive is a travel blogger who believes that with even an elementary or intermediate knowledge of the local language, you can enjoy your travel more.

(a) Destination (b) knowledge
(c) Believes (d) Elementary

160. Select the most appropriate idiom that can substitute the underlined segment in the given sentence.

Popular cosmetics brands in India are <u>very expensive</u>

(a) take it with a pinch of salt
(b) up in arms
(c) cost an arm and a leg
(d) flog a dead horse

161. Underlined word in the sentence is not spelt correctly. Identify the correct spelling from the options given below.

Raman had been living a <u>reklusive</u> life since he had lost his job.

(a) Reslusive (b) Reclusive
(c) Recslusive (d) Reclucive

162. Select the most appropriate option that can substitute the underlined words in the given sentence.

Though very informative, Shweta's article <u>was mercilessly rejected</u> of the editor.

(a) was mercilessly rejected of
(b) was mercilessly rejected by
(c) was mercilessly rejected each
(d) was mercilessly rejected on

163. What is the most appropriate Antonym of the word 'fluctuate'?

(a) Deflect (b) Stabilise
(c) Vacillate (d) Fickle

164. Select the most appropriate option that can substitute the underlined segment in the given sentence.
Last night, I failed to sleep because of some familiar issues that couldn't be avoided.
(a) incapable (b) unthinkable
(c) unsolvable (d) unavoidable

165. Identify the most appropriate antonym of the given word.
Rapid
(a) Smart (b) Active
(c) Slow (d) Lately

166. Select the most appropriate idiom to fill in the blank.
When I went to Egypt and lost my wallet and passport, I was ......
(a) putting my nose to the grindstone
(b) working my fingers to the bone
(c) up in a creek without a paddle
(d) rolling up my sleeves

167. Select the incorrectly spelt word.
(a) Mystery (b) Bycycle
(c) Justice (d) Academy

168. Select the most appropriate meaning of the given idiom.
Gift of the Gab
(a) A talent for speaking
(b) A gift for a person named Gab
(c) A talent for singing
(d) A talent for lying

169. Select the option that can be used as a one-word substitute for the given group of words.
A lover of mankind
(a) Recluse (b) Philanthropist
(c) Cynic (d) Psychiatrist

170. Parts of the following sentence have been given as options. Select the option that contains an error.
My neighbours were serious injured in the car accident.
(a) serious injured
(b) the car accident
(c) in
(d) My neighbours were

171. Parts of the given sentence have been underlined. One of them contains an error.Select the option that has the segment with a grammatical error.
The art historian argued that the painting's value has been greatly underestimated, and that its unique style and technique deserved recognition from the Art community and the public alike
(a) has been greatly underestimated
(b) and the public alike
(c) recognition from the art community
(d) its unique style and technique

172. Select the most appropriate antonym of the given word.
Confound
(a) Discern (b) Suppress
(c) Assure (d) Expire

173. Select the most appropriate option that can substitute the underlined segment in the given sentence. If there is no need to substitute it, select 'No substitution'.
If I was very rich, I would spend all my time and money for the poor.
(a) If I were very rich
(b) No substitution
(c) If I have much riches
(d) If I am very rich

174. Select the incorrectly spelt word.
(a) Perseverance (b) Hierarchy
(c) Knowledgeable (d) Neccessity

175. Select the most appropriate segment to substitute the underlined words in the given sentence.
After he leave, we discussed his suggestion.
(a) he had left (b) he will be leaving
(c) he was leaving (d) he has left

176. Select the option that can be used as a one-word substitute for the given group of words.
An area/place in which dead bodies are buried
(a) Clementi (b) Cemetery
(c) Mansion (d) Demise

177. The following sentence has been split into four segments. Identify the segment that contains a spelling error.
The dried raisons / have an intoxicating /effect on humans as / well as flora and fauna.
(a) The dried raisons
(b) well as flora and fauna.
(c) have an intoxicating
(d) effect on humans as

178. Select the most appropriate synonym of the given word.
Mourn
(a) Dread (b) Amuse
(c) Grieve (d) Approve

179. Select the most appropriate meaning of the given idiom.
To leave no stone unturned
(a) To treat someone/something as if of no importance
(b) To do everything possible to achieve something
(c) To control a person completely
(d) To win everything that is available

180. Select the incorrectly spelt word in the given sentence.
Every season the river overflows its banks and when it goes down it leaves silt for crops to be gruwn.
(a) Silt (b) Gruwn
(c) Season (d) Overflows

181. Select the most appropriate antonym of the given word.
Oral
(a) Dejected (b) Verbal
(c) Obligatory (d) Inscribed

182. Select the option that rectifies the spelling error in the given sentence.
The phone rang, but nobody awnsered.
(a) answord
(b) awmsered
(c) answered
(d) ansvered

183. Select the most appropriate antonym of the given word.
Convalesce
(a) Corrupt (b) Collapse
(c) Confront (d) Conceal

184. The following sentence has been divided into four segments. Identify the segment that has a grammatical error.
I am working with him since 2002, / but even today / I am unable / to understand his motives.
(a) but even today
(b) I am working with him since 2002
(c) I am unable
(d) to understand his motives.

185. Select the word from the sentence below, which is an antonym for the word 'resolve'.
My cousin Nisha's curiosity about life will never be satisfied because no one knows all the answers to all her questions.
(a) Satisfied (b) About
(c) Questions (d) Knows

186. Select the most appropriate idiomatic expression that can substitute the underlined segment in the given sentence.
He is very strict with his students but good-natured.
(a) his eyes are bigger than his stomach
(b) his heart misses a beat
(c) he has a big mouth
(d) his heart is in the right place

187. Select the most appropriate idiom to fill in the blank.
John was always ...... about becoming a millionaire without doing any hard work.
(a) a storm in a tea cup
(b) building castles in the air
(c) eating like a horse
(d) having an ace up his sleeve

188. Select the option that will improve the underlined part of the given sentence.
My friend vanished when the goons came to fight with me.
(a) attacked when the thugs arrived
(b) mobilised when the thugs arrived
(c) disappeared when the thugs arrived
(d) condemned when the thugs arrived

189. Select the most appropriate synonym of the underlined word in the given sentence.
The environmental organisation issued a statement to condemn the deforestation happening in the protected area.
(a) Persuade (b) Compel
(c) Foster (d) Censure

190. Parts of the following sentences have been given as options. Select the option that contains a grammatical error.
Ms. Malathi is living lonely in an apartment.
(a) Ms. Malathi (b) an apartment
(c) is living (d) lonely in

Directions (Q. Nos. 191-195) *In the following passage, some words have been deleted. Read the passage carefully and select the most appropriate option to fill in each blank.*

Why do people yawn? No one seems to know the exact ...(1).... Some people believe that we yawn ...(2)... we do not have enough oxygen in our bodies. In ...(3)... words, we yawn to breathe in ...(4)... oxygen. People also believe that yawning is associated ...(5)... boredom.

191. Select the correct option to fill the blank no. 1.
(a) reality (b) explanation
(c) reason (d) basis

192. Select the correct option to fill blank no. 2.
(a) when (b) why
(c) while (d) as

193. Select the correct option to fill blank no. 3.
(a) some (b) other
(c) rather (d) new

194. Select the correct option to fill blank no. 4.
(a) much (b) less
(c) more (d) little

195. Select the correct option to fill blank no. 5.
(a) in (b) with
(c) on (d) by

Directions (Q. Nos. 196-200) *Read the given passage and answer the questions that follow.*

Ahoy there, matey! Today, we're going to talk about something near and dear to my heart:pirates. You know, those swashbuckling scallywags who pillage and plunder on the high seas.

Now, when you think of pirates, you might picture them as these tough, intimidating figures.But let me tell you, there's a lot more to these buccaneers than meets the eye. For one thing,have you ever noticed that pirates seem to have an unusual fondness for parrots? I mean,come on. They're birds. What use could a pirate possibly have for a bird?

And then there's the whole eyepatch thing. Yes, pirates are known for wearing eye patches,but did you ever stop to wonder why? Some people think it's because they lost an eye in battle, but the real reason is much simpler: it's so they can switch the patch from eye to eye and maintain night vision in both eyes. Genius, right ?

But my favourite pirate quirk has got to be their love of treasure. I mean, who doesn't love a good treasure hunt? But the way pirates go about it is just hilarious. They'll spend months,even years, searching for that one elusive chest of gold, only to bury it on some deserted island and forget where they put it. It's like they're playing an eternal game of hide and seek with themselves.

And let's not forget about their vocabulary. Pirates have a whole language all their own, full of terms like 'shiver me timbers', 'avast', and 'yo-ho-ho'. I mean, what does any of that even mean? It's like they're speaking a different language entirely.

So, there you have it, folks. Pirates might be fierce, but they're also pretty darn funny. Who knows? Maybe we could all learn a thing or two from these salty dogs.

196. Which of the following would be the most appropriate title for this passage ?
(a) The Humorous Quirks of Pirates
(b) The Mysterious Language of Pirates
(c) The Fierce and Intimidating Pirate Culture
(d) The Serious World of Pirates

197. Which of the following options best describes the tone of the passage?
(a) Angry (b) Serious
(c) Sarcastic (d) Humorous

198. Why do pirates wear eyepatches?
(a) Because they lost an eye in battle
(b) To intimidate their enemies
(c) To cover up an embarrassing birthmark
(d) To maintain night vision in both eyes

199. What is a common phrase used in pirate language?
(a) Shiver me timbers
(b) Howdy, partner!
(c) Yo, dude!
(d) Greetings, friend!

200. What is one of the pirate quirks mentioned in the passage?
(a) Their fondness for cats
(b) Their love of gardening
(c) Their love for basketball
(d) Their tendency to forget where they buried their treasure.

Know Correct Answers

1. (c)	2. (b)	3. (a)	4. (b)	5. (b)	6. (a)	7. (b)	8. (a)	9. (d)	10. (b)
11. (d)	12. (b)	13. (d)	14. (a)	15. (a)	16. (a)	17. (c)	18. (a)	19. (d)	20. (d)
21. (d)	22. (c)	23. (c)	24. (c)	25. (a)	26. (c)	27. (d)	28. (c)	29. (a)	30. (a)
31. (c)	32. (d)	33. (b)	34. (b)	35. (b)	36. (a)	37. (c)	38. (a)	39. (d)	40. (c)
41. (c)	42. (c)	43. (c)	44. (d)	45. (c)	46. (d)	47. (b)	48. (d)	49. (d)	50. (b)
51. (d)	52. (a)	53. (b)	54. (d)	55. (a)	56. (a)	57. (b)	58. (c)	59. (d)	60. (c)
61. (b)	62. (c)	63. (a)	64. (d)	65. (c)	66. (b)	67. (a)	68. (d)	69. (a)	70. (d)
71. (d)	72. (c)	73. (c)	74. (d)	75. (d)	76. (b)	77. (c)	78. (a)	79. (c)	80. (c)
81. (c)	82. (c)	83. (c)	84. (b)	85. (a)	86. (d)	87. (b)	88. (b)	89. (c)	90. (b)
91. (d)	92. (d)	93. (b)	94. (b)	95. (a)	96. (c)	97. (b)	98. (c)	99. (d)	100. (d)
101. (a)	102. (b)	103. (c)	104. (c)	105. (d)	106. (d)	107. (d)	108. (a)	109. (a)	110. (c)
111. (a)	112. (c)	113. (b)	114. (b)	115. (d)	116. (b)	117. (c)	118. (d)	119. (b)	120. (d)
121. (c)	122. (c)	123. (c)	124. (b)	125. (c)	126. (a)	127 (b)	128. (b)	129. (c)	130. (c)
131. (d)	132. (b)	133. (a)	134. (b)	135. (a)	136. (a)	137 (b)	138. (c)	139. (b)	140. (b)
141. (b)	142. (b)	143. (a)	144. (b)	145. (c)	146. (c)	147. (c)	148. (b)	149. (a)	150. (c)
151. (b)	152. (a)	153. (d)	154. (b)	155. (d)	156. (b)	157. (a)	158. (a)	159. (d)	160. (c)
161. (b)	162. (b)	163. (b)	164. (d)	165. (c)	166. (c)	167. (b)	168. (a)	169. (b)	170. (a)
171. (b)	172. (c)	173. (a)	174. (d)	175. (a)	176. (b)	177. (a)	178. (c)	179. (b)	180. (b)
181. (d)	182. (c)	183. (b)	184. (b)	185. (c)	186. (d)	187. (b)	188. (c)	189. (d)	190. (d)
191. (c)	192. (a)	193. (b)	194. (c)	195. (b)	196. (a)	197. (d)	198. (d)	199. (a)	200. (d)

Answer & Solutions

1. **(c)** Pattern of the series is as follows,

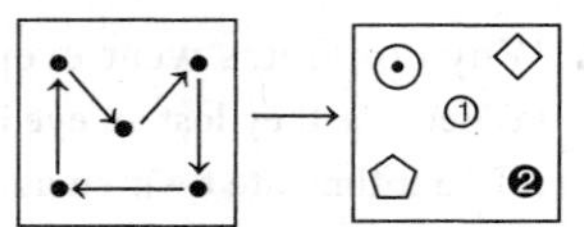

Hence, option figure (c) will replace the question mark.

2. **(b)** The correct mirror image of the given figure is option (b), when the mirror is placed at MN.

M

G w B 7 4 A | A 4 7 B w G

N

3. **(a)** As,

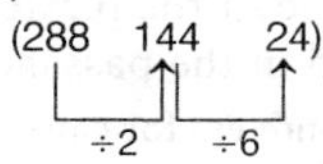

and

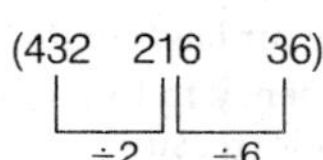

Similarly,

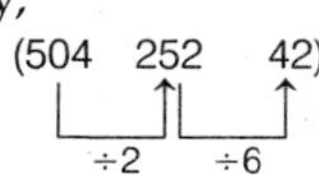

4. **(b)** As,

$F \xrightarrow{+3} I \xrightarrow{+2} K$

$O \xrightarrow{+3} R \xrightarrow{+2} T$

$D \xrightarrow{+3} G \xrightarrow{+2} I$

But, $\boxed{J \xrightarrow{+3} M \xrightarrow{+3} P}$

5. **(b)** As, BASIC = 25 + 26 + 8 + 18 + 24 = 101

[∵ opposite positional value]

and MAGIC = 14 + 26 + 20 + 18 + 24 = 102

Similarly,

LIGHT = 15 + 18 + 20 + 19 + 7 = $\boxed{79}$

6. **(a)** As, (16 4 20)

÷4 ×5

and

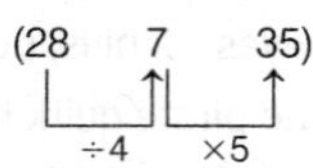

Similarly, (52 13 65)

÷4 ×5

7. **(b)** Given equation, 8 – 6 + 10 = ?

After interchange the numbers and signs '+' and '–' and '8' and '6', we get

= 6 + 8 – 10

[on applying VBODMAS rule]

= 14 – 10 = 4

8. **(a)** After unfolding the paper it will appear as option figure (a).

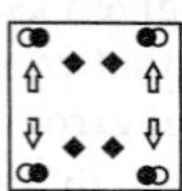

9. **(d)** As, I S L A N D

A N D I S L

and

Similarly,

10. **(b)** Given equation,

[(18 S 5) Q 4] P 2 R 22 Q 3 S 24 R 9 = ?

After interchange the signs, we get

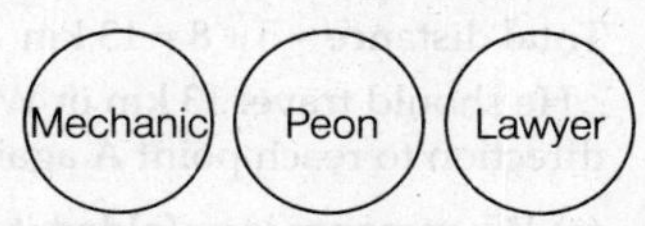

P ⟶ ÷	Q ⟶ ×
R ⟶ +	S ⟶ −

$= [(18 - 5) \times 4] \div 2 + 22 \times 3 - 24 + 9$

$= [13 \times 4] \div 2 + 66 - 24 + 9$

[on applying VBODMAS rule]

$= 26 + 66 - 24 + 9 = \boxed{77}$

11. **(d)** According to the given question,

Here, all are different profession from each other.

12. **(b)** Given equation,

$154 \times 11 - 24 \div 3 + 19 = ?$

After interchange the signs '+ and −' and '× and ÷', we get

$154 \div 11 + 24 \times 3 - 19$

[on applying VBODMAS rule]

$= 14 + 72 - 19$

$= 86 - 19 = \boxed{67}$

13. **(d)** As per the given series, pattern follows here respectively,

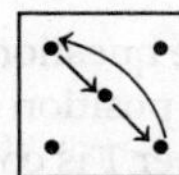

From fig. (1)-(2) and fig. (3)-(4) ; From fig. (2)-(3) and fig. (4)-(5)

14. **(a)** Pattern of the series is as follow,

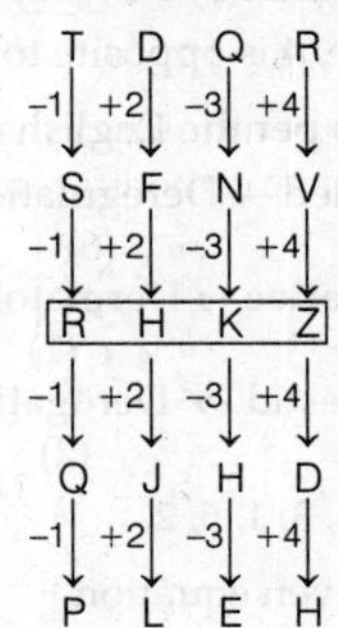

15. **(a)** Pattern of the series is as follows,

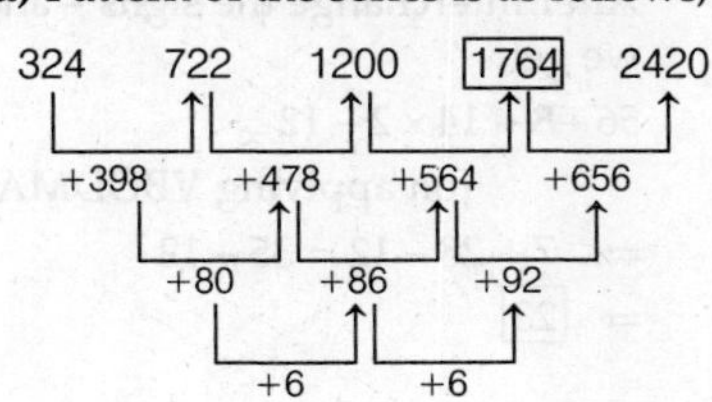

16. **(a)** According to the given statement,

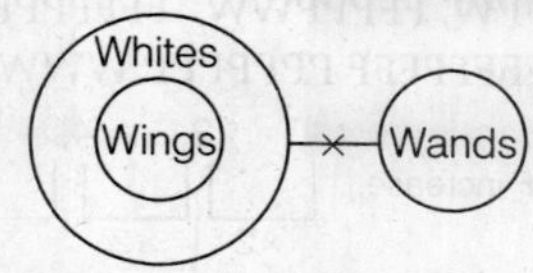

Conclusions I. (✗) II. (✓)

Hence, only Conclusion II follows.

17. **(c)** Given equation,

45R(26Q2) P4R19S32 = ?

After interchanging the signs, we get;

P ⟶ ÷	Q ⟶ ×
R ⟶ +	S ⟶ −

$45 + (26 \times 2) \div 4 + 19 - 32$

$= 45 + 13 + 19 - 32 = \boxed{45}$

18. **(a)** As, (21 , 3 , 15)

÷7 ×5

and (49 , 7 , 35)

÷7 ×5

Similarly, (84 , 12 , 60)

÷7 ×5

19. **(d)** According to the given question,

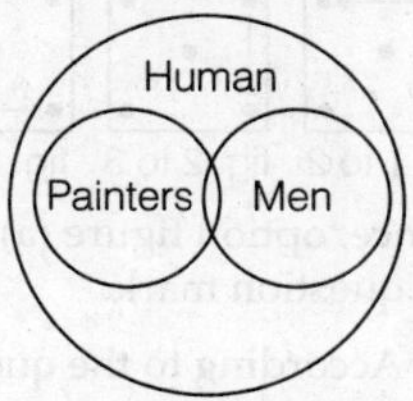

As, all painter and men are human. And some painter are men.

20. **(d)** According to the question,

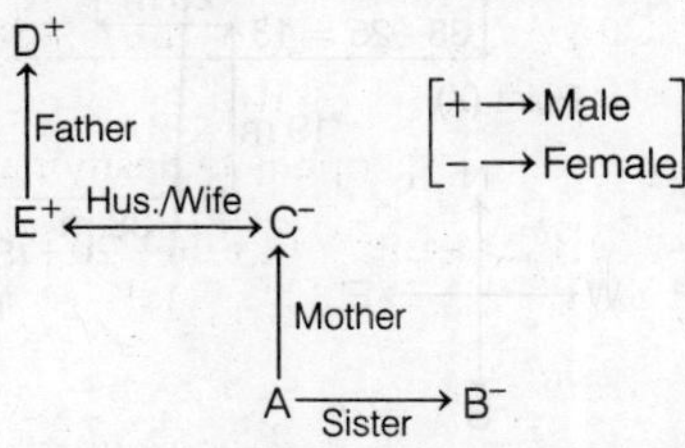

Hence, B is the daughter of E.

21. **(d)** Pattern of the series is as follow,

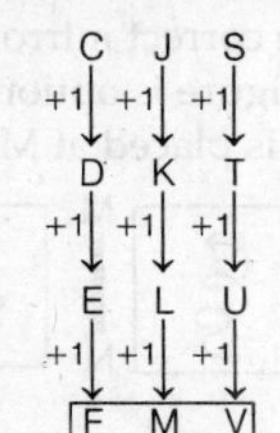

22. **(c)** The problem figure is embedded in option figure (c).

23. **(c)** Pattern of the series is as follow,

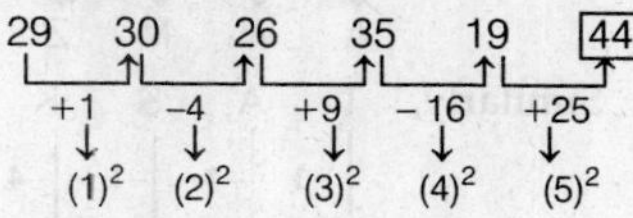

24. **(c)** Pattern of the series is as follow,

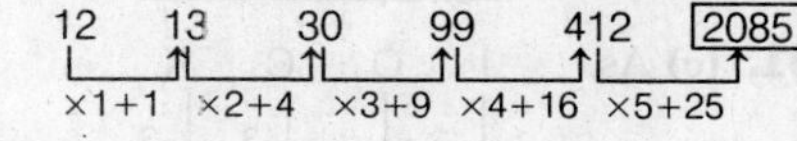

25. **(a)** As, (14 28 84)

×2 ×3

and (17 34 102)

×2 ×3

Similarly, (21 42 126)

×2 ×3

26. **(c)** As, FOX = 14

Number of letters = 3

$(3)^2 + 5 = 14$

and GOAT = 21

Number of letters = 4

$(4)^2 + 5 = 21$

Similarly, TOMMY

Number of letters = 5

$(5)^2 + 5 = \boxed{30}$

27. **(d)** Pattern of the series is as follow,

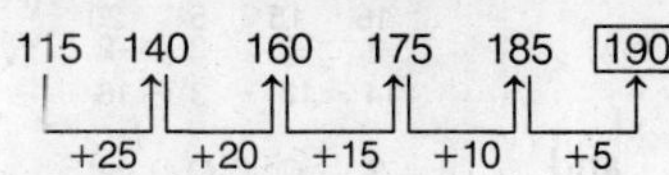

28. **(c)** Given equation,

(121 S 46) R 19 Q 5 R 126 P 6 S 38 = ?

After interchanging the signs,

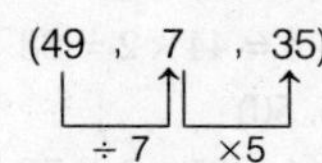

P ⟶ ÷	Q ⟶ ×
R ⟶ +	S ⟶ −

$\Rightarrow (121 - 46) + 19 \times 5 + 126 \div 6 - 38$

$= 75 + 95 + 21 - 38 = \boxed{153}$

29. **(a)** As, MAP = 102

Opposite position value of letter

$(14 + 26 + 11) \times 2 = 51 \times 2 = 102$

and ROT = 56

Opposite position value of letter

$(9 + 12 + 7) \times 2 = 28 \times 2 = 56$

Similarly, SEC

Opposite position value of letter

$(8 + 22 + 24) \times 2 = 54 \times 2 = \boxed{108}$

30. **(a)** As,

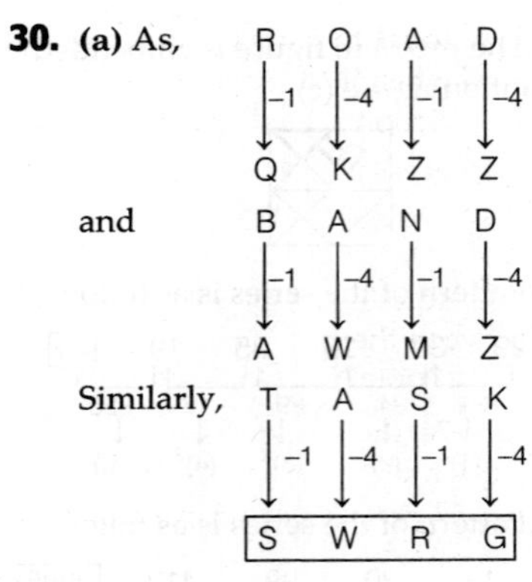

31. **(c)** As,

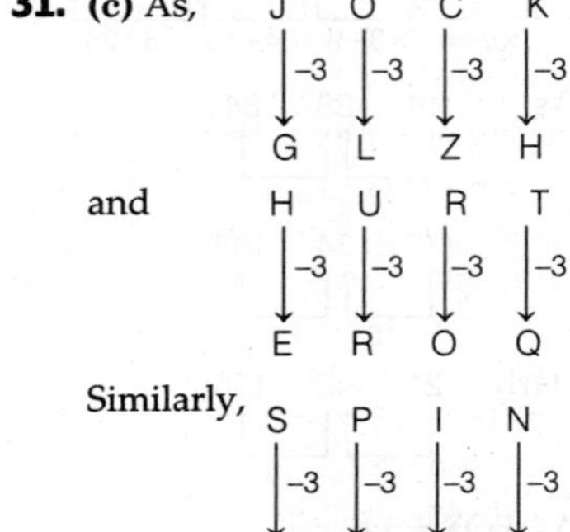

32. **(d)** The problem figure is embedded in option figure (d).

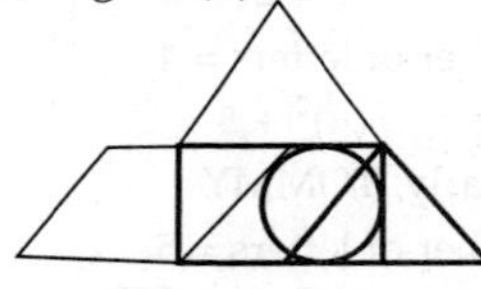

33. **(b)** As,

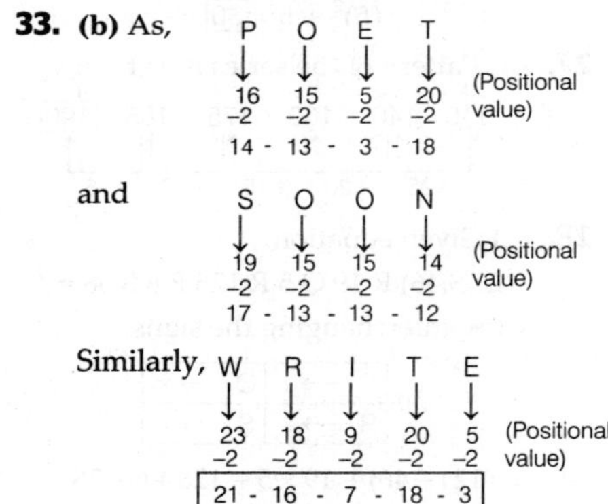

34. **(b)** According to the question,

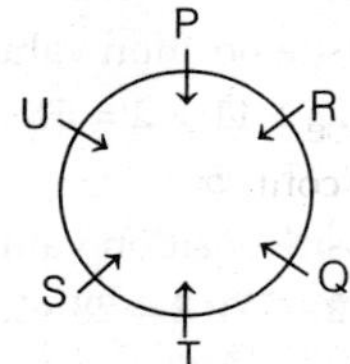

∴ Q sits second to the left of P.

35. **(b)** Accoding to the question,
FPW, FFPPPWW, FFFFPPPPPWWW, FFFFFFFF PPPPPPP WWWW

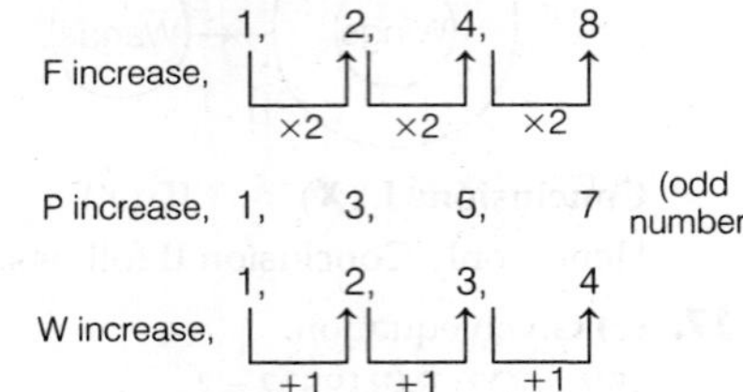

36. **(a)** Given equation,
905 B 2 C 47 D 903 A 3 = ?
After interchange the signs,

A ⟶ ÷	B ⟶ ×
C ⟶ +	D ⟶ −

$\Rightarrow 905 \times 2 + 47 - 903 \div 3$
$\Rightarrow 1810 + 47 - 301 = \boxed{1556}$

37. **(c)** As, (45,88)
$\Rightarrow$ $45 - 1 = 44 \times 2 = 88$
and (26, 50)
$\Rightarrow$ $26 - 1 = 25 \times 2 = 50$
Similarly, (22, 42)
$\Rightarrow$ $22 - 1 = 21 \times 2 = 42$

38. **(a)** In the given series, pattern follows,

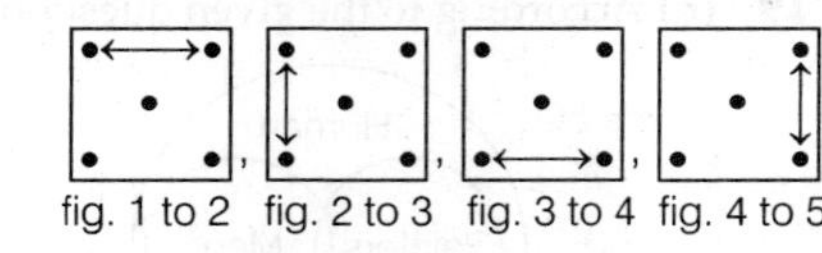

Hence, option figure (a) will replace the question mark.

39. **(d)** According to the question,

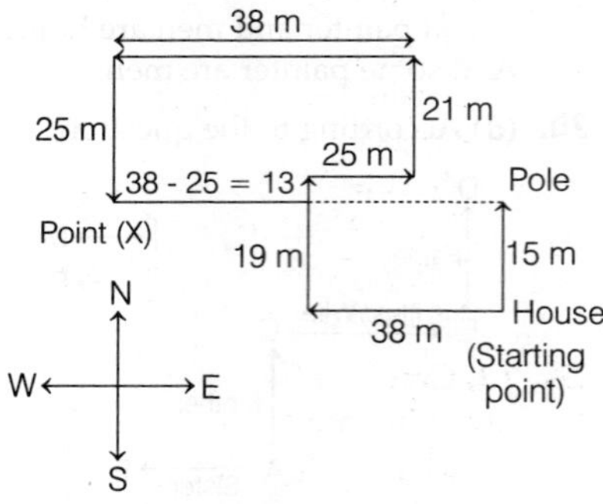

Point X = 38 + 13 = 51 m
Hence, she is 51 m far from the pole.

40. **(c)** The correct mirror image of the given figure is option (c), when the mirror is placed at MN.

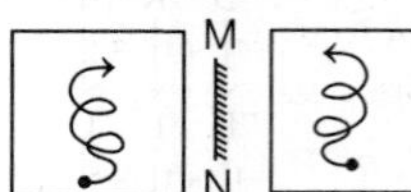

41. **(c)** According to the question,

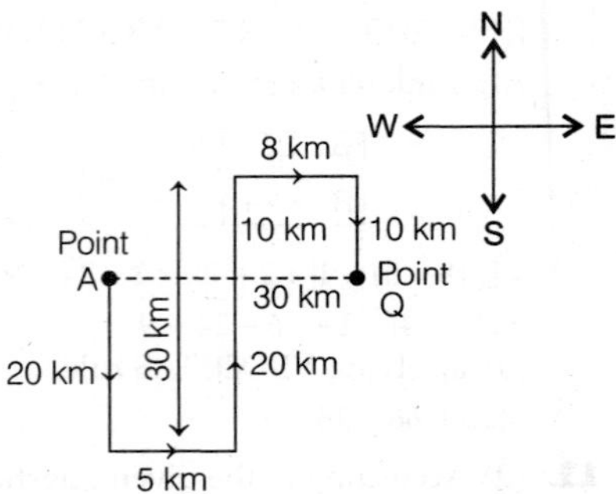

Total distance = 5 + 8 = 13 km
∴ He should travel 13 km in West direction to reach point A again.

42. **(c)** When paper is unfolded it will look like as option (c).

43. **(c)** As per the English dictionary order,
Temperament → Temperature → Temptation → Tenant → Tender → Tenure
(1) (6) (5) (3) (4) (2)
$\Rightarrow$ 1, 6, 5, 3, 4, 2

44. **(d)** According to the question,
From the given two position of dice 1 and 3 we find number 1 is common. So, moving in a clockwise direction from common.
From dice (1) 1 3 | 2 |
From dice (3) 1 5 | 4 |
Hence, 4 is opposite to 2.

45. **(c)** As per the English dictonary order.
Derailed → Deregulation → Derivative → Dermatology → Dermestid → Derogation
(4) (6) (3) (1) (5) (2)
$\Rightarrow$ 4, 6, 3, 1, 5, 2

46. **(d)** Given equation,
$56 \div 8 - 14 \times 2 + 12 = 23$
After interchange the signs − and + we get;
$56 \div 8 + 14 \times 2 - 12$
[on applying VBODMAS rule]
$\Rightarrow$ $7 + 28 - 12 = 35 - 12$
$\Rightarrow$ $\boxed{23}$

47. **(b)** According to the question,

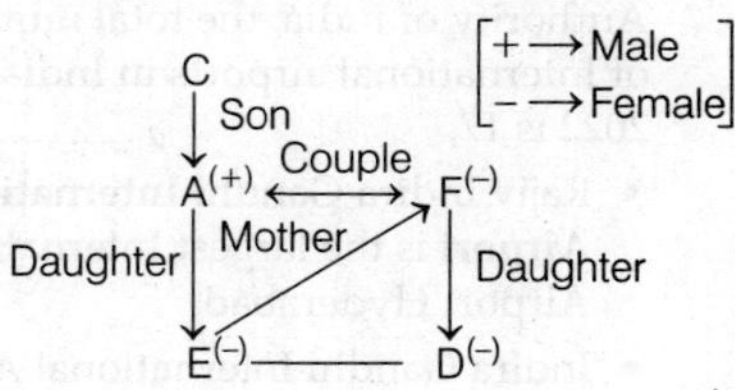

D and E pairs are the grand children of the parents.

48. **(d)** According to the venn diagram,

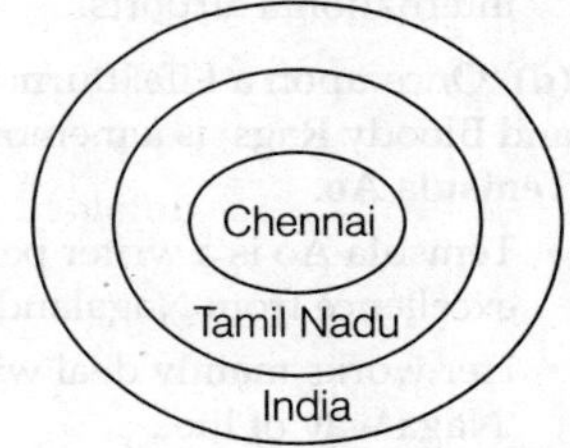

Chennai is in Tamil Nadu and Tamil Nadu is the state of India.

49. **(d)** According to the question, From the given two positions of dice 1 and 2. We find number 2 is common. So, moving in a clockwise direction from common.

From dice (1)	2	12	10
	↕	↕	↕ Opposite
From dice (2)	2	6	8

Hence, 2 is opposite to 4.

50. **(b)** As, P I G = 29

(16 + 9 + 7) – (Number of letter) = 32 – 3 = 29

and C O W = 38

(3 + 15 + 23) – (Number of letter) = 41 – 3 = 38

Similarly,

C A M E L = 29

(3 + 1 + 13 + 5 + 12) – (Number of letter) = 34 – 5 = **29**

51. **(d)** In 1596, Abraham Ortelius suggested in his work 'Thesaurus Geographicus' that the continents of the earth were not always located in their present positions.

- The Dutch Cartographer, **Abraham Ortelius**, first suggested in 1596 that the Americans were 'torn away from Europe and Africa'.
- **German meteorologist Alfred Wegener** proposed in 1912 that the continents were all joined in a common landmass he named Pangaea, which began breaking up approximately 200 million years ago.

52. **(a)** Gobinda Chandra Pal is an awardee of the Sangeet Natak Akademi Amrit Award for the year 2022.

- He contributed to the field of **Odissi Dance** (Gotipua).
- They were honoured for their contribution to the field of performing arts.

53. **(b)** MUDRA provides loan in three categories namely **'Shishu'**, **'Kishore'** and **'Tarun'** to signify the stage of growth and funding needs of the beneficiary.

- Pradhan Mantri MUDRA Yojana (PMMY) is a scheme launched by the Prime Minister Narendra Modi on **8th April, 2015**.
- Under the MUDRA loan scheme, loan is provided in three categories. MUDRA stands for Micro Units Development and Refinance Agency Ltd.
- MUDRA has been initially formed as a wholly owned subsidiary of Small Industries Development bank of India (SIDBI) with 100% capital being contributed by it.
- As of 2025 rule, Government added 4th types of MUDRA loan, i.e. Tarun Plus, for providing loans up to ₹ 20 lakh.

  Other Three are

  Shishu Covering loans up to ₹ 50,000.

  Kishore Covering loans above ₹ 50,000 and up to ₹ 5 lakh.

  Tarun Covering loans above ₹ 5 lakh up to ₹ 10 lakh.

54. **(d)** **Credit rationing** is a selective credit instrument.

- Selective credit control is a qualitative tool that restrict credit and expand it for the priority sectors.
- Under this method, the Central Bank fixes a maximum limit for loans that a Commercial Bank can provide to a particular sector or for all purposes.
- This method restricts the flow of credit in undesirable sectors and diverts it into the most desirable sector.

55. **(a)** **Frictional force** can only be applied when in contact with an object. Friction is a **contact force.**

- It is necessary for two bodies to be in contact for the friction to act on them.
- Therefore, no frictional force acts between the two bodies unless they are in contact with each other.

56. **(a)** In 1976, the four new Directive Principles added to the original list Article 39, Article 39A, Article 43A and Article 48A, by the 42nd Amendment Act.

- It introduced certain changes in the part IV of the Constitution by adding new directives.
- **Article 39** States that the state will make sure that they provide sufficient sources of subsistence to all people, along with women, equal wages for equiralent work.
- **Article 39A** To provide free legal aid to the poor.
- **Article 43A** Participation of workers in management of Industries.
- **Article 48A** To protect and improve the environment.

57. **(b)** With progressive delicensing of industries as part of liberalisation, **coal and lignite** industry is removed from the requirement of license.

- Liberalisation means removing all unnecessary controls and restrictions like permits, licences, quotas, etc imposed by the government.

58. **(c)** **Chathunni Panicker** is a distinguished and experienced scion of the famous Kavungal family associated with **'Kathakali'** for six generations.

- Kathakali is a famous classical dance form of India.
- It is performed in the state of Kerala.
- It uses various colours on the face to symbolise the characters.
- It comlines dance, acting and music to tell stories.

59. **(d)** Kamalini Asthana and Nalini Asthana, veteran dancers who represent **Banaras Gharana** of Kathak, were conferred with third highest award **Padma Shri** in the year 2022.

- **Kamalini Asthana and Nalini Asthana** are a sister duo from Agra in Uttar Pradesh.
- Pandit Gopal Mishra was the founder of Banaras Gharana of Khayal singing.

60. **(c) Germany** won the 15th Men's Hockey World Cup-2023 title.
- Germany won the World Cup by defeating Belgium in the finals held at Kalinga Stadium, Bhubaneswar.
- Germany has won the World Cup title for the third time.
- **Niklas Wellen** of **Germany** was conferred with Best Player Award.
- The Indian hockey team finished Ninth at the FIH Men's Hockey World Cup 2023.

61. **(b) Lord Metcalfe** was the Governor-General of British India who was in favour of free press and repealed the press regulations of 1823.
- He earned the epithet of **'Liberator of Indian press'**.
- The result of this liberal press policy level policies which continued unchanged till 1865 was the rapid growth of newspapers all over the country.

62. **(c)** There are **5 types of makeup** (vesham) used for the performers of Kathakali dance.
- The five major Veshams in Kathakali are **Kathi** (Knife)**, Pacha** (Green), **Thaadi** (Beard), **Minukku** (radiant) and **Kari** (Black).
- It is a classical dance performed in the state of Kerala 'Katha' meaning story and 'Kali' meaning drama 'play of a story'.
- It uses various colours on the face to symbolise the characters.
- Guru Gopinath is a famous Kathakali dancer.

63. **(a)** Epilimnetic, Metalimnetic and Hypolimnetic water strata are examples of **typical thermal stratification of a lake.**
- Thermal stratification of lakes refers to the formation of distinct layers of water due to temperature differences, primarily by solar heating.
- The warmer upper layer of a lake is known as **eplilimnion.**
- Between Epilimnetic Hypolimnetic layer is the **metalimnion,** a zone of rapid temperature change.
- The **hypolimnion** or under lake is the dense, bottom layer of water in a thermally-stratified lake.

64. **(d) Sultan Khan** is associated with Sarangi and is correctly matched **Hariprasad Chaurasia** is associated with flute, Zakir Hussain is an Indian tabla player, Bismillah Khan is associated with Shehnai.
- Sultan Khan was awarded the Padma Bhushan in 2010.

65. **(c)** Anup Rag Vilas is a book written by **Pandit Kumar Gandharva**.
- A famous classical singer known for his unique vocal style. He is famous in the music world.
- He has been conferred with Kalidas Samman, Padma Vibhushan and Sangeet Natak Akademi Award etc.

66. **(b) Aquaporins** is an integral membrane protein that forms the tetramer and facilitates the diffusion of water and some small, unmodified solutes across cellular membranes.
- Different Aquaporins have different sized water channels, the smallest types allowing nothing but water through.
- X-ray profiles show that Aquaporins have two conical entrances.
- In humans, Aquaporins play a key role in kidney functions.

67. **(a) Plastids** is the organelle present in plant cell. Algae and other eukaryotic organism that is not there in an animal cell.
- Plastids contain chlorophyll which gives green colour to plants.
- It performs photosynthesis and is called chloroplasts.

68. **(d) Alessandro Volta** was the physicist who invented the voltaic pile, the forerunner of the modern battery, in 1800.
- With this invention volta proved that electricity could be generated chemically.
- It consists of alternating metal copper and zinc discs separated by pieces of cloth or cardboard soaked in an electrolyte solution.

69. **(a) Pandit Ravi Shankar**, founder of National Orchestra of India,was a sitar player.
- He was honoured with Bharat Ratna in 1999.
- He won the Sangeet Natak Akademi Award in 1962.
- He won UNESCO International Music Council Award in 1975.

70. **(d)** According to the Airports Authority of India, the total number of International airports in India as of 2022 is 17.
- Rajiv Indira Gandhi **International Airport** is the largest International Airport Hyderabad.
- Indira Gandhi International Airport is the busiest airport in India followed by the **Chhatrapati Shivaji** International Airport.
- As of May 2025, India has 35 international airports.

71. **(d)** 'Once upon a Life: Burnt Curry and Bloody Rags' is a memoir of **Temsula Ao**.
- Temsula Ao is a writer par excellence from Nagaland.
- Her works mainly deal with the 'Naga way of life'.

72. **(c)** Statements (A) and (C) are correct regarding the Jurisdiction of supreme court of India.
- Original Jurisdiction extends to any dispute between the Government of India and one or more states or between the government of India and any state or states on one side and one or more states on the other or between two or more States.
- **Under Articles 129 and 142** of the Constitution, the Supreme Court has been vested with the power to punish for contempt of court.
- Statements (B) and (D) are incorrect because **Appellate Jurisdiction** (Article 132 to 136) is the power of a court to review and modify the decisions of lower court.
- Under the Arbitration and Conciliation Act, 1996, International Commercial Arbitration can also be initiated in the Supreme Court.

73. **(c)** Directive Principles of State Policy in India have been taken from the Constitution of **Ireland**.
- Parliamentary system, rule of law and single citizenship have been taken from **Britain.**
- **Fundamental Duty** is inspired from the **USSR.**
- **Fundamental rights**, independent judiciary, impeachment of the President, Preamble have been inspired from the Constitution of **USA.**

74. (d) **Anaphase** is the fourth step in mitosis where non-kinetochore spindle fibres lengthen and elongate the cell.

- **Metaphase** is a stage during the process of cell division (mitosis or meiosis).
- **Prophase** is the first phase of mitosis, the process that separates the duplicated genetic material carried in the nucleus of a parent cell into two identical daughter cells.
- **Telophase** is the fifth stage in Telophase, **Cytokinesis** is the **sixth** and final step of Mitosis.

75. (d) **Aniline (C_6H_5)**, an organic compound, is a benzenoid.

- **The NH_2** group attached to the benzene ring means that there is a lone pair of electrons that can enter into conjugation with the benzene ring resulting in delocalisation in the aniline.

76. (b) According to the Census of India 2011, 'Other Religions and Persuasions' formed **0.7%** of the country's population.

- Hindu 96.63 crores (79.8%); Muslim 17.22 crores (14.2%); Christian 2.78 crores (2.3%); Sikh 2.08 crores (1.7%); Buddhist 0.84 crores (0.7%); Jain 0.45 crores (0.4%).

77. (c) India will host the World Badminton Championship event 2026. The 2026 BWF World Championships will be the 30th edition of the prestigious badminton tournament of BWF held annually.

- The host city for 2023 BWF World Championship was held in Copenhagen, Denmark.
- The host city for 2025 BWF World Championship will be Paris, France.

78. (a) Coasts (2) and (3) i.e., Malabar and Konkan are running along the Arabian Sea.

- Konkan coast is a 720 km long coastline that forms and is a rugged section of the Western coastline of India.
- South of the Konkan coast is the Malabar coast in the State of Kerala.
- Coromandel coast, located in Eastern Tamil Nadu, extended over an area of about 22,800 sq. km.
- The Northern cincars consisted of narrow slip of territory lying along **Bay of Bengal**.

79. (c) Statements (1) and (3) are correct regarding light year.

- Light year is a unit of distance. A light year is the distance that light travels in one Earth year.
- Light moves at a velocity of about 300,000 kilometres (km) each second.
- So in one year, it can travel about 10 trillion km.

80. (c) According to Agricultural Statistics at a Glance 2022, Government of India, Uttar Pradesh (44.8%) followed by Maharashtra (22.5%) have the highest sugarcane producing states with 177 million tonnes and 111 million tonnes of production respectively.

81. (c) Kerala receives initial rainfall by the Arabian Sea branch of monsoon.

- The Arabian Sea branch of the South-West monsoon first hits the Western Ghats of the coastal state of Kerala, thus making this area first to receive rain from the South-West monsoon.

82. (c) Abolition of titles is mentioned in Article 18 of the Indian Constitution.

- It mentions that no title, not being a military or academic.
- Distinction, shall be conferred by the State.
- No citizen of India shall accept any title from any foreign state.

83. (c) In Morley-Minto Act, 1909, Delhi was declared the capital of British India in place of Calcutta.

- It is also known as the Indian Councils Act of 1909.
- The capital of British India was officially shifted from Calcutta to Delhi on 12th December, 1911 during the Delhi Darbar.
- The decision to shift capital was made by King George V.

84. (b) Article 97 mentions about the salaries and allowances of the Chairman and Deputy Chairman of the Rajya Sabha and the Speaker and Deputy Speaker of the Lok Sabha are determined by Parliament and are charged on the Consolidated Fund of India.

85. (a) **Article 89** of the Indian Constitution mentions that the Vice-President of India shall be the Ex-Officio Chairman of the Council of States.

- If the Constitutional setup of India, the holder of the office of the Vice-President is part of the executive but as the Chairman of the Rajya Sabha, he is a part of Parliament.

86. (d) Under Aurangzeb's rule, the Mughal empire achieved its largest territorial limits spanning nearly the entire Indian sub-continent from the Deccan in the South to Afghanistan in the North-West.

- Aurangzeb was the sixth Mughal emperor, reigning from 1658 until his death in 1707.

87. (b) Under the Bahmani kingdom, the provinces were administered by Tarafdars.

- The Sultans in the Bahamani Kingdom followed a feudal type of administration.
- The kingdom was divided into many provinces called Tarafs.
- The Governor who controlled Tarafs were called Tarafdars.
- Bahmani kingdom was a Muslim state of the Deccan in Southern India and was one of the great medieval Indian kingdoms.
- It was founded by Alauddin Hasan in 1347.

88. (b) **Roger Binny** has been elected as the 36th President of BCCI.

- Roger Michael Humphrey Binny is a former Indian international cricketer. He replaced Sourav Ganguly.

89. (c) Goga Navami, which is primarily celebrated in the Indian state of Rajasthan, is dedicated to the snake God, Gogaji.

- As per legends, Guga was a powerful Rajput prince (Rajasthan) who had supernatural powers to control venomous snakes.
- It is celebrated in the Northern regions of India, most importantly in Himachal Pradesh, Haryana and Punjab.

90. (b) Hyderabad was founded by Nizam-ul-Mulk Asaf Jah or Chin-Qilich Khan in 1724.

- He was one of the most powerful members of the court of the Mughal Emperor Farrukhsiyar.

91. (d) The 2026 Winter Olympics will be held in Italy. The first Winter Olympic Games, the 1924, Winter Olympics, were held in Chamonix, France.

- The Games were held every four years from 1924 to 1936, interrupted in 1940 and 1944 by World War II and resumed in 1948.
- Five main sports Bobsleigh, Curling, Ice Hockey, Nordic skiing and Skating are played in the Winter Olympics.
- 2022 Winter Olympics was held at Beijing, China.
- 2030 Winter Olympics will be held at French Alps, France.

92. (d) Statements (i) and (ii) are correct.

- In the Tenth Plan period, the Indian economy grew at 7.7%per year.
- The targeted growth for the Eleventh Five-Year Plan was 9% per year.
- Statement (iii) is incorrect because, in the Ninth Plan period, India realised a growth of 6.5% per year.

93. (b) Damodar Mauzo, who received the 57th Jnanpith Award, primarily a Konkani writer.

- He is a Goa-based poet and won the Sahitya Akademi Award in 1983 for his novel 'Karmelin'.

94. (b) Korkai was the capital, principal centre of trade and important port of the Early Pandyan Kingdom.

- At that time, it was located on the banks of the Thamirabarani river and at the sea coast, forming a natural harbour.

95. (a) Nor Westers are the dreaded evening thunderstorms in Bengal and Assam.

- Their notorious nature can be understood from the local nomenclature of **Kalbaisakhi**, a calamity of the month of Baisakh.
- These showers are useful for tea, jute and rice cultivation.

96. (c) Rheostat is the device used to change the resistance in an electric circuit.

- It is used to adjust the magnitude of the current in a circuit by changing the length of resistance included in the circuit.

97. (b) A choice of goals has been made in each plan due to limitation of resources, which makes it necessary to prioritise goals.

- Limited resources are essential materials and services that are finite supply and are necessary for Human life and development.

98. (c) Yamuna is joined by river Chambal from the South.

- The Chambal river flows through the boundary of Sawai Madhopur and Dholpur districts with the Madhya Pradesh State of India.
- Then, it finally enters Uttar Pradesh and flows 32 kilometres before joining the Yamuna River near Etawah.
- River Chambal, the biggest tributary of Yamuna rises in Vindhyan range near Mhow in Indore District of Madhya Pradesh.
- Yamuna is the longest tributary of the Ganges.
- It originates from Yamunotri Glacier.

99. (d) According to the Global Hunger Index 2022, Bangladesh ranked 84th out of 121 countries. India ranked 107th out of 121 countries in 2022.

- The Global Hunger Index (GHI) is a tool for comprehensively measuring and tracking hunger at global, regional and national levels.
- It is published by Concern Worldwide and Welthungerhilfe.
- As of 2025 Global Hunger Index Report India was ranked 111 among 125.

100. (d) Good Friday is a Christian holy day observing the crucifixion of Jesus and his death at Calvary.

- Christians across the world observe Good Friday as the day when Jesus Christ died on the cross for humanity so that he could save them from their sins.

101. (a) If ΔXYZ and ΔLMN are similar, then

X, Z, Y — L, N, M

$$\frac{\text{Area }(\Delta XYZ)}{\text{Area }(\Delta LMN)} = \left(\frac{XY}{LM}\right)^2 = \left(\frac{YZ}{MN}\right)^2 = \left(\frac{XZ}{LN}\right)^2$$

$$\Rightarrow \frac{16}{25} = \left(\frac{YZ}{MN}\right)^2$$

$$\Rightarrow \frac{16}{25} = \left(\frac{2.4}{MN}\right)^2$$

$$\Rightarrow \frac{4}{5} = \frac{2.4}{MN}$$

$$\Rightarrow MN = 3 \text{ cm}$$

102. (b) Speed of the train

$$= \frac{\text{Distance}}{\text{Time}} = \frac{56 \text{ km}}{35 \text{ min}} = \left(\frac{56}{\frac{35}{60}}\right)$$

$$= \frac{56 \times 60}{35} = 96 \text{ km/h}$$

Now, Time taken to cover 720 m

$$= \left(\frac{720}{96 \times \frac{5}{18}}\right) = \frac{720 \times 18}{96 \times 5} = 27 \text{ sec}$$

103. (c) $\dfrac{92736}{(274 + 830) \text{ of } \frac{7}{4}} + 513$

$$= \frac{92736}{1104 \times \frac{7}{4}} \times 513$$

$$= \frac{92736}{276 \times 7} + 513$$

$$= 48 + 513 = 561$$

104. (c) Given, $\tan\theta = \dfrac{3}{10}$

Now, $\dfrac{(1+\sin\theta)(1-\sin\theta)}{(1+\cos\theta)(1-\cos\theta)}$

$[\because a^2 - b^2 = (a+b)(a-b)]$

$$= \frac{1-\sin^2\theta}{1-\cos^2\theta} (\because \sin^2\theta + \cos^2\theta = 1)$$

$$= \frac{\cos^2\theta}{\sin^2\theta} = \cot^2\theta = \frac{1}{\tan^2\theta} = \frac{100}{9}$$

105. (d) Total number of students in science in all the cities in 2022-2023 = 11200

Total number of cities = 5

$\therefore$ Required Average $= \dfrac{11200}{5} = 2240$

106. (d) Let the total distance be $2x$ km.

According to the question,

$$\frac{x}{12} + \frac{x}{8} = 3 \text{ h } 45 \text{ min}$$

$$\Rightarrow \frac{x}{12} + \frac{x}{8} = 3\frac{3}{4}$$

$$\Rightarrow \frac{8x + 12x}{96} = \frac{15}{4}$$

$$\Rightarrow \frac{20x}{96} = \frac{15}{4}$$

$$\Rightarrow x = 18 \text{ km}$$

$\therefore$ Total distance $= 2x = 2 \times 18 = 36$ km

107. (d) Given, $\tan\theta = \frac{7}{24}$

Now, $(\cos^2\theta - \sin^2\theta)$

$$= \cos 2\theta = \frac{1-\tan^2\theta}{1+\tan^2\theta}$$

$$= \frac{1-\left(\frac{7}{24}\right)^2}{1+\left(\frac{7}{24}\right)^2} = \frac{1-\frac{49}{576}}{1+\frac{49}{576}} = \frac{527}{625}$$

108. (a) Length of the rectangular sheet = 60 cm

Breadth of the rectangular sheet = 25 cm

Now, length of the box formed

= 60 − (5 + 5) = 60 − 10 = 50 cm

Breadth of the box formed

= 25 − (5 + 5) = 25 − 10 = 15 cm

Height of the box formed = 5 cm

∴ Volume of the box = $l \times b \times h$

= 50 × 15 × 5 = 3750 cm^3

109. (a) Given, 40% of A = 60% of B = $\frac{1}{6}$ of C

$$\Rightarrow \frac{40}{100}A = \frac{60}{100}B \Rightarrow \frac{A}{B} = \frac{3}{2} \Rightarrow B = \frac{2}{3}A$$

Now, $\frac{40}{100}A = \frac{1}{6}C$

$$\Rightarrow \frac{A}{C} = \frac{5}{12} \Rightarrow C = \frac{12}{5}A$$

$$\therefore \quad A : B : C = A : \frac{2}{3}A : \frac{12}{5}A$$

= 15 : 10 : 36

110. (c) Number of employees in 2017 = 500

Number of employees in 2018 = 1000

∴ Percentage increase from 2017 to

$$2018 = \frac{(1000-500)}{500} \times 100$$

$$= \frac{500}{500} \times 100 = 100\%$$

111. (a) 35 − [30 + {10 + (12 − 10 − 4)}]

= 35 − [30 + {10 + (− 2)}]

= 35 − [30 + 8]

= 35 − 38 = − 3

112. (c) Let the amount spent on transportation be ₹ x.

Now, according to the question,

130% of cost price = Selling price

$$\Rightarrow \frac{130}{100} \times (700 + x) = 1400$$

$$\Rightarrow \quad (700 + x) = \frac{1400 \times 100}{130}$$

$$\Rightarrow \quad (700 + x) = 1077$$

$$\Rightarrow \quad x = 1077 - 700$$

$\Rightarrow \quad x =$ ₹ 377

113. (b) Given, $r_1 = 35$ cm, $r_2 = 25$ cm

AB = Direct common tangent (DCT)

Length of DCT = $\sqrt{d^2 - (r_1 - r_2)^2}$

Where d = Distance between the centers

$$= \sqrt{(35+25)^2 - (35-25)^2}$$

$$= \sqrt{(60)^2 - (10)^2} = \sqrt{3600 - 100}$$

$$= \sqrt{3500} = 59.16 \text{ cm}$$

114. (b) Given, $16x^4 + \frac{1}{16x^4} = 14159$

Formula used

Adding 2 on both the sides,

$$16x^4 + \frac{1}{16x^4} + 2 = 14159 + 2$$

$$\Rightarrow \quad 4x^2 + \frac{1}{4x^2} = \sqrt{14161} = 119$$

$[\because (a+b)^2 = a^2 + b^2 + 2ab]$

Now, adding 2 on both the sides,

$$4x^2 + \frac{1}{4x^2} + 2 = 119 + 2$$

$$\Rightarrow \quad \left(2x + \frac{1}{2x}\right)^2 = 121$$

$$\Rightarrow \quad 2x + \frac{1}{2x} = \sqrt{121}$$

$$\Rightarrow \quad 2x + \frac{1}{2x} = 11$$

115. (d) Let the speed of stream/current be x km/h.

∴ Speed of boat = $(x + 4)$ km/h

Now, according to the question,

$$\frac{45}{x + (x+4)} + \frac{35}{(x+4) - x} = 10$$

$$\Rightarrow \quad \frac{45}{2x+4} + \frac{35}{4} = 10$$

$$\Rightarrow \quad \frac{45}{2x+4} = 10 - \frac{35}{4}$$

$$\Rightarrow \quad \frac{45}{2x+4} = \frac{5}{4} \Rightarrow 2x + 4 = 36$$

$$\Rightarrow \quad 2x = 32 \Rightarrow x = 16$$

Hence, speed of man in still water

= x + 4 = 16 + 4

= 20 km/h

116. (b) Given, Marked price = ₹ 82500

Selling price = ₹ 79200

∴ Discount percentage

$$= \frac{(MP - SP)}{MP} \times 100$$

$$= \frac{(82500 - 79200)}{82500} \times 100$$

$$= \frac{3300}{82500} \times 100$$

= 0.04 × 100 = 4%

117. (c) We know that,

$$\frac{M_1 \times D_1}{W_1} = \frac{M_2 \times D_2}{W_2}$$

Where, M = Number of men

D = Number of days

W = Work done

$$\therefore \quad \frac{24 \times 25}{90} = \frac{27 \times D_2}{162}$$

$$\Rightarrow \quad D_2 = 40 \text{ days}$$

Hence, (40 − 25) = 15 more days will be required to complete the given work.

118. (d) Surface area of sphere = $4\pi r^2$

Diameter = 28 cm

∴ Radius = 14 cm

Surface area of sphere

$$= 4 \times \frac{22}{7} \times 14 \times 14$$

$= 4 \times 22 \times 2 \times 14 = 2464$ cm^2

119. (b) We know that,

$(a+b)^2 = a^2 + b^2 + 2ab$

And $(a-b)^2 = a^2 + b^2 - 2ab$

$$= \frac{[(525)^2 + (175)^2 + 2 \times 525 \times 175] - [(525)^2 + (175)^2 - 2 \times 525 \times 175]}{525 \times 175}$$

$$= \frac{4 \times 525 \times 175}{525 \times 175} = 4$$

120. (d) According to the question,

Let the population of the town 1 yr ago be x.

∴ Present population = x + 8% of x

= $1.08x$

Now, according to the question,

$1.08x = 142560 \Rightarrow x = 132000$

Hence, population of town 1yr ago was 132000.

121. (c) 5 + [6 + (3 + 5) ÷ 2] ÷ 2

= 5 + [6 + 8 ÷ 2] ÷ 2 = 5 + [6 + 4] ÷ 2

= 5 + 10 ÷ 2 = 5 + 5 = 10

122. (c) Amount of money allocated for Emazon for 2022 = ₹ 13.44 cr

Average salary of Emazon = ₹ 21000

∴ Number of delivery partners in 2022

$$= \frac{13.44 \text{ cr}}{21000} = \frac{134400000}{21000} = 6400$$

Now, Delivery partners in Emazon in 2021 = 5000

∴ Required percentage increase

$$= \frac{(6400 - 5000)}{5000} \times 100$$

$$= \frac{1400}{5000} \times 100 = 28\%$$

123. (c) Let the value of $x = 1$

$x + \frac{1}{x} = 2$ holds true for $x = 1$

Now, the value of

$\left(x^4 + \frac{4}{x^4}\right)\left(x^3 - \frac{4}{x^3}\right)$

$= \left\{1^4 + \frac{4}{1^4}\right\}\left\{1^3 - \frac{4}{1^3}\right\}$

$= (1 + 4)(1 - 4)$

$= 5 \times (-3) = -15$

124. (b) In ΔABC,

$\angle BAC = 30°, \ \angle BCA = 60°$

$\therefore \angle ABC = 180° - (\angle BAC + \angle BCA)$

$= 180° - 90° = 90°$

Now, in a right angled triangle ABC, $(\text{Hypotenuse})^2 = (\text{Perpendicular})^2 + (\text{Base})^2$

$\Rightarrow (AC)^2 = (AB)^2 + (BC)^2$

$\Rightarrow (13)^2 = (12)^2 + (BC)^2$

$\Rightarrow 169 - 144 = (BC)^2 \Rightarrow 25 = (BC)^2$

$\therefore BC = 5$ cm

125. (c) Total work = Number of workers × Number of days

$18 \times 96 = (18 \times 26) + \{(18 + 10) \times x\}$

$\Rightarrow (18 \times 96) - (18 \times 26) = 28 \times x$

$\Rightarrow 18 \times 70 = 28 \times x$

$\Rightarrow x = 45$ days

$\therefore$ Total time taken to finish the work

$= (26 + 45) = 71$ days

126. (a) Total number of students of Science in all the cities = 11200

Total number of students of MBA in all the cities = 6960

$\therefore$ Required difference

$= 11200 - 6960 = 4240$

127. (b) Let the principal be P.

Amount = $9P$

$\therefore$ Simple Interest (SI) $= 9P - P = 8P$

So, $R = \frac{\text{SI} \times 100}{P \times T} = \frac{8P \times 100}{P \times 20} = 40\%$

Now, time taken to become 13 times the amount will be

$T = \frac{\text{SI} \times 100}{P \times R} \Rightarrow T = \frac{(13P - P) \times 100}{P \times 40}$

$\Rightarrow T = \frac{12P \times 100}{P \times 40} \Rightarrow T = 30$ yr

128. (b) Let the amount of lead and tin in alloy A be $5x$ and $3x$ respectively.

Now, $5x + 3x = 80$ kg

$\Rightarrow 8x = 80 \text{ kg} \Rightarrow x = 10$

$\therefore$ Amount of lead in alloy

$A = 5x = 5 \times 10 = 50$ kg

Amount of tin in alloy

$A = 3x = 3 \times 10 = 30$ kg

Let the amount of lead and tin in alloy B be $3y$ and $1y$, respectively.

So, $3y + y = 100$ kg

$\Rightarrow 4y = 100 \Rightarrow y = 25$

$\therefore$ Amount of lead in alloy $B = 3y = 75$ kg

Amount of tin in alloy $B = y = 25$ kg

Hence, total amount of tin in new alloy = 30 kg + 25 kg = 55 kg

129. (c) Let the winner get x votes.

$\therefore$ Loser gets $(x - 170)$ votes

75 votes were invalid.

$\therefore$ Total number of votes polled

$= x + x - 170 + 75 = 2x - 95$

Now, 10% people did not vote

$\therefore$ 90% people voted.

So, total number of voters

$= (2x - 95) \times \frac{100}{90} = \frac{20x - 950}{9}$

Now, winner got 50% of the votes i.e.

$x = 50\% \text{ of } \frac{(20x - 950)}{9}$

$\Rightarrow 9x = \frac{20x - 950}{2}$

$\Rightarrow 2x = 950 \Rightarrow x = 475$

$\therefore$ Total number of voters

$= \frac{20x - 950}{9} = \frac{20 \times 475 - 950}{9}$

$= \frac{8550}{9} = 950$

130. (c) Let the radius of the sphere = r

New radius = $1.4r$

Change in surface area

$= 4\pi(1.4r)^2 - 4\pi r^2$

$= 4\pi [1.96r^2 - r^2]$

$= 4\pi r^2 \times 0.96$

Now, Percentage increase in surface

area $= \frac{4\pi r^2 \times 0.96 \times 100}{4\pi r^2}$

$= 0.96 \times 100 = 96\%$

131. (d) $(4^2)^2 + 4 \times 4 \div 4 - 4$

$= 4^4 + 4 \times 1 - 4$

$= 4^4 + 4 - 4$

$= 4^4$

132. (b) $\therefore$ Net discount percentage

$= x + y - \frac{xy}{100}$

(where x and y are the two discounts)

$= 10 + 10 - \frac{10 \times 10}{100}$

$= 20 - 1 = 19\%$

Now, selling price = (100 − 19)% of marked price

$\Rightarrow$ Marked price $= \frac{7290 \times 100}{81} = ₹\ 9000$

133. (a) Average speed

$= \frac{\text{Total distance}}{\text{Total time taken}}$

$= \frac{(12.5 + 12.5) \text{ km}}{(30 + 20) \text{ min}}$

$= \frac{25}{\frac{50}{60}}$ km/h

$= \frac{25 \times 60}{50}$ km/h

$= 30$ km/h

134. (b) $1 + \cfrac{1}{1 + \cfrac{1}{5 + \cfrac{1}{2 + \cfrac{1}{3}}}} = 1 + \cfrac{1}{1 + \cfrac{1}{5 + \cfrac{3}{7}}}$

$= 1 + \cfrac{1}{1 + \cfrac{1}{\frac{38}{7}}} = 1 + \cfrac{1}{1 + \frac{7}{38}}$

$= 1 + \cfrac{1}{\frac{45}{38}} = 1 + \frac{1 \times 38}{45} = 1\frac{38}{45}$

135. (a) Let his goods contain 1 kg = 1000 gm

It's actual weight is 25% less of 1000 gm = 750 gm

Let cost price of each gm = ₹ 1

$\therefore$ Cost price of 750 gm = ₹ 750

Selling price = 80% of CP of 1 kg

$= \frac{80}{100} \times 1000 = ₹\ 800$

Profit = 800 − 750 = ₹ 50

$\therefore$ Required profit percentage

$= \frac{50}{750} \times 100 = 6.67\%$

136. (a) Let $A = 45°$

Now, $x = \sin A + \cos A$

$\Rightarrow x = \sin 45° + \cos 45°;$

$y = \sec A + \text{cosec} A$

$y = \sec 45° + \text{cosec } 45°$

$\Rightarrow x = \frac{1}{\sqrt{2}} + \frac{1}{\sqrt{2}}$ and $y = \sqrt{2} + \sqrt{2}$

$\Rightarrow x = \sqrt{2}$ and $y = 2\sqrt{2}$

Now, putting these values in the given options, we need to verify.

Option 1. $y + 2x = x^2 y$

$\Rightarrow 2\sqrt{2} + 2\sqrt{2} = (\sqrt{2})^2 \times 2\sqrt{2}$

$\Rightarrow 2\sqrt{2} + 2\sqrt{2} = 2 \times 2\sqrt{2}$

$\Rightarrow 4\sqrt{2} = 4\sqrt{2}$

Since LHS = RHS

Hence, $y + 2x = x^2 y$ is true.

137. **(b)** Let the total number of votes be $100x$.

19% did not cast their votes

$\therefore$ Total votes casted = 81% of $100x = 81x$

Now, A received 27% of the votes

$\therefore B$ received $(81-27)\% = 54\%$ of votes

Now, A received $\frac{125982 \times 27}{54} = 62991$

138. **(c)** $[\{38-(-6)\} \times \{9-(8-1)\}] \div [4 \times \{6+(-4)\}]$

$= [\{38+6\} \times \{9-7\}] \div [4 \times \{6-4\}]$

$= [44 \times 2] \div [4 \times 2]$

$= 88 \div 8 = 11$

139. **(b)** Let the total work be 12 units.

$\therefore$ Efficiency of Mitu $= \frac{12}{12} = 1$

Efficiency of (Titu + Situ) $= \frac{12}{2} = 6$

Efficiency of (Mitu + Situ) $= \frac{12}{3} = 4$

Now, efficiency of (Titu + Situ) − (Mitu + Situ) = 6 − 4 = 2

$\therefore$ Efficiency of Titu − Mitu = 2

Hence, efficiency of Titu = 2 + 1 = 3

($\because$ efficiency of Mitu = 1)

So, time taken by Titu to do the work alone $= \frac{12}{3} = 4$ h

140. **(b)** Here,

a = Side of the triangle = 12 cm

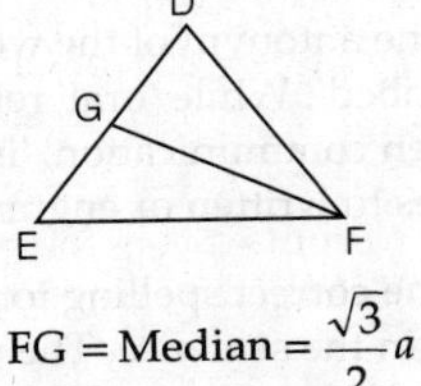

$FG = \text{Median} = \frac{\sqrt{3}}{2}a$

$= \frac{\sqrt{3}}{2} \times 12 = 6\sqrt{3}$

141. **(b)** Let the marks of A and B be $3x$ and $4x$ respectively.

Let the marks of B and $C = 4x$ and $5x$, respectively.

So, $A:B:C = 3x:4x:5x$

Difference of marks of C and A

$= 5x - 3x = 2x$

$\Rightarrow \quad 2x = 30 \Rightarrow x = 15$

$\therefore B$'s marks $= 4x = 4 \times 15 = 60$

142. **(b)** $\frac{1}{4} + \frac{2}{5} \div \left[\left\{2\frac{1}{5} - 2\right\} \times 5\right] - \frac{2}{3} \text{ of } \frac{3}{5}$

$= \frac{1}{4} + \frac{2}{5} \div \left[\left\{\frac{11}{5} - 2\right\} \times 5\right] - \frac{2}{5}$

$= \frac{1}{4} + \frac{2}{5} \div \left[\frac{1}{5} \times 5\right] - \frac{2}{5}$

$= \frac{1}{4} + \left(\frac{2}{5} \div 1\right) - \frac{2}{5}$

$= \frac{1}{4} + \frac{2}{5} - \frac{2}{5} = \frac{1}{4}$

143. **(a)** Number of non-trained male teachers in College A

$= (100-44)\%$ of 225

$= 56\%$ of $225 = 126$

Number of non-trained female teachers in College B

$= (100-25)\%$ of 128

$= 75\%$ of $128 = 96$

$\therefore$ Required sum = 126 + 96 = 222

144. **(b)** $(19 \sin\theta + 6 \cot\theta \sin\theta)$

$= \left(19 \sin\theta + \frac{6 \cos\theta}{\sin\theta} \cdot \sin\theta\right)$

$= 19 \sin\theta + 6 \cos\theta = a \sin\theta + b \cos\theta$

Now, we know that,

Maximum value of

$(a \sin\theta + b \cos\theta) = \sqrt{a^2 + b^2}$

$\therefore$ Maximum value of

$(19 \sin\theta + 6 \cos\theta) = \sqrt{(19)^2 + (6)^2}$

$= \sqrt{361 + 36} = \sqrt{397}$

145. **(c)** Length/Height of cylindrical shell = 42 cm

Inside radius $(r) = \frac{8}{2}$ cm = 4 cm

Outside radius $(R) = \frac{14}{2}$ cm = 7 cm

$\therefore$ Volume of clay required

$= \pi R^2 h - \pi r^2 h = \pi h (R^2 - r^2)$

$= \frac{22}{7} \times 42 [(7)^2 - (4)^2]$

$= 22 \times 6 \times (49 - 16)$

$= 22 \times 6 \times 33 = 4356 \text{ cm}^3$

146. **(c)** $22 \times 10 \div 5 \times 2 + 12$

$= 22 \times 2 \times 2 + 12 = 22 \times 4 + 12$

$= 88 + 12 = 100$

147. **(c)** Total production of P and Q cars in 1993 = 21 + 12 = 33

Total production of R and S cars in 1993 = 13 + 20 = 33

Hence, In 1993, the total production of cars of types P and Q is equal to the total production of cars of types R and S.

148. **(b)** From the given pie-chart,

Savings = 60° = ₹ 8000

$\therefore$ Total monthly expenditure

= 360° − Savings

= 360° − 60° = 300°

Now, Since 60° represents ₹ 8000.

$\therefore$ 300° represents $= \frac{8000}{60} \times 300$

= ₹ 40000

149. **(a)** Surface area of sphere $= 4\pi r^2$

Given, $\frac{4\pi r_1^2}{4\pi r_2^2} = \frac{9}{49}$

$\Rightarrow \quad \frac{r_1}{r_2} = \frac{3}{7}$

Now, volume of sphere $= \frac{4}{3}\pi r^3$

$\therefore$ Required ratio of volume

$= \frac{\frac{4}{3}\pi (r_1)^3}{\frac{4}{3}\pi (r_2)^3}$

$= \frac{(r_1)^3}{(r_2)^3} = \frac{(3)^3}{(7)^3}$

$= \frac{27}{343} = 27:343$

150. **(c)** $9 \times 9 + 9 \div 9 - 9 \times 9 + 9 + 9 \times 9 - 9 - 9 \times 9$

$= 81 + 1 - 81 + 9 + 81 - 9 - 81$

$= 81 - 81 + 81 - 81 + 9 - 9 + 1$

$= 1$

151. **(b)** The most fitting idiom for this situation is 'to take a rain check'. It implies that they are declining the invitation now but may consider attending at a later time.

152. **(a)** For the phrase 'careful nature and hard-working efforts, the most fitting one-word substitute is 'diligence'. It encapsulates the quality of being both careful and persistent in one's work or duties.

153. **(d)** To describe a lively, cheerful and outgoing person, we can use the term 'Extrovert'. An extrovert thrives on social interactions and enjoys being around others.

154. **(b)** For the words 'weak and cowardly', the suitable one-word substitute is 'Pusillanimous'. It precisely conveys the idea of lacking courage or being timid.

155. **(d)** The idiom that best fits the sentence 'The players like the coach because he is honest, realistic and practical in dealing with them' is 'down to earth'. This expression describes someone who is genuine, unpretentious and practical in their approach, which aligns with the coach's qualities.

156. **(b)** To complete the sentence 'It is important to take this opportunity to make a name for yourself - beat around the bush', the appropriate idiom is 'strike while the iron is hot'. This means seizing an opportunity promptly without hesitation or delay.

157. **(a)** The error in the divided sentence 'Mr. Vinu / has never / slept in /a igloo' lies in the phrase 'a igloo'. The correct form should be 'an igloo' because the indefinite article 'an' is used before words starting with a vowel sound (like 'igloo').

158. **(a)** The correct option to substitute the underlined segment in the sentence is 'than she received'.

159. **(d)** The antonym for the word 'advance' is 'Elementary'. In the context of Clive's travel blog, having only basic or elementary knowledge of the local language can still enhance the travel experience.

160. **(c)** The idiom that can substitute the underlined segment in the sentence 'Popular cosmetics brands in India are very expensive' is 'cost an arm and a leg'. This idiom emphasises high costs or exorbitant prices.

161. **(b)** The correct spelling of the underlined word is 'Reclusive'. It means seeking solitude or retiring from society.

162. **(b)** To replace the underlined segment in the sentence 'Though very informative, Shweta's article was mercilessly rejected of the editor,' the appropriate option is 'was mercilessly rejected by'. This phrase conveys that the editor rejected the article.

163. **(b)** The antonym of the word 'fluctuate' is 'stabilise'. While 'fluctuate means to vary or change irregularly, 'stabilise' implies maintaining a steady state or preventing fluctuations.

164. **(d)** The most appropriate option to substitute the underlined segment in the sentence 'Last night, I failed to sleep because of some familiar issues that couldn't be avoided, is 'unavoidable'. This word conveys the same meaning as 'couldn't be avoided and fits well in the context.

165. **(c)** The most appropriate antonym for the word 'rapid' is 'slow'. 'Rapid refers to something happening at great speed', while 'slow' denotes a lack of speed or a leisurely pace.

166. **(c)** Option (c) is the correct idiom that fits in the blank. When I went to Egypt and lost my wallet and passport, I was 'up in a creek without a paddle'. This idiom conveys being in a difficult or challenging situation without any means of help or support.

167. **(b)** The incorrectly spelled word is 'Bycycle'. The correct spelling is 'Bicycle'.

168. **(a)** The meaning of the idiom 'Gift of the Gab' is 'A talent for speaking'. It refers to the ability to speak eloquently and persuasively.

169. **(b)** The one-word substitute for the given group of words 'A lover of Mankind' is 'Philanthropist'. A philanthropist is someone who actively promotes the welfare of others and supports charitable causes.

170. **(a)** The error in the divided sentence 'My neighbours were serious injured in the car accident' lies in the phrase 'serious injured'. The correct form should be 'seriously injured'.

171. **(b)** The correct form should be 'and the public' because the word 'alike' is redundant when used with 'the public' since it already includes everyone.

172. **(c)** The antonym of the word 'confound' is 'assure'. While 'confound' means to cause surprise, confusion, or bewilderment, 'assure' means to give confidence or certainty.

173. **(a)** The most appropriate option to substitute the underlined segment in the sentence 'If I was very rich, I would spend all my time and money for the poor' is 'If I were very rich'. The subjunctive mood requires using 'were' instead of 'was' in this hypothetical condition.

174. **(d)** The incorrectly spelled word is 'neccessity'. The correct spelling is 'necessity' .

175. **(a)** The most appropriate segment to substitute the underlined words in the sentence 'After he leave, we discussed his suggestion' is 'he had left'. This corrects the tense and maintains proper grammar.

176. **(b)** The one-word substitute for 'An area/place in which dead bodies are buried' is 'cemetery'. A cemetery is a place where deceased individuals are interred.

177. **(a)** The segment with the spelling error in the sentence 'The dried raisons have an intoxicating effect on humans as well as flora and fauna' is 'raisins'. The correct spelling should be 'raisins'.

178. **(c)** The most appropriate synonym for the word 'mourn' is 'grieve'. It means to feel or show deep sorrow or regret for someone or something.

179. **(b)** The idiom 'To leave no stone unturned 'means' 'To do everything possible to (achieve something)'. When someone leaves no stone unturned, they make every effort, explore all options, and exhaust all possibilities to achieve their goal.

180. **(b)** The incorrectly spelled word in the sentence 'Every season the river overflows its banks and when it goes down it leaves silt for crops to be gruwn' is 'gruwn'. The correct spelling is 'grown'.

181. **(d)** The antonym of the word 'oral' is 'inscribed'. While 'oral' refers to spoken communication, 'inscribed' relates to written or engraved words.

182. **(c)** The correct spelling to rectify the error in the sentence 'The phone rang. but nobody awnsered is 'answered'. So the corrected sentence would be 'The phone rang, but nobody answered'.

183. **(b)** The antonym of the word 'convalesce' is 'collapse'. While 'convalesce' means to recover or recuperate, 'collapse' refers to a sudden failure or breakdown.

184. **(b)** The phrase 'since 2002' indicates an action that started in the past and continuous to the present. For such situations, we use the present perfect continuous tense, not the present continuous. So the correct sentence is 'I have been working with him. ......'.

185. (c) 'Resolve' means to settle or find a solution to something. Questions (as a verb or noun) implies doubt, incertainty, or lock of resolution, which is the opposite of 'resolving'.

186. (d) The idiomatic expression that can substitute the underlined segment in the sentence 'He is very strict with his students but good-natured' is 'his heart is in the right place'. This expression conveys that despite being strict, he has good intentions.

187. (b) The most appropriate idiom to fill in the blank in the sentence 'John was always about becoming a millionaire without doing an hard work' is 'building castles in the air'. It means having unrealistic dreams or plans.

188. (c) To improve the underlined part of the sentence 'My friend vanished when the goons came to fight with me,' the option that works best is 'disappeared when the thugs arrived'. This choice maintains clarity and conciseness.

189. (d) The synonym for the underlined word in the sentence is 'censure'. It means expressing strong disapproval or criticism.

190. (d) The segment that contains a grammatical error in the sentence is 'lonely in'. The correct form should be 'alone in' to convey the intended meaning.

191. (c) The correct option to fill the blank no. 1 is 'reason'.

192. (a) The correct option to fill the blank no. 2 is 'when'.

193. (b) The correct option to fill the blank no. 3 is 'other'.

194. (c) The correct option to fill the blank no. 4 is 'more'.

195. (b) The correct option fill the blank no. 5 is 'with'.

196. (a) The most appropriate title for this passage would be 'The Humorous Quirks of Pirates'. The passage highlights various amusing aspects of pirates, making this title fitting.

197. (d) The tone of the passage is 'Humorous'. The author playfully discusses pirate quirks and language, creating a lighthearted atmosphere.

198. (d) Pirates wear eyepatches not because they lost an eye in battle, but rather 'to' maintain night vision in both eyes'. The passage explains this practical reason behind the eyepatch tradition.

199. (a) A common phrase used in pirate language is 'Shiver me timbers'. This expression is part of their unique vocabulary.

200. (d) One of the pirate quirks mentioned in the passage is 'their tendency to forget where they buried their treasure'. Despite spending significant time searching for gold, they often end up misplacing it.

CPO SI P-1 SP 08

PAPER-1

SSC CPO SI SOLVED PAPER

27 June 2024 (Shift II)

Instructions

1. This paper contains 200 questions.
2. It has 4 Parts, **Part I** General Intelligence and Reasoning, **Part II** General Knowledge and General Awareness, **Part III** Quantitative Aptitude and **Part IV** English Comprehension.
3. Each question carries **1 marks**.

MM : 200 **Time : 2 hr**

Part I

General Intelligence and Reasoning

1. Manish starts from Point A and drives 12 km towards East. He then takes a left turn,drives 5 km, turns left and drives 30 km. He then takes a left turn and drives 20 km. He takes a final left turn, drives 18 km and stops at Point Q. How far (shortest distance)and towards which direction should he now drive to reach Point A again? (All turns are 90° turns only.)

(a)10 km towards South
(b)15 km towards North
(c)10 km towards North
(d)15 km towards South

2. Select the Venn diagram that best illustrates the relationship between the following classes. Father, Pilots, Women

(a) (b) (c) (d)

3. In a code language, 'HAND' is written as 'GYMB' and 'FOOD' is written as 'EMNB'.How will 'TEXT' be written in that language?

(a) RWSC (b) SCWR
(c) SCRW (d) SWRC

4. Which two signs should be interchanged to make the given equation correct?

$5 + 156 - 12 \times 15 \div 15 = 185$

(a) + and × (b) – and +
(c) ÷ and – (d) × and –

5. Select the Venn diagram that best illustrates the relationship between the following classes. Musical Instrument, Kathak, Xylophone.

(a) (b) (c) (d)

6. Select the option that indicates the correct arrangement of the given words in the order in which they appear in an English dictionary.

1. Elate 2. Election
3. Elbow 4. Elastic
5. Electoral

(a) 1, 3, 4, 2, 5 (b) 4, 3, 2, 1, 5
(c) 1, 4, 5, 2, 3 (d) 4, 1, 3, 2, 5

7. In a certain code language,
'A + B' means 'A is the father of B',
'A – B' means 'A is the husband of B',
'A × B' means 'A is the mother of B',
'A ÷ B' means 'A is the brother of B'.
How is P related to T if 'P + Q – R × S ÷ T'?

(a) Mother's father (b) Father's brother
(c) Father's father (d) Mother's brother

8. Select the correct combination of mathematical signs to replace the *signs and balance the given equation.

16 * 17 * 14 * 2 * 3 * 251

(a) –,–,÷,×,= (b) ×,–,÷,– =
(c) ×,–,÷,×,= (d) ×,–,+,×,=

9. Select the option that is related to the fifth letter-cluster in the same way as the second letter-cluster is related to the first letter-cluster and the fourth letter-cluster is related to the third letter-cluster.

PURE : IDGT :: COOL : VJJM :: LIPS : ?

(a) PIFM (b) MPIF
(c) RKHO (d) KHOR

10. In a certain code language, 'FAVORITE' is written as 'ETIROVAF' and 'MINIMIZE' is written as 'EZIMINIM'. How will 'RESEMBLE' be written in that language?

(a) ELBRESEM
(b) ELBMESER
(c) ERLBMESR
(d) ERESLMBE

11. In a code language, 'COOL' is written as 'EMQJ' and 'CARD' is written as 'EYTB'. How will 'STAR' be written in that language?

(a) URCP (b) UCPR
(c) PCUR (d) URPC

12. A dice has its faces marked by numbers 5, 6, 7, 8, 9 and 10. Two positions of the same dice are given below. Which face is opposite to face 6?

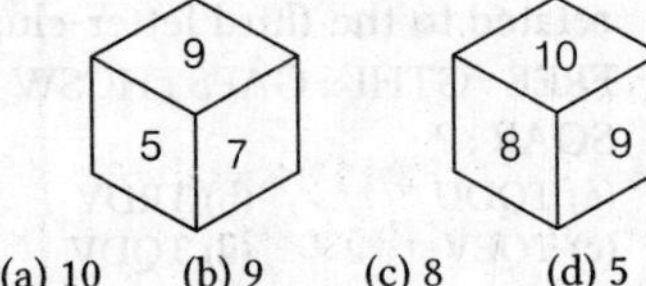

(a) 10 (b) 9 (c) 8 (d) 5

13. Select the correct mirror image of the given figure when the mirror is placed at MN as shown below.

M
Rp37aw
N

(a) wɐ7Ɛqᴙ (b) wɐ37qᴙ
(c) ʍɐ7Ɛdᴙ (d) ʍɐ7ƐqR

14. 36 is related to 70 following a certain logic. Following the same logic, 41 is related to 80. Which of the following numbers is related to 76 related using the same logic?
(a) 39 (b) 38 (c) 37 (d) 42

15. Select the option in which the given figure (X) is embedded as its part. (Rotation is not allowed.)

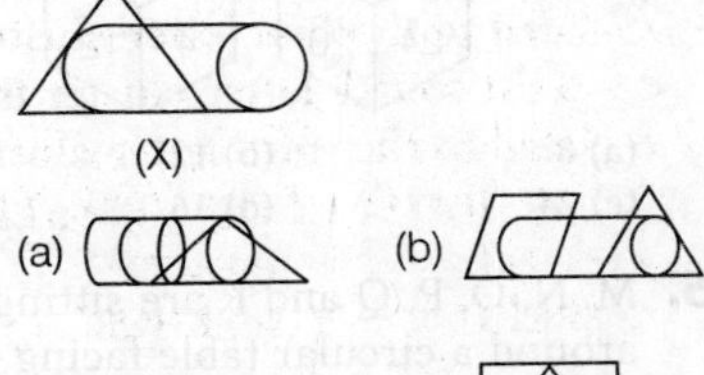

(a) (b)
(c) (d)

16. Select the set in which the numbers are related in the same way as are the numbers of the following sets. (**Note** Operations should be performed on the whole numbers, without breaking down the numbers into its constituent digits. E.g. 13-Operations on 13 such as adding/subtracting/multiplying etc. to 13 can be performed. Breaking down 13 into 1 and 3 and then performing mathematical operations on 1 and 3 is not allowed.)
(108, 27, 9)
(132, 33, 11)
(a) (180, 45, 10) (b) (190, 45, 15)
(c) (180, 45, 15) (d) (180, 55, 15)

17. Select the correct mirror image of the given figure when the mirror is placed at MN as shown below.

M
7GJ3de
N

(a) ɘb3ᒧᘐ٢ (b) ɘb3ᒧᘐ٢
(c) ɘdƐᒧᘐ٢ (d) ɘbƐᒧᘐ٢

18. If 'A' stands for '÷', 'B' stands for '×', 'C' stands for '+' and 'D' stands for '–', what will come in place of the question mark (?) in the following equation?
70 D 11 B 5 C 45 A 9 = ?
(a) 10 (b) 25 (c) 15 (d) 20

19. What will come in place of the question mark (?) when + and – are interchanged and 5 and 18 are also interchanged?
5 –18 + 12 = ?
(a) 12 (b) 13
(c) 10 (d) 11

20. Select the correct mirror image of the given figure when the mirror is placed at MN as shown below.

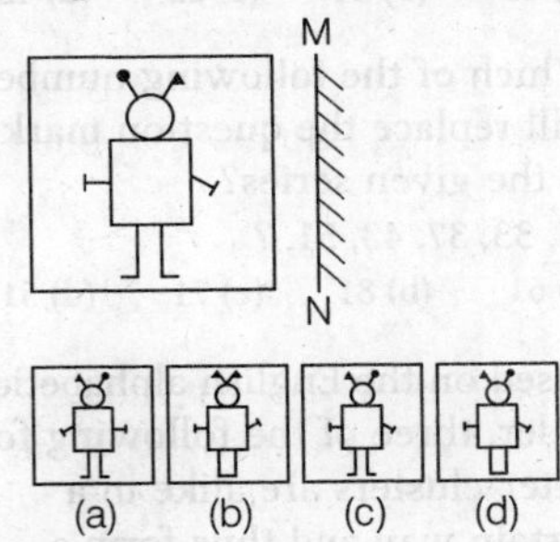

(a) (b) (c) (d)

21. What will come in place of the question mark (?) in the following equation, if '+' and '–' are interchanged and '×' and '÷' are interchanged ?
$110 \times 10 - 175 \div 5 + 29 = ?$
(a) 599 (b) 857
(c) 856 (d) 589

22. Identify the figure given in the options, which when put in place of the question mark(?) will logically complete the series.

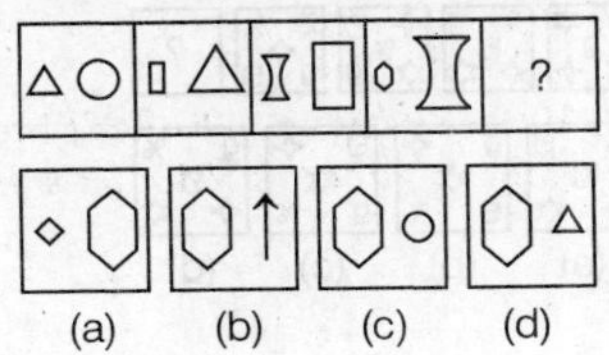

(a) (b) (c) (d)

23. Which of the following terms will replace the question mark (?) in the given series?
AFM, DIP, GLS,?
(a) OST (b) REW
(c) JOV (d) FHG

24. If + means ×,– means ÷,× means –, and ÷ means +, what will be the value of the following expression?
$9 + 7 \times 15 - 5 \div 5 = ?$
(a) 55 (b) 60
(c) 52 (d) 65

25. Aman drives 5 km from point A towards the South. He then takes a left turn and drives 5 km. He then takes a right turn and drives 5 km. He again takes a right turn and drives10 km. He finally takes a right turn and drives 10 km to reach Point B. How much and in which direction does he have to drive to return to Point A?
(All the turns are 90° turns only.)
(a) 5 km towards the West
(b) 5 km towards the North
(c) 5 km towards the East
(d) 5 km towards the South

26. Which of the following letters will sequentially replace the question marks (?) in the given series ?
G, Z, I, X, K, V, ?, ?
(a) Q, R (b) M, T (c) L, N (d) M, S

27. In a code language, 'HELLO' is coded as 83 and 'SHELL' is coded as 79. How will 'MATCH' be coded in the same language?
(a) 87 (b) 96 (c) 92 (d) 90

28. In a certain code language,
'A + B' means 'A is the father of B';
'A – B' means 'B is the sister of A';
'A × B' means 'A is the wife of B' and
'A ÷ B' means 'A is the mother of B'.
Based on the above information, how is T related to V if 'R × S – T ÷ P + V'?
(a) Father's mother (b) Father's father
(c) Sister (d) Mother

29. In a certain code language, 'WHILE' is written as '2167103' and 'DEPTH' is written as'2314186'. How will 'ROUND' be written in that language ?
(a) 15112021 (b) 171520145
(c) 161319122 (d) 181521154

30. Two statements are given, followed by two conclusions numbered I and II. Assuming the statements to be true, even if they seem to be at variance with commonly known facts, decide which of the conclusions logically follow(s) from the statements.

Statements

All tablets are medicines.

Some medicines are ointments.

Conclusions

I. Some tablets are ointments.

II. All ointments are medicines.

(a) Neither Conclusion I nor II follows
(b) Only Conclusion II follows
(c) Both conclusions I and II follow
(d) Only Conclusion I follows

31. Select the correct mirror image of the given figure when the mirror is placed at MN as shown below.

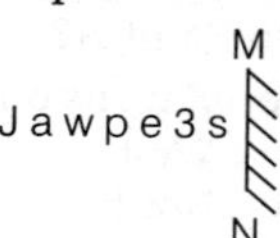

(a) s 3 ə d w e ɾ
(b) ƨ Ɛ ɘ q w ƨ L
(c) ƨ 3 ɘ q ʍ ƨ L
(d) ƨ Ɛ p e a w L

32. Which of the following numbers will replace the question marks (?) in the given series?

2, ?, ?, 17, 26, 37, 50, 65, 82

(a) 3, 4 (b) 5, 10
(c) 2, 5 (d) 3, 5

33. If + means –,– means ×,× means ÷,÷ means +, what will come in place of the question mark (?) in the given equation.

$168 \times 14 - 8 + 90 \div 4 = ?$

(a) 20 (b) 10
(c) 15 (d) 18

34. A sheet of paper is folded along the dotted line successively along the directions shown and is then punched in the last. How would the paper look when unfolded?

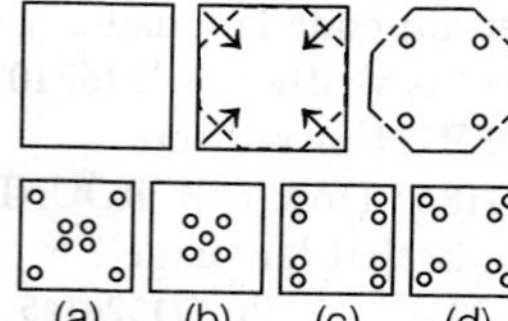

(a) (b) (c) (d)

35. Select the option that represents the correct order of the given words as they would appear in an English dictionary.

1. Ferocious 2. Fervor
3. Fiction 4. Faith
5. Feign 6. Ferment

(a) 6, 5, 2, 1, 4, 3
(b) 6, 4, 5, 3, 2, 1
(c) 4, 6, 5, 2, 1, 3
(d) 4, 5, 6, 1, 2, 3

36. Identify the figure given in the options which when put in place of '?' will logically complete the series.

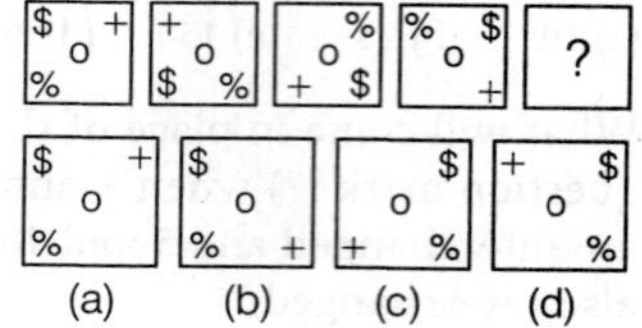

(a) (b) (c) (d)

37. Select the number from among the given options that can replace the question mark(?) in the following series.

1, 2, 4, 8, 10, 20, ?

(a) 40 (b) 24 (c) 22 (d) 42

38. Which of the following numbers will replace the question mark (?) in the given series?

31, 33, 37, 43, 51, ?

(a) 61 (b) 81 (c) 71 (d) 51

39. Based on the English alphabetical order, three of the following four letter-clusters are alike in a certain way and thus form a group. Which letter-cluster does not belong to that group?
(**Note** The odd letter-cluster is not based on the number of consonants/vowels or their position in the letter-cluster)

(a) CGE (b) MQO
(c) GKI (d) KON

40. Select the figure from among the given options that can logically replace the question mark (?) in the following series

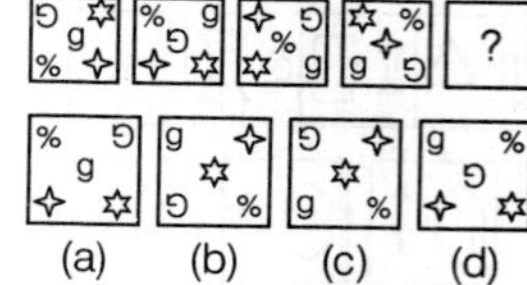

(a) (b) (c) (d)

41. Select the option that is related to the fifth letter-cluster in the same way as the second letter-cluster is related to the first letter-cluster and the fourth letter-cluster is related to the third letter-cluster.

FREE : GTHI :: GAPS : HCSW :: SOAR : ?

(a) TQDU (b) TRDV
(c) TQEV (d) TQDV

42. Select the option in which the numbers share the same relationship as that shared by the given pair of numbers.

40 – 9

(a) 90 – 4 (b) 120 – 4
(c) 60 – 5 (d) 100 – 6

43. Which of the following numbers will replace the question mark (?) in the given series?

45, 90, 154, ?, 347

(a) 256 (b) 273
(c) 248 (d) 239

44. A dice has its faces marked by numbers 4, 8, 12, 16, 20 and 24. Two positions of the same dice are given below. Which face is opposite to face 16?

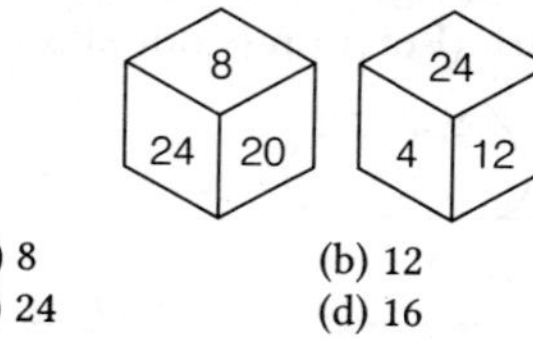

(a) 8 (b) 12
(c) 24 (d) 16

45. M, N, O, P, Q and R are sitting around a circular table facing the centre. O is an immediate neighbour of M. Only two people sit between O and Q. P sits second to the left of R. N is an immediate neighbour of P. Who is sitting second to the right of M?

(a) N (b) Q (c) R (d) P

46. Select the set in which the numbers are related in the same way as are the numbers of the following sets.
(**Note** Operations should be performed on the whole numbers, without breaking down the numbers into its constituent digits. e.g.13- Operations on 13 such as adding /subtracting /multiplying etc. to 13 can be performed. Breaking down 13 into 1 and 3 and

performing mathematical operations on 1 and 3 is not allowed).
(144, 12, 24)
(216, 18, 36)
(a) (324, 29, 54) (b) (324, 27, 50)
(c) (324, 27, 54) (d) (320, 27, 54)

47. In a certain code language, 'join the class' is written as 'yq pt dm' and 'the music class'is written as 'rj yq dm'. How is 'music' written in the given language?
(a) yg (b) rj (c) dm (d) pt

48. Which letter cluster will replace the question mark (?) to complete the given series?
TWEZ, XBYG, ?, FLMU, JQGB
(a) BJEN (b) TWKN
(c) BGSN (d) TWEH

49. Two statements are given, followed by two conclusions numbered I and II. Assuming the statements to be true, even if they seem to be at variance with commonly known facts, decide which of the conclusions logically follow(s) from the statements.
Statements
All pineapples are papayas.
All papayas are pears.
Conclusions
I. All pineapples are pears.
II. Some pears are pineapples.
(a) Only Conclusion II follows
(b) Neither Conclusion I nor II follows
(c) Only Conclusion I follows
(d) Both conclusions I and II follow

50. Select the set in which the numbers are related in the same way as are the numbers of the following sets.
(**Note** Operations should be performed on the whole numbers, without breaking down the numbers into its constituent digits. E.g. 13- Operations on 13 such as adding/subtracting/multiplying etc. to 13 can be performed. Breaking down 13 into 1 and 3 then performing mathematical operations on 1 and 3 is not allowed)
(76, 152, 38)
(84, 168, 42)
(a) (84, 178, 42) (b) (96, 184, 46)
(c) (62, 132, 33) (d) (68, 136, 34)

Part II

General Knowledge and General Awareness

51. Which Greek term was first used by Ernst Haeckel in 1866 to refer to 'the relation of animals to both the organic as well as the inorganic environment'?
(a) Oekologie (b) Ecophagie
(c) Ethnologie (d) Oologie

52. The depositional pattern of $CaCO_3$ and other materials that extend upwards from the floor of a limestone cavern is known as
(a) tactile (b) stalagmite
(c) stalactite (d) dripstone

53. Fundamental Duties of the Indian Constitution are mentioned in which Article?
(a) Article 42 A (b) Article 51
(c) Article 51 A (d) Article 42

54. Thiyam Suryamukhi Devi who received the Sangeet Natak Akademi Awards 2003, is known for her contribution to the
(a) Odissi dance (b) Gotipua dance
(c) Manipuri dance (d) Kathak dance

55. Which of the followings statements is/are true about private goods?
I. Rivalrous in consumption
II. Non-excludability
III. Negative marginal cost
Codes
(a) Only II (b) Only III
(c) Both II and III (d) Only I

56. What is the national female workforce participation rate as per the Census of India 2011?
(a) 53.26% (b) 30.02%
(c) 53.03% (d) 25.51%

57. Who among the following is a Padma Shri Awardee for her contribution to Manipuri dance?
(a) Darshana Jhaveri
(b) Shovana Narayan
(c) Mrinalini Sarabhai
(d) Aditi Rao Hydari

58. Who among the following Padma Vibhushan awardees belongs to Kalka-Bindadin Gharana of Kathak?
(a) Damyanti Devi
(b) Kelucharan Mohapatra
(c) Birju Maharaj
(d) Sitara Devi

59. 'Vasanta', 'Grishma' and 'Varsha' are names of .... in India.
(a) traditional seasons
(b) cyclones
(c) local winds
(d) local storms

60. In which of the following regions is the tropical evergreen forests found in India?
(a) Thar Desert (b) Western Ghats
(c) Eastern Ghats (d) Rann of Kutch

61. Which of the following folk dances is not associated with Goa?
(a) Dashavatara (b) Dekhni
(c) Ghumura (d) Dhangar

62. In 1905, who concluded with Thomas Chamberlain that the planets of the Solar System originated from an encounter between the Sun and another star?
(a) Inge Lehmann
(b) Forest Moulton
(c) Charles Lyell
(d) James Hutton

63. What is the name of the aromatic compound in the given figure?

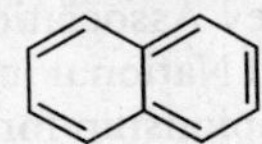

(a) Tropone
(b) Naphthalene
(c) Tetrahydrofuran
(d) Cyclohexene

64. Which of the following is the characteristics of epilimnion?
(a) Top-most layer in a thermally stratified lake
(b) Bottom layer of a river
(c) Bottom layer of a lake
(d) Middle layer of a pond

65. Vijay Kichlu belongs to the .... .
(a) Patiala Gharana
(b) Bhendi Bazaar Gharana
(c) Agra Gharana
(d) Gwalior Gharana

66. From which of the following Constitutions is the idea of 'Charter of Fundamental Rights' adopted in the Indian Constitution?
(a) French Constitution
(b) United States of America's Constitution
(c) Brazilian Constitution
(d) Spanish Constitution

67. Which Article of the Indian Constitution mentions that the law declared by the Supreme Court shall be binding on all the courts within the territory of India?
(a) Article 147 (b) Article 137
(c) Article 141 (d) Article 151

68. Choose the correct statements about the islands of India.
A. Lakshadweep islands are composed of coral islands.
B. Andaman and Nicobar islands are composed of coral islands.
C. It is believed that Lakshadweep islands are an elevated portion of submarine mountains.
D. It is believed that Andaman and Nicobar islands are an elevated portion of submarine mountains.
(a) A and D (b) A and B
(c) C and D (d) B and C

69. Whose autobiography is titled 'A Life Apart'?
(a) Vinita Agarwal
(b) Bindu Bhatt
(c) Mannu Bhandari
(d) Prabha Khaitan

70. The 12th edition of the Ice Hockey Association of India's (IHAI) National Ice Hockey Championship for Men (2023) was organised in ....
(a) Ladakh
(b) Uttarakhand
(c) Jammu and Kashmir
(d) Himachal Pradesh

71. Who among the following was granted the title of 'Chief of the Merchants' or Malik-ut-Tujjar by the Bahamani ruler, Humayun Shah?
(a) Ahmed III
(b) Aladdin Imad Shah
(c) Yusuf Adil Shah
(d) Mahmud Gawan

72. What is pro-vitamin A or the anti-cancer compound present in carrots called?
(a) Alpharesins
(b) Beta-carotene
(c) Alpha-terpenoid
(d) Delta-terpenes

73. Which of the following parts of the Indian Constitution is commonly referred to as the'Magna Carta of India'?
(a) Part II (b) Part I
(c) Part III (d) Part IV

74. Under the Charter Act of 1833 in British India, the East India Company's monopoly on trade with which of the following countries was abolished?
(a) Nepal (b) China
(c) Burma (d) Sri Lanka

75. Which of the following options is correctly matched?
(a) Herbivores - Secondary consumers
(b) Omnivorous - Green plants
(c) Carnivores - Primary consumers
(d) Decomposers - Bacteria

76. The term 'Libero' is used in ....
(a) basketball (b) badminton
(c) volleyball (d) snooker

77. What is the height of the stump from the ground in cricket?
(a) 28 inch (b) 27 inch
(c) 25 inch (d) 26 inch

78. In which of the following states of India is Onam, a harvest festival, primarily celebrated?
(a) Sikkim (b) Madhya Pradesh
(c) Odisha (d) Kerala

79. Which sector promotes modernisation and stable employment in the economy?
(a) Service sector
(b) Energy sector
(c) Agriculture sector
(d) Industrial sector

80. Who among the following started the ceremony of 'Sijda' (prostration) and 'Paibos'(kissing of the monarch's feet), in the court?
(a) Muhammad bin Tughlaq
(b) Ghiyas-ud-din Balban
(c) Iltutmish
(d) Alauddin Khalji

81. In which year did the annexation of Awadh by Lord Dalhousie take place?
(a) 1857 (b) 1850
(c) 1856 (d) 1858

82. As of June 2023, which of the following is India's largest airport in terms of total passengers?
(a) Indira Gandhi International Airport
(b) Netaji Subhas Chandra Bose International Airport
(c) Chhatrapati Shivaji International Airport of Mumbai
(d) Sardar Vallabhbhai Patel International Airport

83. Who is the highest run scorer in an over in a test match cricket?
(a) Virat Kohli (b) Brian Lara
(c) Kapil Dev (d) Jasprit Bumrah

84. Reserve ratio and money supply have .... relationship.
(a) a negative (b) a linear
(c) a symmetrical (d) no

85. Identify the number of electrons found in the outermost shell of halogen.
(a) Two (b) Seven (c) Five (d) One

86. As of June 2023, which of the following is the longest train route in India?
(a) Dibrugarh-Kanyakumari
(b) Jammu Tawi-Kanyakumari
(c) Amritsar-Kochuveli
(d) Guwahati-Trivandrum

87. Who wrote the patriotic song 'Sare Jahan Se Achha Hindustan Hamara' that was published in the weekly journal Ittehad on 16th August, 1904?
(a) Muhammad Iqbal
(b) Chandra Sekhar Azad
(c) Sardar Bhagat Singh
(d) Rabindranath Tagore

88. What is the full form of 'PM-SYM'?
(a) Pradhan Mantri Mukhya Suraksha Yojana
(b) Pradhan Mantri Sanyukt Yojana Maandyan
(c) Pradhan Mantri Shreshtha Yojana Mulyankan
(d) Pradhan Mantri Shram Yogi Maandhan

89. Who among the following Indian musicians is known for his contribution to the field of Hindustani music for the classification of Ragas into ten Thaats?
(a) Pandit Vishnu Digambar Paluskar
(b) Pandit Vishnu Narayan Bhatkhande
(c) Allauddin Khan
(d) Abdul Karim Khan

90. Which of the following statements are correct regarding conditions required to recognise as a political party in India?
A. If a political party is treated as a recognised political party in four or more states, it shall be known as a 'National Party' throughout the whole of India.

B. If a political party is treated as a recognised political party in less than four states, it shall be known as a 'State Party' in the State or States in which it is so recognised.

C. National Parties need only one proposer for filing the nomination and are also entitled for two sets of electoral rolls free of cost.

Codes

(a) A and B (b) A, B and C
(c) A and C (d) B and C

91. Which of the following was true with regard to the Green Revolution?

(a) Its method of cultivation required less quantity of water.
(b) It involved use of organic fertilisers and pesticides.
(c) It involved use of high-yielding variety of seeds.
(d) It was targeted mainly at the pulses-growing areas.

92. How many Mandalas were in Rigveda Samhita?

(a) 11 (b) 12
(c) 20 (d) 10

93. How many electrons does a hydrogen molecule have in its K-shell?

(a) 1 (b) 4
(c) 2 (d) 3

94. Which of the following is used for determining the value of 1 ampere.

(a) A=2C/s (b) A=1C/s
(c) C= A/2s (d) C= A × 2s

95. Which of the following is a feature of globalisation?

(a) Restrictions on expansion of public sector
(b) Liberalisation of import licensing
(c) Disinvestment
(d) Self-reliance

96. Which Article of the Indian Constitution mentions about the right of the Governor to address and to send messages to the House (or Houses) of the state legislature?

(a) Article 176 (b) Article 172
(c) Article 171 (d) Article 175

97. Ambubachi fair is celebrated in which of the following states?

(a) Manipur (b) Nagaland
(c) Mizoram (d) Assam

98. Bhajan Sopori, a Padma Shri awardee, is a .... player.

(a) tabla (b) violin
(c) santoor (d) sitar

99. Truth, Love and a Little Malice is the autobiography of

(a) Khushwant Singh
(b) Phoolan Devi
(c) Satyajit Ray
(d) Arjun Singh

100. Which of the following polyhalogen compounds is used in the production of the freon refrigerant R-22?

(a) Chloroform
(b) Dichlorodiphenyltrichloroethane
(c) Methylene Chloride
(d) Carbon Tetrachloride

Part III

Quantitative Aptitude

101. Two circles with centers *B* and *D* have radii *DA* = 8 cm and *BC* = *x* cm, respectively. *AC* is tangent to both circles. If *DB* and *AC* intersect at the Point *E*, *AE* = 12 cm and *EC* = 18cm, then find the value of *x* (in cm).

(a) 12 (b) 11
(c) 10 (d) 13

102. Find the fourth proportion to 10, 12 and 15.

(a) 20 (b) 22
(c) 16 (d) 18

103. Find the total surface area of a hemisphere with a radius of 11 cm?

(a) $242\pi cm^2$ (b) $313\pi cm^2$
(c) $363\pi cm^2$ (d) $273\pi cm^2$

104. Simplify

$5\times[14\div13\times\{13\times14\div(14\times14)\}]$

(a) 10 (b) 15
(c) 5 (d) 20

105. In an election, the winner was supported by 46% of all the voters in the list and he got 410 votes more than his only rival. 10% of the voters on the voters' list did not cast their votes, and 60 voters cast their ballot papers blank. How many voters were on the list?

(a) 17500 (b) 15750
(c) 17445 (d) 16550

106. Based on the following table which shows production of the number of scooters by a company during the first half of 1992.

Type/ Month	Jan	Feb	Mar	April	May	June
X	25	25	18	40	20	15
Y	25	27	50	45	30	20
Z	25	27	15	25	30	20
T	25	26	25	0	30	35
Total	100	105	108	110	110	90

In which month, did the company produce an equal number of all types of scooters?

(a) January (b) March
(c) June (d) May

107. Arvind works 4 times as fast as Suresh. If Suresh can complete a work in 20 days indpendently, then find the number of days in which Arvind and Suresh can together finish the work.

(a) 6 (b) 5
(c) 3 (d) 4

108. What is the length of the arc of a circle whose radius is 35 cm and whose arc subtends an angle of 72° at the centre of the circle?

(a) 38 cm (b) 56 cm
(c) 44 cm (d) 28 cm

109. If $\alpha+\beta+\gamma=0$ then

$$\frac{3\beta^2+\alpha^2+\gamma^2}{2\beta^2-\alpha\gamma}=?$$

(a) $\frac{1}{4}$ (b) 1 (c) $\frac{1}{2}$ (d) 2

110. Study the given pie-chart answer the question that follows.

The pie-chart shows the amount of money (in ₹) spent (in degrees) on various sports by a school administration in a particular year.

Amount of money (in ₹) spent (in degrees) on verious sports by a school administration in a particular year.

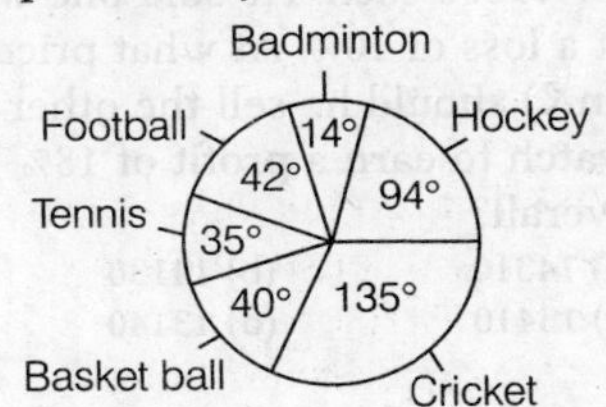

If ₹ 21000 was spent on Football, then the money spent on Tennis and Basketball taken together is what percentage (rounded off to 2 decimal places) of money spent on Hockey and Cricket taken together?
(a) 39.65% (b) 47.25%
(c) 23.50% (d) 32.75%

111. Find the value of $\text{cosec}\,\theta\,(1-\cos\theta)(\text{cosec}\,\theta+\cot\theta)$.
(a) 2 (b) −1
(c) 1 (d) 0

112. Simplify : $9^{18} \div 3^{14}$ of $27^3 \times \sqrt{6561}$
(a) 3^{16} (b) 3^{18}
(c) 3^{15} (d) 3^{17}

113. The marked price of an article is 35% more than its cost price. If a discount of 15% is given, what will be the profit percentage ?
(a) $12\frac{3}{4}$% (b) $10\frac{1}{4}$5%
(c) $14\frac{3}{4}$% (d) $13\frac{2}{3}$%

114. Find the value of $(1+\cot A-\text{cosec}\,A)(1+\tan A+\sec A)-3(\sin^2 A+\cos^2 A)$.
(a) −1 (b) 1
(c) −2 (d) 2

115. The length of the largest possible rod that can be placed in a cubical room is $42\sqrt{3}$m. The surface area (in m^2) of the largest possible sphere that fit within the cubical room is
$\left[\text{Use}, \pi = \frac{22}{7}\right]$
(a) 5544 (b) 2564
(c) 3590 (d) 4589

116. Find the value of $(13.49+12.51)\times 13$.
(a) 438 (b) 238
(c) 138 (d) 338

117. A merchant bought two watches for ₹9000 each. He sold one watch at a loss of 10%. At what price (in ₹) should he sell the other watch to earn a profit of 18% overall?
(a) 14310 (b) 14130
(c) 13410 (d) 13140

118. The volumes of two spheres are in the ratio of 512 : 3375. The ratio of their surface areas is
(a) 27 : 144 (b) 68 : 125
(c) 49 : 325 (d) 64 : 225

119. If $x = 3y + 4$, then what is the value of $(x^3 - 27y^3 - 36xy)$?
(a) 8 (b) 1 (c) 64 (d) 27

120. In a class, the numbers of boys and girls are in the ratio of 3 : 5. What is the percentage of boys in the class?
(a) 60% (b) 12.5%
(c) 42.5% (d) 37.5%

121. A bus covers the first 50 km of its journey in 40 min and covers the remaining 75km in 40 min. What is the average speed (in km/h) of the bus?
(a) $101\frac{1}{4}$ (b) $105\frac{3}{4}$
(c) $93\frac{3}{4}$ (d) $95\frac{1}{4}$

122. Study the given table and answer the question that follows.
The table shows the yearly production (in thousands) of scooters in five different factories (P, Q, R, S and T) from 1985 to 1989.
Yearly production (in thousands) in different factories.

Factory	1985	1986	1987	1988	1989
P	20	15	24	13	17
Q	16	23	41	20	15
R	14	21	30	16	12
S	25	17	15	12	22
T	40	32	39	41	35
Total	115	108	149	102	101

In which year was the production of scooters in all factories equal to the yearly average number of scooters produced from 1985 to 1989 ?
(a) 1986 (b) 1987 (c) 1985 (d) 1988

123. A copper sphere of diameter 12 cm is drawn into a wire of diameter 4 mm. What is the length (in cm) of the wire? $\left(\text{Where}, \pi = \frac{22}{7}\right)$
(a) 7823 (b) 8342 (c) 9000 (d) 7200

124. A and B can do a work in 13 days and 26 days, respectively. If they work for a day alternately, starting with A, then in how many days will the work be completed?
(a) 16 (b) 17 (c) 14 (d) 13

125. Find the area of a minor sector of a circle whose circumference is 88 cm and the length of its minor arc is 22 cm $\left(\text{Use}, \pi = \frac{22}{7}\right)$.
(a) 415 cm^2 (b) 154 cm^2
(c) 451 cm^2 (d) 145 cm^2

126. A 255-m long train is running at a speed of 72 km/h. It crosses a platform of length 745m in
(a) 50 sec (b) 53 sec
(c) 51 sec (d) 40 sec

127. Ashu can row 7.5 km an hour in still water. He finds that it takes four times as much time to row upstream, as it takes to row downstream. The speed of the stream is
(a) 2.5 km/h (b) 4.5 km/h
(c) 3.5 km/h (d) 1.5 km/h

128. The value of $1-\cfrac{7}{1-\cfrac{1}{1+\cfrac{1}{1-7}}}$ is
(a) −1 (b) 2 (c) 1 (d) 0

129. A mixture of 750 kg of alloy of copper and tin contains 25% tin. How much tin must be added, so that it becomes 70% of the mixture?
(a) 956 kg (b) 1125 kg
(c) 1097 kg (d) 895 kg

130. If $\sin\alpha = \frac{5}{13}$, then the value of $\cos\alpha \cdot \text{cosec}\,\alpha \cdot \cot\alpha$ is
(a) $\frac{12}{5}$ (b) $\frac{25}{144}$
(c) $\frac{144}{25}$ (d) $\frac{5}{12}$

131. Find the value of the given expression.
$\frac{1}{4}\times\frac{4}{3}\div\frac{5}{3}+\frac{1}{2}$
(a) 0.7 (b) 1.3
(c) 1.5 (d) 2.1

132. Study the given table answer the question that follows. The table shows the percentage population of four states below poverty line and proportion of male of female.

State	Percentage of population below poverty line	Proportion of male of female	
		Below poverty line	Above poverty line
		Male : Female	Male : Female
A	36	5 : 3	3 : 4
B	27	6 : 7	4 : 7
C	46	2 : 3	3 : 1
D	32	1 : 2	2 : 7

If the population of States A and D is 18000 each, then what is the total number of females below poverty line in these states?

(a) 6250 (b) 6270 (c) 6120 (d) 6050

133. Aarav owns a watch worth ₹ 10000. He sells it to Bhavin at a profit of 15%. After some days, Bhavin sells it back to Aarav at 15% loss. Find the percentage profit or loss faced by Aarav.

(a) 17.25% loss (b) 18.75% loss
(c) 18.25% profit (d) 17.25% profit

134. The strength of a school increases and decreases every alternate year by 15%. If it started with an increase in 2012, then the strength of the school in the beginning of 2015, as compared to that in 2012, had (correct to two decimal places).

(a) Decreased by 13.85 % (b) Increased by 12.41 %
(c) Decreased by 12.41% (d) Increased by 13.85 %

135. The value of $30+180\div30\times6-15-16-60\div3-15$ is

(a) 2 (b) 1 (c) 0 (d) 3

136. Find the value of

$$\frac{12+3\frac{2}{3}\div\left[1\frac{3}{4}\div\left\{5\frac{1}{4}\times\left(3\frac{3}{5}\div4\frac{1}{2}\right)\right\}\right]}{1\frac{1}{3}\times5\frac{1}{5}}$$

(a) 1 (b) 3 (c) 5 (d) 2

137. The table represents marks obtained by students A, B, C, D and E in five subjects in an examination. The maximum marks for each subject are 100.

Student	English	Math	Physics	Chemistry	Information Technology
A	94	100	97	100	100
B	87	93	85	96	95
C	92	100	98	95	100
D	79	92	91	76	97
E	77	85	94	99	98

In how many subjects have the students scored 100% marks?

(a) 5 (b) 2 (c) 3 (d) 4

138. Three boys, on an average, are 25 yr old, and their age are in the ratio of 3 : 5 : 7.What is the age of youngest boy?

(a) 21 yr (b) 12 yr (c) 15 yr (d) 24 yr

139. The savings and expenditure of family in a month on different heads is shown in the given pie-chart. The family saves ₹ 8000 per month.

Monthly Expenditure of a family

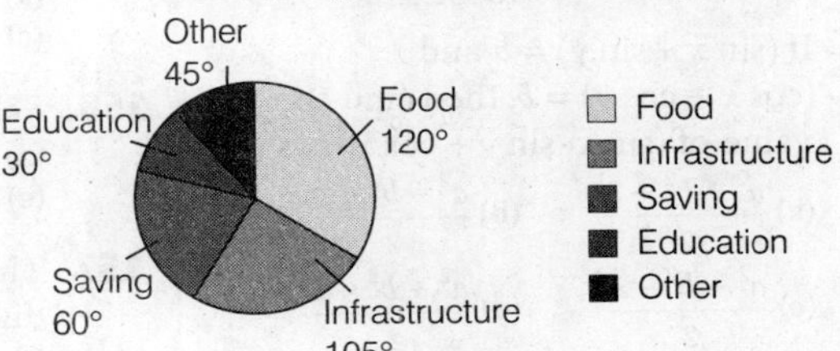

Find the expenditure (in ₹) on education.

(a) 2500 (b) 4000 (c) 3500 (d) 3000

140. Simplify the following expression

$25\times25+9\times9+6\times6+2\times25\times9+2\times9\times6+2\times25\times6$

(a) 2500 (b) 1200 (c) 1600 (d) 900

141. The value of $3+2\times[7+(5+7)\div2]$ is equal to

(a) 29 (b) 65 (c) 39 (d) 47

142. The given pie-chart shows the percentage distribution of a mathematics book in 5 different stores.

Total number of books = 6500

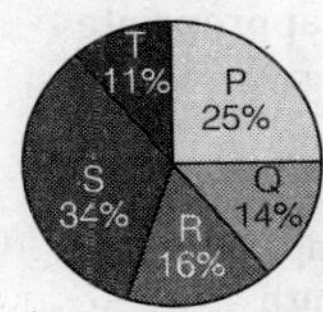

Find the central angle for the book in store S.

(a) 107.3° (b) 122.4° (c) 118.9° (d) 117.5°

143. What annual instalment will discharge a debt of ₹ 10,192 due in 3 yr at 10% simple interest?

(a) ₹ 3044.48 (b) ₹ 3088.48 (c) ₹ 3144.48 (d) ₹ 3188.48

144. The volume of a cube is four times the volume of a cuboid. If the sides of the cuboid are 32 cm, 8 cm and 4 cm, then find the ratio of the total surface area of the cube to that of the cuboid.

(a) 24 : 13 (b) 22 : 13 (c) 21 : 13 (d) 23 : 13

145. Simplify: $8.2+2.6+3.2-4.5\div0.9\times1.2$

(a) 6 (b) 10 (c) 4 (d) 8

146. If L is the mid-point of the side YZ of ΔXYZ, and the area of XYL is 13 cm^2, then the area (in cm^2) of XYZ is

(a) 24 (b) 22 (c) 20 (d) 26

147. Two cars run to a place at the speeds of 45 km/h and 55 km/h, respectively. If the second car takes 40 min less than the first for the journey, then what is the length of the journey (in km)?

(a) 180 (b) 165 (c) 99 (d) 145

148. On account of corona virus, 5% of the population of a village died. Out of the remaining population, 20% fled due to panic. If the present population is 4655, then what was the population of the village before the corona attack?
(a) 6000 (b) 6125 (c) 5995 (d) 5985

149. If $(\sin x + \sin y) = a$ and $(\cos x + \cos y) = b$, then find the value of $(\sin x \cdot \sin y + \cos x \cdot \cos y)$.
(a) $\frac{a^2+b^2+2}{2}$ (b) $\frac{a^2-b^2-2}{2}$
(c) $\frac{a^2+b^2-2}{2}$ (d) $\frac{a^2+b^2-1}{2}$

150. A doll is marked for ₹ 2500. A customer pays ₹ 1800 for it. If the customer got a series of two discounts and the rate of the first discount is 10%, then the rate of the second discount is
(a) 15% (b) 20% (c) 25% (d) 18%

Part IV
English Comprehension

151. Select the most appropriate meaning of the given idiom.
Go down in flames
(a) To fail spectacularly
(b) To destroy completely
(c) To crash and burn
(d) To burn down completely

152. Select the most appropriate meaning of the underlined idiom in the given sentence.
Only those having blue blood can dethrone the evil autocrat and restore equilibrium.
(a) Political ideology
(b) Vigilant nature
(c) Aristocratic lineage
(d) Bitter relations

153. Parts of the following sentence have been given as options. Select the option that contains an error.
We were driving home when suddenly a deer runs across the road.
(a) home
(b) We were driving
(c) a deer runs across the road
(d) when suddenly

154. Select the most appropriate synonym of the given word.
Condemn
(a) Uphold (b) Elevate
(c) Tolerate (d) Denounce

155. Select the option that can be used as a one-word substitute for the underlined group of words.
Rahul has done a study of statistics that contributed to the research.
(a) Demography (b) Choreography
(c) Cartography (d) Cinematography

156. Select the incorrectly spelt word.
(a) Disseminate (b) Enterpreneur
(c) Dilemma (d) Accommodate

157. The following sentence has been divided into four segments. Identify the segment that has a grammatical error.
His energetic attitude / showed that he had / soundly slept / the previous night.
(a) His energetic attitude
(b) showed that he had
(c) the previous night.
(d) soundly slept

158. Select the most appropriate synonym of the underlined word in the given sentence.
The cacophony in the theatre was too much for us.
(a) silence (b) smell
(c) noise (d) laughter

159. In the question four alternatives are given for the underlined word in the sentence.
Choose the alternative which best expresses the opposite meaning of the word.
"Well, what if it is? You are not afraid of anything, you know," returned the boy, looking wicked.
(a) Clean (b) Evil
(c) Righteous (d) Improper

160. Select the most appropriate option to substitute the underlined segment in the given sentence.
Though Kalpana listened to Sheetal carefully, she knew that she should take it with a grain of salt.
(a) accept it as really useful and worthy
(b) move according to the trend
(c) regard it as exaggerated and not completely true
(d) be do it meticulously as taking salt

161. Identify the incorrectly spelt word in the given sentence and select the option that rectifies the spelling error.
Many promote bamboo planting for erosion prevention and to riverse the effects of global warming.
(a) Reverse (b) Bambboo
(c) Efeccts (d) Prevension

162. Select the option that can be used as a one-word substitute for the given group of words.
The doctor who deals with the female reproductive system.
(a) Ophthalmologist
(b) Orthodontist
(c) Cardiologist
(d) Gynaecologist

163. Select the option that can be used as a one-word substitute for the given group of words.
An open space usually rectangular and enclosed in a building
(a) Quadruped (b) Quinton
(c) Quadrangle (d) Quintessential

164. Select the most appropriate synonym of the underlined word in the given sentence.
Mr. Satterthwaite was shrewd enough to penetrate her meaning.
(a) Aged (b) Funny
(c) Innocent (d) Smart

165. Choose the most appropriate meaning of the given idiom.
At the drop of a hat
(a) Consecutively (b) Eventually
(c) Certainly (d) Immediately

166. Identify the meaning of the idiom in the given situation.
I will always stand by my friend.
(a) Be in a queue
(b) Stand next to
(c) Support in difficult situation
(d) Work together

167. Select the most appropriate option that rectifies the error(s) in the following sentence.
One must do his/her duty proparly.
(a) One must do one's duti proprly.
(b) One must do ones duty properly.
(c) One must do one's duty properly.
(d) One must do once duty proparly.

168. Underlined word in the sentence is not spelt correctly. Identify the correct spelling from the options given below.
A congragation of monks reached Shimla for the convention.
(a) Congregetion (b) Cangregation
(c) Congretettion (d) Congregation

169. Select the most appropriate option that can substitute the underlined word in the given sentence.
The culprit had been shot <u>from</u> the back by the police inspector.
(a) to (b) in
(c) by (d) off

170. Select the most appropriate idiom that can substitute the underlined segment in the given sentence.
Read the books of APJ Abdul Kalam, who was <u>a scholar</u>.
(a) a queer fish (b) a man of letters
(c) a dare devil (d) a man of straw

171. Select the most appropriate synonym of the word in brackets to fill in the blank.
Queen Gulnaar of Arabia mourned her .... beauty. (waning)
(a) false (b) frightening
(c) fading (d) futile

172. Identify the most appropriate antonym of the given word.
Summary
(a) Abrupt (b) lengthy
(c) elliptical (d) significant

173. Select the phrase/idiom that will improve the underlined part of the given sentence.
After two hours of wandering in the desert, we realised we were on a <u>wild horse race.</u>
(a) wild goose chase
(b) wild jackal hunt
(c) wild carpet rug
(d) wild shadow chase

174. The following sentence has an error in its tense. Identify the error and select the correct sentence from the given options.
I will be arrange all the necessary materials for the programme.
(a) I was arrange all the necessary materials for the programme.
(b) I would arranging all the necessary materials for the programme.
(c) I is arrange all the necessary materials for the programme.
(d) I will be arranging all the necessary materials for the programme.

175. The following sentence has been divided into four segments. Identify the segment that contains an adverbial usage error.
Mrs. Gomathi was / that tired and weak / that she could / scarcely walk.
(a) Mrs. Gomathi was
(b) that she could
(c) scarcely walk.
(d) that tired and weak

176. Select the most appropriate synonym of the underlined word.
Ramya is an <u>ardent</u> follower of secularism.
(a) committed (b) forced
(c) temporary (d) unhappy

177. Select the option that can be used as a one-word substitute for the given group of words.
A deal of agreement done in a company or firm.
(a) Concurrence (b) Acceptance
(c) Contract (d) Conformity

178. Select the most appropriate option that can substitute the underlined segment in the given sentence.
The author's writing style is characterised by its <u>poetic language.</u>
(a) lyrical language (b) simple language
(c) lucid language (d) prosaic language

179. Select the most appropriate synonym for the given word.
Immune
(a) Resistant (b) Asleep
(c) Variable (d) Safe

180. The following sentence has been split into four segments. Identify the segment that contains a grammatical error.
It is a cheap reasonably / restaurant in this part of the town / where you can eat / delicious food.
(a) delicious food
(b) restaurant in this part of the town
(c) It is a cheap reasonably
(d) where you can eat

181. Select the option that can be used as a one-word substitute for the given group of words.
The act or process of going from the simple or basic to the complex or advanced.
(a) Wither (b) Ennoblement
(c) Evolution (d) Flourishing

182. Select the option that can be used as a one-word substitute for the given group of words.
One who believes in the existence of God.
(a) Fatalist (b) Atheist
(c) Theist (d) Protagonist

183. Based on the situation in the sentence, select the most appropriate idiom for the underlined segment.
After the Pandemic, his business crumbled and he is in a <u>difficult situation</u>.
(a) Bolt from the blue
(b) Give a cold shoulder
(c) Pull the last straw
(d) Be in a tight corner

184. Select the option that can be used as a one-word substitute for the given group of words.
An unpleasant mixture of loud sounds.
(a) Harmony (b) Hegemony
(c) Irony (d) Cacophony

185. Select the incorrectly spelt word.
(a) Cheerfull (b) Tsunami
(c) Efficient (d) Responsibilities

186. Select the most appropriate meaning of the given idiom.
Ignoring his father's warnings, he said, "an elephant in the room" to his mother.
(a) The elephant got stuck in the room
(b) There is an obvious problem
(c) Someone begins to suspect
(d) Someone hiding in the room

187. Select the option that can be used as a one-word substitute for the given group of words.
A story intended to teach moral lessons
(a) Parboil (b) Parable
(c) Parole (d) Parasite

188. Select the most appropriate antonym of the given word.
Mighty
(a) Weak (b) Forcible
(c) Forceful (d) Haughty

189. Select the incorrectly spelt word in the given sentence.
The islands of Japan were connected to the Asian landmass about 12,000 years ago; the first Japanese travelled across the water in serch of animals to hunt.
(a) Landmass (b) Serch
(c) Connected (d) Islands

190. Select the option that can be used as a one-word substitute for the given group of words.
Feeling of being in a place before having already experienced the present situation
(a) Deja-vu (b) Illusion
(c) Spirituality (d) Delusion

Directions (Q. Nos. 191-195) *In the following passage, some words have been deleted. Read the passage carefully and select the most appropriate option to fill in each blank.*

A series of ...(1)... of shell or ivory or thin metal clothed her left upper arm all the way down to her fingers. A necklace ...(2)... three pendants bunched together and a few bangles above the elbow and ...(3)... on the right hands display an almost modern art. She speaks of the ...(4)..., ever hopeful human spirit. She reminds us that it is important to visit museums in our country to experience the ...(5)... that a work of art leaves on our senses, to find among all the riches one particular vision of beauty that speaks to us alone.

191. Select the most appropriate option to fill in blank no. 1.
(a) bangles (b) toe-rings
(c) anklets (d) ear-rings

192. Select the most appropriate option to fill in blank no. 2.
(a) by (b) with (c) upon (d) in

193. Select the most appropriate option to fill in blank no. 3.
(a) toe (b) wrist (c) waist (d) ankle

194. Select the most appropriate option to fill in blank no. 4.
(a) unbelievable (b) ungrateful
(c) unsafe (d) undaunted

195. Select the most appropriate option to fill in blank no. 5.
(a) affect (b) result
(c) blow (d) impact

Directions (Q. Nos. 196-200) *Read the given passage and answer the questions that follow.*

Every minute, the equivalent of one garbage trucks worth of plastic is dumped into our ocean. Plastic pollution is a global problem. Approximately 7 billion of the 9.2 billion metric tonnes of plastic produced from 1950-2017 became plastic waste, ending up in landfills or being dumped. Plastic pollution can alter habitats and natural processes, reducing ecosystems ability to adapt to climate change, directly affecting millions of livelihoods, food production capabilities and social well-being.

UNEPs body of work demonstrates that the problem of plastic pollution doesn't exist in a vacuum. The environmental, social, economic and health risks of plastics need to be assessed alongside other environmental stressors, like climate change, ecosystem degradation and resource use

196. Which of the following is the best description of the tone of the passage?
(a) Populist (b) Laudatory
(c) Informative (d) Patronising

197. Which of the following represents the structure of the passage?
(a) Definition (b) Sequence
(c) Cause-effect (d) Time order

198. Select the most appropriate antonym of the given word.
Exist
(a) Prevail (b) Cease
(c) Imprint (d) Resent

199. Which of the following most accurately states the main idea of the passage?
(a) Plastic pollution (b) Climate change
(c) Plastic waste (d) UNEP

200. Select the most appropriate antonym of the given word.
Alter
(a) Alight (b) Change
(c) Preserve (d) Absorb

Know Correct Answers

1. (b)	2. (c)	3. (b)	4. (c)	5. (b)	6. (d)	7. (c)	8. (c)	9. (b)	10. (b)
11. (a)	12. (b)	13. (a)	14. (a)	15. (d)	16. (c)	17. (d)	18. (d)	19. (d)	20. (a)
21. (b)	22. (a)	23. (c)	24. (d)	25. (c)	26. (b)	27. (d)	28. (a)	29. (c)	30. (a)
31. (b)	32. (b)	33. (b)	34. (d)	35. (d)	36. (a)	37. (c)	38. (a)	39. (d)	40. (b)
41. (d)	42. (a)	43. (d)	44. (c)	45. (a)	46. (c)	47. (b)	48. (c)	49. (d)	50. (d)
51. (a)	52. (b)	53. (c)	54. (c)	55. (d)	56. (d)	57. (a)	58. (c)	59. (a)	60. (b)
61. (c)	62. (b)	63. (b)	64. (a)	65. (c)	66. (b)	67. (c)	68. (a)	69. (d)	70. (a)
71. (d)	72. (b)	73. (c)	74. (b)	75. (d)	76. (c)	77. (a)	78. (d)	79. (d)	80. (b)
81. (c)	82. (a)	83. (d)	84. (a)	85. (b)	86. (a)	87. (a)	88. (d)	89. (b)	90. (b)
91. (c)	92. (d)	93. (a)	94. (b)	95. (b)	96. (d)	97. (d)	98. (c)	99. (a)	100. (a)
101. (a)	102. (d)	103. (c)	104. (c)	105. (a)	106. (a)	107. (d)	108. (c)	109. (d)	110. (d)
111. (c)	112. (d)	113. (c)	114. (a)	115. (a)	116. (d)	117. (d)	118. (d)	119. (c)	120. (d)
121. (c)	122. (c)	123. (d)	124. (b)	125. (b)	126. (a)	127 (b)	128. (d)	129. (b)	130. (c)
131. (a)	132. (b)	133. (d)	134. (b)	135. (c)	136. (b)	137 (c)	138. (c)	139. (b)	140. (c)
141. (a)	142. (b)	143. (b)	144. (a)	145. (d)	146. (d)	147. (b)	148. (b)	149. (c)	150. (b)
151. (a)	152. (c)	153. (c)	154. (d)	155. (a)	156. (b)	157. (d)	158. (c)	159. (c)	160. (c)
161. (a)	162. (d)	163. (c)	164. (d)	165. (d)	166. (c)	167. (c)	168. (d)	169. (b)	170. (b)
171. (c)	172. (b)	173. (a)	174. (d)	175. (d)	176. (a)	177. (c)	178. (a)	179. (a)	180. (c)
181. (c)	182. (c)	183. (d)	184. (d)	185. (a)	186. (b)	187. (b)	188. (a)	189. (b)	190. (a)
191. (a)	192. (b)	193. (b)	194. (d)	195. (d)	196. (c)	197. (c)	198. (b)	199. (a)	200. (c)

Answer & Solutions

1. (b) According to the question ,

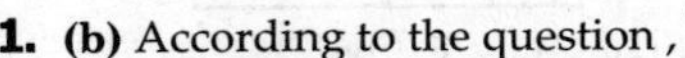

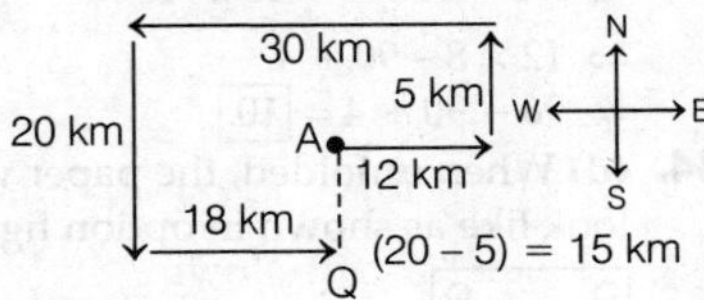

∴ He will drive 15 km towards North to reach point A again.

2. (c) According to the Venn diagram,

(Women (Pilots) Father)

Some women and some father are pilots.

3. (b) As,

H A N D
–1 –2 –1 –2
G Y M B

and

F O O D
–1 –2 –1 –2
E M N B

Similarly,

T E X T
–1 –2 –1 –2
S C W R

4. (c) Given equation,

$5 + 156 - 12 \times 15 \div 15 = 185$

From option (c),

After interchanging '+' and '–' ,we get

$5 + 156 \div 12 \times 15 - 15$

[on applying BODMAS rule]

$\Rightarrow 5 + 195 - 15$

$\Rightarrow 200 - 15 = \boxed{185}$

5. (b) According to the question,

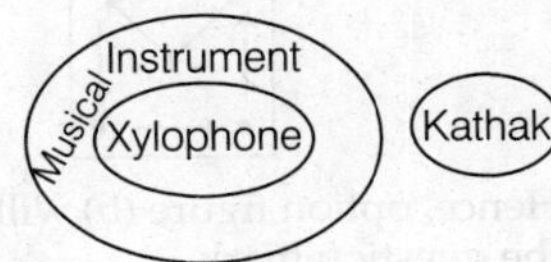

As, xylophone is the music instrument, whereas kathak is dance.

6. (d) As per the english dictionary,

Elastic → Elate → Elbow → Election →
(4) (1) (3) (2)
Electoral
(5)

⇒ 4,1,3,2,5

7. (c) Given equation,

$P + Q - R \times S \div T$

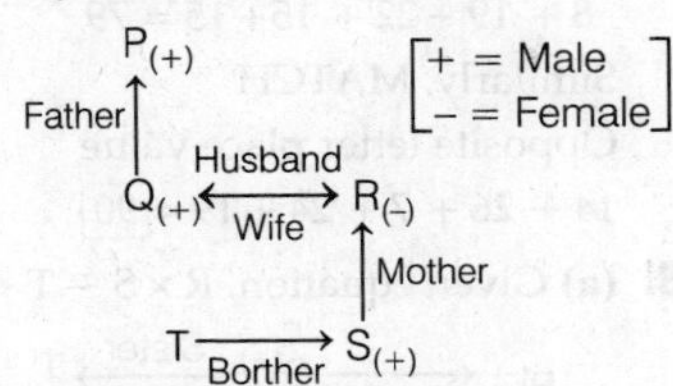

∴ P is Father's of Father T.

8. (c) Given equation,

16 * 17 * 14 * 2 * 3 * 251

From option (c),

$16 \times 17 - 14 \div 2 \times 3 = 251$

$\Rightarrow \quad 272 - 21 = 251$

9. (b) As,

P U R E
Opposite letters K F I V
–2 –2 –2 –2
I D G T

and

C O O L
Opposite letters X L L O
–2 –2 –2 –2
V J J M

Similarly,

L I P S
Opposite letters O R K H
–2 –2 –2 –2
M P I F

10. (b) As,

FAVORITE → ETIROVAF
12345678 87654321

and

MINIMIZE → EZIMINIM
12345678 87654321

Similarly,

RESEMBLE → ELBMESER
12345678 87654321

11. (a) As,

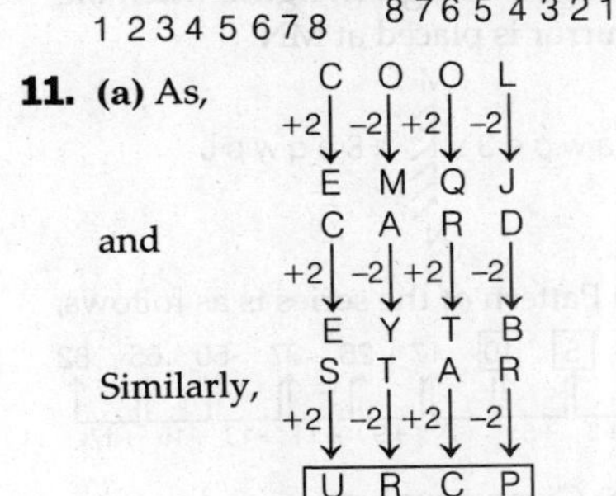

12. (b) Here, 9 is common in both positions of given dice.

Now, write the remaining number of each position in clockwise direction.

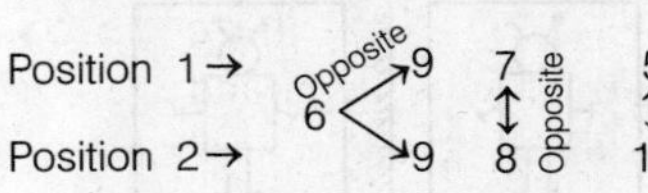

Position 1 → 6 Opposite 9, 7 ↕ 8 Opposite, 5 ↕ 10 Opposite
Position 2 → 9

Hence, 9 is opposite to face 6.

13. (a) As per the figure, option (a) is the correct mirror image as shown in figure placed at MN.

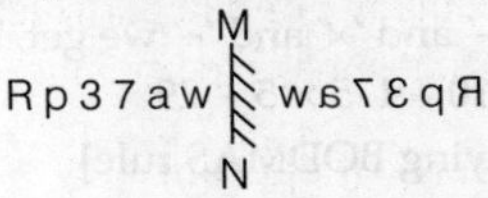

14. (a) As, 36 : 70

$36 - 1 = 35 \times 2 = 70$

and 41 : 80

$41 - 1 = 40 \times 2 = 80$

Similarly, 39 : 76

$\boxed{39} - 1 = 38 \times 2 = 76$

15. (d) Figure (X) is embedded in figure given in option (d).

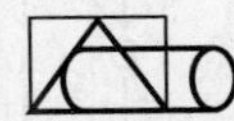

16. (c) As, (108, 27, 9)

$\Rightarrow 9 \times 3 = 27; 9 \times 12 = 108$

and (132, 33, 11)

$\Rightarrow \quad 11 \times 3 = 33; 11 \times 12 = 132$

Similarly, (180, 45, 15)

$\Rightarrow \quad 15 \times 3 = 45; 15 \times 12 = 180$

17. (d) Option (d) is the correct mirror image of the given figure when the mirror is placed at MN.

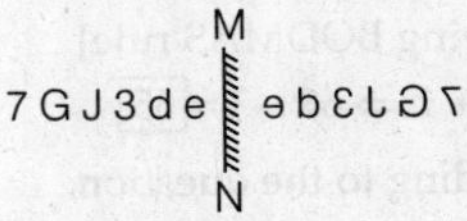

18. (d) Given equation,

70 D 11 B 5 C 45 A 9 = ?

After interchanging the signs, we get

A ⇒ ÷	C ⇒ +
B ⇒ ×	D ⇒ –

$\Rightarrow 70 - 11 \times 5 + 45 \div 9$

[on applying BODMAS rule]

$\Rightarrow 70 - 55 + 5 \Rightarrow 75 - 55 = \boxed{20}$

19. **(d)** Given equation, $5 - 18 + 12 = ?$
After interchanging signs and numbers, '+' and '–' and '5' and '18', we get, $18 + 5 - 12 \Rightarrow 23 - 12 = \boxed{11}$

20. **(a)** Option (a) is the correct mirror image of the given figure when the mirror is placed at MN.

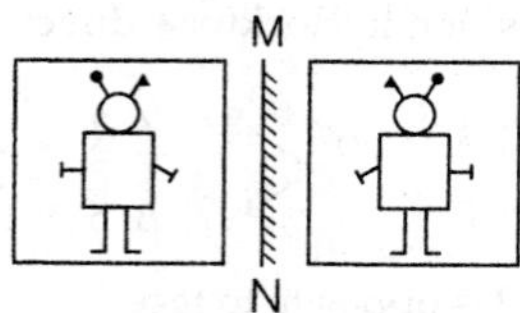

21. **(b)** Given equation,
$110 \times 10 - 175 \div 5 + 29 = ?$
After interchanging the signs, '+' and '–' and '×' and '÷' we get,
$\Rightarrow 110 \div 10 + 175 \times 5 - 29$
[On applying BODMAS rule]
$\Rightarrow 11 + 875 - 29$
$\Rightarrow 886 - 29 = \boxed{857}$

22. **(a)** In the figure series, left side symbol move right side and change the size in next box and new element is add in next box on the left side.
Hence, option (a) is the answer.

23. **(c)** Pattern of the series is as follows,

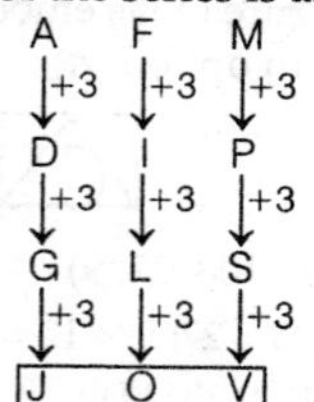

24. **(d)** Given equation,
$9 + 7 \times 15 - 5 \div 5 = ?$
After interchanging the signs, we get

$+ \Rightarrow \times$	$- \Rightarrow \div$
$\times \Rightarrow -$	$\div \Rightarrow +$

$\Rightarrow 9 \times 7 - 15 \div 5 + 5$
[On applying BODMAS rule]
$\Rightarrow 63 - 3 + 5 \Rightarrow 68 - 3 = \boxed{65}$

25. **(c)** According to the question,

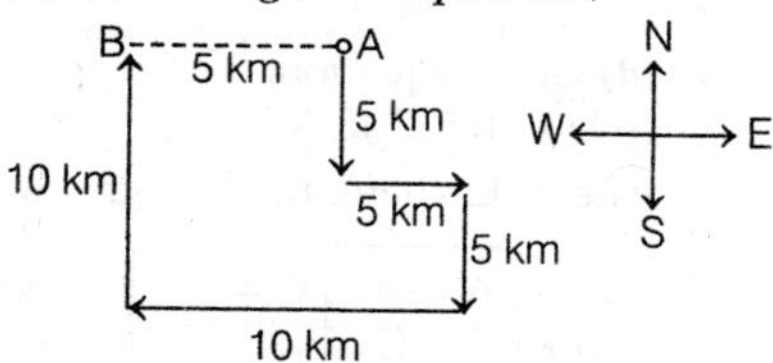

∴ He will drive 5 km towards East direction to reach point A again.

26. **(b)** Pattern of the series is as follows,

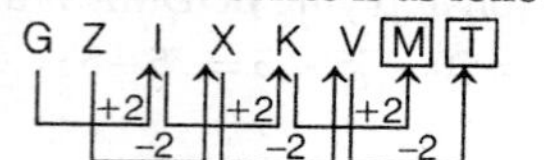

27. **(d)** As, HELLO = 83
Opposite letter place value
$19 + 22 + 15 + 15 + 12 = 83$
and SHELL = 79
Opposite letter place value
$8 + 19 + 22 + 15 + 15 = 79$
Similarly, MATCH
Opposite letter place value
$14 + 26 + 7 + 24 + 19 = \boxed{90}$

28. **(a)** Given equation, $R \times S - T \div P + V$

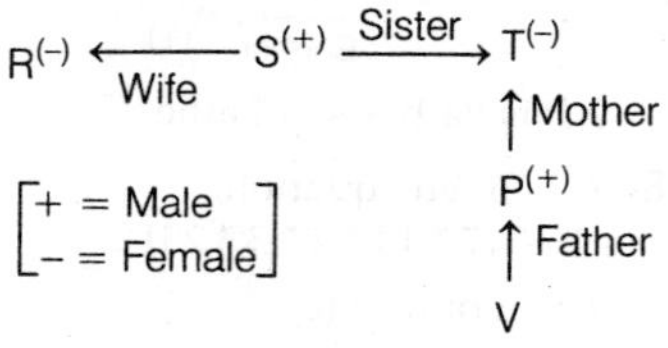

$R^{(-)} \xleftarrow{\text{Wife}} S^{(+)} \xrightarrow{\text{Sister}} T^{(-)}$
↑ Mother
$P^{(+)}$
↑ Father
V

[+ = Male
– = Female]

∴ T is father's of father V.

29. **(c)** As,

W	H	I	L	E
23	8	9	12	5
–2	–2	–2	–2	–2
21	6	7	10	3

and

D	E	P	T	H
4	5	16	20	8
–2	–2	–2	–2	–2
2	3	14	18	6

Similarly,

R	O	U	N	D
18	15	21	14	4
–2	–2	–2	–2	–2
16	13	19	12	2

30. **(a)** According to the statements,

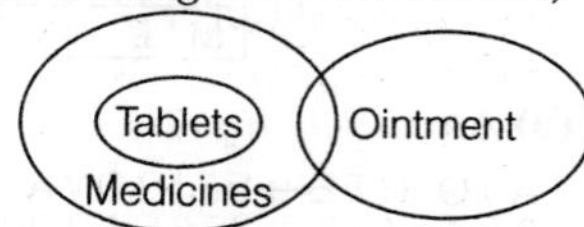

Conclusions
I. (✗) II. (✗)
Hence, neither Conclusion I nor II follows.

31. **(b)** Option (b) is the correct mirror image of the given figure when the mirror is placed at MN.

M
Jawpe3s | ƨƐǝqwɒ˥
N

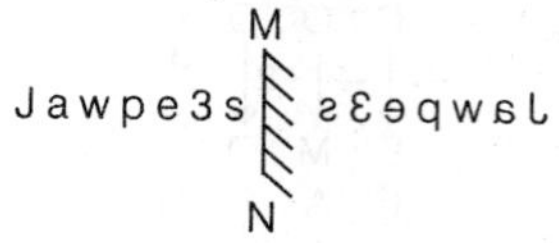

32. **(b)** Pattern of the series is as follows,

2 $\boxed{5}$ $\boxed{10}$ 17 26 37 50 65 82
+3 +5 +7 +9 +11 +13 +15 +17

33. **(b)** Given equation,
$168 \times 14 - 8 + 90 \div 4$

After interchanging the signs, we get,

$+ \Rightarrow -$	$- \Rightarrow \times$
$\times \Rightarrow \div$	$\div \Rightarrow +$

$\Rightarrow 168 \div 14 \times 8 - 90 + 4$
$\Rightarrow 12 \times 8 - 90 + 4$
$\Rightarrow 96 - 90 + 4 = \boxed{10}$

34. **(d)** When unfolded, the paper will look like as shown in option figure(d).

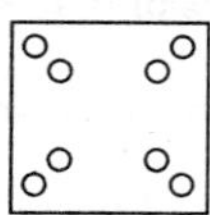

35. **(d)** As per the english dictionary order,
Faith → Feign → Ferment →
(4) (5) (6)
Ferocious → Fervor → Fiction
(1) (2) (3)
⇒ 4,5,6,1,2,3

36. **(a)** In the given series, symbols rotates corner to corner in anti-clockwise direction and symbol 'O' in the center.
Hence, option (a) will replace the question mark.

37. **(c)** Pattern of the series is as follows,

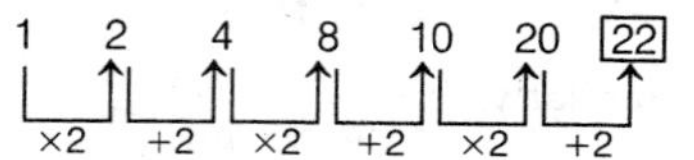

38. **(a)** Pattern of the series is as follows,

31 33 37 43 51 $\boxed{61}$
+2 +4 +6 +8 +10

39. **(d)** As, $G \xrightarrow{+4} K \xrightarrow{-2} I$
$M \xrightarrow{+4} Q \xrightarrow{-2} O$
$C \xrightarrow{+4} G \xrightarrow{-2} E$
But, $K \xrightarrow{+4} O \xrightarrow{\boxed{-1}} N$

40. **(b)** In the given figure series, pattern is followed.

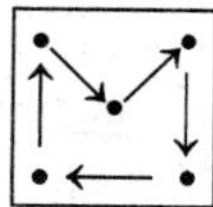

Hence, option figure (b) will replace the question mark.

41. **(d)** As,

F	R	E	E
+1	+2	+3	+4
G	T	H	I

and

G	A	P	S
+1	+2	+3	+4
H	C	S	W

Similarly,

S	O	A	R
+1	+2	+3	+4
T	Q	D	V

42. **(a)** As, 40 – 9

$\Rightarrow \quad 40 \times 9 = 360$

Similarly, 90 – 4

$\Rightarrow \quad 90 \times 4 = 360$

43. **(d)** Pattern of the series is as follows,

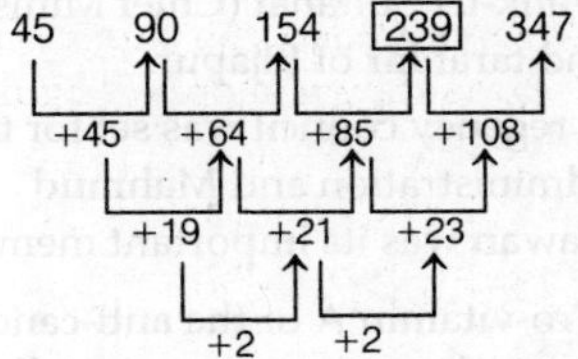

44. **(c)** Here, 24 is common in both positions of given dice.

Now, write the remaining number of each position in clockwise direction.

Position 1 → 24 8 20

Position 2 → 24 12 4

Common Opposite Opposite

Hence, 24 is opposite to face 16.

45. **(a)** According to the question,

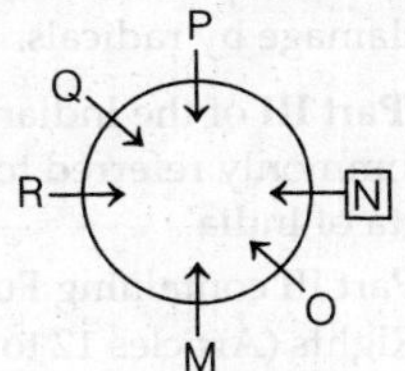

∴ N is sitting second to the right of M.

46. **(c)** As, 144 12 24

÷12 ×2

and 216 18 36

÷12 ×2

Similarly, 324 27 54

÷12 ×2

47. **(b)** According to the question,

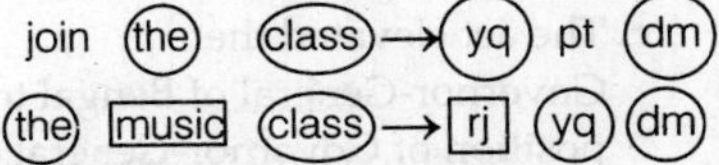

Hence, music is coded as rj.

48. **(c)** Pattern of the series is as follows,

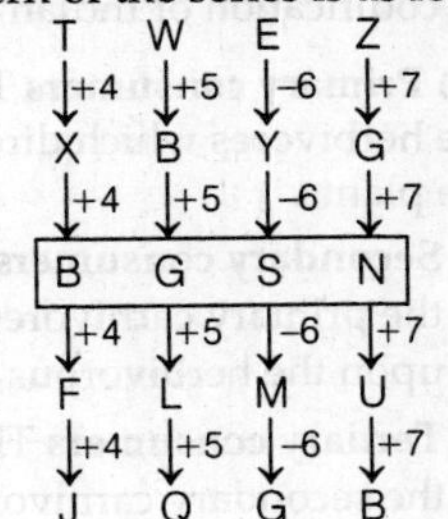

49. **(d)** According to the statement,

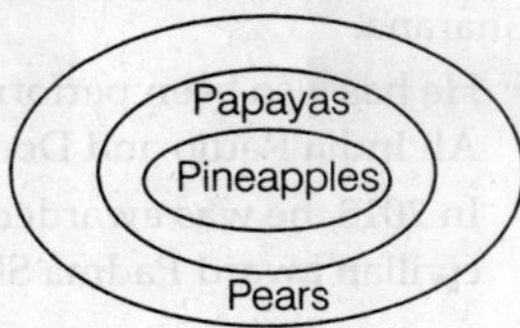

Conclusions

I. (✓) II. (✓)

Hence, both Conclusions I and II follow.

50. **(d)** As, 76 152 38

×2 ÷4

and 84 168 42

×2 ÷4

Similarly, 68 136 34

×2 ÷4

51. **(a)** Ernst Haeckel used the Greek term **Oekologie** in 1866 to refer 'the relation of animals to both the organic as well as the inorganic environment'.

- The word comes from the Greek oikos, meaning 'household', 'home' or 'place to live'. Thus, ecology deals with the organism and its environment.
- The concept of environment includes both other organisms and physical surroundings.

52. **(b)** The depositional pattern of $CaCO_3$ and other materials that extend upwards from the floor of a limestone cavern is known as stalagmite.

- The columns of dripstones hanging from the cave ceiling are called **stalactites.**
- The calcareous columns of dripstones growing upward from the cave floor are known as **stalagmites.**

53. **(c)** Fundamental Duties of the Indian Constitution are mentioned in **Article 51A.**

- The Swaran Singh Committee in 1976 recommended Fundamental Duties.
- The 42nd Amendment Act of 1976 added 10 Fundamental Duties to the Indian Constitution.
- The 86th Amendment Act, 2002 later added the 11th Fundamental Duty to the list.

54. **(c)** Thiyam Suryamukhi Devi who received the Sangeet Natak Akademi Awards 2003, is known for her contribution to the **Manipuri dance.**

- She was among the earliest Manipuri dancers to be part of an Indian cultural delegation visiting other countries in the 1950s.
- Manipuri dance is an Indian classical dance practised in North-East India.
- Ras, Sankirtana and Thang-Ta (war dance) are the popular forms of Manipuri dance.
- Radha, Krishna and Gopis are the main characters in Manipuri dance.
- 'Pung' or 'Dhol' is used as the main instrument in Manipuri dance.

55. **(d)** There is rivalrous consumption of **private goods.**

- Private goods are those goods whose ownership is restricted to the group or individual that purchased the good for their own consumption.
- A private good is not shared with anybody else, but can be sold along with transferring rights to use or consume it.

56. **(d)** As per the Census of India 2011, there is **25.51%** national female workforce participation rate.

- The national male workforce participation rate is 53.26%.
- Rural sector has a better female workforce participation rate of 30.02% compared with 53.03% for males whereas for the urban sector.

57. **(a)** **Darshana Jhaveri** is a Padma Shri Awardee for her contribution to Manipuri dance.

- She is a renowned Manipuri dancer.
- She has been awarded with the Padma Shri in 2007 for her contribution to with the field of dance.

58. **(c)** **Birju Maharaj** was born into a well-known Kathak dancing family.

- Birju Maharaj is a Padma Vibhushan awardee in 1986, belongs to Kalka- Bindadin Gharana of Kathak (community of musicians sharing a distinctive musical style) of Lucknow.

59. **(a)** Vasanta (Spring), Grishma (Summer), Varsha (Monsoon), Sharad (Autumn), Hemanta (pre-winter) and Shishira (winter) are names of traditional season in India. These seasons are also called as **Ritu**.

60. **(b)** The tropical evergreen forests is found in the Western Ghats.
- Tropical evergreen forests are found in regions where temperature is very high and rainfall is also very high.
- It is found on the Western slopes of the Western Ghats, the islands of Lakshadweep, Andaman and Nicobar, North-East India and some parts of the Tamil Nadu coast.

61. **(c)** Ghumura is not associated with **Goa**.
- Ghumura dance is famous in the Kalahandi district of Odisha.
- It is classified as folk dance of Odisha.
- The tribals of Kalahandi mainly perform this dance during religious and traditional festivals like Nuakhai or Dussehara.

62. **(b)** In 1905, Forest Moulton with Thomas Chamberlain concluded that the planets of the solar system originated from an encounter between the Sun and another star.
- It is an important theory to understand the formation of the solar system.

63. **(b)** Naphthalene is the name of the aromatic compound in the given figure.
- The naphthalene is a bicyclic compound having two benzene rings joint at one-two positions.
- According to Huckle rule, if naphthalene is an aromatic compound it should posses $(4n+2)\pi$ electrons delocalised in the ring.

64. **(a)** Top-most layer in a thermally stratified lake is the characteristics of epilimnion.
- The warmer upper layer of a lake is known as epilimnion. Between Epilimnetic Hypolimnetic layers is the metalimnion, a zone of rapid temperature change.
- The hypolimnion or under lake is the dense, bottom layer of water in a thermally stratified lake.

65. **(c)** **Vijay Kichlu** belongs to the Agra Gharana.
- He has also been performing over All India Radio and Doordarshan.
- In 2018, he was awarded with the civilian award Padma Shri.

66. **(b)** Charter of Fundamental Rights, has been adopted from the Constitution of the **United States of America**.
- Fundamental rights are basic rights provided to the people in order to live with dignity and integrity.
- They are enshrined in Part III of the Indian Constitution.

67. **(c)** **Article 141** of the Indian Constitution mentions that the law declared by the Supreme Court shall be binding on all the courts within the territory of India.
- Supreme Court is highest Court in India.
- **Article 137** It grants the Supreme Court the power to review any of its judgement or orders.
- **Article 147** It focuses on the interpretation of the Constitution particularly in the context of Chapter IV and Chapter V of Part-VI.
- **Article 151** It outlines the procedure of submitting and presenting the audit reports of the CAG to the President and the Governor.

68. **(a)** Statement A and D are incorrect regarding the islands of India.
- Lakshadweep islands are composed of coral islands.
- It is believed that Andaman and Nicobar islands are an elevated portion of submarine mountains.

69. **(d)** 'A Life Apart' is an autobiography of **Prabha Khaitan**.
- Prabha Khaitan writer of her feeling, her sense of discomfort and unease at not being the legitimate woman.
- She founded a company **Eigurette**.

70. **(a)** The 12th edition of the Ice Hockey Association of India's (IHAI) National Ice Hockey Championship for Men (2023) was organised in Ladakh.
- The central ice hockey team of the Indo-Tibetan Border Police (ITBP) has won the 12th edition.

71. **(d)** Mahmud Gawan was granted the title of 'Chief of the Merchants' or Malik-ut-Tujjar by the Bahamani ruler, Humayun Shah.
- The sudden death of Humayun led to the coronation of his minor son Ahmad III as Sultan.
- He was also appointed as Walik-us-Sultanat (Chief Minister) and tarafdar of Bijapur.
- A regency council was set for the administration and Mahmud Gawan was its important member.

72. **(b)** Pro-vitamin A or the anti-cancer compound present in carrots called Beta-carotene.
- Beta-carotene is a carotenoid, a natural precursor of vitamin A obtained from various fruits and vegetables like orange, green leafy vegetables, tomatoes, spinach, etc., with antineoplastic potential and chemopreventive activity.
- This carotenoid is an antioxidant that is capable of inhibiting DNA damage by radicals.

73. **(c)** **Part III** of the Indian Constitution is commonly referred to as the 'Magna Carta of India'.
- Part III containing Fundamental Rights (Articles 12 to 35) is described as the Magna Carta of India.
- Magna Carta is the Charter of rights issued by King John of England.
- It is the first written document on the Fundamental Rights of the citizens.

74. **(b)** Under the Charter Act of 1833 in British India, the East India Company's monopoly on trade with China was abolished.
- The act elevated the Governor-General of Bengal to the position of Governor-General of India.
- It established a law commission for codification of Indian laws.

75. **(d)** **Primary consumers** These include the herbivores which directly eat upon the plants.
- **Secondary consumers** It includes the primary carnivores that eat upon the herbivorous animals.
- **Tertiary consumers** These include the secondary carnivores that eat upon secondary consumers.

- **Quaternary consumers** It includes the tertiary or top carnivores that eat upon the tertiary consumers.
- **Microconsumers** These are also called decomposers or saprotrophs or reducers that break down the complex organic compounds of dead bodies of both plants and animals, e.g., bacteria.

76. (c) The term 'Libero' is used in volleyball.
Player on an indoor volleyball team who serves as a defensive specialist.
- It is not allowed to serve or rotate to the front line.
- Volleyball is a team sport where two teams of six players are separated by a net.
- It has been a part of the official programme of the Summer Olympics Games since 1964.

77. (a) The height of the stump from the ground in cricket is **28 inch**.
- The stumps are three vertical posts which support two bails.
- The stumps and bails are usually made of wood, most commonly ash and together form a wicket at each end of the pitch.
- The small wooden pieces that sit on top of the stumps are called bails, they are 4.37 inches long.

78. (d) Onam is a harvest festival, primarily celebrated in Kerala.
- It is a harvest festival celebrated by Malayalis that falls on the 22nd Nakshatra Thiruvonam in the month Chingam of the Malayalam calendar, which coincides with August- September in the Gregorian calendar.

79. (d) Industrial sector promotes modernisation and stable employment in the economy.
- Hence, five-year plans focused on the development of the industrial sector in India.
- It aimed to expand the industrial base with a variety of industries for economic growth after Independence.

80. (b) Ghiyas-ud-Din Balban started the ceremony of 'Sijda' (prostration) and 'Paibos' (kissing of the monarch's feet), in the court.
- He introduced the festival of Nauroz.
- Balban appointed spies who were called 'Diwan-i-Barid'.
- The adopted by Balban was 'Zil-i-illahi'(Shadow of God).

81. (c) In 1856, the annexation of Awadh by Lord Dalhousie took place.
- According to Lord Dalhousie's Doctrine Lapse, the first state to be annexed was Satara.
- In 1856 AD, accusing Oudh of misrule, the Resident Outram of Lucknow got Awadh merged with the British Empire.
- At that time the Nawab of Awadh was 'Wajid Ali Shah'.

82. (a) As of June 2023, Indira Gandhi International Airport was India's largest airport in terms of total passengers.
- Indira Gandhi International Airport is the largest International Airport.
- It is also the busiest airport in India followed by the Chhatrapati Shivaji International Airport.

83. (d) Jasprit Bumrah is the highest run scorer in an over in a test match cricket.
- Bumrah is the fastest Indian pacer to take 150 wickets in test cricket and the second fastest Indian bowler to reach 100 wickets in One Day International (ODI) cricket.
- He is the first bowler to have achieved the number one ranking in the ICC men's player rankings in all three formats of the game.

84. (a) Reserve ratio and money supply have a negative relationship.
- Reserve ratio is the amount of money banks must keep on hand as cash.
- There exists an inverse relationship between the required reserve ratio and the money supply such that as the required reserve ratio rises then money supply falls and as the required reserve ratio falls then money supply rises.

85. (b) The outermost shell of halogen has seven electrons.
- They lie in the 17th group before inert gas. For example, the atomic number of fluorine is 9.
- Its electronic configuration is 2, 7.

86. (a) Dibrugarh-Kanyakumari is the longest train route in India.
- Its runs from Dibrugarh in India's North-Eastern state Assam to Kanyakumari in Tamil Nadu the Southern most state of India.
- The train covers a distance of 4189 kilometres and traverses through nine states in India.

87. (a) 'Sare Jahan Se Achha Hindustan Hamara' was written by **Muhammad Iqbal**.
- It was published in the weekly journal Ittehad on 16th August, 1904.
- It is included in Iqbal's work 'Bang-e-Dara'.

88. (d) The full form of 'PM-SYM' is Pradhan Mantri Shram Yogi Maandhan.
- It ensure old age protection for unorganised workers at the entry age of 18 to 40 years with a maximum monthly income of ₹15,000 or less.

89. (b) Pandit Vishnu Narayan Bhatkhande is known for his contribution to the field of Hindustani music for the classification of Ragas into ten Thaats.

90. (b) All the given statments i.e., A, B and C are correct regarding the conditions required to recognise as a political party in India.
- If a political party is treated as a recognised political party in four or more states, it shall be known as a 'National Party' throughout the whole of India.
- If a political party is treated as a recognised political party in less than four states, it shall be known as a 'State Party' in the State or States in which it is so recognised.
- National parties need only one proposer for filing the nomination and are also entitled for two sets of electoral rolls free of cost.

91. (c) Statement (c) is correct regarding Green revolution.
- Introduced high-yielding variety seeds in Indian agriculture.
- The HYV seeds were highly effective in regions that had rich irrigation facilities and were more successful with the wheat crop.
- It emphasised food grains such as wheat and rice.

- The Green revolution increased the availability and use of fertilisers, weedicides and pesticides to reduce any damage or loss to the crops.
- The introduction of machinery and technology like harvesters, drills, tractors, etc.

92. (d) There are 10 Mandalas in Rigveda Samhita.

- The Rigveda Samhita contains about 10552 Mantras.
- The first and tenth Mandalas are the youngest and the longest.
- The 10th mandala contains the Purusha Sukta which explains the 4 Varnas that were born from the mouth, arms, thighs and feet of the Brahma or Purusha.

93. (a) Hydrogen electronic configuration is $1s^1$,so the K-shell contains only one electron.

- The atomic structure defines how electrons revolve around the nucleus.
- The closest shell to nucleus is called the first shell or K-shell and each shell can accommodate maximum of two electrons.

94. (b) A=1C/s is used for determining the value of 1 ampere.

- Where 'C' is the unit of electric charge and 'S' is the unit of time.
- 1 ampere is defined as the current that flows with electric charge of 1 coulomb per second.
- Ampere or amp is the unit of electrical current.

95. (b) Liberalisation of import licensing is a feature of globalisation.

- It relaxed the rules and regulations for performing trade between countries.
- It allows more freedom and exposure to the countries and thereby promotes development of trade, technology and improving foreign investment.

96. (d) Article 175 of the Indian Constitution mentions the right of the Governor to address.

- He can addressed House (or Houses) of the State Legislature or both Houses to assembled together and may for that purpose require the attendance of members.

97. (d) Ambubachi fair is celebrated in **Assam.**

- It is the most important festival of the Kamakhya temple.
- It is believed that Goddess Kamakhya goes through the annual cycle of menstruation during this time.

98. (c) Bhajan Sopori, a Padma Shri awardee, is a santoor player.

- He belonged to the Sufiana Gharana of Indian classical music.
- Sopori was awarded with the Sangeet Natak Akademi Award in 1992, the Padma Shri in 2004 and in 2009 he was honoured with the Baba Allauddin Khan Award.

99. (a) Truth, Love and a Little Malice is the autobiography of **Khushwant Singh**.

- He is a famous Indian writer, journalist and columnist who is also a qualified Barrister from the King's College, London.

100. (a) Chloroform compound is used in the production of the freon refrigerant R-22.

- R-22 refrigerant is one the most commonly used refrigerant in the air conditioning systems.

101. (a)

In ΔBCE and ΔAED,

$\angle C = \angle A$ (90°)

$\angle BEC = \angle AED$ (vertically opposite angles)

$\therefore \angle CBE = \angle ADE$

So, $\Delta BCE \sim \Delta AED$

$$\therefore \frac{8}{x} = \frac{12}{18}$$

$$\Rightarrow x = 12 \text{ cm}$$

102. (d) Let fourth proportional to 10, 12 and 15 be x.

$$\frac{10}{12} = \frac{15}{x}$$

$$\Rightarrow x = \frac{15 \times 12}{10}$$

$$\Rightarrow x = \frac{180}{10}$$

$$\Rightarrow x = 18$$

103. (c) Total surface area of hemisphere

$$= 3\pi r^2$$

$$= 3 \times \pi \times (11)^2 = 3 \times \pi \times 121$$

$$= 363\ \pi \text{ cm}^2$$

104. (c) $5 \times [14 \div 13 \times \{13 \times 14 \div (14 \times 14)\}]$

$$= 5 \times \left[14 \div 13 \times \left\{\frac{13}{14}\right\}\right]$$

$$= 5 \times \left[\frac{14}{13} \times \frac{13}{14}\right]$$

$$= 5 \times 1 = 5$$

105. (a) Let the winner get x votes and his rival get $(x - 410)$ votes.

So, total number of votes

$$= x + x - 410 + 60$$

$$= (2x - 350) \quad \ldots(i)$$

10% of voters did not cast their vote.

Hence, total number of listed voters

$$= (2x - 350) \times \frac{100}{90}$$

$$= \frac{20x - 3500}{9}$$

Now, winner got

$$x = 46\% \text{ of } \left(\frac{20x - 3500}{9}\right)$$

$$\Rightarrow 900x = 920x - 161000$$

$$x = 8050$$

Now, total listed voters

$$= \frac{20x - 3500}{9}$$

$$= \frac{(20 \times 8050) - 3500}{9} = 17500$$

106. (a) According to the table, the company produces 25 scooters of each type in the month of January.

107. (d) Let the efficiency of Suresh be 1.

$\therefore$ Efficiency of Arvind = 4

Now, total work = 20

$\therefore$ Time taken by Arvind and Suresh to finish the work together

$$= \frac{20}{(4 + 1)} = \frac{20}{5} = 4 \text{ days}$$

108. (c) We know that,

$$\text{Length of an arc} = 2\pi r \times \frac{\theta}{360°}$$

Now, radius (r) = 35 cm

And $\theta = 72°$

$\therefore$ Length of the arc

$$= 2 \times \frac{22}{7} \times 35 \times \frac{72}{360°}$$

$$= 2 \times 22 \times 5 \times \frac{1}{5} = 44 \text{ cm}$$

109. (d) Let, $\alpha = 1, \beta = -1$ and $\gamma = 0$

Then, $\frac{3\beta^2 + \alpha^2 + \gamma^2}{2\beta^2 - \alpha\gamma}$

$= \frac{3(-1)^2 + (1)^2 + 0}{2(-1)^2 - 1 \times 0}$

$= \frac{3+1}{2} = \frac{4}{2} = 2$

110. (d) Total money (in degrees) spent on Tennis + Basketball = 35° + 40° = 75°

Total money (in degrees) spent on Hockey + Cricket = 94° + 135° = 229°

∴ Required percentage

$= \frac{75}{229} \times 100 = 32.75\%$

111. (c) $\operatorname{cosec}\theta(1-\cos\theta)(\operatorname{cosec}\theta + \cot\theta)$

$= \operatorname{cosec}\theta(1-\cos\theta)\left(\frac{1}{\sin\theta} + \frac{\cos\theta}{\sin\theta}\right)$

$= \frac{1}{\sin\theta}(1-\cos\theta)\left(\frac{1+\cos\theta}{\sin\theta}\right)$

$= (1-\cos\theta)(1+\cos\theta) \times \frac{1}{\sin^2\theta}$

$= \frac{1-\cos^2\theta}{\sin^2\theta} = \frac{\sin^2\theta}{\sin^2\theta} = 1$

112. (d) $9^{18} \div 3^{14}$ of $27^3 \times \sqrt{6561}$

$= (3^2)^{18} \div (3)^{14}$ of $(3^3)^3 \times 81$

$= (3)^{36} \div (3)^{14}$ of $(3)^9 \times (3)^4$

$= (3)^{36} \div (3)^{23} \times (3)^4$

$= (3)^{13} \times (3)^4 = (3)^{17}$

113. (c) Let the cost price (CP) be ₹100.

∴ Marked price (MP) = ₹135

Now, Discount = 15%

∴ MP × 85% = SP

⇒ $135 \times \frac{85}{100} = SP$

SP = ₹114.75

∴ Profit % $= \frac{114.75 - 100}{100} \times 100$

$= 14.75\% = 14\frac{3}{4}\%$

114. (a) $(1 + \cot A - \operatorname{cosec} A)(1 + \tan A + \sec A) - 3(\sin^2 A + \cos^2 A)$

$= \left(1 + \frac{\cos A}{\sin A} - \frac{1}{\sin A}\right)\left(1 + \frac{\sin A}{\cos A} + \frac{1}{\cos A}\right) - 3 \times 1$

$= \left(\frac{\sin A + \cos A - 1}{\sin A}\right)\left(\frac{\cos A + \sin A + 1}{\cos A}\right) - 3$

$= \frac{(\sin A + \cos A)^2 - 1^2}{\sin A \cos A} - 3$

[∵ $a^2 - b^2 = (a+b)(a-b)$]

$= \frac{1 + 2\sin A\cos A - 1}{\sin A\cos A} - 3$

$= \frac{2\sin A\cos A}{\sin A\cos A} - 3$

$= 2 - 3 = -1$

115. (a) The largest possible rod that can be placed in a cubical room

$= a\sqrt{3} = 42\sqrt{3}$

⇒ $a = 42$ m

The largest possible sphere that can fit inside the cubical room will have

$2r = a \Rightarrow r = \frac{a}{2}$

Now, its surface area $= 4\pi r^2$

$= 4 \times \frac{22}{7} \times \left(\frac{a}{2}\right)^2$

$= 4 \times \frac{22}{7} \times \frac{42}{2} \times \frac{42}{2}$ (∵ $a = 42$ m)

$= 5544$ m^2

116. (d) (13.49 + 12.51) × 13

= (26.00) × 13

= 26 × 13 = 338

117. (d) Total cost price of both the watches = ₹18000

Now, profit = 18% (overall)

$= 18000 \times \frac{18}{100} = ₹3240$

On first watch, a loss of 10% is incurred = 10% of 9000 = ₹900

Hence, the second watch should be sold at a profit

= ₹(3240 + 900) = ₹4140

∴ Selling price of second watch

= ₹(9000 + 4140) = ₹13140

118. (d) Volume of sphere $= \frac{4}{3}\pi r^3$

According to the question,

$\frac{\frac{4}{3}\pi(r_1)^3}{\frac{4}{3}\pi(r_2)^3} = \frac{512}{3375}$

⇒ $\frac{(r_1)^3}{(r_2)^3} = \frac{512}{3375}$

⇒ $\frac{r_1}{r_2} = \frac{8}{15}$

Now, surface area of sphere $= 4\pi r^2$

∴ Ratio of their surface areas

$= \frac{4\pi(r_1)^2}{4\pi(r_2)^2} = \frac{(r_1)^2}{(r_2)^2} = \frac{64}{225}$ or 64 : 225

119. (c) Given, $x = 3y + 4$

⇒ $x - 3y = 4$

Cubing on both the sides,

$(x - 3y)^3 = (4)^3$

⇒ $x^3 - 27y^3 - 3(x)(3y)(x - 3y) = 64$

⇒ $x^3 - 27y^3 - 9xy \times 4 = 64$

∴ $x^3 - 27y^3 - 36xy = 64$

120. (d) Let the number of boys and girls be $3x$ and $5x$, respectively.

∴ Percentage of boys in the class

$= \frac{3x}{8x} \times 100 = 37.5\%$

121. (c) Here, total distance

= 50 km + 75 km

= 125 km

Total time taken = (40 + 40) min

$= 80 \text{ min} = \frac{80}{60}$ h

∴ Average speed $= \frac{\text{Total distance}}{\text{Total time taken}}$

$= \frac{125}{\frac{80}{60}} = \frac{125 \times 3}{4} = 93\frac{3}{4}$

122. (c) Sum of scooters produced from 1985 to 1989

= 115 + 108 + 149 + 102 + 101

= 575

Average of scooters produced from 1985 to 1989 $= \frac{575}{5} = 115$

Now, it is equal to the total production of all the scooters in all the factories in 1985 = 115

123. (d) Volume of sphere = Volume of wire

⇒ $\frac{4}{3}\pi r^3 = \pi R^2 h$

⇒ $\frac{4}{3}\pi(6)^3 = \pi(0.2)^2 \times h$

∴ h (i.e., length of wire) = 7200 cm

124. (b) Let the total work be 26 units (LCM of 13, 26)

∴ Efficiency of $A = \frac{26}{13} = 2$

Efficiency of $B = \frac{26}{26} = 1$

∴ 2 day work if they work alternately = 3 units

∴ In 16 days (2 × 8), 24 units (3 × 8) work is completed.

Remaining work = 26 − 24 = 2 units

Now, A will work on 17th day to complete the remaining work.

∴ Total days required to complete the work = 17

125. **(b)** Circumference of the circle

$= 2\pi r = 88$ cm

$\therefore \quad r = 14$ cm

Now, length of minor arc

$= 2\pi r \times \frac{\theta}{360°} = 22$ cm

$\Rightarrow 2 \times \frac{22}{7} \times 14 \times \frac{\theta}{360°} = 22 \Rightarrow \theta = 90°$

Now, area of minor sector

$= \frac{\theta}{360°} \times \pi r^2$

$= \frac{90}{360°} \times \frac{22}{7} \times 14 \times 14$

$= 154 \text{ cm}^2$

126. **(a)** Given, length of the train = 255 m

Speed of train = 72 km/h

$= \left(72 \times \frac{5}{18}\right)$ m/s

= 20 m/s

Time taken to cross the platform of length 745 m $= \frac{255 + 745}{20}$

$= \frac{1000}{20} = 50$ sec

127. **(b)** Let the speed of stream = S

Speed of boat $(B) = \frac{7.5 \text{ km}}{1 \text{ h}} = 7.5$ km/h

According to the question,

$\frac{\text{Distance}}{B - S} = 4 \times \frac{\text{(Distance)}}{B + S}$

$\Rightarrow \quad (B + S) = 4(B - S)$

$\Rightarrow \quad 3B = 5S$

$\therefore \quad S = \frac{3B}{5}$

$= \frac{3 \times 7.5}{5} = 4.5$ km/h

$\therefore$ Speed of stream = 4.5 km/h.

128. **(d)** $1 - \cfrac{7}{1 - \cfrac{1}{1 + \cfrac{7}{1-7}}}$

$= 1 - \cfrac{7}{1 - \cfrac{1}{1 + \cfrac{7}{(-6)}}}$

$= 1 - \cfrac{7}{1 - \cfrac{1}{\cfrac{(-6+7)}{-6}}} = 1 - \cfrac{7}{1 - \cfrac{1}{\cfrac{1}{(-6)}}}$

$= 1 - \frac{7}{1-(-6)} = 1 - \frac{7}{7}$

$= 1 - 1 = 0$

129. **(b)** 750 kg of mixture contains 25% tin.

$\therefore$ Amount of tin $= \frac{25}{100} \times 750 = 187.5$ kg

Now, let the amount of tin added be x kg.

$\therefore$ According to the question,

$\frac{187.5 + x}{750 + x} = \frac{70}{100}$

$\Rightarrow \quad 1875 + 10x = 5250 + 7x$

$\Rightarrow \quad 3x = 3375$

$\therefore \quad x = 1125$ kg

130. **(c)** Given, $\sin\alpha = \frac{5}{13}$

$\therefore \cos\alpha \operatorname{cosec}\alpha \cot\alpha$

$= \cos\alpha \times \frac{1}{\sin\alpha} \times \frac{\cos\alpha}{\sin\alpha} = \frac{\cos^2\alpha}{\sin^2\alpha}$

$= \frac{1-\sin^2\alpha}{\sin^2\alpha} \quad [\because \sin^2\alpha + \cos^2\alpha = 1]$

$= \frac{1-\left[\frac{5}{13}\right]^2}{\left[\frac{5}{13}\right]^2} = \frac{1-\frac{25}{169}}{\frac{25}{169}}$

$= \frac{169-25}{25} = \frac{144}{25}$

131. **(a)** $\frac{1}{4} \times \frac{4}{3} \div \frac{5}{3} + \frac{1}{2}$

$= \frac{1}{4} \times \frac{4}{3} \times \frac{3}{5} + \frac{1}{2}$

$= \frac{1}{5} + \frac{1}{2} = \frac{7}{10} = 0.7$

132. **(b)** Number of females below poverty line in state A

$= \frac{3}{8} \times \frac{36}{100} \times 18000 = 2430$

Number of females below poverty line in state D

$= \frac{2}{3} \times \frac{32}{100} \times 18000 = 3840$

$\therefore$ Required total number of females

= 2430 + 3840

= 6270

133. **(d)** Aarav sells a watch to Bhavin at 15% profit = ₹10000 $\times \frac{15}{100}$ = ₹1500

$\therefore$ Aarav sells the watch to Bhavin at profit = (10000 + 1500) = ₹11500

Now, Bhavin sells it back to Aarav at 15% loss = ₹11500 $\times \frac{85}{100}$ = ₹9775

$\therefore$ Percentage profit of Aarav

$= \frac{(11500 - 9775)}{10000} \times 100$

= 17.25% profit

134. **(b)**

2012	2013	2014
+15%	−15%	+15%

Resultant increase/decrease of 2012 and 2013 $= x - y - \frac{xy}{100}$

$= 15 - 15 - \frac{15 \times 15}{100}$

$= -(2.25\%)$

$\therefore$ It is decreased.

Now, resultant increase/decrease of −2.25% and +15%

$= 15 - 2.25 - \frac{15 \times 2.25}{100}$

$= 12.75 - 0.34 + (12.41\%)$

$\therefore$ It is increased.

Hence, net increase = 12.41%

135. **(c)** $30 + 180 \div 30 \times 6 - 15 - 16 - 60 \div 3 - 15$

$= 30 + 6 \times 6 - 15 - 16 - 20 - 15$

$= 30 + 36 - 15 - 16 - 20 - 15$

$= 30 + 36 - 30 - 36 = 0$

136. **(b)**

$\frac{12 + 3\frac{2}{3} \div \left[1\frac{3}{4} \div \left\{5\frac{1}{4} \times \left(3\frac{3}{5} \div 4\frac{1}{2}\right)\right\}\right]}{1\frac{1}{3} \times 5\frac{1}{5}}$

$= \frac{12 + \frac{11}{3} \div \left[\frac{7}{4} \div \left\{\frac{21}{4} \times \left(\frac{18}{5} \div \frac{9}{2}\right)\right\}\right]}{\frac{4}{3} \times \frac{26}{5}}$

$= \frac{12 + \frac{11}{3} \div \left[\frac{7}{4} \div \left\{\frac{21}{4} \times \frac{4}{5}\right\}\right]}{\frac{4}{3} \times \frac{26}{5}}$

$= \frac{12 + \frac{11}{3} \div \left[\frac{7}{4} \times \frac{5}{21}\right]}{\frac{4}{3} \times \frac{26}{5}}$

$= \frac{12 + \frac{11}{3} \times \frac{12}{5}}{\frac{4}{3} \times \frac{26}{5}} = \frac{\frac{104}{104}}{3} = 3$

137. **(c)** 100% marks have been scored in 3 subjects i.e., Maths, Chemistry and Information Technology.

138. **(c)** Sum of the ages of three boys

$= 25 \times 3 = 75$

Ratio of their ages = 3 : 5 : 7

Let their ages be $3x$, $5x$ and $7x$ respectively.

Now, $(3x + 5x + 7x) = 75$

$15x = 75 \Rightarrow x = 5$

$\therefore$ Age of youngest boy $= 3x = 3 \times 5$

= 15 yr

139. (b) Given savings = 60° = ₹8000

∴ Expenditure on education

$= 30° = \frac{8000}{60°} \times 30° = ₹4000$

140. (c) $25 \times 25 + 9 \times 9 + 6 \times 6 + 2 \times 25 \times 9 + 2 \times 9 \times 6 + 2 \times 25 \times 6$

$= (25)^2 + (9)^2 + (6)^2 + 2 \times 25 \times 9 + 2 \times 9 \times 6 + 2 \times 6 \times 25$

$[\because a^2 + b^2 + c^2 + 2ab + 2bc + 2ca = (a + b + c)^2]$

$= (25 + 9 + 6)^2 = (40)^2 = 1600$

141. (a) $3 + 2 \times [7 + (5 + 7) \div 2]$

$= 3 + 2 \times [7 + 6]$

$= 3 + 2 \times 13$

$= 3 + 26 = 29$

142. (b) In the given pie chart,

100% represents 6500

$\therefore$ 34% represents $= \frac{6500}{100} \times 34 = 2210$

Now, 6500 represents 360°

$\therefore$ 2210 represents $= \frac{360}{6500} \times 2210 = 122.4°$

∴ Central angle for the book in store

$S = 122.4°$

143. (b) Let each installment be ₹ x.

1st year $= \left[x + \frac{x \times 10 \times 2}{100}\right]$

2nd year $= \left[x + \frac{x \times 10 \times 1}{100}\right]$

3rd year $= x$

Now,

$x + x + \frac{x \times 10 \times 2}{100} + x + \frac{x \times 10 \times 1}{100} = 10192$

$\Rightarrow 3x + \frac{x \times 10 \times 2}{100} + \frac{x \times 10 \times 1}{100} = 10192$

$\Rightarrow x = \frac{10192}{3.3}$

$\Rightarrow x = ₹3088.48$

144. (a) Volume of cube with side $a = a^3$

Volume of cuboid $= l \times b \times h$

Now, $a^3 = 4(l \times b \times h)$

$\Rightarrow a^3 = 4(32 \times 8 \times 4)$

$\Rightarrow a^3 = 4096$

$\Rightarrow a = 16$ cm

Now, total surface area of cube

$= 6a^2 = 6 \times (16)^2$

Total surface area of cuboid

$= 2(lb + bh + hl)$

$= 2(32 \times 8 + 8 \times 4 + 4 \times 32)$

∴ Required ratio

$= \frac{6 \times 16 \times 16}{2(32 \times 8 + 8 \times 4 + 4 \times 32)}$

$= \frac{1536}{2 \times (256 + 32 + 128)}$

$= \frac{1536}{2 \times 416} = \frac{1536}{832}$

$= 24 : 13$

145. (d) $8.2 + 2.6 + 3.2 - 4.5 \div 0.9 \times 1.2$

$= 8.2 + 2.6 + 3.2 - 5 \times 1.2$

$= 8.2 + 2.6 + 3.2 - 6$

$= 14 - 6 = 8$

146. (d)

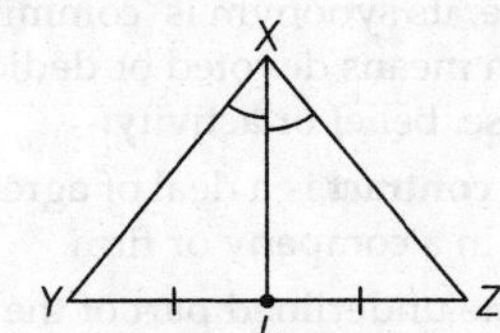

$\because L$ is the mid-point of YZ.

$\therefore XL$ will be the median.

Given, area of $XYL = 13$ cm^2

We know that, median divides a triangle into two equal parts.

$\therefore$ Area of $XYZ = (2 \times 13)$ cm^2

$= 26$ cm^2

147. (b) Let the total distance be x km.

Now, according to the question,

$\frac{x}{45} - \frac{x}{55} = \frac{40}{60}$

$\Rightarrow \frac{55x - 45x}{45 \times 55} = \frac{40}{60}$

$\Rightarrow \frac{10x}{45 \times 55} = \frac{4}{6}$

$\therefore x = 165$ km

148. (b) Let the population of the village before the corona attack be $100x$.

Now, 5% died in corona

∴ Remaining population

$= 100x - 5\%$ of $100x$

$= 95x$

Now, 20% fled due to panic

∴ Remaining population

$= 95x - 20\%$ of $95x$

$= 95x - 19x = 76x$

According to the question,

$76x = 4655$

$\Rightarrow x = 61.25$

∴ Original population $= 100x$

$= 100 \times 61.25 = 6125$

149. (c) Given, $(\sin x + \sin y) = a$,

$(\cos x + \cos y) = b$

On squaring and adding them,

$\sin^2 x + \sin^2 y + 2\sin x \sin y + \cos^2 x + \cos^2 y + 2\cos x \cos y = b^2 + a^2$

$\Rightarrow 2 + 2(\sin x \sin y + \cos x \cos y) = a^2 + b^2$

$\Rightarrow \sin x \sin y + \cos x \cos y = \frac{a^2 + b^2 - 2}{2}$

150. (b) Given,

Marked price of doll = ₹2500

First discount = 10%

Let the second discount = x%

Now, according to the question,

$2500 \times 90\% \times (100 - x)\% = ₹1800$

$\Rightarrow 2500 \times \frac{90}{100} \times \frac{(100 - x)}{100} = 1800$

$\Rightarrow (100 - x) = 80$

$\therefore x = 20\%$

151. (a) To go down in flames means to 'to fail spectacularly; to end suddenly and completely; be utterly ruined or wrecked'.

152. (c) The idiom **blue blood** refers to someone of noble or aristocratic lineage.

153. (c) Part (c) 'A deer runs across the road' contains an error. As the sentence is in past tense, 'ran' should be used.

154. (d) The synonym of 'Condemn' is Denounce, which means to criticise of speak against something strongly. Other options do not convey disapproval.

155. (a) Demography is the study of statistical changes in numbers of births, deaths, marriages and cases of disease in a community over a period of time.

156. (b) The correct spelt word is 'entrepreneur'.

157. (d) Part (d) 'soundly slept' contains an error. The correct phrase should be 'slept soundly' to maintain proper adverb placement as adverb of manner is placed after the verb.

158. (c) The word 'Cacophony' means a harsh, discordant mixture of sounds noise.

159. (c) Wicked' means moral wrongdoing or mischievous behaviour. Hence, its antonym is 'Righteous' which means morally upright, virtuous and adhering to ethical principles.

160. **(c)** The idiom 'to take it with a grain of salt' means regard something as exaggerated; believe only part of something.

161. **(a)** The correct spelling is 'reverse'.

162. **(d)** A **gynaecologist** is a specialist doctor who manages conditions that affect the female reproductive system.

163. **(c)** A **quadrangle** is an open space usually rectangular and enclosed in a building.

164. **(d)** The word 'Shrewd' means having or showing sharp powers of judgement; smart.

165. **(d)** The idiom 'at the drop of a hat' means to do something immediately or without hesitation.

166. **(c)** The idiom 'stand by' in the context of the given situation means to support someone, especially in difficult times.

167. **(c)** This is the correct form. One must be follwed by one's for consistency and properly is the correct spelling.

168. **(d)** The correct spelling is 'congregation'.

169. **(b)** The underlined part of the sentence contains an error. Use 'in' in place of 'from' to correct the sentence.

170. **(b)** The idiom **a man of letters** refers to 'someone who is a scholar or well-educated in literature and scholarly works.'

171. **(c)** **Waning** means to decrease in size, extent or degree; to diminish gradually in power, intensity or importance. Hence, its synonym is 'Fading' which means to gradually becoming less bright, intense or clear; synonymous with 'waning.'

172. **(b)** **Summary** is short description of a story. Hence, its antonym is 'lengthy'.

173. **(a)** The correct idiom to improve the underlined part of the given sentence is 'wild goose chase,' which means a futile or hopeless pursuit.

174. **(d)** The error in the original sentence is in the tense used. 'I will be arrange' is incorrect because it combines 'will be' (future continuous tense) with 'arrange' (which should be in the present participle form 'arranging' for future continuous tense).

The correct sentence from the options provided is 'I will be arranging all the necessary materials for the programme.' This option correctly uses the future continuous tense ('will be arranging') to indicate an action that will be ongoing in the future.

175. **(d)** Part (d) 'that tired and weak' contains an adverbial usage error. The correct adverbial usage should be 'so tired and weak that she could scarcely walk.'

176. **(a)** The word 'Ardent' means passionate, enthusiastic or dedicated. Hence, its synonym is 'committed' which means devoted or dedicated to a cause, belief or activity.

177. **(c)** A **contract** is a deal of agreement done in a company or firm.

178. **(a)** The underlined part of the sentence contains an error.
This sentence maintains the sense that the authors writing style is characterised by using language that is poetic or expressive in nature.
'Lyrical' suggests a style that is melodious, expressive and artistic, similar to 'poetic.'
The most appropriate option that can substitute the underlined segment is 'lyrical language.'

179. **(a)** The word **Immune** refers to being resistant to or protected against a disease or condition.

180. **(c)** Part (c) 'It is a cheap reasonably' contains the error. The correct phrase should be 'reasonably priced' instead of 'cheap reasonably.'
Ms. Malathi is living lonely in an apartment.

181. **(c)** **Evolution** refers to the process of changing or going from the simple or basic to the complex or advanced.

182. **(c)** A *Theist* is someone who believes in the existence of God. An *Atheist* does not and *Fatalist* believes in fate, not necessarily in God.

183. **(d)** The idiom **be in a tight corner** means 'to be in a difficult situation.' It describes a scenario where someone is facing problems or challenges that are hard to overcome.

184. **(d)** A **cacophony** is an unpleasant mixture of loud sounds.

185. **(a)** The correct spelt word is 'cheerful'.

186. **(b)** The idiom 'an elephant in the room' refers to an obvious problem or issue that everyone is aware of but chooses to ignore or avoid discussing.

187. **(b)** A **parable** is a simple story used to illustrate a moral or spiritual lesson.

188. **(a)** **Mighty** means possessing great power or strength. Hence, its antonym is 'Weak'.

189. **(b)** The correct spelling is 'search'.

190. **(a)** **Deja-vu** refers to the feeling of being in a place before having already experienced the present situation.

191. **(a)** 'Bangles' means circular bracelets, fitting the context of bangles on her upper arm.

192. **(b)** 'With' means accompanied by, fitting the context of a necklace with three pendants.

193. **(b)** 'Wrist' means the joint connecting the hand with the forearm, fitting the context of bangles on the wrist.

194. **(d)** 'Undaunted' means not intimidated, fitting the context of the ever hopeful human spirit.

195. **(d)** 'Impact' means a strong effect, fitting the context of the impact a work of art leaves on our senses.

196. **(c)** The passage has an informative tone.

197. **(c)** The passage discusses the causes (plastic pollution) and its effects (altering habitats, affecting livelihoods, etc.).

198. **(b)** The word 'exist' means to have actual being. Hence, its opposite is 'cease' which means to come to an end or to stop existing.

199. **(a)** The passage primarily discusses the issue of plastic pollution, including its scale, impact on ecosystems and human life and the need for comprehensive assessment alongside other environment issues.

200. **(c)** The word 'alter' means to change or modify something. Hence, its antonym is 'preserve' which means to maintain or keep something unchanged.

CPO SI P-1 SP 09

PAPER-1

SSC CPO SI SOLVED PAPER

27 June 2024 (Shift I)

Instructions

1. This paper contains 200 questions.
2. It has 4 Parts, **Part I** General Intelligence and Reasoning, **Part II** General Knowledge and General Awareness, **Part III** Quantitative Aptitude and **Part IV** English Comprehension.
3. Each question carries 1 marks.

MM : 200 **Time : 2 hr**

Part I

General Intelligence and Reasoning

1. The sequence of folding a paper and the manner in which the folded paper is cut is shown in the following figures. How would this paper look, when unfolded?

Question Figures

Answer Figures

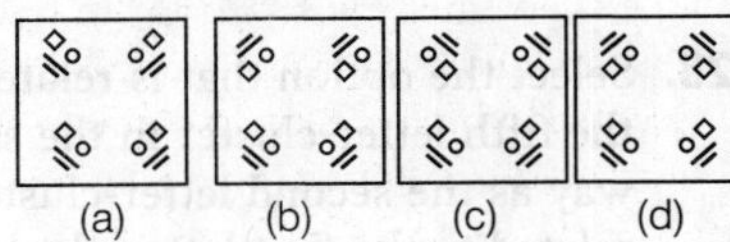

2. Identify the figure given in the options, which when put in place of (?) will logically complete the series.

Question Figures

Answer Figures

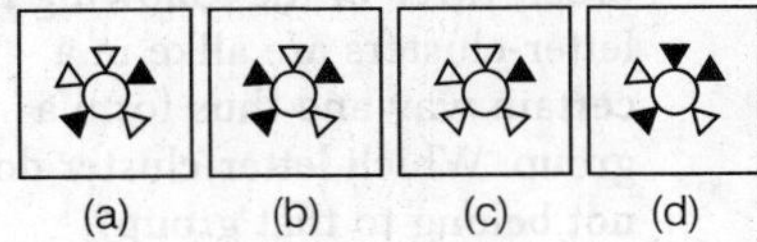

3. Select the venn diagram that best illustrates the relationship between the following classes.

Potatoes, Vegetables, Grapes

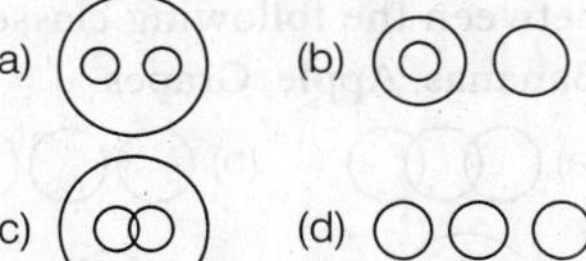

4. 15 is related to 45 following a certain logic. Following the same logic, 25 is related to 125. Which of the following numbers is related to 80 using the same logic?

(a) 20 (b) 21
(c) 18 (d) 22

5. In a code language, 'DINESH' is coded as 12-27-42-15-57-24 and 'VIRAT' is coded as 66-27-54-3-60. How will 'GAUTAM' be coded in the same language?

(a) 24-7-61-34-5-31
(b) 26-7-25-67-4-37
(c) 21-3-63-60-3-39
(d) 29-9-55-47-8-28

6. Select the option figure in which the given figure is embedded as its part (rotation is not allowed).

Question Figure

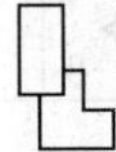

Answer Figures

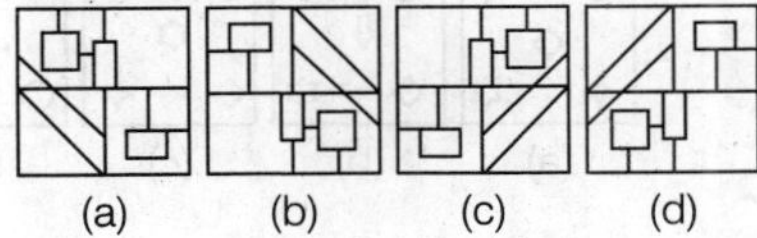

7. Select the set in which the numbers are related in the same way as are the numbers of the following sets. (**Note** Operations should be performed on the whole numbers, without breaking down the numbers into its constituent digits. E.g. 13 – Operations on 13 such as adding /subtracting /multiplying etc. to 13 can be performed. Breaking down 13 into 1 and 3 and then performing mathematical operations on 1 and 3 is not allowed).

(247, 349)
(261, 363)

(a) (282, 382) (b) (294, 396)
(c) (253, 358) (d) (265, 369)

8. Which of the following terms will replace the question mark (?) in the given series?

CHO, DIP, EJQ, ?

(a) EJL (b) FKR (c) DIL (d) HMR

9. Select the correct combination of mathematical signs to replace the * signs and balance the given equation.

13 * 7 * 12 * 4 * 15 * 65

(a) –, +, ÷, ×, = (b) +, ÷, ×, +, =
(c) +, +, ÷, ×, = (d) +, ×, ÷, ×, =

10. At a wedling reception, a man pointed to the groom and said that he was the brother of the son of his grand father Son, What does the groom look like to that man ?

(a) Uncle (b) Father
(c) Brother (d) Brother-in-law

11. Which two signs should be interchanged to make the given equation correct?

$10 \div 63 \times 7 + 90 - 80 = 100$

(a) – and ÷ (b) × and –
(c) + and – (d) × and ÷

12. If + means –, – means ×, × means ÷ , ÷ means +, what will come in place of the question mark (?) in the given equation?

$22 \times 11 - 450 \div 50 + 500 = ?$

(a) 350 (b) 650
(c) 550 (d) 450

13. Select the option that is related to the fifth letter-cluster in the same way as the second letter-cluster is related to the first letter-cluster and the fourth letter-cluster is related to the third letter-cluster.

CARS : HFWX :: BOAT: GTFY :: FUSE : ?

(a) LAYK (b) KZWI
(c) LAXJ (d) KZXJ

14. Two different positions of the same dice are given below. Which is the number on the face opposite the face containing 1?

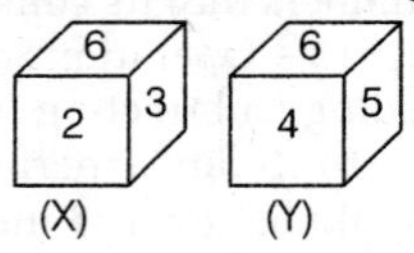

(a) 3 (b) 4
(c) 2 (d) 6

15. Six students - Aman, Bobby, Chintu, Gita, Pranay and Ram - are sitting around a circular table, facing the centre.

Ram is sitting second to the right of Gita. Pranay is the immediate neighbour of Gita and Bobby. Aman is sitting third to the right of Gita. Who among the following is the immediate neighbour of both Ram and Bobby?

(a) Pranay (b) Chintu
(c) Aman (d) Gita

16. Sally drives a mini school bus. She starts at the school gate and drives 7 km North for her first pick-up. She, then turns right and drives 10 km picking up children along the way. She takes another right turn and drives 5 km. She then takes a final right to return to the school. How far would Sally need to drive to reach back to the school gate again?

(a) 17 km (b) 22 km
(c) 10 km (d) 12 km

17. Select the venn diagram that best represent the relationship between the following classes.

Leopard, Bird, Eagle

(a) (b)

(c) (d)

18. Which of the following numbers will replace the question marks (?) in the given series?

1, 6, 15, 28, ?, ?, 91

(a) 40, 60 (b) 42, 54 (c) 45, 66 (d) 44, 54

19. Select the venn-diagram that best illustrates the relationship between the following classes.

Bananas, Apple, Grapes

(a) (b)

(c) (d)

20. In a code language, 'LAND' is written as 'IWKZ' and 'GOLD' is written as 'DKIZ'. How will 'TEAM' be written in that language?

(a) QAXI (b) XJQB
(c) QXJB (d) JXQB

21. Select the number that will replace the question mark (?) in the following number series.

1, 1, 2, 3, 5, 8, 13, ?

(a) 22 (b) 21
(c) 24 (d) 20

22. Identify the option figure that, when put in place of the question mark (?) will logically complete the series.

Question Figures

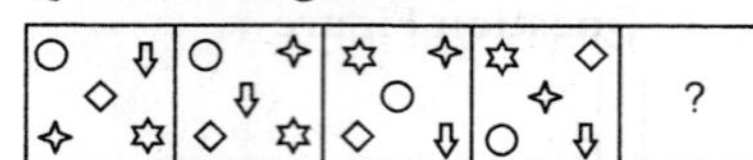

Answer Figures

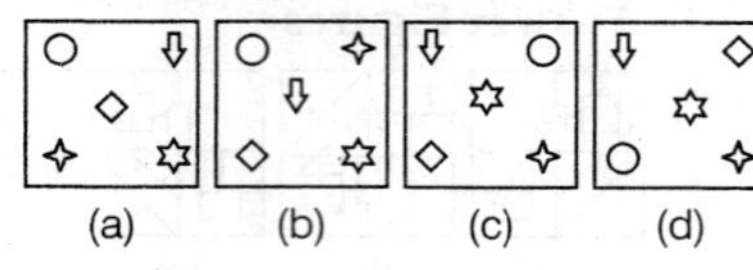

23. Select the correct mirror image of the given figure, when the mirror is placed at MN as shown below.

M

RkgEyw

N

(a) ywƎgkR (b) wyƎgkR
(c) wʎEgkR (d) ʍʎEgkR

24. Find the two signs to be interchanged for making the following equation correct.

$2 + 10 \times 12 - 4 \div 24 = 8$

(a) ÷ and + (b) ÷ and –
(c) × and ÷ (d) – and +

25. Preeti starts from Point A and drives 7 km towards South. From here, she takes a left turn and drives 9 km. She then takes a final left turn and drives 7 km to reach Point B. How far should Preeti drive to reach Point A from Point B?

(a) 9 km (b) 6 km
(c) 7 km (d) 8 km

26. In a code language, 'CUTE' is written as 'FQWA' and 'BLUE' is written as 'EHXA'. How will 'VOTE' be written in that language?

(a) AYWK (b) YWAK
(c) YKAW (d) YKWA

27. Which letter cluster will replace the question mark (?) to complete the given series?

HEWC, KIRI, ?, QQHU, TUCA

(a) NMMO (b) PRZO
(c) NBTO (d) JLSO

28. Select the option that is related to the fifth letter-cluster in the same way as the second letter-cluster is related to the first letter-cluster and the fourth letter-cluster is related to the third letter-cluster.

ABUSE : ASUBE :: BEGIN : BIGEN :: OTHER : ?

(a) ORTHE (b) OHTER
(c) OTHRE (d) OEHTR

29. Based on the English alphabetical order, three of the following four letter-clusters are alike in a certain way and thus form a group. Which letter-cluster does not belong to that group?

(**Note** The odd letter-cluster is not based on the number of

consonants/vowels or their position in the letter-cluster.)
(a) PMS (b) URX
(c) JGM (d) SPU

30. Select the number from among the given options that can replace the question mark(?) in the following series.
25, 40, 70, 115, 175, ?
(a) 200 (b) 275 (c) 250 (d) 225

31. Select the set in which the numbers are related in the same way as are the numbers of the following sets.
(**Note** Operations should be performed on the whole numbers, without breaking down the numbers into its constituent digits. E.g. 13 – Operations on 13 such as adding /Subtracting /multiplying etc. to 13 can be performed. Breaking down 13 into 1 and3 and then performing mathematical operations on 1 and 3 is not allowed).
(12, 36, 6)
(18, 54, 9)
(a) (28, 84, 16) (b) (28, 86, 14)
(c) (28, 84, 14) (d) (26, 84, 14)

32. Select the correct combination of mathematical signs to replace the * signs and balance the given equation.
10 * 2 * 1 * 8 * 11 * 8
(a) ÷, –, ×, –, = (b) ÷, –, –, +, =
(c) +, –, ×, +, = (d) ÷, –, ×, +, =

33. Select the option figure in which the given figure is embedded as its part (rotation is not allowed).
Question Figure

Answer Figures

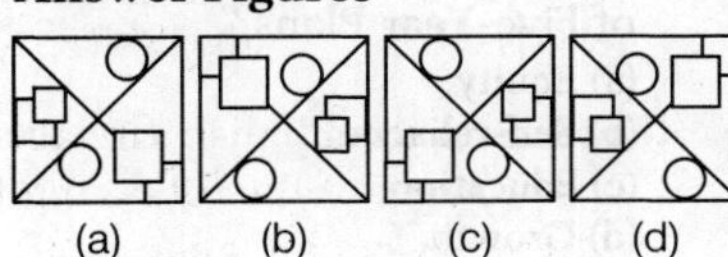
(a) (b) (c) (d)

34. Which of the following numbers will replace the question mark (?) in the given series?
7, 16, 43, 124, 367, ?
(a) 1086 (b) 1096
(c) 1066 (d) 1076

35. In a certain code language, A + B means 'A is the brother's wife of B'. A – B means 'A is the sister of B', A × B means 'A is the wife of B' and A ÷ B means 'A is the daughter of B'. Based on the above, how is G related to Q, if 'G + K – L ÷ M × Q'?
(a) Daughter (b) Sister
(c) Wife's sister (d) Son's wife

36. In a certain code language, 'FIND' is written as 'CLFB' and 'HOW' is written as 'VME'.How will 'WILL' be written in that language?
(a) KSFJ (b) SJFK
(c) SFJK (d) KJFS

37. A dice has its faces marked by numbers 10, 20, 30, 40, 50 and 60. Two positions of the same dice are given below. Which face is opposite to face 50?

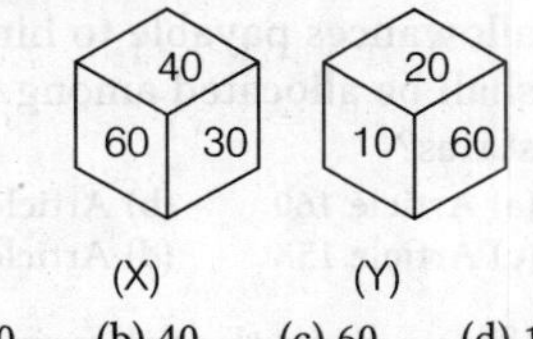

(a) 30 (b) 40 (c) 60 (d) 10

38. Select the option that represents the correct order of the given words as they would appear in an English dictionary.
1. Consistence 2. Conscience
3. Conflagration 4. Consequence
5. Considerable 6. Consignment
(a) 4, 3, 2, 5, 6, 1 (b) 4, 2, 3, 5, 1, 6
(c) 3, 4, 2, 5, 6, 1 (d) 3, 2, 4, 5, 6, 1

39. What will come in place of the question mark (?) in the following equation, if '+' and '×'are interchanged and '–' and '÷' are interchanged?
$14 - 7 \times 10 \div 1 + 7 = ?$
(a) 5 (b) 26 (c) 45 (d) 77

40. In a certain code language, 'DICE' is written as 'EKFI' and 'PLAN' is written as 'QNDR'.How will 'LUDO' be written in that language?
(a) NXES (b) NWES
(c) MWGS (d) MXES

41. 12 is related to 40 following a certain logic. Following the same logic, 9 is related to 31. To which of the following is 16 related using the same logic?
(a) 52 (b) 51 (c) 61 (d) 63

42. Which letter cluster can replace the question mark (?) to complete the given series?
FDKI, GCMG, ?, IAQC
(a) HBNF (b) HBOE
(c) HBPF (d) HBLE

43. Select the set in which the numbers are related in the same way as are the numbers of the given sets.
(**Note** Operations should be performed on the whole numbers, without breaking down the numbers into its constituent digits. E.g. 13 – Operations on 13 such as adding/subtracting/multiplying, etc. to 13 can be performed. Breaking down 13 into 1 and 3 and then performing mathematical operations on 1 and 3 is not allowed.)
(9, 36, 12)
(12, 48, 16)
(a) (21, 84, 24) (b) (21, 81, 28)
(c) (21, 81, 24) (d) (21, 84, 28)

44. Select the correct mirror image of the given figure when the mirror is placed at MN as shown below.
M
L 2 7 A ɘ f
N
(a) ɟ ɘ A ꓶ S ⅃
(b) ɟ ɘ A 2 7 ⅃
(c) ɟ ɘ A ∠ Ƨ ꓶ
(d) ɟ ɘ A ꓶ S ⅃

45. In a code language, 'RACE' is written as 'VWGA' and 'BANK' is written as 'FWRG'.How will 'STEM' be written in that language?
(a) IIWP (b) WIPI (c) WIIP (d) WPII

46. Select the option that indicates the correct arrangement of the given words in the order in which they appear in an English dictionary.
1. Literacy 2. Literature
3. Litany 4. Listen
5. Lithograph
(a) 4, 3, 1, 2, 5 (b) 3, 4, 1, 2, 5
(c) 1, 4, 3, 2, 5 (d) 4, 1, 3, 5, 2

47. Select the correct combination of mathematical signs to sequentially place from left to right in the blanks below to balance the given equation.
6_2_0_8 = 20
(a) +, ×, ÷ (b) +, ÷, ×
(c) ×, ÷, + (d) –, ×, ÷

48. A dice has numbers 2, 3, 5, 6, 7 and 8 on its sides. Two different positions of the same dice are shown below. Select the number that will be on the face opposite to the one having 8.

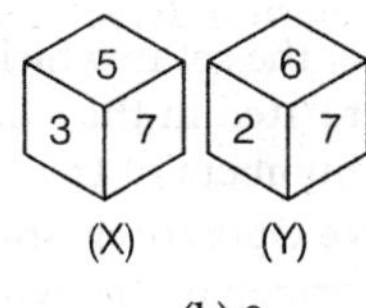

(a) 6 (b) 2
(c) 3 (d) 7

49. Select the figure from among the given options that can logically replace the question mark (?) in the following series.

Question Figures

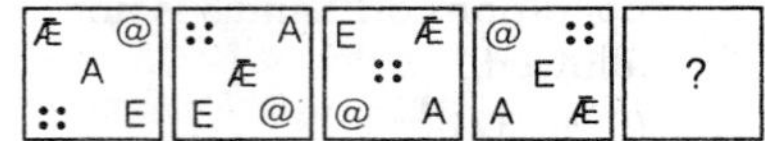

Answer Figures

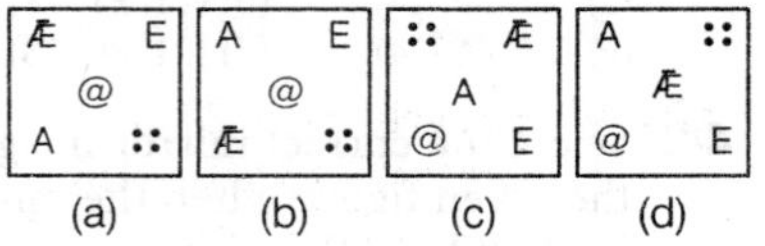

50. Select the venn diagram that best illustrates the relationship between the following classes.
Dogs, Cats, Labradors

(a) 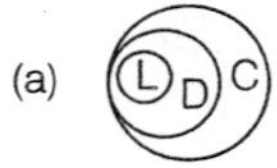

(b) 

(c) 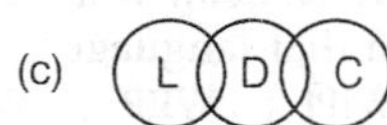

(d) 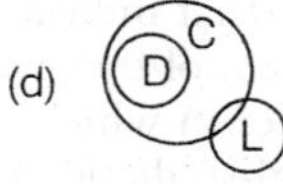

Part II
General Knowledge and General Awareness

51. Under the Sukanya Samriddhi Account Yojana, minimum how much money needs to be deposited in one financial year?
(a) ₹ 250 (b) ₹150
(c) ₹ 100 (d) ₹ 200

52. The Central Government launched the National Air Sports Policy in the year.......... .
(a) 2020 (b) 2021
(c) 2019 (d) 2022

53. Which phenomenon is opposite to solidification?
(a) Fusion (b) Vaporisation
(c) Sublimation (d) Condensation

54. The Commonwealth Fencing Championship 2022 was hosted by
(a) Australia
(b) United Kingdom
(c) Canada
(d) India

55. Which Article of the Indian Constitution mentions that, where the same person is appointed as the Governor of two or more states, the emoluments and allowances payable to him/her shall be allocated among those states?
(a) Article 160 (b) Article 155
(c) Article 158 (d) Article 157

56. Who among the following is the author of the book 'The Guide'?
(a) RK Narayan
(b) Vikram Chandra
(c) Shashi Tharoor
(d) Rohinton Mistry

57. Which of the following dances is not a part of the Odia culture?
(a) Kathakali (b) Gotipua
(c) Paika (d) Dalkhai

58. What are the thin filamentous extensions that the motile bacterial cells have from their cell wall called?
(a) Flagella (b) Pili
(c) Fimbriae (d) Lamellae

59. Famous musician Bhupen Hazarika was awarded the 'Bharat Ratna' in which of the following years?
(a) 2017 (b) 2015
(c) 2011 (d) 2019

60. Over 5,000 athletes were competed in .... sports for 1,936 medals in the 5th edition of Khelo India Youth Games in 2023.
(a) 25 (b) 24
(c) 26 (d) 27

61. In which year was 'Self Help Group – Bank Linkage Programme' (SHG-BLP) introduced in India?
(a) 1996 (b) 2000
(c) 1992 (d) 1984

62. According to Hindu calendar, Diwali falls in which of the following months?
(a) Magha
(b) Ashwin
(c) Chaitra
(d) Kartika

63. In which Article does the Finance Commission of India find a mention?
(a) Article 370
(b) Article 280
(c) Article 375
(d) Article 292

64. Biological Diversity Act, 2002 was passed by the Government of India. It fulfilled ideals of which article of Directive Principles of State Policy in the Constitution of India?
(a) Article 48
(b) Article 48A
(c) Article 49
(d) Article 47

65. What are the two main parts corresponding to Lasya and Tandava elements in Manipuri dance?
(a) Bhangi and Stri
(b) Jagoi and Cholom
(c) Varnam and Paran
(d) Vira and Toda

66. Shyamamani Devi was awarded the Padma Shri in 2022 for her contributions to .... music.
(a) Odissi (b) Gujarati
(c) Tamil (d) Malayali

67. Which of the following is not one of the four primary explicit goals of Five-Year Plans?
(a) Equity
(b) Self-reliance
(c) Education
(d) Growth

68. As per .... of the Indian Constitution, the Council of Ministers are collectively responsible to the Lok Sabha.
(a) Article 75(3) (b) Article 74(1)
(c) Article 73(2) (d) Article 72(1)

69. Which of the following figures accurately depicts the inter-conversion of the three-states of matter?

(a)
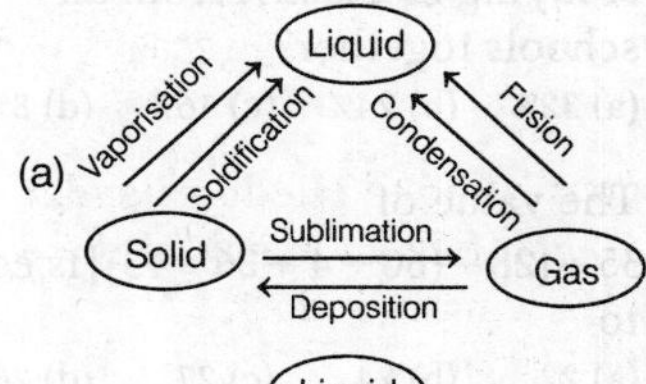

(b)
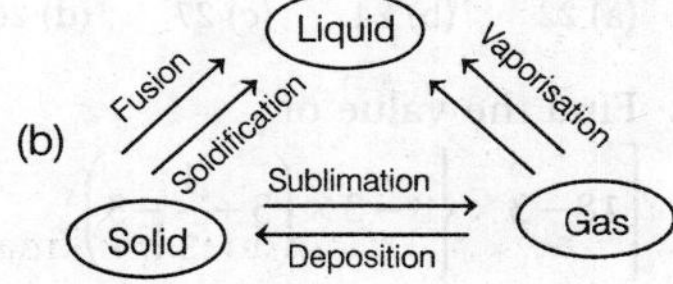

(c)
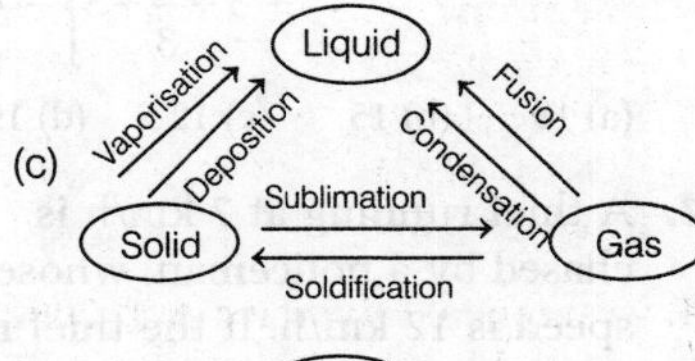

(d)
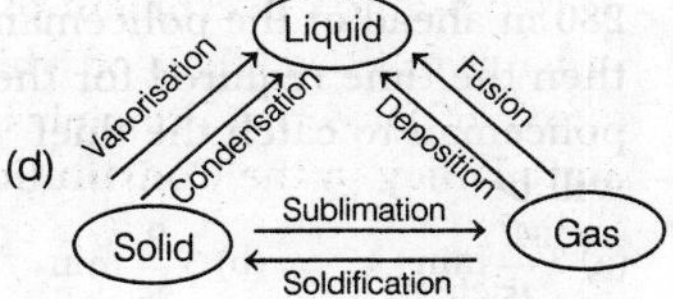

70. Which of the following factors does not control the climate of a place?
(a) Latitude
(b) Distance between two cities
(c) Ocean currents
(d) Relief features

71. The Shailendra kings who had close contacts with the Indian rulers were followers of which of the following religions?
(a) Jainism (b) Vaishnavism
(c) Shaivism (d) Buddhism

72. Select the name of the hydrocarbon with a structural formula
$CH_3 - CH_2 - CH_2 - CH_2 - CH_2 - CH$
(a) 2,2-Dimethylbutane
(b) 3-methyl hexane
(c) n-Hexane
(d) 2-Methylpentane

73. What is the average elevation of the Eastern Ghats of India?
(a) 400 metres (b) 200 metres
(c) 900 metres (d) 600 metres

74. Who among the following envoys was sent by Seleucus I to the court of Chandragupta Maurya?
(a) Fa-Hien (b) Deimachus
(c) Al-Biruni (d) Megasthenes

75. What does 'M' stand for in MUDRA yojana?
(a) Micro (b) Money
(c) Major (d) Macro

76. Chitra Visweswaran is a famous dancer of which of the following dance genres?
(a) Kuchipudi (b) Kathakali
(c) Bharatanatyam (d) Sattriya

77. Which Article of the Indian Constitution pertains to the Fundamental Duties?
(a) Article 51-A (b) Article 50-A
(c) Article 53-A (d) Article 52-A

78. Ustad Asad Ali Khan was one of the masters of the ....
(a) Mridangam (b) Rudra Veena
(c) Sarangi (d) Tanpura

79. Which of the following programmes is not a part of the Tenth Five-Year Plan?
(a) Jute Technology Mission
(b) Drought Prone Area Programme
(c) National Horticulture Mission
(d) Micro Irrigation Programme

80. Which of the following is not included in the Indian Food Guide Pyramid for healthy eating?
(a) Fats and sugar
(b) Pulses and legumes
(c) Milk, meat and products
(d) Alcoholic beverages

81. Which biosphere of Southern Andhra Pradesh is home to many endemic species including the famous Red Sanders and Slender Loris?
(a) Cold Desert (b) Seshachalam
(c) Pachmarhi (d) Agasthyamalai

82. Which of the following is not a fundamental duty of an Indian citizen?
(a) To value and preserve the rich heritage of our composite culture.
(b) To vote in public elections.
(c) To safeguard public property and to abjure violence.
(d) To uphold and protect the sovereignty, unity and integrity of India.

83. Which of the following mountain peaks is located in the Karakoram Range?
(a) Trishul (b) Nanda Devi
(c) K2 (d) Kamet

84. With regard to the component of population density, which state is the odd one out of the following?
(a) Uttar Pradesh
(b) Tamil Nadu
(c) Arunachal Pradesh
(d) Bihar

85. ...., a tribal dancer from the Baiga community, received the Padma Shri Award in 2022.
(a) Arjun Singh Dhurve
(b) Shyamamani Devi
(c) S. Ballesh Bhajantri
(d) Lourembam Bino Devi

86. Vasco da Gama, who discovered the sea route from Europe to India, belonged to which nation?
(a) Spain (b) Portugal
(c) England (d) Germany

87. Which cycle consists of sedimentary and gaseous cycles?
(a) Biogeochemical cycle
(b) Biogeogaseous cycle
(c) Biochemical cycle
(d) Biogeo cycle

88. Kathasaritsagara, a literary work, was originally composed in which of the following languages?
(a) Tamil (b) Prakrit
(c) Sanskrit (d) Pali

89. Who among the following was the pioneer of widow remarriages in Maharashtra and also started a girls' school in Poona along with his wife?
(a) BR Ambedkar
(b) Jyotirao Govindrao Phule
(c) Gopal Hari Deshmukh Lokahitwadi
(d) Mahatma Gandhi

90. What is the total length of Golden Quadrilateral, built by the National Highways Authority of India (NHAI)?
(a) 4,658 km (b) 5,790 km
(c) 5,978 km (d) 5,846 km

91. Identify the crop which is grown in Kharif cropping season in Northern States of India.
(a) Mustard (b) Rice
(c) Gram (d) Barley

92. In which of the following games is the term 'Dribbling' used?
(a) Basketball (b) Volleyball
(c) Baseball (d) Cricket

93. Which of the following states has the lowest literacy rate as per Census of India 2011?
(a) Odisha (b) Bihar
(c) Jharkhand (d) Tamil Nadu

94. Which of the following figures represents Mendeléev's Periodic Table that was published in a German journal in 1872?

(a)
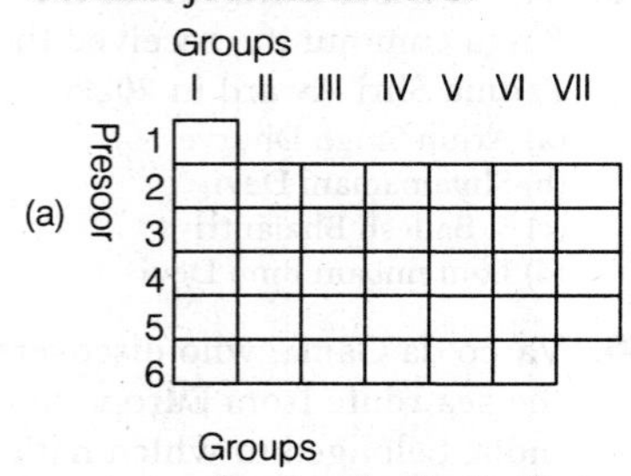

(b)
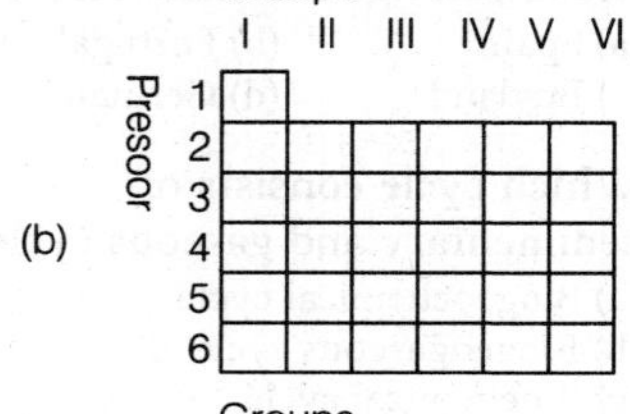

(c)
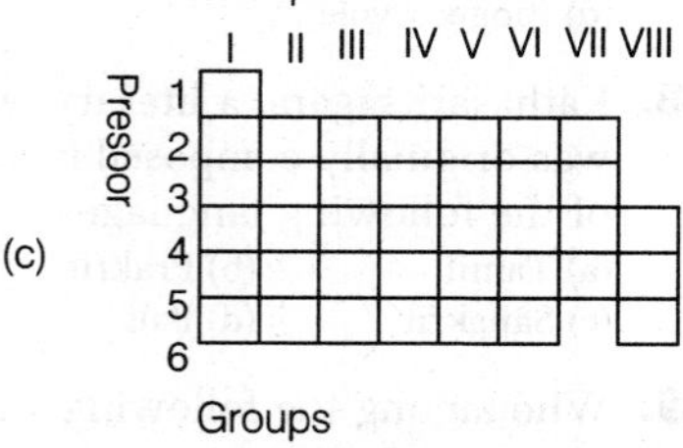

(d)
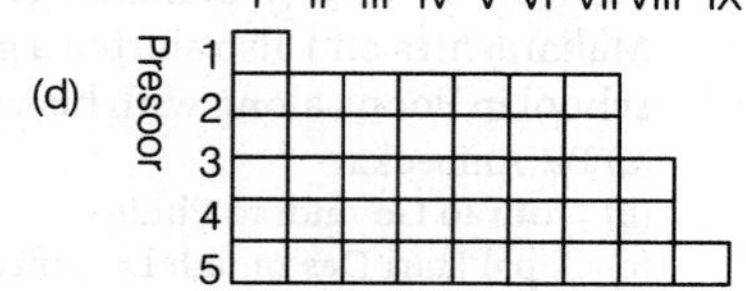

95. Dussehra is celebrated in .... month of the Hindu calendar.
(a) Chaitra (b) Ashwin
(c) Kartika (d) Asada

96. Match the following dams with the rivers on which they are builts.

A.	Hirakud Dam	(i)	Chambal river
B.	Nagarjuna Sagar Dam	(ii)	Narmada river
C.	Sardar Sarovar Dam	(iii)	Krishna river
D.	Tehri Dam	(iv)	Mahanadi river
E.	Rana Pratap Sagar Dam	(v)	Bhagirathi river

Codes
(a) A-iii, B-iv, C-ii, D-v, E-i
(b) A-iv, B-iii, C-ii, D-v, E-i
(c) A-iv, B-iii, C-ii, D-i, E-v
(d) A-i, B-iii, C-ii, D-v, E-iv

97. Which of the following is not an example of inertia at rest?
(a) Falling down of dust particle while dusting a cloth.
(b) Falling down backward when a vehicle starts immediately.
(c) The detachment of leaves/fruits due to shaking.
(d) The sudden application of brakes in a vehicle.

98. Which actor's autobiography is titled 'Bad Man'?
(a) Amrish Puri
(b) Ashish Vidyarthi
(c) Raza Murad
(d) Gulshan Grover

99. Match the following movements with their respective founders.

A.	Faraizi Movement	(i)	Sayyid Ahmad of Raebareli
B.	Mohammedan Literary Society	(ii)	Sir Syed Ahmad Khan
C.	Indian Patriotic Association	(iii)	Nawab Abdul Latif
D.	Wahabi Movement	(iv)	Haji Shariatullah

Codes
(a) A - iii, B - iv, C - ii, D - i
(b) A - i, B - ii, C - iii, D - iv
(c) A - ii, B - i, C - iv, D - iii
(d) A - iv, B - iii, C - ii, D - i

100. Which protein is found in grains?
(a) Gluten (b) Gum protein
(c) Delta protein (d) Arginine

Part III
Quantitative Aptitude

101. Study the given table and answer the question that follows.
The table shows the number of students studying in 6 different classes of 6 different schools.

School	V	VI	VII	VIII	IX	X
P	152	160	145	156	147	144
Q	148	166	150	155	157	143
R	161	152	140	145	143	165
S	159	142	149	140	142	168
T	147	144	158	163	154	150
U	150	160	162	160	161	140
Total	917	924	904	919	904	910

The number of students studying in Class X from School P form approximately what percentage of the total number of students studying in Class X from all schools together?
(a) 32% (b) 24% (c) 16% (d) 8%

102. The value of
$35-[28-(60\div 4+26\div 13)]$ is equal to
(a) 22 (b) 24 (c) 27 (d) 26

103. Find the value of
$$\left[18-3\times\left\{3-3\times\left(3\div\frac{1}{3}-3\right)+3\div\frac{1}{3}+3\right\}-4\times 2\right]$$
(a) 18 (b) 15 (c) 12 (d) 19

104. A thief running at 7 km/h is chased by a policeman, whose speed is 12 km/h. If the thief is 280 m ahead of the policeman, then the time required for the policeman to catch the thief will be
(a) $3\frac{1}{25}$ min (b) $3\frac{9}{25}$ min
(c) $4\frac{9}{25}$ min (d) $3\frac{2}{25}$ min

105. The cost price of 36 articles is the same as the selling price of N articles. If the profit is 20%, then the value of N is
(a) 40 (b) 30
(c) 25 (d) 42

106. A can do a work in 20 days and B in 30 days. If they work on it together for 2 days,then what is the fraction of the work that is left?
(a) $\frac{5}{8}$ (b) $\frac{3}{5}$
(c) $\frac{5}{7}$ (d) $\frac{5}{6}$

107. A man wishes to cover 1 km distance in river water. In still water he takes 12 min to cover it, but in the flowing river he takes 13 min. The speed of the flowing water of the river is
(a) 22 km/h (b) $\frac{7}{12}$ km/h
(c) 25km/h (d) $\frac{5}{13}$ km/h

108. Study the given bar-graph and answer the question that follows.
The bar-graph gives the sales and profit (both in ₹ crore) of Company Z across four years.

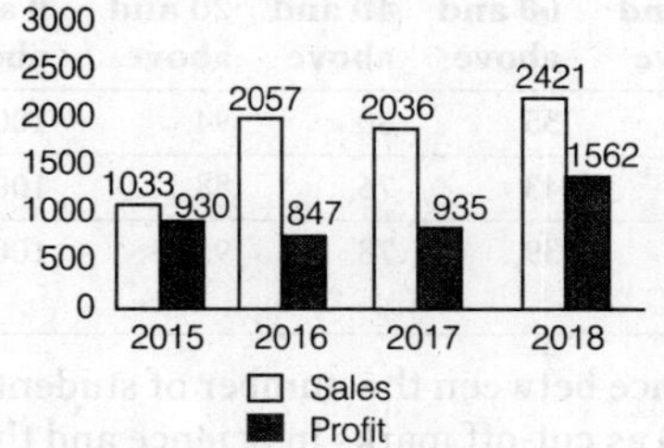

What was the approximate percentage profit margin on revenue of Company Z in 2016 ?
(a) 70% (b) 54.64%
(c) 41.18% (d) 60%

109. A train covers 60 km at a speed of 80 km/h, 100 km at a speed of 90 km/h and another 140 km at a speed of 120 km/h. Find the average speed for the complete journey round to the nearest integer.
(a) 115 km/h (b) 99 km/h
(c) 90 km/h (d) 105 km/h

110. From external point A, tangents AP and AQ are drawn to a circle with centre O. If $\angle APQ = 40°$, then find $\angle POQ$.
(a) 60° (b) 100°
(c) 110° (d) 80°

111. The base of a parallelogram is twice its height. If the area of the parallelogram is 338 cm^2, then find its height (in cm).
(a) 11 (b) 13
(c) 14 (d) 12

112. 57% of Ranita's weekly income is equal to 76% of Bhaskar's weekly income. If Ranita's weekly income was reduced by ₹ 400, while Bhaskar's weekly income did not change the ratio of the weekly incomes of Ranita and Bhaskar, respectively, would have been 6 : 5. What is Bhaskar's weekly income (in ₹)?
(a) 3000 (b) 4000
(c) 2800 (d) 3200

113. A person borrowed ₹ 1760 at 6% p.a. and ₹ 2240 at 9% p.a. at simple interest for the same period. He had to pay ₹ 1536 in all as interest. Find the time (in years).
(a) 2 (b) 3 (c) 4 (d) 5

114. Simplify : $(1+\tan^2 A)+\left(1+\frac{1}{\tan^2 A}\right)$
(a) $\frac{1}{\cot^2 A-\tan^4 A}$
(b) $\frac{1}{\sin^2 A-\sin^4 A}$
(c) $\frac{1}{\sin^2 A-\cos^4 A}$
(d) $\frac{1}{\cos^2 A-\sin^4 A}$

115. The possible value of x satisfying $\frac{(143+13\times x-3\times 3)}{(6^2-7\times 5+x^2)}=1$ is
(a) 4 (b) 1
(c) 3 (d) 2

116. Find the value of $12+24\div 2-7\times 30\div 6 +(5+4)\times 8+8\div 8-8$.
(a) 45 (b) 54
(c) 85 (d) 58

117. The percentage distribution of the number of tires of different brands produced in a year by a certain factory is shown in the given pie-chart. The total number of tires sold is 1350.

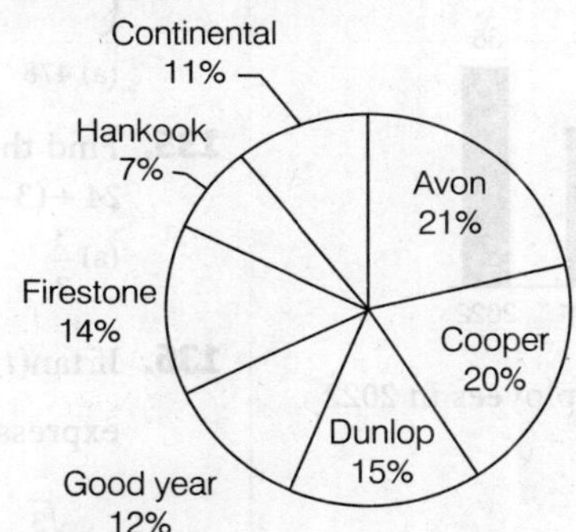

What is the different between the average number of Avon and Firestone tires sold together and the average number of Good year and Dunlop tires sold together?
(a) 55 (b) 54 (c) 46 (d) 45

118. Simplify the given expression.
$25\div 5\times 7$ of $(5+7)-13(6\times 4)$
(a) 108 (b) 138
(c) 126 (d) 112

119. Ramanna purchased raw materials for a certain price to manufacture a product. However, owing to shortage of labour, 22.5% of the raw materials could not be utilised and got wasted. 80% of the cost of raw materials used was added as the cost of manufacturing. If Ramanna could sell his product at a price to earn an overall profit of 20% after offering a discount of 20%, how many times of the total cost of the raw materials purchased was the marked price of the product?
(a) 2.43 times (b) 2.40 times
(c) 2.44 times (d) 4.42 times

120. Simplify the following expression.
$3\frac{1}{5}$ of $2\frac{3}{4}\div\frac{11}{3}+\left(2\frac{1}{5}\div 1\frac{2}{5}\text{ of } 1\frac{3}{7}-2\frac{1}{3}\right)$
(a) $2\frac{1}{6}$ (b) $4\frac{1}{6}$
(c) $1\frac{1}{6}$ (d) $3\frac{1}{6}$

121. A shopkeeper offers 3 schemes of discounts to his customers. Which of the following schemes will fetch the minimum discount percentage?
(A)Two successive discounts of 24% and 27%.
(B) Buy 5 get 3 free.
(C) Buy 6 and get 10.
(a) B (b) A
(c) C (d) Both A and C

122. If the radius of a sphere is 2.1 cm, then the volume of sphere is equal to
(a) 38.088 cm^3 (b) 36.808 cm^3
(c) 38.808 cm^3 (d) 36.088 cm^3

123. Study the given table (pictograph) and answer the question that follows.
The table (pictograph) shows that number of scouts in a school.

Class/Number of scouts	☺ = 15 scouts
IV	☺☺☺☺☺☺
V	☺☺
VI	☺☺☺☺☺☺☺☺
VII	☺☺☺☺
VIII	☺☺☺

What is the total number of scouts in classes VI to VIII?
(a) 225 (b) 320
(c) 200 (d) 195

124. If $\cot\theta = 28/45$, then find the value of $(\sin\theta-\cos\theta)$.
(a) 7/53 (b) 17/53
(c) 28/53 (d) 45/28

125. Find the single discount rate percentage equivalent to the successive discounts of 10%, 20% and 20%.
(a) 40% (b) 42.4% (c) 50% (d) 54.6%

126. *A* can complete a piece of work alone in 200 days, while *B* can complete the same piece of work alone in 100 days. In every three-day cycle, both *A* and *B* work on day 1,only *A* works on day 2 and only *B* works on day 3. This cycle continues till the work is completed. How many days in all does it take the duo to complete the work?
(a) 100 (b) $99\frac{2}{3}$ (c) $100\frac{1}{2}$ (d) $100\frac{1}{3}$

127. A 12 L solution of acid and water contains 30% acid. How much water (in litres) must be added to get a solution having 20% acid?
(a) 3 (b) 6 (c) 5 (d) 4

128. The value of
$52-[18\div3+3+(18-11)\text{of}\,4]$ is equal to
(a) 18 (b) 15
(c) 21 (d) 22

129. Study the given graph and answer that question that follows.
The following bar-graph shows the strength of employees (in lakhs) in a company during five different years.

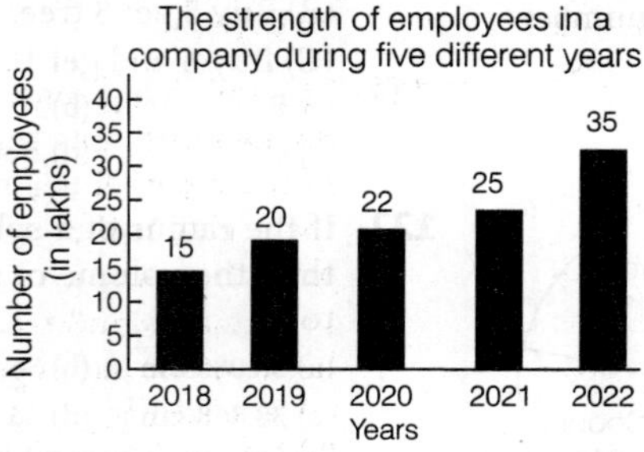

What was the percentage increase in employees in 2022 over 2019?
(a) 70% (b) 75%
(c) 25% (d) 20%

130. The sum of two numbers *x* and *y* (where *x* is greater than *y*) is equal to four times of their difference. Find the value of $\frac{5xy}{3(x^2-y^2)}$.
(a) $\frac{25}{16}$ (b) 16
(c) $2\frac{3}{16}$ (d) 25

131. If the sum of two numbers *x* and *y* is 12 and their product is 27, then find the sum of their cubes.
(a) 576 (b) 657
(c) 756 (d) 765

132. The following table shows the classification of 100 students based on the marks obtained by them in Maths and Science in an examination.

Subjects	Marks out of 100				
	80 and above	60 and above	40 and above	20 and above	0 and above
Maths	12	35	80	94	100
Science	16	43	76	88	100
Average (Aggregate)	14	39	78	91	100

What is the difference between the number of students. who passed with 60 as cut-off marks in Science and those, who passed with 60 as cut-off marks in aggregate?
(a) 5 (b) 3 (c) 6 (d) 4

133. What is the total surface area of a cone, whose radius is $\frac{r}{4}$ and slant height is $4l$?
(a) $4\pi r(l+r)$ (b) $\pi r\left(l+\frac{r}{4}\right)$
(c) $\pi r\left(l+\frac{r}{16}\right)$ (d) $8\pi r(l+r)$

134. How many metres of cloth will be required to make a conical tent, the radius of whose base is 21 m and height is 28 m. The width of the cloth is 5 m.
$\left(\text{where, } \pi=\frac{22}{7}\right)$
(a) 478 (b) 462 (c) 456 (d) 470

135. Find the value of
$24\div(3-8\times3+27)+3$.
(a) $\frac{3}{2}$ (b) 7 (c) $\frac{1}{2}$ (d) $\frac{6}{5}$

136. If $\tan(t)+\cot(t)=1$, then one of the values of the expression $\frac{1}{\sin(t)+\cos(t)}$ is......
(a) $\frac{\sqrt{3}}{2}$ (b) $\frac{2}{\sqrt{3}}$ (c) $\frac{1}{\sqrt{3}}$ (d) $\sqrt{3}$

137. A sum of money at compound interest doubles itself in 4 yr. In how many years does the sum become 8 times of itself at the same rate of interest?
(a) 10 (b) 15 (c) 12 (d) 8

138. The chord length of a chord made on an arc of a circle is equal to the radius of the circle. The length of the arc is ....(in units), if the radius of the circle is 21 units.
$\left(\text{take, } \pi=\frac{22}{7}\right)$
(a) 21 (b) 24
(c) 22 (d) 20

139. In an election, 12% of the voters in the voter list did not cast their votes, where as 84 voters cast their ballot papers blank. There were only two candidates, Ramagya and Shravan. The winner, Ramagya was supported by 54% of all the voters in the list. He got 1456 more votes than his rival, Shravan. Find the total number of voters in the list.
(a) 5690 (b) 6860 (c) 6670 (d) 7860

140. The value of

$$3\frac{2}{3}\div 2\frac{1}{5}\times\frac{1}{4}\times\left(1+\frac{3}{1-\frac{2}{5}}\right) \text{ is}$$

(a) $2\frac{1}{4}$ (b) $1\frac{3}{4}$ (c) $3\frac{1}{2}$ (d) $2\frac{1}{2}$

141. A hemispherical bowl is 88 cm round the brim. Assuming it to be full, how many persons may be served from it in hemispherical glasses, 7 cm in diameter at the top? $\left(\text{where, } \pi = \frac{22}{7}\right)$
(a) 68 (b) 64 (c) 74 (d) 70

142. If $x+y+z=1, xy+yz+zx=-1$ and $xyz=-1$, then $(x^3+y^3+z^3)$ is equal to.......
(a) 1 (b) 3 (c) 2 (d) 0

143. Refer the below data and answer the following question

Partners	Present% share
Singh	10
Pandey	5
Anil	15
Sunil	25
Varma	30
Rajesh	15

If the company has issued 8 lakh shares between its 6 partners and if varma offers to sell 10000 of his shares to Pandey, then how many shares will pandey have?
(a) 40000 (b) 50000
(c) 20000 (d) 30000

144. If $\sec 6A = \text{cosec}(A-29°)$, where $2A$ is an acute angle, then the measure of $\angle A = ...°$
(a) 18 (b) 19
(c) 17 (d) 21

145. In ΔABC, P is a point on AB such that $PB : AP = 3 : 4$ and PQ is parallel to AC. If AR and QS are perpendicular to PC and $QS = 9$ cm, what is the length (in cm) of AR?
(a) 35 (b) 28
(c) 21 (d) 14

146. The fourth proportional to 4, a and $16a$ is 81. What is the value of a?
(a) $\frac{13}{2}$ (b) $\frac{5}{2}$
(c) $\frac{9}{2}$ (d) $\frac{11}{2}$

147. In an election between two candidates, one got 60% of the total valid votes. 25% of the votes were invalid. If the total number of votes was 15000, then find the number of valid votes that the other candidate got.
(a) 5000 (b) 4500
(c) 5550 (d) 6750

148. In ΔABC, AD is the internal bisector of $\angle A$, meeting the side BC at D. If $BD = 5$ cm, $BC = 7.5$ cm, then $AB : AC$ is
(a) 2 : 1 (b) 1 : 3
(c) 1 : 2 (d) 3 : 1

149. Two numbers are in the ratio of 3 : 7. If 11 is subtracted from each, the ratio between the numbers becomes 7 : 20. Find the smaller number.
(a) 39 (b) 27
(c) 36 (d) 21

150. A car covers 20 km in the first quarter of an hour, 25 km in the second quarter of that hour and 15 km in the third quarter. The average speed of the car (in km/h) over the entire journey is
(a) 80 (b) 70 (c) 65 (d) 75

Part IV
English Comprehension

151. Select the word from the sentence below, which is an antonym for the word 'uniformity'
A great variety of birds is found in the sanctuaries of India.
(a) Great (b) Variety
(c) Found (d) Sanctuaries

152. Select the most appropriate meaning of the given phrase.
Hit the sack
(a) Running on the beach
(b) Cracking the exams
(c) Going to sleep
(d) Making money quickly

153. Select the incorrectly spelt word.
(a) Mountan (b) Weekend
(c) Dessert (d) Journey

154. Select the incorrectly spelt word.
(a) Equally (b) Unwilling
(c) Argument (d) Occured

155. Select the option that can be used as a one-word substitute for the given group of words.
Attempting to impress by affecting greater importance or merit than is actually possessed
(a) Pretentious (b) Imperious
(c) Airy (d) Glorious

156. Select the incorrectly spelt word.
(a) Ettiquete
(b) Rationalisation
(c) Elopement
(d) Occasion

157. The following sentence has been divided into four segments. One of them contains an error. Select the segment that contains the error from the given options.
I am understanding;/ you like her/ because she has /a generous nature.
(a) you like her
(b) I am understanding
(c) a generous nature
(d) because she has

158. Select the most appropriate antonym of the underlined word.
The repetitive and <u>monotonous</u> task of data entry made the work seem incredibly long and tedious.
(a) pious
(b) interesting
(c) precarious
(d) threatening

159. Parts of the following sentence have been given as options. Select the option that contains a spelling error.
Joe was so tired that he could scarely stand.
(a) he could
(b) so tired that
(c) scarely stand
(d) Joe was

160. Select the option that can be used as a one-word substitute for the given group of words.
A woman having more than one husband at the same time
(a) Endogamy (b) Polymathy
(c) Polyandry (d) Monogamy

161. Select the most appropriate idiom for the underlined part in the given sentence.
Sohan was very much perplexed to find that his younger brother Mohan had taken poison.
(a) At any rate
(b) At his wit's end
(c) At logger heads
(d) At his disposal

162. Select the most suitable expression that can substitute the underlined part of the sentence without any change in meaning.
Planning to go for a movie just before the final-year examination is nothing but skating on thin ice.
(a) doing hard work
(b) being in a risky situation
(c) enjoying the moment
(d) going to hill stations

163. Select the word which means the same as the group of words given.
A society or company provides these convenient features.
(a) Equipment (b) Facilitate
(c) System (d) Amenities

164. Select the most appropriate antonym of the underlined word in the given sentence.
The speaker delivered a profound speech that left the audience deeply moved.
(a) Deep (b) Inventive
(c) Shallow (d) Occult

165. Select the most appropriate synonym of the underlined word in the following sentence.
He behaved ruthlessly with his junior, to say the least.
(a) Unexpectedly (b) Inhumanly
(c) Weirdly (d) Politely

166. Select the most appropriate antonym of the highlighted word
The worker is known to **exert** himself a lot.
(a) crouch (b) emerge
(c) relax (d) stress

167. Select the most appropriate segment to substitute the underlined words in the given sentence.
The referee declared that the participant who will score the highest points in the tally will take away the cash prize of .50 lakh.
(a) who can score the highest point
(b) who scores the highest point
(c) who could score the highest point
(d) who settles scores the highest point

168. Select the most appropriate option that can substitute the underlined segment in the given sentence.
My friends are on a trip to the world.
(a) in the world
(b) by the world
(c) within the world
(d) around the world

169. Select the most appropriate meaning of the given idiom.
Yeoman's service
(a) Excellent work done
(b) A thankless and tedious job
(c) Working under a cruel master
(d) Fraudulent service

170. Select the most appropriate option that can substitute the underlined segment in the given sentence.
The Government must strive to provide a/an fair and square deal to the citizen of its country.
(a) exclusive and unreal
(b) honest and straightforward
(c) violent and immoral
(d) forward and backward

171. The following sentence has been divided into four segments. Identify the segment that has a grammatical error.
When he resigned, / the company offered him / a huge sum of money but / he refused to agree to it.
(a) a huge sum of money but
(b) When he resigned,
(c) he refused to agree to it.
(d) the company offered him

172. Three segments of the following sentence have been underlined and given as options.
One of them may contain an error. Select the option that contains the error. If you don't find any error, mark 'No error' as your answer.
Since his son has not yet completed the age of eighteen, he was reluctant to fulfil his son's demand of getting a motorbike.
(a) of getting a motorbike
(b) No error
(c) to fulfil his son's demand
(d) he was reluctant

173. Identify the most appropriate antonym of the given word.
Freezing
(a) Summery (b) Brisk
(c) Gnawing (d) Tropical

174. In the following sentence, four words are underlined, out of which one word is misspelt. Select the misspelt word.
The shedule followed by my sister ultimately leads to stress and other adverse effects.
(a) ultimately (b) adverse
(c) followed (d) shedule

175. Select the option that can be used as a one-word substitute for the given group of words.
A professional rider in horse races
(a) Jockey (b) Stuntman
(c) Southpaw (d) Batsman

176. Select the most appropriate option to substitute the underlined segment in the given sentence.
An awkward neither grammatically accurate sentence is the result of centre implanting.
(a) awkward but grammatically
(b) awkward either grammatically
(c) awkward beyond grammatically
(d) awkward unless grammatically

177. Parts of the following sentence have been given as options. Select the option that contains an error.
Can we go visit a Statue of Liberty on our trip to the United States?
(a) on our trip to
(b) Can we go
(c) the United States?
(d) visit a Statue of Liberty

178. Select the option that is similar in meaning to the underlined word in the following sentence.
A good critic should also be a person of great candour.
(a) will (b) resolution
(c) honesty (d) power

179. Select the word which means the same as the group of words underlined in the given sentence.
These glass windows are so old and one can't even see through them, they need to be replaced.
(a) Opaque
(b) Dirty
(c) Transparent
(d) Black

180. The following sentence has been split into four segments. Identify the segment that contains a spelling error.
The precarious case of juvenile / deliquency against him / was dismissed by the / jury in the first hearing.
(a) The precarious case of juvenile
(b) jury in the first hearing.
(c) deliquency against him
(d) was dismissed by the

181. Select the most appropriate meaning of the given idiom.
By leaps and bounds
(a) Unknowingly
(b) Normally
(c) Slowly
(d) Rapidly

182. Select the sentence that uses the given idiom correctly.
Skating on thin ice
(a) They were on thin ice when they skated on the frozen lake.
(b) She was on thin ice while trying to balance on a tightrope.
(c) He was on thin ice after making a controversial statement.
(d) They were on thin ice due to the icy conditions on the road

183. Select the most appropriate segment to substitute the underlined words in the given sentence.
Youth is the time when the seeds of character is sown.
(a) the seeds of character will have been sowing
(b) the seeds of character had been sown
(c) the seeds of character were sown
(d) the seeds of character are sown

184. Select the most appropriate antonym of the given word from the following sentence.
Confusing
The stars twinkled in the dark sky, guiding travellers on their journey.
(a) Guiding
(b) Twinkled
(c) Travellers
(d) Journey

185. Select the most appropriate option that can substitute the underlined segment in the given sentence.
I prefer walking than riding.
(a) walking to riding
(b) walking above riding
(c) walking from riding
(d) walking with riding

186. Parts of the following sentence have been given as options. Select the option that contains an error.
We were grateful for a book they gave us.
(a) they gave us
(b) We were
(c) grateful for
(d) a book

187. Select the most appropriate meaning of the given idiom.
Be in seventh heaven
(a) To be ignored
(b) To start performing better
(c) To be in a state of extreme happiness
(d) To avoid talking about what's important

188. Select the most appropriate option that can substitute the underlined segment in the given sentence.
Shakespeare is great than any other English poet.
(a) was great than (b) was greater than
(c) is greater than (d) is greatest than

189. Select the most appropriate synonym of the given word.
Reckon
(a) Merit (b) Assess
(c) Count (d) Imagine

190. Identify the most appropriate meaning of the given idiom.
Bread and butter
(a) Comfortable living
(b) Means of livelihood
(c) The breakfast
(d) Money making

Directions (Q. Nos. 191-195) *In the following passage, some words have been deleted. Read the passage carefully and select the most appropriate option to fill in each blank.*

Superheroes are fictional characters with ...(1)... powers who use their powers to fight crime and protect the public. Some popular superheroes include Superman, Batman, Spider- Man and Wonder Woman. Superheroes often have backstories that ...(2)... how they have gained their powers, ...(3)... being born with special powers, being bitten by a radioactive spider or being exposed to cosmic radiation. They usually have a specific outfit or clothing that they wear to hide their identity and protect ...(4)... while fighting crime. Superheroes have been a staple of popular culture ...(5)... decades, appearing in comics, movies, television shows, and video games.

191. Select the most appropriate option to fill in blank no. 1.
(a) extraordinary (b) pragmatic
(c) hereditary (d) familiar

192. Select the most appropriate option to fill in blank no. 2.
(a) explaining (b) was explain
(c) explain (d) had explain

193. Select the most appropriate option to fill in blank no. 3.
(a) therefore (b) subsequently
(c) instead (d) such as

194. Select the most appropriate option to fill in blank no. 4.
(a) themselves (b) ourselves
(c) herself (d) himself

195. Select the most appropriate option to fill in blank no. 5.
(a) for (b) on
(c) under (d) above

Directions (Q. Nos. 196-200) *Read the passage given below and answer the questions that follow*

There are no ancient nations anywhere in the world. All nations are modern. Ancient Greece, ancient Egypt, ancient India – all of them may have had great civilizations whose architecture, art, and literature are objects of admiration. But they are not nations. To realize this truth, you will have to forget for the time being the history you were taught at school. Because it is that history, drilled into your heads from the time you were children, and constantly renewed by national festivals and ceremonies, the speeches of your leaders, and novels, films, and television serials, that make it seem obvious to you that your nation is ancient. In actual fact, it is not true. Your nation is not – indeed no nation on earth is – ancient. Only modern people can imagine that way.

196. Find out the correct antonym of the following word.
Realise
(a) Misunderstand (b) Understand
(c) Comprehend (d) Grasp

197. Which of the following statements is correct?
(a) Only modern people can imagine the existence of ancient nations.
(b) History books should be read again and again because they celebrate ancient nations.
(c) Ancient India is an ancient civilisation but not an ancient nation.
(d) Novels, films and speeches of leaders celebrate the modernity of nations

198. Find out the correct synonym of the following word.
Obvious
(a) Dubious (b) Clear
(c) Ambiguous (d) Doubtful

199. Why does the author of the passage ask us to forget the history that we were taught at school?
(a) Because the history book taught us that our nation is ancient.
(b) Because only the modern people can imagine that way.
(c) Because the history book taught us that there are no ancient nations in the world.
(d) Because the history book asks us to celebrate festivals which make us believe that our nation is modern.

200. What does the expression 'drill into your heads' mean?
(a) Make someone learn or understand something by repeating it.
(b) Threaten someone repeatedly drill machine.
(c) Force someone to move his/her head in a particular direction.
(d) Repeatedly question someone regarding a certain issue.

Know Correct Answers

1. (d)	2. (a)	3. (b)	4. (a)	5. (c)	6. (b)	7. (b)	8. (b)	9. (c)	10. (c)
11. (d)	12. (d)	13. (d)	14. (d)	15. (c)	16. (d)	17. (c)	18. (c)	19. (b)	20. (a)
21. (b)	22. (d)	23. (b)	24. (b)	25. (a)	26. (d)	27. (a)	28. (d)	29. (d)	30. (c)
31. (c)	32. (d)	33. (c)	34. (b)	35. (d)	36. (d)	37. (c)	38. (d)	39. (a)	40. (c)
41. (a)	42. (b)	43. (d)	44. (d)	45. (d)	46. (a)	47. (c)	48. (d)	49. (b)	50. (b)
51. (a)	52. (d)	53. (a)	54. (b)	55. (c)	56. (a)	57. (a)	58. (a)	59. (d)	60. (d)
61. (c)	62. (d)	63. (b)	64. (b)	65. (b)	66. (a)	67. (c)	68. (a)	69. (b)	70. (b)
71. (d)	72. (c)	73. (d)	74. (d)	75. (a)	76. (c)	77. (a)	78. (b)	79. (b)	80. (d)
81. (b)	82. (b)	83. (c)	84. (c)	85. (a)	86. (b)	87. (a)	88. (c)	89. (b)	90. (d)
91. (b)	92. (a)	93. (b)	94. (a)	95. (b)	96. (b)	97. (d)	98. (d)	99. (d)	100. (a)
101. (c)	102. (b)	103. (d)	104. (b)	105. (b)	106. (d)	107. (d)	108. (c)	109. (b)	110. (d)
111. (b)	112. (a)	113. (d)	114. (b)	115. (b)	116. (b)	117. (b)	118. (a)	119. (a)	120. (c)
121. (a)	122. (c)	123. (a)	124. (b)	125. (b)	126. (b)	127 (b)	128. (b)	129. (b)	130. (a)
131. (c)	132. (d)	133. (c)	134. (b)	135. (b)	136. (c)	137 (c)	138. (c)	139. (b)	140. (d)
141. (b)	142. (a)	143. (b)	144. (c)	145. (c)	146. (c)	147. (b)	148. (a)	149. (a)	150. (a)
151. (b)	152. (c)	153. (a)	154. (d)	155. (a)	156. (a)	157. (b)	158. (b)	159. (c)	160. (c)
161. (b)	162. (b)	163. (d)	164. (c)	165. (b)	166. (c)	167. (b)	168. (d)	169. (a)	170. (b)
171. (c)	172. (d)	173. (d)	174. (d)	175. (a)	176. (a)	177. (d)	178. (c)	179. (a)	180. (c)
181. (d)	182. (c)	183. (d)	184. (a)	185. (a)	186. (d)	187. (c)	188. (c)	189. (d)	190. (b)
191. (a)	192. (c)	193. (d)	194. (a)	195. (a)	196. (a)	197. (c)	198. (b)	199. (a)	200. (a)

Answer & Solutions

1. **(d)** As per the question, the sequence of folding a paper and the manner in which the folded paper is cut is shown in the figures option (d) paper look, when unfolded.

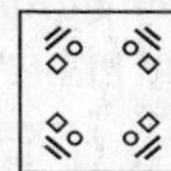

2. **(a)** In the given figure series, add one △ and ▼ alternatively in clockwise direction in the every next figure.

Hence, figure of opiton (a) will logically complete the series.

3. **(b)** As per the given data,

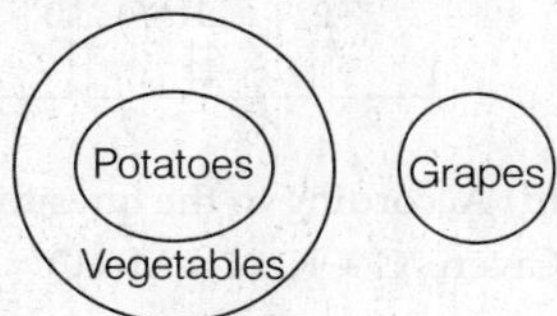

As, potatoes is vegetable and grapes are fruit.

4. **(a)** As, $15 : 45 \Rightarrow (15)^2 \div 5 = 45$

and $25 : 125 \Rightarrow (25)^2 \div 5 = 125$

Similarly, $20 : 80 \Rightarrow (20)^2 \div 5 = 80$

5. **(c)** As,

D	I	N	E	S	H
4	9	14	5	19	8
×3↓	×3↓	×3↓	×3↓	×3↓	×3↓
12 –	27 –	42 –	15 –	57 –	24

and

V	I	R	A	T
22	9	18	1	20
×3↓	×3↓	×3↓	×3↓	×3↓
66 –	27 –	54 –	3 –	60

Similarly,

G	A	U	T	A	M
7	1	21	20	1	13
×3↓	×3↓	×3↓	×3↓	×3↓	×3↓
21 –	3 –	63 –	60 –	3 –	39

6. **(b)** The given figure is embedded in the figure of option (b).

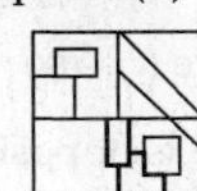

7. **(b)** As, (247, 349)

$\Rightarrow \quad 247 + 102 = 349$

and (261, 363)

$\Rightarrow \quad 261 + 102 = 363$

Similarly, (294, 396)

$\Rightarrow \quad 294 + 102 = 396$

8. **(b)** The pattern of given series is as follow,

$C \xrightarrow{+1} D \xrightarrow{+1} E \xrightarrow{+1} \boxed{F}$

$H \xrightarrow{+1} I \xrightarrow{+1} J \xrightarrow{+1} \boxed{K}$

$O \xrightarrow{+1} P \xrightarrow{+1} Q \xrightarrow{+1} \boxed{R}$

9. **(c)** Given,

13*7*12*4*15*65

From option (c),

$13 + 7 + 12 \div 4 \times 15 = 65$

$\Rightarrow \quad 13 + 7 + 3 \times 15 = 65$

$\Rightarrow \quad 20 + 45 = 65$

$\Rightarrow \quad 65 = 65$

10. **(c)** According to the question,

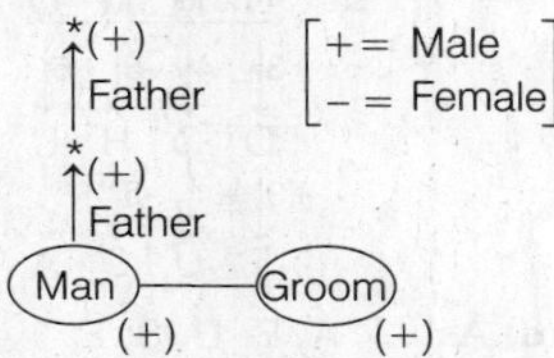

Hence, groom is brother of man.

11. **(d)** Given,

$10 \div 63 \times 7 + 90 - 80 = 100$

Form option (d),

$10 \times 63 \div 7 + 90 - 80 = 100$

$\Rightarrow \quad 10 \times 9 + 90 - 80 = 100$

$\Rightarrow \quad 90 + 90 - 80 = 100$

$\Rightarrow \quad 180 - 80 = 100 \Rightarrow 100 = 100$

12. **(d)** Given,

$22 \times 11 - 450 \div 50 + 500 = ?$

After substituting the sign we get,

$? = 22 \div 11 \times 450 + 50 - 500$

$= 2 \times 450 + 50 - 500$

$= 900 + 50 - 500 = 450$

13. **(d)** As,

C	A	R	S
↓+5	↓+5	↓+5	↓+5
H	F	W	X

and

B	O	A	T
↓+5	↓+5	↓+5	↓+5
G	T	F	Y

Similarly,

F	U	S	E
↓+5	↓+5	↓+5	↓+5
K	Z	X	J

14. **(d)** According to the question,

From figure (X) 6 [3 ↕ 5]

From figure (Y) 6 [2 ↕ 4] Opposite

So, 1 is opposite to 6.

15. **(c)** According to the question,

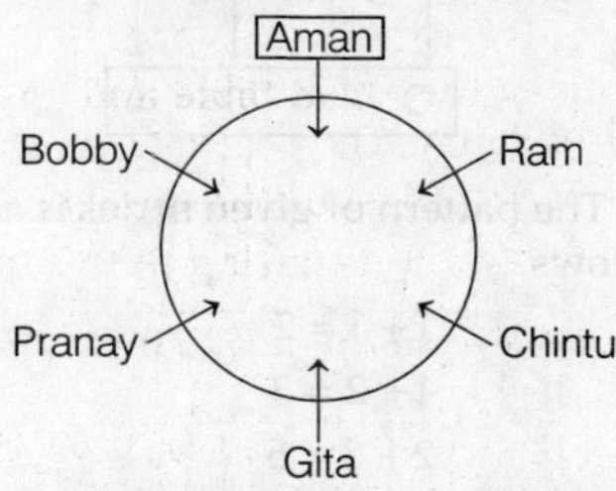

Hence, Aman is the immediate neighbour of Ram and Bobby.

16. **(d)** According to the question,

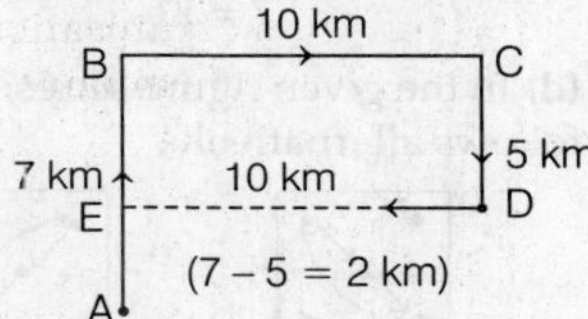

Required distance = DE + EA

= 10 + 2

[∴ EA = AB – CD]

= 12 km

17. **(c)** As per the given data

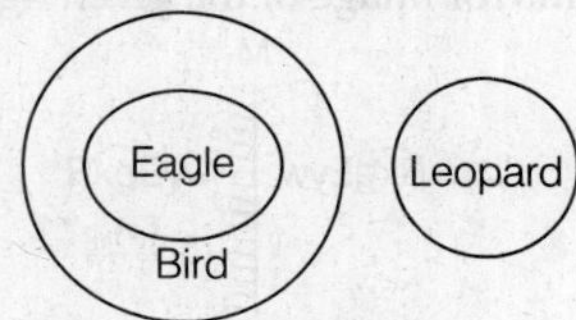

As eagle is the bird and leopard is animal.

18. **(c)** Pattern of the given series is,

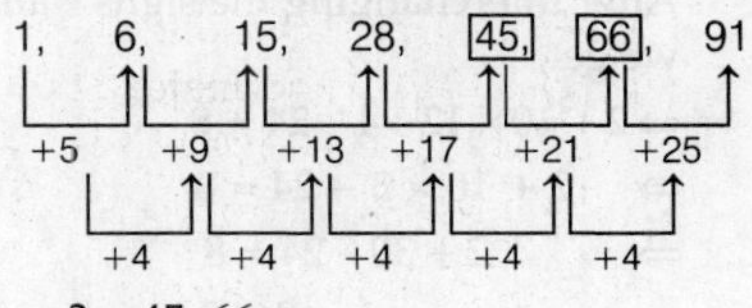

∴ ? = 45, 66

19. **(b)** According to the question,

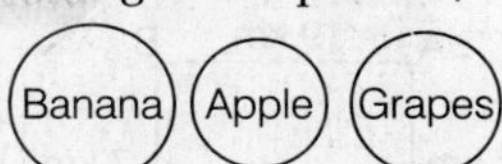

Banana, apple and grapes all are different from each other.

20. **(a)** As, L A N D $\xrightarrow{-3,\,-4,\,-3,\,-4}$ I W K Z

and G O L D $\xrightarrow{-3,\,-4,\,-3,\,-4}$ D K I Z

Similarly, T E A M $\xrightarrow{-3,\,-4,\,-3,\,-4}$ **Q A X I**

21. **(b)** The pattern of given series is as follows.

$$1+1=2$$
$$1+2=3$$
$$2+3=5$$
$$3+5=8$$
$$5+8=13$$
$$8+13=\boxed{21}$$
$$\therefore \quad ?=21$$

22. **(d)** In the given figure series, pattern follows alternatively,

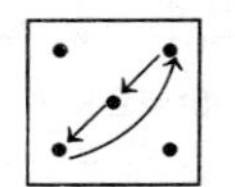

From Fig. (1) to (2) and Fig. (3) to (4) ; From Fig. (2) to (3) and Fig. (4) to (5)

Hence, figure of option (d) will logicallly complete the series.

23. **(b)** Figure of option (b) is the correct mirror image of the given figure,

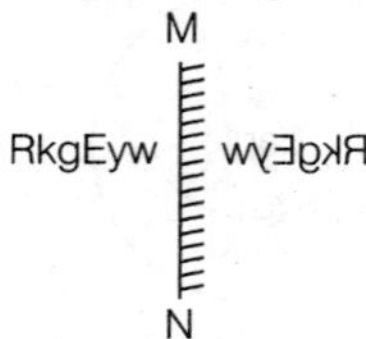

24. **(b)** Given,

$2+10\times 12-4\div 24=8$

After interchanging the signs ÷ and − we get,

$\Rightarrow 2+10\times 12\div 4-24=8$

$\Rightarrow \quad 2+10\times 3-24=8$

$\Rightarrow \quad 2+30-24=8$

$8=8$

25. **(a)** According to the question,

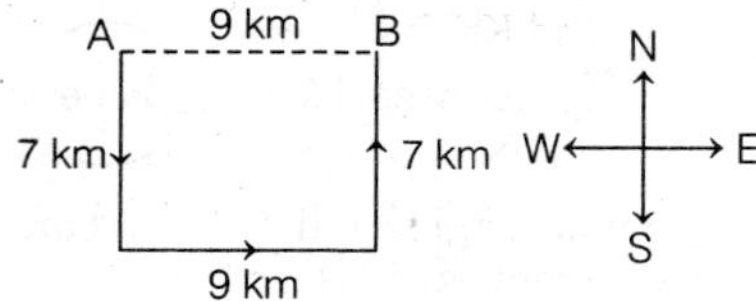

Hence, required distance = 9 km

26. **(d)** As, C U T E $\xrightarrow{+3,\,-4,\,+3,\,-4}$ F Q W A

and B L U E $\xrightarrow{+3,\,-4,\,+3,\,-4}$ E H X A

Similarly, V O T E $\xrightarrow{+3,\,-4,\,+3,\,-4}$ **Y K W A**

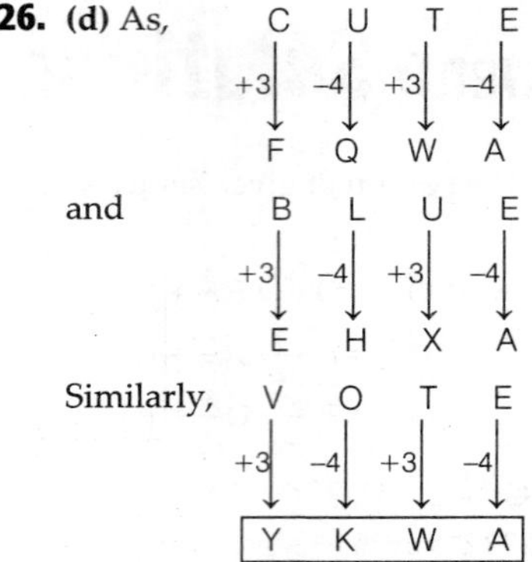

27. **(a)** The pattern of the given series is as follow,

H E W C $\xrightarrow{+3,\,+4,\,-5,\,+6}$ K I R I $\xrightarrow{+3,\,+4,\,-5,\,+6}$ **N M M O** $\xrightarrow{+3,\,+4,\,-5,\,+6}$ Q Q H U $\xrightarrow{+3,\,+4,\,-5,\,+6}$ T U C A

28. **(d)** As, A B U S E → A S U B E

and B E G I N → B I G E N

Similarly, O T H E R → **O E H T R**

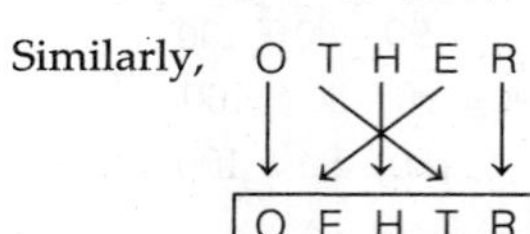

29. **(d)** As, $P\xrightarrow{-3}M\xrightarrow{+6}S$; $U\xrightarrow{-3}R\xrightarrow{+6}X$

$J\xrightarrow{-3}G\xrightarrow{+6}M$ But, $S\xrightarrow{-3}P\xrightarrow{\boxed{+5}}U$

Hence, SPU does not belong to that group.

30. **(c)** The pattern of given series is as follows,

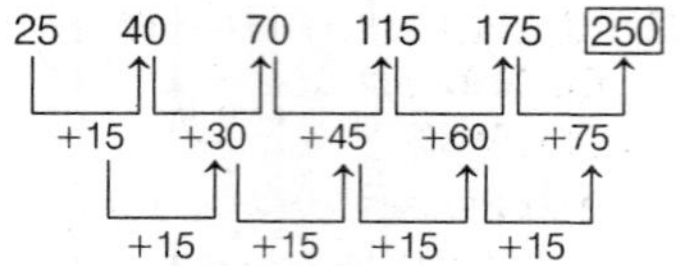

31. **(c)** As, 12 36 6 (×3, ×6)

and 18 54 9 (×3, ×6)

Similarly, 28 84 14 (×3, ×6)

32. **(d)** Given, 10*2*1*8*11*8

From option (d),

$10\div 2-1\times 8+11=8$

$\Rightarrow 5-1\times 8+11=8$

$\Rightarrow \quad 5-8+11=8$

$\Rightarrow \quad 16-8=8$

$\therefore \quad 8=8$

33. **(c)** The given figrue is embedded in the figure of option (c).

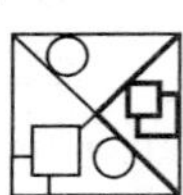

34. **(b)** The pattern of given series is as follows,

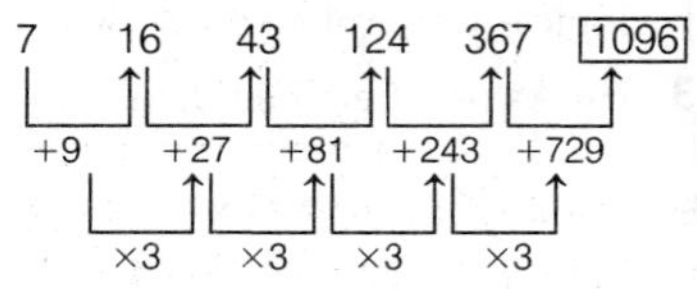

35. **(d)** According to the quesiton ,

Given, 'G + K − L ÷ M × Q'

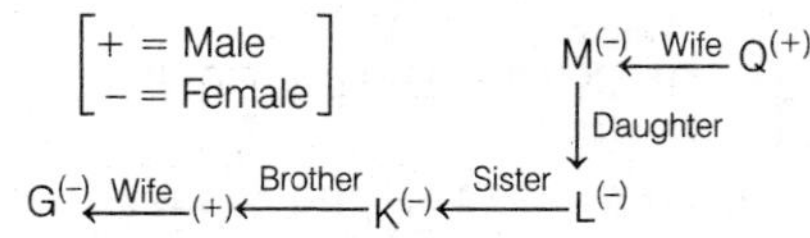

Hence, G is son's is wife of Q.

36. **(d)** As,

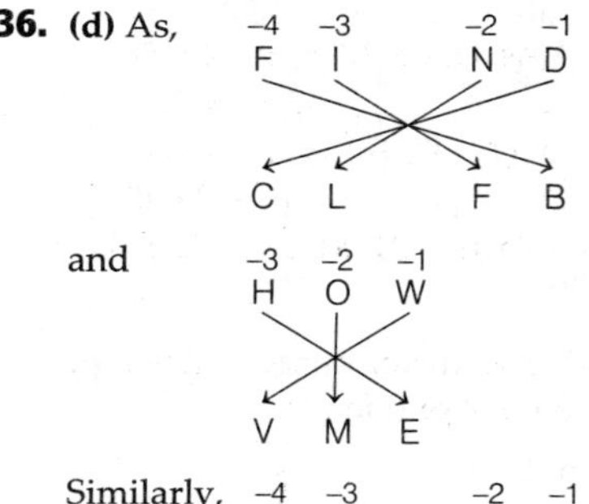

37. **(c)** According to the question,

From figure (x)⟶60 | 40 ↔ 10 | 30 ↔ 20 | Opposite

From figure (y)⟶60

Hence, 50 is opposite to 60.

38. **(d)** As per the English dictionary order,

Conflagration ⟶ Conscience ⟶ Consequence ⟶ Considerable ⟶ Consignment ⟶ Consistence

(3) (2) (4) (5) (6) (1)

Hence, option (d) is the correct answer.

39. **(a)** Given, $14-7\times 10\div 1+7=?$

After interchanging the sign we get,

$? = 14\div 7+10-1\times 7$

$= 2+10-1\times 7$

$= 2+10-7=5$

40. **(c)** As,

D I C E
+1 +2 +3 +4
E K F I

and

P L A N
+1 +2 +3 +4
Q N D R

Similarly,

L U D O
+1 +2 +3 +4
M W G S

41. **(a)** As, $12:40 \Rightarrow 12\times 3+4=40$

and $9:31 \Rightarrow 9\times 3+4=31$

Similarly, $16:52 \Rightarrow 16\times 3+4=\boxed{52}$

42. **(b)** The pattern of given series is as follows,

F $\xrightarrow{+1}$ G $\xrightarrow{+1}$ H $\xrightarrow{+1}$ I

D $\xrightarrow{-1}$ C $\xrightarrow{-1}$ B $\xrightarrow{-1}$ A

K $\xrightarrow{+2}$ M $\xrightarrow{+2}$ O $\xrightarrow{+2}$ Q

I $\xrightarrow{-2}$ G $\xrightarrow{-2}$ E $\xrightarrow{-2}$ C

43. **(d)** As, $(9, 36, 12) \Rightarrow 9\times 4=36$

$12\times 3=36$

and $(12, 48, 16) \Rightarrow 12\times 4=48$

$16\times 3=48$

Similarly, $(21, 84, 28) \Rightarrow 21\times 4=84$

$28\times 3=84$

44. **(d)** The mirror image of given figure is figure of option (d).

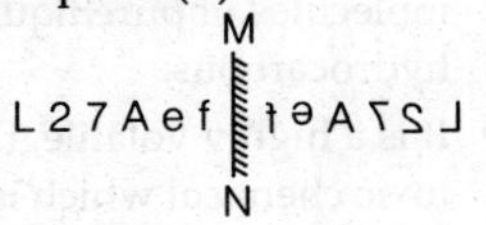

M

L 2 7 A e f | f e A 7 2 L

N

45. **(d)** As,

R A C E
+4 −4 +4 −4
V W G A

and

B A N K
+4 −4 +4 −4
F W R G

Similarly,

S T E M
+4 −4 +4 −4
W P I I

46. **(a)** According to the English dictionary order,

Listen (4) → Litany (3) → Literacy (1) → Literature (2) → Lithograph (5)

47. **(c)** Given, 6_2_0_8 = 20

From option (c), we get

$6\times 2+0+8=20$

$\Rightarrow 12+8=20$

$\Rightarrow 20=20$

48. **(d)** According to the question,

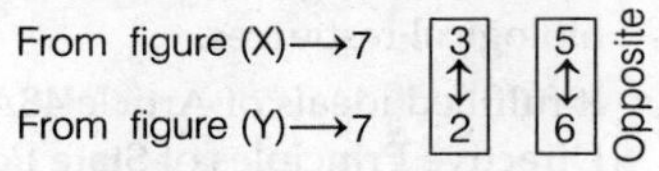

From figure (X) ⟶ 7 | 3 ↕ 2

From figure (Y) ⟶ 7 | 5 ↕ 6 Opposite

Hence, 8 is opposite to 7.

49. **(b)** The pattern of given figure series is as follows,

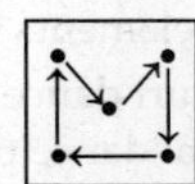

Hence, figure of option (b) can replace the question mark in the given figure series.

50. **(b)** According to the data,

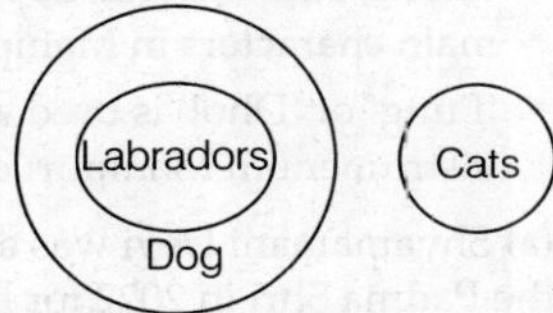

As, Labradors is the breed of dogs, while cat is different.

Hence, option (b) is the answer.

51. **(a)** Under the Sukanya Samriddhi Account Yojana, minimum ₹ 250, maximum deposit ₹1.5 lakh needs to be deposited in one financial year.

- Account can be opened in the name of a girl child till she attains the age of 10 years.
- Only one account can be opened in the name of a girl child.
- Account can be opened in post offices and in authorised banks.
- Tge account matures after 21 years from the date of opening.

52. **(d)** The Central Government launched the National Air Sports Policy in the year **2022**.

- It focuses on promoting air sports in India by making it more safe, affordable, accessible, sustainable and enjoyable.
- The Government of India plans to make India one of the top air sports nations by 2030.

53. **(a)** Fusion is the opposite to solidification. Fusion is the process of conversion of solid to liquid.

- The reverse process will be the conversion of liquid to solid and this is known as solidification.

54. **(b)** The Commonwealth Fencing Championship 2022 was hosted by the **United Kingdom**.

- It is a fencing event held in the Commonwealth of Nations.
- The event included senior, veteran junior cadet and para-fencing competitions.
- England topped the overall medal table with 22 gold, 10 silver and 25 bronze medals.
- The Championships are managed by the Commonwealth Fencing Federation.

55. **(c)** **Article-158** of the Indian Constitution mentions that, where the same person is appointed as the Governor of two or more states, the emoluments and allowances payable to him/her shall be allocated among those states.

- 7th Constitutional Amendment Act of 1956 promoted the appointment of the same person as a governor for two or more states.

56. **(a)** RK Narayan is the author of the book 'The Guide'.

- RK Narayan is one of the most eminent Indian authors of the 20th century.
- Narayan is awarded the National Prize of the Indian Literary Academy, India's chief literary honour.
- He is known for his work set in the fictional South Indian town of Malgudi.

57. **(a)** **Kathakali** is not a part of Odia culture. Gotipua, Paika, Dalkhai are part of Odia culture.

- Dalkhai is one of the most famous folk dances of Western Odisha it signifies woman love.
- Gotipua is a traditional dance form in the state of Odisha, India and the precursor of Odissi classical dance, performed by young boys, who dress as women to praise Jagannath and Krishna.
- Paikas of Odisha were the landed militia who were involved in performing policing functions for the Gajapati rulers.
- Performed by the Munda tribe. It is type of a martial art.

58. **(a)** The thin filamentous extensions that the motile bacterial cells have from their cell wall called Flagella.

- Bacteria show a range in the number and arrangement of flagella.
- Bacterial flagellum is composed of three parts - filament, hook and basal body.

59. **(d)** Famous musician Bhupen Hazarika was awarded the 'Bharat Ratna' in the year 2019.

- He was an Indian playback singer, lyricist, musician, singer, poet and film-maker from Assam, widely known as Sudhakantha.
- In 2024, Karpoori Thakur, MS Swaminathan, PV Narasimha Rao, Lal Krishna Advani and Chaudary Charan Singh was awarded Bharat Ratna.

60. **(d)** Over 5,000 athletes competed in 27 sports for 1,936 medals in the 5th edition of Khelo India Youth Games in 2023.

- Maharashtra emerged as the champion of the Khelo India Youth Games, 2023.
- Tamil Nadu finished second.
- In 2025, Bihar will host Youth Khelo India.

61. **(c)** In the year 1992s, 'Self-Help Group - Bank Linkage Programme' (SHG-BLP) introduced in India.

- The SHG- BLP was first introduced by the National Bank for Agriculture and Rural Development (NABARD) in February 1992.
- Under this programme, banks were linked to Self-Help Groups (SHGs) to distribute credit as well as savings.

62. **(d)** According to Hindu calendar, Diwali falls in the month of Kartika.

- It is the festival of lights. The ancient calendar states that Diwali is celebrated annually on Amavasya or the fifteenth day of the month of Kartika.

63. **(b)** Finance Commission is constituted by the President under Article 280 of the Constitution. It recommend on distribution of tax revenues between the Union and the States and amongst the States themselves.

64. **(b)** Biological Diversity Act, 2002 was passed by the Government of India.

- This is for the conservation of biological diversity and the sustainable use of its components.
- It also ensures fair sharing of the benefits arising out of the use of biological resources.
- It fulfilled ideals of Article 48A of Directive Principles of State Policy in the Constitution of India.

65. **(b)** Jagoi and Cholom are the two main parts corresponding to Lasya and Tandava elements in **Manipuri dance**.

- Manipuri dance is an Indian classical dance practised in North-East India.
- Ras, Sankirtana and Thang-Ta (war dance) are the popular forms of Manipuri dance.
- Radha, Krishna and Gopis are the main characters in Manipuri dance.
- 'Pung' or 'Dhol' is used as the main instrument in Manipuri dance.

66. **(a)** Shyamamani Devi was awarded the Padma Shri in 2022 for her contributions to Odissi music.

- Odissi is one of the 8 recognised classical dances of India.
- The dance originated from the dance of the Devadasis who danced in the temples of Odisha.

67. **(c)** Education is not one of the four primary explicit goals of Five-Year Plans.

- Planning Commission had suggested that India should prepare a plan covering a period of five years.
- The planning commission was established in 1950 on the recommendation of advisory planning board.
- It has four main objectives: growth, modernisation, self-reliance and equity.

68. **(a)** As per Article-75(3) of the Indian Constitution, the Council of Ministers are collectively responsible to the Lok Sabha.

- The Prime Minister and other ministers are collectively known as the Council of Ministers.
- Three categories of the Ministers *viz* Cabinet Ministers, Minister of State and Deputy Ministers.
- All of them are appointed by the President of India.
- The total number of ministers cannot exceed 15% of the total strength of the Lok Sabha.

69. **(b)** Option (b) depicts the inter conversion of the three states of matter.

- The interconversion from solid to liquid is fusion or melting and from liquid to solid is termed as freezing.
- The interconversion from liquid to gas is termed as vaporisation and from gas to liquid is termed as condensation.
- The interconversion from gas to solid and *vice-versa* is sublimation.

70. **(b)** Distance between two cities does not control the climate of a place.

- Whereas , the climate of a place is controlled by latitude, ocean currents and relief features.

71. **(d)** The Shailendra kings who had close contacts with the Indian rulers were followers of Buddhism.

- The kings of this empire, built a monastery at Nalanda in the 9th century and at his request the Pala king Devapala of Bengal granted five villages for its upkeep.

72. **(c)** The name of the hydrocarbon with a structural formula
$CH_3-CH_2-CH_2-CH_2-CH_2-CH_3$
is *n*-Hexane.

- Hexane is a non-polar molecule with a weak intermolecular interactions occur between the molecules of pure liquid hydrocarbons.
- It is a highly volatile, flammable toxic chemical which is a by-product made from crude oil.

73. **(d)** The average elevation of the Eastern Ghats of India is 600 metres.

- Javadi Hills, Palkonda Range, Nallamala Hills, Mahendragiri Hills are some of the important hills of Eastern Ghats.

74. **(d)** **Megasthenes** was the envoys sent by Seleucus I to the court of Chandragupta Maurya.

- Seleucus I Nicator was one of the generals of Alexander the Great who, after Alexander's death, took control of the Eastern part of his empire, which included territories in Asia Minor, Persia and parts of India.

- Megasthenes wrote **Indica**.

75. (a) 'M' stands for Micro in MUDRA yojana.

- MUDRA stands for Micro Units Development and Refinance Agency Ltd. Mudra provides loans into 4 categories.

  Shishu loan upto 50,000.
- **Kishore** loans above 50,000 and upto 5 lakh.
- **Tarun** loan above 5 lakh and upto 10 lakh.
- **Tarun plus** loans above 10 lakh and upto 20 lakh.
- Pradhan Mantri MUDRA Yojana (PMMY) is a scheme launched by the Prime Minister Narendra Modi on 8th April, 2015, for providing loans upto ₹ 20 lakh to the non-corporate, non-farm small/micro-enterprises.

76. (c) Chitra Visweswaran is a famous dancer of **Bharatanatyam** dance genre.

- She has been honoured with Padma Shri Award (1992) and the title of 'Mahila Shiromani' and 'Stree Ratna'.
- She was the first dancer to be invited to occupy the Rabindranath Tagore 'Chair of Fine Arts' in the University of Madras.

77. (a) Article 51-A of the Indian Constitution pertains to the fundamental.

- The Swaran Singh Committee in 1976 recommended Fundamental Duties.
- The 42nd Amendment Act of 1976 added 10 Fundamental Duties to the Indian Constitution.
- The 86th Amendment Act, 2002 later added the 11th Fundamental Duty to the list.

78. (b) Ustad Asad Ali Khan was one of the masters of the **Rudra Veena**.

- He performed in the style dhrupad and was described as the best living Rudra Veena player in India.
- He was awarded the Indian civilian honour Padma Bhushan in 2008.

79. (b) Drought Prone Area Programmes is not a part of the Tenth Five-Year Plan, was a part of the Fourth Five-Year Plan.

- The Tenth Five-Year Plan was to promote inclusive growth and equitable development and intended for an 8% GDP growth per year.
- It aimed at reducing poverty by half and creating employment for 80 million people.
- It also emphasised reducing the gender gaps in the field of education and wage rates by 2007.

80. (d) Alcoholic beverages are not included in the Indian Food Guide Pyramid for healthy eating.

- Balanced diet is the key to staying healthy.
- Follow the 'Healthy Eating Food Pyramid' guide as you pick your food.
- Grains should be taken as the most. Eat more fruit and vegetables. Have a moderate amount of meat, fish, egg, milk and their alternatives. Reduce fat/ oil, salt and sugar.
- Trim fat from meat before cooking.

81. (b) Seshachalam biosphere of Southern Andhra Pradesh is home to many endemic species including the famous Red Sanders and Slender Loris. (endangered species).

- The Seshachalam hills are hilly ranges part of the Eastern Ghats in Andhra Pradesh.
- In 2010 it was designated as Biosphere Reserve. Tirupati, a major Hindu pilgrimage town and the Sri Venkateswara National Park are located in these ranges.
- The native population of the reserve includes the tribes of Yanadis.

82. (b) To vote in public elections is not a Fundamental Duty of an Indian citizen.

- The Fundamental Duties were incorporated in Part IV-A of the Constitution by the 42nd Constitutional Amendment Act, 1976 on the recommendations of the Swaran Singh Committee.

83. (c) K2 is located in the Karakoram Range.
Trisul is a group of three Himalayan mountain peaks of Western Kumaun, Uttarakhand.

- The three peaks resemble a trident. Nanda Devi is the second highest mountain in India, after Kangchenjunga, and the highest located entirely within the country and Kamet.
- Kamet is the second highest mountain in the Garhwal region of Uttarakhand, India, after Nanda Devi.

84. (c) With regard to the component of population density, Arunachal Pradesh is the odd one out.

- Arunachal Pradesh has the lowest population density with 17 persons per sq.km.
- Delhi has the highest population density with 11,320 persons per sq.km.

85. (a) **Arjun Singh Dhurve** is a tribal dancer from the Baiga community, received the Padma Shri Award in 2022.

- Baiga dance form is a traditional dance form of the Baiga tribe, which is an indigenous community residing in the Central Indian State of Madhya Pradesh.

86. (b) Vasco da Gama, who discovered the sea route from Europe to India, belonged to **Portugal**.

- In 1498,Vasco da Gama, a Portuguese sailor, found a sea route directly from Europe to India.
- Vasco da Gama arrives at Calicut at Malabar Coast. Zamorin was the King of Calicut at the time of arrival of Vasco da Gama.

87. (a) **Biogeochemical cycle** consists of sedimentary and gaseous cycles.

- Gaseous cycles include those of nitrogen, oxygen, carbon and water; sedimentary cycles include those of iron, calcium, phosphorus and other more earthbound elements.

88. (c) Kathasaritsagara, a literary work, was originally composed in **Sanskrit**.

- The Kathasaritsagara is also known as Ocean of the Streams of Stories is a famous 11th century.
- It is a collection of Indian legends, fairy tales and folk tales as retold in Sanskrit by **Somadeva**.

89. (b) **Jyotirao Govindrao Phule** was the pioneer of widow remarriages in Maharashtra and also started a girls' school in Poona along with his wife.

- Gulamgiri is written by Jyotiba Phule.
- He, along with his followers, formed the Satyashodhak Samaj (Society of Truth Seekers) to attain equal rights for people from exploited castes.

90. (d) The total length of the Golden Quadrilateral, built by the National Highways Authority of India (NHAI) is 5,846 km.

- It is the largest highway project in India and the fifth longest highway in the world.
- It is the first phase of the National Highways Development Project.
- It connects Delhi, Mumbai, Chennai, Kolkata, etc., and passing through 13 states.

91. (b) Rice is the crop which is grown in Kharif cropping season.

- In Northern States of India during the South-West monsoon season.
- Cotton, Groundnut, Maize and Rice are examples of other Kharif crops.

92. (a) The term 'Dribbling' is used in Basketball.

- Dribbling is bouncing the ball on the floor continuously with one hand at a time.
- It is the only legal way that a player may maintain possession of the ball while walking or running.

93. (b) As per Census of India 2011, Bihar has the lowest literacy rate (male 71.2%, female 51.5%).

- Kerala has the highest literacy rate (male 96.1%, female 92.1%).
- The Census of India pegged the average literacy rate in India to be 73% in 2011.

94. (a) Figure (a) represents Mendeleev's Periodic Table that was published in a German journal in 1872.

- Mendeleev had proposed a periodic table based on the mass number and properties of elements.
- Elements with similar properties were placed in the same group and arranged to increase atomic masses.

95. (b) Dussehra is celebrated in Ashwin month of the Hindu calendar.

- The tenth day after Sharad Navratri is celebrated as Dussehra or Vijayadashmi.
- Vijayadashami , more commonly known as Dussehra, is a major Hindu festival celebrated every year at the end of Durga Puja and Navratri.
- It is observed on the tenth day of the month of Ashwin, the seventh in the Hindu lunisolar calendar.

96. (b) The correct matching is A–iv, B–iii, C–ii, D–v, E–i.

- **Hirakud Dam** is built on Mahanadi river.
- **Nagarjuna Sagar Dam** is built on Krishna river.
- **Sardar Sarovar Dam** is built on Narmada river.
- **Tehri Dam** is built on Bhagirathi river.
- **Rana Pratap Sagar Dam** has been built on Chambal river.

97. (d) The sudden application of brakes in a vehicle is not an example of inertia at rest.

- Inertia of rest is defined as the property of a body to resist any change in its state of rest.
- For example to remove the dust particles the mat is hit with the stick or against the wall.

98. (d) Gulshan Grover's autobiography is titled 'Bad Man'.

- The book which traced the journey of the Delhi boy who moved to Mumbai and faced several hardships before making a mark for himself in cinema not as an actor but as a villain who achieves global success.

99. (d) The correct matching is A–iv, B–iii, C–ii, D–i.

- Founder of Faraizi Movement was Haji Shariatullah.
- The founder of Mohammedan Literary Society was Nawab Abdul Latif.
- The founder of Indian Patriotic Association was Sir Syed Ahmad Khan.
- The founder of Wahabi Movement was Syed Ahmad of Raebareli.

100. (a) Gluten is the protein which is found in grains.

- Gluten is naturally occurring, but it can be extracted, concentrated and added to food and other products to add protein, texture and flavour.
- It also works as a binding agent to hold processed foods together and give them shape.

101. (c) Number of students in Class X from School P = 144

Total number of students studying in Class X = 910

$$\therefore \text{Required percentage} = \frac{144}{910} \times 100 = 15.82 \approx 16\,\%$$

102. (b) $35 - [28 - (60 \div 4 + 26 \div 13)]$

$$= 35 - [28 - (15 + 2)]$$
$$= 35 - [28 - 17]$$
$$= 35 - 11 = 24$$

103. (d) $\left[18 - 3 \times \left\{3 - 3 \times \left(3 \div \frac{1}{3} - 3\right) + 3 \div \frac{1}{3} + 3\right\} - 4 \times 2\right]$

$$= [18 - 3 \times \{3 - 3 \times (3 \times 3 - 3) + 3 \times 3 + 3\} - 4 \times 2]$$
$$= [18 - 3 \times \{3 - (3 \times 6) + 9 + 3\} - 8]$$
$$= [18 - 3 \times \{3 - 18 + 9 + 3\} - 8]$$
$$= [18 - 3 \times (-3) - 8]$$
$$= [18 + 9 - 8] = 19$$

104. (b) Relative speed $= (12 - 7) = 5$ km/h

$$= \left(5 \times \frac{5}{18}\right) \text{m/s}$$

$$\therefore \text{Required} = \left(\frac{280}{5 \times \frac{5}{18}}\right) \text{sec}$$
$$= \left(\frac{280 \times 18}{25 \times 60}\right) \text{min}$$
$$= \left(\frac{84}{25}\right) \text{min} = 3\frac{9}{25} \text{ min}$$

105. (b) According to the question,

$$CP \times 36 = SP \times N$$
$$\Rightarrow \quad \frac{SP}{CP} = \frac{36}{N} \quad \text{...(i)}$$

Now, profit percentage

$$= \frac{SP - CP}{CP} \times 100$$
$$\Rightarrow \quad 20 = \left(\frac{SP}{CP} - 1\right) \times 100$$
$$\Rightarrow \quad \frac{1}{5} = \frac{SP}{CP} - 1$$

$\Rightarrow \frac{SP}{CP} = \frac{1}{5} + 1$

$\Rightarrow \frac{36}{N} = \frac{6}{5}$ [from Eq. (i)]

$\therefore N = 30$

106. (d) Let total work be 60 units (LCM of 20, 30).

$\therefore$ Efficiency of $A = \frac{60}{20} = 3$

Efficiency of $B = \frac{60}{30} = 2$

$\therefore$ Total work done by $(A + B)$ in 2 days $= (3 + 2) \times 2 = 10$ units

Remaining work = 60 − 10 = 50 units.

$\therefore$ Fraction of work that is left $= \frac{50}{60} = \frac{5}{6}$

107. (d) Speed of man in still water

$= \frac{1}{12} \times 60 = 5$ km/h

Let, speed of water = x km/h

Now, $\frac{1}{5 - x} = \frac{13}{60}$

$65 - 13x = 60$

$\therefore x = \frac{5}{13}$ km/ h

108. (c) Sales in 2016 = 2057

Profit in 2016 = 847

$\therefore$ Approximate profit percent margin in 2016 $= \frac{847}{2057} \times 100$

$= 41.18\%$

109. (b) Average speed $= \frac{60 + 100 + 140}{\frac{60}{80} + \frac{100}{90} + \frac{140}{120}}$

$= \frac{300}{\frac{3}{4} + \frac{10}{9} + \frac{7}{6}}$

$= \frac{300}{\frac{27 + 40 + 42}{36}}$

$= \frac{300 \times 36}{109} \approx 99$ km/h

110. (d) $\angle APQ = 40°$

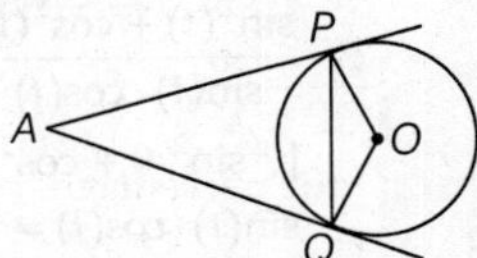

$\therefore \angle AQP = 40°$ ($\because AP = AQ$)

$\therefore \angle PAQ = 180° - 80° = 100°$

Now, $\angle APO = 90°$ and $\angle APQ = 40°$

[Angle made by radius, to the tangent = 90°]

$\therefore \angle QPO = 50°$

Similarly, $\angle PQO = 50°$

$\therefore$ In ΔPOQ,

$\angle QPO + \angle PQO + \angle POQ = 180°$

$50° + 50° + \angle POQ = 180°$

$\therefore \angle POQ = 80°$

111. (b) Given, base (b) of parallelogram = 2 × Height (h) of parallelogram

$\Rightarrow b = 2h$ ...(i)

$\because$ Area of parallelogram $= b \times h$

$\therefore 338 \text{ cm}^2 = b \times h$

$\Rightarrow 338 = 2h \times h$ [from Eq. (i)]

$\Rightarrow 169 = h^2 \Rightarrow h = 13$ cm

112. (a) Given,

57% of Ranita's income = 76% of Bhaskar's income

$\Rightarrow \frac{\text{Ranita's income}}{\text{Bhaskar's income}} = \frac{76}{57} = \frac{4}{3}$

Let Ranita's and Bhaskar's income be $4x$ and $3x$ respectively.

Now, $\frac{4x - 400}{3x} = \frac{6}{5}$

$\Rightarrow 20x - 18x = 2000$

$\therefore x = 1000$

Therefore, Bhaskar's weekly income $= 3x = 3 \times 1000 = ₹ 3000$

113. (d) Interest at 6% p.a. for 1 yr

$= \frac{P \times R \times T}{100}$

$= \frac{1760 \times 6 \times 1}{100} = ₹ 105.6$

Interest at 9% p.a. for 1 yr

$= \frac{2240 \times 9 \times 1}{100} = ₹ 201.6$

$\therefore$ Total interest in 1 yr

$= 105.6 + 201.6 = ₹ 307.2$

$\therefore$ Required time $= \frac{1536}{307.2} = 5$ yr

114. (b) $(1 + \tan^2 A) + \left(1 + \frac{1}{\tan^2 A}\right)$

$= \sec^2 A + 1 + \cot^2 A$

[$\because \sec^2 A - \tan^2 A = 1$]

$= \sec^2 A + \text{cosec}^2 A$

[$\because \text{cosec}^2 A - \cot^2 A = 1$]

$= \frac{1}{\cos^2 A} + \frac{1}{\sin^2 A}$

$= \frac{\sin^2 A + \cos^2 A}{\cos^2 A \sin^2 A}$

$= \frac{1}{(1 - \sin^2 A) \sin^2 A}$

($\because \sin^2 \theta + \cos^2 = 1$)

$= \frac{1}{\sin^2 A - \sin^4 A}$

115. (b) $\frac{(143 \div 13 \times x - 3 \times 3)}{(6^2 - 7 \times 5 + x^2)} = 1$

$\Rightarrow \frac{(11 \times x - 9)}{(36 - 35 + x^2)} = 1$

$\Rightarrow 11x - 9 = 1 + x^2$

$x^2 - 11x + 10 = 0$

$\Rightarrow (x - 1)(x - 10) = 0$

$\Rightarrow x = 1, x = 10$

Now, According to the given option, (b) $x = 1$.

116. (b) $12 + 24 \div 2 - 7 \times 30 \div 6 + (5 + 4) \times 8 + 8 \div 8 - 8$.

$= 12 + 12 - 7 \times 5 + 9 \times 8 + 1 - 8$

$= 12 + 12 - 35 + 72 + 1 - 8$

$= 97 - 43 = 54$

117. (b) Average of Avon and Firestone tires $= \frac{(21 + 14)\%}{2} = \frac{35}{2}\%$

Average of Good year and Dunlop tires $= \frac{(12 + 15)\%}{2} = \frac{27}{2}\%$

Difference $= \left(\frac{35}{2} - \frac{27}{2}\right)\% = \frac{8}{2} = 4\%$

Hence, required difference

$= \frac{4}{100} \times 1350 = 54$

118. (a) $25 \div 5 \times 7$ of $(5 + 7) - 13(6 \times 4)$

$= 25 \div 5 \times 7$ of $12 - 13 \times 24$

$= 5 \times 7$ of $12 - 13 \times 24$

$= 5 \times 84 - 13 \times 24$

$= 420 - 312 = 108$

119. (a) Let Remanna purchased 100 kg of raw materials for ₹ 100.

Now, 22.5% of it got wasted.

$\therefore$ Remaining raw material

$= 100 - 22.5 = 77.5$ kg

Now, According to the question,

80% of 77.5 $= \frac{80}{100} \times 77.5 = 62$

So, ₹ 62 was added as the cost of manufacturing.

Total cost = 100 + 62 = ₹ 162

Now, 120% of 162 = 80% of marked price (MP)

$\Rightarrow \frac{6}{5} \times 162 = \frac{4}{5} \times \text{MP}$

$\Rightarrow$ M.P = ₹ 243

Now, 243 = 2.43 times of 100.

120. (c) $3\frac{1}{5}$ of $2\frac{3}{4} \div \frac{11}{3} + \left(2\frac{1}{5} \div 1\frac{2}{5} \text{ of } 1\frac{3}{7} - 2\frac{1}{3}\right)$

$= \frac{16}{5}$ of $\frac{11}{4} \div \frac{11}{3} + \left(\frac{11}{5} \div \frac{7}{5} \text{ of } \frac{10}{7} - \frac{7}{3}\right)$

$= \frac{44}{5} \times \frac{3}{11} + \left(\frac{11}{5} \div 2 - \frac{7}{3}\right)$

$= \frac{12}{5} + \left(\frac{11}{5} \times \frac{1}{2} - \frac{7}{3}\right)$

$= \frac{12}{5} + \frac{11}{10} - \frac{7}{3} = \frac{35}{10} - \frac{7}{3}$

$= \frac{105 - 70}{30} = \frac{35}{30} = \frac{7}{6} = 1\frac{1}{6}$

121. (a) (A) Successive discounts

$= x + y - \frac{xy}{100}$

$= 24 + 27 - \frac{24 \times 27}{100} = 44.52\%$

(B) Buy 5 get 3 free

Discount percentage $= \frac{\text{Free}}{\text{Total}} \times 100$

$= \frac{3}{(5+3)} \times 100 = \frac{3}{8} \times 100 = 37.5\%$

(C) Buy 6 and get 10 which means buy 6 get 4 free.

Discount Percentage

$= \frac{4}{(6+4)} \times 100 = \frac{4}{10} \times 100 = 40\%$

∴ Scheme B will give minimum discount percentage.

122. (c) Given, radius of sphere (r) = 2.1 cm

Volume of sphere $= \frac{4}{3}\pi r^3$

$= \frac{4}{3} \times \frac{22}{7} \times 2.1 \times 2.1 \times 2.1$

$= 38.808 \text{ cm}^3$

123. (a) Given, ☺ = 15 scouts

Total scouts in class VI = 15 × 8 = 120

Total scouts in class VII = 15 × 4 = 60

Total scouts in class VIII = 15 × 3 = 45

∴ Required total scouts

= 120 + 60 + 45 = 225

124. (b) Given, $\cot\theta = \frac{28}{45}$

By Pythagoras theorem,

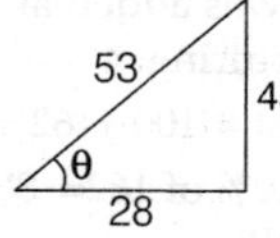

Hypotenuse $= \sqrt{(28)^2 + (45)^2}$

$= \sqrt{784 + 2025}$

$= \sqrt{2809} = 53$

$\therefore \sin\theta - \cos\theta = \frac{45}{53} - \frac{28}{53} = \frac{17}{53}$

125. (b) Successive discount for 10% and 20% $= 10 + 20 - \frac{10 \times 20}{100}$

$= 30 - 2 = 28\%$

Now, successive discount for 28% and 20% $= 28 + 20 - \frac{28 \times 20}{100}$

$= 48 - 5.6 = 42.4\%$

126. (b) Let the total work be 200 units (LCM of 100 and 200).

∴ Efficiency of $A = \frac{200}{200} = 1$

Efficiency of $B = \frac{200}{100} = 2$

3 days of work = 1 + 2 + 1 + 2 = 6 units

Now, 99 days of work

$= \frac{99}{3} \times 6 = 198$ units

Remaining work = 200 − 198 = 2 units

Time taken to complete remaining work by $(A + B) = \frac{2}{3}$.

∴ Total time required $= 99\frac{2}{3}$ days

127. (b) Given,

A 12 L solution has 30% acid.

∴ Amount of acid $= \frac{30}{100} \times 12 = 3.6$ L

Now, According to the question,

⇒ 20% of (12 + water) = 3.6

⇒ $12 + \text{Water} = \frac{3.6 \times 100}{20}$

⇒ Water = 18 − 12 = 6 L

∴ Amount of water added = 6 L

128. (b) 52 − [18 ÷ 3 + 3 + (18 − 11) of 4]

= 52 − (18 ÷ 3 + 3 + 7 of 4)

= 52 − [6 + 3 + 7 of 4]

= 52 − [9 + 28]

= 52 − 37 = 15

129. (b) Employees in 2019 = 20 lakhs

Employees in 2022 = 35 lakhs

∴ Percentage increase in 2022 over 2019

$= \frac{(35 - 20) \times 100}{20}$

$= \frac{15}{20} \times 100 = 75\%$

130. (a) According to the question,

$x + y = 4(x - y)$

⇒ $x + y = 4x - 4y$

⇒ $3x = 5y$

Now, The value of $\frac{5xy}{3(x^2 - y^2)}$

$= \frac{5 \times \frac{5y}{3} \times y}{3\left[\left(\frac{5}{3}y\right)^2 - y^2\right]} = \frac{\frac{25y^2}{3}}{3\left[\frac{25}{9}y^2 - y^2\right]}$

$= \frac{25y^2}{9\left[\frac{25y^2 - 9y^2}{9}\right]} = \frac{25y^2 \times 9}{9 \times 16y^2} = \frac{25}{16}$

131. (c) Let the two numbers are x and y.

Now, $x + y = 12$ and $xy = 27$

$x^3 + y^3 = (x + y)^3 - 3xy(x + y)$

$= (12)^3 - 3 \times 27 \times 12$

$= 1728 - 81 \times 12$

$= 1728 - 972 = 756$

132. (d) Number of students who passed with 60 as cut-off marks in Science = 43

Number of students who passed with 60 as cut-off marks in Aggregate = 39

∴ Required difference = 43 − 39 = 4

133. (c) Given, $r = \frac{r}{4}$

and slant height $= l = 4l$

Total surface area of cone

$= \pi r(r + l)$

$\therefore \pi r(r + l) = \pi \times \frac{r}{4}\left(\frac{r}{4} + 4l\right)$

$= \frac{\pi r^2}{16} + \frac{\pi r}{4} \times 4l$

$= \frac{\pi r^2}{16} + \pi rl = \pi r\left(\frac{r}{16} + l\right)$

134. (b) Radius (r) of base = 21 m

Height (h) = 28 m

∴ Slant height $(l) = \sqrt{(21)^2 + (28)^2}$

$= \sqrt{441 + 784}$

$= \sqrt{1225} = 35$

Now, required cloths

= Curved surface area of cone

$= \pi rl = \frac{22}{7} \times 21 \times 35 = 2310 \text{ m}^2$

Now, width of the cloth = 5 m

∴ Required length of cloth $= \frac{2310}{5}$

= 462 m

135. (b) 24 ÷ (3 − 8 × 3 + 27) + 3

= 24 ÷ (3 − 24 + 27) + 3

= 24 ÷ 6 + 3 = 4 + 3 = 7

136. (c) Given, $\tan(t) + \cot(t) = 1$

⇒ $\frac{\sin(t)}{\cos(t)} + \frac{\cos(t)}{\sin(t)} = 1$

⇒ $\frac{\sin^2(t) + \cos^2(t)}{\sin(t) \cdot \cos(t)} = 1$

$[\because \sin^2\theta + \cos^2\theta = 1]$

⇒ $\sin(t) \cdot \cos(t) = 1$ ...(i)

Now, $[\sin(t) + \cos(t)]^2 = \sin^2(t) + \cos^2(t) + 2\sin(t) \cdot \cos(t)$

$= 1 + 2 \times 1 = 1 + 2 = 3$

$\therefore \sin(t) + \cos(t) = \sqrt{3}$

Hence, $\frac{1}{\sin(t) + \cos(t)} = \frac{1}{\sqrt{3}}$

137. (c) Given, A sum of money 'P' becomes '2P' in 4 yr.

i.e., $P\left(1+\frac{r}{100}\right)^4 = 2P$

$\Rightarrow \left(1+\frac{r}{100}\right)^4 = 2$

Now, To become 8 times *i.e*, 2^3, we have

$$\left[\left(1+\frac{r}{100}\right)\right]^t = (2)^3 = \left[1+\frac{r}{100}\right]^{4\times 3}$$

$\therefore \quad t = 4\times 3 = 12$ yr

138. (c) Given, length of chord AB = Radius (r) of the circle

Hence, ΔAOB is an equilateral triangle.

$\therefore \angle AOB = 60°$

Hence, length of arc $= 2\pi r \frac{\theta}{360°}$

$= 2\times\frac{22}{7}\times 21\times\frac{60°}{360°} = 22$ units

139. (b) Let total number of voters $= x$

Total number of casted votes $= \frac{88x}{100}$

$\therefore$ Valid votes $= \frac{88x}{100} - 84$

Votes got by Ramagya $= \frac{54x}{100}$

$\therefore$ Votes gots by Sbravan

$= \frac{88x}{100} - 84 - \frac{54x}{100} = \frac{34x}{100} - 84$

According to the question,

$\frac{54x}{100} - \frac{34x}{100} + 84 = 1456$

$\Rightarrow \frac{20x}{100} = 1372$

$\therefore \quad x = 6860$

140. (d) $3\frac{2}{3}\div 2\frac{1}{5}\times\frac{1}{4}\times\left(1+\frac{3}{1-\frac{2}{5}}\right)$

$= \frac{11}{3}\div\frac{11}{5}\times\frac{1}{4}\times\left(1+\frac{3}{\frac{3}{5}}\right)$

$= \frac{11}{3}\times\frac{5}{11}\times\frac{1}{4}\times\left(1+\frac{15}{3}\right)$

$= \frac{11}{3}\times\frac{5}{11}\times\frac{1}{4}\times 6$

$= \frac{5}{2} = 2\frac{1}{2}$

141. (b) Given, Circumference = 88 cm

$\Rightarrow \quad 2\pi r = 88 \Rightarrow r = 14$ cm

Now, According to the question, let '*n*' number of persons be served.

$\therefore$ Volume of hemispherical bowl $= n\times$ Volume of hemispherical glass

$\Rightarrow \frac{2}{3}\pi(14)^3 = n\times\frac{2}{3}\pi\left(\frac{7}{2}\right)^3$

$\Rightarrow (14)^3 = n\times\left(\frac{7}{2}\right)^3$

$\therefore \quad n = 64$

Hence, 64 persons can be served.

142. (a) $x + y + z = 1$

On squaring both the sides,

$(x+y+z)^2 = 1^2$

$\Rightarrow x^2 + y^2 + z^2 + 2(xy + yz + zx) = 1$

$\Rightarrow x^2 + y^2 + z^2 = 1 - 2(xy + yz + zx)$

$= 1 - 2(-1) = 1 + 2 = 3$

$\Rightarrow x^2 + y^2 + z^2 = 3$

Now, $x^3 + y^3 + z^3 - 3xyz$

$= (x+y+z)(x^2 + y^2 + z^2 - xy - yz - zx)$

$= 1\times(3+1) = 4$

So, $x^3 + y^3 + z^3 - 3xyz = 4$

$\Rightarrow x^3 + y^3 + z^3 - 3(-1) = 4$

$\Rightarrow \quad x^3 + y^3 + z^3 = 4 - 3$

$\Rightarrow \quad x^3 + y^3 + z^3 = 1$

143. (b) Total shares = 8 lakhs

Present share of Panday = 5% of 8 lakhs

= 40000

Now, Varma sells ₹ 10000 to Pandey.

$\therefore$ Total shares with Panday

= 40000 + 10000 = 50000

144. (c) When, $\sec A = \operatorname{cosec} B$

Then, $A + B = 90°$

So, $\sec 6A = \operatorname{cosec}(A - 29°)$

$\therefore \quad 6A + (A - 29°) = 90°$

$\Rightarrow \quad 7A - 29° = 90°$

$\therefore \quad 7A = 119°$

$\Rightarrow \quad A = 17°$

145. (c) Given, $\frac{PB}{AP} = \frac{3}{4}$

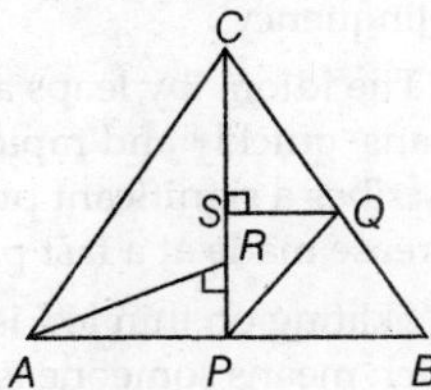

And $PQ \parallel AC$

So, $\Delta BQP \sim \Delta BCA$

$\therefore \quad \frac{BQ}{BC} = \frac{QP}{AC} = \frac{BP}{AB} = \frac{3}{7}$

Now, In ΔACR and ΔQSP

$\angle ARC = \angle QSP = 90°$

$\angle ACR = \angle QPS$ (alternate angles)

$\therefore \angle CAR = \angle SQP$

$\therefore \Delta ARC \sim \Delta QSP$ (*A-A-A* similarity)

$\therefore \quad \frac{AR}{QS} = \frac{RC}{SP} = \frac{AC}{QP} \Rightarrow \frac{AR}{QS} = \frac{RC}{SP} = \frac{7}{3}$

$\therefore \quad AR = \frac{7}{3}\times QS = \frac{7}{3}\times 9$

$\therefore \quad AR = 21$ cm

146. (c) Given, $4 : a :: 16a : 81$

$\Rightarrow \quad \frac{4}{a} = \frac{16a}{81} \Rightarrow a^2 = \frac{81}{4}$

$\therefore \quad a = \frac{9}{2}$

147. (b) Given,

Total number of votes = 15000

$\therefore$ Total number of valid votes

$= \frac{15000\times 75}{100} = 11250$

Hence, the number of valid votes that other candidate got

$= \frac{11250\times(100-60)}{100} = 4500$

148. (a) Given,

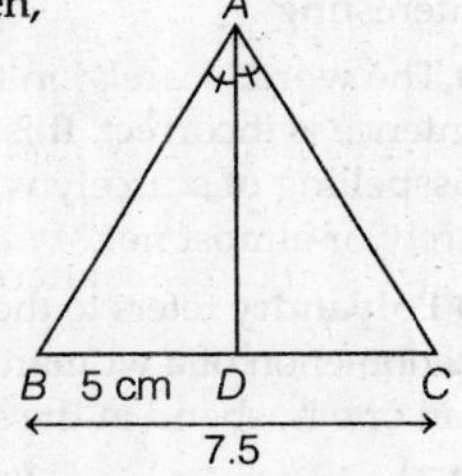

$\therefore \quad DC = (7.5 - 5) = 2.5$ cm

Now, According to angle bisector theorem,

$\frac{AB}{BD} = \frac{AC}{DC}$

$\Rightarrow \quad \frac{BD}{DC} = \frac{AB}{AC}$

$\therefore \quad \frac{AB}{AC} = \frac{5}{2.5} = \frac{2}{1} = 2:1$

149. (a) Let the number be $3x$ and $7x$.

Now, $\frac{3x - 11}{7x - 11} = \frac{7}{20}$

$\Rightarrow \quad 60x - 220 = 49x - 77$

$\Rightarrow \quad 11x = 143 \Rightarrow x = 13$

$\therefore$ Smaller number $= 3x = 3\times 13 = 39$

150. (a) Average speed $= \frac{\text{Total distance}}{\text{Total time taken}}$

Quarter of an hour = 15 min

$\therefore$ Average speed $= \frac{(20 + 25 + 15)\text{ km}}{(15 + 15 + 15)\text{ min}}$

$= \left(\frac{60}{\frac{45}{60}}\right)\text{km/h} = \left(\frac{60\times 60}{45}\right)\text{km/h}$

= 80 km/h

151. (b) The word 'Uniformity' means 'similarity between all things'. Hence, its antonym is 'Variety' which means 'different'.

152. (c) The idiom 'Hit the sack' means 'to go to sleep.' It implies going to bed and resting.

153. (a) The incorrectly spelt word is 'Mountan' The correct spelling of the word is 'Mountain'.

154. (d) The incorrectly spelt word is 'occured'. The correct spelling of the word is 'occurred'.

155. (a) Pretentious means attempting to impress by affecting greater importance or merit than is actually possessed.

156. (a) The incorrectly spelt word is 'etiquette'.

157. (b) Part (b) 'I am understanding' contains an error. Use 'I understand' to correct the sentence.

158. (b) Monotonous means repetitive and boring. Hence, its antonym is 'Interesting'.

159. (c) The word 'scarely' in the given sentence is incorrect. It is a misspelling of scarcely which means barely or almost not.

160. (c) Polyandry refers to the phenomenon of a woman having more than one husband at the same time.

161. (b) The idiom 'at his wit's end' means 'to be completely puzzled and perplexed, not knowing what to do. .

162. (b) The idiom 'skating on thin ice' means to be doing something that is dangerous or involves risks.

163. (d) 'Convenient features' provided by society or company are called amenities.

164. (c) Profound means deep and thoughtful. Hence, its antonym is 'Shallow' which means not deep.

165. (b) The underlined word **ruthlessly** means 'rudely and harshly'. Hence, its synonym is 'inhumanly' which means lacking warmth and love.

166. (c) Exert means to force or stress. Hence, its antonym is 'to relax'.

167. (b) The underlined part of the sentence contains error. The use of future tense is incorrect in the underlined part. It should be 'who scores the highest point'.

168. (d) The underlined part of the sentence contains error. Use 'around' in place of 'to'.

169. (a) The idiom 'yeoman's service' means very good, hard and valuable work that someone does especially to support a cause, to help a team, etc.

170. (b) The idiom 'fair and square' means in an honest way and without any doubt.

171. (c) Part (c) 'he refused to agree to it' contains an error.
The use of 'agree to' is incorrect in the context of the sentence. It should be 'accept.'

172. (d) Part (d) 'he was reluctant' contains an error. As the given sentence is in present tense, 'is' should be used in place of 'was.'

173. (d) The antonym of 'Freezing' is 'Tropical' which means characteristic of a region or climate that is frost-free with temperatures high enough to support year-round plant growth given sufficient moisture.

174. (d) The incorrectly spelt word is 'shedule'. The correct spelling of the word is 'schedule'.

175. (a) A **jockey** is a professional rider in horse races.

176. (a) The underlined part of the sentence contains error. Use 'awkward but grammatically'.

177. (d) Part (d)'visit a Statue of Liberty' contains an error. As 'Statue of Liberty' is a unique monument, article 'the' will be used with it.

178. (c) The underlined word **candour** means the quality of being open and honest.

179. (a) The word that correctly substitutes the given phrase is 'opaque'.

180. (c) Part (c) contains a spelling error. The word 'deliquency' is incorrectly spelt. The correct spelling is 'delinquency'.

181. (d) The idiom 'by leaps and bounds' means 'quickly and rapidly.' It describes a significant progress or increase made at a fast pace.

182. (c) 'Skating on thin ice' is an idiom which means someone is in a risky or dangerous situation, often because of their actions. Sentence (c) correctly uses the idiom.

183. (d) The underlined part of the sentence contains an error. As the subject 'seeds' is plural, plural verb 'are' should be used.

184. (a) The antonym of 'Confusing' in the sentence is 'Guiding'.

185. (a) The underlined part of the sentence contains error. We use preposition 'to' with the word 'prefer'.

186. (d) Part (d) 'a book' contains an error. As we are referring to a specific book, article 'the' will be used with it.

187. (c) The idiom 'be in seventh heaven' means 'to be in a state of extreme happiness.' It expresses a feeling of great joy and bliss.

188. (c) The underlined part of the sentence contains error. Use 'is greater than' as the sentence refers to comparison between two categories.

189. (d) The word **reckon** means 'imagine consider or think about'.
Assess means to test.

190. (b) The idiom 'bread and butter' means the way of earning a livelihood or money.

191. (a) 'Extraordinary' means very special, fitting the context of superheroes having extraordinary powers.

192. (c) 'Explain' means to make clear, fitting the context of backstories explaining how superheroes gained their powers.

193. (d) 'Such as' means for example, fitting the context of examples of how superheroes gained their powers.

194. (a) 'Themselves' means the persons referred to, fitting the context of superheroes protecting themselves while fighting crime.

195. (a) 'For' indicates duration, fitting the context of superheroes being a staple of popular culture for decades.

196. (a) The word 'realise' means to understand. Hence, its antonym is 'misunderstand'.

197. (c) The given passage indicates that no nation can be called ancient. It is only the thinking of the modern people which can think of any nation as ancient.

198. (b) The word 'obvious' means clear and direct.

199. (a) The author of the given passage wants us to forget what we have read in history in schools because these books teach us that our nation can be ancient.

200. (a) The phrase 'drill into your heads' indicates to make someone learn or understand something by repeating it.

CPO SI P-2 SP 10

PAPER-2

SSC CPO SI SOLVED PAPER

8 March 2025 (Shift I)

Instructions

1. This paper contains **200** questions.
2. This paper is based on **English Language and Comprehension.**
3. Each question carries **1 marks**.
4. There will be a negative marking of **0.25 marks** for each wrong answer.

MM : 200 **Time : 2 hr**

Directions (Q. Nos. 1-10) *In the following passage, some words have been deleted. Read the passage carefully and select the most appropriate option to fill in each blank.*

Located 10 miles off Scotland's North-Eastern coast, the Orkney islands are a treasure trove of history. When I visited one of Orkney's famous pre-historic ...(1)..., the Maeshowe tomb, my first impression was of an unremarkable green mound ...(2)... by a ditch. Despite its appearance, this 5,000-year-old ...(3)... place is actually a masterpiece of ...(4)... design and engineering, and a testament ...(5)... the skill of Orkney's pre-historic residents. That's because, ...(6)... around three weeks either side of the winter solstice (which takes ...(7)... on 21st or 22nd December, each year), visitors have the chance to see something truly magical ...(8).... here. During this time of year, the narrow passage into the ...(9)... becomes more than just an entrance: it was deliberately designed ...(10)... with the setting of the midwinter Sun. Just as the last rays start to disappear – which is at around 15:10 at this deepest, darkest time of midwinter – a shaft of light creeps down the passageway, slips across the floor of the tomb and illuminates the back wall like a golden, glowing doorway to another world.

1. Select the most appropriate option to fill in blank no. 1.
(a) sights (b) sites
(c) scenes (d) seats

2. Select the most appropriate option to fill in blank no. 2.
(a) surround
(b) surrounding
(c) surrounded
(d) surrounds

3. Select the most appropriate option to fill in blank no. 3.
(a) burying (b) burry
(c) buried (d) burial

4. Select the most appropriate option to fill in blank no. 4.
(a) chronological (b) historical
(c) antiquated (d) ancient

5. Select the most appropriate option to fill in blank no. 5.
(a) at (b) by
(c) on (d) to

6. Select the most appropriate option to fill in blank no. 6.
(a) with (b) about
(c) in (d) for

7. Select the most appropriate option to fill in blank no. 7.
(a) room (b) abode
(c) place (d) home

8. Select the most appropriate option to fill in blank no. 8.
(a) retire (b) perform
(c) occur (d) arise

9. Select the most appropriate option to fill in blank no. 9.
(a) memorial (b) graveyard
(c) grave (d) tomb

10. Select the most appropriate to fill in blank no. 10.
(a) aligning (b) align
(c) to align (d) aligned

Directions (Q. Nos. 11-20) *In the following passage, some words have been deleted. Read the passage carefully and select the most appropriate option to fill in each blank.*

Air India showcased its first A350 to the world on Thursday (18th January) at the Begumpet Airport in Hyderabad as part of the ongoing air show Wings 2024. The first aircraft of a ...(1)... of 20 arrived on 23rd December, 2023 from Toulouse in France and was ...(2)... for the first time on 18th January. Five more ...(3).... premium passenger aircrafts are scheduled ...(4)... by March this year. This makes Air India ...(5)... first Indian carrier to be operating the A350. Commercial operations for the same are scheduled to begin ...(6)... 22nd January later this month. With the induction of the A350, Air India is ...(7)... to overhaul its image and service to the passengers. The A350 comes equipped ...(8)... a powerful and fuel-efficient Rolls-Royce Trent xwb engine. Once you ...(9)... inside the aircraft, you can immediately ...(10)...the three-class cabin configuration: business, premium economy and economy spread across 316 seats.

11. Select the most appropriate option to fill in blank no. 1.
(a) batch (b) gang
(c) team (d) flock

12. Select the most appropriate option to fill in blank no. 2.
(a) showcase (b) showcased
(c) showcasing (d) showcases

13. Select the most appropriate option to fill in blank no. 3.
(a) such (b) as
(c) same (d) so

14. Select the most appropriate option to fill in blank no. 4.
(a) to arrive (b) arrival
(c) arriving (d) arrived

15. Select the most appropriate option to fill in blank no. 5.
(a) the (b) an
(c) a (d) one

16. Select the most appropriate option to fill in blank no. 6.
(a) to (b) on
(c) at (d) in

17. Select the most appropriate option to fill in blank no. 7.
(a) hoping (b) believing
(c) supposing (d) accepting

18. Select the most appropriate option to fill in blank no. 8.
(a) in (b) with
(c) for (d) to

19. Select the most appropriate option to fill in blank no. 9.
(a) step (b) forward
(c) skip (d) advance

20. Select the most appropriate option to fill in blank no. 10.
(a) see (b) watch
(c) look (d) get

Directions *(Q. Nos. 21-25) In the following passage, some words have been deleted. Read the passage carefully and select the most appropriate option to fill in each blank.*

Organic farming ...(1)... that nature stays clean and rich. If we visit an organic farm, we will notice a ...(2)... of animal, bird and insect activity. Research shows that around 30% more wildlife and plants thrive ...(3)... ecologically produced fields compared to conventional farming. This is because there are no pesticides, and fertiliser is used ...(4)... . Covid-19 pandemic has changed the ...(5)... of organic food, with the spotlight now on safety and healthy food that is nutritious to build a strong immune system.

21. Select the most appropriate option to fill in blank no. 1.
(a) cherish (b) envy
(c) contradict (d) ensures

22. Select the most appropriate option to fill in blank no. 2.
(a) loathe (b) jog
(c) buzz (d) sense

23. Select the most appropriate option to fill in blank no. 3.
(a) up (b) out
(c) downstairs (d) near

24. Select the most appropriate option to fill in blank no. 4.
(a) far away (b) far better
(c) far less (d) far off

25. Select the most appropriate option to fill in blank no. 5.
(a) argument (b) evolution
(c) perception (d) practice

Directions (Q. Nos. 26-30) *Read the given passage and answer the questions that follow.*

In 1600, the East India Company acquired a charter from the ruler of England, Queen Elizabeth I, granting it the sole right to trade with the East. This meant that no other trading group in England could compete with the East India Company. With this charter, the Company could venture across the oceans, looking for new lands from which it could buy goods at a cheap price and carry them back to Europe to sell at higher prices. The Company did not have to fear competition from other English trading companies.

Mercantile trading companies in those days made profit primarily by excluding competition, so that they could buy cheap and sell dear. The Royal Charter, however, could not prevent other European powers from entering the Eastern markets. By the time the first English ships sailed down the West coast of Africa, round the Cape of Good Hope, and crossed the Indian Ocean, the Portuguese had already established their presence in the Western coast of India, and had their base in Goa. In fact, it was Vasco da Gama, a Portuguese explorer, who had discovered this sea route to India in 1498. By the early 17th century, the Dutch too were exploring the possibilities of trade in the Indian Ocean. Soon the French traders arrived on the scene.The problem was that all the companies were interested in buying the same things. The fine qualities of cotton and silk produced in India had a big market in Europe. Pepper, cloves, cardamom and cinnamon too were in great demand. Competition amongst the European companies inevitably pushed up the prices at which these goods could be purchased, and this reduced the profits that could be earned. The only way the trading companies could flourish was by eliminating rival competitors. The urge to secure markets, therefore, led to fierce battles between the trading companies.

26. How did Mercantile companies make profit in the 17th century?
(a) They traded with the East.
(b) They fought wars with other companies.
(c) They discovered new countries to trade with.
(d) They eliminated competition to buy cheap goods and sell them at higher prices.

27. What did East India Company do in India to exclude competition with other European companies?
A. Fought fierce battles with them.
B. Bought goods at higher prices than them.
(a) Both A and B are false
(b) Both A and B are true
(c) A is true and B is false.
(d) B is true and A is false

28. Which Europeans came first to India to trade?
(a) The Dutch (b) The French
(c) The English (d) The Portuguese

29. This passage is mainly about
(a) the coming of East India Company to India.
(b) the discovery of India by Vasco da Gama.
(c) the elimination of rivals by different companies.
(d) the trading mechanism of the foreign companies.

30. The charter of 'the sole right to trade with the East' meant for the East India Company that
(a) among the English companies, only East India Company could trade in the East.
(b) other English companies could trade in the East along with the East India Company.
(c) the East India Company could trade in certain specified goods only in the East.
(d) no other European company except for the East India Company could trade in the East.

Directions (Q. Nos. 31-35) *Read the given passage and answer the questions that follow.*

Rock paintings, which could be four to six thousand years old, have been discovered in a pre-historic cave in the Berinag sub-division of Uttarakhand's Pithoragarh district, an Archaeological Survey of India (ASI) official said. Eleven human figures, both men and women, can be seen in the cave paintings, the official said. "The rock paintings seem over four to six thousand years old like the ones first discovered in the Lakhu Udiyar pre-historic caves near Almora in the year 1965," regional archaeological officer in Almora, Chandra Singh Chauhan said.

This is the first cave with rock paintings to be found in the Pithoragarh district, he said. "Nine such caves in Almora, one in Nainital and three in Garhwal region have been found earlier. They bear testimony to the presence of humans in the Himalayan region in pre-historic times," Chauhan said.

Chauhan said he has received pictures of the rock paintings in the newly discovered cave and will soon visit it to gather more information about them. The cave and the paintings on its walls were discovered by Tarun Mehra, a young adventure tourism entrepreneur.

During a rock climbing expedition, Mehra and his team saw a tunnel-like structure and went inside it out of curiosity.

"When we went inside the cave after discovering it on a hill near PG College Berinag, we were surprised to see rock paintings on its walls in various colours," Mehra said.

A cup mark has also been spotted some 20 feet up the hill, he said. A wild animal has also been depicted below the paintings of the 11 humans the wall, Mehra said.

"Presence of wide space inside the cave also indicates that it was used by pre-historic human groups as their habitation", he said.

31. The passage is mainly about
(a) the discovery of pre-historic rock paintings in a cave in Pithoragarh.
(b) the pre-historic human beings in Himalayan regions.
(c) the rock- climbing expedition of Tarun Mehra.
(d) the caves found in Almora, Nainital and Garhwal regions.

32. What shows that the cave discovered in Pithoragarh was also used as living space by pre-historic human groups?
(a) The paintings of human beings
(b) The presence of rock paintings in the cave
(c) The presence of wide space in the cave
(d) A cup mark

33. Which of the following is not a part of the paintings found in the cave in Pithoragarh?
(a) Wild animal
(b) Female figures
(c) Cup mark
(d) Male figures

34. Where were the first caves found with paintings in Uttarakhand?
(a) Almora (b) Pithoragarh
(c) Garhwal (d) Nainital

35. Identify the option that arranges the following events in the correct sequence.
a. Finding a tunnel.
b. Discovering a cup mark on the hill
c. Exploring the cave
d. Climbing the rocks near the PG College, Berinag
e. Discovering the colourful rock paintings
(a) d c b a e (b) d a c e b
(c) b d c e a (d) a c e d b

Directions (Q. Nos. 36-40) *Read the given passage and answer the questions that follow.*

New Delhi : Forty-two per cent of children in the age group of 14 to 18 years in rural India cannot read easy sentences in English, while more than half of them struggle with simple division problems, according to the Annual Status of Education Report (ASER) 2023 released on Wednesday.

The ASER 2023 'Beyond Basics' survey was conducted in 28 districts across 26 states, reaching a total of 34,745 youths in the age group 14-18 years. One rural district was surveyed in each major state. The annual report published by the Pratham Foundation found that more than half of the students in the 14-18 age group struggle with division problems. About 25 per cent of this age group still cannot read a Class 2 level text fluently in their regional language. More than half struggle with division (3-digit by 1-digit) problems. Only 43.3 per cent of 14-18-year olds are able to do such problems correctly. This skill is usually expected in class 3 and 4.

ASER reports are also used by the government while formulating policies. Across enrollment categories, females (76 per cent) do better than males (70.9 per cent) in reading a Class 2 level text in their regional language. In contrast, males do better than their female counterparts in arithmetic and English reading. The report says that around 45 per cent of the students surveyed could calculate the number of hours a child had slept based on the time she went to bed at night and woke up in the morning.

In another everyday task of measuring an object with a scale, 85 per cent of those surveyed could calculate the length of an object correctly if it was placed at the '0' mark on the ruler. But, when the object was moved and placed elsewhere on the ruler, less than 40 per cent could give the right answer. Two-thirds of the surveyed youths (65.1 per cent) were able to read functional instructions on a packet of ORS solution, the report said.

According to the report, low levels of foundational numeracy affect the ability of youth in tackling everyday calculations where they need to apply measurement or use the unitary method in practical situations, or even do simple financial computations (managing a budget, applying a discount or calculating interest rates or repayment of a loan).

36. According to ASER 2023, how much percentage of 14-18 year olds could divide a three-digit number by a one-digit number correctly?
(a) 25 per cent
(b) 65.1 per cent
(c) 45 per cent
(d) 43.3 per cent

37. Which of the following is better done by girls than boys, according to the passage?
(a) Reading a Class 2 level text in their regional language
(b) Carrying out a simple division sum
(c) Calculating arithmetical problems
(d) Reading simple English sentences

38. The survey was conducted mainly to know

(a) the reading abilities of Class 3 to 4 children.
(b) the simple calculation skills of boys and girls.
(c) the reading level and numeracy abilities of 14-18 year olds.
(d) the level of foundational numeracy among the youth.

39. How many youths could calculate the length of an object correctly if it was placed at the '0' mark on the ruler?

(a) 85 per cent (b) 40 per cent
(c) 45 per cent (d) 76 per cent

40. The given passage is

(a) a news report about an educational survey.
(b) the executive summary of the Annual Status of Education Report.
(c) a press release by Pratham Foundation.
(d) a survey report on rural districts.

Directions (Q. Nos. 41-45) *Read the given passage and answer the questions that follow.*

I had four notes of introduction in London: to Dr. PJ Mehta, to Sjt. Dalpatram Shukla, to Prince Ranjit Singhji and to Dadabhai Naoroji. Someone on board had advised us to put up at the Victoria Hotel in London. Sjt. Mazmudar and I accordingly went there. Dr. Mehta, to whom I had wired from Southampton, called at about 8 o'clock the same evening. He gave me a hearty greeting. As we were talking, I casually picked up his top-hat, and trying to see how smooth it was, passed my hand over it the wrong way and disturbed the fur. Dr. Mehta looked somewhat angrily at what I was doing and stopped me. But the mischief had been done. The incident was a warning for the future. This was my first lesson in European etiquette, into the details of which Dr. Mehta humorously initiated me. "Do not touch other people's things," he said. "Do not ask questions as we usually do in India on first acquaintance; do not talk loudly; never address people as 'sir' whilst speaking to them as we do in India; only servants and subordinates address their masters that way." And so on and so forth. He also told me that it was very expensive to live in a hotel and recommended that I should live with a private family. We deferred consideration of the matter until Monday. Sjt. Mazmudar and I found the hotel to be a trying affair. It was also very expensive. There was, however, a Sindhi fellow-passenger from Malta who had become friends with Sjt. Mazmudar, and as he was not a stranger to London, he offered to find rooms for us. We agreed, and on Monday, as soon as we got our baggage, we paid up our bills and went to the rooms rented for us by the Sindhi friend. I remember my hotel bill came to £3, an amount which shocked me. And I had practically starved in spite of this heavy bill! For I could relish nothing. When I did not like one thing, I asked for another, but had to pay for both just the same. The fact is that all this while I had depended on the provisions which I had brought with me from Bombay.

41. The main theme of the passage is

(a) expensive hotel stay in London.
(b) appreciating European etiquette.
(c) craving for home food in foreign land.
(d) the author's early days in London.

42. Why did Dr. Mehta get a little irritated with the author?

(a) He was late in coming to meet him.
(b) He asked irrelevant questions.
(c) He was talking too loudly.
(d) He touched his hat the wrong way.

43. Who initiated the author in European manners?

(a) Sjt. Majumdar
(b) Dr. PJ Mehta
(c) Sjt. Dalpatram Shukla
(d) Dadabhai Naoroji

44. After reading the above passage it can be inferred that it is an extract from

(a) a biography
(b) an article
(c) a travelogue
(d) an autobiography

45. How did the Author survive during his first day in London?

(a) He ordered and ate food at the hotel.
(b) He ate at Indian restaurants.
(c) He got food from friends.
(d) He used the food he had brought from Bombay.

Directions (Q. Nos. 46-50) *Read the given passage and answer the questions that follow.*

Rivers in the heart of the Amazon rainforest in Brazil fell to their lowest levels in over a century on Monday as a record drought upends the lives of hundreds of thousands of people and damages the jungle ecosystem.

The port of Manaus, the region's most populous city, at the meeting of the Rio Negro and the Amazon River, recorded 13.59 metres (44.6 feet) of water on Monday, compared to 17.60 a year ago, according to its website.

That is the lowest level since records began in 121 years ago in 1902, passing a previous all-time low set in 2010.

Rapidly drying tributaries to the mighty Amazon have left boats stranded, cutting-off food and water supplies to remote villages, while high water temperatures are suspected of killing more than 100 endangered river dolphins.

Some areas of the Amazon have seen the least rain from July to September since 1980, according to the Brazilian Government disaster alert centre, Cemaden.

Brazil's Science Ministry blames the drought on the onset of the El Niño climate phenomenon this year, which is driving extreme weather patterns globally. In a statement earlier this month, the ministry said it expects the drought will last until at least December, when El Niño's effects are forecast to peak.

Underlying El Niño is the long-term trend of global warming, which is leading to more frequent and more intense extreme weather events, like drought and heat.

The drought has affected 4,81,000 people as of Monday, according to the Civil Defence Agency in the state of Amazonas, where Manaus is located.

Late last week, workers from Brazilian NGO Fundacao Amazonia Sustentável fanned out across the parched region near Manaus to deliver food and supplies to vulnerable villages.

The drought has threatened their access to food, drinking water and medicines, which are usually transported by river.

46. The passage is mainly about

(a) the lives of people living in the rainforest of Amazon.
(b) the damage to the jungle's ecosystem.
(c) the El Niño climate phenomenon.
(d) the worst drought conditions in Amazon rainforest area.

47. Which of the following statements is not true?
(a) Food, drinking water and medicines are delivered to remote villages of the rainforest region by boats.
(b) On Monday, the lowest water level since 1902 in the Amazon river was recorded at 17.60 metres.
(c) High water temperatures are suspected of killing more than 100 endangered river dolphins.
(d) Port of Manaus is the most populated city of the Amazon rainforest region.

48. "Workers from Brazilian NGO Fundação Amazônia Sustentável fanned out across the parched region." Here 'fanned out' means
(a) found fans in the area
(b) distributed fans
(c) cooled the area with fans
(d) spread apart in the area

49. Identify the option that arranges the following in the correct sequence.
A. Boats stranded
B. Tributaries dried
C. Food and water supply to remote villages cut-off
D. Very less rain in the Amazon region
(a) ABCD (b) BDAC
(c) DBAC (d) DACB

50. After reading the given passage, it can be inferred that it is
(a) a news report
(b) a research report
(c) a scientific report
(d) a survey report

51. Select the most appropriate option to fill in the blank.
If the weather forecast proves accurate, we .... heavy snowfall in the region tomorrow.
(a) should have (b) need to have
(c) must have (d) are having

52. Select the option that expresses the given sentence in passive voice.
The director organised a meeting to discuss the upcoming projects.
(a) A meeting was organised by the director to discuss the upcoming projects.
(b) A meeting has been organised by the director to discuss the upcoming projects.
(c) A meeting is organised by the director to discuss the upcoming projects.
(d) The upcoming projects were organised by the director to discuss the meeting.

53. Select the most appropriate option to fill in the blank.
She meticulously followed the intricate instructions; ...., the delicate balance of the experiment would have been irreversibly disrupted.
(a) in case (b) otherwise
(c) so that (d) moreover

54. Select the most appropriate option to fill in the blank.
After the storm ...., the explorers realised that their campsite had been completely flooded.
(a) had subsided (b) was subsiding
(c) subsides (d) is subsiding

55. Select the option that expresses the given sentence in active voice.
Let a statement addressing the recent controversy be issued by the company.
(a) The company can issue a statement addressing the recent controversy.
(b) The company is issuing a statement addressing the recent controversy.
(c) The company should issue a statement addressing the recent controversy.
(d) Let the company issue a statement addressing the recent controversy.

56. Select the option that will improve the underlined part of the given sentence. In case no improvement is needed, select 'No improvement required'.
<u>In case</u> everybody has left the office, Ashutosh is still busy at his laptop.
(a) Even though
(b) In spite of
(c) But for
(d) No improvement required

57. Select the option that expresses the given sentence in direct speech.
They exclaimed sadly that India had lost the match in the World Cup finals.
(a) They said, "They are so sorry! India has lost the match in the World Cup finals."
(b) They said, "Hurrah! India has lost the match in the World Cup finals."
(c) They said, "India has sadly lost the match in the World Cup finals."
(d) They said, "What a loss! India has lost the match in the World Cup finals."

58. Select the option that expresses the given sentence in active voice.
A state-of-the-art software program is being designed by our team to enhance the efficiency of our business operations.
(a) Our team is designing a state-of-the-art software program to enhance the efficiency of our business operations.
(b) Our team has designed a state-of-the-art software program to enhance the efficiency of our business operations.
(c) Our team will be designing a state-of-the-art software program to enhance the efficiency of our business operations.
(d) Our team has been designing a state-of-the-art software program to enhance the efficiency of our business operations.

59. Select the option that will improve the underlined part of the given sentence. In case no improvement is needed, select 'No improvement required'.
The schoolroom into which he took me was the most forlorn and desolate place <u>I am ever seeing.</u>
(a) No improvement required
(b) I have ever seeing
(c) I have ever seen
(d) I am ever seen

60. Parts of the following sentence have been given as options. Select the option that contains an error.
The Board of Directors held a meeting sorting out the issue of the NPAs of the bank.
(a) the NPAs of the bank.
(b) the issue of
(c) The Board of Directors held
(d) a meeting sorting out

61. Select the option that expresses the given sentence in active voice.
This cake was baked by Mary for your birthday.
(a) Mary has baked this cake for your birthday.
(b) Mary baked this cake for your birthday.
(c) Mary bakes this cake for your birthday.
(d) Mary has been baking this cake for your birthday.

62. Select the option that expresses the given sentence in passive voice.

The author wrote a compelling novel, weaving together multiple storylines that captivated readers until the last page.

(a) A compelling novel has been written by the author, weaving together multiple storylines that captivated readers until the last page.
(b) A compelling novel was written by the author, weaving together multiple storylines that captivated readers until the last page.
(c) A compelling novel was written by the reader, weaving together multiple storylines that captivated the author until the last page.
(d) A compelling novel was writing the author, weaving together multiple storylines that captivated readers until the last page.

63. Select the option that will improve the underlined part of the given sentence. In case no improvement is needed, select 'No improvement required'.

Mine grandmother need a helper to keep her terrace garden in order.

(a) Mine grandmother needed
(b) No improvement required
(c) My grandmother needs
(d) Mine grandmother needs

64. Parts of the following sentence have been given as options. Select the option that contains an error.

I was with the impression that I had returned the books that I had borrowed from you.

(a) that I had returned
(b) I was with the impression
(c) the books that I had
(d) borrowed from you

65. Select the option that expresses the given sentence in reported speech.

Mother said to Rahul, "Don't forget that the last date for geo-tagging our apartment is tomorrow."

(a) Mother reminded Rahul that the last date for geo-tagging their apartment is the next day.
(b) Mother told Rahul that do not forget that the last date for geo-tagging their apartment was the next day.
(c) Mother reminded Rahul that the last date for geo-tagging their apartment was the next day.
(d) Mother told Rahul not to forget that the last date for geo-tagging our apartment is tomorrow.

66. Select the option that expresses the given sentence in direct speech.

Mohit told his father that he could not solve that sum as it was very difficult.

(a) Mohit said to his father, "I cannot solve this sum as it is very difficult.
(b) Mohit said to his father, "I cannot solve that sum as it had been very difficult."
(c) Mohit said to his father, "He could not solve that sum as it was very difficult."
(d) Mohit said to his father, "You cannot solve that sum as it was very difficult."

67. Select the option that expresses the given sentence in indirect speech.

The tourist said to me, "Can you give me the directions to the temple?"

(a) The tourist asked me if you could give me the directions to the temple.
(b) The tourist asked me if I could give him the directions to the temple.
(c) The tourist asked me if you could give him the directions to the temple.
(d) The tourist asked me if I can give him the directions to the temple.

68. Select the option that expresses the given sentence in passive voice.

Do we have to accept this deal?

(a) This deal has to be accepted?
(b) Does this deal have to be accepted?
(c) Why is this deal to be accepted?
(d) Is this deal to be accepted?

69. Select the option that expresses the given sentence in passive voice.

The company will launch a new product next month.

(a) A new product will be launched by the company next month.
(b) A new product should be launched by the company next month.
(c) A new company will be launched by the product next month.
(d) A new product is to be launched by the company next month.

70. Parts of the following sentence have been given as options. One of them may contain an error. Select the part that contains the error from the given options. If you don't find any error, mark 'No error' as your answer.

My mother give me fresh carrot juice every evening.

(a) No error
(b) fresh carrot juice
(c) My mother give me
(d) every evening

71. Select the option that expresses the given sentence in reported speech.

Sandhya said to me, "Would you like to have some herbal tea?"

(a) Sandhya asked me if I would like to have some herbal tea.
(b) Sandhya told me that she would give me some herbal tea.
(c) Sandhya told me to have some herbal tea.
(d) Sandhya asked me that would you like to have some herbal tea.

72. Select the option that expresses the given sentence in indirect speech.

"Let's go for a walk in the park," he said.

(a) He suggested that they should go for a walk in the park.
(b) He requested that we should go for a walk in the park.
(c) He said that let's go for a walk in the park.
(d) He told us to go for a walk in the park.

73. Select the option that expresses the given sentence in reported speech.

Aditya said to Kavya, "What do you prefer to do in your free time – painting or basketball practice?"

(a) Aditya asked Kavya that what you prefer to do in your free time – painting or basketball practice.
(b) Aditya asked Kavya what does she prefer to do in her free time – painting or basketball practice.
(c) Aditya asked Kavya what she preferred to do in her free time – painting or basketball practice.
(d) Aditya asked Kavya what did she prefer to do in her free time – painting or basketball practice.

74. Select the option that expresses the given sentence in indirect speech.

She said, "I am going to the park."

(a) She said that she is going to the park.
(b) She said she will go to the park.
(c) She said that she was going to the park.
(d) She said she may be going to the park.

75. Select the option that expresses the given sentence in reported speech.
Avika says, "I have completed the math assignment."
(a) Avika says that she had completed the math assignment.
(b) Avika says that I have completed the math assignment.
(c) Avika says that she has completed the math assignment.
(d) Avika said that she has completed the math assignment.

76. Select the option that will improve the underlined part of the given sentence. In case no improvement is needed, select 'No improvement required'.
Since last evening, the boy has been complaining <u>with</u> pain in his legs.
(a) from (b) of (c) for
(d) No improvement required

77. Select the option that expresses the given sentence in indirect speech.
My daughter said, "I might go out to the Mall with my friends tonight."
(a) My daughter said that I might go out to the Mall with her friends tonight.
(b) My daughter said that she may go out to the Mall with her friends that night.
(c) My daughter said that she might go out to the Mall with her friends that night.
(d) My daughter said that she might go out to the Mall with my friends tonight.

78. Select the option that expresses the given sentence in reported speech.
She said, "I don't want to attend the meeting."
(a) She said that she doesn't want to attend the meeting.
(b) She told that she did not want to attend the meeting.
(c) She said that she did not want to attend the meeting.
(d) She said that I don't want to attend the meeting.

79. Select the option that expresses the given sentence in passive voice.
The mechanic did not fix the car yesterday.
(a) The mechanic was not fixed by the car yesterday.
(b) The car had not been fixed by the mechanic yesterday.
(c) The car was not fixed by the mechanic yesterday.
(d) The car did not fix by the mechanic yesterday.

80. Select the option that expresses the given sentence in passive voice.
Are the students discussing the upcoming exam in the library?
(a) Has the upcoming exam been discussed by the students in the library?
(b) Is the upcoming exam being discussed by the students in the library?
(c) What upcoming exam is being discussed by the students in the library?
(d) Was the upcoming exam being discussed by the students in the library?

81. The following sentence has been split into four segments. Identify the segment that contains a grammatical error.
Imagine taking a trip to Northern India / a century or so before the Common Era / using the recently discovering technology / of time travel.
(a) using the recently discovering technology
(b) of time travel
(c) Imagine taking a trip to Northern India
(d) a century or so before the Common Era

82. Select the option that will improve the underlined part of the given sentence. In case no improvement is needed, select 'No improvement required'.
A questionnaire <u>will distributing</u> to all the participants at the end of the session.
(a) will distribute
(b) will be distributed
(c) will be distributing
(d) No improvement required

83. Parts of the following sentence have been given as options. One of them may contain an error. Select the part that contains the error from the given options. If you don't find any error, mark 'No error' as your answer.
We had coffee to the university café last evening.
(a) to the university café
(b) last evening.
(c) We had coffee
(d) No error

84. Select the most appropriate option to fill in the blanks.
He walked .... the park and later strolled .... the riverbank.
(a) besides; about
(b) over; through
(c) against; across
(d) through; along

85. Select the option that expresses the given sentence in reported speech.
Mother said to Amayra, "Did you finish your homework?"
(a) Mother asked Amayra if she had finished her homework.
(b) Mother asked Amayra if she has finished her homework.
(c) Mother asked Amayra have you finished your homework.
(d) Mother asked Amayra did you finished your homework.

86. Select the most appropriate option to fill in the blanks.
.... team of two girls succeeded in reaching .... top of K2, the second highest mountain in the world.
(a) A; the
(b) A; a
(c) The; No word required
(d) The; a

87. Select the most appropriate option to fill in the blanks.
He gave .... the gift before .... left for the airport.
(a) I; she (b) her; she
(c) her; her (d) she; her

88. Select the option that expresses the given sentence in passive voice.
The chef prepared a delicious meal for the guests.
(a) A delicious meal was prepared for the guests by the chef.
(b) A delicious meal is prepared for the guests by the chef.
(c) A delicious meal was preparing for the guests by the chef.
(d) A delicious meal was being prepared for the guests by the chef.

89. Select the option that expresses the given sentence in direct speech.
Mother asked Rubani if she was sorry for what she had done.
(a) Mother said to Rubani, "Are you sorry for what she did?"
(b) Mother said to Rubani, "Were you sorry for what you have done?"
(c) Mother said to Rubani, "Are you sorry for what you have done?"
(d) Mother said to Rubani, "Do you feel sorry for what you are doing?"

90. Select the option that expresses the given sentence in indirect speech.
"I love the way you have decorated the room," she said, smiling warmly.
(a) Smiling warmly, she said that she had loved the way I had decorated the room.
(b) Smiling warmly, she said that I love the way you decorated the room.
(c) Smiling warmly, she said that she loves the way I decorated the room.
(d) Smiling warmly she said that she loved the way I had decorated the room.

91. Select the option that expresses the given sentence in indirect speech.
"Don't forget to bring your umbrella," he said to her.
(a) He told her don't forget to bring her umbrella.
(b) He reminded her to bring her umbrella.
(c) He reminded her not to forget to bring your umbrella.
(d) He told her to bring your umbrella.

92. Parts of the following sentence have been given as options. Select the option that contains an error.
The ancient trees of this forest did not propagate in the release of seeds.
(a) the release of seeds
(b) this forest did not
(c) The ancient trees of
(d) propagate in

93. The following sentence has been divided into parts. One of them may contain an error. Select the part that contains the error from the given options. If you don't find any error, mark 'No error' as your answer.
She use to eat / a lot of chocolates / when she was a child.
(a) when she was a child
(b) No error
(c) a lot of chocolates
(d) She use to eat

94. Select the most appropriate option to fill in the blank.
She decided .... the challenging task of learning a new language during her summer break.
(a) undertook
(b) to undertake
(c) undertake
(d) to undertaking

95. Select the option that expresses the given sentence in direct speech.
Rahul asked his mother if she had prepared the carrot halwa for him.
(a) Rahul said to his mother, "Have you prepared the carrot halwa for me?
(b) Rahul said to his mother, "Had she prepared the carrot halwa for him?
(c) Rahul said to his mother, "Are you preparing the carrot halwa for him?
(d) Rahul told to his mother, "Has she prepared the carrot halwa for me?

96. Select the option that will improve the underlined part of the given sentence. In case no improvement is needed, select 'No improvement required'.
<u>No sooner as I saw</u> the boy running across the road, I applied the brakes.
(a) As soon as I saw
(b) No improvement required
(c) No soon as I saw
(d) No sooner I see

97. Select the option that will improve the underlined part of the given sentence. In case no improvement is needed, select 'No improvement required'.
The movie was not only interesting <u>but also it was very suspenseful.</u>
(a) but also very suspenseful
(b) but also it is very suspenseful
(c) but also was more suspenseful
(d) No improvement required

98. The following sentence has been divided into parts. One of them may contain an error. Select the part that contains the error from the given options. If you don't find any error, mark 'No error' as your answer.
Kavya finishes / her homework / before having dinner.
(a) her homework
(b) Kavya finishes
(c) before having dinner
(d) No error

99. Select the most appropriate option to fill in the blank.
Anna decided to embark on a challenging journey to learn Mandarin, hoping .... the language fluently within a year.
(a) for speaking (b) to speak
(c) to speaking (d) to have spoken

100. Parts of the following sentence have been given as options. One of them may contain an error. Select the part that contains the error from the given options. If you don't find any error, mark 'No error' as your answer.
There were frequent landslides in the Jammu-Srinagar Highway during the monsoons.
(a) There were frequent landslides
(b) during the monsoons
(c) in the Jammu-Srinagar Highway
(d) No error

101. The following sentence has been split into four segments. Identify the segment that contains a grammatical error.
The teacher asked the class / to be quiet while she / explained the new assignment, / but nobody is listening.
(a) to be quiet while she
(b) explained the new assignment
(c) but nobody is listening
(d) The teacher asked the class

102. Select the option that expresses the given sentence in reported speech.
They say, "We are working on a new project."
(a) They say that we are working on a new project.
(b) They say that they are working on a new project.
(c) They say that they were working on a new project.
(d) They say that we were working on a new project.

103. Select the option that expresses the given sentence in indirect speech.
The mother said, "I am busy today".
(a) The mother said that she was busy that day.
(b) The mother said that she is busy today.
(c) The mother told that I am busy today.
(d) The mother told that she was busy today.

104. Select the option that expresses the given sentence in passive voice.
The courier gave my parcel to my neighbour in my absence.
(a) My parcel needs to be given to my neighbour by the courier in my absence.

(b) My neighbour was given to my parcel by the courier in my absence.
(c) My parcel was given to my neighbour by the courier in my absence.
(d) My parcel had been given to my neighbour by the courier in my absence.

105. Select the option that expresses the given sentence in direct speech.
I told my daughter that I would pick her up from school that week.
(a) I said to my daughter, "I would pick her up from school that week."
(b) I said to my daughter, "I will pick you up from school this week."
(c) I said to my daughter, "I will pick her up from school that week."
(d) I said to my daughter, "I will be picking her up from school this week."

106. Select the option that will improve the underlined part of the given sentence. In case no improvement is needed, select 'No improvement required'.
Linguists say that <u>this method helps accelerate</u> language learning.
(a) this method helping accelerating
(b) this method help accelerate
(c) No improvement required
(d) this method helps accelerated

107. Select the option that expresses the given sentence in active voice.
All the arrangements will have been completed by the hotel staff by the time the PM reaches here.
(a) The hotel staff have completed all the arrangements by the time the PM reaches here.
(b) The hotel staff will have completed all the arrangements by the time the PM reaches here.
(c) The hotel staff will complete all the arrangements by the time the PM reaches here.
(d) The hotel staff will be completing all the arrangements by the time the PM reaches here.

108. Select the option that will improve the underlined part of the given sentence. In case no improvement is needed, select 'No improvement required'.
<u>I saw that movie</u> last week and it was really interesting.
(a) I see that movie
(b) No improvement required
(c) I was seeing that movie
(d) I seen that movie

109. Select the option that expresses the given sentence in passive voice.
The scientist conducted a series of ground-breaking experiments, revealing new insights into the nature of dark matter.
(a) A series of ground-breaking experiments are conducted by the scientist, revealing new insights into the nature of dark matter.
(b) A series of ground-breaking insights were conducted by the scientist, revealing new experiments into the nature of dark matter.
(c) A series of ground-breaking experiments were conducted by the scientist, revealing new insights into the nature of dark matter.
(d) A series of ground-breaking experiments have been conducted by the scientist, revealing new insights into the nature of dark matter.

110. Select the option that expresses the given sentence in active voice.
Was the food finished by Kavya?
(a) Does Kavya finish the food?
(b) Has Kavya finished the food?
(c) Had Kavya finished the food?
(d) Did Kavya finish the food?

111. Select the option that expresses the given sentence in active voice.
The dinner will have been prepared by my sisters.
(a) My sisters will have prepared the dinner.
(b) My sisters will be preparing the dinner.
(c) The dinner will have prepared my sisters.
(d) My sisters will prepare the dinner.

112. The following sentence has been split into four segments. Identify the segment that contains a grammatical error.
India's coastline stretches / for over 7,500 kilometres, / to offer a plethora of / must visit beaches and coastal destinations.
(a) for over 7,500 kilometres
(b) must visit beaches and coastal destinations
(c) India's coastline stretches
(d) to offer a plethora of

113. Select the option that will improve the underlined part of the given sentence. In case no improvement is needed, select 'No improvement required'.
She <u>runs more faster than</u> her brother in the track events.
(a) runs fast than
(b) No improvement required
(c) runs faster than
(d) runs more fast than

114. Select the option that will improve the underlined part of the given sentence. In case no improvement is needed, select 'No improvement required'.
She had hoped that she <u>would be able qualifying</u> the CAT with a high percentile, but something went amiss.
(a) No improvement required
(b) would be able to be qualifying
(c) would be able to qualify
(d) will be able to qualify

115. Select the option that expresses the given sentence in passive voice.
The gardener is planting flowers in the garden.
(a) Flowers will be planted in the garden by the gardener.
(b) Flowers are planted in the garden by the gardener.
(c) Flowers have been planted in the garden by the gardener.
(d) Flowers are being planted in the garden by the gardener.

116. Select the option that expresses the given sentence in active voice.
Yesterday all the culprits were arrested.
(a) Yesterday the police were arresting all the culprits.
(b) Yesterday the police was arresting all the culprits.
(c) Yesterday the police had arrested all the culprits.
(d) Yesterday the police arrested all the culprits.

117. Select the option that will improve the underlined part of the given sentence. In case no improvement is needed, select 'No improvement required'.
<u>When I received</u> the appointment letter from the college of Arts and Humanities, I was exhilarated.
(a) While I received
(b) When I receive
(c) No improvement required
(d) When I have received

118. Select the option that will improve the underlined part of the given sentence. In case no improvement is needed, select 'No improvement required'.
Each of the students were asked to submit the project by the following day.
(a) Every of the students was asked
(b) No improvement required
(c) Each of the student was asked
(d) Each of the students was asked

119. Select the option that expresses the given sentence in indirect speech.
Avika said to her father, "I have to stay back at school for dance practice today."
(a) Avika told her father that I have to stay back at school for dance practice today.
(b) Avika told her father that she had to stay back at school for dance practice that day.
(c) Avika told her father that she will have to stay back at school for dance practice that day.
(d) Avika told her father that she has to stay back at school for dance practice today.

120. Select the option that expresses the given sentence in active voice.
This book was loved by the students.
(a) The students are loving this book.
(b) The students have loved this book.
(c) The students love this book.
(d) The students loved this book.

121. Select the option that expresses the given sentence in direct speech.
The teacher asked the students which lines of the poem they had not understood.
(a) The teacher said to the students, "Which lines of the poem they had not understood?"
(b) The teacher said to the students, "Which lines of the poem had you not understood?"
(c) The teacher said to the students, "Which lines of the poem you have not understood?"
(d) The teacher said to the students, "Which lines of the poem have they not understood?"

122. Select the option that expresses the given sentence in passive voice.
My grandmother called me to the worship place.
(a) The worship place was called by me to the grandmother.
(b) I called my grandmother to the worship place.
(c) I was called by my grandmother to the worship place.
(d) The grandmother was called by me to the worship place.

123. The following sentence has been split into four segments. Identify the segment that contains a grammatical error.
Most than half of / the 14-18 year old children / in rural India can't solve / a simple division problem.
(a) Most than half of
(b) the 14-18 year-old children
(c) a simple division problem
(d) in rural India can't solve

124. Select the option that expresses the given sentence in indirect speech.
She said, "I will meet you at the cafe at 3 pm".
(a) She told me that she will meet you at the cafe at 3 pm.
(b) She asked me if she would meet me at the cafe at 3 pm.
(c) She told me that she would meet me at the cafe at 3 pm.
(d) She told me that I will meet you at the cafe at 3 pm.

125. Select the option that expresses the given sentence in direct speech.
The official from the Metrological Department predicted that there would be heavy fog in Delhi the next day.
(a) The official from the Metrological Department said, "Delhi will experience heavy fog tomorrow."
(b) The official from the Metrological Department said, "Heavy fog will descend in Delhi tomorrow."
(c) The official from the Metrological Department said, "There would be heavy fog in Delhi the next day."
(d) The official from the Metrological Department said, "There will be heavy fog in Delhi tomorrow."

126. Select the option that will improve the underlined part of the given sentence. In case no improvement is needed, select 'No improvement required'.
He asked the speaker some questions until the session.
(a) during
(b) through
(c) No improvement required
(d) while

127. Select the option that will improve the underlined part of the given sentence. In case no improvement is needed, select 'No improvement required'.
The teacher along with the students were crossing the river, when the boat capsized.
(a) as well as the students were crossing
(b) with the students were crossing
(c) No improvement required
(d) along with the students was crossing

128. Select the option that expresses the given sentence in passive voice.
Open the window to let in some fresh air.
(a) The window is to be open to let in some fresh air.
(b) Let the window be opened to let in some fresh air.
(c) Let the window open to let in some fresh air
(d) You can open the window to let in some fresh air.

129. Select the option that will improve the underlined part of the given sentence. In case no improvement is needed, select 'No improvement required'.
Last evening I have gone to the theatre to see a performance.
(a) No improvement required
(b) I was going
(c) I am gone
(d) I went

130. The following sentence has been split into four segments. Identify the segment that contains a grammatical error.
People under eighteen / do not have / the right to vote, / don't they?
(a) don't they?
(b) People under eighteen
(c) do not have
(d) the right to vote

131. Select the option that expresses the given sentence in indirect speech.
The little girl said to her friend, "I have brought a chocolate for you."
(a) The little girl told her friend that I have brought a chocolate for you.
(b) The little girl told her friend that she has brought a chocolate for you.
(c) The little girl told her friend that I had brought a chocolate for her.
(d) The little girl told her friend that she had brought a chocolate for her.

132. The following sentence has been divided into parts. One of them may contain an error. Select the part that contains the error from the given options. If you don't find any error, mark 'No error' as your answer.
You may discussing / your problem / in tomorrow's meeting.
(a) in tomorrow's meeting
(b) You may discussing
(c) your problem
(d) No error

133. Select the option that expresses the given sentence in active voice.
The complex math problem was being explained to the students by the teacher.
(a) The teacher explained the complex math problem to the students.
(b) The teacher has explained the complex math problem to the students.
(c) The teacher will be explaining the complex math problem to the students.
(d) The teacher was explaining the complex math problem to the students.

134. Select the option that will improve the underlined part of the given sentence. In case no improvement is needed, select 'No improvement required'.
Shimla is <u>the more beautiful</u> hill station in Himachal Pradesh.
(a) a more beautiful
(b) No improvement required
(c) the very beautiful
(d) a very beautiful

135. Select the option that will improve the underlined part of the given sentence. In case no improvement is needed, select 'No improvement required'.
John was absent from the meeting because he was sick, <u>nor did he inform anyone</u>.
(a) nor did he informed anyone
(b) No improvement required
(c) and did not he inform anyone
(d) but he did not inform anyone

136. Parts of the following sentence have been given as options. One of them may contain an error. Select the part that contains the error from the given options. If you don't find any error, mark 'No error' as your answer.
Her parents did not allowed her to learn western music.
(a) No error
(b) Her parents
(c) to learn Western music
(d) did not allowed her

137. Select the option that expresses the given sentence in reported speech.
"Please listen carefully to what I am teaching," said Madam Mahima to the students.
(a) Madam Mahima asked the students to listen carefully to what she is teaching.
(b) Madam Mahima requested the students to listen carefully to what she has been teaching.
(c) Madam Mahima told the students to listen carefully to what she was teaching.
(d) Madam Mahima said to the students please listen carefully to what I am teaching.

138. Select the option that will improve the underlined part of the given sentence. In case no improvement is needed, select 'No improvement required'.
Traffic <u>is always remaining</u> heavy in this part of Delhi.
(a) No improvement required
(b) have always remained
(c) has always been remaining
(d) always remains

139. The following sentence has been split into four segments. Identify the segment that contains a grammatical error.
A ground-breaking discovery has been made / in a deserting quarry near New York, / where researchers have unearthed / the planet's most ancient forest.
(a) A ground-breaking discovery has been made
(b) where researchers have unearthed
(c) in a deserting quarry near New York,
(d) the planet's most ancient forest.

140. Parts of the following sentence have been given as options. Select the option that contains an error.
It is estimating that this forest once covered an area of approximately 400 km.
(a) approximately 400 km
(b) It is estimating that
(c) covered an area of
(d) this forest once

141. Select the option that expresses the given sentence in active voice.
A remarkable discovery in Paestum, an ancient Greek city, has been made by archaeologists.
(a) Archaeologists made a remarkable discovery in Paestum, an ancient Greek city.
(b) Archaeologists are making a remarkable discovery in Paestum, an ancient Greek city.
(c) Archaeologists make a remarkable discovery in Paestum, an ancient Greek city.
(d) Archaeologists have made a remarkable discovery in Paestum, an ancient Greek city.

142. Select the option that expresses the given sentence in passive voice.
The team completed the project ahead of schedule.
(a) The project had completed ahead of schedule by the team.
(b) The project has been completed ahead of schedule by the team.
(c) The schedule was completed ahead of project by the team.
(d) The project was completed ahead of schedule by the team.

143. The following sentence has been split into four segments. Identify the segment that contains a grammatical error.
Akasa Air planning to acquire /150 Boeing 737 planes in order to / expand the airline's reach in / both domestic and international operations.
(a) 150 Boeing 737 planes in order to
(b) both domestic and international operations
(c) expand the airline's reach in
(d) Akasa Air planning to acquire

144. Select the option that expresses the given sentence in indirect speech.
I said to Bhawna, "Have the monkeys eaten up our cauliflowers?"
(a) I asked Bhawna that have the monkeys eaten up our cauliflowers.
(b) I asked Bhawna if the monkeys had eaten up our cauliflowers.
(c) I asked Bhawna if the monkeys have eaten up our cauliflowers.
(d) I asked Bhawna if the monkeys had eaten up their cauliflowers.

145. Select the most appropriate option to fill in the blank.
If you diligently study the intricacies of the language, you ...... that your proficiency in it improves significantly.
(a) will be finding (b) found
(c) have found (d) will find

146. Select the option that expresses the given sentence in active voice.
The concert will be attended by us.
(a) We are attending the concert.
(b) We will have attended the concert.
(c) We will attend the concert.
(d) We have attended the concert.

147. Select the option that expresses the given sentence in passive voice.
The manager gave the employee a bonus.
(a) The employee was given the manager by the bonus.
(b) The employee had been given a bonus by the manager.
(c) The bonus was given to the employee by the manager.
(d) The employee was given a bonus by the manager.

148. Select the option that expresses the given sentence in direct speech.
Manya said that she didn't want any breakfast.
(a) Manya said, "You didn't want any breakfast."
(b) Manya says, "She doesn't want any breakfast."
(c) Manya said, "I don't want any breakfast."
(d) Manya said, "She didn't want any breakfast."

149. Select the option that will improve the underlined part of the given sentence. In case no improvement is needed, select 'No improvement required'.
<u>She is allergic from peanuts</u>, so she always checks food labels carefully.
(a) She is allergic to peanuts
(b) No improvement required
(c) She is allergical from peanuts
(d) She is allergic with peanuts

150. Parts of the following sentence have been given as options. Select the option that contains an error.
Traditional practices are ways of knowing, learning and to generate a distinct experience of the world around us.
(a) and to generate a distinct experience
(b) ways of knowing, learning
(c) of the world around us
(d) Traditional practices are

151. The following sentence has been divided into parts. One of them may contain an error. Select the part that contains the error from the given options. If you don't find any error, mark 'No error' as your answer.
Human activity often / has a negatively effect / on the ecosystem of wetlands.
(a) Human activity often
(b) No error
(c) has a negatively effect
(d) on the ecosystem of wetlands

152. Select the option that expresses the given sentence in indirect speech.
"The Sun is shining brightly today", he said, looking out of the window.
(a) Looking out of the window, he said that the Sun is shining brightly today.
(b) Looking out of the window, he said that the Sun was shining brightly today.
(c) Looking out of the window, he says that the Sun is shining brightly that day.
(d) Looking out of the window, he said that the Sun was shining brightly that day.

153. Select the option that will improve the underlined part of the given sentence. In case no improvement is needed, select 'No improvement required'.
<u>She don't like</u> chocolate, so I bought a vanilla cake for her birthday.
(a) She don't likes
(b) She doesn't like
(c) She don't liked
(d) No improvement required

154. Select the option that will improve the underlined part of the given sentence. In case no improvement is needed, select 'No improvement required'.
The doctor <u>prescribes</u> antibiotics and a cough syrup to me when I had severe cough and cold.
(a) was prescribing
(b) prescribed
(c) No improvement required
(d) are prescribing

155. Select the most appropriate antonym of the given word.
Mitigate
(a) Diminish (b) Alleviate
(c) Intensify (d) Weaken

156. Select the most appropriate synonym of the given word.
Exuberance
(a) Lethargy (b) Excitement
(c) Depression (d) Indifference

157. Select the most appropriate antonym of the given word.
Extravagant
(a) Restrained (b) Enrich
(c) Lavish (d) Righteous

158. Select the option that can be used as a one-word substitute for the given group of words.
A complete, usually alphabetical list of items, often with notes giving details.
(a) Catalogue (b) Brochure
(c) Pamphlet (d) Monograph

159. Select the most appropriate option to complete the given idiom.
Spill the ....
(a) beads (b) beans
(c) tea (d) milk

160. Select the option that can be used as a one-word substitute for the given group of words.
Not able to be changed or adapted.
(a) Austere (b) Rigid
(c) Permissive (d) Harsh

161. Select the most appropriate synonym of the given word.
Devour
(a) Receive (b) Preserve
(c) Consume (d) Abstain

162. Select the incorrectly spelt word.
(a) Irregular (b) Irresponsible
(c) Irrelevent (d) Irritable

163. Select the most appropriate option to fill in the blank and complete the given idiom.
Piece of ....
(a) cake (b) bread
(c) sweet (d) apple

164. Select the most appropriate synonym of the given word.
Frigid
(a) Futile (b) Facile
(c) Flexible (d) Freezing

165. Select the most appropriate meaning of the given idiom.
Be in apple-pie order
(a) Be in a happy mood
(b) Be in chronological order
(c) Be perfectly arranged and tidy
(d) Be extra sweet to people

166. Select the most appropriate antonym of the given word.
Oaf
(a) Smart (b) Simpleton
(c) Blockhead (d) Magnificient

167. Select the option that can be used as a one-word substitute for the given group of words.
The person who presents and coordinates a show on stage or television.
(a) Reporter (b) Anchor
(c) Jockey (d) Broadcaster

168. Select the option that can be used as a one-word substitute for the given group of words.
Lasting for a very short while
(a) Perpetual (b) Reliable
(c) Eternal (d) Ephemeral

169. Select the most appropriate synonym of the given word.
Feasible
(a) Practical (b) Worthless
(c) Energetic (d) Tentative

170. Select the most appropriate synonym of the given word.
Munificence
(a) Shrewdness (b) Generousness
(c) Quietness (d) Liveliness

171. Select the option that can be used as a one-word substitute for the given group of words.
Not active but has the ability to be active anytime later.
(a) Jubilant (b) Dormant
(c) Ambiguous (d) Conscious

172. Select the most appropriate option to complete the given idiom.
Sitting on the ....
(a) boundary (b) wall
(c) tree (d) fence

173. Select the option that can be used as a one-word substitute for the given group of words.
Protect from a danger, risk or unpleasant experience.
(a) Scare (b) Sever
(c) Seize (d) Shield

174. Select the most appropriate meaning of the given idiom.
Be on the same page
(a) Having the same understanding
(b) Doing things with a partner
(c) Staying in the same place
(d) Reading something together

175. Select the incorrectly spelt word.
(a) Hurdle (b) Humour
(c) Hundred (d) Hungery

176. Select the most appropriate meaning of the given idiom.
To get someone's goat
(a) To have affection for somebody
(b) To steal something
(c) To make one feel good
(d) To irritate someone

177. Select the most appropriate option to fill in the blank and complete the given idiom.
Bite the ....
(a) bread (b) bullet (c) barb (d) bean

178. Select the incorrectly spelt word.
(a) Obstinate (b) Odorous
(c) Occasional (d) Observence

179. Select the most appropriate synonym of the given word.
Genesis
(a) Inception (b) Symbolism
(c) Conclusion (d) Infatuation

180. Select the most appropriate meaning of the given idiom.
Split one's sides
(a) To roar with laughter
(b) To overeat
(c) To undergo surgery
(d) To scream in agony

181. Select the most appropriate meaning of the given idiom.
Cut from the same cloth
(a) To share resources
(b) To have very similar qualities
(c) To belong to the same family
(d) To have the same origin

182. Select the most appropriate option to fill in the blank and complete the given idiom.
Hit the ....
(a) bag (b) head
(c) bay (d) sack

183. Select the option that can be used as a one-word substitute for the given group of words.
An eloquent and skilled public speaker.
(a) Elector (b) Orator
(c) Spokesperson (d) Leader

184. Sentences of a paragraph are given below. While the first and the last sentences (A and F) are in the correct order, the sentences in between are jumbled up. Arrange the sentences in the correct order to form a meaningful and coherent paragraph.
A. The races were something of a disappointment.
B. As we left the grounds, Dad said with satisfaction: It'll be good to get back to the hotel and relax.
C. Dad was not eager.
D. But we were going to the botanical gardens, Mother reminded him.
E. I'd like to have just a peek at them.
F. Those places cover a lot of territory, you know, he said.
(a) ECDB (b) BCED
(c) BDEC (d) CBED

185. Sentences of a paragraph are given below. While the first and the last sentences (A and F) are in the correct order, the sentences in between are jumbled up. Arrange the sentences in the correct order to form a meaningful and coherent paragraph.
A. When I joined the B.Sc. degree course at St. Joseph's, I was unaware of any other option for higher education.
B. Nor did I have any information about career opportunities available to a student of science.
C. I could have joined the Engineering course long ago, right after finishing my Intermediate course.
D. Only after obtaining a B.Sc. did I realise that physics was not my subject.
E. I had to go into engineering to realise my dreams.
F. Better late than never, I told myself as I made the detour, applying for admission into the Madras Institute of Technology (MIT), regarded as the crown jewel of technical education in South India at that time.
(a) CBED (b) BDEC
(c) BCED (d) ECDB

186. Sentences of a paragraph are given below. While the first and the last sentences (A and F) are in the correct order, the sentences in between are jumbled up. Arrange the sentences in the correct order to form a meaningful and coherent paragraph.

A. Whenever I teach my class, I make sure that everyone participates in the question-answer session.

B. Sometimes their questions are so difficult that I am not able to answer.

C. Many times I have learnt a lot from my students during these sessions.

D. I normally teach for forty minutes and keep the last twenty minutes open for debates, questions and answers.

E. This way, students learn to express their opinions in front of others and the teacher also understands how much the students have learnt.

F. Then I tell them that I will refer to my books and answer the next day.

(a) CBED (b) DECB
(c) DCBE (d) ECDB

187. Sentences of a paragraph are given below. While the first and the last sentences (A and F) are in the correct order, the sentences in between are jumbled up. Arrange the sentences in the correct order to form a meaningful and coherent paragraph.

A. When I was a child, I had a teacher called Gowramma.

B. She used to teach us Sanskrit.

C. She was kind and warm and always cheerful.

D. Students usually took Sanskrit as an optional language, in order to score marks like math.

E. She was a great teacher and would tell lots of stories in the class.

F. They only wanted to get good grades and were not interested in Gowramma's old epics.

(a) CBED (b) ECDB
(c) CBDE (d) BDEC

188. Given below are six sentences of a paragraph. Sentence A is the beginning whereas sentence F is the last sentence of the para. The middle four sentences (B-E) are jumbled up. Select the option that gives their correct order forming a meaningful and coherent paragraph.

A. A youngster quit Facebook in December after spending over three years on the social networking site.

B. Like almost everyone from his 'friend's circle', the 20-year-old was a regular on the site.

C. Last week a new feature on Facebook called Timeline forced him to reconsider the pros and cons of being on the networking site.

D. With that one act, he bid a silent adieu to more than 300 contacts that he had added to his account during the period.

E. He visited it every day to post photos and status updates.

F. "Everyone has some skeletons in their closet and I am just not comfortable with Facebook digging up and displaying all the facets of my life on a bulletin board", said the youngster.

(a) CEBD (b) EDBC
(c) BCDE (d) DBEC

189. Sentences of a paragraph are given below. While the first and the last sentences (A and F) are in the correct order, the sentences in between are jumbled up. Arrange the sentences in the correct order to form a meaningful and coherent paragraph.

A. There are about eighty houses in the village, which is the seat of two district governors who administer thirty villages.

B. We were told that we were the first Europeans who had ever come to Kyirong, and the inhabitants watched our entry with astonishment.

C. This time we were quartered in the house of a farmer, which reminded me of our Tyrolese houses.

D. The only difference was that instead of chimneys, the roofs of the houses were decorated with prayer flags.

E. As a matter of fact, the whole of the village might have been transplanted from the Alps.

F. These were always in the five colours, which represented different aspects of life in Tibet.

(a) BDEC (b) CBED
(c) ECDB (d) BCED

190. Sentences of a paragraph are given below in jumbled order. Arrange the sentences in the correct order to form a meaningful and coherent paragraph.

A. 'Who goes there?' shouted the Hodja.

B. One night, Hodja Nasreddin awoke, thinking he had heard a strange noise outside his window.

C. Hearing no reply, Nasreddin reached for his bow, set an arrow to the string, took aim and shot in the direction of the mysterious figure.

D. Looking out, he saw a suspicious white figure.

(a) CBAD (b) BCAD
(c) BDAC (d) ACDB

191. Sentences of a paragraph are given below. While the first and the last sentences (A and F) are in the correct order, the sentences in between are jumbled up. Arrange the sentences in the correct order to form a meaningful and coherent paragraph.

A. Some twelve or fifteen years ago there lived in his own house in the main street of the town a certain official by the name of Gromov, a steady well-to-do man.

B. Sergei, after completing three years of study at the University, contracted galloping consumption and died and this death was the beginning of a series of disasters which overtook the Gromov family.

C. He had two sons: Sergei and Ivan.

D. His house and property were sold at auction, and Ivan Dmitrich and his mother were left without any means of support.

E. A week after Sergei's funeral the old man was sued for forgery and embezzlement, and died soon after of typhus in the prison hospital.

F. While his father was alive Ivan Dmitrich lived in Petersburg, studying at the University, and receiving 60 or 70 roubles from home every month.

(a) BDEC (b) ECDB
(c) CBDE (d) CBED

192. Sentences of a paragraph are given below. While the first and the last sentences (A and F) are in the correct order, the sentences in between are jumbled up. Arrange the sentences in the correct order to form a meaningful and coherent paragraph.

A. Soon, we were treated like members of the family.

B. Once she invited us to come into her room and look at her jewels.

C. Mrs. Thangme talked over her problems with us and was delighted when we paid her compliments on her good looks and good taste.

D. Her treasures were worth looking at.

E. These she kept in a great chest in which her treasures were stored either in small jewel cases or in fine silk wrappings.

F. She had a glorious tiara of corals, turquoise and pearls and many rings as well as diamond earrings and some little Tibetan amulet lockets, which are hung round the neck by a coral chain.

(a) BDEC (b) CDBE
(c) CBED (d) ECDB

193. Sentences of a paragraph are given below in jumbled order. Arrange the sentences in the correct order to form a meaningful and coherent paragraph.

A. Leo Tolstoy, a great Russian novelist, was born in the village of Yasnaya Polyana in Russian Empire, on 9th September, 1828.

B. His mother died before Tolstoy turned two, and his father died in 1837.

C. His parents, Count Nikolay Ilich Tolstoy and Princess Mariya Nikolaevna Volkonskaya, came from distinguished families of the Russian nobility.

D. After his grandmother and an aunt died, Tolstoy and his four siblings were raised by another aunt in Western Russia.

(a) ADBC (b) CDBA
(c) BDAC (d) ACBD

194. Sentences of a paragraph are given below. While the first and the last sentences (A and F) are in the correct order, the sentences in between are jumbled up. Arrange the sentences in the correct order to form a meaningful and coherent paragraph.

A. When I had a house in Sri Lanka, my parents came out one winter to see me.

B. Originally, I had felt some qualms about encouraging their visit.

C. Any one of several things – the constant heat, the unaccustomed food and drinking water, even the presence of a leprosy clinic a quarter of a mile from the house – might easily have an adverse effect on them in one way or another.

D. They claimed not to mind the lack of running water in the bathrooms and regularly praised the curries prepared by Appuhami, the resident cook.

E. But I had underestimated their resilience; they made a greater show of adaptability than I had thought possible and seemed entirely content with everything.

F. Both of them being in their seventies, they were not tempted by the more distant or inaccessible points of interest.

(a) CBED (b) BCED
(c) BDEC (d) ECDB

195. Sentences of a paragraph are given below. While the first and the last sentences (A and F) are in the correct order, the sentences in between are jumbled up. Arrange the sentences in the correct order to form a meaningful and coherent paragraph.

A. Swaminathan and Mani were nervously walking up the short drive leading to Rajam's house.

B. A policeman in uniform cried to them to stop and came running towards them.

C. The policeman asked what they were doing there.

D. Swaminathan felt like turning and fleeing on seeing him.

E. He appealed to Mani to speak to the policeman.

F. Mani replied in a tone in which overdone carelessness was a trifle obvious: If Rajam is in the house, we are here to see him.

(a) CBED (b) ECDB
(c) BDEC (d) BCED

196. Sentences of a paragraph are given below in jumbled order. Arrange the sentences in the correct order to form a meaningful and coherent paragraph.

A. He usually spent such an interval in running round the school or in playing the Digging Game under the huge Tamarind tree.

B. But to-day he sat apart sunk in thought.

C. Next day, Swaminathan was at school early.

D. There was still half an hour before the bell.

(a) BDAC (b) ACBD
(c) CDAB (d) CABD

197. Sentences of a paragraph are given below. While the first and the last sentences (A and F) are in the correct order, the sentences in between are jumbled up. Arrange the sentences in the correct order to form a meaningful and coherent paragraph.

A. Colombo, where all the people I knew lived, was less than a hundred miles away from my place.

B. These weekends in the city were hot and exhausting, and my parents were always happy to get back to the house, where they could change into comfortable clothing.

C. One Sunday not long before they were due to return to America, we decided to take in the horse races at Gintota, where there are also some botanical gardens that Mother wanted to see.

D. There we had tea on the wide verandas of certain houses in Cinnamon Gardens, and sat at dinners with professors from the university, Protestant ministers, and assorted members of the government.

E. Several times me and my parents (who had come from America to visit me) went up for weekends, which I arranged with friends by telephone beforehand.

F. I engaged rooms at the New Oriental in Galle and we had lunch there before setting out to see the botanical gardens.

(a) CBDE (b) ECDB
(c) BDEC (d) EDBC

198. Sentences of a paragraph are given below in jumbled order. Arrange the sentences in the correct order to form a meaningful and coherent paragraph.

A. "I'll forget it for sure", said the Hodja, "Write it on a piece of paper for me."

B. Hodja Nasreddin purchased a piece of meat at the market, and on his way home he met a friend.

C. The friend obliged him, and the Hodja continued on his way, the piece of meat in one hand and the recipe in the other.

D. Seeing the Hodja's purchase, the friend told him an excellent recipe for stew.

(a) BDAC (b) BCAD
(c) ACDB (d) CBAD

199. Sentences of a paragraph are given below. While the first and the last sentences (A and F) are in the correct order, the sentences in between are jumbled up. Arrange the sentences in the correct order to form a meaningful and coherent paragraph.

A. In 1928, Salim Ali went to Germany and trained under Professor Erwin Streseman at the Zoological Museum of Berlin.

B. Then, suddenly one day the female arrives and takes possession of a husband and the half-finished home!

C. Here, he studied the breeding biology of baya birds which won him recognition as a world class ornithologist.

D. He found that it is the male baya which builds the nest.

E. In 1930, finding no suitable employment he moved to Kihim a coastal village near Mumbai.

F. He found that the thousands of baby bayas were fed on soft bodied insects as the young are incapable of digesting hard grain.

(a) CBDE (b) ECDB
(c) EDBC (d) BDEC

200. Sentences of a paragraph are given below in jumbled order. Arrange the sentences in the correct order to form a meaningful and coherent paragraph.

A. He reflected for a while, dipped the pen in ink, and wrote the address: To Grandfather in the Village.

B. Then he scratched his head and thought for a while, and added the words: Konstantin Makarich.

C. Vanka twice folded the sheet of paper and then he put it in an envelope bought the previous day for a kopeck.

D. Pleased because no one interrupted him when he was writing, he threw on his cap, and without troubling to put on a coat, he ran out into the street in his shirt sleeves.

(a) BDAC (b) ACBD
(c) CDBA (d) CABD

Know Correct Answers

1. (b)	2. (c)	3. (d)	4. (d)	5. (d)	6. (d)	7. (c)	8. (c)	9. (d)	10. (c)
11. (a)	12. (b)	13. (a)	14. (a)	15. (a)	16. (b)	17. (a)	18. (b)	19. (a)	20. (a)
21. (d)	22. (c)	23. (d)	24. (c)	25. (c)	26. (d)	27. (c)	28. (d)	29. (a)	30. (a)
31. (a)	32. (c)	33. (c)	34. (a)	35. (b)	36. (d)	37. (a)	38. (c)	39. (a)	40. (a)
41. (d)	42. (d)	43. (b)	44. (d)	45. (d)	46. (d)	47. (b)	48. (d)	49. (c)	50. (a)
51. (a)	52. (a)	53. (b)	54.. (a)	55. (d)	56. (a)	57. (d)	58. (a)	59. (c)	60. (d)
61. (b)	62. (b)	63. (c)	64. (b)	65. (c)	66. (a)	67. (b)	68. (b)	69. (a)	70. (c)
71. (a)	72. (a)	73. (c)	74. (c)	75. (a)	76. (b)	77. (c)	78. (a)	79. (c)	80. (b)
81. (a)	82. (b)	83. (a)	84. (d)	85. (a)	86. (a)	87. (b)	88. (a)	89. (c)	90. (d)
91. (b)	92. (d)	93. (d)	94. (b)	95. (a)	96. (a)	97. (a)	98. (d)	99. (b)	100. (c)
101. (c)	102. (c)	103. (a)	104. (c)	105. (b)	106. (c)	107. (b)	108. (b)	109. (c)	110. (d)
111. (a)	112. (d)	113. (c)	114. (c)	115. (d)	116. (d)	117. (c)	118. (d)	119. (b)	120. (d)
121. (b)	122. (c)	123. (a)	124. (c)	125. (d)	126. (a)	127. (d)	128. (b)	129. (d)	130. (a)
131. (d)	132. (b)	133. (d)	134. (a)	135. (d)	136. (d)	137. (c)	138. (d)	139. (c)	140. (b)
141. (d)	142. (d)	143. (d)	144. (b)	145. (d)	146. (c)	147.. (d)	148. (c)	149. (a)	150. (a)
151. (c)	152. (d)	153. (b)	154. (b)	155. (c)	156. (b)	157. (a)	158. (a)	159. (b)	160. (b)
161. (c)	162. (c)	163. (a)	164. (d)	165. (c)	166. (a)	167. (b)	168. (d)	169. (a)	170. (b)
171. (b)	172. (d)	173. (d)	174. (a)	175. (d)	176. (d)	177. (b)	178. (d)	179. (d)	180. (a)
181. (b)	182. (d)	183. (b)	184. (c)	185. (b)	186 (b)	187 (a)	188. (d)	189. (d)	190 (c)
191. (d)	192. (c)	193. (d)	194. (b)	195. (c)	196 (c)	197 (d)	198. (a)	199. (b)	200 (d)

Answer & Solutions

1. (b) The word 'sites' refers to specific locations of historical, archaeological or cultural significance. In the passage, the Maeshowe tomb is being described as a historical location, making 'sites' the most appropriate choice.

2. (c) The word 'surrounded' is the correct form here as it is the past participle of 'surround' used to describe something that is enclosed or enclosed by something else. The green mound is enclosed by a ditch and 'surrounded' fits this context.

3. (d) The word 'burial' is a noun and refers to the act or process of burying something, especially a body or an object. In this context, 'burial' correctly describes the act of placing the tomb in the ground. The sentence is referring to the place being used for burial, so 'burial' fits best.

4. (d) The word 'ancient' refers to something that is very old, often with historical significance. In this context, the tomb is 5,000 years old, making 'ancient' the most appropriate choice to describe the place. The word emphasises the age and historical depth of the tomb, fitting well with the passage's context.

5. (d) The phrase 'a testament to' is a common expression used to indicate that something serves as proof or evidence of something else, in this case, the skill of Orkney's pre-historic residents. 'To' correctly links the 'testament' to the skill being demonstrated.

6. (d) The word 'for' is used here to indicate the duration of time. The phrase 'for around three weeks' correctly expresses the period of time during which the phenomenon occurs around the winter solstice. It implies that this period extends on either side of the solstice.

7. (c) The word 'place' is the most fitting option because it refers to a location or area, which aligns with the context of the passage discussing a historical site, the Maeshowe tomb. 'Place' is commonly used to refer to a specific geographical location, making it the most appropriate word to describe the tomb.

8. (c) The word 'occur' means 'to happen' or 'to take place', which is the most appropriate choice in this context. The passage is describing a phenomenon that happens during the winter solstice, making 'occur' the correct term to describe this event.

9. (d) The word 'tomb' is the most appropriate choice as it refers to a place where a person is buried, which fits the context of the Maeshowe tomb in the passage. The passage describes a pre-historic burial site and 'tomb' is the correct term to describe such a place.

10. (c) The phrase 'designed to align' is the most appropriate choice. The infinitive form 'to align' is used after 'designed' to indicate the purpose of the design. In this context, the passage is explaining that the passage was intentionally designed with the purpose (or intention) of aligning with the setting of the midwinter Sun.

11. (a) The word 'batch' refers to a group of items or people that are treated or produced together. In this context, 'batch of 20' refers to a group of 20 aircrafts arriving together. This is a common usage when discussing a quantity of items produced or delivered in one go.

12. (b) The word 'showcased' is the correct past tense form of the verb 'showcase', which is used here to indicate that the aircraft was presented or displayed for the first time on 18th January. The sentence is describing a past event, so the past tense 'showcased' is appropriate.

13. (a) The word 'such' is used to refer to a specific type or category of something, often implying the uniqueness or significance of the item. In this context, it emphasises that the five more aircrafts are of the same kind or type as the first A350. The phrase 'such premium passenger aircrafts' correctly points to a specific type of aircraft, highlighting their premium nature.

14. (a) The phrase 'scheduled to arrive' is grammatically correct because it uses the infinitive form to express a planned or expected event. In this context, it refers to the aircraft's scheduled arrival.

15. (a) 'The' is the correct definite article because we are referring to a specific first Indian carrier, which is Air India. The article 'the' points to a unique entity.

16. (b) The preposition 'on' is used to refer to specific dates and days, such as 22nd January in this case.

17. (a) The word 'hoping' is used here because it indicates a desire or expectation for something to happen. The sentence suggests that Air India is expecting to overhaul its image and service.

18. (b) The correct preposition is 'with' because it indicates that the A350 is equipped with a powerful engine. 'With' is used to express the tools or features something has.

19. (a) The word 'step' is the correct option, meaning to move or enter into the aircraft. The phrase 'step inside' is commonly used when describing entering a space.

20. (a) The word 'see' is the most appropriate choice, meaning to observe or notice something. It is commonly used in contexts where something is visually perceived.

21. (d) The word 'ensures' is correct because it means to make certain that something happens. In the context of the passage organic farming guarantees that nature stays clean and rich.

22. (c) The word 'buzz' is correct here as it refers to the sound or activity made by animals, birds and insects, commonly associated with a lively, active environment like an organic farm.

23. (d) The word 'near' is most appropriate here, meaning in close proximity. The phrase suggests that wildlife and plants thrive close to ecologically produced fields, indicating a positive impact on the surrounding area.

24. **(c)** The phrase 'far less' correctly indicates a significantly lower usage of fertiliser in organic farming compared to conventional farming. It emphasises that less fertiliser is used in organic farming.

25. **(c)** The word 'perception' refers to how something is viewed or understood by people. In this context, it reflects how organic food is now perceived differently, focusing more on safety and health due to the pandemic.

26. **(d)** Mercantile companies during the 17th century made profits primarily by excluding their competitors. By eliminating competition, these companies could buy goods at a cheaper price and sell them at higher prices, thus ensuring their profitability. This practice was central to their business strategy.

27. **(c)** The East India Company excluded competition by fighting fierce battles with other European companies to secure markets. However, it did not buy goods at higher prices than its competitors. Instead, it sought to buy cheap goods and sell them at higher prices, which is the core of mercantile profit-making strategies.

28. **(d)** The Portuguese were the first Europeans to establish a presence in India for trade, having set up their base in Goa. Vasco da Gama, a Portuguese explorer, was the one who discovered the sea route to India in 1498.

29. **(a)** The passage discusses the role of the East India Company in the context of trade with the East, including the exclusive rights granted to the company, its venture across the oceans and its rivalry with other European powers. The focus is on the East India Company's establishment and its monopoly in trading, which is the main theme of the passage.

30. **(a)** The Royal Charter granted the East India Company the exclusive right to trade with the East, meaning no other English company could compete with it in the Eastern markets.

31. **(a)** The passage primarily focuses on the discovery of pre-historic rock paintings in a cave in Pithoragarh district. The paintings are described as being thousands of years old and the discovery is highlighted as a significant find in the region.

32. **(c)** The passage indicates that the wide space inside the cave is a clue that suggests the cave was used as a habitation by pre-historic human groups.

33. **(c)** The passage mentions that a cup mark was spotted 20 feet up the hill, which is not part of the rock paintings inside the cave.

34. **(a)** The passage mentions that nine caves in Almora, one in Nainital and three in the Garhwal region were found with rock paintings before the discovery in Pithoragarh. However, the first caves with paintings in Uttarakhand were discovered in Almora, not Pithoragarh.

35. **(d)** This sequence correctly reflects the flow of events as described in the passage.

36. **(d)** The passage mentions that "Only 43.3 per cent of 14-18-year olds are able to do such problems correctly". These problems involve dividing a three-digit number by a one-digit number, which is a skill expected around Class 3 and 4.

37. **(a)** The passage mentions that "females (76 per cent) do better than males (70.9 per cent) in reading a Class 2 level text in their regional language". This clearly shows that girls outperform boys in reading fluency in their regional language.

38. **(c)** The passage describes how the ASER 2023 survey assessed both reading abilities and numeracy skills among 14-18-year-olds, specifically their ability to read Class 2 level texts and perform basic division, making this the primary focus of the survey.

39. **(a)** The passage states that "85 per cent of those surveyed could calculate the length of an object correctly if it was placed at the '0' mark on the ruler". This refers to the ability to measure objects accurately when they are placed at the '0' mark.

40. **(a)** The passage provides detailed information about the findings from the ASER 2023 survey, which is a report on educational status in rural India. The passage discusses the survey's findings on the reading abilities and numeracy skills of 14-18-year-olds in rural India.

41. **(d)** The passage details the author's initial experiences in London, including his first lessons in European etiquette, staying at an expensive hotel and adjusting to the new environment. These events depict the author's early days in London.

42. **(d)** Dr. Mehta got irritated when the author picked up his top-hat and disturbed the fur by passing his hand over it the wrong way. This incident led to the author's first lesson in European etiquette.

43. **(b)** Dr. Mehta is the one who humorously initiated the author into European manners and etiquette, as indicated in the passage.

44. **(d)** The passage is written in a personal narrative style where the author recounts specific personal experiences from their early days in London. This fits the characteristics of an autobiography, where an individual reflects on their own life and experiences.

45. **(d)** The passage mentions that the author had depended on the provisions brought from Bombay during his early days in London, as he found the hotel food unappetising.

46. **(d)** The passage describes the significant impact of the record drought in the Amazon, focusing on how it has affected rivers, wildlife and human lives, marking the worst drought in over a century. This is the main theme of the passage.

47. **(b)** The passage states that on Monday, the port of Manaus recorded a water level of 13.59 metres, which is the lowest since records began in 1902. The statement in option (b) about the water level being 17.60 metres on Monday is incorrect.

48. **(d)** The phrase 'fanned out' means to spread out in different directions or over an area. In this context, it refers to the workers from the NGO who distributed themselves across the region to deliver food and supplies.

49. **(c)** The sequence begins with the least rain in the Amazon region (D), followed by drying tributaries (B), boats being stranded (A) and food and water supplies being cut-off (C).

50. (a) The passage is reporting on the current situation regarding the Amazon drought, the environmental impacts and the government's response, which is typical of a news report.

51. (a) The sentence discusses a weather forecast that predicts a future event (heavy snowfall). When expressing an expectation or prediction about something in the future, we often use the phrase 'should have' to indicate what is expected or likely to happen.

Grammar Concept The phrase 'should have' is used to express a prediction or expectation about a future event, which fits the context of the weather forecast. It suggests that the snowfall is something expected, based on the forecast.

52. (a) This sentence is in passive voice, where the focus is shifted from the doer of the action (the director) to the action itself (the organisation of the meeting). In passive voice, the subject of the sentence receives the action rather than performing it. The structure of a passive sentence is [Object] + [Auxiliary Verb] + [Past Participle] + [by + Subject]

In the active voice, the sentence is 'The director organised a meeting'.

In the passive voice, it becomes 'A meeting was organised by the director'.

53. (b) 'Otherwise' is used to indicate the consequence of not doing something. In this sentence, it explains what would have happened if the person had not followed the instructions.

Grammar Concept 'Otherwise' is a conjunctive adverb that introduces an alternative or result. It is used to indicate that if one action is not done, something undesirable will happen. 'Otherwise' connects the two clauses by showing cause and effect.

54. (a) In this sentence, we are referring to two actions that occurred in the past. The storm subsiding (ceasing or becoming less intense) happened before the explorers realised the flood. This is why the past perfect tense (had subsided) is the correct choice.

55. (d) This sentence is an example of the active voice where the subject (the company) is doing the action (issuing a statement). The phrase 'Let the company issue' correctly expresses the active voice in an imperative form, asking or allowing the company to take action.

Grammar Concept In the active voice, the subject of the sentence performs the action. 'Let' is used to suggest or allow someone to do something. The structure is Let + Subject + Base form of verb.

56. (a) 'Even though' is used to show contrast. The sentence suggests that despite the fact that everyone left the office, Ashutosh was still working. 'Even though' introduces the contrast between the two clauses (everybody leaving the office and Ashutosh still being busy).

57. (d) This sentence in direct speech expresses an exclamation about the loss. 'What a loss!' correctly reflects the sadness or disappointment in the context of the World Cup finals.

Grammar Concept Direct speech is used to quote someone's exact words. In direct speech, punctuation marks like commas and quotation marks are important. The exclamation 'What a loss!' is appropriate for expressing strong feelings of disappointment, fitting the context of the sentence.

58. (a) In the active voice, the subject 'Our team' is performing the action. The present continuous tense (is designing) is used because the action (designing the software) is happening at the present moment. This tense is appropriate for ongoing actions.

Grammar Concept The present continuous tense is used to describe actions that are happening now or around the present time. It is formed with 'am/is/are' + the base form of the verb + '-ing'.

59. (c) The correct phrase is 'I have ever seen' because it correctly uses the present perfect tense. The present perfect tense is used to talk about experiences in life up until now. The word 'ever' indicates that the experience is something that has happened at any point in the past, but it is relevant now.

Grammar Concept The present perfect tense is formed using 'have/has' + the past participle of the verb. In this case, the verb 'see' changes to its past participle form 'seen'. 'Ever' is used to refer to any time before now.

60. (d) The phrase 'a meeting sorting out' is incorrect because it uses a gerund (sorting out) as a noun modifier, which sounds awkward. The correct expression should be 'a meeting to sort out', where 'to sort out' is an infinitive verb that describes the purpose of the meeting.

Grammar Concept When we describe the purpose of something (in this case, the meeting), we typically use an infinitive verb (to + base form of the verb). The phrase 'sorting out' as a gerund does not fit naturally in this context.

61. (b) In this question, the sentence is converted from passive to active voice. Voice in grammar indicates whether the subject performs the action or receives it.

- **Passive voice** The subject (cake) is the recipient of the action (baked by Mary).
- **Active voice** The subject (Mary) performs the action (baked).

The sentence 'This cake was baked by Mary for your birthday' is in passive voice.

To convert it to active voice, we change the focus from the object (the cake) to the subject (Mary) and adjust the verb accordingly.

The past tense verb 'was baked' is changed to 'baked' to make it active. Therefore, the correct active voice is 'Mary baked this cake for your birthday'.

62. (b) In this sentence, passive voice is used. Passive voice focuses on the action (what happened) or the recipient of the action, instead of the person performing it.

- In active voice, the subject (the author) performs the action (wrote a compelling novel).
- In passive voice, the object (the compelling novel) becomes the subject of the sentence and the verb 'was written' is used to indicate the action.

Thus, to convert from active to passive

- The object of the action (a compelling novel) becomes the subject of the sentence.
- The verb is changed to a form of the verb 'to be' + the past participle of the main verb (was written).

63. **(c)** This question involves the possessive pronoun 'mine' vs. the possessive adjective 'my'.

- Possessive pronouns (mine, yours, hers, etc.), replace a noun and stand alone.
- Possessive adjectives (my, your, his, etc.), modify a noun and describe ownership.

In the sentence 'Mine grandmother needs a helper', the use of 'Mine' is incorrect. The correct form is 'My grandmother', as 'my' is the possessive adjective modifying 'grandmother'.

64. **(b)** This sentence contains an idiomatic expression 'under the impression', which means 'believing something'.

The correct phrase is 'under the impression', not 'with the impression'. The sentence should be

- 'I was under the impression that I had returned the books..'.
- 'With' is used to show physical proximity or association, but 'under' is the correct preposition in this idiomatic phrase.

65. **(c)** In direct speech, we quote the exact words spoken

"Don't forget that the last date for geotagging our apartment is tomorrow".

- In indirect speech, we change the pronouns, verb tense and sometimes the time expressions
  - 'tomorrow' changes to 'the next day'.
  - 'Is' changes to 'was' (since we are reporting something in the past).

The reported speech version is

"Mother reminded Rahul that the last date for geo-tagging their apartment was the next day".

66. **(a)** This is a case of direct speech, where the speaker's exact words are quoted. In direct speech, the words spoken are enclosed in quotation marks.

In direct speech, we report what someone said without changing the tense or pronouns.

The original direct speech is

Mohit said to his father, 'I cannot solve this sum as it is very difficult'.

The correct option directly conveys the speaker's words without any change in meaning or structure.

67. **(b)** This is indirect speech (or reported speech). In indirect speech, we report what someone said without using their exact words.

- In direct speech, the question is 'Can you give me the directions to the temple?'
- In indirect speech, we change the word 'can' to 'could' (for past tense) and adjust pronouns accordingly (from 'me' to 'him' and 'you' to 'I').

Thus, the correct indirect speech version is

'The tourist asked me if I could give him the directions to the temple'.

68. **(b)** In this question, we are looking at passive voice in a question structure. Let's break it down

Active voice 'Do we have to accept this deal?' (The subject 'we' is performing the action 'accept').

Passive voice The subject (the deal) is now the focus of the sentence and the action (accepting) is done to it. The correct passive construction is 'Does this deal have to be accepted?'

In passive voice, we use 'does' (because the subject 'deal' is singular) and the structure 'have to be accepted' is correct for a passive construction of the verb phrase.

So, the correct transformation into passive voice is

'Does this deal have to be accepted?' This sentence shifts the focus from the action performed by the subject (we) to the action done to the object (the deal).

69. **(a)** In this question, we are looking at passive voice.

- In active voice, the subject performs the action 'The company will launch a new product next month'.
- In passive voice, the object (new product) becomes the subject and the verb is adjusted accordingly

'A new product will be launched by the company next month'.

The correct passive voice form uses the auxiliary verb 'will be' and the past participle 'launched'.

70. **(c)** The error in this sentence is with the verb 'give'. The correct form is 'gives' because the subject 'my mother' is singular. In English, the verb must agree with the subject in number (singular or plural).

71. **(a)** This is a question in reported speech. In reported speech, the question is often transformed by changing the structure of the sentence.

- **In direct speech** 'Would you like to have some herbal tea?'
- **In reported speech** The question becomes a statement where we use 'if' to introduce the reported question.

So, the correct transformation is 'Sandhya asked me if I would like to have some herbal tea'.

This is because the sentence is a yes/no question, so 'if' is used to join the reported speech.

72. **(a)** In indirect speech, when reporting a suggestion made by someone, we often use the verb 'suggest' followed by a clause with 'that'.

- **The direct speech** 'Let's go for a walk in the park'.
- **The indirect speech becomes** 'He suggested that they should go for a walk in the park'.

73. **(c)** In reported speech, a question that is asked about preferences should use the appropriate past tense form. The correct transformation would be

- **Direct speech** 'What do you prefer to do in your free time - painting or basketball practice?'
- **Indirect speech** 'Aditya asked Kavya what she preferred to do in her free time - painting or basketball practice'.

The word 'do' changes to 'preferred' in the reported speech as the verb tense changes to the past tense.

74. **(c)** In reported speech, when the verb in the direct speech is in the present continuous tense, we change it to the past continuous tense in the indirect speech.

- **Direct speech** 'I am going to the park'.
- **Indirect speech** 'She said that she was going to the park'.

This change happens because the action is in progress and is being reported in the past.

75. (a) The sentence in the direct speech is in the present perfect tense (I have completed). In reported speech, if the reporting verb is in the present tense (in this case, 'says'), the present perfect in direct speech remains unchanged. Therefore, the correct conversion is

- **Direct speech** 'I have completed the math assignment'.
- **Indirect speech** 'Avika says that she had completed the math assignment'.

This shows that the action (completion of the assignment) is recent and still relevant at the time of speaking.

76. (b) In this sentence, the preposition 'of' is the correct one to use. 'Complaining of' is the correct expression when referring to experiencing or suffering from pain or illness.

- 'Complaining of' is the correct preposition to use when talking about experiencing pain, discomfort or other issues.

77. (c) In reported speech, when converting a sentence that uses the word 'might' in the direct speech, the tense remains the same. Additionally, time expressions like 'tonight' change to 'that night' when moving to indirect speech.

78. (a) This is a reported speech conversion. The sentence in direct speech is in the present tense (I don't want to). In reported speech, when the reporting verb is in the past tense, the present tense in the direct speech usually shifts to the past tense. However, if the statement is still true in the present context, we sometimes retain the present tense in reported speech.

79. (c) In passive voice, the subject of the sentence (the car) becomes the focus, and the action is done by the agent (the mechanic).The auxiliary verb 'was' is used to show the past tense and the action is done to the object 'the car'.

80. (b) In passive voice, we focus on the action being done to the object (the exam) and the auxiliary verbs are used appropriately.Notice the use of 'being discussed' to show the ongoing action in passive voice.

81. (a) The error in the sentence lies in the use of 'discovering' instead of the correct form 'discovered'.

Concept Present Participle v/s Past Participle

- Present Participle (discovering) is used to describe an ongoing action (e.g., 'She is discovering new things').
- Past Participle (discovered) is used to describe a completed action (e.g., 'She has discovered new things').

In this case, since 'technology' is already discovered and the phrase is referring to the completed discovery, the past participle form 'discovered' should be used.

82. (b) The sentence describes an action that will happen in the future and it is written in the passive voice.

Concept Passive Voice in Future Tense

In passive voice, the subject of the sentence is the receiver of the action rather than the doer.
The future tense passive voice uses the structure 'will be' followed by the past participle of the verb.

83. (a) The error is in the preposition 'to' used after the verb 'had coffee'.

Concept Prepositions with Verbs of Eating/Drinking

After verbs like 'have', 'eat' and 'drink', the correct preposition to use is 'at' when referring to the location where the activity occurs.

- **Correct Usage** 'I had coffee at the café'.
- **Incorrect Usage** 'I had coffee to the café'. (This is not correct because 'to' suggests movement towards place, which is not applicable here.)

Hence, the correct sentence is 'We had coffee at the university café'.

84. (d) The choice of prepositions is based on the specific movement and location described in the sentence.

Concept Prepositions of Movement

- 'Through' is used when moving within a place or space, such as walking through a park, a forest, etc.
- 'Along' is used when moving next to or beside a line, such as a riverbank, a road, etc.

85. (a) This sentence involves a yes/no question that has been transformed into reported speech.

Concept Reporting Yes/No Questions in Reported Speech

When reporting yes/no questions, we use 'if' or 'whether' to introduce the reported speech. Also, the verb tense changes according to the reporting verb

Direct Speech 'Did you finish your homework?'

Reported Speech 'Mother asked Amayra if she had finished her homework'.

The change from 'did' (present tense) to 'had' (past perfect tense) is necessary because we are reporting a question that happened in the past.

86. (a) In this sentence, we are dealing with the use of articles in English. There are two types of articles in English: the indefinite article (a, an) and the definite article (the).

- 'A' is used when referring to something non-specific or general. In this case, the phrase 'a team' refers to one team, but not a specific or previously identified one.
- 'The' is used when referring to something specific or already known. The phrase 'the top of K2' refers to a particular location that is well known, making it specific.

87. (b) The sentence involves the use of pronouns in the correct grammatical form.

Concept Pronouns - Objective v/s Subjective Case

- 'Her' is the objective case of the pronoun, used when the pronoun is the receiver of the action.
- 'She' is the subjective case, used when the pronoun is the doer of the action.

88. (a) This is a passive voice construction.

Concept Passive Voice

In passive voice, the focus is on the action or the recipient of the action, not on the doer. The structure for past tense in passive voice is

Subject + was/were + past participle + by + agent (if mentioned).

89. (c) This is a direct speech sentence.

Concept Direct Speech

In direct speech, we quote the exact words spoken by the speaker, using quotation marks. The structure typically includes

- Reporting verb (e.g., said)
- The quoted words (exactly as spoken)
- The sentence punctuation and capitalisation are also important.

The sentence 'Mother asked Rubani if she was sorry for what she had done' can be converted into direct speech as 'Mother said to Rubani, 'Are you sorry for what you have done?'

90. (d) This sentence involves reported speech and uses a backshift of tenses because the reporting verb (said) is in the past tense.

Concept Reported Speech - Backshift of Tenses

In reported speech, when the reporting verb is in the past tense, we shift the tense of the direct speech one step back (called 'backshifting')

- Present simple → Past simple
- Present continuous → Past continuous
- Present perfect→ Past perfect
- Will → Would

91. (b) This question involves reported speech where the direct speech is 'Don't forget to bring your umbrella.' When transforming imperative sentences (commands, requests or suggestions) into reported speech, the verb 'reminded' is used to indicate that someone is being prompted to do something. Additionally, the infinitive form 'to bring' is used after 'reminded.'

In reported speech, commands often use 'told', 'asked', or 'reminded'. Followed by an infinitive verb (e.g., to do, to bring, etc.).

92. (d) The error in the sentence lies in the phrase 'propagate in the release of seeds.' The correct preposition to use with the verb 'propagate' in this context is 'by', not 'in'.

- 'Propagate by' is used when referring to the method by which something is spread or reproduced. The word 'in' is not appropriate here, as it changes the meaning and does not follow the expected grammatical structure.
- Thus, the correct phrase should be
- 'The ancient trees of this forest did not propagate by the release of seeds.'

93. (d) This error involves the use of the verb 'use' in the past tense. The correct form of the verb is 'used to' when referring to past habitual actions.

In English, 'used to' is the correct expression to describe something that was done regularly in the past but no longer happens. It is often followed by the base form of the verb.

94. (b) In this sentence, the verb 'decided' is followed by the infinitive form of the verb. When verbs like 'decide', 'plan', 'want', etc., are used, they are typically followed by 'to' + base form of the verb.

The correct form here is 'to undertake', as it correctly follows the verb 'decided'.

95. (a) This question involves direct speech. The sentence 'Rahul asked his mother if she had prepared the carrot halwa for him' is in reported speech. To convert this back into direct speech, we need to ensure that the question remains in its original interrogative form.

- "The direct speech question 'Have you prepared the carrot halwa for me?" The correct format for the question in direct speech is Rahul said to his mother, 'Have you prepared the carrot halwa for me?'

96. (a) This question involves the expression 'No sooner'. The structure for 'No sooner' is No sooner + auxiliary verb + subject + main verb. It is used in sentences that indicate one action happened immediately after another.

The correct form here is 'As soon as I saw' because it follows the correct word order.

97. (a) This question involves the coordinating conjunction 'not only... but also.' In English, 'not only' is used to introduce one idea and 'but also' is used to add another idea that is related but different.

The correct form is 'but also very suspenseful' because 'it' should be omitted after 'but also'.

98. (d) The sentence 'Kavya finishes her homework before having dinner' is grammatically correct.

99. (b) In this sentence, the verb 'hoping' is followed by an infinitive verb. After verbs like 'hope', we use the infinitive form (e.g., 'to speak') to show the purpose or intention behind the action.

100. (c) The error in this sentence is the preposition 'in'. When referring to a road or highway, we use the preposition 'on', not 'in.'

101. (c) The error in the sentence lies in the phrase 'but nobody is listening'. The subject of the sentence refers to an event in the past (the teacher's instruction to be quiet), but the verb tense used is present continuous (is listening), which is not consistent with the rest of the sentence. Since the rest of the sentence is in the past tense (the teacher asked), the correct tense should also be in the past tense.

The correct version should be

'but nobody was listening'.

This ensures the sentence is consistent in tense, specifically the past continuous tense.

102. (c) The sentence 'They say, 'We are working on a new project' is a statement in the present tense. When reporting this in indirect speech, we need to shift the verb 'are working' (present continuous) to 'were working' (past continuous), since the reporting verb 'say' is in the present tense but the action is being reported from the past.

Thus, the indirect speech is

'They say that they were working on a new project.'

Concept Reported Speech - Backshift of Tenses

When reporting a statement in reported speech, we follow these rules

- Present continuous changes to past continuous.
- Present simple changes to past simple.
- Present perfect changes to past perfect.
- Will changes to would.

In this case, the present continuous (are working) becomes past continuous (were working).

103. **(a)** In reported speech, when the reporting verb (e.g., 'said') is in the past tense, we apply backshifting of tenses. This means that the present tense used in direct speech changes to past tense in reported speech.

In this case, 'I am busy today' becomes 'she was busy that day'. This involves two changes

- The present tense 'am' becomes past tense 'was'.
- 'Today' changes to 'that day' because we are reporting what was said on a different day.

104. **(c)** In passive voice, the object of the active sentence becomes the subject of the passive sentence. The sentence 'The courier gave my parcel to my neighbour in my absence' is an active voice sentence and to change it to passive, we need to make the object 'my parcel' the subject and adjust the verb accordingly.

- The active voice verb 'gave' is changed to the passive form 'was given'.
- The original subject 'the courier' becomes the agent in the passive sentence, introduced by 'by'.

105. **(b)** In direct speech, the speaker's exact words are quoted. The sentence 'I would pick her up from school that week' is reported speech and the original speech was made in the present tense (I will pick).

In direct speech, we maintain the original tense. So, 'I will pick her up from school' is the correct expression. Additionally, in direct speech, the pronouns should also reflect the speaker's intent. Since the speaker is referring to 'my daughter', the correct pronoun here should be 'you'.

106. **(c)** The sentence 'Linguists say that this method helps accelerate language learning.' is grammatically correct.

Concept Subject-Verb Agreement and Verb Usage In this sentence, 'helps' is correctly used as the third-person singular form of the verb and it is correctly followed by the base verb 'accelerate'. This is a typical structure for sentences using 'help' followed by another verb in its base form.

107. **(b)** The sentence describes an event that will be completed in the future, before another future event takes place. This requires the future perfect tense.

The future perfect tense is used to show that an action will be completed before a certain time in the future. In this case, the hotel staff will have completed the arrangements by the time the PM reaches.

Thus, the correct form is

' The hotel staff will have completed all the arrangements by the time the PM reaches here.'

Concept Future Perfect Tense

The future perfect tense is formed using 'will have' + the past participle of the verb. It is used to describe actions that will be completed at some point in the future before another action or event occurs.

108. **(b)** The sentence 'I saw that movie last week and it was really interesting' is grammatically correct.

Concept Tense Usage and Conjunctions

The past simple tense 'saw' is correctly used to describe a completed action in the past. The conjunction 'and' properly connects two related ideas, making the sentence clear and coherent.

109. **(c)** The sentence is in the passive voice, so the object 'A series of ground-breaking experiments' becomes the subject and the verb 'were conducted' is in the past tense.

- The correct passive voice construction is

'A series of ground-breaking experiments were conducted by the scientist.'

This maintains proper grammatical structure for passive voice and ensures the sentence remains clear and correct.

Concept Passive Voice

When converting from active to passive voice, the object of the active sentence (here 'a series of ground-breaking experiments') becomes the subject of the passive sentence. The verb is changed to the correct form of 'to be' + the past participle and the subject of the active voice sentence becomes the agent (here 'by the scientist').

110. **(d)** In this sentence, we are converting a passive voice question into its active voice form. The original sentence 'Was the food finished by Kavya?' is in the passive voice and to convert it to the active voice, we follow these steps

1. The subject (in this case, Kavya) becomes the subject of the sentence.
2. The verb 'was finished' (past tense) changes to 'finish' (simple past tense) to form the active voice.
3. The sentence structure changes to form a proper question 'Did Kavya finish the food?'

Thus, the correct active voice form is 'Did Kavya finish the food?'

111. **(a)** In active voice, the subject performs the action. In the passive sentence 'The dinner will have been prepared by my sisters', the subject is the object (dinner). To convert this into active voice, we place the subject 'my sisters' before the verb 'will have prepared' and remove the auxiliary 'been'.

The correct active voice form is 'My sisters will have prepared the dinner.'

112. **(d)** The error lies in the phrase 'to offer a plethora of.' The correct phrase should be 'offering a plethora of', as 'stretches' (which is in the present tense) is followed by an 'ing' verb form when used to show an ongoing action or purpose.

Thus, the correct version is 'India's coastline stretches for over 7,500 kilometres, offering a plethora of must-visit beaches and coastal destinations.'

Concept Parallel Structure and Verb Forms

In this sentence, parallel structure needs to be maintained. After a verb like 'stretches', we use the '-ing' form of the verb when describing what is happening simultaneously. The incorrect form 'to offer' is in the infinitive, which disrupts the parallel construction.

113. **(c)** The error in the sentence is in the comparison structure 'more faster'. The comparative form of 'fast' is 'faster' and it should not be used with the word 'more'.

Thus, the correct phrase is 'runs faster than'.

The sentence should read

'she runs faster than her brother in the track events.'

Concept Comparative Adjectives

In English, when we make comparisons, we use the comparative form of the adjective

- If the adjective is a one-syllable word, we generally add '-er' (e.g., fast → faster).
- For adjectives with two or more syllables, we typically use more (e.g., beautiful → more beautiful), but in this case, 'fast' is a one-syllable adjective, so we use 'faster' without 'more'.

114. (c) The error lies in the use of 'able qualifying'. The correct phrase should be 'able to qualify' because after 'able to', we need the base form of the verb (in this case, 'qualify').

Thus, the sentence should read 'She had hoped that she would be able to qualify the CAT with a high percentile.'

Concept Modals and Infinitives

When using the phrase 'able to', it is followed by the base form of the verb (infinitive). This structure is used to express ability or possibility in a future context. The word 'able' is followed by 'to' and the verb in its base form.

115. (d) In the passive voice, we focus on the action being done to the object rather than who is performing the action. The original sentence 'The gardener is planting flowers in the garden' is in the active voice. To convert it to passive voice

- The object 'flowers' becomes the subject.
- The verb 'is planting' is converted into 'are being planted', which is the present continuous form in passive voice.
- The agent 'by the gardener' is included at the end of the sentence.

116. (d) The sentence 'Yesterday all the culprits were arrested' is in the passive voice. To convert it to the active voice

- Subject 'the police' becomes the subject of the sentence.
- The verb 'were arrested' becomes 'arrested' in the active voice, maintaining the past tense.
- The sentence is then

'Yesterday the police arrested all the culprits'.

117. (c) The sentence 'When I received the appointment letter from the college of Arts and Humanities, I was exhilarated'. is grammatically correct.

- 'When I received' is correct because the sentence talks about an event that happened in the past.
- 'I was exhilarated' also uses the correct past tense to indicate the feeling after receiving the letter.

118. (d) The error is in 'Each of the students were asked'. The phrase 'Each of' requires the singular form of the verb, not plural. The correct form is 'was' instead of 'were'.

Thus, the correct sentence is 'Each of the students was asked to submit the project by the following day'.

Concept Subject-Verb Agreement

When the subject is 'each', it is treated as singular. Therefore, the verb that follows should also be singular. Even though 'students' is plural, the subject 'each' requires a singular verb.

119. (b) The original sentence is in the present tense 'I have to stay back', but since the reporting verb 'told' is in the past tense, we apply backshifting to the present verb 'have', changing it to the past form 'had'.

Additionally, 'today' is changed to 'that day' to indicate that the statement was made in the past.

120. (d) In active voice, the subject performs the action. The original passive sentence 'This book was loved by the students' can be changed to active voice by making 'The students' the subject and using the verb 'loved' in the simple past tense.

Thus, the active voice version is 'the students loved this book'.

121. (b) In reported speech, when transforming questions from direct to indirect, the word order changes and the subject and auxiliary verb are inverted. In this case, the original direct speech question is

'Which lines of the poem you have not understood?'

In reported speech, we apply the correct question word order

- The subject (you) and the auxiliary verb (have) are inverted.
- The present perfect 'have understood' becomes past perfect 'had understood' due to the backshift of tenses.

122. (c) In passive voice, we focus on the action and the receiver of the action rather than the performer. The sentence 'My grandmother called me to the worship place' in the passive voice should be

'I was called by my grandmother to the worship place.'

Concept Passive Voice Construction

To convert an active voice sentence into passive voice

1. The object of the active sentence becomes the subject in the passive sentence.
2. The verb is changed into the appropriate form (e.g., 'called' becomes 'was called').
3. The agent (performer) is introduced using 'by' if needed.

123. (a) The error in the sentence lies in 'Most than half of'. The correct phrase should be 'More than half of' because 'more' is used in comparisons, especially when comparing amounts or numbers.

Concept Comparative Form of 'More'

In English, 'more' is used when comparing quantities, amounts or numbers. We use 'more' with comparative adjectives or nouns, while 'most' is used in superlative forms.

124. (c) The sentence 'She said, 'I will meet you at the cafe at 3 pm' is in direct speech, but in indirect speech, we need to apply the backshift of tense. The present 'will' becomes 'would' in reported speech and the time expression 'tomorrow' becomes 'that day.'

Concept Reported Speech - Backshift of Tenses

In reported speech, when the reporting verb is in the past tense, the verb in the reported speech typically shifts one tense back. For instance

- Will changes to would.
- Present simple changes to past simple.
- Present continuous changes to past continuous.

125. (d) Concept Direct Speech - Reporting Future Events

In direct speech, when reporting something that is expected or predicted to happen in the future, we use 'will' (present simple for future tense) in the direct speech. The time expression 'the next day' changes to 'tomorrow' to keep it in the present context.

126. (a) The sentence 'He asked the speaker some questions until the session' uses the word 'until', which implies a time up to a point, but the word 'during' would be more appropriate when referring to an event or action happening throughout a specific period. The correct sentence should read, 'He asked the speaker some questions during the session'.

Concept Prepositions of Time

In this case, we are dealing with prepositions that denote time periods. 'During' is used when referring to an action that takes place at any point in a given time frame. 'Until' is used when referring to an action that stops at a certain point in time, not something that happens throughout. Therefore, during is the correct preposition here to indicate that the questions were asked while the session was ongoing.

127. (d) The sentence involves a subject 'the teacher along with the students', and in English, when the phrase 'along with' is used, the verb must agree with the main subject, which is 'the teacher' (singular). Therefore, the correct verb form is 'was crossing', not 'were crossing'.

Concept Subject-Verb Agreement

When compound subjects are joined by 'along with', 'as well as' or similar expressions, the verb agrees with the main subject (not the noun that follows the conjunction). Here, 'the teacher' is the main subject and so the singular verb 'was' is required.

128. (b) The sentence uses an imperative structure. In passive voice, the action (opening the window) is directed towards the subject (the window). In this case, 'Let the window be opened' is the correct passive form because we are focusing on the action being done to the subject (the window). The verb 'open' changes to 'be opened' to maintain the passive voice structure.

129. (d) The sentence 'Last evening I have gone to the theatre to see a performance' contains an incorrect tense usage. The phrase 'have gone' is the present perfect tense, which is used for actions that have relevance to the present. Since the sentence clearly refers to a completed action in the past (last evening), the simple past tense 'went' is required.

Concept Tense Consistency

When referring to a completed action in the past, we use the simple past tense (e.g., 'I went'). The present perfect tense is used when the action has a connection to the present moment or when the exact time of the action is not specified. Here, since 'last evening' is a specific time in the past, we should use the simple past tense.

130. (a) The sentence 'People under eighteen do not have the right to vote, don't they?' contains an error in the tag question. The correct form for the tag question should be 'do they?' because the main sentence is negative and tag questions for negative sentences are positive.

Concept Tag Questions

Tag questions are added to the end of a statement to confirm or check information.

If the main sentence is positive, the tag question is negative and if the main sentence is negative, the tag question is positive.

Since the main sentence is negative (do not have), the tag question should be positive (do they?). Hence, the correct tag question is 'do they?' and not 'don't they?'

131. (d) When converting direct speech into indirect speech, the pronouns and tenses must be adjusted accordingly. The direct speech 'I have brought a chocolate for you' becomes 'she had brought a chocolate for her' in indirect speech, where 'I' changes to 'she' and 'you' changes to 'her'. Additionally, the present perfect tense (have brought) shifts to the past perfect tense (had brought) in reported speech.

Concept Reported Speech - Pronoun and Tense Change

In reported speech, pronouns change based on the perspective of the speaker. Moreover, the tense usually shifts backward. For example

- Present perfect becomes Past perfect.
- 'I' changes to 'she' (or the third person) and 'you' changes to 'her' (or the third person in the object form).

132. (b) The sentence 'You may discussing your problem in tomorrow's meeting' contains an error in the verb form. The correct form of the verb after 'may' is the base form (infinitive form) of the verb. Therefore, 'discussing' should be changed to 'discuss'.

Concept Modal Verbs and Base Form of Verb

When using modal verbs like may, can, must, should, etc., the verb that follows the modal must always be in its base form (the infinitive form without 'to').

Modal verbs do not require the use of the present participle (the '-ing' form) or the past tense form. In this case, 'may discuss' is the correct form.

133. (d) The sentence 'The complex math problem was being explained to the students by the teacher' is in passive voice and the question asks for a conversion into active voice. To change the sentence into the active voice, the subject (the teacher) becomes the doer of the action and the object (the complex math problem) becomes the receiver of the action. The verb 'was being explained' is converted into the active voice form 'was explaining', which is in the past continuous tense. The correct sentence is 'The teacher was explaining the complex math problem to the students.'

Concept Active Voice

In active voice, the subject of the sentence performs the action. The structure for active voice sentences is subject + verb + object. Here, the subject (the teacher) performs the action of explaining the math problem to the students.

The past continuous tense (was explaining) is used to describe an action that was ongoing in the past. In active voice, the focus is on the subject performing the action, as opposed to passive voice, where the focus is on the object receiving the action.

134. (a) The original sentence uses 'the more beautiful' which is incorrect. We do not use article 'the' with comparative degree of adjectives. Comparative degree is used to compare two specific things.

Concept Degree of adjective

Degrees of adjectives are used to make comparison. They have specified rules followed in each degree- positive, comparative, superlative. 'The' is not used with comparative degree of adjectives.

135. (d) The sentence 'John was absent from the meeting because he was sick, nor did he inform anyone' contains a problem with the conjunction. The conjunction 'nor' is typically used to continue a negative idea after another negative clause. However, it should be paired with a positive auxiliary or verb ('but' is more suitable here).

Concept Conjunctions in Negative Sentences

In negative sentences, 'nor' is used after a negative clause to connect ideas or actions that both share a negative quality. The use of 'but' is appropriate when connecting a negative statement with a contradiction, especially when it indicates that the second part of the sentence contrasts with the first part. Here, 'but he did not inform anyone' properly connects with the previous statement.

136. (d) The sentence 'Her parents did not allowed her to learn western music' contains an error in the verb form. After the auxiliary verb 'did', the main verb should always be in the base form (i.e., allow), not the past tense form 'allowed'.

Concept Verb Form After 'Did'

When 'did' is used as an auxiliary verb in the past tense, the main verb must be in its base form (infinitive form). The auxiliary verb 'did' already conveys the past tense, so it is incorrect to use the past form of the main verb. The correct form is 'did not allow', not 'did not allowed.'

137. (c) The sentence 'Please listen carefully to what I am teaching', said Madam Mahima to the students is an example of a command or request in direct speech. In indirect speech, commands or requests are generally reported using 'told' or 'asked' followed by 'to' and the verb in the base form (listen). Additionally, the tense changes (present continuous 'am teaching' changes to past continuous 'was teaching').

Concept Reported Speech - Commands and Requests

When reporting a command or request, we generally use the verb 'tell' or 'ask' followed by the infinitive form (e.g., 'to listen'). The pronoun and verb tense in the direct speech also change to reflect the backshift of tenses. In this case, the verb 'am teaching' changes to 'was teaching'.

138. (d) The sentence 'Traffic is always remaining heavy in this part of Delhi' contains an error because the verb 'remaining' is not used correctly with 'is always'. The correct form should be 'remains' since we are describing a state of being that is generally true and ongoing, not an action that is happening continuously.

Concept Verb Forms for State of Being

The verb 'remain' is used to describe a continuing state or condition. When referring to something that is always true, we use the present simple tense (e.g., 'remains'). The continuous form (-ing) is not appropriate here because 'remain' is not an action but a state or condition. Therefore, 'always remains' is the correct expression.

139. (c) The sentence 'A ground-breaking discovery has been made in a deserting quarry near New York' contains an error with the word 'deserting'. The correct word should be 'deserted', which means 'abandoned or empty', as opposed to 'deserting', which refers to an action (someone leaving something behind).

140. (b) The sentence 'It is estimating that this forest once covered an area of approximately 400 km' contains a grammatical error because 'estimating' is not used correctly. The correct form should be 'It is estimated that'. The subject 'it' refers to the passive construction, meaning the action is being done by an unspecified agent.

Concept Passive Voice in Reporting Verbs

In sentences that report something that is being estimated, predicted or considered, the passive voice is often used. For example, 'It is estimated' is a standard passive construction. The verb 'estimate' in this context should be in the passive form 'is estimated' because the action is being performed on the subject (the forest), not by the subject.

141. (d) The sentence 'A remarkable discovery in Paestum, an ancient Greek city, has been made by archaeologists' is in the passive voice, but we need to convert it into the active voice. In the active voice, the subject (archaeologists) performs the action. The correct transformation is 'Archaeologists have made a remarkable discovery in Paestum, an ancient Greek city.' The verb 'have made' is in the present perfect tense, as the discovery is recent.

Concept Active Voice

In active voice, the subject of the sentence performs the action. The active voice form of a sentence is structured as Subject + verb + object. In this case, 'archaeologists' is the subject, 'have made' is the verb and 'a remarkable discovery' is the object. Converting passive to active voice often requires changing the order of the sentence and adjusting the verb tense accordingly.

142. (d) The sentence 'The team completed the project ahead of schedule' is in the active voice, and we are asked to convert it to the passive voice. In passive voice, the object (the project) becomes the subject and the verb 'completed' is changed to the past tense 'was completed'. The subject (the team) is retained at the end, introduced by 'by'. The correct passive voice construction is 'The project was completed ahead of schedule by the team'.

Concept Passive Voice

In passive voice, the subject receives the action rather than performing it. The passive voice structure is subject + form of 'be' + past participle of verb + (by + agent). In this case, 'the project' becomes the subject, 'was completed' is the passive form and 'by the team' is the agent performing the action.

143. (d) The sentence 'Akasa Air planning to acquire 150 Boeing 737 planes' contains a grammatical error. The correct form should be 'Akasa Air is planning to acquire', as the auxiliary verb 'is' is required to form the present continuous tense. The present continuous tense is used to describe an ongoing action or future plan. The verb 'planning' needs to be accompanied by the auxiliary verb 'is.'

Concept Present Continuous Tense

Thepresent continuous tense is used to describe actions that are currently happening or planned for the future. The structure for the present continuous tense is Subject + am/is/are + verb(-ing). In this case, 'Akasa Air' is the subject, 'is' is the auxiliary verb and 'planning' is the main verb in the -ing form. This construction expresses an action that is ongoing or happening in the near future.

144. (b) The sentence 'I said to Bhawna, 'Have the monkeys eaten up our cauliflowers?' is a direct question. When converting this to indirect speech, we follow the rules for reporting questions. In indirect speech, the verb tense in the question changes (backshifting) and the question is not introduced with 'if' or 'whether'. In this case, 'Have' changes to 'had' because the reporting verb 'said' is in the past tense and the reported question needs to reflect this.

Concept Indirect Speech - Questions

In indirect speech, questions are typically reported by using 'if' or 'whether' for yes/no questions. Additionally, the verb tense shifts one step back (known as backshifting). Here, 'have eaten' (present perfect) becomes 'had eaten' (past perfect) because the reporting verb is in the past tense. The structure is [reporting verb] + [if/whether] + [subject] + [verb in past tense].

145. (d) The sentence 'If you diligently study the intricacies of the language, you .... that your proficiency in it improves significantly' involves a first conditional. The first conditional is used to talk about real and possible situations in the present or future. In the first conditional, the main clause uses will + base verb. The correct form here is 'will find' because it indicates a result of the action in the condition.

Concept First Conditional

Thefirst conditional is used to talk about possible future events or actions that depend on a condition. It follows the structure If + present simple, + will + base verb. This form is used when the outcome is likely or possible. In this case, 'If you study', the expected result is that 'you will find' the improvement in proficiency.

146. (c) The sentence 'The concert will be attended by us' is in the passive voice, and we need to convert it into the active voice. The subject in the active voice becomes 'we' (the doers of the action) and the verb 'will attend' is used in its base form. The active voice construction is 'We will attend the concert'. This change correctly reflects that 'we' are doing the action of attending the concert.

Concept Active Voice

In active voice, the subject performs the action. The structure of an active voice sentence is Subject + verb + object. In this case, 'we' is the subject, 'will attend' is the verb in future tense and 'the concert' is the object. The passive voice sentence is converted by making the object of the passive sentence (the concert) the subject in the active sentence.

147. (d) The sentence 'The manager gave the employee a bonus' is in the active voice and we need to convert it to the passive voice. In passive voice, the object (the bonus) becomes the subject of the sentence. The verb 'gave' changes to 'was given', and the agent (the manager) is introduced by 'by'. The correct passive voice construction is 'The employee was given a bonus by the manager'.

Concept Passive Voice

In passive voice, the focus shifts from the subject performing the action to the object receiving the action. The passive voice structure is subject (object in active voice) + form of 'be' + past participle of verb + (by + agent). In this case, 'the employee' is the subject, 'was given' is the passive verb and 'by the manager' is the agent performing the action.

148. (c) The sentence 'Manya said that she didn't want any breakfast' is reported speech. To change it into direct speech, we need to use quotation marks to directly report Manya's words. The correct form is 'I don't want any breakfast', as this is how Manya expressed her desire in the present tense.

Concept Direct Speech

In direct speech, the exact words of the speaker are quoted and the sentence is enclosed in quotation marks. The verb tense remains the same as in the original spoken words.

In this case, the present tense (don't want) is retained in the direct speech and it is placed within quotation marks to reflect the exact speech of the speaker.

149. (a) The sentence 'She is allergic from peanuts, so she always checks food labels carefully' contains an error in the preposition. The correct preposition used with 'allergic' is 'to', not 'from'. The correct sentence is 'She is allergic to peanuts'.

Concept Prepositions with Adjectives

Certain adjectives are followed by specific prepositions. 'Allergic' is one such adjective and it is always followed by the preposition 'to'. This usage is standard and conveys the idea that someone has an allergy to something, such as peanuts. Using 'from' is incorrect in this context. Other common examples include 'interested in,'good at' and 'afraid of'.

150. (a) The sentence 'Traditional practices are ways of knowing, learning and to generate a distinct experience of the world around us' contains a grammatical error in the phrase 'and to generate a distinct experience'. The error lies in the use of 'to generate', which does not parallel the earlier verbs 'knowing' and 'learning' in the list. The verb forms should all be consistent in their structure. Therefore, 'to generate' should be changed to 'generating' to maintain parallelism in the list of verbs.

Concept Parallel Structure

Parallel structure (also called parallelism) refers to the use of the same grammatical structure in a list or series. When multiple actions are listed, all the verbs in the series must be in the same form. In this case, 'knowing' and 'learning' are in the gerund (verb+ing) form, so 'to generate' must be changed to 'generating' to match the structure of the other verbs. The corrected structure ensures grammatical consistency and clarity in the sentence.

151. (c) The error in this sentence lies in the phrase 'has a negatively effect'. The word 'negatively' is an adverb, but it is incorrectly used here. What is needed is the adjective form, 'negative', to modify the noun 'effect'. The correct form should be 'has a negative effect'.

Concept Adjective vs Adverb

In English, adverbs and adjectives have distinct roles

- Adjectives modify nouns (e.g., 'The negative effect').
- Adverbs modify verbs, adjectives or other adverbs (e.g., 'She sings beautifully').

Here, 'effect' is a noun, so it requires an adjective to describe it, not an adverb. Therefore, the correct phrase is 'has a negative effect'.

152. **(d) Concept** Reported Speech (Tense Backshift)

In reported speech, when the reporting verb is in the past tense (as in 'said'), the tenses in the reported speech typically shift one step back

- Present simple → Past simple
- Present continuous → Past continuous
- Present perfect → Past perfect
- 'Will' → 'Would'

In this case, 'is shining' becomes 'was shining' and 'today' becomes 'that day'.

153. **(b)** The sentence contains the incorrect form 'She don't like'. The verb 'do' is an auxiliary verb and in the third person singular (she/he/it), we use 'doesn't' (not 'don't). The correct form is 'She doesn't like'.

Concept Subject-Verb Agreement

In English, the subject and verb must agree in number and person

- For singular third-person subjects (he, she, it), we use 'does' (and 'doesn't' for negative sentences) with the base form of the main verb.
- For plural subjects and I/you/we (e.g., 'I don't like'), we use 'do' (and 'don't' for negatives).

154. **(b)** In the sentence 'The doctor prescribes antibiotics and a cough syrup to me when I had severe cough and cold', the tense is incorrect. The sentence starts in the present tense (prescribes), but then shifts to the past tense (had).

Since the action of the doctor prescribing the antibiotics happened at the same time as the past event (having a severe cough and cold), the correct verb tense for the prescription should be the simple past tense 'prescribed'.

Concept Tense Consistency

When narrating a sequence of events in the past, the tenses should remain consistent unless there is a specific reason for a shift.

Here, the doctor's action (prescribing) and the state of the illness (having a severe cough) both occurred in the past, so 'prescribes' should be changed to 'prescribed' to maintain tense consistency.

155. **(c)** The word 'mitigate' means to make something less severe or to reduce its impact. Therefore, its antonym would be a word that means to increase or worsen something. The word 'intensify' fits as it means to make something stronger or more intense, which is the opposite of mitigating or reducing something.

- **Mitigate** to lessen or reduce.
- **Intensify** to make something stronger or more intense, which is the opposite of reducing.

156. **(b)** The word 'exuberance' refers to the quality of being full of energy, excitement and cheerfulness. Its synonym would be a word that conveys similar meaning. 'Excitement' matches this definition, as it also refers to a state of enthusiasm and high energy.

157. **(a)** The word 'extravagant' refers to someone or something characterised by excessive or lavish spending, behaviour or appearance. The antonym would be a word that describes something moderate or controlled. 'Restrained' fits this definition, as it refers to something that is held back, controlled or not excessive.

- Extravagant means excessive, while
- Restrained means controlled or moderate.

158. **(a)** The given definition describes something that is 'a complete, usually alphabetical list of items, often with notes giving details'. This is exactly what a 'catalogue' is - a complete list of items with detailed descriptions, typically in an ordered format.

159. **(b)** The idiom 'Spill the beans' means to accidentally reveal a secret or disclose something that was meant to be kept confidential.

It is a widely known idiom and is used when someone reveals a piece of information they were not supposed to.

160. **(b)** The phrase 'Not able to be changed or adapted' refers to something that is inflexible, unyielding or not subject to change. The word 'rigid' fits this definition as it means something that is stiff or fixed and cannot be easily changed or adapted.

- Rigid means stiff and unchanging.
- Other options like 'austere', 'permissive' and 'harsh' don't quite match the idea of being unchangeable or fixed.

161. **(c)** The word 'devour' means to eat something eagerly and in large amounts. Its synonym would therefore be 'consume', which also means to eat or drink something, often in a large quantity or with great eagerness.

- Devour and consume both refer to eating or taking in something eagerly.
- Preserve, receive and abstain are not synonyms for devour, as they imply saving, getting or refraining from something, which is opposite in meaning.

162. **(c)** The word 'irrelevant' is spelled incorrectly in 'irrelevent'. The correct spelling is 'irrelevant' with only one 'e' after the 'r'. The term means something that is not related or pertinent to the matter at hand.

163. **(a)** The idiom 'Piece of cake' means something that is very easy to do. It is often used to describe tasks or activities that are simple and require little effort.

164. **(d)** The word 'frigid' means extremely cold and its most appropriate synonym is 'freezing', which also refers to something very cold, often below freezing point.

- Frigid and freezing both refer to extreme cold.
- Futile, facile and flexible do not convey the meaning of 'cold' in any way.

165. **(c)** The idiom 'Be in apple-pie order' means to be perfectly organised or tidy. It is used to describe something that is neat, well-arranged or in good order.

166. **(a)** The word 'oaf' refers to a clumsy, foolish or awkward person. Its antonym would be someone who is 'smart', meaning clever, intelligent or well-dressed.

- Oaf is a term used for someone who is clumsy or foolish.
- Smart means someone who is intelligent or well-dressed, making it the opposite of 'oaf'.

167. **(b)** The group of words 'The person who presents and coordinates a show on stage or television' refers to someone who introduces or leads a broadcast, typically known as an 'anchor'. An anchor is a person who presents news or entertainment programs on TV or stage.

- Anchor refers specifically to someone who presents or hosts shows, whether on television, radio or live events.
- Reporter and broadcaster can be related, but they are not as specific as anchor in the context of someone presenting and coordinating a show.

168. **(d)** The phrase 'lasting for a very short while' refers to something that is brief or temporary. The word 'ephemeral' perfectly matches this definition, as it means lasting for a very short time.

- Ephemeral means something that is short-lived or fleeting.
- Perpetual, reliable and eternal all suggest something long-lasting or permanent, which is the opposite of the given description.

169. **(a)** The word 'feasible' means something that is possible, practical or achievable. 'Practical' is the best synonym because it refers to something that is doable or sensible in real-world situations.

- Feasible and practical both suggest that something is achievable and workable.
- Worthless, energetic and tentative have different meanings and do not align with 'feasible'.

170. **(b)** The word 'munificence' refers to the quality of being very generous, especially with money or resources. Therefore, its synonym is 'generousness', which means the quality of being willing to give or share.

- Munificence and generousness both relate to the act of being generous or giving.
- Shrewdness, quietness and liveliness are unrelated to munificence and do not fit the definition.

171. **(b)** The phrase 'Not active but has the ability to be active anytime later' refers to something that is currently inactive but has the potential to become active at any time. The correct term for this is 'dormant', which means temporarily inactive or asleep but capable of becoming active in the future.

- Dormant refers to something that is not currently active but has the potential to become active.
- Jubilant, ambiguous and conscious do not fit the meaning of something being temporarily inactive.

172. **(d)** The idiom 'Sitting on the fence' means to be undecided or not taking sides in a situation. It is commonly used when someone avoids making a decision or taking a stance on an issue.

173. **(d)** The phrase 'Protect from a danger, risk or unpleasant experience' refers to something that guards or defends against harm. The correct one-word substitute is 'shield', which means to protect or defend from harm or danger.

- Shield is something that protects or guards against danger or unpleasant experiences.
- Scare, sever and seize do not fit the context of protection.

174. **(a)** The idiom 'Be on the same page' means to have a shared understanding or agreement about something. It is commonly used to indicate that everyone is thinking in the same way or has the same perspective.

175. **(d)** The word 'hungry' is spelled incorrectly as 'hungery'. The correct spelling is 'hungry', which refers to the feeling of needing food.

- 'Hurdle', 'humour' and 'hundred' are spelled correctly.

176. **(d)** The idiom 'To get someone's goat' means to irritate or annoy someone. It is commonly used when someone's actions or behaviour are causing irritation or frustration.

177. **(b)** The idiom 'Bite the bullet' means to endure something painful or unpleasant that is unavoidable. It originates from the historical practice of soldiers biting a bullet during surgery to endure pain.

178. **(d)** The word 'observence' is incorrectly spelled. The correct spelling is 'observance', which refers to the act of following or adhering to a rule, law or tradition.

- 'Observence' is an incorrect form of 'observance'.
- 'Obstinate' (stubborn), 'odorous' (having a smell) and 'occasional' (happening from time to time) are all correctly spelled words.

179. **(d)** The word 'genesis' refers to the origin or beginning of something, often used in contexts such as the creation or emergence of ideas, movements or even life. The correct synonym for 'genesis' in this case is 'inception', which means the starting point of something. However, 'infatuation' is an incorrect choice because it refers to an intense but short-lived feeling of love or attraction, which is unrelated to the meaning of 'genesis'.

- 'Inception' is the most appropriate synonym because it signifies the origin or start of something, just like 'genesis'.
- 'Symbolism' refers to the use of symbols to represent ideas, which is unrelated to 'genesis'.
- 'Conclusion' refers to the end or closing part of something, which contrasts with the meaning of 'genesis'.
- 'Infatuation' refers to intense but often short-term feelings of love or passion, which does not relate to 'genesis' in any way.

180. **(a)** The idiom 'Split one's sides' means to laugh very hard or uncontrollably, often due to something extremely funny. It is usually used when someone is laughing so hard that they feel as though their sides might burst.

181. **(b)** The idiom 'Cut from the same cloth' means that two people or things are very similar, often in terms of characteristics, behaviour or nature. It suggests that they share the same qualities, almost as if they were made from the same fabric.

182. **(d)** The idiom 'Hit the sack' means to go to bed or to go to sleep. It is commonly used when someone is tired and ready to sleep.

183. **(b)** An 'orator' is a skilled public speaker who is known for giving eloquent speeches.

The description 'An eloquent and skilled public speaker' matches the definition of an orator perfectly.

- Elector (a voter), spokesperson (a representative) and leader (someone in charge) are not the best substitutes for 'eloquent public speaker'.

184. **(c)** This sequence correctly reflects the flow of events as described in the passage.

185. **(b)** This sequence correctly reflects the flow of events as described in the passage.

186. **(b)** This sequence correctly reflects the flow of events as described in the passage.

187. **(a)** This sequence correctly reflects the flow of events as described in the passage.

188. **(d)** This sequence correctly reflects the flow of events as described in the passage.

189. **(d)** This sequence correctly reflects the flow of events as described in the passage.

190. **(c)** This sequence correctly reflects the flow of events as described in the passage.

191. **(d)** This sequence correctly reflects the flow of events as described in the passage.

192. **(c)** This sequence correctly reflects the flow of events as described in the passage.

193. **(d)** This sequence correctly reflects the flow of events as described in the passage.

194. **(b)** This sequence correctly reflects the flow of events as described in the passage.

195. **(c)** This sequence correctly reflects the flow of events as described in the passage.

196. **(c)** This sequence correctly reflects the flow of events as described in the passage.

197. **(d)** This sequence correctly reflects the flow of events as described in the passage.

198. **(a)** This sequence correctly reflects the flow of events as described in the passage.

199. **(b)** This sequence correctly reflects the flow of events as described in the passage.

200. **(d)** This sequence correctly reflects the flow of events as described in the passage.

CPO SI P-1 SP 11

PAPER-1

SSC CPO SI SOLVED PAPER

5 October 2023 (Shift III)

MM : 200

Time : 2 hr

Instructions

1. This paper contains 200 questions.
2. It has 4 Parts, **Part I** General Intelligence and Reasoning, **Part II** General Knowledge and General Awareness, **Part III** Quantitative Aptitude and **Part IV** English Comprehension.
3. Each question carries **1 marks**.

Part I

General Intelligence and Reasoning

1. A paper is folded and cut as shown. How will it appear when unfolded?

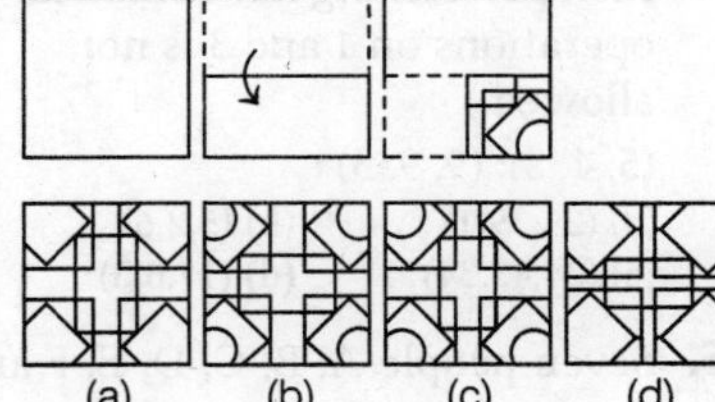

(a) (b) (c) (d)

2. Select the set in which the numbers are related in the same way as are the numbers of the following sets.
(**Note** Operations should be performed on the whole numbers, without breaking down the numbers into its constituent digits. E.g. 13-Operations on 13 such as adding/subtracting/multiplying etc. to 13 can be performed. Breaking down 13 into 1 and 3 and then performing mathematical operations on 1 and 3 is not allowed.)

(53, 36, 25)

(71, 54, 43)

(a) (41, 23, 18) (b) (99, 82, 71)
(c) (66, 53, 41) (d) (32, 14, 7)

3. Six characters A, B,C, 1, 2 and 3 are written on different faces of a dice. Two positions of this dice are shown in the figure. Find the character on the face opposite to C.

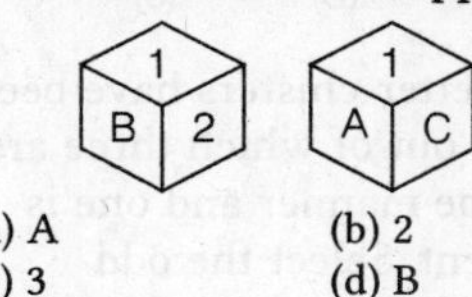

(a) A (b) 2
(c) 3 (d) B

4. Select the figure that will come next in the following figure series.

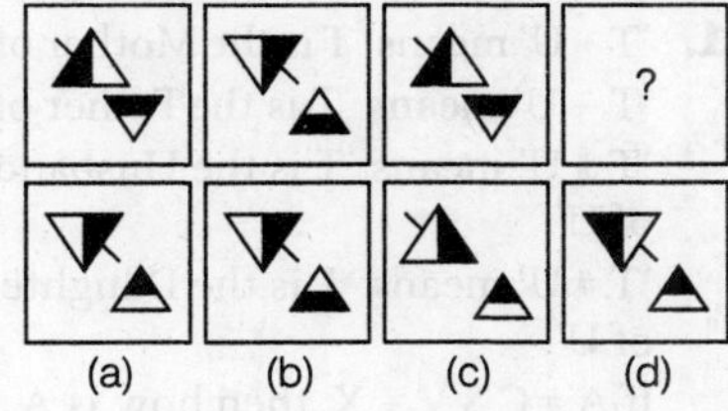

(a) (b) (c) (d)

5. Select the option that represents the letters that, when sequentially placed in the blanks below, will complete the letter-series.

a, b, a, b, b, _, a, b, a, b, _, a, a, b, a, b, b, _

(a) b, a, b (b) a, b, a
(c) b, b, b (d) a, a, a

6. Select the number from among the given options that can replace the question mark (?) in the following series.

144, 171, 200, ?, 264

(a) 240 (b) 256
(c) 225 (d) 231

7. Which letter-cluster will replace the question mark (?) to complete the given series?

FOHV, CKER, ?, WCYJ, TYVF

(a) XHBM (b) ZGBN
(c) AFCP (d) AHCO

8. Six characters A,B, C, 1, 2 and 3 are written on different faces of a dice. Two positions of this dice are shown in the figure. Find the character on the face opposite to 3.

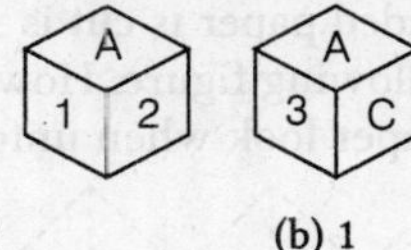

(a) B (b) 1
(c) 2 (d) C

9. In a certain code language, 'BLOCK' is coded as LBCON and 'CABIN' is coded as ACIBQ. How will 'SUITE' be coded in the same language?

(a) USTIH (b) UTSEH
(c) ETHUS (d) USHTI

10. Select the option in which the given figure is embedded (Rotation is not allowed).

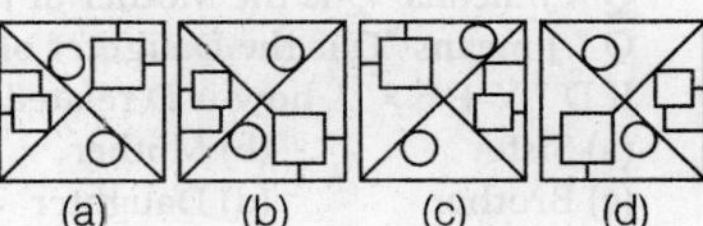

(a) (b) (c) (d)

11. In a certain code language, 'MOBILE' is written as 'NQEMQK' and 'BISHOP' is written as 'CKVLTV'. How will 'CHARGE' be written in that language?
(a) DJEVLJ (b) DJDWLK
(c) DJDVLK (d) DJDVKL

12. Select the correct option that indicates the arrangement of the given words in the order in which they appear in an English dictionary.
1. Warehouse 2. Warden
3. Warship 4. Wardrobe
5. Warrant 6. Warfare
(a) 4, 2, 1, 6, 5, 3 (b) 2, 4, 1, 6, 5, 3
(c) 2, 4, 6, 5, 1, 3 (d) 2, 4, 1, 5, 6, 3

13. Select the Venn diagram that best illustrates the relationship between the following classes.
Clothes, Shoes, Shirts
(a) 
(b)
(c)
(d)

14. The sequence of folding a piece of paper and the manner in which the folded paper is cut is shown in the following figure. How would this paper look when unfolded

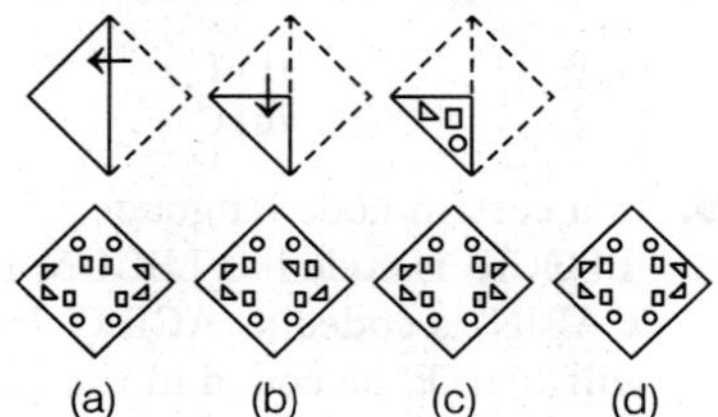

15. If A denotes '+', B denotes '×', C denotes '–', and D denotes '÷', then what will be the value of the following equation?
11 B 12 C 144 D 24 A 57 = ?
(a) 180 (b) 183 (c) 186 (d) 160

16. Q + J means "Q is the Husband of J"
Q – J means "Q is the Father of J"
Q × J means "Q is the Mother of J"
Q * J means "Q is the Daughter of J"
If D * V + B × U, how is D related to U?
(a) Sister (b) Mother
(c) Brother (d) Daughter

17. Q is to the East of S. E is to the South of S. P is to the North-East of Q and North of T. If T is to the South-East of Q, what is the position of S with respect to T? (All positions are arranged in grid pattern)
(a) South-East (b) South-West
(c) West (d) North-West

18. In a certain code language, 'SPAM' is coded as '36' and 'JUG' is coded as '27'. How will 'FROCK' be coded in that language?
(a) 72 (b) 45
(c) 90 (d) 48

19. Select the option figure in which the given figure is embedded as its part (Rotation is not allowed.)

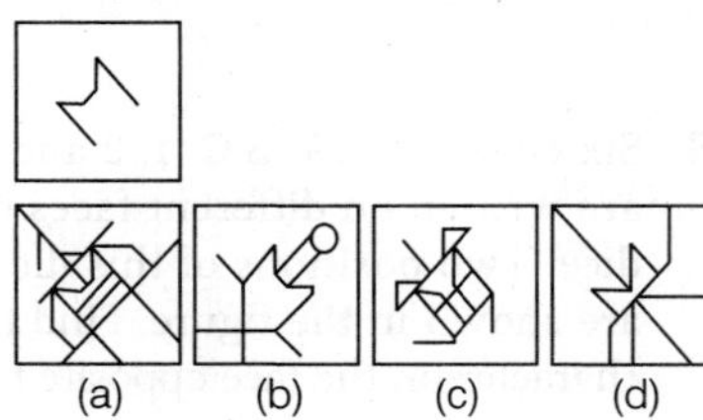

20. Four letter-clusters have been given, out of which three are alike in some manner and one is different. Select the odd letter-cluster.
(a) SRWX (b) HGLM
(c) POTU (d) DBGH

21. 'T + U' means 'T is the Mother of U'.
'T – U' means 'T is the Father of U'.
'T $ U' means 'T is the Husband of U'.
'T # U' means 'T is the Daughter of U'.
If A # C $ V + X, then how is A related to X?
(a) Brother
(b) Sister
(c) Father
(d) Daughter

22. A paper is folded and cut as shown below. How will it appear when unfolded?

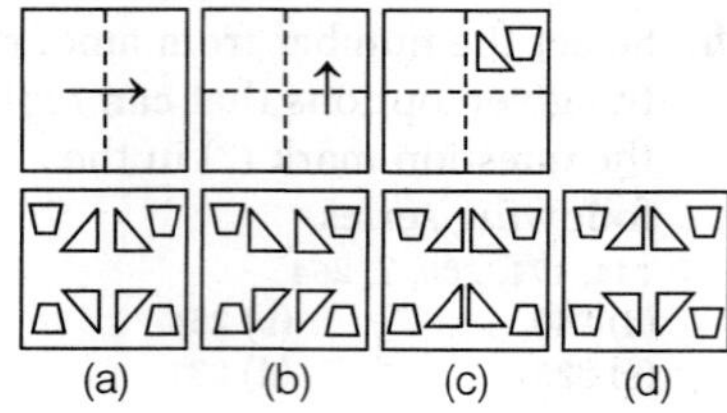

23. Select the set in which the numbers are related in the same way as are the numbers of the following sets.
(**Note** Operations should be performed on the whole numbers, without breaking down the numbers into its constituent digits. E.g. 13 – Operations on 13 such as adding /subtracting /multiplying etc. to 13 can be performed. Breaking down 13 into 1 and 3 and then performing mathematical operations on 1 and 3 is not allowed.)
(112, 327, 215), (98, 254, 156)
(a) (108, 209, 184) (b) (105, 347, 322)
(c) (126, 268, 142) (d) (281, 490,309)

24. Select the set in which the numbers are related in the same way as are the numbers of the following set.
(**Note** Operations should be performed on the whole numbers, without breaking down the numbers into its constituent digits. E.g. 13 – Operations on 13 such as adding/ subtracting/ multiplying etc to 13 can be performed. Breaking down 13 into 1 and 3 and then performing mathematical operations on 1 and 3 is not allowed.)
(5, 4, 2); (9, 9, 3)
(a) (21,39,1) (b) (5,2,6)
(c) (24,43,34) (d) (17,6,5)

25. Seven people A, B, C, D, E, F and G, are sitting in a straight row, facing North. Only two people sit to the right of D. G is an immediate neighbour of D. Only three people sit between A and G. Only two people sit between B and C. E is not an immediate neighbour of C. F sits to the immediate right of G. Who sits to the immediate left of A?
(a) E (b) C (c) D (d) B

26. Select the option that represents the correct order of the given words as they would appear in an English dictionary?
1. Brochure 2. Brine
3. Bright 4. Brief
5. Brocade
(a) 1, 2, 3, 4, 5 (b) 1, 2, 3, 5, 4
(c) 4, 3, 2, 5, 1 (d) 3, 2, 5, 4, 1

27. If '+' means '–', '–' means '×', '×' means '÷' and '÷' means '+', what will come in place of '?' in the following equation?

$79 \div 64 \times 8 - 7 + 12 = ?$

(a) 123 (b) 117 (c) 138 (d) 147

28. Two statements are given followed by three conclusions numbered I, II and III. Assuming the statements to be true, even if they seem to be at variance with commonly known facts, decide which of the conclusions logically follow(s) from the statements.

Statements

All keys are locks.

No door is a lock.

Conclusions

I. Some locks are doors.

II. Some locks are keys.

III. No key is a door.

(a) Both Conclusions I and II follow
(b) Conclusions I, II and III follow
(c) Both Conclusions II and III follow
(d) Both Conclusions I and III follow

29. In a certain code language, 'Live long' is coded as 'mu ae', 'Road is long' is coded as 'ae si du' and 'Game is live' is coded as 'si mu zt'. What is the code for the word Game'?

(a) si (b) mu (c) zt (d) ae

30. Which two signs should be interchanged to make the given equation correct?

$42 \div 7 + 11 \times 87 - 12 = 141$

(a) ÷ and – (b) ÷ and +
(c) × and + (d) – and ×

31. Select the option that is related to the third word in the same way as the second word is related to the first word.

(The words must be considered as meaningful words and must not be related to each other based on the number of letters/number of consonants/vowels in the word).

Pressure : Barometer :: Electricity : ?

(a) Cyclotron (b) Bolometer
(c) Audiometer (d) Multimeter

32. Which of the following numbers will replace the question mark (?) in the given series?

270, 241, 212, ?, 154, 125

(a) 198 (b) 186 (c) 183 (d) 192

33. Select the option that is related to the third term in the same way as the second term is related to the first term and the sixth term is related to the fifth term.

25 : 18 :: 37 : ? :: 49 : 36

(a) 29 (b) 32
(c) 30 (d) 27

34. Six students Meera, Jigyasa, Tarun, Naina, Shambhavi and Avni are sitting around a circular table facing the centre (Not necessarily in the same order). Shambhavi is an immediate neighbour of both Jigyasa and Avni. Tarun is sitting third to the left of Jigyasa. Meera is sitting second to the right of Avni. Who is sitting second to the left of Jigyasa?

(a) Meera (b) Naina
(c) Avni (d) Tarun

35. Which letter-cluster will replace the question mark (?) to complete the given series?

BRCQ, EPFO, ?, KLLK, NJOI

(a) HINO
(b) GNMI
(c) HNIM
(d) GINO

36. Select the Venn diagram that best illustrates the relationship between the following classes.

Animal, Jungle, Wild Animal

(a)  (b) 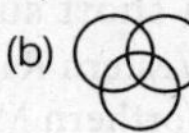

(c) (d)

37. When the following figure is folded to form a cube, which letter-number will be on the face opposite to the face showing the letter-number 'A1'?

(The elements are shown to indicate the sides only.)

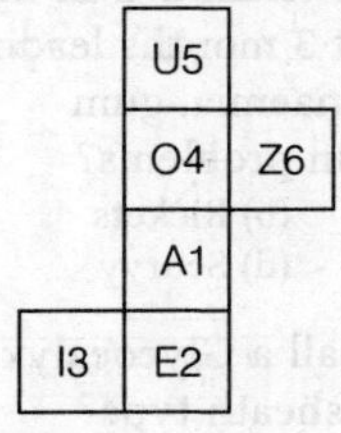

(a) U5 (b) O4
(c) I3 (d) E2

38. Which of the given figures when placed in the 5th position would continue the series that is established by the first four figures?

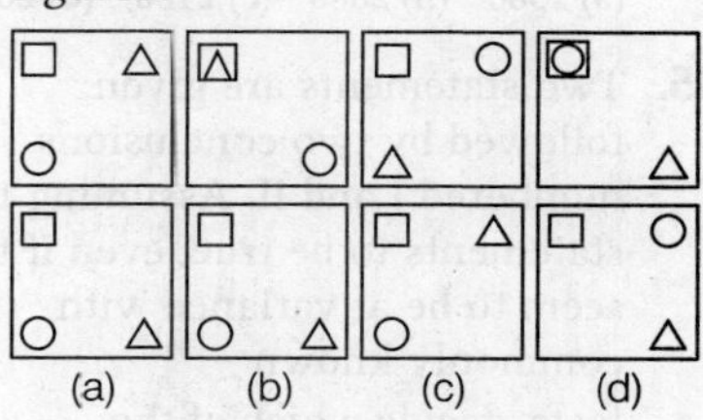

39. Select the option that is related to the third word in the same way as the second word is related to the first word.

(The words must be considered as meaningful words and must not be related to each other based on the number of letters/number of consonants/vowels in the word.)

Centre : Focus :: Vicar : ?

(a) Life (b) Priest
(c) Building (d) Riddle

40. Three of the following four letter-clusters are alike in a certain way and one is different. Pick the odd one out.

(a) MOKN (b) SQUH
(c) GIET (d) CEAX

41. Which two signs should be interchanged to make the given equation correct?

$39 \div 3 - 11 + 57 \times 29 = 171$

(a) – and ×
(b) – and +
(c) ÷ and +
(d) ÷ and –

42. Stanley starts cycling from point A. He cycles x km towards the West and then turns right and cycles 3 km. He again turns right and cycles for x+1 km. He again turns right and cycles for 2x+1 km. He takes a final right turn and cycles for 1 km to stop at point B. Point B is 6 km South of point A. What is the value of x?

(a) 9 (b) 3
(c) 4 (d) 5

43. In a certain code language, 'PIN' is coded as 9 and 'CHARGER' is coded as 49. How will 'CABLE' be coded in the same language?

(a) 27 (b) 25 (c) 18 (d) 36

44. Which of the following numbers will replace the question mark (?) in the given series?
5, 20, 60, 240, 720, ?
(a) 2580 (b) 2880 (c) 2160 (d) 2675

45. Two statements are given, followed by two conclusions numbered I and II. Assuming the statements to be true, even if they seem to be at variance with commonly known facts, decide which of the conclusions logically follow(s) from the statements.
Statements
All rivers are lakes.
Some seas are rivers.
Conclusions
I. Some seas are lakes.
II. All lakes are rivers.
(a) Neither Conclusion I nor II follows
(b) Only Conclusion II follows
(c) Only Conclusion I follows
(d) Both Conclusions I and II follow

46. If '+' means '–', '–' means '×', '×' means '÷', '÷' means '+', then what will come in place of the question mark (?) in the following equation?
$39 \times 3 - 11 \div 57 + 29 = ?$
(a) 163 (b) 190 (c) 185 (d) 171

47. Which figure from the given options would replace the question mark (?) if the following figure series were to be continued?

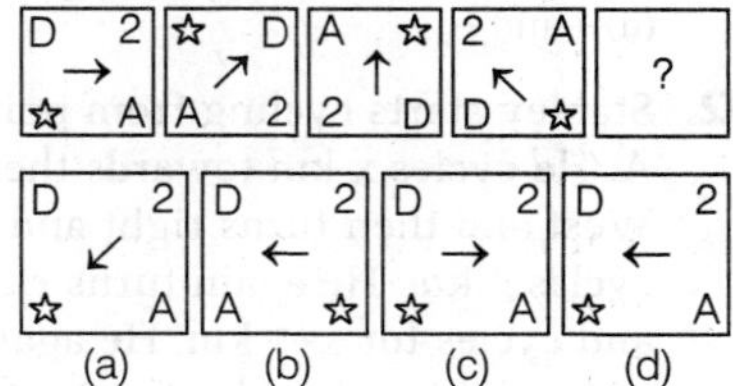

48. If M denotes '–', N denotes '÷', O denotes '×' and P denotes '+', then what will come in place of '?' in the following equations?
21 O 5P69 N3 P $\sqrt{225}$ M 88 = ?
(a) 61 (b) 65 (c) 55 (d) 50

49. Which of the following numbers will replace the question mark (?) in the given series?
69, 65, 67, 63, ?, 61
(a) 65 (b) 60 (c) 62 (d) 64

50. Which two mathematical signs should be interchanged to make the given equation correct?
$(45 \times 2) \div 15 - (6 \times 3) + 10 - (63 \div 21) = 17$
(a) ÷ and + (b) × and –
(c) – and + (d) ÷ and ×

Part II
General Knowledge and General Awareness

51. Lavani is a traditional dance of which of the following states?
(a) Uttar Pradesh
(b) Maharashtra
(c) Himachal Pradesh
(d) Madhya Pradesh

52. Which of the following scientists provided the Law of Octaves?
(a) Galileo Galilei
(b) John Newlands
(c) Michael Faraday
(d) Marie Curie

53. Who among the following Bahmani sultan was noted for cruelty and hence, got the title as 'Zalim'?
(a) Humayun (b) Firoz Shah
(c) Mujahid Shah (d) Ahmad Shah

54. According to the Koppen classification, which regions experience cold humid winter with short summers?
(a) Western Rajasthan
(b) Northern Madhya Pradesh
(c) South of Goa
(d) Arunachal Pradesh

55. The Rajpath was decided to be a permanent venue for the Republic Day parade from which of the following year onwards?
(a) 1959 (b) 1951
(c) 1955 (d) 1958

56. Which disease is caused by not having enough vitamin C in the diet for at least 3 months leading to weakness, anaemia, gum disease and skin problems?
(a) Pellagra (b) Rickets
(c) Beriberi (d) Scurvy

57. What do you call a Glycocalyx that is a loose sheath type?
(a) Mesosomes (b) Capsule
(c) Tubules (d) Slime layer

58. Assessment of the country's GDP growth, external balance and fiscal balance are presented in which part of the budget document?
(a) Medium-term Fiscal Policy Statement
(b) Appropriation Bill
(c) Fiscal Policy Strategy Statement
(d) Macro-economic Framework Statement

59. The seven years of war in the 18th century was fought between Britain and ....
(a) Spain (b) France
(c) Germany (d) Portugal

60. At the time of launch of the Smart Cities Mission, how many cities were proposed to be covered under this scheme?
(a) 100 (b) 50 (c) 75 (d) 25

61. What is the standard weight of a hockey ball?
(a) 156 gm - 161 gm
(b) 156 gm - 162 gm
(c) 156 gm - 160 gm
(d) 156 gm - 163 gm

62. Choose the correct statements related to 'continentality'.
A. The sea exerts a moderating influence on climate.
B. As the distance from the sea increases, the people experience extreme weather conditions.
C. As one goes from the surface of the Earth to higher altitudes, the atmosphere becomes less dense and temperature decreases.
(a) Both A and C (b) Only C
(c) Both B and C (d) Both A and B

63. The Arms Act was passed in......... that prevented Indians from keeping arms without an appropriate license.
(a) 1909 (b) 1897
(c) 1878 (d) 1912

64. Who takes the salute during the Republic Day parade at New Delhi?
(a) Governor (b) President
(c) Chief Justice (d) Prime Minister

65. According to the Census of India 2011, which of the following states has the highest Hindu population percentage of total population?
(a) Madhya Pradesh
(b) Haryana
(c) Himachal Pradesh
(d) Uttar Pradesh

66. Which Article of the Indian Constitution mentions that all the authorities civil and judicial in the Territory of India shall act in aid of the Supreme Court?
(a) Article 143 (b) Article 144
(c) Article 142 (d) Article 141

67. .... river has the least storage capacity of usable water.
(a) Godavari (b) Ganges
(c) Brahmaputra (d) Krishna

68. Dihang and Lohit are rivers in which of the following regions?
(a) Sikkim and Manipur
(b) Punjab and Himachal
(c) Arunachal Pradesh and Assam
(d) Jammu and Kashmir

69. With which of the following dance forms is Thumri music associated?
(a) Sattriya (b) Kathakali
(c) Kathak (d) Bharatanatyam

70. Who among the following Mauryan king fasted to death and died at Shravanabelagola?
(a) Bindusara
(b) Dasharatha
(c) Chandragupta Maurya
(d) Ashoka

71. Shifting agriculture is known as .... in the Western Ghats.
(a) kumari (b) dahiya
(c) koman (d) waltre

72. In which of the following states are Aus, Boro and Aman paddy crops grown in a year?
(a) Punjab (b) Odisha
(c) Haryana (d) Uttarakhand

73. The measure of the force that can cause an object to rotate about an axis is called
(a) moment of inertia
(b) power
(c) torque
(d) centripetal force

74. Who among the following classical poets of the Sultanate period in India popularised Qawwali, a form of music which derived its name from the Arabic word 'qaul', meaning 'to speak'?
(a) Nizam al-Din Awliya
(b) Jalal al-Din Muhammad Rumi
(c) Amir Khusrau
(d) Shams al-Din Muhammad Hafiz

75. What is the name of the 1,3-isomer (or meta-isomer) of benzenediol with the chemical formula $C_6H_4(OH)_2$?
(a) m-Cresol (b) Resorcinol
(c) Catechol (d) Glycerol

76. Who was/were the founders of the Theosophical Society?
(a) HP Blavatsky and Colonel Olcott
(b) Madam Bhikaji Cama
(c) Annie Besant
(d) Charles W. Leadbeater and Emily Lutyens

77. Which Articles of the Indian Constitution describe Fundamental Rights?
(a) Articles 5 to 11
(b) Articles 12 to 35
(c) Articles 36 to 51
(d) Articles 52 to 62

78. Which of the following organisms belongs to phylum Apicomplexa?
(a) Sponge (b) Physalia
(c) Hydra (d) Plasmodium

79. Select the incorrect pair of a famous minaret and its construction year in India.
(a) Shaheed Minar–1828 CE
(b) Chand Minar–1435 CE
(c) Charminar–1664 CE
(d) Jhulta Minar–1452 CE

80. In 1932, who discovered the positron, a particle described as 'carrying a positive charge but having a mass of the same order of magnitude as that normally possessed by a free negative electron'?
(a) Niels Bohr
(b) Paul Dirac
(c) Ernest Rutherford
(d) Carl Anderson

81. Which of the following rights forbids employment of children below the age of 14 years in dangerous jobs?
(a) Right to Equality
(b) Right to Constitutional Remedies
(c) Right against Exploitation
(d) Right to Freedom

82. Which of the following is not the manifestation of Iron-Deficiency Anaemia (IDA)?
(a) Soft palate
(b) Blindness
(c) General pallor
(d) Paleness of conjunctiva of eyes

83. Which of the following books is an autobiography of the Indian politician LK Advani?
(a) Wings of Fire: An Autobiography
(b) My Country My Life
(c) My Times: An Autobiography
(d) In Pursuit of Justice: An Autobiography

84. From which Five-Year Plan did India start its journey of industrialisation?
(a) Third Five-Year Plan
(b) Second Five-Year Plan
(c) Fifth Five-Year Plan
(d) Fourth Five-Year Plan

85. Which of the following statements about Green Revolution is/are correct?
I. Green Revolution began in the 1960s.
II. HYV of a seed made Green Revolution a success.
III. Extensive use of cattle was also one constituent of Green Revolution.
(a) Both II and III (b) Both I and II
(c) Only I (d) Only II

86. Ghanakanta Bora Borbayan has been conferred the Padma Shri award for his contribution to which of the following fields?
(a) Bhortal (b) Bagurumba
(c) Sattriya (d) Chhau

87. The masculine aspect of the Manipuri classical dance is known as
(a) Ras (b) Choloms
(c) Pareng (d) Maiba

88. Which of the following Articles of the Constitution of India lays down the establishment of Public Service Commissions for the Union and for the States?
(a) Article 315 (b) Article 316
(c) Article 317 (d) Article 318

89. Which of the following is an indirect tax?
(a) Death duty
(b) Interest tax
(c) Goods and Services tax
(d) Capital gains tax

90. The ball colour in the sport of Ball Badminton should be
(a) yellow (b) green (c) pink (d) red

91. What is the bicameral legislature of the Indian Constitution?
(a) It is legislative body with three houses.
(b) It is legislative body with two houses.
(c) It is legislative body with one house.
(d) It is legislative body with four houses.

92. Neeru Swamy Pillai and Rajaratanam Pillai are exponents of which musical instrument?
(a) Nadaswaran (b) Mandolin
(c) Mridangam (d) Sarangi

93. Living organisms have been on Earth for how much percent of Earth's history?
(a) 80% (b) 20% (c) 60% (d) 40%

94. According to the 2011 Census, which state recorded the lowest literacy rate?
(a) Arunachal Pradesh
(b) Bihar
(c) Andhra Pradesh
(d) Jharkhand

95. Which Article of the Indian Constitution refers to the Rights of Ministers with respect to the State Legislature?
(a) Article 178 (b) Article 177
(c) Article 175 (d) Article 176

96. In Ball Badminton, players change the ends in each game, when a side first scores all of the following, except
(a) 18 (b) 9 (c) 27 (d) 11

97. In 1928, which equation was derived and combines quantum theory and special relativity to describe the behaviour of an electron moving at a relativistic speed?
(a) Bernoulli's equation
(b) Lorentz equation
(c) Helmholtz equation
(d) Dirac equation

98. The term 'Dribble' is generally associated with ....
(a) cricket (b) baseball
(c) basketball (d) tennis

99. Which of the following Sultans of Delhi was appointed as Amir-i-Tuzuk (Master of Ceremonies) before becoming the Sultan?
(a) Muhammad Bin Tughlaq
(b) Alauddin Khilji
(c) Balban
(d) Iltutmish

100. Who is the author of the book 'The Soul of a Butterfly: Reflections on Life's Journey'?
(a) Jake LaMotta (b) Eugene J Bullard
(c) Roberto Duran (d) Muhammad Ali

Part III
Quantitative Aptitude

101. Find the fourth proportional of 22, 66 and 11.
(a) 23 (b) 33 (c) 17 (d) 39

102. An article is sold at a discount of 25% and an additional discount of 28% is allowed on cash payment. If Ramendra purchased the article by paying ₹ 10800 in cash, then what was the marked price of the article?
(a) ₹ 19800 (b) ₹ 20800
(c) ₹ 20000 (d) ₹ 18000

103. A shopkeeper marked the price as ₹ 15000 on an article, and a successive discount of 5%, 10% and 20% was allowed on it. What is the selling price?
(a) ₹ 10260 (b) ₹ 13520
(c) ₹ 11520 (d) ₹ 9850

104. The value of a washing machine depreciated from ₹ 40960 to ₹ 21970 in 3 yr. Find the yearly rate of depreciation.
(a) 25% (b) 16.25%
(c) 18.75% (d) 20%

105. A and B are equally efficient, and each can individually complete a piece of work in 36 days, if none takes any holiday. A and B started working together on this piece of work, but A took a day off after every five days of work, while B took a day off after every seven days of work. If the duo had started work on 1 July, 2021, on which date was the work completed?
(a) 22nd July, 2021 (b) 19th July, 2021
(c) 21st July, 2021 (d) 20th July, 2021

106. The radius of a metallic spherical ball is 3 cm. If the metallic ball is melted and recast into x number of hemispheres of radius equal to half the radius of the metallic spherical ball, then find the value of x.
(a) 15 (b) 14 (c) 16 (d) 13

107. Some ice pieces, spherical in shape, of diameter 6 cm are dropped in a cylindrical container containing some juice and are fully submerged. If the diameter of the container is 18 cm and level of juice rises by 40 cm, then how many ice pieces are dropped in the container?
(a) 95 (b) 85 (c) 80 (d) 90

108. If the slant height of a cone is 29 cm and its height is 20 cm, find the ratio between the magnitudes of total surface area and the volume.
(a) 5 : 14 (b) 7 : 15 (c) 3 : 7 (d) 3 : 14

109. In ΔABC with sides 8 cm, 9 cm and 12 cm, the angle bisector of the largest angle divides the opposite sides into two segments. What is the length of the shorter segment?
(a) $5\frac{11}{17}$ cm (b) $4\frac{11}{17}$ cm
(c) $6\frac{13}{17}$ cm (d) $3\frac{9}{17}$ cm

110. If $\cot^2\theta = 1 - e^2$, then the value of $\operatorname{cosec}\theta + \cot^3\theta \sec\theta$ is
(a) $(2-e^2)^{\frac{1}{2}}$ (b) $(1-e^2)^{\frac{3}{2}}$
(c) $(1-e^2)$ (d) $(2-e^2)^{\frac{3}{2}}$

111. If $\frac{2\sin A - \cos A}{\sin A + \cos A} = 1$, then find the value of cot A.
(a) 1 (b) $\frac{1}{2}$
(c) $\frac{1}{3}$ (d) 2

112. A, B and C can do a piece of work in 11 days, 20 days and 55 days respectively. How soon can the work be done if A works with B on first day, A works with C on second day and so on?
(a) $8\frac{1}{2}$ days (b) $9\frac{1}{2}$ days
(c) 8 days (d) 9 days

113. Study the given table and answer the question that follows.

Number of children	Number of families
0	4
1	22
2	15
3	6
4	2

The average number of children per family is
(a) 1.47 (b) 1.59
(c) 1.23 (d) 1.72

114. A fast local of Mumbai takes 45 min less than a slow local for a journey of 150 km. If the speed of the fast local is 10 km/h more than that of the slow local, find the speed (in km/h) of the slow local train.
(a) 30 (b) 35 (c) 45 (d) 40

115. In a school of 720 students, the ratio of boys to girls is 3 : 5. Find how many new boys may be allowed to the school if 18 new girls are admitted, so that the ratio of boys to girls changes to 2 : 3.
(a) 42 (b) 44 (c) 50 (d) 38

116. The given graph shows the income and expenditure of a family. Study the graph and answer the question that follows.

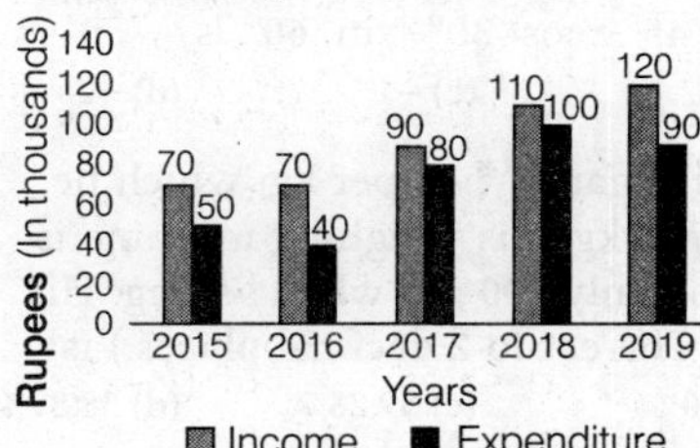

The expenditure of the family increased by .... from 2017 to 2018.
(a) 25% (b) 11% (c) 22% (d) 20%

117. Which of the following is the greatest four-digit number that is divisible by 15, 25, 40, and 75?
(a) 9200 (b) 9500 (c) 9600 (d) 9000

118. What is the average of the first six prime numbers?
(a) $6\frac{1}{3}$ (b) $6\frac{5}{6}$ (c) $6\frac{2}{3}$ (d) $6\frac{1}{6}$

119. Ayush spends 25% of an amount of money on an insurance policy, 26% on food, 23% on children's education and 19% on recreation. He deposits the remaining amount of ₹ 26600 in the bank. What is the total amount (in ₹) that he spends on food and recreation together?
(a) 195000 (b) 171000
(c) 162000 (d) 183000

120. Study the given pie-chart carefully and answer the question that follows.
Degreewise break-up of expenditure of a family in a month

Total amount spent in a month = ₹ 56800

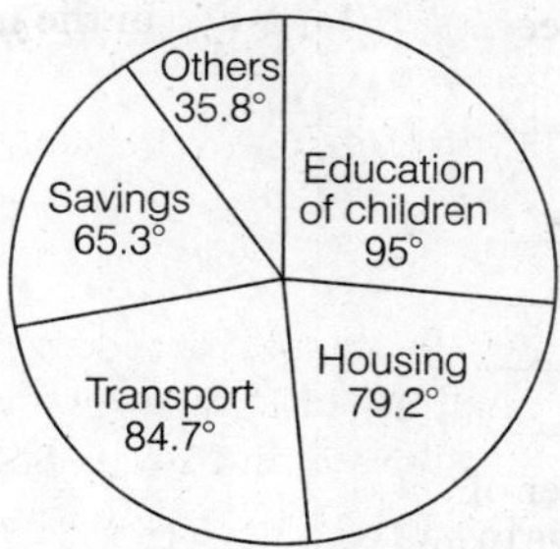

What is the amount spent by the family on housing?
(a) ₹ 11814 (b) ₹ 6248
(c) ₹ 10615 (d) ₹ 12496

121. The number of balls, each one is 4 cm in the diameter that can be made from a solid metallic sphere of diameter 32 cm is
(a) 256 (b) 64
(c) 512 (d) 1024

122. Simplify the given expression.
$b + 2a - [(3b + a) - (2a + b) + 2a] - a$
(a) $-a$ (b) b
(c) $-b$ (d) a

123. In a store, Arun has two options to buy a mobile phone, either he can pay the full amount of ₹ 2500 or he may buy at an installment scheme, *i.e.* ₹ 520 in down payment and four equal installments, rate of interest being charged at 25% p.a. simple interest. Arun buys a mobile phone on the installment scheme. What is the monthly installment for Arun?
(a) ₹ 510 (b) ₹ 530
(c) ₹ 550 (d) ₹ 520

124. In a 1200 m race, Rakesh reaches the final point in 36 sec and Rajesh reaches in 40 sec. By how much distance does Rakesh beat Rajesh?
(a) 130 m (b) 120 m
(c) 140 m (d) 150 m

125. Rakesh runs a coaching institute having 50 faculty members. The average monthly salary of 35 faculty members is ₹ 37500. What will be the average monthly salary (in ₹) of the other 15 faculty members, if the average monthly salary of all the 50 faculty members is found to be ₹ 30000?
(a) 13000 (b) 13500
(c) 12500 (d) 12000

126. If $\sin\theta + \cos\theta = \sqrt{2}\cos\theta$, then find $\frac{\sin\theta - \cos\theta}{\sin\theta}$
(a) $-\sqrt{2}$ (b) -1 (c) 1 (d) $\sqrt{2}$

127. Ankita sold three toys. The first toy was sold for ₹1500 at a profit of 25%; the second toy was sold for ₹2800 at a loss of 50% and the third toy was sold for ₹3500 at a profit of 25%. Find her total profit or loss percentage.
(a) 15.25% loss (b) 15.25% profit
(c) 18.75% profit (d) 18.75% loss

128. Study the given pie-chart and answer the question that follows.
The pie-chart shows the expenditure of a family on different items and their saving throughout the year 2021.

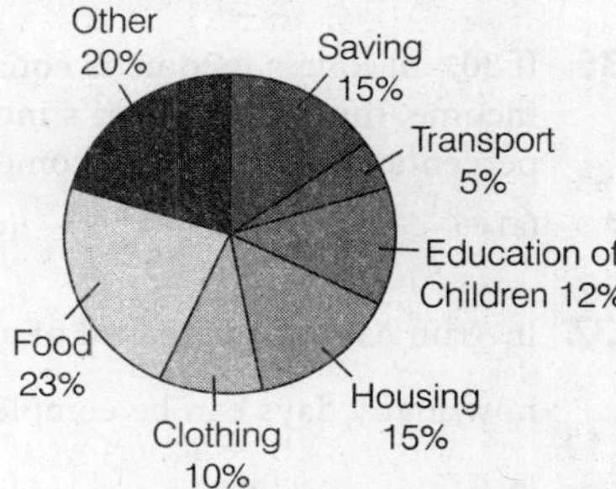

If the total income for the year was ₹ 100000, then the difference in the expenses (in ₹) between housing and transport was
(a) 9500 (b) 10500 (c) 9000 (d) 10000

129. Simplify the given expression.
$(x - 2y)(y - 3x) + (x + y)(x - y) + (x - 3y)(2x + y)$
(a) $2y(x - 3y)$ (b) $2y(x + 3y)$
(c) $2x(x - 3y)$ (d) $2x(x + 3y)$

130. The least number of five digits which is exactly divisible by 9, 12, 15, 25 and 27 is
(a) 10800 (b) 10250 (c) 10700 (d) 10600

131. The LCM of two numbers is five times their HCF. If the product of the two numbers is 20480,then find their HCF and LCM, respectively.
(a) 46 and 230 (b) 48 and 240
(c) 64 and 320 (d) 56 and 280

132. Find the HCF of 125, 250 and 750.
(a) 50 (b) 25 (c) 125 (d) 75

133. The LCM of 8, 12 and 18 is
(a) 24 (b) 80 (c) 72 (d) 36

134. Study the given table and answer the question that follows.
The table shows the number of employees in three organisations during three years.

Year / Organisation	2018	2019	2020
P	75	69	85
Q	96	81	74
R	85	63	90

What is the respective ratio between total number of employees in organisations P and R together in 2019 and total number of employees in organisations Q and R together in 2020?
(a) 23 : 41 (b) 33 : 41
(c) 41 : 31 (d) 33 : 23

135. The ratio of monthly income and expenditure of a man is 7: 3. If his expenditure is ₹ 5400, find his monthly income.
(a) ₹ 12600 (b) ₹13300 (c) ₹ 11500 (d) ₹ 10400

136. If 30% of Ravi's income is equal to 40% of Suresh's income, then 50% of Ravi's income is equal to what percentage of Suresh's income?
(a) $66\frac{1}{3}\%$ (b) $33\frac{1}{3}\%$ (c) $33\frac{2}{3}\%$ (d) $66\frac{2}{3}\%$

137. If Arun can complete $\frac{2}{3}$ rd of a work in 12 days, then in how many days can be complete $\frac{1}{6}$ th of the same work?
(a) 3 (b) 4 (c) 5 (d) 2

138. The chord of a circle is equal to its radius. Find the difference between the angle subtended by this chord at the minor arc and major arc of the circle.
(a) 30° (b) 120° (c) 60° (d) 150°

139. The length of the common chord of two intersecting circles is 24 cm. If the diameter of the circles are 30 cm and 26 cm, then the distance between the centres (in cm) is
(a) 16 cm (b) 14 cm (c) 18 cm (d) 12 cm

140. Study the given table and answer the question that follows.
The table shows the number of students in various courses in various cities A, B, C, D and E in India during the academic years 2022-2023.

City	MBA	Science	Engineering	Medicine	MCA	Total
A	1200	2560	4520	1100	960	10340
B	1350	2650	5100	1050	850	11000
C	1250	2640	4580	1120	750	10340
D	1960	1250	3500	1850	1600	10160
E	1200	2100	3500	960	540	8300

During the academic years 2022-2023, which city had the largest number of students?
(a) C (b) D (c) A (d) B

141. Study the given bar graph carefully and answer the question that follows. Increment of four employees (in ₹) in the months of May, June and July.

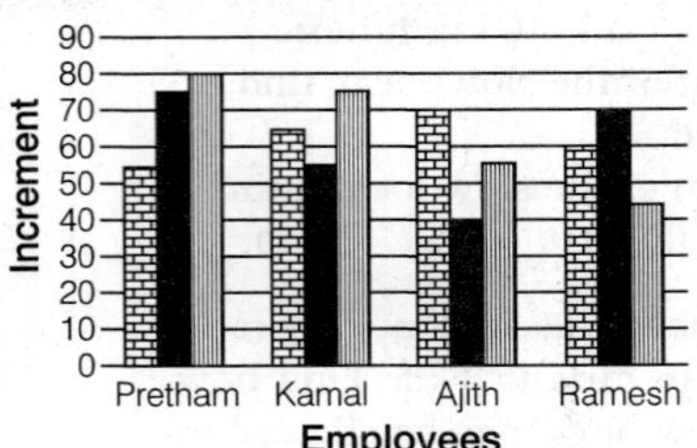

What is Kamal's overall average increment in three months?
(a) ₹ 60 (b) ₹ 70 (c) ₹ 75 (d) ₹ 65

142. A hollow cylindrical tube made of plastic is 3 cm thick. If the external diameter is 20 cm and length of the tube is 49 cm, find the volume of the plastic.
(a) 7238 cm^3 (b) 7644 cm^3 (c) 7546 cm^3 (d) 7854 cm^3

143. The value of $2\tan^2 45° + \cos^2 30° - \sin^2 60°$ is
(a) 2 (b) 1 (c) −1 (d) −2

144. A shopkeeper sells sugar at ₹ 40 per kg, which he purchased at ₹ 36 per kg. His weighing machine is faulty and it weighs only 800 gm while selling. His percentage profit (Correct to 2 decimal places.) is
(a) 37.58% (b) 40% (c) 39.28% (d) 38.89%

145. PQR is right angled at Q such that $PQ = (x - y)$, $QR = x$ amd $PR = (x + y)$. S is a point on QR such that $QS = PQ$. The ratio $QS : SR$ for any values of x and y is
(a) 3 : 1 (b) 2 : 1 (c) 1 : 2 (d) 1 : 3

146. The following table represents the number of scooters sold by 5 stores in 4 different months in the year 2022

Stores / Months	A	B	C	D	E
January	212	168	133	182	190
February	312	250	212	175	182
March	280	275	265	255	245
April	270	280	290	305	275

Find the ratio between the total number of scooters sold by stores A and B together in January and the total number of scooters sold by stores D and E together in March?
(a) 20 : 23 (b) 18 : 23 (c) 17 : 25 (d) 19 : 25

147. A man covers a certain distance by bike. If he covers 25% of the distance at the speed of 25 km/h, 50% of the distance at the speed of 50 km/h and the remaining distance at the speed of 12.5 km/h, find his average speed over the whole journey.
(a) 20 km/h (b) 30 km/h (c) 25 km/h (d) 35 km/h

148. If the sum of two numbers is 60 and their HCF and LCM are 5 and 60 respectively, then the sum of the reciprocals of the numbers will be
(a) $\frac{1}{11}$ (b) $\frac{1}{6}$ (c) $\frac{1}{4}$ (d) $\frac{1}{5}$

149. The following table givens the number of different types of batteries sold by a company over the years numbers in innards

Type of battery Year	7AH	32AH	35AH	55AH
2018	20	30	40	50
2019	40	35	45	45
2020	50	40	40	40
2021	40	50	50	45
2022	45	45	35	55

What is the difference in the number of 7AH batteries sold in 2021 and 2022?
(a) 200 (b) 700 (c) 300 (d) 500

150. The HCF and LCM of two numbers are 9 and 126, respectively. Find the larger number, if the ratio between the numbers is 2 : 7.
(a) 42 (b) 63 (c) 77 (d) 21

Part IV

English Comprehension

151. Select the most appropriate option that can substitute the underlined segment in the given sentence.
The concert was filled with rapt teenage listeners.
(a) really fashionable
(b) boldly dressed
(c) truly energetic
(d) fully attentive

152. Select the most appropriate antonym of the given word.
Decline
(a) Escape (b) Ascend
(c) Demonstrate (d) Traverse

153. Select the most appropriate option that can substitute the underlined segment in the given sentence. If there is no need to substitute it, select 'No substitution required'.
It was a quite afternoon so, Dan decided to take a nap.
(a) an quiet
(b) an quite
(c) No substitution required
(d) a quiet

154. Select the most appropriate option to fill in the blank.
This is not .... exhaustive list of words.
(a) many (b) an
(c) a (d) No word required

155. Select the most appropriate meaning of the highlighted idiom in the given sentence.
She said she liked my hair but it turned out to be a **left-handed compliment**.
(a) A joke (b) A flattery
(c) An insult (d) A praise

156. Select the most appropriate antonym of the given word.
Redemption
(a) Salvation (b) Blasphemy
(c) Corrugation (d) Conjunction

157. Parts of the following sentence have been underlined and given as options. Select the option that contains an error.
Have they been work in that particular shop for several years?
(a) work (b) been
(c) for (d) Have

158. Select the correct spelling of the incorrectly spelt word.
He had a round face made jovial by bright, almost boyish eyes and eyebrows ridiculusly small for a man his size.
(a) ridicolusly (b) jouvial
(c) juvial (d) ridiculously

159. Select the word segment that substitutes (replaces) the bracketed word segment correctly and completes the sentence meaningfully.
Unless you (do will not prepare) well you will not perform well.
(a) would not prepare
(b) prepare
(c) will do not prepare
(d) will prepare

160. Select the most appropriate meaning of the given idiom.
Bite the bullet
(a) Decide to do what is good
(b) To bite something very hard
(c) Decide to do the inevitable which you were avoiding
(d) Decide to take the easier way out

161. Select the most appropriate antonym of the given word.
Resolute
(a) Serious (b) Wavering
(c) Steadfast (d) Brave

162. The following sentence has been split into four segments. Identify the segment that contains a grammatical error.
Roger went / to an United Kingdom / with his wife / to celebrate Christmas.
(a) Roger went
(b) to an United Kingdom
(c) to celebrate Christmas
(d) with his wife

163. Some words in the following sentences have been underlined and given as options. Select the option that contains a spelling error.
Why is everyone so, dressed up? What's the occaseon? Is it a wedding?
(a) wedding (b) occaseon
(c) everyone (d) dressed

164. Select the option that can be used as a one-word substitute for the given group of words.
To restrain or compel a person to do something by force.
(a) Convoy (b) Consensus
(c) Coerce (d) Casualty

165. Select the most appropriate option that can substitute the underlined segment in the given sentence.
Health insurance are important today since, anyone can face a medical emergency without warning.
(a) will be important
(b) has been important
(c) was important
(d) is important

166. Select the most appropriate meaning of the given idiom.
Spill the beans
(a) To make anything visible
(b) To reveal secret information
(c) To ruin someone's plan
(d) To talk randomly

167. Select the option that will improve the underlined part of the given sentence.
People say different things at different times.
(a) should say fanciful things at different times.
(b) says delectable things at different times.
(c) says whimsical things at different times.
(d) say diverse things at different times.

168. Select the most appropriate antonym of the given word.
Together
(a) Apart (b) United
(c) Freight (d) Engulf

169. Select the most appropriate antonym of the given word.
Magnificent
(a) Impressive (b) Peaceful
(c) Quiet (d) Modest

170. Select the most appropriate idiom to fill in the blank.
I have all the technical and communication skills necessary to crack any interview; it will be ....
(a) a storm in a tea cup
(b) a chip on my shoulder
(c) a hard nut to crack
(d) a piece of cake for me

171. Select the most appropriate idiom for the underlined word segment.
He seems to be undecided about whether to move to another city for better prospects.
(a) bouncing off the walls
(b) running out of steam
(c) sitting on the fence
(d) counting down the days

172. The following sentence has been split into four segments. Identify the segment that contains a grammatical error.
I have a dog and a cow. /A dog is black/44e cow is/black and white.
(a) A dog is black
(b) black and white
(c) but the cow is
(d) I have a dog and a cow

173. Select the most appropriate synonym of the underlined word.
Improved rail transport is essential for business.
(a) Recommended (b) Trivial
(c) Crucial (d) Technical

174. Select the most appropriate synonym of the given word.
Desolate
(a) Fortunate (b) Sturdy
(c) Depressive (d) Hopeful

175. Select the option that can be used as a one-word substitute for the given group of words.
An act of exchanging information
(a) Collaboration (b) Communication
(c) Touch (d) Hold

176. Select the correct spelling of the incorrectly spelt word.
They were more often abnoxious than not, impatient with me because my services had been essentially imposed upon them.
(a) obnoxious (b) impatint
(c) servises (d) essentialy

177. Select the most appropriate antonym of the underlined word in the given sentence.
All members of the association adhere to a strict code of practice.
(a) observe (b) cling
(c) flout (d) comply

178. Select the most appropriate antonym for the highlighted word.
She has a **penchant** for art and craft.
(a) anxiety (b) hatred
(c) fear (d) joy

179. Select the most appropriate option that can substitute the underlined segment in the given sentence.
The team leader tried to remain positive or optimistic in the situation, even though they were facing tough competition and limited resources.
(a) to put a strong hand forward
(b) to put on a strong exterior
(c) to put a strong desire in front of
(d) to put a brave face on

180. Select the most appropriate antonym of the given word.
Superb
(a) Infallible (b) Incorrigible
(c) Inferior (d) Splendid

181. Choose the most appropriate meaning of the underlined phrase.
He was carried off his feet when he was declared to have won the prize.
(a) was wild with excitement
(b) was dizzy
(c) bcame delirious
(d) danced on his toes

182. Select the most appropriate phrasal verb to fill in the blank.
It took seven years for Harish to............his migraine.
(a) shake down (b) shake up
(c) shake out (d) shake off

183. Select the most appropriate meaning of the underlined idiom that can be substituted in the following sentence.
The new routine will suit you to a T.
(a) nicely (b) a little bit
(c) exactly (d) very poorly

184. Select the most appropriate meaning of the given idiom.
Spill the beans
(a) Sound familiar
(b) Fail to make an impact
(c) To be very expensive
(d) Give away a secret

185. Replace the underlined segment with the most appropriate idiom/phrase from the following options.
This is the critical point of the issue. One should always be focused on it.
(a) Chip off the old block
(b) A black sheep
(c) The crux of the matter
(d) Don't cry over spilt milk

186. Select the most appropriate option that can substitute the underlined segment in the given sentence.
I like all games instead of cricket.
(a) rather (b) exclude
(c) object (d) except

187. Select the option that can be used as a one-word substitute for the given group of words.
Requiring exceptional skill or caution in performance or handling
(a) Blunt (b) Tricky
(c) Sustainable (d) Abstract

188. The following sentence has been divided into parts. One of them may contain an error. Select the part that contains the error from the given options. If you don't find any error, mark 'No error' as your answer.
(1) He could / (2) be pass his exams / (3) if he studied harder. / (4) No error
(a) 2 (b) 1 (c) 3 (d) 4

189. Select the most appropriate option that can substitute the underlined word which has been incorrectly spelt. They have begun to study in sepparate rooms.
(a) saperate (b) separate
(c) seprate (d) saparate

190. Select the sentence that has a spelling error.
A. One has to understand the rudimentery fact that intelligence and intellect are at two opposite poles.
B. An intellectual person may have all the knowledge of the world but won't know how to give it a shape.
C. Knowledge will plague the individual if he does not have the intelligence to express it.
D. Without basic intelligence, an individual is trapped within himself manifesting conflicts and ignorance in the external world.

(a) Without basic intelligence, an individual is trapped within himself, manifesting conflicts and ignorance in the external world.
(b) An intellectual person may have all the knowledge of the world but won't know how to give it a shape.
(c) Knowledge will plague the individual if he does not have the intelligence to express it.
(d) One has to understand the rudimentery fact that intelligence and intellect are at two opposite poles.

Directions (Q. Nos. 191-195) *In the following passage some words have been deleted. Read the passage carefully and select the most appropriate option to fill in each blank.*

Rabindranath Tagore founded a small school at Santiniketan in 1901 and Kala Bhavan, an art school, in 1919 which ...(1)... became a part of the Visvabharati University founded in 1921. Located in an ...(2)... village some distance from the city of Calcutta, Kala Bhavan presented an alternative methodology of art training, in which studio based practice was ...(3)... in favour of learning through observation and living as a part of nature. The natural surroundings with the ...(4)... of bare red earth dotted with trees, the colours of the changing seasons, the animals and birds ...(5)... inspiration to students.

191. Select the most appropriate option to fill in blank no. 1.
(a) better (b) later
(c) faster (d) slower

192. Select the most appropriate option to fill in blank no. 2.
(a) normal (b) magical
(c) reliable (d) idyllic

193. Select the most appropriate option to fill in blank no. 3.
(a) accepted (b) rejected
(c) investigated (d) aspired

194. Select the most appropriate option to fill in blank no. 4.
(a) vistas (b) murk (c) haze (d) band

195. Select the most appropriate option to fill in blank no. 5.
(a) groomed (b) refused
(c) provided (d) agreed

Directions (Q. Nos. 196-200) *Read the given passage carefully and answer the questions that follow.*

Mountains occupy about a quarter of the Earth's land, harbour most of its biodiversity hotspots and supply fresh water to an estimated half of humanity. Present on every continent, mountains include a multitude of ecosystems holding many unique species such as snow leopards and mountain gorillas. They are also home to great cultural diversity among people adapted to the challenges of mountain life. Their special traditions and breath-taking scenery attract ever-growing numbers of tourists.

Mountain regions are particularly sensitive to degradation from both human pressures and climate change. Steep slopes mean the clearing of forest for farming, settlements or infrastructure can cause serious soil erosion as well as the loss of habitat. Erosion and pollution harm the quality of water flowing downstream. Climate change threatens the quantity and timing of water supplies to farms, cities, industry and power stations. Fast-rising temperatures are forcing mountain species, ecosystems and the people that depend on them to adapt or migrate.

196. What is the antonym for the word 'Diversity' from the passage?
(a) Block (b) Dilemma
(c) Uniformity (d) Heritage

197. What is the antonym for the word 'Migrate' from the passage?
(a) Stay (b) Run (c) Die (d) Assume

198. Which is the best description of the tone of the passage?
(a) Laudatory (b) Emotional
(c) Biased (d) Humanistic

199. Which of the following represents the structure of the passage?
(a) Chronological
(b) Definition
(c) Compare and contrast
(d) Cause-effect

200. Which of the following most accurately states the central idea of the passage?
(a) Pollution
(b) Mountain Ecosystem
(c) Bio-degradation
(d) Climate change

Know Correct Answers

1. (b)	2. (b)	3. (b)	4. (b)	5. (b)	6. (d)	7. (b)	8. (b)	9. (a)	10. (c)
11. (c)	12. (b)	13. (b)	14. (d)	15. (b)	16. (a)	17. (d)	18. (b)	19. (a)	20. (d)
21. (b)	22. (a)	23. (c)	24. (a)	25. (b)	26. (c)	27. (a)	28. (c)	29. (c)	30. (c)
31. (d)	32. (c)	33. (d)	34. (a)	35. (c)	36. (a)	37. (a)	38. (c)	39. (b)	40. (b)
41. (a)	42. (c)	43. (b)	44. (b)	45. (c)	46. (d)	47. (d)	48. (c)	49. (a)	50. (c)
51. (b)	52. (b)	53. (a)	54. (d)	55. (c)	56. (d)	57. (d)	58. (d)	59. (b)	60. (a)
61. (d)	62. (d)	63. (c)	64. (b)	65. (c)	66. (b)	67. (c)	68. (c)	69. (c)	70. (c)
71. (a)	72. (b)	73. (c)	74. (c)	75. (b)	76. (a)	77. (b)	78. (d)	79. (c)	80. (d)
81. (c)	82. (b)	83. (b)	84. (b)	85. (b)	86. (c)	87. (b)	88. (a)	89. (c)	90. (a)
91. (b)	92. (a)	93. (a)	94. (b)	95. (b)	96. (d)	97. (d)	98. (c)	99. (b)	100. (d)
101. (b)	102. (c)	103. (a)	104. (c)	105. (c)	106. (c)	107. (d)	108. (a)	109. (a)	110. (d)
111. (b)	112. (c)	113. (b)	114. (d)	115. (a)	116. (a)	117. (c)	118. (b)	119. (b)	120. (d)
121. (c)	122. (c)	123. (d)	124. (b)	125. (c)	126. (a)	127 (d)	128. (d)	129. (a)	130. (a)
131. (c)	132. (c)	133. (c)	134. (b)	135. (a)	136. (d)	137 (a)	138. (b)	139. (b)	140. (d)
141. (d)	142. (d)	143. (a)	144. (d)	145. (a)	146. (d)	147. (c)	148. (d)	149. (d)	150. (b)
151. (d)	152. (b)	153. (d)	154. (b)	155. (c)	156. (b)	157. (a)	158. (d)	159. (b)	160. (c)
161. (b)	162. (b)	163. (b)	164. (c)	165. (d)	166. (b)	167. (a)	168. (d)	169. (d)	170. (d)
171. (c)	172. (a)	173. (c)	174. (c)	175. (b)	176. (a)	177. (c)	178. (b)	179. (d)	180. (c)
181. (a)	182. (d)	183. (c)	184. (d)	185. (c)	186. (d)	187. (b)	188. (a)	189. (b)	190. (d)
191. (b)	192. (d)	193. (b)	194. (a)	195. (c)	196. (c)	197. (a)	198. (d)	199. (d)	200. (b)

Answer & Solutions

1. **(b)** The option figure (b) will appear when given paper is unfolded after cutting.

2. **(b)** As, (53, 36, 25)

$53 - 17 = 36$

$36 - 11 = 25$

And, (71, 54, 43)

$71 - 17 = 54$

$54 - 11 = 43$

Similarly, (99, 82, 71)

$99 - 17 = 82$

$82 - 11 = 71$

3. **(b)** In both position of dice number '1' is common.

Dice I. 1 [2] B
Dice II. 1 [C] A

Hence, on opposite of C, 2 will come.

4. **(b)** In each next figure of the given figure series the whole figure is rotated 180°. So, option figure (b) will next figure of the series.

5. **(b)** The pattern of the given series as follows.

a, b, a, b, b, a/a, b, a, b, b, a/a, b, a b, b, a

⇒ aba

6. **(d)** The pattern of the given series as follows,

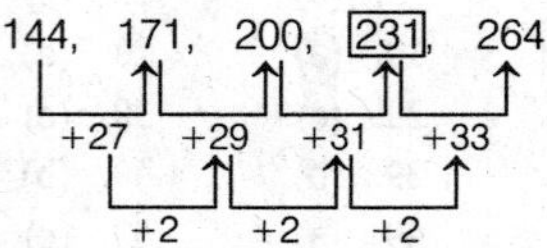

7. **(b)** The pattern of the given series as follows,

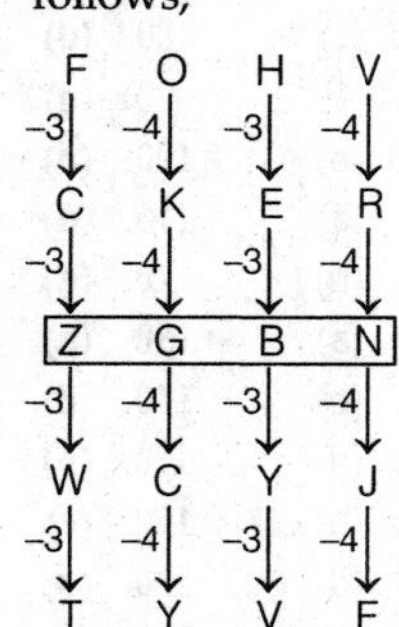

8. **(b)** In both position of dice letter 'A' is common

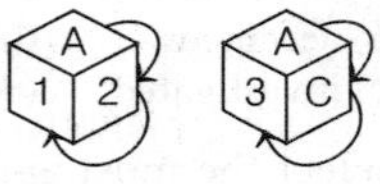

Position I. A 2 [1]
Position II. A C [3]

Hence, on the opposite face of 3,1 will appear.

9. **(a)** As,

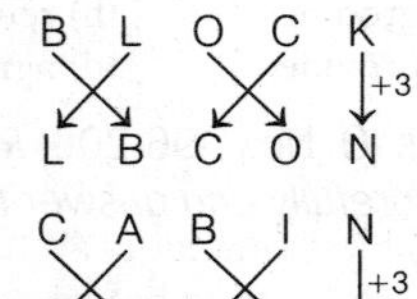

Similarly,

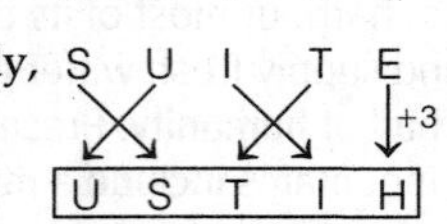

10. **(c)** Given question figure is hidden in option figure (c).

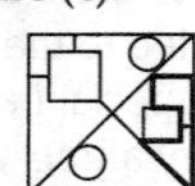

11. **(c)** As,

M O B I L E
+1 +2 +3 +4 +5 +6
N Q E M Q K

and

B I S H O P
+1 +2 +3 +4 +5 +6
C K V L T V

Similarly,

C H A R G E
+1 +2 +3 +4 +5 +6
[D J D V L K]

12. **(b)** The correct dictionary order of the given words,

Warden → Wardrobe → Warehouse →
(2) (4) (1)
Warfare → Warrant → Warship.
(6) (5) (3)

⇒2,4,1,6,5,3

13. **(b)** According to the question,

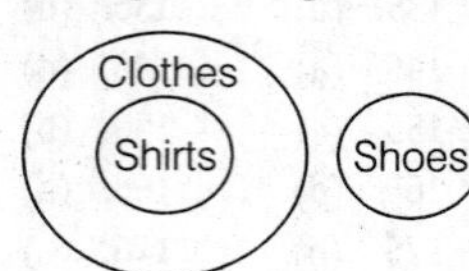

14. **(d)** The option figure (d) will appear, when it is unfolded after cutting.

15. **(b)** Given equation,

11 B 12 C 144 D 24 A 57 = ?

After replace the signs,

A ⇒ +	B ⇒ ×
C ⇒ −	D ⇒ ÷

$= 11 \times 12 - 144 \div 24 + 57$

$= 132 - 6 + 57 = 189 - 6 = 183$

16. **(a)** According to the question,

Given, D * V + B × U

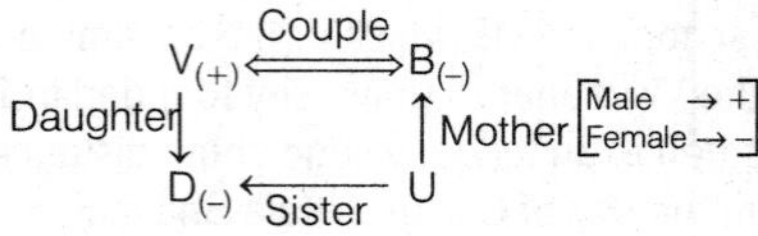

∴ D is sister of U.

17. **(d)** According to the question,

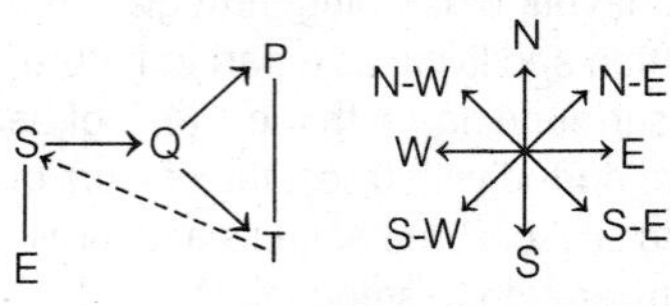

Hence, S is in the North-West direction of T.

18. **(b)** As, SPAM = 36

⇒ $4 \times 9 = 36$
↑
Numbers of letters in word

and JUG = 27

⇒ $3 \times 9 = 27$
↑
Numbers of letters in word

Similarly, FROCK = 45

$5 \times 9 =$ [45]
↑
Numbers of letters in word

19. **(a)** The given question figure is embedded in option figure (a).

20. **(d)** As,

S $\xrightarrow{-1}$ R $\xrightarrow{+5}$ W $\xrightarrow{+1}$ X

H $\xrightarrow{-1}$ G $\xrightarrow{+5}$ L $\xrightarrow{+1}$ M

P $\xrightarrow{-1}$ O $\xrightarrow{+5}$ T $\xrightarrow{+1}$ U

But, [D $\xrightarrow{-2}$ B $\xrightarrow{+5}$ G $\xrightarrow{+1}$ H]

21. **(b)** According to the question,

A # C $ V + X

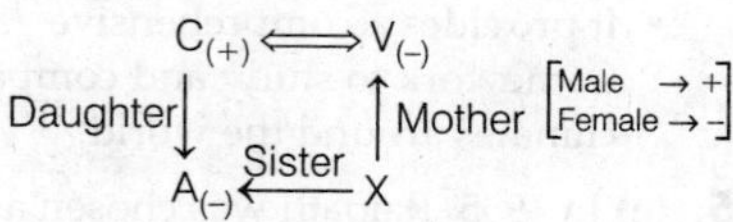

∴ A is sister of X.

22. **(a)** The option figure (a) will appear when it is unfolded after cutting.

23. **(c)** As (112, 327, 215)

⇒ 112 + 215 = 327

And, (98, 254, 156)

98 + 156 = 254

Similarly, (126, 268, 142)

126 + 142 = 268

24. **(a)** As (5, 4, 2)

⇒(5 × 2) – (2 × 3) = 10 – 6 = 4

And (9, 9, 3)

⇒(9 × 2) – (3 × 3) = 18 – 9 = 9

Similarly, (21, 39, 1)

⇒(21 × 2) – (1 × 3) = 42 – 3 = 39

25. **(b)** As per the question,

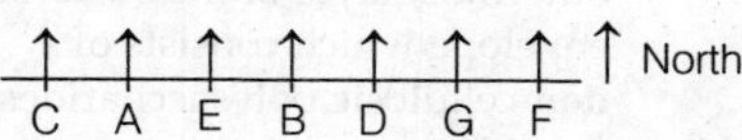

Hence, C sits to the immediate left of A.

26. **(c)** The correct dictionary order of given words.

Brief → Bright → Brine → Brocade →
(4) (3) (2) (5)

Brochure.
(1)

⇒ 4, 3, 2, 5, 1

Hence, option (c) is the correct answer.

27. **(a)** Given equation,

79 ÷ 64 × 8 – 7 + 12 = ?

After replace the signs,

+ ⇒ –	– ⇒ ×
× ⇒ ÷	÷ ⇒ +

79 + 64 ÷ 8 × 7 – 12

= 79 + 8 × 7 – 12

= 79 + 56 – 12 = 123

28. **(c)** According to the statement,

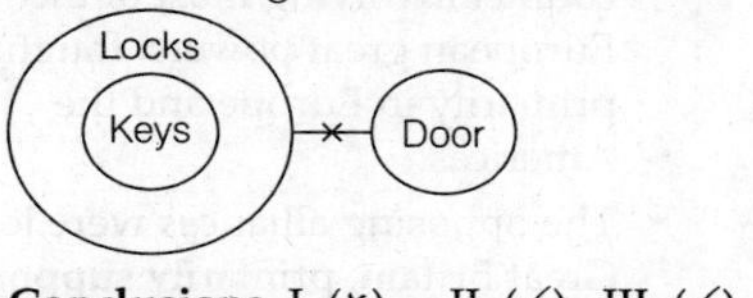

Locks

Keys

Door

Conclusions I. (×) II. (✓) III. (✓)

Hence, both Conclusions II and III follow.

29. **(c)** According to the question,

[Live] Long ⇒ [mu] ae

Road (is) Long ⇒ ae (si) du

{Game} (is) [Live] ⇒ (si) [mu] {zt}

Hence, Game is coded as zt.

30. **(c)** Given equation,

42 ÷ 7 + 11 × 87 – 12 = 141

From option (c) interchange the signs × and +,

42 ÷ 7 × 11 + 87 – 12 = 141

⇒ 6 × 11 + 87 – 12 = 141

⇒ 66 + 87 – 12 = 141

⇒ 153 – 12 = 141 ⇒ 141 = 141

LHS = RHS

31. **(d)** As, barometer is an instrument which is used to measure pressure. Similarly, multimeter is used to measure electricity.

32. **(c)** The pattern of the given series is as follows,

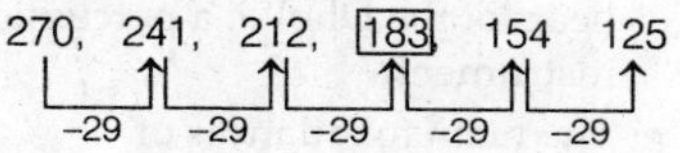

270, 241, 212, [183] 154 125

–29 –29 –29 –29 –29

33. **(d)** As, 25 : 18

⇒ 25 – (2 + 5) = 25 – 7 = 18

And 49 : 36

⇒ 49 – (4 + 9) = 49 – 13 = 36

Similarly, 37 : [27]

37 – (3 + 7) = 37 – 10 = 27

34. **(a)** According to the question,

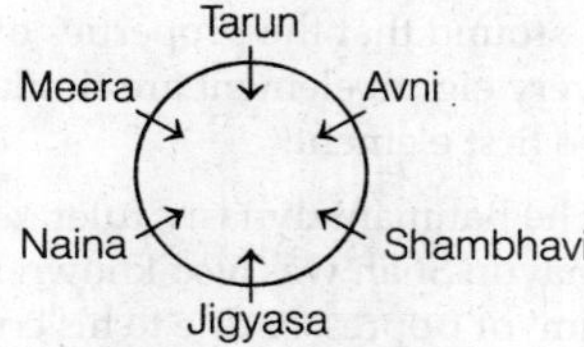

Hence, Meera is sitting second to the left of Jigyasa.

35. **(c)** The pattern of the given series as follows.

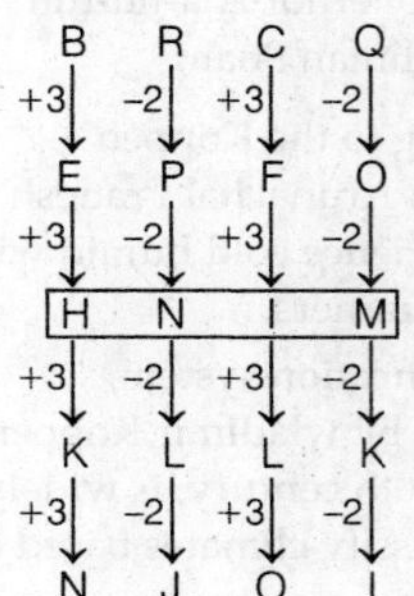

36. **(a)** According to the question,

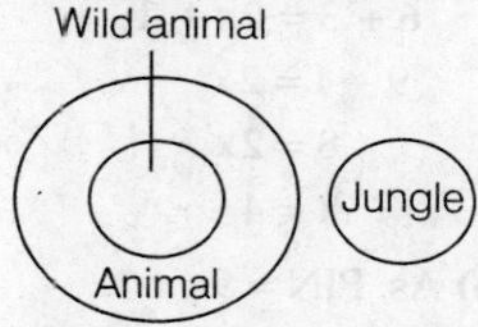

37. **(a)** According to the question,

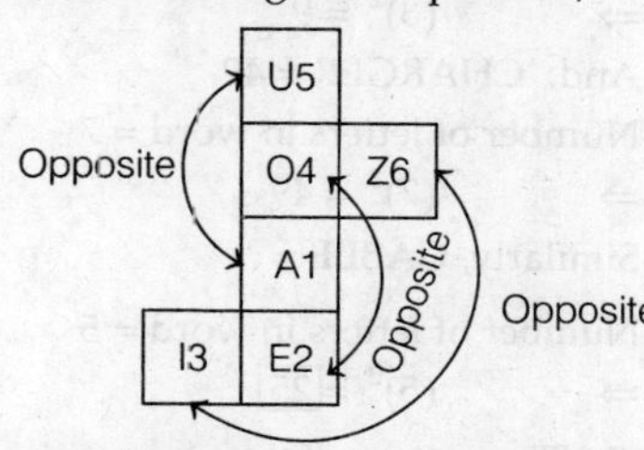

Hence, the face opposite to face showing the letter number A1 is U5.

38. **(c)** In each step of the given figure series triangle and circle are moved 90° in anti-clockwise direction so, option figure (c) will placed the 5th position to continue the given series.

39. **(b)** As, centre is a synonym of focus. Similarly, vicar is a synonym of Priest.

40. **(b)**

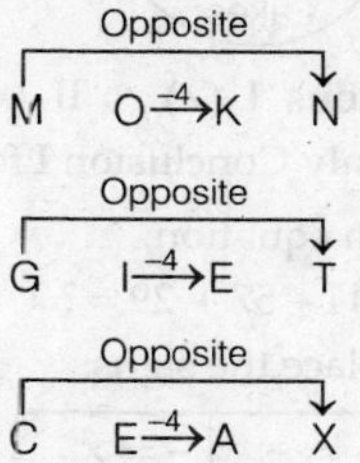

Opposite
M O $\xrightarrow{-4}$ K N

Opposite
G I $\xrightarrow{-4}$ E T

Opposite
C E $\xrightarrow{-4}$ A X

But, Opposite
S Q $\xrightarrow{+4}$ U H

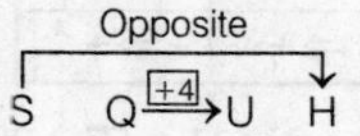

41. **(a)** Given equation,

39 ÷ 3 – 11 + 57 × 29 = 171

From option (a) interchange the signs – and ×,

39 ÷ 3 × 11 + 57 – 29 = 171

⇒ 13 × 11 + 57 – 29 = 171

⇒ 143 + 57 – 29 = 171

⇒ 200 – 29 = 171

⇒ 171 = 171

LHS = RHS

42. **(c)** According to the question,

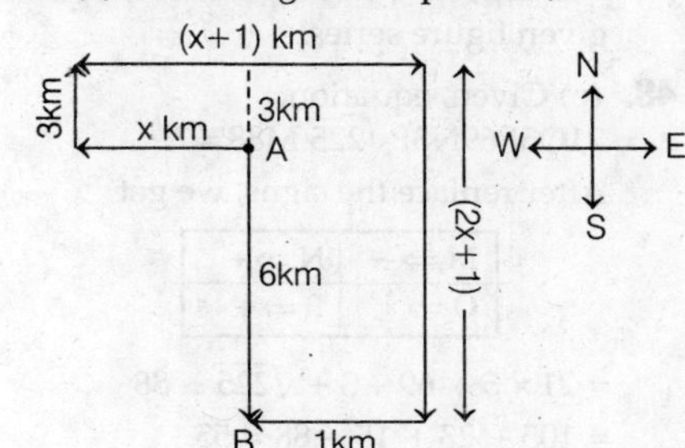

From the above diagram,

$6 + 3 = 2x + 1$

$\Rightarrow \quad 9 - 1 = 2x$

$\Rightarrow \quad 8 = 2x$

$\Rightarrow \quad x = 4$

43. (b) As, PIN = 9

Number of letters in word = 3

$\Rightarrow \quad (3)^2 = 9$

And, CHARGER = 49

Number of letters in word = 7

$\Rightarrow \quad (7)^2 = 49$

Similarly, CABLE = ?

Number of letters in word = 5

$\Rightarrow \quad (5)^2 = \boxed{25}$

44. (b) The pattern of the given series as follows

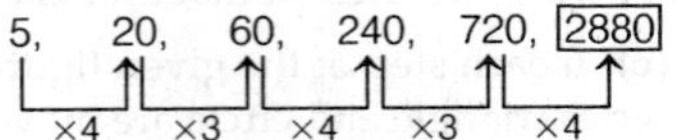

45. (c) According to the statements.

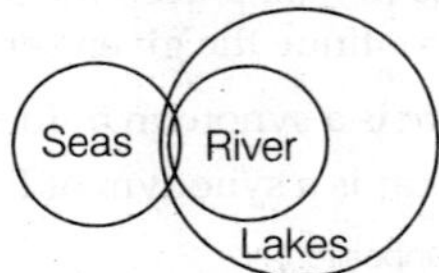

Conclusions I. (✓) II. (✗)

Hence, only Conclusion I follows.

46. (d) Given equation,

$39 \times 3 - 11 \div 57 + 29 = ?$

After replace the signs,

$+ \Rightarrow -$	$- \Rightarrow \times$
$\times \Rightarrow \div$	$\div \Rightarrow +$

$= 39 \div 3 \times 11 + 57 - 29$

$= 13 \times 11 + 57 - 29$

$= 143 + 57 - 29$

$= 200 - 29 = 171$

47. (d) The pattern of the given figure series as follows.

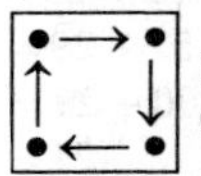

Rotate 45° in anti-clockwise direction

From this pattern option figure (d) will replace question mark (?) of the given figure series.

48. (c) Given, equation,

21O5P69N3P$\sqrt{225}$ M88 = ?

After replace the signs, we get

$M \Rightarrow -$	$N \Rightarrow \div$
$O \Rightarrow \times$	$P \Rightarrow +$

$= 21 \times 5 + 69 \div 3 + \sqrt{225} - 88$

$= 105 + 23 + 15 - 88 = 55$

49. (a) The pattern of the given series is as follows

69, 65, 67, 63, $\boxed{65}$ 61

−4 +2 −4 +2 −4

50. (c) Given, equation,

$(45 \times 2) \div 15 - (6 \times 3) + 10 - (63 \div 21) = 17$

From option (c) interchange the sign '−' and '+' we get,

$(45 \times 2) \div 15 + (6 \times 3) - 10 + (63 \div 21) = 17$

$\Rightarrow 90 \div 15 + 18 - 10 + 3 = 17$

$\Rightarrow \quad 6 + 18 - 10 + 3 = 17$

$\Rightarrow \quad 27 - 10 = 17$

$\Rightarrow \quad 17 = 17$

LHS = RHS

51. (b) Lavani is a famous folk-dance form of Maharashtra State.

- Lavani is a combination of traditional song and dance, which is particularly performed to the beats of the Dholki, a percussion instrument.
- The main folk dances of Maharashtra are Lavani, Dhangarigaja, Lezim, Koli, Gondhal and Tamasha.
- Surekha Punekar is a Lavani dancer from Maharashtra.

52. (b) John Newlands provided the Law of Octaves.

- John Alexander Newlands arranged the elements in increasing order of their atomic mass.
- He found that the properties of every eighth element are similar to the first element.

53. (a) The Bahmani dynasty ruler, Humayun Shah was also known as 'Zalim' or oppressor due to his cruelty.

- Humayun Shah ruled between 1458 and 1461.
- The Bahmani Kingdom came to power in August, 1347 AD, led by Turkish Governor Ala-ud-din Hassan Bahman Shah.

54. (d) According to the Koppen classification, Arunachal Pradesh regions experience cold humid winter with short summers.

- This classification system, developed by wladimir Koppen in the early 20th century, is widely used to classify climates based on temperature, precipitation and vegetation patterns.
- It provides a comprehensive framework to study and compare climates around the world.

55. (c) In 1955, Rajpath was chosen as the permanent venue for Republic Day celebrations.

- Rajpath, officially named Kartavya Path and formerly known as Kingsway, is a ceremonial boulevard in New Delhi.

56. (d) Scurvy is caused by not having enough vitamin C in the diet for at least 3 months leading to weakness, anaemia, gum disease and skin problems.

- Vitamin C (also known as ascorbic acid and ascorbate) is a water-soluble vitamin found in citrus and other fruits, berries and vegetables.

57. (d) Glycocalyx that is a loose sheath type called Slime layer.

- Glycocalyx (mucilage sheath) is the outermost layer of the bacterial cell envelope which consists of non-cellulosic polysaccharides with or without proteins.
- If it is a thick covering, it is called capsule.
- Glycocalyx gives sticky character to the cell and is not absolutely essential for survival of bacteria.

58. (d) Assessment of the country's GDP growth, external balance and fiscal balance represented in Macro-economic Framework Statement part of the budget document.

- Every year, a macro-economic framework statement is presented before Parliament at the time of Union Budget presentation.
- This is under Section 3(5) of the Fiscal Responsibility and Budget Management (FRBM) Act, 2003.

59. (b) The seven years of war in the 18th century was fought between Britain and France (1756-1763).

- The Seven Years' War was a global conflict involving most of the European great powers, fought primarily in Europe and the Americas.
- The opposing alliances were led by Great Britain, primarily supported by Prussia and France, backed by Spain, Saxony, Sweden and Russia.

60. (a) At the time of launch of the Smart Cities Mission, 100 cities were proposed to be covered under this scheme with the deadline for completion of the projects set between 2019 and 2023.

- As of September 2023, 6,188 out of total 7,960 tendered projects have been completed, utilising 1,13,721 crores out of total tendered amount of 1,71,432 crore.

61. (d) 156 gm - 163 gm is the standard weight of a hockey ball.

- Hockey game is played by two teams of 11 players on a rectangular ground.
- The field is 100 yards (91.4 metres) long and 60 yards (55 metres) wide and it is marked with a centre line and two 25-yard lines.
- The goals are 4 yards (3.66 metres) wide and 7 feet (2.13 metres) high.

62. (d) A and B are correct. Large bodies of water like oceans absorb heat during summer and release it during winter, reducing temperature extremes.

- Due to lower air pressure, temperatures tend to drop with increasing altitude.

63. (c) The Arms Act was passed in 1878 that prevented Indians from keeping arms without an appropriate license.

- Under this act, manufacture and sale of guns in the country were regulated. No Indian was allowed to manufacture, sell or even carry a weapon without a license from the government.
- During this period the Viceroy of India was Lord Lytton.

64. (b) President takes the salute during the Republic Day parade at New Delhi.

- Republic Day commemorates the adoption of the Constitution of India on 26th January, 1950.
- The Constitution was adopted by the Constituent Assembly of India on 26th November, 1949 and came into effect on 26th January, 1950.
- 2025 Republic Day parade chief guest was Indonesia's President Prabowo Subianto.

65. (c) According to the Census of India 2011, Himachal Pradesh has the highest Hindu population percentage of total population.

- Himachal Pradesh takes the top spot with 95.17% Hindu population.
- Hinduism is the largest religious grouping in India, with around 966 million adherents as of 2011, composing 79.8% of the population.

66. (b) Article 144 of the Indian Constitution mentions that all the authorities civil and judicial in the territory of India shall act in aid of the Supreme Court.

- This essentially means that all these authorities have a duty to assist the Supreme Court in carrying out its functions effectively.

67. (c) Brahmaputra river has the least storage capacity of usable water.

- This is due to high sediment filling reservoirs quickly, steep terrain limiting dam construction and its braided river system making storage infrastructure difficult.

68. (c) Dihang and Lohit are rivers in Arunachal Pradesh and Assam regions.

- Dihang river is the upper course of the Brahmaputra river in India.
- It originates in Tibet and enters India in Arunachal Pradesh.
- Lohit river also originates in Tibet and flows through Arunachal Pradesh before joining the Dihang to form the Brahmaputra river in Assam.

69. (c) Thumri music is most closely associated with Kathak, a classical dance form from North India.

- It originated in Eastern Uttar Pradesh, mainly in Lucknow and Banaras, around 18th century.
- Three main gharanas of thumri are Banaras, Lucknow and Patiala.
- Begum Akhtar is one of the most popular singers of thumri style.

70. (c) Chandragupta Maurya fasted to death and died at Shravanabelagola.

- Chandragupta Maurya (321-297 BCE) is the founder of the Mauryan Empire.
- Chandragupta Maurya is believed to have adopted Jainism in his later years and fasted to death (Sallekhana) at Shravanabelagola, a Jain pilgrimage site in Karnataka, India.

71. (a) Shifting agriculture is known as kumari in the Western Ghats.

- Shifting cultivation is an agricultural practice in which a plot of land was cultivated temporarily and is abandoned to allow vegetation to grow freely while the cultivator moves to another plot.

72. (b) In Odisha, Aus, Boro and Aman paddy crops are grown in a year.

- Aus refers July- August season.
- Aman refers to the December-January seasons.
- Boro refers March-May seasons, these are the varieties of rice.

73. (c) The measure of the force that can cause an object to rotate about an axis is called torque.

- And the value of this is equal to the product of the product of the magnitude of the force applied on the object and the perpendicular distance of the line of action of the force from a fixed point.
i.e., Torque $(\tau) = F \times d$

74. (c) Amir Khusrau, classical poets of the Sultanate period in India, popularised Qawwali.

- Qawwali is a form of music which derived its name from the Arabic word 'qaul', meaning 'to speak'.
- Khusrau is sometimes referred to as 'India's Parrot'.
- His music may be heard in a number of dargahs throughout the country. Khusrau is known for being the 'Father of Qawwali'.
- Amir Khusrau was renownede Sufi musician, poet and scholar during the time of Alauddin Khilji.

75. (b) The name of the 1,3-isomer (or meta-isomer) of benzenediol is Resorcinol with the chemical formula $C_6H_4(OH)_2$.

76. (a) HP Blavatsky and Colonel Olcott were the founders of the Theosophical Society.

- Theosophical Society, founded in 1875 in New York, aimed to promote theosophy.
- The Society gained significant traction in the Indian community, leading to the establishment of its headquarters in Adyar, near Madras (now Chennai), India, in 1882.

77. **(b)** Articles 12 to 35 of the Indian Constitution describe Fundamental Rights.

- **Fundamental Rights** The Constitution of India provides for six **Fundamental Rights,** Right to equality (Articles 14-18), Right to freedom (Articles 19-22), Right against exploitation (Articles 23-24), Right to freedom of religion (Articles 25-28), Cultural and educational rights (Articles 29-30), Right to constitutional remedies (Article 32).
- The Concept of Fundamental rights is inspired from the Constitution of the USA.

78. **(d)** Apicomplexa are a diverse obligate intracellular parasities group that includes organisms such as the **plasmodium,** coccidia, gregarines, piroplasma, haemogregarines.

79. **(c) Charminar** was built by Sultan **Mohammed Quli Qutb Shah** in 1591.

- It was built in honour of his wife, Bhagmati.
- Charminar has been built with granite and lime mortar and pulverised marble.
- The Charminar is situated on the East bank of Musi River.

80. **(d)** In 1932, Carl Anderson discovered the positron, a particle described as 'carrying a positive charge but having a mass of the same order of magnitude as that normally possessed by a free negative electron' and the symbol of this is e^-.

81. **(c)** Right against Exploitation forbids employment of children below the age of 14 years in dangerous jobs. Right against Exploitation is enshrined in Articles 23 and 24 of the Indian Constitution.

82. **(b)** Blindness is not the manifestation of Iron-Deficiency Anaemia (IDA).

- Vitamin A deficiency is the most common cause of blindness in children worldwide.
- It can cause vision loss and blindness and the leading cause of preventable blindness in children.

83. **(b)** My Country My Life is an autobiography of the Indian politician LK Advani.

- He served as the 7th Deputy Prime Minister of India from 2002 to 2004.
- The Prime Minister announced that LK Advani will be conferred Bharat Ratna 2024, India's highest civilian award.

84. **(b)** From Second Five-Year Plan India started its journey of industrialisation. This plan prioritised the development of heavy industries like steel, iron and machinery, aiming to build a strong foundation for future industrial growth.

85. **(b)** Both I and II are correct about Green revolution.

- The revolution began in 1960 and HYV of a seed made Green revolution a success.
- While some aspects of traditional agriculture continued, the Green Revolution focused heavily on mechanised farming and increased use of chemical fertilisers and pesticides.
- Extensive use of cattle wasn't a primary feature.

86. **(c)** Ghanakanta Bora Borbayan has been conferred the Padma Shri award for his contribution **Sattriya** dance.

- The Sattriya dance form was introduced in the 15th century AD by the great Vaishnava saint and reformer of Assam, Mahapurusha.
- Sankaradeva as a powerful medium for propagation of the Vaishnava fait.

87. **(b)** The masculine aspect of the Manipuri classical dance is known as Choloms.

- Manipuri dance is especially noted for themes based on Vaishnavism and spectacular execution of 'Ras Lila', dance dramas based on love between Radha and Krishna.
- This classical dance form primarily originated in the North-Eastern state of Manipur.

88. **(a)** Article 315 of the Constitution of India lays down the establishment of Public Service Commissions for the Union and for the States.

- As per Article 312 of the Indian Constitution, the Parliament is entitled to create one or more.
- All India services common to the Union and the States.

89. **(c) Goods and services tax is an indirect tax.**

- Indirect taxes are levied on suppliers of goods and services but the tax is passed on to the consumers, who are indirectly paying the tax.
- Examples of Indirect tax include customs duty, sales tax, excise duty, service tax, value-added tax and dividend distribution tax.

90. **(a)** The ball colour in the sport of Ball Badminton should be yellow.

- Ball badminton is a sport native to India.
- It is a racket sport game, played with a yellow ball made of wool, on a court of fixed dimensions (12 by 24 metres) divided by a net.

91. **(b)** The bicameral legislature of the Indian Constitution legislative body with two houses.

- The Constitution establishes a bicameral legislature with an Upper House (Rajya Sabha) and a Lower House (Lok Sabha).

92. **(a)** Neeru Swamy Pillai and Rajaratanam Pillai are exponents of Nadaswaran musical instrument.

- The Nadaswaram is a double reed wind instrument from South India.
- It is used as a traditional classical instrument in Tamil Nadu, Andhra Pradesh, Telangana, Karnataka and Kerala and in the North and East of Sri Lanka.

93. **(a)** Earth is estimated to be roughly 4.6 billion years old.

- Evidence suggests life emerged around 3.8 billion years ago.
- Therefore, living organisms have been on Earth for % ≈ 82.6% of Earth's history.

94. **(b)** As per the 2011 Census, among states, Bihar has the lowest literacy rate of 47%.

- The male and female literacy rate is the lowest in Bihar (**male** 71.2%, **female** 51.5%) and highest in Kerala (**male** 96.1%, **female** 92.1%).
- **Further Reading** Census of India 2011, 15th Census of India.

95. **(b)** Article 177 of the Indian Constitution refers to the Rights of Ministers with respect to the State Legislature.

- Under Article 178 of the Indian Constitution, every Legislative Assembly of a state shall, choose one of its Members as Speaker.

96. (d) In Ball Badminton, players change the ends in each game when a side first scores 9, 18, 27, except 11.

- In a game of badminton, under the current rules set by the Badminton World Federation, a singles match is won by the player who first scores 21 points, unless the score reaches 20 all.

97. (d) In 1928, Dirac equation was derived which combines quantum theory and special relativity to describe the behaviour of an electron moving a relativistic speed.

- This equation is used to predict the existence of antiparticles.

98. (c) The term 'Dribble' is associated with basketball.

- Down Screen, Dribble, Drive and Dunk are associated with Basketball.
- Basketball is indoor game.
- It is played between two teams of five players each on a rectangular court, Basketball is National game of Servia.

99. (b) Alauddin Khilji Sultans of Delhi was appointed as Amir-i-Tuzuk (Master of Ceremonies) before becoming the Sultan.

- Alauddin Khilji, who goes by the common name Alauddin Khilji was a Turco-Afghan born under the name of Ali Gurshasp.
- He was the leader and emperor of the Khalji dynasty.
- Under the rule of Alauddin, he made major changes in administration, revenues, society and prices.

100. (d) Muhammad Ali is the author of the book 'The Soul of a Butterfly: Reflections on Life's Journey.

- The Soul of a Butterfly (2003) is the autobiography of Muhammad AIi, born Cassius Marcellus Clay sr., a former heavyweight boxer who was a three-time World.
- Heavyweight Champion and is considered by many to be the greatest heavyweight of all time.

101. (b) The fourth proportional of 22, 66 and 11.

By formula,

Fourth proportional

$$= \frac{\text{Third number} \times \text{Second number}}{\text{First number}}$$

So, fourth proportional $= \frac{11 \times 66}{22}$

$= 11 \times 3 = 33$

Hence, the correct answer is 33.

102. (c) Let the marked price of the article $= x$

According to the question,

On article a discount of 25% and an additional discount of 28%.

By formula,

$$SP = MP \times \frac{(100 - D_1)}{100} \times \frac{(100 - D_2)}{100}$$

Here, SP = 10800, $D_1 = 25\%$, $D_2 = 28\%$, MP $= x$

$$10800 = x \times \frac{100 - 25}{100} \times \frac{100 - 28}{100}$$

$$\Rightarrow \quad x = \frac{10800 \times 100 \times 100}{75 \times 72}$$

$\Rightarrow \quad x =$ ₹ 20000

Hence, the marked price of the article is ₹ 20000.

103. (a) Given, marked price = 15000

By formula,

$$MP \times \frac{(100 - D_1\%)}{100} \times \frac{(100 - D_2\%)}{100} \times \frac{(100 - D_3\%)}{100} = SP$$

Here, $D_1 = 5\%$, $D_2 = 10\%$, $D_3 = 20\%$

$$SP = 15000 \times \frac{(100 - 5)}{100} \times \frac{(100 - 10)}{100} \times \frac{(100 - 20)}{100}$$

$$SP = 15000 \times \frac{95}{100} \times \frac{90}{100} \times \frac{80}{100}$$

Selling price, SP = ₹ 10260

Hence, the correct answer is 10260.

104. (c) From ratio method. The value of a washing machine depreciated

Old		New	
40960	:	21970	
4096	:	2197	{time is 3 yr}
$\sqrt[3]{4096}$	:	$\sqrt[3]{2197}$	
16	:	13	

$$\text{Depreciation} = \frac{16 - 13}{16} \times 100$$

$$= \frac{3}{4} \times 25 = \frac{75}{4}\% = 18.75\%$$

Hence, the correct answer is 18.75%.

105. (c) Let the total work = 36 unit

So, Efficiency of A and $B = 1$ unit/day

According to the question,

A and B started working together but A took a day off after every five days of work. While B took a day off after every seven days of work.

So, per day work A and B

$= 1 + 1 = 2$ unit

So, work done on each day

$= 2 + 2 + 2 + 2 + 2 + 1 + 2 + 1 + 2 + 2 + 2 + 1 + 2 + 2 + 2 + 1 + 2 + 1 + 2 + 2 + 1$

$= 36$ units

So, the work will be completed on 21st July, 2021.

106. (c) Formula used,

Number of hemisphere

$$(x) = \frac{\text{Volume of a metallic spherical ball}}{\text{Volume of a hemisphere}}$$

$$x = \frac{\frac{4}{3}\pi r^3}{\frac{2}{3}\pi R^3} \Rightarrow x = \frac{2r^3}{R^3}$$

Given, $\left(r = 3 \text{ cm}, R = \frac{3}{2}\right)$

$$x = \frac{2(3)^3 \times (2)^3}{(3)^3}$$

$x = 2 \times 8$

$x = 16$

Hence, the correct answer is 16.

107. (d) The radius of a ice piece,

$$r = \frac{d}{2} = \frac{6}{2} = 3 \text{ cm}$$

The radius of a cylindrical container

$$R = \frac{d}{2} = \frac{18}{2} = 9 \text{ cm}$$

The height of a cylindrical container

$h = 40$ cm

Formula used,

Number of ice pieces

$$(n) = \frac{\text{Volume of a cylindrical container}}{\text{Voulme of an ice piece}}$$

$$n = \frac{\pi R^2 h}{\frac{4}{3}\pi r^3}$$

$$\Rightarrow n = \frac{3 \times R^2 h}{4 \times r^3} = \frac{3 \times (9)^2 \times 40}{4 \times (3)^3}$$

$$n = \frac{3 \times 9 \times 9 \times 40}{4 \times 3 \times 3 \times 3}$$

$\Rightarrow n = 9 \times 10 \Rightarrow n = 90$

Hence, 90 ice pieces are dropped in the container.

108. (a) From given,

Slant height of a cone, $l = 29$ cm

Height of a cone, $h = 20$ cm

We know that,

Radius $r^2 = l^2 - h^2$

$r = \sqrt{(29)^2 - (20)^2}$

$= \sqrt{841 - 400} = \sqrt{441}$

$r = 21$ cm

According to the question,

$\dfrac{\text{Total surface area of a cone}}{\text{Volume of a cone}}$

$= \dfrac{\pi r(r + l)}{\frac{1}{3}\pi r^2 h} = \dfrac{3(r + l)}{h \times r}$

$= \dfrac{3(21 + 29)}{20 \times 21} = \dfrac{5}{14}$

Hence, the correct answer is 5 : 14.

109. **(a)** Here, $\Delta ABD \cong \Delta ADC$

So, $\dfrac{AB}{BD} = \dfrac{BD}{DC} = \dfrac{AB}{AC}$

$\dfrac{a}{b} = \dfrac{8}{9}$

Where, $a = 8$ (Shorter segment)

$b = 9$ (Larger segment)

Shorter segment $= \dfrac{12}{17} \times 8 = \dfrac{96}{17} = 5\dfrac{11}{17}$

Hence, the shorter segment is $5\dfrac{11}{17}$.

110. **(d)** $\cot^2 \theta = 1 - e^2$

We know that, $\cot^2 \theta = \operatorname{cosec}^2 \theta - 1$

$\therefore \quad \operatorname{cosec}^2 \theta - 1 = 1 - e^2$

$\Rightarrow \quad \operatorname{cosec}^2 \theta = 2 - e^2$

$\Rightarrow \quad \operatorname{cosec} \theta = (2 - e^2)^{\frac{1}{2}}$ ...(i)

$\therefore \operatorname{cosec} \theta + \cot^3 \theta \sec \theta$

$= \operatorname{cosec} \theta + \dfrac{\cos^3 \theta}{\sin^3 \theta} \times \dfrac{1}{\cos \theta}$

$\left[\because \cot \theta = \dfrac{\cos \theta}{\sin \theta}, \sec \theta = \dfrac{1}{\cos \theta}\right]$

$= \dfrac{1}{\sin \theta} + \dfrac{\cos^2 \theta}{\sin^3 \theta} \left(\operatorname{cosec} \theta = \dfrac{1}{\sin \theta}\right)$

$= \dfrac{\sin^2 \theta + \cos^2 \theta}{\sin^3 \theta} \quad [\because \sin^2 \theta + \cos^2 \theta = 1]$

$= \dfrac{1}{\sin^3 \theta} = \operatorname{cosec}^3 \theta$

From Eq. (i)

$= [(2 - e^2)^{1/2}]^3 = (2 - e^2)^{3/2}$

Hence, the correct answer is $(2 - e^2)^{3/2}$.

111. **(b)** $\dfrac{2 \sin A - \cos A}{\sin A + \cos A} = 1$

$\Rightarrow 2 \sin A - \cos A = \sin A + \cos A$

$\Rightarrow 2 \sin A - \sin A = \cos A + \cos A$

$\Rightarrow \quad \sin A = 2 \cos A$

$\Rightarrow \quad 2 \cos A = \sin A$

$\dfrac{\cos A}{\sin A} = \dfrac{1}{2}$

We know that, $\left(\dfrac{\cos A}{\sin A} = \cot A\right)$

$\therefore \cot A = \dfrac{1}{2}$

Hence, the correct answer is $\dfrac{1}{2}$.

112. **(c)** Given,

Time	Efficiency
A = 11 days	20 Unit/day
B = 20 days	11 — LCM (11, 20, 55)
C = 55 days	4 — Total work = 220 Unit

According to the question,

In Ist day A and B together complete 31 unit work.

In IInd day A and C together complete 24 unit work.

Total units of work in 2 days

$= (31 + 24)$ units $= 55$ units

$\therefore$ 220 units of work is done in

$= \dfrac{220}{55} = 4$

$\therefore$ Total time $= 4 \times 2 = 8$ days

Hence, the correct answer is 8 days

113. **(b)** We know that,

$\text{Average} = \dfrac{\text{Total children}}{\text{Total families}}$

Average

$= \dfrac{n_1 a_1 + n_2 a_2 + n_3 a_3 + n_4 a_4 + n_5 a_5}{a_1 + a_2 + a_3 + a_4 + a_5}$

$= \dfrac{0 \times 4 + 1 \times 22 + 2 \times 15 + 3 \times 6 + 4 \times 2}{4 + 22 + 15 + 6 + 2}$

$= \dfrac{0 + 22 + 30 + 18 + 8}{49} = \dfrac{78}{49} = 1.59$

Hence, the correct answer is 1.59.

114. **(d)** Used formula,

Distance (D)

$= \dfrac{\text{Speed [Speed + Difference in speed]}}{\text{Difference in speed}} \times \text{Difference in time}$

$150 = \dfrac{S(S + 10)}{10} \times \dfrac{45}{60} \quad [\because 1\text{h} = 60 \text{ min}]$

$\Rightarrow \quad \dfrac{150 \times 10 \times 60}{45} = S(S + 10)$

$\Rightarrow \quad S(S + 10) = 2000$

$\Rightarrow S^2 + 10S - 2000 = 0$

$\Rightarrow (S + 50)(S - 40) = 0$

$\Rightarrow \quad S = -50, S = 40$

$\because$ Speed can't be in minus, so eliminating $S = -50$

$\therefore \quad S = 40$ km/h

Hence, the correct answer is 40 km/h.

115. **(a)** Given,

The ratio of boys to girls = 3: 5

So, let the number of boys $= 3x$

and the number of girls $= 5x$

But, according to the question,

$3x + 5x = 720$

$\Rightarrow \quad 8x = 720$

$\Rightarrow \quad x = 90$

So, number of boys

$= 3 \times 90 = 270$

and number of girls

$= 5x = 5 \times 90 = 450$

According to question,

Number of new boys and girls

$= 2x$ and $3x$

But, $\quad 3x = 450 + 18$

$\Rightarrow \quad 3x = 468$

$\Rightarrow \quad x = 156$

Number of new boys

$= 2x = 2 \times 156 = 312$

Number of old boys = 270

Hence, the number of new boys may be allowed to the school

$= 312 - 270 = 42$

Hence, the correct answer is 42.

116. **(a)** From the given graph, we observed that

In 2017, the expenditure of a family $= 80000$

In 2018, the expenditure of a family $= 100000$

Increased expenditure %

$= \dfrac{100000 - 80000}{80000} \times 100\%$

$= \dfrac{20000}{80000} \times 100$

$= \dfrac{1}{4} \times 100\% = 25\%$

Hence, the expenditure of the family increased by 25% from 2017 to 2018.

117. (c) Used concept,

Largest number of whose divisible by 15, 25, 40, 75 = LCM (15, 25, 40, 75)

3	15, 25, 40, 75
5	5, 25, 40, 25
5	1, 5, 8, 5
8	1, 1, 8, 1
	1, 1, 1, 1

LCM (15, 25, 40, 75) = 3 × 5 × 5 × 8

= 600

Now, we check the option, which is completely divisible by 600. 9600 is completely divisible by 600.

Hence, the correct answer is 9600.

118. (b) We know that,

The first six prime numbers

= 2, 3, 5, 7, 11, 13

$\therefore$ Average $= \dfrac{\text{Total sum of numbers}}{\text{Total numbers}}$

$= \dfrac{2+3+5+7+11+13}{6}$

$= \dfrac{41}{6} = 6\dfrac{5}{6}$

Hence, the correct answer is $6\frac{5}{6}$.

119. (b) Let the total income = 100 unit

According to the question,

Ayush spends total money = 93 unit

So, Ayush saved money = (100 – 93)

= 7 unit

But, Ayush spends on food and recreation = 45 unit

According to the question,

7 unit = 26600

45 unit $= \dfrac{26600}{7} \times 45$

= 3800 × 45 = 171000

Hence, the correct answer is ₹ 171000.

120. (d) Total amount spent in a month = 56800

From pie-chart, total amount spent = 360°

So, 360° = 56800

$1° = \dfrac{56800}{360°}$

According to question,

Total spent by the family on housing

$= \dfrac{56800}{360°} \times 79.2°$

= 568 × 22 = ₹ 12496

121. (c) Used formula,

The number of balls,

$n = \dfrac{\text{Volume of a solid metallic sphere}}{\text{Volume of a small ball}}$

$n = \dfrac{\frac{4}{3}\pi R^3}{\frac{4}{3}\pi r^3}; \; n = \dfrac{R^3}{r^3}$

Here, R = radius of a solid metallic sphere $= \dfrac{32}{2} = 16$ cm

r = Radius of a solid ball $= \dfrac{4}{2} = 2$ cm

$n = \dfrac{(16)^3}{(2)^3} \Rightarrow n = \dfrac{4096}{8} \Rightarrow n = 512$

Hence, the correct answer is 512.

122. (c) $b + 2a - [(3b + a) - (2a + b) + 2a] - a$

$b + 2a - [3b + a - 2a - b + 2a] - a$

$= b + 2a - (2b + a) - a$

$= b + 2a - 2b - a - a$

$= 2a - 2a - b = -b$

Hence, the correct answer is $-b$.

123. (d) Given, total cost of mobile phone

= ₹ 2500

He pay in down payment = ₹ 520

Remaining amount = ₹ (2500 – 520)

= ₹ 1980

Then, SI on ₹ 1980 at 25% per annum

$SI = \dfrac{P \times R \times T}{100} = \dfrac{1980 \times 25 \times 4}{100 \times 12} = ₹\ 165$

Amount due = 1980 + 165 = ₹ 2145

Let monthly installment be ₹ x.

So, at the end of 4th month.

Ist installment $= ₹\left(x + \dfrac{x \times \frac{0}{12} \times 25}{100}\right)$

$= ₹\ x$ ...(i)

IInd installment $= ₹\left(x + \dfrac{x \times \frac{1}{12} \times 25}{100}\right)$

$= ₹\left(x + \dfrac{x}{48}\right)$ ...(ii)

IIIrd installment $= ₹\left(x + \dfrac{x \times \frac{2}{12} \times 25}{100}\right)$

$= ₹\left(x + \dfrac{x}{24}\right)$ ...(iii)

IVth installment $= ₹\left(x + \dfrac{x \times \frac{3}{12} \times 25}{100}\right)$

$= ₹\left(x + \dfrac{x}{16}\right)$ ...(iv)

So, total installment at the end of 4th month

$x + x + \dfrac{x}{48} + x + \dfrac{x}{24} + x + \dfrac{x}{16} = 2145$

$\Rightarrow 4x + \dfrac{x + 2x + 3x}{48} = 2145$

$\Rightarrow 4x + \dfrac{6x}{48} = 2145$

$\Rightarrow \dfrac{32x + x}{8} = 2145$

$\therefore x = \dfrac{2145 \times 8}{33} = ₹\ 520$

Hence, monthly installment of mobile phone is ₹ 520.

124. (b) Here, distance is constant.

So, speed depend on $\dfrac{1}{\text{time}}$.

or Speed $\propto \dfrac{1}{\text{Time}}$

So, Rakesh's speed is 40 m/s.

Rajesh's speed is 36 m/s.

Distance = 1200 m

Distance by which Rakesh beat Rajesh

$= \dfrac{1200}{40} \times 4 = 120$ m

Hence, the correct answer is 120 m.

125. (c) Used concept, 15 faculty members average monthly salary

$= \dfrac{\text{50 faculty monthly salary} - \text{35 faculty monthly salary}}{15}$

$= \dfrac{50 \times 30000 - 35 \times 37500}{15}$

$= \dfrac{1500000 - 1312500}{15} = \dfrac{187500}{15}$

Average = 12500

Hence, the correct answer is 12500.

126. (a) Given,

$\sin\theta + \cos\theta = \sqrt{2}\cos\theta$ ...(i)

Squaring on both sides of Eq. (i),

$(\sin\theta + \cos\theta)^2 = (\sqrt{2}\cos\theta)^2$

$\Rightarrow \sin^2\theta + \cos^2\theta + 2\sin\theta\cos\theta = 2\cos^2\theta$

$\Rightarrow 2\sin\theta\cos\theta = 2\cos^2\theta - \cos^2\theta - \sin^2\theta$

$\Rightarrow 2\sin\theta\cos\theta = \cos^2\theta - \sin^2\theta$

$\Rightarrow 2\sin\theta\cos\theta = -(\sin\theta - \cos\theta)(\sin\theta + \cos\theta)$

Put the value from Eq. (i),

$\dfrac{2\sin\theta\cos\theta}{\sqrt{2}\cos\theta} = -(\sin\theta - \cos\theta)$

$\therefore \dfrac{\sin\theta - \cos\theta}{\sin\theta} = -\sqrt{2}$

127. **(d)** For first toy,

$$CP = \frac{SP}{(100 + P\%)} \times 100$$

$$= \frac{1500}{125} \times 100 = ₹\,1200$$

For second toy

$$CP = \frac{SP}{(100 - L\%)} \times 100$$

$$= \frac{2800}{50} \times 100 = ₹\,5600$$

For third toy,

$$CP = \frac{SP}{(100 + P\%)} \times 100$$

$$= \frac{3500}{125} \times 100 = ₹\,2800$$

Then, total CP = 1200 + 5600 + 2800 = ₹ 9600

And total SP = 1500 + 2800 + 3500 = ₹ 7800

Here, CP > SP

Then, overall loss % $= \frac{CP - SP}{CP} \times 100$

$$= \frac{9600 - 7800}{9600} \times 100 = 18.75\%$$

128. **(d)** Given, total income = ₹ 100000

Then, expenses in housing = 15% of 100000

$$= \frac{15}{100} \times 100000 = ₹\,15000$$

Then, expenses in transport = 5% of 100000

$$= \frac{5}{100} \times 100000 = ₹\,5000$$

Then, difference = 15000 − 5000 = ₹ 10000

129. **(a)** $(x - 2y)(y - 3x) + (x + y)(x - y) + (x - 3y)(2x + y)$

$$= xy - 3x^2 - 2y^2 + 6xy + x^2 - y^2 + 2x^2 + xy - 6xy - 3y^2$$

$$= 3x^2 - 3x^2 - 2y^2 - y^2 - 3y^2 + xy + 6xy + xy - 6xy$$

$$= -6y^2 + 2xy = 2y(x - 3y)$$

130. **(a)** For least number divisible, we have to find LCM of 9, 12, 15, 25 and 27.

Then,

3	9, 12, 15, 25, 27
3	3, 4, 5, 25, 9
3	1, 4, 5, 25, 3
4	1, 4, 5, 25, 1
5	1, 1, 5, 25, 1
5	1, 1, 1, 5, 1
	1, 1, 1, 1, 1

LCM = 3 × 3 × 3 × 4 × 5 × 5 = 2700

From option (a), 10800 is multiple of 2700.

So, it is a least number which is divisible by 9, 12, 15, 25 and 27.

131. **(c)** Let HCF = x, Then, LCM = $5x$

We know, product of two numbers = HCF × LCM

$\Rightarrow \quad 20480 = x \times 5x \Rightarrow x^2 = 4096$

$\therefore \quad x = 64$

Hence, HCF = 64

and LCM = $5 \times x = 5 \times 64 = 320$

132. **(c)** For HCF find the factor

125 = 5 × 5 × 5
250 = 2 × 5 × 5 × 5
750 = 2 × 3 × 5 × 5 × 5

HCF = 5 × 5 × 5 = 125

133. **(c)** LCM of 8, 12 and 18

2	8, 12, 18
2	4, 6, 9
2	2, 3, 9
3	1, 3, 9
3	1, 1, 3
	1, 1, 1

∴ LCM = 2 × 2 × 2 × 3 × 3 = 72

134. **(b)** Ratio

$$= \frac{\text{Total number of employees in P and R together, in 2019}}{\text{Total number of employees in } Q \text{ and } R \text{ together in 2020}}$$

$$= \frac{69 + 63}{74 + 90} = \frac{132}{164} = \frac{33}{41}$$

Hence, ratio = 33 : 41

135. **(a)** Let monthly income = $7x$

and expenditure = $3x$

Given, expenditure = 5400

$\Rightarrow \quad 3x = ₹\,5400$

$\Rightarrow \quad x = 1800$

Then, monthly income = $7x$ = 7 × 1800 = ₹ 12600

136. **(d)** According to question,

30% of Ravi's income = 40% of Suresh's income

$$\therefore \frac{\text{Ravi's income}}{\text{Suresh's income}} = \frac{4}{3}$$

Let Ravi's income = $4x$ and Suresh's income = $3x$

Then, 50% of Ravi's income

$$= \frac{50}{100} \times 4x = 2x$$

Hence, Suresh's income

$$= \frac{2x}{3x} \times 100 = 66\frac{2}{3}\%$$

137. **(a)** If Arun can complete $\frac{2}{3}$rd of a work in 12 days.

Then, they can complete total work in

$$= \frac{3}{2} \times 12 = 18 \text{ days}$$

Hence, he can complete $\frac{1}{6}$th of the same work in $= \frac{1}{6} \times 18$ days = 3 days

138. **(b)** If chord of a circle = Radius of circle, then ΔAOB is a equilateral triangle.

So, all angles are 60°.

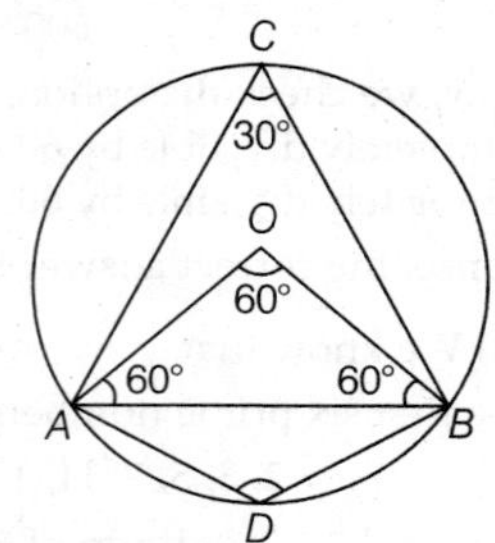

According to theorem,

$$\angle ACB = \frac{\angle AOB}{2} = \frac{60°}{2} = 30°$$

And, in quadrilateral sum of opposite angles are 180°.

Then, $\angle ADB = 180° - 30° = 150°$

Then, difference between the angle subtended by this chord at the minor arc and major arc of the circle

$$= \angle ADB - \angle ACB = 150° - 30° = 120°$$

139. **(b)** Given, $AB = 24$ cm

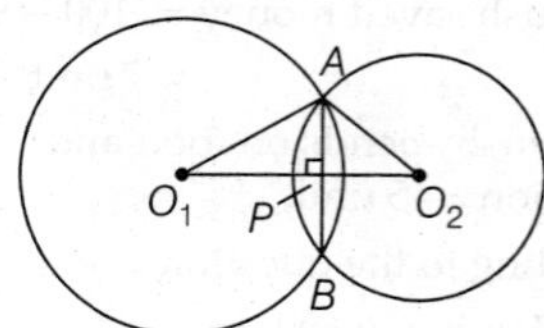

Then, $AP = \frac{AB}{2} = \frac{24}{2} = 12$ cm

And $O_1A = \frac{30}{2}$ cm = 15 cm

and $O_2A = \frac{26}{2}$ cm = 13 cm

So, in ΔAO_1P

$$(O_1A)^2 = (O_1P)^2 + (AP)^2$$

$$(O_1P)^2 = (15)^2 - (12)^2 = 225 - 144$$

$$O_1P = \sqrt{81} = 9 \text{ cm}$$

Similarly, in ΔAO_2P,

$$(O_2P)^2 = (O_2A)^2 - (AP)^2$$

$$(O_2P)^2 = (13)^2 - (12)^2 = 169 - 144$$

$$O_2P = \sqrt{25} = 5 \text{ cm}$$

Then, distance between two centres

$$= O_1P + PO_2 = 9 + 5 = 14 \text{ cm}$$

140. (d) We can clearly see from the table city B had the largest number of students. City B had = 11000 students.

141. (d) Kamal's overall average increment

$= \frac{65+55+75}{3} = \frac{195}{3} = ₹\, 65$

142. (d) Given, height of cylinder = 49 cm

And outer radius $= \frac{20}{2} = 10$ cm

And inner radius = 10 − 3 = 7 cm

∴ Volume of plastic = Volume of hollow cylinder

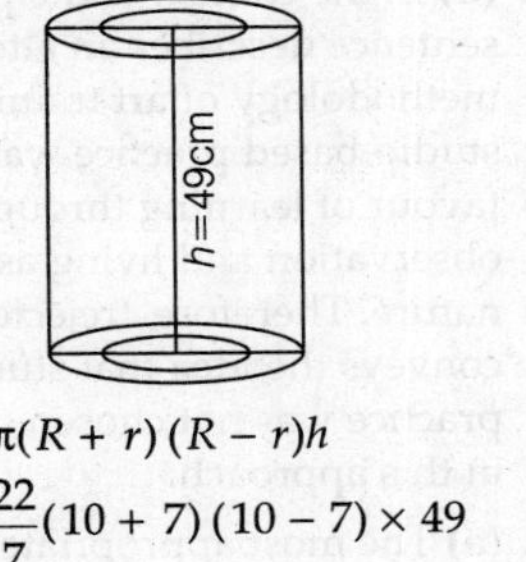

$= \pi(R+r)(R-r)h$

$= \frac{22}{7}(10+7)(10-7)\times 49$

$= 22 \times 17 \times 3 \times 7 = 7854 \text{ cm}^3$

143. (a) Given,

$2\tan^2 45° + \cos^2 30° - \sin^2 60°$

$= 2\times(1)^2 + \left(\frac{\sqrt{3}}{2}\right)^2 - \left(\frac{\sqrt{3}}{2}\right)^2 = 2$

144. (d) Ratio of CP and SP of Sugar

$= \frac{\text{CP of sugar} \times \text{weighs}}{\text{SP of sugar} \times \text{weighs}}$

$\frac{36 \times 800}{40 \times 1000}$

$\therefore \frac{CP}{SP} = \frac{36}{50}$

Then, profit% $= \frac{50-36}{36} \times 100$

$= \frac{14}{36} \times 100 = 38.89\%$

145. (a) According to question,

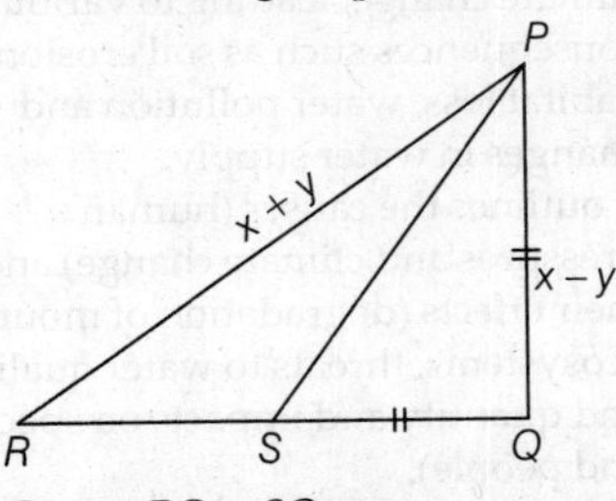

Given, $PQ = SQ$

Let $PQ = 3,\ QR = 4,\ PR = 5$

All are triplets

Then, $QS : SR = 3 : (RQ - SQ)$

$= 3 : (4-3) = 3 : 1$

146. (d) Ratio

$= \frac{\text{Total number of scooters sold by } A \text{ and } B \text{ in January}}{\text{Total number of scooters sold by } D \text{ and } E \text{ in March}}$

$= \frac{212+168}{255+245} = \frac{380}{500} = \frac{19}{25}$

Then, ratio = 19 : 25

147. (c) Let total distance = 100 km

According to the question,

25% of total distance covered by 25 km/h and 50% of total distance covered by 50 km/h.

Then, remaining 25% of total distance covered by 12.5 km/h.

Now, time taken for 25% of total distance $= \frac{25}{25} = 1$ h

Time taken for 50% of total distance

$= \frac{50}{50}$ 1h

Time taken for 25% of total distance

$= \frac{25}{12.5} = 2$ h

Then, average speed $= \frac{\text{Total distance}}{\text{Total time}}$

$= \frac{100}{1+1+2} = \frac{100}{4} = 25$ km/h

148. (d) Let the numbers be a and b.

Then, according to the question,

$a + b = 60$ ...(i)

and $a \times b = 5 \times 60$ [I × II = HCF × LCM]

$ab = 300$ ...(ii)

Now, $\frac{1}{a} + \frac{1}{b} = \frac{b+a}{ab} = \frac{60}{300} = \frac{1}{5}$

Hence, sum of the reciprocals of the numbers will be $\frac{1}{5}$.

149. (d) Difference of 7 AH batteries sold in 2021 and 2022

= 4500 − 4000 = 500

150. (b) Let the numbers be $2x$ and $7x$.

We know,

Product of two numbers = HCF × LCM

$\Rightarrow 2x \times 7x = 9 \times 126$

$\Rightarrow 14x^2 = 9 \times 126$

$\Rightarrow x^2 = 9 \times 9$

$\therefore x = 9$

Hence, larger number

$= 7x = 7 \times 9 = 63$

151. (d) The term 'rapt' typically means fully attentive or completely engrossed in something.

152. (b) The word 'decline' typically means to decrease or to move downward. The antonym of 'decline' would be 'Ascend' that means to increase or to move upward.

153. (d) The word 'quite' is incorrect in the context of the sentence. It should be replaced with 'quiet' which is an adjective that means making little or no noise, which correctly describes the afternoon in the sentence.

154. (b) The indefinite article 'an' is used before words that begin with a vowel sound like 'exhaustive'.

155. (c) A 'left-handed compliment' is an idiom used to describe a statement that, despite being superficially complimentary, actually carries a hidden insult or criticism.

156. (b) The word 'Redemption' refers to the act of being saved or rescued from sin, error, or evil. Its antonym is 'blasphemy' which refers to the act of speaking disrespectfully or irreverently about sacred things.

157. (a) As the given sentence is in present perfect continuous tense, the correct form should be 'working' instead of 'work'.

158. (d) The correct spelling is option (d), 'ridiculously'.

159. (b) In the given sentence, the phrase 'do will not prepare' is incorrect. The correct construction should be 'prepare' '(do will not prepare)' to make the sentence grammatically correct and meaningful.

160. (c) The idiom 'Bite the bullet' means to bravely endure a difficult or unpleasant situation, especially when there is no other choice.

161. (b) The word 'Resolute' means to be firmly determined or steadfast in purpose. The most appropriate antonym for 'resolute' would be 'wavering' as it conveys indecision or lack of determination.

162. (b) The part containing the error is 'to an United Kingdom'. We use 'the' with the names of places which comprises more than one country.

163. (b) The incorrectly spelt word is 'occaseon'. The correct spelling is 'occasion'.

164. (c) The word 'coerce' means to persuade or compel (someone) to do something by using force or threats.

165. **(d)** In the given sentence, the verb should agree with the subject 'health insurance', which is singular. Therefore, the correct form of the verb is 'is'. Additionally, the sentence is discussing the present importance of health insurance so, the present tense 'is important' is the most appropriate option.

166. **(b)** The idiom 'spill the beans' means to reveal secret or confidential information.

167. **(a)** The given sentence is already clear and grammatically correct. However, to enhance the sentence, the word 'diverse' can be used instead of 'different' to add a bit more sophistication and specificity to the statement.

168. **(d)** The antonym of 'together' is 'apart.'

169. **(d)** The antonym of 'magnificent', which means splendid or grand, would be 'modest', which means humble or simple.

170. **(d)** The idiom 'a piece of cake' means something that is very easy to do.

171. **(c)** The person is undecided about moving to another city, hesitating to make a decision, which is described figuratively as 'sitting on the fence'.

172. **(a)** 'A dog is black' is grammatically incorrect. The correct form would be 'The dog is black' as article 'the' is used with nouns already mentioned.

173. **(c)** The word 'essential' in the given sentence means absolutely necessary or extremely important. A synonym for essential in this context is 'crucial', as it also means extremely important or indispensable.

174. **(c)** The word 'desolate' means barren, empty or bleak, often describing a place that is deserted or showing signs of abandonment. A synonym for 'desolate' would be 'depressive', which conveys a similar sense of emptiness or bleakness.

175. **(b)** Communication is the process of exchanging information or ideas between individuals or groups.

176. **(a)** The correct spelling is 'obnoxious', not 'abnoxious'.

177. **(c)** The word 'adhere' means to stick to or follow closely. Therefore, the antonym for 'adhere' would be 'flout' which means to disregard or disobey.

178. **(b)** The word 'penchant' refers to a strong liking or preference for something. An antonym for 'penchant' would be a word indicating a strong dislike or aversion to something. Among the given options, 'hatred' fits this definition best.

179. **(d)** The phrase 'to put a brave face on' means to try to appear cheerful and confident despite difficulties or adversity. In the given sentence, the team leader is trying to remain positive and optimistic despite facing tough competition and limited resources. This aligns with the meaning of 'to put a brave face on', making it the most appropriate option to substitute the underlined segment in the sentence.

180. **(c)** The antonym of 'superb', which means excellent or outstanding, would be 'inferior', which means of lower quality or standard

181. **(a)** The phrase 'carried off his feet' means to be overwhelmed with excitement or emotion.

182. **(d)** The phrasal verb 'shake off' means to get rid of something unwanted or unpleasant. In the given sentence, Harish is trying to get rid of his migraine so, the appropriate phrasal verb to fill in the blank would be 'shake off'.

183. **(c)** The idiom 'to a T' means exactly or precisely suited to someone or something. Therefore, option (c), 'exactly', is the most appropriate meaning for the underlined idiom in this context.

184. **(d)** The idiom 'spill the beans' means to give away a secret or disclose confidential information, often unintentionally or without permission.

185. **(c)** The phrase 'the crux of the matter' refers to the central or most important point of an issue or situation.

186. **(d)** The most appropriate option to substitute the underlined segment in the given sentence is 'except' to make the sentence contextually meaningful and correct.

187. **(b)** The word 'tricky' means something that is difficult to deal with or requires careful handling due to its complexity or unpredictability. Therefore, it accurately captures the meaning of the given group of words.

188. **(a)** The use of 'be' is incorrect in 'Be pass his exam'. Remove it to correct the sentence.

189. **(b)** The incorrectly spelt word is 'sepparate'. The correct spelling is 'separate'.

190. **(d)** The word with incorrect spelling is - One has to understand the rudimentery fact that intelligence and intellect are at two opposite poles. The correct spelling is rudimentary.

191. **(b)** The word 'later' fits appropriately in the context of the passage, indicating the sequence of events.

192. **(d)** The word 'idyllic' means extremely pleasant, beautiful or peaceful. In the context of the passage, it describes the village where Kala Bhavan, the art school, is located.

193. **(b)** In the context of the passage, the sentence describes an alternative methodology of art training where studio-based practice was rejected in favour of learning through observation and living as a part of nature. Therefore, 'rejected' accurately conveys the idea that studio-based practice was not chosen or preferred in this approach.

194. **(a)** The most appropriate option to fill in the blank is 'vistas'.

195. **(c)** The word 'provided' indicates that these elements offer inspiration to the students.

196. **(c)** The antonym for the word 'diversity' from the passage is 'Uniformity'.

197. **(a)** The word 'migrate' means to move to a different place for better opportunities. Its antonym is 'stay'.

198. **(d)** The given passage presents the need to protect mountain ecosystems. It takes a humanistic tone to present how mountain ecosystems are facing problems in the current situation of climate change.

199. **(d)** The passage discusses how mountains, as ecosystems, are affected by human pressures and climate change, leading to various consequences such as soil erosion, habitat loss, water pollution and changes in water supply.
It outlines the causes (human pressures and climate change) and their effects (degradation of mountain ecosystems, threats to water quality and quantity and impacts on species and people).
This cause-effect structure is evident throughout the passage, making option (d) the most appropriate choice.

200. **(b)** The passage primarily focuses on the significance of mountain ecosystems.

CPO SI P-1 SP 12

PAPER-1

SSC CPO SI SOLVED PAPER

5 October 2023 (Shift II)

Instructions

1. This paper contains 200 questions.
2. It has 4 Parts, **Part I** General Intelligence and Reasoning, **Part II** General Knowledge and General Awareness, **Part III** Quantitative Aptitude and **Part IV** English Comprehension.
3. Each question carries **1 marks.**

MM : 200 **Time : 2 hr**

Part I

General Intelligence and Reasoning

1. Select the correct mirror image of the given figure, when the mirror is placed at line MN as shown.

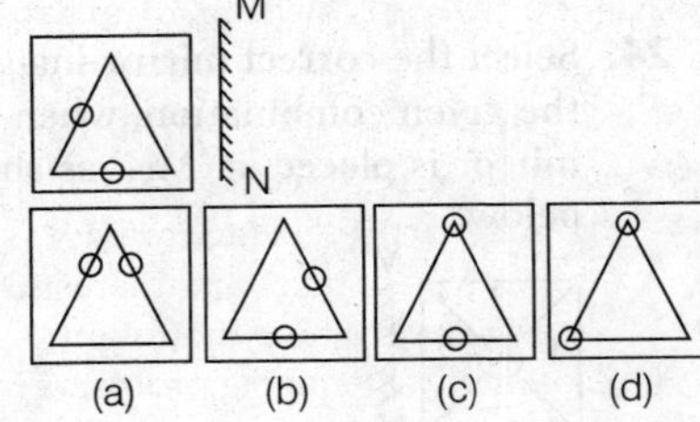

2. Two statements are given followed by three conclusions numbered I, II and III.
Assuming the statements to be true, even if they seem to be at variance with commonly known facts, decide which of the conclusions logically follow(s) from the statements.

Statements

All knives are guns.
Some bullets are knives.

Conclusions

I. Some guns are bullets.
II. No bullet is a gun.
III. Some guns are knives.

(a) Both Conclusions II and III follow
(b) Both Conclusions I and III follow
(c) Conclusions I, II and III follow
(d) Both Conclusions I and II follow

3. Select the correct option that indicates the arrangement of the given words in the order in which they appear in an English dictionary.

1. Channel 2. Chariot
3. Charcoal 4. Chapel
5. Chamber 6. Chance

(a) 5, 6, 1, 4, 3, 2 (b) 5, 1, 6, 4, 3, 2
(c) 5, 1, 6, 4, 2, 3 (d) 5, 6, 1, 4, 2, 3

4. Select the option that represents the correct order of the given words as they would appear in an English dictionary?

1. Sermonize 2. Serious
3. Servant 4. Session
5. Serrated

(a) 3, 1, 5, 2, 4 (b) 2, 3, 5, 1, 4
(c) 3, 2, 5, 1, 4 (d) 2, 1, 5, 3, 4

5. Select the option that is related to the third word in the same way as the second word is related to the first word.
(The words must be considered as meaningful words and must not be related to each other based on the number of letters/number of consonants/vowels in the word.)
Pamper : Gratify :: Devour : ?

(a) Build (b) Ravage
(c) Receive (d) Abstain

6. In a certain code language, 'CANADA' is written as 'XZMZWZ' and 'AFRICA' is written as 'ZUIRXZ'. How will 'DEPRESSION' be written in that language?

(a) XVKIVGGPLM
(b) WVKIVHHRLM
(c) XVKIVGGRLM
(d) WVKIVGGPLM

7. Which letter-cluster will replace the question mark (?) to complete the given series?
FMQX, DJSA, ?, ZDWG, XAYJ

(a) BFUC (b) BGDU
(c) BGUD (d) BEDF

8. Which of the following letters will replace the question mark (?) in the given series?
B, D, G, K, P, ?

(a) V (b) R
(c) Q (d) S

9. Amsterdam is located to the South of Barcelona. Munich is to the West of Amsterdam.
Detroit is to the East of Munich.
Toronto is to the South of Detroit and to the South-East of Barcelona.
What is the position of Amsterdam with respect to Detroit? (All positions are arranged in GRID pattern)

(a) West (b) North
(c) South (d) East

10. Select the option that is related to the third term in the same way as the second term is related to the first term and the sixth term is related to the fifth term.

98 : 115 :: 74 : ? :: 67 : 84

(a) 85 (b) 91
(c) 95 (d) 80

11. Six students P, Q, R, S, T and U are sitting around a circular table facing the centre. R is an immediate neighbour of both T and U. P is sitting third to the right of U. Q is sitting to the immediate left of S. S is sitting second to the right of P. Who is the immediate neighbour of both R and S?

(a) T (b) Q
(c) U (d) P

12. A @ B means 'A is the husband of B'. A & B means 'A is the mother of B'. A # B means 'A is the daughter of B'. If J # L @ Y & K @ Z, then how is J related to Z?

(a) Brother's wife
(b) Sister's husband
(c) Husband's sister
(d) Mother

13. Select the correct mirror image of the given figure, when the mirror is placed at line MN as shown.

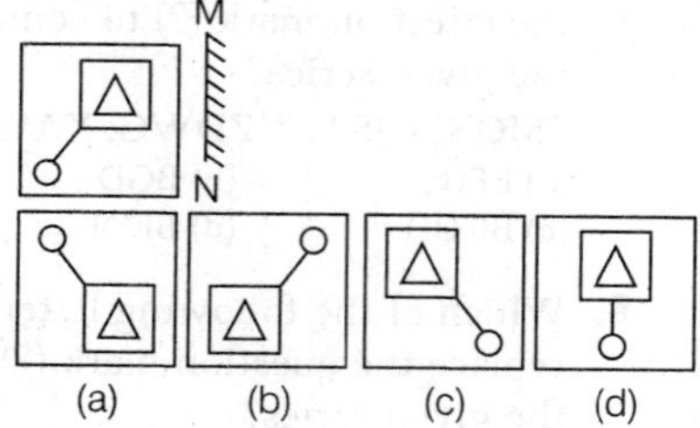

14. If '+' means '–', '–' means '÷', '÷' means '×' and '×' means '+', then what will come in place of the question mark (?) in the following equation?

$300 - 2 + 50 \times 3 \div 2 = ?$

(a) 23 (b) 106
(c) 61 (d) 661

15. In a certain code language, 'BAKED' is written as 'CCNII' and 'COOK' is written as 'DQRO'. How will 'EATING' be written in that language?

(a) FDVMRM (b) FCWMTM
(c) GDXNTN (d) FCWMSM

16. Select the option that is related to the fourth term in the same way as the first term is related to the second term and the fifth term is related to the sixth term.

7 : 40 :: ? : 667 :: 39 : 1512

(a) 34 (b) 25
(c) 47 (d) 26

17. Select the option figure that is embedded in the given figure as its part (rotation is not allowed)

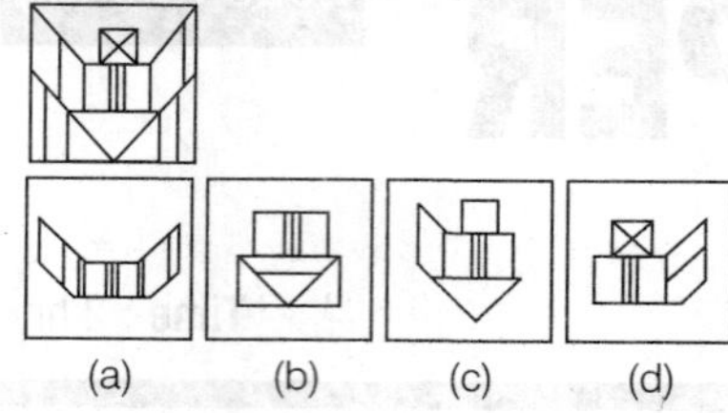

18. Select the correct mirror image of the given figure, when the mirror is placed at line MN as shown.

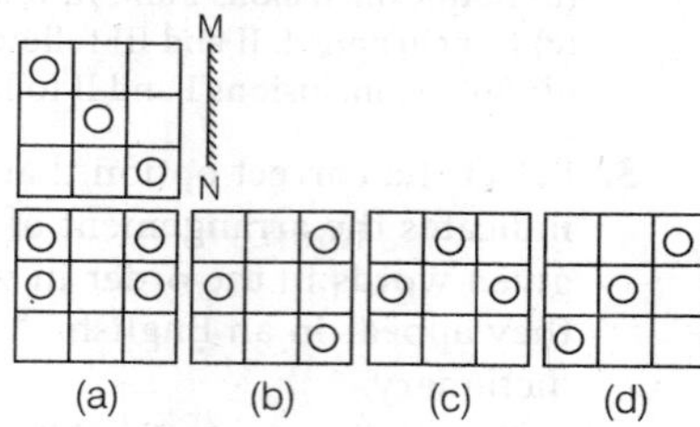

19. 'A # B' means 'A is the brother of B'. 'A * B' means 'A is the wife of B'. 'A $ B' means 'A is the daughter of B'. 'A = B' means 'A is the father of B'. If P * V # D $ B = Z, then how is B related to P?

(a) Wife (b) Husband
(c) Husband's father (d) Brother

20. Select the set in which the numbers are related in the same way as are the numbers of the following set.

(**Note** Operations should be performed on the whole numbers, without breaking down the numbers into its constituent digits. e.g. 13 – Operations on 13 such as adding /subtracting /multiplying, etc. to 13 can be performed. Breaking down 13 into 1 and 3 and then performing mathematical operations on 1 and 3 is not allowed.)

(6, 15, 1)
(5, 6, 3)

(a) (12,46,5) (b) (7,42,5)
(c) (5,32,7) (d) (15,21,8)

21. In a certain code language, 'RING' is coded as 64 and 'WATCH' is coded as 125. How will 'BRACELET' be coded in the same language?

(a) 512 (b) 504 (c) 478 (d) 343

22. In a certain code language, 'CHALK' is coded as 6-16-2-24-22 and 'BOARD' is coded as 4-30-2-36-8. How will 'PAPER' be coded in the same language?

(a) 32-2-32-12-36 (b) 32-2-32-10-36
(c) 36-2-36-12-32 (d) 36-2-36-10-32

23. Two statements are given, followed by two conclusions numbered I and II. Assuming the statements to be true, even if they seem to be at variance with commonly known facts, decide which of the conclusions logically follow(s) from the statements.

Statements

All actors are singers.
Some musicians are dancers.

Conclusions

I. All dancers are musicians.
II. Some singers are actors.

(a) Neither Conclusion I nor II follows
(b) Only Conclusion II follows
(c) Both Conclusions I and II follow
(d) Only Conclusion I follows

24. Select the correct mirror image of the given combination, when the mirror is placed at 'MN' as shown below.

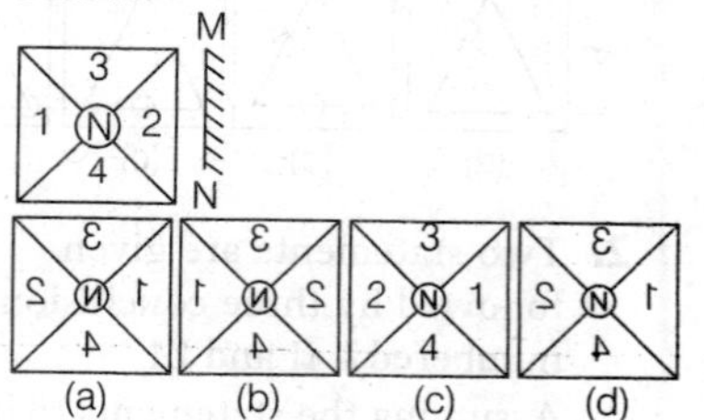

25. 6 friends are sitting around a circular table. Vini, Urja and Tanvi are sitting facing the centre and two out of Abhay, Bala and Chan are not sitting facing the centre. Vini is sitting second to the left of Chan. Urja is sitting second to the right of Abhay. Bala is sitting third to the left of Tanvi. Chan is sitting second to the right of Tanvi. Abhay is sitting next to Vini.

Who is sitting fourth to the right of Chan?

(a) Tanvi (b) Urja (c) Vini (d) Bala

26. If P denotes '×', Q denotes '÷', R denotes '+', and S denotes '–', then what will come in place of '?' in the following equation?

$\sqrt{256}$ P 3 S 66 Q 11 P 5 R 43 = ?

(a) 72 (b) 58
(c) 61 (d) 69

27. Which of the given figures, when placed in the 5th position would continue the series that is established by the first four figures?

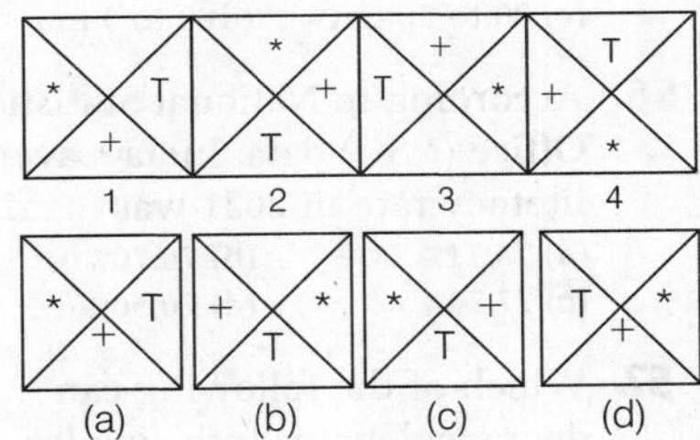

28. In a certain code language, 'BABY' is coded as '29' and 'GENDER' is coded as '52'. How will 'CRIPPLE' be coded in that language?

(a) 74 (b) 84
(c) 78 (d) 88

29. Which of the following numbers will replace the question mark (?) in the given series?

98, 126, 165, 216, 280, ?

(a) 344 (b) 358
(c) 356 (d) 348

30. Three of the following letter-clusters are alike in some manner and one is different. Select the one that is different.

(a) NPOQ (b) XZYA
(c) QSRT (d) PKQJ

31. Three of the following letter-clusters are alike in some manner and one is different. Select the one that is different.

(a) AZBY (b) ZUYV
(c) FAEB (d) UPTQ

32. If '+' means '–', '–' means '×', '×' means '÷' and '÷' means '+', what will come in place of '?' in the following equation?

137 ÷ 80 × 5 – 4 + 34 = ?

(a) 167 (b) 235
(c) 184 (d) 141

33. The sequence of folding a piece of paper and the manner in which the folded paper is cut is shown in the following figures. How would this paper look when unfolded?

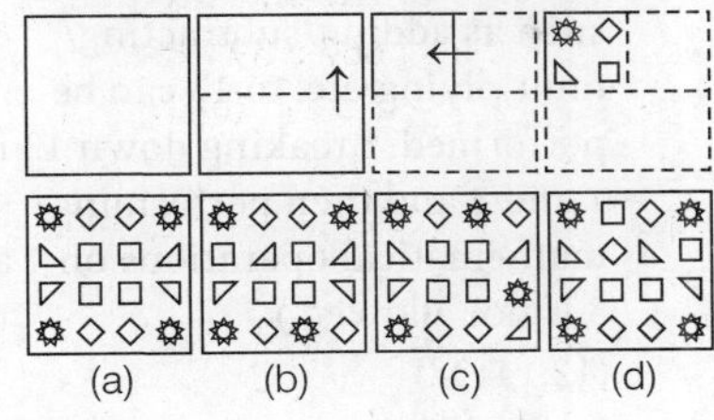

34. If '+' means '×', '×' means '–', '–' means '÷' and '÷' means '+', then what will come in place of the (?) in the following equation?

150 – 5 + 3 ÷ 23 × 3 = ?

(a) 145 (b) 111
(c) 155 (d) 110

35. Which of the following terms will replace the question mark (?) in the given series?

EQUE, ? ,GOWC, HNXB, IMYA

(a) FDVD (b) FIVD
(c) FPVD (d) FEVD

36. Select the figure that will come next in the following figure series?

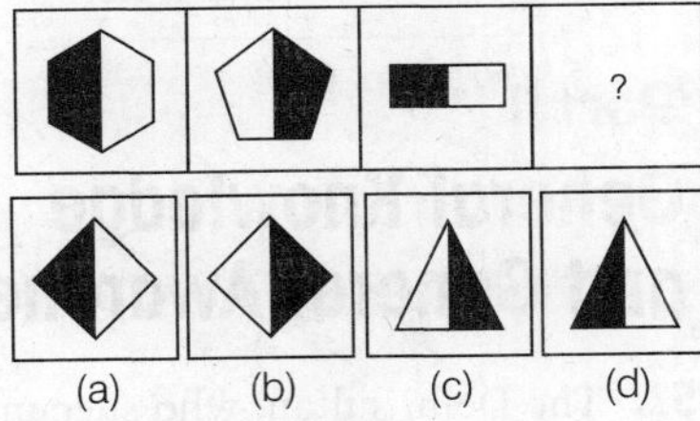

37. Two statements are given, followed by two conclusions numbered I and II. Assuming the statements to be true, even if they seem to be at variance with commonly known facts, decide which of the conclusions logically follow(s) from the statements.

Statements

All cardiologists are doctors.
Some cardiologists are neurologists.

Conclusions

I. Some doctors are cardiologists.
II. Some doctors are neurologists.

(a) Both Conclusions I and II follow
(b) Neither Conclusion I nor II follows
(c) Only Conclusion I follows
(d) Only Conclusion II follows

38. If '+' means '÷', '–' means '+', '×' means '–' and '÷' means '×', then what will come in place of (?) in the given equation?

5 ÷ 2 – 20 + 5 × 2 = ?

(a) 12 (b) 15 (c) 20 (d) 10

39. Which of the following numbers will replace the question mark (?) in the given series?

96, 12, $\frac{3}{2}$, ?, $\frac{3}{128}$

(a) $\frac{3}{12}$ (b) $\frac{1}{128}$ (c) $\frac{3}{64}$ (d) $\frac{3}{16}$

40. A paper is folded and cut as shown. How will it appear when unfolded?

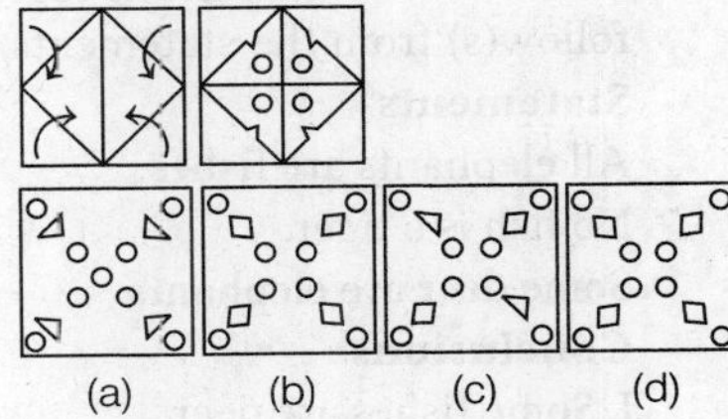

41. Which of the following numbers will replace the question mark (?) in the given series?

18, 6, 2, ?, $\frac{2}{9}$

(a) $\frac{1}{3}$ (b) $\frac{1}{9}$ (c) $\frac{2}{3}$ (d) 1

42. A paper is folded and cut as shown. How will it appear when unfolded?

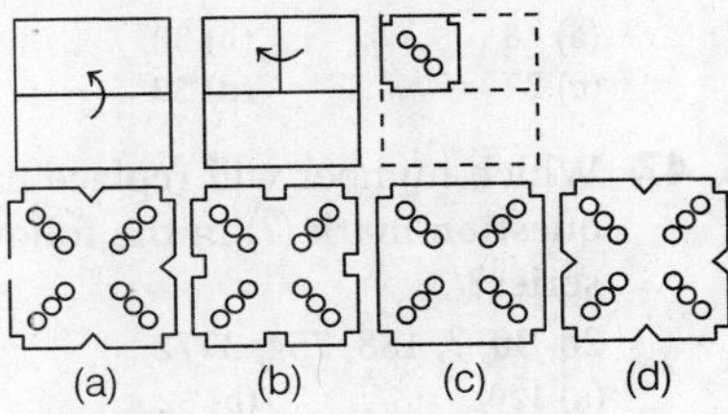

43. Param drives 8 km towards North from point A. He takes a right turn and drives 8 km. Again he takes a right turn and drives 4 km. Finally, he takes a right turn and drives 8 km to reach point B. How far and towards which direction should he drive in order to reach point A again?

(a) 5 km towards North
(b) 4 km towards South
(c) 6 km towards East
(d) 3 km towards West

44. Select the figure that will replace the question mark (?) in the following figure series.

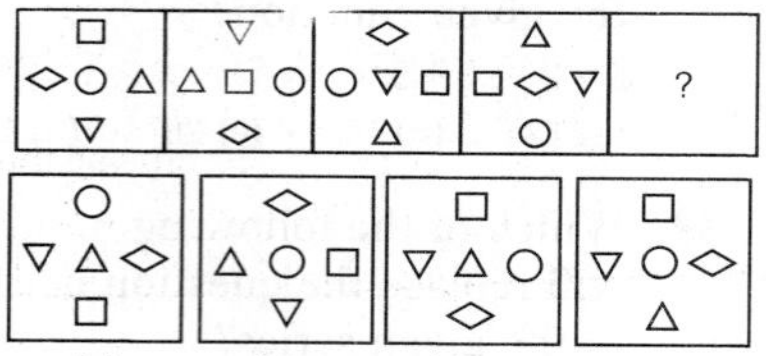

□ ◇ ○ △ ▽	▽ △ □ ○ ◇	◇ ○ ▽ □ △	△ □ ◇ ▽ ○	?

○ ▽ △ ◇ □	◇ △ ○ □ ▽	□ ▽ △ ○ ◇	□ ▽ ○ ◇ △
(a)	(b)	(c)	(d)

45. Three statements are given followed by three conclusions numbered I, II and III. Assuming the statements to be true, even if they seem to be at variance with commonly known facts, decide which of the conclusions logically follow(s) from the statements.

Statements

All elephants are fishes.

No fish is a tiger.

Some deer are elephants.

Conclusions

I. Some fishes are deer.

II. No elephant is a deer.

III. Some tigers are fishes.

(a) Both Conclusions I and III follow
(b) Only Conclusion II follows
(c) Both Conclusions I and II follow
(d) Only Conclusion I follows

46. If A denotes '+', B denotes '×', C denotes '–' and D denotes '÷', then what will be the value of the following equation?

17 B 3 A 14 D 7 C 5 = ?

(a) 48 (b) 38
(c) 29 (d) 57

47. Which number will replace the question mark (?) in the following series?

28, 30, ?, 188, 754, 3772

(a) 120 (b) 62
(c) 60 (d) 122

48. Which of the following interchange of numbers (not digit) would make the given equation correct?

$16 \times 5 \div 20 + 6 + 50 = 40$

(a) 40, 50 (b) 6, 40
(c) 20, 40 (d) 5, 40

49. Select the set in which the numbers are related in the same way as are the numbers of the following sets.

(**Note** Operations should be performed on the whole numbers, without breaking down the numbers into its constituent digits. e.g. 13- Operations on 13 such as adding/subtracting/ multiplying etc. to 13 can be performed. Breaking down 13 into 1 and 3 and then performing mathematical operations on 1 and 3 is not allowed.)

(12,14, 38)

(6, 23, 35)

(a) (8, 10, 24)
(b) (19, 9, 38)
(c) (16, 11, 43)
(d) (4, 5, 20)

50. Select the option that is related to the third word in the same way as the second word is related to the first word. (The words must be considered as meaningful words and must not be related to each other based on the number of letters/number of consonants/vowels in the word.)

Pencil : Lead :: Pen : ?

(a) Black (b) Gas
(c) Ink (d) Water

Part II

General Knowledge and General Awareness

51. The Delhi sultan, who succumbed to injuries as a result of his fall from horse was ....

(a) Iltutmish
(b) Balban
(c) Behram Shah
(d) Qutb-ud-din Aibak

52. M Balamuralikrishna is associated with which form of music?

(a) Folk music
(b) Carnatic Sangeet
(c) Haveli Sangeet
(d) Hindustani Sangeet

53. Who among the following had written 'The Dark Room' that presents an Indian woman in stiff opposition to male domination?

(a) Kuldip Nayyar
(b) RK Narayan
(c) Kazi Nazrul Islam
(d) Mulk Raj Anand

54. Which of the following is responsible for attending to disputes concerning recruitment and conditions of service of public personnel at the Centre?

(a) Joint Administrative Tribunal
(b) The Settlement and Appellate Tribunal
(c) The Competition Appellate Tribunal
(d) Central Administrative Tribunal

55. What is the length of a bacterial cell?

(a) 3 to 5 μm (b) 1 to 40 μm
(c) 30 to 50 μm (d) 0 to 3 μm

56. According to National Statistical Office (NSO) data, India's average literacy rate in 2021 was ....

(a) 78.71% (b) 76.70%
(c) 77.70% (d) 70.50%

57. Which of the following can degrade detritus into simpler inorganic substances?

(a) Lichens (b) Fungal enzymes
(c) Algae (d) Phytoplankton

58. The food component present in sugar is

(a) protein (b) vitamins
(c) carbohydrates (d) fats

59. Which of the following states has the lowest literacy rate in India according to census 2011?

(a) Bihar (b) Andhra Pradesh
(c) Odisha (d) Haryana

60. In test match cricket, how many minimum overs can a team play in a day?

(a) 80 (b) 90 (c) 70 (d) 60

61. In a basketball game, how many players from one team play on the court at any given time?

(a) 5 (b) 6 (c) 4 (d) 7

62. Which of the following places experiences extreme cold in winter and pleasant weather in summer?

(a) Amritsar (b) Leh
(c) Chennai (d) New Delhi

63. French possessions in India were restored after the Battle of Wandiwash by the Treaty of .... signed in the year 1763 between Britain and France.

(a) Paris (b) Surat
(c) Tordesillas (d) Purandar

64. When did Heinrich Hertz discover the photoelectric effect and observe that shining ultraviolet light on the electrodes caused a change in voltage between them?
(a) 1916 (b) 1902
(c) 1990 (d) 1887

65. Which of the following statements is correct?
(a) Zinc oxide is a form of rust.
(b) Copper can also turn into rust upon hydration.
(c) Chemically rust is hydrated ferric oxide.
(d) Chemically rust is non-hydrated ferric oxide.

66. Ugadi is a .... New Year celebrated in the month of March.
(a) Marathi (b) Bengali
(c) Telugu (d) Punjabi

67. Ustad Asad Ali Khan is famous for which of the following schools of Dhrupad as an instrumentalist?
(a) Gauri (b) Dagar
(c) Nauhar (d) Khandarbani

68. The drainage system formed when rivers discharge their waters from all directions in a lake or depression, as in the case of Loktak Lake in Manipur, is called ....
(a) centripetal (b) radial
(c) trellis (d) dendritic

69. Which report is not associated with Fundamental Rights?
(a) Tej Bahadur Sapru Report
(b) Sarkaria Commission Report
(c) JB Kripalani Report
(d) Motilal Nehru Report

70. The preferred IUPAC name of Allyl bromide is:
(a) 3-Bromopropene
(b) 3-Bromobutene
(c) 2-Bromopropene
(d) 1-Bromopantene

71. Kanaka Raju has been awarded Padma Shri in 2021 for which of the following folk dances?
(a) Gussadi (b) Ganagor
(c) Bhavai (d) Fugdi

72. Articles 36 to 51 of the Indian Constitution deal with ....
(a) fundamental rights
(b) fundamental duties
(c) directive principles of state policy
(d) preamble of Indian constitution

73. Calculate the GDP at factor cost given in the following data.
GDP at market price = 600 crores
Consumption of fixed capital = 100 crores
Indirect taxes = 200 crores
Subsidies = 50 crores
(a) 350 crores (b) 850 crores
(c) 950 crores (d) 450 crores

74. Which of the following was the major export item from India in 2021?
(a) Automobiles
(b) Jewellery
(c) Petroleum products
(d) Pharmaceuticals

75. Tomb of Iltutmish was built in which year?
(a) 1388 AD (b) 1458 AD
(c) 1235 AD (d) 1199 AD

76. Which of the following events took place in 1398?
(a) Humayun's flight to Persia
(b) Timur invasion of india
(c) Babur's invasion of Delhi
(d) Battle of Haldighati

77. After how many days of absence from Parliament without permission will a Member of Parliament be disqualified?
(a) 30 days (b) 50 days
(c) 20 days (d) 60 days

78. Which of the following statements is incorrect with regard to the Green Revolution?
(a) It was funded by international agencies.
(b) It was introduced in areas that were rain-fed.
(c) It was targeted mainly at the wheat and rice-growing areas.
(d) It was a government programme of agricultural modernisation.

79. The Fundamental Rights in the Indian Constitution are inspired by the 'Bill of Rights' of which of the following countries?
(a) Australia (b) Japan
(c) The USSR (d) The USA

80. Who succeeded Alivardi Khan as Nawab of Bengal?
(a) Mir Jaffar
(b) Siraj-ud-Daulah
(c) Mir Kasim
(d) Shaukat Jang

81. Identify the correct statement about gravity.
(a) The unit of g is the same as that of velocity.
(b) The unit of g is the same as that of friction.
(c) The unit of g is the same as that of mass.
(d) The unit of g is the same as that of acceleration.

82. Which of the following sets of statements are correct about Inter Tropical Convergence Zone (ITCZ)?
A. The ITCZ is a broad trough of low pressure in equatorial latitudes.
B. This is where the North-East and the South-East trade winds converge.
C. The ITCZ is the equatorial trough normally positioned about 5°N of the equator and remain there throughout the year.
D. The ITCZ moves over to the plane of Ganga in summer.
(a) A, B and C (b) Only A and C
(c) A, B and D (d) Only B and C

83. 'Wings of Fire' is the autobiography of ....
(a) Zakir Husain
(b) Rajendra Prasad
(c) APJ Abdul Kalam
(d) KR Narayanan

84. The Harshacharita is written in Sanskrit by ....
(a) Harisena
(b) Banabhatta
(c) Harshavardhana
(d) Nagasena

85. Which of the following policy measures is not a step towards liberalisation?
(a) Increase in equity limit of foreign investment.
(b) Enhancement in tariffs.
(c) Removal of industrial licensing for certain industries.
(d) Removal of requirement of registration for certain industries.

86. The Madhya Pradesh government conferred the Dhananjay, a celebrated .... couple from Chennai, with the prestigious Rashtriya Kalidas Samman for 2019-2020.
(a) Sattriya
(b) Kathakali
(c) Kuchipudi
(d) Bharatanatyam

- The overall literacy rate of Bihar was approximately 61.8%.
- Male literacy stood at 71.2%, while female literacy was significantly lower at 51.5%.
- The state faced challenges like poverty, lack of infrastructure and low female education contributing to the low rate.

Knowledge Booster
- Kerala had the highest literacy rate in Census 2011 with 94%.
- The national average literacy rate in 2011 was 74.04%.

60. **(b)** As per the rules of Test match cricket, a team must bowl a minimum of 90 overs in a day.
- The day's play typically spans 6 hours, divided into three sessions.
- If the 90-over quota is not completed in the allotted time, play is extended to meet the minimum requirement.
- The over rate is expected to be 15 overs per hour.

61. **(a)** A standard basketball team fields 5 players on the court at a time.
- These include 2 guards 2 forwards and 1 center, forming the starting lineup.
- Substitutions are allowed during stoppages, but only 5 can play simultaneously.
- This rule applies across professional leagues like the NBA, FIBA and Olympics.

62. **(b)** Leh is located in the Union Territory of Ladakh, situated at a high altitude of over 3,500 meters.
- It experiences extreme cold during winter, with temperatures dropping below -20°C.
- Summers in Leh are mild and pleasant, with daytime temperatures ranging between 15°C to 25°C.
- The region has a cold desert climate, receiving minimal rainfall due to the rain shadow effect of the Himalayas.

Knowledge Booster
- Leh lies in the Trans-Himalayan zone, making it one of the coldest inhabited regions in India.
- Due to its unique climate and terrain, it is a key location for high-altitude acclimatisation for the Indian Armed Forces.

63. **(a)** The Treaty of Paris (1763) was signed between Britain and France after the conclusion of the Seven Years' War.
- As per the treaty, French possessions in India like Pondicherry and Chandernagore were restored.
- The French, however, were allowed only trading activities in India and political ambitions were curbed.
- The Third Carnatic War (1756–1763) in India was part of the larger Seven Years' War.

64. **(d)** In 1887, Heinrich Hertz first observed the photoelectric effect while experimenting with ultraviolet light and metal electrodes.
- He noticed that shining UV light on the electrodes produced a spark, indicating a change in voltage due to emitted electrons.
- This phenomenon revealed that light can influence electrical properties of materials.
- Though discovered by Hertz, the explanation for the photoelectric effect came later through Albert Einstein in 1905.

Knowledge Booster
- Albert Einstein received the Nobel Prize in Physics (1921) for explaining the photoelectric effect, not for relativity.
- The photoelectric effect provided experimental evidence for the quantum nature of light.

65. **(c)** Rust is the hydrated form of ferric oxide ($F_2O_3 \cdot xH_2O$), formed when iron reacts with oxygen and water.
- The process is an example of a slow chemical reaction known as oxidation or corrosion.
- Zinc oxide is not rust; it forms a white powder and acts as a protective coating on galvanised iron.
- Copper does not rust like iron; instead, it forms a green layer of copper carbonate (patina) on exposure to air and moisture.

Knowledge Booster
- Rust formation is accelerated in the presence of salts or acids, making coastal areas more prone to corrosion.
- Stainless steel resists rusting due to the presence of chromium, which forms a passive oxide layer.

66. **(c)** Ugadi is the Telugu New Year, primarily celebrated in Andhra Pradesh, Telangana and Karnataka.
- The festival marks the beginning of the Chaitra month, which usually falls in March or early April.
- It is associated with the beginning of a new lunar calendar and is a major cultural celebration.
- Ugadi is known as Gudi Padwa in Maharashtra and as Navreh in Kashmir.

67. **(d)** Ustad Asad Ali Khan was a renowned rudra veena player and one of the last great exponents of the Khandarbani school of Dhrupad.
- The Khandarbani style is one of the four principal banis (styles) of the Dhrupad tradition.
- This style emphasises precision in rhythm and clarity in swaras (notes).
- The other three main Dhrupad banis are Gaurihar, Dagarbani and Nauharbani.

68. **(a)** A centripetal drainage system forms when rivers flow inward from all directions into a common depression or basin.
- It is observed in inland drainage basins, where water does not flow into the sea.
- Loktak Lake in Manipur is a prominent example of this drainage pattern.
- This type of drainage is generally associated with endorheic basins, which have no external outlet.

Knowledge Booster
- The Radial pattern is found on volcanic cones or domes where rivers radiate outward.
- The Trellis pattern develops in folded topography, where tributaries join main rivers at right angles.

69. **(b)** The Sarkaria Commission Report (1983) focused on Centre-State relations, not on Fundamental Rights.
- It was established to examine the balance of power between the Union and States in the Indian federal structure.
- The Motilal Nehru Report (1928) was the first to propose a bill of rights, including fundamental rights.
- Tej Bahadur Sapru and JB Kripalani Reports also discussed civil liberties and fundamental rights.

110. Arbind has 650 kg of wheat. A part of which he sells at 9% profit and the rest at 19% profit to get 15% profit on the whole. What is the quantity (in kg) of wheat sold by Arbind at 9% profit?
(a) 260 (b) 195 (c) 455 (d) 390

111. What is the LCM of 0.15, 0.18 and 0.45?
(a) 0.9 (b) 0.09 (c) 0.81 (d) 0.6

112. A train of length 180 m takes 40 sec. to cross a tunnel of length 500 m. What is the speed of the train, in km/h?
(a) 71.2 (b) 61.2 (c) 80.5 (d) 52.5

113. Find the value of
$$\frac{\sin^2 39°+\sin^2(90°-39°)}{\cos^2 35°+\cos^2(90°-35°)}+3\tan 25°\tan 75°$$
(a) 2 (b) 4 (c) 3 (d) 1

114. Which of the following ratios is the greatest?
(a) 2 : 5 (b) 7 : 10
(c) 5 : 6 (d) 1 : 3

115. Find the LCM of 20, 30, 45 and 65.
(a) 2000 (b) 2340 (c) 2240 (d) 180

116. The greatest possible length that can be used to measure exactly the lengths of 3 m 15 cm, 5 m and 6 m 85 cm is
(a) 9 cm (b) 11 cm
(c) 7 cm (d) 5 cm

117. If $\frac{x}{4y}=\frac{3}{4}$, then the value of $\frac{2x+3y}{x-2y}$ is
(a) 7 (b) 9 (c) 6 (d) 8

118. The difference between a discount of 30% on ₹5000 and two successive discounts of 15% and 25% on the same amount is
(a) ₹ 315.50 (b) ₹ 350.50
(c) ₹ 312.50 (d) ₹ 412.50

119. Two circles with centres P and Q of radii 6 cm and 4 cm, respectively touch each other internally. If the perpendicular bisector of PQ meets the bigger circle in A and B, then the value of AB is
(a) $\sqrt{5}$ cm (b) $2\sqrt{35}$ cm
(c) $\sqrt{35}$ cm (d) $2\sqrt{5}$ cm

120. The monthly income of an employee was ₹26500 and his monthly expenditure was ₹22000. Next year his income increased by 20% and his expenditure increased by 15%. Find the percentage increase in his savings.
(a) $44\frac{7}{9}$% (b) $44\frac{8}{9}$%
(c) $44\frac{5}{9}$% (d) $44\frac{4}{9}$%

121. Find the value of
$\sin(50°+A)-\cos(40°-A)$.
(a) 2 (b) 0
(c) −1 (d) 1

122. A sum amounts to ₹7656 in 4 yr and to ₹8120 in 5 yr at a certain simple interest rate per cent per annum. The rate of interest is
(a) 4% (b) 3%
(c) 7% (d) 8%

123. If $a-\frac{1}{a}=4$, then the value of $a+\frac{1}{a}$ is
(a) $5\sqrt{5}$ (b) $4\sqrt{5}$
(c) $2\sqrt{5}$ (d) $3\sqrt{5}$

124. Vipin can do a piece of work in 2 days; Vaibhav can do the same work in 3 days and Chirag can do the same work in 6 days. If they start working together, how many days will they take to complete the work?
(a) 3 (b) 1
(c) 5 (d) 4

125. Two successive discounts of 30% and 20% are equivalent to a single discount of
(a) 44% (b) 52%
(c) 45% (d) 50%

126. The LCM of $x^2-8x+15$ and x^2-5x+6 is
(a) $(x-2)(x-3)^2(x-5)$
(b) $(x+5)(x+2)(x+3)$
(c) $(x+5)(x-2)(x-3)$
(d) $(x-5)(x-2)(x-3)$

127. The average of 45 numbers was found to be 39. Later on, it was detected that a number 65 was misread as 56. Find the correct average of the given numbers.
(a) 39.2 (b) 37.2
(c) 38.2 (d) 36.2

128. Robert takes twice as much time as Tom and thrice as much time as George to complete a work. If working together, they can complete it in 23 hours, then find the time that Tom will take to complete the work.
(a) 46 h (b) 69 h
(c) 11 h (d) 39 h

129. Two metallic balls P and Q are such that the diameter of P is four times the diameter of Q. What is the ratio between the volumes of P and Q?
(a) 32 : 1 (b) 16 : 1
(c) 8 : 1 (d) 64 : 1

130. A runner runs a 750 m race in 54 sec. Find the runner's speed (in km/h).
(a) 40 (b) 30 (c) 14 (d) 50

131. Out of two concentric circles, the radius of the outer circle is 6 cm and the chord PQ of the length 10 cm is a tangent to the inner circle. Find the radius (in cm) of the inner circle.
(a) 4 (b) $\sqrt{7}$
(c) $\sqrt{13}$ (d) $\sqrt{11}$

132. Simplify the following.
$9\times2\div3$ of $24-3\div2\times(6-7)\times2+3\div3$ of 5
(a) 3 (b) $\frac{9}{20}$ (c) 4 (d) $\frac{69}{20}$

133. What will be the area of a plot of quadrilateral shape, one of whose diagonals is 20 m and lengths of the perpendiculars from the opposite vertices on it are 12 m and 18 m, respectively?
(a) 400 m^2 (b) 250 m^2
(c) 200 m^2 (d) 300 m^2

134. In a survey, 200 respondents were asked whether they owned a vehicle or not. Their response are tabulated below. What percentage of respondents do not own a car?

		Men	Women
Own Vehicle	Scooter	30	20
	Car	25	10
	Both	15	5
Do not own vehicle		50	45

(a) 68.5% (b) 75%
(c) 65% (d) 72.5%

135. Study the given table and answer the questions that follows.

The table shows the number of students studying in six different classes of six different schools.

School	Class V	Class VI	Class VII	Class VIII	Class IX	Class X
P	152	160	145	156	147	144
Q	148	166	150	155	157	143
R	161	152	140	145	143	165
S	159	142	149	140	142	168
T	147	144	158	163	154	150
U	150	160	162	160	161	140
Total	917	924	904	919	904	910

The number of students studying in class VII from School U is what percentage of the total number of students from all the classes together from that school (rounded off to 2 digits after decimal)?

(a) 16.48% (b) 18.25% (c) 15.63% (d) 17.36%

136. Study the following table carefully and answer the questions based on it.

The following table shows the domestic sales of vehicles of four manufacturers from 2010 to 2015.

Manufacturer	2010	2011	2012	2013	2014	2015
A	560000	580000	600000	620000	650000	680000
B	540000	590000	570000	630000	710000	550000
C	610000	580000	620000	680000	690000	630000
D	630000	570000	700000	690000	700000	640000

With respect to which of the following combination is the sales of vehicles lowest over the given period?

(a) A, 2010 (b) B, 2015 (c) B, 2010 (d) A, 2011

137. If $\sin\theta + \cos\theta = \frac{\sqrt{11}}{3}$, then what is $\sin\theta - \cos\theta$?

(a) $\frac{\sqrt{7}}{4}$ (b) $\frac{\sqrt{7}}{3}$ (c) $\frac{\sqrt{5}}{3}$ (d) $\frac{\sqrt{5}}{2}$

138. The following table shows the marks obtained out of 100, by 5 students in 5 different subjects.

Students	Hindi	English	Maths	Science	Social
Ravi	78	84	88	75	79
Abhishek	84	86	78	89	80
Ayush	88	80	90	82	85
Rohit	72	85	88	89	78
Aryan	86	88	77	79	89

What are the marks scored by Ayush in all the subject?

(a) 435 (b) 465 (c) 445 (d) 425

139. A family earns ₹75000, out of which 10% is saved. 30% of the expenditure is incurred on education, while ₹30375 is spent on health and the remaining amount is spent on food. What is the percentage of food expenditure to the total income?

(a) 32.5% (b) 22.5% (c) 20% (d) 21.5%

140. Study the given table and answer the question that follows.

The table shows the number of employees in five different organisations A, B, C, D and E in different departments.

Dept ↓ Org →	A	B	C	D	E
HR	1050	1015	976	888	1004
Finance	1017	960	786	1025	963
Marketing	1382	1384	1275	1300	1290
Production	1542	1545	4550	1570	1580
Account	786	745	801	800	735
Legal	48	54	36	30	53
Total	5825	5703	5424	5613	5625

Which organisation has maximum number of employees?

(a) A (b) B (c) D (d) E

141. Find the amount (integral value only) if a sum of ₹6,500 is being borrowed at 10% interest per annum for 2 years if interest is compounded half-yearly.

(a) ₹ 8250 (b) ₹ 7650 (c) ₹ 8150 (d) ₹ 7900

142. A can do a certain piece of work in 2·4 times the number of days in which B and C together can do it. If A and B together can do the said piece of work in 27 days and C alone can do it in 75 days, then how many days will B take to do this piece of work alone?

(a) 54 (b) 48 (c) 45 (d) 42

143. Two circles touch each other externally at C. AB is a direct common tangent to the two circles, A and B are points of contact and $\angle CAB = 55°$. Then $\angle ACB$ is

(a) 35° (b) 90° (c) 55° (d) 45°

144. The following table shows the data of 10th grade students of Portland High School

	Boys	Girls
Enrolled in Science	25	20
Not enrolled in Science	20	30

What is the approximate percentage of the 10th grade boys at Portland High School who are not enrolled in Science?

(a) 22.22% (b) 55.55% (c) 33.33% (d) 44.44%

145. Study the given pie-chart and answer the question that follows.

The pie-chart shows the sale of different fruits in a shop in a day.

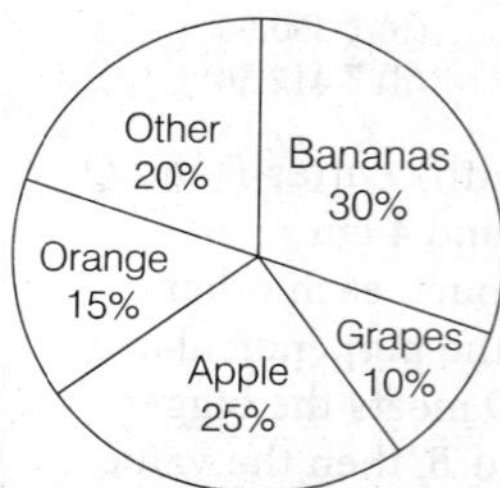

If a total of 1200 kg of fruits were sold in a day, find the difference between sales of grapes and oranges (in kg).

(a) 60 (b) 55 (c) 65 (d) 45

146. Study the given table chart carefully and answer the question that follows. The given table represents the number of employees in five different organisations, i.e. *A*, *B*, *C*, *D* and *E* in 2019, 2020, 2021 and 2022.

Organisation	Years			
	2019	2020	2021	2022
A	4000	7800	2600	5200
B	3800	9200	9100	7300
C	4500	5500	7800	3250
D	7000	3800	8000	4650
E	6600	6200	7600	2880

The ratio of the number of employees in 2019 in Organisations *D* and *E* taken together to that in 2021 in the same organisations is

(a) 9 : 14 (b) 39 : 34
(c) 14 : 9 (d) 34 : 39

147. If $\tan\theta + \cot\theta = 2$, θ is an acute angle, then find the value of $2\tan^{25}\theta + 3\cot^{20}\theta + 5\tan^{30}\theta\cot^{15}\theta$.

(a) 8 (b) 6
(c) 10 (d) 12

148. In an equilateral ΔPQR, *S* is point on the side *QR* such that $QR = 3QS$. If $PQ = 9$ cm, then what will be the length (in cm) of *PS*?

(a) $\sqrt{60}$ (b) $\sqrt{63}$
(c) $\sqrt{62}$ (d) $\sqrt{61}$

149. By selling a table for ₹1596, Aarav loses 24%. At what price (in ₹) should he sell it to gain 24%?

(a) 3196 (b) 3024
(c) 1979 (d) 2604

150. What will be the least number which when doubled will be exactly divisible by 12, 14, 16 and 18?

(a) 636 (b) 428
(c) 504 (d) 226

Part IV

English Comprehension

151. Select the most appropriate antonym for the highlighted word.

They drank some **spurious** drink and fainted.

(a) curious
(b) artificial
(c) nefarious
(d) genuine

152. Select the option that can be used as a one-word substitute for the underlined group of words.

Children and adolescents with a <u>morbid compulsion to steal</u> experience a growing sense of tension just before stealing, followed by pleasure, relief or gratification during or just after stealing.

(a) Pyromania (b) Kleptomania
(c) Dipsomania (d) Megalomania

153. Select the most appropriate idiom for the given situation focusing on the underlined segment.

I know every detail of his accident because <u>I heard the facts directly</u> from him.

(a) Speak of the devil
(b) Get something out of your system
(c) Pour one's heart out
(d) Straight from horse's mouth

154. Select the option that can be used as a one-word substitute for the given group of words.

Study of coins

(a) Philately (b) Antiquary
(c) Numismatics (d) Apothecary

155. Select the most appropriate option that can substitute the underlined segment in the given sentence. If there is no need to substitute it, select 'No substitution'.

The teacher asked the students to <u>be quite</u> during the exam.

(a) No substitution (b) be quiet
(c) have quiet (d) been quiet

156. Select the most appropriate option that can substitute the underlined segment in the given sentence.

The platter was <u>insipid</u>, so we refused to pay the bill.

(a) full of flavours (b) filled with dirt
(c) full of spices (d) lacking taste

157. Select the most appropriate meaning of the underlined idiom.

Doctors are raising <u>hue and cry</u> against the RTH bill.

(a) Enquire (b) Protest
(c) Postpone (d) Abandon

158. Select the most appropriate meaning of the underlined idiom.

Technology has become <u>a part and parcel</u> of modern lifestyle.

(a) an obstacle (b) a myth
(c) a useless part (d) an integral part

159. Select the most appropriate synonym of the given word.

Major

(a) Diligent (b) Shallow
(c) Considerable (d) Creviced

160. Select the most appropriate option to fill in the blank.

Being courteous .... costs you nothing.

(a) No article required
(b) an (c) a (d) the

161. Select the most appropriate meaning of the given idiom.

Hear someone out

(a) Let someone complete what they are saying
(b) Hear from far away
(c) Dismiss someone from listening to you
(d) Keep someone out

162. Select the most appropriate antonym of the given word.

Ethical

(a) Discord (b) Joyous
(c) Mourning (d) Immoral

163. Select the most appropriate synonym of the given word.

Vagrancy

(a) Vagueness (b) Exploration
(c) Vagabond (d) Fragrance

164. Select the most appropriate meaning of the given idiom.

Build castles in the air

(a) To make useless efforts
(b) To talk pointlessly
(c) To make imaginary schemes
(d) To build a palatial house

165. Select the most appropriate meaning of the given idiom.

Bite your tongue

(a) To scold someone verbally
(b) To drink very heavily
(c) To avoid saying something
(d) To have something explored

166. Select the option that will improve the underlined part of the given sentence. In case no improvement is needed, select 'No improvement required'.

Lily <u>has dedicate</u> her life towards becoming a doctor.

(a) had dedicate
(b) is dedicate
(c) No improvement required
(d) has dedicated

167. Select the most appropriate synonym of the given word.
Diabolical
(a) Malicious (b) Sycophant
(c) Celestial (d) Sophisticated

168. Select the incorrectly spelt word
(a) Legitimate (b) Exagerate
(c) Propagate (d) Promulgate

169. Select the most appropriate antonym of the underlined word in the given sentence.
The court absolved the defendant of all charges due to lack of evidence.
(a) accused (b) condemned
(c) attacked (d) criticised

170. Select the correctly spelt sentence.
(a) The country's GDP bloomed despite the ongoing war situation.
(b) The country's GDP bloomed dispete the ongoing war situation.
(c) The country's GDP bloomed despete the ongoing war sitution.
(d) The country's GDP bloomed dispite the ongoing war situation.

171. Select the most appropriate antonym of the given word.
Calm
(a) Turbulent (b) Shocked
(c) Variable (d) Confused

172. Select the most appropriate option that can substitute the underlined segment in the given sentence. If there is no need to substitute it, select 'No substitution required'.
The cat climbed a tree and perched itself on a branch.
(a) parched
(b) No substitution required
(c) perked
(d) perished

173. Select the incorrectly spelt word from the underlined words in the following sentence.
But he waited with the inconceivable patience and persistancy of the race; besides, he was certain, the cat was a creature of absolute convictions and his faith in his deductions never wavered.
(a) inconceivable
(b) deductions
(c) convictions
(d) persistancy

174. The following sentence has been divided into parts. One of them may contain an error. Select the part that contains the error from the given options. If you don't find any error, mark 'No error' as your answer.
I am sure Helena / would passes / with flying colours.
(a) would passes
(b) No error
(c) I am sure Helena
(d) with flying colours

175. Select the most appropriate option that can substitute the underlined segment in the given sentence.
The manager noticed a discrepancy between the two audit reports.
(a) deliberate mistake
(b) selfish interest
(c) major difference
(d) great similarity

176. Select the most appropriate option that can substitute the underlined segment in the given sentence. If there is no need to substitute it, select 'No substitution required'.
Despite of an injury, he won the match.
(a) No substitution required
(b) In spite off
(c) Despite
(d) In despite of

177. Identify the error in tense and choose the correct form of the verb in present tense from the following options.
My teacher often forget the name of students.
(a) was forgetting
(b) have been forgetting
(c) forgot
(d) forgets

178. Select the most appropriate idiom to fill in the blank and complete the meaning of the sentence.
Most of the ministers are concerned with the .... of office than the service of man.
(a) leaps and bounds
(b) loaves and fishes
(c) wear and tear
(d) Herculean task

179. Select the most appropriate meaning of the given idiom.
To let the cat out of the bag
(a) To hide the truth
(b) To be in a hurry
(c) To be careful
(d) To reveal a secret

180. Select the most appropriate antonym of the given word.
Sluggish
(a) Abnormal (b) Utterly
(c) Swift (d) Slow

181. Select the most appropriate meaning of the given idiom.
Pull yourself together
(a) Feel agitated
(b) Encourage the rich
(c) Calm down after an upsetting incident
(d) Discourage the orph

182. The following sentence has been divided into parts. One of them may contain an error. Select the part that contains the error from the given options. If you don't find any error, mark 'No error' as your answer.
He are very thirsty / Give him / a little water to drink.
(a) Give him
(b) a little water to drink
(c) He are very thirsty
(d) No error

183. Select the most appropriate meaning of the underlined idiom.
I did not even listen to him; he was only talking through his hat.
(a) Talking non-stop
(b) Talking garrulously
(c) Talking nonsense
(d) Talking ignorantly

184. Select the option that can be used as a one-word substitute for the given group of words.
A person who eats too much
(a) Glutton (b) Garrulous
(c) Greedy (d) Gullible

185. Select the most appropriate antonym of the given word.
Profane
(a) Perverse (b) Immaterial
(c) Divine (d) Barnyard

186. Select the most appropriate option that can substitute the underlined segment in the given sentence.
Fifty rupees feels too much for such a pen.
(a) looks (b) minds
(c) price (d) seems

187. Select the most appropriate antonym of the given word.
Hideous
(a) Attractive
(b) Restorative
(c) Lament
(d) Healthful

188. Identify the option that rectifies the underlined spelling error in the given sentence.
Mountainering is now looked upon as the king of sports.
(a) Mounteineering
(b) Mountainearing
(c) Mountaineering
(d) Mountainouring

189. The following sentence has been split into four segments. Identify the segment that contains a grammatical error.
One of their freighters, / a Neptune, / will be leaving/ in two weeks.
(a) One of their freighters
(b) will be leaving
(c) in two weeks
(d) a Neptune

190. Select the incorrectly spelt word.
(a) Commission
(b) Comutter
(c) Committee
(d) Camouflage

Directions (Q. Nos. 191-195) *In the following passage some words have been deleted. Read the passage carefully and select the most appropriate option to fill in each blank.*

The concept of motivation focuses on explaining what 'moves' behaviour. In fact, the term ...(1)... is derived from the Latin word 'movere', referring to movement of activity. Most of our everyday explanation of ...(2)... is given in terms of motives. Motives also help in making ...(3)... about behaviour. A person will work hard in school, in sports, in business, in music and in many other situations, if he/she has a very strong need for ...(4)... . Hence, motives are the general states that enable us to make predictions about behaviour in many different situations. In other words, motivation is one of the ...(5)... of behaviour. Instincts, drives, needs, goals and incentives come under the broad cluster of motivation.

191. Select the most appropriate option to fill in blank no. 1.
(a) psychology (b) human behaviour
(c) instinct (d) motivation

192. Select the most appropriate option to fill in blank no. 2.
(a) behaviour (b) goal
(c) incentive (d) motivation

193. Select the most appropriate option to fill in blank no. 3.
(a) clarifications (b) predictions
(c) directions (d) decisions

194. Select the most appropriate option to fill in blank no. 4.
(a) achievements (b) motivation
(c) desire (d) grow

195. Select the most appropriate option to fill in blank no. 5.
(a) meaning (b) causes
(c) ways (d) determinants

Directions (Q. Nos. 196-200) *Read the given passage carefully and answer the questions that follow.*

The rise of social media has undoubtedly changed the way we communicate with one another. It has connected people from all over the world and provided a platform for voices that were once silenced. However, as with any form of communication, social media has its down sides.

One of the most significant down sides is the spread of misinformation. With the rise of social media, anyone can become a content creator, which me that anyone can share information without fact-checking or considering the consequences. This has led to a proliferation of false information, from conspiracy theories to hoaxes, that can quickly spread and cause harm.

One recent example of this is the COVID-19 pandemic. Social media has played a significant role in the spread of misinformation about the virus and the vaccines. False claims about the safety and effectiveness of the vaccines have caused many people to be hesitant or outright refuse to get vaccinated. This, in turn, has led to the prolongation of the pandemic and the loss of many lives.

The spread of misinformation on social media is not a new phenomenon. In fact, it has been around for centuries. However, the speed and ease with which misinformation can spread on social media have made it a particularly pernicious problem in our modern world.

Throughout history, misinformation has been used to sow discord and manipulate people. For example, during World War II, the Nazi regime used propaganda to spread false information about Jews, Roma and other targeted groups in order to justify their persecution and ultimately their extermination. Similarly, during the Cold War, both the United States and the Soviet Union used propaganda to demonise one another and sway public opinion.

The difference now is that social media has made it easier than ever to spread false information. A single post or tweet can reach millions of people within seconds and it can be difficult to counteract the effects of that misinformation once it has spread. So, what can we do about it? The answer is not simple, but it starts with education.

We need to teach people how to think critically, how to fact-check and how to discern between credible sources and fake news. We also need to hold social media companies accountable for the content on their platforms and ensure that they are doing their part to combat the spread of misinformation.

In short, the rise of social media has given us a powerful tool for communication, but we must use it wisely. We must be vigilant against the spread of misinfor- mation and work together to ensure that the information we consume and share is accurate and reliable.

196. What is the antonym of the word 'accurate', as used in the passage?
(a) Correct (b) Inexact
(c) Precise (d) Reliable

197. Identify the main theme of the passage.
(a) The role of education in combating misinformation.
(b) The dangers of spreading false information on social media.
(c) The significance of propaganda and misinformation.
(d) The benefits of social media for communication.

198. According to the passage, which of the following is not a cause of the spread of false information on social media?

(a) Lack of education and critical thinking skills among social media users.
(b) Inability to discem between credible sources and fake news.
(c) Social media companies 'failure to regulate false information on their platforms.
(d) The desire of people to engage in controversial and sensational content.

199. What is the author's opinion of social mecia in this passage?

(a) Social media was has had a mostly positive impact on society, despite some drawbacks.
(b) Social media is responsible for the spread of false information, but its impact on society is otherwise neutral.
(c) Social media has changed the way we communicate, but has also brought about significant negative consequences.
(d) Social media is a powerful tool for communication that has many benefits.

200. What is the author's purpose is writing this passage?

(a) To warn readers of the dangers of spreading false information on social media.
(b) To provide an in-depth analysis of the benefits of social media for communication.
(c) To explain the history of propaganda and misinformation and its impact on society.
(d) To persuade readers to delete their social media accounts.

Know Correct Answers

1. (b)	2. (b)	3. (a)	4. (d)	5. (b)	6. (b)	7. (c)	8. (a)	9. (a)	10. (b)
11. (c)	12. (c)	13. (c)	14. (b)	15. (d)	16. (d)	17. (c)	18. (d)	19. (c)	20. (d)
21. (a)	22. (b)	23. (b)	24. (a)	25. (c)	26. (c)	27. (a)	28. (c)	29. (b)	30. (d)
31. (a)	32. (a)	33. (a)	34. (d)	35. (c)	36. (c)	37. (a)	38. (a)	39. (d)	40. (c)
41. (c)	42. (b)	43. (b)	44. (a)	45. (d)	46. (a)	47. (b)	48. (a)	49. (c)	50. (c)
51. (d)	52. (b)	53. (b)	54. (d)	55. (a)	56. (c)	57. (b)	58. (c)	59. (a)	60. (b)
61. (a)	62. (b)	63. (a)	64. (d)	65. (c)	66. (c)	67. (d)	68. (a)	69. (b)	70. (a)
71. (a)	72. (c)	73. (d)	74. (c)	75. (c)	76. (b)	77. (d)	78. (b)	79. (d)	80. (b)
81. (d)	82. (c)	83. (c)	84. (b)	85. (b)	86. (d)	87. (d)	88. (c)	89. (b)	90. (d)
91. (a)	92. (c)	93. (c)	94. (b)	95. (c)	96. (d)	97. (a)	98. (c)	99. (b)	100. (b)
101. (d)	102. (b)	103. (d)	104. (d)	105. (c)	106. (c)	107. (c)	108. (d)	109. (b)	110. (a)
111. (a)	112. (b)	113. (b)	114. (c)	115. (b)	116. (d)	117. (b)	118. (c)	119. (b)	120. (d)
121. (b)	122. (d)	123. (c)	124. (b)	125. (a)	126. (d)	127 (a)	128. (b)	129. (d)	130. (d)
131. (d)	132. (d)	133. (d)	134. (d)	135. (d)	136. (c)	137 (b)	138. (d)	139. (b)	140. (a)
141. (d)	142. (c)	143. (b)	144. (d)	145. (a)	146. (d)	147. (c)	148. (b)	149. (d)	150. (c)
151. (d)	152. (b)	153. (d)	154. (c)	155. (b)	156. (d)	157. (b)	158. (d)	159. (c)	160. (a)
161. (a)	162. (d)	163. (c)	164. (c)	165. (c)	166. (d)	167. (a)	168. (b)	169. (a)	170. (a)
171. (a)	172. (b)	173. (d)	174. (a)	175. (c)	176. (c)	177. (d)	178. (b)	179. (d)	180. (c)
181. (c)	182. (c)	183. (c)	184. (a)	185. (c)	186. (d)	187. (a)	188. (c)	189. (d)	190. (b)
191. (d)	192. (a)	193. (b)	194. (a)	195. (d)	196. (b)	197. (b)	198. (d)	199. (c)	200. (a)

Answer & Solutions

1. (b) Option figure (b) is the correct mirror image of the given figure, when the mirror is placed at the 'MN' line.

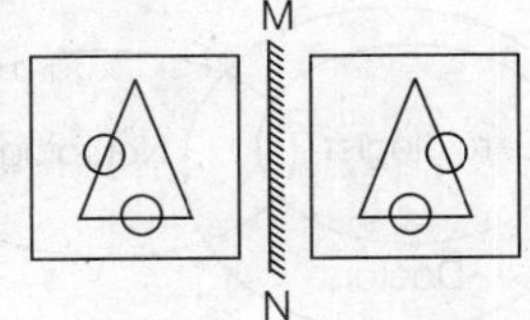

2. (b) According to the statements,

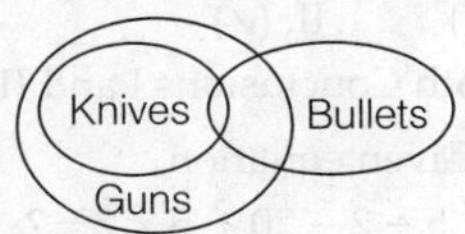

Conclusions

I. (✓) II. (✗) III. (✓)

∴ Both Conclusions I and III follow.

3. (a) The order of the words in dictionary is

Chamber (5) → Chance (6) → Channel (1) → Chapel (4) → Charcoal (3) → Chariot (2)

⇒ 5, 6, 1, 4, 3, 2

4. (d) The order of the words in dictionary is

Serious (2) → Sermonize (1) → Serrated (5) → Servant (3) → Session(4)

⇒ 2,1,5,3,4

5. (b) Here, the first word is a synonym of the second word, and both relate to satisfying desire(s) or indulging someone.

Therefore, Ravage is the correct answer.

6. (b) As,

Similarly,

7. (c) Pattern of the series is as follows,

F $\xrightarrow{-2}$ D $\xrightarrow{-2}$ B $\xrightarrow{-2}$ Z $\xrightarrow{-2}$ X

M $\xrightarrow{-3}$ J $\xrightarrow{-3}$ G $\xrightarrow{-3}$ D $\xrightarrow{-3}$ A

Q $\xrightarrow{+2}$ S $\xrightarrow{+2}$ U $\xrightarrow{+2}$ W $\xrightarrow{+2}$ Y

X $\xrightarrow{+3}$ A $\xrightarrow{+3}$ D $\xrightarrow{+3}$ G $\xrightarrow{+3}$ J

8. (a) Pattern of the series is as follows,

B $\xrightarrow{+2}$ D $\xrightarrow{+3}$ G $\xrightarrow{+4}$ K $\xrightarrow{+5}$ P $\xrightarrow{+6}$ V

9. (a) According to the question,

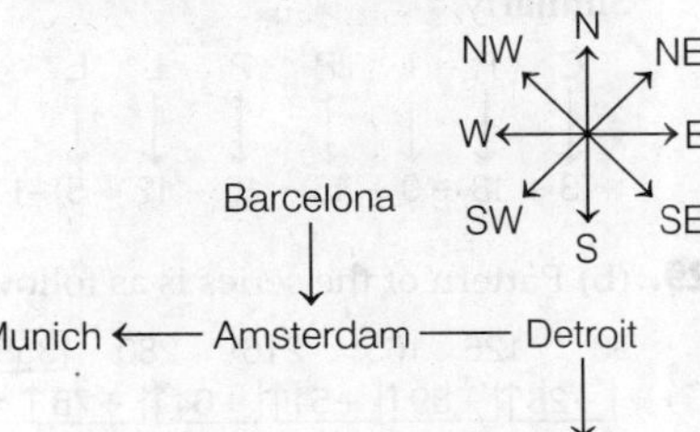

∴ It is clearly shown that Amsterdam is in the West direction of Detroit.

10. (b) As, 98 + 17 = 115

and 67 + 17 = 84

Similarly, 74 + 17 = 91

11. (c) According to the question,

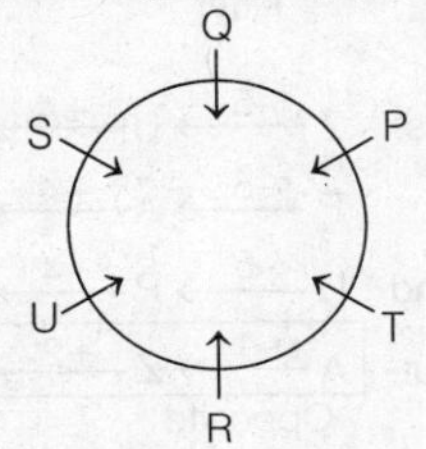

∴ U is the immediate neighbour of both R and S.

12. (c) According to the question,

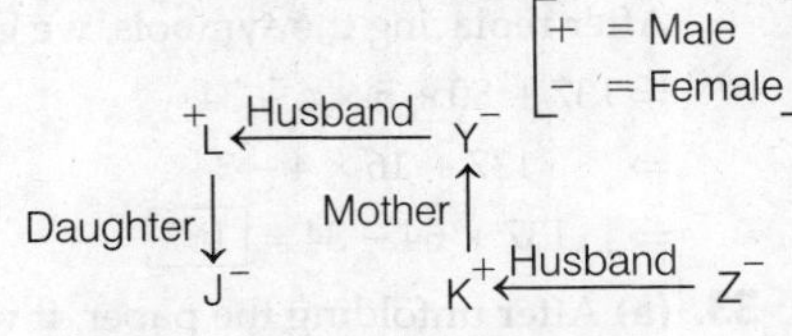

∴ J is the husband's sister of Z.

13. (c) Option figure (c) is the correct mirror image of the given figure, when the mirror is placed at the 'MN' line.

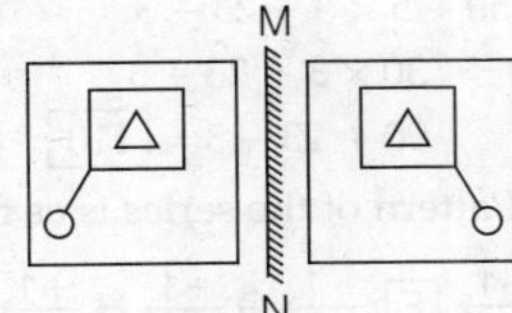

14. (b) Given equation,

300 – 2 + 50 × 3 ÷ 2 = ?

After replacing the signs, we get

300 ÷ 2 – 50 + 3 × 2

⇒ 150 – 50 + 3 × 2

⇒ 150 – 50 + 6

⇒ 100 + 6

∴ ? = 106

15. (d) As,

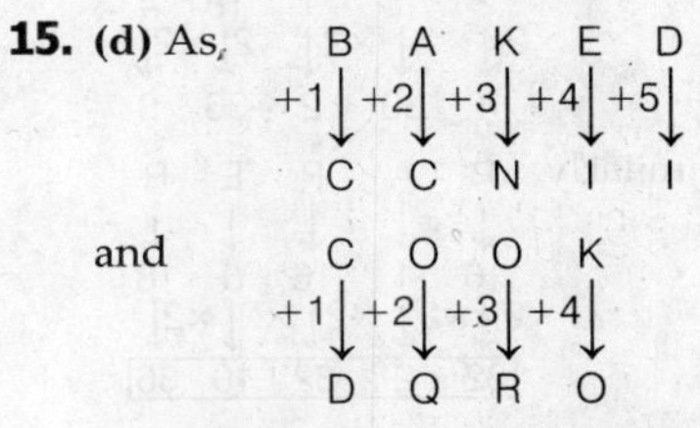

Similarly, E A T I N G

+1 +2 +3 +4 +5 +6

F C W M S M

16. (d) As, $7^2 - 9 = 40$

and $39^2 - 9 = 1512$

Similarly, $26^2 - 9 = 667$

17. (c) The option figure (c) is embedded in the question figure.

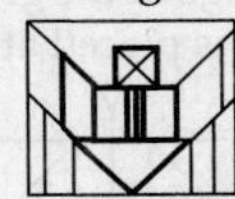

18. (d) Option figure (d) is the correct mirror image of the given figure, when the mirror is placed at the 'MN' line.

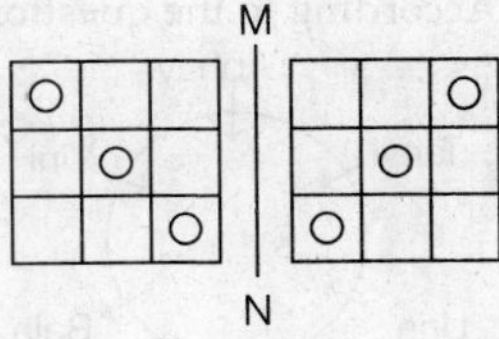

19. (c) According to the question,

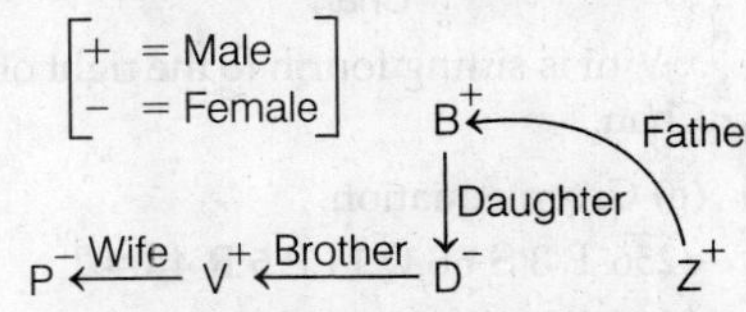

∴ B is the husband's father of P.

20. (d) As, (6 – 1) × 3 = 15

and (5 – 3) × 3 = 6

Similarly, (15 – 8) × 3 = 21

21. (a) As,

The number of letters in RING is

$4 \to 4^3 = 64$

and The number of letter in WATCH is

$5 \to 5^3 = 125$

Similarly,

The number of letters in BRACELET is

$8 \to 8^3 = 512$

22. **(b)** As,

C H A L K
↓ ↓ ↓ ↓ ↓
3 8 1 12 11
×2↓ ×2↓ ×2↓ ×2↓ ×2↓
6 16 2 24 22

and

B O A R D
↓ ↓ ↓ ↓ ↓
2 15 1 18 4
×2↓ ×2↓ ×2↓ ×2↓ ×2↓
4 30 2 36 8

Similarly,

P A P E R
↓ ↓ ↓ ↓ ↓
16 1 16 5 18
×2↓ ×2↓ ×2↓ ×2↓ ×2↓
| 32 2 32 10 36 |

23. **(b)** According to the statements,

Conclusions I. (✗) II. (✓)

∴ Only Conclusion II follows.

24. **(a)** Option figure (a) is the correct mirror image of the given figure, when the mirror is placed at the 'MN' line.

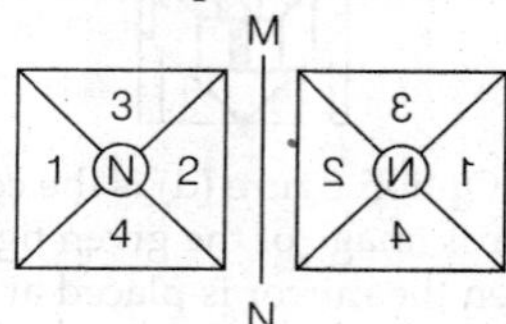

25. **(c)** According to the question,

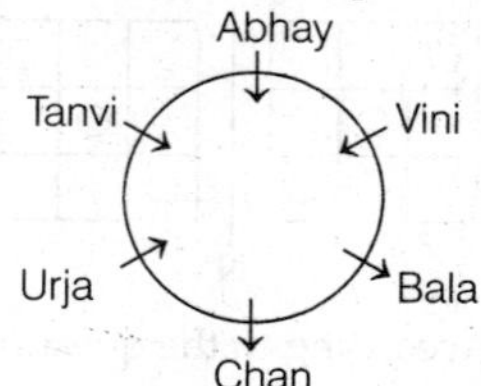

∴ Vini is sitting fourth to the right of Chan.

26. **(c)** Given equation,

$\sqrt{256}$ P 3 S 66 Q 11 P 5 R 43 = ?

After putting given sign we get,

$\sqrt{256} \times 3 - 66 \div 11 \times 5 + 43$

$\Rightarrow \quad 16 \times 3 - 6 \times 5 + 43$

$\Rightarrow \quad 48 - 30 + 43$

$\Rightarrow \quad 91 - 30 = \boxed{61}$

27. **(a)** In the given figure series, the symbols '*' and '+' move one step clockwise, and the symbol 'T' moves one step in an anticlockwise direction in each step.

Hence, the figure in option (a) is the correct answer.

28. **(c)** As,

B A B Y
↓ ↓ ↓ ↓
(2 + 1 + 2 + 25) −1 = 29

and

G E N D E R
↓ ↓ ↓ ↓ ↓ ↓
(7 + 5 + 14 + 4 + 5 + 18) −1 = 52

Similarly,

C R I P P L E
↓ ↓ ↓ ↓ ↓ ↓ ↓
(3 + 18 + 9 + 16 + 16 + 12 + 5) −1 = (78)

29. **(b)** Pattern of the series is as follows,

98 126 165 216 280 | 358 |
+28 +39 +51 +64 +78
+11 +12 +13 +14

30. **(d)** As, N $\xrightarrow{+2}$ P $\xrightarrow{-1}$ O $\xrightarrow{+2}$ Q

X $\xrightarrow{+2}$ Z $\xrightarrow{-1}$ Y $\xrightarrow{+2}$ A

and Q $\xrightarrow{+2}$ S $\xrightarrow{-1}$ R $\xrightarrow{+2}$ T

But, | P ⟶ K $\xrightarrow{+6}$ Q ⟶ J |

Opposite letter   Opposite letter

31. **(a)** As, Z $\xrightarrow{-5}$ U $\xrightarrow{+4}$ Y $\xrightarrow{-3}$ V

F $\xrightarrow{-5}$ A $\xrightarrow{+4}$ E $\xrightarrow{-3}$ B

and U $\xrightarrow{-5}$ P $\xrightarrow{+4}$ T $\xrightarrow{-3}$ Q

But, | A $\xrightarrow{-1}$ Z $\xrightarrow{+2}$ B $\xrightarrow{-3}$ Y |

Opposite letter   Opposite letter

32. **(a)** Given equation,

$137 \div 80 \times 5 - 4 + 34 = ?$

After replacing the symbols, we get,

$\Rightarrow 137 + 80 \div 5 \times 4 - 34$

$\Rightarrow \quad 137 + 16 \times 4 - 34$

$\Rightarrow \quad 137 + 64 - 34 = \boxed{167}$

33. **(a)** After unfolding the paper, it will appear as the option figure (a).

34. **(d)** Given equation,

$150 - 5 + 3 \div 23 \times 3 = ?$

After interchanging the signs we get,

$\Rightarrow 150 \div 5 \times 3 + 23 - 3$

$\Rightarrow \quad 30 \times 3 + 23 - 3$

$\Rightarrow \quad 90 + 23 - 3 = \boxed{110}$

35. **(c)** Pattern of the series is as follows,

E $\xrightarrow{+1}$ | F | $\xrightarrow{+1}$ G $\xrightarrow{+1}$ H $\xrightarrow{+1}$ I

Q $\xrightarrow{-1}$ | P | $\xrightarrow{-1}$ O $\xrightarrow{-1}$ N $\xrightarrow{-1}$ M

U $\xrightarrow{+1}$ | V | $\xrightarrow{+1}$ W $\xrightarrow{+1}$ X $\xrightarrow{+1}$ Y

E $\xrightarrow{-1}$ | D | $\xrightarrow{-1}$ C $\xrightarrow{-1}$ B $\xrightarrow{-1}$ A

36. **(c)** In the figure, series number of sides is reduced by one, and the shaded part is shifted from left to right and right to left in each figure. Hence, figure in option (c) is the correct answer.

37. **(a)** According to the statements,

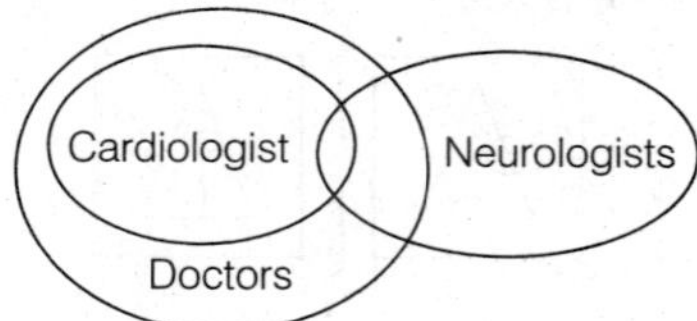

Conclusions

I. (✓) II. (✓)

∴ Both Conclusions I and II follow.

38. **(a)** Given equation,

$5 \div 2 - 20 + 5 \times 2 = ?$

After replacing the signs, we get

$\Rightarrow 5 \times 2 + 20 \div 5 - 2$

$\Rightarrow \quad 10 + 4 - 2$

$\therefore \quad \boxed{12}$

39. **(d)** Pattern of the series is as follows,

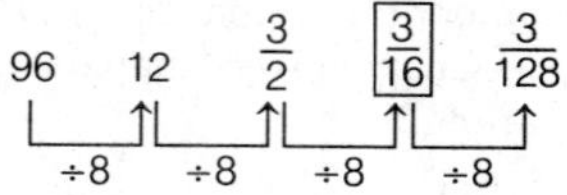

40. **(c)** After unfolding the paper, it will appear as the option figure (c).

41. **(c)** Pattern of the series is as follows,

18 6 2 $\boxed{\frac{2}{3}}$ $\frac{2}{9}$
÷3 ÷3 ÷3 ÷3

42. **(b)** After unfolding the paper, it will appear as the option figure (b).

43. **(b)** According to the question,

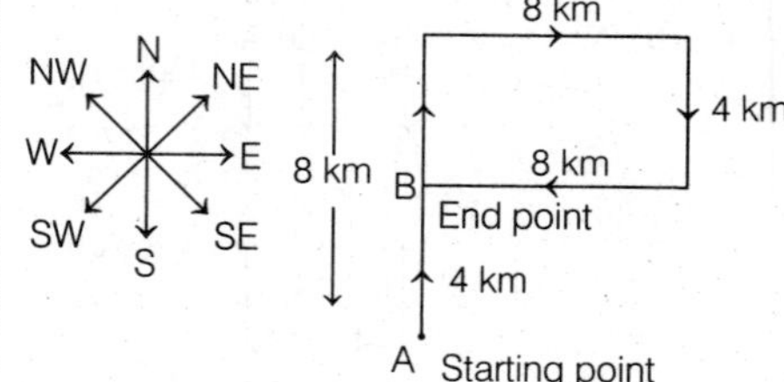

∴ It is clear that Param has to move 4 km towards the south direction to reach the starting point.

44. **(a)** The given series follows the pattern as shown below,

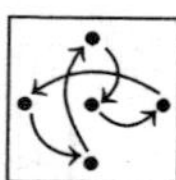

Hence, option figure (a) will replace the question mark.

45. (d) According to the statements,

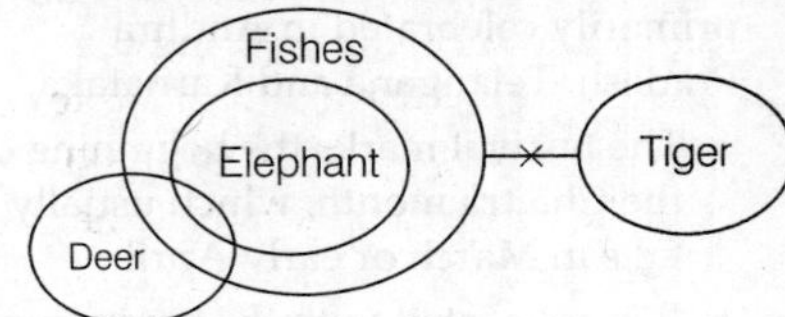

Conclusions

I. (✓) II. (✗) III.(✗)

∴ Only Conclusion I follows.

46. (a) Given equation,

17 B 3 A 14 D 7 C 5 = ?

After replacing the signs we get,

$\Rightarrow 17 \times 3 + 14 \div 7 - 5$

$\Rightarrow 17 \times 3 + 2 - 5$

$\Rightarrow \quad 51 + 2 - 5$

$\therefore \quad 48 = ?$

47. (b) Pattern of the series is as follows,

28, 30, [62], 188, 754, 3772

×1+2 ×2+2 ×3+2 ×4+2 ×5+2

48. (a) Given equation,

$16 \times 5 \div 20 + 6 + 50 = 40$

After interchanging the number 40 and 50, we get,

$\Rightarrow 16 \times 5 \div 20 + 6 + 40 = 50$

$\Rightarrow \quad 16 \times 0.25 + 6 + 40 = 50$

$\Rightarrow \quad 4 + 6 + 40 = 50$

$\therefore \quad 50 = 50$

49. (c) As, $(12, 14, 38) \Rightarrow 12 \times 2 + 14 = 38$

and $(6, 23, 35) \Rightarrow 6 \times 2 + 23 = 35$

Similarly, (16, 11, 43)

$\Rightarrow 16 \times 2 + 11 = 43$

50. (c) The second word is the material for the first word. As Lead is used in Pencil.

Similarly, Ink is used in Pen.

51. (d) Qutb-ud-din Aibak was the founder of the Slave Dynasty and the first Sultan of Delhi (1206–1210 CE).

- He died in 1210 CE after falling from a horse while playing polo (chaugan) in Lahore.
- He initiated the construction of Qutub Minar, which was later completed by Iltutmish.
- He earned the title 'Lakh Baksh' (Giver of Lakhs) due to his generosity.

52. (b) M. Balamuralikrishna was a legendary vocalist and multi-instrumentalist of Carnatic Sangeet, the classical music of South India.

- He was known for his mastery over raga improvisation and creation of new ragas such as Mahati and Lavangi.
- Apart from singing, he played instruments like the violin, veena, and mridangam.
- He was conferred with prestigious awards like Padma Vibhushan, Padma Bhushan and Sangeet Natak Akademi Award.

53. (b) 'The Dark Room' is a novel written by RK Narayan, published in 1938.

- It explores the plight of Indian women in a male-dominated society through the story of Savitri, the protagonist.
- The book highlights gender inequality, emotional suffering, and silent resistance within a traditional Indian household.
- He was awarded the Sahitya Akademi Award and honoured with the Padma Vibhushan for his literary contributions.

Knowledge Booster

- RK Narayan is also the creator of the fictional town Malgudi, featured in many of his works.

54. (d) The Central Administrative Tribunal (CAT) was established in 1985 under Article 323A of the Indian Constitution.

- It adjudicates disputes and complaints related to recruitment and service conditions of persons appointed to public services and posts under the Union Government.
- The CAT was set up under the Administrative Tribunals Act, 1985.
- CAT exercises original jurisdiction and functions independently of the judiciary, although its decisions can be appealed in the High Courts.

55. (a) The average length of a bacterial cell typically ranges from 3 to 5 micrometers (μm).

- Most bacteria are unicellular prokaryotes and are not visible to the naked eye.
- Some of the smallest bacteria measure around 0.1 μm, while giant bacteria like Epulopiscium can reach up to 500 μm.

Knowledge Booster

- Micrometer (μm) is one-millionth of a meter (1 μm = 10^{-6} m), a standard unit for measuring microorganisms.
- Size can vary depending on the type of bacteria, environment and function.

56. (c) As per National Statistical Office (NSO) data for 2021, India's average literacy rate stood at 77.7%.

- The male literacy rate was 84.7%, while the female literacy rate was 70.3%.
- The data was collected under the National Sample Survey (NSS) 2017–18 and later updated.
- Kerala recorded the highest literacy rate, while Andhra Pradesh was among the lowest.

57. (b) Fungal enzymes play a crucial role in decomposition, breaking down complex organic matter into simpler inorganic substances.

- They secrete hydrolytic enzymes such as cellulase, protease and lipase to degrade detritus.
- Fungi act as saprophytes, thriving on dead and decaying organisms.
- This process helps in nutrient cycling, enriching the soil ecosystem.

Knowledge Booster

- Dewnposition is a vital step in the detritus food chain, initiated primarily by bacteria and fungi.
- Fungi such as Aspergillus and Penicillium are well-known for their detritus-degrading capacity.

58. (c) Carbohydrates are the primary nutrient found in sugar, providing quick energy to the body.

- Sugars are classified as simple carbohydrates, consisting of monosaccharides like glucose and disaccharides like sucrose.
- These simple carbs are rapidly absorbed into the bloodstream, causing a quick rise in blood sugar levels.
- Excessive intake of simple sugars can lead to obesity and insulin resistance.

59. (a) As per Census 2011, Bihar recorded the lowest literacy rate among Indian states.

- The overall literacy rate of Bihar was approximately 61.8%.
- Male literacy stood at 71.2%, while female literacy was significantly lower at 51.5%.
- The state faced challenges like poverty, lack of infrastructure and low female education contributing to the low rate.

Knowledge Booster
- Kerala had the highest literacy rate in Census 2011 with 94%.
- The national average literacy rate in 2011 was 74.04%.

60. **(b)** As per the rules of Test match cricket, a team must bowl a minimum of 90 overs in a day.
- The day's play typically spans 6 hours, divided into three sessions.
- If the 90-over quota is not completed in the allotted time, play is extended to meet the minimum requirement.
- The over rate is expected to be 15 overs per hour.

61. **(a)** A standard basketball team fields 5 players on the court at a time.
- These include 2 guards 2 forwards and 1 center, forming the starting lineup.
- Substitutions are allowed during stoppages, but only 5 can play simultaneously.
- This rule applies across professional leagues like the NBA, FIBA and Olympics.

62. **(b)** Leh is located in the Union Territory of Ladakh, situated at a high altitude of over 3,500 meters.
- It experiences extreme cold during winter, with temperatures dropping below -20°C.
- Summers in Leh are mild and pleasant, with daytime temperatures ranging between 15°C to 25°C.
- The region has a cold desert climate, receiving minimal rainfall due to the rain shadow effect of the Himalayas.

Knowledge Booster
- Leh lies in the Trans-Himalayan zone, making it one of the coldest inhabited regions in India.
- Due to its unique climate and terrain, it is a key location for high-altitude acclimatisation for the Indian Armed Forces.

63. **(a)** The Treaty of Paris (1763) was signed between Britain and France after the conclusion of the Seven Years' War.
- As per the treaty, French possessions in India like Pondicherry and Chandernagore were restored.
- The French, however, were allowed only trading activities in India and political ambitions were curbed.
- The Third Carnatic War (1756–1763) in India was part of the larger Seven Years' War.

64. **(d)** In 1887, Heinrich Hertz first observed the photoelectric effect while experimenting with ultraviolet light and metal electrodes.
- He noticed that shining UV light on the electrodes produced a spark, indicating a change in voltage due to emitted electrons.
- This phenomenon revealed that light can influence electrical properties of materials.
- Though discovered by Hertz, the explanation for the photoelectric effect came later through Albert Einstein in 1905.

Knowledge Booster
- Albert Einstein received the Nobel Prize in Physics (1921) for explaining the photoelectric effect, not for relativity.
- The photoelectric effect provided experimental evidence for the quantum nature of light.

65. **(c)** Rust is the hydrated form of ferric oxide ($F_2O_3 \cdot xH_2O$), formed when iron reacts with oxygen and water.
- The process is an example of a slow chemical reaction known as oxidation or corrosion.
- Zinc oxide is not rust; it forms a white powder and acts as a protective coating on galvanised iron.
- Copper does not rust like iron; instead, it forms a green layer of copper carbonate (patina) on exposure to air and moisture.

Knowledge Booster
- Rust formation is accelerated in the presence of salts or acids, making coastal areas more prone to corrosion.
- Stainless steel resists rusting due to the presence of chromium, which forms a passive oxide layer.

66. **(c)** Ugadi is the Telugu New Year, primarily celebrated in Andhra Pradesh, Telangana and Karnataka.
- The festival marks the beginning of the Chaitra month, which usually falls in March or early April.
- It is associated with the beginning of a new lunar calendar and is a major cultural celebration.
- Ugadi is known as Gudi Padwa in Maharashtra and as Navreh in Kashmir.

67. **(d)** Ustad Asad Ali Khan was a renowned rudra veena player and one of the last great exponents of the Khandarbani school of Dhrupad.
- The Khandarbani style is one of the four principal banis (styles) of the Dhrupad tradition.
- This style emphasises precision in rhythm and clarity in swaras (notes).
- The other three main Dhrupad banis are Gaurihar, Dagarbani and Nauharbani.

68. **(a)** A centripetal drainage system forms when rivers flow inward from all directions into a common depression or basin.
- It is observed in inland drainage basins, where water does not flow into the sea.
- Loktak Lake in Manipur is a prominent example of this drainage pattern.
- This type of drainage is generally associated with endorheic basins, which have no external outlet.

Knowledge Booster
- The Radial pattern is found on volcanic cones or domes where rivers radiate outward.
- The Trellis pattern develops in folded topography, where tributaries join main rivers at right angles.

69. **(b)** The Sarkaria Commission Report (1983) focused on Centre-State relations, not on Fundamental Rights.
- It was established to examine the balance of power between the Union and States in the Indian federal structure.
- The Motilal Nehru Report (1928) was the first to propose a bill of rights, including fundamental rights.
- Tej Bahadur Sapru and JB Kripalani Reports also discussed civil liberties and fundamental rights.

70. **(a)** The IUPAC name of Allyl bromide is 3-Bromopropene, as it consists of a three-carbon chain with a double bond and a bromine substituent.

- The double bond begins at carbon 1 and the bromine is attached to the third carbon.
- The structure is: $CH_2 = CH - CH_2Br$, which confirms the name 3-Bromopropene.
- Allyl bromide is commonly used in organic synthesis and alkylation reactions.

71. **(a)** Kanaka Raju, a tribal dance teacher from Telangana, was conferred the Padma Shri in 2021 for Gussadi dance.

- He is known for his contribution to Gussadi, a traditional tribal folk dance of the Raj Gond tribe.
- Gussadi is performed by men during Diwali, especially in the tribal belts of Adilabad district.
- The dance includes elaborate headgear made of peacock feathers and is accompanied by drums and flutes.

72. **(c)** Articles 36 to 51 of the Indian Constitution form Part IV, which deals with the Directive Principles of State Policy (DPSP).

- These principles aim to create a welfare state by guiding the state in the formulation of laws and policies.
- They are non-justiciable, meaning they are not enforceable by courts, but are fundamental in governance.
- DPSPs are inspired by the Irish Constitution, which adopted them from the Spanish Constitution.

73. **(d)** GDP at factor cost = GDP at market price - Indirect taxes + Subsidies

Given,

GDP at market price = 600 crores

Indirect taxes = 200 crores

Subsidies = 50 crores

Substituting,

600 - 200 + 50 = 450 crores

Knowledge Booster

- GDP at factor cost reflects the actual income received by factors of production.
- It excludes indirect taxes as they are not retained by the producers and includes subsidies as government support to production.

74. **(c)** Petroleum products were India's top export item in 2021, contributing a significant share to the overall merchandise exports.

- These include refined petroleum, diesel and aviation turbine fuel.
- India exports petroleum products mainly to countries like the UAE, Singapore and the Netherlands.
- The sector is supported by India's large refining capacity, especially at major ports like Jamnagar (Gujarat).

75. **(c)** The Tomb of Iltutmish was constructed in 1235 AD, shortly after his death.

- It is located in the Qutub Complex in Delhi, near the Qutub Minar.
- The tomb is one of the earliest examples of Indo-Islamic architecture in India.
- Iltutmish was the founder of the Delhi Sultanate's administrative and a ruler of the Slave Dynasty framework.

76. **(b)** The Timur invasion of India occurred in 1398 AD, during the reign of Nasir-ud-Din Mahmud Tughlaq of the Delhi Sultanate.

- Timur crossed the Indus River near Attock and defeated the Tughlaq army near Delhi.
- His invasion was marked by widespread massacre and destruction, especially in Delhi.
- The invasion severely weakened the Tughlaq dynasty and Delhi's political structure.

77. **(d)** A Member of Parliament is liable for disqualification if absent from all meetings of the House without permission for 60 consecutive days.

- This provision is laid down under Article 101(d) of the Indian Constitution.
- The House may excuse the absence if valid reasons are presented and accepted.
- This rule applies individually to each House of Parliament – Lok Sabha and Rajya Sabha.

Knowledge Booster

- Article 190(d) similarly governs the disqualification of State Legislature members.
- A 'session' is excluded from the 60-day calculation if the House is not sitting continuously.

78. **(b)** The Green Revolution in India was not introduced in rain-fed areas but in irrigated regions with access to water and infrastructure.

- It began in the 1960s to increase agricultural productivity through HYV seeds, fertilizers and irrigation.
- The initial focus was on Punjab, Haryana and Western Uttar Pradesh, where conditions were suitable.
- MS Swaminathan is known as the Father of the Green Revolution in India.

79. **(d)** The Fundamental Rights in the Indian Constitution are inspired by the Bill of Rights of the USA.

- These rights are enshrined in Part III (Articles 12 to 35) of the Indian Constitution.
- Dr BR Ambedkar called Fundamental Rights the 'Conscience of the Constitution.'
- They are enforceable by the courts and considered essential for the development of the individual.

80. **(b)** Siraj-ud-Daulah succeeded his maternal grandfather Alivardi Khan as the Nawab of Bengal in 1756.

- He was the last independent Nawab of Bengal before British control began post the Battle of Plassey.
- His rule was marked by conflict with the British East India Company, especially regarding fortification of Calcutta.
- Siraj-ud-Daulah was defeated by Robert Clive and betrayed by Mir Jafar in the Battle of Plassey (1757).

Knowledge Booster

- The Battle of Plassey is considered a turning point in Indian history as it laid the foundation of British rule in India.
- Mir Jafar became the puppet Nawab of Bengal after Siraj-ud-Daulah's defeat.

81. **(d)** The acceleration due to gravity (g) has the same unit as acceleration, which is metres per second squared (m/s^2).

- It represents the rate at which an object accelerates when falling freely near the Earth's surface.

- The standard value of g on Earth is approximately 9.8 m/s^2.
- g is a vector quantity, having both magnitude and direction (towards the Earth's center).

Knowledge Booster
- g decreases with height, depth and latitude—it is highest at the poles and lowest at the equator.
- Universal gravitational constant (G) is a constant, while g varies with location.

82. **(c)** Statements (A), (B) and (D) are correct because
- The Inter Tropical Convergence Zone (ITCZ) is a broad trough of low pressure located near the equator.
- It is the region where the North-East and South-East trade winds converge, causing air to rise and form clouds.
- During summer, the ITCZ shifts Northwards and moves over the Ganga plains in India.
- The ITCZ is not fixed at 5°N, as it shifts with the apparent movement of the Sun.

Knowledge Booster
- The shifting of the ITCZ is a major factor responsible for the onset of the Indian monsoon.
- The ITCZ is also referred to as the doldrums, due to the calm winds and low pressure in this region.

83. **(c)** 'Wings of Fire' is the autobiography of Dr. APJ Abdul Kalam, the 11th President of India and a renowned aerospace scientist.
- The book was co-authored by Arun Tiwari, one of Kalam's close associates.
- It highlights Kalam's journey from a humble childhood in Rameswaram to becoming the 'Missile Man of India'.
- The book was first published in 1999 and has inspired millions across India.

Knowledge Booster
- Dr. Kalam played a pivotal role in India's missile and space programs, particularly AGNI and PRITHVI.
- He was awarded the Bharat Ratna in 1997 for his contributions to science and public service.

84. **(b)** 'Harshacharita' is a Sanskrit biography written by Banabhatta, the court poet of Emperor Harshavardhana.
- It provides a detailed account of Harsha's early life, ancestry and political achievements.
- The work is considered the first historical biography in Sanskrit literature.

85. **(b)** Liberalisation refers to reducing government restrictions to promote private enterprise and market forces.
- Enhancement in tariffs implies increasing taxes or duties on imports, which is a protectionist measure, not liberalisation.
- Liberalisation typically involves reducing tariffs and duties to allow free trade.
- India's liberalisation reforms began in 1991 under Finance Minister Dr. Manmohan Singh.

86. **(d)** The Rashtriya Kalidas Samman is one of the most prestigious arts awards given by the Madhya Pradesh Government.
- In 2019–2020, it was awarded to the Dhananjayans, a famous dancing couple from Chennai.
- They are renowned exponents of Bharatanatyam, a classical dance form originating from Tamil Nadu.
- The Dhananjayans have also received the Padma Bhushan and Sangeet Natak Akademi Award.

87. **(d)** The Fifth Five-Year Plan (1974–1979) was the first to explicitly focus on gender issues and women's empowerment.
- It emphasised poverty alleviation, self-reliance and reducing regional and inter-state disparities.
- The plan was launched under the leadership of Indira Gandhi, following the concept of 'Garibi Hatao".
- The plan laid the foundation for inclusive growth, recognising women as crucial contributors to development.

Knowledge Booster
- The Integrated Rural Development Programme (IRDP) was launched during this plan.
- This plan was later terminated in 1978 by the Janata Government and a rolling plan system was introduced.

88. **(c)** Manoj Sinha was serving as the Lieutenant Governor of Jammu and Kashmir in October 2022.
- He assumed office on 7th August 2020, after the resignation of Girish Chandra Murmu.
- The post of Lieutenant Governor in Jammu and Kashmir was created after the abrogation of Article 370 and the reorganisation of the state in August 2019.
- The Lieutenant Governor is appointed by the President of India and functions as the administrative head of the Union Territory.

89. **(b)** Customs duties are taxes imposed on imports and exports and are a major source of tax revenue for the government.
- These duties are regulated under the Customs Act, 1962 and administered by the Central Board of Indirect Taxes and Customs (CBIC).
- Customs duties aim to protect domestic industries, regulate the movement of goods and raise revenue.
- Tax revenue is classified into direct taxes (like income tax) and indirect taxes (like GST, excise and customs).

90. **(d)** Aquifers are underground layers of water-bearing permeable rock or sediment that store groundwater, not surface water.
- Unlike rivers, lakes, or oceans, aquifers lie beneath the Earth's surface and are accessed through wells or springs.
- They play a crucial role in providing freshwater for drinking and irrigation, especially in arid regions.
- Overexploitation of aquifers can lead to groundwater depletion and land subsidence.

91. **(a)** Bharatanatyam is one of the oldest classical dance forms of India, traditionally performed to Carnatic music.
- It originated in Tamil Nadu, particularly in temples, where it was performed as a form of devotional offering.
- The musical compositions for Bharatanatyam often include

Sanskrit and Tamil hymns, set to Carnatic ragas and talas.

- Famous Carnatic musicians like M. Balamuralikrishna and Lalgudi Jayaraman have contributed compositions used in Bharatanatyam.
- Renowned Bharatanatyam exponents include Rukmini Devi Arundale and Padma Subrahmanyam.

92. **(c)** The Imperial Cricket Conference (ICC) was founded in the year 1909 by representatives from England, Australia and South Africa.

- In 1965, it was renamed the International Cricket Conference and in 1989, it became the International Cricket Council (ICC).
- The first official ICC tournament was the Cricket World Cup held in 1975 in England.
- The headquarters of ICC is currently located in Dubai, United Arab Emirates.

93. **(c)** The Littoral Zone refers to the coastal zone of a water body, especially lakes and oceans, where sunlight penetrates to the sediment, allowing plant growth.

- It is rich in dissolved oxygen, nutrients and sunlight, making it highly productive biologically.
- This zone supports aquatic plants, algae and diverse animal life and is ecologically crucial for food chains.
- The intertidal subzone within the littoral zone experiences alternating submergence and exposure due to tidal action.

Knowledge Booster

- The limnetic zone lies just beyond the littoral zone but lacks rooted vegetation due to depth.
- The benthic zone, located at the bottom of water bodies, contains decomposers and low oxygen levels.

94. **(b)** Anju Bobby George became the first Indian to win a medal at the World Athletics Championships in 2003.

- She won the bronze medal in the long jump event held in Paris.
- Anju achieved a jump of 6.70 m, creating history for Indian athletics.
- Anju Bobby George was honoured with the Arjuna Award (2002) and Khel Ratna Award (2003–04)

Knowledge Booster

- Her performance marked India's entry onto the global stage in track and field events.
- In 2021, she received the BBC Lifetime Achievement Award for her contribution to Indian sports.

95. **(c)** The Deep sea hydro-thermal ecosystem does not rely on solar energy for its functioning.

- It is found around hydro-thermal vents on the ocean floor, where sunlight cannot penetrate.
- These ecosystems depend on chemosynthesis, where bacteria convert hydrogen sulfide and other minerals into energy
- Organisms like tubeworms, clams and crabs survive through a symbiotic relationship with chemosynthetic bacteria.

Knowledge Booster

- Chemosynthesis is the process used by organisms in such ecosystems instead of photosynthesis.
- These ecosystems were discovered in 1977 near the Galápagos Rift by scientists exploring the ocean floor.

96. **(d)** Nauroz (also spelled Nowruz) is celebrated by the Parsi community in India as a festival marking the Persian New Year.

- It symbolises renewal and rebirth, falling around March 21, the vernal equinox.
- Nauroz has Zoroastrian roots and is recognised by UNESCO as Intangible Cultural Heritage
- The celebration includes cleaning homes, wearing new clothes and offering special prayers at fire temples.

97. **(a)** The correct maching is 1-B, 2-A, 3-C.

- Tuticorin Port (now VO Chidambaranar Port) is located in Tamil Nadu, on the South-Eastern coast of India.
- Haldia Port lies in West Bengal and serves as an important riverine port on the Hooghly River.
- Mangalore Port, also known as New Mangalore Port, is located in the state of Karnataka, along the Arabian Sea.
- These ports are significant for international trade, bulk cargo handling and regional connectivity.

Knowledge Booster

- Haldia Port acts as a feeder port for Kolkata Port Trust.
- Tuticorin Port was declared a major port in 1974 and is one of the fastest-growing ports in India.

98. **(c)** Aluna Kabuini is a renowned exponent of Manipuri dance, one of the major classical dance forms of India.

- Manipuri dance originates from the North-Eastern state of Manipur, with strong influences from Vaishnavism.
- Manipuri is recognised as one of the eight classical dance forms of India.
- It includes dance forms like Ras Leela, Pung Cholom and Lai Haraoba, showcasing religious and folk traditions.

99. **(b)** The Universal Law of Gravitation, formulated by Sir Isaac Newton, states that ' every object attracts every other object with a force proportional to their masses and inversely proportional to the square of the distance between them".

- It is the force that binds us to the Earth and is responsible for the weight of all objects.
- The mathematical expression of Newton's gravitational law is $F = G\,(m1m2)\,/\,r^2$.
- This gravitational force also governs the motion of celestial bodies, such as the Moon around Earth and planets around the Sun.

100. **(b)** In the Interim Government formed on 2nd September 1946, Liaquat Ali Khan was appointed as the Finance Member, equivalent to today's Finance Minister.

- The Interim Government was headed by Jawaharlal Nehru and included representatives from both the Indian National Congress and the Muslim League.
- Liaquat Ali Khan's Finance Budget of 1947 introduced heavy taxes on business profits, causing tensions with the Congress.

Knowledge Booster

- Liaquat Ali Khan later became the first Prime Minister of Pakistan after the country's creation in 1947.
- The Interim Government acted as a transitional body until independence and Partition were finalised in August 1947.

101. (d) Expenses on Rent

$= ₹\left(300000 \times \frac{20}{100}\right) = ₹\,60000$

Expenses on others

$= ₹\left(300000 \times \frac{10}{100}\right) = ₹\,30000$

Difference between expenses

$= ₹(60000 - 30000) = ₹30000$

$\%\text{ More} = \left(\frac{\text{Difference}}{\text{Expenses on others}} \times 100\right)\%$

$= \left(\frac{30000}{30000} \times 100\right)\%$

% More = 100%

Speedy Method

Difference between % distribution between rent and others

= (20 – 10) = 10%

% More

$= \left(\frac{\text{Difference}}{\%\text{ Distribution on others}} \times 100\right)\%$

$\%\text{ More} = \left(\frac{10}{10} \times 100\right)\% = 100\%$

102. (b) SP of two cars = ₹ 60000 each

Let the CP be ₹ x.

Profit on the first car = 20%

$\text{CP of first car} = 60000 \times \frac{100}{(100 + 20)}$

$= 60000 \times \frac{100}{120}$

= ₹ 50000

$\text{CP of second car} = 60000 \times \left(\frac{100}{100 - 20}\right)$

$= 60000 \times \frac{100}{80}$

= ₹ 75000

Total CP of both car

= ₹ (50000 + 75000)

= ₹ 125000

Total SP of both car = ₹ 120000

⇒ Loss = ₹ (125000 – 120000) = ₹ 5000

$\Rightarrow \text{Loss }\% = \left(\frac{5000}{125000} \times 100\right)$

⇒ Loss % = 4%

103. (d) Factors of

96 = 2 × 2 × 2 × 2 × 2 × 3

Factors of 132 = 2 × 2 × 3 × 11

Factors of 438 = 73 × 2 × 3

LCM of 96, 132, 438

= 2 × 2 × 2 × 2 × 2 × 3 × 11 × 73

= 77088

104. (d) Total votes = 1136 + 7636 + 11628

= 20400

Votes get by winning candidate

= 11628

% of votes winning candidate got

$= \left(\frac{11628}{20400} \times 100\right) = 57\%$

105. (c) Ram has 12 hens and 5 cows.

Ratio of $H : C = 12 : 5$ $\left(\text{i.e. } \frac{12}{5} = 2.4\right)$

Shyam has 18 hens 9 cows.

Ratio of $H : C = 18 : 9 = 2 : 1$

$\left(\text{i.e, } \frac{2}{1} = 2\right)$

Preetham has 4 hens and 8 cows

⇒ Ratio of $H : C = 4 : 8 = 1 : 2$

$\left(\text{i.e, } \frac{1}{2} = 0.5\right)$

Vinay has 10 hens and 7 cows

⇒ Ratio of $H : C = 10 : 7$

$\left(\text{i.e, } \frac{10}{7} = 1.42\right)$

Hence, Ram has greater ratio of hens to cows.

106. (c) Let the radius of sphere and hemisphere be r_1 and r_2, respectively.

Surface area of sphere $= 4\pi r_1^2$

Surface area of hemisphere

$= 2\pi r_2^2 + \pi r_2^2 = 3\pi r_2^2$

$\text{Volume of sphere} = \frac{4}{3}\pi r_1^3$

$\text{Volume of hemisphere} = \frac{2}{3}\pi r_1^3$

According to questions

$\Rightarrow \quad 4\pi r_1^2 = 3\pi r_2^2$

$\Rightarrow \quad r_1^2 = \frac{3r_2^2}{4}$

$\Rightarrow \quad r_1 = \frac{\sqrt{3}}{2} r_2$

Ratio of their volume

$= \frac{\frac{4}{3}\pi r_1^3}{\frac{2}{3}\pi r_2^3} = \frac{4r_1^3}{2r_2^3} = \frac{2r_1^3}{r_2^3}$

$= \frac{2\left(\frac{\sqrt{3}r_2}{2}\right)^3}{r_2^3} = \frac{3\sqrt{3}r_2^3}{4r_2^3}$

$\text{Ratio of their volume} = \frac{3\sqrt{3}}{4}$

107. (c) CSA of cylinder = 660 cm^2

Height of cylinder = h = 15 cm

Let r be the radius of cylinder.

⇒ CSA of cylinder = $2\pi rh$

$\Rightarrow 660 = 2 \times \frac{22}{7} \times r \times 15$

$\Rightarrow \frac{660 \times 7}{2 \times 15 \times 22} = r \Rightarrow r = 7\text{ cm}$

Volume of cylinder $= \pi r^2 h$

$= \frac{22}{7} \times (7 \times 7) \times 15$

$= 2310\text{ cm}^3$

108. (d) Radius of cone = 3 cm = r

Height of cone = 4 cm = h

$\Rightarrow l = \text{Slant height of cone} = \sqrt{h^2 + r^2}$

$= \sqrt{3^2 + 4^2} = \sqrt{25}$

$\Rightarrow l = 5\text{ cm}$

⇒ TSA of cone $= \pi r(l + r)$

$= \frac{22}{7} \times 3 \times (5 + 3)$

$= \frac{22}{7} \times 3 \times 8$

$\Rightarrow \text{TSA of cone} = \frac{528}{7}\text{ cm}^2$

109. (b) Let the speed of Soma = x km/h

Julie's speed = $(x + 4)$ km/h

Distance covered by Soma in 4 h

= $4x$ km

Distance covered by Julie in 4 h

= $4(x + 4)$ km

According to question,

⇒ Total distance between them

$= 4x + 4x + 16$

$\Rightarrow \quad 40 = 8x + 16$

$\Rightarrow \quad 24 = 8x$

$\Rightarrow \quad x = 3\text{ km}$

Speed of Soma = 3 km/h

Speed of Julie = $x + 3$ = 7 km/h

110. (a) Let the quantity of wheat Arbind sells at 9% profit be x kg.

Remaining quantity he sells at 19% profit is = $(650 - x)$ kg

Profit earned on overall sale = 15%

According to question,

$\Rightarrow \frac{9x}{100} + \frac{19}{100}(650 - x) = \frac{15}{100} \times 650$

$\Rightarrow 9x + 650 \times 19 - 19x = 15 \times 650$

$\Rightarrow 650 \times 19 - 15 \times 650 = 10x$

$\Rightarrow \quad 65\,(19 - 15) = x$

$\Rightarrow \quad x = 65 \times 4 = 260\text{ kg}$

Speedy Method

Let the x kg of wheat sells at a profit of 9%.

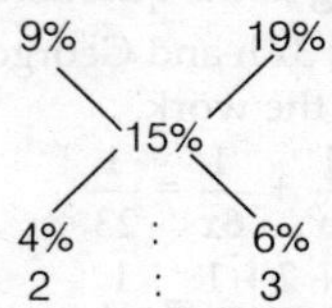

Total profit = 2% + 3% = 5%

Given, 5% = 650 kg

$\Rightarrow$ 1% = 130 kg

For 2% i.e, 2% = 260 kg

260 kg of wheat is sold at a profit of 9%.

111. (a) $0.15 = \frac{15}{100}$

$0.18 = \frac{18}{100}$

$0.45 = \frac{45}{100}$

LCM of 0.15, 0.18 and 0.45

$= \left(\frac{15}{100}, \frac{18}{100}, \frac{45}{100}\right)$

$= \frac{\text{LCM}(15,18,45)}{\text{HCF}(100,100,100)}$

$= \frac{90}{100} = 0.9$

112. (b) Length of train = 180 m

Length of tunnel = 500 m

Total length = (500 + 180) = 680 m

Time taken to cross tunnel = 40 sec

$\Rightarrow$ Speed of train $= \frac{\text{Distance}}{\text{Time}}$

$= \frac{680}{40} = 17$ m/sec

$\Rightarrow$ Speed of train $= \left(17 \times \frac{18}{5}\right)$ km/h

= 61.2 km/h

113. (b) Let $y = \frac{\sin^2 39° + \sin^2(90° - 39°)}{\cos^2 35° + \cos^2(90° - 35°)} + 3\tan 25° \tan 75°$

$\Rightarrow \quad y = \frac{\sin^2 39° + \cos^2 39°}{\cos^2 35° + \sin^2 35°} + 3\tan 25° \tan(90° - 25°)$

$\Rightarrow y = 1 + 3\tan 25° \cot 25°$

$\{\because \sin^2\theta + \cos^2\theta = 1$, $\tan A \times \cot A = 1\}$

$\Rightarrow y = 1 + 3 = 4$

114. (c) $\frac{2}{5} = 0.4$, $\Rightarrow \frac{7}{10} = 0.7$

$\Rightarrow \frac{5}{6} = 0.833$, $\Rightarrow \frac{1}{3} = 0.33$

Hence, (c) is the greater in all given ratio.

115. (b) Factors of 20 = 2 × 2 × 5

Factors of 30 = 2 × 3 × 5

Factors of 45 = 3 × 3 × 5

Factors of 65 = 5 × 13

LCM of 20, 30, 45 and 65

= 2 × 2 × 3 × 3 × 5 × 13 = 2340

116. (d) Factors of 3 m, 15 cm or 315 cm

= 3 × 3 × 7 × 5

Factors of 500 cm = 5 × 5 × 5 × 2 × 2

Factors of 6 m 85 cm or 685 cm = 5 × 137

Greater possible length that can be used to measure exactly the length is HCF (315,500,685) i.e.5 cm.

117. (b) If $\frac{x}{4y} = \frac{3}{4} \Rightarrow \frac{x}{y} = \frac{3}{1} \Rightarrow x = 3y$

The value of $\frac{2x + 3y}{x - 2y}$ is i.e.

$= \frac{2x + 3y}{x - 2y} = \frac{2(3y) + 3y}{3y - 2y}$

$= \frac{9y}{y} = 9$

118. (c) Discount amount after the discount of 30% be D_1.

$\Rightarrow D_1$ = Discount amount on ₹ 5000

$= ₹\ 5000 \times \frac{30}{100} = ₹\ 1500$

Net discount of two successive discount 15% and 25% is

$\Rightarrow \left(15 + 25 - \frac{15 \times 25}{100}\right)\% = \frac{145}{4}\%$

Discount amount of the discount of $\frac{145}{4}$% be D_2.

Discount amount on ₹ 5000

$= ₹\left(5000 \times \frac{145}{400}\right) \Rightarrow D_2 = ₹\ \frac{3625}{2}$

$\Rightarrow$ Difference between discount

$= D_2 - D_1 = ₹\left(\frac{3625}{2} - 1500\right)$

= ₹ 312.50

Speedy Method

First discount, D_1 = 30%

Second discount is two successive discount of 15% and 25%.

So, net second discount i.e.,

$D_2 = \left(15 + 25 - \frac{15 \times 25}{100}\right)\% = \frac{145}{4}\%$

Overall discount on amount = $D_2 - D_1$

$= \left(\frac{145}{4} - 30\right)\% = \frac{25}{4}\%$

Discount amount

$= ₹\left(5000 \times \frac{25}{400}\right) = ₹\ 312.50$

119. (b) Two circle of radii 6 cm and 4 cm respectively with centre P and Q.

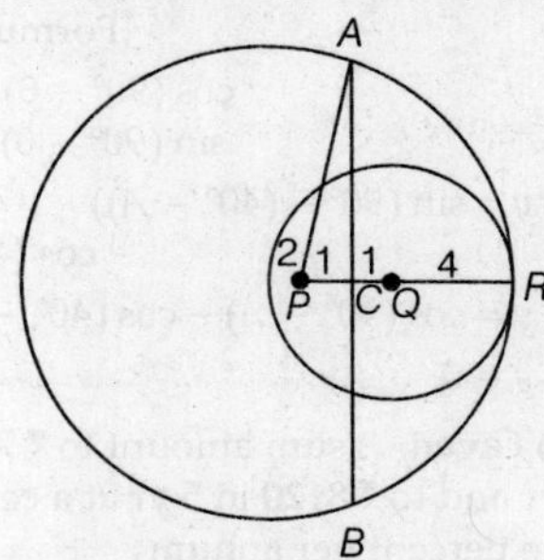

Perpendicular bisector of PQ meet the bigger circle at A and B.

$\Rightarrow PQ = 6 - 4 = 2$ cm

$\Rightarrow PC = \frac{PQ}{2} = \frac{2}{2} = 1$ cm

In ΔPCA, using Pythagoras theorem

$(AP)^2 = (PC)^2 + (AC)^2$

$\Rightarrow (AC)^2 = (AP)^2 - (PC)^2$

$\Rightarrow AC^2 = 6^2 - (1)^2$

$\Rightarrow AC = \sqrt{35}$ cm

Length or value of $AB = 2AC$

$= 2\sqrt{35}$ cm

120. (d) Monthly income of employee

= ₹ 26500

Monthly expenditure of employee

= ₹ 22000

Monethly saving of employee

= ₹ (26500 22000)

= ₹ 4500

Next year, his income is increased by 20%, then his income

$= ₹\left(26500 + 26500 \times \frac{20}{100}\right)$

= ₹ 31800

Expenditure is increased by 15%, the expenditure amount

$= ₹\left(22000 + 22000 \times \frac{15}{100}\right)$

= ₹ 25300

$\Rightarrow$ His saving will become

= ₹ (31800 – 25300)

= ₹ 6500

$\Rightarrow$ Increased amount in saving

= ₹ (6500 – 4500)

= ₹ 2000

$\Rightarrow$ % increase in saving

$= \left(\frac{\text{Difference}}{\text{Saving of Ist year}} \times 100\right)\%$

$= \left(\frac{2000}{4500} \times 100\right) = 44\frac{4}{9}\%$

121. **(b)** Let, $y = \sin(50° + A) - \cos(40° - A)$

$\Rightarrow y = \sin(50° + A) - \cos(40° - A)$

{Formula used $\because \cos(90° - \theta) = \sin\theta$, $\sin(90° - \theta) = \cos\theta$}

$\Rightarrow y = \sin(90° - (40° - A)) - \cos(40° - A)$

$\Rightarrow y = \cos(40° - A) - \cos(40° - A)$

$\Rightarrow y = 0$

122. **(d)** Given, A sum amount to ₹ 7656 in 4 yr and to ₹ 8120 in 5 yr at a certain SI rate percent per annum

$\Rightarrow$ Interest for 1 yr = ₹ (8120 − 7656) = ₹ 464

$\Rightarrow$ Interest for 4 yr = ₹ (464 × 4) = 1856

So, principle = ₹ (7656 − 1856) = ₹ 5800

We know that,

$\Rightarrow \quad SI = \frac{P \times R \times T}{100}$

$\Rightarrow \quad 1856 = \frac{5800 \times R \times 4}{100}$

$\Rightarrow \quad R = \frac{1856 \times 100}{5800 \times 4}$

$\Rightarrow \quad R = 8\%$ per annum

123. **(c)** If $a - \frac{1}{a} = 4$

On squaring both sides, we get

$\Rightarrow \left(a - \frac{1}{a}\right)^2 = 16$

$\Rightarrow a^2 + \frac{1}{a} - 2 = 16$

$\Rightarrow a^2 + \frac{1}{a^2} = 18$

$\Rightarrow \left(a + \frac{1}{a}\right)^2 = a^2 + \frac{1}{a^2} + 2$

$\Rightarrow \left(a + \frac{1}{a}\right)^2 = 18 + 2$

$\Rightarrow \left(a + \frac{1}{a}\right)^2 = 20$

$\Rightarrow \quad a + \frac{1}{a} = \sqrt{20} = 2\sqrt{5}$

124. **(b)** Vipin can do a piece of work in 2 days.

Vipin's one day work $= \frac{1}{2}$

Vaibhav can do same work = 3 days

$\Rightarrow$ Vaibhav's one day work $= \frac{1}{3}$

Chirag can do the same work = 6 day

$\Rightarrow$ Chirag's one day work $= \frac{1}{6}$

Total work = LCM (2, 3, 6) = 6

Efficiency of Vipin $= \frac{6}{2} = 3$ unit/day

Efficiency of Vaibhav $= \frac{6}{3} = 2$ unit/day

Efficiency of Chirag $= \frac{6}{6} = 1$ unit/day

If the work together, then their efficiency = (3 + 2 + 1) = 6 units/day

$\therefore$ Required number of days $= \frac{6}{6} = 1$ day

Speedy Method

Total work

Vipin 2		3 unit/day
Vaibhav 3	6	2 unit/day
Chirag 6		1 unit/day

Total efficiency (Vipin + Vaibhav + Chirag) = 3 + 2 + 1 = 6 units/day

Required Days $= \frac{\text{Total work}}{\text{Total efficiency}}$

$= \frac{6}{6} = 1$ day

125. **(a)** Let $D_1 = 30\%$, $D_2 = 20\%$

Single discount

$= \left(30 + 20 - \frac{30 \times 20}{100}\right)\%$

$= (50 - 6) = 44\%$

{**Formula Used**

For successive discount $x\%$ and $y\%$

Single discount $= \left(x + y - \frac{xy}{100}\right)\%$}

126. **(d)** We have two quadratic equation $(x^2 - 8x + 15)$ and $x^2 - 5x + 6$

$\Rightarrow x^2 - 8x + 15$

$= x^2 - 5x - 3x + 15$

$= (x - 5)(x - 3)$

Factors of $(x^2 - 8x + 15)$ is $(x - 5)(x - 3)$

Now, $(x^2 - 5x + 6)$

$= x^2 - 3x - 2x + 6$

$= (x - 3)(x - 2)$

Factors of $(x^2 - 5x + 6)$ is $(x - 3)(x - 2)$

LCM of $(x^2 - 8x + 15)$ and $(x^2 - 5x + 6)$ is $(x - 5)(x - 3)(x - 2)$.

127. **(a)** The average of 45 number = 39

$\Rightarrow$ The sum of 45 numbers

= 45 × 39 = 1755

According to the question

The correct sum of 45 numbers

= 1755 − 56 + 65

= 1764

The correct average of 45 numbers

$= \frac{1764}{45} = 39.2$

128. **(b)** Let Robert took $6x$ h to complete the work.

According to the question,

Tom took $3x$ h and George took $2x$ h to complete the work.

$\therefore \frac{1}{2x} + \frac{1}{3x} + \frac{1}{6x} = \frac{1}{23}$

$\Rightarrow \quad \frac{3 + 2 + 1}{6x} = \frac{1}{23}$

$\Rightarrow \quad 6x = 23 \times 6$

$\Rightarrow \quad x = 23$

$\therefore$ Required time taken by Tom $= 3x$

$= 3 \times 23 = 69$ h

129. **(d)** Let the diameter of metallic ball Q be d_Q.

Then diameter of metallic ball $Q = 4d_Q$

i.e., $d_P = 4d_Q$

Radius of metallic ball $Q = \frac{d}{2}$ i.e.,

$r_Q = \frac{d_Q}{2}$

Radius of metallic ball $P = r_P = 4r_Q$

$\left\{\because \text{Volume of sphere} = \frac{4}{3}\pi r^3\right\}$

$\Rightarrow$ Required volume ratio

$= \frac{\frac{4}{3}\pi r_P^3}{\frac{4}{3}\pi r_Q^3} = \frac{r_P^3}{r_Q^3} = \frac{(4r_Q)^3}{r_Q^3} = \frac{64}{1}$

$\therefore$ Required volume ratio = 64 : 1

130. **(d)** Distance covered by runner = 750 m

Time take by runner = 54 sec

Speed of runner $= \frac{750}{54}$ m/sec

$\Rightarrow$ Speed of runner $= \left(\frac{750}{54} \times \frac{18}{5}\right)$ km/h

= 50 km/h

131. **(d)** Radius of outer circle = 6 cm

Length of chord PQ = 10 cm

$\Rightarrow \quad PA = \frac{PQ}{2} = \frac{10}{2} = 5$ cm

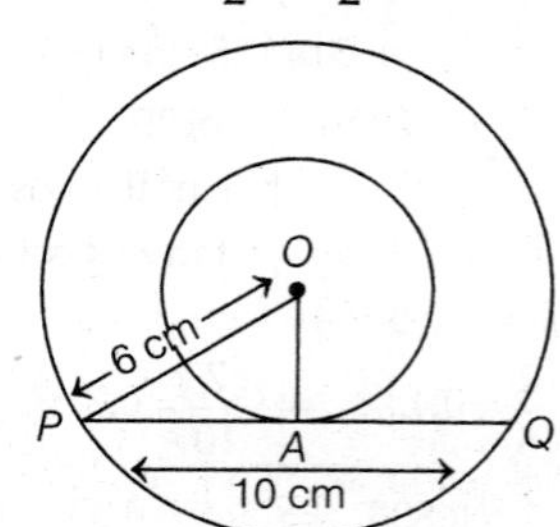

Let the radius of inner circle be r cm

$\Rightarrow OA = r$ cm

In ΔOPA, Using Pythagoras theorem

$\Rightarrow OA^2 + AP^2 = OP^2$

$\Rightarrow OA^2 = OP^2 - AP^2$

$\Rightarrow OA = \sqrt{6^2 - 5^2} = \sqrt{36 - 25}$

$\Rightarrow OA = \sqrt{11}$ cm

Radius of inner circle is $\sqrt{11}$ cm.

132. (d) We have,

$= 9 \times 2 \div 3 \text{ of } 24 - 3 \div 2 \times (6 - 7) \times 2 + 3 \div 3 \text{ of } 5$

$= \frac{9 \times 2}{72} - \frac{3}{2}(-1) \times 2 + \frac{3}{15}$

$= \frac{1}{4} + 3 + \frac{1}{5} = \frac{5 + 60 + 4}{20}$

$= \frac{69}{20}$

133. (d) Diagonal of quadrilateral = 20 m

Length of perpendiculars from the opposite vertices on it are 12 m and 18 m respectively

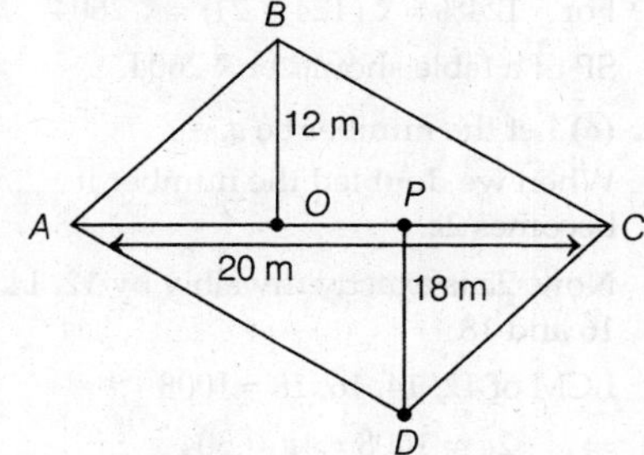

In ΔABC,

Area of $\Delta ABC = \frac{1}{2} \times AC \times OB$

$= \frac{1}{2} \times 20 \times 12 = 120 \text{ m}^2$

In ΔADC

Area of $\Delta ADC = \frac{1}{2} \times AC \times PD$

$= \frac{1}{2} \times 20 \times 18 = 180 \text{ m}^2$

The area of quadrilateral = Area of ΔABC + Area of ΔADC

$= (120 + 180) = 300 \text{ m}^2$

134. (d) From the given table,

Number of respondents do not own a car

$= 30 + 20 + 50 + 45 = 145$

Total number of respondents = 200

% of respondent do not own a car

$= \left(\frac{145}{200} \times 100\right) = 72.5\%$

135. (d) From the given table,

The number of student studying in class VIII from school U = 162

Total number of student studying in school U in all classes

$= 150 + 160 + 162 + 160 + 161 + 140$

$= 933$

Required % $= \left(\frac{162}{933} \times 100\right)\%$

$= \left(\frac{54}{311} \times 100\right)\%$

$= 17.36\%$

136. (c) From the given table, we concluded that manufacturer B has lowest vehicles in year 2010 over the given period as compare to other manufacturer.

137. (b) $\sin\theta + \cos\theta = \frac{\sqrt{11}}{3}$

On squaring both side,

$\Rightarrow \sin^2\theta + \cos^2\theta + 2\sin\theta\cos\theta = \frac{11}{9}$

$\Rightarrow \quad 1 + 2\sin\theta\cos\theta = \frac{11}{9}$

$\Rightarrow 2\sin\theta\cos\theta = \frac{11}{9} - 1 = \frac{2}{9}$

$\Rightarrow (\sin\theta - \cos\theta)^2 = \sin^2\theta + \cos^2\theta - 2\sin\theta\cos\theta$

$= 1 - 2\sin\theta\cos\theta = 1 - \frac{2}{9} = \frac{7}{9}$

$\Rightarrow \quad \sin\theta - \cos\theta = \frac{\sqrt{7}}{3}$

138. (d) Marks obtained by Ayush in various subject as Hindi = 88, English = 80, Maths = 90, Science = 82, Social = 85

Total Marks scored by Ayush

$= 88 + 80 + 90 + 82 + 85$

$= 425$

139. (b) Income of family = ₹ 75000

Saving of family is 10% i.e.

₹$\left(75000 \times \frac{10}{100}\right)$ = ₹ 7500

Expenditure of family

= ₹ (75000 − 7500)

= ₹ 67500

30% expenditure is incurred on education i.e. ₹ $67500 \times \frac{30}{100}$

= ₹ 20,250

Remaining amount

= ₹ (67500 − 20250)

= ₹ 47250

Amount left after ₹ 30375 spen on health = ₹ (47250 − 30375)

= ₹ 16875

Amount spent on food = ₹ 16875

% of food expenditure

$= \left(\frac{\text{Amount spent on food}}{\text{Total income}} \times 100\right)\%$

$= \left(\frac{16875}{75000} \times 100\right) = 22.5\%$

140. (a) From the given data, we concluded that organisation A has maximum number of employee than any other organisations

Number of employee in organisation A = 5825

141. (d) Sum of money i.e., P = ₹ 6500

Rate of interest = 10% per annum

Time = 2 yr

According to questions,

Interest is compounded half yearly then

$n = \frac{2}{1} \times 2 = 4$

$r = \frac{10}{2}\% = 5\%$ per half year

$\Rightarrow \quad A = P\left(1 + \frac{r}{100}\right)^n$

$= 6500\left(1 + \frac{5}{100}\right)^4$

$\Rightarrow A = 6500\left(1 + \frac{1}{20}\right)^4$

$= 6500 \times \frac{21}{20} \times \frac{21}{20} \times \frac{21}{20} \times \frac{21}{20}$

$\Rightarrow A$ = ₹ 7900

142. (c) Given,

Days Efficiency
A+B 27 25
675 Work
C 75 9

Again Let efficiency of A in x unit/day

$\therefore$ Efficiency of $B + C$ is $2.4x$ unit/day.

Now, Efficiency of

$A + B + C = 25 + 9 = 34$

$\Rightarrow x + 2.4x = 34$

$\Rightarrow 3.4x = 34$

$\Rightarrow x = 10$

$\therefore$ Efficiency of A = 10 unit/day

and Efficiency of B

= 25 − 10 = 15 unit/day

$\therefore$ Required no. of days

$= \frac{675}{15} = 45$ days.

143. **(b)** *AB* is common tangent to the two circle.

A and *B* are point of contact.

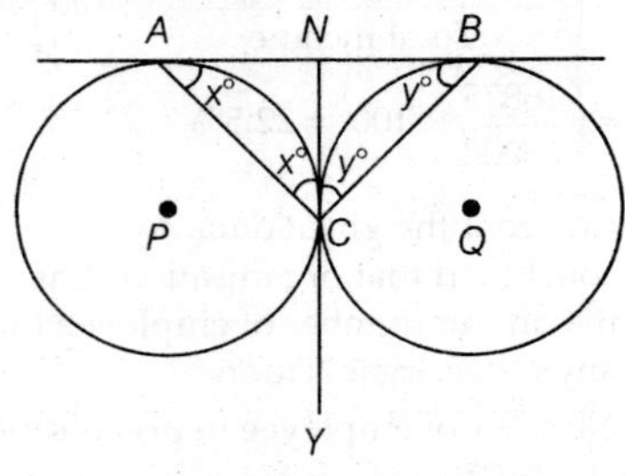

$\angle CAB = 55°$

Let *C* meet *AB* at point *N*.

Now, *NA* and *NC* are two tangents to the circle with centre *P*.

$\Rightarrow NA = NC$

$\Rightarrow NAC$ is an isosceles Δ.

$\Rightarrow \angle NAC = \angle NCA = x°$ (say) $= 55°$

Similarly, consideration *NB* and *NC* are tangents from *N* to circle with centre *Q*.

So, ΔNBC is isosceles with $NB = NC$ and $\angle NBC = \angle NCB = y$ (say)

In ΔABC

$\Rightarrow \angle A + \angle B + \angle C = 180°$

$\Rightarrow x° + y° + x° + y° = 180°$

$\Rightarrow 2(x + y) = 180°$

$\Rightarrow x + y = 90°$

$\Rightarrow y = (90° - 55°) = 35°$

$\{\because x = 55° = \angle NAC\}$

$\Rightarrow \angle NCB = 35°$

$\angle ACB = \angle ACN + \angle NCB = x° + y°$

$\angle ACB = 35° + 55° = 90°$

144. **(d)** Number of boys who are not enrolled in science = 20

Total number of students = 45

Required %

$$= \frac{\text{Student not enrolled in science}}{\text{Total students}} \times 100$$

$$= \left(\frac{20}{45} \times 100\right) = 44.44\%$$

145. **(a)** Sales of grapes in a day

$$= 1200 \times \frac{10}{100} = 120 \text{ kg}$$

Sales of oranges in a day

$$= \left(1200 \times \frac{15}{100}\right) = 180 \text{ kg}$$

Difference between sales of both fruits

$= (180 - 120)$ kg $= 60$ kg

146. **(d)** Number of employee in organisation *D* in 2019 = 70003

Number of employee in organisation *D* in 2021 = 8000

Number of employee in organisation *E* in 2019 = 6600

Number of employee in organisation *E* in 2021 = 7600

According to question

$$\text{Required ratio} = \frac{D_{2019} + E_{2019}}{D_{2021} + E_{2021}}$$

$$= \frac{7000 + 6600}{8000 + 7600}$$

$$= \frac{13600}{15600} = \frac{34}{39}$$

$\therefore$ Ratio = 34 : 39

147. **(c)** If $\tan\theta + \cot\theta = 2$

$\Rightarrow \tan\theta + \frac{1}{\tan\theta} = 2$

$\Rightarrow \tan^2\theta + 1 = 2\tan\theta$

$\Rightarrow (\tan\theta - 1)^2 = 0$

$\Rightarrow \tan\theta = 1$

$\Rightarrow \theta = \frac{\pi}{4}$

Then,

$2\tan^{25}\theta + 3\cot^{20}\theta + 5\tan^{30}\theta\cot^{15}\theta$

$= 2(1)^{25} + 3(1)^{20} + 5(1)^{30}(1)^{15}$

$= 2 + 3 + 5 = 10$

$\left\{\because \tan\theta = \tan\frac{\pi}{4} = 1, \cot\theta = \frac{1}{\tan\theta} = 1\right\}$

148. **(b)** *PQR* is an equilateral Δ, *S* is a point on *QR* such that $QR = 3QS$, $PQ = 9$ cm

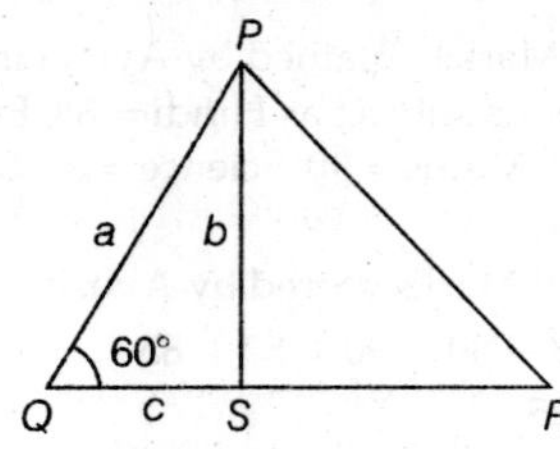

$\Rightarrow QS = \frac{QR}{3} = \frac{9}{3} = 3$ cm

In ΔPQS, Using cosine rule

$\Rightarrow \cos\theta = \frac{a^2 + c^2 - b^2}{2ac}$,

Here, $a = 9$, $c = 3$, $b = PS$

$\Rightarrow \cos 60° = \frac{9^2 + 3^2 - PS^2}{2 \times 9 \times 3}$

$\Rightarrow \frac{1}{2} = \frac{90 - PS^2}{2 \times 27}$

$\Rightarrow PS^2 = 90 - 27$

$\Rightarrow PS = \sqrt{63}$ cm

Length of $PS = \sqrt{63}$ cm

149. **(d)** Let the CP of a table be ₹ x

SP of a table = ₹ 1596

Loss incurred by Aarav = 24%

$\Rightarrow$ Loss = CP – SP = $(x - 1596)$ ₹

$\Rightarrow \text{Loss\%} = \frac{L}{\text{CP}} \times 100$

$\Rightarrow 24 = \frac{(x - 1596)}{x} \times 100$

$\Rightarrow x = ₹ 2100$

CP of a table is ₹ 2100

To gain 24%, Aarav should sell a table

$= ₹\left(2100 + 2100 \times \frac{24}{100}\right)$

$= ₹ 2604$

Speedy Method

Let the CP be ₹ x

Let incurred is 24$ on selling a table at₹ 1596.

According to question,

$\Rightarrow \frac{76}{100} = 1596$

$\Rightarrow 1\% = ₹ 21$

For $1\% = ₹ 21$

For $124\% = ₹ (124 \times 21) = ₹ 2604$

SP of a table should be ₹ 2604.

150. **(c)** Let the number be *a*.

When we doubled the number it becomes 2*a*.

Now, 2*a* is exactly divisibly by 12, 14, 16 and 18

LCM of 12, 14, 16, 18 = 1008

$\Rightarrow 2a = 1008 \Rightarrow a = 504$

151. **(d)** The word 'spurious' means false, fake, or not genuine.

So, the antonym is 'genuine', which means authentic or real.

152. **(b)** 'Kleptomania' is a psychological condition where a person has an irresistible urge to steal items, even if they're not needed.

This exactly matches the underlined description.

153. **(d)** The phrase 'straight from the horse's mouth' means to get information directly from the source. Since, the speaker heard the facts directly from him,' this idiom is the most appropriate fit.

154. **(c)** The one-word substitution for the 'study of coins' is numismatics.

155. **(b)** The sentence says 'The teacher asked the students to be quite during the exam'.

'Quite' is incorrect here. The correct word is 'quiet' (not noisy).

So, the correct substitution is 'be quiet'.

156. (d) 'Insipid' means bland, dull or lacking in flavour.

So, the correct substitution for the underlined segment is 'lacking taste'.

157. (b) 'Hue and cry' means a loud public outcry or protest, especially about an issue or injustice.

In the sentence, doctors are protesting against the RTH bill, so protest is the correct choice.

158. (d) 'Part and parcel' means an essential or inseparable part of something.

So, 'an integral part' is the most appropriate meaning.

159. (c) 'Major' means important, significant or large in scope.

'Considerable' means large in amount or extent, making it a suitable synonym.

160. (a) The correct sentence is 'Being courteous costs you nothing'.

The gerund being courteous acts as a general concept here and does not require an article.

161. (a) The idiom 'hear someone out' means to allow a person to speak without interruption until they've fully expressed their thoughts.

This is about patience and attentiveness in conversation.

162. (d) 'Ethical' means morally right or virtuous.

The opposite of that is 'immoral', which means lacking moral principles or being unethical.

163. (c) 'Vagrancy' refers to the state of living without a settled home, often wandering and being homeless.

'Vagabond' means a person who wanders without a home, making it the closest synonym.

164. (c) 'Build castles in the air' refers to making unrealistic or fanciful plans that are not grounded in reality.

Hence, 'To make imaginary schemes' is the most appropriate meaning.

165. (c) The idiom 'bite your tongue' means to stop yourself from saying something that you might regret, often to avoid conflict or being rude.

So, 'To avoid saying something' is the correct interpretation.

166. (d) The original sentence uses the present perfect form incorrectly.

'Lily has dedicate' is grammatically incorrect. The correct past participle of 'dedicate' is 'dedicated'.

So, the correct sentence is 'Lily has dedicated her life towards becoming a doctor'.

167. (a) 'Diabolical' means extremely evil or wicked, often associated with the devil.

'Malicious', meaning having the intention to harm, is the closest synonym.

168. (b) The incorrectly spelt word is 'Exagerate'. The correct spelling is 'exaggerate' (with a double 'g').

169. (a) The word 'absolved' means to be declared free from guilt or blame. The most direct antonym is 'accused', which refers to someone who has been formally charged with wrongdoing.

170. (a) 'The country's GDP bloomed despite the ongoing war situation' is the only sentence with correct spelling throughout 'despite' is correctly spelled and 'war situation' is also correct.

171. (a) The word 'calm' refers to a state of peace or tranquility. Its antonym would be 'turbulent', which indicates disorder, chaos or agitation - the opposite of calm.

172. (b) The sentence 'The cat climbed a tree and perched itself on a branch' is correct.

173. (d) The correct spelling is 'persistence.

'Persistancy' is an incorrect or obsolete form.

The other words - inconceivable, convictions, and deductions - are all correctly spelled.

174. (a) The correct form should be 'would pass', not 'would passes'.

'Would' is a modal verb and should be followed by the base form of the verb (pass).

So, the error lies in the verb form used.

175. (c) The word 'discrepancy' means a lack of compatibility or similarity, typically between facts or figures.

'Major difference' is the most accurate substitute.

176. (c) The phrase 'Despite of' is incorrect. It is a common grammatical error.

The correct usage is either

'Despite an injury...'

or

'In spite of an injury...'.

177. (d) The subject 'My teacher' is third person singular and the sentence is in the present tense.

Therefore, the verb should be in the simple present form with -s: 'forgets'.

178. (b) The idiom 'loaves and fishes' refers to material or selfish benefits obtained from a position of power rather than service.

Sentence meaning 'Ministers are more interested in the benefits of office than genuinely serving people'.

179. (d) The idiom 'to let the cat out of the bag' means to disclose a secret or a surprise unintentionally.

Example, He let the cat out of the bag about the surprise party.

180. (c) 'Sluggish' means slow-moving or lacking energy.

The antonym is 'swift', which means quick or fast.

181. (c) The idiom 'pull yourself together' means to regain control of your emotions, especially after being upset or disturbed.

Example, After hearing the bad news, she needed a moment to pull herself together.

182. (c) There is a subject-verb agreement error. The correct form is 'He is very thirsty' (not are).

'He' is singular, so it should be followed by 'is', not 'are.'

183. (c) The idiom 'talking through his hat' means talking nonsense or saying things without knowing the facts.

It implies that the person is speaking in a silly or meaningless way.

While 'ignorantly' is close, 'nonsense' is the more accurate and commonly accepted interpretation.

184. (a) A 'glutton' is a person who eats or consumes excessively, especially food.

185. (c) 'Profane' means not sacred, disrespectful to religion or the sacred. The opposite is 'divine', which relates to godliness or sacredness.

186. (d) Fifty rupees seems too much' is the correct usage. Even though 'fifty rupees' is plural in form, it refers to a single amount of money and hence takes a singular verb - 'seems' fits grammatically and contextually.

'Feels' is not the right verb for expressing judgement of value here.

187. (a) The word 'hideous' means extremely ugly or unpleasant.

The opposite would be 'attractive', which refers to something pleasing or beautiful.

188. (c) The correct spelling is 'Mountaineering', which refers to the sport of climbing mountains.

The underlined word 'Mountainering' is incorrect.

189. (d) The article 'a' is incorrect before a proper noun or specific name like 'Neptune' if it refers to a named ship or spacecraft.

Correct usage would be 'the Neptune', not 'a Neptune'.

190. (b) The correct spelling is 'commuter', referring to someone who travels regularly. 'Comutter' is incorrectly spelt.

191. (d) The word 'motivation' best fits in blank number 1.

192. (a) The word 'behaviour' best fits in blank number 2.

193. (b) The word 'predictions' best fits in blank number 3.

194. (a) The word 'achievements' best fits in blank number 4.

195. (d) The word 'determinants' best fits in blank number 5.

196. (b) The word 'accurate' means correct, precise or free from error. Its antonym is 'inexact', which means not accurate or not precise.

197. (b) The passage discusses how social media contributes to the spread of misinformation, its effects (such as during COVID-19), historical parallels and possible solutions like education and platform accountability.

198. (d) The passage attributes the spread of misinformation to factors like lack of fact-checking, poor critical thinking skills, inability to distinguish credible sources, and lack of platform accountability. It does not mention people's desire for sensational or controversial content as a cause, making this the correct answer to the 'NOT' question.

199. (c) The author acknowledges the benefits of social media, such as global connectivity and giving a voice to the unheard.

However, the bulk of the passage focuses on its negative consequences, especially the rapid and harmful spread of misinformation.

This balanced viewpoint is best reflected in option 3.

200. (a) The passage outlines the negative impact of misinformation, gives historical context and suggests solutions like education and platform responsibility.

The author's tone is cautionary, aiming to raise awareness and warn readers about the consequences of unchecked misinformation in the digital age.

CPO SI P-1 SP 13

PAPER-1

SSC CPO SI SOLVED PAPER

5 October 2023 (Shift I)

Instructions

1. This paper contains 200 questions.
2. It has 4 Parts, **Part I** General Intelligence and Reasoning, **Part II** General Knowledge and General Awareness, **Part III** Quantitative Aptitude and **Part IV** English Comprehension.
3. Each question carries **1 marks.**

MM : 200 **Time : 2 hr**

Part I

General Intelligence and Reasoning

1. Three of the following letter-clusters are alike in some manner and one is different. Select the one that is different.
(a) LOKP (b) HMIL
(c) KPLO (d) SXTW

2. If the given sheet is folded to form a cube, which of the given figures are possible?
The elements are shown to indicate the sides only.)

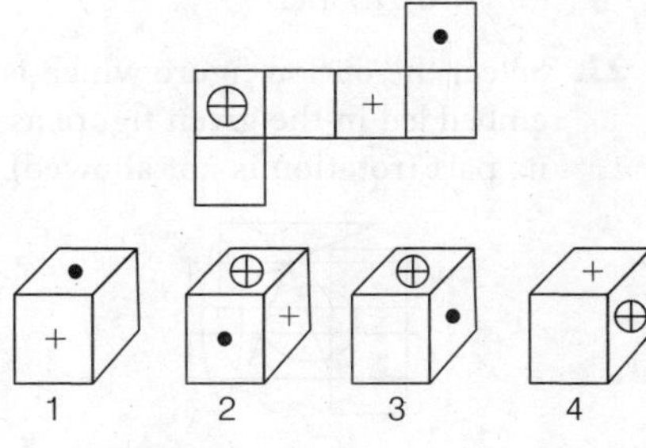

(a) Only 2 and 3
(b) Only 2 and 4
(c) Only 1 and 3
(d) Only 1 and 4

3. Select the correct mirror image of the given figure, when the mirror is placed at line MN as shown.

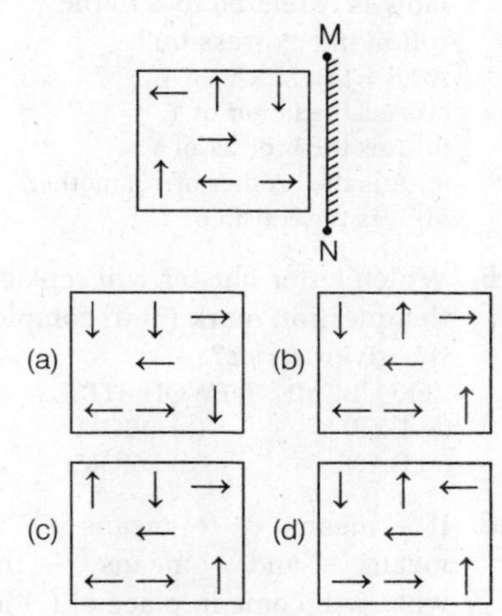

4. If A denotes '+', B denotes '×', C denotes '−', and D denotes '÷', then what will be the value of the following equation?
94 C 12 B 6 A 216 D 9 = ?
(a) 46 (b) 52
(c) 47 (d) 68

5. Which of the following numbers will replace the question mark (?) in the given series?
42, 53, 46, ?, 53, 66
(a) 58 (b) 51
(c) 55 (d) 48

6. Select the correct mirror image of the given figure when the mirror is placed at line MN as shown.

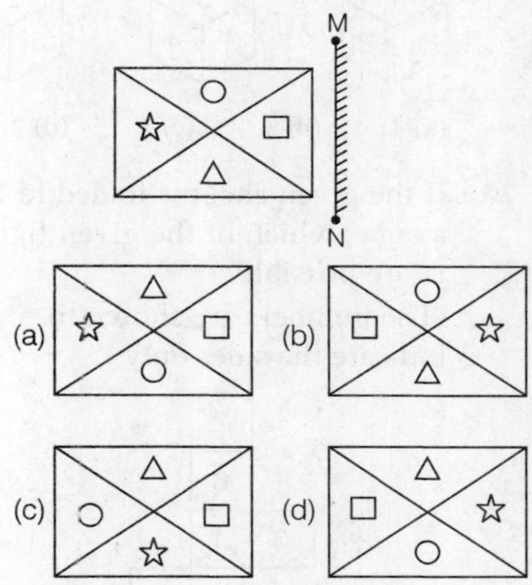

7. Six friends are sitting in a circle facing the centre. Sumit sits second to the right of Amit. Karan is an immediate neighbour of Param. Tony sits third to the right of Amit. Dharam is an immediate neighbour of Amit and Sumit. Karan sits second to the right of Sumit.
Who sits fourth to the right of Param?
(a) Karan (b) Sumit
(c) Dharam (d) Tony

8. Select the option that is related to the fifth number in the same way as the first number is related to the second number and the third number is related to the fourth number.
32 : 10 :: 24 : 12 :: 98 : ?
(a) 25 (b) 24 (c) 43 (d) 34

9. Select the set in which the numbers are related in the same way as are the numbers of the following sets.
(**Note** Operations should be performed on the whole numbers, without breaking down the numbers into its constituent digits. e.g. 13 . Operations on 13 such as adding /subtracting /multiplying etc. to 13 can be performed. Breaking down 13 into 1 and 3 and then performing mathematical operations on 1 and 3 is not allowed)
(7, 52), (9, 84)

(a) (13, 172) (b) (11, 125)
(c) (14, 196) (d) (8, 65)

10. Three different positions of the same dice are shown. Find the number on the face opposite the face showing '6'.

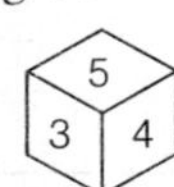

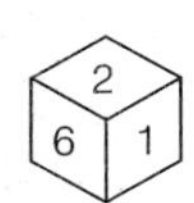

(a) 4 (b) 3 (c) 1 (d) 2

11. If the given sheet is folded to form a cube, which of the given figures is/are possible?
(The numbers are shown to indicate the sides only.)

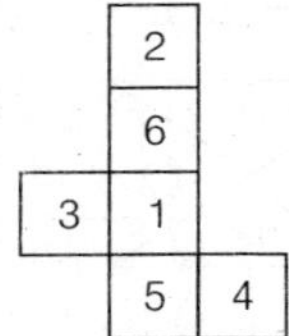

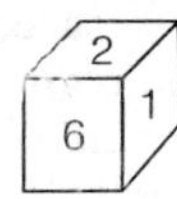
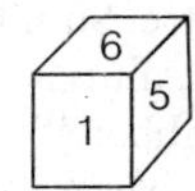
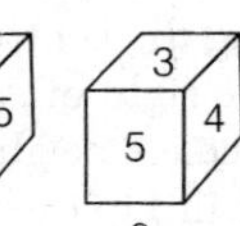
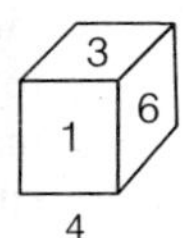

(a) Only 4 (b) Only 3
(c) Only 1 and 4 (d) Only 2

12. In a certain code language, 'COLD' is coded as '6428' and 'TIDE' is coded as '9673'. What is the code for 'D' in the given code language?

(a) 2 (b) 6 (c) 3 (d) 9

13. Select the venn diagram that best illustrates the relationship between the following classes.
Europe, United Kingdom, London

(a)

(b)

(c)

(d)

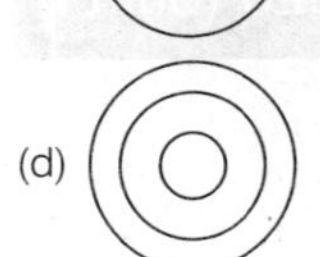

14. 'Z @ A' means 'Z is the son of A'.
'Z * A' means 'Z is the brother of A'.
'Z × A' means 'Z is the father of A'.
'Z # A' means 'Z is the sister of A'.
'Z $ A' means 'Z is the daughter of A'.
'Z = A' means 'Z is the mother of A'.
How is A related to Y in the following expression?
A * S = J @ M × Y

(a) A is the father of Y.
(b) A is the brother of Y.
(c) A is the brother of Y's mother.
(d) A is the cousin of Y.

15. Which letter-cluster will replace the question mark (?) to complete the given series?
ZFKQ, BCMN, ?, FWQH, HTSE

(a) DZPJ (b) DBOM
(c) DAOL (d) DZOK

16. If '+' means '÷', '−' means '+', '×' means '−' and '÷' means '×' , then what will come in place of (?) in the given equation?
$8 \div 5 - 5 \times 10 + 2 = ?$

(a) 40 (b) 30 (c) 35 (d) 45

17. Select the figure will come next in the following figure series?

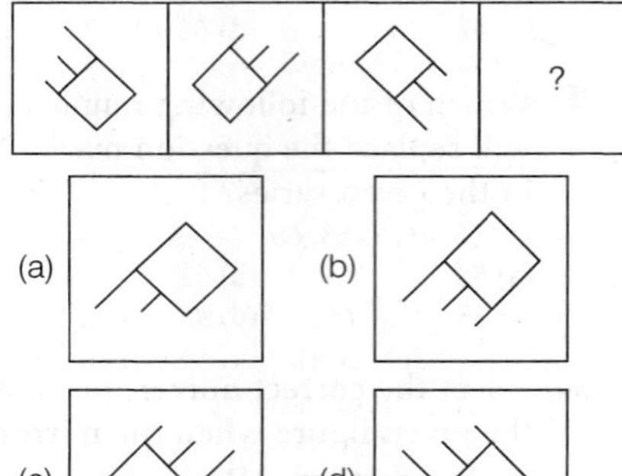

18. Select the correct mirror image of the given pattern when the mirror is placed at 'MN' as shown below.

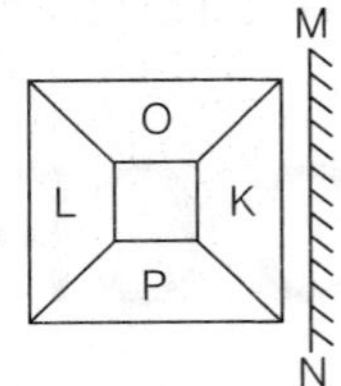

(a) 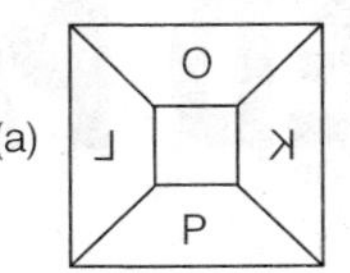 (b) 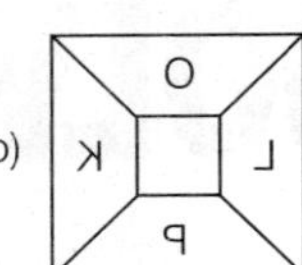

(c) 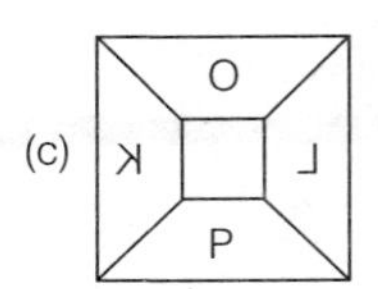 (d) 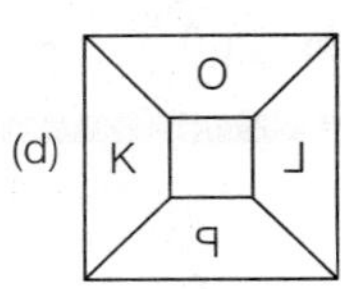

19. F is the brother of J. E is the sister of D. K is the sister of L. D is the son of L. J is the father of E. How is D related to F?

(a) Sister's husband
(b) Brother's son
(c) Wife
(d) Brother's daughter

20. In a certain code language, 'EDUCATION' is written as 'FCVBBSJNO' and 'MICROSOFT' is written as 'NHDQPRPEU'. How will 'SEMICIRCLE' be written in that language?

(a) TDNHDHSBMD
(b) TDNHHDSBFM
(c) TDHNDHSFBD
(d) TDNHHDSBFD

21. Select the option figure which is embedded in the given figure as its part (rotation is not allowed).

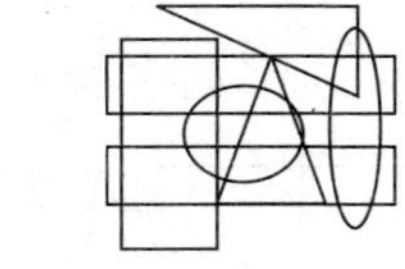

(a)  (b) 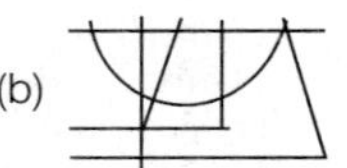

(c) 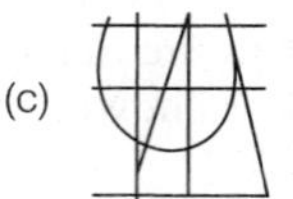 (d) 

22. Select the option that is related to the third word in the same way as the second word is related to the first word.
(The words must be considered as meaningful words and must not be related to each other based on the number of letters/number of consonants/vowels in the word.)
Pedal : Bicycle :: Oar : ?
(a) Car (b) Television
(c) Canoe (d) Motorcycle

23. P is to the North of Q. T is to the East of Q and S is to the East of P. S is to the North-East of T and South-West of R. What is the position of R with respect to Q? (All positions are arranged in GRID pattern)
(a) North-East
(b) South-West
(c) East
(d) South

24. Choose one of the following correct combinations of mathematical signs which can be filled to balance the following equation.
86 ◯ 42 ◯ 12 ◯ 3 ◯ 12 ◯ 3 ◯ 4
(a) +, −, ÷, ×, =, + (b) −, −, ÷, =, ×, +
(c) −, +, ÷, ×, =, + (d) −, +, ×, =, ÷, +

25. Six students are sitting around a circular table facing the centre. A is an immediate neighbour of both E and D. E sits third to the right of C. D sits third to the left of F. E is an immediate neighbour of F. B sits second to the left of E. Who is the immediate neighbour of both A and C ?
(a) E (b) D
(c) F (d) B

26. If '+' means '−', '−' means '÷', '÷' means '×', and '×' means '+', then what will come in place of the (?) in the following equation?
$15 \times 30 + 15 - 3 \div 2 = ?$
(a) 15 (b) 30
(c) 35 (d) 40

27. Which of the following terms will replace the question mark (?) in the given series?
HKOE , KNOE , ? , QTOE , TWOE
(a) NQOE (b) QNOE
(c) NQEO (d) NOQE

28. Select the option that is related to the third word in the same way as the second word is related to the first word. (The words should be considered as meaningful word and should not be related to each other on the basis of number of betters/consonants/vouls in the word.)
Yearn : Crave :: Haste : ?
(a) Alacrity (b) Hanker
(c) Delay (d) Leisure

29. Select the set in which the numbers are related in the same way as are the numbers of the following sets.
(**Note** Operations should be performed on the whole numbers, without breaking down the numbers into its constituent digits. E.g. 13- Operations on 13 such as adding/subtracting /multiplying etc. to 13 can be performed. Breaking down 13 into 1 and 3 and then performing mathematical operations on 1 and 3 is not allowed.)
(23, 6, 35)
(13, 5, 23)
(a) (24, 5, 33) (b) (16, 4, 20)
(c) (25, 8, 41) (d) (13, 7, 28)

30. If '+' means '−', '−' means '×' '×' means '÷' and '÷' means '+', what will come in place of '?' in the following equation?
$42 \times 6 - 7 \div 13 + 28 = ?$
(a) 43 (b) 27 (c) 34 (d) 39

31. In a certain code language, 'GRAPE' is coded as 21-54-3-48-15 and 'MELON' is coded as 39-15-36-45-42. How will 'PEACH' be coded in the same language?
(a) 48-15-3-8-27 (b) 48-15-3-9-24
(c) 49-15-3-9-27 (d) 45-16-3-9-24

32. Which number will replace the question mark (?) in the following series?
6, 20, 42, ?, 110, 156
(a) 80 (b) 72 (c) 50 (d) 64

33. Which of the following numbers will replace the question mark (?) in the given series?
473, 517, 561, ?, 649, 693
(a) 607 (b) 598 (c) 603 (d) 605

34. Select the option that represents the letters which, when sequentially placed from left to right in the blanks below, will complete the letter series.
_ L _ _ K S _ T U _ S L _ _ K
(a) L U S K T U K
(b) U T S K T L U
(c) S T U L K T U
(d) K T U L U T S

35. Select the option that represents the correct order of the given words as they would appear in an English dictionary?
1. Flint 2. Flec
3. Flaw 4. Fleet
5. Flight
(a) 3, 5, 4, 2, 1 (b) 2, 3, 4, 5, 1
(c) 3, 2, 4, 5, 1 (d) 3, 4, 2, 5, 1

36. Which figure from the given options would replace the question mark (?) if the following figure series were to be continued?

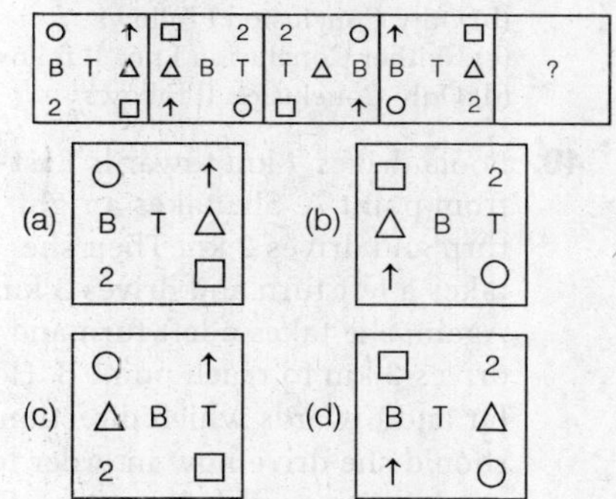

37. Select the set in which the numbers are related in the same way as are the numbers of the following set.
(**Note** Operations should be performed on the whole numbers without breaking down the numbers into its constituent digits. E.g. 13 . Operations on 13 such as adding /subtracting /multiplying etc. to 13 can be performed. Breaking down 13 into 1 and 3 and then performing mathematical operations on 1 and 3 is not allowed)
(2, 5, 341)
(1, 7, 510)
(a) (8,2,140) (b) (1,2,25)
(c) (2,5,56) (d) (3,6,64)

38. Six characters A, B, C, 1, 2 and 3 are written on different faces of a dice. Two positions of this dice are shown in the figure. Find the character on the face opposite to C.

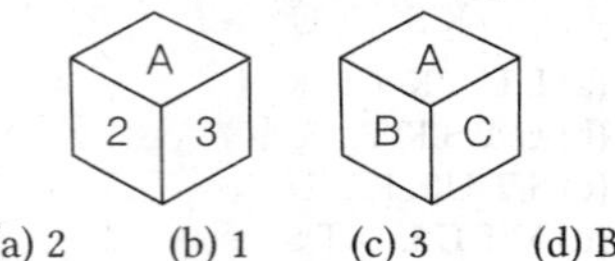

(a) 2 (b) 1 (c) 3 (d) B

39. Given below are two statements and two conclusions. Take the statements to be true even if they are at variance with commonly known facts, and decide whether the conclusion(s) follow(s) the given statements.

Statements

Some dates are hazelnuts.

All hazelnuts are walnuts.

Conclusions

I. Some dates are walnuts.

II. Some walnuts are hazelnuts.

(a) Both the conclusions follow
(b) Only Conclusion I follows
(c) Neither Conclusion I nor II follows
(d) Only Conclusion II follows

40. Pooja drives 4 km towards East from point A. She takes a right turn and drives 2 km.Then she takes a left turn and drives 3 km. Again, she takes a left turn and drives 2 km to reach point B. How far and towards which direction should she drive now in order to reach point A again?

(a) 7 km towards West
(b) 4 km towards South
(c) 4 km towards East
(d) 5 km towards North

41. In this question, three statements are given, followed by two conclusions numbered I and II. Assuming the statements to be true, even if they seem to be at variance with commonly known facts, decide which of the conclusions logically follows/follow from the statements.

Statements

All teas are coffees.

All coffees are beverages.

Some teas are drinks

Conclusions

I. All teas are beverages.

II. No drink is a coffee.

(a) Only Conclusion I follows
(b) Only Conclusion II follows
(c) Both Conclusions I and II follow
(d) Neither Conclusion I nor II follows

42. Given below are two statements and two conclusions. Take the statements to be true even if they are at variance with commonly known facts, and decide whether the conclusion(s) follow(s) the given statements.

Statements

All irons are coppers.

All coppers are aluminiums.

Conclusions

I. Some aluminiums are irons

II. Some aluminiums are coppers

(a) Only Conclusion II follows
(b) Neither Conclusion I nor II follows
(c) Only Conclusion I follows
(d) Both the Conclusions I and II follow

43. Select the correct option that indicates the arrangement of the given words in the order in which they appear in an English dictionary.

1. Desperate 2. Desolate
3. Destruction 4. Desire
5. Descend 6. Destination

(a) 5, 4, 2, 1, 3, 6 (b) 5, 4, 1, 6, 2, 3
(c) 5, 4, 2, 1, 6, 3 (d) 5, 4, 1, 2, 6, 3

44. In a certain code language, 'YATCH' is coded as 67 and 'DINE' is coded as 40. How will 'MANGO' be coded in that language?

(a) 57 (b) 60
(c) 62 (d) 65

45. Which of the given figure when placed in the 5th position would continue the series that is established by the first four figures?

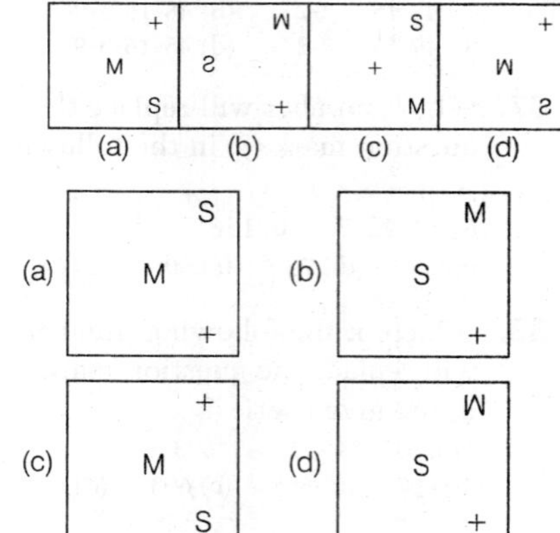

46. If '+' means '–', '–' means '×', '×' means '÷' and '÷' means '+', what will come in place of '?' in the following equation?

$45 - 3 \div 144 \times 12 + 38 = ?$

(a) 123 (b) 109 (c) 91 (d) 95

47. Three of the following letter-clusters are alike in some manner and one is different. Select the one that is different.

(a) OKNL (b) JQAZ
(c) FBEC (d) HDGE

48. In a certain code language, 'STORY' is coded as '97' and 'PULL' is coded as '61'. How will 'INCOME' be coded in that language?

(a) 54 (b) 49 (c) 59 (d) 47

49. Which of the following numbers will replace the question mark (?) in the given series

32, 32, 32, 34, ?, 106, 530

(a) 96 (b) 38 (c) 102 (d) 34

50. Which two signs should be interchanged to make the given equation correct?

$729 \times 9 - (56 - 6) \times 5 \div 2 + 152 \times 19 = 69$

(a) × and + (b) × and ÷
(c) ÷ and – (d) + and –

Part II

General Knowledge and General Awareness

51. Ashtadhyayi, is a Sanskrit treatise on grammar, written in the 6th to 5th century BCE by ....

(a) Panini (b) Patanjali
(c) Agastya (d) Vishvamitra

52. The provision of fundamental duties in the Indian Constitution is inspired by..........

(a) the Constitution of USSR
(b) the Constitution of France
(c) the Constitution of Canada
(d) the Constitution of USA

53. Which of the following is not included in inventory investment when calculating national income?

(a) Change in sales during the year.
(b) Change in stock of raw material.
(c) Change in stock of semi-finished goods.
(d) Change in stock of finished goods.

54. The .... birth rate indicates the number of live births occurring during the year per 1000 population estimated at midyear.
(a) crude (b) positive
(c) negative (d) neutral

55. The shape of a basketball court is a.......... .
(a) square (b) rectangle
(c) triangle (d) circle

56. Under which Article of the Indian Constitution shall the executive power of the Union be vested in the President?
(a) Article 53 (b) Article 55
(c) Article 58 (d) Article 56

57. What do you call those types of drugs which replicate natural messengers by switching on the receptor?
(a) Antidepressants (b) Agonist
(c) Depressonts (d) Antagonist

58. In which of the following years did the government opt for a plan holiday after the Seventh Five-Year Plan?
(a) From 1991 to 1993
(b) From 1990 to 1992
(c) From 1992 to 1993
(d) From 1989 to 1991

59. Which of the following did not emerge as a result of disintegration of the Bahmani kingdom during the 16th century?
(a) Ahmadnagar (b) Gaur
(c) Golconda (d) Bidar

60. When was the 8th round of the General Agreement on Tariffs and Trade (GATT), the so-called 'Uruguay Round' which led to the establishment of World Trade Organisation (WTO) completed?
(a) 1993 (b) 1994
(c) 1991 (d) 1992

61. In which of the following languages is 'Childhood Days - A Memoir' by Satyajit Ray written?
(a) Hindi (b) Telugu
(c) Kannada (d) Bengali

62. Which of the following dance forms originated in South-Eastern India?
(a) Chhau (b) Sattriya
(c) Kathak (d) Kuchipudi

63. Where is Red Lake found?
(a) USA (b) UK
(c) China (d) Japan

64. How many Fundamental Duties are listed in the Indian Constitution as of 2022?
(a) 13 (b) 10
(c) 12 (d) 11

65. Which of the following is not an example of small savings?
(a) Mutual Funds
(b) National Savings Certificates
(c) Kisan Vikas Patras
(d) Post Office Deposits

66. .... land is suitable for cropping on a regular basis.
(a) Urban (b) Barren
(c) Arable (d) Marginal

67. Who among the following had written the novel Coolie, that concentrated on social misery caused by inhumanity?
(a) RK Narayan
(b) Vijay Tendulkar
(c) VS Naipaul
(d) Mulk Raj Anand

68. Which of the following dance forms traces its lineage to the ancient dance of Sadir Aṭṭam?
(a) Bharatanatyam (b) Kuchipudi
(c) Mohiniyattam (d) Kathakali

69. What percentage of jobs in India are at risk of automation, as per World Bank data,2016?
(a) 77% (b) 40%
(c) 69% (d) 55%

70. Which of the following is a round worm?
(a) Planaria (b) Ascaris
(c) Liver fluke (d) Taenia

71. Which of the following indicates the system introduced by Lord Cornwallis granting legal ownership of land to the zamindars in Bengal in order to get a fixed revenue by a fixed date?
(a) The Ryotwari System
(b) Mahalwari System
(c) Taluqdari System
(d) The Permanent Settlement

72. Vultures are
(a) carnivores (b) omnivores
(c) decomposers (d) herbivores

73. Which of the following is not an example of a minor industrial region of India?
(a) Durg-Raipur region
(b) Ambala-Amritsar region
(c) Northern Malabar region
(d) Hugli region

74. Jagjit Singh is associated with which form of singing?
(a) Ghazal (b) Thumri
(c) Dhrupad (d) Tappa

75. By observing the motion of objects on an inclined plane ...... deduced that objects move with a constant speed when no force acts on them.
(a) Michael Faraday
(b) Johannes Kepler
(c) Galileo
(d) Archimedes

76. In which type of rainfall, winds move out from a high-pressure area with wind direction clockwise in the Northern Hemisphere, and anti-clockwise in the Southern Hemisphere?
(a) Orography
(b) Cyclones
(c) Anticyclone
(d) Convection

77. From the given options, choose the one which is not a product of the decomposition reaction of Lead nitrate.
(a) Nitrogen dioxide
(b) Oxygen
(c) Nitrogen
(d) Lead oxide

78. The Eastern Ghats stretch from the ...... to the Nigiris in the south.
(a) Damodar Valley
(b) Son Valley
(c) Mahanadi Valley
(d) Godavari Valley

79. When was the Atmiya Sabha founded to attack the evils within Hinduism?
(a) 1845 (b) 1814
(c) 1839 (d) 1828

80. The 'Servants of India Society' was the brainchild of which of the following leaders?
(a) Chittaranjan Das
(b) Gopal Krishna Gokhale
(c) BR Ambedkar
(d) Lala Lajpat Rai

81. The President of which of the following countries was invited as the Chief Guest for the Republic Day parade on 26th January, 2020?
(a) New Zealand (b) Australia
(c) Brazil (d) Indonesia

82. 1 kilowatt is equivalent to
(a) 3600 KJ/h (b) 3600 calorie
(c) 7200 KJ/h (d) 7200 Joule

83. The star-shaped temples were built during the reign of
(a) Chalukaya (b) Badami
(c) Cholas (d) Hoysala

84. Hara Shankar Bhattacharya is a maestro of ....
(a) sitar (b) sarangi
(c) violin (d) santoor

85. Which radioactive element with atomic number 43 in the modern periodic table is unstable, and the half-lives of all its isotopes are relatively short, from 4.2 million years to 5.0 s?
(a) Nobelium (b) Promethium
(c) Neptunium (d) Technetium

86. The Himalayas have been divided on the basis of regions from West to East. The correct order of regions from West to east is
(a) Punjab Himalayas, Nepal Himalayas, Kumaon Himalayas and Assam Himalayas
(b) Punjab Himalayas, Kumaon Himalayas, Nepal Himalayas and Assam Himalayas
(c) Punjab Himalayas, Kumaon Himalayas, Assam Himalayas and Nepal Himalayas
(d) Punjab Himalayas, Nepal Himalayas, Assam Himalayas and Kumaon Himalayas

87. How many times has India won the ICC T20 Men's World Cup in cricket?
(a) 3 (b) 2 (c) 1 (d) 4

88. Which chemical element of Group 18 of the periodic table is produced by the natural radioactive decay of uranium in soils and rocks?
(a) Oganesson (b) Krypton
(c) Radon (d) Neon

89. Chad Sukra festival is celebrated by the Jaintia tribe of ....
(a) Jharkhand (b) Assam
(c) Punjab (d) Meghalaya

90. Which of the following industries was not in Schedule A of Industrial Policy 1956?
(a) Air transport (b) Mining of salt
(c) Mineral oils (d) Iron and steel

91. Which Article of the Constitution of India states that the Prime Minister is appointed by the President of India?
(a) Article 73 (b) Article 75
(c) Article 74 (d) Article 76

92. Ammannur Madhava Chakyar was conferred the Padma Shri for his contribution to which of the following dance forms?
(a) Kutiyattam (b) Kuchipudi
(c) Kathakali (d) Yakshagana

93. Which cell organelle appears as rounded or sausage-shaped structures under electron microscopy, measuring about 0.5-1.0μm in diameter and 2-8 μm in length?
(a) Ribosomes (b) Lysosomes
(c) Mitochondria (d) Plastids

94. When was Khandesh merged into the Mughal empire by Akbar?
(a) 1601 (b) 1595
(c) 1597 (d) 1605

95. How many types of the amendment are mentioned by the Indian Constitution as per Article 368?
(a) Five (b) Four
(c) Two (d) Three

96. In the game of Ice hockey, during normal play how many players are there in each team on the ice at any one time to compete?
(a) 12 (b) 6 (c) 10 (d) 5

97. Siachen in Himalayas is
(a) a glacier (b) a national park
(c) a dam (d) a lake

98. Maimata is a popular folk dance of which of the following states?
(a) Tripura (b) Uttarakhand
(c) Haryana (d) Punjab

99. To which feature of the Constitution of India does the appointment of the Governor by the Centre belong?
(a) Federal feature
(b) Directive Principles
(c) Supremacy of the Constitution
(d) Unitary system

100. The term 'inning' is related to which of the following sports?
(a) Volleyball (b) Kho-Kho
(c) Hockey (d) Basketball

Part III
Quantitative Aptitude

101. Find the fourth proportional to 0.48, 0.84 and 32.
(a) 65 (b) 34
(c) 56 (d) 43

102. Study the given table and answer the question that follows.
The table shows data of population and literacy/illiteracy rate among the population in three different villages.

Village	Respective ratio between number of males and females	Percentage of literates (Males and females) out of total population	Number of illiterates (Males and females cut of total population)
P	2 : 5	45	380
Q	3 : 7	65	270
R	1 : 3	80	150

The number of illiterates in village R is what percentage less than that in village P?
(a) $60\frac{11}{19}\%$ (b) $60\frac{9}{19}\%$
(c) $60\frac{10}{19}\%$ (d) $60\frac{8}{19}\%$

103. In a circle of radius 42 cm, an arc subtends an angle of 60° at the centre. Find the length of the arc. (Take $\pi = \frac{22}{7}$)
(a) 44 cm (b) 21 cm
(c) 22 cm (d) 42 cm

104. Mihir buys a book for ₹625. However, because of certain urgency, he sells it for ₹550.Find his loss percentage.
(a) 12% (b) 14%
(c) 10% (d) 15%

105. The salary of Arpit fell by 5% after 1 yr and further fell by 8% after the second year due to bad performance. Initially, his salary was ₹ 80000. What is his current salary (in ₹)?
(a) 69620 (b) 69920
(c) 70920 (d) 65720

106. Study the given graph and answer the question that follows. The graph shows data related to number of students of enrolled for a vocational course in two institutes (X and Y) during three years.

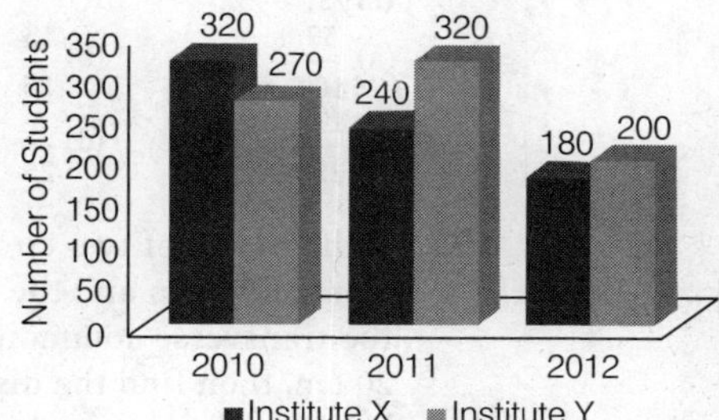

What is the difference between the average number of students enrolled in institute X in 2010 and 2011 and that in institute Y in 2011 and 2012?

(a) 20 (b) 15 (c) 18 (d) 22

107. The total surface area of a solid hemisphere is 4158 cm^2. Find its volume (in cm^3).

(a) 462 (b) 9702 (c) 1848 (d) 19404

108. The average weight of 8 students is 48 kg. If four students of average weight 44 kg and four students of average weight 58 kg is also added, then find the average weight of 16 students.

(a) 49.5 kg (b) 48 kg (c) 49 kg (d) 48.5 kg

109. Simplify the given expression.

$(1-2x)^2 - (1+2x)^2$

(a) $8x$ (b) $-8x$ (c) $-(2+8x^2)$ (d) $2+8x^2$

110. The table below shows the number of laptops sold by the 4 sellers and the ratio of Brand 1 laptops sold to Brand 2 laptops sold.

Seller	Total laptops sold	Brand 1 laptops sold : Brand 2 laptops sold
A	4000	3 : 1
B	6000	2 : 1
C	8000	5 : 3
D	5000	1 : 4

The number of Brand 1 laptops sold by A seller is how many more than the number of Brand 2 laptops sold by B seller?

(a) 1200 (b) 800 (c) 1000 (d) 600

111. A boy goes from home to school at a speed of 30 km/h and returns back at a speed of 70 km/h. What is his average speed for the journey?

(a) 42 km/h (b) 48 km/h (c) 38 km/h (d) 36 km/h

112. Rupu's income is 20% more than Madhu's income. Madhu's income is less than Rupu's income by

(a) $17\frac{2}{3}\%$ (b) 20% (c) $18\frac{2}{3}\%$ (d) $16\frac{2}{3}\%$

113. What annual instalment (in ₹) will discharge a debt of ₹9429 due in three years at12.25% simple interest per annum? [**Note** Instalments will be paid at the end of Year 1,Year 2 and Year 3.]

(a) 2840 (b) 2800 (c) 2700 (d) 2760

114. Study the given table and answer the question that follows.

The table shows the number of students studying in 6 different classes of 6 different schools.

Which class has the minimum number of students from all schools together?

Schools	Class V	Class VI	Class VII	Class VIII	Class IX	Class X
P	152	160	145	156	147	144
Q	148	166	150	155	157	143
R	161	152	140	145	143	165
S	159	142	149	140	142	168
T	147	144	158	163	154	150
U	150	160	162	160	160	140
Total	917	924	904	919	903	910

(a) VIII (b) IX (c) VII (d) X

115. Find the least number which is exactly divisible by 20, 28, 34, 60 and 75.

(a) 36220 (b) 35900 (c) 34500 (d) 35700

116. The mean proportional between 0.03 and 0.0003 is

(a) 0.0003 (b) 0.0013 (c) 0.003 (d) 0.033

117. If $a+b+c=5$ and $ab+bc+ca=7$, then the value of $a^3+b^3+c^3-3abc$ is

(a) 15 (b) 20 (c) 25 (d) 30

118. The given pie-chart represent the survey report on favourite games of a group of young people.

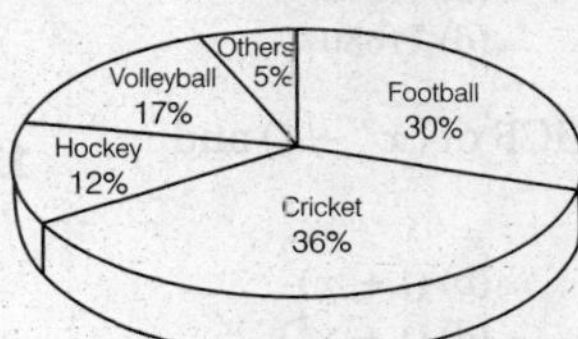

If a total of 4980 people were surveyed, then what is the central angle produced by the sector indicating football?

(a) 108° (b) 105° (c) 100° (d) 90°

119. The following table shows the income of a company in a year from various sectors

Sectors	Finance	Communication	Production	Sales	Transportation
Amount (in lakh ₹)	85	60	67	115	75

What is the difference (in lakh ₹) between the income from the maximum earning sector and the minimum earning sector?

(a) 48 (b) 40 (c) 30 (d) 55

120. An item with a marked price of Z was sold for ₹ 6622, after a discount of 12% was offered. What was the value of Z?
(a) ₹7425 (b) ₹7500
(c) ₹7525 (d) ₹7575

121. Study the given bar graph carefully to answer the question that follows.
Marks obtained by four students in Mid-I and Mid-II.

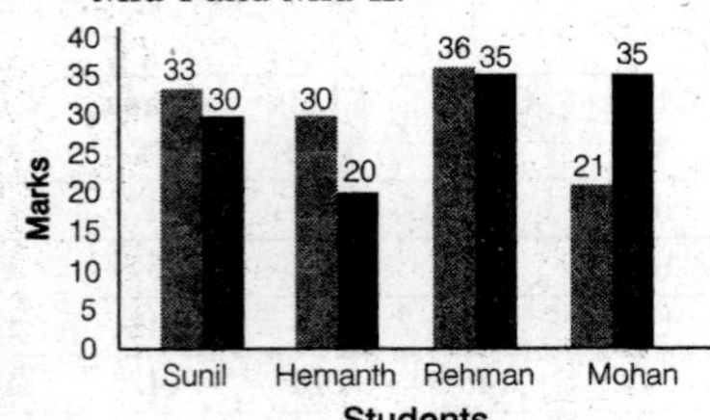

Marks obtain by Hemanth in Mid-I are what percentage of the total marks obtained by all the students in Mid-I?
(a) 30% (b) 15% (c) 20% (d) 25%

122. A shopkeeper increases the cost price of an item by 50% and offers a discount of 40% on this marked price. What is his loss percentage?
(a) 15% (b) 20% (c) 10% (d) 5%

123. If interest be compounded half-yearly, then find the compound interest on ₹8,000 at 20% p.a. for 1 yr.
(a) ₹1675 (b) ₹1690
(c) ₹1685 (d) ₹1680

124. What is the HCF of $(x^6 + 1)$ and $(x^4 - 1)$?
(a) 1 (b) $(1 + x)$
(c) $(1 - x^2)$ (d) $(1 + x^2)$

125. The value of $\dfrac{1\frac{1}{2} \div 3\frac{1}{4} + \frac{1}{2} \div \frac{13}{14} + \frac{1}{5}}{\frac{1}{5} \times 3\frac{1}{2} - \frac{1}{3} \div 1\frac{3}{4} \times 3\frac{1}{2}}$ is
(a) 33 (b) 36 (c) 38 (d) 40

126. If 2 men or 4 women can build a wall in 34 days, in how many days can 6 men and 5 women build the same wall?
(a) 24 (b) 8 (c) 12 (d) 16

127. Find the HCF of 78, 84, 90 and 112.
(a) 1 (b) 2 (c) 5 (d) 7

128. Study the given graph and answer the question that follows. The following graph shows the distribution of the cost percentage of different items.

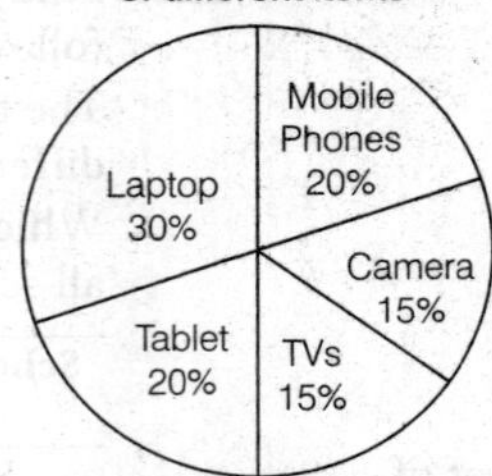

If a person purchased all the items for ₹ 300000, then the cost of a TV is less than that of a laptop by
(a) ₹40000 (b) ₹55000
(c) ₹50000 (d) ₹45000

129. If $\cos A = \frac{1}{2}, 0 \le A \le 90°$, then what is the value of $\sin(180 - A)$?
(a) $\frac{1}{2}$ (b) $\frac{\sqrt{3}}{2}$
(c) $\frac{1}{\sqrt{3}}$ (d) 1

130. Mahesh agreed to sell rice with 24% loss, as the rice got rotten. However, he cheated customers and gave only 19 gm of rice in place of 50 gm of rice. What is the percentage of his profit or loss?
(a) 100% loss (b) $\frac{100}{3}$% loss
(c) $\frac{100}{3}$% profit (d) 100% profit

131. A cylinder has some water in it at a height of 16 cm. If a sphere of radius 9 cm is put into it, then find the rise in the height of the water if the radius of the cylinder is 12 cm.
(a) 8 cm (b) 6 cm
(c) 8.75 cm (d) 6.75 cm

132. A can do $\frac{1}{5}$ of a piece of work in 20 days, B can do 30% of the same work in 36 days, while C can do 80% of the same work in 160 days. B and C together started and worked for x days. After x days B left the work, and A joined C and both completed the remaining work in $(x - 41)$ days. If the ratio between the work done by $(B + C)$ together to the work done by $(A + C)$ together is 19 : 6, then what fraction of the same work can be completed by C alone in $2x$ days?
(a) $\frac{57}{100}$ (b) $\frac{13}{25}$
(c) $\frac{19}{25}$ (d) $\frac{6}{25}$

133. If the radius of two circles be 6 cm and 9 cm and the length of the transverse common tangent be 20 cm, then find the distance between the two centres.
(a) 25 cm (b) 22 cm
(c) 24 cm (d) 27 cm

134. Nikunj goes 4 kilometres against the current of a stream in 1 h, and 2 km along the current in 15 min. How long will it take him to go 7 km in stationary water?
(a) 1 h 15 min
(b) 1 h 20 min
(c) 1 h 10 min
(d) 1 h 5 min

135. At 7: 30 P.M. the owner of a Cycle noticed that a thief is taking away his cycle from his home and is cycling in a particular direction at an estimated speed of 10 km/h. He informed the police about the theft and the policeman started from the same point,half an hour later than the time of the theft but with a speed of 12 km/h. At what time will Policeman catch the thief?
(a) 10:45 P.M. (b) 9: 30 P.M.
(c) 10:00 P.M. (d) 10:30 P.M.

136. The pie-chart below shows the spending of a state on various sports during a particular year

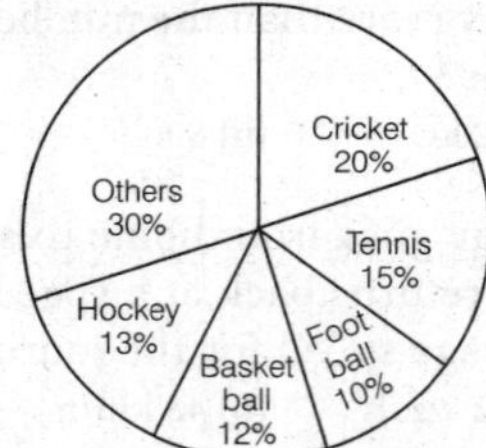

If the total amount spent on sports during the year was ₹ 7500000 then how much (in ₹) was spent on cricket and hockey together?
(a) ₹1875000 (b) ₹2680000
(c) ₹2475000 (d) ₹2155000

137. In a ΔABC, the bisectors of angle ABC and angle ACB intersect each other at point O. If the angle BOC is 125°, then the angle BAC is equal to

(a) 75° (b) 78°
(c) 70° (d) 82°

138. Two trains Mumbai Rajdhani and Kissan Express of lengths 850 m and 700 m are 1050m apart, and are running on parallel tracks towards each other. Mumbai Rajdhani is running at 62 km/h and Kissan Express is running at 55 km/h. In how much time (in sec) will the trains cross each other?

(a) 70 (b) 45
(c) 75 (d) 80

139. If $\sin\beta = \frac{1}{3}$, $(\sec\beta - \tan\beta)^2$ is equal to

(a) $\frac{3}{4}$ (b) $\frac{2}{3}$
(c) $\frac{1}{2}$ (d) $\frac{1}{3}$

140. A right square pyramid having lateral surface area is 624 cm^2. If the length of the diagonal of the square is $24\sqrt{2}$, then the volume of the pyramid is

(a) 1150 cm^3 (b) 780 cm^3
(c) 1083 cm^3 (d) 960 cm^3

141. The sides of a rectangle are in the ratio of 3 : 8 and its area is 1944 cm^2. What is its perimeter?

(a) 189 cm (b) 208 cm
(c) 198 cm (d) 308 cm

142. A and B complete a work in 24 and 30 days, respectively, working 10 h per day.The work is to be done in two shifts. The morning shift is for 6 h and the evening shift is for 4 hours. On the first day, A works in the morning and B works in the evening, and they interchange their shifts every day. On which day did the work get completed?

(a) 21st day (b) 24th day
(c) 30th day ((d) 27th day

143. If $\sin A = \frac{\sqrt{3}}{2}, 0 < A < 90°$, then find the value of $2(\text{cosec } A + \cot A)$.

(a) $2\sqrt{3}$ (b) $\sqrt{3}$
(c) $\frac{2}{\sqrt{3}}$ (d) $\frac{1}{\sqrt{3}}$

144. The height and the radius of the base of a right circular cone are in the ratio of 12 : 5. If its volume is 314 cm^3, then what is the slant height of the cone? (Use $\pi = 3.14$)

(a) 12 cm (b) 11 cm
(c) 13 cm (d) 14 cm

145. Three numbers are in the ratio of 5 : 7 : 9 and their LCM is 34650. Their HCF is

(a) 315 (b) 55
(c) 110 (d) 99

146. Which is the largest number that divides each of 1036, 1813 and 3885 without leaving any remainder?

(a) 333 (b) 111
(c) 259 (d) 37

147. If $\sin A = \frac{2}{3}$, then find the value of $(7 - \tan A)(3 + \cos A)$.

(a) $\frac{61}{3} + \frac{17}{3\sqrt{5}}$ (b) $\frac{61}{3\sqrt{5}} + \frac{17}{3}$
(c) $\frac{61}{3} + \frac{17}{\sqrt{5}}$ (d) $\frac{61}{3} - \frac{17}{3\sqrt{5}}$

148. In an election between two candidates, 20% of the voters on the voters list did not cast their votes and 80 voters cast their ballot papers blank. The winner secured 45% of all the voters in the list and he got 280 votes more than his rival. The number of voters on the list was

(a) 1500 (b) 2800
(c) 2500 (d) 2000

149. Find the LCM of 73 and 657.

(a) 73 (b) 657
(c) 146 (d) 365

150. In a circle, chords AB and CD intersect internally at E. If $CD = 18$ cm, $DE = 5$ cm, $AE = 13$ cm, then the length of BE is

(a) 4 cm (b) 7 cm
(c) 3 cm (d) 5 cm

Part IV

English Comprehension

151. Select the most appropriate meaning of the given idiom.
Fit as a fiddle

(a) To be extremely excited and energetic
(b) To be in good health
(c) Something is perfect
(d) A good and useful invention

152. Select the most appropriate meaning of the underlined word.
She has become a <u>familiar</u> figure in the world of politics.

(a) Known (b) Legend
(c) Elevated (d) Fancy

153. Select the most appropriate antonym of the given word.
Authentic

(a) Genuine (b) Fake
(c) Basic (d) Different

154. Select the most appropriate antonym of the given word.
Inquisitive

(a) Innocent (b) Indifferent
(c) Curious (d) Studious

155. Select the incorrectly spelt word from the underlined words in the following sentence.
It is important to see school <u>holistically</u>, it is not a set of atomic items of rooms, library,assembly halls, canteen and playgrounds; it is all of these but in <u>symbiotic</u> relationship with each other, the <u>contors</u> of which are often far too obvious and often simply <u>mysterious</u>.

(a) mysterious
(b) symbiotic
(c) contors
(d) holistically

156. The following sentence has been split into four segments. Identify the segment that contains an error.
Will Ramya / had completed / that work / by 2025?

(a) by 2025
(b) that work
(c) had completed
(d) Will Ramya

157. Select the most appropriate meaning of the given idiom.
Apple of discord
(a) Practical
(b) Distant love
(c) Bone of contention
(d) Centre of attraction

158. Fill in the blank by selecting the meaningful and correctly spelt word from the given options.
They knew that the stock of the food was getting reduced and the fund .... for that was not enough for the next week.
(a) asserted (b) allotted
(c) alerted (d) abandoned

159. Select the most appropriate option that can substitute the underlined segment in the given sentence. If there is no need to substitute it, select 'No substitution required'
The unexpected turn beside the project put the company in a big financial crisis.
(a) in the project
(b) until the project
(c) No substitution required
(d) between the project

160. Select the most appropriate option that can substitute the underlined segment in the given sentence.
We all should respect each other.
(a) every other
(b) all other
(c) one another
(d) all of us

161. Select the most appropriate one-word substitution of the given group of words.
A form of government in which the supreme power is vested in the people and exercised by their elected agents under a free electoral system.
(a) Democracy
(b) Anarchy
(c) Monarchy
(d) Autocracy

162. Select the most appropriate meaning of the given idiom.
Come what may
(a) To be among the latest
(b) No matter what happens
(c) To get frightened
(d) Meeting someone

163. Select the most appropriate option that can substitute the underlined segment in the given sentence.
The decision to engage in an armed conflict is tacit.
(a) incomprehensible for some
(b) ineffective completely
(c) regretted by everyone
(d) implied without being stated

164. The following sentence has been divided into parts. One of them may contain an error. Select the part that contains the error from the given options. If you don't find any error, mark 'No error' as your answer.
My elder brother / yesterday had took / my Facebook password.
(a) my Facebook password
(b) yesterday had took
(c) My elder brother
(d) No error

165. Select the option that can be used as a one-word substitute for the given group of words.
To tell the nature of a disease by its symptoms.
(a) Design (b) Diagnosis
(c) Decisive (d) Dosage

166. Select the most appropriate meaning of the given idiom.
Fit as a fiddle
(a) At the last moment
(b) To ignore what someone is saying
(c) To betray a close person
(d) In good health

167. The following sentence has been split into four segments. Identify the segment that contains a grammatical error.
The students / are expected / to come / in the right time.
(a) in the right time
(b) The students
(c) to come
(d) are expected

168. Select the option that best expresses the meaning of the underlined idiom.
Christy should discuss this with her face to face.
(a) With another person in their presence rather than, say, by phone or letter
(b) Come to fully accept or understand something
(c) Remained normal and realistic
(d) Almost always

169. Select the most appropriate option that can substitute the underlined segment in the given sentence.
The book narrated the athlete's prowess in a lucid manner.
(a) refined arguments
(b) exceptional mastery
(c) difficult situation
(d) affluent days

170. Select the most appropriate meaning of the underlined word.
She has no desire for money.
(a) Disgust
(b) Despise
(c) Care
(d) Wish

171. Select the most appropriate meaning of the underlined phrase.
She can't make up her mind where to go for her summer vacation.
(a) Decide between alternatives or come to a decision
(b) Decide on a suitable parlour
(c) Decide how to do her makeup
(d) Engage her mind in creative activities

172. Select the most appropriate antonym of the underlined word.
He is so stingy that I have never seen him spending money on basic necessities.
(a) Wicked
(b) Extravagant
(c) Obnoxious
(d) Indecent

173. Select the option that can be used as a one-word substitute for the given group of words.
A book published after author's death.
(a) Posthuman publication
(b) Posthumous publication
(c) Supernatural publication
(d) Predecessor publication

174. Select the most appropriate synonym of the given word.
Rehabilitate
(a) Reinstall (b) Develop
(c) Absolve (d) Decline

175. Select the most appropriate option that can substitute the underlined segment in the given sentence.
You can become confident to speak English within one year.
(a) convinced to speaking
(b) reassured of speaking
(c) assured of speaking
(d) confident in speaking

176. Select the option that can be used as a one-word substitute for the given group of words.
Centre of public attention
(a) Ambiguity
(b) Obscurity
(c) Fuzziness
(d) Limelight

177. The following sentence has been divided into parts. One of them may contain an error.Select the part that contains the error from the given options. If you don't find any error, mark 'No error' as your answer.
We will / have been know the result / of the CAT exam by next week.
(a) of the CAT exam by next week
(b) We will
(c) have been know the result
(d) No error

178. Select the most appropriate meaning of the given idiom.
Break a leg
(a) To hurt someone
(b) To avoid someone
(c) To wish someone good luck
(d) To love someone

179. Select the most appropriate meaning of the given idiom.
To hit the nail on the head
(a) To hit something accurately
(b) To be indecisive
(c) To miss an opportunity
(d) To express an idea with great precision

180. Select the most appropriate option that can substitute the underlined segment in the given sentence.
Rajib's habit of sneering at the beliefs of others often hurts others' sentiments.
(a) manipulation (b) cynicism
(c) certainty (d) cleverness

181. Select the most appropriate option that can substitute the underlined segment in the given sentence. If there is no need to substitute it, select 'No substitution required'.
Politics and money go together in this country.
(a) go arm in arm
(b) go holding hands
(c) go hand in hand
(d) No substitution required

182. Select the most appropriate antonym of the underlined word in the given sentence.
After losing his job and his home, he found himself destitute and living on the streets.
(a) glorious (b) disturbed
(c) affluent (d) ridiculous

183. Select the most appropriate synonym of the highlighted word in the given sentence.
The plane crash was a **harrowing** experience for everyone involved.
(a) Exterminate
(b) Excruciating
(c) Awesome
(d) Sad

184. Identify the option that rectifies the spelling of the incorrectly spelt word in the given sentence.
Students should have a good vocabulary to write an essay efectively.
(a) Gud
(b) Effectively
(c) Wriite
(d) Voicabulary

185. Select the most appropriate synonym of the word 'factual' in the given sentence and choose the correct option.
The scientist's hypothesis was based on empirical evidence and rigorous experimentation.
(a) Rigorous (b) Hypothesis
(c) Evidence (d) Empirical

186. Select the incorrectly spelt word in the given sentence.
It is beyond my cognative capacity to solve the mathematical problems.
(a) problems (b) cognative
(c) mathematical (d) capacity

187. Select the most appropriate option that can substitute the underlined word which has been incorrectly spelt.
Mrs. Lal taught me English gramar.
(a) grammar (b) gramarr
(c) gramerr (d) gramer

188. Select the most appropriate meaning of the underlined idiom.
Sanchit stands by his friends through thick and thin.
(a) In winter and summer
(b) In favourable situations
(c) In crowded areas
(d) Under all circumstances

189. Select the option that can be used as a one-word substitute for the given phrase.
One who goes from place to place, begging
(a) Misogamist (b) Malleable
(c) Meticulous (d) Mendicant

190. Select the most appropriate synonym of the given word.
Reminiscence
(a) Harsh (b) Remembrance
(c) Benevolence (d) Oblivion

Directions (Q.Nos. 191-195) *In the following passage, some words have been deleted. Read the passage carefully and select the most appropriate option to fill in each blank.*

Swigspans are large waterbirds that ...(1)... to the family Anatidae, which also includes ducks and geese. They ...(2)... for their beauty and grace and are often used as symbols of love, fidelity, and elegance. They are also famous for their ...(3)... features,such as their long necks, large wings p, and striking white feathers. ...(4)... not all swan species are white; the Black Swans, ...(5)..., has black feathers with a red bill. Swans are found on every continent and are known for their strong pair bonds. They mate for life and can live up to 20 years.

191. Select the most appropriate option to fill in blank number 1.
(a) belonged (b) belonging
(c) belong (d) belongs

192. Select the most appropriate option to fill in blank number 2.
(a) were known (b) have knowing
(c) had know (d) are known

193. Select the most appropriate option to fill in blank number 3.
(a) finite (b) similar
(c) popular (d) distinctive

194. Select the most appropriate option to fill in blank number 4.
(a) Consequently (b) Because
(c) Formerly (d) However

195. Select the most appropriate option to fill in blank number 5.
(a) for example (b) of course
(c) after all (d) in addition

Directions (Q.Nos. 196-200) *Read the given passage carefully and answer the questions that follow.*

As the world's population approaches 8 billion and resource use intensifies, pollution is ever more extensive, pervasive and persistent. It affects our health through the food we eat, the water we drink and the air we breathe. By 2025, the world's cities will produce 2.2 billion tonnes of waste every year, more than three times the amount produced in 2009. That said,pollution is not a new phenomenon and is largely controllable and often avoidable, as shown in some countries and cities that have succeeded in decoupling economic growth from pollution and waste accumulation.

With the end goal to eradicate all forms of pollution by 2030, the UN Environment Programme was tasked by the UN Environment Assembly to coordinate the implementation of a global plan reiterating that pollution is not only an environmental priority, it's a priority for the achievement of the Sustainable Development Goals.

196. Which is the best description of the tone of the passage?
(a) Technical (b) Sarcastic
(c) Dogmatic (d) Humanistic

197. Which of the following most accurately states the central idea of the passage?
(a) United Nations
(b) Pollution free planet
(c) Population explosion
(d) Economic growth

198. Which of the following represents the structure of the passage?
(a) Definition
(b) Cause-effect
(c) Critique
(d) Chronology

199. What is the antonym for the word 'pervasive' from the passage?
(a) Clear (b) Emotional
(c) Limited (d) Offensive

200. What is the antonym for the word 'priority' from the passage?
(a) Factor (b) Last
(c) Part (d) Task

Know Correct Answers

1. (a)	2. (c)	3. (b)	4. (a)	5. (a)	6. (b)	7. (d)	8. (d)	9. (a)	10. (a)
11. (a)	12. (b)	13. (d)	14. (c)	15. (d)	16. (a)	17. (b)	18. (b)	19. (b)	20. (a)
21. (a)	22. (c)	23. (a)	24. (b)	25. (b)	26. (c)	27. (a)	28. (a)	29. (c)	30. (c)
31. (b)	32. (b)	33. (d)	34. (c)	35. (c)	36. (b)	37. (b)	38. (c)	39. (a)	40. (a)
41. (a)	42. (d)	43. (c)	44. (b)	45. (b)	46. (b)	47. (b)	48. (c)	49. (c)	50. (b)
51. (a)	52. (a)	53. (a)	54. (a)	55. (b)	56. (a)	57. (b)	58. (b)	59. (b)	60. (b)
61. (d)	62. (d)	63. (a)	64. (d)	65. (a)	66. (c)	67. (d)	68. (a)	69. (c)	70. (b)
71. (d)	72. (a)	73. (d)	74. (a)	75. (c)	76. (c)	77. (c)	78. (c)	79. (b)	80. (b)
81. (c)	82. (a)	83. (d)	84. (a)	85. (d)	86. (b)	87. (c)	88. (c)	89. (d)	90. (b)
91. (b)	92. (a)	93. (c)	94. (a)	95. (c)	96. (b)	97. (a)	98. (a)	99. (d)	100. (b)
101. (c)	102. (c)	103. (a)	104. (a)	105. (b)	106. (a)	107. (d)	108. (a)	109. (b)	110. (c)
111. (a)	112. (d)	113. (b)	114. (b)	115. (d)	116. (c)	117. (b)	118. (a)	119. (d)	120. (c)
121. (d)	122. (c)	123. (d)	124. (d)	125. (b)	126. (b)	127 (b)	128. (d)	129. (b)	130. (d)
131. (d)	132. (a)	133. (a)	134. (c)	135. (d)	136. (c)	137 (c)	138. (d)	139. (c)	140. (d)
141. (c)	142. (d)	143. (a)	144. (c)	145. (c)	146. (c)	147. (a)	148. (d)	149. (b)	150. (d)
151. (b)	152. (a)	153. (b)	154. (b)	155. (c)	156. (c)	157. (c)	158. (b)	159. (a)	160. (c)
161. (a)	162. (b)	163. (d)	164. (b)	165. (b)	166. (d)	167. (a)	168. (a)	169. (b)	170. (d)
171. (a)	172. (b)	173. (b)	174. (a)	175. (d)	176. (d)	177. (c)	178. (c)	179. (d)	180. (b)
181. (c)	182. (c)	183. (b)	184. (b)	185. (d)	186. (b)	187. (a)	188. (d)	189. (d)	190. (b)
191. (c)	192. (d)	193. (d)	194. (d)	195. (a)	196. (d)	197. (b)	198. (b)	199. (c)	200. (b)

Answer & Solutions

1. (a) As, H $\xrightarrow{+5}$ M $\xrightarrow{-4}$ I $\xrightarrow{+3}$ L
K $\xrightarrow{+5}$ P $\xrightarrow{-4}$ L $\xrightarrow{+3}$ O
and S $\xrightarrow{+5}$ X $\xrightarrow{-4}$ T $\xrightarrow{+3}$ W
But, L $\xrightarrow{+3}$ O $\xrightarrow{-4}$ K $\xrightarrow{+5}$ P

2. (c) From the unfolded cube, the opposite faces are shown below,

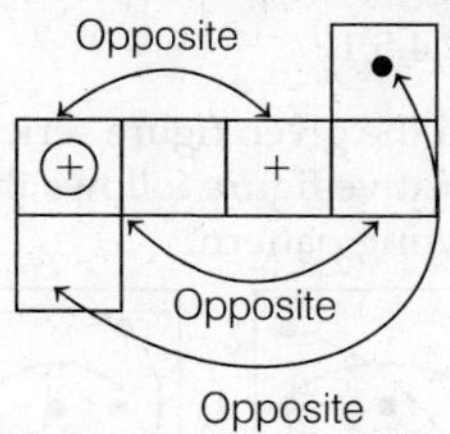

According to the property of dice, opposite sides can not be adjacent to each other.
∴ Only figure 1 and 3 are possible.

3. (b) Mirror image of the given figure, when the mirror is placed at the 'MN' line.

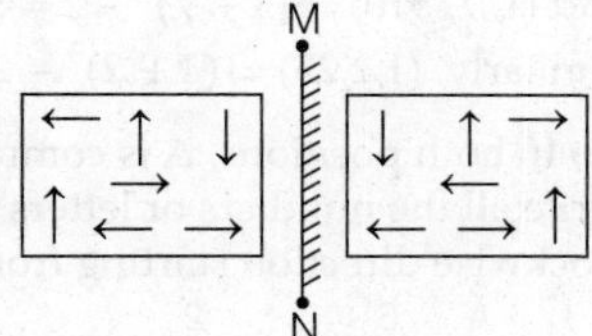

4. (a) Given equation,
94 C 12 B 6 A 216 D 9 = ?

A → +	C → −
B → ×	D → ÷

After putting signs we get,
⇒ 94 − 12 × 6 + 216 ÷ 9
⇒ 94 − 72 + 24
∴ 46 = ?

5. (a) Pattern of the series is as follows,

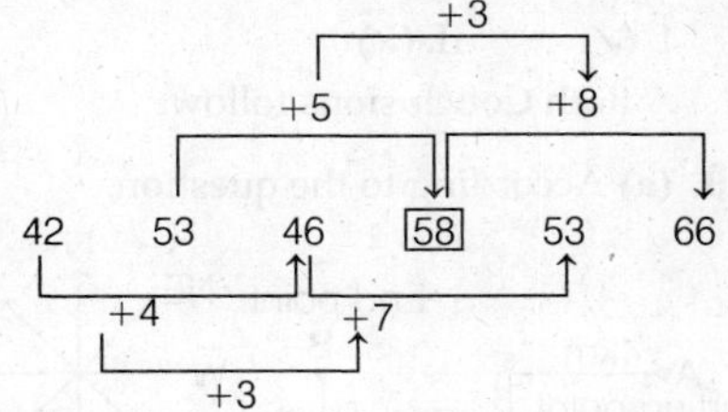

6. (b) Mirror image of the given figure when the mirror is placed at the 'MN' line.

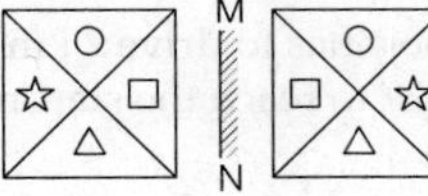

7. (d) According to the question,

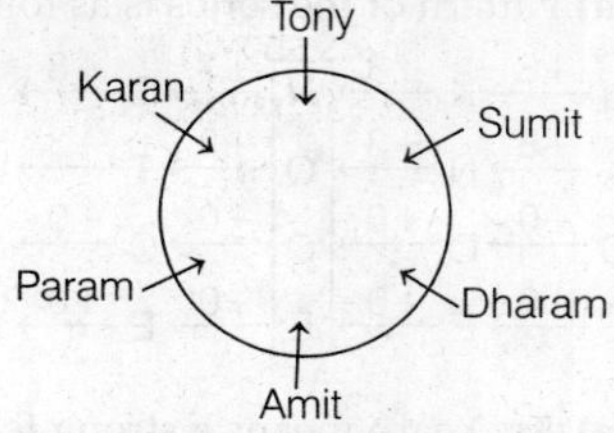

Hence, Tony sits fourth to the right of Param.

8. (d) As, 32 : 10 ⇒ (3 + 2) × 2 = 10
and 24 : 12 ⇒ (2 + 4) × 2 = 12
Similarly, 98 : ? ⇒ (9 + 8) × 2 = 34

9. (a) As, (7, 52) ⇒ $7^2 + 3 = 52$
and (9, 84) ⇒ $9^2 + 3 = 84$
Similarly, (13, 172) ⇒ $13^2 + 3 = 172$

10. (a) According to the properties of dice, if two different positions of the same dice are given and have two common faces, then the third face will be opposite of each other.
∴ 4 is the opposite of 6.

11. (a) From the question figure, the opposite faces are

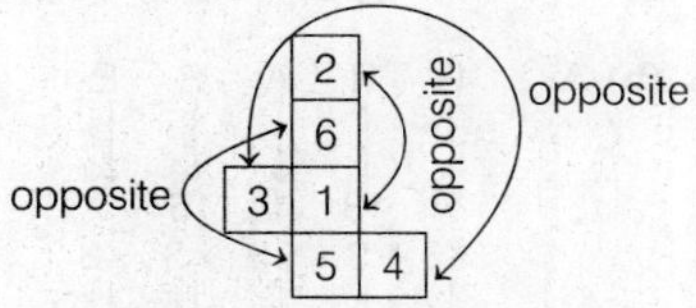

(2 and 1), (6 and 5) and (3 and 4)
According to the properties of dice, opposite faces can not be adjacent to each other.

12. (b) According to the statement,
C O L (D) ⟶ (6) 4 2 8
T I (D) E ⟶ 9 (6) 7 3
∴ The code for "D" is "6".

13. (d) According to the venn diagram,

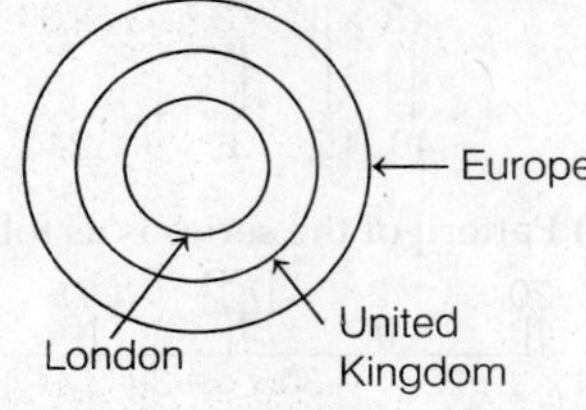

London is in the United kingdom and the united kingdom is in Europe.

14. (c) According to the question,
A * S = J@M × Y

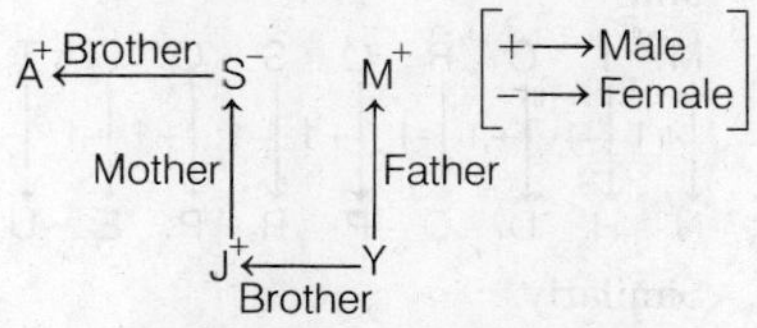

∴ A is the brother of Y's mother.

15. (d) Pattern of the series is as follows,

Z $\xrightarrow{+2}$ B $\xrightarrow{+2}$ D $\xrightarrow{+2}$ F $\xrightarrow{+2}$ H
F $\xrightarrow{-3}$ C $\xrightarrow{-3}$ Z $\xrightarrow{-3}$ W $\xrightarrow{-3}$ T
K $\xrightarrow{+2}$ M $\xrightarrow{+2}$ O $\xrightarrow{+2}$ Q $\xrightarrow{+2}$ S
Q $\xrightarrow{-3}$ N $\xrightarrow{-3}$ K $\xrightarrow{-3}$ H $\xrightarrow{-3}$ E

16. (a) Given equation,
8 ÷ 5 − 5 × 10 + 2 = ?

+ → ÷	− → +
× → −	÷ → ×

If '+' means '÷', '−' means '+', '×' means '−' and '÷' means '×', then what will come in place of (?) in the given equation
After interchanging the signs, we get:
⇒ 8 × 5 + 5 − 10 ÷ 2
⇒ 40 + 5 − 5
∴ 40 = ?

17. (b) In the given figure series, the figure in the box is rotated by 90 degrees in a clockwise direction in each step.
Hence, the figure in option (b) will complete the figure series.

18. (b) Mirror image of the given figure, when the mirror is placed at the 'MN' line.

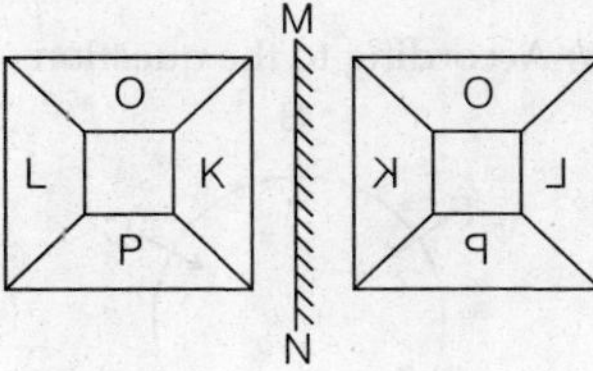

19. (b) According to the question,

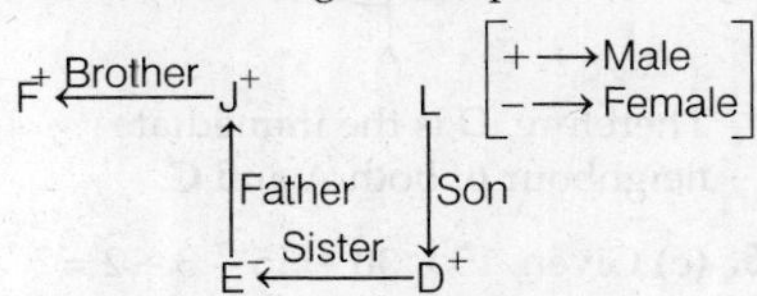

∴ D is Brother's son of F.

20. **(a)** As,

E D U C A T I O N
+1 −1 +1 −1 +1 −1 +1 −1 +1
F C V B B S J N O

and

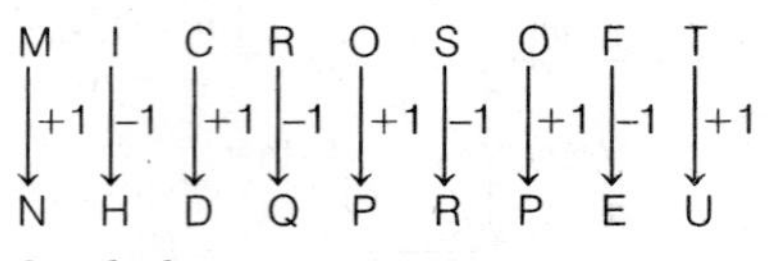

Similarly,

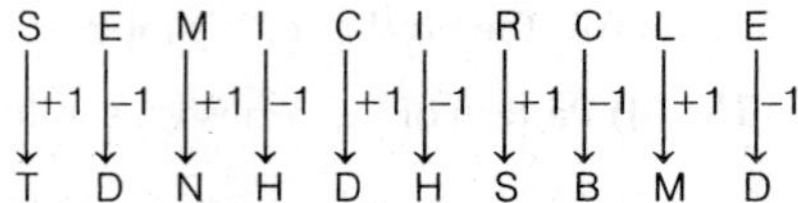

21. **(a)** The option figure (a) is embedded in the question figure.

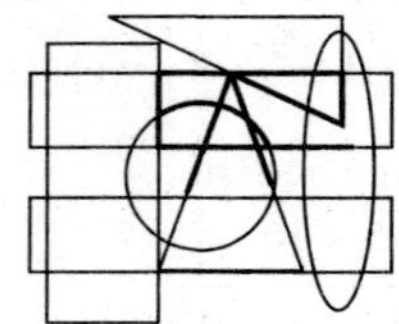

22. **(c)** As, Pedal is used in Bicycle to control the bicycle movement. Similarly, Oar is used in Canoe to steer through the water.

23. **(a)** According to the question,

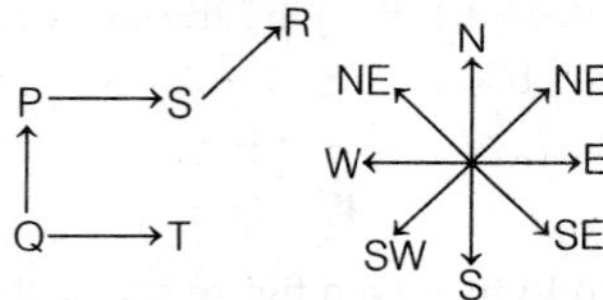

∴ R is in north-east Q.

24. **(b)** Given equation,

86 ◯ 42 ◯ 12 ◯ 3 ◯ 12 ◯ 3 ◯ 4

From option (b),

$\Rightarrow 86 - 42 - 12 \div 3 = 12 \times 3 + 4$

$\Rightarrow 86 - 42 - 4 = 36 + 4$

$\Rightarrow 40 = 40$

25. **(b)** According to the question,

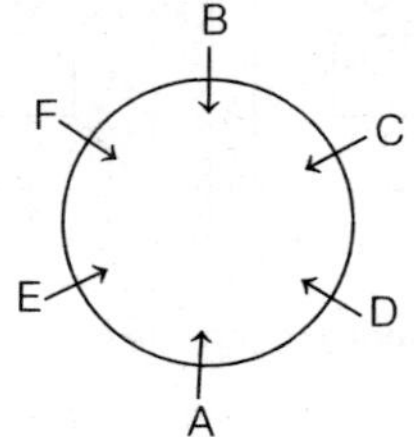

Therefore, D is the immediate neighbour of both A and C.

26. **(c)** Given, $15 \times 30 + 15 - 3 \div 2 = ?$

After replacing sign, we get

$\Rightarrow 15 + 30 - 15 \div 3 \times 2$

$\Rightarrow 15 + 30 - 5 \times 2$

$\Rightarrow 15 + 30 - 10$

$\Rightarrow 35 = ?$

27. **(a)** Pattern of the series is as follows,

H →(+3) K →(+3) **N** →(+3) Q →(+3) T

K →(+3) N →(+3) **Q** →(+3) T →(+3) W

O →(+0) O →(+0) **O** →(+0) O →(+0) O

E →(+0) E →(+0) **E** →(+0) E →(+0) E

28. **(a)** As, Yearn means a strong feeling of wishing for something and crave is the synonym of yearn. Similarly, Haste means excessive speed and alacrity is a synonym of haste.

29. **(c)** As, $(23, 6, 35) \Rightarrow 23 + 6 \times 2 = 35$

and $(13, 5, 23) \Rightarrow 13 + 5 \times 2 = 23$

Similarly, $(25, 8, 41) \Rightarrow 25 + 8 \times 2 = 41$

30. **(c)** Given equation,

$42 \times 6 - 7 \div 13 + 28 = ?$

+ → −	÷ → +
× → ÷	− → ×

After substituting symbols, we get

$\Rightarrow 42 \div 6 \times 7 + 13 - 28$

$\Rightarrow 7 \times 7 + 13 - 28$

$\Rightarrow 49 + 13 - 28$

$\Rightarrow 34 = ?$

31. **(b)** As,

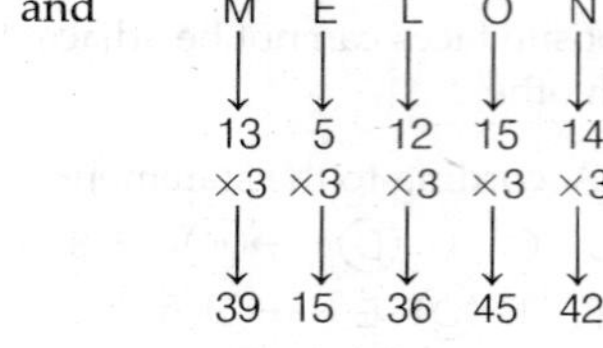

and

M E L O N
13 5 12 15 14
×3 ×3 ×3 ×3 ×3
39 15 36 45 42

Similarly,

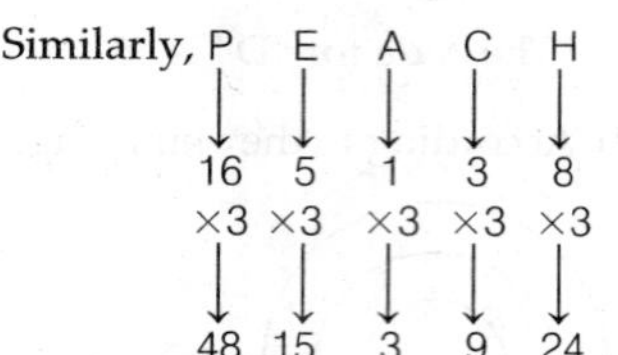

32. **(b)** Pattern of the series is as follows,

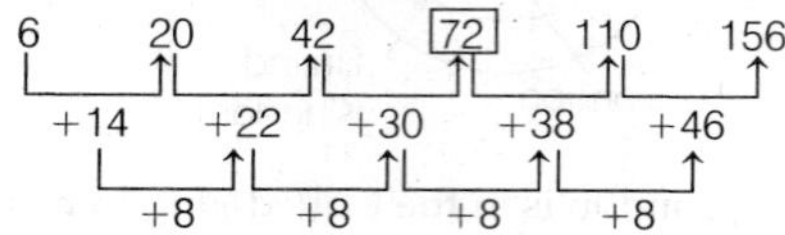

33. **(d)** Pattern of the series is as follows,

473 517 561 **605** 649 693

+44 +44 +44 +44 +44

34. **(c)** The series will be as shown below

S L T U K / S L T U K / S L T U K

⇒ STULKTU

35. **(c)** The correct dictionary order is,

Flaw (3) → Flec (2) → Fleet (4) → Flight (5) → Flint (1)

⇒ 3,2,4,5,1

36. **(b)** In the given figure series, each alternative figure follows the following pattern,

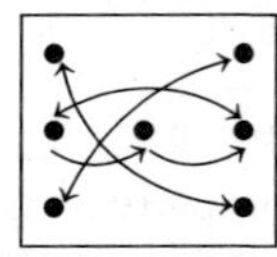
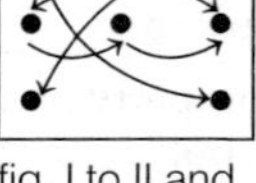

fig. I to II and fig. II to III

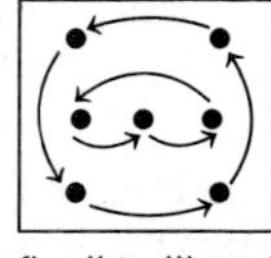

fig. II to III and fig. IV to V

Hence, the figure in option (b) will complete the question series.

37. **(b)** As, $(2, 5, 341) \Rightarrow (2 + 5)^3 - 2 = 341$

and $(1, 7, 510) \Rightarrow (1 + 7)^3 - 2 = 510$

Similarly, $(1,2,25) \Rightarrow (1 + 2)^3 - 2 = 25$

38. **(c)** In both positions, A is common, so write all the numbers or letters in a clockwise direction starting from A.

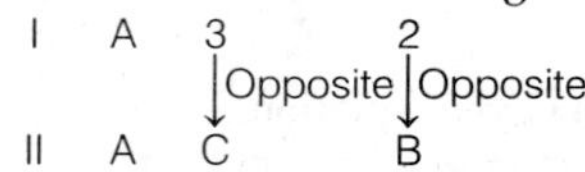

Therefore, c is the opposite of 3.

39. **(a)** According to the statements,

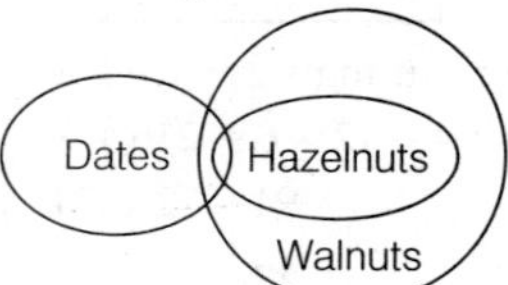

Conclusions

I. (✓) II. (✓)

∴ Both Conclusions follow.

40. **(a)** According to the question,

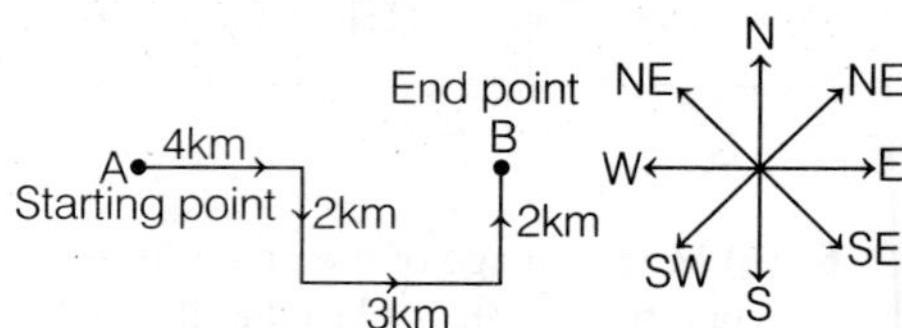

So, Pooja has to drive 7 km towards the west to reach the starting point.

41. **(a)** According to the statements,

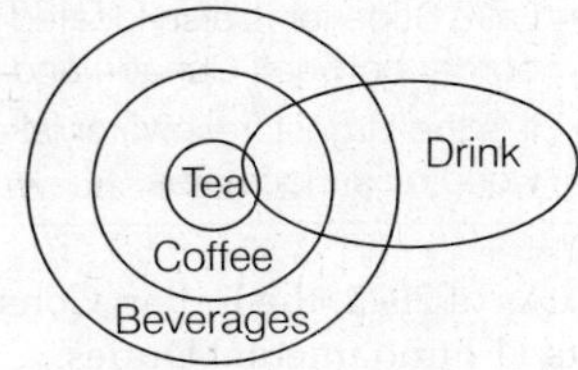

Conclusions

I. (✓) II. (✗)

∴ Only Conclusion I follows.

42. **(d)** According to the statements,

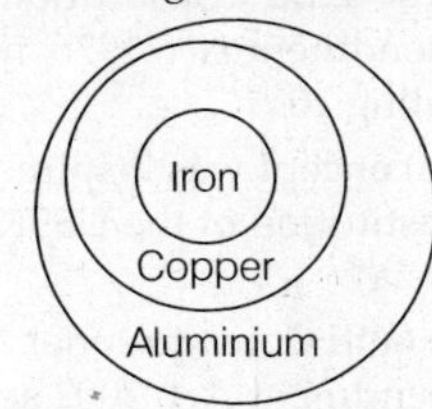

Conclusions

I. (✓) II. (✓)

∴ Both Conclusions I and II follow.

43. **(c)** The correct dictionary order is,
Descend (5) → Desire (4) → Desolate (2) → Desperate (1) → Destination (6) → Destruction (3)
⇒ 5,4,2,1,6,3

44. **(b)** As,

Y A T C H (Number of letter)
(25 + 1 + 20 + 3 + 8) + 5 × 2 = 67

and D I N E (Number of letter)
(4 + 9 + 14 + 5) + 4 × 2 = 40

Similary,

M A N G O (Number of letter)
(13 + 1 + 14 + 7 + 15) + 5 × 2 = 60

45. **(b)** In the given figure series, S, M and + shifted to one position in a clockwise direction and flipped vertically in each step.
Hence, the figure in option (b) will complete the figure series.

46. **(b)** Given equation,
45 – 3 ÷ 144 × 12 + 38 = ?

+ → –	÷ → +
× → ÷	– → ×

After interchanging signs, we get
⇒ 45 × 3 + 144 ÷ 12 – 38
⇒ 135 + 12 – 38
⇒ 109 = ?

47. **(b)** As, O $\xrightarrow{-4}$ K $\xrightarrow{+3}$ N $\xrightarrow{-2}$ L
F $\xrightarrow{-4}$ B $\xrightarrow{+3}$ E $\xrightarrow{-2}$ C
and H $\xrightarrow{-4}$ D $\xrightarrow{+3}$ G $\xrightarrow{-2}$ E
But, J $\xrightarrow{+7}$ Q $\xrightarrow{+10}$ A $\xrightarrow{-1}$ Z

48. **(c)** As, S T O R Y
(19 + 20 + 15 + 18 + 25) = 97

and P U L L
(16 + 21 + 12 + 12) = 61

Similarly,
I N C O M E
(9 + 14 + 3 + 15 + 13 + 5) = 59

49. **(c)** Pattern of the series is as follows,

32 32 32 34 [102] 106 530
+0 ×1 +2 ×3 +4 ×5

50. **(b)** Given that
729 × 9 – (56 – 6) × 5 ÷ 2 + 152 × 19 = 69
From option (b),
⇒ 729 ÷ 9 – (56 – 6) ÷ 5 × 2 + 152 ÷ 19 = 69
⇒ 81 – 50 ÷ 5 × 2 + 8 = 69
⇒ 81 – 10 × 2 + 8 = 69
⇒ 81 – 20 + 8 = 69
⇒ 69 = 69
∴ The correct answer is 69.

51. **(a)** **Panini** was an ancient Sanskrit grammarian who authored the Ashtadhyayi, a comprehensive treatise on Sanskrit grammar.

- It was composed around the 6th to 5th century BCE, making it one of the earliest known works of descriptive linguistics.
- The Ashtadhyayi consists of nearly 4,000 sutras (aphoristic rules) and is known for its systematic and scientific approach to grammar.
- Panini's grammar laid the foundation for modern linguistic theory and is considered a landmark in the history of human thought

Knowledge Booster
- Patanjali later wrote the Mahabhashya, a commentary on Panini's grammar.
- Agastya is associated with ancient Tamil and Vedic traditions, not grammar.

52. **(a)** The provision of Fundamental Duties in the Indian Constitution is inspired by the Constitution of the USSR (now Russia).

- These duties were added by the 42nd Constitutional Amendment Act, 1976 during the Emergency period.
- Initially, 10 Fundamental Duties were incorporated under Article 51A in Part IV-A of the Constitution.
- In 2002, the 86th Constitutional Amendment added the 11th Fundamental Duty which provide opportunities for education to children aged 6 to 14 years.

53. **(a)** **Change in sales during the year** is not included in inventory investment when calculating national income.

- Inventory investment refers to the net change in the stock of unsold goods, such as raw materials, semi-finished goods and finished goods.
- It reflects the production not immediately sold and is part of gross domestic capital formation.
- Sales represent final consumption or demand, not an accumulation of goods, hence they are excluded from inventory investment.

54. **(a)** The **crude** birth rate indicates the number of live births occurring during a year per 1000 people estimated at midyear.

- It is called 'crude' because it does not take into account age or sex composition of the population.
- It is one of the most basic and widely used indicators for studying population growth.

55. **(b)** A basketball court is **rectangular** in shape, as defined by international standards.

- In the NBA, the court measures 94 feet by 50 feet (approximately 28.65 m × 15.24 m).
- The rectangular shape allows for organised play zones, such as the three-point arc, free-throw lane and half-court line.

56. **(a)** **Article-53** of the Indian Constitution states that the executive power of the Union shall be vested in the President of India.

- Although the President is the nominal executive head, real executive powers are exercised by the Council of Ministers, headed by the Prime Minister.
- Article 53 also emphasises that the executive power shall be exercised in accordance with the Constitution.

Knowledge Booster

- Articles 52 to 78 in Part V of the Constitution deal with the Union Executive, which includes the President, Vice-President, Prime Minister and the Council of Ministers.
- Article 74 mandates that the President shall act according to the advice of the Council of Ministers

57. **(b)** Agonists bind to a specific receptor and activate it to produce a biological response.

- They mimic natural ligands like hormones or neurotransmitters.
- Used in treatment where stimulation of a receptor is needed, e.g., in asthma (ß2 agonists).
- Examples include morphine, adrenaline and salbutamol.

Knowledge Booster

- Antagonists, in contrast, block the action of natural messengers.
- Agonist drugs are essential in neurotransmission and hormone therapy.

58. **(b)** After the completion of the Seventh Five-Year Plan (1985–1990), the Indian government observed a plan holiday from **1990 to 1992**.

- During this period, no new Five-Year Plan was launched due to political instability and economic crisis.
- Instead, the government introduced Annual Plans (1990–91 and 1991–92) to maintain continuity in development efforts.
- India has witnessed three major plan holidays: after the Third Plan (1966–69), Fifth Plan (1978–80) and Seventh Plan (1990–92).

59. **(b)** **Gaur** did not emerge as a result of the disintegration of the Bahmani Kingdom in the 16th century.

- Gaur was the capital of medieval Bengal and was unrelated to the Deccan Sultanates that arose from the Bahmani breakup.
- The Bahmani Kingdom disintegrated into five independent Deccan Sultanates: Ahmadnagar, Bijapur, Berar, Bidar and Golconda.

60. **(b)** The Uruguay Round, the 8th round of the General Agreement on Tariffs and Trade (GATT), was completed in 1994.

- It began in 1986 in Punta del Este, Uruguay and concluded with the Marrakesh Agreement in April 1994.
- The Uruguay Round led to the formation of the World Trade Organisation (WTO) in 1995.

Knowledge Booster

- The Marrakesh Agreement (1994) was signed by 123 countries, marking the formal conclusion of the Uruguay Round.
- The WTO aims to facilitate global trade, resolve trade disputes and enforce trade agreements.

61. **(d)** The book 'Childhood Days – A Memoir' by Satyajit Ray was originally written in **Bengali**.

- Its original Bengali title is 'Jakhan Chhoto Chilam', which translates to 'When I Was Small.'
- Satyajit Ray (1921–1992) was a renowned Indian filmmaker, writer and illustrator and a recipient of the Bharat Ratna (1992).

62. **(d)** **Kuchipudi** is a classical dance form that originated in South-Eastern India, specifically in Andhra Pradesh.

- The dance form combines fast rhythmic footwork, sculpturesque body movements and dramatic characterisation.
- Famous exponents include Yamini Krishnamurthy, Raja-Radha Reddy and Vempati Chinna Satyam.
- Kuchipudi is one of the eight classical dance forms recognised by the Sangeet Natak Akademi.

63. **(a)** Red Lake is located in the state of Minnesota, **USA**.

- It is the largest natural freshwater lake entirely within the borders of Minnesota.
- It is known for its rich fishing grounds, particularly for walleye.

Knowledge Booster

- Lake Superior is also located on the border between Canada and USA.
- It is the largest freshwater lake in the world by surface area.

64. **(d)** As of 2022, the Indian Constitution lists 11 Fundamental Duties.

- These duties are enshrined under Article 51A, Part IV-A of the Constitution.
- Fundamental Duties were added by the 42nd Constitutional Amendment Act, 1976, initially totaling 10.
- The concept was inspired by the Constitution of the USSR (now Russia).
- The 86th Constitutional Amendment Act, 2002 added the 11th duty, related to the education of children.

65. **(a)** **Mutual Funds** are market-linked investment schemes, not classified under small savings schemes.

- Small savings schemes are managed by the National Small Savings Fund (NSSF) under the Ministry of Finance.
- Examples of small savings are National Savings Certificates (NSC), Kisan Vikas Patra (KVP) and Post Office Deposits.
- Mutual funds are managed by Asset Management Companies (AMCs) and are regulated by SEBI, not by the Ministry of Finance.

66. **(c)** **Arable land** is defined as land capable of being ploughed and used to grow crops.

- It is fertile, well-drained and regularly used for agricultural cultivation.
- Arable land is a key resource in agricultural economies and is crucial for food security.

Knowledge Booster

- India has around 160 million hectares of arable land, one of the largest in the world.
- Arable land supports seasonal cropping and intensive farming practice

67. **(d)** The novel 'Coolie' was written by **Mulk Raj Anand**, a prominent Indian English writer.

- The novel highlights social injustice, caste-based discrimination and the exploitation of the working class.
- Mulk Raj Anand is also the author of another famous novel 'Untouchable', which deals with the plight of Dalits.

Knowledge Booster
- He was influenced by Mahatma Gandhi's ideas and used literature as a tool for social reform.
- 'Coolie' is considered a pioneer work in Indian English literature addressing social realism

68. (a) **Bharatanatyam** is the classical dance form that traces its origin to the ancient temple dance Sadir Attam, which was traditionally performed by the Devadasis in Tamil Nadu.
- The dance combines nritta (pure dance), nritya (expressive dance) and natya (dramatic art), with themes often centered around Hindu mythology.
- Today, Bharatanatyam is one of the most popular and widely practiced classical dance forms of India, especially in Tamil Nadu.

69. (c) According to World Bank data (2016), approximately 69% of jobs in India are at risk of automation.
- This high percentage is attributed to the labour-intensive nature of many Indian industries and the increasing adoption of technologies like AI, robotics and machine learning.
- Sectors like manufacturing, retail, transport and customer service are considered highly vulnerable.

70. (b) **Ascaris** belongs to the phylum Aschelminthes (also called Nematoda).
- It is a parasitic roundworm found in the intestine of humans.
- The body is cylindrical, bilaterally symmetrical and unsegmented.
- It causes the disease Ascariasis, which spreads through contaminated food or water.

71. (d) **The Permanent Settlement** was introduced in 1793 by Lord Cornwallis in the Bengal Presidency.
- It gave legal ownership of land to zamindars, making them responsible for collecting and paying fixed revenue to the British government.
- The system ensured a permanent and stable revenue for the British but ignored changes in agricultural output.

Knowledge Booster
- The Ryotwari System involved direct settlement with individual cultivators in Madras and Bombay Presidencies.
- The Mahalwari System was implemented in North-Western Provinces, where revenue was settled with village communities.

72. (a) Vultures are classified as **carnivores** because they feed exclusively on animal flesh, especially carrion (dead animals).
- Omnivore: An omnivore is an organism that consumes both plants and animals for food like a bear.
- Herbivore: A herbivore is an organism that primarily feeds on plants such as a cow.
- Decomposer: A decomposer is an organism that breaks down dead organic matter, recycling nutrients back into the ecosystem like fungi.

73. (d) **The Hugli region** is not a minor industrial region, rather it is considered a major industrial region of India.
- It includes industrial hubs such as Kolkata, Howrah and Haldia, known for jute, engineering, petrochemical and textile industries.
- In contrast, regions like Durg-Raipur, Ambala-Amritsar and Northern Malabar are recognised as minor industrial regions.
- The region was historically important for jute manufacturing, making India a global leader in jute exports.

74. (a) Jagjit Singh was a legendary Indian singer, composer and musician, best known for popularising the **Ghazal** genre.
- His singing brought Ghazals to the masses, blending classical depth with modern instruments.
- Jagjit Singh was honoured with the Padma Bhushan in 2003 for his contribution to music
- Some of his iconic albums include 'The Unforgettable' (1976) and 'Mirage', which became widely popular.

75. (c) **Galileo Galilei**, by studying objects on an inclined plane, concluded that they move at a constant speed in the absence of external force.
- He laid the foundation for the first law of motion, which was later developed by Isaac Newton.
- Galileo is considered the father of modern physics and experimental science.
- Galileo's experiments refuted Aristotle's belief that a force is required to maintain motion.

76. (c) An **anticyclone** is a system of high atmospheric pressure with winds circulating outward.
- In the Northern hemisphere, winds move clockwise and in the southern hemisphere, they move anti-clockwise due to the Coriolis effect.
- Anticyclones are opposite in nature to cyclones, which are low-pressure systems with converging winds.

77. (c) Nitrogen gas (N_2) is not produced in this decomposition reaction.
- The reaction is
$2Pb(NO_3)_2 \rightarrow 2PbO + 4NO_2 + O_2$
- On heating, Lead nitrate ($Pb(NO_3)_2$) undergoes thermal decomposition.
- The products formed are Lead oxide (PbO), Nitrogen dioxide (NO_2) and Oxygen (O_2).

Knowledge Booster
- The brown fumes observed during the decomposition of Lead nitrate are due to Nitrogen dioxide (NO_2).
- Lead nitrate is often used in labs to demonstrate thermal decomposition reactions.

78. (c) The Eastern Ghats are a discontinuous range of mountains along the Eastern coast of India.
- They stretch from the **Mahanadi Valley** in Odisha to the Nilgiris in Tamil Nadu.
- These hills are lower in elevation compared to the Western Ghats.

- Rivers like the Godavari, Krishna and Kaveri cut through the Eastern Ghats

79. **(b)** The Atmiya Sabha was founded in 1814 by Raja Ram Mohan Roy in Kolkata (then Calcutta).
- Its aim was to reform Hinduism and oppose social evils like idol worship and caste discrimination.
- It promoted monotheism and emphasised the use of reason and logic in religious discussions.
- The Sabha was one of the first socio-religious reform movements in modern India.

80. **(b)** The Servants of India Society was founded in 1905 by **Gopal Krishna Gokhale**, a senior leader of the Indian National Congress.
- Its objective was to train Indians to dedicate themselves to the service of the nation.
- The society operated from Pune, Maharashtra and emphasised social reform along with political work.

Knowledge Booster
- Gokhale was a political mentor to Mahatma Gandhi.
- The motto of the Society was "Service before Self".

81. **(c)** The President of **Brazil**, Jair Bolsonaro, was invited as the Chief Guest for India's Republic Day parade on 26th January, 2020.
- This was the third time a Brazilian President was invited for Republic Day celebrations.
- The first Brazilian President to attend Republic Day as Chief Guest was Fernando Henrique Cardoso in 1996.
- The tradition of inviting a foreign dignitary for Republic Day started in 1950 with President Sukarno of Indonesia.

82. **(a)** 1 kilowatt (kW) is a unit of power, equivalent to 1000 joules per second.
- When converted over one hour, it equals 1 kilowatt-hour (kWh), which is equal to **3600** kilojoules (KJ/h).
- 1 kWh = 1000 J/s × 3600 seconds = 3.6 million joules = 3600 KJ.
- This is the standard unit used in electricity bills to measure energy consumption.

Knowledge Booster
- In the SI system, joule is the derived unit of energy and work.
- 1 calorie = 4.184 joules, so 3600 calories # 3600 KJ.

83. **(d)** The **Hoysala dynasty** ruled parts of present-day Karnataka between the 10th and 14th centuries CE.
- They are best known for constructing star-shaped temples using soapstone, especially in Belur and Halebidu.
- These temples are examples of Vesara-style architecture, a mix of Dravidian and Nagara styles.
- Detailed carvings, multiple shrines and intricately designed star-like bases were their hallmark features.

84. **(a)** Hara Shankar Bhattacharya is a renowned **sitar** maestro from India.
- He is known for his deep knowledge and mastery of the Hindustani classical music tradition.
- The sitar has been popularised globally by Pandit Ravi Shankar.

85. **(d)** **Technetium** has the atomic number 43 in the modern periodic table.
- It is the lightest radioactive element and none of its isotopes are stable.
- The half-lives of its isotopes range from 4.2 million years to just a few seconds.
- It was the first element to be artificially produced discovered in 1937.

86. **(b)** The Himalayas are classified into longitudinal and regional divisions. Based on regional classification (West to East), the order is:
- **Punjab Himalayas** (Indus to Sutlej)
- Kumaon Himalayas (Sutlej to Kali)
- Nepal Himalayas (Kali to Tista)
- Assam Himalayas (Tista to Dihang)
- These divisions are based on river valleys and states they pass through.

Knowledge Booster
- Punjab Himalayas are also called Kashmir Himalayas.
- The Assam Himalayas include Arunachal Himalayas in the Eastern most region.

87. **(c)** India has won the ICC T20 Men's World Cup only once.
- The victory came in the inaugural edition of the tournament held in 2007.
- The final match was played against Pakistan at Wanderers Stadium, Johannesburg.
- M. S. Dhoni captained the Indian team during this historic win.

Knowledge Booster
- India has reached the final only once and the semi-finals three times (2007, 2014 and 2016).

88. **(c)** **Radon** (Rn) is a noble gas that belongs to Group 18 of the periodic table.
- It is produced naturally through the radioactive decay of uranium in soils and rocks.
- Radon is a colourless, odourless and radioactive gas.
- It is considered the second leading cause of lung cancer after smoking due to prolonged exposure.

89. **(d)** Chad Sukra is a spring festival celebrated by the Jaintia tribe in the Indian state of **Meghalaya**.
- It marks the beginning of the sowing season and is observed with traditional dances, songs and rituals.
- The festival is organised by the Doloi (traditional chief) of the Elaka (administrative unit).
- The Jaintia tribe is one of the three major tribal groups of Meghalaya, along with the Khasi and Garo tribes.

90. **(b)** **Mining of salt** was not included in Schedule A, although it remained under government control via other regulations.
- Schedule A of the Industrial Policy Resolution of 1956 included industries that were to be exclusively owned and operated by the State (Public Sector).
- It listed 17 industries, such as arms and ammunition, atomic energy, iron and steel, mineral oils, etc.

Knowledge Booster
- Schedule B included industries that the state would progressively take over, while Schedule C was open to the private sector.

91. **(b)** Article 75(a) of the Constitution clearly states that the Prime Minister shall be appointed by the President of India.

- The Council of Ministers is also appointed by the President on the advice of the Prime Minister.
- The ministers hold office during the pleasure of the President, as mentioned in Article 75(b).
- The Council of Ministers is collectively responsible to the Lok Sabha, under Article 75(c).

92. **(a) Kutiyattam** is a traditional Sanskrit theatre form from Kerala, recognised as one of India's oldest surviving theatrical forms.

- Ammannur Madhava Chakyar was a legendary Kutiyattam performer, known for reviving and popularising the art globally.
- He was honoured with the Padma Shri in 1981 for his immense contribution to Indian classical theatre.
- Kutiyattam has been recognised by UNESCO as a Masterpiece of the Oral and Intangible Heritage of Humanity.

93. **(c) Mitochondria** are known as the 'powerhouses of the cell', producing energy in the form of ATP via cellular respiration.

- Under electron microscopy, they appear rounded or sausage-shaped, measuring about 0.5–1.0 μm in diameter and 2–8 μm in length.
- Mitochondria have a double membrane structure, with the inner membrane folded into cristae.
- They contain their own DNA, enabling them to replicate independently within the cell.

94. **(a)** The Khandesh region was annexed into the Mughal Empire by Emperor Akbar in the year 1601.

- It was ruled by Bahadur Khan, a descendant of the Faruqi dynasty, who resisted Mughal authority.
- The Mughal army defeated Bahadur Khan and captured Asirgarh Fort, the key stronghold in Khandesh.
- After the conquest, Akbar renamed the region as Dandes and incorporated it under Mughal administration.

95. **(c)** Article 368 of the Indian Constitution provides the procedure for amendment of the Constitution.

- It mentions two types of amendments (i) by special majority of Parliament and (ii) by special majority of Parliament with ratification by half of the states.
- Amendments can be made to various parts of the Constitution, but basic structure cannot be altered.

Knowledge Booster

- The concept of "Basic Structure Doctrine" was established in the Kesavananda Bharati Case (1973).
- First Constitutional Amendment Act (1951) was the first amendment to the Indian Constitution

96. **(b)** In ice hockey, each team has 6 players on the ice during normal play.

- The team consists of 1 goaltender and 5 skaters — typically 3 forwards and 2 defensemen.
- The game is played on an ice rink, with three main zones — defensive, neutral and offensive.
- Ice hockey is governed internationally by the International Ice Hockey Federation (IIHF).
- The sport is particularly popular in Canada, USA, Russia, Sweden and Finland.

97. **(a) Siachen Glacier** is located in the Eastern Karakoram range of the Himalayas, in the union territory of Ladakh, India.

- It is the longest glacier in the Karakoram and the second-longest in the world's non-polar areas (approx. 76 km long).
- The glacier feeds the Nubra River, a tributary of the Shyok River, which ultimately joins the Indus.

Knowledge Booster

- The Siachen Conflict began in 1984 with Operation Meghdoot, when India gained control over the glacier.
- Situated at an altitude of over 5,400 meters, it is one of the highest battlefields on Earth.

98. **(a)** Maimata is a traditional folk dance of **Tripura**, performed by the Halam tribe of the state.

- The dance includes graceful body movements, accompanied by folk music and drums.
- It reflects the agrarian culture and seasonal cycles, especially post-harvest celebrations.
- Tripura is known for its ethnic diversity, with over 19 tribal communities preserving their own unique art forms.

99. **(d)** The appointment of the Governor by the President (Centre) reflects the **unitary system** of the Indian Constitution.

- Article 155 of the Constitution empowers the President to appoint the Governor of a state.
- The Governor acts as the Centre's representative, highlighting central control over states.
- The Sarkaria Commission suggested limiting the Centre's discretion in appointing governors.

100. **(b)** The term 'inning' in **Kho-Kho** refers to a turn of play for attacking and defending teams.

- Each team gets two innings, comprising both chasing and defending roles.
- In standard matches, each inning lasts 9 minutes as per official Kho-Kho rules.
- Kho-Kho originated in Maharashtra and is a popular traditional Indian sport.
- The game is governed by the Kho-Kho Federation of India (KKFI), established in 1955.

101. **(c)** Let the fourth proportional be x.

The numbers are 0.48, 0.84 and 32.

According to question,

The product of the extrems equal the product of the means

$\Rightarrow 0.48 : 0.84 :: 32 : x$

$$\Rightarrow \frac{0.48}{0.84} = \frac{32}{x} \Rightarrow \frac{48}{84} = \frac{32}{x} \Rightarrow x = 56$$

102. **(c)** Number of illiterates in village $R = 150$

Number of illiterates in village $P = 380$

According to question,

Difference between illiterates in village R and P

$= 380 - 150 = 230$

$$\text{Less\%} = \frac{\text{Difference}}{\text{Number of illiterates in village } P} \times 100\ \%$$

$$\text{Less } \% = \left(\frac{230}{380} \times 100\right)\% = 60\frac{10}{19}\%$$

103. **(a)** Radius of circle = 42 cm

Angle subtend by an arc at the centre = 60°.

$\Rightarrow$ Length of arc $OAB = \dfrac{\theta}{360°}(2\pi r)$

$= \dfrac{60°}{360°} \times 2 \times \dfrac{22}{7} \times 42$

Length of arc OAB = 44 cm

104. **(a)** CP of book buys by Mihir = ₹ 625

SP of book = ₹ 550.

$\Rightarrow$ Loss = ₹ (625 – 550) = ₹ 75

$\Rightarrow$ Loss % $= \left(\dfrac{\text{Loss}}{\text{CP}} \times 100\right)\%$

$= \left(\dfrac{75}{625} \times 100\right)\%$

$\Rightarrow$ Loss % = 12%

105. **(b)** Initial salary of Arpit = ₹ 80000.

After 1 year, Salary of Arpit fell by 5% then salary after 1 year

$=$ ₹$\left(80000 - 80000 \times \dfrac{5}{100}\right) =$ ₹ 76000

Salary after 2 year, 8% fell due to bad performance i.e.

₹$\left(76000 \times \dfrac{92}{100}\right) =$ ₹ 69920

Speedy Method

Initial salary of Arpit = ₹ 80000.

Salary after successive deduction of 5% in first year and 8% in second year

$=$ ₹$\left(80{,}000 \times \left(1 - \dfrac{5}{100}\right) \times \left(1 - \dfrac{8}{100}\right)\right)$

$=$ ₹$\left(80{,}000 \times \dfrac{95}{100} \times \dfrac{92}{100}\right)$

Current salary = ₹ 69920.

106. **(a)** Number of students enrolled in institute X in 2010 = 320

Number of students enrolled in institute X in 2011 = 240

Average number of students

$= \dfrac{320 + 240}{2} = \dfrac{560}{2} = 280$

Number of students enrolled in institute in Y in 2011 = 320

Number of students enrolled in institute in Y in 2012 = 200

Average number of students

$= \dfrac{320 + 200}{2} = \dfrac{520}{2} = 260$

Their difference = 280 – 260 = 20

107. **(d)** TSA of hemisphere = 4158 cm^2

Let the radius of hemisphere be r.

According to question,

$\Rightarrow$ TSA of hemisphere = 4158

$\Rightarrow \quad 3\pi r^2 = 4158$

$\Rightarrow \quad r^2 = \dfrac{4158 \times 7}{22 \times 3}$

$\Rightarrow \quad r = \sqrt{441} = 21$ cm

Volume of hemisphere $= \dfrac{2}{3}\pi r^3$

$\Rightarrow$ Volume of hemisphere

$= \dfrac{2}{3} \times \dfrac{22}{7} \times 21 \times 21 \times 21$

Volume of hemisphere = 19404 cm^3

108. **(a)** The average weight of 8 students = 48 kg

The weight of 8 students = (48 × 8) kg = 384 kg

The average weight of first four student = 44 kg

The total weight of first four student = (44 × 4) = 176 kg

The total weight of second four students = (58 × 4) = 232 kg

Total weight of 16 students

= (384 + 232 + 176) = 792 kg

Average weight of 16 students

$= \left(\dfrac{792}{16}\right) = 49.5$ kg

109. **(b)** Let the expression by y

$\Rightarrow y = (1 - 2x)^2 - (1 + 2x)^2$

$\Rightarrow y = 1 + 4x^2 - 4x - (1 + 4x^2 + 4x)$

$\Rightarrow y = 1 + 4x^2 - 4x - 1 - 4x^2 - 4x$

$\Rightarrow y = -8x$

110. **(c)** Total laptop sold by A = 4000

Number of brand 1 laptop sold by

$A = \dfrac{3}{4} \times 4000 = 3000$

Number of brand 2 laptop sold by

$B = \dfrac{1}{3} \times 6000 = 2000$

Difference between brand 1 laptop sold by A and brand 2 laptop sold by

$B = 3000 - 2000 = 1000$

111. **(a)** Going speed of a boy from home to school = 30 km/h

Returning speed of a boy from school to home = 70 km/h

Average speed $= \dfrac{2 \times S_1 \times S_2}{S_1 + S_2}$

Here, S_1 = 30 km/h, S_2 = 70 km/h

Average speed

$= \left(\dfrac{2 \times 30 \times 70}{30 + 70}\right) = 42$ km/h

112. **(d)** Let the Madhu's income be ₹ x.

According to question,

Rupu's income

$=$ ₹$\left(x + x \times \dfrac{20}{100}\right) =$ ₹ $\dfrac{6x}{5}$

Difference between income

$=$ ₹$\left(\dfrac{6x}{5} - x\right) =$ ₹ $\dfrac{x}{5}$

$\Rightarrow$ Loss % $= \left(\dfrac{\text{Difference}}{\text{Rupu's income}} \times 100\right)\%$

$= \left(\dfrac{\frac{x}{5}}{\frac{6x}{5}} \times 100\right)\%$

$\Rightarrow$ Loss % $= 16\dfrac{2}{3}\%$

Madhu's income is less than Rupu's income by $16\dfrac{2}{3}\%$.

113. **(b)** Let the required annual installment be ₹ x. The calculated equation for first year is equal to the sum of installments and interest of the remaining two years as follows:

$\Rightarrow$ ₹$\left[x + \dfrac{x \times 12.25 \times 2}{100}\right]$

The calculate equation for the second year is equal to the sum of installment and interest of the remaining year is a follow:

$\Rightarrow$ ₹$\left[x + \dfrac{x \times 12.25 \times 1}{100}\right]$

The calculated equation for the third year is equal to the installment only as no other year remains is ₹ x

According to question,

$\Rightarrow \left[x + \dfrac{x \times 12.25 \times 2}{100}\right] + \left[x + \dfrac{x \times 12.25 \times 1}{100}\right] + x$

= 9429

$\Rightarrow 3x + \dfrac{24.50x}{100} + \dfrac{12.25x}{100} = 9429$

$\Rightarrow \dfrac{336.75x}{100} = 9429$

$\Rightarrow x = \dfrac{9429 \times 100}{336.75} = \dfrac{9429 \times 4}{13.47}$

$\Rightarrow x = 2800$

Annual installment is ₹ 2800.

Speedy Method

Here, principle = ₹ 9429, $R = 12.25\%$,

Time = 3 years

Annual payment

$= ₹\left(\frac{100 \times P}{100T + RT(T-1)/2}\right)$

$= ₹\left(\frac{100 \times 9429}{100 \times 3 + 3 \times 12.25(3-1)/2}\right)$

$= ₹\left(\frac{942900}{336.75}\right) = ₹\ 2800$

114. **(b)** From the given table, we concluded that class IX has the minimum number of students from all schools together.

115. **(d)** Factors of 20 = 2 × 2 × 5

Factors of 24 = 2 × 2 × 2 × 3

Factors of 34 = 2 × 17

Factors of 60 = 2 × 2 × 3 × 5

Factors of 75 = 3 × 5 × 5

LCM of (20, 24, 34, 60 and 75)

= 2 × 3 × 2 × 5 × 5 × 7 × 17 = 35700

Last number which is exactly divisible is 35700.

116. **(c)** Let x be the mean proportional value

Let $a = 0.03$, $b = 0.0003$

According to question,

$\Rightarrow \frac{a}{x} = \frac{x}{5} \Rightarrow x = \sqrt{ab}$

$\Rightarrow x^2 = \sqrt{0.03 \times 0.0003}$

$\Rightarrow x = 0.003$

117. **(b)** Here, $a + b + c = 5$

$ab + bc + ca = 7$

from, $a + b + c = 5$

On squaring both sides

$\Rightarrow (a + b + c)^2 = 25$

$\Rightarrow a^2 + b^2 + c^2 + 2ab + 2bc + 2ca = 25$

$\Rightarrow a^2 + b^2 + c^2 + 2(ab + bc + ca) = 25$

$\Rightarrow a^2 + b^2 + c^2 = 25 - 2 \times 7$

$= 25 - 14$

$\Rightarrow a^2 + b^2 + c^2 = 11$

We know that,

$(a + b + c)^3 = (a + b + c)(a^2 + b^2 + c^2 - ab - bc - ca) + 3abc$

As, $a + b + c = 5, bc + ca + ab = 7$

$\Rightarrow (a + b + c)^3 = 5(11 - 7) + 3abc$

$\Rightarrow (a + b + c)^3 - 3abc = 20$

118. **(a)** Total number of people = 4980

Favourite games of group of young people who like football = 30%

$\therefore$ Central angle $= \frac{\text{Percentage}}{100} \times 360°$

$= \frac{30 \times 360°}{100}$

Central angle of football = 108°

119. **(d)** Maximum earning sector is sales = ₹ 155 lakh

Minimum earning sector is communication = ₹ 60 lakh

Their difference = Maximum earning sector – Minimum earning sector

= ₹ (115 – 60) lakh

⇒ ₹ 55 lakh

120. **(c)** MRP of an item = ₹ Z

SP of an item = ₹ 6622

Discount offered = 12%

According to question, SP of an item

=(MRP – MRP × D%)

$\Rightarrow Z - Z \times \frac{12}{100} = 6622$

$\Rightarrow \frac{22Z}{25} = 6622$

$\Rightarrow Z = \frac{6622 \times 25}{22}$

$\Rightarrow Z = ₹ 7525$

Speedy Method

MRP of an item = ₹ Z

SP of an item = ₹ 6622

Discount offered = 12%

$D\% = \frac{D}{\text{MRP}} \times 100$

$\Rightarrow \frac{D}{\text{MRP}} = \frac{12}{100} = \frac{3}{25}$

Let the ratio be x.

$\Rightarrow$ SP = MRP – $D = (25 - 3)x = 22x$

Given, SP = ₹ 6622

$\Rightarrow Z = \frac{6622}{22} = ₹301$

Then, MRP = $25x = Z$

$\Rightarrow Z = 25 \times 301$

$\Rightarrow Z = ₹\ 7525$

121. **(d)** Marks obtained by students in Mid-1.

Sunil = 33

Hemanth = 30

Rehman = 36

Mohan = 21

Total marks = 33 + 30 + 36 + 21 = 120

Hemanth %

$= \left(\frac{\text{Hemanth marks}}{\text{Total marks}} \times 100\right)\%$

$= \left(\frac{30 \times 100}{120}\right)\% = 25\%$

122. **(c)** Let the CP be ₹ $100x$

A shopkeeper increases price of an item by 50%, then it become MRP

$= \left(100x + 100x \times \frac{50}{100}\right) ₹ = 150x$

Discount offered on MRP

$= ₹\ \frac{150x \times 40}{100} = 60x$

SP of an item = $(150x - 60x)$ = ₹ $90x$

Loss = ₹ $(100x - 90x)$ = ₹ $10x$

Loss % $= \left(\frac{\text{Loss}}{\text{CP}} \times 100\right)\%$

$= \left(\frac{10x}{100} x \times 100\right)\%$

Loss % = 10%

Speed Method

Let the CP be $100x$.

According to question, MRP become = ₹ $150x$

Discount offered = 40%

$\Rightarrow 150x(100 - 40) = 100x(100 - L\%)$

$\Rightarrow 3x \times 60 = 2x(100 - L\%)$

$\Rightarrow 90 = 100\ L\%$

$\Rightarrow L\% = 10\%$

123. **(d)** Principle = ₹ 8000,

Rate = 30% p.a. for 1 year

Interest be compounded half yearly

i.e. $t = 2n$, $r = \frac{20}{2}\% = 10\%$ p.a.

$\Rightarrow$ A = P + CI

$\Rightarrow$ CI = A – P = $P\left[\left(1 + \frac{r/2}{100}\right)^{2n} - 1\right]$

$\Rightarrow$ CI $= 8000\left[\left(1 + \frac{20/2}{100}\right)^2 - 1\right]$

$\Rightarrow$ CI $= 8000\left[\left(1 + \frac{1}{10}\right)^2 - 1\right]$

$= 8000\left(\frac{121}{100} - 1\right)$

$\Rightarrow$ CI $= 8000 \times \frac{21}{100}$

$\Rightarrow$ CI = ₹ 1680

124. **(d)** We have, $(x^6 + 1)$ and $(x^4 - 1)$

Using, $(a^3 + b^3) = (a + b)(a^2 - ab + b^2)$

$a^2 + b^2 = (a + b)(a - b)$

$(x^6 + 1) = (x^2)^3 + (1)^3$

$= (x^2 + 1)(x^4 - x^2 + 1)$

and $(x^4 - 1) = (x^2 + 1)(x^2 - 1)$

So, HCF of $(x^6 + 1)$ and $(x^4 - 1)$ is $(x^2 + 1)$

125. **(b)** Let $y = \dfrac{1\frac{1}{2} \div 3\frac{1}{4} + \frac{1}{2} \div \frac{13}{14} + \frac{1}{5}}{\frac{1}{5} \times 3\frac{1}{2} - \frac{1}{3} \div 1\frac{3}{4} \times 3\frac{1}{2}}$

$\Rightarrow y = \dfrac{\frac{3}{2} \times \frac{4}{13} + \frac{1}{2} \times \frac{14}{13} + \frac{1}{5}}{\frac{1}{5} \times \frac{7}{2} - \frac{1}{3} \times \frac{4}{7} \times \frac{7}{2}}$

$\Rightarrow y = \dfrac{\frac{6}{13} + \frac{7}{13} + \frac{1}{5}}{\frac{7}{10} - \frac{2}{3}} = \dfrac{\frac{30 + 35 + 13}{65}}{\frac{21 - 20}{30}}$

$\Rightarrow y = \dfrac{\frac{78}{65}}{\frac{1}{30}} = \dfrac{78}{65} \times 30$

$\Rightarrow y = 36$

126. **(b)** If 2 men can build the wall in 34 days, then 1 men can build the wall $= 2 \times 34$ days.

$\Rightarrow$ Rate of work done of 1 man $= \dfrac{1}{2 \times 34}$ per day

If 4 women can build the wall in 34 days, then 1 women can build it in (4×34) days

$\Rightarrow$ Rate of work done of 1 woman $= \dfrac{1}{4 \times 34}$ per day

Now, 6 men and 5 women working together combined.

$= 6 \times \dfrac{1}{2 \times 34} + 5 \times \dfrac{1}{4 \times 34}$

$= \dfrac{6}{68} + \dfrac{5}{136} = \dfrac{17}{136}$

Number of days required

$= \dfrac{1}{\text{Combined work rate}}$

$= \dfrac{1}{\frac{17}{136}} = \dfrac{136}{17} = 8$ days.

Speedy Method

Let the efficiency of one man be m and one women be n work done

$= 2 \times m \times 34 = 4 \times w \times 34$

$\Rightarrow$ Ratio of efficiency of man to women, $m : w = 2 : 1$

Let the efficiency of man and women be x and $2x$.

Number of days by which 6 men and 5 women can finish the work

$= \dfrac{(2 \times 2 \times 34)}{(6 \times 2 + 5 \times 1)}$

$= \dfrac{136}{17} = 8$ days

127. **(b)** Factors of $78 = 2 \times 3 \times 13$

Factors of $84 = 2 \times 2 \times 3 \times 7$

Factors of $90 = 2 \times 3 \times 3 \times 5$

Factors of $112 = 2 \times 2 \times 2 \times 2 \times 7$

HCF of 78, 84, 90 and 112 is 2.

128. **(d)** Cost % distribution of laptop $= 30\%$

If a person purchased all the items for ₹ 300000

Then cost of laptop $= ₹\left(300000 \times \dfrac{30}{100}\right)$

$= ₹\ 90000.$

Cost of a TV $= ₹\left(300{,}000 \times \dfrac{15}{100}\right)$

$= ₹\ 45000$

Difference $= ₹\ (90000 - 45000)$

$= ₹\ 45000$

Cost of a TV is ₹ 45000 less than a laptop is cost.

Speedy Method

Cost % distribution of a laptop = 30%

Cost % of distribution of a TV = 15%.

Total cost of all items = ₹ 300000

Cost difference $= \left\{\dfrac{300000 \times (30 - 15)}{100}\right\}$

$= ₹\ 45000$

129. **(b)** We have, $\cos A = \dfrac{1}{2}$

$\Rightarrow \sin (180° - A) = \sin A$

$\cos A = \dfrac{1}{2} = \dfrac{B}{H}$

Here, $P = ?, B = 2, H = 2$

$\Rightarrow \quad P = \sqrt{H^2 - B^2} = \sqrt{(2)^2 - (1)^2}$

$= \sqrt{4 - 1} = \sqrt{3}$

$\sin A = \dfrac{P}{H} = \dfrac{\sqrt{3}}{2}$

$\Rightarrow \sin (180° - A) = \sin A = \dfrac{\sqrt{3}}{2}$

130. **(d)** Let the CP of 50 gm of rice is ₹ $100x$.

Then, SP of 50 gm of rice with 24%

Loss $= \left(100 - \dfrac{24 \times 100x}{100}\right) = 76x$

The CP of 19 gm of rice

$= \dfrac{100x}{50} \times 19 = 38x$

$\Rightarrow$ Profit or Loss

$\% = \left(\dfrac{\text{SP} - \text{CP}}{\text{CP}} \times 100\right)\%$

$= \left\{\dfrac{(76x - 38x)}{38x} \times 100\right\}\%$

$= 100\%$ profit

131. **(d)** Radius of sphere = 9 cm

Radius of cylinder = 12 cm

Let h be the rise in the height of water.

$\Rightarrow$ Volume of sphere $= \dfrac{4}{3}\pi r^3$

$= \dfrac{4}{3} \times \pi \times 9 \times 9 \times 9$

$= 972\pi\ \text{cm}^3$

Volume of displaced water is equal to the volume of sphere

$\Rightarrow \quad \dfrac{4}{3}\pi r^3 = \pi r^2 h$

$\Rightarrow \quad 972\pi = \pi \times (12)^2 \times h$

$\Rightarrow \quad h = \dfrac{972}{144}$

$\Rightarrow \quad h = 6.75$ cm

132. **(a)** A can do $\dfrac{1}{5}$ of a piece of work in 20 days.

$\Rightarrow$ Time taken by A to do complete work $= (5 \times 20)$ days

= 100 days

$\Rightarrow B$ can complete 30% of work in 36 days than B can finish the work

$= \left(\dfrac{36 \times 100}{30}\right)$ days = 120 days

$\Rightarrow C$ can complete 80% of the work in 160 days, then time taken by C to finish the work $= \left(\dfrac{160 \times 100}{80}\right)$ days

= 200 days.

According to question,

B and C togetehr started and work for x days

i.e. Efficiency of B and $C = \dfrac{1}{120} + \dfrac{1}{200}$

$= \dfrac{8}{600} = \dfrac{1}{75}$

In x days, work done by B and $C = \dfrac{x}{75}$

A and C togther worked for $(x-41)$ days

$\Rightarrow$ Efficiency of A and $C = \dfrac{1}{100} + \dfrac{1}{200}$

$= \dfrac{3}{200}$

In $(x - 41)$ days, work done by A and $C = \dfrac{3}{200}(x - 41)$

According to question,

$\Rightarrow \quad \dfrac{x}{75} : \dfrac{3(x - 41)}{200} = 19 : 6$

$\Rightarrow \quad \dfrac{6x}{75} = \dfrac{19 \times 3(x - 41)}{200}$

$\Rightarrow \quad 16x = 57x - 57 \times 41$

$\Rightarrow \quad 41x = 57 \times 41$

$\Rightarrow \quad x = 57$ days

Now, the part of work be completed by C alone in $2x$ days

i.e. $\dfrac{2 \times 57 \times 1}{200} = \dfrac{57}{100}$ part

133. (a) Radii of two circles be 6 cm and 9 cm.

i.e., $r_1 = 6$ cm and $r_2 = 9$ cm

Let d be the distance between the centre of two circle.

L = Length of transverse common tangent = 20 cm

We know that, $L = \sqrt{d^2 - (r_1 + r_2)^2}$

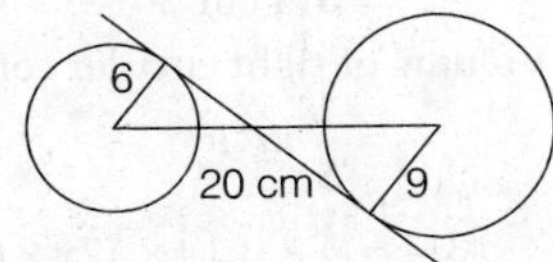

$\Rightarrow (20)^2 = d^2 - (6+9)^2$

$\Rightarrow \quad d^2 = 400 + 225$

$\Rightarrow \quad d^2 = 625 \Rightarrow d = 25$ cm

134. (c) Let x be the speed of Nikunj and y be the speed of stream.

According to question,

$\Rightarrow \quad x - y = \dfrac{4}{1}$

$\Rightarrow \quad x - y = 4$ km/h ...(i)

$\Rightarrow \quad x + y = \dfrac{2}{\frac{15}{60}}$

$\Rightarrow x + y = 8$ km/h ...(ii)

From Eqs. (i) and (ii)

$\Rightarrow \quad x = 6$ km/h

Time taken for a distance of 7km,

$\Rightarrow \text{Time} = \dfrac{\text{Distance}}{\text{Speed}} = \dfrac{7}{6} = 1$ h 10 min

135. (d) Speed of theif = 10 km/h

Speed of policeman = 12 km/h

Relative speed in same direction

$= (12 - 10) = 2$ km/h

Distance travelled by their with a speed of 10 km/h in 30 min

$\left(\text{i.e, } \dfrac{1}{2}\text{ h}\right) = 30 \times \dfrac{1}{2} = 5$ km

$\Rightarrow \quad \text{Time} = \dfrac{\text{Distance}}{\text{Speed}} = \dfrac{5}{2} = 2.5$ h

The policeman started at 8 : 00 p.m. after 2.5 hour the caught the thief (8 : 00 + 2 : 30) = 10 : 30 p.m.

136. (c) Total amount spent on sport during the year = ₹ 7500000.

% Distribution of amount spent on sports i.e.

Cricket = 20%

Hockey = 13%

Amount spent on cricket

$= \left(\dfrac{20}{100} \times 7500000\right) = ₹\,1500000$

Amount spent on hockey

$= \left(\dfrac{13}{100} \times 7500000\right) = ₹\,975000.$

Amount spent on cricket and hockey

$= ₹\,(1500000 + 975000) = ₹\,2475000$

Speedy Method

Total amount spent on sports

$= ₹\,75{,}00{,}000.$

Total % distribution of amount an cricket and Hokay

$= 20\% + 13\% = 33\%$

Amount spent on cricket and Hockey

$= \left(\dfrac{33}{100} \times 7500000\right) = ₹\,2475000$

137. (c) In ΔBOC,

$\angle BOC = 125°$

We know that, the sum of angle is 180°.

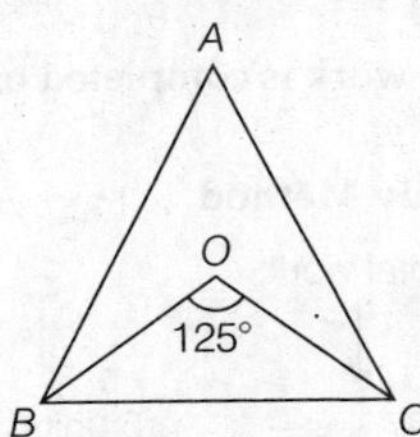

$\Rightarrow \angle BOC + \angle OBC + \angle OCB = 180°$

$\Rightarrow \angle OCB + \angle OBC = 180° - 125°$

$\Rightarrow \angle OCB + \angle OBC = 55°$

Since, BO and CO are angle bisector

$\Rightarrow \angle ABC = 2\angle OBC$

$\Rightarrow \angle ACB = 2\,OCB$

$\Rightarrow \angle ABC + \angle ACB = 2(\angle OBC + \angle OCB)$

$\Rightarrow \angle ABC + \angle ACB = 2 \times 55°$

$\Rightarrow \angle ABC + \angle ACB = 110°$

In ΔABC, the sum of angle is 180°

$\Rightarrow \angle BAC + \angle ABC + \angle ACB = 180°$

$\Rightarrow \angle BAC = 180° - 110°$

$\Rightarrow \angle BAC = 70°$

Speedy Method

We have, $\angle BOC = 125°$

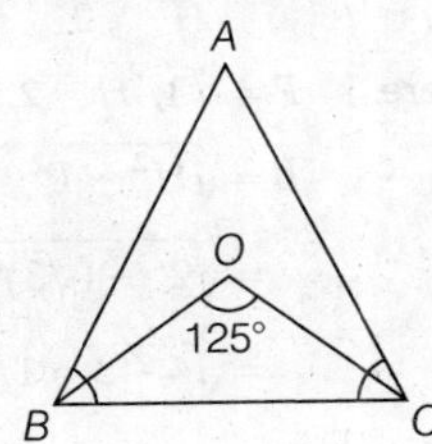

BO and OC is angle bisector.

Now, by angle bisector theorem,

$\Rightarrow \angle BOC = 90° + \dfrac{1}{2}\angle BAC$

$\Rightarrow \quad 125° = 90° + \dfrac{1}{2}\angle BAC$

$\Rightarrow \angle BAC = 70°$

138. (d) MR 62 km/h → 1050 m ← 55 km/h KE

Length of Mumbai Rajdhani = 850 m

Length of Kissan express = 700 m

Distance between them = 1050 m

S_1 = Speed of Mumbai Rajdhani = 62 km/h

$= 62 \times \dfrac{5}{18} = \dfrac{155}{9}$ km/s

S_2 = Speed of Kissan Express = 55 km/h

$= 55 \times \dfrac{5}{18} = \dfrac{275}{18}$ m/s

Relative speed $= S_1 + S_2$

$= \left(\dfrac{155}{9} + \dfrac{275}{18}\right) = \dfrac{195}{6}$ m/s

Time taken to cross each other

$= \dfrac{\text{Total distance}}{\text{Total time}}$

$= \dfrac{850 + 1050 + 700}{\frac{195}{6}}$

$= \dfrac{2600 \times 6}{195} = 80$ sec.

139. (c) If $\sin\beta = \dfrac{1}{3}$

$\Rightarrow (\sec\beta - \tan\beta)^2 = \left(\dfrac{1}{\cos\beta} - \dfrac{\sin\beta}{\cos\beta}\right)^2$

$= \left(\dfrac{1 - \sin\beta}{\cos\beta}\right)^2$

$= \dfrac{(1-\sin\beta)^2}{\cos^2\beta} = \dfrac{(1-\sin\beta)^2}{1-\sin^2\beta}$

$= \dfrac{(1-\sin\beta)^2}{1-(\sin\beta)^2} = \dfrac{\left(1-\frac{1}{3}\right)^2}{1-\left(\frac{1}{3}\right)^2}$

$= \dfrac{\left(\frac{2}{3}\right)^2}{1-\frac{1}{9}} = \dfrac{\frac{4}{9}}{\frac{8}{9}}$

$\Rightarrow (\sec\beta - \tan\beta)^2 = \dfrac{1}{2}$

140. (d) Given, length of diagonal of a square = $24\sqrt{2}$

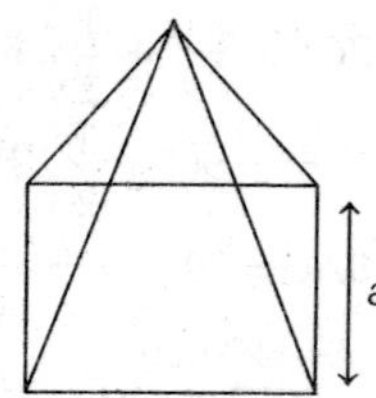

Let the side of square be a cm.

$\Rightarrow$ Length of diagonal = $24\sqrt{2}$

$\Rightarrow \quad a\sqrt{2} = 24\sqrt{2}$

$\Rightarrow \quad a = 24$ cm

Perimeter of square

$= 4a = 4 \times 24 = 96$ cm

Area of square

$= a^2 = (24)^2 = 576 \text{ cm}^2$

Lateral surface area of pyramid

$= 624 \text{ cm}^2$

We know that,

Lateral surface area of pyramid

$= \frac{1}{2} \times$ Perimeter of base $\times$ Slant height

$\Rightarrow 624 = \frac{1}{2} \times 96 \times$ Slant height

$\Rightarrow$ Slant height $= \frac{624 \times 2}{96} = 13$ cm

Now, $(\text{Height})^2 = (\text{Slant height})^2 - \left(\frac{\text{Side of square}}{2}\right)^2$

$\Rightarrow \text{Height} = \sqrt{(13)^2 - (24/2)^2}$

$\Rightarrow \text{Height} = \sqrt{169 - 144} = \sqrt{25}$

$\Rightarrow$ Height = 5 cm

Volume of pyramid

$= \frac{1}{3} \times$ Area of base $\times$ Height

$= \frac{1}{3} \times 576 \times 5 = 960 \text{ cm}^3$

141. (c) Let the ratio be x.

Side of rectangle are in ratio 3 : 8.

Area of rectangle = 1944 cm^2

$\Rightarrow 3x \times 8x = 1944$

$\Rightarrow \quad x^2 = \frac{1944}{24}$

$\Rightarrow \quad x^2 = 81$

$\Rightarrow \quad x = 9$ cm

Perimeter of rectangle

$= 2(l + b) = 2(3x + 8x)$

$= 2 \times 11x$

$= 22x = 22 \times 9$

= 198 cm

142. (d) A can complete the whole work in 24 days in (10 hour/day)

B can complete the whole work in 30 days (i.e. 10 hours/day)

Total work = LCM of 24 and 30 = 120.

$\Rightarrow$ Efficiency of $A = \frac{120}{24} = 5$ units/day

$\Rightarrow$ Efficiency of $B = \frac{120}{30} = 4$ units/day

Work done by A and B in 10 hours of one day is 5 and 4 respectively.

Work done of A and B in 2 days $= 5 + 4 = 9$ units

A and B repeat the same process on all 26 days.

Work done by A and B is 26 days $= 9 \times 13 = 117$ units

Remaining work = (120 – 117) units = 3 units

3 part work will be completed in

$= \frac{2}{3}$ days.

Total time taken to complete the work $= 26\frac{2}{3}$ days.

Total work is completed on the 27th day.

Speedy Method

Total work

↓

A – 24 day, B – 30 day → 120 → 5 units, 4 units → Working 10 hour/day

↓

Efficiency

Efficiency of ($A + B$) in two shift in 2 days working in alternate shift = (5 + 4) units = 9 units.

So, they work on alternate shift, then in 26 days, working together = 9 × 13 units = 117 units

Remaining work = (120 – 117) units = 3 units

So, the work get completed on 27th day.

143. (a) If $\sin A = \frac{\sqrt{3}}{2}, 0 < A < 90°$.

$\sin A = \frac{P}{H} = \frac{\sqrt{3}}{2}$.

Here, $P = \sqrt{3}, H = 2, B = ?$

$\Rightarrow \quad B = \sqrt{H^2 - P^2}$

$= \sqrt{2^2 - (\sqrt{3})^2}$

$= \sqrt{4 - 3} = 1$

$\text{cosec } A = \frac{1}{\sin A} = \frac{2}{\sqrt{3}}$.

$\cot A = \frac{B}{P} = \frac{1}{\sqrt{3}}$

Then, $2(\text{cosec } A + \cot A)$

$= 2\left(\frac{2}{\sqrt{3}} + \frac{1}{\sqrt{3}}\right)$

$= 2\left(\frac{3}{\sqrt{3}}\right) = 2\sqrt{3}$

144. (c) Height and radius of a base of a right circular cone are in the ratio = 12 : 5

Volume of right circular cone $= 314 \text{ cm}^3$

$\Rightarrow$ Volume of right circular cone

$= \frac{1}{3} \pi r^2 h$

$\Rightarrow \quad 314 = \frac{1}{3} \times 3.14 \times 12x \times (5x)^2$

$\Rightarrow \quad \frac{314 \times 3}{3.14 \times 12 \times 25} = x^3$

$\Rightarrow \quad x = 1$

Height of cone = $12x$ = 12 cm

Radius of cone = $5x$ = 5 cm

Slant height of cone

$= \sqrt{\text{Height}^2 + \text{Radius}^2}$

$= \sqrt{12^2 + 5^2}$

$= \sqrt{144 + 25} = \sqrt{169}$

Slant height of cone = 13 cm

145. (c) Three number are in ratio 5 : 7 : 9.

LCM of the number = 34650.

Let the number be $5x$, $7x$ and $9x$

LCM of be $5x$, $7x$ and $9x = 315x$

According to question,

$\Rightarrow 315x = 34650$

$\Rightarrow x = \frac{34650}{315} = 110$

HCF of $5x$, $7x$ and $9x$ is 110.

146. (c) HCF of 1036, 1813 and 3885 are as follows.

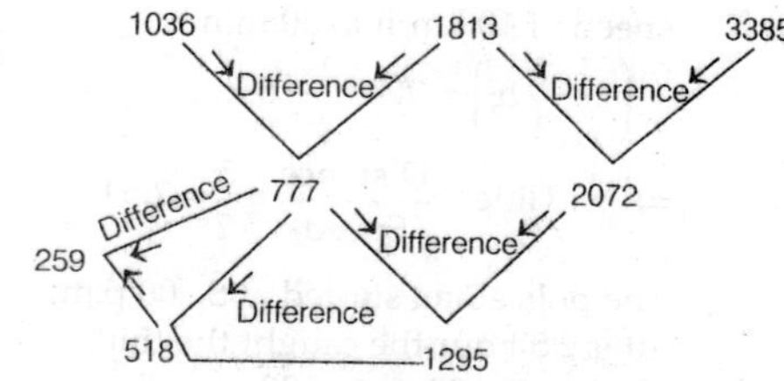

259 is the largest number that divides each number without leaving remainder. i.e., difference between each number show that 259 divides each number completely.

147. (a) If $\sin A = \frac{2}{3} \Rightarrow \sin A = \frac{2}{3} = \frac{P}{H}$

Here, $P = 2, H = 3, B = ?$

$\Rightarrow \quad B = \sqrt{H^2 - B^2}$

$= \sqrt{9-4} = \sqrt{5}$

$\Rightarrow \cos A = \frac{B}{H} = \frac{\sqrt{5}}{3},$

$\tan A = \frac{P}{B} = \frac{2}{\sqrt{5}}$

$\Rightarrow (7 - \tan A)(3 + \cos A)$

$= \left(7 - \frac{2}{\sqrt{5}}\right)\left(3 + \frac{\sqrt{5}}{3}\right)$

$= 21 + \frac{7\sqrt{5}}{3} - \frac{6}{\sqrt{5}} - \frac{2\sqrt{5}}{3\sqrt{5}}$

$\Rightarrow (7 - \tan A)(3 + \cos A) = \frac{61}{3} + \frac{17}{3\sqrt{5}}$

148. (d) Let the total number of votes in the voting list be $100x$.

Total cast votes $= 100x \times \frac{80}{100} = 80x.$

As 20% didn't cast their votes, votes who cast votes are 80%

Total valid votes $= 80x - 80$

Number of votes winner got

$= 100x \times \frac{45}{100} = 45x.$

Number of votes loser got $= 45x - 280.$

According to question,

$\Rightarrow 45x + 45x - 280 = 80x - 80$

$\Rightarrow 10x = 200 \Rightarrow x = 20$

Number of votes in voting list is $100x$ i.e., 2000.

149. (b) We have,

Two numbers, 73 and 657.

Factors of 73 is 73×1.

Factors of 657 is 73×9.

LCM of 73 and 657 is 657.

150. (d) Given, $AE = 13$ cm, $ED = 5$ cm and $EC = 13$ cm

Let $BE = x$ cm

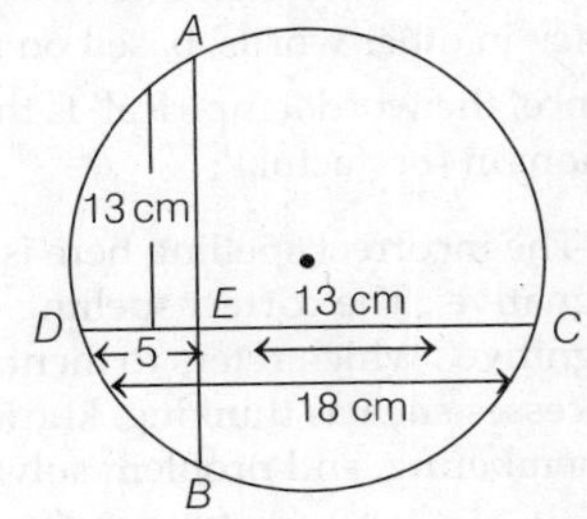

AB and CD are two chords intersect internally at E.

$AE \times BE = CE \times DE$

$\Rightarrow \quad 13 \times x = 13 \times 5$

$\Rightarrow \quad x = 5$ cm

$BE = 5$ cm

151. (b) The idiom 'fit as a fiddle' means to be in good health.

152. (a) The word 'familiar' in the sentence refers to someone who is well-known or recognisable. In this context, it means that she has become a well-known figure in the world of politics.

153. (b) The word 'authentic' means genuine, real or true. The opposite of authentic, in this case, is 'fake', which refers to something that is not real or is made to deceive.

154. (b) The word 'Inquisitive' means eager to learn or curious, especially about things that are not one's immediate concern. The antonym of inquisitive is 'Indifferent', which means having little or no interest or concern.

155. (c) The word 'contors' is incorrectly spelt. The correct spelling is 'contours', which refers to the outlines or shapes of something.

156. (c) The error lies in the phrase 'had completed'. The sentence is in the future tense because of 'Will Ramya', so it should use 'will have completed' instead of 'had completed'. The past perfect tense ('had completed') is not appropriate here.

Corrected sentence

Will Ramya have completed that work by 2025?

157. (c) The idiom 'Apple of discord' refers to something that causes disagreement or conflict. It is similar in meaning to 'bone of contention,' which refers to a subject or issue that causes prolonged dispute or argument.

158. (b) The correct word here is 'allotted', which means to assign or distribute something (in this case, funds) for a particular purpose. The sentence suggests that the funds assigned for food were insufficient for the upcoming week.

159. (a) 'In the project' could indeed work depending on the context you're aiming for. If the unexpected turn is something that happened within the project itself (for example, a key event or decision within the project led to the financial crisis), then 'in the project' would make sense.

'In the project' suggests that the issue arose directly within the project, which might indeed be a more precise expression depending on the situation described.

160. (c) The phrase 'respect each other' is most appropriately substituted with 'respect one another'. The phrase 'one another' is used when referring to mutual actions or feelings between two or more people, which fits the context of respect between individuals.

161. (a) The description provided refers to 'democracy', which is a form of government where supreme power is vested in the people and is exercised by their elected representatives under a free electoral system.

162. (b) The idiom 'come what may' is a phrase that expresses determination and resilience. It means that regardless of the challenges, difficulties or unforeseen circumstances, the person will continue on their path or will take action as planned.

It conveys a sense of persistence, suggesting that whatever happens, the individual will not back down or change course.

For example, if someone says, 'I will finish my project, come what may,' they are saying that they will complete the project no matter what obstacles or difficulties they face.

163. (d) The word 'tacit' means something that is understood or implied without being directly stated. It refers to a situation where something is conveyed through actions or mutual understanding rather than being explicitly mentioned. In this case, 'tacit' is describing the decision to engage in armed conflict, which suggests that the decision is implied or understood, even if not directly spoken out loud.

164. .**(b)** The error is in the phrase 'yesterday had took.' The correct form should be 'yesterday took'. The verb 'took' is the simple past tense, and when referring to an action completed in the past, we do not need the auxiliary verb 'had' unless we're using the past perfect tense. Since the sentence talks about an action that happened 'yesterday,' the simple past tense 'took' is correct.

Corrected sentence

My elder brother yesterday took my Facebook password.

165. **(b)** The correct one-word substitute for 'to tell the nature of a disease by its symptoms' is 'diagnosis'. Diagnosis refers to the identification or determination of the nature of a disease based on the symptoms presented.

166. **(d)** The idiom 'Fit as a fiddle' means to be in good health or physically well. The phrase refers to someone who is healthy, energetic, and physically capable, much like a well-maintained violin (a fiddle) that produces good music.

167. **(a)** The error lies in the phrase 'in the right time.' The correct expression should be 'on time', which refers to being punctual or arriving at the correct time. The phrase 'in the right time' is incorrect because 'in' is not the appropriate preposition when talking about punctuality.

168. **(a)** The idiom 'face to face' refers to meeting or discussing something directly with someone in person, rather than through other means like phone calls, letters or digital communication. It suggests having a personal, direct interaction.

169. **(b)** The word 'prowess' refers to exceptional skill or ability, especially in a particular area. In the context of the sentence, it is describing the athlete's exceptional abilities or mastery in their field. The most suitable substitution for 'prowess' would be 'exceptional mastery', as it conveys the same meaning of extraordinary skill.

170. **(d)** The word 'desire' in the sentence refers to a strong feeling of wanting something or a wish. In this context, it indicates that the person does not wish or long for money.

171. **(a)** The phrase 'make up her mind' means to come to a decision after considering choices.

172. **(b)** The antonym of 'Stingy' (which means unwilling to spend money) is extravagant, meaning someone who spends lavishly.

173. **(b)** A posthumous publication is a work published after the author's death.

174. **(a)** Rehabilitate means to restore to a former state or condition, often used in the context of health, status or function. Reinstall fits best in this context.

175. **(d)** The correct preposition with 'confident' in this context is 'in', making the phrase 'confident in speaking English' grammatically accurate.

This question tests knowledge of correct adjective-preposition collocations. Certain adjectives are commonly followed by specific prepositions. The adjective 'confident' is typically followed by the preposition 'in' when used before a gerund (verb ending in -ing).

The correct structure is

confident in + gerund/noun

176. **(d)** 'Limelight' refers to the center of attention or focus, especially in a public setting. Originally a type of stage lighting, it now metaphorically describes someone or something that is receiving a lot of attention or praise. It fits perfectly as a one-word substitute for 'centre of public attention'.

177. **(c)** This part is grammatically incorrect. The sentence intends to express that the result will be known by a future time (next week), so it requires the future perfect tense:

'Will have known' (Subject + will have + past participle).

'Have been know' is incorrect:

'Know' should be in its past participle form 'known'.

The helping verbs are misused - 'have been' implies a present perfect continuous or passive structure, which doesn't fit here.

178. **(c)** 'Break a leg' is an idiom used mainly in the context of performing arts to wish someone good luck, especially before a performance. It's based on theatrical superstition where saying 'good luck' directly is believed to bring bad luck, so performers say 'break a leg' instead.

179. **(d)** 'To hit the nail on the head' means to say or do exactly the right thing. It's used when someone gives an accurate or precise explanation or insight into a situation, especially when identifying the core issue.

180. **(b)** The sentence describes someone who sneers at others' beliefs, showing contempt or lack of respect.

'Cynicism' accurately captures this attitude - it reflects a general distrust of others' motives and often involves sarcasm or ridicule.

181. **(c)** The phrase 'Go hand in hand' is a commonly used idiom that means two things are closely related or happen together. In this context, 'Politics and money go hand in hand' accurately conveys the idea that both are deeply interconnected in the country.

182. **(c)** The word 'destitute' means extremely poor and lacking the basic necessities of life. Its antonym is 'affluent', which means having a lot of wealth and financial resources.

183. **(b)** The word 'harrowing' describes something extremely distressing or painful. The closest synonym is 'excruciating', which means intensely painful or emotionally distressing.

184. **(b)** The sentence contains the spelling error 'efectively'.

The correct spelling is 'effectively', meaning in a way that produces the desired result.

185. **(d)** In the sentence, the word 'empirical' is used to describe evidence based on observation or experience rather than theory or pure logic - in other words, based on facts.

Hence, the word 'empirical' is the synonym for 'factual'.

186. **(b)** The incorrect spelling here is 'cognative'. The correct spelling is 'cognitive', which refers to mental processes such as thinking, knowing, remembering, and problem-solving.

All other words - problems, mathematical, and capacity - are spelled correctly.

187. (a) The misspelt word in the sentence is 'gramar'. The correct spelling is 'grammar', which refers to the rules and structure of a language.

188. (d) The idiom 'through thick and thin' means to remain loyal and supportive in all situations, whether good or bad.

So, 'Under all circumstances' is the most appropriate meaning.

189. (d) A mendicant is a person who lives by begging from place to place.

190. (b) Reminiscence means the act of recalling past experiences or memories.

The closest synonym is 'remembrance', which also relates to remembering or thinking back on past events.

191. (c) The sentence is in the present tense and refers to a general fact about swans.

'Belong' is the base form of the verb, appropriate for the relative clause beginning with 'that.' 'Belongs' (Option d) is incorrect because the subject 'swans' is plural. 'Belonged' (past tense) and 'Belonging' (present participle) do not fit grammatically here.

192. (d) This is again a general truth or fact. The passive voice 'are known' is used to indicate what swans are generally recognised for they are known for their beauty and grace.

193. (d) The passage is highlighting the unique features of swans.

'Distinctive' means characteristic or unique, which fits perfectly with 'such as their long necks, large wingspans...'

194. (d) The sentence introduces a contrast - not all swans are white. So, the appropriate linking word is 'However':

195. (a) This sentence gives a specific example of a swan species that isn't white.

196. (d) The tone of the passage is concerned with human well-being and the environment, emphasising the effects of pollution on health, the planet and efforts being made to control it.

197. (b) The central idea of the passage revolves around pollution, its growing threat and efforts to eradicate it by 2030 under UN coordination. Hence, 'Pollution free planet' is the most accurate reflection of the core message.

198. (b) The passage begins with the cause - increasing population and resource use and then explains the effects - pollution and its impacts. It also talks about the solution via the UN's global plan. So, the cause-effect structure best represents the organisation of ideas.

199. (c) Pervasive means widespread or present everywhere. The opposite of that is limited something that is restricted in extent or presence.

200. (b) Priority means something of high importance or urgency.

The antonym would be 'last', as in something of least importance.

PAPER-1

SSC CPO SI SOLVED PAPER

4 October 2023 (Shift III)

Instructions

1. This paper contains 200 questions.
2. It has 4 Parts, **Part I** General Intelligence and Reasoning, **Part II** General Knowledge and General Awareness, **Part III** Quantitative Aptitude and **Part IV** English Comprehension.
3. Each question carries **1 marks**.

MM : 200

Time : 2 hr

Part I

General Intelligence and Reasoning

1. In a certain code language, 'ACTION' is written as 'TXANLI' and 'DEBATE' is written as 'BVDEGA'. How will 'CHANGE' be written in that language?
(a) ATHFN
(b) HRPEIU
(c) BJDLER
(d) ASCETN

2. Which of the following numbers will replace the question mark (?) in the given series?
38, 57, 40, 59, 42, ?
(a) 59 (b) 62 (c) 60 (d) 61

3. Which of the following numbers will replace the question mark (?) in the given series?
112, 129, 150, 175, 204, ?
(a) 240 (b) 234
(c) 237 (d) 245

4. In a certain code language, 'COACH' is coded as 'XAOHC' and 'BERTH' is coded as 'WREHT'. How will 'TRAIN' be coded in the same language?
(a) OARNI (b) PARNI
(c) PARIN (d) ONIAR

5. If '+' means '–', '–' means '×', '×' means '÷' and '÷' means'+', what will come in place of question mark '?' in the following equation?
$121 \times 11 \div 28 - 3 + 46 = ?$
(a) 49 (b) 43
(c) 65 (d) 71

6. Which of the following terms will replace the question mark (?) in the given series?
LDEA, NGIF, ?, RMQP, TPUU
(a) PMJK (b) PIMK
(c) PMIK (d) PJMK

7. If '+' means '–' , '–' means '×' , '×' means '÷' and '÷' means '+', then what will come in place of question mark (?) in the given equation?
$30 + 5 - 2 \times 10 \div 2 = ?$
(a) 50 (b) 31
(c) 80 (d) 60

8. A paper is folded and cut as shown below. How will it appear when unfolded?

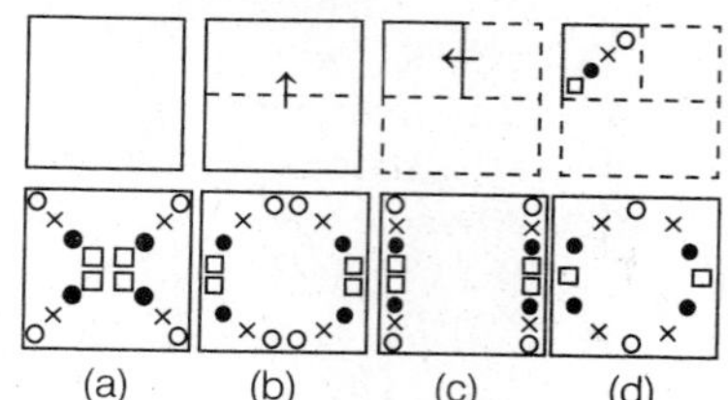

9. In a certain code language, 'HORSE' is coded as 75 and 'MOVE' is coded as 63. How will 'RACE' be coded in that language?
(a) 46 (b) 32
(c) 48 (d) 35

10. Select the option that is related to the third word in the same way as the second word is related to the first word. (The words should be considered as meaninful words, and should not be related to each other on the basic of number of letters, consonants, vowels in the words).
Alas: Woe :: Beauty:?
(a) Expunge (b) Inelegance
(c) Crudeness (d) Charm

11. Sona goes to a park every day for walking. One morning, she started walking from her home and walked 40 km towards the North. Then, she turned to the right and walked 60 km. Again, she turned right and walked 40 km. Lastly, she took a left turn and walked 60 km. In which direction and how far is she from her home?
(a) East, 90 km
(b) West, 120 km
(c) West, 60 km
(d) East, 120 km

12. Which of the following numbers will replace the question mark (?) in the given series?

3, 5, 7, 12, 37, 69, 357, ?

(a) 656 (b) 645 (c) 665 (d) 654

13. Three statements are given followed by three conclusions numbered I, II and III.

Assuming the statements to be true, even if they seem to be at variance with commonly known facts, decide which of the conclusions logically follow(s) from the statements.

Statements

All plains are mountains.

No sea is a mountain.

Some valleys are seas.

Conclusions

I. Some valleys are plains.

II. No valley is a mountain.

III. No sea is a plain.

(a) Only Conclusion III follows
(b) Only Conclusion II follows
(c) Both Conclusions I and II follow
(d) Only Conclusion I follows

14. Select the option that represents the letters that, when placed from left to right in the blanks below, will complete the letter series.

P _ R R _ P Q _ _ S _ Q R _ S P _ R R S

(a) R Q P Q R S Q
(b) S Q R R Q P R
(c) S Q Q R R P Q
(d) Q S R R P R Q

15. If A denotes '+', B denotes '×', C denotes '–' and D denotes '÷', then what will be the value of the following equation?

16 B 5 A 112 D 8 C 32 = ?

(a) 65 (b) 72 (c) 62 (d) 57

16. Six students Shree, Dayal, Sharda, Tripti, Shrishti and Manju are sitting around a circular table facing the centre (not necessarily in the same order). Shree is an immediate neighbour of both Dayal and Tripti. Manju is sitting second to the right of Dayal. Shrishti is an immediate neighbour of both Manju and Tripti. Who is an immediate neighbour of Sharda?

(a) Dayal (b) Shree
(c) Tripti (d) Shrishti

17. Select the option that is related to the fourth term in the same way as the first term is related to the second term and the fifth term is related to the sixth term.

2 : 26 :: ? : 152 :: 27 : 1026

(a) 6 (b) 8 (c) 24 (d) 13

18. Select the figure that will replace the question mark (?) in the following figure series.

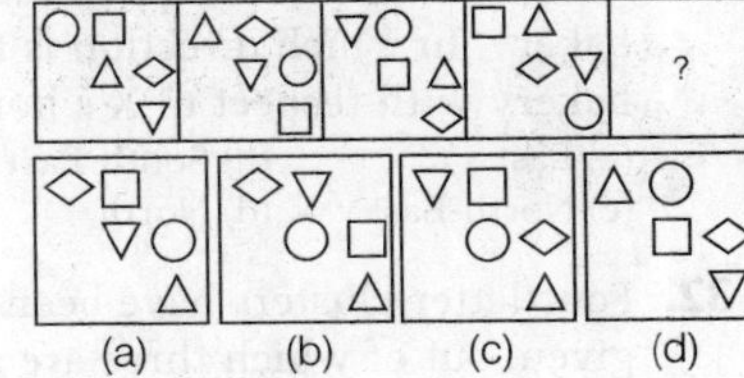

19. Select a suitable figure from the answer figures, which would replace the question mark (?).

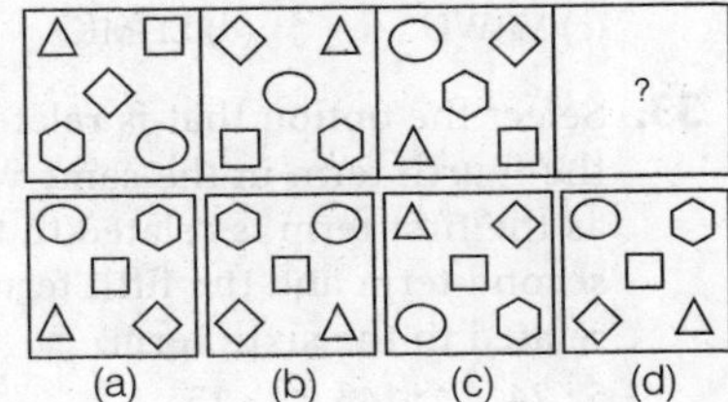

20. If '+' means '–', '–' means '×', '×' means '÷' and '÷' means '+', what will come in place of question mark (?) in the following equation?

83 ÷ 12 – 65 × 13 + 47 = ?

(a) 92 (b) 96 (c) 79 (d) 108

21. In a certain code language, "GBTA" is coded as "24" and "ZWQVI" is coded as "30". How will "DLUCPR" be coded in that language?

(a) 30 (b) 28 (c) 24 (d) 36

22. In this question, three statements are given, followed by two conclusions numbered I and II. Assuming the statements to be true, even if they seem to be at variance with commonly known facts, decide which of the conclusions logically follows/follow from the statements.

Statements

Some rooms are cages.

Some cages are enclosures.

All enclosures are houses.

Conclusions

I. Some houses are cages.

II. All rooms are enclosures.

(a) Both Conclusions I and II follow
(b) Only Conclusion I follows
(c) Neither Conclusion I nor II follows
(d) Only Conclusion II follows

23. If the given sheet is folded to form a cube, which of the given figures are possible?

(The numbers are shown to indicate the sides only.)

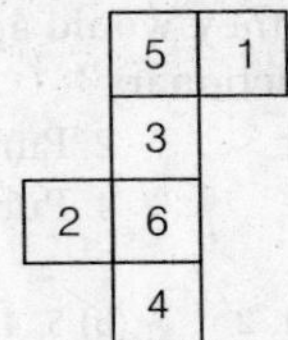

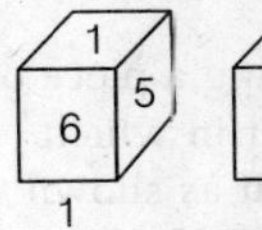
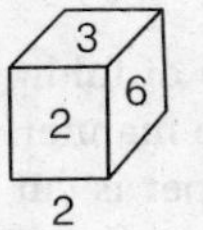
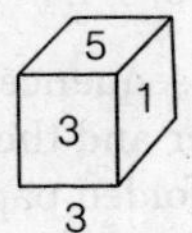
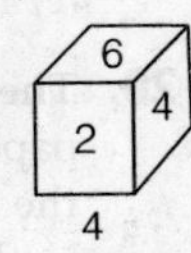

(a) All 1, 2, 3 and 4
(b) Only 2 and 3
(c) Only 1, 2 and 3
(d) Only 2, 3 and 4

24. If '+' means '–', '–' means '×', '×' means '÷', '÷' means '+', then what will come in place of the question mark (?) in the following equation?

14 – 7 ÷ 42 × 6 + 33 = ?

(a) 72 (b) 84
(c) 68 (d) 56

25. A paper is folded and cut as shown below. How will it appear when unfolded?

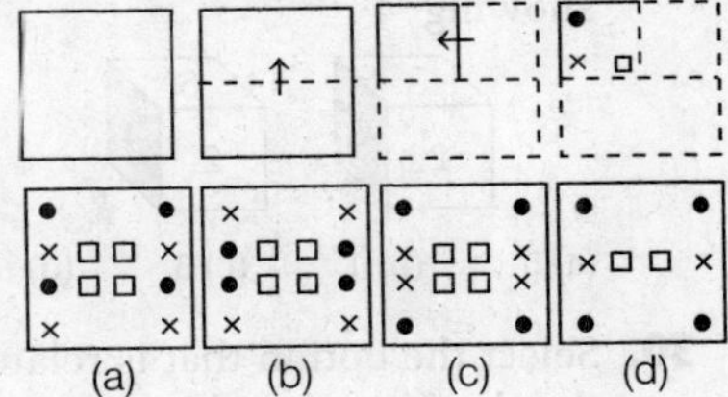

26. Two statements are given, followed by two conclusions numbered I and II. Assuming the statements to be true, even if they seem to be at variance with commonly known facts, decide which of the conclusion(s) logically follow(s) from the statements.

Statements
All kids are small.
Some funny are kids.
Conclusions
I. Some funny are small.
II. Some small are kids.
(a) Only Conclusion I follows
(b) Both Conclusions I and II follow
(c) Only Conclusion II follows
(d) Neither Conclusion I nor II follows

27. Select the option that represents the correct order of the given words as they would appear in an English dictionary?
1. Puritan 2. Purpose
3. Purge 4. Purgatory
5. Purify
(a) 3, 4, 5, 1, 2 (b) 5, 4, 3, 1, 2
(c) 4, 5, 3, 1, 2 (d) 4, 3, 5, 1, 2

28. The sequence of folding a piece of paper and the manner in which the folded paper is cut as shown in the following figure. How would this paper look when unfolded?

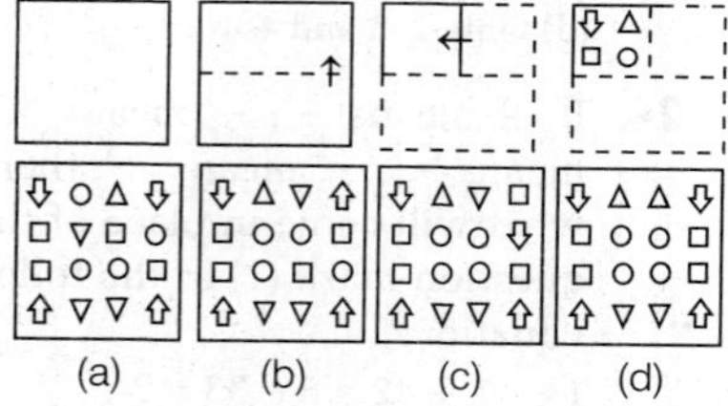

29. Two different positions of the same dice are shown, the six faces of which are numbered from 1 to 6. Select the number that will be on the face opposite to the one showing '4'.

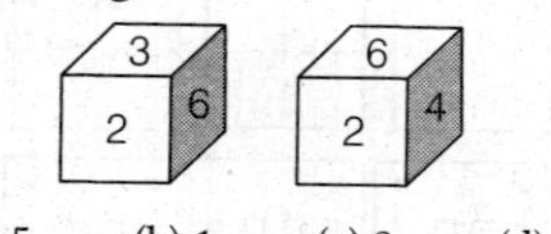

(a) 5 (b) 1 (c) 3 (d) 6

30. Select the option that is related to the third word in the same way as the second word is related to the first word. (The words should be considered as meaninful words, and should not be related to each other on the basic of number of letters, consonants, vowels in the words).
Whale : Mammals :: Crocodile : ?
(a) Rodent (b) Amphibian
(c) Sea (d) Reptiles

31. X, from his house, ran 200 steps towards the East and then ran 30 steps after turning to his right to reach a monastery. He then ran 30 steps towards his right and reached a point W. He then turned again towards his right and ran 30 steps. From there, turning towards his right he ran 130 steps. He then turned towards his left and ran 10 steps to reach a bakery. In which direction is the bakery with respect to X's house?
(a) East (b) South-East
(c) North-East (d) North

32. Four letter-clusters have been given, out of which three are alike in some manner and one is different. Select the odd letter-cluster.
(a) NJPM (b) EAFD
(c) VRWU (d) LHMK

33. Select the option that is related to the fourth term in the same way as the first term is related to the second term and the fifth term is related to the sixth term.
5 : 24 :: ? : 143 :: 4 : 15
(a) 7 (b) 12
(c) 8 (d) 11

34. If '+' means'divided by', '–' means'added to','×'means 'subtracted from' and '÷' means 'multiplied by', then what will be the value of the following expression?
[{(23 × 15) – (2 ÷ 2)} + (2 – 4)] ÷ 2`
(a) 8 (b) 2
(c) 6 (d) 4

35. Which of the following numbers will replace the question mark (?) in the given series?
261, 232, 203, ?, 145, 116
(a) 174 (b) 188
(c) 192 (d) 186

36. In a certain code language, 'HUSTLE' is written as 'SFHEOT' and 'BRIGHT' is written as 'IIBTSG'. How will 'TUNNEL' be written in that language?
(a) NRTPEN (b) NGTYPN
(c) NFTLVN (d) RNLPED

37. Select the Venn diagram that best illustrates the relationship between the following classes.
Spoon, Soup, Rice

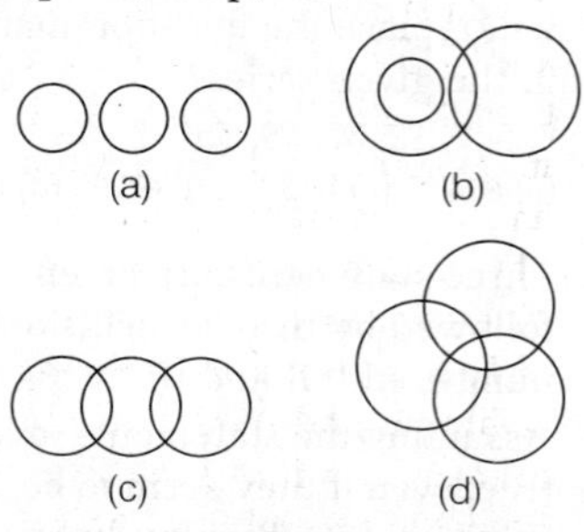

38. Select the option figure in which the given figure is embedded as its part (rotation is not allowed).

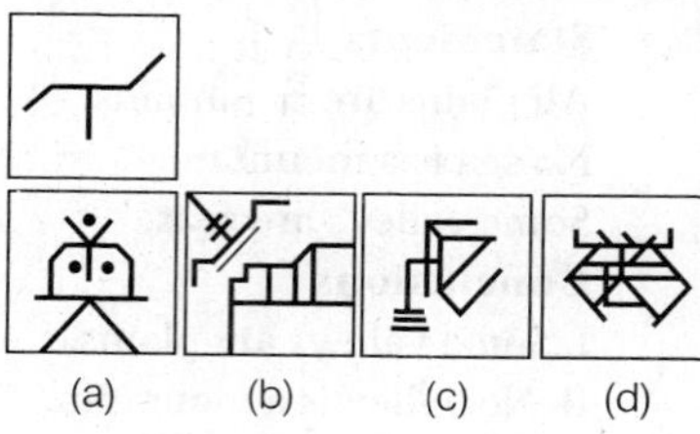

39. 'P $ Q' means'P is the daughter of Q'. 'P ? Q' means'P is the son of Q'. 'P * Q' means'P is the sister of Q'. 'P = Q' means'P is the father of Q'. If 'D $ G * U ? F', how is G related to F?
(a) Father's sister
(b) Mother's sister
(c) Brother
(d) Daughter

40. Select the set in which the numbers are related in the same way as are the numbers of the following sets.
(Note Operations should be performed on the whole numbers, without breaking down the numbers into its constituent digits. E.g. 13- Operations on 13 such as adding /subtracting /multiplying etc. to 13 can be performed. Breaking down 13 into 1 and 3 and then performing mathematical operations on 1 and 3 is not allowed.)
(13, 18, 21)
(11, 25, 8)
(a) (6, 10, 12) (b) (4, 12, 24)
(c) (8, 16, 23) (d) (14, 33, 9)

41. Which two signs should be interchanged to make the given equation correct?
31 ÷ 48 × 7 – 322 + 23 = 353
(a) ÷ and – (b) – and ×
(c) × and + (d) ÷ and +

42. Seven students A, B, C, D, E, F and G are sitting around a circular table facing the centre. C is an immediate neighbour of both E and F. D is sitting third to the left of C and to the immediate right of A. A is sitting second to the right of E. B is an immediate neighbour of both E and A. G is to the immediate left of F. Who is the immediate neighbour of both C and G?

(a) E (b) F]
(c) A (d) D

43. Select the correct option that indicates the arrangement of the given words in the order in which they appear in an English dictionary.

1. Stoop 2. Stoke
3. Storage 4. Stock
5. Storey 6. Stomach

(a) 2, 4, 6, 3, 1, 5
(b) 2, 4, 6, 1, 3, 5
(c) 4, 2, 6, 3, 1, 5
(d) 4, 2, 6, 1, 3, 5

44. Three of the following letter-clusters are alike in some manner and one is different. Select the one that is different.

(a) JEAX (b) DYUR
(c) WDXC (d) QLHE

45. Select the figure from among the given options that can replace the question mark (?) in the following series.

(a) (b) (c) (d)

46. Select the option figure in which the given figure is embedded as its part (rotation is not allowed).

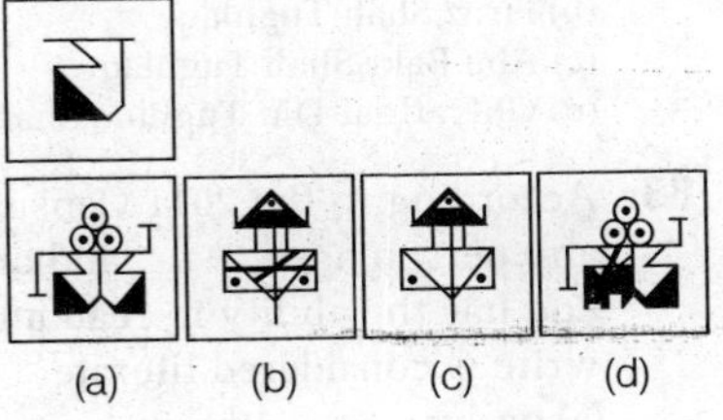

(a) (b) (c) (d)

47. Select the set in which the numbers are related in the same way as are the numbers of the following set.

(**Note** Operations should be performed on the whole numbers, without breaking down the numbers into its constituent digits. E.g. 13 – Operations on 13 such as adding /subtracting /multiplying etc. to 13 can be performed. Breaking down 13 into 1 and 3 and then performing mathematical operations on 1 and 3 is not allowed)

(1, 16 , 3)
(21, 529, 2)

(a) (5, 189, 8) (b) (7, 364, 12)
(c) (11, 429, 2) (d) (8, 100, 2)

48. If the given sheet is folded to form a cube, which of the following figures is possible?

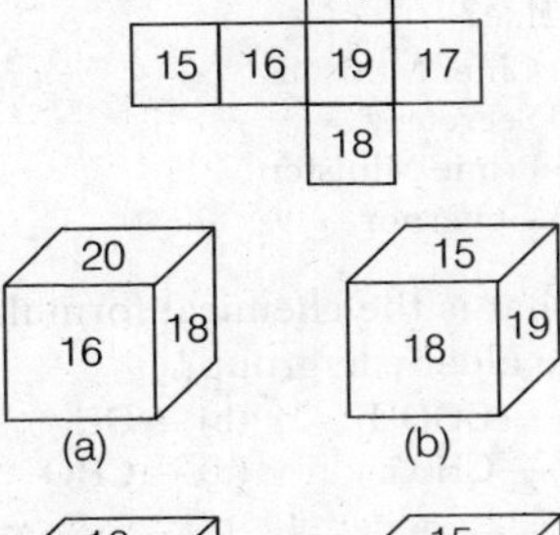

(a) (b) (c) (d)

49. Select the option that represents the letters that, when sequentially placed from left to right in the blanks below, will complete the letter series.

P _ _ ON _ LB _ NPL _ O _ PL _ _ N

(a) L B P O B N B O
(b) L B P B O N B O
(c) L P B O B N N O
(d) L B P O B B N O

50. A @ B means'A is the husband of B'. A & B means'A is the mother of B'. A # B means'A is the daughter of B'. If L @ M & K @ J # P, then how is J related to L?

(a) Son's wife
(b) Daughter's husband
(c) Mother
(d) Son

Part II
General Knowledge and General Awareness

51. Choose the incorrect statement out of the following.

(a) Most parts of the country receive rainfall from June to September.
(b) The annual precipitation in Meghalaya is over 400 cm.
(c) Some parts like the Tamil Nadu's coast gets a large portion of its rains during October and November.
(d) There is increase in rainfall generally from East to West in the Northern Plains.

52. How many cities are covered under the Atal Mission for Rejuvenation and Urban Transformation (AMRUT) scheme?

(a) 200 (b) 300
(c) 400 (d) 500

53. Select the correct combination of the temple and the state in which it is located.

(a) Mahakaleshwar Jyotirlinga–Uttarakhand
(b) Kamakhya Temple–Assam
(c) Jagannath Temple–West Bengal
(d) Somnath Jyotirlinga Temple–Maharashtra

54. The liability to pay the tax and the actual burden of which of the following taxes lie on two different persons?

(a) Corporation Tax
(b) Income Tax
(c) Capital Gains Tax
(d) Goods and Services Tax

55. Which of the following cannot be grouped under physiographic divisions of India?

(a) The Himalayas
(b) Appalachian Mountains
(c) The Indian Desert
(d) The Island

56. Why do pickles last longer?

(a) Only beneficial bacteria can grow in the pickle.
(b) The water content of the pickle protect the pickle from spoilage.
(c) Pickle is prepared in a vacuum so that no harmful bacteria can grow on it.
(d) Bacterial and fungal cells get plasmolysed in high salt concentration of pickle.

57. When was the Prime Minister's Employment Generation Programme (PMEGP) launched?
(a) 2006 (b) 2008
(c) 2012 (d) 2009

58. Which state among the following started the Hornbill Festival to encourage interaction among the tribes and to promote the cultural heritage of the state?
(a) Chhattisgarh (b) West Bengal
(c) Assam (d) Nagaland

59. The agricultural land below the main canal water level forms the ....
(a) flow system (b) lift system
(c) command area (d) warebandi

60. Identify the pigment that gives blood its colour.
(a) Ferritin (b) Chlorophyll
(c) Xanthophyll (d) Haemoglobin

61. Who was the teacher of the famous musician Tansen?
(a) Ravidas (b) Swami Haridas
(c) Kalidas (d) Surdas

62. Pandit Ram Narayan a famous instrumentalist, is known for playing which of the following instruments?
(a) Ghatam (b) Veena
(c) Sarod (d) Sarangi

63. Which scientist synthesised an organic compound (urea), from an inorganic compound, ammonium cyanate?
(a) F Wohler (b) Kolbe
(c) Berthelot (d) Berzelius

64. Which of the following is an autobiography of the international tennis player Andre Agassi?
(a) Open: An Autobiography
(b) Becoming
(c) Too Many Reasons to Live
(d) Me

65. The Bishnu Rabha Award 2019 went to the noted .... dance exponent Kumari Laitjonam Ebampisok Devi.
(a) Odissi (b) Manipuri
(c) Kuchipudi (d) Kathakali

66. Which of the following rights was deleted from the list of Fundamental Rights by the 44th Constitutional Amendment Act?
(a) Right to Freedom of Religion
(b) Right to Property
(c) Right to Freedom
(d) Right to Equality

67. Which Manipuri dance expert founded Govindji Nartanalaya dance school for women in Imphal ?
(a) Guru Bipin Singh
(b) Rajkumar Singhajit Singh
(c) Guru Amubi
(d) Phanjoubam Iboton Singh

68. Who was the eldest of four sons of Babur?
(a) Hindal (b) Askari
(c) Kamran (d) Humayun

69. As per Article 361 of the Constitution of India, who among the following shall not be answerable to any court for the exercise and performance of the powers and duties of his/her office?
(a) Chief Minister
(b) Secretary
(c) Prime Minister
(d) Governor

70. What is the chemical formula for the aldehyde group?
(a) —COOH (b) —OH
(c) —CH_2O (d) —CHO

71. How many balls are there in an over in cricket?
(a) 4 (b) 6
(c) 7 (d) 5

72. In which year did Ernst Haeckel introduced the term 'ecology' to describe the economies of living forms?
(a) 1888 (b) 1884
(c) 1887 (d) 1866

73. Which schedule of the Constitution of India contains provisions for disqualification of legislator on the ground of defection?
(a) Schedule-X (b) Schedule-IX
(c) Schedule-XI (d) Schedule-VIII

74. When was the first World Weightlifting Championship organised by the World Weightlifting Federation in London, UK?
(a) March 1891 (b) March 1991
(c) March 2000 (d) March 1895

75. Which of the following years was declared as the International Year of Microcredit by the UN?
(a) 2008 (b) 2004
(c) 2002 (d) 2005

76. Chapchar Kut festival is predominantly celebrated in ....
(a) Nagaland (b) Mizoram
(c) Manipur (d) Meghalaya

77. The age of the Earth is currently thought to be
(a) 4.5 billion years
(b) 4 billion years
(c) 3.5 billion years
(d) 5 billion years

78. When did the First Five-Year Plan end?
(a) March 1956
(b) January 1956
(c) December 1955
(d) February 1956

79. Which Article of the Constitution clarifies that policies like 'reservation' is not a violation of right to equality?
(a) Article-16 (4) (b) Article-14 (1)
(c) Article-21 (d) Article-15 (2)

80. Which of the following is not a correct match?
(a) Voltage - Volts
(b) Resistance - Ohm
(c) Conductance - Siemens
(d) Capacitance - Dyne

81. Who first observed ribosomes in the mid-1950s and described them as small particles in the cytoplasm that were preferentially attached to the endoplasmic reticulum membrane?
(a) Ernst Abbe (b) Albert Kolliker
(c) Carl Zeiss (d) George E. Palade

82. Who among the following was the successor of Muhammad-bin Tughlaq to the throne?
(a) Nais-ud-Din Mahmud Shah Tughlaq
(b) Firuz Shah Tughlaq
(c) Abu Bakr Shah Tughlaq
(d) Ghiyath-al-Din Tughluq Shah II

83. According to the 2011 Census, any person aged .... and above and has the ability to read and write is considered literate.
(a) twelve (b) six
(c) seven (d) ten

84. Kuchipudi originated in which of the following states?
(a) Kerala (b) Tamil Nadu
(c) Gujarat (d) Andhra Pradesh

85. Padma Bhushan awardee Kumudini Lakhia is renowned for which of the following dance forms?
(a) Bharatanatyam (b) Kathak
(c) Kuchipudi (d) Odissi

86. The black soil of the Deccan Plateau lacks which of the following minerals?
(a) Phosphorous (b) Potash
(c) Iron (d) Lime

87. Which Article of the Constitution of India prohibits forced labour?
(a) Article 23 (b) Article 21
(c) Article 22 (d) Article 20

88. Consider the following statements regarding the Indo Greeks.
1. The most celebrated Indo-Greek ruler was Menander.
2. Menander has been identified with King Milinda mentioned in the famous Buddhist text Milindapanho.
3. Milindapanho contains philosophical questions that Milinda asked Amrapali.
4. Impressed by the answers, King Milinda accepted Buddhism as his religion.

Which among the above statements are correct ?
(a) Only 1, 2 and 3
(b) Only 1, 3 and 4
(c) Only 1, 2 and 4
(d) Only 3, 2 and 4

89. Which of the following options are homogeneous mixtures?
(a) Solution, colloid, suspension, milk, toothpaste, salt water, brass
(b) Solution, salt water, brass
(c) Solution, colloid, milk, toothpaste, salt water, brass
(d) Colloid, suspension, milk, toothpaste

90. Match List I to List II.

List I		List II
A. Second Five-Year Plan	(i)	1974-1979
B. Fifth Five-Year Plan	(ii)	1956-1961
C. Eight Five-Year Plan	(iii)	1992-1997

(a) A-iii, B-i, C-ii (b) A-i, B-ii, C-iii
(c) A-i, B-iii, C-ii (d) A-ii, B-i, C-iii

91. Which Article of the Indian Constitution lays the condition that the President, once elected, shall not be a member of the either House of Parliament or State Legislature?
(a) Article-62
(b) Article-59
(c) Article-80
(d) Article-79

92. Which of the following books has been written by the Booker Prize winner Kiran Desai?
(a) A Fine Balance
(b) The Year of Runaways
(c) The Inheritance of Loss
(d) Shantaram

93. Who among the following was not associated with 'Prarthana Sabha'?
(a) Govind Ranade
(b) Atmaram Pandurang
(c) RG Bhandarkar
(d) Motilal Nehru

94. Identify the group of major jute producing states of India.
(a) Kerala, Tamil Nadu, Telangana, Madhya Pradesh
(b) West Bengal, Bihar, Assam, Odisha
(c) Punjab, Haryana, Uttarakhand, Himachal Pradesh
(d) Rajasthan, Maharashtra, Karnataka, Gujarat

95. Which trend is found about the distance between the galaxies?
(a) Constant
(b) Increasing
(c) Unpredictable
(d) Decreasing

96. Under the Regulating Act of 1773, the King-in-Council created a Supreme Court in which of the following places?
(a) Calcutta (b) Delhi
(c) Madras (d) Bombay

97. The Landholder's Society was founded to look after the interests of which class?
(a) Landlords (b) Labour
(c) Farmers (d) Traders

98. Which of the following is a primary arylamine in which an amino functional group is substituted for one of the benzene hydrogens?
(a) Quinoline (b) Aniline
(c) Pyridine (d) Toluidine

99. Which of the following states hosted 2023 Men's Hockey World Cup?
(a) Chhattisgarh (b) Jharkhand
(c) Maharashtra (d) Odisha

100. In football, a kick is awarded to the opposition player when a player has committed a foul. What is the kick called?
(a) Bicycle kick (b) Free kick
(c) Wide kick (d) Goal kick

Part III

Quantitative Aptitude

101. Two mixtures A and B have the following compositions:
Mixture A has copper and tin in a ratio of 1:2.
Mixture B has copper and tin in a ratio of 1:3.
If equal quantities of mixtures A and B are used for producing mixture C, then find the ratio of copper and tin in mixture C.
(a) 2:5 (b) 1:5 (c) 7:17 (d) 7:12

102. If the volume of a sphere is 38808 cm^3, then its surface area is
(a) 5554 cm^2 (b) 5574 cm^2
(c) 5564 cm^2 (d) 5544 cm^2

103. The area of a rhombus having one side measuring 17 cm and one diagonal measuring 16 cm is
(a) 280 cm^2 (b) 180 cm^2
(c) 240 cm^2 (d) 210 cm^2

104. By selling 42 m of cloth, Vijay gains the selling price of 7 m of cloth. Find the profit percentage.
(a) 15% (b) 30%
(c) 20% (d) 25%

105. Ramesh gives 15% additional discount along with a discount of 25% on the marked price of a sofa set. If the selling price of the sofa set is ₹12750, then find the marked price of the sofa set.
(a) ₹20000 (b) ₹23000
(c) ₹22000 (d) ₹24000

106. Two pipes can fill a cistern in 12 h and 16 h, respectively. The pipes are opened simultaneously and it is found that due to leakage at the bottom, it takes 90 min more to fill the cistern. How much time will the leakage take to empty the completely filled tank?

(a) $36\frac{29}{49}$ h (b) $38\frac{10}{49}$ h

(c) $39\frac{13}{49}$ h (d) $37\frac{15}{49}$ h

107. A sum of money amounts to ₹1200 in 2 yr and becomes ₹1260 in 3 yr at compound interest, when interest is compounded annually. What is the rate of compound interest per annum?

(a) 5% (b) 3%

(c) 4% (d) 6%

108. Find the least value of $16\operatorname{cosec}^2\theta + 25\sin^2\theta$.

(a) 40 (b) 42

(c) 35 (d) 38

109. In a megastore, the following data reveals the units purchased during the years.

What is the percentage growth in total units purchased (of all the three products) from 2015 to 2020?

Year	Tea	Coffee	Cold drink
2015	650	450	1008
2016	730	402	1092
2017	710	354	770
2018	570	438	812
2019	820	390	1043
2020	830	501	1330

(a) 21.68 % (b) 22.75 %

(c) 26.23 % (d) 25.76 %

110. If $\cos A = \frac{1}{11}$, then find the value of $\cot A$.

(a) $\frac{2\sqrt{30}}{11}$ (b) $2\sqrt{30}$

(c) $\frac{1}{2\sqrt{30}}$ (d) $\frac{11}{2\sqrt{30}}$

111. The following bar graph shows tha milk production (in million tonnes) details for 4 yr for three brands (P, Q, R):

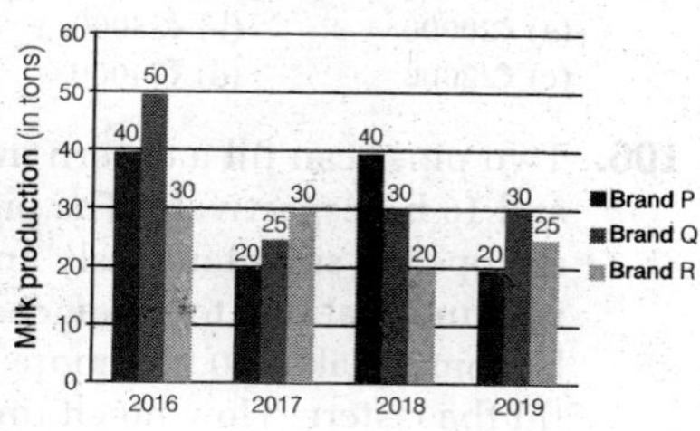

What was the average production of milk (in million tonnes) per year over the period of 4 yr?

(a) 90 (b) 50

(c) 30 (d) 70

112. If $\operatorname{cosec} A + \cot A = 3, 0 \le A \le 90°$, then find the value of $\cos A$.

(a) $\frac{3}{4}$ (b) $\frac{2}{5}$

(c) $\frac{3}{5}$ (d) $\frac{4}{5}$

113. 36 equally efficient workers can paint 25 identical walls in 48 days. In how many days can 45 such workers paint 60 such walls?

(a) 92.36 (b) 92.16

(c) 91.96 (d) 91.16

114. Which of the following numbers leaves the remainder equal to the highest common factor of 6, 8 and 9, when divided by 6, 8 and 9?

(a) 291 (b) 575

(c) 506 (d) 433

115. Simplify the given expression $(1+x)^3 + (1-x)^3 + (-2)^3$

(a) $6(1-x^2)$ (b) $-3(1-x^2)$

(c) $-6(1-x^2)$ (d) $3(1-x^2)$

116. If $1\frac{1}{3} \div \frac{2}{5} \times \frac{x}{5} = 1\frac{1}{4} \times \frac{2}{3} \div \frac{1}{6}$, then the value of x is

(a) 5.5 (b) 7.5

(c) 7.0 (d) 15

117. The average weight of 49 students is 53 kg. When a new student is admitted to the class, the average decreases by 500 g. Find the weight of the new student.

(a) 48 kg (b) 18 kg

(c) 28 kg (d) 38 kg

118. In an election between two candidates, the difference between the candidates who won and lost was 2500 votes. The candidate who won got 75% of the votes and there were no invalid votes. The total number of votes polled of the losing candidate was

(a) 1875 (b) 5000

(c) 1250 (d) 3750

119. In an election between two candidates,30% of the electorate did not cast their votes. 20% of the votes polled were found invalid. The winning candidate got 64% of the valid votes and won by a majority of 3136 votes. Find the number of voters enrolled in the voter list.

(a) 20000 (b) 25000

(c) 24000 (d) 30000

120. Find the mean proportion of x^3y and xy^3.

(a) x^2y^2 (b) x^3y^3

(c) xy (d) x^4y^4

121. The least common multiple of 12, 18 and 27 is

(a) 54 (b) 216

(c) 27 (d) 108

122. Jimmy has to cover a distance of 88 km in 16 h. If she covers half of the journey in $\frac{3}{4}$ time, then what should be her speed to cover the remaining distance in the time left?

(a) 12 km/h (b) 10 km/h

(c) 11 km/h (d) 13 km/h

123. What is the smallest perfect square number which is completely divisible by 4, 6, 9, 12 and 15?

(a) 784 (b) 900

(c) 961 (d) 841

124. A vehicle is going at one-fourth of its usual speed and it takes an extra 45 min to reach its destination. Its usual time to cover the same distance is

(a) 15 min (b) 10 min

(c) 30 min (d) 20 min

125. Kanchan lent ₹10000 for 2 yr and ₹5000 for 4 yr at the same rate of simple interest. If the total interest received by Kanchan is ₹2000, then what was the rate of interest?

(a) 5% (b) 2%

(c) 3% (d) 4%

126. The average weight of A, B and C is 77 kg. If the average weight of A and B is 68 kg and that of B and C is 83 kg, then the weight (in kg) of B is

(a) 74 (b) 71

(c) 73 (d) 67

127. The diameter of a hemisphere is equal to the diagonal of a rectangle of length 4 cm and breadth 3 cm. Find the total surface area (in cm^2) of the hemisphere.

(a) 25π (b) $\frac{75\pi}{4}$
(c) $\frac{50\pi}{4}$ (d) $\frac{25\pi}{4}$

128. A cylindrical metallic rod of diameter 2 cm and length 45 cm is melted and converted into wire of uniform thickness and length 5 m. The diameter of the wire is

(a) 3 mm (b) 2 mm
(c) 6 mm (d) 5 mm

129. If the base radius and the height of a right circular cone are increased by 10%, then the percentage increase in the volume is

(a) 30.2% (b) 22.1%
(c) 33.1% (d) 20.2%

130. The given pie chart shows the distribution of land under various food crops. The expenditure invested on these food crops is ₹25000 per annum. Study the pie chart carefully and answer the question that follows.

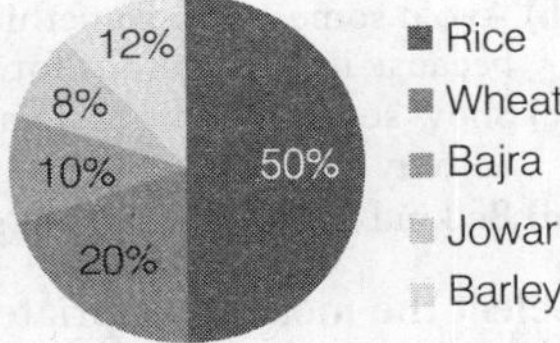

The expenditure invested in Rice and Barley is what percentage (correct to 2 decimal places) of the expenditure invested in Wheat and Bajra?

(a) 206.55% (b) 206.66%
(c) 260.66% (d) 260.55%

131. If perimeter of the circle is 13.2 cm, then the radius of the circle is ....

$\left(\text{Take } \pi = \frac{22}{7}\right)$

(a) 6.6 cm (b) 4.2 cm
(c) 2.1 cm (d) 3.3 cm

132. A goods train 350 m long passes through a tunnel of 1250m in 80 sec. What is the speed of the train?

(a) 72 km/h (b) 64 km/h
(c) 78 km/h (d) 56 km/h

133. Study the given table and answer the question that follows.

The table shows the number of employees in five different organisations A, B, C, D and E in different departments.

Dept↓ Org→	A	B	C	D	E
HR	1050	1015	976	888	1004
Finance	1017	960	786	1025	963
Marketing	1382	1384	1275	1300	1290
Production	1542	1545	4550	1570	1580
Accounts	786	745	801	800	735
Legal	48	54	36	30	53
Total	5825	5703	5424	5613	5625

Which department has a minimum number of employees in each organisation?

(a) Marketing (b) Production
(c) Accounts (d) Legal

134. The value of

$$\frac{a^2-(b-c)^2}{(a+c)^2-b^2}+\frac{b^2-(a-c)^2}{(a+b)^2-c^2}+\frac{c^2-(a-b)^2}{(b+c)^2-a^2} \text{ is}$$

(a) 1 (b) 2
(c) −1 (d) 3

135. In a triangle LMN, OP is a line segment drawn parallel to the side MN. OP intersects the sides LM and LN at O and P, respectively. If $LM = 15$ cm, $OM = 4$ cm and $PN = 5$ cm, then what is the length (in cm) of the side LN?

(a) 16.25 (b) 18.75
(c) 20.25 (d) 22.75

136. The value of $\sqrt{\frac{1+\sin A}{1-\sin A}}$ is

(a) $\sec A - \tan A$
(b) $\operatorname{cosec} A + \cot A$
(c) $\sec A + \tan A$
(d) $\operatorname{cosec} A - \cot A$

137. Determine the LCM of two numbers if their HCF is 12 and their ratio is 13 : 15.

(a) 1780 (b) 2450
(c) 1890 (d) 2340

138. Study the given graph and answer the question that follows.

The graph shows data regarding number of boys and girls studying in class 5 in four different schools.

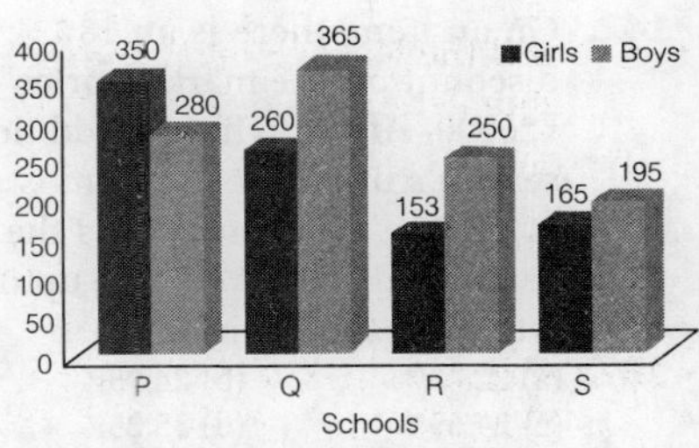

What is the difference between total number of boys studying in school P and Q together and the total number of girls in the same schools together?

(a) 38 (b) 45
(c) 40 (d) 35

139. Study the given bar-graph and answer the question that follows.

The bar-graph displays the number of bicycles produced at a factory from 1998 to 2002.

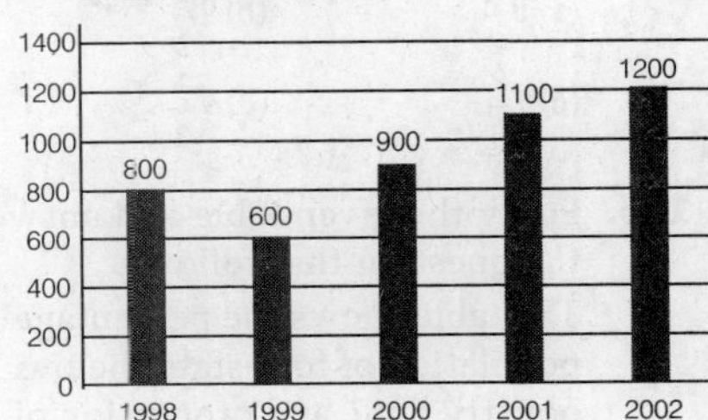

What was the average number of bicycles produced at the factory per year from 1998-2002?

(a) 940 (b) 960
(c) 920 (d) 880

140. Find the least number which when divided by 4, 9, 12 and 15 leaves the remainder 3 in each case.

(a) 360 (b) 183
(c) 193 (d) 180

141. The table below shows the number of trees planted by the government in 4 different years.

Year	Neem	Oak	Birch
2019	2000	3000	4000
2020	3000	4000	5000
2021	5000	6000	7000
2022	7000	8000	9000

Find the ratio between the number of neem trees planted in the year 2021 and the number of birch trees planted in the year 2022.

(a) 5:9 (b) 3:7
(c) 5:8 (d) 3:8

142. On an item, there is an 18% discount on the marked price of ₹26000. After giving an additional season's discount, the item is sold at ₹16000. How much was the season's discount correct upto two places of decimal?
(a) 22.45% (b) 24.95%
(c) 24.65% (d) 35.25%

143. In a ΔPQR, $\angle P = 90°$, $\angle R = 47°$ and $PS \perp QR$. Find the value of $\angle QPS$.
(a) 43° (b) 47°
(c) 45° (d) 40°

144. Sanjay and Rohan can complete a work in 8 days and 12 days, respectively. Starting with Sanjay, they work on alternate days. In how many days will the work be completed?
(a) $8\frac{1}{2}$ (b) $9\frac{1}{2}$
(c) $9\frac{2}{3}$ (d) $9\frac{1}{3}$

145. Study the given table and answer the question that follows.
The table shows the percentage population of four states below poverty lione and proportion of male to female.

States	Percentage of population below poverty line	Proportion of male to female	
		Below poverty line	Above poverty line
		Male : Female	Male : Female
P	28	3:2	7:3
Q	15	4:7	6:5
R	24	5:3	3:3
S	13	2:5	1:3

If the total population of state R is 26,000, then what is the number of females above poverty line in state R?
(a) 9780 (b) 9880
(c) 9560 (d) 9950

146. AB is a chord of a circle having radius 1.7 cm. If the distance of this chord AB from the centre of the circle is 0.8 cm, then what is the length (in cm) of the chord AB?
(a) 4 (b) 1
(c) 3 (d) 2

147. The monthly budget of an average household is given in the following table.

Category	Food	Clothing	Rent	Savings
Amount	8000	2000	6000	4000

The percentage of the monthly budget spent on clothing is
(a) 10% (b) 12%
(c) 8% (d) 4%

148. If the HCF of 45 and 55 is expressible in the form of $55 \times 5 + 45\,m$, then what is the value of m?
(a) −6 (b) 5
(c) 6 (d) −5

149. The monthly salary of a person is ₹50000. He spends 40% of his salary on household expenses, 25% on rent and 15% on transportation and saves the remaining amount. What is his yearly savings?
(a) ₹100000 (b) ₹110000
(c) ₹120000 (d) ₹90000

150. The cost price of pulses is 12% less than the selling price. Using a faulty weighing machine, shopkeeper is able to earn 25% profit. How much per cent of the faulty machine shows more weight as compared to the actual weight (Rounded off to the nearest integer)?
(a) 13% (b) 15%
(c) 10% (d) 14%

Part IV

English Comprehension

151. Select the option that can be used as a one-word substitute for the given group of words.
A collection of historical documents or records providing information about a place, institution or group of people.
(a) Museum (b) Apostate
(c) Asylum (d) Archive

152. Select the most appropriate idiom for the given situation focusing on the underlined segment.
The modern era statistics data provides useful advantage to the players at competent level.
(a) Cost an arm and a leg
(b) Grist to the mill
(c) Put something on ice
(d) Play it by ear

153. The following sentence has been divided into parts. One of them may contain an error. Select the part that contains the error from the given options. If you don't find any error, mark 'No error' as your answer.
We should/not make an noise/in the class.
(a) in the class
(b) We should
(c) No error
(d) not make an noise

154. Identify the antonym of the following word in the given sentence.
Languid
The animated infantry was marching forward for another rehearsal.
(a) infantry (b) rehearsal
(c) forward (d) animated

155. Select the most appropriate meaning of the given idiom.
Steer clear of
(a) Loose temper and react furiously to someone
(b) Avoid someone or something because it is dangerous for you
(c) Show someone how to do a job or activity
(d) Be kind and empathetic to someone

156. Select the most appropriate antonym for the highlighted word.
The **malice** he developed for all caused a lot of damage.
(a) avarice
(b) grace
(c) oppression
(d) sympathy

157. The following sentence has been divided into parts. One of them may contain an error.
Select the part that contains the error from the given options. If you don't find any error, mark 'No error' as your answer.
I was wish/to meet her/on her birthday.
(a) I was wish
(b) No error
(c) to meet her
(d) on her birthday

158. The following sentence has been split into four segments. Identify the segment that contains a grammatical error.
It is take/a couple of minutes/for the computer/to boot up.
(a) for the computer
(b) to boot up
(c) a couple of minutes
(d) It is take

159. You are preparing a speech for an upcoming function. Select a synonym for the highlighted word to make it better.
Sexual assault is a severe and **pervasive** issue that can have a significant impact on a victim's life.
(a) Retrospective (b) Longitudinal
(c) Widespread (d) Equatorial

160. Select the incorrectly spelt word.
(a) Adjourn (b) Addict
(c) Abdact (d) Advise

161. Choose the option which means the same as the underlined segment.
The boss wanted to finish the case before the arrival of the Inspection team.
(a) be over and done with
(b) be over one's head
(c) be over and over
(d) be over a barrel

162. Select the most appropriate synonym of the given word.
Cruise
(a) Bounce (b) Fall
(c) Distance (d) Voyage

163. Select the most appropriate meaning of the highlighted idiom in the given sentence.
Nancy held a grudge against her teacher for a long time, but she finally decided to **let bygones be bygones**.
(a) Change the past (b) Take revenge
(c) Flatter someone (d) Ignore the past

164. Select the option that will improve the underlined part of the given sentence.
Farmers have harvested wheat by using whatever labour that was available to them.
(a) by using amalgamated labour
(b) by using limited labour
(c) by using dispersed labour
(d) by using united labour

165. Select the most appropriate meaning of the underlined idiom in the following sentence.
Rahim had to eat a humble pie in starting a row with his neighbour over a trifle.
(a) To remain without food
(b) To be punished for doing something wrong
(c) To take simple food
(d) To feel sorry and apologise for a mistake

166. Select the most appropriate option that can substitute the underlined segment in the given sentence.
Malati has a difficult job, but she does it good.
(a) better (b) well
(c) best (d) nice

167. Select the most appropriate synonym of the given word.
Fierce
(a) Lame (b) Lavish
(c) Strange (d) Furious

168. Select the most appropriate synonym of the given word.
Faithful
(a) Daring (b) Unfaithful
(c) Cheerful (d) Loyal

169. Select the most appropriate meaning of the underlined idiom.
Yamini is a great singer. She will make it big one day.
(a) Succeed and become famous
(b) Become financially sound
(c) Educated and rich
(d) Migrate and settle

170. Select the most appropriate antonym of the given word.
Malice
(a) Torsion
(b) Haughtiness
(c) Kindness
(d) Tremor

171. Select the most appropriate option that can substitute the underlined segment in the given sentence. If there is no need to substitute it, select 'No substitution required'.
He travelled the whole world, but found piece at home.
(a) peach
(b) No substitution required
(c) prize
(d) peace

172. Select the most appropriate meaning of the given word.
Trousseau
(a) Being true to oneself
(b) The clothes, linen and other belongings collected by a bride for her marriage
(c) A large cabinet full of expensive clothes
(d) Single leg side of a trouser

173. Select the option that can be used as a one-word substitute for the underlined group of words.
Since God is an all-powerful creator, he has absolute control over those whom he has created.
(a) Voracious
(b) Omnipotent
(c) Incorrigible
(d) Omniscient

174. Select the most appropriate option to substitute the underlined segment in the given sentence.
At some point in the past, there were rows of temporary shops that used to display various cooking utensils.
(a) One upon a time
(b) Before now
(c) In the past few years
(d) Long ago

175. Select the option that can be used as a one-word substitute for the given group of words.
A structure in the garden where climbing plants can grow and people can walk under
(a) Tomb (b) Outhouse
(c) Pergola (d) Treehouse

176. Select the most appropriate option that can substitute the underlined segment in the given sentence.
She was yearning for a trip to the mountains.
(a) leaving for
(b) deeply repenting
(c) keenly desiring
(d) saving money for

177. Select the most appropriate idiom for the given situation.
You wanted to speak but you controlled yourself and became patient. What have you done?
(a) Pin drop silence
(b) Dragged your feet
(c) Herculean task
(d) Hold your horses

178. Select the most appropriate meaning of the given idiom.
Step up to the plate
(a) Think about a crisis
(b) Plan for better performance
(c) Implement a plan
(d) Take control of a situation

179. Select the most appropriate meaning of the underlined idiom.
He ate the whole bunch of grapes under the nose of all of us.
(a) After much persuasion
(b) In full view of somebody
(c) Sharing equally
(d) Secretly

180. Select the incorrectly spelt word.
(a) Prefered (b) Revered
(c) Answered (d) Reference

181. Select the option that can be used as a one-word substitute for the given group of words.
Extremely beautiful, elaborate or impressive
(a) Proficient
(b) Magnificent
(c) Transient
(d) Deficient

182. Select the most appropriate meaning of the given idiom.
To burn the midnight oil
(a) To waste time
(b) To stay up late working or studying
(c) To overthink
(d) To be relaxed and calm

183. Select the most appropriate synonym of the underlined word.
It was inevitable that the team management would sack him after his rude behaviour.
(a) impassionate (b) amiable
(c) measurable (d) unavoidable

184. Select the incorrectly spelt word from the underlined words in the following sentence.
As affidevit is a statement or declaration in writing an oath or affirmation, sworn before a person having authority to administer oath.
(a) affidevit
(b) administer
(c) authority
(d) affirmation

185. The following sentence has been split into four segments. Identify the segment that contains a grammatical error.
We have being / arranged the stay / for the guests at / a hillside resort.
(a) a hillside resort
(b) We have being
(c) arranged the stay
(d) for the guests at

186. Select the most appropriate synonym of the given word.
Extravagance
(a) Simplicity (b) Love
(c) Fortune (d) Self-indulgence

187. Select the most appropriate synonym of the given word.
Antique
(a) Ancient (b) New
(c) Gothic (d) Modern

188. Select the incorrectly spelt word in the given sentence.
The Egyptian Pharohs were the Kings of ancient Egypt and were considered as the literal embodiment of God himself.
(a) literal (b) ancient
(c) pharohs (d) embodiment

189. Select the incorrectly spelt word.
(a) Isle (b) Braed
(c) Achieve (d) Amicable

190. Select the most appropriate option that can substitute the underlined segment in the given sentence.
Naina is leaving and I am think to apply for her job.
(a) thinking in applying
(b) thinking about applying
(c) thinking about apply
(d) thinking on applying

Directions (Q. Nos.191-195) *In the following passage, some words have been deleted. Read the passage carefully and select the most appropriate option to fill in each blank.*

Discrimination refers to the inequitable or ...(1)... treatment of individuals or collectives on the basis of attributes such as ethnicity, sex, age and sexual orientation. Studies have indicated that the perception of discrimination can ...(2)... a series of stress-induced alterations in an individual's mental, physiological and behavioural responses. The experience of stress is known to elicit unfavourable emotional reactions, including but not limited to ...(3)..., despair and resentment. Furthermore, anxiety has been linked to a rise in health-compromising behaviours such as smoking, drinking and ...(4)... drug use, while simultaneously causing a ...(5)... in health-promoting activities such as quality sleep and vigorous exercise.

191. Select the most appropriate option to fill in blank no. 1.
(a) systematic (b) biased
(c) pathetic (d) tragic

192. Select the most appropriate option to fill in blank no. 2.
(a) support (b) inspire
(c) trigger (d) motivate

193. Select the most appropriate option to fill in blank no. 3.
(a) death (b) anxiety
(c) deafness (d) impairment

194. Select the most appropriate option to fill in blank no. 4.
(a) prescribed (b) mandatory
(c) illicit (d) legitimate

195. Select the most appropriate option to fill in blank no. 5.
(a) rise (b) unfruitful
(c) decline (d) upheaval

Directions (Q. Nos. 196-200) *Read the given passage carefully and answer the questions that follow.*

The world of social media is a strange and wondrous place. It's a world where you can connect with people from all over the globe, share your thoughts and opinions, and maybe even go viral if you're lucky. But let's be real, it's also a world filled with endless cat videos, oversharing, and drama.

One of the most interesting things about social media is the way it's changed the way we communicate. We ve gone from long, thoughtful emails to quick, abbreviated messages with emojis and acronyms. And don't even get me started on the whole hashtag phenomenon. It's like we're all speaking a different language now.

But there are also some downsides to this constant connection. It's easy to get sucked into the world of social media and forget about the real world around us. We're so busy scrolling through our feeds that we forget to enjoy the little moments in life. And let's not forget about the pressure to present the perfect life online. It's like we're all in a competition to see who can be the most popular, the most successful, the most enviable. Despite all of this, I have to admit, I'm still a fan of social media. It's a great way to stay connected with friends and family, and I've even made some new friends through various online communities. Plus, let's face it, sometimes you just need a good laugh at a ridiculous meme.

196. What is the antonym of the word 'perfect', as used in the passage?
(a) Troublesome (b) Limited
(c) Unsatisfactory (d) Laughable

197. Which of the following is not mentioned as a way social media has changed the way we communicate?
(a) Quick, abbreviated messages with emojis and acronyms.
(b) Video conferencing for more meaningful conversations.
(c) Connecting with people from all over the world.
(d) The use of hashtags.

198. Which of the following would be the most appropriate title for this passage?
(a) The Joys and Sorrows of Social Media
(b) The Benefits of Social Media
(c) The Dark Side of Social Media
(d) Mastering the Art of Social Media

199. What is one of the downsides of social media mentioned in the passage?
(a) It can help connect with people all over the globe.
(b) It's a great way to stay connected with friends and family.
(c) It encourages people to enjoy the little moments in life.
(d) It can lead to pressure to present a perfect life online.

200. What is the theme of the passage?
(a) The dangers of spending too much time online.
(b) The importance of social media for businesses.
(c) The positive and negative effects of social media.
(d) The history of social media.

Know Correct Answers

1. (d)	2. (d)	3. (c)	4. (a)	5. (a)	6. (d)	7. (b)	8. (b)	9. (d)	10. (d)
11. (d)	12. (a)	13. (a)	14. (d)	15. (c)	16. (a)	17. (b)	18. (b)	19. (b)	20. (b)
21. (d)	22. (b)	23. (d)	24. (a)	25. (c)	26. (b)	27. (d)	28. (d)	29. (c)	30. (d)
31. (c)	32. (a)	33. (b)	34. (d)	35. (a)	36. (c)	37. (a)	38. (d)	39. (d)	40. (d)
41. (d)	42. (b)	43. (d)	44. (c)	45. (a)	46. (a)	47. (d)	48. (d)	49. (a)	50. (a)
51. (d)	52. (d)	53. (b)	54. (d)	55. (b)	56. (d)	57. (b)	58. (d)	59. (c)	60. (d)
61. (b)	62. (d)	63. (a)	64. (a)	65. (b)	66. (b)	67. (a)	68. (d)	69. (d)	70. (d)
71. (b)	72. (d)	73. (a)	74. (a)	75. (d)	76. (b)	77. (a)	78. (a)	79. (a)	80. (d)
81. (d)	82. (b)	83. (c)	84. (d)	85. (b)	86. (a)	87. (a)	88. (c)	89. (b)	90. (d)
91. (b)	92. (c)	93. (d)	94. (b)	95. (b)	96. (a)	97. (a)	98. (b)	99. (d)	100. (b)
101. (c)	102. (d)	103. (c)	104. (c)	105. (a)	106. (b)	107. (a)	108. (a)	109. (c)	110. (c)
111. (a)	112. (d)	113. (b)	114. (d)	115. (c)	116. (b)	117. (c)	118. (c)	119. (a)	120. (a)
121. (d)	122. (c)	123. (b)	124. (a)	125. (a)	126. (b)	127 (b)	128. (c)	129. (c)	130. (b)
131. (c)	132. (a)	133. (d)	134. (a)	135. (b)	136. (c)	137 (d)	138. (d)	139. (c)	140. (b)
141. (a)	142. (b)	143. (b)	144. (b)	145. (b)	146. (c)	147. (a)	148. (a)	149. (c)	150. (c)
151. (d)	152. (b)	153. (d)	154. (d)	155. (b)	156. (d)	157. (a)	158. (d)	159. (c)	160. (c)
161. (a)	162. (d)	163. (d)	164. (b)	165. (d)	166. (b)	167. (d)	168. (d)	169. (a)	170. (c)
171. (d)	172. (b)	173. (b)	174. (d)	175. (c)	176. (c)	177. (d)	178. (d)	179. (b)	180. (a)
181. (b)	182. (b)	183. (d)	184. (a)	185. (b)	186. (d)	187. (a)	188. (c)	189. (b)	190. (b)
191. (b)	192. (c)	193. (b)	194. (c)	195. (c)	196. (c)	197. (b)	198. (a)	199. (d)	200. (c)

Answer & Solutions

1. (d) As,

A C T → T X A (Opposite letter)   I O N → N L I (Opposite letter)

and

D E B → B V D (Opposite letter)   A T E → E G A (Opposite letter)

Similarly,

C H A → A S C (Opposite letter)   N G E → E T N (Opposite letter)

2. (d) Pattern of the series is as follows,

38, 57, 40, 59, 42, [61]

+2 (57 → 59), +2 (59 → 61); +2 (38 → 40), +2 (40 → 42)

3. (c) Pattern of the series is as follows,

112, 129, 150, 175, 204, [237]

+17, +21, +25, +29, +33

+4, +4, +4, +4

4. (a) As,

C O A C H → X A O H C (C –5 → X)

and

B E R T H → W R E H T (B –5 → W)

Similarly,

T R A I N → O A R N I (T –5 → O)

5. (a) Given equation,

$121 \times 11 \div 28 - 3 + 46 = ?$

After interchanging the signs, we get:

$121 \div 11 + 28 \times 3 - 46 = ?$

$\Rightarrow 11 + 84 - 46 = ?$

$\therefore 49 = ?$

6. (d) Pattern of the series is as follows,

L $\xrightarrow{+2}$ N $\xrightarrow{+2}$ [P] $\xrightarrow{+2}$ R $\xrightarrow{+2}$ T

D $\xrightarrow{+3}$ G $\xrightarrow{+3}$ [J] $\xrightarrow{+3}$ M $\xrightarrow{+3}$ P

E $\xrightarrow{+4}$ I $\xrightarrow{+4}$ [M] $\xrightarrow{+4}$ Q $\xrightarrow{+4}$ U

A $\xrightarrow{+5}$ F $\xrightarrow{+5}$ [K] $\xrightarrow{+5}$ P $\xrightarrow{+5}$ U

7. (b) Given equation,

$30 + 5 - 2 \times 10 \div 2 = ?$

After interchanging the signs, we get

$\Rightarrow 30 - 5 \times 2 \div 10 + 2 = ?$

$\Rightarrow 30 - 5 \times 0.2 + 2 = ?$

$\Rightarrow 30 - 1 + 2 = ?$

$\therefore ? = 31$

8. (b) After unfolding the paper, it will appear as the option figure (b).

9. (d) As,

H O R S E

$(8 + 15 + 18 + 19 + 5) + (2 \times 5) = 75$

and

M O V E

$(13 + 15 + 22 + 5) + (2 \times 4) = 63$

Similarly,

R A C E

$(18 + 1 + 3 + 5) + (2 \times 4) = 35$

10. (d) Alas is used to express grief, and woe is a synonym for alas.

Similarly, Beauty is the combination of quality and charm is the synonym of Beauty.

11. (d) According to the question,

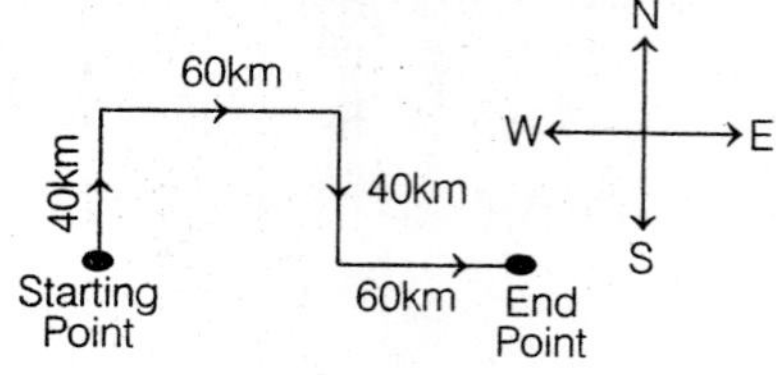

$\therefore$ The distance from home to end point of Sona is $60 + 60 = 120$ km.

12. (a) Pattern of the series is as follows,

3, 5, 7, 12, 37, 69, 357, [656]

+2, +2, +5, +25, +32, +288, +299

×1, +3, ×5, +7, ×9, +11

13. (a) According to the statements,

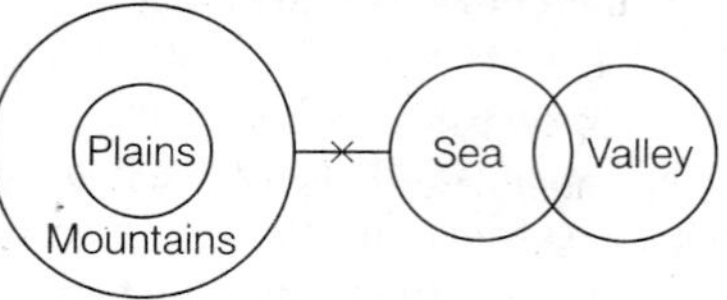

Conclusions

I. (✗)   II. (✗)   III. (✓)

14. (d) The series will be as shown below,

P Q R R S / P Q R R S / P Q R R S / P Q R R S

15. (c) Given equation,

16 B 5 A 112 D 8 C 32

After putting the signs, we get

$16 \times 5 + 112 \div 8 - 32 = ?$

$\Rightarrow 80 + 14 - 32 = ?$

$\therefore 62 = ?$

16. (a) According to the question,

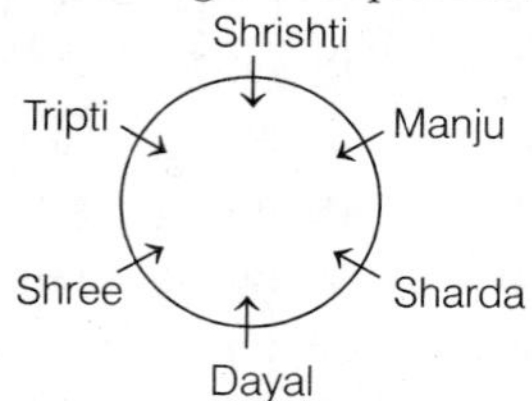

$\therefore$ Dayal is an immediate neighbour of Sharda.

17. (b) As, $2 : 26 \Rightarrow 2 \times (2 + 11) = 26$

and $27 : 1026 \Rightarrow 27 \times (27 + 11) = 1026$

Similarly, $? : 152 \Rightarrow ? \times (? + 11) = 152$

$\Rightarrow ? = 8$

18. (b) In the given fig. series, each figure follows the following pattern.

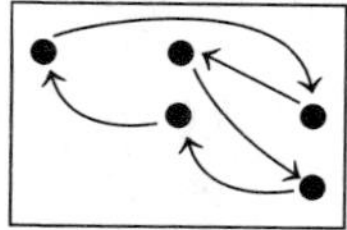

19. (b) In the given figure series, each figure follows the following pattern,

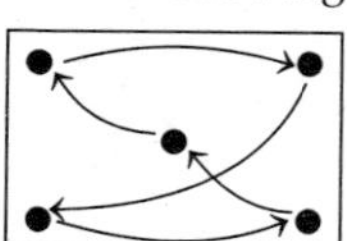

20. (b) Given equation,

$83 \div 12 - 65 \times 13 + 47 = ?$

After interchanging signs we get,

$83 + 12 \times 65 \div 13 - 47 = ?$

$\Rightarrow \quad 83 + 12 \times 5 - 47 = ?$

$\Rightarrow \quad 83 + 60 - 47 = ?$

$\therefore \quad 96 = ?$

21. (d) As, GBTA
Number of letters in GBTA is 4 and
$4 \times 6 = 24$
and ZWQVI
Number of letters in ZWQVI is 5 and
$5 \times 6 = 30$
Similarly, DLUCPR
Number of letters in DLUCPR is 6 and
$6 \times 6 = 36$

22. (b) According to the statements,

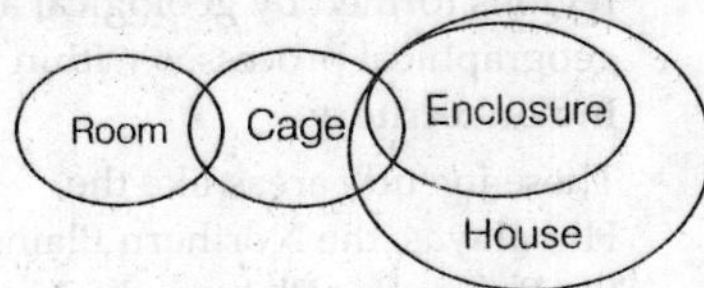

Conclusions
I. (✓) II. (✗)
$\therefore$ Only Conclusion I follows.

23. (d) In the given unfolded dice, the opposite faces are, (3 and 4), (5 and 6) and (1 and 2).
And opposite faces can not be adjacent to each other.
$\therefore$ Only 2, 3, and 4 cubes are possible.

24. (a) Given equation,
$14 - 7 \div 42 \times 6 + 33 = ?$
After interchanging signs, we get
$14 \times 7 + 42 \div 6 - 33 = ?$
$\Rightarrow \quad 98 + 7 - 33 = ?$
$\therefore \quad 72 = ?$

25. (c) After unfolding the figure, it will appear as the answer figure (c).

26. (b) According to the statements,

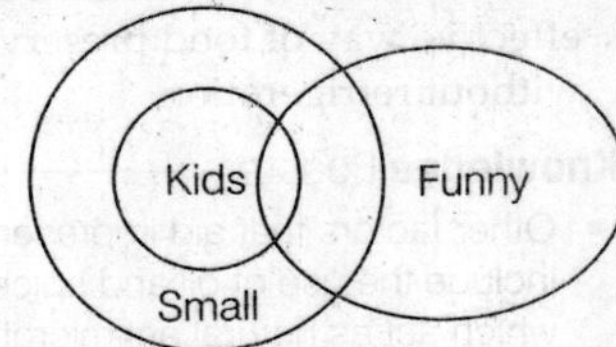

Conclusions
I. (✓) II. (✓)
$\therefore$ Both Conclusions I and II follow.

27. (d) The order of the words in dictionary will be as follows,
Purgatory (4) $\rightarrow$ Purge (3) $\rightarrow$ Purify (5) $\rightarrow$ Puritan(1) $\rightarrow$ Purpose (2)
$\Rightarrow$ 4,3,5,1,2

28. (d) After unfolding the figure, it will appear as the answer figure (d).

29. (c) Since, two faces (6 and 2) are common in two dices, hence, the remaining face i.e., '3' will be opposite to '4'.

30. (d) As, Whale are Mammal. Similarly, crocodiles is the type of reptile.
$\therefore$ Reptile is the correct answer.

31. (c) According to the statement, the movement of X is as follows,

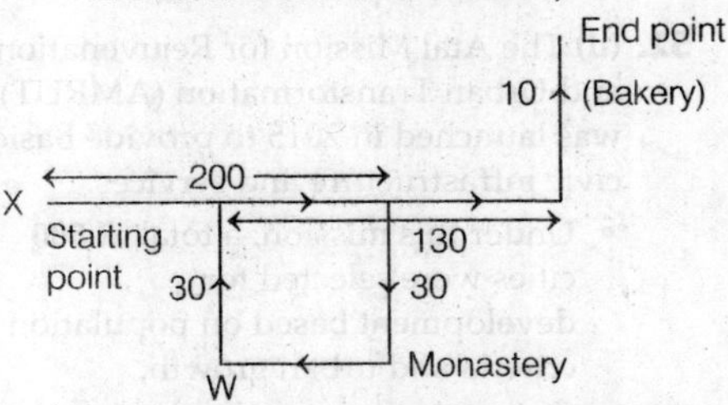

Hence, the bakery is in the north east direction to X's house.

32. (a) As, $E \xrightarrow{-4} A \xrightarrow{+5} F \xrightarrow{-2} D$

and $V \xrightarrow{-4} R \xrightarrow{+5} W \xrightarrow{-2} U$

$L \xrightarrow{-4} H \xrightarrow{+5} M \xrightarrow{-2} K$

But, $N \xrightarrow{-4} J \xrightarrow{-6} P \xrightarrow{-3} M$

33. (b) As, $5 : 24 \Rightarrow 5^2 - 1 = 24$
and $4 : 15 \Rightarrow 4^2 - 1 = 15$
Similarly, $? : 143$
$\Rightarrow ?^2 - 1 = 143 \Rightarrow 12$

34. (d) Given equation,
$[\{(23 \times 15) - (2 \div 2)\} + (2 - 4)] \div 2$
After interchanging the signs, we get
$\Rightarrow [\{(23 - 15) + (2 \times 2)\} \div (2 + 4)] \times 2$
$\Rightarrow [\{(8) + (4)\} \div (6)] \times 2$
$\Rightarrow [12 \div 6] \times 2$
$\Rightarrow 2 \times 2 \Rightarrow 4$

35. (a) Pattern of the series is as follows,

261, 232, 203, 174, 145, 116
(each step −29)

36. (c) As,

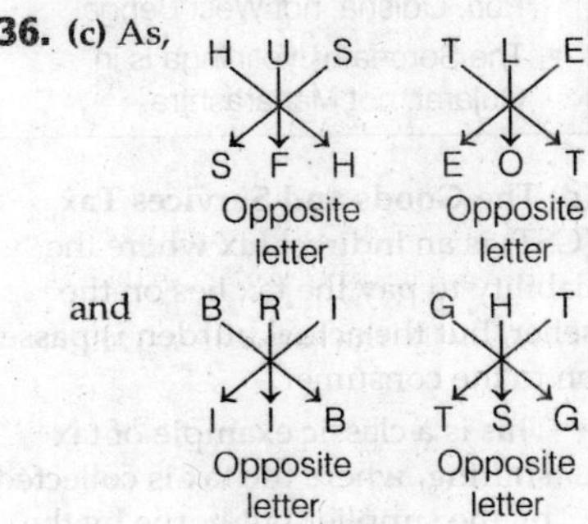

Similarly,

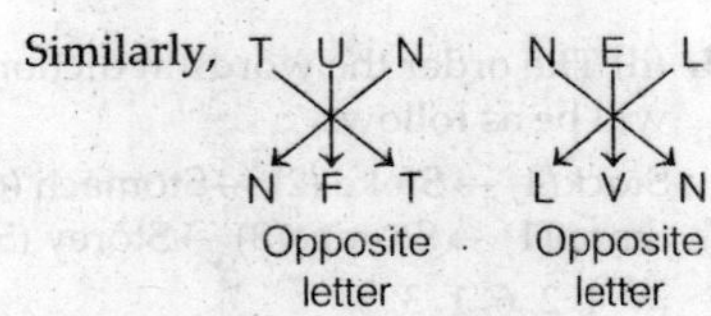

37. (a) According to the quesion,

Spoon, Soup and Rice are not related to each other.
So, the diagram in option (a) shows the correct relationship.

38. (d) The question figure is embedded in the option figure (d).

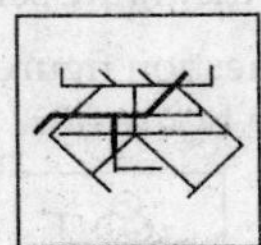

39. (d) According to the question,

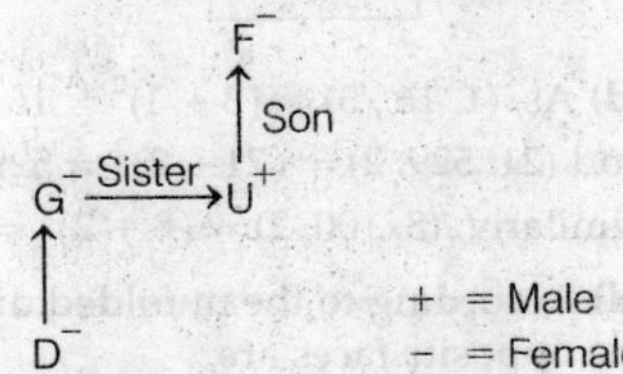

G is the daughter of F.

40. (d) As, $(13, 18, 21) \Rightarrow \frac{(18 + 21)}{3} = 13$

and $(11, 25, 8) \Rightarrow \frac{(25 + 8)}{3} = 11$

Similarly, $(14, 33, 9) \Rightarrow \frac{(33 + 9)}{3} = 14$

41. (d) Given equation,
$31 \div 48 \times 7 - 322 + 23 = 353$
From option(d),
$31 + 48 \times 7 - 322 \div 23 = 353$
$\Rightarrow \quad 31 + 336 - 14 = 353$
$\therefore \quad 353 = 353$

42. (b) From the statements, the arrangement is as follows,

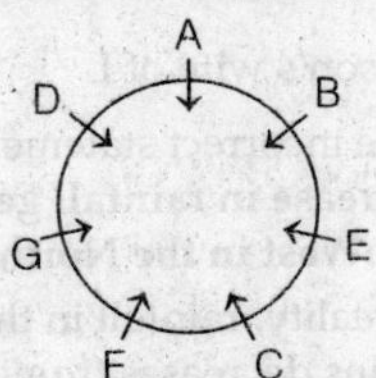

Hence, F is the immediate neighbour of both C and G

43. **(d)** The order the words in dictionary will be as follows,

Stock(4) $\rightarrow$ Stoke (2) $\rightarrow$ Stomach (6) $\rightarrow$ Stoop(1) $\rightarrow$ Storage(3) $\rightarrow$ Storey (5)

$\Rightarrow$ 4, 2, 6, 1, 3, 5

44. **(c)** As, $J \xrightarrow{-5} E \xrightarrow{-4} A \xrightarrow{-3} X$

and $D \xrightarrow{-5} Y \xrightarrow{-4} U \xrightarrow{-3} R$

$Q \xrightarrow{-5} L \xrightarrow{-4} H \xrightarrow{-3} E$

But $\boxed{W \xrightarrow{+7} D \xrightarrow{-6} X \xrightarrow{+5} C}$

45. **(a)** In the given figure series, one cross(x) symbol is removed from the right side in each step, and one zero (0) is added in each step.

Hence, the figure in option(a) will complete the figure series.

46. **(a)** The question figure is embedded in the option figure (a).

47. **(d)** As, (1, 16 , 3) $\Rightarrow (3 + 1)^2 = 16$

and (21, 529, 2) $\Rightarrow (21 + 2)^2 = 529$

Similarly, (8, 100, 2) $\Rightarrow (8 + 2)^2 = 100$

48. **(d)** According to the unfolded dice, the opposite faces are,

(15, and 19), (16 and 17) and (20 and 18)

As, opposite faces can not be adjacent to each other.

Therefore, only the dice given in option (d) is possible.

49. **(a)**The series will be as shown below,

P $\underline{L}$ $\underline{B}$ O N / $\underline{P}$ L B $\underline{O}$ N/ P L $\underline{B}$ O $\underline{N}$ /P L $\underline{B}$ $\underline{O}$ N

$\Rightarrow$LBPOBNBO

50. **(a)** According to the question,

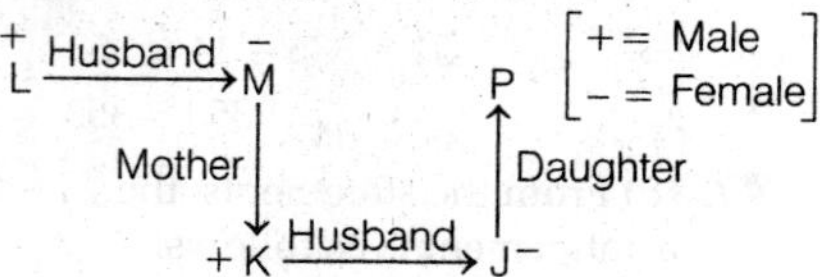

$\therefore$ J is son's wife of L.

51. **(d)** The incorrect statement is **There is an increase in rainfall generally from East toWest in the Northern Plains.**

- In reality, rainfall in the Northern Plains decreases from East to West, as the South-West monsoon weakens while moving Westward.
- Eastern regions like West Bengal and Bihar receive higher rainfall, while Western regions like Punjab and Haryana receive much less.

Knowledge Booster

- Meghalaya, especially Mawsynram and Cherrapunji, receives more than 1100 cm of annual rainfall - among the highest in the world.
- Tamil Nadu receives most of its rain from the North-East monsoon, especially in October and November.

52. **(d)** The Atal Mission for Rejuvenation and Urban Transformation (AMRUT) was launched in 2015 to provide basic civic infrastructure and services.

- Under this mission, a total of **500** cities were selected for development based on population criteria and urban growth.
- The scheme aims to ensure access to tap water supply, sewerage, urban transport and green spaces in urban areas.
- AMRUT is administered by the Ministry of Housing and Urban Affairs (MoHUA) and supports urban reforms through incentive-based frameworks.

53. **(b)** The **Kamakhya Temple** is a famous Hindu temple dedicated to Goddess Kamakhya (a form of Shakti), located in Guwahati, Assam.

- It is considered one of the most sacred of the 51 Shakti Peethas in India.
- The temple is known for the annual Ambubachi Mela, which celebrates the menstruation cycle of the goddess.

Knowledge Booster

- The Mahakaleshwar Jyotirlinga is actually located in Ujjain, Madhya Pradesh, not Uttarakhand.
- The Jagannath Temple is located in Puri, Odisha, not West Bengal.
- The Somnath Jyotirlinga is in Gujarat, not Maharashtra.

54. **(d)** The **Goods and Services Tax** (GST) is an indirect tax where the liability to pay the tax lies on the seller, but the actual burden is passed on to the consumer.

- This is a classic example of tax shifting, where the tax is collected by the supplier but borne by the end user.
- GST was introduced in India on 1st July, 2017, replacing multiple indirect taxes like VAT, excise duty and service tax.
- It is implemented as a dual model: Central GST (CGST) and State GST (SGST) or Integrated GST (IGST) for interstate supply.

55. **(b)** The **Appalachian Mountains** are located in North America, not in India and hence cannot be grouped under the physiographic divisions of India.

- The physiographic divisions of India refer to distinct physical regions formed by geological and geographical processes within Indian territory.
- These include areas like the Himalayas, the Northern Plains, the Peninsular Plateau, the Indian Desert, the Coastal Plains and the Islands.
- The Appalachians stretch across Eastern USA and Canada and are much older than the Himalayas.

56. **(d)** Pickles last longer because their high **salt concentration causes plasmolysis in bacterial and fungal cells**, leading to their death or inactivation.

- Plasmolysis is the process in which cells lose water in a hypertonic environment, causing the cell membrane to shrink away from the cell wall.
- The salty and acidic conditions create an inhospitable environment for microbial growth, thus preserving the pickle.
- This method is a traditional and effective way of food preservation without refrigeration.

Knowledge Booster

- Other factors that aid in preservation include the use of oil and spices, which act as natural antimicrobials.
- Osmosis is the scientific principle behind this preservation technique - water moves out of microbial cells due to high external salt concentration.

57. **(b)** The Prime Minister's Employment Generation Programme (PMEGP) was **launched in 2008** by the Ministry of Micro, Small and Medium Enterprises (MSME).

- PMEGP provides a subsidy of 15% to 35% on project costs, depending on location and category of the entrepreneur.
- The scheme merges two earlier schemes Prime Minister's Rozgar Yojana (PMRY) and Rural Employment Generation Programme (REGP).
- It is implemented by the Khadi and Village Industries Commission (KVIC) at the national level.

58. (d) The Hornbill Festival is celebrated in the state of **Nagaland**, starting from 1st December every year.

- It was initiated by the Government of Nagaland in 2000 to encourage interaction among the tribes and promote their rich cultural heritage.
- The Hornbill Festival is often called the 'Festival of Festivals' and attracts both national and international tourists.
- The festival is named after the Hornbill bird, which is respected and revered by the Naga tribes.

59. (c) The **command area** refers to the agricultural land that lies below the water level of the main canal, enabling irrigation through gravity flow.

- It is the total area that can be irrigated using water supplied from a canal system, without requiring lifting mechanisms.
- The command area is further divided into Gross Command Area (GCA), Culturable Command Area (CCA) and Irrigated Area.
- This system ensures efficient use of water for irrigation in canal-based agricultural regions.

60. (d) **Haemoglobin** is the iron-containing respiratory pigment found in Red Blood Cells (RBCs) that gives blood which is in red colour.

- It binds with oxygen in the lungs and carries it to tissues throughout the body.
- The red colour of blood is due to the presence of iron in the heme group of haemoglobin, which forms oxyhaemoglobin when combined with oxygen.
  Each haemoglobin molecule can carry upto four oxygen molecules.

61. (b) **Swami Haridas** was the guru (teacher) of the legendary Indian classical musician Tansen, who later became one of the Navratnas (Nine Gems) in the court of Mughal Emperor Akbar.

- Swami Haridas was a saint, poet and a musician from the Bhakti movement and a devotee of Lord Krishna.
- He belonged to the Vaishnavite tradition and is considered a pioneer of Dhrupad music, one of the oldest forms of Hindustani classical music.
- Swami Haridas taught music in Vrindavan, where Tansen received his early musical training.

Knowledge Booster

- Tansen is credited with creating several ragas and was said to possess mystical abilities through his music, like bringing rain (Raga Megh Malhar) or lighting lamps (Raga Deepak).

62. (d) Pandit Ram Narayan is a renowned Indian classical musician famous for playing the **Sarangi**, a bowed string instrument.

- He is credited with reviving the Sarangi as a solo concert instrument, which was earlier primarily used for accompaniment in vocal performances.
- He was awarded the Padma Vibhushan in 2005 for his contributions to Indian classical music.

63. (a) **Friedrich Wöhler**, a German chemist, was the first scientist to synthesise an organic compound (urea) from an inorganic compound, ammonium cyanate in 1828.

- This experiment is considered a milestone in the history of chemistry, as it disproved the concept of vitalism, which claimed that organic compounds could only be produced by living organisms.
- Vitalism was a widely accepted theory before Wohler's discovery, asserting that a 'vital force' was needed to make organic matter.

64. (a) **'Open: An Autobiography** is the critically acclaimed memoir of Andre Agassi, a former world No. 1 professional tennis player from the USA.

- Published in 2009, the book gives a candid and introspective look into Agassi's personal life, struggles and tennis career.
- Some of the important autobiographies
  - 'Becoming' is the memoir of Michelle Obama.
  - 'Too Many Reasons to Live' is written by Rob Burrow.
  - 'Me' is the autobiography of Elton John.

65. (b) The Bishnu Rabha Award 2019 was conferred upon Kumari Laitjonam Ebampisok Devi, a renowned **Manipuri** dance exponent.

- She was recognised for her exceptional contribution to Manipuri classical dance, one of the eight classical dance forms of India.
- The Bishnu Rabha Award is named after Kalaguru Bishnu Prasad Rabha, a cultural icon of Assam.
- The award honours artists who have made significant contributions to arts, culture and literature in Assam and the North-East.

Knowledge Booster

- Manipuri dance is known for its graceful movements, devotional themes and mythological story-telling, often based on Vaishnavism.
- Manipuri dance originated in Manipur and often features Rasa Lila, depicting the love stories of Radha and Krishna.

66. (b) The **Right to Property** was deleted from the list of Fundamental Rights by the 44th Constitutional Amendment Act, 1978.

- It was originally a Fundamental Right under Article-31, but post-amendment, it was made a legal right under Article-300A.
- Article 300A now states 'No person shall be deprived of his property save by authority of law.'

67. (a) **Guru Bipin Singh**, a celebrated Manipuri dance exponent, founded the Govindji Nartanalaya in Imphal, specifically for training women in the classical dance form.

- He is known for his significant contributions in reviving, promoting and choreographing Manipuri dance on stage.
- Guru Bipin Singh also established Manipuri Nartanalaya in Kolkata to

spread Manipuri dance outside the North-East.

- Manipuri dance is one of the eight classical dance forms of India, known for its devotional themes, fluid movements and mythological story-telling.

68. **(d)** **Humayun** was the eldest of the four sons of Babur, the founder of the Mughal Empire in India.

- He was born in 1508 and succeeded Babur as the second Mughal emperor in 1530.
- After Humayun's death, his son Akbar ascended the throne and became one of the greatest rulers of the Mughal dynasty.

69. **(d)** As per Article-361 of the Constitution of India, the **Governor** (and also the President) is not answerable to any court for the exercise and performance of the powers and duties of their office.

- Article-361 also states that no criminal proceedings can be initiated against the Governor or President during their term of office.
- However, the actions of the Governor can be challenged indirectly if they affect Fundamental Rights or are contrary to constitutional provisions.
- The Governor can be removed by the President and holds office during the pleasure of the President (Article-156).

70. **(d)** The chemical formula for the aldehyde group is —**CHO**, which consists of a carbonyl group ($C=O$) bonded to a hydrogen atom.

- The general formula for an aldehyde is R—CHO, where R is an alkyl or aryl group.
- Aldehydes are widely used in organic synthesis, perfumes, dyes and preservatives.

Knowledge Booster

- —COOH represents a carboxylic acid group.
- —OH denotes a hydroxyl group (as found in alcohols).
- —CH_2O is not a valid representation of any specific functional group.
- A common example of an aldehyde is formaldehyde (HCHO).

71. **(b)** An over in cricket consists of **6** legal deliveries (balls) bowled by a bowler from one end of the pitch.

- After completing an over, a different bowler delivers the next over from the opposite end.
- The system of 6-ball overs is followed in all formats of international cricket - Test, ODI, and T20.
- Any wide or no-ball does not count as one of the six and must be re-bowled.

Knowledge Booster

- Historically, the number of balls in an over has varied; for example, Australia and South Africa once used 8-ball overs.
- The 6-ball over became the standard internationally by the 1970s and remains the norm today.

72. **(d)** The term 'Ecology' was first introduced in **1866** by the German biologist Ernst Haeckel.

- He used the term to describe the relationship of organisms with their environment, referring to it as the 'economy of nature.'
- The word is derived from the Greek 'oikos' (household) and 'logos' (study), meaning the study of the household (environment) of living beings.

73. **(a)** **Schedule-X** of the Constitution of India contains provisions related to the disqualification of legislators on the ground of defection.

- It was added by the 52nd Constitutional Amendment Act, 1985, also known as the Anti-Defection Law.
- The 91st Amendment Act, 2003 further strengthened the anti-defection provisions by removing protection for splits and limiting the size of the Council of Ministers.
- The Speaker or Chairman of the respective House decides on disqualification under this schedule.

74. **(a)** The first World Weightlifting Championship was organised in **March 1891** by the World Weightlifting Federation in London, UK.

- It marked the beginning of organised international competition in the sport of weightlifting.
- The International Weightlifting Federation (IWF) was officially founded later, in 1905, to oversee international competitions.
- Women's weightlifting was included in the World Championships starting from 1987 and in the Olympics from 2000.

75. **(d)** The United Nations declared the year **2005** as the International Year of Microcredit to recognise the importance of microfinance in eradicating poverty.

- The initiative aimed to promote microcredit and microfinance institutions as tools for financial inclusion and sustainable development.
- Microcredit is a key component of SDG Goal 1: No Poverty, and plays a role in entrepreneurship, job creation and gender equality.

Knowledge Booster

- Muhammad Yunus and the Grameen Bank were awarded the Nobel Peace Prize in 2006 for pioneering microcredit.

76. **(b)** Chapchar Kut is the most popular spring festival of **Mizoram**, celebrated with great enthusiasm by the Mizo community.

- It marks the completion of the jhum (slash-and-burn) cultivation clearing phase and is a time for celebration before the sowing season.
- Other major festivals of Mizoram include Pawl Kut and Mim Kut, which are also linked to agriculture.

77. **(a)** The age of the Earth is scientifically estimated to be about **4.5 billion** years (approximately 4.54 ± 0.05 billion years).

- This estimate is based on the dating of the oldest rocks on Earth, Moon rocks and meteorites using radiometric methods.
- Uranium-lead dating and isotope analysis are among the most reliable techniques used to determine Earth's age.
- The solar system, including Earth, formed about 4.6 billion years ago, shortly after the Sun's formation.

Knowledge Booster
- The oldest rocks found on Earth are around 4 billion years old, while zircon crystals from Australia are dated to about 4.4 billion years.

78. (a) The First Five-Year Plan in India ended in **March 1956**, after being launched in 1951.
- The plan focused on agriculture, irrigation, power and price stability, with an emphasis on community development and land reforms.
- The First Five-Year Plan aimed for a growth rate of 2.1%, but achieved around 3.6% annually.
- It was heavily influenced by the Harrod-Domar model and was considered a success in terms of achieving its growth targets.

79. (a) Article-16(d) of the Constitution of India allows the state to make provisions for reservation in appointments or posts in favour of any backward class of citizens.
- It clarifies that such affirmative action is not a violation of the Right to Equality enshrined in Article-14.
- This article empowers the state to uplift socially and educationally backward classes and ensure equal opportunity in public employment.

Knowledge Booster
- Article-15(4) allows for special provisions for the advancement of socially and educationally backward classes in education.
- Article-14 guarantees equality before the law, while Article-21 ensures the Right toLife.
- Article-16(4) is a constitutional safeguard for the implementation of positive discrimination policies and personal liberty.

80. (d) The incorrect match is **Capacitance - Dyne.** The correct unit of capacitance is the Farad (F).
- Dyne is a unit of force, part of the Centimeter-Gram-Second (CGS) system, not related to electrical measurements.
- The correct physical quantity-unit pairs are
  – Voltage - Volt
  – Resistance - Ohm
  – Conductance - Siemens

81. (d) George E. Palade, a Romanian-American cell biologist, was the first to observe and describe ribosomes in the mid-1950s.
- He identified them as small particles in the cytoplasm that are often attached to the Endoplasmic Reticulum (ER), later termed rough ER due to this association.
- For his pioneering work in cell structure and function, George E. Palade received the Nobel Prize in Physiology or Medicine in 1974, alongwith Albert Claude and Christian de Duve.
- His discovery of ribosomes laid the foundation for understanding protein synthesis in eukaryotic cells..

82. (b) Firuz Shah Tughlaq succeeded Muhammad-bin-Tughlaq to the throne of the Delhi Sultanate in 1351 CE.
- Firuz Shah is known for his welfare-oriented rule, including canal construction, building of new towns and establishment of charitable institutions.
- Firuz Shah founded several cities, including Firozabad and built structures like the Hauz Khas complex and Firoz Shah Kotla in Delhi.

83. (c) According to the 2011 Census of India, any person aged 7 years and above who can both read and write with understanding in any language is considered literate.
- The state with the highest literacy rate was Kerala (94%), while the lowest was Bihar (61.8%).
- As per the 2011 Census, India's overall literacy rate was 74.04%, with 82.14% for males and 65.46% for female.

Knowledge Booster
- The literacy criteria do not include the ability to speak or basic education level-only the ability to read and write is essential.
- This definition helps in uniformly assessing the literacy rate across rural and urban areas.

84. (d) Kuchipudi is a classical dance form that originated in **Andhra Pradesh,** specifically from the village of Kuchipudi in Krishna district.
- It is one of the eight classical dance forms of India, combining fast rhythmic footwork, sculpturesque body movements and dramatic story-telling.
- Siddhendra Yogi, a 14th-century saint and scholar, is credited with formalising and developing Kuchipudi as a dance-drama tradition.
- The dance is deeply rooted in Natya Shastra and is closely associated with Vaishnavism, often depicting stories of Lord Krishna.

85. (b) Kumudini Lakhia is a renowned Indian classical dancer and choreographer, best known for her contribution to the **Kathak** dance form.
- Kumudini Lakhia has been honoured with prestigious awards like the Padma Shri (1987) and the Padma Bhushan (2010).
- Lakhia blended classical structure with contemporary themes, making Kathak more expressive and relevant to modern audiences.

86. (a) The black soil of the Deccan Plateau, also known as Regur soil, is rich in iron, lime, calcium, alumina, and magnesium, but lacks in **phosphorous.**
- It is known for its moisture-retaining capacity and is highly suitable for cotton cultivation, hence often called black cotton soil.
- This soil is formed by the weathering of volcanic rocks, particularly basalt and is predominantly found in Maharashtra, Madhya Pradesh, Gujarat and parts of Karnataka and Andhra Pradesh.

Knowledge Booster
- Phosphorous is an essential macronutrient for plant growth, especially for root development and flowering.
- Other major soils in India include alluvial, red, laterite, desert and mountain soils, each with distinct characteristics and mineral content.

87. (a) Article 23 of the Constitution of India prohibits traffic in human beings, begar (forced labour) and other similar forms of forced labour.
- It is a Fundamental Right under Part III of the Constitution and is enforceable by law.
- Any contravention of Article 23 is an offense punishable under the law, including provisions in the

Indian Penal Code (IPC) and specific acts like the Bonded Labour System (Abolition) Act, 1976.

88. **(c)** Statements (a), (b) and (c) are correct became the most celebrated Indo-Greek ruler was Menander I (Milinda), who ruled large parts of North-Wstern India.

- He has been identified with King Milinda, mentioned in the Buddhist text 'Milindapanho' (The Questions of Milinda).
- It is believed that King Milinda was impressed by Nagasena's answers and embraced Buddhism.
- Statement c is incorrect: The philosophical dialogue in Milindapanho is between King Milinda and the Buddhist monk Nagasena, not Amrapali.

Knowledge Booster

- The Milindapanho is an important Pali text composed in the form of a question-and-answer dialogue and reflects the fusion of Hellenistic and Indian philosophies.
- The Indo-Greek rule is known for introducing Hellenistic culture to India and for the spread of Mahayana Buddhism.

89. **(b)** Homogeneous mixtures have a uniform composition throughout and the components are not visibly distinguishable.

- Among the given options, **solution, salt water** and **brass** are homogeneous mixtures.
- A true solution is homogeneous as the solute is completely dissolved in the solvent.

Knowledge Booster

- Colloid, suspension, milk and toothpaste are heterogeneous mixtures
- Colloid has particles dispersed but not dissolved.
- Suspension has visible particles that settle over time.
- Milk is an emulsion (colloid).
- Toothpaste is a gel (also heterogeneous).

90. **(d)** The correct matching of Five-Year Plans with their corresponding periods is

- Second Five Year Plan (ii) 1956-1961
- Fifth Five Year Plan (i) 1974-1979
- Eighth Five Year Plan (iii) 1992-1997.
- The Second Five-Year Plan focused on rapid industrialisation, following the Mahalanobis model.
- The Fifth Plan aimed at poverty alleviation and self-reliance with programmes like Garibi Hatao.
- The Eighth Plan was launched after a gap (due to economic crisis and liberalisation reforms), focusing on modernisation, privatisation and economic growth.

91. **(b) Article-59** of the Indian Constitution lays down the conditions of the President's office, including the provision that once elected, the President shall not be a member of either House of Parliament or of a State Legislature.

- Article-59 also prohibits the President from holding any other office of profit during the term of office.
- The article ensures the neutrality and independence of the President, who is the constitutional head of the Republic.
- Article-58 outlines the qualifications for election as President.

92. **(c)** Kiran Desai is the author of the acclaimed novel 'The Inheritance of Loss', which won the Man Booker Prize in 2006.

- The novel explores themes of migration, identity, post-colonialism and the conflict between tradition and modernity.
- Some of the important novels :
  - 'A Fine Balance' is by Rohinton Mistry.
  - 'The Year of Runaways' is by Sunjeev Sahota.
  - 'Shantaram' is authored by Gregory David Roberts.
  - Kiran Desai's debut novel was 'Hullabaloo in the Guava Orchard', which also received international recognition.

93. **(d) Motilal Nehru** was not associated with the Prarthana Samaj. He was a prominent Congress leader and freedom fighter and the Father of Jawaharlal Nehru.

- The Prarthana Samaj was a socio-religious reform movement founded in 1867 in Bombay (now Mumbai), inspired by the Brahmo Samaj.
- The Prarthana Samaj was influenced by Raja Ram Mohan Roy's Brahmo Samaj and emphasised monotheism and rationalism.
- The movement aimed to reform Hindu religious practices, oppose caste discrimination and promote women's education and widow remarriage.

Knowledge Booster

- Reformers like Atmaram Pandurang, Govind Ranade and RG Bhandarkar were closely associated with the Prarthana Samaj.
- Justice MG Ranade, a key member, also played a vital role in establishing institutions like the Widow Marriage Association.

94. **(b)** The major jute producing states of India are West Bengal, Bihar, Assam and Odisha.

- West Bengal leads in jute cultivation, contributing over 75% of the total jute production in the country.
- India and Bangladesh are the top two producers of jute globally.
- The Jute Corporation of India (JCI) is responsible for procurement of raw jute at minimum support prices.

Knowledge Booster

- Jute, also called the 'Golden Fibre,' is mainly used in gunny bags, ropes, carpets and textiles.
- The jute industry in India is centered around the Hooghly River belt in West Bengal.

95. **(b)** The distance between galaxies is found to be **increasing**, indicating that the universe is expanding.

- This discovery was first made by Edwin Hubble in the 1920s through observations that galaxies are moving away from us.
- The farther a galaxy is, the faster it appears to be receding, a phenomenon described by Hubble's Law.
- This observation laid the foundation for the Big Bang Theory of the origin of the universe.

96. (a) The Regulating Act of 1773 led to the establishment of the Supreme Court at **Calcutta** (now Kolkata), the first Supreme Court in British India.

- The court had original and appellate jurisdiction over civil, criminal, admiralty and ecclesiastical matters.
- The first Chief Justice of the Supreme Court at Calcutta was Sir Elijah Impey.

Knowledge Booster
- The court was later replaced by the High Court of Calcutta in 1862 under the Indian High Courts Act of 1861.
- Similar Supreme Courts were later established in Madras (1801) and Bombay (1823).

97. (a) The **Landholder's** Society, also known as the Zamindari Association, was established in 1838 in Calcutta.

- It was founded to protect the interests of landlords (zamindars), especially those under the Permanent Settlement system introduced by the British.
- Prominent founders included Dwarkanath Tagore, Radhakanta Deb and other wealthy zamindars of Bengal.
- It was the first political association of modern India, marking the beginning of organised political activity.

98. (b) **Aniline** is a primary arylamine in which an amino group ($-NH_2$) is directly attached to a benzene ring, replacing one of its hydrogen atoms.

- Its chemical formula is $C_6H_5NH_2$, making it the simplest aromatic amine.
- Aniline is an important industrial chemical used in the production of dyes, drugs, rubber chemicals and polymers.

99. (d) The 2023 Men's Hockey World Cup was hosted by the state of **Odisha**, India.

- The tournament took place in two cities: Bhubaneswar (Kalinga Stadium) and Rourkela (Birsa Munda Hockey Stadium).
- This was the second consecutive time that Odisha hosted the event, having also hosted the 2018 edition.
- The 2023 edition marked the 15th Men's Hockey World Cup and featured 16 international teams.

Knowledge Booster
- The Birsa Munda Hockey Stadium in Rourkela is now the largest hockey stadium in the world in terms of seating capacity.
- Odisha has a long-standing partnership with Hockey India and has adopted several national teams for training and support.

100. (b) In football (soccer), when a player commits a foul, a **free kick** is awarded to the opposition team.

- A free kick can be either direct (a goal can be scored directly) or indirect (another player must touch the ball before a goal is scored).
- The kick is taken from the spot of the foul and opposing players must stay at least 10 yards away.
- A bicycle kick is an acrobatic move, not a type of awarded kick.
- A wide kick is not a recognised term in football rules.

101. (c) Let the quantity of copper and tin in mixture A and B be x and y units respectively

In mixture A,

Quantity of copper $= \frac{x}{3}$ units

Quantity of tin $= \frac{2y}{3}$ units

In mixture B,

Quantity of copper $= \frac{x}{4}$ units

Quantity of tin $= \frac{3y}{4}$ units

According to question, equal quantities of A and B are mixed to form C.

Then, total quantity of copper and tin in mixture C.

$$\text{Copper} = \left(\frac{x}{3} + \frac{x}{4}\right) \text{units} = \frac{7}{12}x \text{ units}$$

$$\text{Tin} = \left(\frac{2y}{3} + \frac{3y}{4}\right) \text{units} = \frac{17}{12}y \text{ units}$$

So, the ratio of copper to tin in mixture C.

$$\text{i.e. } \frac{\frac{7x}{12}}{\frac{17y}{12}} = \frac{7}{17} \Rightarrow x:y = 7:17$$

102. (d) Let the radius of sphere be r.

$$\because \text{Volume of sphere} = \frac{4}{3}\pi r^3$$

$$\Rightarrow \quad 38808 = \frac{4}{3}\pi r^3$$

$$\Rightarrow \quad r^3 = \frac{38808 \times 3 \times 7}{22 \times 4}$$

$$\Rightarrow \quad r^3 = 21 \times 21 \times 21$$

$$\Rightarrow \quad r = 21 \text{ cm}$$

$$\because \text{Surface area of sphere} = 4\pi r^2$$

$$= 4 \times \frac{22}{7} \times 21 \times 21$$

$$\therefore \text{Surface area of sphere} = 5544 \text{ cm}^2$$

103. (c) We have, diagonal and side of rhombus is 16 cm and 17 cm, respectively.

Let the other diagonal be d (i.e. $d = d_2$)

$d_1 = 16$ cm and $a = 17$ cm

Then, $(d_1)^2 + (d_2)^2 = 4a^2$

$$\Rightarrow \quad (16)^2 + (d)^2 = 4 \times (17)^2$$

$$\Rightarrow \quad d^2 = 4 \times 289 - 256$$

$$\Rightarrow \quad d^2 = 1156 - 256 = 900$$

$$\Rightarrow \quad d = 30 \text{ cm}$$

$$\therefore \text{Area of rhombus} = \frac{1}{2} \times d_1 \times d_2$$

$$= \frac{1}{2} \times 30 \times 16$$

$$= 240 \text{ cm}^2$$

104. (c) Given, Vijay sell 42 m of cloth.

Let the SP of 1 m cloth be ₹ x

So, the SP of 42 m cloth = ₹ $42x$

Profit earn of SP = ₹ $7x$

So, CP of cloth = ₹$(42 - 7)x$

= ₹ $35x$

$$\therefore \quad P\% = \left(\frac{P}{CP} \times 100\right)\%$$

$$= \left(\frac{7x}{35x} \times 100\right)\%$$

$$\Rightarrow \quad P\% = 20\%$$

105. (a) Let the MRP of sofa set be $100x$.

Ramesh gives 25% discount on MRP

i.e. $\left(100x - 100x \times \frac{25}{100}\right) = 75x$

Also, given 15% additional discount on MRP, then SP of a sofa set

$$= \left(75x - 75x \times \frac{15}{100}\right)$$

$$= \left(75x - \frac{45x}{4}\right)$$

$$= ₹\,\frac{255x}{4}$$

Given, SP of sofa set = ₹ 12750

$$\Rightarrow \quad \frac{255x}{4} = 12750$$

$$\Rightarrow \quad x = \left(\frac{12750 \times 4}{255}\right)$$

$$\Rightarrow \quad x = ₹\,200$$

$\therefore$ The MRP of sofa set is ₹ 20000.

Speedy Method

Let MRP be x

SP after discount of 25% along with additional discount of 15% i.e.,

$$\Rightarrow \text{SP} = \left(x \times \frac{75}{100} \times \frac{85}{100}\right) = \frac{255x}{400}$$

{Formula used SP = MRP $(1 - D_1\%)(1 - D_2\%)\ldots(1 - D_r\%)$}

Given, SP = ₹ 12750

$$\Rightarrow \frac{255x}{400} = 12750$$

$$\Rightarrow x = \frac{12750 \times 400}{255} = \left(\frac{12750 \times 400}{255}\right)$$

$$\Rightarrow x = ₹\,200000$$

106. (b) Speedy Method

$P_1 = 12$ hour $\quad P_2 = 16$ hour

Rate of filing per hour

P_1 12 ⟩ 48 ⟨ 4

P_2 16 ⟩ ⟨ 3

Time taken without leakage $= \frac{48}{7}$ h

Time taken with leakage

$$= \left(\frac{48}{7} + \frac{90}{60}\right)\text{h} = \frac{117}{14}\text{ h}$$

$$\text{Leakage rate} = \left(\frac{14}{117} - \frac{7}{48}\right) = \left(\frac{-147}{5616}\right)$$

$$= \frac{49}{1872} \text{ per hour}$$

{∵ time can't be '−' ve}

Time taken to empty the tank

$$= \frac{1872}{49} = 38\frac{10}{49}\text{ h.}$$

107. (a) Given, amount after 2 yr = ₹ 1200 and amount after 3 yr = ₹ 1260

Amount after 2 yr become principal for 3rd yr.

P = ₹ 1200, T = 1 yr and A = ₹ 1260

Let the rate of interest be r%.

$$\therefore \quad A = P\left(1 + \frac{r}{100}\right)^1$$

$$\Rightarrow 1260 = 1200\left(\frac{1 + r}{100}\right)^1$$

$$\Rightarrow \frac{1260}{1200} = 1 + \frac{r}{100}$$

$$\Rightarrow \frac{21}{20} - 1 = \frac{r}{100}$$

$$\Rightarrow \frac{1}{20} = \frac{r}{100}$$

$$\Rightarrow r = 5\%$$

Speedy Method

Interest for 1 yr = (Amount after 3 yr) − (Amount after 2 yr) = ₹ (1260 − 1200) = ₹ 60

P = ₹ 1200

$$\Rightarrow \text{CI} = \frac{P \times R}{100}$$

$$\Rightarrow 60 = \frac{1200 \times R}{100}$$

$$\Rightarrow R = 5\%\text{ p.a.}$$

108. (a) Let $f(x) = 16\,\text{cosec}^2\theta + 25\sin^2\theta$

Formula used,

Minimum of $f(x) = a\sin^2\theta + b\,\text{cosec}^2\theta$ is $2\sqrt{ab}$.

Here, $a = 25$ and $b = 16$

Least or minimum value $= 2\sqrt{16 \times 25} = 2 \times 4 \times 5 = 40$

109. (c) Total units purchased in year 2015 = 650 + 450 + 1008 = 2108

Total unit purchased in year 2020 = 830 + 501 + 1330 = 2661

∴ Difference = (2661 − 2108) units = 553 units

∴ Percentage increased

$$= \left(\frac{\text{Difference}}{\text{Total purchased in 2015}} \times 100\right)\%$$

$$= \left(\frac{553}{2108} \times 100\right)\% = 26.23\%$$

110. (c) We have, $\cos A = \frac{1}{11}$

We know that, $\cos\theta = \frac{B}{H}$

Here, $B = 1$, $H = 11$, then $P = \sqrt{H^2 - B^2}$

$$\Rightarrow P = \sqrt{(11)^2 - (1)^2} = \sqrt{121 - 1} = \sqrt{120}$$

$$\Rightarrow P = 2\sqrt{30}$$

$$\therefore \cot A = \frac{B}{P} = \frac{1}{2\sqrt{30}}$$

111. (a) Total production in year 2016 = Production of (Brand P + Brand Q + Brand R) = (40 + 50 + 30) million

Total production in year 2017 = Production of (Brand P + Brand Q + Brand R)

= 20 + 25 + 30 = 75 million

Total production in year 2018 = Production of (Brand P + Brand Q + Brand R)

= (40 + 30 + 20) = 90 million

Total production in Year 2019 = Production of (Brand P + Brand Q + Brand R)

= (20 + 30 + 25) = 75 million

Average production of milk

$$= \frac{120 + 75 + 90 + 75}{4} = \frac{360}{4} \text{ million}$$

Average production of milk = 90 million

112. (d) We have, $\text{cosec}\,A + \cot A = 3$, $0 \le A \le 90°$

$$\Rightarrow \frac{1}{\sin A} + \frac{\cos A}{\sin A} = 3$$

$$\Rightarrow \frac{1 + \cos A}{\sin A} = 3$$

$$\Rightarrow 1 + \cos A = 3\sin A$$

On squaring both sides, we get

$$(1 + \cos A)^2 = (3\sin A)^2$$

$$\Rightarrow 1 + \cos^2 A + 2\cos A = 9\sin^2 A$$

$$\Rightarrow 1 + \cos^2 A + 2\cos A = 9(1 - \cos^2 A)$$

$$\Rightarrow 1 + \cos^2 A + 2\cos A = 9 - 9\cos^2 A$$

$$\Rightarrow 10\cos^2 A + 2\cos A - 8 = 0$$

$$\Rightarrow 5\cos^2 A + \cos A - 4 = 0$$

$$\Rightarrow (5\cos A - 4)(\cos A + 1) = 0$$

$$\Rightarrow 5\cos A - 4 = 0 \text{ or } (\cos A + 1) = 0$$

$$\Rightarrow \cos A = \frac{4}{5} \text{ or } \cos A = -1$$

Since, $\cos A = -1$ is not in range.

Then, the value of $\cos A = \frac{4}{5}$

113. (b) Given, 36 equally efficient workers can paint 25 identical walls in 48 days.

Then one worker can paint 25 walls = (48 × 36) days

⇒ One worker can paint one wall

$$= \frac{48 \times 36}{25} \text{ days} = \frac{1728}{25} \text{ days}$$

45 workers can paint 1 wall

$$= \left(\frac{\frac{1728}{25}}{45}\right) \text{ days} = \frac{1728}{25 \times 45} \text{ days}$$

⇒ 45 workers can paint 60 walls

$$= \frac{1728}{25 \times 45} \times 60 = \frac{1728 \times 12}{5 \times 45} = 92.16 \text{ days}$$

Speedy Method

Given, 36 equally efficient workers can paint 25 identical walls in 48 days.

Using formula,

$$\frac{M_1 \times D_1}{W_1} = \frac{M_2 \times D_2}{W_2}$$

Here, $M_1 = 36$, $D_1 = 48$, $W_1 = 25$

and $M_2 = 45, D_2 = ?, W_2 = 60$

$\Rightarrow \frac{36 \times 48}{25} = \frac{45 \times D}{60}$

$\Rightarrow D = \frac{36 \times 48 \times 60}{25 \times 45} = 92.16$ days

114. **(d)** Remainder when 433 divided by 6 = 1

Remainder when 433 divided by 8 = 1

Remainder when 433 divided by 9 = 1

If satisfies the condition for the highest common factor.

Hence, 433 is the number leaves remainder equal HCF of 6, 8, 9 and divided by 6, 8 and 9.

115. **(c)** Let $y = (1 + x)^3 + (1 - x)^3 + (-2)^3$

$\Rightarrow y = (1 + x^3 + 3x + 3x^2) + (1 - 3x + 3x^2 - x^3) + (-8)$

$\Rightarrow y = 1 + x^3 + 3x + 3x^2 + 1 - 3x + 3x^2 - x^3 - 8$

$\Rightarrow y = 2 + 6x^2 - 8$

$\Rightarrow y = 6x^2 - 6$

$\Rightarrow y = 6(x^2 - 1)$

$y = -6(1 - x^2)$

116. **(b)** We have, $1\frac{1}{3} \div \frac{2}{5} \times \frac{x}{5} = 1\frac{1}{4} \times \frac{2}{3} \div \frac{1}{6}$

$\Rightarrow \frac{4}{3} \times \frac{5}{2} \times \frac{x}{5} = \frac{5}{4} \times \frac{2}{3} \times 6$

$\Rightarrow \frac{2x}{3} = 5$

$\Rightarrow x = \frac{15}{2} = 7.5$

$\Rightarrow x = 7.5$

117. **(c)** The average weight of 49 students = 53 kg

Total weight of 49 students = (49 × 53) kg = 2597 kg

Let the weight of new student be x kg.

Now, total number of student = 50

According to question,

$\frac{2597 + x}{50} = (53 - 0.5)$ kg

$\Rightarrow 2597 + x = 50(53 - 0.5)$

$\Rightarrow 2597 + x = (2650 - 25)$

$\Rightarrow 2597 + x = 2625$

$\therefore x = 28$ kg

118. **(c)** Let the total votes be x.

Total votes of candidate who won

$= x \times \frac{75}{100} = \frac{75x}{100}$ votes

Total votes of candidate who loss

$= \left(x - \frac{75x}{100}\right) = \frac{25x}{100}$ votes

Difference between them = 2500 votes

$\Rightarrow \frac{75x}{100} - \frac{25x}{100} = 2500$

$\Rightarrow 50x = 2500 \times 100$

$\Rightarrow x = \frac{2500 \times 100}{50} = 5000$ votes

Total number of votes polled of the losing candidate was

$= \frac{25}{100} \times 5000 = 1250$ votes

119. **(a)** Given, 30% votes didn't cast their votes and 20% are declared as invalid.

Winner get = 64% of valid votes

Let the total number of votes in the voting list be x.

According to question,

30% didn't csst their vote

$= x \times \frac{30}{100} = \frac{30x}{100}$

Remaining votes $= x - \frac{30x}{100} = \frac{70x}{100}$

Invalid votes $= \frac{70x}{100} \times \frac{20}{100} = \frac{14x}{100}$

Valid votes $= \frac{70x}{100} - \frac{14x}{100} = \frac{56x}{100}$

Winner get 64% of the valid votes

$= \frac{56x}{100} \times \frac{64}{100}$

Losser get 36% of the valid votes

$= \frac{36}{100} \times \frac{56x}{100}$

According to question,

$\frac{56x}{100} \times \frac{64}{100} - \frac{56x}{100} \times \frac{36}{100} = 3136$

$\Rightarrow \frac{56x}{100 \times 100}(64 - 36) = 3136$

$\Rightarrow x = \frac{3136 \times 100 \times 100}{56 \times 28}$

$\Rightarrow x = \frac{784 \times 25 \times 100}{14 \times 7}$

$\therefore x = 20,000$

Numbers of votes enrolled 20000 voters.

Speedy Method

Let the total votes be x

Valid votes $= x \times \frac{70}{100} \times \frac{80}{100} = \frac{56x}{100}$

According to question,

$\frac{56x}{100} \frac{(64 - 36)}{100} = 3136$

$\Rightarrow x = \frac{3136 \times 100 \times 100}{28 \times 56}$

$\therefore x = 20000$ voters

120. **(a)** Let the mean proportion be A.

So, $x^3y : A :: A : xy^3$

Product of means $= A \times A = A^2$

Product of extremes $= x^3y \times xy^3 = x^4y^4$

In proportion, the product of means is equal to the product of extremes.

$\Rightarrow A^2 = x^4y^4$

$\Rightarrow A = \sqrt{x^4y^4} = x^2y^2$

Mean proportional is x^2y^2

121. **(d)** Factors of 12 is 2 × 2 × 3.

Factors of 18 is 3 × 3 × 2.

Factors of 27 is 3 × 3 × 3.

LCM of 12, 18 and 27 is 108.

122. **(c)** Given, Distance covered by Jimmy = 88 km in 16 h

Distance covered by Jimmy in $\frac{3}{4}$ times

$= \frac{88}{2} = 44$ km

$\therefore$ Time taken $= \left(16 \times \frac{3}{4}\right)$h = 12 h

Remaining distance = 44 km

$\therefore$ Remaining time $= 16 \times \frac{1}{4} = 4$ h

Speed of Jimmy to cover remaining distance $= \frac{44}{4} = 11$ km/h

123. **(b)** LCM of 4, 6, 9, 12 and 15 is 180.

The LCM are found is 180 to find the least perfect square divisible by 180. We need to adjust the prime factorisation of 180 to make all the exponent even.

Prime factorisation of

$180 = 2^2 \times 5^1 \times 3^2$

New perfect square

$= 2^2 \times 5^2 \times 3^2 = 900$

The least perfect square number that is divisible by 4, 6, 9, 12 and 15 is 900.

124. **(a)** Let s be usual speed and t be the time taken to cover the distance.

According to question,

$\Rightarrow s \times t = s \times \frac{1}{4} \times (t + 45)$

$\Rightarrow st = \frac{s}{4}(t + 45)$

$\Rightarrow t = \frac{(t + 45)}{4}$

$\Rightarrow 4t = t + 45$

$\Rightarrow 3t = 45$

$\therefore t = 15$ min

125. **(a)** Let R be the rate of interest.

Kanchana lent ₹ 10000 for 2 yr and ₹ 5000 for 4 yr.

Total interest received is ₹ 2000

According to question,

$\Rightarrow$ SI after 6 yr = SI after 2 yr + SI after 4 yr

$$\Rightarrow \quad 2000 = \frac{10000 \times 2 \times R}{100} + \frac{5000 \times 4 \times R}{100}$$

$\Rightarrow 2000 \times 100 = 40000 \times R$

$$\Rightarrow \quad \frac{200000}{40000} = R$$

$\therefore \quad R = 5\%$

126. **(b)** Average weight of A, B and $C = 77$ kg

Total weight of A, B and $C = (77 \times 3)$ kg $= 231$ kg

Average weight of B and $A = 68$ kg

Total weight of A and B $= (68 \times 2) = 136$ kg

Average weight of B and $C = 83$ kg

Total weight of B and C $= (83 \times 2) = 166$ kg

Weight of A = Weight of $(A + B + C)$ – Weight of $(B + C)$

$= (231 - 166) = 65$ kg

Weight of C = Weight of $(A + B + C)$ – Weight of $(A + B)$

$= (231 - 136) = 95$ kg

Weight of B = Weight of $(A + B + C)$ – Weight of C – Weight of A

$= (231 - 95 - 65)$ kg

Weight of $B = 71$ kg

127. **(b)** Length and breadth of rectangle 4 cm and 3 cm, respectively.

Let the radius of hemisphere be r.

According to question,

$\Rightarrow \quad 2r = \sqrt{l^2 + b^2}$

$\Rightarrow \quad 2r = \sqrt{(4)^2 + (3)^2}$

$\Rightarrow \quad 2r = \sqrt{16 + 9} = \sqrt{25}$

$\Rightarrow \quad 2r = 5 \Rightarrow r = \frac{5}{2}$ cm

Surface area of hemisphere

$= 2\pi r^2 + \pi r^2$

$= 3\pi r^2 = 3 \times \pi \times \left(\frac{5}{2}\right)^2$

Surface area of hemisphere $= \frac{75\pi}{4}$ cm^2

128. **(c)** Let the diameter of wire be d.

Given, diameter of metallic rod = 2 cm

r_1 = Radius of metallic rod $= 1$ cm $= 10$ mm

h_1 = Length of metallic rod $= 45$ cm $= 450$ mm

Let the radius of wire be r_2 and h_2 $= 5$ m $= 5000$ mm

According to question,

$\pi r_1^2 h_1 = \pi r_2^2 h_2$

$\Rightarrow \pi \times (10)^2 \times 450 = \pi \times (r_2)^2 \times (5000)$

$\Rightarrow r_2^2 = 9 \Rightarrow r = 3$ mm

$\therefore$ Diameter of the wire is 6 mm.

129. **(c)** Let the initial base radius and initial height of right circular cone be r_1 and h_1, respectively.

Final base radius i.e.

$$r_2 = r_1 + \frac{10}{100} \times r_1 = \frac{11r_1}{10}$$

Final height of right circular cone i.e.,

$$h_2 = h_1 + \frac{10}{100} \times h_1 = \frac{11h_1}{10}$$

Volume of initial right circular cone

$$= \frac{1}{3}\pi r_1^2 h_1$$

Volume of final right circular cone

$$= \frac{1}{3}\pi\left(\frac{11r_1}{10}\right)^2\left(\frac{11h_1}{10}\right)$$

$$= \frac{1}{3}\pi \times \left(\frac{121r_1^2}{100}\right) \times \left(\frac{11h_1}{10}\right)$$

$$= \frac{1331}{1000}\left(\frac{1}{3}\pi r_1^2 h_1\right)$$

Difference between volume $= V_E - V_I$

$$= \frac{1331}{1000}\left(\frac{1}{3}\pi r_1^2 h_1\right) - \frac{1}{3}\pi r_1^2 h_1$$

$$= \frac{331}{1000}\left(\frac{1}{3}\pi r_1^2 h_1\right)$$

$\therefore$ Percentage Increased

$$= \frac{\frac{331}{1000}\left(\frac{1}{3}\pi r_1^2 h_1\right)}{\left(\frac{1}{3}\pi r_1^2 h_1\right)} \times 100$$

$\Rightarrow$ Percent Increased = 33.1%

130. **(b)** Expenditure invested on

Rice = ₹ $25000 \times \frac{50}{100}$ = ₹ 12500

Wheat = ₹ $25000 \times \frac{20}{100}$ = ₹ 5000

Bajra = ₹ $25000 \times \frac{10}{100}$ = ₹ 2500

Jowar = ₹ $25000 \times \frac{8}{100}$ = ₹ 2000

Barley = ₹ $25000 \times \frac{12}{100}$ = ₹ 3000

According to question,

$$= \frac{\text{Expenditure of (Rice + Barley)}}{\text{Expenditure of (Wheat + Bajra)}} \times 100$$

$$= \left(\frac{15500}{7500} \times 100\right) = 206.66\%$$

131. **(c)** Perimeter of circle = 13.2 cm

Let r be radius of circle.

According to question,

$2\pi r = 13.2$ cm

$\Rightarrow \quad 2 \times \frac{22}{7} \times r = 13.2$

$\Rightarrow \quad r = \frac{13.2 \times 7}{22 \times 2}$

$\therefore \quad r = 2.1$ cm

132. **(a)** Length of train = 350 m

Length of tunnel = 1250 m

Time taken to pass the tunnel = 80 sec

Speed of train $= \frac{D}{T} = \frac{1250 + 350}{80}$

$= \frac{1600}{80} = 20$ m/sec

$\therefore$ Speed of train $= \left(20 \times \frac{18}{5}\right)$ km/h

$= 72$ km/h

133. **(d)** Legal department has a minimum number of employees in each organisation, as compare to other department.

134. **(a)** Let

$$y = \frac{a^2 - (b - c)^2}{(a + c)^2 - b^2} + \frac{b^2 - (a - c)^2}{(a + b)^2 - c^2} + \frac{c^2 - (a - b)^2}{(b + c)^2 - a^2}$$

{Using $a^2 - b^2 = (a + b)(a - b)$}

$$\Rightarrow y = \frac{(a + b - c)(a - b + c)}{(a + c - b)(a + b + c)} + \frac{(b - a + c)(b + a - c)}{(a + b + c)(a + b - c)} + \frac{(c - a + b)(c + a - b)}{(b + c + a)(b + c - a)}$$

$$\Rightarrow y = \frac{(a + b - c)}{(a + b + c)} + \frac{(b - a + c)}{(a + b + c)} + \frac{(c + a - b)}{(a + b + c)}$$

$$\Rightarrow y = \frac{a + b - c + b - a + c + c + a - b}{(a + b + c)}$$

$$\Rightarrow y = \frac{(a + b + c)}{(a + b + c)}$$

$\therefore y = 1$

135. **(b)**

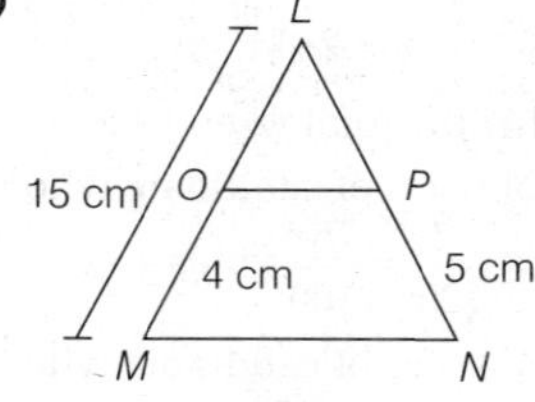

$OP \parallel MN$

Given, $LM = 15$ cm, $OM = 4$ cm and $PN = 5$ cm

$\therefore LO = LM - OM = (15 - 4)$ cm = 11

Let $LN = x$ cm

$\therefore LP = LN - PN = (x - 5)$ cm

In ΔLOP and ΔLMN,

$\angle LOP = \angle LMN$ [corresponding angles]

$\angle O\angle P = \angle MLN$ [common angle]

By AAA similarity, $\Delta LOP \cong \Delta LMN$

$\Rightarrow \dfrac{LO}{LM} = \dfrac{LP}{LN}$

$\Rightarrow \dfrac{11}{15} = \dfrac{x-5}{x}$

$\Rightarrow 11x = 15x - 75$

$\Rightarrow x = \dfrac{75}{4} = 18.75$ cm

Length of LN is 18.75 cm.

136. (c) Let $y = \sqrt{\dfrac{1+\sin A}{1-\sin A}}$

$\Rightarrow y = \sqrt{\dfrac{1+\sin A}{1-\sin A} \times \dfrac{(1+\sin A)}{(1+\sin A)}}$

$\Rightarrow y = \sqrt{\dfrac{(1+\sin A)^2}{1^2 - (\sin A^2)^2}}$

$\Rightarrow y = \sqrt{\dfrac{(1+\sin A)^2}{\cos^2 A}}$

$\{\because 1 - \sin^2\theta = \cos^2\theta\}$

$\Rightarrow y = \dfrac{1+\sin A}{\cos A}$

$= \dfrac{1}{\cos A} + \dfrac{\sin A}{\cos A}$

$\Rightarrow y = \sec A + \tan A$

137. (d) HCF of two number is 12.

Ratio of two number = 13 : 15

Let $13x$ and $15x$ and be the two number.

$\therefore x = 12$

LCM of $13x$ and $15x$

$= 13 \times 15 \times 12 = 2340$

138. (d) Number of Boy in school P = 280

Number of Girls in school P = 350

Number of Boys in school Q = 365

Number of Girls in school Q = 260

According to question,

Difference = Boys in school $(P + Q)$ − Girls in school $(P + Q)$

= 645 − 610

$\Rightarrow$ Difference = 35

139. (c) Average number of bicycle product at the factory per year from 1998 to 2002

$= \dfrac{800 + 600 + 900 + 1100 + 1200}{5}$

$= \dfrac{4600}{5} = 920$

140. (b) Factors of $4 = 2 \times 2$

Factors of $9 = 3 \times 3$

Factors of $12 = 2 \times 2 \times 3$

Factors of $15 = 3 \times 5$

LCM of 4, 9, 12, 15

$= 2 \times 2 \times 3 \times 3 \times 5 = 180$

$\therefore$ Remainder = 3

$\therefore$ Required number = 180 + 3 = 183

141. (a) From the given table, are get

Number of neem treesplanted in year 2021 = 5000

Number of birch trees planted in year 2022 = 9000

According to question,

Their ratio = 5000 : 9000 = 5 : 9

142. (b) MP of a item = ₹ 26000

Discount offered on MP is 18%.

Then, price of item

$= \left(26000 - 26000 \times \dfrac{18}{100}\right)$

= ₹ (26000 − 4680) = ₹ 21320

Let the additional seasonal discount be ₹ x

Then, SP of item become

= ₹ (21320 − x).

Given, SP of an item = ₹ 16000

Then, discount amount in

x = ₹ (21320 − 16000) = ₹ 5320

$\therefore$ Season discount D%

$= \left(\dfrac{D}{MP} \times 100\right)\%$

$\Rightarrow D\% = \left(\dfrac{5320}{21320} \times 100\right)\%$

$\Rightarrow D\% = 24.95\%$

143. (b) In ΔPQR, $\angle P = 90°$ and $\angle R = 47°$

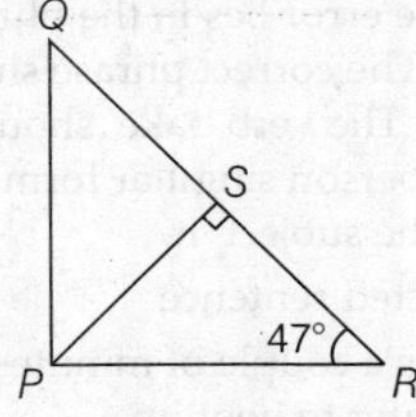

Sum of interior angle of triangle is 180°.

$\Rightarrow 90° + 47° + \angle Q = 180°$

$\angle Q = 180° - 137° = 43°$

In ΔPSQ,

$\angle Q = 43°$ and $\angle S = 90°$

According to question,

$\angle Q + \angle S + \angle P = 180°$

$\Rightarrow 43° + 90° + \angle P = 180°$

$\Rightarrow \angle P = 180° - 133° = 47°$

$\therefore \angle QPS = 47°$

144. (b)

(LCM of 8,12)
Total work

Time		Total work		
Sanjay	8	24	3 Units/day	
Rohan	12		2 Units/day	Efficiency

Efficiency of Rohan and Sanjay for 2 days = 3 + 2 = 5 units/ day

If the work alternate, the work done by both of them is 20 units in 8 days.

Remaining work = (24 − 20) units/day

= 4 units/day

Remaining work first started by Sanjay and then by Rohan total time for remaining work $= 1 + \dfrac{1}{2} = \dfrac{3}{2}$

Total time $= \left(8 + \dfrac{3}{2}\right) = 9\dfrac{1}{2}$ days

145. (b) Total population of state R is 26000.

Population above poverty line

$= 26000 \times \dfrac{76}{100} = 19760$

Ratio of male to female above poverty line = 3:3 = 1:1

Then, according to question

$\Rightarrow x + x = 19760$

$\Rightarrow 2x = 19760$

$\Rightarrow x = 9880$

Number of females above poverty line in state R is 9880.

146. (c) Let AB is a chord

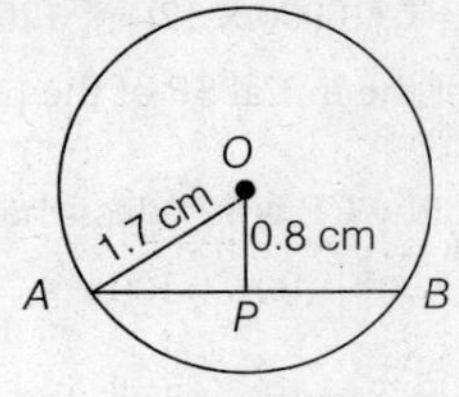

$OP \perp AB$

$OP = 0.8$ cm [given]

OP is distance between centre and chord radius of circle = 1.7 cm

In ΔOPA,

Applying pythagoras theorem,

$OA^2 = AP^2 + PO^2$

$\Rightarrow AP^2 = OA^2 - (PO)^2$

$\Rightarrow AP = \sqrt{(1.7)^2 - (0.8)^2}$

$\Rightarrow AP = \sqrt{2.89 - 0.64} = \sqrt{2.25}$

$\Rightarrow AP = 1.5$ cm

$\therefore$ Length of chord

$= AB = 2AP = 2 \times 1.5$ cm

= 3 cm

147. **(a)** Budget open on clothing = ₹ 2000

Total budget

$= 8000 + 2000 + 6000 + 4000$.

$=$ ₹ 20000

Clothing % $= \left(\frac{2000}{20000} \times 100\right) = 10\%$

Percentage of the monthly budget on clothing is 10%.

148. **(a)** HCF of 45 and 55 is 5.

According to question,

$\Rightarrow \quad 5 = 55 \times 5 + 45\,m$

$\Rightarrow \quad 5 = 275 + 45\,m$

$\Rightarrow \quad -270 = 45\,m \Rightarrow m = -6$

149. **(c)** Monthly salary of a person = ₹ 50000

He spend on Household is 40%, 25% on Rent and 15% on transportation.

Total expense = ₹ $50000 \times \frac{80}{100}$

$=$ ₹ 40000

Remaining amount is saving

$=$ ₹ $(50000 - 40000)$

$=$ ₹ 10000

Yearly saving of a person

$=$ ₹ (10000×12)

$=$ ₹ 120000

Speedy method

Monthly Salary of a person = ₹ 50000

Saving after all expenses

$=$ ₹ $\left(50000 \times \frac{20}{100}\right) =$ ₹ 10000

Person's yearly saving

$=$ ₹ $(10000 \times 12) =$ ₹ 120000

150. **(c)** Let the initial SP of the pulse be $100x$.

Then, the CP is 12% less than SP

$=$ ₹ $\left(100x - 100\,x \times \frac{12}{100}\right) =$ ₹ $88x$

To earn a profit of 25%, the final SP will be

i.e, $\text{SP} = \frac{125}{100} \times \text{CP}$

$\Rightarrow \quad \text{SP} = \frac{125}{100} \times 88$

$\Rightarrow \quad \text{SP} = 110$

$\therefore$ Difference in SP $= 110 - 100 = 10$

$\therefore$ Required % $= \left(\frac{\text{Difference}}{\text{Initial SP}} \times 100\right)\%$

$= \left(\frac{10}{100} \times 100\right)\% = 10\%$

151. **(d)** The phrase describes a collection of historical documents or records. An Archive fits this exactly, as it stores important records.

152. **(b)** The phrase 'provides useful advantage' matches the idiom grist to the mill, which means something that can be used to your benefit or advantage.

153. **(d)** The error lies in the phrase 'an noise'. The word 'noise' begins with a consonant sound, so it should be preceded by 'a' instead of 'an'.

154. **(d)** The word 'languid' means weak, sluggish, or lacking energy. The antonym of 'languid' would be something that conveys liveliness or energy, which in this case is 'animated'. The word 'animated' means full of life, energy, or excitement, making it the opposite of 'languid.'

155. **(b)** The idiom 'Steer clear of' means to avoid someone or something, especially because it is dangerous or harmful. It suggests consciously staying away from a situation or person to prevent trouble or harm.

156. **(d)** The word 'malice' refers to the desire to cause harm or ill will towards others. The antonym of malice would be 'sympathy', which means feeling compassion or concern for others.

157. **(a)** The error is in the phrase 'I was wish'. The correct expression should be 'I wished'because the past tense of the verb 'wish' is used here. The sentence should be in the past tense to maintain proper subject-verb agreement.

Corrected sentence

I wished to meet her on her birthday.

158. **(d)** The error lies in the phrase 'It is take'. The correct phrase should be 'It takes'. The verb 'take' should be in the third-person singular form to agree with the subject 'it.'

Corrected sentence

It takes a couple of minutes for the computer to boot up.

159. **(c)** The word 'pervasive' means something that is spreading widely throughout an area or affecting many people. The synonym 'widespread' fits perfectly in this context as it also means something that is broadly distributed or commonly occurring.

160. **(c)** The word 'Abdact' is incorrectly spelt. The correct spelling is 'Abduct', which means to take someone away illegally, especially by force.

161. **(a)** The phrase 'be over and done with' means to complete or finish something in a straightforward manner. It aligns perfectly with the context of the boss wanting to finish the case before the arrival of the inspection team.

162. **(d)** The word 'cruise' refers to a journey, typically by sea, or moving smoothly and at a steady pace. The synonym 'voyage' also refers to a long journey, especially by sea or in space, making it the most appropriate choice.

163. **(d)** The idiom 'let bygones be bygones' means to forgive and forget past mistakes or grievances and move on, without holding onto resentment or anger. It suggests ignoring the past and not letting it affect the present or future.

164. **(b)** The phrase 'whatever labour that was available to them' indicates that farmers had to make do with the available or limited resources. The most appropriate improvement is to use 'limited labour', which clearly conveys the idea that the amount of labor they had access to was restricted or not abundant.

165. **(d)** The idiom 'eat humble pie' means to admit one's mistakes and apologise for them. It conveys the idea of being humble and recognising that one's actions were wrong.

166. **(b)** The correct word here is 'well', as it is the appropriate adverb to describe how someone performs a task. In this case, Malati does her job in a good manner, so the adverb 'well' is the correct choice.

167. **(d)** The word 'fierce' typically refers to something intensely aggressive, violent, or passionate. It's often used to describe emotions like anger or behaviour that is intense and forceful.

168. **(d)** The word 'Faithful' means remaining loyal and steadfast, especially in relationships, duties or beliefs.

'Loyal directly' reflects this meaning, indicating support, devotion or allegiance.

169. **(a)** The idiom 'make it big' means to achieve great success or fame in a particular field.

In the context, 'Yamini is a great singer' implies her talent will help her rise to success, hence the idiom refers to achieving recognition and popularity.

170. **(c)** The word 'malice' means the intention or desire to cause harm, ill will, or spite.

The opposite of that is Kindness', which involves benevolence, goodwill and a desire to do good to others.

171. **(d)** The word 'piece' (a portion or part) is incorrect in this context.

The correct word is 'peace', which refers to a state of calmness, tranquility, or contentment.

He found peace at home - not a physical 'piece'.

172. **(b)** 'Trousseau' is a French-origin word meaning the collection of clothes and personal possessions a bride brings for her marriage.

173. **(b)** The term 'omnipotent' means all-powerful. In the sentence, God is described as having absolute control, which perfectly matches the meaning of 'omnipotent'.

174. **(d)** 'Long ago' fits best because it refers to something that happened a significant time black matching the idea of ' some point in the past'.

175. **(c)** A 'pergola' is a garden structure made with vertical posts and an open lattice, often covered with climbing plants, providing a shaded walkway or sitting area.

176. **(c)** The phrase 'yearning for' means longing for or keenly desiring something.

177. **(d)** The idiom 'hold your horses' means to wait or be patient, especially when you're eager to act or speak.

In the given situation, the person controlled themselves and remained patient, which perfectly fits the idiom.

178. **(d)** The idiom 'step up to the plate' originates from baseball and means to take responsibility or to take charge of a situation, especially when action is needed. It doesn't mean merely planning or thinking, but actively taking initiative.

179. **(b)** The idiom 'under the nose' means doing something right in front of someone, usually without them noticing or stopping it.

In the sentence, eating the grapes 'under the nose of all of us' implies he did it openly and in full view.

180. **(a)** The incorrectly spelt word is 'prefered'.

The correct spelling is 'Preferred', with double 'r'.

181. **(b)** 'Magnificent' refers to something that is extremely beautiful, elaborate or impressive, which matches the given description.

182. **(b)** The idiom 'to burn the midnight oil' means to work or study late into the night, often used in academic or professional contexts to describe dedication or last-minute effort.

183. **(d)** The word 'inevitable' means something that is certain to happen; unavoidable.

184. **(a)** The incorrectly spelt word is 'affidevit.

The correct spelling is 'affidavit'.

185. **(b)** The correct form should be 'We have been', as 'have been' is the proper present perfect continuous auxiliary.

'Being' is incorrect in this structure.

186. **(d)** 'Extravagance' means excessive or unnecessary spending, often linked to luxury or indulgence.

'Self-indulgence' refers to excessive gratification of one's own desires, making it the closest synonym.

187. **(a)** The word 'antique' refers to something old and often valuable due to its age, especially in the context of art or furniture.

'Ancient' is the closest synonym as it relates to something from a very long time ago.

188. **(c)** The incorrectly spelt word is "pharohs'.

The correct spelling is 'pharaohs'.

189. **(b)** The correct spelling is 'bread', not 'braed'.

190. **(b)** The correct structure is 'thinking about applying', which uses the preposition 'about' followed by a gerund (applying).

191. **(b)** The word ' biased' fits best in blank no. 1

192. **(c)** The word 'trigger' fits best in blank no. 2

193. **(b)** The word ' anxiety' fits best in blank no. 3

194. **(c)** The word 'illicit' fits best in blank no. 4

195. **(c)** The word 'decline' fits best in blank no. 5

196. **(c)** The word 'perfect' in the passage refers to an ideal or flawless life portrayed online. The opposite of perfect in this context would be unsatisfactory, which implies something flawed or lacking.

197. **(b)** The passage mentions quick messages, emojis, acronyms, and hashtags as changes in communication, but it does not mention video conferencing at all.

198. **(a)** The passage reflects both the positives (global connection, memes, friendships) and negatives (pressure, distraction, oversharing) of social media.

199. **(d)** One of the explicit downsides mentioned in the passage is the pressure of portraying an idealised version of life on social media.

200. **(c)** The overall theme of the passage explores both the advantages (connection, laughter, friendships) and drawbacks (distraction, pressure, unrealistic expectations) of social media use.

CPO SI P-1 SP 15

PAPER-1

SSC CPO SI SOLVED PAPER

4 October 2023 (Shift II)

Instructions

1. This paper contains 200 questions.
2. It has 4 Parts, **Part I** General Intelligence and Reasoning, **Part II** General Knowledge and General Awareness, **Part III** Quantitative Aptitude and **Part IV** English Comprehension.
3. Each question carries **1 marks**.

MM : 200 **Time :** 2 hr

Part I

General Intelligence and Reasoning

1. Select the option figure in which the given figure is embedded as its part (rotation is not allowed).

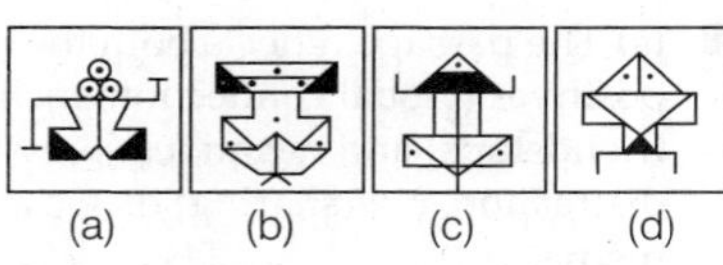

(a) (b) (c) (d)

2. If the given sheet is folded to form a cube, which of the following figures is possible?

7	8	9
	X	
	Y	
	Z	

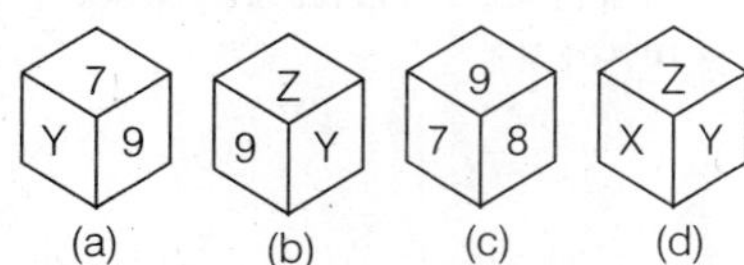

(a) (b) (c) (d)

3. Which letter-cluster will replace the question mark (?) to complete the given series?

AXFN, GCJQ, MHNT, ?, YRVZ

(a) SWMR (b) QRLV

(c) RLQV (d) SMRW

4. 'F $ G' means 'F is the mother of G'.
'F # G' means 'F is the father of G'.
'F @ G' means 'F is the husband of G'.
'F % G' means 'F is the daughter of G'.
If J @ C $ B # R, then how is J related to R?

(a) Mother's brother

(b) Father

(c) Father's sister

(d) Father's father

5. In a certain code language, 'SUGAR' is coded as 81 and 'FILL' is coded as 51. How will 'CREAM' be coded in that language?

(a) 52 (b) 60

(c) 57 (d) 55

6. Select the set in which the numbers are related in the same way as are the numbers of the following sets.

(**Note** Operations should be performed on the whole numbers, without breaking down the numbers into its constituent digits. E.g. 13- Operations on 13 such as adding/subtracting/multiplying etc. to 13 can be performed. Breaking down 13 into 1 and 3 and then performing mathematical operations on 1 and 3 is not allowed.)

(7, 2, 70)

(6, 4, 120)

(a) (3, 8, 120) (b) (13, 4, 208)

(c) (5, 9, 270) (d) (11, 6, 143)

7. Select the option that is related to the third term in the same way as the second term is related to the first term and the sixth term is related to the fifth term.

16 : 106 :: 11 : ? :: 10 : 22

(a) 36 (b) 42 (c) 40 (d) 31

8. Which figure from the given options would replace the question mark (?), if the following figure series were to be continued?

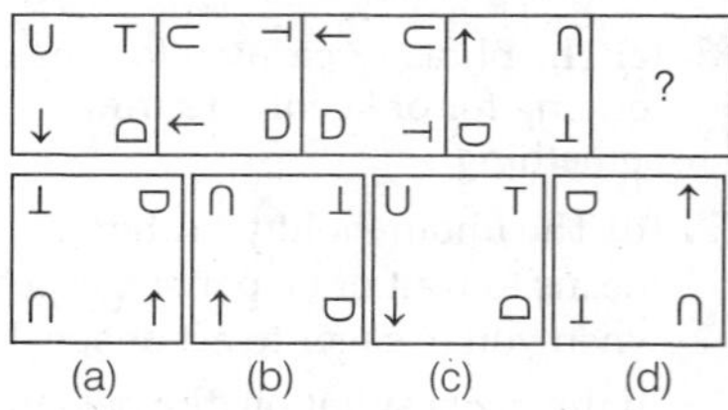

(a) (b) (c) (d)

9. Which letter-cluster will replace the question mark (?) to complete the given series?

PJVG, VBZB, BTDW, HLHR,?

(a) NDLN (b) MDLN

(c) MDLM (d) NDLM

10. Which of the given figures when placed in the 5th position would continue the series that is established by the first four figures?

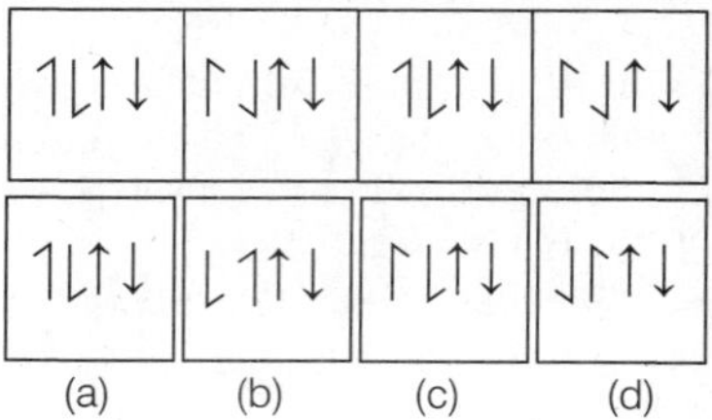

(a) (b) (c) (d)

11. Select the figure that will come next in the following figure series.

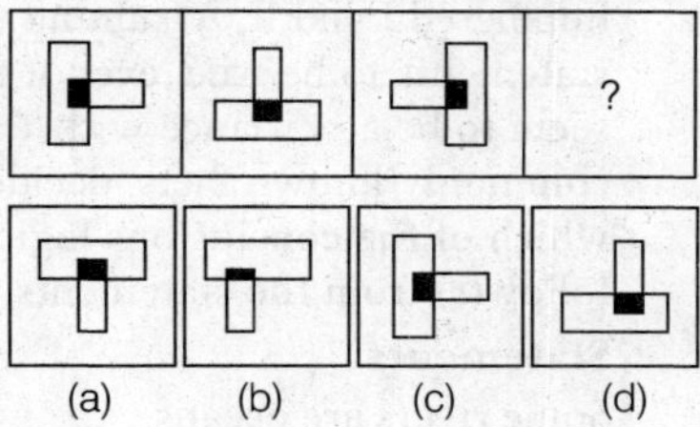

12. Select the correct option that indicates the arrangement of the given words in the order in which they appear in an English dictionary.

1. Doctor 2. Doctorate
3. Docile 4. Documentary
5. Dock 6. Doctrine

(a) 3, 5, 1, 2, 6, 4 (b) 3, 5, 1, 6, 2, 4
(c) 3, 5, 2, 1, 6, 4 (d) 3, 4, 5, 1, 2, 6

13. Six characters A, B, C, 1, 2 and 3 are written on different faces of a dice. Two positions of this dice are shown in the figure. Find the character on the face opposite to A.

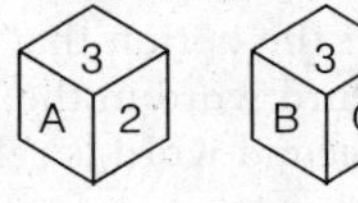

(a) C (b) 2 (c) B (d) 1

14. Which of the following numbers will replace the question mark (?) in the given series?

$\frac{1}{121}, \frac{1}{11}, 1, ?, 121$

(a) 11 (b) 12 (c) 21 (d) 1

15. Two statements are given, followed by two conclusions numbered I and II. Assuming the statements to be true, even if they seem to be at variance with commonly known facts, decide which of the conclusions logically follow(s) from the statements.

Statements

Some movies are dramas.
Some dramas are fiction.

Conclusions

I. Some movies are fiction.
II. All fiction are movies.

(a) Only Conclusion I follows
(b) Only Conclusion II follows
(c) Neither Conclusion I nor II follows
(d) Both Conclusions I and II follow

16. If A denotes '+', B denotes '×', C denotes '–', and D denotes '÷', then what will be the value of the following equation?

22 B 7 C 288 D 12 A 27 = ?

(a) 160 (b) 103
(c) 130 (d) 157

17. Select the option that is related to the fourth term in the same way as the first term is related to the second term and the fifth term is related to the sixth term.

12 : 64 :: ? :116 :: 32 : 144

(a) 25 (b) 46
(c) 35 (d) 14

18. If A denotes '+', B denotes '×', C denotes '–', and D denotes '÷', then what will be the value of the following equation ?

21 B 14 C 154 D 14 A 42 = ?

(a) 357 (b) 325
(c) 342 (d) 352

19. If A denotes '+ ', B denotes '×', C denotes '–', and D denotes '÷', then what will come in place of '?' in the following equation ?

56 D 8 B 7 = ? B 7

(a) 9 (b) 7
(c) 8 (d) 12

20. Aunt Gloria walked out of her house and walked 65 m towards the East. She took a left turn and walked 28 m. Again, she took a left turn and walked 110 m to reach a public library. How far (shortest distance) and in which direction is the library from Aunt Gloria's house?

(a) 48 m, North-East
(b) 48 m, North-West
(c) 53 m, North-East
(d) 53 m, North-West

21. Select the set in which the numbers are related in the same way as are the numbers of the following set. (**Note** Operations should be performed on the whole numbers, without breaking down the numbers into its constituent digits. E.g. 13 – Operations on 13 such as adding /subtracting/ multiplying etc. to 13 can be performed. Breaking down 13 into 1 and 3 and then performing mathematical operations on 1 and 3 is not allowed)

(9, 1, 19)
(5, 2, 14)

(a) (3,5,56) (b) (3,2,10)
(c) (2,5,12) (d) (4,7,37)

22. A cube is made by folding the given sheet. In the cube so formed, which pair of letters will be on the opposite faces?

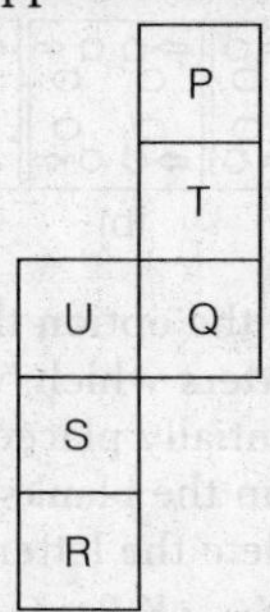

(a) T and S (b) R and P
(c) P and U (d) U and T

23. A @ B means 'A is the husband of B'
A & B means 'A is the mother of B'
A # B means 'A is the daughter f B'.
If Z # L @ P & K @ J # X, then how is K related to Z?

(a) Brother (b) Sister
(c) Mother (d) Brother' wife

24. In a certain code language, 'ALIVE' is coded as 64 and 'HALL' is coded as 45. How will 'MOVIE' be coded in that language?

(a) 71 (b) 80 (c) 79 (d) 58

25. Six students Prateek, Sameer, Kabir, Ziya, Joseph, Kiran are sitting around a circular table facing the centre (not necessarily in the same order). Prateek is an immediate neighbour of both Sameer and Kabir. Ziya is sitting second to the right of Sameer. Kiran is sitting third to the left of Kabir. Joseph is an immediate neighbour of both Ziya and Kabir. Who is an immediate neighbour of Ziya?

(a) Prateek (b) Kabir
(c) Sameer (d) Kiran

26. If A denotes '+', B denotes '×' , C denotes '–', D denotes '÷', then what will be the value of the following expression?

89 A 94 C 35 D 8 B 8 = ?

(a) 148 (b) 189
(c) 169 (d) 135

27. The sequence of folding a piece of paper and the manner in which the folded paper is cut as shown in the following figures. How would this paper look when unfolded?

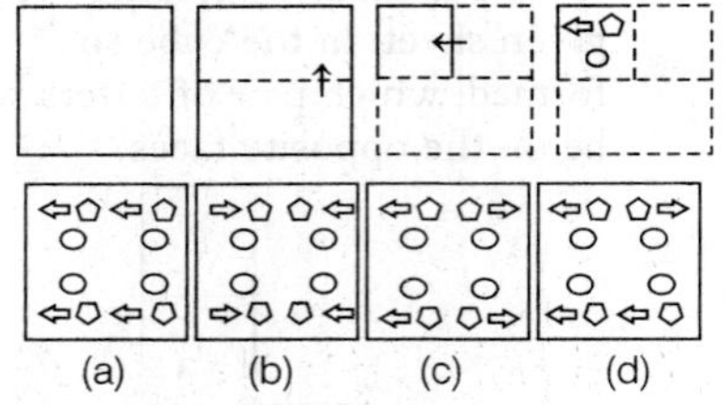

28. Select the option that represents the letters which, when sequentially placed from left to right in the blanks below, will complete the letter series.

F _ _ Y _ _ K B _ O F _ B Y _

(a) O F K B O Y K (b) B Y O K F O K
(c) K B O F Y K O (d) Y O K B F O K

29. Select the option that is related to the fifth letter-cluster in the same way as the second letter-cluster is related to the first letter-cluster and the fourth letter-cluster is related to the third letter-cluster.

INDIA : FKAFX :: ESTONIA : BPQLKFX:: MALAYSIA :?

(a) JPFXXIXV (b) JXVPFXXI
(c) JXIXFXVP (d) JXIXVPFX

30. In a certain code language, 'PAINT' is written as 'ODYTN' and 'BRUSH' is written as 'CMMOZ'. How will 'HOUSE' be written in that language?

(a) WDNOS (b) WPMOC
(c) PHYWS (d) PBOMS

31. Select the option that represents the correct order of the given words as they would appear in an English dictionary?

1. Wrist 2. Wrangle
3. Workable 4. Wrongful
5. Woodland

(a) 3, 5, 2, 1, 4 (b) 3, 2, 5, 1, 4
(c) 5, 2, 3, 1, 4 (d) 5, 3, 2, 1, 4

32. Select the correct mirror image of the given figure when the mirror is placed at MN as shown below.

M
8BEYTK@8 |
N

(a) 8&ꓘTYƎB8 (b) 8@ꓘ⊥⅄ƎB8
(c) 8@ꓘTYƎB8 (d) 8&ꓘ⊥⅄ƎB8

33. Two statements are given, followed by two conclusions numbered I and II. Assuming the statements to be true, even if they seem to be at variance with commonly known facts, decide which of the conclusions logically follow(s) from the statements.

Statements

Some apples are oranges.
All oranges are fruits.

Conclusions

I. All apples are fruits.
II. Some fruits are oranges.

(a) Neither Conclusion I nor II follows
(b) Only Conclusion II follows
(c) Both Conclusions I and II follow
(d) Only Conclusion I follows

34. Manohar cycles x km towards West and then turns right and cycles y km to reach his office. Now, the shortest distance between the starting point and his office is 13 km.

What can be the value of x and y, respectively, (in km)?

(a) 12 and 5 (b) 8 and 5
(c) 11 and 6 (d) 6 and 7

35. In a certain code language, 'EARS' is coded as '4268' and 'NICE' is coded as '9723'. What is the code for 'E' in the given code language?

(a) 3 (b) 2 (c) 9 (d) 4

36. Six people are sitting around a circular table facing the centre. P sits second to the left of Q. S is an immediate neighbour of both Q and U. T sits second to the left of R. Who is the immediate neighbour of both P and U?

(a) T (b) S (c) Q (d) R

37. Based on the position in the English alphabetical order, three of the following letter-clusters are alike in some manner and one is different. Select the odd letter-cluster.

(a) SWYX (b) PTVU
(c) RVXW (d) LOQP

38. Four letter-clusters have been given, out of which three are alike in some manner and one is different. Select the odd letter-cluster.

(a) GCKD (b) UQYR
(c) XOTP (d) NJRK

39. Two statements are given, followed by two conclusions numbered I and II. Assuming the statements to be true, even if they seem to be at variance with commonly known facts, decide which of the conclusions logically follow(s) from the statements.

Statements

Some rivers are oceans.
All oceans are beaches.

Conclusions

I. Some rivers are beaches.
II. All oceans are rivers.

(a) Only Conclusion II follows
(b) Both Conclusions I and II follow
(c) Neither Conclusion I nor II follows
(d) Only Conclusion I follows

40. If '+' means '×', '–' means '÷', '×' means '+', and '÷' means '–', then what will be the value of the following expression ?

$42 \times 168 - 8 \div 4 + 3 = ?$

(a) 62 (b) 45
(c) 56 (d) 51

41. Select the option that is related to the third word in the same way as the second word is related to the first word.

(The words must be considered as meaningful words and must not be related to each other based on the number of letters/number of consonants/vowels in the word.)

Artist : Painting :: Cobbler : ?

(a) Stitching clothes
(b) Fixing shoes
(c) Wooden repair work
(d) Fixes electricity

42. Which two mathematical signs should be interchanged to make the given equation correct?

$15 \times 3 \div 15 - (45 \times 3) - 10 + (13 \div 2) = 76$

(a) ÷ and × (b) × and +
(c) × and – (d) ÷ and +

43. If '+' means '–', '–' means '×', '×' means '÷', '÷' means '+', then what will come in place of the question mark (?) in the following equation ?

$23 - 5 \div 240 \times 8 + 14 = ?$

(a) 145 (b) 119
(c) 131 (d) 124

44. Select the correct mirror image of the given figure when the mirror is placed at line MN as shown.

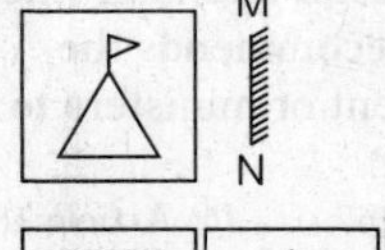

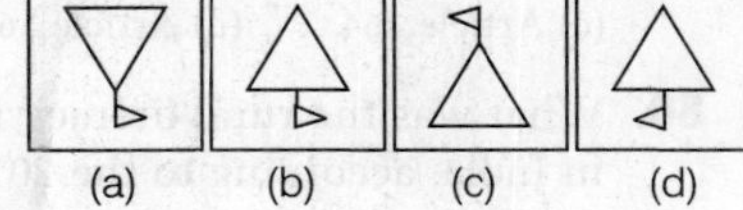

45. Two statements are given followed by two conclusions numbered I and II. Assuming the statements to be true, even if they seem to be at variance with commonly known facts, decide which of the conclusions logically follow(s) from the statements.

Statements

All teas are juices.

All juices are cocktails.

Conclusions

I. All teas are cocktails.

II. All cocktails are definitely juices.

(a) Both Conclusions I and II follow
(b) Only Conclusion II follows
(c) Only Conclusion I follows
(d) Neither Conclusion I nor II follows

46. In a certain code language, 'ACTOR' is coded as ROYCA and 'NURSE' is coded as ESWUN. How will 'JUDGE' be coded in the same language?

(a) EGJUI (b) GEIUJ
(c) EGUIJ (d) EGIUJ

47. Which of the following numbers will replace the question mark (?) in the given series?

76, 99, 135, 185, 250, ?

(a) 330 (b) 331 (c) 328 (d) 315

48. A cube is made by folding the given sheet. In the cube so formed, which letter will be on the face opposite to the face having 'F'?

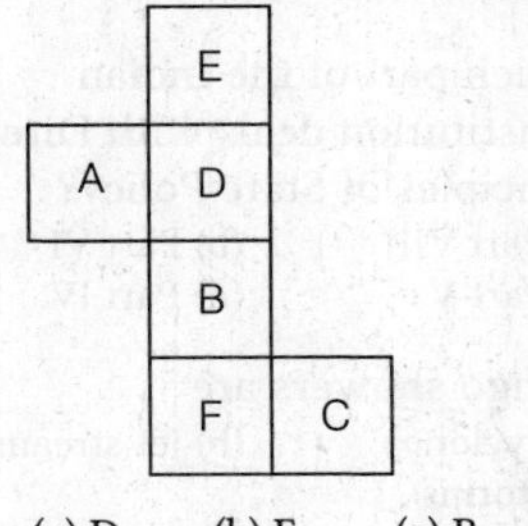

(a) D (b) E (c) B (d) A

49. Which of the following numbers will replace the question mark (?) in the given series?

4, 11, 19, 31, 52, 89, ?

(a) 151 (b) 105
(c) 150 (d) 115

50. Which of the following numbers will replace the question mark (?) in the given series?

134, 129, 122, ?, 102, 89

(a) 117 (b) 113
(c) 111 (d) 115

Part II

General Knowledge and General Awareness

51. Which of the following Articles of the Indian Constitution empowers the Parliament to restrict or abrogate the fundamental rights of the members of the armed forces, paramilitary forces, police forces, intelligence agencies and analogous forces?

(a) Article 35 (b) Article 31
(c) Article 33 (d) Article 37

52. Mohenjodaro site of Harappan Civilisation is situated on the bank of which river?

(a) Jhelum river
(b) Indus river
(c) Ghaghara river
(d) Beas river

53. The Wadali Brothers are ...... singers.

(a) pandavani (b) lavani
(c) sufi (d) bhatiali

54. Rongker festival is celebrated by which of the following tribes?

(a) Karbi (b) Gond
(c) Bhil (d) Ao

55. Who among the following Mauryan kings turned to Buddhism and its tenet of non-violence after the Kalinga War?

(a) Chandragupta Maurya
(b) Bindusara
(c) Ashoka
(d) Dasharatha

56. What is the name of the large supercontinent that existed 200 million years ago when all the continents were together?

(a) Asia (b) India
(c) Pangea (d) America

57. Who explained the structure of protein?

(a) RF Rose
(b) Emil Fischer
(c) Johnson and Cristae
(d) Pauling and Corey

58. According to Census of India 2011, identify the third largest spoken language in India.

(a) Tamil (b) Marathi
(c) Bengali (d) Hindi

59. Which of the following taxes is proportional in nature?

(a) Capital Gains Tax
(b) Income Tax
(c) Corporation Tax
(d) Goods and Services Tax

60. Gopika Varma has won the Sangeet Natak Akademi Award in 2019 in which of the following dance forms?

(a) Kathak (b) Bharatanatyam
(c) Mohiniyattam (d) Kuchipudi

61. What is the IUPAC name of the organic compound depicted in the figure?

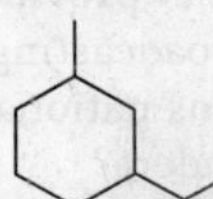

(a) 1-Methyl-1-Propylcyclohexane
(b) 1-Methyl-2-Propylcyclohexane
(c) 1-Methyl-4-Propylcyclohexane
(d) 1-Methyl-3-Propylcyclohexane

62. Identify whether the given statements about ionisation energy are correct or incorrect.

Statement A The ionisation energy of an atom is the amount of energy that is required to remove an electron from a mole of atoms in the gas phase.

Statement B The ionisation energy increases from top to bottom in groups and decreases from left to right across a period.

(a) Both statements A and B are correct.
(b) Only statement A is correct.
(c) Both statements A and B are incorrect.
(d) Only statement B is correct.

63. Which of the following sports does not have its apex national governing body headquartered in New Delhi?

(a) Athletes Federation of India
(b) Badminton Association of India
(c) Volleyball Federation of India
(d) Hockey India

64. Which of the following is an autobiography of a Bengali illiterate woman who secretly acquired literacy skills to read sacred texts in an age when girls and women were denied education and deemed fit only for household chores?
(a) Ente Katha by Kamala Das
(b) Amar Jiban by Rassundari Devi
(c) Jina Amucha by Baby Kamble
(d) Smritichitre by Lakshmibai Tilak

65. The Lucknow Pact was signed in .... by Congress and the Muslim League to work in alliance for representative government.
(a) 1920 (b) 1914
(c) 1916 (d) 1918

66. What is most important health benefits of Vitamin D?
(a) Strengthening of bones and muscles.
(b) Reducing the blood pressure.
(c) Rapid growth after teenage years.
(d) Elevation of heartbeat.

67. What is the name of the geostationary satellite launched by ISRO in 1983 that provides high power TV broadcasting and telecommunications national coverage transponders?
(a) Bhaskara-I
(b) Insat-1B
(c) GSAT-7
(d) RISAT-1

68. Which Article of the Indian Constitution provides for equal opportunity for all citizens in the matter of employment under the state?
(a) Article 17 (b) Article 16
(c) Article 18 (d) Article 15

69. Which Rajput princess belonged to the Bhakti tradition of Medieval India, whose songs were devoted to Lord Krishna?
(a) Mirabai
(b) Muddupalani
(c) Lal Ded
(d) Akka Mahadevi

70. When was the National Interim Government of India formed, under Jawaharlal Nehru?
(a) 2nd September, 1946
(b) 2nd September, 1947
(c) 20th September, 1946
(d) 2nd September, 1945

71. Which among the following is incorrect about the salient features of the 73rd Amendment Act?
(a) The Act gives a Constitutional status to the Panchayati Raj Institutions.
(b) It contains 29 functional items of the Panchayats and deals with Article 243 to 243(O).
(c) The Act has added the Eleventh Schedule to the Constitution of India.
(d) The Act corresponds to Part III of the Constitution of India.

72. Which element of the boron family has a high boiling point, making it ideal for recording temperatures that would vaporise a thermometer?
(a) Thallium (b) Aluminium
(c) Gallium (d) Indium

73. How many medal(s) did India win in the World Athletics Championship 2022?
(a) 4 (b) 2
(c) 3 (d) 1

74. Who became the first Indian to win the prestigious Zurich Diamond League Final 2022 in Switzerland?
(a) Rameshbabu Praggnanandhaa
(b) Mary Kom
(c) Neeraj Chopra
(d) PV Sindhu

75. Which of the following government departments is associated with infrastructure development in India?
(a) Division of Economic Agenda
(b) Division of Electricity Agenda
(c) Department of Energy Affairs
(d) Department of Economic Affairs

76. Identify an anomaly element that belongs to both group 1 and group 17.
(a) Oxygen (b) Hydrogen
(c) Chlorine (d) Nitrogen

77. The Vijayanagara kingdom was established by .... in 1336.
(a) Venkata II
(b) Devaraya II
(c) Krishnadevaraya
(d) Harihara and Bukka

78. Which of the following is the new alluvium deposited by floods in the Ganga plain?
(a) Regur (b) Khadar
(c) Kachhar (d) Bhangar

79. Which of the following Articles of the Constitution of India provides that the Governor appoints the Chief Minister and later, the Chief Minister recommends the appointment of ministers to the Governor?
(a) Article 167 (b) Article 165
(c) Article 164 (d) Article 163

80. What was the rural literacy rate in India, according to the 2011 Census?
(a) 67.00% (b) 68.91%
(c) 67.77% (d) 69.00%

81. FIFA Women's World Cup 2023 will be hosted by ....
(a) Australia and New Zealand
(b) USA and Canada
(c) France and Germany
(d) Brazil and Argentina

82. The President of India decides on the question as to the disqualification of Members of Parliament in consultation with the ....
(a) Supreme Court of India
(b) Parliament
(c) Vice-President
(d) Election Commission of India

83. Mohiniyattam, a classical dance of India belongs to which of the following states?
(a) Uttar Pradesh (b) Kerala
(c) Andhra Pradesh (d) Manipur

84. Which of the following is not an example of manufacturing activity?
(a) Yarn made from cotton.
(b) Sugar made from sugarcane.
(c) Paper made from wood.
(d) Mutual fund product made by combing debt and equity funds.

85. Which of the following is incorrect match?
(a) Pressure – Pascal
(b) Volume – Metre
(c) Force – Newton
(d) Work done – Joule

86. Which part of the Indian Constitution deals with Directive Principles of State Policy?
(a) Part VII (b) Part VI
(c) Part V (d) Part IV

87. Mango showers are
(a) cyclones (b) jet streams
(c) storms
(d) pre-monsoon showers

88. What type of climate is found in North-Western Europe, West Coast of North America, North of California, Southern Chile, South-Eastern Australia and New Zealand?
(a) Marine West coast climate
(b) Cold snow forest climate
(c) Sub-tropical steppe climate
(d) Tropical wet and dry climate

89. Which of the following places of India can have maximum temperature difference between the day and night?
(a) Thiruvananthapuram
(b) Jaisalmer
(c) Port Blair
(d) Kanyakumari

90. Mohiniyattam belongs to which of the following states?
(a) Jharkhand (b) Chhattisgarh
(c) Karnataka (d) Kerala

91. Haripriya Namboodiri is an exponent of which Indian classical dance form?
(a) Kathakali (b) Kuchipudi
(c) Odissi (d) Bharatanatyam

92. During one of the Five-Year Plans, which of the following politicians gave the slogan 'Garibi Hatao'?
(a) Charan Singh
(b) Gaini Zail Singh
(c) Morarji Desai
(d) Indira Gandhi

93. During which phase of the cell, cycle does metabolic changes assemble the cytoplasmic material required for mitosis and cytokinesis?
(a) G2 phase (b) G1 phase
(c) S phase (d) M phase

94. Expenditure of the government on health facilities, education and fixed-asset acquisition is termed as ....
(a) revenue expenditure
(b) plan expenditure
(c) non-plan revenue expenditure
(d) capital expenditure

95. Which of the following is the autobiography of the first Indian President Dr. Rajendra Prasad?
(a) Atmavrittanta
(b) Atmakatha
(c) A Shot at History
(d) My Country My Life

96. Which of the following policy measures is a step towards liberalisation?
(a) Enhancing tariffs.
(b) Eliminating licenses for importing a majority of goods.
(c) Imposing limits on capital accumulation.
(d) Increasing requirements for bank reserves and restrictions on interest rates.

97. Which of the following cultural festivals of South India is associated with the folklore of King Mahabali?
(a) Gudi Padwa (b) Ugadi
(c) Pongal (d) Onam

98. Europeans entered India with a mindset of trading only. This streak was initiated by which of the following European nations?
(a) French (b) Portuguese
(d) British (d) Dutch

99. How big are red blood cells in diameter?
(a) 7.5 μ (b) 2.0 μ (c) 4.0 μ (d) 40.0 μ

100. In which year Timur's invasion of Delhi took place?
(a) 1492 (b) 1221 (c) 1526 (d) 1398

Part III

Quantitative Aptitude

101. Find the value of $\sqrt{\frac{1-\tan A}{1+\tan A}}$.
(a) $\sqrt{\frac{1+\sin 2A}{\cos 2A}}$ (b) $\sqrt{\frac{1-\sin 2A}{\cos 2A}}$
(c) $\sqrt{\frac{1+\sin A}{\cos A}}$ (d) $\sqrt{\frac{1-\sin A}{\cos A}}$

102. If the diameter of a sphere is reduced to its half, then the volume would be
(a) increased by $\frac{1}{4}$ of the former volume
(b) reduced by $\frac{1}{4}$ of the former volume
(c) increased by $\frac{1}{8}$ of the former volume
(d) reduced by $\frac{1}{8}$ of the former volume

103. The HCF of 3888 and 3969 is
(a) 81 (b) 73 (c) 83 (d) 71

104. Which is the smallest natural number that is exactly divisible by each of 96, 108 and 144?
(a) 864 (b) 2592 (c) 1296 (d) 1728

105. Find the HCF of 240, 280 and 560.
(a) 30 (b) 10 (c) 20 (d) 40

106. The following table shows the number of mobile phones sold by four different stores in four different years.

Stores	2012	2013	2014	2015
P	178	183	205	225
Q	133	198	220	235
R	284	250	220	198
S	225	243	199	205

Find the difference between the number of mobile phones sold by Store Q in 2013 and Store S in 2015.
(a) 12 (b) 7 (c) 10 (d) 8

107. The table below shows the production of jute fabric (in lakh metre) by two Companies P and Q during 2001 to 2005.

Year	Company P	Company Q
2001	100	96
2002	120	130
2003	108	100
2004	190	180
2005	240	275

In which year/years, did Company Q produce more fabric than Company P?
(a) 2002 (b) 2005
(c) 2003, 2005 (d) 2002, 2005

108. A car, during its entire journey of 5 h, travels the first 45 min at a certain speed, the next 75 min at a speed of 85 km/h, and the last 3 h at a speed of 70 km/h. During its entire journey, the average speed of the car is found to be 73 km/h. What is the speed (in km/h) of the car during the first 45 min?
(a) 65 (b) 68 (c) 62 (d) 72

109. Peter invested a certain sum of money in a scheme paying 10% simple interest per annum, while Rachel invested half of the sum that Peter invested in a scheme paying 10% interest per annum compounded annually. Also, while Peter invested for 2 yr, Rachel invested for 3 yr. If the difference in the interest earned by Peter and Rachel was ₹ 897, what was the sum that Rachel had invested?
(a) ₹ 13000 (b) ₹ 12900
(c) ₹ 13100 (d) ₹ 12960

110. The price of almonds is increased by 10%. By what percentage should the consumption be decreased, so that the expenditure remains the same?

(a) $9\frac{1}{11}\%$ (b) $5\frac{3}{11}\%$
(c) $8\frac{1}{11}\%$ (d) $10\frac{3}{11}\%$

111. A vendor marked the selling price of a table at ₹ 5670 after adding 35% profit to its cost price. Since, the sale was very low at this price level, he decided to sell the table with 12% profit. Find the new selling price (in ₹).

(a) 4810 (b) 4750
(c) 4704 (d) 4608

112. The time taken to travel the same distance by three cars are in the ratio of 12:15:10. What is the ratio of the speeds of the three cars?

(a) 4 : 5 : 6 (b) 4 : 6 : 5
(c) 5 : 4 : 6 (d) 5 : 6 : 4

113. Find the area of a triangle, whose length of two sides are 4 cm and 5 cm and the angle between them is 45°.

(a) $4\sqrt{2}$ cm^2 (b) $7\sqrt{2}$ cm^2
(c) $5\sqrt{2}$ cm^2 (d) $6\sqrt{2}$ cm^2

114. If a shopkeeper allows a discount of 10% to his customers and still gains 30%, then the marked price of an article which costs ₹ 450 is

(a) ₹ 700 (b) ₹ 650
(c) ₹ 500 (d) ₹ 750

115. The fourth proportional to 0.3, 0.8 and 0.108 is

(a) 0.144 (b) 0.124
(c) 0.288 (d) 0.482

116. Simplify the given expression.

$$\frac{(3.254 \times 3.254 \times 3.254) \times (0.746 \times 0.746 \times 0.746)}{(3.254 \times 3.254) + (0.746 \times 0.746) + (3.254 \times 0.746)}$$

(a) 3.156 (b) 4.508
(c) 2.146 (d) 2.508

117. The price of a land passing through three hands rises on the whole by 65%. The first and second sellers earned 20% and 25% profit, respectively. Find the profit percentage earned by the third seller.

(a) 10% (b) 20% (c) 25% (d) 15%

118. Study the given table and answer the question that follows.

The table shows the number of people, who responded to a survey about their favourite style of music.

Age	18-20	21-30	31+
Classical	8	5	15
Pop	5	11	10
Hip-Hop	6	9	8
Rock	9	7	13
Total	28	32	46

What percentage of the total sample indicated that Rock is their favourite style of music (rounded off to 2 decimal places)?

(a) 27.36% (b) 18.25 %
(c) 29.65% (d) 22.35%

119. The following table shows the percentage population of four towns below poverty line and the proportion of males and females.

Town	Percentage of population below poverty line	Below poverty line	Above poverty line
		Male : Female	Male : Female
A	10	1 : 3	3 : 2
B	15	3 : 4	1 : 2
C	20	2 : 3	5 : 3
D	25	4 : 5	5 : 4

If the total population of Town C is 8000, then what is the number of females above the poverty line in State C?

(a) 2000 (b) 2200 (c) 2400 (d) 2600

120. The value of

$$\frac{(157 \times 157) + (157 \times 133) + (133 \times 133)}{(157 \times 157 \times 157) - (133 \times 133 \times 133)}$$

is

(a) $\frac{1}{24}$ (b) 24 (c) 290 (d) $\frac{1}{290}$

121. The number of hours spent by a student of different activities as shown in the following pie-chart

Number of hours

The central angle corresponding to the sleeping time is what percentage of the whole central angle?

(a) 66.66% (b) 33.33%
(c) 55% (d) 50%

122. The area of a rectangular field is 480 m^2. If the length is 20% more than the breadth, then the length of the rectangular field is

(a) 30 m (b) 20 m (c) 24 m (d) 27 m

123. In a circle centred at O, PQ is a tangent at P. Furthermore, AB is the chord of the circle and is extended to Q. If PQ = 12 cm and QB = 8 cm, then the length of AB is equal to

(a) 20 cm (b) 4 cm
(c) 10 cm (d) 8 cm

124. The upstream speed of a boat is 8 km/h and the downstream is 15 km/h. What is the speed of the boat in still water and the speed of the stream (in km/h), respectively?

(a) 11 and 3 (b) 3 and 11
(c) 11.5 and 3.5 (d) 3.5 and 11.5

125. A number is first decreased by 28% and then increased by 28%. The number so obtained is 784 less than the original number. Find the value of the original number.

(a) 1000 (b) 15000
(c) 10000 (d) 1500

126. The following pie chart shows the number of students who failed in different subjects in an examination. Examine the chart and answer the following question.

The total number of students who have failed is 350.

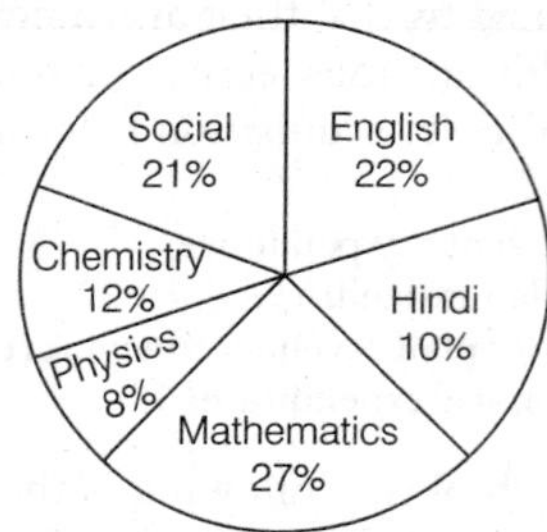

The number of students failed in Mathematics is less than the number of students failed in all other subjects by

(a) 190 (b) 256 (c) 95 (d) 161

127. Simplify the following.
$19 \div 5$ of $(27 - 15 - 21) + 37$
(a) $\frac{6124}{165}$ (b) $\frac{19}{165}$ (c) $\frac{6142}{165}$ (d) $\frac{37}{165}$

128. The price of a stock increased by 30% in the first year and decreased by 20% in the second year. If an investor bought 100 shares of the stock for ₹ 1000, then what is the final value of the investment after 2 yr?
(a) ₹ 960 (b) ₹ 1040 (c) ₹ 1400 (d) ₹ 1020

129. The LCM of two numbers is 660 and their HCF is 5. If one of the numbers is 55, find the other.
(a) 275 (b) 12 (c) 110 (d) 60

130. Some medicine in liquid form is prepared in a hemispherical container of diameter 36 cm. When the container is full of medicine, the medicine is transferred to small cylindrical bottles of diameter 6 cm and height 6 cm. How many bottles are required to empty the container?
(a) 76 (b) 72 (c) 70 (d) 75

131. Tom can do a piece of work in 7 days, whereas Jay can do the same work in 14 days.
How long will they take to finish the work if both work together?
(a) $5\frac{2}{3}$ days (b) $4\frac{2}{3}$ days
(c) $7\frac{2}{3}$ days (d) $2\frac{2}{3}$ days

132. Two trains of lengths 200 m and 250 m are running on parallel rail tracks at speeds of 68 km/h and 50 km/h, respectively. In how much time (In seconds) will they cross each other if they are running in the same direction?
(a) 90 (b) 85 (c) 80 (d) 75

133. Travelling a distance of 1000 km, a train slowed down due to repairs of the tracks. Its average speed for the trip reduced by 75 km/h and the time of travel increased by 3 h. The original duration of the travel is
(a) 6 h (b) 5 h (c) 5.5 h (d) 6.5 h

134. $7\sin^2 A + 3\cos^2 A = 4$, then find $\cot A$.
(a) $\sqrt{3}$ (b) $\sqrt{2}$ (c) $\frac{1}{\sqrt{2}}$ (d) $\frac{1}{\sqrt{3}}$

135. If $\sec A - \tan A = P$, then find the value of $\sec A$.
(a) $\frac{p^2 - 1}{p^2 + 1}$ (b) $\frac{P^2 +}{P^2 - 1}$
(c) $\frac{p^2 + 1}{P}$ (d) $\frac{P^2 + 1}{2P}$

136. $2(\sin 1° \times \sec 89°) + 3(\cos 11° \times \operatorname{cosec} 79°) + 5(\tan 21° \times \tan 69°) = ?$
(a) 11 (b) 12 (c) 20 (d) 10

137. A person has three iron bars whose lengths are 20 m, 30 m and 40 m, respectively. He wants to cut pieces of the same length from each of the three bars. What is the least number of total pieces if he cuts without any wastage?
(a) 8 (b) 10 (c) 9 (d) 11

138. In a ΔPQR, $\angle P : \angle Q : \angle R = 3:4:8$. The shortest side and the longest side of the triangle, respectively, are
(a) PQ and PR (b) QR and PR
(c) PQ and QR (d) QR and PQ

139. In a triangle ABC, if $\angle B = 90°$, $\angle C = 45°$ and $AC = 4$ cm, then the value of BC is
(a) $\sqrt{2}$ cm (b) 4 cm
(c) $2\sqrt{2}$ cm (d) $4\sqrt{2}$ cm

140. Study the given pie-chart and answer the question that follows. The pie-chart shows the number of boys studying in play group of various schools (A, B, C).

Total number of boys=2000

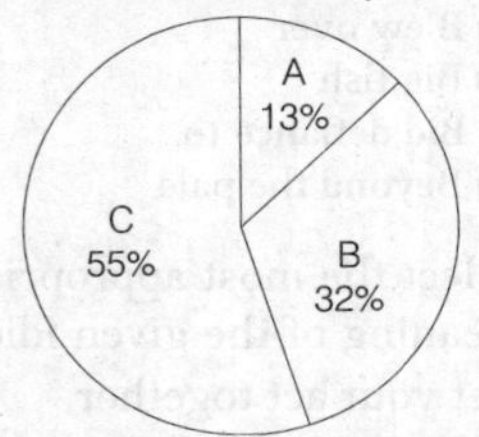

What is the average number of boys studying in schools A and C?
(a) 740 (b) 920 (c) 560 (d) 680

141. In an office, 75 employees can finish a project in 60 days. After few days, 15 employees left the job and the project was completed in 65 days. After how many days did the 15 employees leave?
(a) 50 (b) 45 (c) 30 (d) 40

142. Ramesh borrowed ₹15000 at a certain rate of simple interest from a bank. He repaid (the principal but not interest) ₹ 6000 after 5 yr, and after 5 more years he paid ₹ 18600 and settled his account. Find the rate of simple interest per annum.
(a) 12% (b) 10% (c) 8% (d) 6%

143. Let ABC, PQR be two congruent triangle such that $\angle A = \angle P = 90°$. If $BC = 17$ cm, $PR = 8$ cm, find AB (in cm).
(a) 12 (b) 15 (c) 14 (d) 9

144. Study the pie-chart given below, and answer the question that follows. Percentage-wise break up of students in terms of specialisation in BTech
Total number of students = 6700

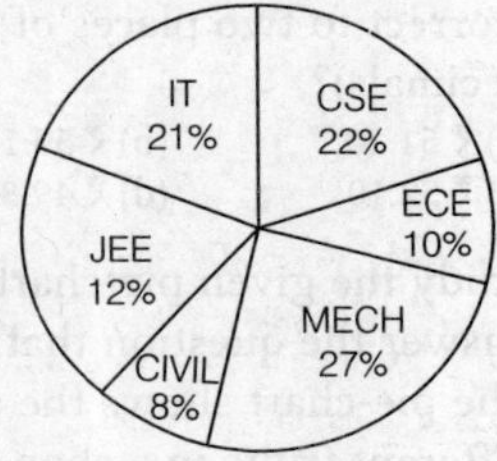

What is the total number of students having specialisation in CSE, ECE and CIVIL?
(a) 2680 (b) 2840
(c) 2860 (d) 2480

145. The LCM and HCF of two numbers are 1105 and 5. If the LCM is 17 times the first number, then find the two numbers.
(a) 65 and 85 (b) 55 and 85
(c) 65 and 75 (d) 60 and 80

146. Akshita and Raina are typing a book, but have only one laptop to work upon. They decided that they will work on alternate basis such that Akshita works for the first day, Raina works for the second day, Akshita for the third day and so on. Akshita alone can finish the typing work in 16 days, while Raina will take 24 days if she works alone on the entire book. How many days will they take to finish the typing work if they work on alternate basis?
(a) 15 (b) 18
(c) 19 (d) 17

147. A train covers a distance of 540 km between two stations in 240 min. It travels at a speed of 90 km/h to another station in 5 h. What is the average speed of the train (in km/h)?
(a) 112 (b) 110
(c) 100 (d) 120

148. The height of two cones are in the ratio 7:5 and their diameters are in the ratio 10:21. What is the ratio of their volumes ? $\left(\text{Where}, \pi = \frac{22}{7}\right)$
(a) 26 : 47 (b) 14 : 19
(c) 20 : 63 (d) 17 : 21

149. What is the difference between a single discount of 35% on ₹ 700 and two successive discounts of 18% and 12% on the same amount (correct to two places of decimals)?
(a) ₹ 51.20 (b) ₹ 50.12
(c) ₹ 52.10 (d) ₹ 49.80

150. Study the given pie-chart and answer the question that follows. The pie-chart shows the sale of different fruits in a shop in a day.

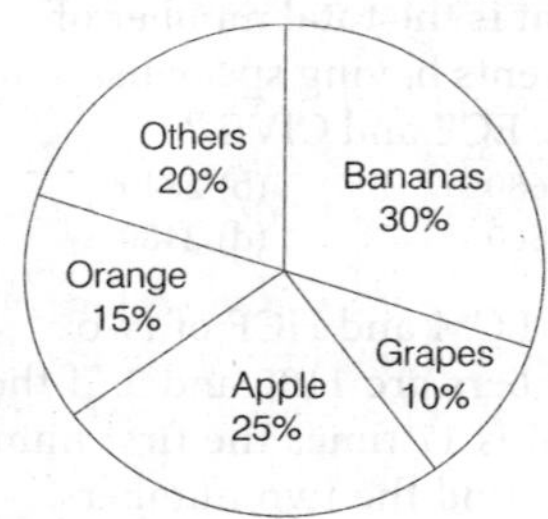

If a total of 1200 kg of fruits were sold in a day, calculate the amount of bananas sold (in kg).
(a) 360 (b) 290
(c) 330 (d) 260

Part IV
English Comprehension

151. Select the most appropriate antonym of the given word.
Transparent
(a) Crossover
(b) Linger
(c) Opaque
(d) Oppress

152. Select the most appropriate meaning of the underlined idiom.
The office management was in dire straits after the financial crash.
(a) To be extremely happy
(b) In a very bad situation
(c) Being direct or fair
(d) To walk on already trodden paths

153. Select the incorrectly spelt word.
(a) Puzzled (b) Nasal
(c) Councel (d) Embezzlement

154. Select the option that can be used as a one-word substitute for the given group of words.
Lasting for a very short time
(a) Eternal (b) Ephemeral
(c) Blasphemy (d) Chronology

155. Select the most appropriate idiom that can substitute the underlined segment in the given sentence.
Do you believe that you have a possibility of getting that job?
(a) spill the beans
(b) snow job
(c) stand a chance
(d) shoot the breeze

156. Select the most appropriate synonym of the given word.
Aggravate
(a) Annoy (b) Mitigate
(c) Enhance (d) Satisfy

157. Choose the idiom that can best substitute the underlined part of the given sentence.
Shelley ignored her father's wish of studying arts and instead took admission in commerce.
(a) Blew over
(b) Big fish
(c) Bid defiance to
(d) Beyond the pale

158. Select the most appropriate meaning of the given idiom.
Get your act together
(a) To ruin one's plans
(b) To organise yourself so, that you can do something properly
(c) To get the conversation going
(d) To understand something complicated

159. Identify from the given options the word most similar in meaning to the underlined word according to its meaning in the following sentence.
He is a person who holds old fashioned opinions.
(a) obsolete (b) ancient
(c) antique (d) senior citizen

160. Select the most appropriate option that can substitute the underlined words in the given sentence.
Kiran's teacher was doubtful on her success.
(a) doubtful beyond
(b) doubtful in
(c) doubtful off
(d) doubtful of

161. Select the correct spelling for the incorrectly spelt word in the given sentence.
The Eustachian tube and vestubular complex in the middle and inner ear, respectively, have an important role to play.
(a) vestibular (b) midle
(c) respictevely (d) importent

162. Select the most appropriate idiom to fill in the blank.
There are others waiting to grab an opportunity, if you don't act fast, you are going to ....
(a) be in the same boat
(b) a full boat
(c) push the boat out
(d) miss the boat

163. The following sentence has been split into four segments. Identify the segment that contains a grammatical error.
Mr. Khanna and family / have visit / Manali during / the summer vacation.
(a) have visit
(b) Mr. Khanna and family
(c) the summer vacation.
(d) Manali during

164. Select the most appropriate idiom for the given situation.
He started with an online company and became a millionaire. Then, he sold it and invested in the share market and earned more money. Now, he has invested in the transportation industry and is generating huge wealth. What does he have?
(a) As genuine as a three-dollar bill
(b) Midas touch
(c) Rule of thumb
(d) Sticky fingers

165. The following sentence has been divided into parts. One of them may contain an error.
Select the part that contains the error from the given options. If you don't find any error, mark 'No error' as your answer.
There was no other book / in the English language / which is as interesting as this one.
(a) There was no other book
(b) in the English language
(c) No error
(d) which is as interesting as this one

166. Select the option that can be used as a one-word substitute for the given group of words.
Very attractive and easy to feel love for
(a) Flamboyant (b) Adorable
(c) Mysterious (d) Laudable

167. Select the most appropriate meaning of the underlined word.
He uses one of the finest <u>ingredients</u> in his cooking.
(a) components (b) mixtures
(c) culinary (d) preparations

168. Select the most appropriate antonym of the given word.
Abhor
(a) Occupy (b) Despise
(c) Danger (d) Love

169. Select the option that can be used as a one-word substitute for the underlined words.
He was <u>not willing</u> to attend the technical session of the conference.
(a) dejecting (b) reluctant
(c) curious (d) comprehensive

170. Select the option that can be used as a one-word substitute for the given group of words.
A disease prevalent in a community or a specific region at a specific time, affecting a large area.
(a) Pandemic (b) Eradicate
(c) Epidemic (d) Endemic

171. Select the most appropriate antonym of the given word.
Apex
(a) Pinnacle (b) Bottom
(c) Farthest (d) Watchful

172. Select the most appropriate meaning of the underlined word.
Ram was <u>abandoned</u> by his parents at a very early age.
(a) loved (b) left
(c) hated (d) disgraced

173. Select the most appropriate meaning of the given idiom.
Part and parcel
(a) Passing blame to someone else
(b) Agreement with someone
(c) A payment system for parcels
(d) Basic or essential element

174. Choose the most appropriate meaning of the underlined phrase.
What we need is skilled and energetic planning and <u>elbow grease</u>.
(a) The grease that is earned through labour.
(b) Hard work that one puts into cleaning one's elbow.
(c) Hard work that one puts into removing grease.
(d) Hard work that one puts into doing something.

175. Select the most appropriate synonym of the given word.
Robe
(a) Robbery (b) Mishap
(c) Success (d) Cloak

176. Select the most appropriate meaning of the given idiom.
A snowball effect
(a) An accelerating growth of magnitude
(b) Trick someone completely
(c) Cold and uncomfortable
(d) Slow movement

177. Some words in the following sentence have been underlined and given as options.
Select the option that contains a spelling error.
Roshni does a <u>fabulouous</u> job at her <u>company</u> and has been offered a <u>promotion</u>.
(a) fabulouous (b) company
(c) promotion (d) offered

178. The following sentence has been split into four segments. Identify the segment that contains a grammatical error.
I have never / come to / such a kind person / like my friend.
(a) such a kind person
(b) like my friend
(c) come to
(d) I have never

179. Select the most appropriate option that can substitute the underlined word in the given sentence.
The Board of Film Analysts <u>vituperated</u> the novice Indonesian film-maker and cancelled its nomination for the 'Golden Globe Award'.
(a) lamented the untimely death of
(b) censured with harsh and abusive language
(c) dealt in a delicate and polite manner
(d) recognised and praised the talent of

180. Select the most appropriate idiom to substitute the underlined segment in the given sentence.
My final round of Spell Bee competition is coming up and to win this event, I need to <u>study hard</u> from today.
(a) burn the books
(b) hit the books
(c) cut to the chase
(d) pour my heart out

181. Select the option that can be used as a one-word substitute for the given group of words.
To have a strong emotional effect on
(a) To forfeit (b) To overwhelm
(c) To smoother (d) To yield

182. Select the incorrectly spelt word.
(a) Ocassion (b) Agreeable
(c) Formulae (d) Waitress

183. Select the most appropriate option that can substitute the underlined segment in the given sentence. If there is no need to substitute it, select 'No substitution required'.
Harry is the one sitting <u>on</u> the corner.
(a) No substitution required
(b) upon
(c) onto
(d) in

184. Select the incorrectly spelt word from the underlined words in the following sentence.
Communities must build their <u>resileince</u>, including adopting <u>appropriate</u> technologies while making the most of traditional knowledge and <u>diversifying</u> their <u>livelihoods</u> to cope with current and future climate stress.
(a) livelihoods (b) diversifying
(c) appropriate (d) resileince

185. The following sentence has been split into four segments. Identify the segment that contains a grammatical error.
The university has putting off / the semester examination / for the second time now / due to technical issues.
(a) the semester examination
(b) due to technical issues
(c) for the second time now
(d) The university has putting off

186. Select the correct option to substitute the underlined segment in the given sentence. If no substitution is required, select 'No substitution'.
Her smile is similar to her mother.
(a) No substitution
(b) her mother's
(c) mother
(d) the mother

187. Select the most appropriate antonym of the given word.
Inquisitive
(a) Careful (b) Dull
(c) Uninterested (d) Indolent

188. Parts of the following sentence have been given as options. One of them may contain an error. Select the part that contains the error from the given options. If you don't find any error, mark 'No error' as your answer.
Anant was telling a story about his most recent exploits when a tree branch break the living room window.
(a) about his most recent exploits
(b) when a tree branch break the living room window
(c) Anant was telling a story
(d) No error

189. Select the option that can be used as a one-word substitute for the given group of words.
An animal or a person that eats all types of food, especially plants and meat
(a) Vegetarian (b) Herbivore
(c) Omnivore (d) Carnivore

190. Select the most appropriate antonym of the given word.
Bombastic
(a) Essential (b) Sarcastic
(c) Plain (d) Rhythmic

Directions (Q. Nos. 191-195) *In the following passage some words have been deleted. Read the passage carefully and select the most appropriate option to fill in each blank.*

Among the largest species of cats in the world, tigers are powerful hunters with ...(1)... teeth, strong jaws and agile bodies. They range across Asia from Russia all the way to Sumatra and mainland South-East Asia. Researchers still have much to learn ...(2)... these beautiful, endangered ...(3)... .

There is currently one recognised species of tiger, Panthera tigris. Scientists have further ...(4)... the tiger into nine sub-species: the extinct Bali, Caspian and Javan sub-species, and the living Malayan, Sumatran, South China, Indochinese, Bengal and Amur (or Siberian) sub-species. Of these six sub-species AZA-accredited zoos currently manage three: Amur, Malayan and Sumatran. The Smithsonian's National Zoo and Conservation Biology Institute is home to Sumatran and Amur tigers, Sumatran tigers are ...(5)... as Critically Endangered on the International Union for Conservation of Nature's Red List and Amur tigers have been classified as Endangered.

191. Select the most appropriate option to fill blank no. 1.
(a) long (b) small
(c) blunt (d) sharp

192. Select the most appropriate option to fill blank no. 2.
(a) with (b) into
(c) about (d) along

193. Select the most appropriate option to fill blank no. 3.
(a) rabbits (b) cats
(c) elephants (d) dogs

194. Select the most appropriate option to fill blank no. 4.
(a) declared (b) restricted
(c) generalised (d) classified

195. Select the most appropriate option to fill blank no. 5.
(a) numerated (b) detailed
(c) recorded (d) listed

Directions (Q. Nos. 196-200) *Read the given passage and answer the questions that follow.*

What if globally designed products could radically change how we work, produce and consume? Several examples across continents show the way we are producing and consuming goods could be improved by relying on globally shared digital resources, such as design, knowledge and software.

Imagine a prosthetic hand designed by geographically dispersed communities of scientists, designers and enthusiasts in a collaborative manner via the web. All knowledge and software related to the hand is shared globally as a digital commons. People from all over the world who are connected online and have access to local manufacturing machines (from 3D printing and CNC machines to low-tech crafts and tools) can, ideally with the help of an expert, manufacture a customised hand. This is the case of the Open Bionics project, which produces designs for robotic and bionic devices.

There are no patent costs to pay for. Less transportation of materials is needed, since a considerable part of the manufacturing takes place locally, maintenance is easier, products are designed to last as long as possible and costs are thus, much lower.

196. Identify the most suitable title for the given passage.
(a) Knowledge Explosion
(b) Customised Hand
(c) Shared Information
(d) Digital Globalisation

197. What is the term used in the passage for globally shared digital things?
(a) Digital commons
(b) Digital information
(c) Digital resources
(d) Digital world

198. What is the tone of the author?
(a) Speculative
(b) Caustic
(c) Acerbic
(d) Belligerent

199. Which of the following is not a globally shared digital resource?
(a) Knowledge
(b) Design
(c) Automobile
(d) Software

200. Select the most suitable word from the passage which means 'Scattered'.
(a) Collaborative
(b) Shared
(c) Customised
(d) Dispersed

Know Correct Answers

1. (b)	2. (b)	3. (d)	4. (d)	5. (d)	6. (a)	7. (d)	8. (d)	9. (d)	10. (a)
11. (a)	12. (a)	13. (c)	14. (a)	15. (c)	16. (d)	17. (a)	18. (b)	19. (b)	20. (d)
21. (b)	22. (a)	23. (a)	24. (c)	25. (d)	26. (a)	27. (c)	28. (c)	29. (d)	30. (b)
31. (d)	32. (c)	33. (b)	34. (a)	35. (b)	36. (a)	37. (d)	38. (c)	39. (d)	40. (d)
41. (b)	42. (a)	43. (c)	44. (c)	45. (c)	46. (d)	47. (b)	48. (a)	49. (a)	50. (b)
51. (c)	52. (b)	53. (c)	54. (a)	55. (c)	56. (c)	57. (d)	58. (b)	59. (d)	60. (c)
61. (d)	62. (b)	63. (c)	64. (b)	65. (c)	66. (a)	67. (b)	68. (b)	69. (a)	70. (a)
71. (d)	72. (c)	73. (d)	74. (c)	75. (d)	76. (b)	77. (d)	78. (b)	79. (c)	80. (c)
81. (a)	82. (d)	83. (b)	84. (d)	85. (b)	86. (d)	87. (d)	88. (a)	89. (b)	90. (d)
91. (a)	92. (d)	93. (a)	94. (d)	95. (b)	96. (b)	97. (d)	98. (b)	99. (a)	100. (d)
101. (b)	102. (d)	103. (a)	104. (a)	105. (d)	106. (b)	107. (d)	108. (a)	109. (a)	110. (a)
111. (c)	112. (c)	113. (c)	114. (b)	115. (c)	116. (d)	117. (a)	118. (a)	119. (c)	120. (a)
121. (b)	122. (c)	123. (c)	124. (c)	125. (c)	126. (d)	127 (a)	128. (b)	129. (d)	130. (b)
131. (b)	132. (a)	133. (b)	134. (a)	135. (d)	136. (d)	137 (c)	138. (d)	139. (c)	140. (d)
141. (d)	142. (c)	143. (b)	144. (a)	145. (a)	146. (c)	147. (b)	148. (c)	149. (b)	150. (a)
151. (c)	152. (b)	153. (c)	154. (b)	155. (c)	156. (a)	157. (c)	158. (b)	159. (a)	160. (d)
161. (a)	162. (d)	163. (a)	164. (b)	165. (a)	166. (b)	167. (a)	168. (d)	169. (b)	170. (c)
171. (b)	172. (b)	173. (d)	174. (d)	175. (d)	176. (a)	177. (a)	178. (c)	179. (b)	180. (b)
181. (b)	182. (a)	183. (d)	184. (d)	185. (d)	186. (b)	187. (c)	188. (b)	189. (c)	190. (c)
191. (d)	192. (c)	193. (b)	194. (d)	195. (d)	196. (d)	197. (c)	198. (a)	199. (c)	200. (d)

Answer & Solutions

1. (b) Given question figure is embedded in option figure (b).

2. (b) According to the question,

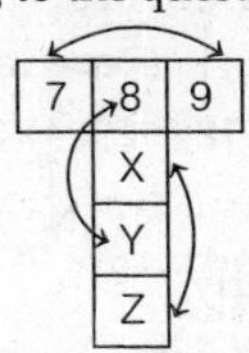

8 is opposite to Y. , X is opposite to Z. 7 is opposite to 9.
Hence, option (b) is the correct answer.

3. (d) Pattern of the series is as follows,

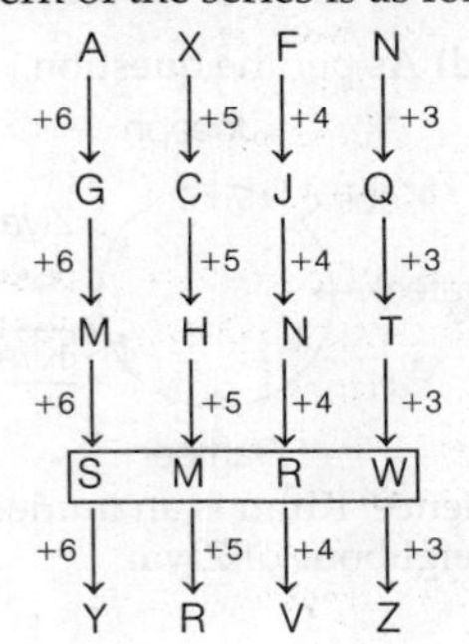

4. (d) According to the question,

J@C$B#R

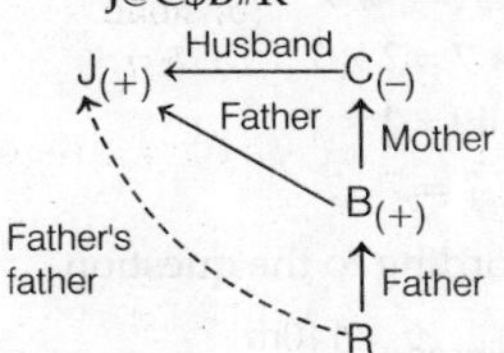

Hence, J is father's father of R.

5. (d) As,

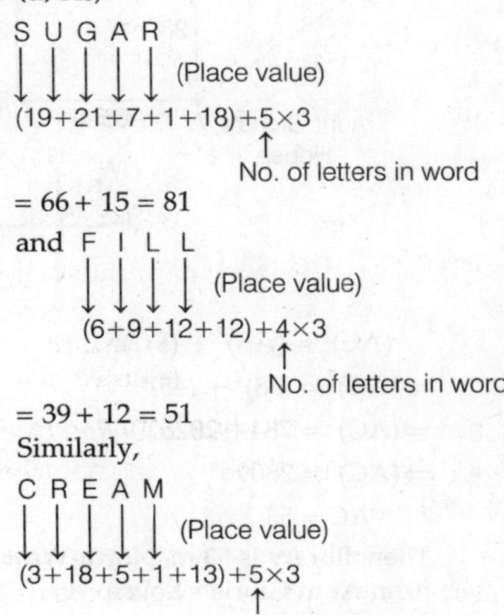

$= 40 + 15 = \boxed{55}$

6. (a) As, (7, 2, 70)

$\Rightarrow \quad 7 \times 2 \times \boxed{5} = 70$

and (6, 4, 120)

$\Rightarrow \quad 6 \times 4 \times 5 = 120$

Similarly, (3, 8, 120)

$\Rightarrow \quad 3 \times 8 \times 5 = 120$

7. (d) As, 16 : 106

$16 - 7 = 9 \Rightarrow 9^2 + 9 + 16 = 106$

and 10 : 22

$10 - 7 = 3 \Rightarrow 3^2 + 3 + 10 = 22$

Similarly, 11 : $\boxed{?}$

$11 - 7 = 4 \Rightarrow 4^2 + 4 + 11 = \boxed{31}$

8. (d) The alternate pattern of the given series are following.

From Ist figure to IInd figure and IIIrd figure to 4th figure all the elements are moving in 90° clockwise direction at its own place.

From IInd to IIIrd figure, 4th figure to 5th figure elements are moving 90° clockwise from one corner to another.

So, the next figure of the given series will be figure (d).

9. **(d)** Pattern of the series is as follows,

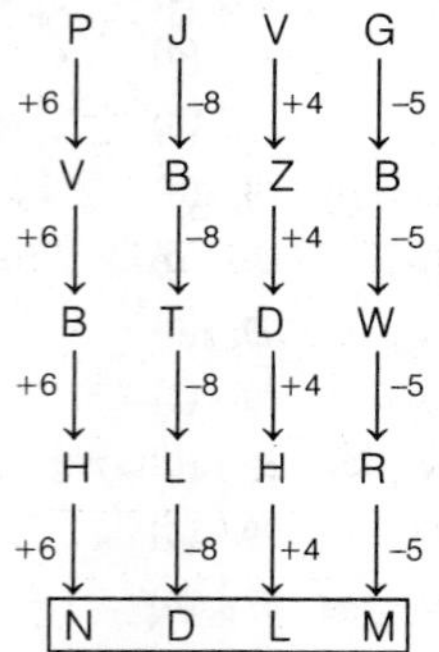

10. **(a)** In each figure of the given figure series, first two design are invested vertically.
So, option figure (a) is the continue continuation of senes the series.

11. **(a)** In each steps of the given figure series optained by rotating whole 90° in anti-clockwise direction.
Hence, option figure (a) is next figure of the given series.

12. **(a)** The correct English dictionary order of the given words.
Docile → Dock → Doctor → Doctorate
(3) (5) (1) (2)
→ Doctrine → Documentary
(6) (4)
⇒3, 5, 1, 2, 6, 4

13. **(c)** In both position of dice number '3' is common.

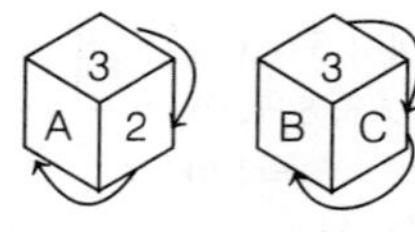

Position I ⟶ 3 | 2 C | A B
Position II ⟶ 3

Hence, B is opposite to A.

14. **(a)** Pattern of the series is as follows,

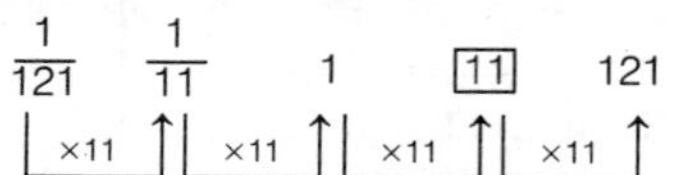

15. **(c)** According to the statements,

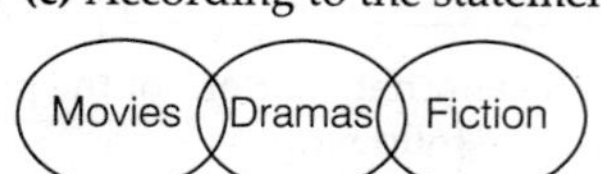

Conclusions I. (✗) II. (✗)
Hence, neither Conclusion I nor II follows.

16. **(d)** Given equation,
22B7C288D12A27 = ?
After replacing the signs,

A → +	C → −
B → ×	D → ÷

$22 \times 7 - 288 \div 12 + 27$
$= 154 - 24 + 27 = 157$

17. **(a)** As, 12 : 64
$\Rightarrow \quad 12 \times 4 + 16 = 48 + 16 = 64$
and 32 : 144
$32 \times 4 + 16 = 128 + 16 = 144$
Similarly, [?] : 116
$? \times 4 + 16 = 116$
$? \times 4 = 100$
$\therefore \quad ? = \frac{100}{4} = \boxed{25}$

18. **(b)** Given equation,
21 B 14 C 154 D 14 A 42 = ?
After replacing the signs,

A ⇒ +	B ⇒ ×
C ⇒ −	D ⇒ ÷

$? = 21 \times 14 - 154 \div 14 + 42$
$= 294 - 11 + 42 = 336 - 11 = 325$

19. **(b)** Given equation,
56 D 8 B 7 = ? B 7
After replacing the signs,

A ⇒ +	B ⇒ ×
C ⇒ −	D ⇒ ÷

$56 \div 8 \times 7 = ? \times 7$
$\Rightarrow \quad 7 \times 7 = ? \times 7$
$\Rightarrow \quad 49 = ? \times 7$
$\therefore \quad ? = 7$

20. **(d)** According to the question,

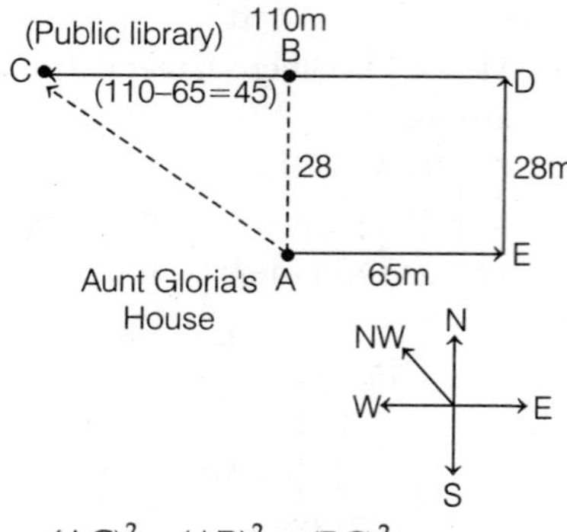

$(AC)^2 = (AB)^2 + (BC)^2$
$\Rightarrow (AC)^2 = (28)^2 + (45)^2$
$\Rightarrow (AC)^2 = 784 + 2025$
$\Rightarrow (AC)^2 = 2809$
$\therefore \quad AC = 53$
Then, library is 53 m, North-West from Aunt Gloria's house.

21. **(b)** As, (9, 1, 19)
$\Rightarrow \quad (9 \times 2) + 1^2 = 18 + 1 = 19$
and (5, 2, 14)
$\Rightarrow \quad (5 \times 2) + 2^2 = 10 + 4 = 14$
Similarly, (3, 2, 10)
$\Rightarrow \quad (3 \times 2) + 2^2 = 6 + 4 = 10$

22. **(a)** According to the question,

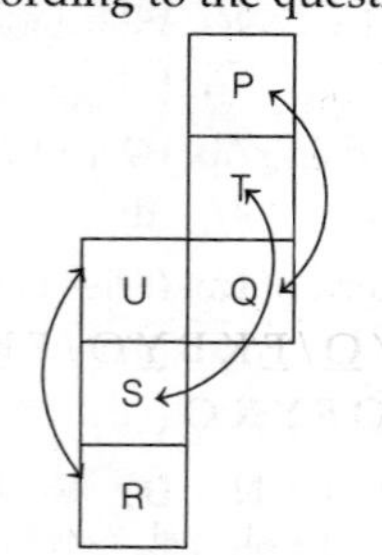

T is opposite to S.
U is opposite to R.
P is opposite to Q.

23. **(a)** According to the question,
Z # L @ P & K @ J # X

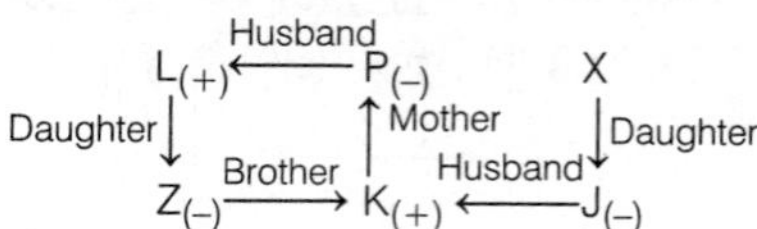

Hence, K is brother of Z.

24. **(c)** As,

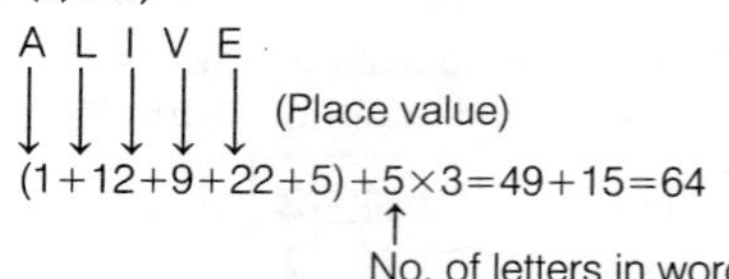

and

Similarly,

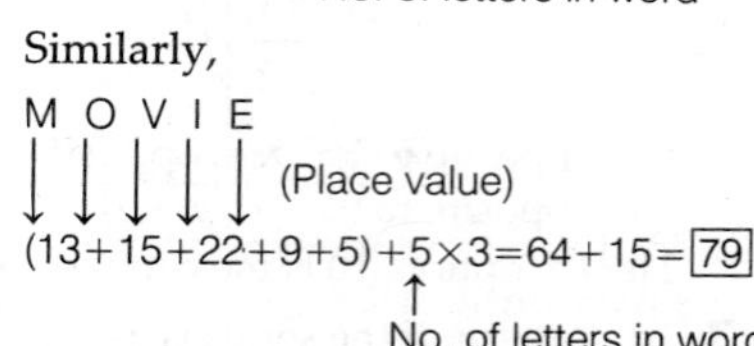

25. **(d)** As per the question,

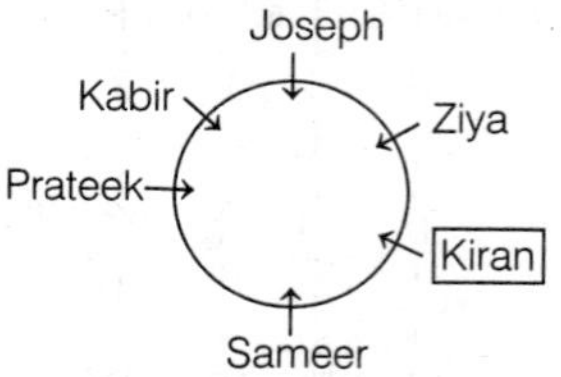

Hence, Kiran is an immediate neighbour of Ziya.

26. (a) Given equation,

89 A 94 C 35 D 8 B 8 = ?

After replace the signs,

A ⇒ +	B ⇒ ×
C ⇒ −	D ⇒ ÷

$89 + 94 - 35 \div 8 \times 8 = ?$

$\Rightarrow \quad ? = 183 - 35 = 148$

27. (c) The option figure (c) will appear, when given paper is unfolded after cutting.

28. (c) Pattern of the series is as follows,

F K B Y O / F K B Y O / F K B Y O

⇒ K B O F Y K O

29. (d) As, I N D I A (−3 each) → F K A F X

and E S T O N I A (−3 each) → B P Q L K F X

Similarly,

M A L A Y S I A (−3 each) → J X I X V P F X

30. (b) As, P A I N T (Opposite) → K Z R M G (+4, +4, +7, +7, +7) → O D Y T N

and B R U S H (Opposite) → Y I F H S (+4, +4, +7, +7, +7) → C M M O Z

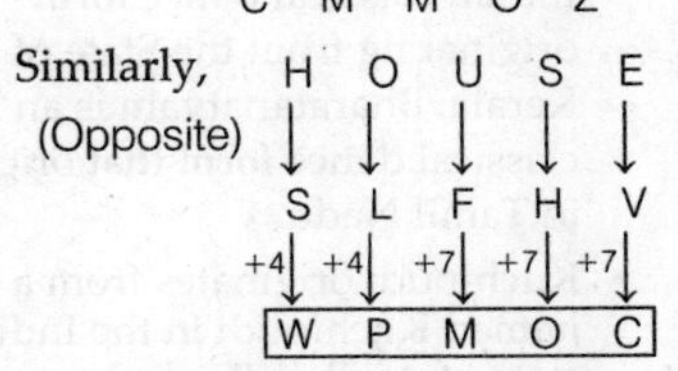

Similarly, H O U S E (Opposite) → S L F H V (+4, +4, +7, +7, +7) → W P M O C

31. (d) The correct dictionary order of the given words is as follows.

Woodland → Workable →
(5) (3)

Wrangle → Wrist → Wrongful
(2) (1) (4)

⇒ 5, 3, 2, 1, 4

32. (c) The correct mirror image of given figure is option figure.

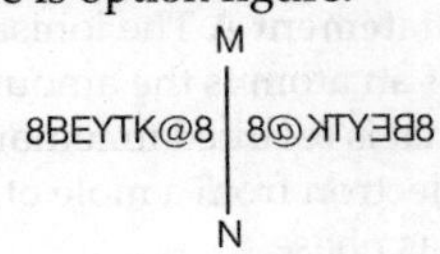

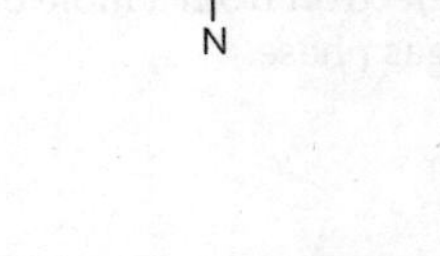

33. (b) According to the statements,

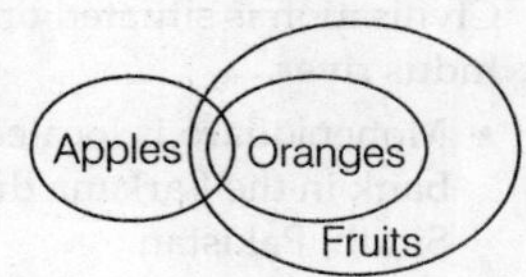

Conclusions I. (✗) II. (✓)

Hence, only Conclusion II follows.

34. (a) As, per the question,

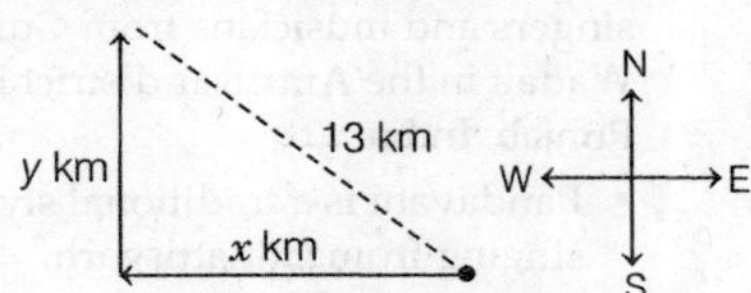

$(x)^2 + (y)^2 = (13)^2$

Put, $x = 12$ and $y = 5$

$\Rightarrow (12)^2 + (5)^2 = 169$

$\Rightarrow 144 + 25 = 169$

$\Rightarrow 169 = 169$

35. (b) According to the question,

[E] A R S = 4 [2] 6 8

N I C [E] = 9 7 [2] 3

So, E is coded as 2.

36. (a) According to the question,

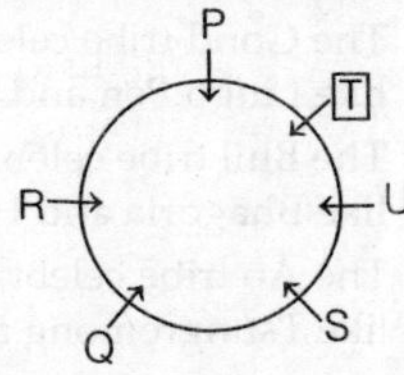

Hence, T is the immediate neighbours of both P and U.

37. (d) S →(+4) W →(+2) Y →(−1) X

P →(+4) T →(+2) V →(−1) U

R →(+4) V →(+2) X →(−1) W

But, L →(+3) O →(+2) Q →(−1) P

38. (c) As,

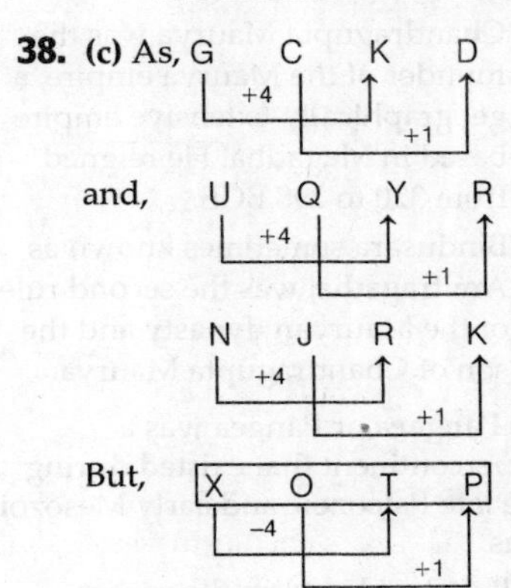

39. (d) According to the statements,

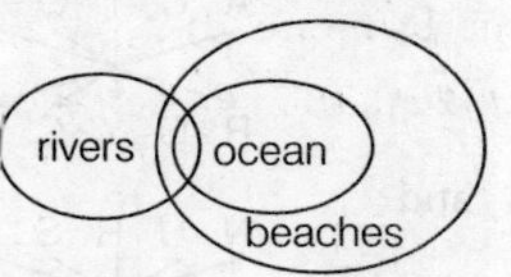

Conclusions I. (✓) II. (✗)

Hence, only Conclusion I follows.

40. (d) Given equation,

$42 \times 168 - 8 \div 4 + 3 = ?$

After replacing the signs,

+ ⇒ ×	× ⇒ +
− ⇒ ÷	÷ ⇒ −

$42 + 168 \div 8 - 4 \times 3 = ?$

$\Rightarrow ? = 42 + 21 - 12$

$= 63 - 12 = 51$

41. (b) As, work of artist is painting. Similarly, work of cobbler is fixing shoes.

42. (a) Given equation,

$15 \times 3 \div 15 - (45 \times 3) - 10 + (13 \div 2) = 76$

From option (a) interchanging the signs, '÷' and '×'.

$15 \div 3 \times 15 - (45 \div 3) - 10 + (13 \times 2) = 76$

$\Rightarrow 75 - 15 - 10 + 26 = 76$

$\Rightarrow \quad 101 - 25 = 76$

$\Rightarrow \quad 76 = 76$

43. (c) Given equation,

$23 - 5 \div 240 \times 8 + 14 = ?$

After replacing the signs,

+ ⇒ −	× ⇒ ÷
− ⇒ ×	÷ ⇒ +

$23 \times 5 + 240 \div 8 - 14 = ?$

$= 115 + 30 - 14$

$= 145 - 14 = 131$

44. (c) Option (c) is the correct mirror image of the given question figure.

45. (c) According to the statement,

Conclusions I. (✓) II. (✗)

Hence, only Conclusion I follows.

46. **(d)** As,

+5
A C T O R

R O Y C A

and

+5
N U R S E

E S W U N

Similarly,

+5
J U D G E

E G I U J

47. **(b)** Pattern of the series is as follows,

76, 99, 135, 185, 250, 331

+23 +36 +50 +65 +81

+13 +14 +15 +16

48. **(a)** According to the question,

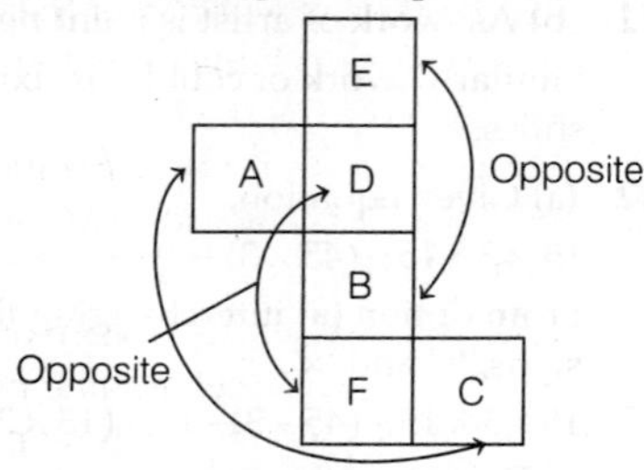

D is opposite to F.

49. **(a)** Pattern of the series is as follows,

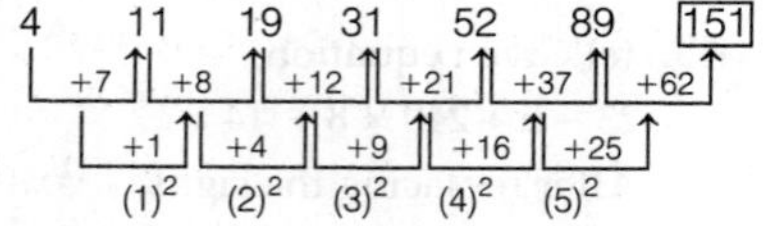

50. **(b)** Pattern of the series is as follows,

134 129 122 113 102 89

−5 −7 −9 −11 −13

51. **(c)** **Article 33** of the Indian Constitution empowers the Parliament to restrict or abrogate the fundamental rights of the members of the armed forces, paramilitary forces, police forces, intelligence agencies and analogous forces.

- **Article 35** It empowers the Parliament to enact laws to give effect to the provisions of Part IV (Directive Principles of State Policy) and Part IVA (Fundamental Duties) of the Constitution.
- **Article 31** repealed by 44th Amendment Act of 1978, dealt with compulsory acquisition of property.
- **Article 37** states that DPSP in Part IV are not enforceable in court, but are fundamental in governance.

52. **(b)** Mohenjodaro site of Harappan Civilisation is situated on the bank of Indus river.

- Mohenjodaro is located on its right bank in the Larkana district of Sindh, Pakistan.
- Mohenjodaro was discovered in 1922 by **RD Banerji**.

53. **(c)** The Wadali Brothers (Puranchand Wadali and Pyarelal Wadali) are **sufi** singers and musicians from Guru Ki Wadali in the Amritsar district in Punjab, India.

- Pandavani is a traditional style of singing from Chhattisgarh.
- Lavani is a traditional style of singing and dancing from Maharashtra.
- Bhatiali is a traditional style of singing from West Bengal.
- Sufi music is a genre of music that is associated with Sufism, a mystical branch of Islam.

54. **(a)** The Rongker festival is celebrated by the **Karbi tribe**, primarily residing in Assam.

- The Karbis have 5 (five) clans called 'KUR'.
- The Gond tribe celebrates festivals like Lingo Pen and Karma.
- The Bhil tribe celebrates festivals like Bhagoria and Holi.
- The Ao tribe celebrates festivals like Tsungremong and Mongmong.

55. **(c)** Ashoka had a change of heart after the Kalinga War, embraced Buddhism and followed its principles of non-violence.

- Ashoka, popularly known as Ashoka the Great, was the third Mauryan emperor of Magadha in the Indian sub-continent during 268 to 232 BCE.
- Chandragupta Maurya was the founder of the Maurya empire, a geographically-extensive empire based in Magadha. He reigned from 320 to 298 BCE.
- Bindusara sometimes known as Amitragatha, was the second ruler of the Mauryan dynasty and the son of Chandragupta Maurya.

56. **(c)** **Pangaea** or Pangea was a supercontinent that existed during the late Paleozoic and early Mesozoic eras.

- It assembled from the earlier continental units of Gondwana, Euramerica and Siberia during the Carboniferous approximately 335 million years ago.
- It began to break apart about 200 million years ago at the end of the Triassic and beginning of the Jurassic.

57. **(d)** Pauling and Corey are widely recognised for their work in elucidating the structure of proteins, particularly the alpha helix and beta sheet conformations.

- Emil Fischer, a German organic chemist, discovered caffeine and other related purines.
- In 1902, he was awarded the Nobel Prize in Chemistry for his work on sugar and purine synthesis.

58. **(b)** Marathi is the third most spoken language based on the 2011 census data.

- Hindi is the most spoken language according to the Census 2011.
- Bengali is the second most spoken language.

59. **(d)** Goods and Services Tax is proportional in nature.

- The Goods and services Tax (GST) is a type of tax levied on most goods and services sold for domestic consumption.
- It is an indirect form of tax.
- It was introduced in 2017.

60. **(c)** Gopika Varma has won the Sangeet Natak Akademi Award in 2019 in **Mohiniyattam dance** forms.

- Mohiniyattam (Malayalam) is an Indian classical dance form originating from the State of Kerala. Bharatanatyam is an Indian classical dance form that originated in Tamil Nadu.
- Kuchipudi originates from a village named Kuchipudi in the Indian state of Andhra Pradesh.
- Kathak is a classical dance of North India.

61. **(d)**

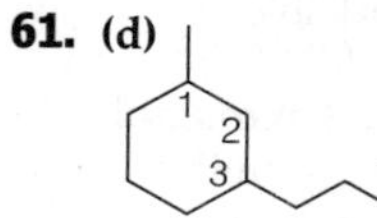

1-Methyl-3-Propylcyclohexane.

62. **(b)** Only Statement A is correct.

- **Statement A** The ionisation energy of an atom is the amount of energy that is required to remove an electron from a mole of atoms in the gas phase.

- **Statement B** The ionisation energy decreases from top to bottom in groups and increases from left to right across a period.

63. (c) Volleyball Federation of India has its apex national governing body headquartered in Chennai, Tamil Nadu.

- It was founded in 1951. Volleyball Federation of India (VFI) is the governing body of volleyball in India.
- Athletics Federation of India is the national governing body for Athletics sport in India formed in 1946.
- Badminton Association of India is the governing body of badminton in India Formed in 1934.
- Hockey India was formed in 2009 after Indian Hockey Federation was dismissed in 2008.

64. (b) **Amar Jiban** by **Rassundari Devi** is an autobiography of a Bengali illiterate woman who secretly acquired literacy skills to read sacred texts in an age when girls and women were denied education and deemed fit only for household chores.

- Ente Katha is an autobiography written by Kamala Surayya from Kerala in the year 1973.
- Lakshmibai Tilak was a Marathi writer, best-known for her memoir, 'Smritichitre'.
- Jina Amucha is an autobiography of Baby Kamble's written in Marathi.

65. (c) The Lucknow Pact was signed in 1916 by Congress and the Muslim League to work in alliance for representative government.

- The main achievements of the Lucknow Pact of 1916 include the moderates and radicals reunited on the idea of self-rule.
- It gave an impression of the Hindu-Muslim unity.

66. (a) Strengthening of bones and muscles is most important health benefits of Vitamin D.

- The main sources of Vitamin D are sunlight, flesh of fatly fish and fish river oils.
- Vitamin C's most important benefit is supporting the immune system by aiding white blood cell function.
- Vitamin A, a fat-soluble vitamin, is crucial for maintaining healthy vision.
- Vitamin K's most important health benefit is its role in blood clotting and preventing excessive bleeding.

67. (b) **Insat-1B** is the geostationary satellite launched by ISRO in 1983 that provides high power TV broadcasting and telecommunications national coverage transponders.

- Bhaskara-I, India's first experimental remote sensing satellite was launched by the Indian Space Research Organisation (ISRO) on 7th June, 1979.
- Radar Imaging Satellite 1 or RISAT-1 was an Indian remote sensing satellite built and operated by the Indian Space Research Organisation.
- GSAT-7 or INSAT-4F is a multi-band military communications satellite developed by the ISRO.

68. (b) **Article 16** of the Indian Constitution provides equal opportunity for all citizens in the matter of employment under the state.

- **Article 15** of the Constitution of India forbids discrimination on grounds only of religion, race, caste, gender or place of birth.
- **Article 17** of the Indian Constitution helps end untouchability against lower castes.
- **Article 18** talks about the abolition of titles.

69. (a) Mirabai was the Rajput princess belonged to the Bhakti tradition of Medieval India, whose songs were devoted to Lord Krishna.

- Mirabai was born in the late 15th century (around 1498 AD) in Rajasthan, India, into the royal family of Merta.
- **Mirabai** was married to Prince Bhoj Raj, the heir of the Chittor kingdom.

70. (a) The National Interim Government of India formed, under Pt. Jawaharlal Nehru was established on 2nd September, 1946.

- Pt. Jawaharlal Nehru became its Vice-President and served as the de-facto Prime Minister.
- It was formed under the recommendations of the Cabinet Mission Plan.
- It lasted till 15th August, 1947 when India became independent and was partitioned into India and Pakistan.

71. (d) The 73rd Amendment Act corresponds to Part IX of the Indian Constitution not Part III.

- The 73rd Amendment Act of the Indian Constitution, passed in 1992, is a landmark legislation that empowered Panchayati Raj Institutions (PRIs) at the village level, also known as the Panchayati Raj Act.
- The amendment aimed to decentralise power and decision-making from the Central and State Governments to the local Panchayats, and empower them to undertake development works in their respective areas.
- 'Panchayats' and 'Municipalities' came under Part IX and IXA of the Constitution.

72. (c) **Gallium** is the only element of the boron family has a high boiling point (1500-2000 °C) and low melting point and is a liquid metal at room temperature.

- It has low toxicity and low pressure, so it is used in high temperature thermameters.

73. (d) India won 1 medal in the World Athletics Championship 2022.

- United States hosted the 2022 World Athletics Championship.
- India won their first silver at the World Athletics Championships since their debut in the games.
- Neeraj Chopra became the first male Indian athlete to win a medal at the World Athletics Championships.

74. (c) **Neeraj Chopra** became the first Indian to win the prestigious Zurich Diamond League Final 2022 in Switzerland.

- Neeraj Chopra is an Indian track and field athlete, who is the reigning Olympic champion and World champion in Men's javelin throw.
- He is the first Asian athlete to win an Olympic gold medal and gold medal at the World Championship in Javelin Throw.

75. **(d)** Department of Economic Affairs is associated with infrastructure development in India.

- Department of Economic Affairs (DEAs) is incharge of Economic Policy as well as the development and filing of the Union budget, which includes the Railways, the budgets of Union territories that do not have legislatures.
- The budgets of states that are governed by the President.

76. **(b)** Hydrogen is an anomaly element that belong to both group 1 and group 17.

- Hydrogen has electronic configuration $1S^1$.
- Assume stable configuration can form H^+ ion by losing one electron from its outer shell like alkalimetal and like halogen is accepts one electron and form H^- ion.

77. **(d)** The Vijayanagara kingdom was established by **Harihara** and **Bukka** in **1336**.

- The most famous king of the Vijayanagara empire was Krishnadevaraya.
- He defeated the king of Odisha and annexed Vijayawada and Rajmahendri.

78. **(b)** **Khadar** is the new alluvium deposited by floods in the Ganga plain.

- It is less fertile compared to Bhangar as it hasn't undergone the weathering process as long.
- Bhangar is the older alluvium deposited away from the floodplains and is generally more fertile than Khadar due to weathering and accumulation of finer particles over time.
- Regur refers to black soil, a type of fertile soil found in the Deccan plateau region of India.

79. **(c)** **Article 164** of the Indian Constitution provides that the Governor appoints the Chief Minister and later, the Chief Minister recommends the appointment of ministers to the Governor.

- **Article 165** is related to the Advocate-General for the State.
- **Article 167** is related to the duties of Chief Minister as respects the furnishing of information to Governor, etc.
- **Article 163** deals with Council of Ministers to aid and advise to Governor.

80. **(c)** According to the 2011 Census of India, the rural literacy rate was 67.77% and Urban areas has 84.98%.

- As per Census 2011, the literacy rate at all India level is 74.04% .
- The literacy rate for females and males are 65.46% and 82.14%, respectively.

81. **(a)** FIFA Women's World Cup 2023 will be hosted by **Australia** and **New Zealand**.

- Spain beat England 1-0 to win their first Women's World Cup title.
- The 2024 FIFA U-20 Women's World Cup will be hosted by Colombia from 31st August to 22nd September, 2024.

82. **(d)** The President of India decides on the question as to the disqualification of Members of Parliament in consultation with the Election Commission of India.

- A person shall be disqualified from membership in either House of Parliament, if he is so disqualified under the Tenth Schedule of the Indian Constitution.
- The 10th Schedule also known as the Anti-Defection law, was added to the Constitution by 52nd Amendment Act of 1985.

83. **(b)** Mohiniyattam is a classical dance of India that belongs to the State of **Kerala**.

- Uttar Pradesh is known for dances like Kathak.
- Andhra Pradesh is known for Kuchipudi.
- Bharatanatyam, Kuchipudi, Kathak, Odissi, Sattriya, Kathakali, Manipuri and Mohiniyattam are the eight styles recognised by the Sangeet Natak Akademi as classical dance.

84. **(d)** Mutual fund product made by combing debt and equity funds is not an example of manufacturing activity.

- Manufacturing refers to the production of items from raw materials on a large scale.
- From bakeries to steel plants, everything falls under manufacturing industries.
- Furniture, heavy machinery, refined petroleum products, ships, steel and tools and dies are some of the examples of manufacturing industries.

85. **(b)** Volume is typically measured in cubic metres (m^3), liters (L) or gallons (gal).

- Pressure is measured in Pascals (Pa).
- Force is measured in Newtons (N).
- Work done is measured in Joules (J).

86. **(d)** Part IV of the Indian Constitution deals with Directive Principles of State Policy.

- The Concept behind the DPSP is to create a 'Welfare State'.
- DPSP are borrowed from Irish Constitution.
- DPSP are included from Article 36 to Article 51 in Indian Constitution.
- These principles aim at ensuring socio-economic justice to the people and establishing India as a Welfare State.

87. **(d)** The pre-monsoon showers that aid in the ripening of mangoes in Karnataka, Kerala, Konkan and Goa are called Mango Showers.

- They go by other names, Such as summer showers or April rains.
- Storms over the Bay of Bengal are what caused the Mango showers.

88. **(a)** Marine West coast climate is found in North-Western Europe, West Coast of North America, North of California, Southern Chile, South-Eastern Australia and New Zealand.

- The Marine West coast climate is a biome characteristic of being located mid-way between the tropics and arctic or antarctic regions of the world, most often between 35° and 60° North.

89. **(b)** Jaisalmer can have maximum temperature difference between the day and night.

- In the summer, the maximum temperature can soar as high as 49°C (120°F), while, nights can be quite pleasant, dropping down to 25°C (77°F).
- This large difference of up to 24°C (43°F) can occur within a single day.

90. **(d)** Mohiniyattam belongs to Kerala. The dance is performed by women in honour of the Hindu God Vishnu in his incarnation as the enchantress Mohini.

- Instruments played during a Mohiniyattam performance usually comprises of Kuzhitalam or cymbals; Veena; Idakka, an hourglass-shaped drum; Mridangam, a barrel-shaped drum with two heads and flute.

91. **(a)** Haripriya Namboodiri is an exponent of Kathakali.

- Dr. Haripriya Namboodiri, the first woman to take a Ph.D in Kathakali. Kathakali comes from South-Western India, around the State of Kerala.
- Like Bharatanatyam, Kathakali is a religious dance. It draws inspiration from the Ramayana and stories from Shaiva traditions.

92. **(d)** During 5th Five-Year Plan, Indira Gandhi gave the slogan "Garibi Hatao'.

- 'Garibi Hatao Desh Bachao' (Remove Poverty, Save the Country) was the theme and slogan of Indira Gandhi's 1971 Election Campaign.

93. **(a)** During G2 phase of the cell, cycle does metabolic changes assemble the cytoplasmic material required for mitosis and cytokinesis.

- The G2 phase, also known as the Gap 2 phase or Growth 2 phase, is a critical period in the cell cycle where the cell prepares for cell division by assembling the necessary cytoplasmic materials for mitosis and cytokinesis.

94. **(d)** Expenditure of the government on health facilities, education and fixed-asset acquisition is termed as **capital expenditure.**

- Revenue expenditure is the part of government spending that does not result in the production of assets.
- Salaries, wages, pensions, subsidies and interest payments are all instances of revenue expenditures.

95. **(b)** Atmakatha is the autobiography of the first Indian President Dr. Rajendra Prasad.

- He officially joined the Indian National Congress in 1911, during its annual session held in Calcutta.
- He presided over the Bombay Session of the Indian National Congress in October 1934.
- In March 1930, Gandhiji launched the Salt Satyagraha.

96. **(b)** Eliminating licenses for importing a majority of goods is a step towards liberalisation.

- Liberalisation is the process or means of removing the state's control over economic activities.
- It gives business enterprises more autonomy in decision-making and eliminates government interference.

97. **(d)** Onam festival of South India is associated with the folklore of King Mahabali.

- Onam is a major harvest festival in Kerala and is celebrated to honour the home-coming of Asura king Mahabali who brought about peace and prosperity in Kerala.
- Onam is celebrated by making Pookkalam (the flower rangolis).

98. **(b)** Europeans entered India with a mindset of trading only. This streak was initiated by **Portuguese**.

- The Portuguese, led by Vasco da Gama in 1498, arrive in India primarily seeking to establish trade routes and acquire spices, textiles and other valuable goods.
- Dutch arrived in India in 1602, British and French arrived in 1608 and 1664.

99. **(a)** Red blood cells are **7.5 μm** in diameter.

- A type of blood cell that is made in the bone marrow and found in the blood.
- Red blood cells contain a protein called Hemoglobin, which carries oxygen from the lungs to all parts of the body.

100. **(d)** Timur's invasion of Delhi took place in 1398.

- On 24th September, he crossed the Indus river and marched on Delhi, leaving a trail of devastation in his wake.
- He invaded India during the reign of Nasiruddin Mahmud, the last king of the Tughlaq dynasty.

101. **(b)** $\sqrt{\dfrac{1-\tan A}{1+\tan A}}$

We know that, $\tan A = \dfrac{\sin A}{\cos A}$

$$\therefore \sqrt{\frac{1-\tan A}{1+\tan A}} = \sqrt{\frac{1-\dfrac{\sin A}{\cos A}}{1+\dfrac{\sin A}{\cos A}}}$$

$$= \sqrt{\frac{\dfrac{\cos A - \sin A}{\cos A}}{\dfrac{\cos A + \sin A}{\cos A}}}$$

$$= \sqrt{\frac{\cos A - \sin A}{\cos A + \sin A} \times \frac{\cos A - \sin A}{\cos A - \sin A}}$$

$$= \sqrt{\frac{(\cos A - \sin A)^2}{\cos^2 A - \sin^2 A}}$$

$$= \sqrt{\frac{\cos^2 A + \sin^2 A - 2\sin A\cos A}{\cos^2 A - \sin^2 A}}$$

$$= \sqrt{\frac{1-\sin 2A}{\cos 2A}}$$

$$\left[\begin{array}{l} \therefore \cos^2 A + \sin^2 A = 1 \\ 2\sin A \cdot \cos A = \sin 2A \\ \cos^2 A - \sin^2 A = \cos 2A \end{array}\right]$$

Hence, the correct answer is $\sqrt{\dfrac{1-\sin 2A}{\cos 2A}}$.

102. **(d)** Let, diameter = x

Then, radius = $\dfrac{x}{2}$

Now, volume of a sphere = $\dfrac{4}{3} \times \pi \times r^3$

$$= \frac{4}{3} \times \pi \times \left(\frac{x}{2}\right)^3$$

$$= \frac{1}{6} x^3 \pi$$

According to the questions,

Diameter = $\dfrac{x}{2}$

Then, radius = $\dfrac{x}{4}$

Now, volume of a sphere

$$= \frac{4}{3}\pi r^3 = \frac{4}{3}\pi\left(\frac{x}{4}\right)^3$$

$$= \frac{4}{3}\pi \times \frac{x}{4} \times \frac{x}{4} \times \frac{x}{4}$$

$$= \frac{1}{48} x^3 \pi$$

We can clearly see that the volume reduced by $\dfrac{1}{8}$ of the former volume.

103. **(a)**

$3888 = 2 \times 2 \times 2 \times 2 \times 3 \times 3 \times 3 \times 3 \times 3$

$3969 = 3 \times 3 \times 3 \times 3 \times 7 \times 7$

HCF (3888, 3969)

$= 3 \times 3 \times 3 \times 3 = 81$

Hence, the correct answer is 81.

104. (a) $96 = 2^5 \times 3$
$108 = 2^2 \times 3^3$
$144 = 2^4 \times 3^2$
Smallest natural number
= LCM of 96,108 and 144
= 864

105. (d) HCF (240, 280, 560)
$240 = 4 \times 6 \times 10$
$280 = 4 \times 7 \times 10$
$560 = 4 \times 2 \times 7 \times 10$
HCF (240, 280, 560) $= 4 \times 10 = 40$
Hence, the correct answer is 40.

106. (b) From the following table,
The number of mobile phone sold by store Q in 2013 = 198
The number of mobile phone sold by store S in 2015 = 205
According to the question,
Difference = 205 ~ 198 = 7
Hence, the correct answer is 7.

107. (d) From the table below shows, we observed that,
In 2002, company Q produce 130 lakh and company P produce 120 lakh .
In 2005, company Q produce 275 lakh and company P produce 240 lakh.
So, in years 2002, 2005 company Q produce more fabric than company P.

108. (a) Given, total time = 5 h
By formula, Time $= \dfrac{\text{Distance}}{\text{Speed}}$
or Average speed $= \dfrac{\text{Total distance}}{\text{Total time}}$
First half distance $= \dfrac{75}{60} \times 85 = \dfrac{425}{4}$ km
= 106 km (approx)
Second half, $D = 3 \times 70 = 210$ km
Let distance = x
$\Rightarrow \quad 73 = \dfrac{x + 316}{5}$
$\Rightarrow x + 316 = 365 \Rightarrow x = 365 - 316$
$\therefore \quad x = 49$
$\therefore$ Speed $= \dfrac{49}{45} \times 60 = \dfrac{196}{3} = 65$ (approx)
Hence, the speed of the car during the first 45 min = 65 km/h.

109. (a) Let Peter invest = ₹ 100
Then, Rachel invest $= \dfrac{100}{2} =$ ₹ 50
Peter's simple interest $= \dfrac{PRT}{100}$
$= \dfrac{100 \times 10 \times 2}{100} =$ ₹ 20

Rachel's compound interest
$= P\left[\left(1 + \dfrac{r}{100}\right)^t - 1\right]$
$= 50\left[\left(1 + \dfrac{10}{100}\right)^3 - 1\right]$
$= 50\left[\left(\dfrac{110}{100}\right)^3 - 1\right]$
$= 50\left[\dfrac{1331}{1000} - 1\right]$
$= 50 \times \dfrac{331}{1000} = 16.55$
Difference = SI – CI
= ₹ 20 – 16.55 = 3.45
According to the question,
$3.45 \rightarrow 897$
$1 \rightarrow \dfrac{897}{3.45}$
Rachel invest money $= \dfrac{897}{3.45} \times 50$
= ₹ 13000
Hence, the correct answer is 13000.

Toppers Tip
In compound interest questions, using successive rate change method can help you solve problems faster than solving the entire question step by step.

110. (a) Let the cost price of almonds = ₹ 100
After 10% increment, then the price of almonds = 100 + 100 of 10% = ₹ 110
$\because$ Expenditure = Price × Consumption
When expenditure remains constant
$\left\{\text{Price} \propto \dfrac{1}{\text{Consumption}}\right\}$
Now, decreased consumption%
$= \dfrac{110 - 100}{110} \times 100\%$
$= \dfrac{10}{110} \times 100 = \dfrac{100}{11}\%$
$= 9\dfrac{1}{11}\%$

111. (c) Let cost price of a table = 100 unit
Adding 35% profit of a table, then Selling price
= 100 + 100 of 35%
$= 100 + 100 \times \dfrac{35}{100} = 135$ unit
According to the question,
135 unit = 5670
1 unit $= \dfrac{5670}{135} =$ ₹ 42
Now, the cost price of a table = 100
= 100 × 42 = ₹ 4200

He decided to sell the table with 12% profit, then the new selling price of a table = 4200 + 4200 of 12%
$= 4200 + 4200 \times \dfrac{12}{100}$
= 4200 + 504 = ₹ 4704
Hence, the correct answer is ₹ 4704.

112. (c) Here, distance = Constant
Then, time $\propto \dfrac{1}{\text{Speed}}$
Ratio of time = 12 : 15 : 10
Then, ratio of speeds $= \dfrac{1}{12} : \dfrac{1}{15} : \dfrac{1}{10}$
$\Rightarrow \quad \left(\dfrac{1}{12} : \dfrac{1}{15} : \dfrac{1}{10}\right) \times 60 = 5 : 4 : 6$
Hence, the correct answer is 5 : 4 : 6.

113. (c) According to the question,

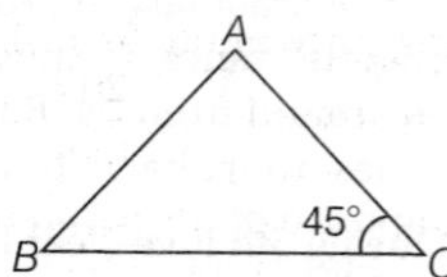

When two sides are given and angle between them.
Area $= \dfrac{1}{2} ab \sin\theta$
where, ($a = 4$, $b = 5$, $\theta = 45°$)
Area of a triangle
$= \dfrac{1}{2} \times 4 \times 5 \times \sin 45°$
$= 2 \times 5 \times \dfrac{1}{\sqrt{2}} \qquad \left[\because \sin 45° = \dfrac{1}{\sqrt{2}}\right]$
$= \sqrt{2} \times \sqrt{2} \times 5 \times \dfrac{1}{\sqrt{2}} = 5\sqrt{2}$ cm^2

114. (b) Given, Discount = 10%,
Profit = 30% and Cost price = 450
Used formula,
$\dfrac{\text{CP}}{\text{MP}} = \dfrac{100 - D\%}{100 + P\%}$
$\Rightarrow \dfrac{450}{\text{Marked price}} = \dfrac{(100 - 10)}{(100 + 30)} = \dfrac{90}{130}$
$\Rightarrow$ Marked price $= \dfrac{13}{9} \times 450$
= 13× 50 = 650
Hence, the correct answer is 650.

115. (c) Fourth proportional
$= \dfrac{\text{Second number} \times \text{Third number}}{\text{First number}}$
$= \dfrac{0.8 \times 0.108}{0.3} = 0.288$
Hence, the correct answer is 0.288.

116. (d) $\dfrac{(3.254 \times 3.254 \times 3.254) - (0.746 \times 0.746 \times 0.746)}{(3.254 \times 3.254) + 0.746 \times 0.746) + (3.254 \times 0.746)}$

Let $a = 3.254$, $b = 0.746$

$= \dfrac{a \times a \times a - b \times b \times b}{a \times a + b \times b + a \times b} = \dfrac{a^3 - b^3}{a^2 + b^2 + ab}$

Used formula,

$a^3 - b^3 = (a - b)(a^2 + b^2 + ab)$

$\therefore \dfrac{(a - b)(a^2 + b^2 + ab)}{(a^2 + b^2 + ab)} = a - b$

Putting value $= 3.254 - 0.746 = 2.508$

Hence, the correct answer is 2.508.

117. (a) Let the price of a land = 100 unit

Increasing the price of a land

$= 100 \times \dfrac{65}{100} + 100 = 165$ unit

Selling price of the first seller

$= 100 + 100 \times \dfrac{20}{100} = 120$ unit

Selling price of the second seller

$= 120 + 25\%$ of 120

$= 120 + \dfrac{25}{100} \times 120 = 150$ unit

But selling price of the third seller

= 165 unit

Profit percentage earned by the third seller $= \dfrac{165 - 150}{150} \times 100$

$= \dfrac{15}{150} \times 100 = 10\%$

Hence, the correct answer is 10%.

118. (a) From the given table,

We observed that,

Total sample indicated $= 28 + 32 + 46 = 106$

Total rock indicated $= 9 + 7 + 13 = 29$

Now, percentage $= \dfrac{29}{106} \times 100$

$= \dfrac{2900}{106} = 27.36\%$

Hence, the correct answer is 27.36%.

119. (c) From the given table,

Total population of town C = 8000

Population of town C below poverty line = 8000 × 20%

$= 8000 \times \dfrac{20}{100} = 1600$

Population of town C above poverty line = 8000 − 1600 = 6400

Let above poverty line in town C male population $= 5x$

Above poverty line in town C female population $= 3x$

According to the question,

$5x + 3x = 6400$

$8x = 6400$

$x = 800$

Now, in town C above poverty line female population

$= 3x = 3 \times 800 = 2400$

Hence, 2400 is the correct answer.

120. (a)

$\dfrac{(157 \times 157) + (157 \times 133) + (133 \times 133)}{(157 \times 157 \times 157) - (133 \times 133 \times 133)}$

Let $a = 157$, $b = 133$

Then, $\dfrac{(a \times a) + (a \times b) + (b \times b)}{(a \times a \times a) - (b \times b \times b)}$

$= \dfrac{a^2 + ab + b^2}{a^3 - b^3}$

$\because a^3 - b^3 = (a - b)(a^2 + ab + b^2)$

Then, $\dfrac{(a^2 + ab + b^2)}{(a - b)(a^2 + ab + b^2)} = \dfrac{1}{a - b}$

Putting a and b value,

$= \dfrac{1}{(157 - 133)} = \dfrac{1}{24}$

Hence, the correct answer is $\dfrac{1}{24}$.

121. (b) Through the pie-chart, we observed that sleeping time = 8

Whole central angle = 24

Then, percentage % $= \dfrac{8}{24} \times 100$

$= \dfrac{100}{3}\% = 33.33\%$

Hence, the correct answer is 33.33%.

122. (c) Let the breadth of the rectangular field $= x$ m

Then, the length of the rectangular field $= x + 20\%$ of x

$= x + x \times \dfrac{20}{100} = \dfrac{120x}{100}$ m

By formula

Area of a rectangle = Length × Breadth

According to the question,

$x \times \dfrac{120}{100} x = 480$

$x^2 = \dfrac{480 \times 100}{120} = 400$

$x = 20$

Hence, the length of the rectangular field

$= \dfrac{120}{100} x = \dfrac{120}{100} \times 20 = 24$ m

Hence, the correct answer is 24 m.

123. (c) According to the question,

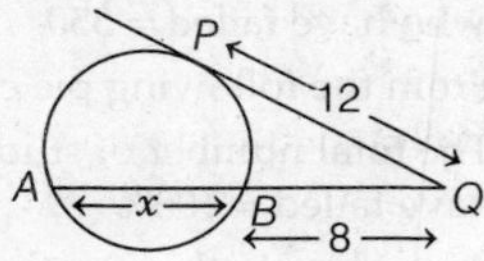

Let $AB = x$

$PQ^2 = AQ \times QB$

$\Rightarrow (12)^2 = (8 + x)\,8$

$\Rightarrow \dfrac{144}{8} = 8 + x$

$\Rightarrow x = 18 - 8$

$\therefore x = 10$ cm

Hence, $AB = 10$ cm is the correct answer.

124. (c) Let the speed of the boat in still water $= x$ km/h

and the speed of the stream $= y$ km/h

According to the question,

The upstream speed of a boat

= 8 km/h

$x - y = 8$ ....(i)

The downstream speed of a boat

= 15 km/h

$x + y = 15$ ...(ii)

Adding Eqs. (i) and (ii),

$2x = 23$

$\Rightarrow x = \dfrac{23}{2} = 11.5$ km/h

Subtract Eqs. (i) and (ii),

$2y = 7$

$y = \dfrac{7}{2} = 3.5$ km/h

Hence, the correct answer is 11.5 and 3.5 km/h.

125. (c) By the ratio method,

According to the question,

First decreased = 28%

$= \dfrac{28}{100} = \dfrac{7}{25}$

Increased $= 28\% = \dfrac{28}{100} = \dfrac{7}{25}$

Now,	Original value	New value
Decreased	= 25	18
Increased	= 25	32
	625	: 576

49

$\therefore 49 \rightarrow 784$

Original (625) $= \dfrac{784}{49} \times 625$

= ₹ 10000

126. **(d)** Given, total number of students who have failed = 350

From the following pie chart shows,

The total number of students who have failed = 100%

According to the question,

The number of students failed in Mathematics $= 350 \times \frac{27}{100} = \frac{189}{2}$

The number of students failed in all other subject $= 350 \times \frac{73}{100} = \frac{511}{2}$

Less than the number of students

$$= \frac{511}{2} - \frac{189}{2} = \frac{322}{2} = 161$$

127. **(a)** $19 \div 5 \text{ of } (27 - \overline{15 - 21}) + 37$

By using VBODMAS rule,

$19 \div 5 \text{ of } [27 - (\overline{15 - 21})] + 37$

$= 19 \div 5 \text{ of } [27 - (-6)] + 37$

$= 19 \div 5 \text{ of } [27 + 6] + 37$

$= 19 \div 5 \text{ of } 33 + 37$

$= 19 \div (5 \times 33) + 37$

$= 19 \div 165 + 37$

$= \frac{19}{165} + 37 = \frac{19 + 37 \times 165}{165}$

$= \frac{19 + 6105}{165} = \frac{6124}{165}$

Hence, the correct answer is $\frac{6124}{165}$.

128. **(b)** An investor bought the stock = ₹ 1000

According to the question,

In first year, the price of a stock increased by 30%.

$\Rightarrow 1000 \times \frac{30}{100} + 1000 =$ ₹ 1300

In second year, the price of a stock decreased by 20%

$= 1300 - 1300$ of 20%

$= 1300 - 1300 \times \frac{20}{100}$

$= 1300 - 260 =$ ₹ 1040

Hence, the final value of the investment after 2 yr at ₹ 1040.

129. **(d)** Let the second number is x.

We Know that,

Product of two number

= HCF of both numbers × LCM of both number

$x \times 55 = 5 \times 660$

$\Rightarrow \quad x = \frac{5 \times 660}{55}$

$\Rightarrow \quad x = \frac{660}{11}$

$\therefore \quad x = 60$

130. **(b)** Number of bottle are required

$= \frac{\text{Volume of hemispherical container}}{\text{Volume of a small cylindrical bottles}}$

$$n = \frac{\frac{2}{3}\pi R^3}{\pi r^2 h} \Rightarrow n = \frac{2R^3}{3r^2 h}$$

$D = 36,\ R = \frac{36}{2} = 18$ cm

(radius of hemispherical container)

$d = 6,\ r = \frac{6}{2} = 3$ cm

(radius of a small cylindrical bottles)

$h = 6$ cm

(height of a small cylindrical bottles)

$n = \frac{2 \times 18 \times 18 \times 18}{3 \times 3 \times 3 \times 6}$

$\therefore n = 72$

Hence, 72 bottles are required to empty the container.

131. **(b)**

Efficiency

Tom = 7 day — 2

Jay = 14 day — 1

LCM (7, 14) = 14

Total work = 14

Together work $\frac{14}{3} = 4\frac{2}{3}$ days

Hence, the correct answer is $4\frac{2}{3}$ days.

132. **(a)** When a train passes another train in same direction.

$$\text{Time} = \frac{\text{Distance covered}}{\text{Relative speed}} = \frac{L_1 + L_2}{S_1 - S_2}$$

$L_1 = 200$ m, $L_2 = 250$ m

$S_1 - S_2 = 68 - 50 = 18$ km/h

[change km/h into m/sec]

$S_1 - S_2 = 18 \times \frac{5}{18} = 5$ m/s

$\text{Time} = \frac{200 + 250}{5}$

$= \frac{450}{5} = 90$ s

Hence, the correct answer is 90 s.

133. **(b)** $\because \text{Speed} = \frac{\text{Distance}}{\text{Time}}$

According to the question,

$T_1 \sim T_2 = 3$ h

Let (Speed = S),

$D = 1000$ km

$$\frac{1000}{S} \sim \frac{1000}{S - 75} = 3$$

$$1000\left[\frac{1}{S} - \frac{1}{S - 75}\right] = 3$$

$$1000\left[\frac{S - S + 75}{S(S - 75)}\right] = 3$$

$$\frac{1000 \times 75}{3} = S(S - 75)$$

$S(S - 75) = 25000$

$S^2 - 75\,S - 25000 = 0$

Solve this quadratic equation,

$S^2 - 200\,S + 125\,S - 25000 = 0$

$\Rightarrow (S - 200)(S + 125) = 0$

$\Rightarrow S = 200$ km/h

Hence, the original duration of the travel $= \frac{1000}{S} = \frac{1000}{200} = 5$ h

Hence, the correct answer is 5h.

134. **(a)** $7\sin^2 A + 3\cos^2 A = 4$

We know that, $[\because \cos^2 A = 1 - \sin^2 A]$

$7\sin^2 A + 3(1 - \sin^2 A) = 4$

$7\sin^2 A + 3 - 3\sin^2 A = 4$

$\Rightarrow \quad 4\sin^2 A = 4 - 3$

$\Rightarrow \quad \sin^2 A = \frac{1}{4}$

$\Rightarrow \quad \sin A = \frac{1}{2} \quad \left[\because \sin 30° = \frac{1}{2}\right]$

$\Rightarrow \quad \sin A = \sin 30°$

$\therefore \quad A = 30°$

According to the question,

$\cot A = \cot 30° \quad [\because \cot 30° = \sqrt{3}]$

Hence, the correct answer is $\sqrt{3}$.

135. **(d)** $\sec A - \tan A = P$ ...(i)

$\because \sec^2 A - \tan^2 A = 1$

$(\sec A - \tan A)(\sec A + \tan A) = 1$

$\Rightarrow \quad \sec A + \tan A = \frac{1}{\sec A - \tan A}$

So, $\sec A + \tan A = \frac{1}{P}$ ...(ii)

From adding Eqs. (i) and (ii),

$2\sec A = P + \frac{1}{P}$

$2\sec A = \frac{P^2 + 1}{P}$

$\therefore \quad \sec A = \frac{P^2 + 1}{2P}$

Hence, the correct answer is $\sec A = \frac{P^2 + 1}{2P}$.

136. **(d)** $2(\sin 1° \times \sec 89°)$

$+ 3(\cos 11° + \operatorname{cosec} 79°)$

$+ 5(\tan 21° \times \tan 69°)$

We know, $\sec\theta = \frac{1}{\cos\theta}$, $\operatorname{cosec}\theta = \frac{1}{\sin\theta}$

and $\tan\theta = \frac{1}{\cot\theta}$

$\cos(90° - \theta) = \sin\theta,$

$\sin(90° - \theta) = \cos\theta,$

$\cot(90° - \theta) = \tan\theta,$

$$= 2\left(\sin 1° \times \frac{1}{\cos 89°}\right) + 3\left(\cos 11° \times \frac{1}{\sin 79°}\right) + 5\left(\tan 21° \times \frac{1}{\cot 69°}\right)$$

$$= 2\left(\sin 1° \times \frac{1}{\cos(90° - 1°)}\right) + 3\left(\cos 11° \times \frac{1}{\sin(90° - 11)}\right) + 5\left(\tan 21° \times \frac{1}{\cot(90° - 21°)}\right)$$

$$= 2\left(\sin 1° \times \frac{1}{\sin 1°}\right) + 3\left(\cos 11° \times \frac{1}{\cos 11°}\right) + 5\left(\tan 21° \times \frac{1}{\tan 21°}\right)$$

$= 2 + 3 + 5 = 10$

137. (c) HCF (20, 30, 40)

$20 = 2 \times 2 \times 5,\ 30 = 2 \times 3 \times 5,$

$40 = 2 \times 2 \times 2 \times 5$

HCF (20, 30, 40) $= 2 \times 5 = 10$

He wants to cut pieces of the same length = 10 m

Hence, the least number of total pieces

$$= \frac{20}{10} + \frac{30}{10} + \frac{40}{10}$$

$= 2 + 3 + 4 = 9$

138. (d) We make figure,

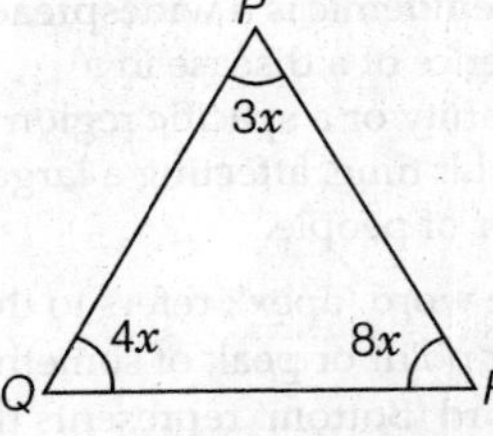

Let $\angle P = 3x$, $\angle Q = 4x$ and $\angle R = 8x$

We know that,

$\angle P + \angle Q + \angle R = 180°$

According to the question,

$3x + 4x + 8x = 180°$

$\Rightarrow \quad 15x = 180°$

$\Rightarrow \quad x = 12°$

$\angle P = 3x = 3 \times 12 = 36°,$

$\angle Q = 4 \times 12 = 48°,$

$\angle R = 8x = 8 \times 12 = 96°$

We can see that,

PQ is the longest side and QR is the shortest side.

Hence, QR and PQ is the correct answer.

139. (c) We make figure,

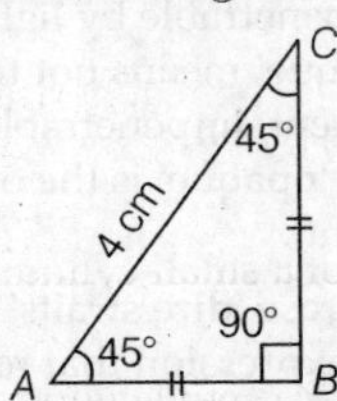

In every triangle have three angle sum 180°.

In ΔABC, $AB = BC$

By Pythagoras theorem,

$AC^2 = AB^2 + BC^2$

$AC^2 = BC^2 + BC^2 \quad [\because AB = BC]$

$BC^2 = \frac{1}{2}AC^2$

$BC = \frac{1}{\sqrt{2}}AC = \frac{1}{\sqrt{2}} \times 4$

$BC = 2\sqrt{2}$

Hence, the correct answer is $2\sqrt{2}$.

140. (d) Given,

Total number of boys = 2000

From given pie-chart

Total number of boys = 100%

So, 100% = 2000

1% = 20

According to the question,

In Schools A and C

Total number of boys = 13% + 55%

= 68%

The total number of boys in Schools A and C = 68% × 20 = 1360

The average number of boys studying in schools A and C $= \frac{1360}{2} = 680$

Hence, the correct answer is 680.

141. (d) Let after x days 15 employees left.

According to the question,

$75 \times 60 = x \times 75 + 60(65 - x)$

$600 = 15x \Rightarrow x = 40$ days

142. (c) Given, borrowed amount = 15000

Time = 5 yr $\quad \left[\because \text{SI} = \frac{PRT}{100}\right]$

According to the question,

SI = (6000 + 18600 − 15000)

SI = 9600

Total interest

$$= \left[\left(\frac{15000 \times 5 \times R}{100}\right) + \left(\frac{9000 \times 5 \times R}{100}\right)\right]$$

$\Rightarrow 750R + 450R \Rightarrow 9600 = 1200R$

$\therefore \ R = 8\%$

143. (b) Given,

ΔABC and ΔPQR are congruent triangles, where $\angle A = \angle P = 90°$.

We make figure.

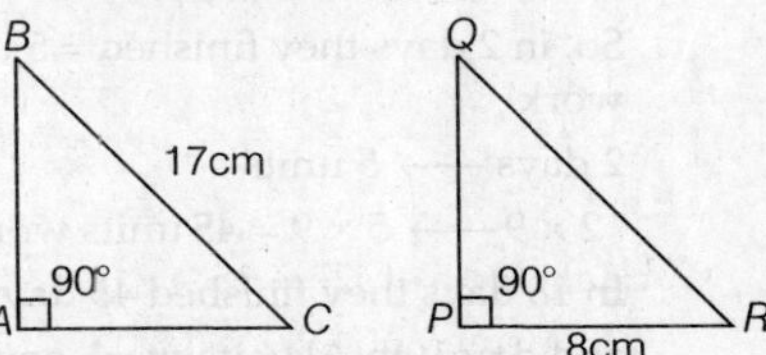

Given that,

$BC = 17$ cm, $PR = 8$ cm

As both are congruent triangles

$\therefore AC = PR$, $AB = PQ$ and $BC = QR$

So, $AC = PR = 8$ cm

$AB = PQ = ?$

$BC = QR = 17$cm

By Pythagoras theorem,

$(BC)^2 = (AB)^2 + (AC)^2$

$\Rightarrow \quad (17)^2 = AB^2 + (8)^2$

$\Rightarrow \quad (AB)^2 = 289 - 64$

$\Rightarrow \quad (AB)^2 = 225$

$\therefore \quad AB = 15$ cm

144. (a) Given, total students = 6700

So, total students having specialisation in CSE, ECE and CIVIL are

= 22% + 10% + 8% = 40%

$= 6700 \times \frac{40}{100} \Rightarrow 2680$

Hence, option (a) is correct answer.

145. (a) Given, LCM and HCF of two numbers are 1105 and 5. And LCM is 17 times of the first number.

Let, first number be x

Then LCM = $17x$.

$17x \longrightarrow 1105$

$x \longrightarrow 65$

So, first number is 65

Now, second number = ?

By formula,

First number × Second number = LCM × HCF

Second number $= \frac{1105 \times 5}{65} = 85$

Hence, two numbers are 65 and 85.

146. (c) Given,

Akshita alone can finish the typing work in 16 days.

Raina alone can finish the typing work in 24 days.

Akshita 16 → 3

>48 (LCM –16,24)

Raina 24 → 2

Let, total work = 48 units

They work on alternate basis, i.e. day 1 Akshita and on day 2 Raina

So, in 2 days they finished = 5 units work

2 days ⟶ 5 units

$2 \times 9 \longrightarrow 5 \times 9 = 45$ units work

In 18 days they finished 45 days work and day 19th Akshita work and entire work will be finished.

So, 19 days they take to finish the typing work if they work on alternate basis.

Hence, option (c) is correct.

147. (b) Given, distance = 540 km

Time = 240 min = 4 h

$S = \frac{D}{T}$

$D = S \times T$

$D = 90 \times 5$

$D = 450$ km

($\because$ Distance between another stations)

$$\text{Average speed} = \frac{\text{Total distance}}{\text{Total time}}$$

$$= \frac{450 + 540}{5 + 4} = \frac{990}{9} = 110 \text{ km/h}$$

148. (c) Let their height be $7x$ and $5x$ and their diameter are $10y$ and $21y$.

So, their radius

$= 5y$ and $10.5y$ $\left[\because R = \frac{D}{2}\right]$

Now, their volumes,

$= \pi r_1^2 h_1 : \pi r_2^2 h_2$

$= 10.5y \times 10.5y \times 5x : 5y \times 5y \times 7x$

$= 551.25 : 175 = 63 : 20$

149. (b) Given, single discount

$\Rightarrow 700 \times \frac{35}{100} = ₹\ 245$

Now, successive discounts

$= 18 + 12 - \frac{18 \times 12}{100}\%$

$\left[\text{formula} \because a + b - \frac{a \times b}{100}\right]$

$= 30 - 2.16\% = 27.84\%$

$\Rightarrow 700 \times \frac{27.84}{100} = 194.88$

So, difference = 245 – 194.88 = ₹ 50.12

150. (a) Given, total fruits sold = 1200 kg

Percentage of Banana sold = 30%

So, sold banana (in kg) $= 1200 \times \frac{30}{100}$

$= 360$ kg

Hence, 360 kg of Banana sold in a day.

151. (c) The word 'transparent' means clear and penetrable by light. The word 'opaque' means not transparent or translucent, impenetrable to light. Therefore, 'opaque' is the opposite of 'transparent'.

152. (b) The phrase 'dire straits' is an idiomatic expression that refers to a very difficult or desperate situation. It comes from the nautical term straits, which are narrow, difficult-to-navigate passages of water. So, being in dire straits means being in a state of serious trouble or adversity.

153. (c) The incorrectly spelled word is 'Councel'. The correct spelling is 'Counsel'.

154. (b) 'Ephemeral' means lasting for a very short time or fleeting.

155. (c) The idiom 'stand a chance' means to have a possibility or likelihood of success in a particular situation.

156. (a) The word 'aggravate' means to irritate or annoy.

157. (c) The idiom 'Bid defiance to' means to openly resist or challenge someone's authority or wishes.

158. (b) The idiom 'Get your act together' essentially means to gather oneself, become organised, or prepare oneself to perform effectively.

159. (a) Both old-fashioned and obsolete refer to something that is no longer in widespread use or that is considered outdated or outmoded.

160. (d) The underlined segment is incorrect. The preposition 'of' is commonly used after the adjective 'doubtful' to indicate the object of doubt or skepticism.

161. (a) The incorrectly spelt word is 'vestubular', The correctly spelt word is 'Vestibular'.

162. (d) The idiom 'miss the boat' means to fail to take advantage of an opportunity because one did not act in time or was not prepared. In the given sentence, the context suggests that there are other people waiting to seize an opportunity and if the person being addressed doesn't act quickly, they will fail to capitalise on it.

163. (a) The correct form should be 'have visited' instead of 'have visit' as we use third form of verb with 'has/have'.

164. (b) The phrase 'Midas touch' refers to the ability to be successful in all endeavors, especially those related to wealth and business.

In the given scenario, the person has consistently succeeded in various ventures and amassed significant wealth, akin to the legendary King Midas, who was able to turn everything he touched into gold. Therefore, Midas touch accurately describes the person's remarkable success and ability to generate wealth.

165. (a) Part (a) 'There was no other book' is incorrect as the presence of the word 'other' is unnecessary. Remove 'other' to correct the sentence.

166. (b) 'Adorable' means inspiring great affection or delightful, it implies something or someone that is charming, attractive and easily evokes feelings of love or affection.

167. (a) The most appropriate meaning of the underlined word ingredients is 'components'.

168. (d) The word 'abhor' means to regard with disgust and hatred so, its opposite would be to feel affection or positive regard towards something, which is represented by Love.

169. (b) Reluctant describes being unwilling or hesitant to do something.

170. (c) An epidemic is a widespread occurrence of a disease in a community or a specific region at a particular time, affecting a large number of people.

171. (b) The word 'apex', refers to the highest point or peak of something. The word 'Bottom' represents the lowest point or base, making it the suitable antonym in this context.

172. (b) 'Abandoned' in this context means to leave someone or something behind, especially in a situation where one has responsibility or an obligation to stay or care for them. Therefore, 'left' accurately conveys the meaning of 'abandoned' in this sentence.

173. (d) Part and parcel refers to something that is an essential or integral component of a whole, something that cannot be separated from the whole. Therefore, it signifies a fundamental or indispensable element of something.

174. (d) The phrase 'elbow grease' means to put hard work into doing something.

175. (d) A 'robe' and a 'cloak' are both garments worn over other clothing, typically for warmth or ceremonial purposes.

176. (a) 'A snowball effect' refers to a situation in which something starts small and then grows or increases at an accelerating rate, similar to a snowball rolling down a hill and getting larger as it picks up more snow.

177. (a) The incorrectly spelt word is 'fabulouous'. The correct spelling should be 'fabulous'.

178. (c) The use of preposition 'to is incorrect in the sentence. Use preposition 'across' is correct in the context of the sentence.

179. (b) 'Vituperated' means to criticise or rebuke someone harshly and with abusive language. Therefore, option (b) accurately captures the meaning conveyed by the word 'vituperated' in the sentence.

180. (b) The idiom 'hit the books' means to study diligently or intensively.

181. (b) To overwhelm means to have a strong emotional effect on someone, typically causing them to feel intense emotions or to be deeply affected by something.

182. (a) The incorrectly spelled word is: 'Ocassion'. The correct spelling is 'Occasion'.

183. (d) The preposition 'on' is incorrect in the sentence. The correct preposition for the sentence is 'in'.

184. (d) The incorrectly spelled word is 'resileince'. The correct spelling is 'resilience'.

185. (d) Part (d) 'the university has putting off' is incorrect as the structure of present perfect continuous tense is has/have+ been+ -ing form of verb. Hence, add 'been' after 'has'.

186. (b) The underlined segment 'her mother' in the given sentence is incorrect. In the context of the sentence, the possessive case of the noun must be used- her mother's.

187. (c) 'Inquisitive' means showing curiosity or interest in learning new things. So, its antonym would be someone who is not interested or curious, which is represented by 'uninterested'.

188. (b) The part that contains the error is 'when a tree branch break the living room window'.
The correct form should be when a tree branch broke the living room window as the given sentence is in past tense.

189. (c) An omnivore is an organism that consumes both plants and animals as part of its diet.

190. (c) 'Bombastic' means high-sounding but with little meaning, inflated. Therefore, its opposite would be something plain or simple in style or expression, which is represented by 'plain'.

191. (d) The word 'sharp' emphasises the idea that tigers have teeth that are keen or capable of causing injury, which aligns with their role as hunters.

192. (c) The word 'about' indicates the direction of learning or the topic being studied, which fits the context of researchers seeking knowledge about tigers.

193. (b) Among the largest species of cats in the world, tigers are powerful hunters with sharp teeth, strong jaws and agile bodies. Therefore, the word 'cats' accurately describes the subject of the passage which is about tigers.

194. (d) The word 'classified' is used here to indicate the categorisation or grouping of the tiger into different sub-species.

195. (d) The word 'listed' here indicates the status of Sumatran tigers as being officially recognised as critically endangered.

196. (d) The passage discusses how globally shared digital resources, such as design, knowledge and software, can impact how goods are produced and consumed worldwide. It highlights the collaborative nature of design projects and the benefits of relying on shared digital resources for manufacturing processes. Therefore, Digital Globalisation accurately captures the overarching theme of the passage.

197. (c) The passage refers to globally shared digital resources, such as design, knowledge, and software, as a digital commons. This term emphasises the idea of shared ownership and accessibility of digital assets across geographical boundaries.

198. (a) The author discusses the potential impact of globally shared digital resources on how goods are produced and consumed, presenting examples and highlighting the benefits of such a model. The tone is forward-looking and exploratory rather than critical or confrontational, indicating a speculative approach to the topic. Therefore, Speculative is the most appropriate choice for describing the author's tone.

199. (c) In the passage, the author discusses globally shared digital resources such as knowledge, design and software. However, 'automobiles' are physical objects and not digital resources.

200. (d) In the passage, the term 'geographically dispersed communities' refers to communities that are spread out or scattered across different geographic locations. Therefore, dispersed accurately conveys the idea of being scattered.

CPO SI P-1 SP 16

PAPER-1

SSC CPO SI SOLVED PAPER

4 October 2023 (Shift I)

MM : 200 **Time** : 2 hr

Instructions

1. This paper contains 200 questions.
2. It has 4 Parts, **Part I** General Intelligence and Reasoning, **Part II** General Knowledge and General Awareness, **Part III** Quantitative Aptitude and **Part IV** English Comprehension.
3. Each question carries **1 marks.**

Part I

General Intelligence and Reasoning

1. Three of the following letter-clusters are alike in some manner and one is different. Select the one that is different.
(a) NQST
(b) GTHS
(c) PSUV
(d) SVXY

2. Three statements are given followed by three conclusions numbered I, II and III. Assuming the statements to be true, even if they seem to be at variance with commonly known facts, decide which of the conclusion(s) logically follow(s) from the statements.

Statements
Some elephants are fishes.
No fish is a tiger.
All deer are tigers.

Conclusions
I. Some elephants are deer.
II. No elephant is a tiger.
III. No deer is a fish.
(a) Only Conclusion III follows.
(b) Both Conclusions I and III follow.
(c) Both Conclusions I and II follow.
(d) Only Conclusion II follows.

3. Select the figure that will come next (?) in the following series.

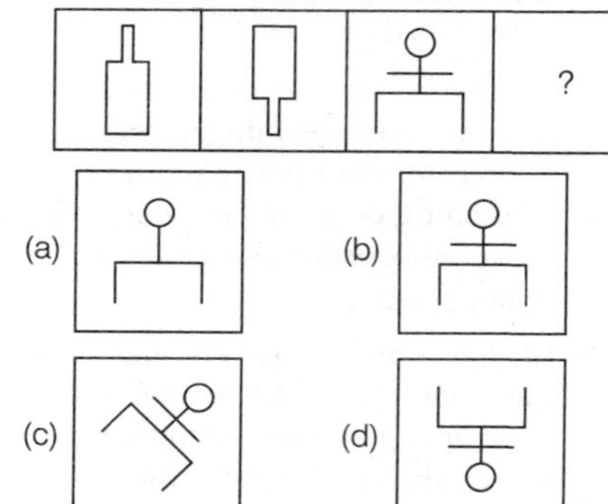

4. Six friends are sitting in a circle. All of them are facing the centre. Kanak sits third to the right of Sona. Kapil is an immediate neighbour of Mani. Goldy sits second to the right of Mani. Sona is an immediate neighbour of Kapil and Suresh.
Who sits second to the left of Kanak?
(a) Suresh (b) Kapil
(c) Goldy (d) Mani

5. In this question, three statements are given, followed by two conclusions numbered I and II. Assuming the statements to be true, even if they seem to be at variance with commonly known facts, decide which of the conclusion(s) logically follows/follow from the statements.

Statements
All buildings are towers.
No tower is a shop.
Some shops are offices.

Conclusions
I. Some offices are towers.
II. No building is a shop.
(a) Both Conclusions I and II follow
(b) Only Conclusion I follows
(c) Only Conclusion II follows
(d) Neither Conclusion I nor II follows

6. Which of the following numbers will replace the question mark (?) in the given series?
239, 274, 309, 354, 399, 454, ?
(a) 499 (b) 474
(c) 539 (d) 509

7. If '+' means '−', '−' means '×', '×' means '÷' and '÷' means '+', what will come in place of question mark (?) in the following equation?
$36 - 5 \div 240 \times 6 + 17 = ?$
(a) 218 (b) 221
(c) 203 (d) 237

8. If A, B, C, D and E denote +, −, ×, ÷ and =, respectively, then which of the following options is correct?
(a) 4A9C6D2E40A9
(b) 4A9C6D2B40E9
(c) 4A9C6D2E40B9
(d) 4A9E6D2C40B9

9. Which of the following numbers will replace the question mark (?) in the given series?
25, 26, 28, 32, 40, ?
(a) 50 (b) 56 (c) 58 (d) 52

10. Which letter-cluster will replace the question mark (?) to complete the given series?
VQSN, ?, ROOL, PNMK, NMKJ
(a) PQMN (b) TPQM
(c) PTMQ (d) TQRN

11. If '+' means '×', '×' means '–', '–' means '÷' and '÷' means '+', then what will come in place of the question mark (?) in the following equation?
$9 + 3 \div 2 \times 135 - 15 = ?$
(a) 22 (b) 25 (c) 18.5 (d) 20

12. Select the correct option that indicates the arrangement of the given words in the order in which they appear in an English dictionary.
1. Realistic 2. Readily
3. Reach 4. Really
5. Reactor 6. Realize
(a) 3, 5, 1, 2, 6, 4 (b) 3, 5, 2, 1, 6, 4
(c) 3, 2, 6, 1, 5, 4 (d) 3, 5, 6, 1, 2, 4

13. Select the option that is related to the third word in the same way as the second word is related to the first word.
(The words must be considered as meaningful words and must not be related to each other based on the number of letters/number of consonants/vowels in the word.)
Derive : Infer :: Urge : ?
(a) Protest (b) Hinder
(c) Censure (d) Exhort

14. Select the correct mirror image of the given figure, when the mirror is placed at line MN as shown.

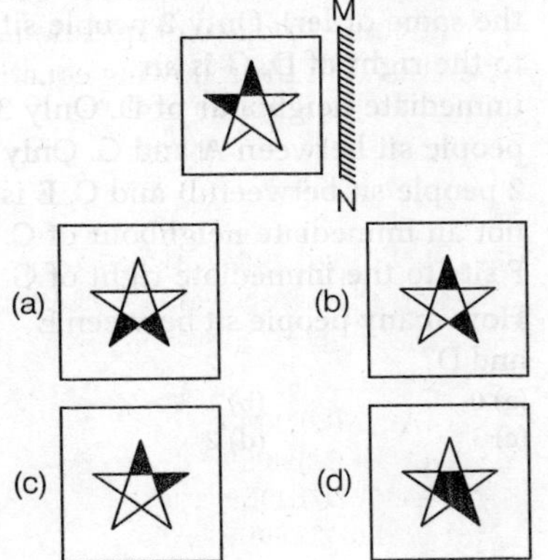

15. 'D @ G' means 'D is the father of G', 'D # G' means 'D is the daughter of G', 'D * G' means 'D is the mother of G' and 'D – G' means 'D is the husband of G'.
If A – Q * B @ R, how is A related to R?
(a) Father (b) Husband
(c) Son (d) Father's father

16. If A denotes '+', B denotes '×', C denotes '–', and D denotes '÷', then what will come in place of question mark (?) in the following equation?
145 A 27 D 3 B ? = 163
(a) 1 (b) 2 (c) 3 (d) 6

17. In a certain code language, 'LIFE' is coded as '9351' and 'NEAR' is coded as '4692'. What is the code for 'E' in the given code language?
(a) 3 (b) 4 (c) 1 (d) 9

18. If '+' means '–', '–' means '×', '×' means '÷', '÷' means '+', then what will come in place of the question mark (?) in the following equation?
$124 \times 4 \div 13 - 3 + 36 = ?$
(a) 31 (b) 34 (c) 45 (d) 42

19. Select the correct mirror image of the given figure, when the mirror is placed at MN as shown below.

M
BK$6GHX |
N

(a) ЯHӘɘ$ꓘB (b) ꓤHᎮ9$ꓘB
(c) XHӘɘ$ꓘB (d) XHᎮ9$ꓘB

20. In a certain code language, 'FIRE' is coded as '7391' and 'AGED' is coded as '8247'. What is the code for 'E' in the given code language?
(a) 2 (b) 7
(c) 4 (d) 3

21. A man is standing in the park facing North. He turns to 90° towards the left and walks 40 km. He again takes a 90° turn towards the right and walks 50 km. He takes the next 90° turn towards the right and walks 60 km. Lastly, he takes 90° turn towards the right and walks 50 km. How much distance is he from the starting point?
(a) 40 km (b) 60 km
(c) 50 km (d) 20 km

22. If the given sheet is folded to form a cube, which of the following figures is not possible?

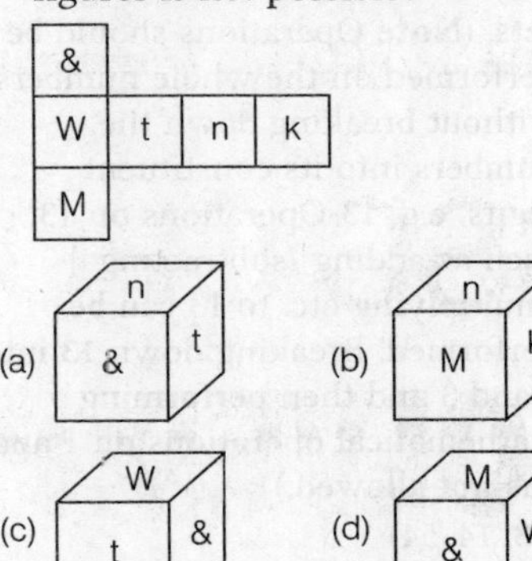

23. Two statements are given, followed by two conclusions numbered I and II. Assuming the statements to be true, even if they seem to be at variance with commonly known facts, decide which of the conclusion(s) logically follow(s) from the statements.

Statements
All cars are vehicles.
All vehicles are trucks.

Conclusions
I. All cars are trucks.
II. All trucks are vehicles.
(a) Neither Conclusion I nor II follows.
(b) Only Conclusion I follows.
(c) Only Conclusion II follows.
(d) Both Conclusions I and II follow

24. Select the option that represents the letters which, when sequentially placed from left to right in the blanks below, will complete the letter series.
P _ _ H _ CE _ ZP _ EH _
(a) H Z C Z P E C (b) C E Z P H C Z
(c) Z C H P Z C E (d) E P Z C H E C

25. Select the figure that will replace the question mark (?) in the following series.

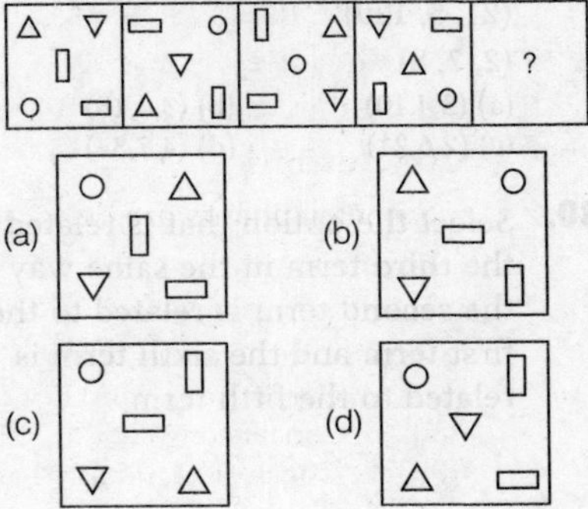

26. Select the set in which the number are related in the same way as the numbers of the given sets. (**Note** Operations should be performed on the whole numbers, without breaking down the numbers into its constituent digits. e.g. 13-Operations on 13 such as adding /subtracting /multiplying etc. to 13 can be performed. Breaking down 13 into 1 and 3 and then performing mathematical operations on 1 and 3 is not allowed.)

(13, 14, 54)

(15, 18, 66)

(a) (11, 13, 52) (b) (15, 17, 66)
(c) (13, 19, 64) (d) (12, 34, 90)

27. Select the number from among the given options that can replace the question mark (?) in the following series.

61, 95, 138, 197, 279, ?

(a) 397 (b) 389
(c) 391 (d) 395

28. Which letter-cluster will replace the question mark (?) to complete the given series?

GOWB, MVEK, SCMT, ?, EQCL

(a) YJUC (b) YJCU
(c) YKUC (d) YKCU

29. Select the set in which the numbers are related in the same way as are the numbers of the following set. (**Note** Operations should be performed on the whole numbers, without breaking down the numbers into its constituent digits. e.g. 13-Operations on 13 such as adding /subtracting /multiplying etc. to 13 can be performed. Breaking down 13 into 1 and 3 and then performing mathematical operations on 1 and 3 is not allowed)

(21, 5, 120)

(2, 7, 8)

(a) (3,4,10) (b) (3,4,16)
(c) (2,6,21) (d) (4,7,34)

30. Select the option that is related to the third term in the same way as the second term is related to the first term and the sixth term is related to the fifth term

142 : 108 :: 185 : ? :: 169 : 135

(a) 157 (b) 148
(c) 151 (d) 162

31. In a certain code language, 'TRAUMA' is coded as '36' and 'STIL' is coded as '24'. How will 'OBEIDEINT' be coded in that language?

(a) 54 (b) 84
(c) 44 (d) 72

32. Which of the following numbers will replace the question mark (?) in the given series?

352, 326, 284, 225, 148, ?

(a) 71 (b) 54
(c) 52 (d) 50

33. A cube is made by folding the given sheet. In the cube so formed, what would be the number on the opposite side of the number '1'.

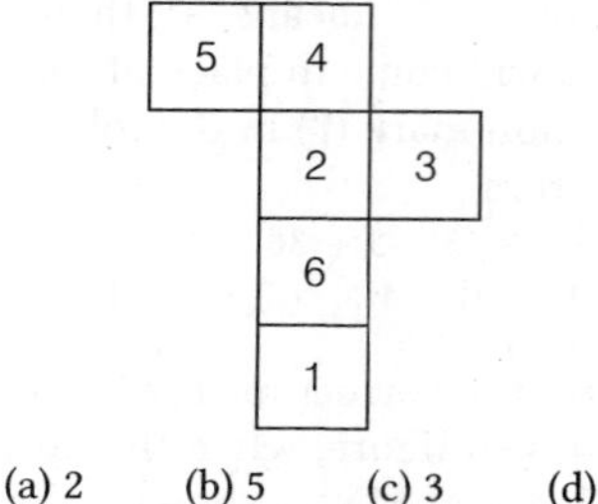

(a) 2 (b) 5 (c) 3 (d) 4

34. Four letter-clusters have been given, out of which three are alike in some manner and one is different. Select the odd letter-cluster.

(a) ZSNK (b) VOJG
(c) WNDD (d) TMHE

35. A paper is folded and cut as shown. How will it appear when unfolded?

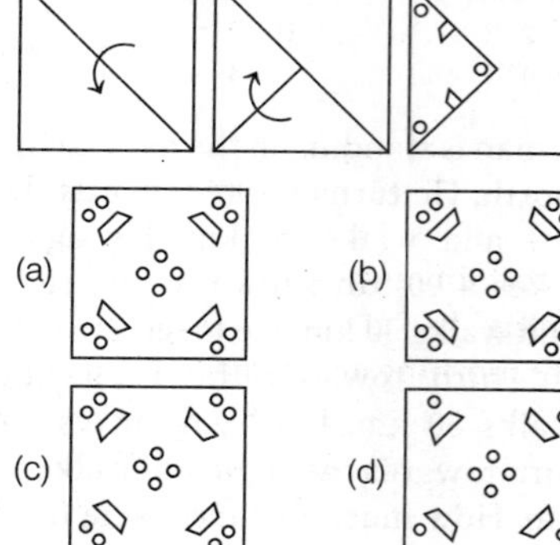

36. Select the set in which the numbers are related in the same way as are the numbers of the following sets.

(**Note** Operations should be performed on the whole numbers, without breaking down the numbers into its constituent digits. e.g. 13. Operations on 13 such as adding /subtracting /multiplying etc. to 13 can be performed. Breaking down 13 into 1 and 3 and then performing mathematical operations on 1 and 3 is not allowed)

(329, 145, 184), (567, 221, 346)

(a) (308, 205, 192)
(b) (506, 302, 224)
(c) (676, 225, 451)
(d) (464, 264, 206)

37. Select the correct mirror image of the given combination, when the mirror is placed at 'MN' as shown below.

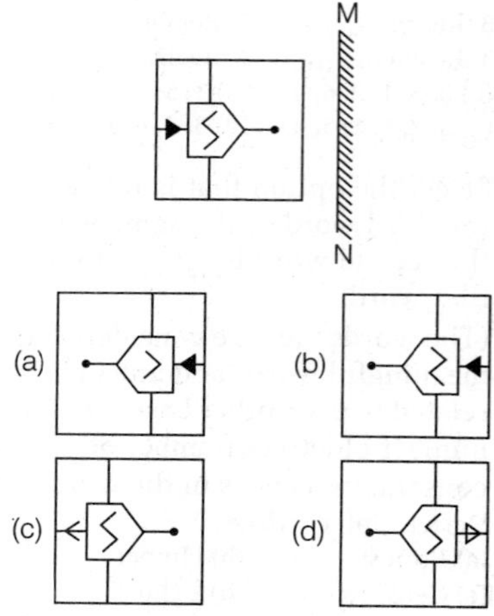

38. Seven people, A, B, C, D, E, F and G, are sitting in a straight row, facing North (not necessarily in the same order). Only 2 people sit to the right of D. G is an immediate neighbour of D. Only 3 people sit between A and G. Only 2 people sit between B and C. E is not an immediate neighbour of C. F sits to the immediate right of G. How many people sit between E and D?

(a) 0 (b) 1
(c) 3 (d) 2

39. Select the option figure which is embedded in the given figure as its part (rotation is not allowed).

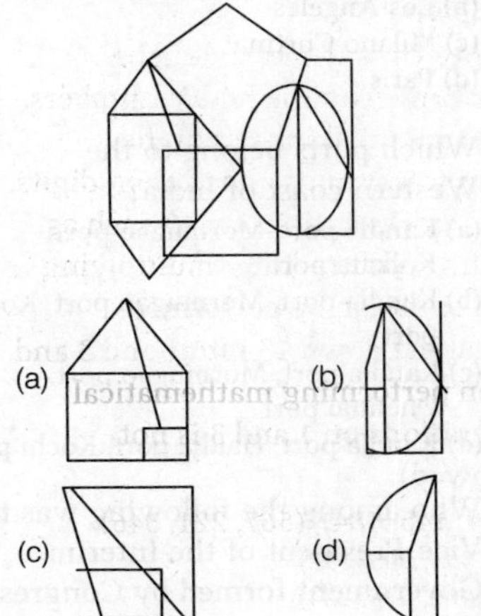

40. B is West of E. A is North-West of B. F is North-East of B. D is South-East of F, such that F is North-West of E and D is South-East of E as well. If C is South-West of E, what is the position of A with respect to E? (All positions are arranged in grid pattern)

(a) South-East (b) North-East
(c) South-West (d) North-West

41. A paper is folded and cut as shown. How will it appear when unfolded?

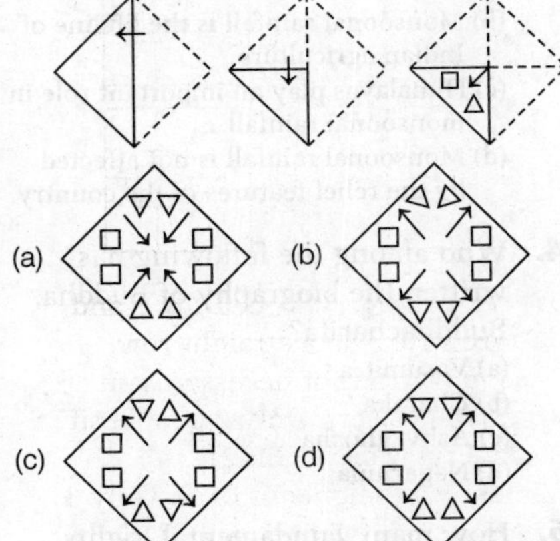

42. In a certain code language, 'ASIA' is written as 'ZHRZ' and 'IRELAND' is written as 'RIVOZMW'. How will 'NORWAY' be written in that language?

(a) NLISZB (b) MLIDZB
(c) NJIDZB (d) MJIDZB

43. If '+' means '–', '–' means '×', '×' means '÷', '÷' means '+', then what will come in place of the question mark (?) in the following equation?

$61 \div 9 \times 3 - 8 + 5 = ?$

(a) 80 (b) 75
(c) 89 (d) 72

44. Given below are two statements and two conclusions. Take the statements to be true even, if they are at variance with commonly known facts and decide whether the conclusion(s) follow(s) the given statements.

Statements

Some rats are mats.
All mats are ants.

Conclusions

I. Some rats are ants.
II. Some ants are mats.

(a) Both the Conclusions follow
(b) Neither Conclusion I nor II follows
(c) Only Conclusion II follows
(d) Only Conclusion I follows

45. Select the figure from among the given options that can replace the question mark (?) in the following series?

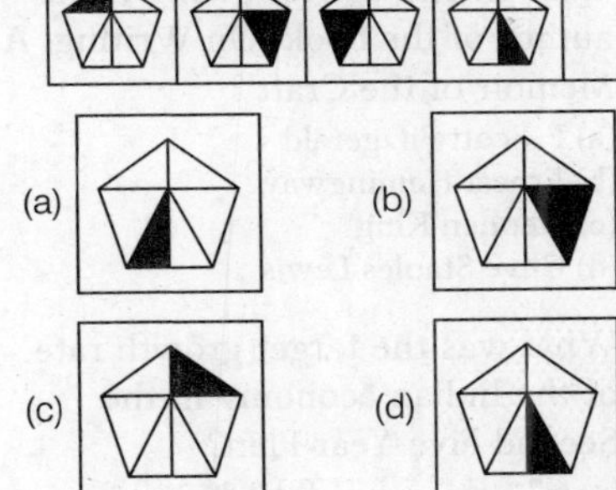

46. Which two signs should be interchanged to make the given equation correct?

$114 \div 85 + 5 \times 4 - 33 = 149$

(a) ÷ and + (b) ÷ and –
(c) + and × (d) – and +

47. In a certain code language, 'good morning' is coded as 'mu du', 'early morning tea' is coded as 'du tu se', 'tea is early' is coded as 'se re tu'. What is the code for the word 'is'?

(a) mu (b) tu
(c) du (d) re

48. Select the option that represents the correct order of the given words as they would appear in an English dictionary?

1. Voice 2. Vocalist
3. Vivisection 4. Void
5.Vogue

(a) 3, 2, 5, 1, 4 (b) 5, 2, 3, 1, 4
(c) 2, 3, 5, 1, 4 (d) 4, 2, 3, 1, 5

49. 'A ? B' means 'A is the son of B'.
'A \$ B' means 'A is the daughter of B'.
'A * B' means 'A is the brother of B'.
'A = B' means 'A is the father of B'.
If H \$ Q * Y * N, then how is Y related to H?

(a) Father
(b) Brother
(c) Father's brother
(d) Father's father

50. Select the option that is related to the third word in the same way as the second word is related to the first word. (The words must be considered as meaningful words and must not be related to each other based on the number of letters/number of consonants/vowels in the word.)

Wrestling : Arena :: Ice-Skating : ?

(a) Track
(b) Rink
(c) Stadium
(d) Ground

Part II

General Knowledge and General Awareness

51. The Karewa formations are found in the ....

(a) North-Eastern Hills
(b) Terai Region
(c) Uttaranchal Himalayas
(d) Kashmir Himalayas

52. In which part of the Constitution are Fundamental Duties added?

(a) Part III-B (b) Part II-B
(c) Part I-A (d) Part IV-A

53. Who among the following applied European theatrical techniques to Indian Classical dance with folk and tribal dance?

(a) Guru Bipin Singh
(b) Uday Shankar
(c) Birju Maharaj
(d) Kelucharan Mohapatra

54. Ravana Phadi Cave and Durga Temple at Aihole portray the architectural style of which dynasty?
(a) Chalukya (b) Pallava
(c) Hoysala (d) Vijaynagara

55. Read the given statements and select the correct option.
(i) The Governor is the real head of the State Government.
(ii) The Chief Minister plays a key role in framing the laws and policies of the State Government.
(iii) Governor of a State is appointed by the President.
(a) Both (i) and (ii)
(b) Only (ii)
(c) Both (ii) and (iii)
(d) Only (i)

56. What do you call the drugs that bind to the receptor site and inhibit its natural function?
(a) Antagonists
(b) Depressants
(c) Antidepressants
(d) Agonist

57. What is the dimension of the Kabaddi play field for men?
(a) 14 m × 10 m
(b) 14 m × 8 m
(c) 12.50 m × 10 m
(d) 13 m × 10 m

58. In which year did the Ministry of Health and Family Welfare of India launch the Weekly Iron and Folic Acid Supplementation (WIFS) programme to meet the challenge of high prevalence and incidence of anaemia among adolescent girls and boys (56% girls and 30% boys)?
(a) 2013 (b) 2011
(c) 2014 (d) 2012

59. Who among the following was the successor of Mughal emperor Shahjahan to the throne?
(a) Shah Shuja
(b) Aurangzeb
(c) Murad Bakhsh
(d) Dara Shikoh

60. Who is the ex-officio Chairman of the Rajya Sabha?
(a) Vice-President
(b) Prime Minister
(c) President
(d) Attorney General of India

61. What is the full form of RIDF?
(a) Rural Infrastructure Development Forum
(b) Road Infrastructure Development Fund
(c) Rural Infrastructure Development Fund
(d) Rural Industries Development Fund

62. Tansen, the music legend was a courtier in which of the following courts before coming to Akbar?
(a) Benaras (b) Gandhara
(c) Rewa (d) Maghad

63. How many Fundamental Rights were provided originally by the Indian Constitution in1950?
(a) Seven (b) Six
(c) Nine (d) Five

64. The Five-Year Plans in India laid down not only specific objectives to be attained in the five years of a plan, but also what was to be achieved over a period of 20 years. This long-term plan is called a ......
(a) perspective plan
(b) twenty-year plan
(c) two-decade plan
(d) perpetual plan

65. Who among the following is the author of the book 'On Writing: A Memoir of the Craft'?
(a) F. Scott Fitzgerald
(b) Ernest Hemingway
(c) Stephen King
(d) Clive Staples Lewis

66. What was the target growth rate of the Indian economy in the Second Five-Year Plan?
(a) 6.7% (b) 2.8%
(c) 5.4% (d) 4.5%

67. Who among the following was the first President of IOC?
(a) Lord Killanin
(b) Pierre, Baron de Coubertin
(c) Demetrius Vikelas
(d) Avery Brundage

68. In which process is a solid substance volatilised by heating and the vapour is condensed back to the solid at a cold surface?
(a) Chromatography
(b) Filtration
(c) Distillation
(d) Sublimation

69. The Olympic Winter Games 2026 would be played in.......
(a) Brisbane
(b) Los Angeles
(c) Milano Cortina
(d) Paris

70. Which ports belong to the Western coast of India?
(a) Kandla port, Mormugao port, Kolkata port
(b) Kandla port, Mormugao port, Kochi port
(c) Kandla port, Mormugao port, Chennai port
(d) Kandla port, Haldia port, Kochi port

71. Who among the following was the Vice-President of the Interim Government formed by Congress in 1946?
(a) Vallabhbhai Patel
(b) Baldev Singh
(c) John Matthai
(d) Jawaharlal Nehru

72. Which East-flowing river basin covers the states of Jharkhand, Chhattisgarh and Odisha and has a drainage area of 39,033 sq km?
(a) Baitarni (b) Brahmani
(c) Nagavali (d) Sarada

73. Which of the following statements is not true for Indian monsoons?
(a) Monsoonal rainfall is affected by jet streams.
(b) Monsoonal rainfall is the lifeline of Indian agriculture.
(c) Himalayas play an important role in monsoonal rainfall.
(d) Monsoonal rainfall is not affected by the relief features of the country.

74. Who among the following has written the biography of Buddha, Buddhacharita?
(a) Vasumitra
(b) Charaka
(c) Ashvaghosha
(d) Nagarjuna

75. How many Fundamental Rights were there at the time of adoption of the Indian Constitution?
(a) Seven (b) Five
(c) Six (d) Eight

76. Linthoi Chanambam is associated with which of the following sports events?
(a) Cricket (b) Chess
(c) Badminton (d) Judo

77. In 1957, who redefined a model that predicted the shape of individual molecules based on the extent of electron-pair electrostatic repulsion?
(a) Nyholm and Gillespie
(b) Heitler and London
(c) Staudinger and Perey
(d) Marcet and Pauling

78. In which of the following states is Bonalu festival celebrated?
(a) Jharkhand (b) Gujarat
(c) Telangana (d) Uttar Pradesh

79. Who among the following designed a campaign that came to be known as the 'Rowlatt Satyagraha'?
(a) Mahatma Gandhi
(b) Feroze Shah Mehta
(c) Mahadev Govind Ranade
(d) Bal Gangadhar Tilak

80. Asad Ali Khan was known for playing which of the following Indian instruments?
(a) Sitar (b) Tabla
(c) Rudra Veena (d) Violin

81. Recoveries of loans and advances, borrowings, are an example of ....
(a) non-tax receipts
(b) capital receipts
(c) revenue receipts
(d) tax receipts

82. Thullal dance originated in which of the following states?
(a) Uttarakhand (b) Kerala
(c) Manipur (d) Gujarat

83. Which winds blow across the Asian continent at latitudes North of the Himalayas roughly parallel to the Tibetan highlands?
(a) Trade winds
(b) South-West winds
(c) Jet streams
(d) North-West winds

84. What is the name of the Comprehensive Household Survey providing labour force statistics in India, which was first conducted in 1955?
(a) Periodic Labour Force Survey (PLFS)
(b) Employment-Unemployment Survey (EUS)
(c) Quarterly Employment Survey (QES)
(d) Area Frame Establishment Survey (AFES)

85. During the British rule in India, which of the following Governor-Generals devised the 'Doctrine of Lapse', a policy of annexation?
(a) Lord Cornwallis
(b) Lord Canning
(c) Warren Hastings
(d) Lord Dalhousie

86. Which compound structure includes a saturated short-chain fatty acid with 4 carbon molecules, commonly found in esterified form in animal fats and plant oils?
(a) Butyric acid (b) Propionic acid
(c) Succinic acid (d) Lactic acid

87. In June ...., the Reserve Bank of India published a 'Consultative Document on Regulation of Microfinance'.
(a) 2021 (b) 2019 (c) 2022 (d) 2020

88. What amount of 'Seed Capital' is provided as support to a Self-Help Group under the Pradhan Mantri Formalisation of Micro Food Processing Enterprises Scheme?
(a) ₹20,000 (b) ₹30,000
(c) ₹50,000 (d) ₹40,000

89. The Beating Retreat ceremony is held at which of the following places?
(a) Chandni Chowk
(b) Connaught Place
(c) India Gate
(d) Vijay Chowk

90. Soparrkar and the logo of his worldwide initiative 'Dance for a Cause' are being printed on an official postage stamp issued by the .... government.
(a) Bangladesh (b) Sri Lanka
(c) Bhutan (d) Nepal

91. Who among the following Bahmani sultans transferred his capital from Gulbarga to Bidar?
(a) Humayun (b) Mujahid Shah
(c) Ahmad Shah (d) Firuz Shah

92. In which of the following cases the Supreme Court, while laying out the 'basic structure' of the Constitution held that the democratic character of the polity was an essential component of the 'basic structure'?
(a) Sajjan Singh *vs* State of Rajasthan
(b) Kesavananda Bharati *vs* State of Kerala
(c) Romesh Thappar vs State of Madras
(d) A K Gopalan *vs* State of Madras

93. In 2015, the eminent danseuse and .... exponent, Padma Subrahmanyam was selected for Kerala's prestigious choreography award 'Nishagandhi Puraskaram' instituted by the state tourism department.
(a) Kathakali
(b) Sattriya
(c) Bharatanatyam
(d) Kuchipudi

94. What do you call the fluid matrix filling in the cell?
(a) Ribosome (b) Plasmid
(c) Cytoplasm (d) Golgi bodies

95. 'A Grain of Sand in the Hourglass of Time' is an autobiography of which Indian politician?
(a) IK Gujral
(b) Arjun Singh
(c) Manmohan Singh
(d) LK Advani

96. Which odourless, colourless, tasteless and chemically unreactive gas was invented by Daniel Rutherford in 1772 and was independently isolated at the same time by CW Scheele and H. Cavendish?
(a) Nitrogen (b) Argon
(c) Fluorine (d) Oxygen

97. ....2005 is referred to as the 'Right to Work' as it guaranteed 100 days of employment in a year by the Indian Government to people who are in need of and who are able to do work.
(a) Mahatma Gandhi Regional Employment Guarantee Act
(b) Mahatma Gandhi Rural Employment Act
(c) Mahatma Gandhi National Rural Employment Guarantee Act
(d) Mohan Gandhi Regional Guarantee Act

98. In which year did Albert Einstein predict a new state of matter, the Bose-Einstein condensate (BEC), based on a quantum formulation by the Indian physicist Satyendra Nath Bose?
(a) 1919 (b) 1935 (c) 1924 (d) 1930

99. The main function of centriole is
(a) to help plant cell for multiplication
(b) to help cell division in animal cell
(c) to maintain rigidity in plant cell
(d) to maintain mineral composition in bacterial cell

100. How many planets are terrestrial planets?
(a) 3 (b) 6 (c) 4 (d) 5

Part III
Quantitative Aptitude

101. The total surface area of a square-based right pyramid is 1536 m^2, of which 37.5% is the area of the base of the pyramid. What is the volume (in m^3) of this pyramid?
(a) 3048 (b) 3072
(c) 3144 (d) 3108

102. If $\sin A + \sin^2 A = 1$, then the value of $\cos^4 A + \cos^6 A$ is
(a) $\cos A$ (b) $\sin A$
(c) 1 (d) 0

103. The radius of a circle is 1.75 cm. What is the circumference of the circle? $\left(\pi = \frac{22}{7}\right)$
(a) 5.5 cm (b) 11 cm
(c) 9.63 cm (d) 22 cm

104. Let the HCF of m and n be 'a' and let $n = ab$, LCM of m and n is given by
(a) bm (b) am
(c) ab (d) mn

105. Study the given pie-chart and answer the question that follows. The pie-chart shows the number of students (boys and girls) studying in standard 10 of various schools (X, Y, Z in the year 2022.)

Total number of students (Boys and Girls) = 3600

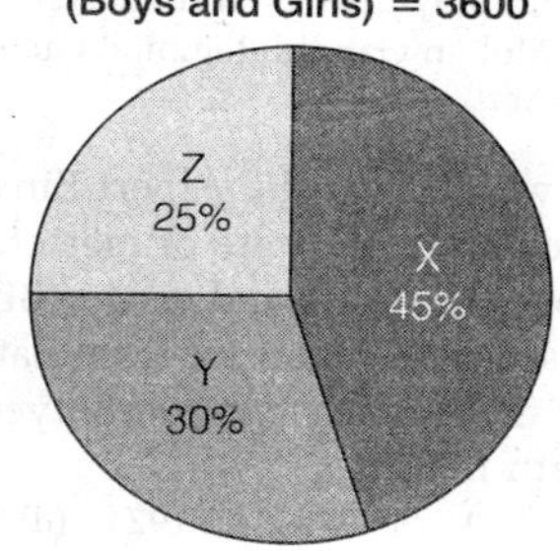

What is the difference between the total number of students (boys and girls) in school Y and Z together and the total number of students (boys and girls) in school X and Y together?
(a) 720 (b) 840 (c) 780 (d) 820

106. The radius of the base of a right circular cone is 5 cm. Its slant height is 13 cm. What is its volume (in cm^3, rounded off to 1 decimal place)? (Take, $\pi = \frac{22}{7}$)
(a) 328.6 (b) 323.4
(c) 314.3 (d) 340.5

107. A sum of money was invested at 10% interest per year, compounded half-yearly, for 18 months. If the amount payable on maturity was ₹ 64827, what was the sum invested?
(a) ₹55600 (b) ₹56000
(c) ₹56800 (d) ₹56500

108. Let C be a circle with centre O and radius 5 cm. Let PQ be a tangent to the circle and A be the point of tangency. Let B be a point on PQ such that the length of AB is 12 cm. If the line joining O and B intersects the circle at R, find the length of BR (in cm).
(a) 2 (b) 13
(c) 6 (d) 8

109. The value of
$$1\frac{2}{5} - \left[3\frac{3}{4} \div \left\{1\frac{1}{4} \div \frac{1}{2}\left(1\frac{1}{2} \times 3\frac{1}{3} \div 1\frac{1}{3}\right)\right\}\right]$$
is
(a) 3 (b) 0 (c) 2 (d) 1

110. When A alone does a piece of work, he takes 25 days more than the time taken by A and B to do the work together. On the other hand, B alone takes 16 days more than the time taken by A and B to do the work together. How many days will A and B, working together, take to do the work?
(a) 24 (b) 20 (c) 23 (d) 22

111. In what proportion should a grocer mix wheat at ₹ 12 per kg and ₹ 25 per kg so as to make a mixture of worth ₹ 20 per kg?
(a) 8 : 3 (b) 3 : 5
(c) 5 : 8 (d) 5 : 7

112. Find the mean proportional between 32 and 162.
(a) 99 (b) 65 (c) 72 (d) 97

113. Rakhi purchased a basket, a wallet and a belt. She got discounts of 5%, 8% and 10% on the basket, the wallet and the belt, respectively, on their respective marked prices of ₹80, ₹150 and ₹ 350. How much amount (in ₹) did she pay in total?
(a) 529 (b) 51 (c) 580 (d) 519

114. In ΔABC, $\angle B = 90°$ and $AB : BC = 1 : 2$. The value of $\cos A + \tan C$ is
(a) $\frac{5+\sqrt{5}}{2\sqrt{5}}$ (b) $\frac{1+\sqrt{5}}{2\sqrt{5}}$
(c) $\frac{2\sqrt{5}}{2+\sqrt{5}}$ (d) $\frac{2+\sqrt{5}}{2\sqrt{5}}$

115. The product of two numbers is 20000. If their LCM is 800, then what is their HCF?
(a) 25 (b) 30 (c) 35 (d) 20

116. If $a + \frac{1}{a} = 3$, then the value of $a^4 + \frac{1}{a^4}$ is.
(a) 48 (b) 81 (c) 27 (d) 47

117. Study the given graph and answer the question that follows. The given graph represents the percentage of books on different subjects that a person has in his library.

Percentage distribution of books on different subjects

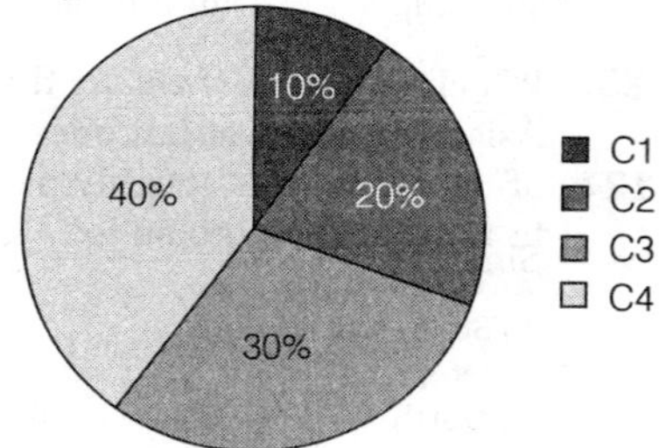

If the total number of books is 60, then what is the ratio of the number of books on subject C_1 to the average number of books per subject?
(a) 3 : 7 (b) 2 : 3 (c) 3 : 5 (d) 2 : 5

118. Find the value of $\frac{\cos 37°}{\sin 53°} - \cos 47° \operatorname{cosec} 43°$.
(a) 0 (b) −1 (c) 2 (d) 1

119. The volume of a sphere is given by 130977 cm^3. Its surface area (in cm^2) is
(a) 16847 (b) 12474
(c) 17424 (d) 14274

120. The speed of a boat in standing water is 6 km/h and the speed of the stream is 2.5 km/h. A man rows to a place at a distance of 59.5 km and comes back to the starting point. The total time taken by him is
(a) 16 h (b) 24 h (c) 22 h (d) 18 h

121. The table below shows the number of students commuting to school by different modes of transport

Modes of transport	School bus	Bicycle	Walking	Other vehicles
No. of boys	80	280	130	200
No. of girls	140	190	90	250

Which mode of transport is used by maximum number of students?
(a) Bicycle (b) Walking
(c) Other vehicles (d) School bus

122. A boat covers a distance of 72 km downstream in 6 h, while it takes 12 h to cover the same distance upstream. What is the speed of the boat in still water?
(a) 6 km/h (b) 9 km/h
(c) 10 km/h (d) 8 km/h

123. Simplify
$$5\frac{1}{3}-\left[4\frac{1}{3}+\left(3\frac{1}{3}\div 2\frac{1}{3}-\overline{\frac{1}{3}}\right)\right]$$
(a) $\frac{2}{3}$ (b) $\frac{1}{3}$ (c) $-\frac{1}{3}$ (d) $-\frac{2}{3}$

124. Simplify : $\dfrac{1-\frac{3}{7}\div\frac{9}{49}\times\frac{3}{14}}{1+\frac{3}{5}\div\frac{1}{25}\times\frac{1}{30}}$
(a) $\frac{1}{7}$ (b) $\frac{1}{6}$ (c) $\frac{1}{3}$ (d) $\frac{1}{5}$

125. In an election between two candidates, 80% of the voters cast their votes, out of which 5% votes were declared invalid. A candidate got 9500 votes, which were 80% of the valid votes. Find the total number of voters enrolled in that election.
(a) 14780 (b) 15100
(c) 15625 (d) 16100

126. An inlet pipe can fill an empty tank in 3.6 h, while an outlet pipe can drain a completely-filled tank in 6.3 h. If both the pipes are opened simultaneously, when the tank is empty, in how many hours will the tank get completely filled?
(a) 9.0 (b) 8.4
(c) 8.1 (d) 8.7

127. Avi sold a house to Bhargav at a gain of 10% and Bhargav sold it to Chetan at a gain of 20%. If Chetan paid ₹ 26400000 for it, then at what price must Avi have purchased it?
(a) ₹20000000
(b) ₹23000000
(c) ₹25000000
(d) ₹17500000

128. The pie-chart 1 given below shows the runs scored by a player against 6 different countries during 2019-2020. Pie-chart 2 shows the runs scored by the same player against the same 6 countries during 2020-2021.

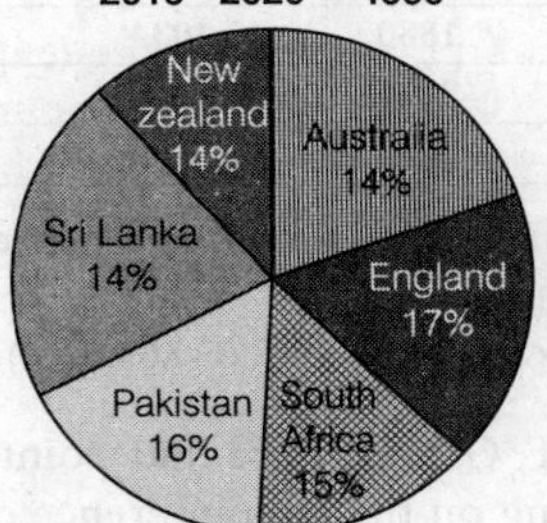

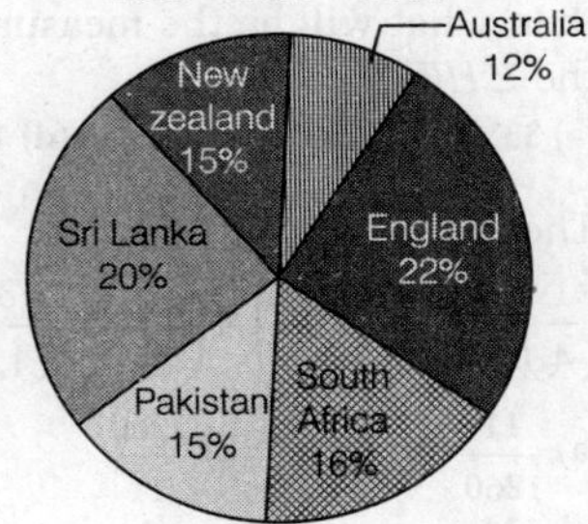

Find the difference between the total runs scored against New Zealand and Pakistan during 2019-2020 and the total runs scored against Sri Lanka and Pakistan during 2020-2021.
(a) 500 (b) 600
(c) 650 (d) 550

129. Find the total surface area of a sphere whose volume is $\frac{256}{3}\pi$ cm^3.
(a) 48 π cm^2
(b) 64 π cm^2
(c) 38 π cm^2
(d) 56 π cm^2

130. If $k(\tan 45^\circ \sin 60^\circ) = \cos 60^\circ \cot 30^\circ$, then the value of k is
(a) 1 (b) 2
(c) $\frac{1}{\sqrt{3}}$ (d) $\sqrt{3}$

131. An inspector is 288 m behind a thief. The inspector runs 42 m and the thief runs 30 metres in a minute. In how much time will the inspector catch the thief?
(a) 24 m (b) 19 m
(c) 21 m (d) 20 m

132. Three boys, on an average, are 25 yr old and their ages are in the ratio of 3 : 5 : 7. What is the age of youngest boy'?
(a) 24 yr (b) 21 yr
(c) 12 yr (d) 15 yr

133. Two numbers are in the ratio 12:7. If their HCF is 25, then find the numbers.
(a) 225, 135 (b) 300, 175
(c) 300, 50 (d) 175, 120

134. A dealer sells his goods at 10% loss on the cost price, but uses 25% less weight. What is his profit percentage?
(a) 35% (b) 20%
(c) 25% (d) 15%

135. A and B undertake a project worth ₹ 36000. A alone can do the work in 25 days. They worked together for 5 days. For the next five days, B worked alone. After that, A substituted B and completed the remaining work in 5 days. The share of A in the earnings is
(a) ₹ 14400 (b) ₹ 21400
(c) ₹ 14600 (d) ₹ 21600

136. A shopkeeper has a sale of ₹5445, ₹5937, ₹5865 and ₹6562 for 4 consecutive days. If he gets an average sale of ₹ 6050 for 5 days, then his sale on the fifth day is
(a) ₹6131 (b) ₹6341
(c) ₹6441 (d) ₹6231

137. Study the given table and answer the question that follows.
The data given in the table is for the month of December 2022.

Company	Total number of employees	Number of female employees
P	4560	2210
Q	4258	1650
R	3052	1280
S	4350	1920

What is the difference between the number of male employees in company P and that in company R?
(a) 592 (b) 578
(c) 605 (d) 580

138. The following table shows the mobile-addicted population of four different cities Hyderabad, Mumbai, Chennai and Pune and the ratio of males to females among them.

City	Mobile-Addicted Population	Male : Female
Hyderabad	220000	7 : 8
Mumbai	350000	12 : 13
Chennai	200000	11 : 9
Pune	150000	9 : 11

Find the total number of addicted males in Chennai.
(a) 110000 (b) 80000
(c) 100000 (d) 120000

139. A company is manufacturing boxes of three types-plastic, wood and glass. The ratio of the numbers of plastic, wood and glass boxes is 2 : 3 : 5. The difference between the numbers of wood and glass boxes is 144. If the number of plastic boxes is increased by 25%, then what will be the number of plastic boxes now?
(a) 144 (b) 360
(c) 216 (d) 180

140. The fraction equivalent to $\frac{1}{5}\%$ is
(a) $\frac{1}{125}$ (b) $\frac{1}{200}$
(c) $\frac{1}{40}$ (d) $\frac{1}{500}$

141. After deducing a commission of 20%, a DVD set costs ₹ 9080. Its marked price is
(a) ₹11200 (b) ₹11350
(c) ₹10000 (d) ₹10100

142. Anandi bought a smart watch from an electronic store for ₹ 4400. Since she had less money, she paid ₹ 2000 for down payment and the shopkeeper offered her an alternative to pay ₹ 2440 after 1 month. Find the rate of interest being charged at simple interest by the shopkeeper in this installment option?
(a) 20% (b) 10% (c) 22% (d) 15%

143. PQR is a triangle. The bisectors of the internal angle $\angle Q$ and external angle $\angle R$ intersect at S. If $\angle QSR = 40°$, then $\angle P$ is
(a) 40° (b) 60° (c) 80° (d) 30°

144. If $x^4 + y^4 = x^2y^2$, then the value of $x^6 + y^6$ is
(a) 2 (b) 0 (c) 1 (d) 3

145. The given table shows the number of students from 4 schools during 2022-2023.

Schools	Total no. of students	Boys	Girls
A	2060	1339	721
B	1880	1034	846
C	2200	990	1210
D	1680	924	756

What is the percentage of girls in school B?
(a) 65% (b) 45% (c) 60% (d) 55%

146. E, F, G, and H are four points lying on the circumference of a circle to make a cyclic quadrilateral. If $\angle FGH = 57°$, then what will be the measure of the $\angle HEF$?
(a) 33° (b) 123° (c) 93° (d) 143°

147. The square root of $\left(\frac{1}{4}\right)\times\left(\frac{1}{9}\right)\times\left(\frac{1}{25}\right)\times\left(\frac{1}{49}\right)\div\left(\frac{36}{121}\right)$ is
(a) $\frac{11}{1260}$ (b) $\frac{1260}{11}$
(c) $\frac{11}{12.60}$ (d) $\frac{1}{1260}$

148. If the radius of a hemispherical balloon increases from 4 cm to 7 cm as air is pumped into it, find the ratio of the surface area of the new balloon to its original.
(a) 16 : 21 (b) 49 : 16
(c) 20 : 49 (d) 21 : 12

149. The sales of batteries (in lakhs) manufactured by a company over the years are shown in the given table.

Year	Types of Batteries					
	4AH	7AH	32AH	35AH	55AH	Total
1992	75	144	114	102	108	543
1993	90	126	102	84	126	528
1994	96	114	75	105	135	525
1995	105	90	150	90	75	510
1996	90	75	135	75	90	465
1997	105	60	165	45	120	495
1998	115	85	160	100	145	605

Which type of battery had the highest total sales over the last seven years?
(a) 32 AH (b) 35 AH
(c) 4 AH (d) 55 AH

150. Study the given table and answer the question that follows.
The table shows the number of students studying in 6 different classes of 6 different schools.

Schools	V	VI	VII	VIII	IX	X
P	152	160	145	156	147	144
Q	148	166	150	155	157	143
R	161	152	140	145	143	165
S	159	142	149	140	142	168
T	147	144	158	163	154	150
U	150	160	162	160	160	140
Total	917	924	904	919	903	910

Which class has the maximum number of students from all schools together?
(a) X (b) VII
(c) VI (d) V

Part IV

English Comprehension

151. Select the most appropriate synonym of the given word.
Spontaneous
(a) Attractive
(b) Exhaustive
(c) Instinctive
(d) Acquisitive

152. Some words in the following sentence have been underlined and given as options.Select the option that contains a spelling error.
The rolling waves on the beach were so trainquil and soothing.
(a) beach (b) trainquil
(c) soothing (d) rolling

153. Parts of the following sentence have been given as options. Select the option that contains an error.

Rani was extreme upset with her results this year.

(a) extreme upset (b) this year
(c) with her results (d) Rani was

154. Four words have been underlined in the given sentence of which one word has a spelling error. Identify the incorrectly spelt word.

The tiger thrshed (A) against his chains (B) in the cage at the circus (C) but nobody paid him any heed (D).

(a) thrshed (b) circus
(c) chains (d) heed

155. Select the most appropriate meaning of the underlined idiom.

We' ve sent a very strong protest letter. That should make them sit up and take notice.

(a) Follow (b) Attend
(c) Observe (d) Consider

156. Select the most appropriate antonym of the given word.

Defunct

(a) Stoicism (b) Extant
(c) Convoluted (d) Redundant

157. You are preparing a speech for the upcoming function. Select a synonym for the highlighted word to make it better.

The education system must evolve to keep pace with the rapid changes in the job market.

(a) Emanate (b) Censor
(c) Demolish (d) Conceal

158. Select the option that will improve the underlined part of the given sentence.

The village Seoni is located 113 km away from the capital city of MP, Bhopal .

(a) adjacent from city capital of MP, Bhopal
(b) far from the capital city of MP, Bhopal
(c) near from the city capital of MP, Bhopal
(d) proximate from capital of MP, Bhopal

159. Select the sentence that has a spelling error.

A. Keeping cities clean and free of germs is particularly essential for keeping their residents healthy.

B. Our health depends not just on our nutrition and personal hygeine but also on how we clean our cities and surroundings.

C. The spread of various diseases is intricately linked to the deteriorating state of public health condition.

D. The good news is that waste management, to keep cities clean, is now getting attention through the Swachh Bharat Mission.

(a) The good news is that waste management, to keep cities clean, is now getting attention through the Swachh Bharat Mission.
(b) The spread of various diseases is intricately linked to the deteriorating state of public health condition.
(c) Keeping cities clean and free of germs is particularly essential for keeping their residents healthy.
(d) Our health depends not just on our nutrition and personal hygeine but also on how we clean our cities and surroundings.

160. Select the most appropriate option that can substitute the underlined word in the given sentence.

The new professor is liked by his students for his amiable approach.

(a) simple (b) strict
(c) academic (d) friendly

161. Select the option that can be used as a one-word substitute for the given group of words.

Spoken or done without any previous thought or preparation

(a) Inaugural (b) Maiden
(c) Extempore (d) Initiative

162. Select the option that can be used as a one-word substitute for the given group of words.

A place where coins are made

(a) Trough (b) Post Office
(c) Grove (d) Mint

163. Select the most appropriate antonym of the given word.

Vague

(a) Elegant (b) Regal
(c) Definite (d) Dwarf

164. Select the option that can be used as a one-word substitute for the given group of words.

Something of monstrous size or power

(a) Bulk (b) Amazon
(c) Heavyweight (d) Behemoth

165. Select the most appropriate idiomatic expression to fill in the blank.

Our Director took a meeting and asked us to express our views on .... of the new HR policy.

(a) the bandwagon (b) the pros and cons
(c) the hook (d) the ups and downs

166. Select the most appropriate idiom that can substitute the underlined segment in the given sentence.

He got a burst of energy and started digging again.

(a) took bull by the horns
(b) a fancy of someone
(c) second wind
(d) heart on the sleeve

167. Select the most appropriate antonym of the given word.

Brave

(a) Elegant (b) Cordial
(c) Cowardly (d) Courageous

168. Select the most appropriate synonym of the given word.

Behold

(a) Look (b) Burden
(c) Fortunate (d) Predict

169. Select the most appropriate option that can substitute the underlined segment in the given sentence.

A gust of wind came abruptly and our sand castle toppled .

(a) tumbled down (b) ran after
(c) turned up (d) blew out

170. Parts of the following sentence have been given as options. One of them may contain an error. Select the part that contains the error from the given options. If you don't find any error, mark 'No error' as your answer.

Luckily, I managed to get a room in the college hostel and I move in there.

(a) and I move in there
(b) Luckily, I managed to get a room
(c) in the college hostel
(d) No error

171. Select the most appropriate meaning of the given idiom.

Open your heart

(a) Immediately think of something
(b) Share your deepest feelings
(c) Feel relieved because the stress is removed
(d) Could do something very easily

172. Select the most appropriate one-word substitution of the given group of words.
A list of source materials that are used or consulted in the preparation of a work or that are referred to in the text.
(a) Bibliography (b) Bibliophile
(c) Bibliotheca (d) Bibliomemoir

173. Select the most appropriate idiom to fill in the blank.
The company had some initial problems, but now it is ....
(a) flying like a rock
(b) flying the nest
(c) flying a kite
(d) flying high

174. Select the most appropriate meaning of the given idiom.
Burn one's bridges
(a) Working very hard
(b) Impossible to return to an earlier state
(c) Having an overnight success
(d) Attack on one's enemy

175. Select the option that can be used as a one-word substitute for the given group of words.
An ability to do several things at the same time.
(a) Indictment (b) Blasphemy
(c) Unit asking (d) Multi-tasking

176. Select the most appropriate meaning of the underlined idiom that can be substituted in the following sentence.
Right now, <u>my hands are full</u>.
(a) My hands are filled up
(b) My hands are swollen
(c) I'm very tired
(d) I'm very busy

177. Select the incorrectly spelt word.
(a) Click (b) Caricature
(c) Cumbersome (d) Cumolative

178. Select the most appropriate antonym of the given word.
Credit
(a) Litigate (b) Install
(c) Debit (d) Impute

179. Select the most appropriate meaning of the given idiom.
Boil the ocean
(a) Something very big
(b) Something which gets hot gradually
(c) Try to do something impossible
(d) To make someone very angry

180. The following sentence has been split into four segments. Identify the segment that contains a grammatical error.
"You look so young!/When did you completed your graduation?"/ asked Rekha/to her neighbour.
(a) to her neighbour
(b) When did you completed your graduation?
(c) asked Rekha
(d) You look so young!

181. Select the correct spelling of the incorrectly spelt word.
Diplomats believe that buraucratic delays are inevitable.
(a) inivitable (b) burocratic
(c) beleave (d) bureaucratic

182. Select the option that can be used as a one-word substitute for the given group of words.
The compulsion to tell lies
(a) Pyromania
(b) Nymphomania
(c) Megalomania
(d) Mythomania

183. Select the most appropriate antonym of the word 'hinderance' in the given sentence and choose the correct option.
The refreshing breeze blew through the open window, bringing relief from the summer heat.
(a) Bringing (b) Blew
(c) Refreshing (d) Relief

184. The following sentence has been divided into parts. One of them may contain an error.Select the part that contains the error from the given options. If you don't find any error, mark 'No error' as your answer.
Neem tastes / a little bitterly, / but is very useful.
(a) a little bitterly (b) Neem tastes
(c) but is very useful (d) No error

185. Select the option that can be used as a one-word substitute for the given group of words.
Someone who pretends to have certain moral standards while secretively that person practices those very moral lapses.
(a) Sinner (b) Actor
(c) Spy (d) Hypocrite

186. Select the most appropriate idiomatic expression to substitute for the underlined segment in the given sentence.
I had <u>to work late in the night</u> for nearly three months to write my first book.
(a) to take a back seat
(b) to burn the midnight oil
(c) to blow a fuse
(d) to look through coloured glasses

187. Select the option that can be used as a one-word substitute for the given group of words.
A person who does not eat any animal product
(a) Vegetarian (b) Veggie
(c) Vegan (d) Non-vegetarian

188. Select the most appropriate meaning of the underlined idiom.
You must <u>lie in the bed you have made</u> .
(a) Face the unpleasant consequences of your own acts
(b) Sleep on the bed you made yourself
(c) Sleep in your own bed
(d) Be contended always

189. The following sentence has been split into four segments. Identify the segment that contains a grammatical error.
The postman/delivers the letters/ through hand,/door to door.
(a) The postman
(b) delivers the letters
(c) door to door
(d) through hand

190. Select the most appropriate antonym of the given word.
Demolish
(a) Inferior (b) Annihilate
(c) Unmethodical (d) Fabricate

Directions (Q. Nos. 191-195) *In the following passage, some words have been deleted. Read the passage carefully and select the most appropriate option to fill in each blank.*

It is said that everyone lives ...(1)... selling something. What you can ...(2)... from this statement is that teachers live by selling knowledge, philosophers live by selling wisdom and priests earn their living by selling spiritual comfort. Though it may be possible to measure the value of material goods in terms of money, it is extremely difficult to ...(3)... the true value of the services which people perform for us. There are times when we would ...(4)... give everything we possess to save our lives, yet we might grudge paying a surgeon a high fee for offering us precisely the same service. The ...(5)... of society are such that skills have to be paid for in the same way that goods are paid for at a shop.

191. Select the most appropriate option to fill in blank no. 1.
(a) by (b) over
(c) of (d) into

192. Select the most appropriate option to fill in blank no. 2.
(a) separate (b) derive
(c) revive (d) choose

193. Select the most appropriate option to fill in blank no. 3.
(a) extort (b) mock
(c) conceal (d) estimate

194. Select the most appropriate option to fill in blank no. 4.
(a) willingly (b) thoroughly
(c) perfectly (d) thoughtfully

195. Select the most appropriate option to fill in blank no. 5.
(a) obstacles (b) interferences
(c) conditions (d) connections

Directions (Q. Nos. 196-200) *Read the given passage carefully and answer the questions that follow.*

As a society, we have come a long way in terms of progress and development. We have eradicated diseases, explored space and created technological wonders that were once thought impossible. Yet, there is still one issue that continues to plague us: stupidity.

Yes, stupidity. The thing that seems to be contagious and has been spreading faster than the common cold. It's everywhere you look - on social media, in politics, in the workplace. You can't escape it.

It's as if we've all collectively decided that intelligence and common sense are no longer important. Why bother using your brain when you can just rely on your gut feelings and conspiracy theories?

Take politics, for example. It used to be that political were expected to be knowledgeable and well-informed about the issues they were dealing with. Now, it seems that all you need is a catchy slogan and some empty promises to win an election.

And don't even get me started on social media. It's a breeding ground for stupidity. People will believe anything they read as long as it confirms their preconceived biases. And don't even think about trying to present them with actual facts and evidence. That's just a waste of time.

But it's not just individuals who are to blame for this epidemic of stupidity. Our education system is failing us as well. We're teaching our kids how to pass tests instead of how to think critically and solve problems. It's no wonder we have a generation of adults who can't even find their way around a basic math problem.

Of course, there are some who would argue that stupidity is just a different way of thinking.That it's a valid perspective that deserves to be respected. To those people, I say this: if you want to be stupid, go ahead. Just don't expect the rest of us to respect your opinions when they're based on nothing but ignorance and misinformation.

It's time for us to take a stand against stupidity. We need to start valuing intelligence and critical thinking again. We need to hold our leaders accountable for their actions and demand that they be knowledgeable and well-informed. We need to teach our children how to think,not just how to memorise.

It won't be easy, but it's a fight worth fighting. Because if we don't, we'll be stuck in a world where stupidity reigns supreme and there's no telling what kind of damage that could do. Solet's all do our part and start using our brains again. It's time to put an end to the epidemic of stupidity once and for all.

196. Which of the following techniques has been used by the author of the passage to convey the message?
(a) Examples and anecdotes
(b) Factual and chronological account
(c) Humour and exaggeration
(d) Parody and mimicry

197. According to the passage, what is the solution to the issue of stupidity in society?
(a) Embracing ignorance and misinformation
(b) Teaching students how to pass tests
(c) Electing politici with catchy slog
(d) Encouraging critical thinking and problem-solving skills

198. What is the tone of the passage?
(a) Sarcastic (b) Serious
(c) Melancholic (d) Joyful

199. According to the author of the passage, who among the following is not responsible for the spread of stupidity?
(a) Politici
(b) Education system
(c) Individuals
(d) Children

200. What could be a suitable title for the passage?
(a) The Evils of Social Media
(b) The Benefits of Stupidity
(c) The Joy of Living in a World of Ignorance
(d) The Importance of Critical Thinking

Know Correct Answers

1. (b)	2. (a)	3. (d)	4. (b)	5. (c)	6. (d)	7. (c)	8. (c)	9. (b)	10. (b)
11. (d)	12. (b)	13. (d)	14. (c)	15. (d)	16. (b)	17. (d)	18. (b)	19. (c)	20. (b)
21. (d)	22. (d)	23. (b)	24. (b)	25. (c)	26. (c)	27. (c)	28. (a)	29. (a)	30. (c)
31. (a)	32. (c)	33. (a)	34. (c)	35. (a)	36. (c)	37. (b)	38. (b)	39. (d)	40. (d)
41. (d)	42. (b)	43. (a)	44. (a)	45. (b)	46. (a)	47. (d)	48. (a)	49. (c)	50. (b)
51. (d)	52. (d)	53. (b)	54. (a)	55. (c)	56. (a)	57. (d)	58. (d)	59. (b)	60. (a)
61. (c)	62. (c)	63. (a)	64. (a)	65. (c)	66. (d)	67. (c)	68. (d)	69. (c)	70. (b)
71. (d)	72. (b)	73. (d)	74. (c)	75. (a)	76. (d)	77. (a)	78. (c)	79. (a)	80. (c)
81. (b)	82. (b)	83. (c)	84. (b)	85. (d)	86. (a)	87. (a)	88. (d)	89. (d)	90. (c)
91. (c)	92. (b)	93. (c)	94. (c)	95. (b)	96. (a)	97. (c)	98. (c)	99. (b)	100. (c)
101. (b)	102. (b)	103. (b)	104. (a)	105. (a)	106. (c)	107. (b)	108. (d)	109. (d)	110. (b)
111. (c)	112. (c)	113. (a)	114. (d)	115. (a)	116. (d)	117. (d)	118. (a)	119. (b)	120. (b)
121. (a)	122. (b)	123. (d)	124. (c)	125. (c)	126. (b)	127 (a)	128. (d)	129. (b)	130. (a)
131. (a)	132. (d)	133. (b)	134. (b)	135. (a)	136. (c)	137 (b)	138. (a)	139. (d)	140. (d)
141. (b)	142. (a)	143. (c)	144. (b)	145. (b)	146. (b)	147. (a)	148. (b)	149. (a)	150. (c)
151. (c)	152. (b)	153. (a)	154. (a)	155. (d)	156. (b)	157. (a)	158. (b)	159. (d)	160. (d)
161. (c)	162. (d)	163. (c)	164. (d)	165. (b)	166. (c)	167. (c)	168. (a)	169. (a)	170. (a)
171. (b)	172. (a)	173. (d)	174. (b)	175. (d)	176. (d)	177. (d)	178. (c)	179. (c)	180. (b)
181. (d)	182. (d)	183. (d)	184. (a)	185. (d)	186. (b)	187. (c)	188. (a)	189. (d)	190. (d)
191. (a)	192. (b)	193. (d)	194. (a)	195. (c)	196. (c)	197. (d)	198. (a)	199. (d)	200. (d)

Answer & Solutions

1. **(b)** As,

$N \xrightarrow{+3} Q \xrightarrow{+2} S \xrightarrow{+1} T,$

$P \xrightarrow{+3} S \xrightarrow{+2} U \xrightarrow{+1} V$

and $S \xrightarrow{+3} V \xrightarrow{+2} X \xrightarrow{+1} Y$

But, $\boxed{G \xrightarrow{+13} T \xrightarrow{+14} H \xrightarrow{+11} S}$

2. **(a)** From the statements,

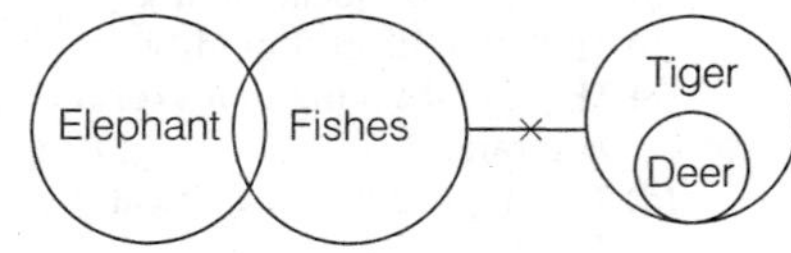

Conclusions

I. (✗) II. (✗) III. (✓)

∴ Only Conclusion III follows.

3. **(d)** In the figure series, the first figure is rotated by 180 degrees to get the second figure; similarly, the third figure is rotated by 180 degrees to get the fourth missing figure in the series.

Therefore, the figure in option (d) is the correct answer.

4. **(b)** According to the question,

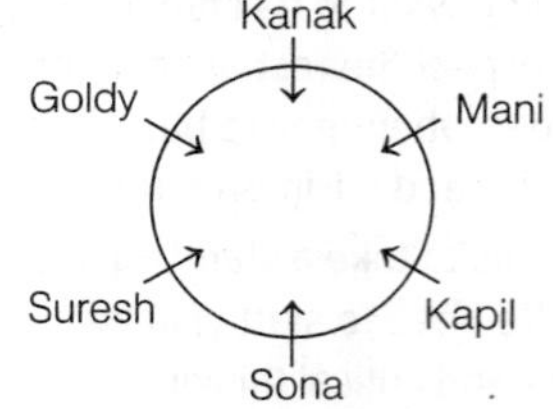

∴ Kapil sits second to the left of Kanak.

5. **(c)** According to the statements,

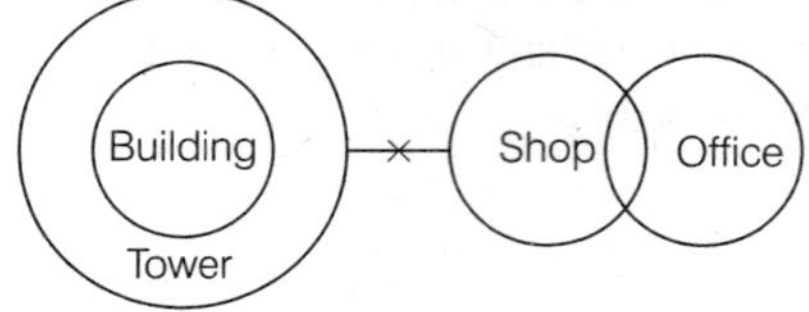

Conclusions

I. (✗) II. (✓)

∴ Only Conclusion II follows.

6. **(d)** Pattern of the series is as follows,

239 274 309 354 399 454 $\boxed{509}$

+35, +35, +45, +45, +55, +55

7. **(c)** Given equation,

$36 - 5 \div 240 \times 6 + 17 = ?$

After interchanging signs, we get

$\Rightarrow 36 \times 5 + 240 \div 6 - 17$

$\Rightarrow 180 + 40 - 17$

$\Rightarrow ? = \boxed{203}$

8. **(c)** From option (c), 4A9C6D2E40B9

After putting signs, we get

$\Rightarrow 4 + 9 \times 6 \div 2 = 40 - 9$

$\Rightarrow 4 + 9 \times 3 = 31$

$\Rightarrow 4 + 27 = 31$

$\Rightarrow 31 = 31$

9. **(b)** Pattern of the series is as follows,

25 26 28 32 40 $\boxed{56}$

+1, +2, +4, +8, +16

×2, ×2, ×2, ×2

10. **(b)** Pattern of the series is as follows,

$V \xrightarrow{-2} \boxed{T} \xrightarrow{-2} R \xrightarrow{-2} P \xrightarrow{-2} N$

$Q \xrightarrow{-1} \boxed{P} \xrightarrow{-1} O \xrightarrow{-1} N \xrightarrow{-1} M$

$S \xrightarrow{-2} \boxed{Q} \xrightarrow{-2} O \xrightarrow{-2} M \xrightarrow{-2} K$

$N \xrightarrow{-1} \boxed{M} \xrightarrow{-1} L \xrightarrow{-1} K \xrightarrow{-1} J$

11. **(d)** Given equation,

$9 + 3 \div 2 \times 135 - 15 = ?$

After interchanging the signs, we get

$\Rightarrow \quad 9 \times 3 + 2 - 135 \div 15$

$\Rightarrow \quad 9 \times 3 + 2 - 9$

$\Rightarrow \quad 27 + 2 - 9$

$\Rightarrow \quad ? = \boxed{20}$

12. **(b)** The order of the words in the dictionary is as follows,

Reach (3) → Reactor (5) → Readily (2) → Realistic (1) → Realize (6) → Really (4)

⇒3,5,2,1,6,4

13. **(d)** As, derive and infer both are synonyms of each other and the meaning of both is conclude. Similarly, the meaning of Urge is to encourage something, and the synonym of urge is exhort.

14. **(c)** Option figure (c) is the correct mirror image of the given figure, when the mirror is placed at the 'MN' line.

M

N

15. **(d)** According to the question,

+A ← Husband → Q−   [+ = Male, − = Female]

Q ↑ Mother — B+

B ↑ Father — R

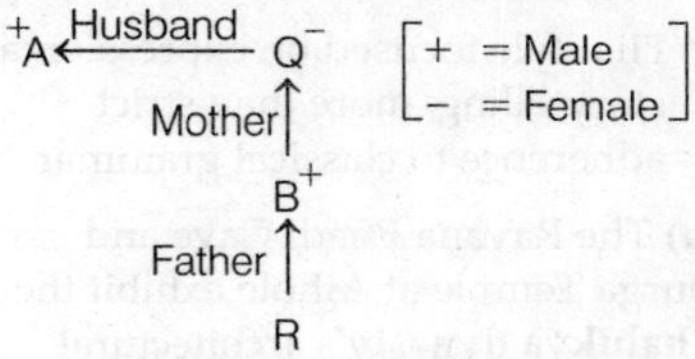

∴ A is the father's father of R.

16. **(b)** Given equation,

145 A 27 D 3 B ? = 163

After replacing the signs we get,

$\Rightarrow 145 + 27 \div 3 \times ? = 163$

$\Rightarrow \quad 145 + 9 \times ? = 163$

$\Rightarrow \quad 9 \times ? = 163 - 145$

$\Rightarrow \quad 9 \times ? = 18$

$\Rightarrow \quad ? = \frac{18}{9}$

$\therefore \quad ? = 2$

17. **(d)** According to the question,

L I F Ⓔ ⟶ ⑨3 5 1

N Ⓔ A R ⟶ 4 6 ⑨ 2

∴ The code for "E" is "9".

18. **(b)** Given equation,

$124 \times 4 \div 13 - 3 + 36 = ?$

After interchanging the signs, we get

$\Rightarrow 124 \div 4 + 13 \times 3 - 36$

$\Rightarrow \quad 31 + 13 \times 3 - 36$

$\Rightarrow \quad 31 + 39 - 36$

$\Rightarrow \quad ? = \boxed{34}$

19. **(c)** Option figure (c) is the correct mirror image of the given figure, when the mirror is placed at the 'MN' line.

M

BK$6GHX | XHG6$KB (mirrored)

N

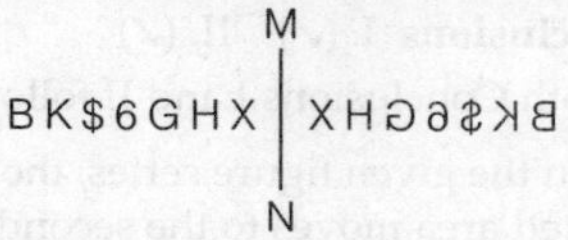

20. **(b)** According to the question,

F I R Ⓔ ⟶ ⑦3 9 1

A G Ⓔ D ⟶ 8 2 4 ⑦

∴ The code for "E" is "7".

21. **(d)** According to the question,

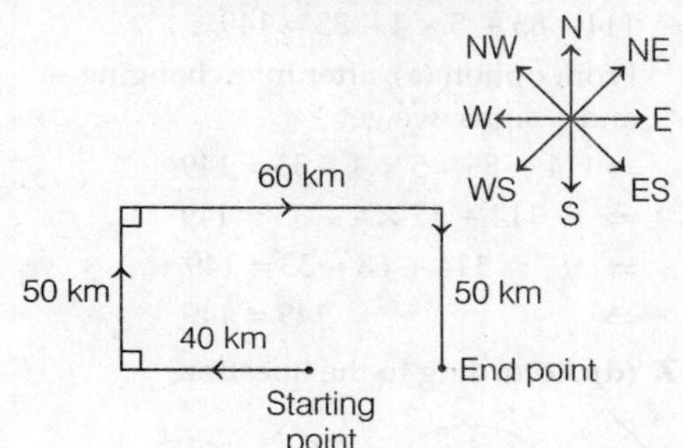

∴ The distance from the starting point is 60 − 40 = 20 km

22. **(d)** In the given figure, the opposite faces are,

(& and M), (W and n), and (t and k)

According to the property of dice, opposite faces can not be adjacent to each other.

∴ The dice in option (d) is not possible.

23. **(b)** According to the statements,

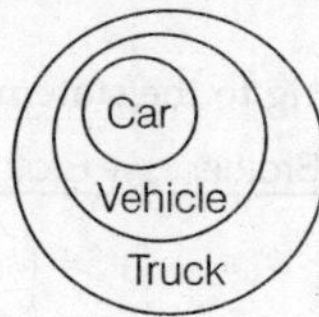

Conclusions

I. (✓) II. (✗)

∴ Only Conclusion I follows.

24. **(b)** The series will be as shown below,

P <u>C</u> E H <u>Z</u> / <u>P</u> C E <u>H</u> Z / P <u>C</u> E H <u>Z</u>

⇒CEZPHCZ

25. **(c)** In the given figure series, each figure follows the following pattern,

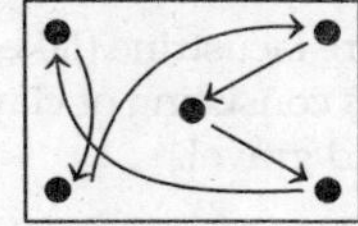

Hence, the figure in option (c) will complete the question series.

26. **(c)** As, (13, 14, 54)

$\Rightarrow (13 + 14) \times 2 = 54$

and (15, 18, 66)

$\Rightarrow (15 + 18) \times 2 = 66$

Similarly, (13, 19, 64)

$\Rightarrow (13 + 19) \times 2 = 64$

27. **(c)** Pattern of the series is as follows,

61 95 138 197 279 $\boxed{391}$

+34 +43 +59 +82 +112

+9 +16 +23 +30

+7 +7 +7

28. **(a)** Pattern of the series is as follows,

G $\xrightarrow{+6}$ M $\xrightarrow{+6}$ S $\xrightarrow{+6}$ $\boxed{Y}$ $\xrightarrow{+6}$ E

O $\xrightarrow{+7}$ V $\xrightarrow{+7}$ C $\xrightarrow{+7}$ $\boxed{J}$ $\xrightarrow{+7}$ Q

W $\xrightarrow{+8}$ E $\xrightarrow{+8}$ M $\xrightarrow{+8}$ $\boxed{U}$ $\xrightarrow{+8}$ C

B $\xrightarrow{+9}$ K $\xrightarrow{+9}$ T $\xrightarrow{+9}$ $\boxed{C}$ $\xrightarrow{+9}$ L

29. **(a)** As, (21, 5, 120)

$\Rightarrow (21 - 1) \times (5 + 1) = 120$

and (2, 7, 8) $\Rightarrow (2 - 1) \times (7 + 1) = 8$

Similarly, (3, 4, 10)

$\Rightarrow (3 - 1) \times (4 + 1) = 10$

30. **(c)** As, 142 : 108 ⇒ 142 − 34 = 108

and 169 : 135 ⇒ 169 − 34 = 135

Similarly, 185 : ? ⇒ 185 − 34 = $\boxed{151}$

31. **(a)** Multiply the number of letters in the word by 6.

As TRAUMA is coded as 36,

Number of letters in TRAUMA is

$6 = 6 \times 6 = 36$

and, STIL is coded as 24.

The number of letters in STIL is

$4 = 4 \times 6 = 24$

Similarly, OBEIDEINT is coded as ?,

The number of letters in OBEIDEINT is $9 = 9 \times 6 = \boxed{54}$

32. **(c)** Pattern of the series is as follows,

352 326 284 225 148 $\boxed{52}$

−26 −42 −59 −77 −96

−16 −17 −18 −19

33. **(a)** The opposite faces are,

(4 and 6), (2 and 1) and (5 and 3)

∴ 2 is the opposite face of 1.

34. **(c)** As, Z $\xrightarrow{-7}$ S $\xrightarrow{-5}$ N $\xrightarrow{-3}$ K

V $\xrightarrow{-7}$ O $\xrightarrow{-5}$ J $\xrightarrow{-3}$ G

T $\xrightarrow{-7}$ M $\xrightarrow{-5}$ H $\xrightarrow{-3}$ E

But, $\boxed{W \xrightarrow{-9} N \xrightarrow{-10} D \xrightarrow{-0} D}$

35. **(a)** After unfolding the figure, it will appear as the answer figure (a).

36. **(c)** As, (329, 145, 184)
$\Rightarrow 145 + 184 = 329$
and (567, 221, 346) $\Rightarrow 221 + 346 = 567$
Similarly, (676, 225, 451)
$\Rightarrow 225 + 451 = 676$

37. **(b)** Option figure (b) is the correct mirror image of the given figure, when the mirror is placed at the 'MN' line.

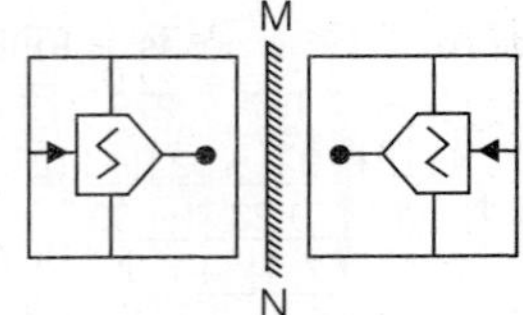

38. **(b)** According to the question,

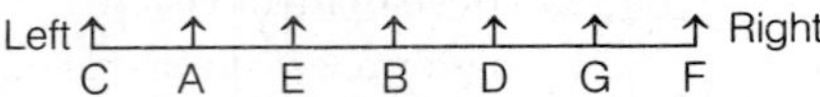

∴ One person sits between E and D.

39. **(d)** The option figure (d) is embedded in the question figure,

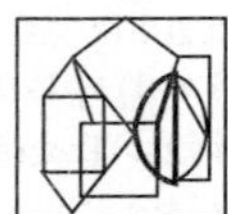

40. **(d)** The arrangement is as follows,

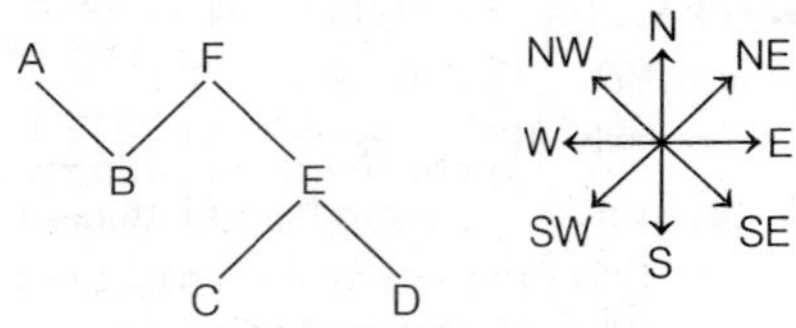

∴ A is in the North-West of E.

41. **(d)** After unfolding the figure, it will appear as the answer figure (d).

42. **(b)** As,

Similarly,

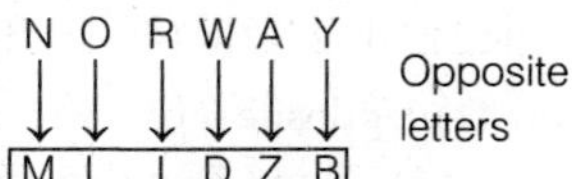

43. **(a)** Given equation,
$61 \div 9 \times 3 - 8 + 5 = ?$
After interchanging signs, we get
$\Rightarrow 61 + 9 \div 3 \times 8 - 5$
$\Rightarrow 61 + 3 \times 8 - 5$
$\Rightarrow 61 + 24 - 5$
$\Rightarrow ? = \boxed{80}$

44. **(a)** According to the statements,

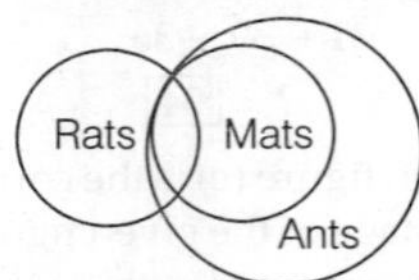

Conclusions I. (✓) II. (✓)
∴ Both Conclusions I and II follow.

45. **(b)** In the given figure series, the shaded area moves to the second, third, and fourth block in a clockwise direction in each step. So, the shaded area moves to the fifth block at last.

Therefore, the figure in option (b) is correct.

46. **(a)** Given equation,
$114 \div 85 + 5 \times 4 - 33 = 149$
From option (a), after interchanging ÷ and + signs, we get
$\Rightarrow 114 + 85 \div 5 \times 4 - 33 = 149$
$\Rightarrow 114 + 17 \times 4 - 33 = 149$
$\Rightarrow 114 + 68 - 33 = 149$
$\Rightarrow 149 = 149$

47. **(d)** According to the question,

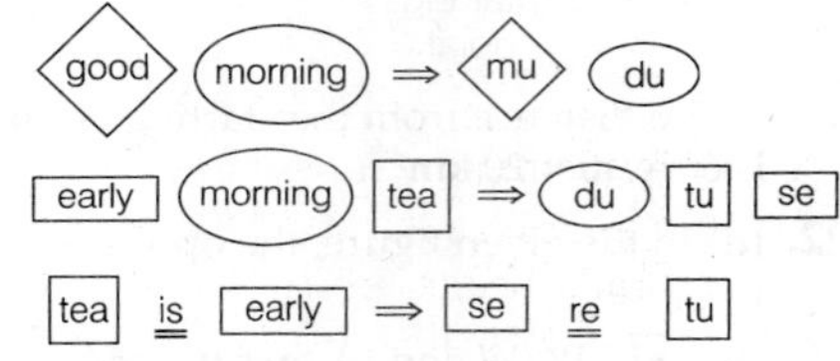

∴ The code of "is" is "re".

48. **(a)** The order of the word in the dictionary is as follows,
Vivisection (3) → Vocalist (2) → Vogue (5) → Voice (1) → Void (4)
$\Rightarrow$ 3,2,5,1,4

49. **(c)** According to the statements,

$\overset{+}{Q} \xleftarrow{\text{Brother}} \overset{+}{Y} \xleftarrow{\text{Brother}} N$
Daughter ↓ $\overset{-}{H}$
[+ = Male, – = Female]

∴ Y is the father's brother of H.

50. **(b)** As, Wrestling is a game played on the ground, called an Arena. Similarly, ice skating is a game that is played on a Rink.

51. **(d)** Karewa formations are found in the **Kashmir Himalayas**, particularly in the Vale of Kashmir.

- These are lacustrine (lake-origin) deposits consisting of clay, silt, sand and gravel.
- It formed during the pleistocene period, they are highly fertile and ideal for agriculture.
- The flat-topped terraced landforms created by Karewas support cultivation of high-value crops.

52. **(d)** Fundamental Duties were incorporated in the Indian Constitution under **Part IV-A** by the 42nd Constitutional Amendment Act, 1976.

- Fundamental Duties are mentioned in Article 51A of the Constitution.
- These duties were based on the recommendations of the Swaran Singh Committee, formed during the Emergency period.
- In 2002, the 86th Amendment added the 11th duty to provide education to children aged 6 to 14 years.
- These duties are inspired by the Constitution of the former USSR, which had a similar provision.

53. **(b)** **Uday Shankar** is known as the pioneer of modern dance in India.

- He innovatively blended Indian classical dance with folk, tribal and European theatrical techniques.
- He was awarded the Padma Vibhushan in 1971.
- His style focused on expression and storytelling, more than strict adherence to classical grammar.

54. **(a)** The Ravana Phadi Cave and Durga Temple at Aihole exhibit the **Chalukya dynasty's** architectural style.

- The Chalukyas ruled parts of Karnataka from the 6th to 8th centuries CE.
- These temples display stories from Ramayana and Mahabharata in detailed carvings.
- Aihole is often called the "Cradle of Indian Temple Architecture".

55. **(c)** Statements (ii) and (iii) are correct because the Chief Minister plays a major role in framing State laws and policies, leading the Council of Ministers and the Governor of a State is appointed by the President of India under Article 155 of the Constitution.

- Statement (i) is incorrect because the Governor is the constitutional head, not the real executive of the State Government. The Chief Minister is the real head.

Knowledge Booster
- The Governor is responsible for reserving bills for the President and can also issue ordinances (Article 213).

56. (a) Drugs that bind to receptors and block their natural function are called **Antagonists.**
- They inhibit the physiological activity of naturally occurring substances like neurotransmitters or hormones.
- Antagonists are used in treating conditions like hypertension, allergies and mental disorders.
- They work by blocking the receptor site without activating it.
- Common types include beta blockers, antihistamines and opioid antagonists.

57. (d) The standard Kabaddi play field dimension for men is **13 metres × 10 metres.**
- For women, the court size is slightly smaller: 12m × 8m.
- The central line, baulk lines and bonus lines divide the zones for raiders and defenders.
- Each half has 7 players and raiding must be completed within 30 sec.
- Kabaddi was included in the Asian Games from 1990 and India has been a dominant team.

58. (d) The WIFS (Weekly Iron and Folic Acid Supplementation) programme was launched in **2012** by the Ministry of Health and Family Welfare.
- The goal is to reduce iron-deficiency anaemia in adolescents.
- It targets adolescents aged 10–19 years, especially girls (66%) and boys (30%) with high anaemia prevalence.
- The programme includes weekly iron (IFA) tablets, biannual deworming, and nutrition counseling.
- It is implemented through schools and anganwadi centres.

59. (b) **Aurangzeb** succeeded Shah Jahan as the Mughal emperor after a war of succession among his brothers.
- He defeated his elder brother Dara Shikoh, who was Shah Jahan's favourite but considered unfit by orthodox factions.
- Shah Shuja and Murad Bakhsh were also eliminated in this struggle.
- Aurangzeb ascended the throne in 1658 and ruled until 1707, becoming the last powerful Mughal emperor.

60. (a) The **Vice-President** of India is the ex-officio Chairman of the Rajya Sabha, as per Article 64 of the Constitution.
- He presides over sessions of the Upper House of Parliament but does not vote except in the case of a tie.
- Unlike the Lok Sabha Speaker, the Vice-President is not a member of the House.
- His role is mostly ceremonial unless there's a tie in voting.
- The first Vice-President of India was Dr. S. Radhakrishnan.

61. (c) RIDF stands for **Rural Infrastructure Development Fund.**
- It was established in 1995 by the Government of India and is managed by NABARD (National Bank for Agriculture and Rural Development).
- It provides low-cost finance to State Governments for rural infrastructure projects.
- Key sectors include irrigation, roads, health centres and schools in rural areas.
- The goal is to strengthen rural connectivity and productivity.

62. (c) Tansen, one of the Navratnas (nine jewels) in Akbar's court, was earlier a musician in the court of **Rewa**, a princely state in Madhya Pradesh.
- His original name was Ramtanu Pandey, and he was trained in Dhrupad music.
- Tansen is credited with developing several ragas, including Miyan ki Todi and Miyan ki Malhar.
- He was conferred the title 'Miyan' by Akbar as a mark of respect.

63. (a) The original Constitution of India (1950) granted **Seven** Fundamental Rights to citizens.
- These were enshrined in Part III (Articles 12–35) of the Indian Constitution.
- The Right to Property was later removed from the list of Fundamental Rights by the 44th Constitutional Amendment Act, 1978, making the count six.
- Right to Property (Article 31) is now a legal right under Article 300A, not a Fundamental Right.

Knowledge Booster
- The concept of Fundamental Rights was inspired by the U.S. Bill of Rights (1791).
- The Supreme Court introduced the Doctrine of Basic Structure in Kesavananda Bharati Case (1973) to protect Fundamental Rights from arbitrary amendments.

64. (a) In India, the Five-Year Plans were designed not only for short-term objectives but also as part of a long-term development vision.
- This long-term vision was called the perspective plan, which outlined economic and social goals for 15 to 20 years.
- It ensured that Five-Year Plans contributed towards a broader national development strategy.
- **Perspective planning** helped in sectoral and regional development in a phased manner.

65. (c) The book 'On Writing: A Memoir of the Craft' was written by **Stephen King** in 2000.
- It is a combination of memoir and writing advice, offering insights into King's early life, struggles and writing process.
- Stephen King is a prolific American author known for horror, suspense and supernatural fiction.
- Some of his most famous books include 'The Shining' (1977), 'IT' (1986), 'Carrie' (1974) and 'The Dark Tower' series.
- King has won multiple awards, including the Bram Stoker Award and National Medal of Arts.

66. (d) The target growth rate of the Indian economy in the Second Five-Year Plan (1956–1961) was **4.5%.**
- This plan was designed based on the Mahalanobis Model, emphasising rapid industrialisation and heavy industries.
- The actual growth rate achieved was 4.27%, slightly below the target.
- The plan aimed to reduce reliance on imports and promote self-reliance in key industries like iron, steel, heavy machinery and engineering goods.

67. (c) The first President of the International Olympic Committee (IOC) was **Demetrius Vikelas**.

- He was a Greek businessman and writer, who served as IOC President from 1894 to 1896.
- Vikelas played a crucial role in reviving the Olympic Games, leading to the first modern Olympics in Athens (1896).

Knowledge Booster

- The International Olympic Committee (IOC) was founded by Pierre de Coubertin in 1894, but he became the second President after Vikelas.
- The first Winter Olympics were held in Chamonix, France (1924).

68. (d) **Sublimation** is the process in which a solid directly converts into gas without passing through the liquid state and then condenses back to solid upon cooling.

- Common examples include dry ice (solid CO_2) and naphthalene balls.
- In laboratory settings, sublimation is used for purification of substances like camphor and iodine.
- This method is widely used in the pharmaceutical and chemical industries.

69. (c) The 2026 Winter Olympics will be hosted in **Milano Cortina**, Italy.

- This will be the fourth time Italy hosts the Olympics and the second time for the Winter Games.
- The event will be held from 6th February to 22nd February, 2026.
- This is the first time two cities (Milan and Cortina) will co-host the Winter Olympics.
- Los Angeles (USA) will host the 2028 Summer Olympics.

70. (b) **Kandla Port** (Gujarat), **Mormugao Port** (Goa), **Kochi Port** (Kerala) are major ports located on the Western coast of India.

- Kolkata, Chennai and Haldia are on the Eastern coast.
- Kandla Port is one of India's busiest commercial ports, handling a large volume of oil and petroleum products.
- Mormugao Port is crucial for iron ore exports.

71. (d) **Jawaharlal Nehru** was the Vice-President of the Interim Government (1946), serving as the de facto Prime Minister.

- The Interim Government (2nd September, 1946 – 15th August, 1947) was led by the Indian National Congress under British rule.
- Vallabhbhai Patel was in charge of Home, Information and Broadcasting.
- Baldev Singh was the first Defence Minister of Independent India.
- John Matthai later became India's Finance Minister (1949).

72. (b) The **Brahmani** river is an East-flowing river covering Jharkhand, Chhattisgarh and Odisha, with a drainage area of 39,033 sq km.

- It originates from the Chota Nagpur Plateau and flows into the Bay of Bengal.
- The Baitarni, Nagavali and Sarada rivers also flow East, but cover different regions.
- Krishna, Kaveri and Mahanadi are major East-flowing rivers in India.

73. (d) Statement (d) is incorrect because relief features impact rainfall; mountains like the Western Ghats enhance rain, while regions like Rajasthan remain dry due to their alignment.

- Statements (a), (b) and (c) are correct because monsoonal rainfall is influenced by jet streams, especially the Tibetan Plateau heating and the Easterly Jet Stream, which triggers monsoon onset and over 60% of Indian agriculture depends on monsoons, making it the lifeline for crops like rice and maize.
- The Himalayas block monsoon winds, causing heavy rainfall on windward slopes (e.g., Meghalaya) and rain-shadow areas (e.g., Rajasthan).

74. (c) **Ashvaghosha**, a Buddhist philosopher and poet, wrote the Buddhacharita, an epic poem on the life of Gautama Buddha.

- He lived during the Kushan Empire under the patronage of Kanishka.
- He was a strong proponent of Mahayana Buddhism and travelled across India to spread Buddhist philosophy.
- His other works include Saundarananda, another Buddhist poetic text.

75. (a) At the time of adoption in 1950, the Indian Constitution guaranteed 7 Fundamental Rights.

- The Right to Property was later removed in 1978 by the 44th Amendment.
- It was removed because it hindered land reforms and nationalisation policies.
- The Right to Constitutional Remedies was called the 'Heart and Soul' of the Constitution by Dr. B.R. Ambedkar.

76. (d) Linthoi Chanambam is an Indian Judoka from Manipur.

- She became the first Indian to win a gold medal at the World Cadet **Judo** Championships in 2022.
- She competes in the 57 kg weight category and has trained under the Target Olympic Podium Scheme (TOPS).

Knowledge Booster

- Judo originated in Japan and was founded by Jigoro Kano in 1882.
- India won its first-ever Judo medal at the Asian Games in 1986.

77. (a) In 1957, **Ronald Gillespie and Ronald Nyholm** proposed the VSEPR (Valence Shell Electron Pair Repulsion) theory.

- The model predicts molecular shape based on electron-pair repulsion in the valence shell.
- It explains why molecules adopt specific geometries like linear, trigonal planar, tetrahedral and bent shapes.
- The concept applies beyond chemistry, helping in drug design and nanotechnology.

78. (c) Bonalu is a Hindu festival celebrated mainly in **Telangana**, especially in Hyderabad and Secunderabad.

- It is dedicated to Goddess Mahakali and involves offering rice cooked with jaggery and milk in decorated pots.
- Bonalu in Telangana's official state festival, declared in 2014 after state formation.

Knowledge Booster

- The word 'Bonalu' comes from 'Bhojanalu', meaning food offerings to the Goddess.
- The celebrations take place in July-August (Ashada month), with Golkonda Fort being the first site where rituals begin.

79. (a) The Rowlatt Satyagraha was initiated by **Mahatma Gandhi** in 1919 to oppose the Rowlatt Act, which permitted the British government to arrest and detain individuals without trial.

- The act was officially known as the Anarchical and Revolutionary Crimes Act of 1919.
- It marked Gandhi's first all-India mass protest movement, introducing Satyagraha (non-violent resistance) on a national scale.

Knowledge Booster

- On 6th April, 1919 a nationwide hartal (strike) was observed as part of the protest.
- The agitation led to the Jallianwala Bagh massacre on 13th April, 1919 a turning point in India's struggle for independence.

80. (c) Asad Ali Khan was a renowned Indian classical musician known for playing the **Rudra Veena**, one of the oldest string instruments in India.

- He belonged to the Khandarbani Dhrupad Gharana and was one of the few musicians who kept the tradition of Rudra Veena alive in modern times.
- He was also a recipient of the Padma Bhushan for his contributions to Indian classical music.

81. (b) **Capital receipts** refer to funds received by the government that lead to either a reduction in assets or an increase in liabilities.

- Recoveries of loans and advances represent money coming back to the government, reducing its financial assets.
- Borrowings from internal or external sources increase the government's liabilities, hence counted as capital receipts.
- In contrast, revenue receipts (like tax and non-tax revenues) are regular and do not create liabilities or reduce assets.

82. (b) Thullal is a classical dance and poetic performance art form that originated in the state of **Kerala**.

- It was introduced by the famous Malayalam poet Kunchan Nambiar in the 18th century as a means to satirize societal norms and injustice.
- Thullal blends storytelling, facial expressions, rhythmic footwork and vibrant costumes.

Knowledge Booster

- The performance is usually based on themes from Indian epics like the Ramayana and Mahabharata, presented in a humorous and relatable manner.

83. (c) Jet streams are high-altitude, fast-moving winds that blow from West to East in the upper layers of the troposphere.

- Over the Asian continent, they blow North of the Himalayas, running roughly parallel to the Tibetan highlands.
- These winds play a critical role in influencing the Indian monsoon system, especially the onset and withdrawal of monsoons.
- Jet streams are also crucial for aviation, as flying with them can reduce travel time and fuel consumption.

84. (b) The **Employment-Unemployment Survey** (EUS) was the comprehensive household survey conducted by the National Sample Survey Office (NSSO).

- It was first conducted in 1955 to collect detailed data on labour force participation, employment, and unemployment in India.
- The survey provided important insights into the nature of employment, helping in policy formulation.
- The EUS was conducted once every five years and has since been replaced by the Periodic Labour Force Survey (PLFS) from 2017–18 onwards.

85. (d) The Doctrine of Lapse was a controversial annexation policy introduced by **Lord Dalhousie**, the Governor-General of India from 1848 to 1856.

- According to this policy, if a ruler of a princely state died without a biological male heir, the territory would be annexed by the British.
- Major states annexed under this doctrine included Satara (1848), Jhansi (1854) and Nagpur (1853).

Knowledge Booster

- This policy was seen as unjust and became one of the causes of resentment leading to the Revolt of 1857.
- Rani Lakshmibai of Jhansi opposed the annexation of her kingdom under this doctrine and became a key figure in the 1857 uprising.

86. (a) Butyric acid is a saturated short-chain fatty acid with a 4 carbon molecule structure.

- It occurs naturally in animal fats and plant oils, usually in esterified form.
- It is a key component responsible for the distinct smell of rancid butter and contributes to the flavour of dairy products.
- Chemically known as butanoic acid, it is used in the manufacture of esters, perfumes and flavouring agents.

87. (a) In **June 2021**, the Reserve Bank of India (RBI) published a 'Consultative Document on Regulation of Microfinance'.

- The document aimed to review and reform the existing regulatory framework for microfinance institutions (MFIs).
- Key areas addressed included interest rate caps, borrower indebtedness and regulatory parity across lenders.
- The purpose was to enhance transparency, borrower protection and financial inclusion in the microfinance sector.

88. (d) Under the Pradhan Mantri Formalisation of Micro Food Processing Enterprises (PMFME) Scheme, each member of a Self-Help Group (SHG) is eligible to receive ₹ 40000 as Seed Capital support.

- This amount helps members to start or upgrade their micro food processing units.
- The PMFME Scheme was launched in 2020 by the Ministry of Food Processing Industries (MoFPI).
- The aim is to promote self-reliance, entrepreneurship and rural development through food processing activities.

Knowledge Booster

- The scheme follows the One District One Product (ODOP) approach to boost local food industries across India.
- The scheme offers financial support of up to ₹ 10 lakh for the modernisation of food processing units, along with interest subvention for loans.

89. **(d)** The Beating Retreat ceremony is held at **Vijay Chowk**, located at the end of Rajpath near the Rashtrapati Bhavan in New Delhi.

- It marks the formal conclusion of the Republic Day celebrations and is held every year on 29th January.
- The event features military bands from the Indian Army, Navy and Air Force playing ceremonial and patriotic tunes.

90. **(c)** The Government of **Bhutan** issued an official postage stamp featuring Soparrkar and the logo of his global initiative 'Dance for a Cause'.

- The initiative combines performing arts and social awareness, using dance as a medium to promote social issues.
- Soparrkar is an internationally recognised Indian Latin and ballroom dancer known for merging dance with humanitarian efforts.

91. **(c)** **Ahmad Shah** I Wali of the Bahmani Sultanate shifted the capital from Gulbarga to Bidar in the early 15th century.

- He ruled from 1422 to 1436 CE and is remembered for his patronage of art, architecture and religious tolerance.
- The shift to Bidar was strategically motivated due to its central location and better climate compared to Gulbarga.
- Ahmad Shah also developed Bidar as a cultural and architectural hub, commissioning several iconic structures.

92. **(b)** The **Kesavananda Bharati** *vs* **State of Kerala** (1973) case is one of the most landmark judgements in Indian constitutional history.

- In this case, the Supreme Court of India laid down the 'Basic Structure Doctrine', ruling that Parliament cannot alter the basic structure of the Constitution.
- It held that the democratic character of the polity is an essential part of the basic structure and thus cannot be amended.
- The Kesavananda Bharati case was decided by a 13-judge constitutional bench, the largest ever in Indian judicial history.
- Secularism, federal structure, judicial revienew and rule of law are also the component of basic structure doctrine.

93. **(c)** In 2015, eminent danseuse and **Bharatanatyam** exponent Padma Subrahmanyam was honoured with Kerala's prestigious 'Nishagandhi Puraskaram'.

- The award is instituted by the Kerala Tourism Department to recognise excellence in dance and music.
- Padma Subrahmanyam is known for her contributions to reviving Bharatanatyam and integrating it with Natya Shastra traditions.
- She is also an accomplished scholar, choreographer and cultural ambassador of Indian classical dance.

94. **(c)** The **cytoplasm** is the fluid matrix that fills the interior of a cell, present between the cell membrane and the nucleus.

- It consists of cytosol (the gel-like substance), organelles and inclusions, enabling cellular processes to occur efficiently.
- It serves as the site for many metabolic reactions, including glycolysis and protein synthesis.
- The cytoplasm also plays a role in cell expansion, growth and structural support.

95. **(b)** "A Grain of Sand in the Hourglass of Time" is the autobiography of Indian politician **Arjun Singh**.

- Arjun Singh was a senior leader of the Indian National Congress and held key positions including Chief Minister of Madhya Pradesh and Union Minister of Human Resource Development.
- The book provides a first-person account of Indian politics, covering his experiences during crucial events like the Emergency and Mandal Commission era.
- Arjun Singh was a prominent supporter of OBC reservations and played a key role in implementing the Mandal Commission recommendations.

96. **(a)** **Nitrogen** is a colourless, odourless, tasteless and chemically unreactive gas that makes up about 78% of Earth's atmosphere.

- It was first discovered by Daniel Rutherford in 1772, who called it 'noxious air' due to its inability to support life or combustion.
- At the same time, it was independently isolated by Carl Wilhelm Scheele and Henry Cavendish.

Knowledge Booster

- Nitrogen is essential for the formation of proteins, nucleic acids (DNA and RNA) and is crucial in the nitrogen cycle.
- Liquid nitrogen is commonly used in cryogenics and food preservation due to its extremely low boiling point.

97. **(c)** The **Mahatma Gandhi National Rural Employment Guarantee Act** (MGNREGA), 2005 is popularly referred to as the 'Right to Work'.

- It guarantees 100 days of wage employment per financial year to every rural household whose adult members are willing to do unskilled manual work.
- The Act was enacted in 2005 and came into force in 2006, aiming to enhance livelihood security in rural areas.

98. **(c)** In **1924**, Albert Einstein predicted a new state of matter called the Bose-Einstein Condensate (BEC) based on the quantum formulations of Indian physicist Satyendra Nath Bose.

- BEC represents a state of matter in which particles occupy the same quantum state, behaving as a single quantum entity.
- The first experimental creation of a BEC was achieved in 1995 by Eric Cornell and Carl Wieman, for which they won the Nobel Prize in Physics (2001).

Knowledge Booster

- BEC typically occurs at near absolute zero temperatures, where quantum effects become observable at a macroscopic level.
- Bosons, the particles governed by Bose-Einstein statistics, are named after Satyendra Nath Bose.

99. **(b)** The main function of the centriole is **to help the cell division in animal cells**, especially during mitosis and meiosis.

- Centrioles are cylindrical structures composed of microtubules, typically found in pairs within the centrosome of animal cells.
- They assist in the formation of the spindle fibers, which help in the movement and segregation of chromosomes during cell division.
- Centrioles also play a role in the formation of cilia and flagella, structures used for cell movement in certain animal cells.

100. **(c)** There are 4 terrestrial planets in our solar system: Mercury, Venus, Earth and Mars.

- Terrestrial planets are rocky planets with solid surfaces and are located closest to the Sun.
- These planets have metallic cores, rocky mantles and thin atmospheres (except Earth which has a thick atmosphere).
- They are distinctly different from gas giants like Jupiter and Saturn or ice giants like Uranus and Neptune.

Knowledge Booster

- The term "terrestrial" comes from the Latin word Terra, meaning Earth-like.
- Among these, Earth is the only planet known to support life due to its atmosphere, water and temperature range.

101. **(b)** Area of base = 37.5% of 1536

$= \frac{3}{8} \times 1536 = 576 \text{ m}^2$

Lateral surface area = Total surface area − Area of base

$= 1536 - 576 = 960 \text{ m}^2$

Now, area of base = 576 m^2

$\Rightarrow \text{Side}^2 = 576$

$\Rightarrow \text{Side} = 24 \text{ m}$

Perimeter of base = $4 \times 24 = 96$ m

We know that,

Lateral surface area of pyramid

$= \frac{1}{2} \times \text{Perimeter of base} \times \text{Slant height}$

$\Rightarrow 960 = \frac{1}{2} \times 96 \times \text{Slant height}$

$\therefore$ Slant height = 20 m

$\text{Height} = \sqrt{\text{Slant height}^2 - \left(\frac{\text{Side}}{2}\right)^2}$

$= \sqrt{20^2 - 12^2}$

$= \sqrt{400 - 144} = 16$

Now, Volume of pyramid

$= \frac{1}{3} \times \text{Area of base} \times \text{Height}$

$= \frac{1}{3} \times 576 \times 16 = 3072 \text{ m}^3$

102. **(b)** $\sin A = 1 - \sin^2 A$

$\sin A = \cos^2 A \quad [\because \sin^2 A + \cos^2 A = 1]$

Now,

$\cos^4 A + \cos^6 A = (\cos^2 A)^2 + (\cos^2 A)^3$

$= (\sin A)^2 + (\sin A)^3$

$= \sin A[\sin A + \sin^2 A]$

$= \sin A[1]$

$= \sin A$

103. **(b)** $r = 1.75$ cm

$\therefore$ Circumference of circle $= 2\pi r$

$= 2 \times \frac{22}{7} \times 1.75$

$= 2 \times 22 \times 0.25$

$= 11$ cm

104. **(a)** We know that,

Product of two numbers

= HCF × LCM

$m \times n = a \times \text{LCM}$

But, $n = ab$

So, $a = \frac{n}{b}$

Now, $m \times n = \frac{n}{b} \times \text{LCM}$

$\Rightarrow \text{LCM} = bm$

105. **(a)** Required difference = Number of students in X and Y together − Number of students in Y and Z together

= [(45% + 30%) − (30% + 25%)] × 3600

= [75% − 55%] × 3600

= 20% × 3600 = 720

106. **(c)** Let height of a cone be 'h' cm.

$r = 5$ cm, $l = 13$ cm

Now, $h^2 = l^2 - r^2$

$\Rightarrow h = \sqrt{13^2 - 5^2}$

$\Rightarrow h = \sqrt{169 - 25}$

$= \sqrt{144} = 12$

$\therefore$ Volume of a cone $= \frac{1}{3}\pi r^2 h$

$= \frac{1}{3} \times \frac{22}{7} \times 5 \times 5 \times 12$

$= \frac{2200}{7} \approx 314.3 \text{ cm}^3$

107. **(b)** Let principal be ₹ 'P'.

$r = 10\%$ p.a.

r for 6 months = 5%

Here, $n = 3$

$A =$ ₹64827

We know, that

$A = P\left(1 + \frac{r}{100}\right)^n$

$\Rightarrow A = P\left[1 + \frac{5}{100}\right]^3$

$\Rightarrow 64827 = P\left[\frac{21}{20}\right]^3$

$\Rightarrow P = 64827\left[\frac{20}{21}\right]^3$

$= 64827 \times \frac{8000}{9261}$

$\Rightarrow P =$ ₹56000

108. **(d)**

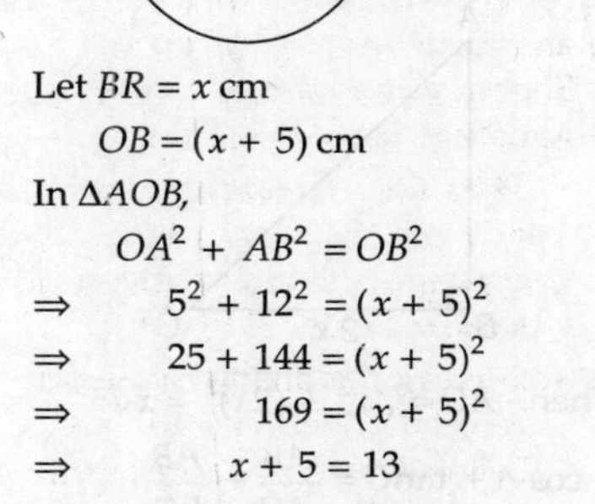

Let $BR = x$ cm

$OB = (x + 5)$ cm

In ΔAOB,

$OA^2 + AB^2 = OB^2$

$\Rightarrow 5^2 + 12^2 = (x + 5)^2$

$\Rightarrow 25 + 144 = (x + 5)^2$

$\Rightarrow 169 = (x + 5)^2$

$\Rightarrow x + 5 = 13$

$\Rightarrow x = 8$ cm

109. **(d)** $\frac{7}{5} - \left[\frac{15}{4} \div \left\{\frac{5}{4} \div \frac{1}{2}\left(\frac{3}{2} \times \frac{10}{3} \div \frac{4}{3}\right)\right\}\right]$

$= \frac{7}{5} - \left[\frac{15}{4} \div \left\{\frac{5}{4} \div \frac{1}{2}\left(\frac{3}{2} \times \frac{10}{3} \times \frac{3}{4}\right)\right\}\right]$

$= \frac{7}{5} - \left[\frac{15}{4} \div \left\{\frac{5}{4} \times 2 \times \frac{15}{4}\right\}\right]$

$= \frac{7}{5} - \left[\frac{15}{4} \div \frac{75}{8}\right]$

$= \frac{7}{5} - \left[\frac{15}{4} \times \frac{8}{75}\right]$

$= \frac{7}{5} - \frac{2}{5} = \frac{5}{5} = 1$

110. **(b)** Let the time taken by A and B together to do the work be 'x' days.

According to the question,

$\frac{1}{x + 25} + \frac{1}{x + 16} = \frac{1}{x}$

$\Rightarrow (2x + 41)x = (x + 25)(x + 16)$

$\Rightarrow 2x^2 + 41x = x^2 + 41x + 400$

$\Rightarrow x^2 = 400$

$\Rightarrow x = 20$

111. (c) According to the rule of alligation,

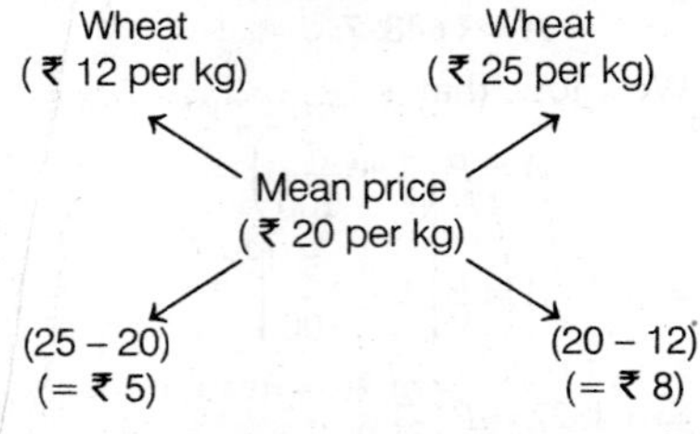

∴ Ratio of mixing of two types of wheat = 5 : 8

112. (c) Let mean proportional be 'x'.

$\therefore \quad x = \sqrt{32 \times 162}$

$= \sqrt{16 \times 2 \times 18 \times 9}$

$= 4 \times 18 = 72$

113. (a) Total amount that Rakhi paid

$= \frac{95}{100} \times 80 + \frac{92}{100} \times 150 + \frac{90}{100} \times 350$

$= 76 + 138 + 315 =$ ₹529

114. (d) Let $AB = x$ and $BC = 2x$

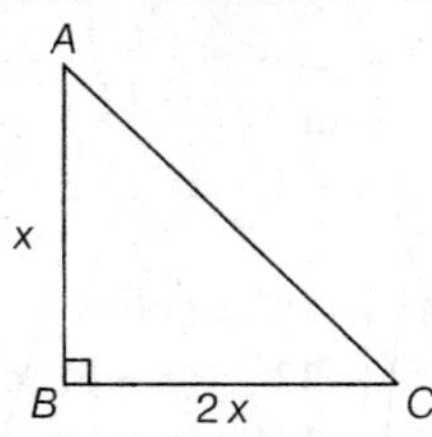

Then, $AC = \sqrt{x^2 + (2x)^2} = x\sqrt{5}$

$\therefore \cos A + \tan C = \frac{AB}{AC} + \frac{AB}{BC}$

$= \frac{x}{x\sqrt{5}} + \frac{x}{2x}$

$= \frac{1}{\sqrt{5}} + \frac{1}{2} = \frac{2 + \sqrt{5}}{2\sqrt{5}}$

115. (a) We know,

Product of two numbers

= LCM × HCF

$\Rightarrow \quad 20000 = 800 \times \text{HCF}$

$\Rightarrow \quad \text{HCF} = \frac{200}{8} = 25$

116. (d) $a + \frac{1}{a} = 3$ (given)

Squaring on both sides, we get

$\left(a + \frac{1}{a}\right)^2 = 3^2$

$\Rightarrow a^2 + \frac{1}{a^2} + 2 = 9$

$\Rightarrow \quad a^2 + \frac{1}{a^2} = 7$

Again squaring on both sides,

$\left(a^2 + \frac{1}{a^2}\right)^2 = 7^2$

$\Rightarrow a^4 + \frac{1}{a^4} + 2 = 49$

$\Rightarrow \quad a^4 + \frac{1}{a^4} = 47$

117. (d) Required ratio $= 10\% : \frac{100}{4}\%$

$= 10\% : 25\%$

$= 10 : 25 = 2 : 5$

118. (a) Given expression,

$\frac{\cos 37^\circ}{\sin 53^\circ} - \cos 47^\circ \operatorname{cosec} 43^\circ$

$\because \quad \sin 53^\circ = \cos 37^\circ$

and $\cos 47^\circ = \sin 43^\circ$

$\therefore \quad \frac{\cos 37^\circ}{\cos 37^\circ} - \sin 43^\circ \operatorname{cosec} 43^\circ$

$= 1 - \sin 43^\circ \times \frac{1}{\sin 43^\circ}$

$= 1 - 1 = 0$

119. (b) Let radius of sphere be 'r' cm.

Volume of sphere = 130977 cm^3

$\Rightarrow \quad \frac{4}{3}\pi r^3 = 130977$

$\Rightarrow \quad \frac{4}{3} \times \frac{22}{7} \times r^3 = 130977$

$\Rightarrow \quad r^3 = \frac{130977 \times 21}{22 \times 4} = \frac{11907 \times 21}{2 \times 4}$

$= \frac{243 \times 49 \times 21}{2 \times 4}$

$r = \sqrt[3]{\frac{729 \times 49 \times 7}{2 \times 4}}$

$= \frac{9 \times 7}{2} = \frac{63}{2}$ cm

∴ Surface area of sphere $= 4\pi r^2$

$= 4 \times \frac{22}{7} \times \frac{63}{2} \times \frac{63}{2}$

$= 63 \times 9 \times 22 = 12474$ cm^2

120. (b) Here, $x = 6$ km/h

and $\quad y = 2.5$ km/h

∴ Downstream speed

$= x + y = 8.5$ km/h

and Upstream speed

$= x - y = 3.5$ km/h

Now, According to the question,

Total time taken

$= \frac{59.5 \text{ km}}{8.5 \text{ km/h}} + \frac{59.5 \text{ km}}{3.5 \text{ km/h}}$

$= \frac{35}{5} + \frac{85}{5} = 7 + 17 = 24$ h

121. (a) School bus used by number of students = 80 + 140 = 220

Bicycle used by number of students

= 280 + 190 = 470

Walking used by number of students

= 130 + 90 = 220

and other vehicles used by number of students = 200 + 250 = 450

Hence, bicycle used by maximum number of students.

122. (b) Downstream speed $= \frac{72}{6} = 12$ km/h

and Upstream speed $= \frac{72}{12} = 6$ km/h

Let speed of boat in still water be 'x' km/h and speed of stream be 'y' km/h

∴ Downstream speed

$= x + y = 12$ ...(i)

and Upstream speed

$= x - y = 6$ ...(ii)

From Eqs. (i) and (ii), we get

$2x = 18 \Rightarrow x = 9$ km/h

123. (d) $\frac{16}{3} - \left\{\frac{13}{3} + \left(\frac{10}{3} \div \frac{7}{3} - \frac{1}{3}\right)\right\}$

$= \frac{16}{3} - \left\{\frac{13}{3} + \left(\frac{10}{3} \div 2\right)\right\}$

$= \frac{16}{3} - \left\{\frac{13}{3} + \left(\frac{10}{3} \times \frac{1}{2}\right)\right\}$

$= \frac{16}{3} - \left\{\frac{13}{3} + \frac{5}{3}\right\}$

$= \frac{16}{3} - \frac{18}{3} = \frac{-2}{3}$

124. (c) $\frac{1 - \frac{3}{7} \div \frac{9}{49} \times \frac{3}{14}}{1 + \frac{3}{5} \div \frac{1}{25} \times \frac{1}{30}} = \frac{1 - \frac{3}{7} \times \frac{49}{9} \times \frac{3}{14}}{1 + \frac{3}{5} \times 25 \times \frac{1}{30}}$

$= \frac{1 - \frac{7}{14}}{1 + \frac{5}{10}} = \frac{1 - \frac{1}{2}}{1 + \frac{1}{2}} = \frac{\frac{1}{2}}{\frac{3}{2}} = \frac{1}{3}$

125. (c) Let the total number of voters be $100x$.

Total number of valid votes

$= 100x \times \frac{80}{100} \times \frac{95}{100}$

$= \frac{7600x}{100} = 76x$

According to the question,

$\frac{80}{100} \times 76x = 9500$

$x = \frac{9500 \times 100}{80 \times 76}$

$= \frac{10000}{64} = 156.25$

$\therefore \quad$ Total number of voters $= 100x$

$= 15625$

126. (b)

Inlet pipe 3.6 h → 7 ; Outlet pipe 6.3 h → –4 ; T.W. (25.2) Units

If both pipes are opened, part of tank filled in one hour = 7 – 4 = 3

∴ Required number of hours

$= \frac{25.2}{3} = 8.4$ hours

127. (a) Let the CP of house = ₹100x

According to the question,

$26400000 = 100x \times \frac{110}{100} \times \frac{120}{100}$

$\Rightarrow x = 200000$

∴ CP of house = ₹ 20000000

128. (d) Total runs scored against New Zealand and Pakistan during 2019-20

$= 4000 \times \frac{(14+16)}{100}$

$= 40 \times 30 = 1200$

Total runs scored against Sri Lanka and Pakistan during 2020-21

$= 5000 \times \frac{(20+15)}{100}$

$= 50 \times 35 = 1750$

∴ Required difference

$= 1750 - 1200 = 550$

129. (b) Volume of sphere $= \frac{256}{3}\pi \text{ cm}^3$

$\frac{4}{3}\pi r^3 = \frac{256}{3}\pi \Rightarrow r^3 = 64$

$\Rightarrow r = 4$ cm

∴ Total surface area $= 4\pi r^2$

$= 4 \times \pi \times (4)^2$

$= 64\pi \text{ cm}^2$

130. (a) $k(\tan 45^\circ \sin 60^\circ) = \cos 60^\circ \cot 30^\circ$

$\Rightarrow k\left(1 \cdot \frac{\sqrt{3}}{2}\right) = \frac{1}{2}\sqrt{3}$

$\Rightarrow k\frac{\sqrt{3}}{2} = \frac{\sqrt{3}}{2}$

$\Rightarrow k = 1$

131. (a) Relative speed (for same direction)

$= 42 - 30 = 12$ m/min

∴ Required time

$= \frac{\text{Distance between them}}{\text{Relative speed}}$

$= \frac{288}{12} = 24$ min

132. (d) Let ages of three boys be $3x$, $5x$ and $7x$, respectively.

According to the question,

$\frac{3x + 5x + 7x}{3} = 25$

$\Rightarrow 15x = 75 \Rightarrow x = 5$

∴ Age of youngest boy $= 3x$

$= 3 \times 5 = 15$ yr

133. (b) Let HCF of two numbers be x.

Then numbers will be in the ratio

$= 12x : 7x$

Here, HCF $= x = 25$ (given)

Hence, two numbers will be

$12 \times 25, 7 \times 25 = 300, 175$

134. (b) Let real weight cost ₹100.

∴ $\text{CP} = \frac{75}{100} \times ₹100 = ₹75$

and $\text{SP} = \frac{90}{100} \times 100 = ₹90$

∴ Profit percent $= \frac{90 - 75}{75} \times 100$

$= \frac{15}{75} \times 100 = 20\%$

135. (a) Let efficiencies of A and B be 'x' and 'y' respectively.

Total work $= 25x$

According to the question,

$5(x + y) + 5y + 5x = 25x$

$\Rightarrow 10x + 10y = 25x$

$\Rightarrow 15x = 10y$

$\Rightarrow \frac{x}{y} = \frac{2}{3}$

∴ A's share in the earnings

$= \frac{2}{5} \times ₹36000$

$= 2 \times 7200 = ₹14400$

136. (c) Total sales for 5 days

$= ₹6050 \times 5 = ₹30250$

And total sales for 4 days

$= ₹5445 + ₹5937 + ₹5865 + ₹6562$

$= ₹23809$

∴ Sales on fifth day

$= ₹[30250 - 23809] = ₹6441$

137. (b) Male employees in company P

$= 4560 - 2210 = 2350$

and Male employees in company R

$= 3052 - 1280 = 1772$

∴ Required difference

$= 2350 - 1772 = 578$

138. (a) Total number of addicted males in Chennai $= \frac{11}{20} \times 200000 = 110000$

139. (d) Let the number of plastic, wood and glass boxes be $2x$, $3x$ and $5x$ respectively.

According to the question,

$5x - 3x = 144 \Rightarrow 2x = 144 \Rightarrow x = 72$

Initially, number of plastic boxes

$= 2x = 72 \times 2 = 144$

∴ Required number of plastic boxes

$= \frac{125}{100} \times 144 = 180$

140. (d) $\frac{1}{5}\% = \frac{1}{500}$

141. (b) According to the question,

$\frac{80}{100} \times \text{Marked price} = ₹9080$

$\text{Marked price} = \frac{9080 \times 100}{80} = ₹11350$

142. (a) Remaining payment after down payment $= 4400 - 2000 = ₹2400$

Installment paid at the end of one month = ₹2440

∴ Interest $= 2440 - 2400 = ₹40$

Let rate of interest be $r\%$ p.a.

We know, $\text{SI} = \frac{P \times r \times t}{100}$

$\Rightarrow 40 = \frac{2400 \times r \times 1}{100 \times 12}$ [∵ $P = ₹2400$]

$\Rightarrow r = \frac{40}{2} = 20$

143. (c) Let $\angle PQR$ be $2a$ and $\angle PRT$ be $2b$.

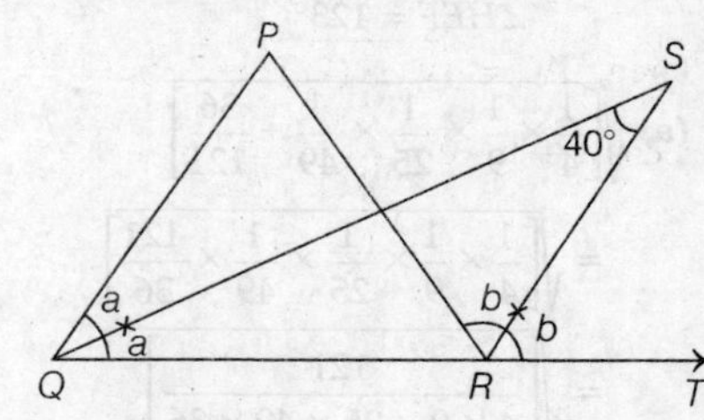

In ΔPQR,

$\angle PRT = \angle PQR + \angle QPR$

(Exterior angle property of a triangle)

$\Rightarrow 2b = 2a + \angle QPR$ ...(i)

In ΔSRQ,

$\angle SRT = \angle SQR + \angle QSR$

(Exterior angle property)

$\Rightarrow b = a + 40$ ...(ii)

From Eq. (i) and (ii), we get

$2[a + 40] = 2a + \angle QPR$

$\Rightarrow 2a + 80 = 2a + \angle QPR$

$\Rightarrow \angle QPR = 80^\circ$

144. (b) We know,

$(x^2 + y^2)^2 = x^4 + y^4 + 2x^2y^2$

$= x^2y^2 + 2x^2y^2$ [∵ $x^4 + y^4 = x^2y^2$]

$\Rightarrow (x^2 + y^2)^2 = 3x^2y^2$

$(x^2 + y^2) = xy\sqrt{3}$

On cubing both sides, we get

$(x^2 + y^2)^3 = (xy\sqrt{3})^3$

$\Rightarrow x^6 + y^6 + 3x^2y^2[x^2 + y^2] = x^3y^3 3\sqrt{3}$

$\Rightarrow x^6 + y^6 + 3x^2y^2[xy\sqrt{3}] = x^3y^3 3\sqrt{3}$

$\Rightarrow x^6 + y^6 + 3\sqrt{3}x^3y^3 = 3\sqrt{3}x^3y^3$

$\Rightarrow x^6 + y^6 = 3\sqrt{3}x^3y^3 - 3\sqrt{3}x^3y^3$

$\Rightarrow x^6 + y^6 = 0$

145. **(b)** Required percentage

$$= \frac{846}{1880} \times 100\% = 45\%$$

146. **(b)**

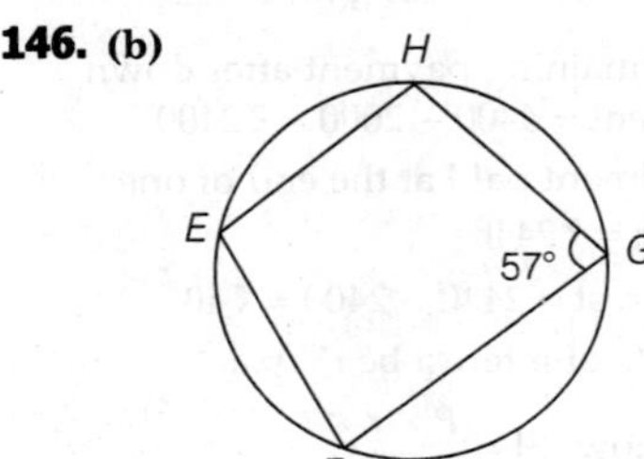

For a cyclic quadrilateral.

Sum of opposite angles = 180°

According to the question,

$\angle HEF + \angle FGH = 180°$

$\angle HEF = 180° - 57°$ $[\because \angle FGH = 57°]$

$\angle HEF = 123°$

147. **(a)** $\sqrt{\left[\frac{1}{4} \times \frac{1}{9} \times \frac{1}{25} \times \frac{1}{49} \div \frac{36}{121}\right]}$

$$= \sqrt{\left[\frac{1}{4} \times \frac{1}{9} \times \frac{1}{25} \times \frac{1}{49} \times \frac{121}{36}\right]}$$

$$= \sqrt{\left[\frac{121}{4 \times 9 \times 25 \times 49 \times 36}\right]}$$

$$= \frac{11}{2 \times 3 \times 5 \times 7 \times 6} = \frac{11}{1260}$$

148. **(b)** Here, $r_1 = 4$ cm and $r_2 = 7$ cm

We know that,

Surface area of hemisphere = $3\pi r^2$

Now,

Ratio of surface area of new balloon to its original

$$= \frac{3\pi r_2^2}{3\pi r_1^2} = \frac{r_2^2}{r_1^2} = \frac{7^2}{4^2} = \frac{49}{16}$$

149. **(a)** Total sales of 4AH battery over the years

= 75 + 90 + 96 + 105 + 90 + 105 + 115

= 676

Total sales of 7H battery over the years

= 144 + 126 + 114 + 90 + 75 + 60 + 85

= 694

Total sales of 32AH battery over the years

= 114 + 102 + 75 + 150 + 135 + 165 + 160 = 901

Total sales of 35AH battery over the years

= 102 + 84 + 105 + 90 + 75 + 45 + 100

= 601

Total sales of 55AH battery over the years

= 108 + 126 + 135 + 75 + 90 + 120 + 145 = 799

∴ 32AH battery has the highest total sales.

150. **(c)** From the table,
It is clear that class VI has the maximum number of students from all schools together.

151. **(c)** The word 'spontaneous' refers to something that happens naturally, without premeditation or planning, often driven by instinct or an impulse. The synonym that best matches this meaning is 'instinctive't which also refers to something that occurs naturally or by instinct.

152. **(b)** The word 'trainquil' is incorrectly spelt. The correct spelling is 'tranquil' which means calm or peaceful.

153. **(a)** The phrase 'extreme upset' is incorrect. The correct phrase should be 'extremely upset' because 'upset' is an adjective and it needs to be modified by an adverb (extremely) to indicate the degree of upset.

154. **(a)** The word 'thrshed' is incorrectly spelt. The correct spelling is 'thrashed' which means to move violently or struggle, especially in a way that causes movement.

155. **(d)** The idiom 'sit up and take notice' means to pay attention or take something seriously after being made aware of it. It suggests that the protest letter will prompt the recipients to start considering the issue seriously.

156. **(b)** The word 'defunct' means no longer existing, operating, or functioning. The antonym of 'defunct' would be 'extant't which means still in existence or active.

157. **(a)** The word 'evolve' in the sentence refers to the idea of gradual development or change over time. A synonym for evolve that would fit the context better is 'emanate', which can mean to emerge or develop naturally. Although it is not the most common synonym, it works well in this context as it reflects the natural progression of the education system.

158. **(b)** The phrase '113 km away from' implies a significant distance, so the most appropriate word choice would be 'far'. The word 'far' is commonly used when referring to distance, making it the best fit here.

159. **(d)** The word 'hygeine' is incorrectly spelt. The correct spelling is 'hygiene't which refers to practices or conditions that help maintain health and prevent the spread of diseases.

160. **(d)** The word 'amiable' means friendly, pleasant or good-natured. The most appropriate substitute in this context would be 'friendly't as it conveys the same meaning of being approachable and likable, especially in a social or academic setting.

161. **(c)** The word 'extempore' means spoken or done without preparation, especially in response to an immediate need or situation. It refers to something done off the cuff, spontaneously or impromptu.

162. **(d)** A 'mint' is a place where coins are produced or manufactured. It is specifically the term used for a facility where money, especially coins, are created.

163. **(c)** The word 'vague' means unclear, indefinite or not clearly expressed. The antonym of 'vague' would be 'definite't which means clear, precise or certain.

164. **(d)** The word 'behemoth' refers to something of enormous size or power, often used to describe something very large or powerful, whether it's a creature or an entity.

165. **(b)** The idiomatic expression 'the pros and cons' refers to the positive and negative aspects or arguments regarding a particular situation or decision. In this context, the Director asked to express views on both the benefits and drawbacks of the new HR policy.

166. (c) The idiom 'second wind' refers to a renewed burst of energy or strength after feeling fatigued or tired. It fits perfectly in the sentence as it describes someone getting a burst of energy and continuing their work.

167. (c) The word 'brave' means having courage or being fearless in the face of danger or difficulty. The opposite of 'brave' is 'cowardly', which means lacking courage or being easily frightened.

168. (a) The word 'behold' means to look at or observe something, often with admiration or wonder. The most appropriate synonym for 'behold' is 'look't which means to direct one's gaze at something.

169. (a) The phrase 'tumbled down' is an appropriate substitute for 'toppled' because it means to fall suddenly or collapse in a disorderly manner, which fits the context of the sand castle falling due to the gust of wind.

170. (a) The error lies in the phrase 'and I move in there'. The sentence is in the past tense ('managed'), so the phrase should also be in the past tense for consistency. The correct phrase would be 'and I moved in there'.

171. (b) The idiom 'open your heart' means to share your innermost feelings, emotions or thoughts, especially in an honest and vulnerable manner.

172. (a) A bibliography is a list of sources or references that are used or consulted in the preparation of a work, such as books, articles or other research materials.

173. (d) The idiom 'flying high' means to be very successful or doing very well. In this context, it suggests that despite initial problems, the company is now thriving and performing successfully.

174. (b) The idiom 'burn one's bridges' means to destroy the possibility of returning to an earlier state or situation. It often refers to making a decision or taking an action that leaves no way of going back or reversing it.

175. (d) Multi-tasking refers to the ability to perform multiple tasks simultaneously, which is the one-word substitute for the given group of words.

176. (d) The idiom 'my hands are full' means that someone is very busy or occupied with tasks and doesn't have time for anything else. It doesn't refer to physical exhaustion or swollen hands, but rather to being engaged or overwhelmed with work or responsibilities.

177. (d) The word 'cumolative' is incorrectly spelt. The correct spelling is 'cumulative', which means increasing or growing by accumulation or successive additions.

178. (c) The word 'credit' refers to the addition of money to an account or the acknowledgement of something positive. The opposite of credit, in accounting terms, is 'debit', which refers to the subtraction of money from an account or a financial charge.

179. (c) The idiom 'boil the ocean' means attempting to do something that is impractical or impossible due to the scale or nature of the task. It refers to a challenge that is overwhelming and unachievable.

180. (b) The error lies in the phrase 'When did you completed your graduation?'. The correct structure in indirect or direct questions after 'did' should use the base form of the verb, not the past tense. Therefore, 'completed' should be replaced with 'complete'.

181. (d) The word 'buraucratic' is incorrectly spelt. The correct spelling is 'bureaucratic', which refers to the administrative system of government or organisations, often associated with complex rules and procedures.

182. (d) Mythomania refers to the compulsion or tendency to tell lies or exaggerate the truth. It is a pathological habit of lying or fabricating stories.

183. (d) The word 'hinderance' refers to something that blocks or obstructs progress or movement. The antonym of 'hinderance' would be something that facilitates or provides comfort or relief, which in this case is 'relief'.

184. (a) The error lies in the phrase 'a little bitterly'. The word 'bitterly' is an adverb describing the manner of tasting, but it is not used correctly here. Instead, 'bitter' (an adjective) should be used to describe the taste.

185. (d) A hypocrite is someone who pretends to have certain moral standards or beliefs but acts in a way that contradicts those standards. This perfectly fits the description of someone who practices the very moral lapses they claim to oppose.

186. (b) The idiomatic expression 'to burn the midnight oil' means to stay up late working on something, usually studying or working hard. In this context, it is the most appropriate substitute as it refers to the effort of working late into the night, which aligns with the task of writing a book.

187. (c) A vegan is a person who does not eat any animal products, including meat, dairy, eggs, or any other product derived from animals.

188. (a) The idiom 'lie in the bed you have made' means that you must face the consequences of your own actions, especially if those actions lead to negative outcomes. It suggests that you are responsible for the situation you find yourself in and you must deal with it.

189. (d) The phrase 'through hand' is grammatically incorrect. The correct expression would be 'by hand', which means that something is delivered manually, not by machine or automation.

190. (d) The word 'demolish' means to destroy or tear down something. The antonym of 'demolish' would be 'fabricate', which means to create or build something, often from scratch.

191. (a) The correct preposition here is 'by'. The phrase 'live by' means to earn a living from a particular activity or profession. In this context, it suggests that everyone earns their livelihood by selling something.

192. (b) The correct word is 'derive', which means to obtain or take something from a source. In this context, it implies that what you can obtain or understand from the statement is that various professions, such as teaching, philosophy and priesthood, earn a living by offering their respective services.

193. (d) The most appropriate word for blank number 3 is 'estimate'. This word fits the context, as it means to judge or calculate the value, amount or extent of something. In this case, the passage is talking about measuring or assessing the true value of services, which is difficult to do.

194. **(a)** The word 'willingly' means freely, without reluctance or hesitation, which fits perfectly in this context. The passage describes a situation where someone might be ready to give everything to save their life, implying that it would be done willingly.

195. **(c)** The most appropriate word to fill in blank number 5 is 'conditions'. In this context, the phrase refers to the circumstances or factors in society that require skills to be compensated in a similar way as goods in a shop.

196. **(c)** The author of the passage uses humour and exaggeration to convey the message about the rise of stupidity in society. The passage contains a sarcastic tone, especially when referring to 'stupidity' as a contagious epidemic and the criticism of various aspects of society like politics, social media and the education system.

The use of humour and exaggeration helps make the serious topic more engaging and emphasises the absurdity of the situation.

197. **(d)** According to the passage, the solution to the issue of stupidity in society is encouraging critical thinking and problem-solving skills.

The author argues that the education system should focus on teaching children how to think critically and solve problems, rather than just memorising information.

This approach will help combat th spread of ignorance and misinformation.

198. **(a)** The tone of the passage is sarcastic. The author uses irony and mockery to criticise the spread of stupidity in society, especially in areas like politics, social media and the education system. Phrases like 'stupidity is contagious' and sarcastically mentioning 'catchy slogans and empty promises' convey a sarcastic tone while highlighting the seriousness of the issue.

199. **(d)** According to the author, children are not directly blamed for the spread of stupidity. Instead, the passage criticises politicians, the education system and individuals for contributing to the epidemic of stupidity.

The author mentions that the education system is failing, individuals are becoming more ignorant and politicians are no longer knowledgeable, but does not place the blame on children.

The focus is on societal structures and behaviours, not the children themselves.

200. **(d)** The passage emphasises the importance of critical thinking and how the lack of it has contributed to the spread of stupidity in various areas of society.

The author argues that intelligence and critical thinking need to be value again, especially in politics, the education system and individual behaviour. The title 'The Importance of Critical Thinking' captures the essence of the passage and its central message.

CPO SI P-1 SP 17

PAPER-1

SSC CPO SI SOLVED PAPER

3 October 2023 (Shift III)

MM : 200 **Time : 2 hr**

Instructions

1. This paper contains 200 questions.
2. It has 4 Parts, **Part I** General Intelligence and Reasoning, **Part II** General Knowledge and General Awareness, **Part III** Quantitative Aptitude and **Part IV** English Comprehension.
3. Each question carries **1 marks.**

Part I

General Intelligence and Reasoning

1. Select the option that represents the letters that, when sequentially placed from left to right in the blanks below, will complete the letter series.

L _ _ A _ _ S _ _ K _ _ L _ _ A

(a) A S L K A L S A K A
(b) K S K K A L S A K A
(c) K S L K A L S A K S
(d) K S L K A L S A K A

2. Select the set in which the numbers are related in the same way as the numbers of the given sets.

(Note Operations should be performed on the whole numbers, without breaking down the numbers into its constituent digits. e.g. 13 . Operations on 13 such as adding /subtracting /multiplying etc. to 13 can be performed. Breaking down 13 into 1 and 3 and then performing mathematical operations on 1 and 3 is not allowed.)

(6, 8, 106)

(7, 11, 177)

(a) (8, 7, 119) (b) (9, 8, 154)
(c) (5, 9, 101) (d) (7, 9, 136)

3. Select the correct mirror image of the given figure when the mirror is placed at MN as shown.

M

Jm45ae

N

(a) əɒƧ4mႱ (b) əɒ45mႱ
(c) əɒƧ4ɯႱ (d) əɐ54mſ

4. A @ B means 'A is the husband of B'.
A & B means 'A is the mother of B'.
A # B means 'A is the daughter of B'.
If D & G @ F & E @ H, then how is G related to H?

(a) Husband's father
(b) Husband's mother
(c) Mother
(d) Father

5. In a certain code language, 'TOWER' is written as 'INGYL' and 'SIGHT' is written as 'JTWVJ'. How will 'BRING' be written in that language?

(a) LWYDB (b) ACTBE
(c) KRPJS (d) AKUPW

6. If '×' means '–', '+' means '÷', '–' means '+' and '÷' means '×', what will be the value of the following expression?

$40 + [\{(24 - 12) \times (2 \div 2)\} + (18 \times 10)]$

(a) 10 (b) 20
(c) 1 (d) 5

7. In this question, three statements are given, followed by two conclusions numbered I and II. Assuming the statements to be true, even if they seem to be at variance with commonly known facts, decide which of the conclusions logically follows/ follow from the statements.

Statements

I. No dean is a teacher.
II. All teachers are professors.
III. No professor is a lecturer.

Conclusion

I. Some deans are lecturers.
II. Some teachers are lecturers.

(a) Only Conclusion II follows
(b) Only Conclusion I follows
(c) Both Conclusions I and II follow
(d) Neither Conclusion I nor II follows

8. Select the correct combination of mathematical signs to sequentially replace the * signs and to balance the given equation.

42 * 7 * 3 * 2 * 13 * 7

(a) ÷, ×, –, =, × (b) +, =, ÷, ×, +
(c) ÷, ×, =, +, + (d) ÷, ×, +, =, +

9. In a certain code language, 'Here we go' is coded as 'asa te du' and 'we can go' is coded as 'du mu asa'. What is the code for the word 'Here'?

(a) mu (b) asa
(c) du (d) te

10. Three of the following letter-clusters are alike in some manner and one is different. Select the one that is different.
(a) QJPK (b) KOLN
(c) MQNP (d) XBYA

11. Select the correct option that indicates the arrangement of the given words in the order in which they appear in an English dictionary.
1. Glory 2. Glossary
3. Globe 4. Gloss
5. Glow 6. Gloomy
(a) 3, 1, 6, 4, 2, 5 (b) 3, 6, 1, 2, 4, 5
(c) 3, 6, 1, 4, 2, 5 (d) 6, 3, 1, 4, 2, 5

12. If '+' means, '–', '–' means '÷','÷' means '×' and '×' means '+', then what will come in place of the (?) in the following equation?
$15 \div 405 - 3 + 25 \times 5 = ?$
(a) 1890 (b) 2000 (c) 2005 (d) 1889

13. Select the option that is embedded in the given figure as its part (rotation is not allowed)

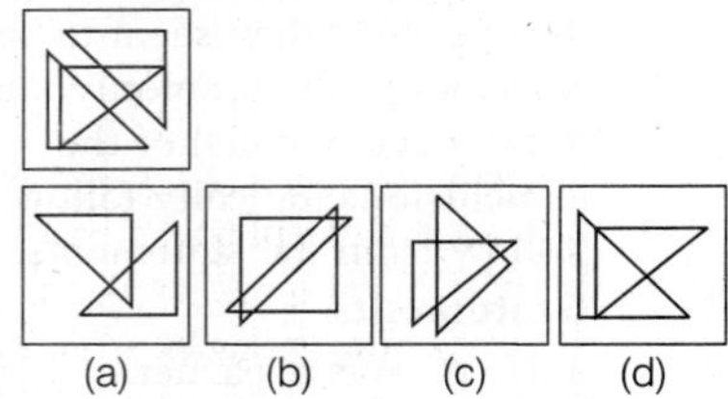

(a) (b) (c) (d)

14. Two statements are given, followed by two conclusions numbered I and II. Assuming the statements to be true, even if they seem to be at variance with commonly known facts, decide which of the conclusions logically follow(s) from the statements.
Statements
All cupboards are shelves.
All shelves are drawers.
Conclusions
I. All cupboards are drawers.
II. All drawers are shelves.
(a) Neither Conclusion I nor II follows
(b) Both Conclusions I and II follow
(c) Only Conclusion II follows
(d) Only Conclusion I follows

15. Which of the following terms will replace the question mark (?) in the given series?
WWVU , USTQ , ? , QKPI , OGNE
(a) SQRM (b) SORW
(c) SORM (d) SROM

16. In a certain code language, 'CARD' is coded as '3597' and 'DOGS' is coded as '8346'. What is the code for 'D' in the given code language?
(a) 4 (b) 9
(c) 5 (d) 3

17. Which figure from the given options would replace the question mark (?) if the following figure series were to be continued?

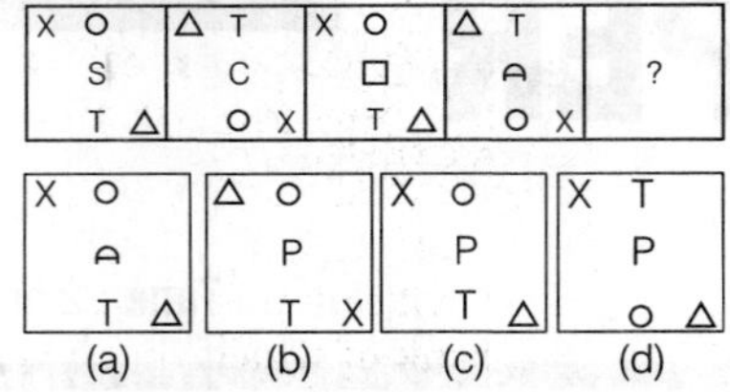

(a) (b) (c) (d)

18. Select the option figure in which the given figure is embedded (rotation is not allowed).

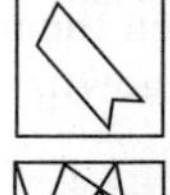

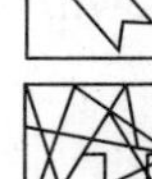

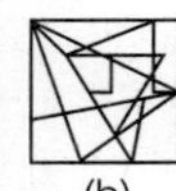

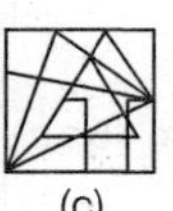

(a) (b) (c) (d)

19. In a certain code language, 'BED' is coded as 9 and 'TABLE' is coded as 25. How will 'RECLINER' be coded in the same language?
(a) 58 (b) 72
(c) 36 (d) 64

20. Six students are sitting around a circular table facing the centre. A is an immediate neighbour of both E and D. E sits third to the right of C. D sits third to the left of F. E is an immediate neighbour of F. B sits second to the left of E. Who sits to the immediate left of C?
(a) B (b) D (c) E (d) A

21. Which of the given figure when placed in the 5th position would continue the series that is established by the first four figures?

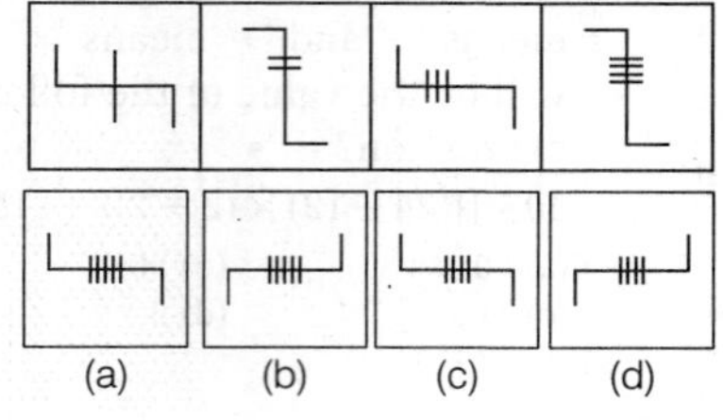

(a) (b) (c) (d)

22. Given below are two statements and two conclusions. Take the statements to be true even if they are at variance with commonly known facts and decide whether the conclusion(s) follow(s) the given statements.
Statements
All dogs are cats.
Some cats are not dolls.
Conclusions
I. All dolls are cats.
II. Some cats are dogs.
(a) Only Conclusion II follows
(b) Only Conclusion I follows
(c) Both the Conclusions follow
(d) Neither Conclusion I nor II follows

23. If A denotes '+', B denotes '×', C denotes '–' and D denotes '÷', then what will be the value of the following equation?
80 C 16 B 4 A 96 D 4 = ?
(a) 37 (b) 54 (c) 120 (d) 40

24. Select the correct mirror image of the given figure when the mirror is placed at line MN as shown.

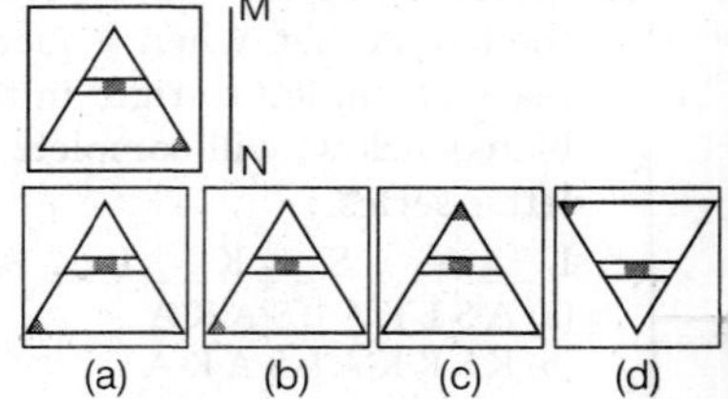

(a) (b) (c) (d)

25. If '+' means '÷', '–' means '×', '×' means '–' and '÷' means '+', then what will be the value of the following expression?
$108 \times 343 + 7 - 2 \div 13 = ?$
(a) 23 (b) 19 (c) 28 (d) 44

26. Four letter-clusters have been given, out of which three are alike in some manner and one is different. Select the odd letter-cluster.
(a) SUPT (b) JLGK
(c) EHBG (d) PRMQ

27. 'C @ D' means 'C is the mother of D'.
'C $ D' means 'C is the brother of D'.
'C # D' means 'C is the sister of D'.
'C * D' means 'C is the father of D'.
If V $ Y @ G * F, then how is Y related to F?
(a) Father's mother (b) Sister
(c) Father's sister (d) Brother

28. Select the option that is related to the third word in the same way as the second word is related to the first word.
(The words must be considered as meaningful words and must not be related to each other based on the number of letters/number of consonants/vowels in the word.)
Cat : Paw :: Crow : ?
(a) Hoff (b) Wings
(c) Beak (d) Claw

29. Which of the following numbers will replace the question mark (?) in the given series?
13, 14, −2, 79, −177, ?
(a) 424 (b) 528
(c) 608 (d) 448

30. In a certain code language, 'How are you' is coded as 'si de tu' and 'You are fine' is coded as 'de mu si'. What is the code for the word 'How'?
(a) mu (b) tu
(c) de (d) si

31. Manoj starts from point A and drives X km towards the South and then turns left and drives Y km. He then takes a right turn and drives for 4 km to reach point D. If Manoj drove a total of 17 km between Points A and D and both X and Y are perfect squares where X > Y, then what is the value of X?
(a) 4 (b) 11
(c) 5 (d) 9

32. If '+' means '−', '−' means '×', '×' means '÷' and '÷ means '+', what will come in place of '?' in the following equation?
$42 \times 7 - 11 \div 57 + 10 = ?$
(a) 133 (b) 113
(c) 103 (d) 123

33. Select the option figure which is embedded in the given figure as its part (rotation is not allowed).

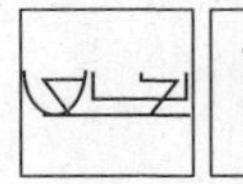

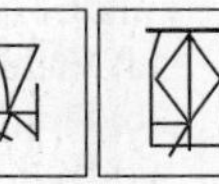
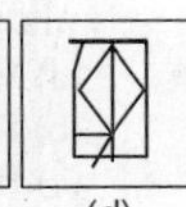

(a) (b) (c) (d)

34. Which of the following terms will replace the question mark (?) in the given series?
PMRO, NKTQ, LIVS, ?, HEZW
(a) JGUX (b) GJXU (c) JGVU (d) JGXU

35. Which of the following numbers will replace the question mark (?) in the given series?
93, ?, 102, 111, 123, 138
(a) 95 (b) 96 (c) 98 (d) 97

36. Select the figure that will come next in the following figure series.

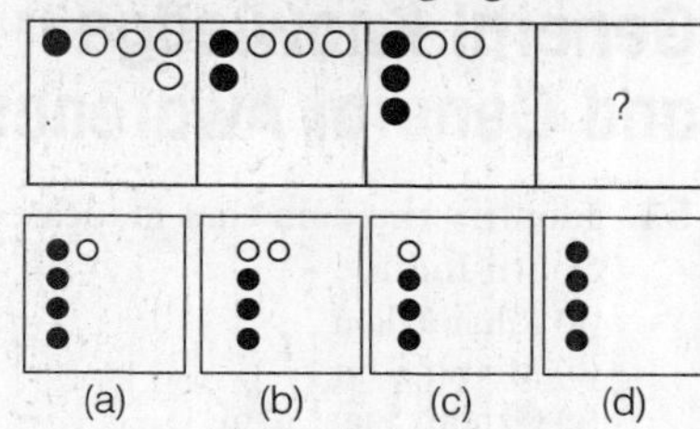

(a) (b) (c) (d)

37. Select the option that represents the correct order of the given words as they would appear in an English dictionary?
1. Jalopy 2. Jabber
3. Jackpot 4. Jackdaw
5.Jackal
(a) 2, 5, 4, 3, 1 (b) 4, 5, 2, 3, 1
(c) 3, 2, 4, 5, 1 (d) 2, 4, 3, 1, 5

38. A boy walks 15 m north, turns right and walks 20 m. Again, he turns right and walks 15m. Finally, he turns to his left and moves 20 m. What is the distance now from his original position?
(a) 40 m (b) 46 m (c) 50 m (d) 45 m

39. Which of the following numbers will replace the question mark (?) in the given series?
38, 64, 98, 140, ?
(a) 190 (b) 186 (c) 188 (d) 192

40. Six students Prateek, Sameer, Kabir, Ziya, Joseph, Kiran are sitting around a circular table facing the centre (not necessarily in the same order). Prateek is an immediate neighbour of both Sameer and Kabir. Ziya is sitting second to the right of Sameer. Kiran is sitting third to the left of Kabir. Joseph is an immediate neighbour of both Ziya and Kabir. Who is sitting to the immediate left of Joseph?
(a) Kabir (b) Ziya
(c) Sameer (d) Kiran

41. Select the set in which the numbers are related in the same way as are the numbers of the following sets.
(**Note** Operations should be performed on the whole numbers, without breaking down the numbers into its constituent digits. e.g. 13 . Operations on 13 such as adding /subtracting /multiplying etc. to 13 can be performed. Breaking down 13 into 1 and 3 and then performing mathematical operations on 1 and 3 is not allowed)
(125, 87, 49)
(236, 198, 160)
(a) (194, 162, 124) (b) (222, 186, 140)
(c) (166, 128, 101) (d) (277, 239, 201)

42. Which two mathematical signs should be interchanged to make the given equation correct?
$(63 \times 21) + 8 + 99 \times 11 \div 16 + (12 \times 4) = 158$
(a) + and − (b) × and +
(c) × and − (d) ÷ and ×

43. Select the option in which the given figure is embedded (rotation is not allowed).

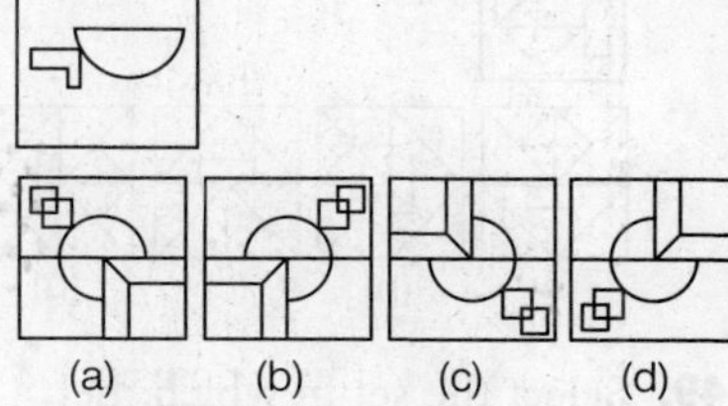

(a) (b) (c) (d)

44. Two statements are given followed by two conclusions numbered I and II. Assuming the statements to be true, even if they seem to be at variance with commonly known facts, decide which of the conclusions logically follow(s) from the statements.
Statements
All goods are services.
No service is a delivery.
Conclusions
I. No good is a delivery.
II. Some goods are deliveries.
(a) Neither Conclusion I nor II follows
(b) Both Conclusions I and II follow
(c) Only Conclusion II follows
(d) Only Conclusion I follows

45. Select the correct mirror image of the given figure when the mirror is placed at line MN as shown.

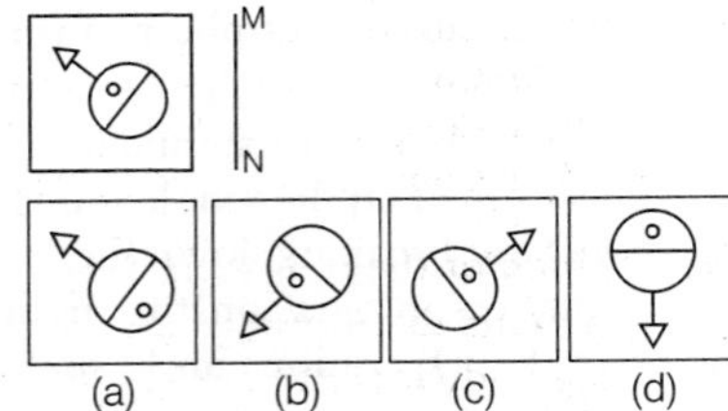

46. Which of the following numbers will replace the question mark (?) in the given series?
1024, 256, 64, ?, 4
(a) 32 (b) 34
(c) 36 (d) 16

47. Select the option that is related to the fourth term in the same way as the first term is related to the second term and the fifth term is related to the sixth term.
5 : 21 :: ? : 252 :: 27 : 725
(a) 26 (b) 10
(c) 16 (d) 12

48. Select the option in which the given figure is embedded (rotation is not allowed).

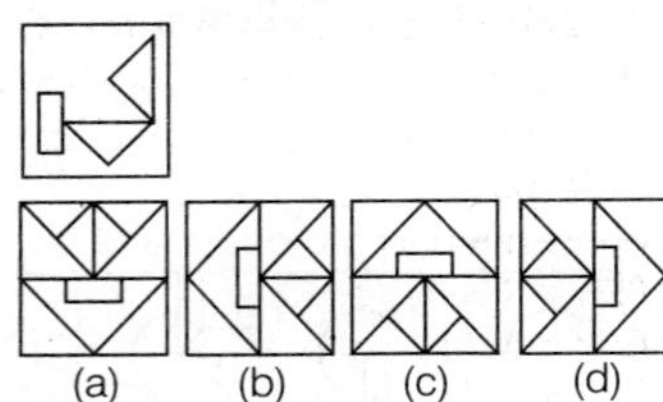

49. Select the set in which the numbers are related in the same way as are the numbers of the following set.
(**Note** Operations should be performed on the whole numbers, without breaking down the numbers into its constituent digits. e.g. 13 . Operations on 13 such as adding /subtracting /multiplying etc. to 13 can be performed. Breaking down 13 into 1 and 3 and then performing mathematical operations on 1 and 3 is not allowed)
(5, 4, 405)
(7, 3, 500)
(a) (4, 1, 125) (b) (3, 2, 145)
(c) (4, 5, 850) (d) (5, 8, 789)

50. Select the option that is related to the fifth letter-cluster in the same way as the second letter-cluster is related to the first letter-cluster and the fourth letter-cluster is related to the third letter-cluster.
CREATION : ETGCVKQP ::
UNIVERSE : WPKXGTUG ::
PLANET :?
(a) RNCPGV (b) RCPNGV
(c) RPGVNC (d) RPCGVN

Part II

General Knowledge and General Awareness

51. Identify the dam that is located in South India.
(a) Rihand dam
(b) Mettur dam
(c) Gandhi Sagar dam
(d) Tilaiya dam

52. Who is the author of the novel 'Before We Visit the Goddess'?
(a) Chitra Banerjee Divakaruni
(b) Kiran Doshi
(c) Arundhati Roy
(d) Jhumpa Lahiri

53. When the President of India keeps a bill (except money bill and constitutional amendment bill) pending for an indefinite period, it is called ....
(a) pocket veto of the President
(b) suspensive veto of the President
(c) absolute veto of the President
(d) amendatory veto of the President

54. Which of the following union territories has the lowest literacy rate according to the 2011 Census?
(a) Delhi
(b) Dadra and Nagar Haveli
(c) Lakshadweep
(d) Daman and Diu

55. Where are Huka Falls located?
(a) Spain (b) Australia
(c) New Zealand (d) Germany

56. A Money Bill under Article-111 of the Constitution of India, presented to the President for assent, has to be endorsed by a Certificate of the .... signed by him/her that it is a Money Bill.
(a) Speaker of the Lok Sabha
(b) Secretary General of the Rajya Sabha
(c) Deputy Chairman of the Rajya Sabha
(d) Secretary General of the Lok Sabha

57. Which state was the host of fifth Khelo India Youth Games 2022?
(a) Madhya Pradesh
(b) Uttarakhand
(c) Haryana
(d) Jharkhand

58. Who among the following is considered as the 'Father of Carnatic Music in India'?
(a) Gopala (b) Purandardas
(c) Narayan Tirtha (d) Krishna Bharati

59. Terrestrial planets are composed of ....
(a) metals and air (b) metals and gas
(c) rocks and gas (d) rocks and metals

60. Which of the following is considered a capital expense?
(a) Payment of salaries
(b) Pension
(c) Construction of school buildings
(d) Subsidies

61. Which Goddess is associated with the Gangaur festival celebrated in Central and Western India?
(a) Goddess Saraswati
(b) Goddess Lakshmi
(c) Goddess Parvati
(d) Goddess Kali

62. In which of the following Indian states does the South-West monsoon set first to give rainfall?
(a) Goa (b) Andhra Pradesh
(c) Kerala (d) Tamil Nadu

63. In which year did the 44th Amendment remove the Right to Property from the list of Fundamental Rights?
(a) 1975 (b) 1978
(c) 1981 (d) 1973

64. In which year was the Small Industries Development Bank of India (SIDBI) set up?
(a) 1990 (b) 1988
(c) 1989 (d) 1987

65. Which Nobel Laureate conducted an experiment in the late 19th century and observed that a glass tube filled with a low-pressure gas emitted radiation when a voltage was applied between two metal plates?
(a) Victor Francis Hess
(b) Philipp Lenard
(c) Paul Dirac
(d) Hideki Yukawa

66. Which of the following Articles of the Indian Constitution mentions that all executive actions of the Government of India shall be expressed to be taken in the name of the President?
(a) Article-81 (b) Article-67
(c) Article-77 (d) Article-48

67. Identify the third germinal layer found in triploblastic animals.
(a) Mesoderm (b) Ectoderm
(c) Coelom (d) Endoderm

68. What is the metric unit of pressure that is equal to 0.986923 atm?
(a) Bar (b) Quart
(c) Gallon (d) Yard

69. Famous musician Talvin Singh is associated with playing the ....
(a) shehnai (b) flute
(c) veena (d) tabla

70. During the year 1991-92, the industrial production recorded a .... growth of ....
(a) negative; 1.1 percent
(b) positive; 0.6 percent
(c) positive; 1.1 percent
(d) negative; 0.9 percent

71. Select the correct pair of classical dance and dancer.
(a) Padma Subrahmanyam-Bharatanatyam
(b) Mallika Sarabhai- Kathak
(c) Jhelum Paranjape - Kuchipudi
(d) K. Uma Rama Rao - Odissi

72. In which type of tax is the marginal tax rate higher than the average tax rate?
(a) Digressive (b) Proportional
(c) Regressive (d) Progressive

73. Which of the following Governor Generals, under the British rule in India, professionalised, bureaucratised and Europeanised the administration of East India Company?
(a) Lord Canning
(b) Lord Cornwallis
(c) Warren Hastings
(d) Lord Dalhousie

74. Which of the following elements is a member of the actinoid series?
(a) Magnesium (b) Lanthanum
(c) Lutetium (d) Thorium

75. 'The Great Indian Novel' is written by .... in which he based 'The Mahabharata' as a framework for his satirical novel.
(a) Shashi Tharoor
(b) Khushwant Singh
(c) Sarojini Naidu
(d) Kuldip Nayyar

76. Alarmel Valli is an Indian classical dancer and choreographer and a foremost exponent of the .... dance form of Bharatanatyam.
(a) Tarangam style
(b) Pandanallur style
(c) Vazhuvoor style
(d) Melattur style

77. In which of the following processes nutrients or contaminants are carried away by water or moved into the lower layer of the soil?
(a) Ploughing (b) Leaching
(c) Sowing (d) Bleaching

78. In July 2018, an experiment aboard the International Space Station cooled a cloud of atoms of which chemical element to one ten-millionth of one Kelvin above absolute zero, forming a Bose-Einstein Condensate in space?
(a) Rubidium (b) Plutonium
(c) Radium (d) Thorium

79. Malavikagnimitram, a drama of the 5th century CE, was written by ....
(a) Pingala (b) Kalidasa
(c) Harisena (d) Bhavabhuti

80. Who was the first winner of the Arjuna Award in Kabaddi?
(a) Sahanand Mahadev Shetty
(b) Manjeet Chhillar
(c) BC Ramesh
(d) Bholanath Guin

81. The number of Pawn in chess is......... .
(a) 16 (b) 14
(c) 17 (d) 15

82. Who made the use of Gun powder common in North India to defeat enemies?
(a) Ibrahim Lodi
(b) Babur
(c) Daulat Khan Lodi
(d) Rana Sanga

83. By which Indian Constitutional Amendment Act was the 11th Fundamental Duty added in the Indian Constitution?
(a) 87th Constitutional Amendment Act
(b) 88th Constitutional Amendment Act
(c) 85th Constitutional Amendment Act
(d) 86th Constitutional Amendment Act

84. Which of the following Acts prevents disrespect to the National Flag and National Anthem?
(a) Protection of National Honour Act, 1996
(b) Civil Liberties Act, 2001
(c) Unlawful Activities (Prevention) Act, 2006
(d) Prevention of Insults to National Honour Act, 1971

85. In alchemy, aqua fortis is the classical name of which chemical compound that is used chiefly in the manufacture of explosives and fertilisers and in organic synthesis?
(a) Nitric acid (b) Formic acid
(c) Chloric acid (d) Hydrobromic acid

86. What is the height of the badminton net?
(a) 6 feet (b) 6.5 feet
(c) 5.1 feet (d) 5.5 feet

87. Which of the following mosques/ masjids was built during the reign of Lodi dynasty of the Delhi Sultanate?
(a) Begumpuri Mosque, Delhi
(b) Lal Masjid, Delhi
(c) Moth ki Masjid, Delhi
(d) Quwwat al-Islam, Delhi

88. Sattriya was recognised in .... as a Classical Dance by Sangeet Natak Akademi.
(a) 2000 (b) 2010
(c) 2020 (d) 2005

89. The synthesis of which chemical is inhibited due to aspirin?
(a) Pyrites (b) Prostaglandins
(c) Histamines (d) Analgesics

90. Who was the first ecologist to describe the specific shape of eco-trophic interactions, which he called the Pyramid of Numbers, in the 1920s?
(a) Charles Elton
(b) Ernst Haeckel
(c) Howard Thomas Odum
(d) Edward O. Wilson

91. Siddheshvara Mahadeva temple in Bengal depicts the architecture of which dynasty?
(a) Chalukya dynasty
(b) Shung dynasty
(c) Hussain Shahi dynasty
(d) Pala dynasty

92. In 2010, considering its outstanding value and vulnerability, UNESCO recognised 'Mudiyettu', an age-old ritual-drama of ...., as an 'Intangible Cultural Heritage of Humanity'.
(a) Tamil Nadu (b) Karnataka
(c) Kerala (d) Telangana

93. Choose the incorrect statement related to monsoon.
(a) The South-West Monsoon winds blow over the warm oceans, gather moisture and bring widespread rainfall over the mainland of India.
(b) The intensity and position of the high-pressure area, East of Madagascar, affects the Indian Monsoon.
(c) The difference in pressure over Tahiti (Pacific Ocean) and Darwin in Northern Australia (Indian Ocean) is computed to predict the intensity of the monsoons.
(d) The Western cyclonic disturbances occur due to withdrawal or the retreat of the monsoon.

94. The natural vegetation of India is broadly divided into .... groups.
(a) 6 (b) 5 (c) 9 (d) 7

95. According to the Census of India 2011, what was the percentage of Sikh communities in the total population in India?
(a) 0.4% (b) 79.8%
(c) 14.2% (d) 1.7%

96. Which of the following is not a food preservative?
(a) Aqua regia
(b) Vinegar
(c) Sodium chloride
(d) Sodium nitrite

97. Losar (a new year festival) is celebrated in which of the following states?
(a) Jharkhand
(b) Arunachal Pradesh
(c) Himachal Pradesh
(d) Uttarakhand

98. Who among the following leaders founded the women's wing of Congress in 1940?
(a) Lakshmi Sahgal
(b) Sarojini Naidu
(c) Sucheta Kripalani
(d) Aruna Asaf Ali

99. Which of the following schemes adopts the One District One Product (ODOP) approach to reap the benefit of scale in terms of procurement of inputs, availing common services and marketing of products?
(a) Pradhan Mantri Kisan Sampada Yojana
(b) Micro and Small Enterprises Cluster Development Programme (MSE-CDP)
(c) Production Linked Incentive Scheme for Food Processing Industry (PLISFPI)
(d) Pradhan Mantri Formalisation of Micro Food Processing Enterprises (PMFME)

100. Which of the following Acts, enacted by the British Parliament, provided for the establishment of a Law Commission for the consolidation and codification of Indian Laws?
(a) Indian Council Act, 1909
(b) Government of India Act, 1919
(c) Charter Act, 1813
(d) Charter Act, 1833

Part III
Quantitative Aptitude

101. What should be the value in place of (?) in $7\frac{5}{8}+\frac{5}{8}$ of $184 \times 15 \div 5 - (?) = 0$.
(a) $-352\frac{5}{8}$ (b) $152\frac{1}{8}$
(c) $-152\frac{1}{8}$ (d) $352\frac{5}{8}$

102. The following table shows the earning of different firms (in ₹ crore) in different years.

Firm/Year	2012	2013	2014	2015	2016
P	50	45	49	56	57
Q	46	48	50	55	62
R	70	65	63	68	73
S	38	47	56	60	69

The earning (in ₹ crore) of which firm was highest in the year 2015?
(a) P (b) S
(c) R (d) Q

103. A shopkeeper allows a discount of 15% on an article and still makes a profit of 20%. What does the shopkeeper pay for an article whose marked price is ₹ 7200?
(a) ₹ 6120 (b) ₹ 5120
(c) ₹ 6100 (d) ₹ 5100

104. If $\tan A = \frac{2}{5}$ find the value of $\frac{\sec^2 A}{\operatorname{cosec}^2 A}$.
(a) $\frac{2}{5}$ (b) $\frac{4}{25}$
(c) $\frac{9}{25}$ (d) $\frac{3}{5}$

105. What is the compound interest on a sum of ₹25000 after three years at a rate of 12 percent per annum interest compounded yearly?
(a) ₹ 9824.00 (b) ₹ 10.520.00
(c) ₹ 9956.86 (d) ₹ 10123.20

106. The least number which should be added to 1351 so that the sum is exactly divisible by 2,4,6 and 8 is
(a) 11 (b) 15 (c) 13 (d) 17

107. In a ΔPQR and ΔABC, $\angle P = \angle A$ and $AC = PR$. Which of the following conditions is true for triangle PQR and ABC to be congruent?
(a) $AB = PQ$ by SSS
(b) $AB = PQ$ by SAS
(c) $BC = QR$ by ASS
(d) $\angle Q = \angle B$ by AAA

108. Study the given pie-chart and answer the question that follows.
The pie-chart shows the expenditure of a family on different items and their savings throughout the year 2021.

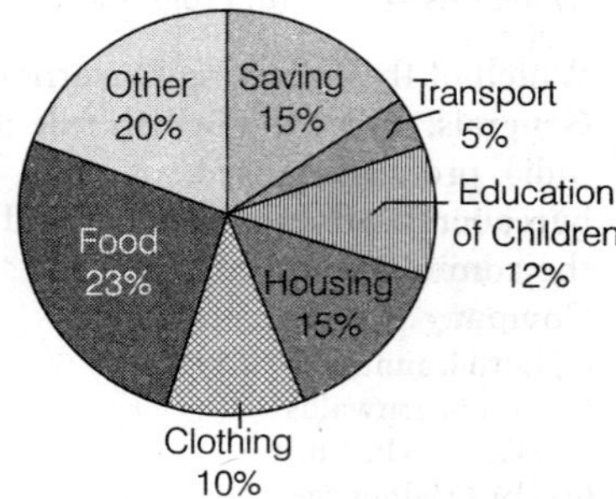

If the total income of the family was ₹ 100000, how much money (in ₹) was spent on the education of the children?
(a) 12500 (b) 12000
(c) 13500 (d) 13000

109. A vendor bought a book marked at ₹ 850 at successive discounts of 20% and 10%, respectively. He spent ₹ 55 on transport and sold the book for ₹ 980. What will be his profit percentage (rounded off to 2 decimal places)?
(a) 45.65% (b) 48.25%
(c) 50.65% (d) 46.93%

110. Two numbers are in the ratio of 4 : 3. The product of their HCF and LCM is 2700. The difference between the numbers is
(a) 15 (b) 30
(c) 25 (d) 105

111. Ramesh borrowed some money at rate of 5% per annum for the first four years, 8% per annum for the next six years and 12% per annum for the period beyond ten years. If the total interest paid by him at the end of twelve years is ₹ 9016, then find the money borrowed by Ramesh.
(a) ₹ 9816 (b) ₹ 9800
(c) ₹ 9016 (d) ₹ 9616

112. The area of an equilateral triangle is $4\sqrt{3}$ cm^2. Find the side (in cm) of the triangle.
(a) 2 (b) 4 (c) $\sqrt{3}$ (d) $2\sqrt{3}$

113. The following table shows the percentage of students passing out of four colleges (A, B, C and D) over four years. Study the table and answer the question the follows.

Years	College A	College B	College C	College D
2019	68	78	56	78
2020	72	86	78	82
2021	78	91	82	85
2022	80	87	84	87

In which college is the average percentage of passing students over the given four years the least?
(a) College D (b) College C
(c) College B (d) College A

114. The average weight of 15 people increases by 3.2 kg when a new person comes in place of one of them weighing 52 kg. The weight of the new person is
(a) 48 kg (b) 96 kg
(c) 100 kg (d) 52 kg

115. Study the given graph and answer the following question.
Number of boys and girls students in each section.

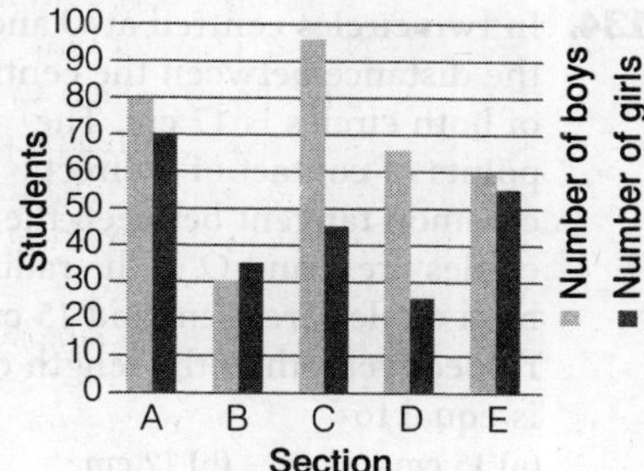

The number of boy students in section B is approximately what percentage of the number of girl students in section E?
(a) 25% (b) 55%
(c) 45% (d) 15%

116. If $x\left(5-\frac{2}{x}\right)=\frac{5}{x}$, then the value of $x^2+\frac{1}{x^2}$ is
(a) $\frac{54}{25}$ (b) $\frac{53}{28}$
(c) $\frac{53}{27}$ (d) $\frac{54}{23}$

117. The length and the breadth of the floor of a rectangular hall are 126 feet and 90 feet, respectively. What will be the area (in square feet) of each of the largest identical square tiles that can be used to tile this floor in a way that no part of the floor remains uncovered?
(a) 484 (b) 256 (c) 324 (d) 196

118. Study the given table and answer the question that follows.

Years	Rice	Wheat	Coarse grains	Pulses
1960-62	161	62	131	61
1970-72	197	81	116	64
1980-82	187	116	103	46
1990-92	189	124	101	44
2000-02	201	137	86	64

The table shows the consumption of food grains per day (in grams) in the given set of following years. For which food grain consumption was there successive increase over the given set of years?
(a) Rice (b) Pulses
(c) Coarse grains (d) Wheat

119. The LCM of two prime numbers x and y $(x > y)$ is 533. The value of $4y - x$ is
(a) 18 (b) 11 (c) 23 (d) 21

120. If $A + B = 90°$, then the expression $\frac{\cot A}{\cot B} + \cos^2 A + \cos^2 B$ is equal to
(a) $\cot^2 B$ (b) $\operatorname{cosec}^2 A$
(c) $\cot^2 A$ (d) $\operatorname{cosec}^2 B$

121. Ramesh does half as much work as Parul in $\frac{4}{5}$ of the time. If together Ramesh and Parul take 24 days to complete the work, then how much time will Parul take to do it?
(a) 38 days (b) 41 days
(c) 37 days (d) 39 days

122. Study the given table and answer the question that follows.
The table shows the number of employees in five different organisations A, B, C, D and E in different departments.

Dept ↓ / Org →	A	B	C	D	E
HR	1050	1015	976	888	1004
Finance	1017	960	786	1025	963
Marketing	1382	1384	1275	1300	1290
Production	1542	1545	4550	1570	1580
Accounts	786	745	801	800	735
Legal	48	54	36	30	53
Total	5825	5703	5424	5613	5625

Which organisation has minimum number of employees?
(a) C (b) B (c) D (d) E

123. If $\sin\theta + \cos\theta = \frac{\sqrt{11}}{3}$, then the value if $(\cos\theta - \sin\theta)$ is
(a) $\frac{\sqrt{5}}{3}$ (b) $\frac{7}{3}$ (c) $\frac{5}{3}$ (d) $\frac{\sqrt{7}}{3}$

124. If $(48 \div 72 \times 3) - [15 \div 8 \times (40 - 32) - 10] + 2P = 6 \div 2$, then find the value of P?
(a) 3 (b) 4 (c) 2 (d) 1

125. Mayur sold a watch at a profit of 7%. If he had sold it for ₹1329 more, he would have gained 57%. Find the cost price (in ₹) of the watch.
(a) 2580 (b) 2658
(c) 2420 (d) 2856

126. If $A + \cfrac{1}{1+\cfrac{1}{2+\cfrac{1}{3}}} = \frac{9}{10}$, then the value of A is
(a) $\frac{1}{5}$ (b) $\frac{3}{10}$ (c) $\frac{2}{5}$ (d) $\frac{1}{10}$

127. Find the area of a rhombus if the perimeter of the rhombus is 52 cm and one of its diagonals is 10 cm long.
(a) 120 cm^2 (b) 164 cm^2
(c) 160 cm^2 (d) 144 cm^2

128. The speed of a boat in still water is 20 km/h, while the river is flowing at a speed of 8 km/h and the time taken to cover a certain distance upstream is 6 h more than the time taken to cover the same distance downstream. Find the distance.
(a) 120 km (b) 336 km
(c) 126 km (d) 125 km

129. In an election between P and Q, P gets 40% of the total votes and thus loses by 10 votes. The total number of votes is
(a) 80 (b) 50
(c) 90 (d) 70

130. The price of a treadmill is marked at ₹ 1250. A shopkeeper earns a profit of 14% after allowing a discount of 14% on the marked price. Find the cost price (to the nearest rupee) of the treadmill.
(a) ₹ 845 (b) ₹ 840
(c) ₹ 1043 (d) ₹ 943

131. Jeevan can do a piece of work alone in 42 days, while Rishi and Jeevan together can do the same piece of work in 27 days. How many days will Rishi take to complete the same piece of work alone?
(a) $74\frac{3}{5}$ (b) $75\frac{1}{5}$ (c) $75\frac{4}{5}$ (d) $75\frac{3}{5}$

132. A person covers 28 km while walking at a speed of 8 km/h. How much distance (in km) will he cover in same time if he walks at a speed of 6 km/h?
(a) 36 (b) 28 (c) 32 (d) 21

133. The area of an equilateral triangle is 173.2 cm^2. Its side will be ....
(a) 20 cm (b) 22 cm
(c) 17.32 cm (d) 21.32 cm

134. In two circles centred at O and O', the distance between the centres of both circles is 17 cm. The points of contact of a direct common tangent between the circles are P and Q. If the radii of both circles are 7 cm and 15 cm, respectively, then the length of PQ is equal to
(a) 15 cm (b) 17 cm
(c) 10 cm (d) 22 cm

135. If 4 men or 6 boys can finish a piece of work in 20 days, then in how many days can 6 men and 11 boys finish the same work?
(a) 5 (b) 6
(c) 7 (d) 8

136. Aditya sold article X at a profit of 23% and article Y at a loss of 13%. He earned a profit of ₹180 in the entire transaction. If article X costs 90 less than article Y, then what is the price of article Y (in ₹)?
(a) 2100 (b) 2007
(c) 2020 (d) 2050

137. If $\sin 2A = \cos 15°$, then the smallest positive value of A is
(a) 75° (b) 37.5°
(c) 7.5° (d) 47.5°

138. In an election, Ajay and Mohan are contesting for the Secretary post in a trade union of 9000 workers. 80% of the workers cast their votes, out of which 20% votes were found invalid. Ajay defeated Mohan by 1152 votes. How many votes did Ajay get?
(a) 3456 (b) 2304
(c) 4480 (d) 3546

139. Find the third proportional to 16 and 20.
(a) 25 (b) 23
(c) 24 (d) 26

140. The area of a sector of a circle of radius 8 cm, formed by an arc of length 4.6 cm, is ....
(a) 6.3 cm^2 (b) 9.2 cm^2
(c) 18.4 cm^2 (d) 12.6 cm^2

141. Following is the figure showing the sales of different items of a stationery shop. Which product recorded the highest percentage changes from 2020 to 2021?

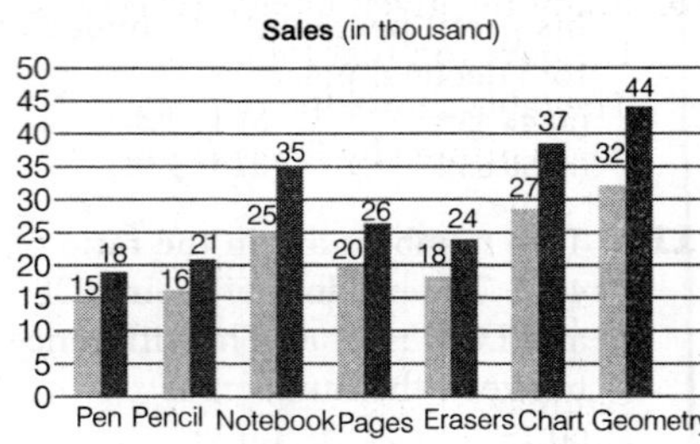

(a) Geometry (b) Notebook
(c) Charts (d) Pages

142. A solid sphere made of wax of radius 12 cm is melted and cast into solid hemispheres of radius 4 cm each. Find the number of such solid hemispheres.
(a) 54 (b) 27
(c) 14 (d) 28

143. The curved surface area (CSA) and the total surface area (TSA) of a hemisphere whose radius is 7 cm are
(a) CSA – 350 cm^2; TSA – 500 cm^2
(b) CSA – 320 cm^2; TSA – 480 cm^2
(c) CSA – 412 cm^2; TSA – 544 cm^2
(d) CSA – 308 cm^2; TSA – 462 cm^2

144. Study the given pie-chart and answer the question that follows. The pie-chart is about Country-wise Global Exports Presentation.

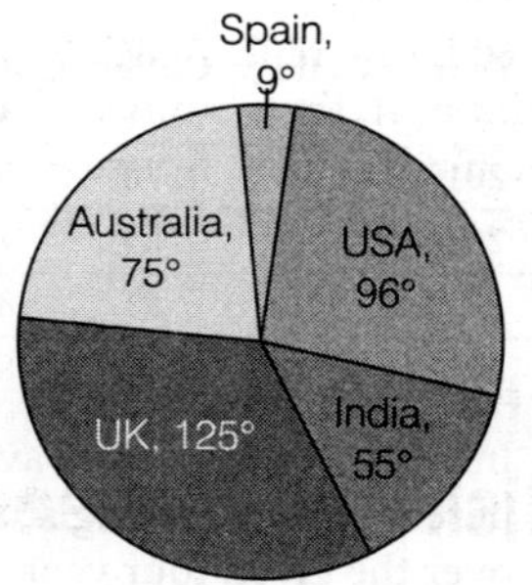

Total export = ₹14400 Billion

By how much does the value of the exports of UK exceed that of Australia (in ₹ billion)?
(a) 1500 (b) 2000
(c) 1440 (d) 2550

145. If the radius of a sphere is doubled, then its surface area will be increased by
(a) 100% (b) 200% (c) 300% (d) 400%

146. Study the given table and answer the question that follows.
The table shows the number of pages printed by four printers in three days.

Days	Printers			
	A	B	C	D
Friday	350	451	412	206
Saturday	420	325	365	251
Sunday	238	198	258	326

What is the respective ratio between total number of pages printed by printer D on Friday and Sunday together and total number of pages printed by printer A on Friday and Saturday together?
(a) 34 : 51 (b) 38 : 55
(c) 51 : 34 (d) 55 : 38

147. Find the third proportional to 23 and 31.
(a) $\frac{31}{23}$ (b) $\frac{961}{23}$ (c) $\frac{23}{31}$ (d) $\frac{23}{961}$

148. A speedboat, whose speed is 20 km/h in still water, goes 35 km downstream and comes back in a total of 8 h. What is the speed of the stream?
(a) 20 km/h (b) 10 km/h
(c) 15 km/h (d) 5 km/h.

149. What is the HCF of 12, 18 and 42?
(a) 123 (b) 12 (c) 6 (d) 60

150. If 60 L of a milk solution has 40% milk in it, then how much milk should be added to make the milk 60% in the solution?
(a) 30 L (b) 25 L (c) 20 L (d) 35 L

Part IV

English Comprehension

151. Select the most appropriate option that can substitute the underlined idiom/phrase in the given sentence.
You cannot throw dust into my eyes.
(a) terrify me
(b) hurt me
(c) abuse me
(d) mislead or deceive me

152. Select the most appropriate option that can substitute the underlined segment in the given sentence.
O' Henry's short stories are read all over the world till now because they are pithy.
(a) fascinating and lengthy
(b) elusive and unreal
(c) exaggerated yet short
(d) concise and expressive

153. Select the most appropriate meaning of the given idiom.
A plum job
(a) An easy and pleasant job
(b) A rare job
(c) A difficult job
(d) A job involving extensive travelling

154. Select the most appropriate option that can substitute the underlined segment in the given sentence.
If there is no need to substitute it, select 'No substitution'.
I like to read books, but my brother prefers to watching movies.
(a) in watching
(b) to watch
(c) on watching
(d) No substitution

155. Select the most appropriate antonym of the given word.
Glad
(a) Keen (b) Loyal
(c) Sad (d) Pleased

156. The following sentence has been split into four segments. Identify the segment that contains a grammatical error.
There is a spectrum / of seas around that / land which attracts / tourists of all aging.
(a) tourists of all aging.
(b) There is a spectrum
(c) land which attracts
(d) of seas around that

157. Select the most appropriate meaning of the underlined word.
Saurabh imitates his boss perfectly.
(a) Admires (b) Worships
(c) Copies (d) Hates

158. Select the most appropriate synonym of the given word.
Unequivocal
(a) Complete (b) Articulate
(c) Unambiguous (d) Doubted

159. In the following sentence, four words are underlined, out of which one word is incorrectly spelt. Identify the incorrectly spelt word.
Traffic accidents are increasing steadily, and large cities are plaged by traffic congestion. Worst of all is the air pollution caused by internal combustion engine, uninterruptedly.
(a) plaged (b) uninterruptedly
(c) congestion (d) combustion

160. Select the most appropriate meaning of the given idiom.
Keep count of
(a) To remind of a deadline
(b) To act more politely
(c) To remember a total
(d) To accept an invitation

161. Select the most appropriate one-word substitution of the given group of words.
A pretence of having a virtuous character, moral or religious beliefs or principles, etc., that one does not really possess.
(a) Shrewdness (b) Naivety
(c) Gullibility (d) Hypocrisy

162. Select the most appropriate idiom that can substitute the underlined segment in the given sentence.
He made a mess of that bookcase he was supposed to be repairing.
(a) made a pig's ear
(b) had a butcher hook
(c) made a clean breast
(d) brought a dog's breast

163. The following sentence has been split into four segments. Identify the segment that contains a grammatical error.
My apartment / in Delhi / is situated / on second floor.
(a) is situated (b) in Delhi
(c) My apartment (d) on second floor

164. Select the most appropriate option that can substitute the underlined segment in the given sentence. If there is no need to substitute it, select 'No substitution'.
This case is serious. You need to look into this matter; otherwise, the situation will get out of control soon.
(a) look up (b) look at
(c) No substitution (d) look after

165. Select the most appropriate meaning of the given idiom.
Keep a straight face
(a) Become very confused
(b) Get on extremely well with someone
(c) Not laugh or change your expression even though you want to laugh
(d) Make more of an effort

166. Select the option that can be used as a one-word substitute for the given group of words.
Huge fire for celebration
(a) Campaign (b) Bonfire
(c) Agenda (d) Crossfire

167. Identify the option that rectifies the spelling of the incorrectly spelt word in the given sentence.
The disadvantages of listening to music at a loud voluume include loss of hearing.
(a) Lissening (b) Lose
(c) Heering (d) Volume

168. Select the most appropriate synonym of the word 'disclosed' in the given sentence and choose the correct option.
The linguist's analysis of the language revealed patterns and structures that were previously unknown.
(a) Linguist (b) Patterns
(c) Revealed (d) Unknown

169. Select the incorrectly spelt word.
(a) Gllidder (b) Airplane
(c) Helicopter (d) Ladybug

170. Select the most appropriate meaning of the underlined word.
We shouldn't blame or <u>envy</u> anyone.
(a) Love (b) Jealousy
(c) Curse (d) Reap

171. Select the option that can be used as a one-word substitute for the given group of words.
Minimum people needed for a meeting
(a) Forum (b) Quorum
(c) Addendum (d) Decorum

172. Select the option that can be used as a one-word substitute for the given group of words.
Detailed list of goods dispatched with quantity and price to the purchaser.
(a) Ledger (b) Sales
(c) Receipt (d) Invoice

173. Select the grammatically correct sentence.
(a) The simple mistake which was committed by the boy haunted her for years.
(b) An simple mistake which was committed by the boy haunted her for years.
(c) A simple mistake which was committed by an boy haunted her for years.
(d) The simple mistake which was committed by an boy haunted her for years.

174. Select the most appropriate synonym of the given word.
Vulnerable
(a) Susceptible (b) Guarded
(c) Amiable (d) Delectable

175. Select the most appropriate synonym of the given word.
Benevolent
(a) Generous (b) Innocent
(c) Cruel (d) Wicked

176. In the following sentence, four words are underlined, out of which one word is incorrectly spelt. Identify the incorrectly spelt word.
The <u>ruins</u> of many structures that still stand tall in their <u>granduer</u> are <u>testimony</u> to the fact that Mewar was not only the land of the <u>courageous</u> .
(a) testimony (b) courageous
(c) granduer (d) ruins

177. Select the option that can be used as a one-word substitute for the given group of words.
To criticise someone severely
(a) Rate (b) Remonstrate
(c) Chastise (d) Scoff

178. Select the most appropriate one-word substitution of the given group of words.
A state of intense happiness and self-confidence.
(a) Euphoria (b) Intoxication
(c) Touche (d) Oblivion

179. Select the option that can be used as a one-word substitute for the given group of words.
To make a low continuous vibratory sound expressing contentment (of a cat).
(a) To meow (b) To purr
(c) To buzz (d) To roar

180. Select the most appropriate meaning of the given idiom.
Face the music
(a) To work every possible way to succeed
(b) To accept punishment for some mistakes which you have done
(c) To be cheated by someone you trust
(d) To have the problems with money

181. Select the most appropriate idiom to fill in the blank.
I was going to mention it, but it ....
(a) brought to mind
(b) changed my mind
(c) bore in mind
(d) slipped my mind

182. Select the most appropriate phrasal verb to fill in the blank.
Though Pradeep .... for Jamaica, he landed up in Nigeria.
(a) set aside (b) set about
(c) set out (d) set up

183. Select the most appropriate antonym of the given word.
Specific
(a) Topple (b) Lawful
(c) Random (d) Stroll

184. Select the most appropriate antonym of the given word.
Beneficent
(a) Cruel (b) Lethargic
(c) Soft (d) Friendly

185. Select the most appropriate meaning of the given idiom.
Grasping at straws
(a) Trying to find the best way to compete with others when nothing you choose is likely to work
(b) Trying to find some way to succeed when you see others are also doing the same
(c) Trying to find some way to succeed when nothing you choose is likely to work
(d) Trying to find manipulative ways to succeed

186. Select the most appropriate antonym of the given word.
Contempt
(a) Mockery (b) Deny
(c) Regard (d) Immoral

187. Select the option that can be used as a one-word substitute for the given group of words.
No longer used because something new has been invented
(a) Classic (b) Ancient
(c) Ornamental (d) Obsolete

188. Select the most appropriate idiom or phrase to complete the given sentence.

I like her because she never likes to make ....

(a) a slap on the wrist
(b) a drop in the bucket
(c) a bed of roses
(d) a quick buck

189. Select the sentence that has a spelling error.

A. A fisherman, enfeebled with age, could no longer go out to sea so he began fishing in the river.

B. Every morning he would go down to the river and sit there fishing the whole day long.

C. In the evening, he would sell whatever he had caught, buy food for himself and go home.

D. One hot afternoon, while he was bemoaning his fate, a large bird alited near him.

(a) One hot afternoon, while he was bemoaning his fate, a large bird alited near him.
(b) In the evening, he would sell whatever he had caught, buy food for himself and go home.
(c) A fisherman, enfeebled with age, could no longer go out to sea so he began fishing in the river.
(d) Every morning he would go down to the river and sit there fishing the whole day long.

190. Choose the most appropriate meaning of the underlined phrase.

Ram could not go to Delhi for vacation since he <u>was banking on</u> his arrears of pay which he did not get in time.

(a) Sloping on
(b) Depending on his bank
(c) Calling on
(d) Relying on

Directions (Q. Nos. 191-195) *In the following passage, some words have been deleted. Read the passage carefully and select the most appropriate option to fill in each blank.*

When another old cave is discovered in the south of France, it is not ...(1)... in news. Rather, it is an ordinary event. Such discoveries are so ...(2)... these days that hardly anybody pays heed to them. However, when the Lascaux cave complex was discovered in 1940, the world was ...(3).... Painted directly on its walls were hundreds of scenes showing how people lived thousands of years ago. The scenes show people hunting animals, such as bison or wild cats. Other images ...(4)... birds and, most noticeably, horses, which appear in more than 300 wall images, by far ...(5)... all other animals.

191. Select the most appropriate option to fill in blank number 1.

(a) suitably (b) nearly
(c) merrily (d) usually

192. Select the most appropriate option to fill in blank number 2.

(a) disorderly (b) frequent
(c) ghastly (d) delusional

193. Select the most appropriate option to fill in blank number 3.

(a) baffled (b) overthrown
(c) encouraged (d) crushed

194. Select the most appropriate option to fill in blank number 4.

(a) imprint (b) depict
(c) require (d) determine

195. Select the most appropriate option to fill in blank number 5.

(a) outnumbering (b) outsourcing
(c) outlasting (d) outreaching

Directions (Q.Nos. 196-200) *Read the given passage and answer the questions that follow.*

Climate policy must now put health at the centre and promote climate change mitigation policies that bring health benefits simultaneously. Health-focused climate policy would help bring about a planet that has cleaner air, more abundant and safer freshwater and food, more effective and fairer health and social protection systems and, as a result, healthier people.

Investment in clean energy will yield health gains that repay those investments twice over. There are proven interventions able to reduce emissions of short-lived climate pollutants, for instance applying higher standards for vehicle emissions, which have been calculated to save approximately 2.4 million lives per year, through improved air quality and reduce global warming by about 0.5°C by 2050. The cost of renewable sources of energy has decreased significantly in the last few years, and solar energy is now cheaper than coal or gas in most major economies.

196. What is the antonym for the word 'intervention', from the passage?

(a) Specific
(b) Evidence
(c) Non-involvement
(d) Data

197. What is the antonym for the word 'promote', from the passage?

(a) Conduct (b) Obstruct
(c) Invade (d) Exclude

198. Which of the following represents the structure of the passage?

(a) Chronology
(b) Critique
(c) Problem-solution
(d) Definition

199. Which of the following most accurately states the central idea of the passage?

(a) Greenhouse gases
(b) Pollution
(c) Climate policy for health
(d) Fossil fuels

200. Which is the best description of the tone of the passage?

(a) Biased
(b) Cynical
(c) Technical
(d) Humanistic

Know Correct Answers

1. (c)	2. (b)	3. (a)	4. (a)	5. (d)	6. (a)	7. (d)	8. (d)	9. (d)	10. (a)
11. (c)	12. (c)	13. (d)	14. (d)	15. (c)	16. (d)	17. (c)	18. (d)	19. (d)	20. (b)
21. (a)	22. (a)	23. (d)	24. (b)	25. (a)	26. (c)	27. (a)	28. (d)	29. (d)	30. (b)
31. (d)	32. (b)	33. (b)	34. (d)	35. (b)	36. (a)	37. (a)	38. (a)	39. (a)	40. (b)
41. (d)	42. (d)	43. (d)	44. (d)	45. (c)	46. (d)	47. (c)	48. (b)	49. (a)	50. (a)
51. (b)	52. (a)	53. (a)	54. (b)	55. (c)	56. (a)	57. (a)	58. (b)	59. (d)	60. (c)
61. (c)	62. (c)	63. (b)	64. (a)	65. (b)	66. (c)	67. (a)	68. (a)	69. (d)	70. (b)
71. (a)	72. (d)	73. (b)	74. (d)	75. (a)	76. (b)	77. (b)	78. (a)	79. (b)	80. (a)
81. (a)	82. (b)	83. (d)	84. (d)	85. (a)	86. (c)	87. (c)	88. (a)	89. (b)	90. (a)
91. (d)	92. (c)	93. (d)	94. (b)	95. (d)	96. (a)	97. (b)	98. (c)	99. (d)	100. (d)
101. (d)	102. (c)	103. (d)	104. (b)	105. (d)	106. (d)	107. (b)	108. (b)	109. (d)	110. (a)
111. (b)	112. (b)	113. (d)	114. (c)	115. (b)	116. (a)	117. (c)	118. (d)	119. (b)	120. (b)
121. (d)	122. (a)	123. (d)	124. (a)	125. (b)	126. (a)	127 (a)	128. (c)	129. (b)	130. (d)
131. (d)	132. (d)	133. (a)	134. (a)	135. (b)	136. (b)	137 (b)	138. (a)	139. (a)	140. (c)
141. (b)	142. (a)	143. (d)	144. (b)	145. (c)	146. (b)	147. (b)	148. (c)	149. (c)	150. (a)
151. (d)	152. (d)	153. (a)	154. (b)	155. (c)	156. (a)	157. (c)	158. (c)	159. (a)	160. (c)
161. (d)	162. (a)	163. (d)	164. (c)	165. (c)	166. (b)	167. (d)	168. (c)	169. (a)	170. (b)
171. (b)	172. (d)	173. (a)	174. (a)	175. (a)	176. (c)	177. (c)	178. (a)	179. (b)	180. (b)
181. (d)	182. (c)	183. (c)	184. (a)	185. (c)	186. (c)	187. (d)	188. (d)	189. (a)	190. (d)
191. (d)	192. (b)	193. (a)	194. (b)	195. (a)	196. (c)	197. (b)	198. (c)	199. (c)	200. (d)

Answer & Solutions

1. (c) The series will be as shown below
L K S A / L K S A / L K S A / L K S A
⇒ KSLKALSAKS

2. (b) As, (6, 8, 106)
$\Rightarrow (6^2 + 8^2) + 6 = 106$
and, (7, 11, 177) $\Rightarrow (7^2 + 11^2) + 7 = 177$
Similarly, (9, 8, 154)
$\Rightarrow (9^2 + 8^2) + 9 = 154$

3. (a) Option figure (a) is the correct mirror image of the given figure, when the mirror is placed at the 'MN' line.

M
Jm45ae | ɘɒ54mJ
N

4. (a) According to the information,

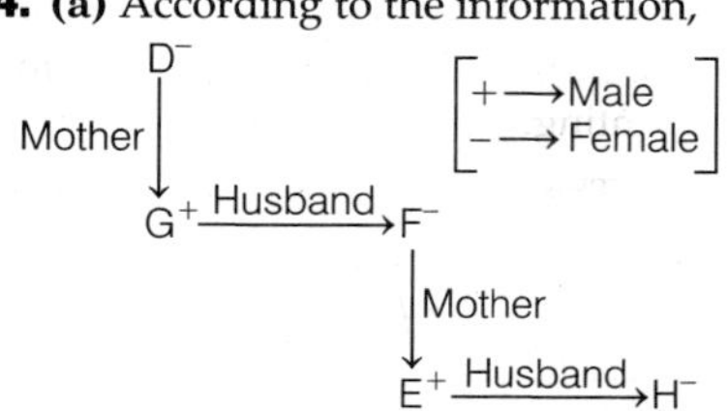

∴ G is the husband's father of H.

5. (d) As,

T O W E R
↓ Opposite letters
G L D V I
+2 +2 +3 +3 +3
I N G Y L

and

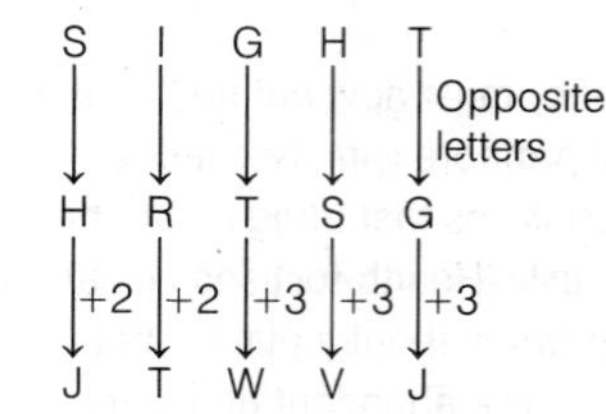

Similarly,

B R I N G
↓ Opposite letters
Y I R M T
+2 +2 +3 +3 +3
A K U P W

6. (a) Given expressions,
$40 + [\{(24 - 12) \times (2 \div 2)\} + (18 \times 10)] = ?$
On interchanging the signs,
$40 \div [\{(24 + 12) - (2 \times 2)\} \div (18 - 10)]$
$\Rightarrow 40 \div [\{36 - 4\} \div (8)]$
$\Rightarrow 40 \div [32 \div 8]$
$\Rightarrow 40 \div 4 = \boxed{10}$

7. (d) According to the statements,

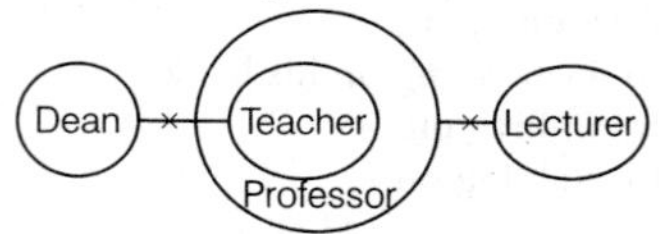

Conclusions
I. (✗) II. (✗)
∴ Neither Conclusion I nor II follows.

8. (d) Given equation,
42 * 7 * 3 * 2 * 13 * 7
From option (d),
After putting the signs we get:
$\Rightarrow 42 \div 7 \times 3 + 2 = 13 + 7$
$\Rightarrow 6 \times 3 + 2 = 20$
$\Rightarrow 18 + 2 = 20$
$\Rightarrow 20 = 20$

9. (d) According to the question,

Here (we) (go) ⟶ (asa) te (du)

(we) can (go) ⟶ (du) mu (asa)

∴ The code for 'Here' is te.

10. (a) As, $K \xrightarrow{+4} O \xrightarrow{-3} L \xrightarrow{+2} N$

$M \xrightarrow{+4} Q \xrightarrow{-3} N \xrightarrow{+2} P$

$X \xrightarrow{+4} B \xrightarrow{-3} Y \xrightarrow{+2} A$

But, $\boxed{Q \xrightarrow{-7} J \xrightarrow{+6} P \xrightarrow{-5} K}$

11. (c) Arranging the words as per dictionary,

Globe (3) ⟶ Gloomy (6) ⟶ Glory (1) ⟶ Gloss (4) ⟶ Glossary (2) ⟶ Glow (5)

⇒ 3, 6, 1, 4, 2, 5

12. (c) Given equation,

$15 \div 405 - 3 + 25 \times 5 = ?$

On interchanging the signs, we get

+ ⇒ −	− ⇒ ÷
÷ ⇒ ×	× ⇒ +

$\Rightarrow 15 \times 405 \div 3 - 25 + 5$

$\Rightarrow 15 \times 135 - 25 + 5$

$\Rightarrow 2025 - 25 + 5$

$\Rightarrow \boxed{2005}$

So, 2005 is the correct answer.

13. (d) The option figure (d) is embedded in the question figure,

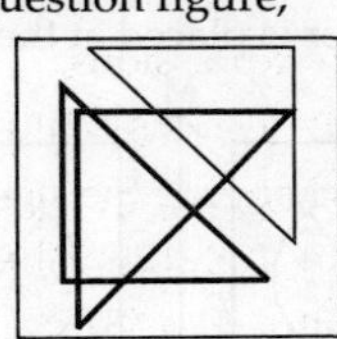

14. (d) From the statements,

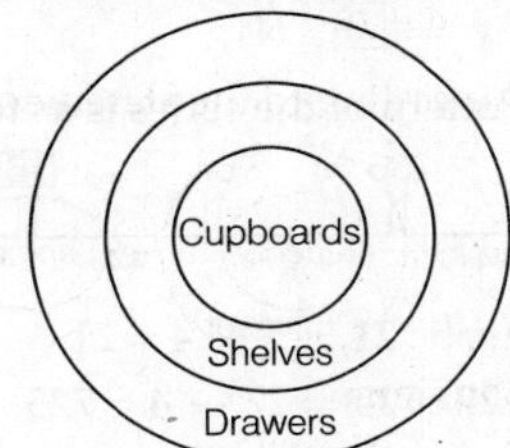

Conclusions

I. (✓) II. (✗)

∴ Only Conclusion I follow.

15. (c) The pattern is as follows,

$W \xrightarrow{-2} U \xrightarrow{-2} \boxed{S} \xrightarrow{-2} Q \xrightarrow{-2} O$

$W \xrightarrow{-4} S \xrightarrow{-4} \boxed{O} \xrightarrow{-4} K \xrightarrow{-4} G$

$V \xrightarrow{-2} T \xrightarrow{-2} \boxed{R} \xrightarrow{-2} P \xrightarrow{-2} N$

$U \xrightarrow{-4} Q \xrightarrow{-4} \boxed{M} \xrightarrow{-4} I \xrightarrow{-4} E$

16. (d) According to the questions,

C A R (D) ⇒ (3) 5 9 7

(D) O G S ⇒ 8 (3) 4 6

∴ The code for 'D' is '3'.

17. (c) In the given figure series, the symbols X and Δ interchange their position and O and T interchange their position in each step and the centre of the box symbol or letter is replaced with a new symbol or letter. Therefore, the figure in option (c) is the required missing figure.

18. (d) The question figure is embedded in the option figure (d).

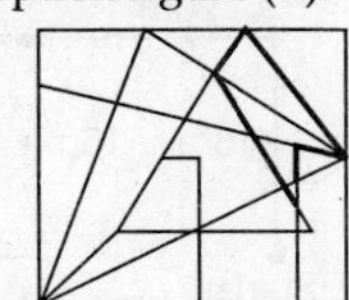

19. (d) As BED is coded as 9,

Number of letters is BED = 3

$3^2 = 9$

And, TABLE is coded as 25,

Number of letters in TABLE = 5

$5^2 = 25$

Similarly, RECLINER is coded as,

Number of letters in RECLINER = 8

$8^2 = \boxed{64}$

20. (b) From the statements, the arrangement is as follows,

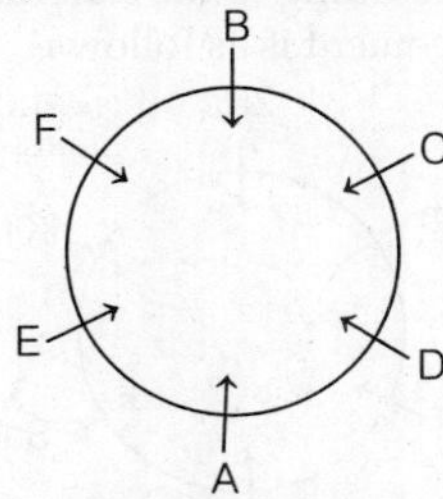

So, D sits immediately left of C.

21. (a) In the given figure series, the symbols at the middle of the box rotated by 90 degrees in a clockwise direction and then flipped horizontally and the number of lines at the middle of the symbol is increased by one in each step.

Therefore, the figure in option (a) is the required missing figure.

22. (a) From the statements,

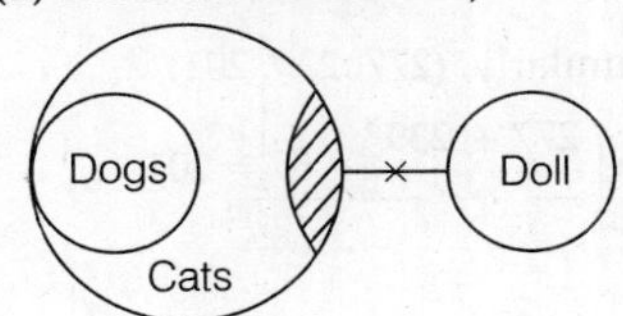

Conclusions

I. (✗) II. (✓)

∴ Only conclusion II follows.

23. (d) Given equation,

80 C 16 B 4 A 96 D 4 = ?

After putting the signs, we get:

$\Rightarrow 80 - 16 \times 4 + 96 \div 4$

$\Rightarrow 80 - 64 + 24$

$\Rightarrow 104 - 64$

$\Rightarrow \boxed{40}$

24. (b) Option figure (b) is the correct mirror image of the given figure, when the mirror is placed at the 'MN' line.

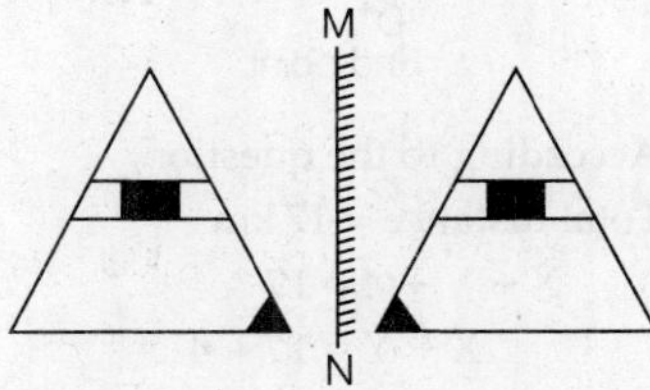

25. (a) Given equation,

$108 \times 343 + 7 - 2 \div 13 = ?$

After interchanging the signs we get,

$\Rightarrow 108 - 343 \div 7 \times 2 + 13$

$\Rightarrow 108 - 49 \times 2 + 13$

$\Rightarrow 108 - 98 + 13$

$\Rightarrow 121 - 98 = \boxed{23}$

26. (c) As, $S \xrightarrow{+2} U \xrightarrow{-5} P \xrightarrow{+4} T$

$J \xrightarrow{+2} L \xrightarrow{-5} G \xrightarrow{+4} K$

$P \xrightarrow{+2} R \xrightarrow{-5} M \xrightarrow{+4} Q$

But, $\boxed{E \xrightarrow{+3} H \xrightarrow{-6} B \xrightarrow{+5} G}$

27. (a) According to the questions,

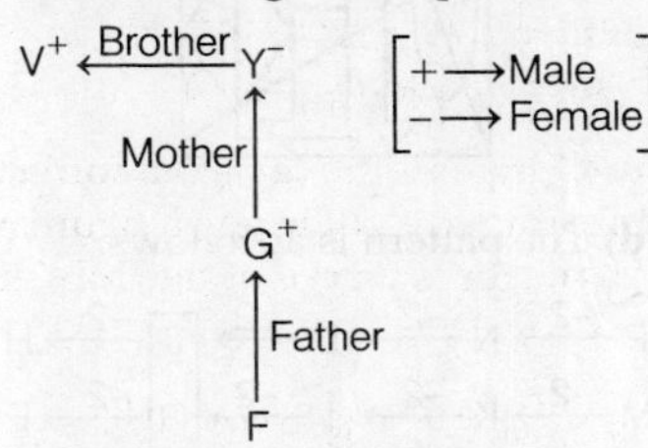

∴ Y is the father's mother of F.

28. (d) As cat uses their paw for hunting. Similarly, crow used their claws for hunting.

29. (d) The pattern of the series is as follows,

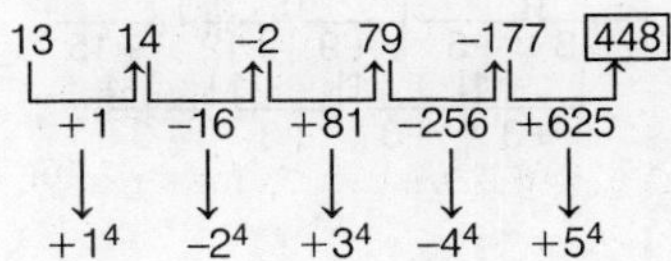

30. **(b)** According to the question,

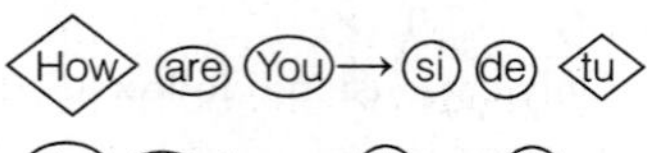

Therefore, 'How' is coded as 'tu'.

31. **(d)** According to the question,

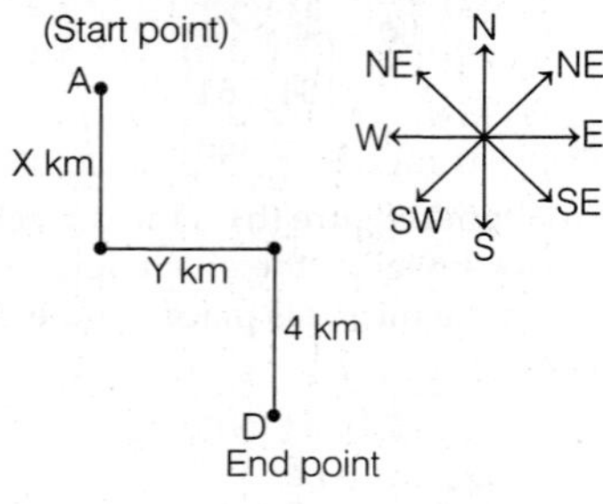

According to the question,
Total distance = 17 km

$$X + Y + 4 = 17$$
$$X + Y = 17 - 4$$
$$X + Y = 13$$

As given X > Y and X a perfect square, so possible value are X = 9, Y = 4

32. **(b)** Given equation,

$42 \times 7 - 11 \div 57 + 10 = ?$

After interchanging the symbols, we get,

$\Rightarrow 42 \div 7 \times 11 + 57 - 10$

$\Rightarrow \quad 6 \times 11 + 57 - 10$

$\Rightarrow \quad 66 + 57 - 10 = \boxed{113}$

33. **(b)** The option figure (b) is embedded in the question figure.

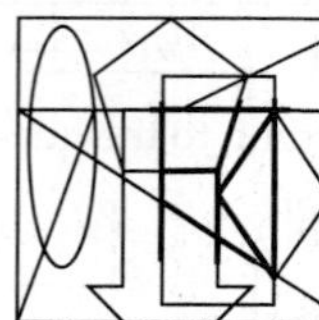

34. **(d)** The pattern is as follows,

P $\xrightarrow{-2}$ N $\xrightarrow{-2}$ L $\xrightarrow{-2}$ J $\xrightarrow{-2}$ H

M $\xrightarrow{-2}$ K $\xrightarrow{-2}$ I $\xrightarrow{-2}$ G $\xrightarrow{-2}$ E

R $\xrightarrow{+2}$ T $\xrightarrow{+2}$ V $\xrightarrow{+2}$ X $\xrightarrow{+2}$ Z

O $\xrightarrow{+2}$ Q $\xrightarrow{+2}$ S $\xrightarrow{+2}$ U $\xrightarrow{+2}$ W

35. **(b)** The pattern of the series is as follows,

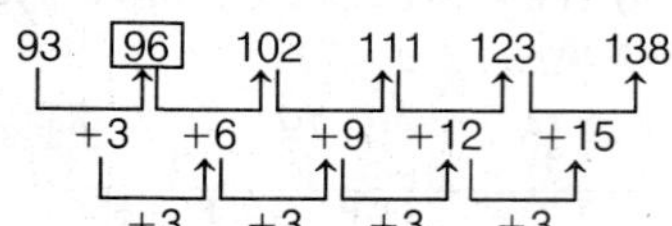

36. **(a)** In the given question figure, the number of white circles is decreased by one from the right side in each step and the number of black circles is increased by one on the left side.

Therefore, the figure in option **(a)** is the correct answer.

37. **(a)** The order of the word in the dictionary is as follows,

Jabber (2) → Jackal (5) → Jackdaw (4) → Jackpot (3) → Jalopy (1)

⇒ 2, 5, 4, 3, 1

38. **(a)** The movement of boy according to the statements is as follows,

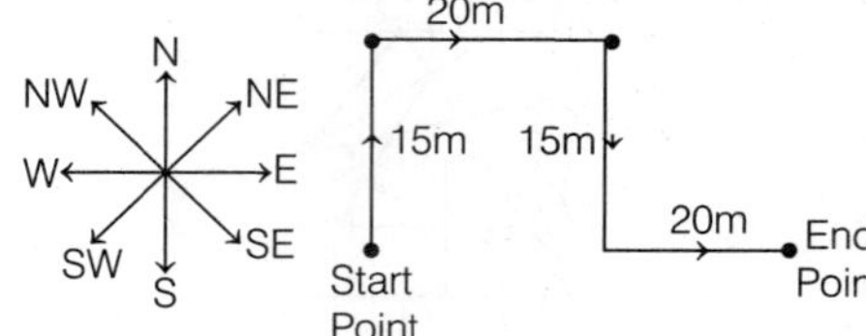

Therefore, the distance from the starting position to the end point is

= 20 + 20 = 40m

39. **(a)** The pattern of the series is as follows,

38 64 98 140 $\boxed{190}$

+26 +34 +42 +50

+8 +8 +8

40. **(b)** According to the statement the arrangement is as follows,

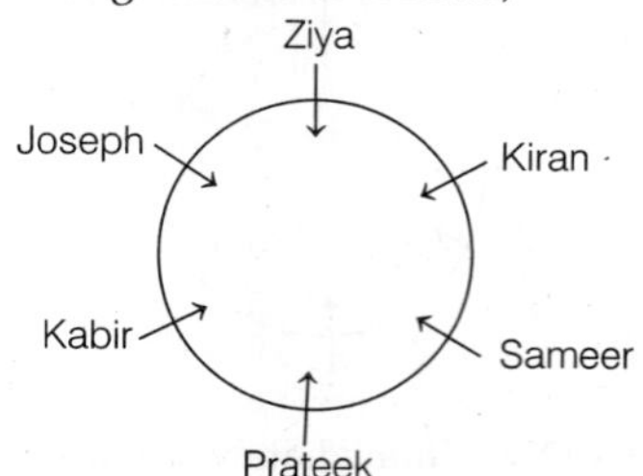

Therefore, Ziya is sitting immediate left of Joseph.

41. **(d)** As, (125, 87, 49)

$$\Rightarrow \left(\frac{125 + 87}{2}\right) - 57 = 49$$

And, (236, 198, 160)

$$\Rightarrow \left(\frac{236 + 198}{2}\right) - 57 = 160$$

Similarly, (277, 239, 201)

$$\Rightarrow \left(\frac{277 + 239}{2}\right) - 57 = 201$$

42. **(d)** Given equation,

$(63 \times 21) + 8 + 99 \times 11 \div 16 + (12 \times 4) = 158$

From option **(d)**, after interchanging symbols ÷ and ×, we get:

$\Rightarrow (63 \div 21) + 8 + 99 \div 11 \times 16 + (12 \div 4) = 158$

$\Rightarrow 3 + 8 + 9 \times 16 + 3 = 158$

$\Rightarrow \quad 3 + 8 + 144 + 3 = 158$

$\Rightarrow \quad 158 = 158$

43. **(d)** The question figure is embedded in the option figure **(d)**,

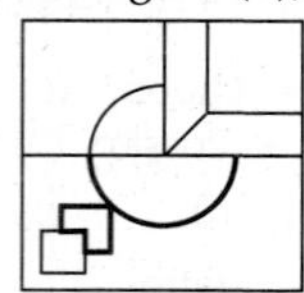

44. **(d)** From the statements,

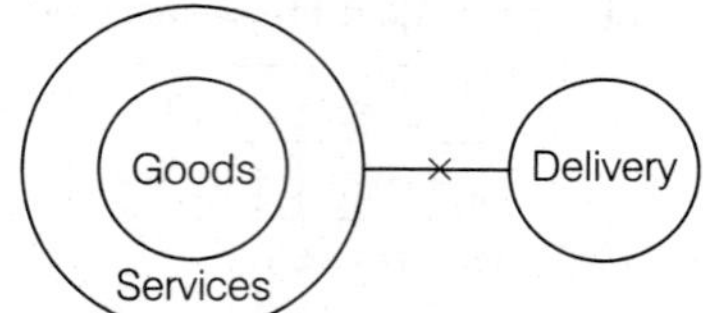

Conclusions

I. (✓) II. (✗)

∴ Only Conclusion I follows.

45. **(c)** Option figure **(c)** is the correct mirror image of the given figure, when the mirror is placed at the 'MN' line.

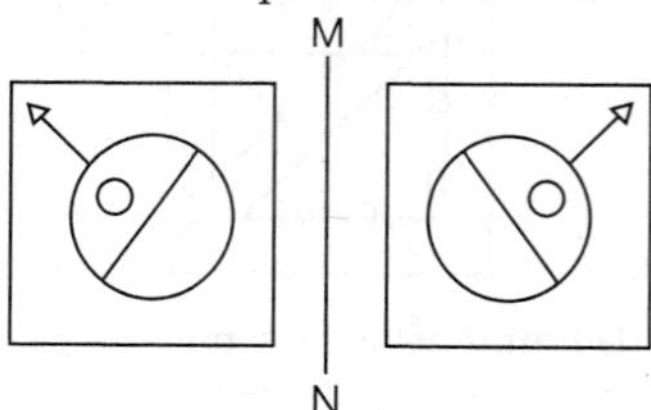

46. **(d)** Pattern of the series is as follows,

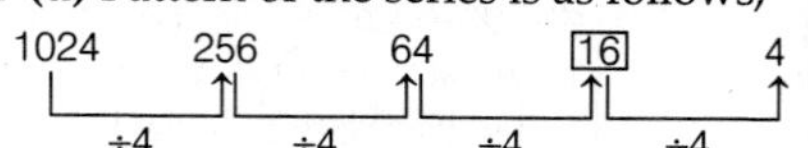

47. **(c)** As, $5 : 21 \Rightarrow 5^2 - 4 = 21$

and $27 : 725 \Rightarrow 27^2 - 4 = 725$

Similarly, $? : 252 \Rightarrow ?^2 - 4 = 252$

$\Rightarrow ?^2 = 252 + 4 = 256$

$? = \sqrt{256} = \boxed{16}$

48. **(b)** The question figure is embedded in option figure (b).

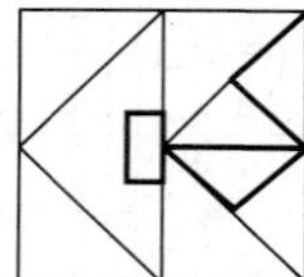

49. **(a)** As, $(5, 4, 405) \Rightarrow (5+4)^2 \times 5 = 405$
and, $(7, 3, 500) \Rightarrow (7+3)^2 \times 5 = 500$
Similarly,
$(4, 1, 125) \Rightarrow (4+1)^2 \times 5 = 125$

50. **(a)** As,

C	R	E	A	T	I	O	N
+2	+2	+2	+2	+2	+2	+2	+2
E	T	G	C	V	K	Q	P

and

U	N	I	V	E	R	S	E
+2	+2	+2	+2	+2	+2	+2	+2
W	P	K	X	G	T	U	G

Similarly,

P	L	A	N	E	T
+2	+2	+2	+2	+2	+2
R	N	C	P	G	V

51. **(b)** The **Mettur Dam** is located in the state of Tamil Nadu, South India.

- It is built across the Kaveri River and was completed in 1934.
- The dam supports irrigation hydroelectric power generation and drinking water supply.
- The reservoir formed by the dam is known as the Stanley Reservoir.
- Other major dams in South India: Krishna Raja Sagara (Karnataka), Nagarjuna Sagar (Telangana/Andhra), Tungabhadra Dam (Karnataka), Srisailam Dam (Andhra Pradesh).

Knowledge Booster
- Mettur Dam plays a key role in the Kaveri water-sharing dispute between Tamil Nadu and Karnataka.

52. **(a)** The novel 'Before We Visit the Goddess' is written by **Chitra Banerjee Divakaruni.**

- She is an Indian-American author, known for portraying strong female characters.
- The novel explores mother-daughter relationships across generations.
- It blends immigrant experiences with Indian cultural elements.

53. **(a)** The **pocket veto** is when the President of India keeps a bill pending without acting on it indefinitely.

- This is not defined in the Constitution but is used in practice.
- It applies to non-money and non-constitutional amendment bills.
- It was first used by President Zail Singh in 1986.
- India's President enjoys three types of vetoes: absolute, suspensive and pocket veto.

54. **(b)** As per the 2011 Census, **Dadra and Nagar** Haveli had the lowest literacy rate among Union Territories.

- Its overall literacy rate was around 76.2%, lower than Lakshadweep and Delhi.
- The region had a large tribal population with lower educational outreach.
- Significant efforts have been made post-2011 to improve literacy there.

Knowledge Booster
- In 2020, Dadra and Nagar Haveli were merged with Daman and Diu to form a single union territory.
- The highest literacy rate among UTs was in Lakshadweep (91.85%).

55. **(c)** Huka Falls is a famous waterfall located in **New Zealand.**

- It is situated on the Waikato River, near the town of Taupo in the North Island.
- The waterfall is known for its intense water flow and stunning blue colour.
- The Waikato River is the longest river in New Zealand.

56. **(a)** A Money Bill is defined under Article 110 of the Constitution.

- Before being sent to the President under Article 111, it must be certified by the **Speaker of the Lok Sabha.**
- The Speaker's decision is final on whether a bill is a Money Bill.
- Money Bills can only be introduced in the Lok Sabha.

Knowledge Booster
- The Rajya Sabha cannot amend a Money Bill - it can only make recommendations.
- The President cannot return a Money Bill for reconsideration.

57. **(a)** The fifth Khelo India Youth Games (KIYG) 2022 were hosted by Madhya Pradesh.

- The mascot of KIYG 2022 was Asha the Cheetah, symbolising speed and energy.
- The games were held from 30th January to 11th February, 2023.
- Events took place across eight cities, including Bhopal, Indore, Gwalior and Jabalpur.
- Over 5,000 athletes participated in more than 25 sports disciplines.

58. **(b)** **Purandardas** is regarded as the 'Father of Carnatic Music'.

- He systematised the teaching methods in Carnatic music using graded lessons.
- He introduced swaravalis (scale exercises) and alankaras (pattern exercises).
- Lived during the 16th century and composed thousands of devotional songs.
- He composed in Kannada and used the pen name 'Purandara Vittala' in his songs.

59. **(d)** Terrestrial planets are composed primarily of **rocks and metals.**

- These include Mercury, Venus, Earth and Mars.
- They have solid surfaces and are located closer to the Sun.
- These planets have higher density compared to gas giants.

Knowledge Booster
- Earth is the largest of the terrestrial planets.
- The word 'terrestrial' is derived from the Latin word 'Terra', meaning Earth.

60. **(c)** Capital expenses are used to create long-term assets like buildings and infrastructure.

- **Construction of school buildings** is a capital expenditure as it adds value over time.
- These expenses appear in the capital budget of the government.
- Unlike revenue expenses, they are non-recurring and not for daily operations.

61. **(c)** **Goddess Parvati** is associated with the Gangaur Festival, mainly celebrated in Rajasthan, Madhya Pradesh and Gujarat.

- The word 'Gangaur' is a combination of Gana (Shiva) and Gauri (Parvati).
- The festival symbolises marital love and devotion, especially among newly married women.
- Women pray for the prosperity and long life of their husbands.
- It involves processions, songs and traditional attire.

62. **(c)** The South-West monsoon first hits the Indian mainland at **Kerala**, usually around 1st June.

- It arrives through the Arabian Sea branch and spreads across the country.
- Kerala receives heavy rainfall due to its coastal location and Western Ghats.
- It marks the beginning of the monsoon season in India.
- The progress of the monsoon is monitored by the Indian Meteorological Department (IMD).

63. **(b)** The 44th Constitutional Amendment Act (1978) removed the Right to Property(earlier a part of Article 31) from the list of Fundamental Rights.

- It was moved to Article 300A as a legal right instead.
- The amendment was passed during Morarji Desai's government.
- The objective was to prevent misuse of the property right against land reforms.

64. **(a)** Small Industries Development Bank of India (SIDBI) was set up in the year **1990**.

- It functions as the principal financial institution for Micro, Small and Medium Enterprises (MSMEs).
- SIDBI promotes financing, development and support to small businesses.
- It works under the Ministry of Finance.

Knowledge Booster

- SIDBI also regulates Non-Banking Financial Companies (NBFCs) dealing with MSMEs.
- It plays a major role in employment generation and entrepreneurship development.

65. **(b)** **Philipp Lenard**, a Nobel Laureate in Physics (1905), conducted an experiment with low-pressure gas in a glass tube.

- He observed that radiation (cathode rays) was emitted when voltage was applied between metal plates.
- His work contributed to the discovery of the electron.
- This experiment helped establish the foundation of atomic and quantum physics.

66. **(c)** Article 77 of the Indian Constitution states that all executive actions of the Government of India shall be taken in the name of the President.

- It also deals with the authentication of orders and instruments made in the President's name.
- It ensures legal and formal validity of executive decisions.
- This article is a part of the Union Executive provisions.

67. **(a)** The **mesoderm** is the third germinal layer found in triploblastic animals.

- It lies between the ectoderm and endoderm.
- It gives rise to muscles, bones, blood, kidneys and reproductive organs.
- Triploblastic animals have three primary cell layers during embryonic development.
- Animals like flatworms and above (e.g., humans, frogs) are triploblastic.

Knowledge Booster

- Diploblastic animals (like jellyfish) have only ectoderm and endoderm

68. **(a)** 1 bar is the metric unit of pressure equal to approximately 0.986923 atm.

- It is commonly used in meteorology and engineering to measure pressure.
- 1 bar = 100,000 Pascals (Pa).
- It is slightly less than standard atmospheric pressure.

Knowledge Booster

- Standard atmospheric pressure is 1 atm = 101325 Pa.
- Bar is not an SI unit, but is still widely used for practical and industrial purposes.

69. **(d)** Talvin Singh is a world-renowned musician associated with the **tabla**.

- He is known for blending Indian classical music with electronic and fusion genres.
- Talvin is one of the pioneers of the Asian Underground music movement.
- He won the Mercury Music Prize in 1999 for his album 'OK'.

70. **(b)** In 1991-92, India's industrial production recorded a **positive growth of 0.6%.**

- This was during a time of economic crisis and liberalisation reforms.
- The New Economic Policy (1991) introduced Liberalisation, Privatisation and Globalisation (LPG).
- Industrial growth was low due to balance of payments issues and fiscal deficit.
- Dr. Manmohan Singh, then Finance Minister, was the key architect of these reforms.

71. **(a)** Padma Subrahmanyam is an iconic Indian classical dancer of Bharatanatyam.

- She reintroduced Karanas (dance movements) from the Natya Shastra into Bharatanatyam.
- Also a scholar, she has contributed to the revival of traditional dance texts.
- She founded the Nrithyodaya school of dance in Chennai.
- Padma Subrahmanyam received Padma Shri (1981) and Padma Bhushan (2003) for her contribution to Indian art.

Knowledge Booster

- Correct Matches
  1. Padma Subrahmanyam - Bharatanatyam
  2. Mallika Sarabhai - Bharatanatyam and Kuchipudi
  3. Jhelum Paranjape - Odissi
  4. K . Uma Rama Rao - Kuchipudi

72. **(d)** In a **progressive** tax system, the marginal tax rate increases as income increases.

- The tax burden rises more than proportionately with income.
- Higher earners pay a larger percentage of their income in taxes.
- This system aims to reduce income inequality.
- Income Tax in India is a progressive tax.

73. **(b)** **Lord Cornwallis** introduced major bureaucratic, judicial and police reforms in British India.

- He is known for implementing the Cornwallis Code (1793).
- Lord Cornwallis is often called the 'Father of Civil Services in India'.
- He also introduced the Permanent Settlement in Bengal.

74. **(d)** Thorium is a member of the actinoid (actinide) series in the periodic table.

- The actinoids are a series of elements from atomic number 89 to 103, including examples like Uranium, Thorium and Plutonium.
- It is a radioactive metal, atomic number 90.
- Found naturally in monazite sands, especially in India's coastal regions.
- Used in nuclear reactors as an alternative to uranium.

Knowledge Booster

- India has one of the largest reserves of thorium in the world.
- The Indian nuclear programme includes a three-stage plan where thorium plays a key role in Stage III.

75. **(a) Shashi Tharoor** is the author of the satirical novel 'The Great Indian Novel'.

- The novel uses the Mahabharata as an allegorical framework to retell Indian political history.
- It cleverly blends mythology with modern political events, especially around the Indian Independence Movement.
- Published in 1989, it is one of Tharoor's most acclaimed works.
- He has also authored other works like 'Why I Am a Hindu' and 'Inglorious Empire'.

76. **(b)** Alarmel Valli is a renowned Bharatanatyam dancer and choreographer.

- She is a foremost exponent of the **Pandanallur style** of Bharatanatyam.
- Known for her graceful expressions and subtle abhinaya, she has performed worldwide.
- She received numerous awards including Padma Shri and Padma Bhushan.

Knowledge Booster

- The Pandanallur style is characterised by linear movements, strong footwork and precision.
- Alarmel Valli was trained under Guru Pandanallur Chokkalingam Pillai and his son Subbaraya Pillai.

77. **(b) Leaching** is the process where nutrients or contaminants are washed away from the topsoil to lower layers by water.

- It reduces the fertility of soil, especially in regions with heavy rainfall.
- Leaching is a key concern in agriculture and soil conservation.
- It can also cause groundwater contamination.

78. **(a)** In July 2018, the International Space Station (ISS) created a Bose-Einstein Condensate using **rubidium** atoms.

- The atoms were cooled to just above absolute zero (one ten-millionth of a kelvin).
- It helped scientists study quantum phenomena in microgravity.
- Rubidium is ideal for such experiments due to its low melting point and stable isotopes.

79. **(b)** The Sanskrit drama 'Malavikagnimitram' was written by **Kalidasa**.

- It is a romantic play that tells the story of King Agnimitra and his love for Malavika.
- This play belongs to the 5th century CE.
- Kalidasa is considered one of the greatest classical poets of India.
- Other famous works by Kalidasa include 'Shakuntala' and 'Meghaduta'.

80. **(a) Sahanand Mahadev Shetty** was the first recipient of the Arjuna Award in Kabaddi.

- The award honours outstanding performance in sports.
- He received it in the early years of the Arjuna Awards, which started in 1961.
- His contribution helped in the popularisation of Kabaddi.

Knowledge Booster

- The Arjuna Award is India's second-highest sports honour after the Major Dhyan Chand Khel Ratna.
- Kabaddi became an Asian Games sport in 1990, further boosting its prominence.

81. **(a)** Each player in chess has 8 pawns, totaling **16** pawns on the board.

- Pawns are placed in the second rank (row) from each player's side.
- A pawn is sometimes called the 'soul of chess' due to its strategic role.
- They move one step forward and capture diagonally.
- Pawns can be promoted upon reaching the opponent's last rank.

82. **(b) Babur**, the founder of the Mughal Empire in India, popularised the use of gunpowder in warfare.

- He used cannons and matchlocks effectively in the First Battle of Panipat (1526).
- This technological advantage helped defeat Ibrahim Lodi, despite being outnumbered.
- Babur's tactics introduced modern warfare in North India.

83. **(d)** The **86th Constitutional Amendment Act, 2002** added the 11th Fundamental Duty to the Indian Constitution.

- It made it a duty for parents or guardians to provide opportunities for education to children between 6-14 years.
- This amendment also inserted Article 21A as a Fundamental Right.
- It aimed to promote universal elementary education.

84. **(d)** The **Prevention of Insults to National Honour Act, 1971** prohibits disrespect to the National Flag, Anthem and Constitution.

- Disrespect includes burning, mutilating, defacing or publicly insulting them.
- Violations can lead to imprisonment and fines.
- It ensures the dignity and respect of national symbols.

85. **(a)** In alchemy, aqua fortis refers to **Nitric Acid** (HNO_3).

- It is a strong acid used in making explosives, fertilisers and nitration reactions.
- It reacts violently with many substances and is highly corrosive.
- The term 'aqua fortis' means 'strong water' in Latin.

Knowledge Booster

- Nitric acid was historically used with hydrochloric acid to form aqua regia, which dissolves gold.
- It plays a key role in the manufacture of TNT (trinitrotoluene) and other explosives.

86. **(c)** The standard height of a badminton net at the center is **5 feet 1 inch** (1.55 metres).

- At the posts, it is slightly higher at 5 feet 1 inch and 5 feet at the center.
- This height is maintained in both singles and doubles games.
- Ensures fair play and standardisation across matches.

Knowledge Booster
- The official governing body of badminton is the Badminton World Federation (BWF), which formed in 1934

87. **(c)** The **Moth ki Masjid in Delhi** was built during the Lodi Dynasty of the Delhi Sultanate.

- It was constructed by Wazir Miya Bhoiya, a minister under Sikandar Lodi.
- The mosque is known for its Lodi-style architecture and symmetry.
- Located in South Delhi, it is a protected monument today.
- The Lodi Dynasty ruled from 1451 to 1526, the last dynasty of the Delhi Sultanate.

88. **(a)** Sattriya was recognised as a Classical Dance by the Sangeet Natak Akademi in the year **2000.**

- Originating from Assam, Sattriya was introduced by Srimanta Sankardev, a Vaishnavite saint.
- It was traditionally performed by male monks (Bhakats) in Satras (monasteries).
- Today, both men and women perform it on stage.

Knowledge Booster
- Sattriya is one of the eight recognised classical dances of India.
- It combines elements of bhakti, drama, music and story-telling.

89. **(b)** Aspirin works by inhibiting the synthesis of prostaglandins, which are responsible for pain, inflammation and fever.

- It blocks the enzyme cyclooxygenase (COX) involved in the production of prostaglandins.
- This is why aspirin is used as an analgesic (pain reliever), antipyretic (fever reducer) and anti-inflammatory drug.
- It is one of the most commonly used Non-Steroidal Anti-Inflammatory Drugs (NSAIDs).

90. **(a) Charles Elton** was the first ecologist to describe the Pyramid of Numbers in the 1920s.

- He introduced the concept to explain the trophic levels and energy flow in an ecosystem.
- The pyramid shows how the number of organisms decreases as one moves up the food chain.
- It laid the foundation for modern ecological studies.

Knowledge Booster
- Charles Elton also contributed to invasion ecology and niche theory.
- He authored the book 'Animal Ecology' (1927), which shaped ecological science.

91. **(d)** The Siddheshvara Mahadeva Temple in Bengal reflects the architectural style of the **Pala dynasty**.

- The Pala dynasty ruled Bengal and Bihar from the 8th to the 12th century CE.
- Their temple architecture includes curvilinear shikharas, carved stone panels and Buddhist influences.
- The Palas were also great patrons of Buddhism and art.

92. **(c)** In 2010, UNESCO recognised 'Mudiyettu' of **Kerala** as an Intangible Cultural Heritage of Humanity.

- It is a ritual dance drama based on the mythological battle between Goddess Kali and Darika, a demon.
- Performed in Bhagavathy temples, it combines music, dance, painting and drama.
- Mudiyettu is part of Kerala's temple festival traditions.
- Other UNESCO-tagged intangible heritages from India include Koodiyattam, Chhau dance and Yoga.

93. **(d)** Statement (d) is incorrect. Western cyclonic disturbances are not related to monsoon withdrawal.

- South-West monsoon winds blow over warm oceans, pick up moisture and cause rainfall over India.
- The intensity and position of the high-pressure area East of Madagascar (Mascarene High) influences the Indian Monsoon.
- The pressure difference between Tahiti (Pacific Ocean) and Darwin (Indian Ocean) is used in the Southern Oscillation Index (SOI) to predict monsoon strength.
- They are winter systems originating from the Mediterranean region, affecting North-West India with rain and snow, not monsoon rains.

94. **(b)** The natural vegetation of India is broadly classified into 5 major groups.

- These include Tropical Evergreen Forests, Tropical Deciduous Forests, Thorny Shrubs, Montane Forests and Mangrove Forests.
- Classification is based on climate, rainfall and altitude.
- Each group supports unique flora and fauna.

Knowledge Booster
- Tropical Deciduous forests are the most widespread in India.
- Mangroves are found in coastal areas, especially in Sundarbans, West Bengal.

95. **(d)** As per Census 2011, Sikh population accounts for approximately **1.7%** of India's total population.

- Punjab has the highest concentration of Sikhs, with over 75% of its population following Sikhism.
- Sikhs are the fourth-largest religious group in India.
- Sikhism was founded in the 15th century by Guru Nanak Dev Ji.
- The largest religious group in India is Hindus (around 79.8%), followed by Muslims (14.2%).

96. **(a)** Aqua regia is not a food preservative; it is a highly corrosive mixture of nitric acid and hydrochloric acid.

- It is used in laboratories to dissolve noble metals like gold and platinum.
- Vinegar (acetic acid), sodium chloride (table salt) and sodium nitrite are used as common food preservatives.
- These substances prevent bacterial growth and spoilage.

97. (b) Losar is a traditional New Year festival celebrated in **Arunachal Pradesh.**

- It is observed by the Monpa tribe, marking the beginning of the Tibetan lunar calendar.
- The festival involves Buddhist rituals, folk dances and cultural performances.
- It usually takes place between January and February.

Knowledge Booster
- Losar is also celebrated in other Himalayan regions like Ladakh and Sikkim.
- It reflects the Tibetan Buddhist cultural influence in Arunachal Pradesh.

98. (c) Sucheta Kripalani founded the women's wing of the Indian National Congress in 1940.

- She was an active participant in the Quit India Movement and a close aide of Mahatma Gandhi.
- Later, she became the first woman Chief Minister in India, leading Uttar Pradesh (1963-67).
- She worked tirelessly for women's empowerment and social welfare.

99. (d) The **Pradhan Mantri Formalisation of Micro Food Processing Enterprises (PMFME)** scheme supports the One District One Product (ODOP) approach.

- It was launched in 2020 under the Atmanirbhar Bharat Abhiyan.
- PMFME is implemented by the Ministry of Food Processing Industries (MoFPI).
- The scheme also emphasises cluster-based development and skill training for food processors.
- ODOP promotes specialisation of a single product per district for better market access.

100. (d) The **Charter Act of 1833** provided for the establishment of the Law Commission in India.

- Its purpose was the consolidation and codification of Indian laws under British rule.
- The Charter Act of 1833 also made the Governor-General of Bengal into the Governor-General of India.
- The first Law Commission was headed by Lord Macaulay.
- This Act marked a major shift towards centralised legislation in British India.

Knowledge Booster
- It was responsible for drafting the Indian Penal Code (IPC), later enacted in 1860.

101. (d) $7\frac{5}{8} + \frac{5}{8}$ of $184 \times 15 \div 5 - (?) = 0$

$\Rightarrow \frac{61}{8} + \frac{5}{8} \times 184 \times \frac{15}{5} - (?) = 0$

$\Rightarrow \frac{61}{8} + 345 = x \Rightarrow x = \frac{2821}{8}$

$\Rightarrow x = 352\frac{5}{8}$

102. (c) From the given table, we get the result that R earned more than by any firm in 2015, R = ₹68 crore

103. (d) Let the cost price of an article be x.

We have, marked price of an article = ₹ 7200

Profit = 20%, Discount = 15%

Applying formula,

$CP(100 + P\%) = MRP(100 - D\%)$

$\Rightarrow x(100 + 20) = 7200(100 - 15)$

$\Rightarrow x(120) = 7200 \times 85$

$\Rightarrow x = \frac{7200 \times 85}{120}$

$\Rightarrow x = ₹\ 5100$

Shopkeeper pay ₹ 5100 for an article.

104. (b) We have, $\tan A = \frac{2}{5}$

$\Rightarrow \frac{\sec^2 A}{\text{cosec}^2 A} = \frac{1}{\cos^2 A} \times \sin^2 A$

$\left\{\because \sec A = \frac{1}{\cos A}, \text{cosec}A = \frac{1}{\sin A}\right\}$

$= \left(\frac{\sin A}{\cos A}\right)^2 = (\tan A)^2 = \left(\frac{2}{5}\right)^2 = \frac{4}{25}$

105. (d) We have, P = ₹ 25000

Time = t = 3 yr, R = 12% per annum

$\Rightarrow A = CI + P$

$\Rightarrow CI = A - P = P\left[1 + \frac{r}{100}\right]^n - P$

$\Rightarrow CI = P\left[\left(1 + \frac{r}{100}\right)^n - 1\right]$

$\Rightarrow CI = 25000\left[\left(1 + \frac{12}{100}\right)^3 - 1\right]$

$\Rightarrow CI = 25000\left[\left(1 + \frac{3}{25}\right)^3 - 1\right]$

$\Rightarrow CI = 25000\left[\left(\frac{28}{25}\right)^3 - 1\right]$

$\Rightarrow CI = 25000\left[\frac{21952 - 15625}{15625}\right]$

$\Rightarrow CI = \frac{25000 \times 6327}{15625} = ₹\ 10123.20$

106. (d) We have, the number 1351.

According to conditions

A number is divisible by 2 if last digit is 0, 2, 4, 6, 8.

A number is divisible by 4 if last two digit is divisible by 4.

A number is divisible by 6 if the number is divisible by 2, 3.

A number is divisible by 8 if last 3 digit is divisible by 8.

Then, the least number which should be added to 1351 is 17.

107. (b) Given, ΔPQR and ΔABC

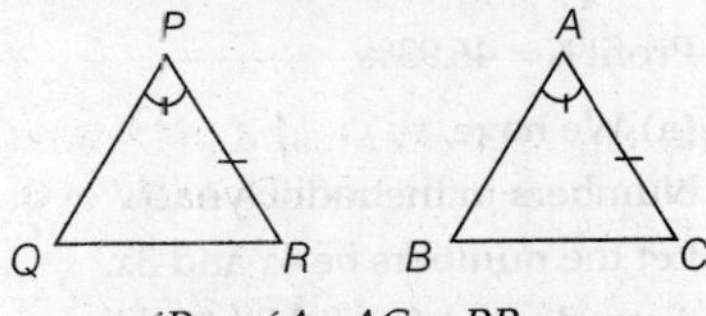

$\angle P = \angle A$, $AC = PR$

For ΔPQR and ΔABC to be congruent.

If $AB = PQ$, then they will be congruent by SAS rule.

If two sides and the included angle of a triangle is equal to the two sides and the included angle of another triangle, then the two triangles are said to congruent by SAS congruence criteria.

108. (b) We have, total income of family, ₹ 100000.

According to table, money spent on the education of children was 12%

then = Total income × 12%

$= \left(100000 \times \frac{12}{100}\right) = ₹\ 12000$

109. (d) We have, MRP of book = ₹ 850

and two successive discount

$d_1 = 20\%$, $d_1 = 10\%$

Then, price after 20% discount,

i.e. $\left(850 - 850 \times \frac{20}{100}\right)$

$= (850 - 170) = ₹\ 680$

Then, price after d_2 = 10% discount i.e.

$\left(680 - 680 \times \frac{10}{100}\right) = (680 - 68) = ₹\ 612$

A vendor ₹ 55 on transport, then cost price of book become

= ₹ (612 + 55) = ₹ 667

But book sold at ₹ 980, then profit on Book = 980 − 667 = ₹ 313

Profit% = $\frac{P}{CP} \times 100 = \frac{313}{667} \times 100$

Speedy Method

Vendor allow two successive discount 20% and 10% then, total discount

$= \left(20 + 10 - \frac{20 \times 10}{100}\right)\% = 28\%$

Price after discount

$= \left(850 - 850 \times \frac{28}{100}\right) = ₹\ 612$

Transportation cost = ₹ 55

CP of book become

$= (612 + 55) = ₹\ 667$

Profit = $(980 - 667) = ₹\ 313$

Profit% $= \left(\frac{P}{CP} \times 100\right)\%$

$= \left(\frac{313}{667} \times 100\right)\%$

Profit% = 46.93%

110. (a) We have,

Numbers in the ratio is 4 : 3.

Let the numbers be $4x$ and $3x$.

According to formula,

$\Rightarrow$ HCF $(a, b) \times$ LCM (a, b) = Product of two number $(a \times b)$

$\Rightarrow \quad 4x \times 3x = 2700$

$\Rightarrow \quad 12x^2 = 2700$

$\Rightarrow \quad x^2 = 225$

$\Rightarrow \quad x = \sqrt{225} = 15$

Their difference $= 4x - 3x = x = 15$

111. (b) Let the borrowed money be P.

Then, interest after first four year at the rate of 5% per annum i.e.,

$SI_1 = \frac{P \times 5 \times 4}{100} = \frac{P}{5}$

Interest after next six year at the rate of 8% per annum, i.e.

$SI_2 = \frac{P \times 8 \times 6}{100} = \frac{12P}{25}$

Interest after ten years at the rate of 12% per annum i.e.

$SI = \frac{P \times 2 \times 12}{100} = \frac{6P}{25}$

$SI = SI_1 + SI_2 + SI_3$

$= \frac{P}{5} + \frac{6P}{25} + \frac{12P}{25} = \frac{23P}{25}$

Total interest paid by Ramesh = ₹ 9016

$\Rightarrow \quad \frac{23P}{25} = ₹\ 9016$

$\Rightarrow \quad P = \frac{9016 \times 25}{23}$

$\Rightarrow \quad P = ₹\ 9800$

112. (b) We have, area of equilateral triangle is $4\sqrt{3}$ cm^2.

We know that, area of equilateral

$\Delta = \frac{\sqrt{3}a^2}{4} = \frac{\sqrt{3}a^2}{4} = 4\sqrt{3}$

$\Rightarrow \quad a^2 = 16 \Rightarrow a = 4$

113. (d) For college A,

average % of passing student for

collage $A = \frac{68 + 72 + 78 + 80}{4} = 74.5$

Average % of passing students for

college $B = \frac{78 + 86 + 91 + 87}{4} = 85.5$

Average % of passing student for

college $C = \frac{56 + 78 + 82 + 84}{4} = 75$

Average % of passing student for

college $D = \frac{78 + 82 + 85 + 87}{4} = 83$

Hence, College A have least average percentage of passing students.

114. (c) Number of people = 15

Increase in average weight = 3.2 kg.

Weight of replaced person = 52 kg.

Let the weight of new person be x.

According to question,

Total increase in weight of 15 people

$= 15 \times 3.2 = 48$ kg

Then, the weight of new person

$= (52 + 48) = 100$ kg

115. (b) Number of boy in section B = 30

Number of girls in section E = 55

According to question,

$= \left(\frac{30}{55} \times 100\right)\%$

$= 54.54\% = 55\%$ approx.

116. (a) We have,

$\Rightarrow \quad x\left(5 - \frac{2}{x}\right) = \frac{5}{x}$

$\Rightarrow \quad 5x - 2 = \frac{5}{x}$

$\Rightarrow \quad x - \frac{1}{x} = \frac{2}{5}$

Let $\quad x - \frac{1}{x} = a$

Then, $x^2 + \frac{1}{x^2} = a^2 + 2$

Then, $x^2 + \frac{1}{x^2} = \left(\frac{2}{5}\right)^2 + 2 = \frac{54}{25}$

117. (c) Length and Breadth of rectangular hall is 126 feet and 90 feet respectively.

Factors of $126 = 2 \times 3 \times 3 \times 7$

Factors of $90 = 2 \times 3 \times 3 \times 5$

HCF $(126, 90) = 2 \times 3 \times 3 = 18$

So, the area of the square

$= (\text{side})^2 = (18)^2$

= 324 square feet.

118. (d) From the given data, the consumption of wheat was there in successive increase over the given set of years.

119. (b) We have, LCM of two prime numbers x and y is 533.

Prime factorisation of $533 = 13 \times 41$

Since, $x > y$ (given) then $x = 41$, $y = 13$

The value of

$4y - x = 4 \times 13 - 41 = 52 - 41$

$4y - x = 11$

120. (b) We have, $A + B = 90°$

Then, $\frac{\cot A}{\cot B} + \cos^2 A + \cos^2 B$

$= \frac{\cot(90° - B)}{\cot B} + \cos^2(90° - B) + \cos^2 B$

$= \frac{\tan B}{\cot B} + \cos^2 B + \sin^2 B$

$= \tan^2 B + 1 = \sec^2 B$

$= \sec^2(90° - A) = \operatorname{cosec}^2 A$

121. (d) Let the time taken by Parul to complete the work be x days.

Work done by Parul in one day $= \frac{1}{x}$

Time taken by Ramesh $= 2 \times \frac{4x}{5} = \frac{8x}{5}$

Work done by Ramesh in one day

$= \frac{5}{8x}$

Together they complete work in 24 days.

According to question,

$\frac{1}{x} + \frac{5}{8x} = \frac{1}{24} \Rightarrow \frac{13}{8x} = \frac{1}{24}$

$\Rightarrow \quad x = 13 \times 3 = 39$ days

122. (a) C has minimum number of employee.

123. (d) We have, $\sin\theta + \cos\theta = \frac{\sqrt{11}}{3}$

Then, on squaring both side, we get

$\Rightarrow (\sin\theta + \cos\theta)^2 = \left(\frac{\sqrt{11}}{3}\right)^2$

$\Rightarrow \sin^2\theta + \cos^2\theta + 2\sin\theta\cos\theta = \frac{11}{9}$

$\{\because \sin^2\theta + \cos^2\theta = 1\}$

$\Rightarrow 1 + 2\sin\theta\cos\theta = \frac{11}{9}$

$\Rightarrow 2\sin\theta\cos\theta = \frac{11}{9} - 1 = \frac{2}{9}$

As we know that,

$\Rightarrow (\cos\theta - \sin\theta)^2 = \cos^2\theta + \sin^2\theta - 2\sin\theta\cos\theta$

$= 1 - 2\sin\theta\cos\theta = 1 - \frac{2}{9} = \frac{7}{9}$

$\Rightarrow (\cos\theta - \sin\theta) = \frac{\sqrt{7}}{3}$

124. (a) We have,

$\Rightarrow (48 \div 72 \times 3) - [15 \div 8 \times (40 - 32) - 10] + 2P = 6 \div 2$

$\Rightarrow \left(\frac{48}{72} \times 3\right) - \left[\frac{15}{8} \times (40 - 32) - 10\right] + 2P = \frac{6}{2}$

$\Rightarrow 2 - \left[\frac{15}{8} \times 8 - 10\right] + 2P = 3$

$\Rightarrow \quad 2 - 5 + 2P = 3$

$\Rightarrow \quad 2P = 6 \Rightarrow P = 3$

125. (b) Let the CP of watch be x.

Profit earn on watch = 7%

i.e. $\frac{7x}{100} = P$

Selling price of watch

$= x + \frac{7x}{100} = \frac{107x}{100}$ ...(i)

If watch is sold at ₹ 1329 more, he would have 57% profit, then

According to question

Profit = $\frac{57x}{100}$

Selling price of watch become

$= x + \frac{57x}{100} = \frac{157x}{100}$

Then, $\frac{157x}{100} - \frac{107x}{100} = 1329$

$\Rightarrow \frac{50x}{100} = 1329 \Rightarrow x = 2658$

Speedy Method

Using ratio and proportion method, Profit earn on watch when it sold is 7% means,

Profit% = $\frac{P}{CP} \times 100$

$= \frac{7}{100} \times 100$

Here, ratio of $\frac{CP}{SP} = \frac{100}{107}$ ...(i) $\begin{cases} P = SP - CP \\ SP = P + CP \end{cases}$

When he sold the watch at ₹ 1329 more he would gain 57%, then P = ratio of

$\frac{CP}{SP} = \frac{100}{157}$ ...(ii)

In both case 1 and 2, CP is same then, according to question, difference of SP have 50 units and the value for 100 units = 2 × 1329 = ₹ 2658

126. (a) We have,

$A + \cfrac{1}{1 + \cfrac{1}{2 + \cfrac{1}{3}}} = \frac{9}{10}$

$\Rightarrow A + \cfrac{1}{1 + \cfrac{3}{7}} = \frac{9}{10} \Rightarrow A + \frac{7}{10} = \frac{9}{10}$

$\Rightarrow A = \frac{9}{10} - \frac{7}{10} = \frac{2}{10} = \frac{1}{5}$

127. (a) Perimeter of rhombus = 52 cm

We know that,

Perimeter of rhombus = $4a$

i.e., $4a = 52$ cm $\Rightarrow a = 13$ cm

Length of diagonal (d_1) = 10 cm

Then, $(d_1)^2 + (d_2)^2 = 4a^2$

$\Rightarrow (d_2)^2 = 4a^2 - (d_1)^2 = 4(13)^2 - (10)^2$

$\Rightarrow (d_2)^2 = 4 \times 169 - 100 = 676 - 100 = 576$

$\Rightarrow \quad d_2 = 24$ cm

Area of rhombus = $\frac{1}{2} \times d_1 \times d_2$

$= \frac{1}{2} \times 24 \times 10$

$= 120 \text{ cm}^2$

128. (c) Speed of boat in still water (x) = 20 km/h

Speed of stream (y) i.e., speed of flowing river = 8 km/h

Upstream speed (u) = Speed of boat − Speed of stream = $x - y$

$= (20 - 8) = 12$ km/h

Downstream speed (v) = Speed of boat + Speed of stream

$= x + y = (20 + 8) = 28$ km/h

Let the distance be D km.

According to question,

$\Rightarrow \quad \frac{D}{u} = \frac{D}{v} + 6$

$\Rightarrow \quad D\left(\frac{1}{u} - \frac{1}{v}\right) = 6$

$\Rightarrow \quad D\left(\frac{1}{12} - \frac{1}{28}\right) = 6$

$\Rightarrow \quad D\left(\frac{7 - 3}{84}\right) = 6$

$\Rightarrow \quad D = \frac{6 \times 84}{4} = 126$ km

129. (b) Let the total votes be x.

P get 40% of votes i.e., $P = \frac{40x}{100}$

Then, Q got 60% of votes i.e., $Q = \frac{60x}{100}$

According to question,

$\Rightarrow \frac{60x}{100} - \frac{40x}{100} = 10$

$\Rightarrow \quad \frac{20x}{100} = 10$

$\Rightarrow \quad x = 50$

Total number of votes is 50.

Speedy Method

P got 40% of total votes, then Q got 60% of total votes.

i.e. P loss by a difference 20% of votes.

According to question,

$\Rightarrow x \times 20\% = 10$

$\Rightarrow \quad x = \frac{100}{2}$

Total votes = $\frac{100}{2} = 50$

130. (d) MRP of treadmill = ₹ 1250

Profit earn by shopkeeper = 14%

Discount given by shopkeeper = 14%

Selling price of treadmill

$= ₹\left(1250 - 1250 \times \frac{14}{100}\right)$

$= ₹ 1075$

Let the cost price be x.

$\Rightarrow$ Profit% = $\frac{P}{CP} \times 100$

$\Rightarrow \quad 14 = \frac{SP - CP}{CP} \times 100$

$\Rightarrow \quad 14 = \frac{(1075 - x)}{x} \times 100$

$\Rightarrow \quad 14x = 107500 - 100x$

$\Rightarrow \quad 114x = 107500 = x = 942.98$

$\Rightarrow \quad x \cong ₹ 943$

CP of treadmill is ₹ 943.

Speedy Method

MRP of treadmill = ₹ 1250

Profit% = 14% and Discount = 14%

Using formula

= MRP (100 − D%) = CP(100 + P%)

$\Rightarrow \quad 1250(100 - 14) = CP(100 + 14)$

$\Rightarrow \quad \frac{1250 \times 86}{114} = CP$

$\Rightarrow \quad CP = ₹ 942.98$

$\Rightarrow \quad CP = ₹ 943$

131. (d) Jeevan can do a piece of work in 42 days.

Jevan's one day work = $\frac{1}{42}$

Jevan and Rishi together can do same work in 27 days,

Then, Jevan and Rishi one day work

$= \frac{1}{27}$

Total work = LCM (42, 27) = 378

Efficiency of Jeevan's one day work

$= \frac{378}{42} = 9$ units/day

Efficiency of Jeevan and Rishi together

$= \frac{378}{27} = 14$ units/day

Efficiency of Rishi = (Efficiency of Jevan and Rishi together) – (Efficiency of Jevan)]

$= (14 - 9)$ unit/day

= 5 units/day

Time taken by Rishi to complete the same work alone $= \frac{378}{5}$ days

i.e. $75\frac{3}{5}$ days

Speedy Method

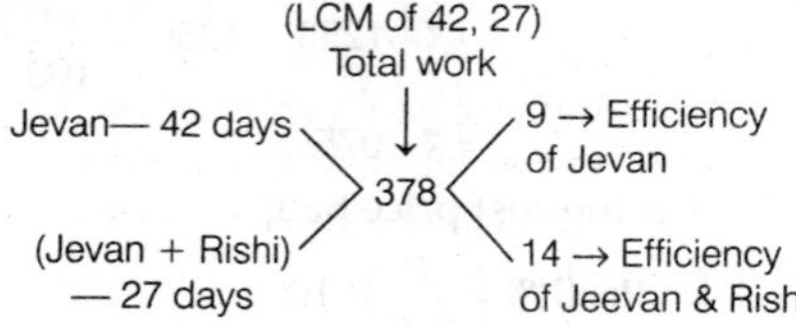

Efficiency of Rishi = (Efficiency of Jevan and Rishi) – (Efficiency of Jevan)

$= (14 - 9) = 5$ units/day

Time taken by Rishi to complete the work alone $= \frac{378}{5} = 75\frac{3}{5}$ days

132. (d) Let the distance be x.

Time taken by person to cover 28 km at a speed of 8 km/h $= \frac{28}{8}$ h $\left\{\because t = \frac{D}{S}\right\}$

If he walk at 6 km/h, speed in $\frac{28}{8}$ h,

then distance covered will be

i.e., $D = S \times t = 6 \times \frac{28}{8} = 21$ km

133. (a) Area of equilateral triangle $= 173.2$ cm^2

Let the side of equilateral triangle be a.

Area of equilateral triangle $= \frac{\sqrt{3}}{4}a^2$

$\Rightarrow \quad 173.2 = \frac{\sqrt{3}}{4}a^2$

$\Rightarrow \quad a^2 = \frac{173.2 \times 4}{\sqrt{3}}$

$\Rightarrow \quad a^2 = \frac{173.2 \times 4 \times 100}{173.2}$

$\Rightarrow \quad a^2 = 4 \times 100 \Rightarrow a = 20$ cm

134. (a)

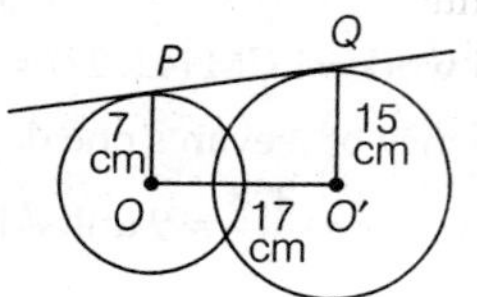

{Distance between the circles = 17 cm Radii of two circle is 7 cm and 15 cm respectively}

Length of direct common tangent PQ

$= \sqrt{(\text{Distance between centres of circle})^2 - (\text{Difference between radius of two circle})^2}$

$= \sqrt{(17)^2 - (15-7)^2}$

$= \sqrt{289 - (8)^2} = \sqrt{289 - 64} = \sqrt{225}$

Length of direct common tangent

= 15 cm

135. (b) Given, 4 mens or 6 boys can finish work in 20 days.

Let the time taken by them be x days.

Then, 4 Men = 6 Boys

$\Rightarrow \quad 1 \text{ Boy} = \frac{4}{6}$ Men

$\Rightarrow \quad \text{Boy} = \frac{2}{3}$ Men

Then, for 11 boys.

$\Rightarrow \quad 11 \text{ Boys} = \frac{2}{3} \times 11 = \frac{22}{3}$ Mens

Then, 6 Mens + 11 Boys $= \left(6 + \frac{22}{3}\right)$

Men $= \frac{40}{3}$ Men

Since, total work done is same.

Total work = 4 mens × 20 days

i.e., $4 \times 20 = \frac{40}{3} \times x \Rightarrow x = 6$ days

136. (b) Let the CP of Y be x, then CP of x be $(x - 90)$.

Profit earn on selling on article x = 23%

$\Rightarrow \quad \text{Profit\%} = \frac{P}{CP} \times 100$

$\Rightarrow \quad 23 = \frac{P}{x - 90} \times 100$

$\Rightarrow \quad \frac{23(x - 90)}{100} = P$

Loss earn on selling an article y = 13%

$\Rightarrow \quad \text{Loss\%} = \frac{L}{CP} \times 100$

$\Rightarrow \quad 13 = \frac{L}{x} \times 100$

$\Rightarrow \quad L = \frac{13x}{100}$

Net profit in the entire transcantion = ₹ 180

$\Rightarrow \frac{23(x - 90)}{100} - \frac{13x}{100} = 180$

$\Rightarrow 23x - 2070 - 13x = 18000$

$\Rightarrow \quad 10x = 20070$

$\Rightarrow \quad x =$ ₹ 2007

CP of article y is ₹ 2007.

137. (b) We have,

$\sin 2A = \cos 15°$

$\Rightarrow \quad \sin 2A = \cos 15°$

$\Rightarrow \cos(90° - 2A) = \cos 15°$

$[\cos(90° - \theta) = \sin\theta]$

$\Rightarrow \cos(90° - 2A) = \cos 15°$

On equating, we get,

$\Rightarrow \quad 90° - 2A = 15°$

$\Rightarrow \quad 90 - 15° = 2A$

$\Rightarrow \quad A = \frac{75°}{2} = 37.5°$

138. (a) Total workers = 9000

Number of voters who caste their votes

$= 9000 \times \frac{80}{100} = 7200$

Number of invalid votes

$= 7200 \times \frac{20}{100} = 1440$

Number of valid votes

$= 7200 - 1440 = 5760$

Let the vote get by Ajay be x, then Mohan get $(x - 1152)$ votes.

According to question,

$\Rightarrow x + x - 1152 = 5760$

$\Rightarrow \quad 2x = 6912$

$\Rightarrow \quad x = 3456$

139. (a) Let the third proportional be x.

$\therefore$ 16, 20 and x are in proportion

$\Rightarrow 16 : 20 = 20 : x$

Product of means = Product of extremes

$\Rightarrow \quad 20 \times 20 = 16x$

$\Rightarrow \quad 400 = 16x$

$\Rightarrow \quad 25 = x$

Third proportional is 25.

140. (c) We have, arc of length = 4.6 cm and radius 8 cm

Area of sector $= \frac{1}{2} \times r \times l$

$= \frac{1}{2} \times 8 \times 4.6$

Area of sector = 18.4 cm^2

141. (b) Notebook recorded the highest percentage change from 2020 to 2021

Difference = 10

Increase $= \left(\frac{10}{25} \times 100\right)\% = 40\%$

142. (a) Let x be number of solid hemisphere casted by melting solid sphere made of wax.

(R) Radius of sphere = 12 cm

(r) Radius of hemisphere = 4 cm

According to question,

Volume of solid sphere = $n \times$ (Volume of hemisphere)

$$\Rightarrow \frac{4}{3}\pi R^3 = n \times \frac{2}{3}\pi r^3$$

$$\Rightarrow \frac{R^3}{r^3} = n$$

$$\Rightarrow \frac{2 \times 12 \times 12 \times 12}{4 \times 4 \times 4} = n$$

$$\Rightarrow n = 54$$

143. (d) Radius of hemisphere (r) = 7 cm

CSA of hemisphere

$$= 2\pi r^2 = 2 \times \frac{22}{7} \times 7 \times 7 = 308 \text{ cm}^2$$

TSA of hemisphere = $2\pi r^2 + \pi r^2 = 3\pi r^2$

$$= 3 \times \frac{22}{7} \times 7 \times 7$$

$$= 462 \text{ cm}^2$$

144. (b) From the given pie chart,

$$\text{Spain} = \frac{9^\circ}{360} \times 14400 = 360 \text{ billion}$$

$$\text{Australia} = \frac{75^\circ}{360} \times 14400 = 3000 \text{ billion}$$

$$\text{USA} = \frac{96 \times 14400}{360} = 3840 \text{ billion}$$

$$\text{India} = \frac{55 \times 14400}{360} = 2200 \text{ billion}$$

$$\text{UK} = \frac{125^\circ \times 14400}{360} = 5000 \text{ billion}$$

Difference = E_{UK} $E_{Australia}$

= (5000 − 3000) billion

= ₹ 2000 billion

Speedy Method

From the given pie chart,

UK = 125°

Australia = 75°

Difference = ($E_{UK} - E_{Australia}$) $\times \frac{14400}{360}$ billion

$$= ₹\,(125^\circ - 75^\circ) \times \frac{14400}{360} \text{ billion}$$

= ₹ (50 × 40) = ₹ 2000 billion

145. (c) Let the radius of sphere be r.

Surface area of sphere (S_1) = $4\pi r^2$

When radius is doubled, then $r_1 = 2r$

Surface area of sphere (S_2) = $4\pi r_1^2$

$= 4\pi(2r)^2 = 16\pi r^2$

Difference = $16\pi r^2 - 4\pi r^2 = 12\pi r^2$

% Increased in surface area

$$= \frac{\text{Difference}}{\text{Initial SA}} \times 100$$

$$= \frac{12\pi r^2}{4\pi r^2} \times 100$$

% Increased in surface area = 300%

146. (b) From the given table,

Number of pages printed by D on Friday = 206

Number of pages printed by D on Sunday = 326

Number of pages printed by A on Friday = 350

Number of pages printed by A on Saturday = 420

According to question,

$\Rightarrow D$ (Friday + Sunday) : A (Friday + Saturday)

$\Rightarrow 532 : 770 \Rightarrow 266 : 385$

$\Rightarrow$ Ratio become 38 : 55.

147. (b) Let the third proportional be x.

Since, 23, 31 and x are in proportion,

$\Rightarrow 23 : 31 = 31 : x$

Product means = Product of extremes

$$\Rightarrow \frac{23}{21} = \frac{31}{x}$$

$$\Rightarrow 23x = 31 \times 31$$

$$\Rightarrow x = \frac{961}{23}$$

Hence, the third proportional is $\frac{961}{23}$.

148. (c) Speed of boat (x) = 20 km/h

Distance covered in downstream = 35 km

Time taken to cover the distance = 8 h

Downstream speed = $x + y$

Let speed of stream be y km/h

According to question,

$$\Rightarrow \frac{35}{x+y} + \frac{35}{x-y} = 8$$

$$\Rightarrow \frac{35}{20+y} + \frac{35}{20-y} = 8$$

$$\Rightarrow 35\left[\frac{20 - y + 20 + y}{400 - y^2}\right] = 8$$

$$\Rightarrow \frac{35 \times 40}{400 - y^2} = 8$$

$$\Rightarrow 175 = 400 - y^2$$

$$\Rightarrow y^2 = 225$$

$$\Rightarrow y = 15 \text{ km/h}$$

Hence, speed of stream is 15 km/h.

149. (c) We have number, 12, 18 and 42.

Factor of 12 = 2 × 2 × 3

Factor of 18 = 3 × 2 × 3

Factor of 42 = 2 × 3 × 7

HCF of (12, 18, 42) = 2 × 3 = 6

150. (a) Quantity of milk solution = 60 l

Quantity of milk in solution = 40%

i.e., $\frac{60 \times 40}{100} = 24\ l$

Quantity of other solution in milk solution = $(60 - 24)\ l = 36\ l$

Let $x\ l$ of milk be added in solution to make 60% milk in solution.

Then,

According to question,

$$\Rightarrow \frac{24 + x}{36} = \frac{60}{40}$$

$$\Rightarrow \frac{24 + x}{36} = \frac{3}{2}$$

$$\Rightarrow 48 + 2x = 108$$

$\Rightarrow 2x = 60 \Rightarrow x = 30\ l$

151. (d) The idiom 'throw dust into someone's eyes' means to 'deceive or mislead someone intentionally', often by hiding facts or presenting false appearances. Just as dust obstructs clear vision, this idiom refers to preventing someone from seeing the truth.

152. (d) The word 'pithy' refers to language or writing that is brief, concise and full of meaning. It is often used to describe statements or expressions that are short yet impactful. O. Henry's short stories are admired for their brevity and depth, which aligns perfectly with the meaning of concise and expressive.

153. (a) The idiom 'A' plum job refers to a highly desirable job that is well-paid, easy to do or has many advantages. It is often used to describe a position that many people would want because of its comfort, prestige or benefits.

154. (b) The correct grammatical structure after the verb prefers when followed by another verb is either:

- prefers + verb-ing (e.g., prefers watching)
- prefers + to + base verb (e.g., prefers to watch)

In the given sentence, the incorrect phrase is prefers to watching, which mixes both patterns incorrectly. The correct form should be my brother prefers to watch movies

This follows the structure: prefers + to + base verb = prefers to watch.

155. (c) The word 'Glad' is an adjective that means happy, pleased or delighted. It expresses a feeling of joy or satisfaction.

The word 'Sad' directly expresses the opposite feeling of being glad, making it the correct antonym.

156. **(a)** The error lies in the phrase tourists of all aging. The word 'aging' is a verb form or gerund, meaning the process of growing old and it is incorrect in this context.

The correct expression should be: tourists of all ages. Here, ages is a noun referring to different age groups, which is appropriate when talking about a variety of people.

Correct sentence
There is a spectrum of seas around that land which attracts tourists of all ages.

157. **(c)** The word imitates is a verb that means to copy someone's actions, speech, behaviour or mannerisms, often in order to resemble them or mock them. In the sentence, it suggests that Saurabh behaves in the same way as his boss, indicating mimicry or replication.

158. **(c)** The word 'Unequivocal' is an adjective that means leaving no doubt, clear or unambiguous. It refers to something stated in a way that is definite and cannot be misunderstood or misinterpreted.

'Unambiguous' is the direct synonym as it also means clear and not open to multiple interpretations.

159. **(a)** The word 'plaged' is incorrectly spelt. The correct spelling is plagued, which means to trouble or afflict persistently, often with problems or difficulties.

160. **(c)** The idiom 'Keep count of' means to keep a record or remember the number or amount of something, such as occurrences, people, items, etc.

Example She kept count of the number of books she read last year.

161. **(d)** The correct one-word substitution for a pretence of having a virtuous character, moral or religious beliefs or principles that one does not really possess is hypocrisy. It refers to the act of pretending to have moral standards or beliefs which one's own behaviour does not conform to.

162. **(a)** The idiom 'made a pig's ear' (of something) means to do something very badly or to mess it up completely. In the sentence, the person was supposed to repair the bookcase but instead ruined it, which fits the meaning of this idiom perfectly.

163. **(d)** The error lies in the phrase on second floor. In English grammar, when using ordinal numbers like first, second, third, etc., an article (the) is required before the noun.

The correct phrase should be: on the second floor

164. **(c)** The phrasal verb 'look into' means to investigate or examine a matter carefully, which is perfectly appropriate in the context of the sentence. The sentence talks about a serious case that requires attention and investigation, so look into is the correct usage.

165. **(c)** The idiom 'keep a straight face' means to avoid laughing or showing amusement, especially in a situation where it is difficult to control laughter. It refers to maintaining a serious or neutral expression even when something is funny or ridiculous.

Example He told such a ridiculous story, but I somehow managed to keep a straight face.

166. **(b)** A bonfire is a large open-air fire, typically built for celebration, festive events, or ceremonial purposes. It is often associated with traditional celebrations like festivals, camp gatherings, or historical commemorations.

167. **(d)** The word 'voluume' in the sentence is incorrectly spelt. The correct spelling is volume, which refers to the loudness or intensity of sound.

168. **(c)** The word 'disclosed' means made known, uncovered, or revealed something that was previously hidden or secret.

Hence, the synonym of 'disclosed' in the sentence is 'revealed'.

169. **(a)** The word 'Gllidder' is incorrectly spelt. The correct spelling is Glider, which refers to a type of aircraft that does not have an engine and is designed to glide through the air.

170. **(b)** The word 'envy' means a feeling of jealousy towards someone who has something that one desires or lacks. It indicates a negative emotional response to someone else's success or possessions.

171. **(b)** The term 'quorum' refers to the minimum number of members required to be present for a meeting or decision-making process to be valid. It is often used in the context of formal meetings, such as in legislative bodies or board meetings.

172. **(d)** An invoice is a detailed list of goods or services provided, along with the quantity and price for each item. It is typically issued by the seller to the purchaser as a record of the transaction.

173. **(a)** The sentence is grammatically correct when using 'The simple mistake' because:

- 'The' is the correct article to use before 'simple mistake' when referring to a specific mistake.
- 'The boy' is also correct, as 'boy' refers to a specific individual who committed the mistake.

174. **(a)** The word 'Vulnerable' means susceptible to harm or damage, or easily hurt or affected. 'Susceptible' is the closest synonym as it also means likely to be influenced or harmed by something.

175. **(a)** The word 'Benevolent' means kind, charitable, or showing goodwill. It refers to someone who is generous and caring towards others. Therefore, generous is the most appropriate synonym.

176. **(c)** The word 'Granduer' is incorrectly spelt. The correct spelling is grandeur, which means greatness or magnificence, especially in terms of appearance or scale.

177. **(c)** The term 'Chastise' means to criticise or rebuke someone severely for their actions or behaviour. It implies a strong reprimand or correction, which is the most fitting one-word substitute for the given group of words.

178. **(a)** The word 'Euphoria' refers to a state of intense happiness, excitement, or self-confidence. It captures the idea of a positive emotional state of joy and well-being, which fits the description provided in the question.

179. **(b)** The word 'purr' refers to the low, continuous, vibratory sound that cats make, typically when they are content or relaxed. It is a distinctive sound that expresses a state of satisfaction, commonly heard when a cat is happy.

180. **(b)** The idiom 'Face the music' means to accept the consequences or punishment for something you have done wrong or for a mistake you made. It is used when someone must confront the unpleasant outcome of their actions.

181. **(d)** The idiom 'Slipped my mind' means to forget something. In this context, it indicates that the speaker intended to mention something but forgot to do so.

182. **(c)** The phrasal verb 'set out' means to begin a journey or endeavor with a specific goal or destination in mind. In this context, Pradeep began his journey with the intention of going to Jamaica, but ended up in Nigeria.

183. **(c)** The word 'Specific' means clear, definite, or precise in detail. The antonym of 'Specific' would be random, which refers to something without a particular pattern, order, or purpose.

184. **(a)** The word 'Beneficent' means doing good or being charitable; it refers to a person or action that is kind and helpful. The antonym of beneficent would be cruel, which refers to being unkind, harsh, or causing pain or suffering.

185. **(c)** The idiom 'Grasping at straws' refers to making desperate attempts to find a solution or trying to achieve something when all options seem unlikely to work or are inadequate. It conveys the idea of clinging to any possibility, no matter how unlikely, in times of desperation.

186. **(c)** The word 'Contempt' refers to a feeling of disdain, disrespect, or scorn toward someone or something.
The antonym of 'Contempt' would be regard, which means to respect, honour, or have positive feelings toward someone or something.

187. **(d)** The word 'Obsolete' refers to something that is no longer in use because it has been replaced by something newer or more efficient. It perfectly fits the description of something that is no longer used due to the invention of something new.

188. **(d)** The sentence is referring to the person's character and behaviour. 'A quick buck' refers to making money in a quick, often unscrupulous way.
So, the sentence 'She never likes to make a quick buck' would suggest that she doesn't like to engage in opportunistic or dishonest ways to make money, emphasizing integrity and ethics.

189. **(a)** The word 'alited' is incorrectly spelt. The correct spelling is 'alighted', which means to land or descend, usually referring to birds.

190. **(d)** The phrase 'banking on' means relying on or depending on something, often used to express the expectation that something will happen or provide support. In this sentence, Ram is depending on the arrears of pay to go to Delhi but did not receive it in time.

191. **(d)** The word 'usually' fits best in blank number 1.

192. **(b)** The word 'frequent' means occurring often or regularly fits best in blank number 2.

193. **(a)** The word 'baffled' means confused or astonished fits best in blank number 3.

194. **(b)** The word 'depict' fits best in blank number 4.

195. **(a)** The word 'outnumbering' fits perfectly in blank number 5.

196. **(c)** The word 'intervention' refers to the act of taking action to influence or change a situation. The antonym of this would be 'non-involvement', which means not participating or taking action in a particular situation.

197. **(b)** The word 'promote' means to encourage, advance or support something.
The antonym of promote would be 'obstruct', which means to block or hinder progress or development.

198. **(c)** The passage presents a problem-solution structure. It first discusses the issue of climate change and its impact on health and then suggests a solution by focusing on health-centered climate policies, clean energy investments and proven interventions to mitigate climate pollutants.

199. **(c)** The central idea of the passage focuses on the importance of health-centered climate policies that not only address climate change but also bring health benefits simultaneously. The passage emphasises the need to invest in clean energy and interventions to improve air quality and reduce global warming, which directly impacts health.

200. **(d)** The tone of the passage is humanistic, as it focuses on health, well-being and the positive impacts of climate policy on people's lives. It emphasises how climate change mitigation can benefit people by providing cleaner air, safer water, better health systems and ultimately healthier lives, which reflects a concern for human welfare.

PAPER-1

SSC CPO SI SOLVED PAPER

3 October 2023 (Shift II)

MM : 200 **Time : 2 hr**

Instructions

1. This paper contains 200 questions.
2. It has 4 Parts, **Part I** General Intelligence and Reasoning, **Part II** General Knowledge and General Awareness, **Part III** Quantitative Aptitude and **Part IV** English Comprehension.
3. Each question carries **1 marks.**

Part I

General Intelligence and Reasoning

1. Which of the following numbers will replace the question mark (?) in the given series?

91, 111, 133, ?, 183, 211

(a) 149 (b) 156
(c) 167 (d) 157

2. Three statements are given followed by three conclusions numbered I, II and III.

Assuming the statements to be true, even if they seem to be at variance with commonly known facts, decide which of the conclusions logically follow(s) from the statements.

Statements

All valleys are mountains.
No sea is a mountain.
Some plains are seas.

Conclusions

I. Some valleys are plains.
II. No plain is a mountain.
III. No sea is a valley.

(a) Only Conclusion II follows
(b) Only Conclusion III follows
(c) Only Conclusion I follows
(d) Both Conclusions I and II follow

3. Select the set in which the numbers are related in the same way as are the numbers of the following set.
(**Note** Operations should be performed on the whole numbers, without breaking down the numbers into its constituent digits. e.g. 13 – Operations on 13 such as adding /subtracting /multiplying etc. to 13 can be performed. Breaking down 13 into 1 and 3 and then performing mathematical operations on 1 and 3 is not allowed)

(25, 3, 150)
(13, 7, 182)

(a) (5, 8, 184) (b) (6, 13, 234)
(c) (10, 5, 100) (d) (3, 4, 45)

4. Select the correct mirror image of the given figure, when the mirror is placed at line MN as shown.

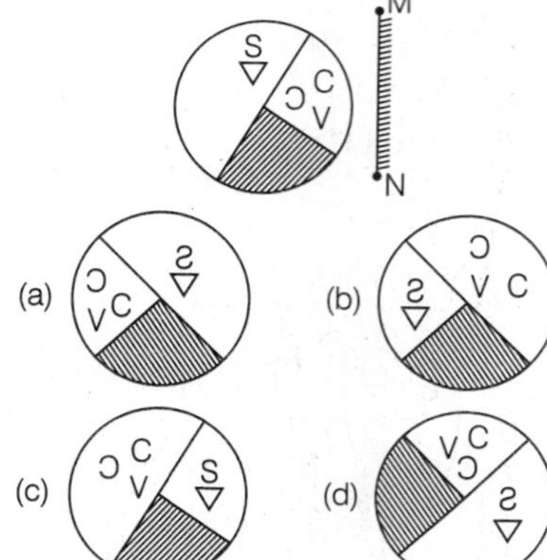

5. In a certain code language, 'COUNTY' is written as 'ULCYGN' and 'FOREST' is written as 'RLFTHE'. How will 'MARGIN' be written in that language?

(a) RJMDSZ (b) ZMTPRH
(c) ZMMRGI (d) RZMNRG

6. Six students Meera, Jigyasa, Tarun, Naina, Shambhavi and Avni are sitting around a circular table facing the centre (not necessarily in the same order). Shambhavi is an immediate neighbour of both Jigyasa and Avni. Tarun is sitting third to the left of Jigyasa. Meera is sitting second to the right of Avni.
Who is sitting third to the right of Meera?

(a) Avni (b) Naina
(c) Jigyasa (d) Shambhavi

7. Shilpa goes to a park every day for walking. One morning, she started walking from her home and walked 40 km towards the North. Then, she turned to the right and walked 60 km. Again, she turned right and walked 40 km. Lastly, she took a left turn and walked 30 km. How far is she from her home?

(a) 140 km (b) 90 km
(c) 100 km (d) 60 km

8. Which two mathematical signs should be interchanged to make the given equation correct?

$(75 + 15) \times 27 \times 1 - 9 \div 7$
$\times (135 + 3) - 10 \div (189 + 63) = 434$

(a) + and ÷ (b) + and –
(c) × and + (d) ÷ and –

9. Select the Venn diagram that best illustrates the relationship between the following classes.

Animals, Cats, Dogs

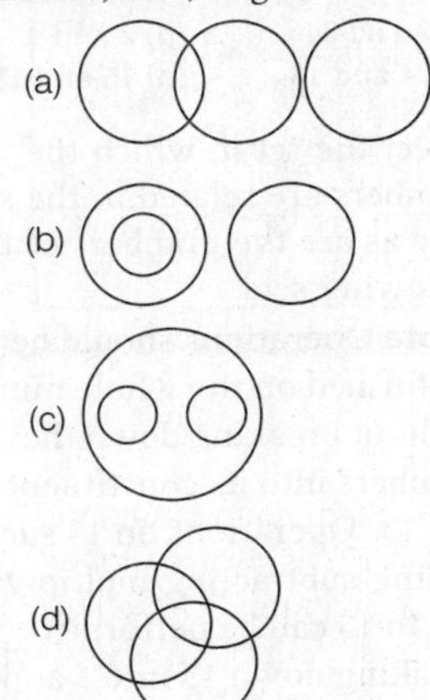

10. A paper is folded and cut as shown below. How will it appear when unfolded?

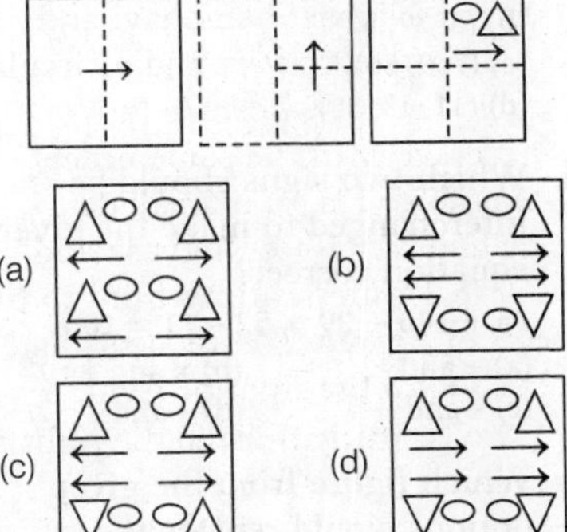

11. Three different positions of the same dice are shown. Find the number on the face opposite the face showing '5'.

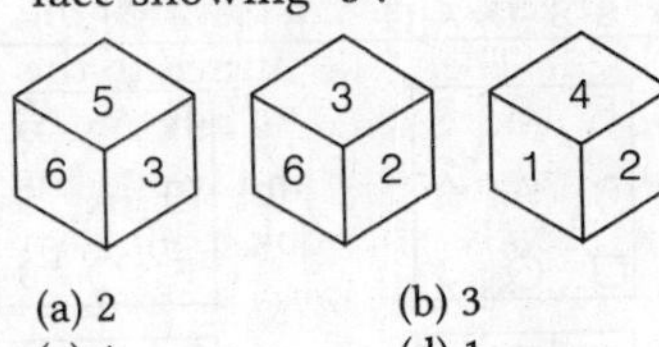

(a) 2 (b) 3
(c) 4 (d) 1

12. In a certain code language, 'DOING' is written as 'BQTOV' and 'ZEBRA' is written as 'FAAKB'. How will 'STORM' be written in that language?

(a) PETBK (b) MKYTS
(c) PRYSK (d) MLNKP

13. Two statements are given followed by two conclusions numbered I and II. Assuming the statements to be true, even if they seem to be at variance with commonly known facts, decide which of the conclusions logically follow(s) from the statements.

Statements

Some shells are pebbles.
All pebbles are rocks.

Conclusions

I. No shell is a rock.
II. Some shells are rocks.

(a) Only Conclusion I follows
(b) Neither Conclusion I nor II follows
(c) Both Conclusions I and II follow
(d) Only Conclusion II follows

14. Select the option figure in which the given figure is embedded (rotation is not allowed).

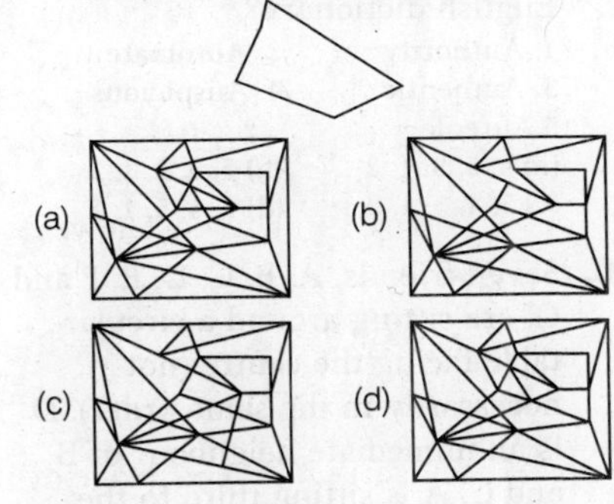

15. Select the figure that will come next in the following figure series.

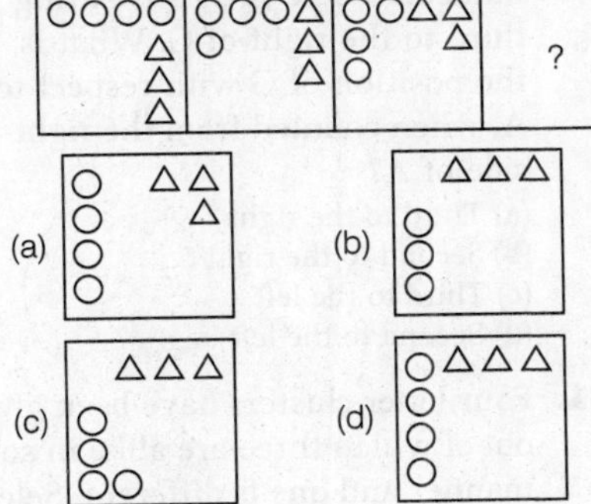

16. Select the correct option that indicates the arrangement of the given words in the order in which they appear in an English dictionary.

1. Formal 2. Foreign
3. Forest 4. Forgotten
5. Forge 6. Forlorn

(a) 2, 3, 5, 4, 6, 1 (b) 2, 3, 6, 1, 5, 4
(c) 2, 3, 4, 5, 6, 1 (d) 2, 3, 5, 6, 4, 1

17. If A denotes '+', B denotes '×', C denotes '–' and D denotes '÷', then what will be the value of the following equation?

13 B 7 A 64 D 4 C 23 = ?

(a) 82 (b) 84 (c) 86 (d) 76

18. Select the option that represents the letters which, when sequentially placed from left to right in the blanks below, will complete the letter series.

A _ _ D F _ K _ _ F A _ L _ _

(a) D L K L F A L D
(b) L A L K D F D K
(c) K L A L D K D F
(d) F D L A K F D L

19. Select the correct mirror image of the given combination, when the mirror is placed at 'MN' as shown below.

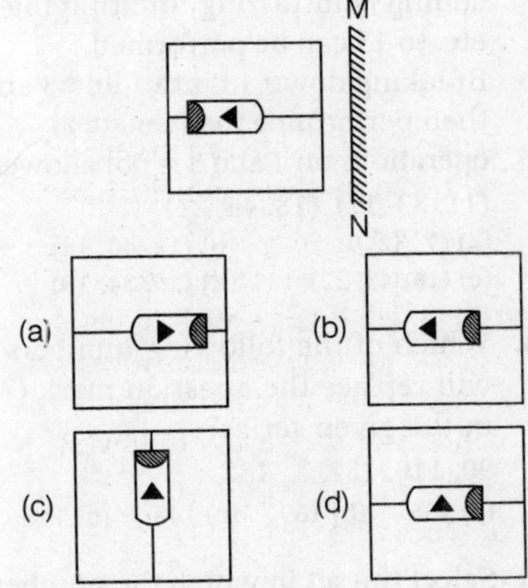

20. Town Q is to the North of Town P. Town R is to the West of Town Q. Town S is to the North of Town R. Town T is to the East of Town S. What is the position of Town T with respect to Town R? (All positions are arranged in grid pattern).

(a) East (b) South
(c) North-East (d) South-East

21. In a certain code language, 'FRIGHT' is written as 'FOCQED' and 'SHREDS' is written as 'OEPPAB'. How will 'UPSETS' be written in that language?
(a) PMRSQB (b) PMROQB
(c) PMRPQB (d) PMSPQB

22. A paper is folded and cut as shown. How will it appear when unfolded?

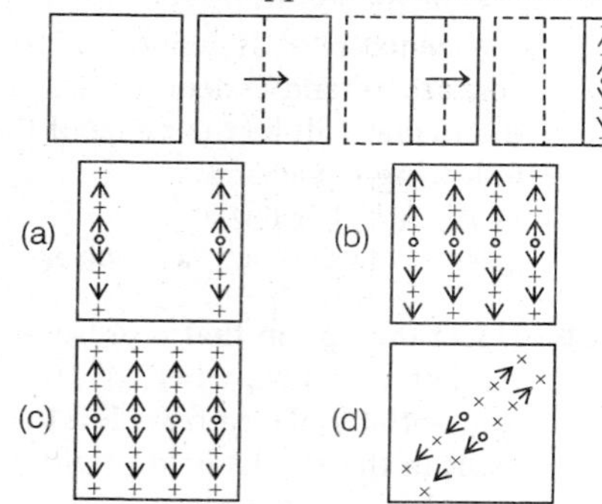

23. Select the set in which the numbers are related in the same way as are the numbers of the following sets.
(**Note** Operations should be performed on the whole numbers, without breaking down the numbers into its constituent digits. e.g. 13 – Operations on 13 such as adding /subtracting /multiplying etc. to 13 can be performed. Breaking down 13 into 1 and 3 and then performing mathematical operations on 1 and 3 is not allowed).
(11, 33, 17), (18, 44, 21)
(a) (7, 32, 9) (b) (12, 40, 18)
(c) (16, 43, 22) (d) (15, 34, 19)

24. Which of the following numbers will replace the question mark (?) in the given series?
90, 110, 132, ? , 182
(a) 156 (b) 169 (c) 148 (d) 146

25. Select the set in which the numbers are related in the same way as are the numbers of the following sets.
(**Note** Operations should be performed on the whole numbers, without breaking down the numbers into its constituent digits. e.g. 13 – Operations on 13 such as adding /subtracting /multiplying etc. to 13 can be performed. Breaking down 13 into 1 and 3 and then performing mathematical operations on 1 and 3 is not allowed)
(13, 104, 16), (9, 63, 14)
(a) (23, 204, 26) (b) (8, 60, 15)
(c) (12, 85, 15) (d) (10, 92, 17)

26. Which of the following numbers will replace the question mark (?) in the given series?
18, 27, 31, 43, 44, 59, 57, ?
(a) 82 (b) 74 (c) 83 (d) 75

27. Which letter-cluster will complete the given series?
BHERZ, DGHTX, FFKVV, ...
(a) HENWT (b) GGNXU
(c) HGMWU (d) HENXT

28. Select the option that is related to the third word in the same way as the second word is related to the first word. (The words must be considered as meaningful words and must not be related to each other based on the number of letters/number of consonants/vowels in the word.)
Nun : Convent :: King : ?
(a) Palace (b) Cottage
(c) Prison (d) Monastery

29. Select the option that represents the correct order of the given words as they would appear in an English dictionary?
1. Authority 2. Automate
3. Authentic 4. Auspicious
5. Aureole
(a) 4, 5, 3, 1, 2 (b) 5, 3, 4, 1, 2
(c) 5, 4, 3, 1, 2 (d) 3, 4, 5, 1, 2

30. Seven friends, A, B, C, D, E, F and G, are sitting around a circular table facing the centre (not necessarily in the same order). D is an immediate neighbour of B and C. A is sitting third to the right of C. E is an immediate neighbour of A and F. G is sitting immediate left of C. B is sitting third to the right of G. What is the position of G with respect to A, when counted from the right side of A?
(a) Third to the right
(b) Second to the right
(c) Third to the left
(d) Second to the left

31. Four letter-clusters have been given, out of which three are alike in some manner and one is different. Select the odd letter-cluster.
(a) KNJZ (b) FIEU
(c) MJLO (d) SVRH

32. Three of the following letter-clusters are alike in some manner and one is different. Select the one that is different.
(a) MRVY (b) GLPS
(c) NSWZ (d) TGQJ

33. Which two numbers (not digits) should be interchanged to make the given equation correct?
$(18 \times 2) - 24 + 10 \times 160 \div 16 + (10 \times 4) = 170$
(a) 2 and 24 (b) 2 and 4
(c) 24 and 18 (d) 16 and 18

34. Select the set in which the numbers are related in the same way as are the numbers of the following sets.
(**Note** Operations should be performed on the whole numbers, without breaking down the numbers into its constituent digits. e.g. 13- Operations on 13 such as adding/subtracting/multiplying etc. to 13 can be performed. Breaking down 13 into 1 and 3 and then performing mathematical operations on 1 and 3 is not allowed.)
(15, 21, 66)
(9, 17, 44)
(a) (2, 4, 12)
(b) (5, 37, 52)
(c) (7, 9, 86)
(d) (11, 13, 35)

35. Which two signs should be interchanged to make the given equation correct?
$13 + 145 \div 29 \times 52 - 11 = 106$
(a) – and × (b) × and +
(c) ÷ and – (d) ÷ and +

36. Which figure from the given options would replace the question mark (?), if the following figure series were to be continued?

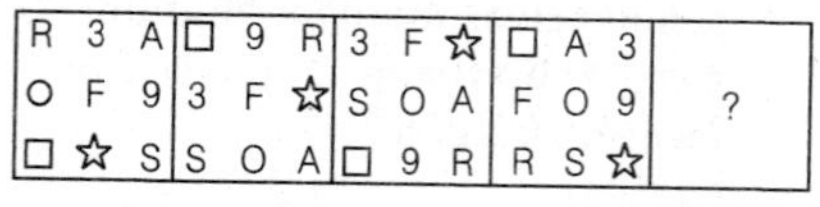

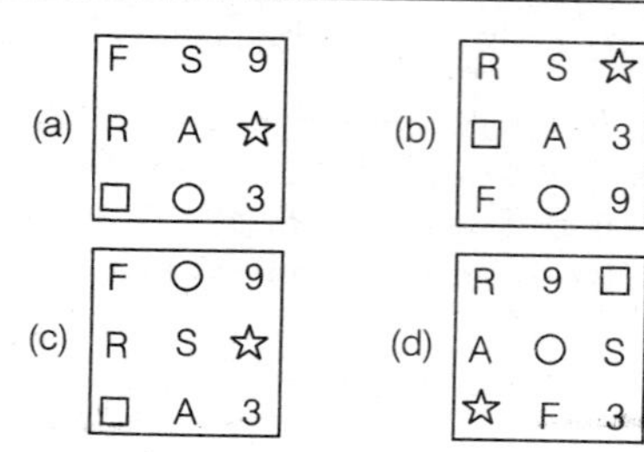

37. If M denotes '–', N denotes '÷', O denotes '×' and P denotes '+', then what will come in place of '?' in the following equation?

255 N 5 O 4 P 16 O 3 M 29 = ?

(a) 223 (b) 216
(c) 211 (d) 230

38. 'PRO5' is related to 'OSQ15' in a certain way. In the same way, 'OPO10' is related to 'NQQ30'. Which of the following is related to 'MAC9' using the same logic?

(a) NZA 3 (b) OZA 3
(c) NZB 3 (d) NZA 27

39. 'M $ K' means 'M is the mother of K'.
'M # K' means 'M is the father of K'.
'M @ K' means 'M is the husband of K'.
'M% K' means 'M is the daughter of K'.
If A $ C @ R, then how is R related to A?

(a) Husband's father
(b) Mother
(c) Son's wife
(d) Daughter

40. If '+' means 'divided by', '–' mean 'added to', '×' means 'subtracted from' and '÷' means 'multiplied by', then what will be the value of the following expression?

$[(25 \times 13) - (3 \div 3) + (3 - 4)] \div 5$

(a) 20 (b) 10 (c) 15 (d) 5

41. Which of the following numbers will replace the question mark (?) and complete the given number series?

15, 19 , 21, 25 , 27, ?

(a) 31 (b) 32
(c) 29 (d) 30

42. Which letter-cluster will replace the question mark (?) to complete the given series?

MMNO, OKPM, ?, SGTI, UEVG

(a) POKI (b) QRIL
(c) QIRK (d) PQIJ

43. In a certain code language, 'OIL' is coded as 27 and 'CREAM' is coded as 125. How will 'POWDER' be coded in the same language?

(a) 225 (b) 216
(c) 198 (d) 169

44. Given below are two statements and two conclusions. Take the statements to be true even, if they are at variance with commonly known facts and decide whether the conclusion(s) follow(s) the given statements.

Statements

Some cakes are biscuits.
Some biscuits are chocolates.

Conclusions

I. Some biscuits are cakes.
II. Some cakes are chocolates.

(a) Both the conclusions follow
(b) Only Conclusion II follows
(c) Neither Conclusion I nor II follows
(d) Only conclusion I follows

45. If I denotes '÷', J denotes '×', K denotes '–' and L denotes '+', then what will come in place of '?' in the following equation?

(35 I 5) J 9 K 23 L 39 K (3 J 8) = ?

(a) 60 (b) 59 (c) 51 (d) 55

46. Which of the given figures, when placed in the 5th position would continue the series that established by the first four figures?

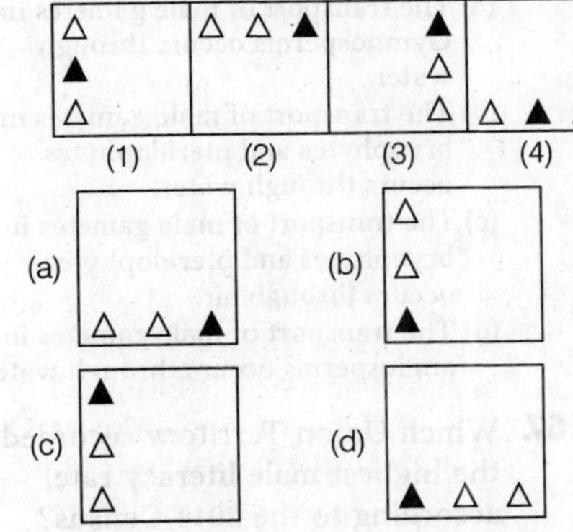

47. A @ B means 'A is the husband of B',
A & B means 'A is the mother of B',
A # B means 'A is the daughter of B'.
If Q @ M & Y @ J # R & Z, then how is Y related to Z?

(a) Brother's wife (b) Father's sister
(c) Sister's husband (d) Father

48. A paper is folded and cut as shown below. How will it appear when unfolded?

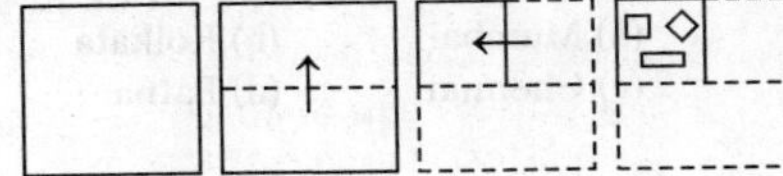

(a) (b)
(c) (d)

49. Select the option figure, which is embedded in the given figure as its part (rotation is not allowed).

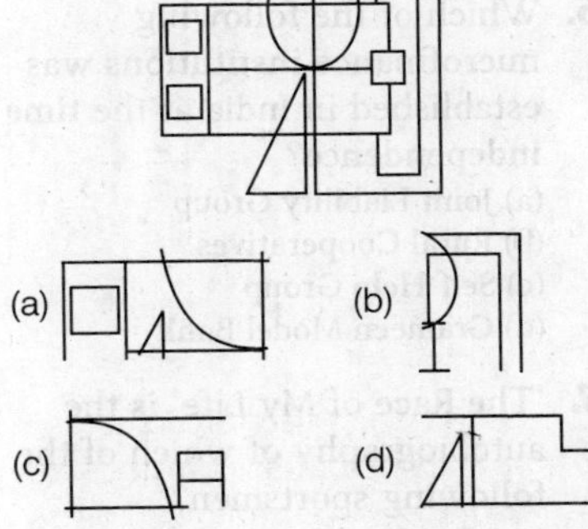

50. In a certain code language, 'HIGHLY' is written as 'GRHYOH' and 'CLEVER' is written as 'EOCRVV'. How will 'HORROR' be written in that language?

(a) JRLPDB (b) RLHRLR
(c) JPRDER (d) RKJPED

Part II

General Knowledge and General Awareness

51. In India, which of the following modes of transportation reduces trans-shipment losses and delays in supply of petroleum and gas?

(a) Pipeline
(b) Roadways
(c) Railways
(d) Waterways

52. From which country has the concept of Martial Law, which restricts Fundamental rights, borrowed?

(a) The UK (b) The USSR
(c) China (d) Japan

53. Copacabana Beach is situated in ....

(a) Peru (b) Australia
(c) Mexico (d) Brazil

54. Which of the following is the most widely used method for refining impure metals?
(a) Vapour-Phase Refining
(b) Poling Refining
(c) Electrolytic Refining
(d) Liquidation Refining

55. Which of the following is the correct statement?
(a) Joule is the unit of work.
(b) The unit of energy is the watt.
(c) Joule/second is also a unit of energy.
(d) The unit of power is joule/newton.

56. Which of the following microfinance institutions was established in India at the time of independence?
(a) Joint Liability Group
(b) Rural Cooperatives
(c) Self-Help Group
(d) Grameen Model Bank

57. 'The Race of My Life' is the autobiography of which of the following sportsmen?
(a) PT Usha
(b) Mary Kom
(c) Milkha Singh
(d) Saurav Ganguly

58. Which of the following has been incorrectly listed as a condition for becoming a citizen of India?
(a) Citizenship by birth
(b) Citizenship by naturalisation
(c) Citizenship through acquisition of property
(d) Citizenship by descent

59. Which British scientist is known for developing the Principle of Holography in 1947 to improve the resolution of the electron microscope?
(a) Werner Heisenberg
(b) Lloyd Cross
(c) Dennis Gabor
(d) Charles Towns

60. The 'Tripartite Struggle' was between Gurjara Pratiharas in North India, Palas in Eastern India and .... in South India.
(a) Marathas (b) Rashtrakutas
(c) Cholas (d) Cheras

61. Who is the author of the novel 'The Moor's Last Sigh'?
(a) VS Naipaul (b) John Keay
(c) Kiran Doshi (d) Salman Rushdie

62. Which of the following dances is based on Rasleela themes of Radha and Krishna?
(a) Manipuri dance
(b) Sattriya dance
(c) Mohiniyattam
(d) Kathak

63. Who among the following was the last Mauryan ruler and was killed by his Commander-in-Chief?
(a) Shatadhanvan (b) Bindusara
(c) Brihadratha (d) Dashratha

64. Which writ is issued when the court finds that there is unlawful arrest of a person?
(a) Prohibition (b) Mandamus
(c) Quo Warranto (d) Habeas Corpus

65. Who among the following founded an expatriate Communist Party of India at Tashkent in 1920?
(a) PC Joshi
(b) Shripad Amrut Dange
(c) Jolly Kaul
(d) MN Roy

66. Which of the following statements is correct?
(a) The transport of male gametes in Gymnosperms occurs through water.
(b) The transport of male gametes in bryophytes and pteridophytes occurs through water.
(c) The transport of male gametes in bryophytes and pteridophytes occurs through air.
(d) The transport of male gametes in angiosperms occurs through water.

67. Which Union Territory recorded the highest male literacy rate, according to the 2011 Census?
(a) Daman and Diu
(b) Delhi
(c) Andaman and Nicobar Islands
(d) Lakshadweep

68. Pandit Ravi Shankar popularised which instrument in particular all over the world?
(a) Sitar (b) Tabla
(c) Veena (d) Harmonium

69. According to the Census of India 2011, which metropolitan city has the highest population?
(a) Mumbai (b) Kolkata
(c) Chennai (d) Patna

70. Ker and Garia Puja are traditional tribal festivals of which state?
(a) Jharkhand (b) Manipur
(c) Odisha (d) Tripura

71. Which company has been given the responsibility of construction, operation and maintenance of the Hazira-Vijaipur-Jagdishpur (HVJ) pipeline project?
(a) TATA Petrodyne Limited (TPL)
(b) Oil and Natural Gas Corporation (ONGC)
(c) Gas Authority of India Limited (GAIL)
(d) Reliance Industries Limited (RIL)

72. Mawsynram, the place that receives the highest rainfall in the world, is situated in which hills?
(a) Patkai Hills (b) Mishmi Hills
(c) Rajmahal Hills (d) Khasi Hills

73. Which of the following organisations was founded in Poona, Satara and other towns of Maharashtra that worked against Brahmanical orthodoxy and tried to reform Hinduism?
(a) Brahmo Samaj
(b) Paramahansa Mandali
(c) Ramakrishna Mission
(d) Arya Samaj

74. In 1784, who discovered the composition of water through his experiment with hydrogen and oxygen?
(a) Henry Cavendish
(b) Herbert C. Brown
(c) Joseph Priestley
(d) John Dalton

75. Under which strata do trees fall?
(a) Second vertical
(b) Top vertical
(c) Middle vertical
(d) Bottom vertical

76. The Fundamental Duties were added in the Indian Constitution on the recommendation of the
(a) Balwant Rai Mehta Committee
(b) Bibek Debroy Committee
(c) LM Singhvi Committee
(d) Sardar Swaran Singh Committee

77. Which of the following is the correct formula for moment of inertia?
(a) $I = mr^2$ (b) $I = rm^2$
(c) $I = m / r^2$ (d) $I = 2mr$

78. Which of the following Articles of the Indian Constitution deals with the relationship between the Prime Minister and the President?
(a) Article 45 (b) Article 25
(c) Article 35 (d) Article 75

79. India's rank in Tokyo Olympic 2020 is
(a) 49 (b) 48
(c) 47 (d) 46

80. In which of the following years was the Muslim League formed?
(a) 1915 (b) 1909
(c) 1906 (d) 1912

81. The Chambal, Hindon and Tons rivers are tributaries of the river
(a) Yamuna (b) Mahanadi
(c) Kaveri (d) Tapi

82. Prabhat Sarma, a recipient of Sangeet Natak Akademi Award, was a.........player from Assam.
(a) Ghatam (b) Flute
(c) Tabla (d) Sarangi

83. Mehrangarh Fort is located in which of the following cities?
(a) Jaipur (b) Kota
(c) Jodhpur (d) Bikaner

84. During a game of hockey, following an offence, if a player is shown a yellow card then he will be sent off the pitch for.......... .
(a) 5 minutes (b) 6 minutes
(c) 4 minutes (d) 3 minutes

85. Trade liberalisation has helped India improve its...........in industries with medium-to-high technology content.
(a) imports
(b) fuel efficiency
(c) labour intensity
(d) comparative advantage

86. Which of the following Five-Year Plans addressed the issue of removal of poverty as a chief objective for the first time?
(a) Fourth Five-Year Plan
(b) Third Five-Year Plan
(c) Sixth Five-Year Plan
(d) Fifth Five-Year Plan

87. Which of the following was the first B vitamin discovered in 1897 that is essential in amino acid and carbohydrate metabolism and is active in energy production reactions?
(a) Biotin (b) Riboflavin
(c) Thiamine (d) Folate

88. Identify the cultural festival on the basis of given clues.
(i) This festival brings together craftsmen like potters, embroiderers, weavers, wood carvers, metal workers, stone smiths and painters from all over India on one platform in Haryana.
(ii) This crafts mela is held in February every year and provides a glimpse of the state's cultural heritage and recent achievements.
(a) Kapil Muni Fair
(b) Shamlaji Fair
(c) Chitra Vichitra Fair
(d) Surajkund Mela

89. The duration of the 12th Five-Year Plan was from.........to ....
(a) 2012 - 2017 (b) 1987 - 1992
(c) 2007 - 2012 (d) 1990 - 1995

90. Manisha Kalyan is associated with which of the following sports events?
(a) Football (b) Hockey
(c) Cricket (d) Chess

91. A Governor shall, notwithstanding the expiration of his term, continue to hold office until ....
(a) the President's consent
(b) the Legislative Secretary takes charge
(c) his/her successor enters his/her office
(d) he/she has aid and advice of the Chief Minister

92. A government budget shows a primary deficit of ₹ 6900 crore. The revenue expenditure on interest payment is ₹ 400 crore. Fiscal deficit is equal to
(a) ₹ 6500 crore
(b) ₹ 7300 crore
(c) ₹ 7100 crore
(d) ₹ 6900 crore

93. The office of Diwan-i-Insha dealt with which affair in administration?
(a) State correspondence
(b) Military
(c) Finance
(d) Religious affairs

94. The Earth's perihelion occurs in
(a) July (b) October
(c) January (d) September

95. Guru Bipin Singh, who received the honour of Sangeet Natak Akademi Award in 1966 and the Kalidas Samman by Madhya Pradesh Government, was an exponent of which of the following Indian classical dance forms?
(a) Odissi (b) Manipuri
(c) Kuchipudi (d) Kathak

96. Who among the following was the youngest recipient of the Padma Vibhushan award in dance in 1984?
(a) Birju Maharaj (b) Rajendra Gangani
(c) Abhimanyu Lal (d) Ehshan Hilal

97. When was the Indian Meteorological Department, which collects data on temperature, rainfall, wind, etc., and makes weather forecasts, established by the Government of India?
(a) 1879 (b) 1876
(c) 1875 (d) 1873

98. What is the percentage of proteins in the cell membrane?
(a) 60-80% (b) 80-100%
(c) 20-40% (d) 40-60%

99. Syed Modi India International is organised in which sporting event?
(a) Kabaddi (b) Volleyball
(c) Chess (d) Badminton

100. Which dance form of Goa is also known as the 'Warrior Dance'?
(a) Bihu (b) Lavani
(c) Ghode Modni (d) Rauf

Part III
Quantitative Aptitude

101. Sukhvir purchased some perishable items for sale but 30% of those items could not be sold and went bad. However, Sukhvir managed to sell the rest of the items at a price that helped him earn an overall profit of 19%. At what percentage above the cost price of each item purchased by Sukhvir did he sell each of the items that did not go bad?
(a) 49% (b) 70%
(c) 63% (d) 75%

102. An item with a marked price of ₹1940 was sold at a discount of 15%. At what price (in ₹) was the item sold?
(a) 1659 (b) 1639
(c) 1649 (d) 1654

103. A hostel mess requires 217 eggs for a week. How many eggs will it require in total for the months of July, August and September?
(a) 2821 (b) 2883
(c) 2852 (d) 2790

104. Find the greatest number, which when divides 261, 853 and 1221, leaves a remainder of 5 in each case.
(a) 19 (b) 18
(c) 17 (d) 16

105. Study the given pie-chart and answer the question that follows.
The pie-chart shows total expenditure of ₹30000000 on different items for constructing a flat in a town.

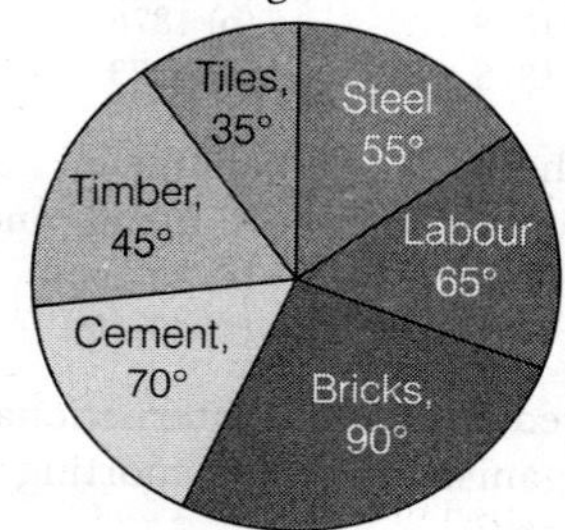

The percentage of the total expenditure on Labour and Timber is
(a) $30\frac{5}{9}\%$ (b) $30\frac{1}{3}\%$
(c) $30\frac{1}{9}\%$ (d) $30\frac{7}{9}\%$

106. What is the number of valid votes cast in favour of a candidate in an election, if the candidate received 75% of the total valid votes, and 5% of the total votes were declared invalid, given that the total number of voters was 146000?
(a) 106650 (b) 110250
(c) 104025 (d) 108850

107. A conical shape vessel has a radius of 21 cm and has a slant height of 25 cm. If the curved part of the vessel is to be painted white, find the cost (in ₹) of painting at the rate of ₹1.5 per cm^2.
(a) 2475 (b) 1650
(c) 825 (d) 1250

108. *P* and *Q* can do a work together in 30 days.
Q and *R* can do the same work together in 24 days and *R* and *P* together in 20 days. They started the work together, but *Q* and *R* left after 10 days. How many more days will *P* take to finish the remaining work?
(a) 23 (b) 21
(c) 18 (d) 19

109. Find the greatest possible length (in metres) that can be used to exactly measure the lengths 6 m, 5 m 25 cm and 12 m 50 cm.
(a) 0.25 m (b) 0.75 m
(c) 0.90 m (d) 0.35 m

110. In a village election, Sharuk got 80% of the total valid votes. 10% of the votes were invalid. If the total number of votes was 4500, then find the number of valid votes the other candidate got.
(a) 620 (b) 450
(c) 530 (d) 810

111. What will be the difference between the total surface area and the curved surface area of a hemisphere having 4 cm diameter?
(a) 5π cm^2 (b) 8π cm^2
(c) 4π cm^2 (d) 4.4π cm^2

112. *A* can do a piece of work in 8 days, while *B* can do it in 7 days. If they work at it alternately beginning with *A*, then in how many days will the work be completed?
(a) 8 (b) $8\frac{1}{2}$
(c) $7\frac{1}{2}$ (d) 7

113. The cost of painting the total surface area of 30 m high solid right circular cylinder at the rate of ₹25 per m^2 is ₹18425. What is the volume (in m^3) of this cylinder $\left[\text{use } \pi = \frac{22}{7}\right]$?
(a) 1145 (b) 1210
(c) 1155 (d) 1122

114. What is the length (in cm) of the transverse common tangent between two circles with radii 6 cm and 4 cm, given that the distance between their centres is 14 cm?
(a) $2\sqrt{6}$ (b) $4\sqrt{6}$ (c) $5\sqrt{6}$ (d) $3\sqrt{6}$

115. The value of $(1 + \sin^4 A - \cos^4 A)\text{cosec}^2 A$ is
(a) −2 (b) 2 (c) 1 (d) −1

116. The table given below shows the number of products sold by 4 shopkeepers A, B, C and D on four different days.

Days/Persons	A	B	C	D
Monday	1000	800	-	750
Tuesday	500	-	900	650
Wednesday	800	1000	700	-
Thursday	-	1200	800	900

If the total products sold by A and B, including all four days, is 3000 and 3500, respectively, the products sold by B on. Tuesday is how many more or less than the products sold by A on Thursday?
(a) 300 more (b) 200 less
(c) 200 more (d) 300 less

117. If an amount of ₹80 becomes ₹96 in 2 yr in a bank account which gives simple annual interest, then an amount of ₹62000 will become ...... in the same account after 5 yr.
(a) ₹ 88200 (b) ₹ 84600
(c) ₹ 82400 (d) ₹ 93000

118. If $a \propto b$, $b \propto \frac{1}{c}$ and $c \propto d$, then the relation between *a* and *d* is
(a) $a \propto \frac{1}{d}$ (b) $a \propto d$
(c) $a \propto d^2$ (d) $a \propto \sqrt{d}$

119. Study the given table and answer the question that follows.
The table shows the production of five types of cars P, Q, R, S and T by a company from the year 1989 to 1994.

Type of Cars	1989	1990	1991	1992	1993	1994	Total
P	8	20	16	17	21	6	88
Q	16	10	14	12	12	14	78
R	21	17	16	15	13	8	90
S	4	6	10	16	20	31	87
T	25	18	19	30	14	27	133
Total	74	71	75	90	80	86	476

During the period 1989-94, which type of car featured a continuous increase in production?
(a) S (b) Q
(c) R (d) P

120. Evaluate $6.9 - [8.6\{6.5 - (5.4 - \overline{4.3 - 2})\}]$
(a) 1.8 (b) 1.9 (c) 1.6 (d) 1.7

121. A thief is noticed by a policeman from a distance of 300 m. The thief starts running and the policeman starts chasing him. The thief and policeman run at the rate of 11 km/h and 13 km/h, respectively. After running for how many kilometres will the policeman be able to catch the thief?
(a) 1.65 (b) 1.85 (c) 1.75 (d) 1.95

122. A sum of ₹100000 was taken from a bank at the rate of 7% p.a to be compounded annually for 5. Calculate the compound interest. (Closest to a ₹)
(a) ₹40000 (b) ₹20963 (c) ₹40567 (d) ₹40255

123. The curved surface area of a cone whose base radius is 7 cm and slant height is 10 cm is:
(a) 280 cm^2 (b) 250 cm^2 (c) 300 cm^2 (d) 220 cm^2

124. A sector of a circle has a central angle of 45° and an arc length of 22 cm.
Find the radius of the circle. $\left(\text{Use } \pi = \frac{22}{7}\right)$
(a) 32 cm (b) 35 cm (c) 28 cm (d) 36 cm

125. The least common multiple of 210, 336 and 504 is
(a) 5040 (b) 3360 (c) 2100 (d) 4560

126. The LCM of $\frac{1}{3}, \frac{3}{5}, \frac{4}{7}$ and $\frac{9}{16}$ is
(a) 36 (b) 49 (c) 38 (d) 81

127. Study the given table and answer the question that follows.
The table shows the number of students doing various courses in various cities.

City	MBA	MCA	M.Sc.	M.Com.	M.A.	Total
Ahmedabad	1234	1384	1440	1289	1332	6679
Bengaluru	1156	1783	1874	1003	1340	7156
Bhopal	1187	1347	1532	1321	1486	6873
Chennai	1342	1473	1129	1765	1666	7375
New Delhi	1230	1098	1128	1865	1777	7098
Hyderabad	1456	1234	1556	1653	1789	7688
Kolkata	1239	1785	1865	1504	1762	8155

In Chennai, the number of students in MBA is nearly what percentage of students in M.A.? (rounded off to 2 digits after decimal)
(a) 76.25% (b) 80.55% (c) 92.12% (d) 99.23%

128. If $\cos A = \frac{15}{17}, 0 \le A \le 90°$, then the value of $\cot(90° - A)$ is
(a) $\frac{8}{15}$ (b) $\frac{2\sqrt{2}}{15}$ (c) $\frac{\sqrt{2}}{15}$ (d) $\frac{7}{15}$

129. Study the given table and answer the question that follows.
The table shows the number of cakes sold by four different bakeries in 4 different months.

Month/Bakery	August	September	October	November
P	250	241	213	168
Q	175	189	201	122
R	164	145	129	168
S	224	154	184	209

What is the difference between the total number of cakes sold by bakeries Q and S together in September and the total number of cakes sold by bakeries P and R together in November?
(a) 7 (b) 9 (c) 10 (d) 8

130. The volume of a right circular cone having a base diameter of 14 cm is 196 π cm^3. Find the perpendicular height of this cone.
(a) 10 cm (b) 12 cm (c) 14 cm (d) 8 cm

131. Find the LCM of $\frac{3}{2}, \frac{81}{16}$ and $\frac{9}{8}$.
(a) $\frac{91}{2}$ (b) $\frac{81}{2}$ (c) $\frac{111}{2}$ (d) $\frac{101}{2}$

132. If $\frac{A}{L} + \frac{M}{B} = 1$ and $\frac{B}{M} + \frac{N}{C} = 1$, then the value of $\frac{L}{A} + \frac{C}{N}$ is
(a) $\frac{B}{M}$ (b) 0 (c) 1 (d) $\frac{M}{B}$

133. The perimeter of a sector of a circle is 24 cm and the radius is 3 cm. Calculate the area (in cm^2) of the sector.
(a) 24 (b) 33 (c) 27 (d) 30

134. Study the given table and answer the question that follows.
The table shows the production of five types of cars P, Q, R, S and T by a company from the year 1989 to 1994.

Type of Cars	1989	1990	1991	1992	1993	1994	Total
P	8	20	16	17	21	6	88
Q	16	10	14	12	12	14	78
R	21	17	16	15	13	8	90
S	4	6	10	16	20	31	87
T	25	18	19	30	14	27	133
Total	74	71	75	90	80	86	476

During the period 1989-94, which type of car featured a continuous decrease in production?
(a) S (b) Q (c) R (d) T

135. Find the value of $\frac{\cos 65°}{\sin 25°} + \frac{5\sin 19°}{\cos 71°} - \frac{3\cos 28°}{\sin 62°}$.
(a) 2 (b) 0 (c) 1 (d) 3

136. Swastik saves 20% of his income, while spends the remaining amount on food, rent, education and shopping. 15% of the income is spent on food, while ₹12800 is spent on rent, ₹32000 on education and ₹7200 on shopping. The amount spent on shopping is 11.25% of the total expenditure. How much money (in ₹) is spent on food?
(a) 9600 (b) 10800 (c) 12000 (d) 15000

137. Simplify the given expression.

$$\frac{a^2 - b^2 - 2bc - c^2}{a^2 + b^2 + 2ab - c^2}$$

(a) $\frac{a+b+c}{a-b-c}$ (b) $\frac{a-b-c}{a+b-c}$

(c) $\frac{a+b-c}{a-b-c}$ (d) $\frac{a-b+c}{a+b-c}$

138. If the marked price is 75% more than the cost price and a discount of 40% is allowed on the marked price, then the percentage profit is

(a) 6% (b) 7% (c) 8% (d) 5%

139. In what ratio must a shopkeeper mix two types of rice worth ₹55 per kg and ₹70 per kg, so that the average cost of the mixture is ₹65 per kg?

(a) 1 : 2 (b) 2 : 3 (c) 3 : 2 (d) 1 : 3

140. What is the value of the given expression?

$$\frac{1}{12} + \frac{1}{16} + \frac{1}{8}$$

(a) $\frac{13}{48}$ (b) $\frac{10}{72}$ (c) $\frac{3}{48}$ (d) $\frac{13}{18}$

141. For a triangle ABC, D and E are two points on AB and AC such that $AD = \frac{1}{6}AB$, $AE = \frac{1}{6}AC$. If $BC = 22$ cm, then DE is .... (Consider up to two decimals)

(a) 1.33 cm (b) 1.67 cm

(c) 3.67 cm (d) 3.33 cm

142. Reema runs $\frac{5}{4}$ times as fast as Rekha. In view of this Reema allows Rekha a lead of 50 m to Rekha in a friendly race competition. What is the distance from the starting point, where both Reema and Rekha meet?

(a) 250 m (b) 225 m

(c) 200 m (d) 240 m

143. The given table shows marks obtained by four students in four subjects.

Subjects/ Students	Maths (100)	English (100)	Science (100)	Hindi (100)
A	75	80	75	85
B	80	70	70	80
C	70	85	85	75
D	85	75	80	70

The average percentage of marks obtained by all students in Hindi is

(a) 77.0% (b) 77.6%

(c) 77.8% (d) 77.5%

144. If $\cot\theta = \frac{4}{3}, 0 < \theta < \frac{\pi}{2}$ and $5p\cos^2\theta\sin\theta = \cot^2\theta$, then the value of p is

(a) $\frac{7}{27}$ (b) $\frac{125}{27}$ (c) $\frac{5}{27}$ (d) $\frac{25}{27}$

145. Train 'A' requires 15 seconds to cross train 'B' of length 300 m moving in the opposite direction at a speed of 36 km/h. Further, train 'A' requires 30 sec to cross a 500 m long stationary train 'C'. Find the length (in m) of train 'A'.

(a) 200 (b) 300

(c) 250 (d) 275

146. If the difference between the selling prices of an article at profits of 10% and 7% is ₹6, then the cost price (in ₹) of the article is

(a) 175 (b) 150

(c) 200 (d) 100

147. Study the given pie-chart and answer the question that follows.

The pie-chart shows the National Budget Expenditure in the year 2019.

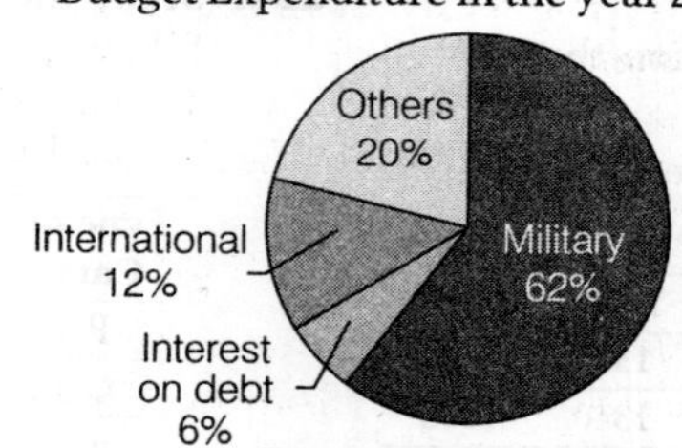

Percentage distribution

If ₹850 billion were spent in year 2019 for interest on debt and military, then what would have been the total expenditure for that year (in ₹ billion)?

(a) 1700 (b) 1300

(c) 1250 (d) 1450

148. John can do a piece of work alone in 20 days, while Ravi can do the same piece of work alone in 28 days. In how many days can the duo complete the same work, if they work together?

(a) $11\frac{1}{3}$ (b) $12\frac{2}{3}$

(c) $11\frac{2}{3}$ (d) $12\frac{1}{3}$

149. At a courier shop, the weights of 8 parcels were found to be 1.5 kg, 1.25 kg, 1.35 kg, 750 gm, 950 gm, 0.7 kg, 0.4 kg and 0.5 kg. Find their average weight.

(a) 875 gm (b) 900 gm

(c) 925 gm (d) 700 gm

150. Study the given pie-chart and answer the question that follows.

The pie-chart shows the percentage of 3600 students enrolled in different hobby classes in a school.

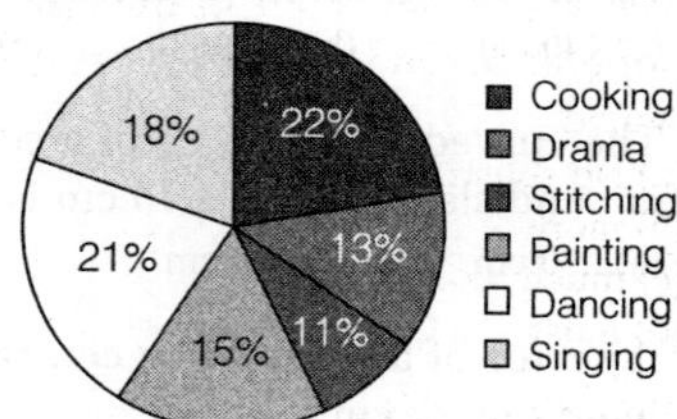

The number of students enrolled in painting classes is approximately what percentage of those enrolled in Singing classes?

(a) 108% (b) 83%

(c) 98% (d) 78%

Part IV

English Comprehension

151. Select the most appropriate option to substitute the underlined segment in the given sentence.

Any sort of unfair conduct is not tolerated in international sports tournaments as it can completely ruin an athlete's career.

(a) straw in the eye

(b) hand in the mud

(c) red handed

(d) foul play

152. Select the most appropriate antonym of the given word.

Placid

(a) Pristine (b) Turbulent

(c) Pensive (d) Destined

153. Select the option that can be used as a one-word substitute for the given group of words.

A person who believes that God does not exist

(a) Hedonistic (b) Fanatic

(c) Epicurean (d) Atheist

154. Select the correct idiom that can substitute the italicised group of words in the given sentence.
He really stinks and smells foul after a hard session at the gym.
(a) an iron will (b) pen and ink
(c) lame excuse (d) an old flame

155. Select the most appropriate option that can substitute the underlined segment in the given sentence. If there is no need to substitute it, select 'No substitution required'.
The Taj Mahal is one of the much popular seven wonders of the world.
(a) No substitution required
(b) more
(c) much more
(d) most

156. Select the correct option to substitute the underlined segment in the given sentence. If no substitution is required, select 'No substitution'.
He is faster than smarter.
(a) faster than being smart
(b) more fast than smart
(c) fast than smart
(d) No substitution

157. Select the most appropriate antonym of the given word.
Rejoinder
(a) Expedite (b) Request
(c) Ordinary (d) Reply

158. Select the most appropriate option that can substitute the underlined segment in the given sentence.
Payal's father was seen desperately searching for the medicine that can counteract the effect of a venomous snakebite in Parul's left hand.
(a) remedy (b) antiseptic
(c) anti-serum (d) antidote

159. Select the option that can be used as a one-word substitute for the given group of words.
The capacity for being useful for some purpose.
(a) Gain (b) Utility
(c) Desirability (d) Aid

160. Parts of the following sentence have been given as options. Select the option that contains an error.
Raman ate the cake and exclaimed that it tasted sweetly.
(a) and exclaimed that
(b) the cake
(c) Raman ate
(d) it tasted sweetly

161. Choose the correct spelling of the underlined word in the given sentence.
He has won the medal for the twelth time.
(a) Twelfth (b) Tweltth
(c) Twwelfth (d) Twellth

162. Identify the sentence that correctly uses the indefinite article.
(a) There are three cars parked outside: an Mercedes, a Jaguar and a Fiat.
(b) There are three cars parked outside: a Mercedes, an Jaguar and a Fiat.
(c) There are three cars parked outside: a Mercedes, a Jaguar and a Fiat.
(d) There are three cars parked outside: a Mercedes, an Jaguar and an Fiat.

163. Select the incorrectly spelt word.
(a) Zenith (b) Merriment
(c) Yearn (d) Miniture

164. Select the most appropriate idiom to fill in the blank.
Choosing not to pursue a degree in computer engineering was ..., as the market for them is extremely limited nowadays.
(a) a cut above
(b) a blessing in disguise
(c) airy fairy
(d) an elevator pitch

165. Select the option that can be used as a one-word substitute for the given group of words.
One who settles in another country
(a) Refugee (b) Traveller
(c) Immigrant (d) Resident

166. Select the most appropriate antonym of the given word.
Asset.
(a) Liability (b) Mole
(c) Refuge (d) Wealth

167. Select the most appropriate antonym of the given word.
Leniency
(a) Sternness (b) Favour
(c) Discard (d) Penalty

168. Select the option that can be used as a one-word substitute for the given group of words.
A keeper or custodian of a museum or other collection.
(a) Curator (b) Calligrapher
(c) Chauffeur (d) Cartographer

169. Select the most appropriate antonym of the given word.
Apathy
(a) Interest (b) Interruption
(c) Ignorance (d) Sincerity

170. Select the correct idiom to replace the underlined segment in the given sentence.
We should ask Emily to join our team. She is as keen as butter.
(a) as keen as a bee
(b) as keen as mustard
(c) as keen as sugar
(d) as keen as salt

171. Select the most appropriate synonym of the 'wordviable' in the given sentence and choose the correct option.
The engineer's design was optimised for efficiency and scalability, with a focus on sustainability.
(a) Scalability (b) Efficiency
(c) Sustainability (d) Optimised

172. Select the most appropriate idiom to fill in the blank.
All my efforts went in vain. The project on which I was working for the last two months has failed and we are ....
(a) back to square one
(b) around the bend
(c) on the fly
(d) all in the seventh heaven

173. Select the most appropriate meaning of the given idiom.
Crack someone up
(a) To make someone laugh
(b) To criticise someone
(c) To make someone angry
(d) To force someone to commit a mistake

174. Choose the most suitable idiom for the given situation.
Ravi has a strong desire to be in college hockey team this year and he is working hard to gain such skills to fulfill his goal of life. He has clearly made up his mind to achieve his target.
(a) To rise to the occasion
(b) Set sights on
(c) To move the goal posts
(d) To make the cut

175. Select the correct idiom to substitute the underlined word segment in the following sentence.

She trusted her husband but he stabbed her in the neck when he usurped her inheritance.

(a) stabbed her in the back
(b) snapped her in the neck
(c) stabbed her with a fork
(d) stabbed her prospects

176. Select the sentence that has a spelling error.

A. The art of living is learnt easily by those who are positive and optimistic.
B. We can learn a lot about the art of living by having a peep into the lives of great men.
C. The daily routines of these great men dissiminate that they are different.
D. Their unique lifestyles help us learn certain habits and practices that they followed.

(a) The art of living is learnt easily by those who are positive and optimistic.
(b) The daily routines of these great men dissiminate that they are different.
(c) Their unique lifestyles help us learn certain habits and practices that they followed.
(d) We can learn a lot about the art of living by having a peep into the lives of great men.

177. Select the most appropriate antonym of the given word.

Denounce

(a) Dainty
(b) Praise
(c) Relieve
(d) Criticise

178. Parts of the following sentence have been given as options. One of them may contain an error. Select the part that contains the error from the given options. If you don't find any error, mark 'No error' as your answer.

You arrived two days ago. By the time you leave, you will have spent nine days here.

(a) you will have spent nine days here
(b) You arrived two days ago
(c) By the time you leave
(d) No error

179. You are preparing a speech for an upcoming function. Select a synonym for the highlighted word to make it better.

Effective public transportation networks may greatly alleviate traffic congestion and enhance inhabitants' quality of life in general.

(a) Amplification (b) Diversion
(c) Laxity (d) Gridlock

180. Select the incorrectly spelt word from the given sentence.

Gandhiji considared untouchability to be one of India's major social ills.

(a) major (b) considared
(c) untouchability (d) social

181. Select the most appropriate antonym of the word 'discordant' in the given sentence and choose the correct option.

The sweet melodious symphony of the piano filled the room, transporting the listeners to a world of beauty and emotion.

(a) Transporting (b) Melodious
(c) Filled (d) Emotion

182. The following sentence has been divided into parts. One of them may contain an error.

Select the part that contains the error from the given options. If you don't find any error, mark 'No error' as your answer.

I wanted to buy a candle holder, / but the store didn't have one. / So, I got a cake.

(a) I wanted to buy a candle holder
(b) but the store didn't have one
(c) No error
(d) So, I got a cake

183. Select the most appropriate idiom to fill in the blank.

I think we should ...... before buying this car.

(a) stop to change horses
(b) eat like a horse
(c) hold our horses
(d) get off our high horse

184. Select the option that can be used as a one-word substitute for the given group of words.

Happening repeatedly

(a) Rapport (b) Recurrent
(c) Recuperate (d) Regression

185. Select the option that can be used as a one-word substitute for the given group of words.

The study of the human mind

(a) Microbiology (b) Anthropology
(c) Psychology (d) Epidemiology

186. Select the most appropriate synonym of the given word.

Captivate

(a) Arrest (b) Study
(c) Allure (d) Envelope

187. Select the option that can be used as a one-word substitute for the given group of words.

Study of science of insects

(a) Entomology (b) Anthropology
(c) Microbiology (d) Ecology

188. Select the incorrectly spelt word.

(a) Noodle (b) Pitza
(c) Pasta (d) Bread

189. The following sentence has been split into four segments. Identify the segment that contains a grammatical error.

A Prime Minister of India / will address / the nation today / on the occasion of Independence Day.

(a) will address
(b) the nation today
(c) A Prime Minister of India
(d) on the occasion of Independence Day

190. Select the most appropriate meaning of the given idiom.

What a small world!

(a) What a beautiful place!
(b) What a coincidence!
(c) The world is great.
(d) The world is a village.

Directions (Q. Nos. 191-195) *In the following passage, some words have been deleted. Read the passage carefully and select the most appropriate option to fill in each blank.*

South Korea is the most cosmetically ...(1)... country on Earth. Beauty editors estimate that it is because of the government's heavy investment ...(2)... industry. It is ahead of its competitors, and its citizens ...(3)... twice as much on skincare products as consumers in the United States, the UK, and France. Korean shoppers are ...(4)... the world's most discerning. Eight out of 10 Korean women in their 20s and 30s use an app that ...(5)... like a cosmetics-specific, to debate the merits of various common ingredients.

191. Select the most appropriate option to fill in blank number (1).
(a) ancient (b) early
(c) advanced (d) primitive

192. Select the most appropriate option to fill in blank number (2).
(a) in the (b) from the
(c) of the (d) by the

193. Select the most appropriate option to fill in blank number (3).
(a) spend (b) propagate
(c) cherish (d) comply

194. Select the most appropriate option to fill in blank number (4).
(a) though (b) perhaps
(c) although (d) maybe

195. Select the most appropriate option to fill in blank number (5).
(a) dissolves (b) functions
(c) malfunctions (d) stops

Directions (Q.Nos. 196-200) *Read the given passage carefully and answer the questions that follow.*

Throughout history, the intricacies of the human mind have been the subject of fascination and inquiry. From ancient philosophers to modern-day neuroscientists, the workings of the brain have been studied and analysed in an attempt to unravel its mysteries. However, despite centuries of research, much remains unknown about the complexities of human cognition and consciousness.

One of the most fascinating aspects of the human mind is its ability to create and imagine.

The human mind has the capacity to conceptualise and bring into being ideas that were previously unknown or unimaginable, from artistic expression to scientific discovery. The process of creativity has captured the attention of scholars and lay people alike and is both enigmatic and awe-inspiring.

There have been many theories proposed to explain the process of creativity. Some suggest that it is a purely subconscious process, while others argue that creativity is a result of conscious effort and intentional problem-solving. Still others suggest that creativity arises from a combination of conscious and subconscious processes.

Despite the ongoing debate over the nature of creativity, one thing is clear: it is a multifaceted and complex phenomenon. Creativity can manifest in a wide range of human activities, from the creation of art and literature to the development of scientific theories and inventions. It can occur in both individual and collective contexts and can be driven by a variety of factors such as curiosity, passion, or the desire for recognition.

Creativity also has the potential to bring about positive change in the world. Throughout history, creative individuals and groups have used their talents to address social, political, and environmental challenges, often inspiring others to take action and make a difference. From the abolitionist movement to the civil rights movement to the environmental movement, creativity has played a crucial role in promoting social justice and positive change.

Despite the many benefits of creativity, it is not without its challenges.

The process of creative expression can be fraught with obstacles, from self-doubt and insecurity to external pressures and constraints. Moreover, not all creative ideas are successful or well-received, and many artists and innovators face rejection and criticism as they seek to bring their ideas to fruition.

Despite these challenges, however, the human drive to create and imagine persists. Individuals and groups continue to harness the power of creativity to make a difference inthe world. From the humblest amateur artist to the most celebrated innovator, the human capacity for creativity remains one of our greatest strengths and sources of inspiration.

196. Select an appropriate title for the passage.
(a) The Role of the Human Mind in Promoting Positive Change
(b) The Power of Creativity
(c) The History of the Human Mind
(d) The Complexities of Human Cognition

197. According to the passage, what is one of the challenges of creative expression?
(a) The over emphasis on conscious problem-solving.
(b) The lack of appreciation for creative ideas.
(c) The limited capacity of the human mind.
(d) The absence of external pressures and constraints.

198. What is the main focus of the passage?
(a) The mysteries of the human mind.
(b) The nature of creativity, its benefits and challenges.
(c) The complexities and challenges of cognitive processes.
(d) The nature of fancy and imagination.

199. Select the most appropriate antonym for the word 'fraught.'
(a) Beset (b) Tranquil
(c) Devoid (d) Calm

200. Which of the following factors can drive creativity?
(a) External pressures and constraints
(b) Fancy and imagination
(c) Self-doubt and insecurity
(d) Curiosity and passion

Know Correct Answers

1. (d)	2. (b)	3. (c)	4. (a)	5. (d)	6. (d)	7. (b)	8. (a)	9. (c)	10. (b)
11. (a)	12. (d)	13. (d)	14. (c)	15. (d)	16. (a)	17. (b)	18. (c)	19. (a)	20. (c)
21. (c)	22. (c)	23. (c)	24. (a)	25. (b)	26. (d)	27. (d)	28. (a)	29. (c)	30. (a)
31. (c)	32. (d)	33. (c)	34. (b)	35. (b)	36. (c)	37. (a)	38. (a)	39. (c)	40. (c)
41. (a)	42. (c)	43. (b)	44. (d)	45. (d)	46. (c)	47. (c)	48. (a)	49. (d)	50. (b)
51. (a)	52. (a)	53. (d)	54. (c)	55. (a)	56. (b)	57. (c)	58. (c)	59. (c)	60. (b)
61. (d)	62. (a)	63. (c)	64. (d)	65. (d)	66. (b)	67. (d)	68. (a)	69. (a)	70. (d)
71. (c)	72. (d)	73. (b)	74. (a)	75. (b)	76. (d)	77. (a)	78. (d)	79. (b)	80. (c)
81. (a)	82. (b)	83. (c)	84. (a)	85. (d)	86. (d)	87. (c)	88. (d)	89. (a)	90. (a)
91. (c)	92. (b)	93. (a)	94. (c)	95. (b)	96. (a)	97. (c)	98. (d)	99. (d)	100. (c)
101. (b)	102. (c)	103. (c)	104. (d)	105. (a)	106. (c)	107. (a)	108. (c)	109. (a)	110. (d)
111. (c)	112. (c)	113. (c)	114. (b)	115. (b)	116. (b)	117. (d)	118. (a)	119. (a)	120. (d)
121. (d)	122. (d)	123. (d)	124. (c)	125. (a)	126. (a)	127 (b)	128. (a)	129. (a)	130. (b)
131. (b)	132. (c)	133. (c)	134. (c)	135. (d)	136. (c)	137 (b)	138. (d)	139. (a)	140. (a)
141. (c)	142. (a)	143. (d)	144. (d)	145. (a)	146. (c)	147. (c)	148. (c)	149. (c)	150. (b)
151. (d)	152. (b)	153. (d)	154. (b)	155. (d)	156. (b)	157. (b)	158 (d)	159. (b)	160. (d)
161. (a)	162. (c)	163. (d)	164. (b)	165. (c)	166. (a)	167. (a)	168. (a)	169. (a)	170. (b)
171. (c)	172. (a)	173. (a)	174. (b)	175. (a)	176. (b)	177. (b)	178. (d)	179. (d)	180. (b)
181. (b)	182. (c)	183. (c)	184. (b)	185. (c)	186. (c)	187. (a)	188. (b)	189. (c)	190. (b)
191. (c)	192. (a)	193. (a)	194. (b)	195. (b)	196. (b)	197. (b)	198. (b)	199. (c)	200. (b)

Answer & Solutions

1. (d) Pattern of the series is as follows,

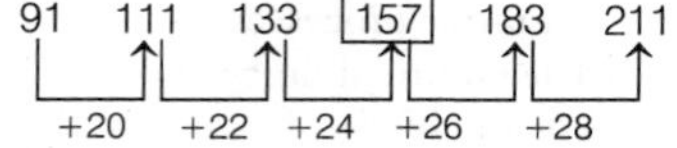

2. (b) As per the given statements,

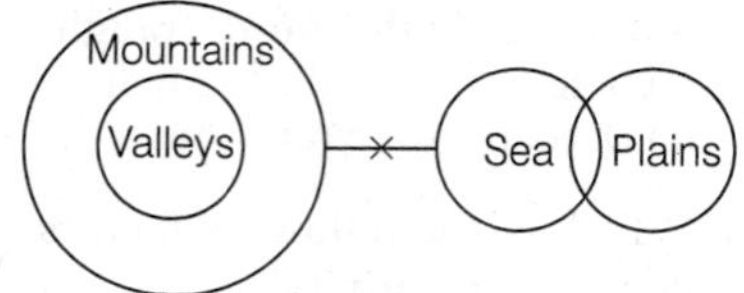

Conclusions

I. (✗) II. (✗) III. (✓)

So, only Conclusion III follows.

3. (c) As, $(25, 3, 150) \Rightarrow 25 \times 3 \xrightarrow{\times 2} 150$

and $(13, 7, 182) \Rightarrow 13 \times 7 \xrightarrow{\times 2} 182$

Similarly $(10, 5, 100) \Rightarrow 10 \times 5 \xrightarrow{\times 2} 100$

4. (a) When the mirror is placed at the line MN, it look like as option **(a)**.

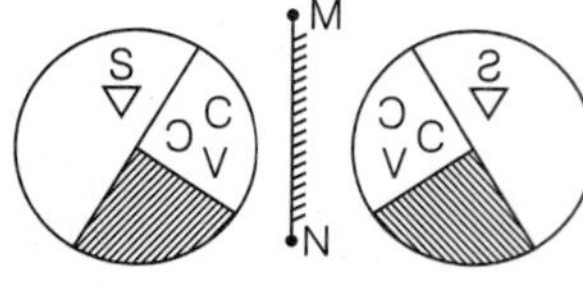

5. (d) As,

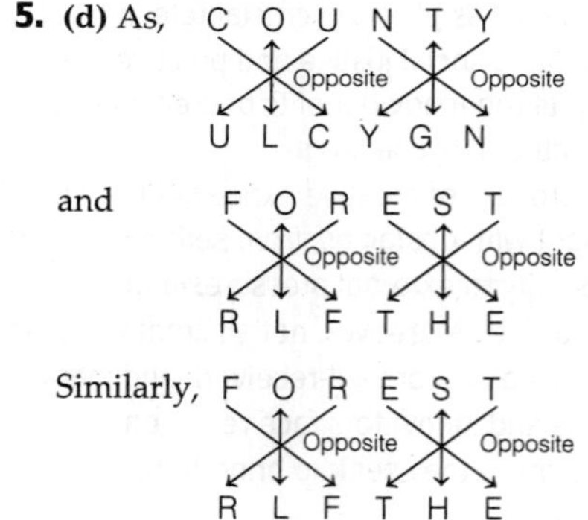

6. (d) According to the question,

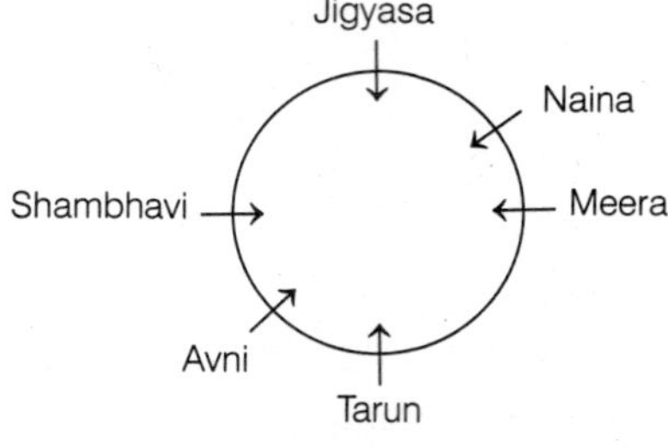

∴ Shambhavi is sitting third to the right of Meera.

7. (b) According to the question,

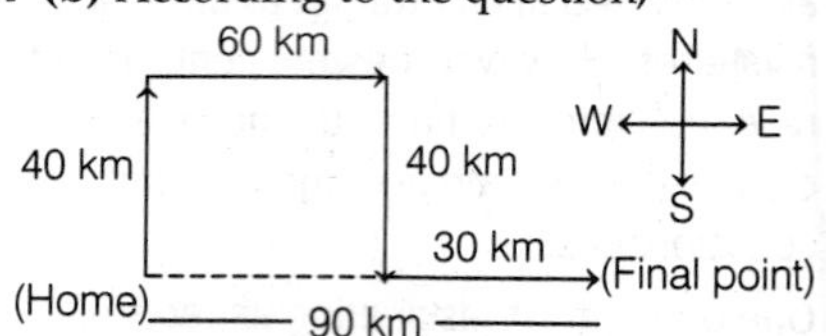

So, she is 90 km from her home.

8. (a) Given, $(75 + 15) \times 27 \times 1 - 9 \div 7 \times (135 + 3) - 10 \div (189 + 63) = 434$

On interchanging + and ÷

$(75 \div 15) \times 27 \times 1 - 9 + 7 \times (135 \div 3) - 10 + (189 \div 63) = 434$

$\Rightarrow (5 \times 27 \times 1) - 9 + 7 \times 45 - 10 + 3 = 434$

$\Rightarrow 135 - 9 + 315 - 10 + 3 = 434$

$\Rightarrow 453 - 19 = 434 \Rightarrow 434 = 434$

9. (c) Venn diagram of the given words is

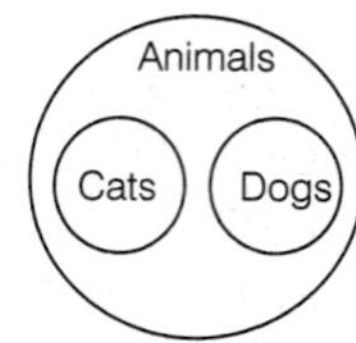

All cats and dogs are animals but cats and dogs are different from each other.

10. (b) When paper is unfolded it look like as option **(b)**.

11. (a) From the Dice I and II, 3 and 6 are common. So, number '2' on the opposite face of '5'.

12. (d) As,

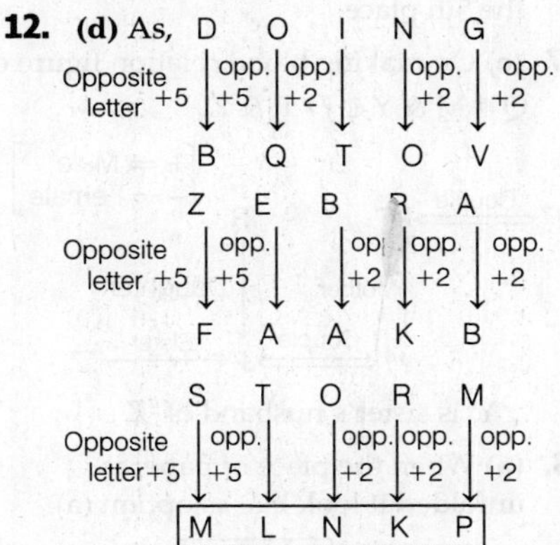

13. (d) As per the given statements,

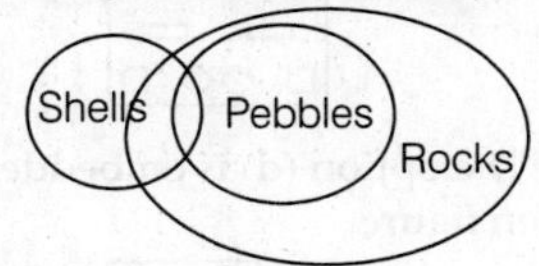

Conclusions I. (✗) II. (✓)

So, only Conclusion II follows.

14. (c) The given figure is embedded in option **(c)**.

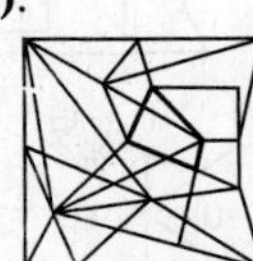

15. (d) The element of the given series moves in anticlockwise wise direction. So, the next term of the series is as option (d).

16. (a) The arrangement of the given words as per the english dictionary is as follows.

Foreign → Forest → Forge →
(2) (3) (5)

Forgotten → Forlorn → Formal
(4) (6) (1)

⇒ 2, 3,. 5, 4, 6, 1

17. (b) Given, 13 B 7 A 64 D 4 C 23 = ?

A ⇒ +, B ⇒ ×, C ⇒ –, and D ⇒ ÷

? = 13 × 7 + 64 ÷ 4 – 23

using VBODMAS rule,

⇒ ? = 91 + 16 – 23 = 107 – 23

∴ ? = 84

18. (c) The correct order of the letter series is as follows;

A K L D F / A K L D F / A K L D F

⇒ KLALDKDF

19. (a) When the mirror is placed at MN it look like as option (a).

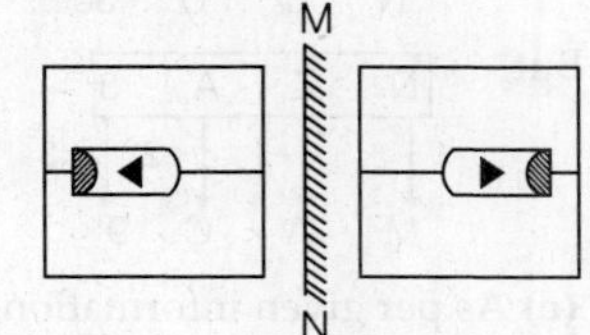

20. (c) As per the given statements,

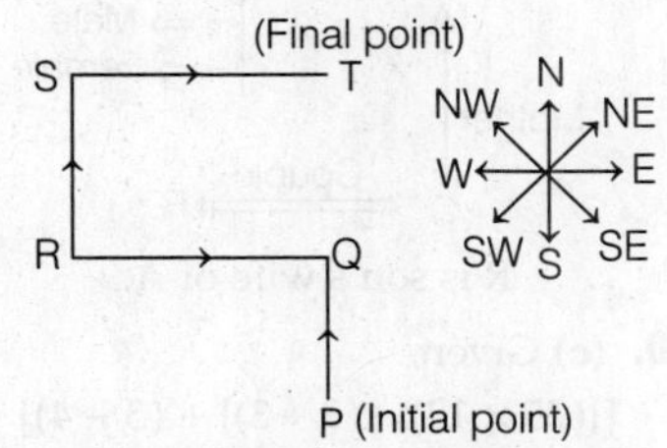

So, the 'Town T' is North-East of 'Town R'.

21. (c) As,

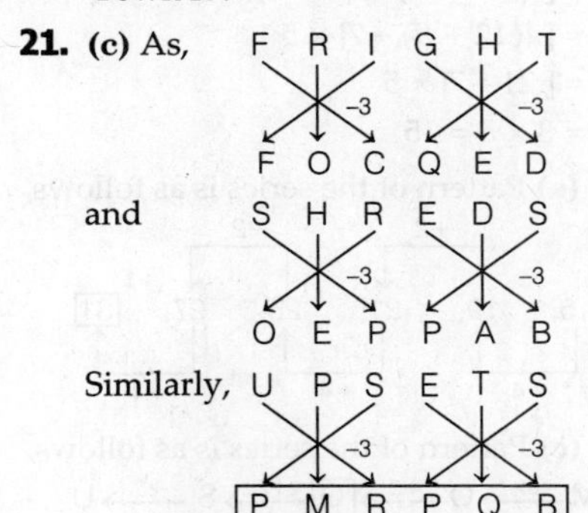

22. (c) When the paper is unfolded it look like as option (c).

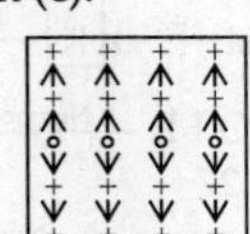

23. (c) As, (11, 33, 17)

⇒ 33 – (11 + 17) = 5

and (18, 44, 21)

⇒ 44 – (18 + 21) = 5

Similarly, (16, 43, 22)

⇒ 43 – (16 + 22) = 5

24. (a) Pattern of the series is as follows,

90 110 132 [156] 182

+20 +22 +24 +26

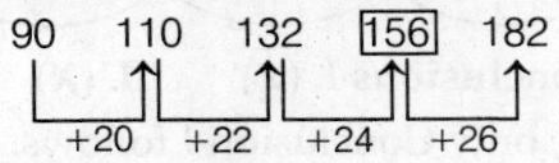

25. (b) As, (13, 104, 16)

⇒ $13 \times \frac{16}{2} = 104$

and (9, 63, 14) ⇒ $9 \times \frac{14}{2} = 63$

Similarly, (8, 60, 15) ⇒ $8 \times \frac{15}{2} = 60$

26. (d) Pattern of the series is as follows,

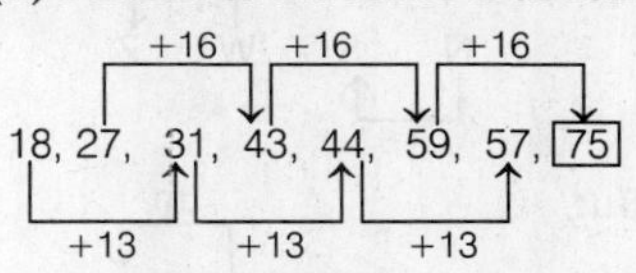

27. (d) Pattern of the series is as follows,

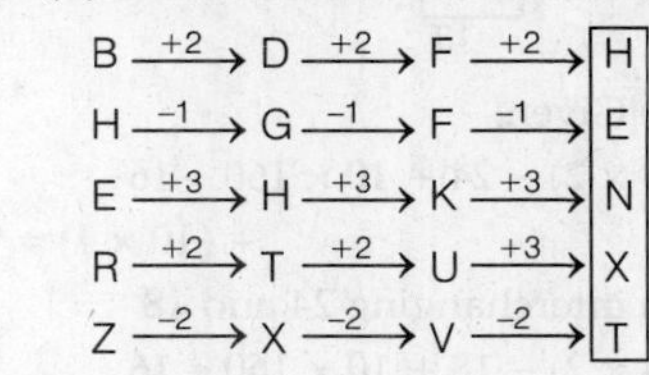

28. (a) As, nun-lives in the convent. Similarly, king lives in the palace.

29. (c) The correct order of the given words as per english dictionary order is as follows;

Aureole → Auspicious → Authentic →
(5) (4) (3)

Authority → Automate
(1) (2)

⇒ 5, 4, 3, 1, 2

30. (a) According to the given information,

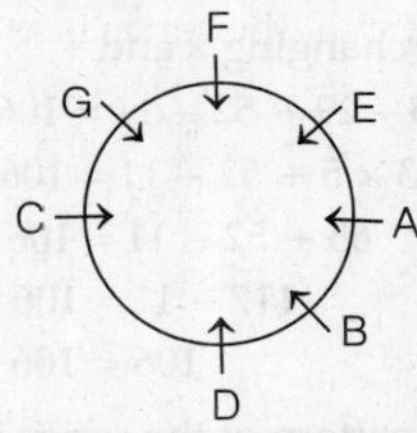

∴ When counted from the right side of A, the position of G is third to the right of A.

31. (c) As,

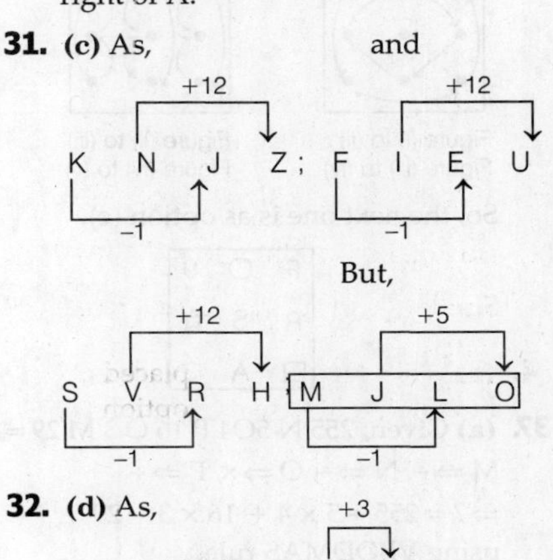

32. (d) As,

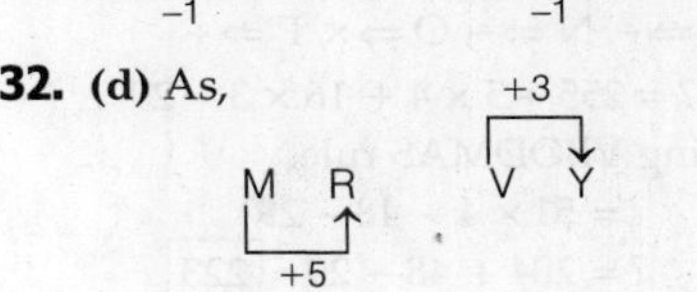

and

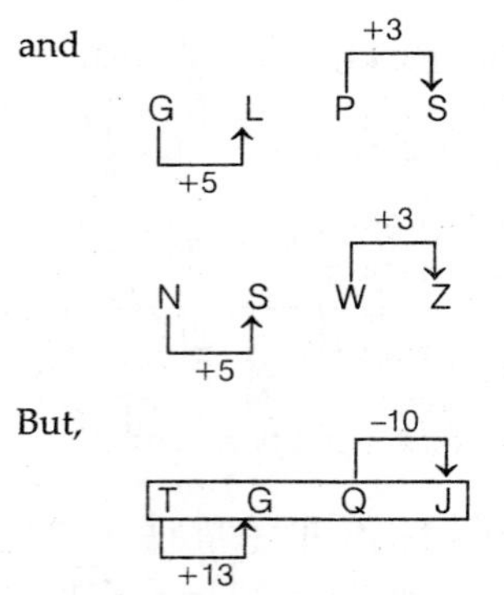

33. **(c)** Given,

$(18 \times 2) - 24 + 10 \times 160 \div 16 + (10 \times 4) = 170$

On interchanging 24 and 18

$(24 \times 2) - 18 + 10 \times 160 \div 16 + (10 \times 4) = 170$

$\Rightarrow 48 - 18 + 100 + 40 = 170$

$\Rightarrow \quad 188 - 18 = 170$

$\Rightarrow \quad 170 = 170$

34. **(b)** As, $(15, 21, 66) \Rightarrow \dfrac{66-21}{3} = 15$

and $(9, 17, 44) \Rightarrow \dfrac{44-17}{3} = 9$

Similarly, $(5, 37, 52) \Rightarrow \dfrac{52-37}{3} = 5$

35. **(b)** Given,

$13 + 145 \div 29 \times 52 - 11 = 106$

On interchanging $\times$ and $+$,

$13 \times 145 \div 29 + 52 - 11 = 106$

$\Rightarrow \quad 13 \times 5 + 52 - 11 = 106$

$\Rightarrow \quad 65 + 52 - 11 = 106$

$\Rightarrow \quad 117 - 11 = 106$

$\Rightarrow \quad 106 = 106$

36. **(c)** The pattern of the series is as follows.

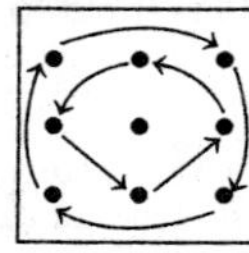

Figure (i) to (ii)
Figure (iii) to (iv)

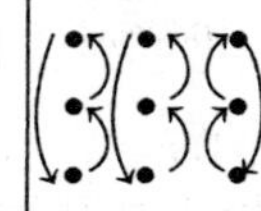

Figure (ii) to (iii)
Figure (iv) to (v)

So, the next one is as option (c).

F	O	9
R	S	☆
□	A	3

37. **(a)** Given, 255 N 504 P 16 O 3 M 29 = ?

M ⇒ −, N ⇒ ÷, O ⇒ ×, P ⇒ +

$\Rightarrow ? = 255 \div 5 \times 4 + 16 \times 3 - 29$

using VBODMAS rule,

$\Rightarrow \quad ? = 51 \times 4 + 48 - 29$

$\Rightarrow \quad ? = 204 + 48 - 29 = \boxed{223}$

38. **(a)** As, P R O 5 → (−1, +1, +2, ×3) → O S Q 15

and O P O 10 → (−1, +1, +2, ×3) → N Q Q 30

But, N Z A 3 → (−1, +1, +2, ×3) → M A C 9

39. **(c)** As per given information, on making blood relation figure of A $ C @ R,

A⁻ ↑ Mother — C⁺ ⟺ (Couple) R⁻

[+ ⇒ Male, − ⇒ Female]

∴ R is son's wife of A.

40. **(c)** Given,

$[\{(25 \times 13) - (3 \div 3)\} + (3 - 4)] \div 5$

$+ \Rightarrow \div, - \Rightarrow +, \times \Rightarrow -, \div \Rightarrow \times$

$= [\{(25 - 13) + (3 \times 3)\} \div (3 + 4)] \times 5$

$= [\{(12 + 9) \div 7\}] \times 5$

$= [21 \div 7] \times 5$

$= 3 \times 5 = 15$

41. **(a)** Pattern of the series is as follows,

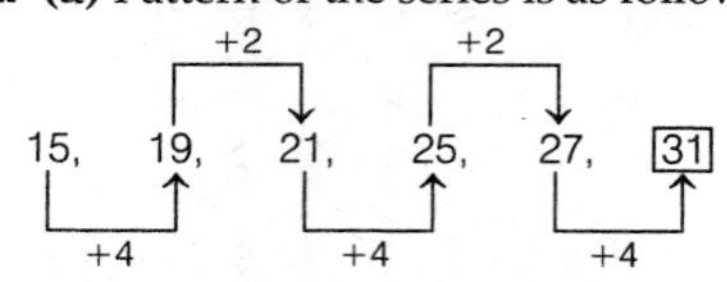

42. **(c)** Pattern of the series is as follows,

M —+2→ O —+2→ **Q** —+2→ S —+2→ U

M —−2→ K —−2→ **I** —−2→ G —−2→ E

N —+2→ P —+2→ **R** —+2→ T —+2→ V

O —−2→ M —−2→ **K** —−2→ I —−2→ G

43. **(b)** As, O I L —Number of letters→ 3

$\Rightarrow 3^3 = 27$

and C R E A M —Number of letters→ 5

$\Rightarrow 5^3 = 125$

Similarly,

P O W D E R —Number of letters→ 6

$\Rightarrow 6^3 = 216$

44. **(d)** As per the given statements,

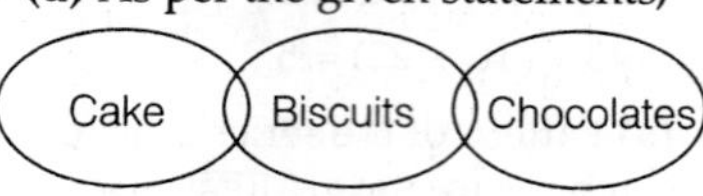

Conclusions I. (✓) II. (✗)

So, only Conclusion I follows.

45. **(d)** Given,

(35 I 5) J 9 K 23 L 39 K (3 J 8) = ?

I ⇒ ÷, J ⇒ ×, K ⇒ −, L ⇒ +

$(35 \div 5) \times 9 - 23 + 39 - (3 \times 8) = ?$

$\Rightarrow ? = (7 \times 9) - 23 + 39 - 24$

$\Rightarrow ? = 63 - 23 + 39 - 24$

$\Rightarrow ? = 102 - 47 = 55$

46. **(c)** In each next figure of the given figure series, the first triangle remains at its place and the other two triangles move 135° clockwise. Thus, in the series the figure of option (c) will be at the 5th place.

47. **(c)** On making blood relation figure of Q @ M & Y @ J # R & Z,

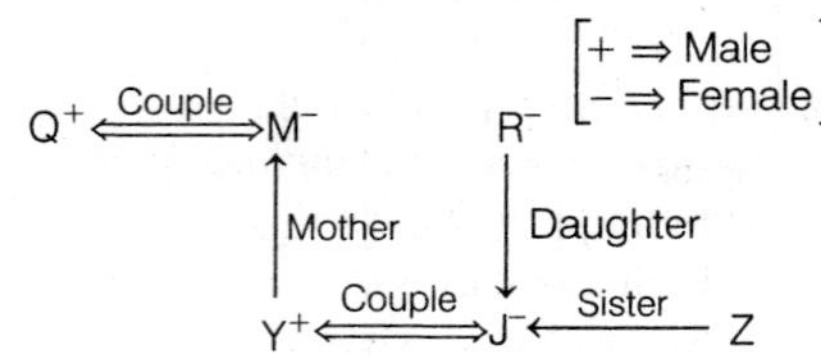

∴ 'Y' is sister's husband of 'Z'.

48. **(a)** When the piece of paper is unfolded it look like as option (a).

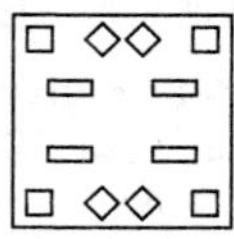

49. **(d)** The option (d) is embedded in the given figure.

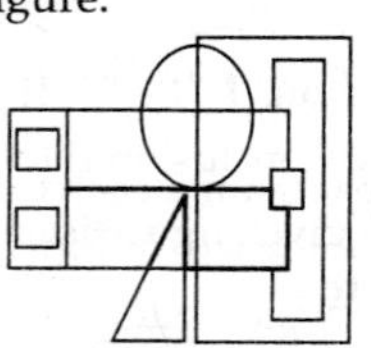

50. **(b)** As,

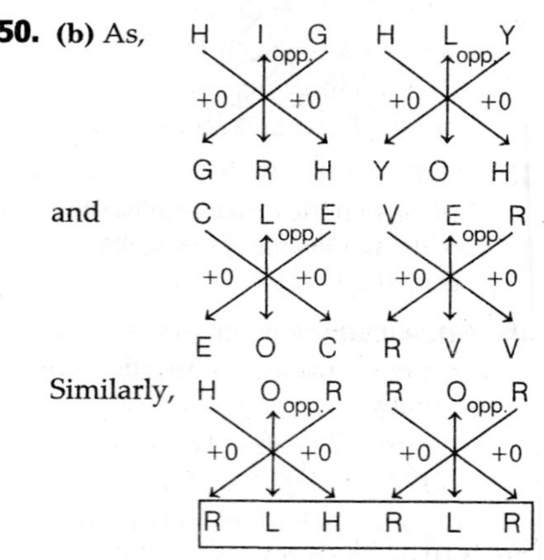

51. **(a)** In India, pipelines are considered the most efficient mode of transportation for petroleum and natural gas.

- They reduce trans-shipment losses (losses during unloading/loading at multiple stages) and help in timely delivery of fuel over long distances.

- Pipelines are also cost-effective, safe and environment-friendly compared to conventional modes like roadways or railways.

Knowledge Booster
- India has major pipelines like the Haldia-Jagdishpur pipeline and the Mumbai High-Hazira-Vijaipur (HVJ) pipeline.
- Pipelines are not just used for petroleum but also for natural gas, water and even milk in some industries.

52. **(a)** The concept of Martial Law is borrowed from the United Kingdom.
- In India, Article 34 allows Parliament to restrict Fundamental Rights during Martial Law.
- It empowers the state to take control through military authority when civil administration fails to function properly.

Knowledge Booster
- Martial Law is not defined in the Constitution but has historical usage in colonial India.
- The Jallianwala Bagh Massacre (1919) happened under Martial Law imposed by the British.

53. **(d)** Copacabana Beach is located in Brazil, in the city of Rio de Janeiro.
- It is one of the most iconic beaches globally, famous for its vibrant culture and scenic beauty.
- It is a popular venue for New Year's Eve celebrations, attracting millions of visitors.
- Copacabana also gained fame during the 2016 Rio Olympics, hosting beach volleyball events.

Knowledge Booster
- Copacabana is a symbol of Brazil's tourism, offering a blend of leisure, sports and cultural events year-round.

54. **(c)** The Electrolytic Refining method is the most widely used technique for purifying impure metals.
- It involves the use of an electrolyte solution and electric current to transfer pure metal onto the cathode.
- Impure metal is made the anode, while a thin sheet of the same pure metal acts as the cathode.
- This method is particularly useful for refining copper, zinc, silver and gold.
- It ensures a high degree of purity, making it ideal for industrial applications.

Knowledge Booster
- Electrolytic refining gives 99.9% purity and is crucial in producing metals for electrical and electronic use.

55. **(a)** The Joule is the standard SI unit of work and energy.
- Work is said to be done when a force of 1 Newton moves an object 1 metre in the direction of the force.
- Work = Force × Displacement
$\Rightarrow$ 1 Joule = 1 Newton × 1 metre.

Knowledge Booster
- 1 Kilo Joule (kJ) = 1000 Joules;
- Joule is a derived unit named after James Prescott Joule, a physicist who studied the relationship between heat and mechanical work.

56. **(b)** Rural Cooperatives were the earliest form of microfinance institutions established in India, even before independence.
- These cooperatives aimed to provide credit and financial services to rural farmers and small-scale producers.
- They were regulated under the Cooperative Societies Act of 1904, Now Rural cooperatives are regulated under both
  - State Cooperative Societies Acts (for those operating within a state)
  - Multi-State Cooperative Societies Act, 2002 (for those operating across states)
- The cooperatives played a key role in inclusive rural financial access and poverty alleviation.

57. **(c)** 'The Race of My Life' is the autobiography of Milkha Singh .
- It captures his journey from Partition struggles to becoming a world-class sprinter.
- It narrates his inspiring journey from a Partition survivor to being called 'The Flying Sikh'.
- Some of the important books by famous personalities are- 'Unbreakable' is the autobiography of Mary Kom, 'A Century is Not Enough' is written by Sourav Ganguly.

Knowledge Booster
- Milkha Singh won gold medals in the 1958 Asian Games (400m, 200m) and the 1958 Commonwealth Games.
- He missed the bronze medal in the 1960 Rome Olympics by just 0.1 sec

58. **(c)** Citizenship through acquisition of property is not a mode of acquiring Indian citizenship and they are given below
- The Constitution and Citizenship Act of 1955 recognise five legal methods for acquiring Indian citizenship and they are given below.
  - **By Birth** Person born in India under specific conditions (based on date of birth and parents' citizenship).
  - **By Descent** Person born outside India to at least one Indian parent, subject to certain rules.
  - **By Registration** Person of Indian origin or spouse of Indian citizen who has stayed in India for 7 yr.
  - **By Naturalisation** Foreigners residing in India for 12 yr (with specific conditions) can apply.
  - **By Incorporation of Territory** Citizens of a territory that becomes part of India automatically become citizens (e.g., Sikkim).

Knowledge Booster
- Articles 5 to 11 of the Indian Constitution and the Citizenship Act, 1955 govern the rules for Indian citizenship.

59. **(c)** Dennis Gabor, a British-Hungarian physicist, developed the Principle of Holography in 1947.
- Holography is a photographic technique that records light scattered from an object and presents it in three dimensions.
- His invention aimed to enhance the resolution of electron microscopes.
- The full potential of holography was realised only after the invention of the laser in the 1960s.

Knowledge Booster
- Gabor was awarded the Nobel Prize in Physics (1971) for his work on holography.

60. **(b)** The Tripartite Struggle was a prolonged conflict in early medieval India for the control of Kannauj, a strategically important city.

- The three main powers involved were the Gurjara Pratiharas (North India), the Palas (Eastern India), and the Rashtrakutas (South India).
- The struggle began in the 8th century and continued into the 10th century.
- The region of Kannauj was prized for its political and commercial significance.
- Eventually, the Gurjara Pratiharas gained temporary control over Kannauj.

Knowledge Booster
- The 'Tripartite Struggle' is also known as the Kannauj Triangle War because of the three dynasties contesting for the same region.
- Kannauj was symbolically important as a seat of imperial power, especially after Harshavardhana's rule.

61. **(d)** Salman Rushdie is the author of the novel 'The Moor's Last Sigh'.

- Published in 1995, the novel explores themes of politics, religion and family across generations in India.
- The book received international acclaim and was shortlisted for the Booker Prize.

62. **(a)** Manipuri dance is the classical dance form based on the Rasleela themes of Radha and Krishna.

- Originates from Manipur, a state in North-Eastern India.
- It is deeply rooted in Vaishnavism, emphasising devotion (bhakti) to Lord Krishna.
- Performances often depict scenes from the life of Krishna, especially his divine love for Radha.

63. **(c)** Brihadratha was the last ruler of the Mauryan dynasty.

- He was killed by his Commander-in-Chief, Pushyamitra Shunga.
- This incident happened around 185 BCE, leading to dynastic change.
- Pushyamitra Shunga established the Shunga dynasty after his assassination.

64. **(d)** Habeas Corpus means 'to have the body' in Latin.

- It is issued by courts when a person is unlawfully arrested or detained.
- It protects the fundamental right to personal liberty under Articles 32 and 226.
- The detained person must be presented before a court within 24 hours to justify the legality of the detention.

Knowledge Booster
- Habeas Corpus is called the 'bulwark of individual freedom' against arbitrary state action.

65. **(d)** MN Roy founded the Communist Party of India in Tashkent in 1920.

- It was the first expatriate communist movement by an Indian.
- This laid the ideological base for communism in India during the freedom struggle.
- India officially recognised the Communist Party of India (CPI) in 1925 at Kanpur, following MN Roy's overseas initiative.

66. **(b)** In bryophytes and pteridophytes, male gametes are motile and require water for fertilisation.

- This process is known as zoidogamy.
- The water medium allows male gametes to reach the female gamete.
- Bryophytes and pteridophytes are often called the 'amphibians of the plant kingdom' due to their dependence on water for reproduction.

67. **(d)** According to the 2011 Census, Lakshadweep had the highest male literacy rate among Union Territories.

- The male literacy rate was around 96.11%.
- Smaller population size and better education initiatives contributed to this.
- It surpassed other UTs like Daman and Diu and Delhi.

68. **(a)** Pandit Ravi Shankar was an iconic Indian musician known for playing the sitar.

- He introduced Indian classical music to the Western world.
- Honoured with India's highest civilian award, the Bharat Ratna, in 1999.

Knowledge Booster
- Ravi Shankar performed at legendary venues like Woodstock and helped create global interest in Indian classical instruments.

69. **(a)** According to the 2011 Census, Mumbai is the most populated metropolitan city in India.

- It had a population of approximately 1.84 crores (18.4 million).
- Mumbai is the financial capital of India and a major urban centre.
- It has the highest population density among metro cities.
- According to the 2011 Census of India, the three most populous cities were Mumbai (12,442,373), Delhi (11,034,555) and Kolkata (4,486,679).

70. **(d)** Ker and Garia Puja are major tribal festivals celebrated in Tripura.

- These festivals are associated with the Tripuri tribes.
- Ker Puja is a protective festival invoking the guardian deity Ker for welfare.
- Garia Puja is celebrated during April to pray for a good harvest and prosperity.

Knowledge Booster
- Garia dance and traditional instruments like Khamb and Sumui are used during these festivals, highlighting Tripura's vibrant tribal culture.

71. **(c)** The Hazira-Vijaipur-Jagdishpur (HVJ) pipeline is India's first major natural gas pipeline.

- The construction, operation and maintenance were entrusted to Gas Authority of India Limited (GAIL).
- It was commissioned in 1987 to transport gas from Hazira (Gujarat) to Uttar Pradesh.
- It plays a vital role in supplying natural gas to fertiliser and power plants.

72. **(d)** Mawsynram is located in the Khasi Hills of Meghalaya.

- It receives an average annual rainfall of over 11,000 mm, making it the wettest place on Earth.

- The orographic effect causes the moisture-laden winds from the Bay of Bengal to release heavy rain.
- It surpasses Cherrapunji in average annual rainfall.

Knowledge Booster
- Mawsynram villagers use grass-covered huts to reduce the thunder's sound from the constant rain.
- Despite such rainfall, the region faces drinking water issues due to lack of proper storage infrastructure.

73. **(b)** Paramahansa Mandali was formed in 1849 in Poona and Satara, Maharashtra.
- It aimed to reform Hinduism by promoting monotheism and social equality.
- Encouraged inter-caste dining and women's education.
- The founders were inspired by Raja Ram Mohan Roy, though they operated independently.
- It was among the first reformist movements in Western India before Arya Samaj and Brahmo Samaj gained popularity.

74. **(a)** In 1784, Henry Cavendish discovered that water is formed by the reaction of hydrogen and oxygen.
- His experiments confirmed that water is a chemical compound, not an element.
- He was one of the earliest scientists to use quantitative methods in chemistry.
- This discovery was foundational to modern chemical understanding.

75. **(b)** Trees belong to the top vertical strata in the forest structure.
- Forests are vertically divided into layers or strata based on vegetation height.
- The top vertical typically includes canopy trees and tall emergents.
- This layer receives the maximum sunlight and plays a key role in photosynthesis.
- The stratification of forests helps in better biodiversity and niche separation.

76. **(d)** Fundamental Duties were added by the 42nd Constitutional Amendment Act, 1976.
- These were based on the recommendations of the Sardar Swaran Singh Committee.
- A total of 10 duties were initially added to Part IV-A of the Constitution.
- One more duty was added later by the 86th Amendment in 2002.

Knowledge Booster
- Fundamental Duties are non-justiciable– they can't be enforced by courts but are morally obligatory.
- India borrowed the idea of Fundamental Duties from the USSR (now Russia).

77. **(a)** The correct formula for moment of inertia is: $I = mr^2$.
- Here, I = moment of inertia, m = mass, r = distance from axis of rotation.
- It is a measure of a body's resistance to angular acceleration.
- This is crucial in rotational mechanics, like in gears or flywheels.
- Moment of inertia is often called the rotational analog of mass.

78. **(d)** Article 75 of the Constitution governs the relationship between the Prime Minister and the President.
- It states that the President appoints the Prime Minister and other ministers are appointed on the advice of the PM.
- The Council of Ministers is collectively responsible to the Lok Sabha.
- The President can act only on the aid and advice of the Council of Ministers (Article 74).

Knowledge Booster
- The real executive power lies with the Prime Minister (real head) and Council of Ministers, not the President (nominal head).
- This structure is inspired by the Westminster model of parliamentary democracy.

79. **(b)** India ranked 48th in the Tokyo Olympics 2020 held in 2021 due to the pandemic.
- It was India's best-ever performance in Olympic history.
- India won a total of 7 medals — 1 gold, 2 silver and 4 bronze.
- The gold medal was won by Neeraj Chopra in Javelin Throw.

Knowledge Booster
- Neeraj Chopra became the first Indian to win an Olympic gold in athletics.
- In 2024 Paris Olympic, Neeraj Chopra won a silver medal.
- India's rank was 71st in Paris Olympic 2024.

80. **(c)** The All India Muslim League was founded in 1906 in Dhaka.
- The Muslim League's formation came after the Partition of Bengal (1905), which increased communal tensions.
- It was formed to safeguard the rights of Muslims in British India.
- Key founders included Nawab Salimullah, Aga Khan and Nawab Mohsin-ul-Mulk.
- It later played a pivotal role in the creation of Pakistan in 1947.

81. **(a)** The Chambal, Hindon and Tons rivers are all tributaries of the Yamuna River.
- Yamuna is the largest tributary of the Ganga River.
- The Tons River is the largest tributary of the Yamuna by volume.
- These rivers originate from the Vindhyan and Himalayan ranges.

Knowledge Booster
- A mnemonic to remember the major tributaries of the Yamuna River is 'Silly People Make Hasty Actions To' representing Sarasvati, Panchganga, Markanda, Hindon, Assan and Ton.

82. **(b)** Prabhat Sarma, a renowned musician from Assam, was a flute player.
- He was a recipient of the Sangeet Natak Akademi Award for his contribution to Indian classical music.
- He played a key role in preserving Assamese folk music and traditions.
- His work is celebrated in both the classical and regional music scenes.

83. **(c)** Mehrangarh Fort is located in Jodhpur, Rajasthan.

- Built in the 15th century by Rao Jodha, the founder of Jodhpur.
- It is one of the largest forts in India, situated 400 feet above the city.
- Known for its massive walls, intricate carvings and museum collection.

84. **(a)** In field hockey, when a player is shown a yellow card, they are suspended for 5 minutes.

- It is a temporary suspension given for serious offenses like rough play.
- The player must leave the field immediately and cannot be substituted.
- Repeated offenses can lead to a red card (permanent expulsion).

Knowledge Booster

- A green card in hockey means a 2-minute suspension, often for minor infractions.
- Yellow cards can escalate to red cards depending on the severity of the foul.

85. **(d)** Trade liberalisation has helped India improve its comparative advantage in medium-to-high technology industries.

- Comparative advantage allows a country to specialise in production where it has efficiency over others.
- This policy shift began post 1991 economic reforms.
- It led to an increase in exports of IT, pharmaceuticals and auto components.

86. **(d)** The Fifth Five-Year Plan (1974–79) gave top priority to the removal of poverty for the first time.

- The Fifth Plan emphasised self-reliance and social justice.
- The slogan 'Garibi Hatao' was popularised during this plan by Prime Minister Indira Gandhi.
- It focused on employment generation and poverty alleviation.
- The plan was later terminated early in 1978 by the Janata Party government.

87. **(c)** Thiamine (Vitamin B1) was the first B vitamin discovered in 1897.

- It plays a vital role in carbohydrate metabolism and energy production.
- Thiamine deficiency causes beri-beri, affecting the nervous and cardiovascular systems.
- It is essential for the metabolism of amino acids and sugars.

88. (d) The described festival is the Surajkund Mela, held in Faridabad, Haryana.

- It showcases traditional artisans, craftsmen and performers from across India.
- Organised every February, it promotes folk art, music and heritage.
- The mela is a major platform for cultural exchange and tourism.

89. **(a)** The 12th Five-Year Plan spanned from 2012 to 2017.

- It focused on 'Faster, More Inclusive and Sustainable Growth'.
- Emphasis was placed on health, education, infrastructure and environmental sustainability.
- It was the last official Five-Year Plan before the NITI Aayog replaced the Planning Commission.

Knowledge Booster

- The Planning Commission was abolished in 2015 and replaced by NITI Aayog.
- The Five-Year Plans were adopted from the Soviet model of planned economy.

90. **(a)** Manisha Kalyan is a professional footballer from India.

- She plays as a midfielder/forward and represents the Indian Women's National Football Team.
- Manisha became the first Indian woman to play in the UEFA Women's Champions League.

Knowledge Booster

- In 2021, Manisha scored a goal against Brazil, becoming the first Indian woman to do so.
- She won the AIFF Women's Emerging Footballer of the Year award in 2020–21.

91. **(c)** As per Article 156(3) of the Constitution, a Governor continues to hold office even after the expiry of term until his/her successor assumes charge.

- The Governor is appointed for a term of five years, but can remain longer if a successor is not appointed.
- The provision ensures continuity in constitutional functioning at the state level.
- This clause avoids an administrative vacuum in the state.

92. **(b)** Fiscal deficit = Primary deficit + Interest payments.

- Given Primary deficit = ₹ 6900 crore, Interest payment
  = ₹ 400 crore
- Thus, Fiscal Deficit
  = ₹ 6900 + ₹ 400
  = ₹ 7300 crore
- Fiscal deficit represents the total borrowing requirement of the government.

93. **(a)** The Diwan-i-Insha was responsible for state correspondence and royal communications in medieval India.

- It managed letters, farmans (royal orders) and official records of the court.
- The head of this office was called Insha-i-Mumalik.
- It was a vital part of administrative machinery under the Delhi Sultanate and Mughals.

Knowledge Booster

- The office ensured proper archival and communication protocols in the empire.
- It worked closely with the Diwan-i-Arz (Military) and Diwan-i-Wizarat (Finance).

94. **(c)** Perihelion is the point when the Earth is closest to the Sun in its elliptical orbit.

- It occurs annually in early January, around 3rd or 4th January.
- The distance is about 147.1 million km, compared to 152.1 million km at aphelion (farthest point).
- Earth's speed is fastest at perihelion due to gravitational pull.

Knowledge Booster

- Despite being closest to the Sun in January, it's winter in the Northern Hemisphere due to Earth's axial tilt, not distance.
- The term 'perihelion' comes from Greek: Peri (near) + Helios (Sun).

95. **(b)** Guru Bipin Singh was a renowned exponent of the Manipuri dance form.
- He received the Sangeet Natak Akademi Award in 1966 and the Kalidas Samman.
- He was instrumental in popularising Manipuri classical dance on national platforms.
- Trained many disciples and established Manipuri Nartanalaya institutions.

96. **(a)** Birju Maharaj, a legendary Kathak dancer, received the Padma Vibhushan in 1984.
- He was the youngest recipient of the award in the field of dance at that time.
- Belonging to the Lucknow Gharana, he blended traditional storytelling with graceful footwork.
- He trained numerous Indian film and classical dancers.

97. **(c)** The Indian Meteorological Department (IMD) was established in 1875.
- It operates under the Ministry of Earth Sciences, Government of India.
- IMD is responsible for weather forecasting, cyclone alerts and climate monitoring.
- It was created during British rule to monitor monsoons after a series of famines.

98. **(d)** The cell membrane is made of lipids and proteins.
- Proteins make up about 40–60% of the membrane's mass.
- These proteins help in transport, communication and support.
- Two types of proteins: integral (inside membrane) and peripheral (on surface).
- The structure of the cell membrane is explained by the fluid mosaic model.

99. **(d)** Syed Modi is a International Badminton tournament.
- It is held annually in Lucknow, Uttar Pradesh.
- The tournament is named after Syed Modi, an Indian badminton champion.
- It is part of the BWF World Tour series and attracts global players.

Knowledge Booster
- Syed Modi was a Commonwealth Games gold medalist in 1982.
- The tournament has been upgraded over the years to a BWF Super 300 event.

100. **(c)** Ghode Modni is a traditional 'Warrior Dance of Goa'.
- It features men in traditional warrior attire, performing with swords and shields.
- Dancers wear wooden horse costumes (ghode) around their waist, symbolising horse-riding warriors.
- Ghode Modni is influenced by Maratha military traditions.

101. **(b)** Let Sukhvir purchased 100 items.

Bad items $= 100 \times \frac{30}{100} = 30$ items

Remaining items $= 100 - 30 = 70$

Let he sell at x% above to remaining items to gain overall 19%.

$$70 \times \frac{100 + x}{100} = 119\%$$

$$\Rightarrow \quad (100 + x) = \frac{119 \times 100}{70} = 170$$

$$\Rightarrow \quad x = 170 - 100 = 70\%$$

102. **(c)** Selling price after discount

$$= \text{MP} \times \frac{(100 - d)}{100}$$

$$= 1940 \times \frac{(100 - 15)}{100}$$

$$= 1940 \times \frac{85}{100} = ₹1649$$

103. **(c)** Hostel mess required 217 egg for, 7 days.

Total days in July, August and September $= 31 + 31 + 30 = 92$ days

In 7 days required egg = 217

In 1 one day required egg $= \frac{217}{7}$

In 92 days required egg

$$= \frac{217}{7} \times 92 = 2852$$

104. **(d)** For greatest number = HCF of $(|1261 - 853|, |853 - 1221|, |1221 - 261|)$

= HCF of [592, 368, 960]

Therefore, $592 = 16 \times 37 = 2^4 \times 37$

$368 = 2^4 \times 23$

$960 = 2^6 \times 3 \times 5$

Thus, required number

= HCF of [592, 368, 960]

$= 2^4 = 16$

105. **(a)** Required percentage of labour and timber $= \frac{(45° + 65°)}{360} \times 100$

$$= \frac{110}{360} \times 100 = \frac{11000}{360}$$

$$= \frac{275}{9} = 30\frac{5}{9}\%$$

106. **(c)** Total votes = 146000

Total valid votes $= 146000 \times \frac{95}{100}$

$= 138700$

Number of valid votes cast in favour of candidates $= 138700 \times \frac{75}{100}$

$= 104025$

107. **(a)** Radius of concical shape vessel = 21 cm

Slant height of vessel = 25 cm

Curve surface of vessel $= \pi rl$

$$= \frac{22}{7} \times 21 \times 25 = 1650 \text{ cm}^2$$

Cost of painting $= 1650 \times ₹1.5$

$= ₹2475$

108. **(c)**
P+Q → 30 days — 4
Q+R → 24 days — 5 → (120) units
R+P → 20 days — 6

Efficiency of $(P + Q + R)$

$$= \frac{(4 + 5 + 6)}{2}$$

$$= \frac{15}{2} = 7.5$$

Work done in 10 days by $(P + Q + R)$

$$= \frac{15}{2} \times 10 = 75 \text{ units}$$

Now, time to finish remaining work by P

$$= \frac{120 - 75}{7.5 - 5} = \frac{45}{2.5} = 18 \text{ days}$$

109. **(a)** Greatest possible length = HCF of (600 cm, 525 cm, 1250 cm)

$600 = 6 \times 25 \times 4 = 2^3 \times 3 \times 5^2$

$525 = 3 \times 7 \times 5^2$

$1250 = 2 \times 5^4$

HCF of 600, 525 and 1250

$= 5^2 = 25$ cm

$= \frac{25}{100} = 0.25$ m

110. **(d)** Total votes = 4500

Total valid votes $= 4500 \times \frac{90}{100} = 4050$

Number of votes obtained by other candidate $= 4050 \times \frac{20}{100} = 810$

111. **(c)** Diameter of hemisphere = 4 cm

Radius of hemisphere = 2 cm

Total surface area = $3\pi r^2$

$= 3 \times \pi \times 2 \times 2$

$= 12\pi \text{ cm}^2$

Surface area of hemisphere = $2\pi r^2$

$= 2 \times \pi \times 2^2 = 8\pi \text{ cm}^2$

Required difference = $12\pi - 8\pi$

$= 4\pi \text{ cm}^2$

112. **(c)** $A \rightarrow$ 8 days — 7; $B \rightarrow$ 7 days — 8; (56) Units

Work done in 2 days by A and B alternately = 7 + 8 = 15 units

Work done in 6 days by A and B alternately = 45 units

Work done by 7th day by A = 7 units

Remaining work done by B

$= \frac{56 - 45 - 7}{8} = \frac{4}{8} = \frac{1}{2}$ days

Hence, total time to finish work

$= 6 + 1 + \frac{1}{2} = 7\frac{1}{2}$ days

113. **(c)** Height of circular cylinder = 30 m

TSA of circular cylinder

$= \frac{18425}{25} = 737 \text{ m}^2$

$2\pi r(h + r) = 737$

$\Rightarrow \quad 2 \times \frac{22}{7} \times r(30 + r) = 737$

$\Rightarrow \quad \frac{4r}{7}(30 + r) = 67$

$\Rightarrow \quad 30r + r^2 = 67 \times \frac{7}{4}$

$\Rightarrow \quad 4r^2 + 120r - 469 = 0$

$\Rightarrow \quad 4r^2 + 134r - 14r - 469 = 0$

$\Rightarrow 2r(2r + 67) - 7(2r + 67) = 0$

$\Rightarrow \quad (2r - 7)(2r + 67) = 0$

$\therefore \quad r = \frac{7}{2}$ cm

We know,

Volume of cylinder = $\pi r^2 h$

$= \frac{22}{7} \times \frac{7}{2} \times \frac{7}{2} \times 30$

$= 1155 \text{ m}^2$

114. **(b)** Length of transverse tangent

$= \sqrt{d^2 - (r_1 + r_2)^2}$

$= \sqrt{14^2 - (6 + 4)^2}$

$= \sqrt{14^2 - 10^2}$

$= \sqrt{24 \times 4}$

Length of transverse tangent = $4\sqrt{6}$ cm

115. **(b)** Given,

$(1 + \sin^4 A - \cos^4 A) \operatorname{cosec}^2 A$

$= (1 + (\sin^2 A)^2 - (\cos^2 A)^2) \operatorname{cosec}^2 A$

$= [1 + (\sin^2 A + \cos^2 A)(\sin^2 A - \cos^2 A)] \operatorname{cosec}^2 A$

$= [1 + \sin^2 A - \cos^2 A] \operatorname{cosec}^2 A$

$= [\operatorname{cosec}^2 A + 1 - \cot^2 A]$

$[\because \operatorname{cosec}^2 A - \cot^2 A = 1]$

$= 1 + 1 = 2$

116. **(b)** Total product sold by A = 3000

Total product sold by B = 3500

Product sold on Thursday by A

= 300 − 1000 − 500 − 800= 700

Product sold on Tuesday by B

= 3500 − 800 − 1000 − 1200 = 500

∴Required difference

= 700 − 500 = 200

117. **(d)** Let rate of interest be r%.

SI for 2 yr = $\frac{80 \times r \times 2}{100}$

$\Rightarrow 96 - 80 = \frac{80 \times r \times 2}{100}$

$\Rightarrow \quad 16 = \frac{8}{5} \times r$

$\Rightarrow \quad r = 10\%$

Again,

SI = $62000 \times \frac{10 \times 5}{100} = 31000$

Required amount after 5 yr

= 62000 + 31000 = ₹93000

118. **(a)** Given, $a \propto b$

$\Rightarrow \quad a = kb \quad \ldots$(i)

$b \propto \frac{1}{c}$

$\Rightarrow \quad b = \frac{h}{c} \quad \ldots$(ii)

and $\quad c \propto d$

$\Rightarrow \quad c = zd \quad \ldots$(iii)

From Eqs. (i), (ii) and (iii)

$\Rightarrow \quad a = k \times \frac{h}{z} \times \frac{1}{d}$

[∵ where k, h and z are constant]

$\Rightarrow \quad a = \left(\frac{kh}{z}\right) \times \frac{1}{d}$

$\Rightarrow \quad a \propto \frac{1}{d}$

119. **(a)** From the table it is very clear that type S car continuous increase from 1989 to 1994.

120. **(d)** $6.9 - [8.6 - \{6.5 - (5.4 - \overline{4.3 - 2})\}]$

[∵ By BODMAS rule]

$= 6.9 - [8.6 - \{6.5 - (5.4 - 2.3)\}]$

$= 6.9 - [8.6 - \{6.5 - 3.1\}]$

$= 6.9 - [8.6 - 3.4]$

$= 6.9 - [5.2] = 1.7$

121. **(d)** Distance between police and thief = 300 m

Relative speed of policeman and thief

= (13 − 11) = 2 km/h

$= 2 \times \frac{5}{18} = \frac{5}{9}$ m/sec

∴Required time to catch thief

$= \frac{300}{\frac{5}{9}} = 540$ sec

∴Required distance travelled by policeman = $13 \times \frac{540}{60 \times 60} = 1.95$ km

122. **(d)** Principal = ₹100000

$r = 7\%$

Amount after 5 yr = $P\left(1 + \frac{r}{100}\right)^5$

$= 100000\left(1 + \frac{7}{100}\right)^5$

$= 100000 \times \left(\frac{107}{100}\right)^5$

= 100000 × 1.40255 = ₹140255

Hence, CI = 140255 − 100000 = ₹40255

123. **(d)** Radius of cone = 7 cm

and slant height of cone = 10 cm

CSA of cone = πrl

$= \frac{22}{7} \times 7 \times 10 = 220 \text{ cm}^2$

124. **(c)** Length of arc = $2\pi r \times \frac{\theta}{360°}$

$22 = 2 \times \frac{22}{7} \times r \times \frac{45°}{360°}$

$\Rightarrow \quad 22 = 2 \times \frac{22}{7} \times r \times \frac{1}{8}$

$\Rightarrow \quad r = \frac{22 \times 7 \times 8}{2 \times 22}$

$\Rightarrow \quad r = 28$ cm

125. **(a)** Given, $210 = 2 \times 3 \times 5 \times 7$

$336 = 2^4 \times 3 \times 7$

$504 = 2^3 \times 3^2 \times 7$

LCM of 210, 336 and 504

$= 2^4 \times 3^2 \times 5 \times 7$

= 5040

126. **(a)** LCM of $\left(\frac{1}{3}, \frac{3}{5}, \frac{4}{7} \text{ and } \frac{9}{16}\right)$

$= \frac{\text{LCM of (1, 3, 4 and 9)}}{\text{HCF of 3, 5, 7 and16}}$

$= \frac{36}{1} = 36$

127. (b) Required percentage

$$= \frac{1342}{1666} \times 100 = 80.55\%$$

128. (a) $\cos A = \frac{15}{17}$

By 15, 8, 17 triplet

$$\sin A = \frac{8}{17}$$

Thus, value of $\cot(90° - A)$

$$= \tan A$$

$$= \frac{\sin A}{\cos A} = \frac{8}{17} \times \frac{17}{15}$$

$$= \frac{8}{15}$$

129. (a) Number of cakes sold by bakeries Q and S together in September

$= 189 + 154 = 343$

and, Number of cakes sold by P and R together in November

$= 168 + 168 = 336$

Required difference $= 343 - 336 = 7$

130. (b) Let the height of circular cone be h.

Volume of cone $= \frac{1}{3}\pi r^2 h$

$$\Rightarrow 196\pi = \frac{1}{3}\pi \times 7 \times 7 \times h$$

$$\Rightarrow h = \frac{196\pi \times 3}{\pi \times 7 \times 7} = 12 \text{ cm}$$

131. (b) LCM of $\frac{3}{2}, \frac{81}{16}$ and $\frac{9}{8}$

$$= \frac{\text{LCM of 3, 81 and 9}}{\text{HCF of 2, 16 and 8}} = \frac{81}{2}$$

132. (c) $\frac{A}{L} + \frac{M}{B} = 1$ and $\frac{B}{M} + \frac{N}{C} = 1$

$$\frac{M}{B} = 1 - \frac{A}{L}$$

$$\frac{M}{B} = \frac{L - A}{L}$$

$$\frac{B}{M} = \frac{L}{L - A}$$

and, $\frac{B}{M} + \frac{N}{C} = 1$

$$\frac{N}{C} = 1 - \frac{B}{M} = 1 - \frac{L}{(L - A)}$$

$$\frac{N}{C} = \frac{L - A - L}{L - A}$$

$$\frac{N}{C} = \frac{-A}{L - A}$$

$$\frac{C}{N} = \frac{L - A}{-A}$$

Required value,

$$\frac{L}{A} + \frac{C}{N} = \frac{L}{A} - \frac{L - A}{A}$$

$$= \frac{L - L + A}{A} = 1$$

133. (c) Perimeter of sector = 24 cm

$2r$ + Length of arc = 24

Length of arc $= 24 - 2 \times 3$

$= 18$ cm

As we know,

Area of sector $= \frac{1}{2} \times l \times r$

$$= \frac{1}{2} \times 18 \times 3$$

$$= 27 \text{ cm}^2$$

134. (c) It is very clear from table that type R continuous decrease through the year.

135. (d) $\frac{\cos 65°}{\sin 25°} + \frac{5\sin 19°}{\cos 71°} - \frac{3\cos 28°}{\sin 62°}$

$$= \frac{\cos(90 - 25)°}{\sin 25°} + \frac{5\sin(90° - 71)°}{\cos 71°} - \frac{3\cos(90° - 62°)}{\sin 62°}$$

$$= \frac{\sin 25°}{\sin 25°} + \frac{5\cos 71°}{\cos 71°} - \frac{3\sin 62°}{\sin 62°}$$

$= 1 + 5 - 3 = 3$

136. (c) Let income be ₹ $100x$.

$\therefore$ Expenditure $= 100x - 20x$

$= ₹\, 80x$

Expenditure on shoping

$= 80x \times 11.25\% = 9x$

$9x = ₹\, 7200$

Expenditure on food $(15x)$

$$\Rightarrow \frac{7200}{9x} \times 15x = ₹\, 12000$$

137. (b) $\frac{a^2 - b^2 - 2bc - c^2}{a^2 + b^2 + 2ab - c^2}$

$$= \frac{a^2 - (b^2 + 2bc + c^2)}{a^2 + b^2 + 2ab - c^2}$$

$$= \frac{a^2 - (b + c)^2}{(a + b)^2 - c^2}$$

$[\because a^2 - b^2 = (a + b)(a - b)]$

$$= \frac{(a + b + c)(a - b - c)}{(a + b + c)(a + b - c)}$$

$$= \frac{(a - b - c)}{(a + b - c)}$$

138. (d) Let the cost price be ₹ 100

Marked price $= 100 \times \frac{175}{100} = ₹\, 175$

Selling price $= 175 \times \frac{(100 - 40)}{100}$

$$= 175 \times \frac{60}{100} = ₹\, 105$$

Profit % $= \frac{105 - 100}{100} \times 100 = 5\%$

139. (a) By Alligation Rule,

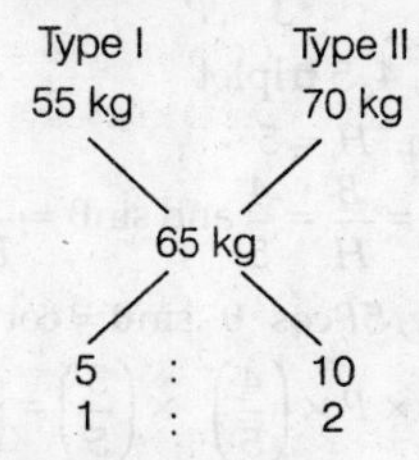

$\therefore$ Required ratio = 1 : 2

140. (a) Given, $\frac{1}{12} + \frac{1}{16} + \frac{1}{8}$

$$= \frac{4 + 3 + 6}{48} = \frac{13}{48}$$

141. (c) $AD = \frac{1}{6}AB$

$$\frac{AD}{AB} = \frac{1}{6}$$

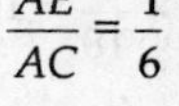

$$\frac{AE}{AC} = \frac{1}{6}$$

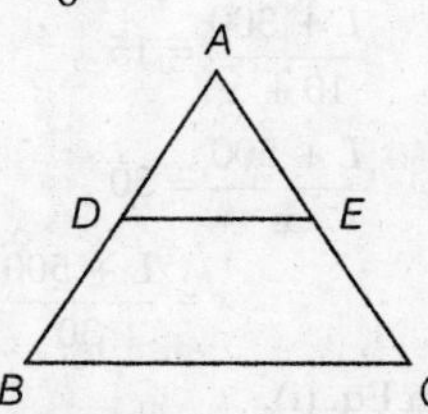

Thus, $\Delta ADE \sim \Delta ABC$

$$\therefore \quad \frac{DE}{BC} = \frac{1}{6}$$

$\therefore$ 6 units → 22 cm

1 unit → $\frac{22}{6} = 3.67$ cm

142. (a) Let distance be D m.

Let Rekha's speed be $4x$ and Reema's speed be $5x$.

We know, Time $= \frac{\text{Distance}}{\text{Speed}}$

$$\Rightarrow \quad \frac{D - 50}{4x} = \frac{D}{5x}$$

$$\Rightarrow \quad 5D - 250 = 4D$$

$$\therefore \quad D = 250 \text{ m}$$

Speedy Method

	Rekha		Reena
Speed	4	:	5
Distance	5	:	4
		1	

$\because$ 1 → 50 m

$\therefore$ Distance = (5) → 250 m

143. (d) Average percentage of marks obtained by all student in Hindi is

$$= \frac{85\% + 80\% + 75\% + 70\%}{4}$$

$$= \frac{310}{4} = 77.5\%$$

144. **(d)** $\cot\theta = \frac{4}{3} = \frac{B}{P}$

By 3, 4, 5 triplet

Then, $H = 5$

$\cos\theta = \frac{B}{H} = \frac{4}{5}$ and $\sin\theta = \frac{P}{H} = \frac{3}{5}$

Now, $5P\cos^2\theta \cdot \sin\theta = \cot^2\theta$

$\Rightarrow 5 \times P \times \left(\frac{4}{5}\right)^2 \times \left(\frac{3}{5}\right) = \left(\frac{4}{3}\right)^2$

$\Rightarrow P = \frac{4 \times 4}{3 \times 3} \times \frac{5}{3} \times \frac{25}{4 \times 4 \times 5}$

$\Rightarrow P = \frac{25}{27}$

145. **(a)** Let the length of train A be L and speed of A be x m/sec.

According to the question,

Speed of train B = 36 km/h

$= 36 \times \frac{5}{18} = 10$ m/sec

$\frac{L + 300}{10 + x} = 15$ ...(i)

and $\frac{L + 500}{x} = 30$

$\Rightarrow x = \frac{L + 500}{30}$

From Eq. (i),

$\frac{L + 300}{10 + \frac{L + 500}{30}} = 15$

$\Rightarrow L + 300 = \frac{(800 + L)}{2}$

$\Rightarrow 2L + 300 = 800$

$\therefore L = 800 - 600 = 200$ m

146. **(c)** Let the cost price be $100x$.

Selling price at 10% profit

$= 100x \times \frac{110}{100} = 110x$

Selling price at 7% profit $= 107x$

$\therefore 110x - 107x = ₹6$

$\Rightarrow 3x = ₹6$

$\Rightarrow x = ₹2$

Thus, CP $= 100x = 100 \times 2$

$= ₹200$

Speedy Method

100 —(+10%)→ 110

100 —(+71)→ 107 —(+1)→ 110

3 ⟶ ₹6

1 ⟶ ₹2

100 ⟶ ₹200

147. **(c)** Let total expenditure be $100x$.

According to question

$100x \times \frac{6}{100} + 100x \times \frac{62}{100} = ₹850$ billion

$\Rightarrow 68x = ₹850$ billion

$\Rightarrow x = 12.5$ billion

Thus, total expenditure $= 100x$

$= 100 \times 12.5$

$= ₹1250$ billion

148. **(c)**

A → 20 days — 7

B → 28 days — 5

(140) Units

Required time to complete work

$= \frac{140}{7 + 5}$

$= \frac{140}{12} = \frac{35}{3} = 11\frac{2}{3}$ days

149. **(c)** Average weight of 8 parcels

$= \frac{1.5 + 1.25 + 1.35 + 0.75 + 0.95 + 0.7 + 0.4 + 0.5}{8}$

$= \frac{7.4}{8} = 0.925$ kg $= 925$ gm

150. **(b)** Number of student enrolled in painting

$= 3600 \times \frac{15}{100} = 36 \times 15 = 540$

Number of students enrolled in singing

$= 3600 \times \frac{18}{100} = 648$

Required % $= \frac{540}{648} \times 100 = 83\%$

151. **(d)** The phrase 'foul play' refers to dishonest, unfair or unethical behaviour, especially in sports or competitions. Since the sentence is about unfair conduct in sports tournaments, 'foul play' is the most suitable replacement.

152. **(b)** **Placid** Calm, peaceful and serene; not easily disturbed.

Turbulent Characterised by conflict, disorder, or confusion; chaotic and unstable. (Correct antonym)

153. **(d)** An Atheist is a person who does not believe in the existence of God or gods. This fits perfectly as the one-word substitute for a person who believes that God does not exist.

154. **(b)** The idiom 'pen and ink' typically refers to writing or drawing, but when used figuratively, it can describe something being 'freshly prepared' or 'newly done,' much like how a smell can be fresh or new after an intense activity like a gym session.

155. **(d)** The phrase 'one of the' is always followed by a superlative adjective to indicate that the subject belongs to a group of the highest-ranked items.

Most popular' is the correct answer because 'one of the' requires a superlative adjective (most popular).

156. **(b)** The sentence 'He is faster than smarter' involves a comparison between two adjectives. When making such comparisons, the comparative form of 'fast' is 'faster' and the comparative form of 'smart' is 'smarter'. However, in English, when comparing two adjectives with different forms of comparison, it's grammatically more natural to say 'more fast' in this context.

So, the correct form is 'more fast than smart' rather than 'faster than smarter'.

157. **(b)** **Rejoinder** A quick, often witty, or sharp reply to a remark or statement.

Request A polite or formal act of asking for something, which is the opposite of a rejoinder (a sharp reply). (Correct antonym)

158. **(d)** The word 'antidote' refers to a substance that counteracts the effects of a poison or venom, especially after a snakebite. This makes it the most appropriate choice for the sentence.

159. **(b)** **Utility** The state of being useful, beneficial, or serving a purpose. (Correct answer)

160. **(d)** The error is in 'it tasted sweetly.' The word 'sweetly' is an adverb, but the verb 'tasted' here is a linking verb. Linking verbs describe a state or condition and should be followed by an adjective, not an adverb.

The correct word should be 'sweet' (an adjective), not 'sweetly.'

Correct sentence: Raman ate the cake and exclaimed that it tasted sweet.

161. **(a)** The correct spelling is 'twelfth', which refers to the ordinal number for 12th.

162. **(c)** There are three cars parked outside a Mercedes, a Jaguar and a Fiat.

The indefinite article 'a' is used before words that begin with a consonant sound, and 'an' is used before words that begin with a vowel sound.

163. **(d)** The correct spelling of the word is 'Miniature', not 'Miniture.' 'Miniature' refers to something in a very small form or a detailed, small-scale model.

164. **(b)** The idiom 'a blessing in disguise' means that something which initially appears to be a negative situation turns out to have positive consequences in the long run. In this context, choosing not to pursue a degree in computer engineering, despite the market being limited, could turn out to be a positive decision, as the person might have avoided potential challenges or limitations in that field.

165. **(c)** **Immigrant** A person who moves to another country to settle there permanently.

166. **(a)** **Asset** An item of value or a resource that is useful or beneficial.

Liability A responsibility or obligation, often involving a burden or something that poses a disadvantage. (Correct antonym)

167. **(a)** The word 'Leniency' refers to mercy, tolerance, or being forgiving in judgement or punishment. The opposite of Leniency is strictness or severity, which is best represented by 'Sternness.'

168. **(a)** A curator is a person who is responsible for managing, preserving, and organising a museum, gallery, or any other collection of valuable items. They oversee exhibitions and ensure that artifacts and artworks are properly maintained.

169. **(a)** **Apathy** Lack of interest, enthusiasm, or concern.

Interest A feeling of curiosity or concern about something. (Correct antonym)

170. **(b)** The correct idiom is 'as keen as mustard', which means to be very eager, enthusiastic, or interested in something.

171. **(c)** The word 'viable' means capable of working successfully, feasible, or sustainable in the long run. In the given sentence, the engineer's design focuses on efficiency, scalability and sustainability, but the word that best matches 'viable' is 'sustainability,' as it directly refers to something being practical and able to last over time.

172. **(a)** The idiom 'back to square one' means to start over again after a failure or setback.
In the context of the sentence, the project has failed, and the speaker needs to restart the process, making 'back to square one' the most appropriate choice.

173. **(a)** The idiom 'Crack someone up' means to make someone laugh very hard. It is commonly used in informal conversations when something is extremely funny.
Example Sentences
His jokes always crack me up.
The comedian's performance was so hilarious that it cracked up the entire audience.

174. **(b)** The idiom 'set sights on' means to focus one's attention and efforts on achieving a particular goal or target. It fits perfectly with Ravi's clear determination and hard work to achieve his goal of being in the college hockey team.

175. **(a)** The correct idiom is 'stabbed her in the back.' This phrase means to betray someone who trusted you. In the given sentence, the woman trusted her husband, but he betrayed her by taking her inheritance.

176. **(b)** The word 'dissiminate' is incorrectly spelled. The correct spelling is 'disseminate', which means to spread or distribute information, ideas, or knowledge.

177. **(b)** The word 'Denounce' means to publicly declare something as wrong or evil or to strongly criticise someone or something.

The opposite of denounce would be to speak positively or approve of something, which is best represented by 'Praise.'

178. **(d)** The sentence is grammatically correct and logically coherent. Here's the breakdown:

You arrived two days ago Correct past tense usage to describe an action that happened in the past.

By the time you leave Correct use of the future perfect tense to describe a time in the future when the action will be completed.

you will have spent nine days here The future perfect tense is correctly used to describe the completion of spending nine days by the time the person leaves.

179. **(d)** In this sentence, the word 'congestion' refers to the overcrowding or traffic jams that are commonly experienced in urban areas. To improve the sentence, we need a synonym that specifically conveys the idea of traffic jams or a standstill in traffic.

Gridlock Refers to severe traffic congestion where vehicles are unable to move, perfectly fitting the context of traffic congestion in the sentence.

180. **(b)** The correct spelling of 'considared' should be 'considered'.

181. **(b)** The word 'discordant' refers to something that is harsh, jarring, or unpleasant to the ear, especially in music. The sentence describes a 'sweet melodious symphony', where 'melodious' means pleasant or harmonious, which is the opposite (antonym) of discordant.

182. **(c)** Let's examine the sentence:

I wanted to buy a candle holder This part is grammatically correct. It properly uses the past tense for expressing a desire in the past.

but the store didn't have one. This part is also correct. It correctly uses 'didn't have' to indicate the past tense of the store not having the item.

So, I got a cake This part is also correct. It logically follows the previous sentence, explaining what the speaker did instead of buying the candle holder.

183. **(c)** The idiom 'hold your horses' means to be patient or to wait before making a decision. Since the sentence suggests caution before buying a car, this idiom fits best.

184. **(b)** The phrase 'happening repeatedly' describes something that occurs over and over again. The correct one-word substitute would be 'recurrent,' which means occurring repeatedly or regularly.

185. **(c)** Psychology is the scientific study of the human mind and behavior. It deals with understanding mental processes, emotions, cognition, and how individuals behave in various situations.

186. **(c)** Captivate means to attract and hold the attention of someone; to charm or fascinate.

Allure means to attract or entice someone in a very appealing way, which is similar to captivate. (Correct answer)

187. **(a)** Entomology - The scientific study of insects. (Correct answer)

188. **(b)** The correct spelling is 'Pizza', not 'Pitza.'

189. **(c)** The phrase 'A Prime Minister of India' is incorrect because India has only one Prime Minister at a time. The correct phrase should be 'The Prime Minister of India' since the definite article 'The' is used when referring to a specific position that is unique within a country.

190. **(b)** The idiom 'What a small world!' is used to express surprise or amazement when two people discover that they know each other or have something in common in an unexpected way. It suggests that the world feels smaller because of the surprising coincidence.

191. **(c)** The word 'advanced' fits best in blank no. 1.

192. **(a)** The option 'in the' fits best in blank no. 2.

193. **(a)** The word 'spend' fits best in blank no. 3.

194. **(b)** The word 'perhaps' fits best in blank no. 4.

195. **(b)** The word ' function' fits best in blank no. 5.

196. **(b)** The passage discusses various aspects of creativity, including its ability to inspire positive change, the challenges that come with it, and how it has been an important part of human history and development. Therefore, the most fitting title is 'The Power of Creativity' because it emphasises the central theme of creativity's influence and potential.

197. (b) The passage mentions that creative expression can be fraught with obstacles such as self-doubt, insecurity, external pressures, and constraints. Additionally, it notes that not all creative ideas are successful or well-received, and many artists and innovators face rejection and criticism as they seek to bring their ideas to fruition. This indicates that the lack of appreciation for creative ideas is one of the challenges of creative expression. Therefore, option (b) is the correct answer.

198. **(b)** The passage primarily discusses the concept of creativity, its multifaceted nature, the ongoing debates around its origins (whether subconscious or conscious), and how it can bring positive changes in the world. It also highlights the challenges faced by individuals in the creative process.

The passage doesn't solely focus on cognitive processes, the mysteries of the human mind, or just fancy and imagination, making option (b) the most appropriate choice.

199. **(c)** Fraught' means something filled with or causing distress or anxiety.

So, the opposite of something being 'fraught' would be something that is lacking or free from such negative qualities or challenges.

'Devoid' means lacking or without something, making it the most fitting antonym to 'fraught.' Thus, Devoid is the correct answer.

200. **(b)** In the passage, it is mentioned that creativity can be driven by factors such as curiosity, passion, or the desire for recognition.

These factors are positive drivers of creativity. On the other hand, self-doubt, insecurity, external pressures, and constraints are described as obstacles to creativity, while 'fancy and imagination' are more about the result or expression of creativity rather than the driving factors.

Therefore, option (b) is the correct answer.

PAPER-1

SSC CPO SI SOLVED PAPER

3 October 2023 (Shift I)

MM : 200 **Time : 2 hr**

Instructions

1. This paper contains 200 questions.
2. It has 4 Parts, **Part I** General Intelligence and Reasoning, **Part II** General Knowledge and General Awareness, **Part III** Quantitative Aptitude and **Part IV** English Comprehension.
3. Each question carries **1 marks.**

Part I

General Intelligence and Reasoning

1. Select the option in which the given figure is embedded (rotation is not allowed).

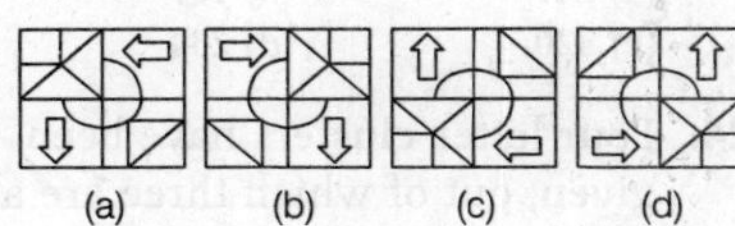

2. Which letter cluster will replace the question mark (?) to complete the given series ?

ELSV, FJVR, GHYN, ?, IDEF

(a) HFJB (b) HBJF
(c) HFBJ (d) GHFJ

3. Three of the following four letter-clusters are alike in a certain way and one is different.

Pick the odd one out.

(a) WVTD (b) JIGQ
(c) SRPH (d) KLNP

4. Seven people, A, B, C, D, E, F and G, are sitting in a straight row, facing North (not necessarily in the same order). Only 1 person sits to the left of D. A is an immediate neighbour of D. Only 2 people sit between F and D. Only 3 people sit between C and G. B is not an immediate neighbour of G. Only 2 people sit between E and A. Who sits at the extreme right end of the row?

(a) A (b) G
(c) C (d) B

5. In a certain code language, 'GAME' is coded as '8426' and 'MUST' is coded as '7853'. What is the code for 'M' in the given code language ?

(a) 8 (b) 2
(c) 3 (d) 7

6. Two statements are given, followed by two conclusions numbered I and II. Assuming the statements to be true, even if they seem to be at variance with commonly known facts, decide which of the conclusions logically follow(s) from the statements.

Statements

All flowers are trees.

All leaves are flowers.

Conclusions

I. All trees are flowers.

II. All leaves are trees.

(a) Only Conclusion I follows
(b) Neither Conclusion I nor II follows
(c) Only Conclusion II follows
(d) Both Conclusions I and II follow

7. Three different positions of the same dice are shown. Find the number on the face opposite the face showing '1'.

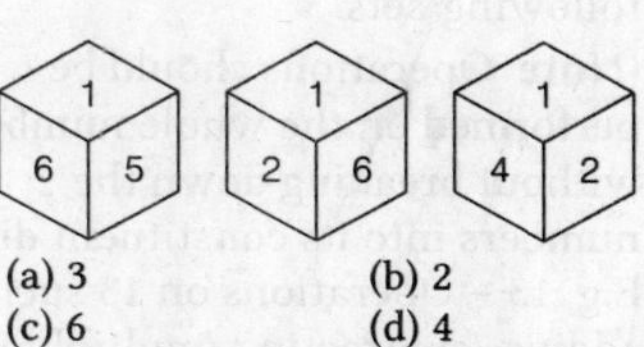

(a) 3 (b) 2
(c) 6 (d) 4

8. Select the correct mirror image of the given figure, when the mirror is placed at line MN as shown.

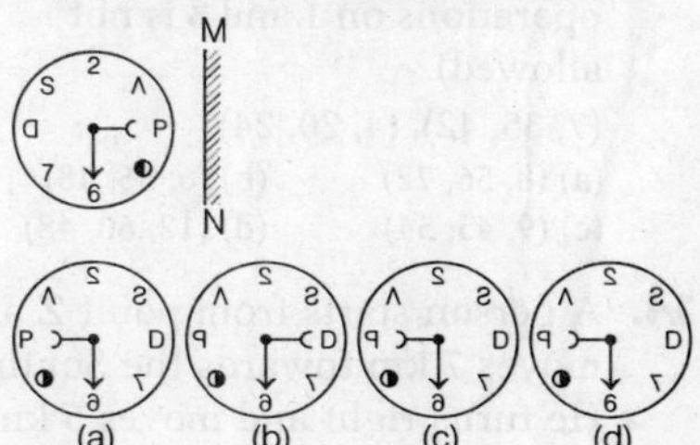

9. If '+' means '–', '–' means '×', '×' means '÷', '÷' means '+', then what will come in place of the question mark (?) in the following equation ?

$137 \div 56 \times 7 - 6 + 31 = ?$

(a) 149 (b) 163
(c) 145 (d) 154

10. Select the option that represents the correct order of the given words as they would appear in an English dictionary ?

1. Lollipop 2. Loincloth
3. Longways 4. Logician
5. Lonely

(a) 3, 2, 1, 5, 4 (b) 4, 3, 1, 5, 2
(c) 4, 2, 1, 5, 3 (d) 3, 4, 1, 5,2

11. Which of the following terms will replace the question mark (?) in the given series?
ABEG, FFHI, KJKK, PNNM, ?
(a) URQO (b) VRQO
(c) RUQO (d) UROQ

12. Select the Venn diagram that best illustrates the relationship between the following classes.
Electrical Appliance, Refrigerator, Freezer

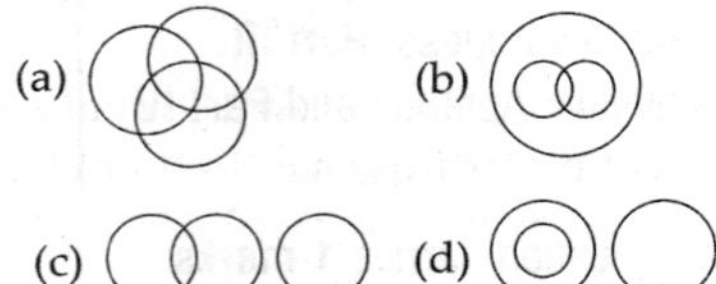

13. Select the set in which the numbers are related in the same way as are the numbers of the following sets.
(**Note** Operations should be performed on the whole numbers, without breaking down the numbers into its constituent digits. E.g. 13 – Operations on 13 such as adding /subtracting /multiplying etc. to 13 can be performed. Breaking down 13 into 1 and 3 and then performing mathematical operations on 1 and 3 is not allowed)
(7, 35, 42), (4, 20, 24)
(a) (8, 56, 72) (b) (6, 36, 48)
(c) (9, 45, 54) (d) (12, 60, 48)

14. A person starts from point Z and moves 7 km towards the South. He turns right and moves 5 km, turns right, and moves 3 km, then turns right and moves 1 km. He takes a left turn and moves 4 km to reach a point X. How much and in which direction does he need to move now to reach point Z?
(a) 4 km, South (b) 4 km, East
(c) 4 km, West (d) 6 km, East

15. Select the figure that will replace the question mark (?) in the following figure series.

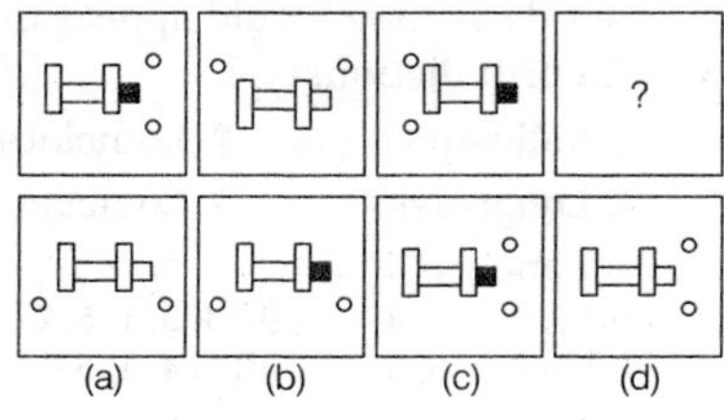

16. Two different positions of the same dice are shown, the six faces of which are numbered from 1 to 6. Select the number that will be on the face opposite to the one showing '1'.

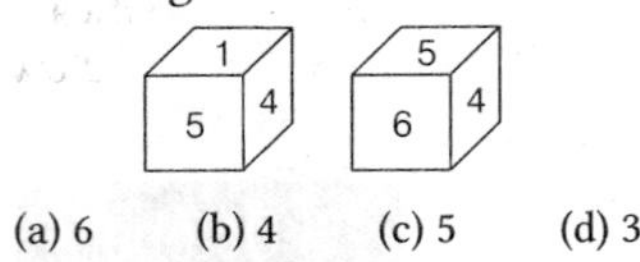

(a) 6 (b) 4 (c) 5 (d) 3

17. Two statements are given, followed by two conclusions numbered I and II. Assuming the statements to be true, even if they seem to be at variance with commonly known facts, decide which of the conclusions logically follow(s) from the statements.

Statements
All plants are vegetables.
Some plants are poisonous.

Conclusions
I. All vegetables are poisonous.
II. Some vegetables are plants.
(a) Neither Conclusion I nor II follows
(b) Only Conclusion I follows
(c) Both Conclusions I and II follow
(d) Only Conclusion II follows

18. Select the correct option that indicates the arrangement of the given words in the order in which they appear in an English dictionary.
1. Desire 2. Destination
3. Descend 4. Destructive
5. Desolate 6. Desperate
(a) 3, 1, 2, 6, 5, 4 (b) 3, 1, 6, 5, 2, 4
(c) 3, 1, 5, 6, 2, 4 (d) 3, 1, 5, 6, 4, 2

19. Select the figure that will come next in the following figure series.

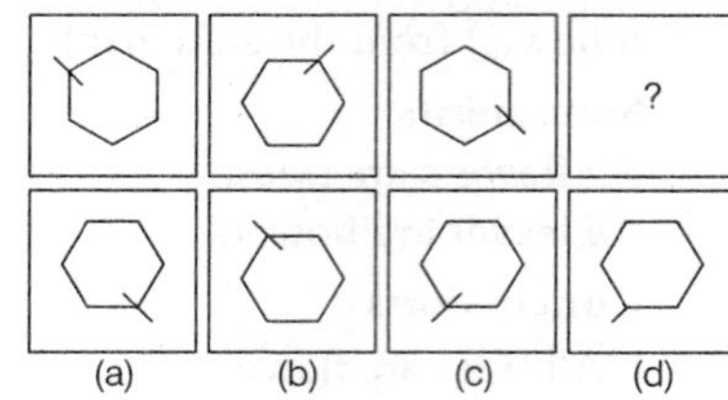

20. Three different positions of the same dice are shown. Find the number on the face opposite the face showing '4'.

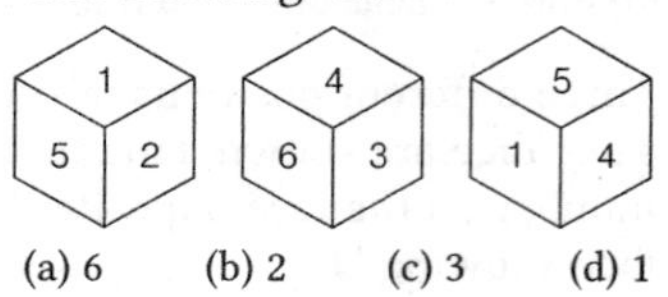

(a) 6 (b) 2 (c) 3 (d) 1

21. Select the set in which the numbers are related in the same way as are the numbers of the following sets.
(**Note** Operations should be performed on the whole numbers, without breaking down the numbers into its constituent digits. E.g. 13 – Operations on 13 such as adding /subtracting /multiplying etc. to 13 can be performed. Breaking down 13 into 1 and 3 and then performing mathematical operations on 1 and 3 is not allowed)
(264, 462), (132, 330)
(a) (211, 340)
(b) (188, 378)
(c) (386, 584)
(d) (282, 496)

22. If A denotes '+' B denotes '×', C denotes '–', and D denotes '÷', then what will come in place of '?' in the following equation ?
$2B?D2 = 4B32D8$
(a) 12 (b) 30
(c) 16 (d) 8

23. If '+' means '×', '×' means '–', '–' means '÷ ', and '÷ ' means '+', then what will come in place of the (?) in the following equation ?
$250 - 10 + 10 \times 5 \div 2 = ?$
(a) 247 (b) 167
(c) 320 (d) 234

24. Four letter-clusters have been given, out of which three are alike in some manner and one is different. Select the odd letter-cluster.
(a) WYRS (b) PSJK
(c) PRKL (d) FHAB

25. In a certain code language, 'VATT' is coded as '65' and 'STOLK' is coded as '79'. How will 'GENEROUS' be coded in that language?
(a) 116 (b) 216 (c) 204 (d) 106

26. Select the option that is embedded in the given figure as its part (rotation is not allowed).

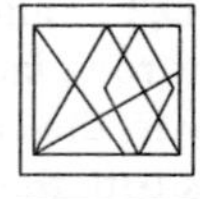

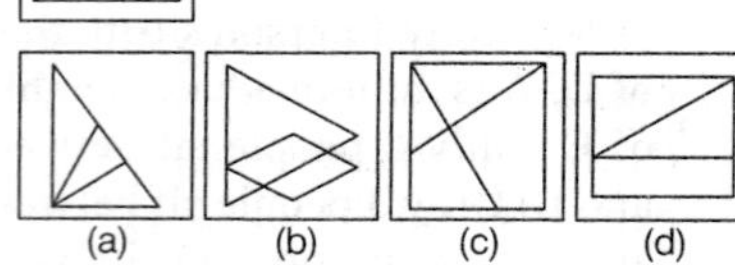

27. If '+' means '÷', '–' means '+', '×' means '–' and '÷' means '×', what will be the value of the following expression ?
$[\{(14\times6)-(4\div3)\}+(6-4)]\div3$
(a) 3 (b) 6
(c) 1 (d) 9

28. Select the option that is related to the fifth letter-cluster in the same way as the second letter-cluster is related to the first letter-cluster and the fourth letter-cluster is related to the third letter-cluster.
TEMPLE : SCJLGY :: CHURCH : BFRNXB :: MOSQUE : ?
(a) LMPYPM (b) LMPYMP
(c) LPYMPM (d) LMPMPY

29. In a certain code language, 'COURT' is coded as OCRTR and 'JUDGE' is coded as UJAEG. How will 'ORDER' be coded in the same language?
(a) LDRRE (b) ROARE
(c) REARO (d) ROBRE

30. Which of the following numbers will replace the question mark (?) in the given series?
115, 130, 122, 137, 129, ?
(a) 144 (b) 142
(c) 148 (d) 150

31. Select the correct mirror image of the given figure when the mirror is placed at line MN as shown.

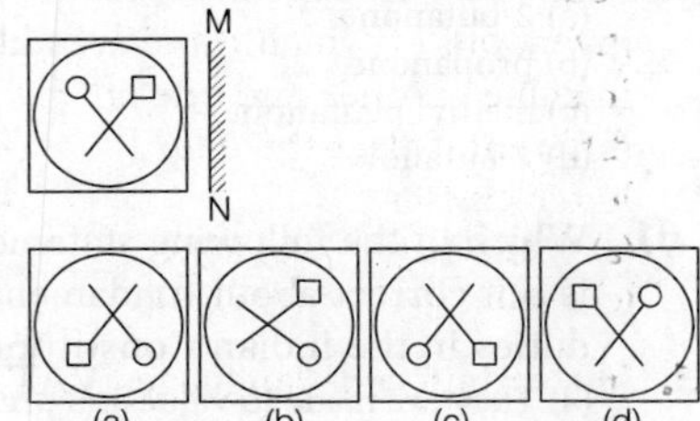

(a) (b) (c) (d)

32. In a certain code language, 'FLORA' is written as 'WQOLC' and 'MONEY' is written as 'PNPYE'. How will 'GOING' be written in that language?
(a) VNUPW (b) RMWEH
(c) VBUDP (d) RHKSR

33. Select the set in which the numbers are related in the same way as are the numbers of the following set.
(**Note** Operations should be performed on the whole numbers, without breaking down the numbers into its constituent digits. E.g. 13 – Operations on 13 such as adding /subtracting/ multiplying etc. to 13 can be performed. Breaking down 13 into 1 and 3 and then performing mathematical operations on 1 and 3 is not allowed)
(6, 2, 96)
(5, 6, 240)
(a) (4,1,6) (b) (12,3,45)
(c) (1,2,16) (d) (8,3,28)

34. Study the given pattern carefully and select the number that can replace the question mark (?) in it.
First row: 19, 6, 37
Second row: 21, 8, 45
Third row: 72, 14, ?
(**Note** Operations should be performed on the whole numbers, without breaking down the numbers into its constituent digits. E.g. 13 – Operations on 13 such as adding /subtracting /multiplying etc. to 13 can be performed. Breaking down 13 into 1 and 3 and then performing mathematical operations on 1 and 3 is not allowed)
(a) 124 (b) 134
(c) 114 (d) 144

35. If A denotes '+', B denotes '×', C denotes '–', and D denotes '÷', then what will be the value of the following expression ?
39 D 13 B 2 C 6 A 8
(a) 10 (b) 8
(c) 12 (d) 9

36. Select the set in which the numbers are related in the same way as are the numbers of the following sets.
(**Note** Operations should be performed on the whole numbers, without breaking down the numbers into its constituent digits. E.g. 13- Operations on 13 such as adding subtracting /multiplying etc. to 13 can be performed. Breaking down 13 into 1 and 3 and then performing mathematical operations on 1 and 3 is not allowed.)
(7, 91, 98)
(4, 52, 56)
(a) (12, 156, 168) (b) (3, 36, 42)
(c) (8, 80, 96) (d) (5, 25, 60)

37. If A denotes '+', B denotes '×', C denotes '–', and D denotes '÷', then what will be the value of the following equation ?
96 D 3 B 8 C 25 A 14 = ?
(a) 217 (b) 234 (c) 254 (d) 245

38. If A denotes '+', B denotes '×', C denotes '–', and D denotes '÷', then what will come in place of '?' in the following equation ?
7 A 3 B 24 D 2 = 20 B ? A 3
(a) 2 (b) 20 (c) 14 (d) 7

39. Which of the following numbers will replace the question mark (?) in the given series?
35, ?, 40, 47, 45, 53
(a) 37 (b) 43 (3) 42 (d) 41

40. If the given sheet is folded to form a cube, which of the given figures is/are possible ?
(The elements are shown to indicate the sides only).

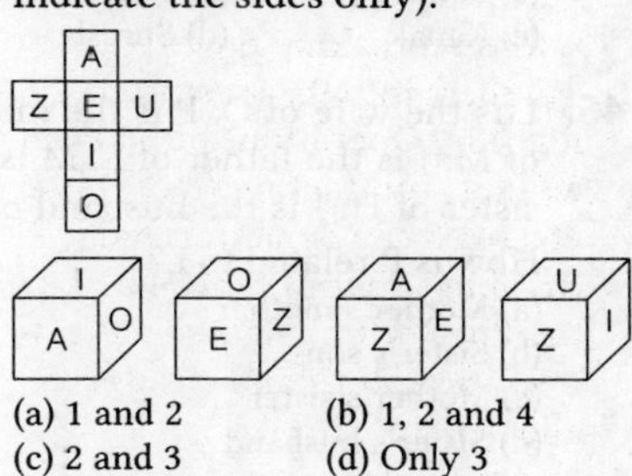

(a) 1 and 2 (b) 1, 2 and 4
(c) 2 and 3 (d) Only 3

41. Which figure from the given options would replace the question mark (?), if the following figure series were to be continued ?

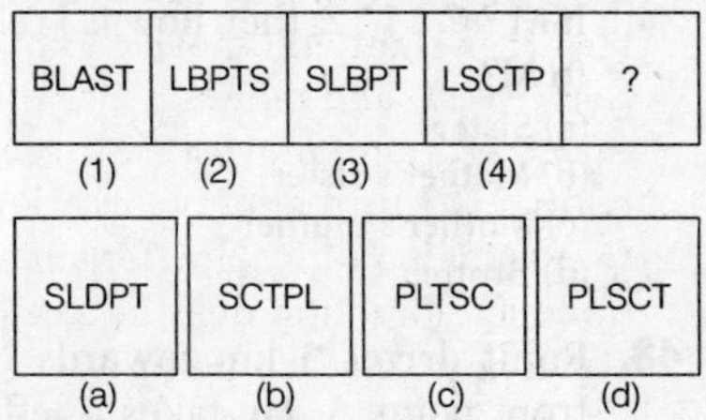

42. Which of the following numbers will replace the question mark (?) in the given series?
$-1/729, -1/81, -1/9, ?$
(a) 1 (b) –1 (c) –1 / 3 (d) 1 / 3

43. Which letter-cluster will replace the question mark (?) to complete the given series?
MKPN, LMOP, ?, JQMT, ISLV
(a) KOLT (b) KNNQ
(c) KNMR (d) KONR

44. Select the option that is related to the third word in the same way as the second word is related to the first word. (The words must be considered as meaningful words and must not be related to each other based on the number of letters/number of consonants/vowels in the word.)
Butterfly : Caterpillar : : Insect : ?
(a) Cygnet
(b) Nymph
(c) Larva
(d) Microbes

45. Six friends are sitting in a circle. All of them are facing the centre. Kanak sits third to the right of Sona. Kapil is an immediate neighbour of Mani. Goldy sits second to the right of Mani. Sona is an immediate neighbour of Kapil and Suresh. Who sits to the immediate right of Goldy?
(a) Sona (b) Kapil
(c) Kanak (d) Suresh

46. L is the wife of Q. P is the mother of M. J is the father of L. M is the sister of H. J is the husband of H. How is P related to L?
(a) Mother's mother
(b) Sister's son
(c) Mother's sister
(d) Sister's husband

47. 'A = B' means 'A is the father of B'.
'A $ B' means 'A is the sister of B'.
'A * B' means 'A is the mother of B'.
'A ? B' means 'A is the son of B'.
If M ? C $ J * Z, then how is J related to M?
(a) Sister
(b) Mother's sister
(c) Mother's mother
(d) Brother

48. Rohit drives 3 km towards North from point A. He takes a left turn and drives 4 km. Again he takes a left turn and drives 6 km. Finally, he takes a left turn and drives 4 km to reach point B. How far and towards which direction should he drive in order to reach point A again?
(a) 4 km towards South
(b) 3 km towards East
(c) 3 km towards North
(d) 2 km towards West

49. In a certain code language, 'FRIEND' is written as 'IIFDME' and 'DEMAND' is written as 'MVDDMA'. How will 'GROUND' be written in that language?
(a) DOTENC (b) PXKRYS
(c) OIGDMU (d) OFTSBU

50. Select the Venn diagram that best illustrates the relationship between the following classes.
Pencil, Eraser, Sharpener

(a) 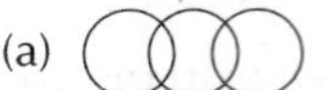

(b) 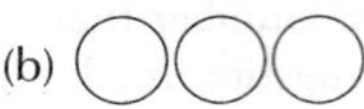

(c) 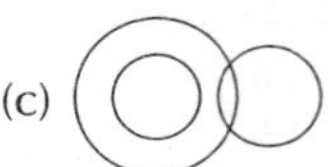

(d) 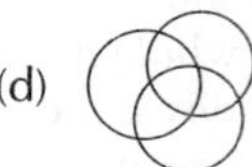

Part II

General Knowledge and General Awareness

51. Which of the following does not belong to the family of organic compounds?
(a) Ammonia (b) Nonane
(c) Furan (d) Decane

52. In November 2020, ... has set a record of becoming the world's fastest piano player ever.
(a) Lydian Nadhaswaram
(b) Anisrinivasan
(c) Gauri Mishra
(d) Shikha Chaurasia

53. For Kharif crops, the temperature required for farming is above 25°C with high humidity and annual rainfall above .... cm.
(a) 16 (b) 100 (c) 35 (d) 50

54. Bhutia dance is performed in which of the following states?
(a) West Bengal (b) Odisha
(c) Sikkim (d) Nagaland

55. With which neighbouring country did India sign the Farakka Treaty in 1996 for sharing of the Ganga Waters and on augmenting its flows?
(a) Bhutan (b) Bangladesh
(c) Nepal (d) Afghanistan

56. Which ruler of the Chahamana dynasty made Ajmer his capital?
(a) Ajayaraja (b) Prithviraj II
(c) Arnoraj (d) Prithviraj III

57. How many Members of Parliament were elected from Punjab to the 17th Lok Sabha?
(a) 14 (b) 15
(c) 13 (d) 17

58. In India, which of the following regulatory mechanisms was not in existence to enforce regulation of the industrial sector?
(a) Industrial licensing under which every entrepreneur had to get permission from government officials to start a firm, close a firm or decide the amount of goods that could be produced.
(b) Controls on price fixation and distribution of selected industrial products.
(c) Private sector was allowed in all industries.
(d) Some goods could be produced only in small-scale industries.

59. Who among the following Indian authors has written the autobiography titled 'My Story'?
(a) Arundhati Roy
(b) Shobha Dey
(c) Kiran Desai
(d) Kamala Das

60. Methyl ethyl ketone is also known as
(a) 2-butanone
(b) propanone
(c) methyl pentanone
(d) 2-butanol

61. Which of the following statements is not correct about fundamental duties in the Indian Constitution?
(a) They are made to value and preserve the rich heritage of our composite culture.
(b) They are made to cherish and follow the noble ideals which inspired our national struggle for freedom.
(c) They are made to develop the scientific temper, humanism and the spirit of inquiry and reform.
(d) They are made justiciable in nature.

62. Who was the first Chairman of Finance Commission of India?
(a) Ashok Kumar Chanda
(b) KC Neogy
(c) K Santhanam
(d) PV Rajamannar

63. The first Commonwealth Games were organised in which of the following years?
(a) 1920 (b) 1930
(c) 1922 (d) 1926

64. Continental Shelf which is the shallowest part of the ocean has an average gradient of
(a) 8° or even less (b) 1° or even less
(c) 5° or even less (d) 2° or even less

65. Dhruvasena II is related to which of the following ruling dynasties?
(a) Vakataka (b) Pushyabhuti
(c) Maitraka (d) Maukhari

66. Under which of the following Acts was the National Commission for Women established?
(a) The National Commission for Women Act, 1989
(b) The National Commission for Women Act, 1987
(c) The National Commission for Women Act, 1990
(d) The National Commission for Women Act, 1988

67. Identify the position of stomata in plants.
(a) Tip of stem
(b) Inside the roots
(c) Inside the flower
(d) Surface of leaves

68. Who among the following has given extraordinary powers during an emergency?
(a) Prime Minister
(b) The Chief Justice
(c) The President
(d) The Governor

69. In India, all loans that are below .... are considered as micro loans.
(a) one lakh rupees
(b) two lakh rupees
(c) four lakh rupees
(d) three lakh rupees

70. Identify whether the given statements about p-block elements are correct or incorrect.
Statement A In p-block elements, the last electron enters the outermost p orbital.
Statement B The non-metals and metalloids exist only in the p-block of the periodic table.
(a) Both Statements A and B are correct.
(b) Only Statement A is correct.
(c) Both Statements A and B are incorrect.
(d) Only Statement B is correct.

71. Vallabhbhai Patel and .... helped Gandhi in Kheda by organising his tour of the villages and urging the peasants to stand firm against the government.
(a) Jamunalal Bajaj
(b) Mohammad Ali Jinnah
(c) Motilal Nehru
(d) Indulal Yajnik

72. The deliberations of the representatives at the Third Round Table Conference was held during the later months of which year?
(a) 1932 (b) 1929
(c) 1930 (d) 1931

73. Which part of the Indian Constitution deals with fundamental rights?
(a) Part III (b) Part II
(c) Part V (d) Part IV

74. At normal temperature and atmospheric pressure, ... has a density of 1.87 kg/m^3, which is 1.5 times heavier than air and exists as a liquid below the critical temperature of 31°C.
(a) carbon dioxide (b) nitrogen
(c) hydrogen (d) lithium

75. Sao Joao festival is celebrated primarily by the Catholic Christians in which of the following Indian states?
(a) Assam (b) Goa
(c) Manipur (d) Nagaland

76. According to the Global Hunger Index 2022, which neighbouring country is only behind India with a rank of 109 out of 121 countries?
(a) Bangladesh
(b) Afghanistan
(c) Nepal
(d) Pakistan

77. Which of the following was established by Jyotirao Govindrao Phule in 1873 to fight against idolatry and caste system?
(a) Shree Narayan Guru Dharma Paripalana (SNDP) Movement
(b) Satyashodhak Samaj
(c) Young Bengal Movement
(d) Arya Samaj

78. Who is the first Indian to participate in a Super Heavyweight Boxing event in the Olympic Games 2020?
(a) Satish Kumar
(b) Manish Harshit
(c) Sakshi Chaudhary
(d) Amit Panghal

79. Prithviraj Raso, an epic poem about the life of the 12th century Indian king, Prithviraj Chauhan, was written by
(a) Banabhatta
(b) Ashvaghosha
(c) Bharavi
(d) Chand Bardai

80. Which is the most widely accepted model to explain the formation and evaluation of the solar system?
(a) Nebular hypothesis
(b) Gas hypothesis
(c) Solar hypothesis
(d) Cloud hypothesis

81. How many controls are there globally that influence the climate of a particular zone?
(a) 8 (b) 6
(c) 3 (d) 5

82. Moatsu festival of Nagaland is celebrated by which of the following tribes?
(a) Bhil tribe (b) Ao tribe
(c) Munda tribe (d) Bodo tribe

83. Which of the following is considered as a good indicator of economic growth?
(a) Steady increase in loan.
(b) Steady increase in international trade.
(c) Steady increase in population.
(d) Steady increase in the GDP.

84. What is the full form of PPLO with respect to bacteria?
(a) Pleuro Pneumonia Like Organisms
(b) Pleuro Platelet Like Organisms
(c) Platelet Prone Like Organisms
(d) Pneumonia Platelet Like Organisms

85. Which of the following algae is also called kelp and found in the deep sea?
(a) Chlamydomona
(b) Fucus
(c) Laminaria
(d) Nostoc

86. Atal Tunnel connects which two places?
(a) Manali and Lahaul-Spiti valley
(b) Shimla and Nainital
(c) Shimla and Mussorie
(d) Manali and Nainital

87. Priorities of the government in the fiscal area and its related policies and deviations are mentioned in which part of the budget document?
(a) Fiscal Policy Strategy Statement
(b) Appropriation Bill
(c) Macroeconomic Framework Statement
(d) Medium-term Fiscal Policy Statement

88. The structure that produces and holds sperm cells in bryophytes (non-vascular plants) and ferns is called
(a) megasporangia
(b) archegonium
(c) antheridium
(d) protonema

89. Shore temple of Mamallapuram was built by
(a) Pallavas (b) Chalukayas
(c) Nagas (d) Cholas

90. Dr.Teejan Bai, a Padma Shri, Padma Bhushan and Padma Vibhushan awardee is globally recognised for her contribution to which of the following art forms?
(a) Gendi
(b) Pandavani
(c) Raut Nacha
(d) Jhirliti

91. In how many phases did the Indian Economy experience the success of the Green Revolution?
(a) Two (b) Three
(c) Five (d) Four

92. Which of the following statement is correct regarding climate of Indian sub-continent?
I. The climate of North India remains similar throughout the year.
II. The Himalayas protect the sub-continent from extremely cold winds from Central Asia.
(a) Only Statement B is correct.
(b) Both Statements A and B are incorrect.
(c) Only Statement A is correct.
(d) Both Statements A and B are correct

93. In a volleyball game, each team comprise of how many players?
(a) 5 (b) 6 (c) 8 (d) 7

94. What is Kalbaisakhi?
(a) Pre-monsoon showers and thunderstorms
(b) Cold waves and rains
(c) Snowfall and hail
(d) Heatwaves and loo

95. Which of the following books is an autobiography of the former American President Bill Clinton?
(a) Becoming
(b) My Life
(c) Long Walk to Freedom
(d) My Country My Life

96. Tansen, the famous musician, often sang in the court of which ruler?
(a) Sher Shah Suri
(b) Akbar
(c) Firoz Shah Tughlaq
(d) Alauddin Khilji

97. Who among the following founded the Kalakshetra Foundation in Chennai that is an important centre for the study and performance of fine arts?
(a) Rukmini Devi Arundale
(b) Yamini Krishnamurthy
(c) Mrinalini Sarabhai
(d) Alarmel Valli

98. Which German chemist was the first to show a graphical representation of the periodicity of an atomic volume plotted against atomic weight?
(a) Lothar Meyer
(b) John Newlands
(c) William Ramsay
(d) Glenn T. Seaborg

99. Which of the following is not an Equestrian discipline?
(a) Dressage
(b) Sprint
(c) Show jumping
(d) Vaulting

100. The Guru Kelucharan Mohapatra Yuva Pratibha Samman, 2021 was presented to Arushi Mudgal for .... dance.
(a) Mohiniyattam (b) Odissi
(c) Kuchipudi (d) Kathak

Part III
Quantitative Aptitude

101. The radii of two cylinders are in the ratio of 4 : 5 and their heights are in the ratio of 5 : 2. The ratio of their volume is
(a) 9 : 4 (b) 2 : 1
(c) 9 : 7 (d) 8 : 5

102. A person crosses a 900 m long street in 6 min. The speed of the person, in km/h, is
(a) 10 (b) 9
(c) 5 (d) 8

103. If 3 goats or 5 sheeps can graze a field in 54 days, then in how many days can 6 goats and 8 sheep graze the same field?
(a) 15 (b) 12
(c) 10 (d) 8

104. An item with a marked price of . ₹ 3800 was sold for . ₹ 3496, after a discount of y% was offered. What was the value of y?
(a) 7.5% (b) 8.5%
(c) 8% (d) 7%

105. A dishonest dealer announces selling his articles with 22% loss, but uses 35% lighter weights. What is the percentage of his profit or loss?
(a) 20% loss (b) 13% profit
(c) 13% loss (d) 20% profit

106. The following table represents the population of four different areas and the percentage of males, females and children among them.

Area	Population	Males	Females	Children
P	10000	40%	40%	20%
Q	20000	30%	40%	30%
R	16000	50%	30%	20%
S	18000	45%	35%	20%

What is the total number of children in areas P and Q together?
(a) 7000 (b) 9000
(c) 6000 (d) 8000

107. If θ is an acute angle and $\sin\theta + \operatorname{cosec}\theta = 2$,then the value of $\sin^5\theta + \operatorname{cosec}^5\theta$ is
(a) 10 (b) 2
(c) 4 (d) 5

108. What is the central angle corresponding to the expenditure spent on Education in the given figure?

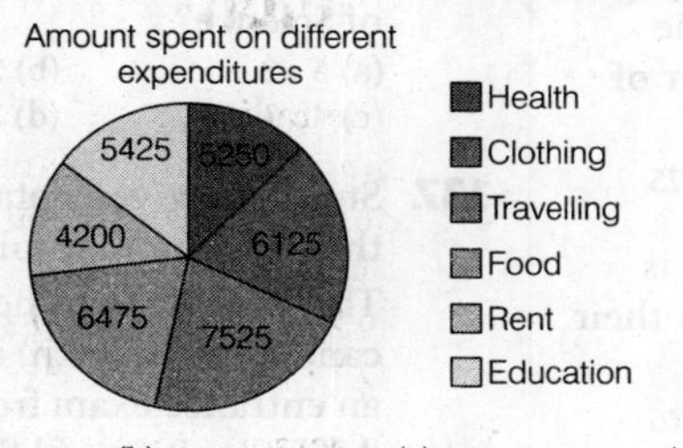

(a) 55.8° (b) 55.2° (c) 52° (d) 42°

109. Evaluate $\frac{0.04}{0.05}$ of $\frac{\left(3\frac{1}{3}-2\frac{1}{2}\right)\div\frac{1}{2}\text{of }1\frac{1}{4}}{\frac{1}{3}+\frac{1}{5}\text{of }\frac{1}{9}}$

(a) 0.3 (b) 5 (c) 3 (d) 0.03

110. If $\tan A = \frac{4}{3}, 0 \le A \ge 90°$, then find the value of $\sin A$.

(a) $\frac{3}{5}$ (b) 1 (c) $\frac{3}{4}$ (d) $\frac{4}{5}$

111. Find the LCM of 15, 24, 35 and 54.

(a) 5670 (b) 7560 (c) 7650 (d) 6570

112. Study the given data and answer the question that follows.

The data shows the number of candidates (in thousand) appearing for Civil Service (CS) and Engineering Service (ES) Examinations in the years 2020, 2021, 2022 in USA.

Year	Civil Service		Engineering Service	
	Total Number of candidates appeared	Graduates out of the total candidates Appeared (in%)	Total Number of candidates appeared	Graduates out of the total candidates appeared (in%)
2020	75	60	89	57
2021	110	64	118	65
2022	120	80	135	78

What is total number of graduates who appeared for both CS and ES together in the year 2022?

(a) 201000 (b) 201100 (c) 201300 (d) 201200

113. Let the speed of the boat in still water be 17 km/h and let the speed of the stream be 5 km/h. What is the time taken by the boat to go 110 km downstream?

(a) 4.5 h (b) 6 h (c) 5.5 h (d) 5 h

114. A number is first increased by 10% and then increased by 20%. The number, so obtained, is now decreased by 12%. What is the net increase or decrease percent in the original number?

(a) 16.16% increase (b) 14.14% decrease
(c) 11.11% decrease (d) 12.12% increase

115. Study the given graph carefully and answer the question that follows.

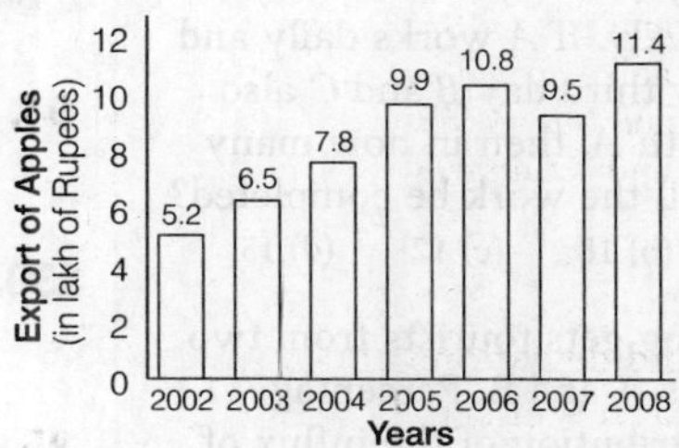

In which year was there maximum percentage increase in the export of apples to that of the previous years?

(a) 2003 (b) 2005 (c) 2006 (d) 2008

116. The following data gives a year-wise outlay (in lakhs of rupees) in a certain 4 year plan (2018-2022) of a state.

Year	Health	Housing	Transport	Education
2018-2019	6200	6500	7100	8000
2019-2020	7000	6600	7200	8100
2020-2021	7300	6800	7400	8200
2021-2022	7400	7000	7500	8400

What was the percentage increase during 2020-2021 over 2018-2019 in Education outlay?

(a) 2.8% (b) 3.2% (c) 2.0% (d) 2.5%

117. The first shirt is sold at twice the selling price of the second shirt. The first shirt is sold at 8% profit and the second shirt is sold at a 3% loss. What is the overall percentage profit on the shirts (rounded off to two decimal place)?

(a) 4.86% (b) 4.07% (c) 4.60% (d) 3.86%

118. The areas of the two triangles are in the ratio 4 : 3 and their heights are in the ratio 6 : 5. Find the ratio of their bases.

(a) 5 : 6 (b) 10 : 9 (c) 6 : 5 (d) 9 : 10

119. The largest number of four digits that is exactly divisible by 17 and 36 is

(a) 7956 (b) 9180 (c) 9792 (d) 8568

120. ΔPQR is an equilateral triangle inscribed in a circle. S is any point on the arc QR. Measure of $\frac{1}{2}\angle PSQ$ is

(a) 20° (b) 15° (c) 30° (d) 60°

121. If $\frac{x}{y}+\frac{y}{x}=1$ and $x+y=2$, then the value of x^3+y^3 is

(a) 1 (b) 3 (c) 0 (d) 2

122. If the height of a cone is 7 cm and the diameter of the circular base is 12 cm, then its volume is (nearest to integer)

(a) 254 cm^3 (b) 284 cm^3
(c) 264 cm^3 (d) 274 cm^3

123. *A*, *B* and *C* can do a piece of work in 20 days, 30 days and 60 days, respectively. If *A* works daily and on every third day *B* and *C* also work with *A*, then in how many days, will the work be completed?
(a) 21 (b) 18 (c) 12 (d) 15

124. Darjeeling gets tourists from two countries A and B. Percentage wise distribution of the influx of tourists is given below for the first six months of the year.

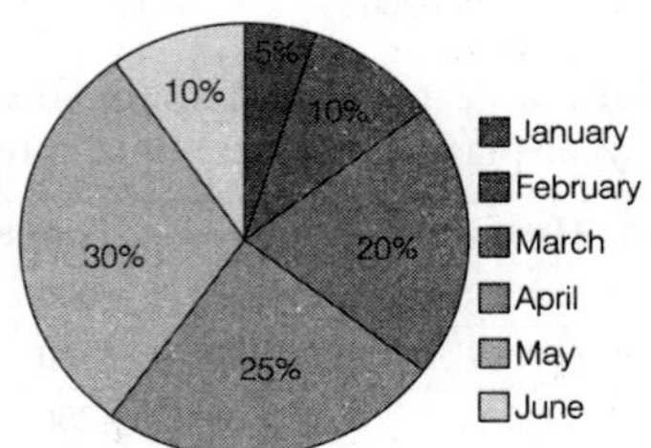

Total number of tourists = 60000	
Months	Ratio A : B
January	5:7
February	6:7
March	3:2
April	8:7
May	4:5
June	3:4

Find the ratio of tourists from country A coming in during March and April.
(a) 4:7 (b) 3:7 (c) 7:10 (d) 9:10

125. The value of $11\times11+11\div11-11\times11+11+11\times11-11-11\times11$ is
(a) 1 (b) 11 (c) 121 (d) 0

126. A man spends 72% of his salary and saves ₹ 5,740 per month. What is 10% of his annual salary (in ₹)?
(a) ₹ 21600 (b) ₹ 24600
(c) ₹ 20500. (d) ₹ 28400

127. The population of a city is 352314. It increases annually at the rate of 15% per annum. What was its population 2 yr ago?
(a) 302400 (b) 306360
(c) 266400 (d) 256400

128. A tourist van travels the distance of 35 km from Dehradun to Mussoorie at an average speed of 36 km/h and returns at 60 km/h. What is the approximate average speed (in km/h) of the tourist van for the entire journey?
(a) 48 (b) 42 (c) 45 (d) 50

129. The HCF and the LCM of two numbers are 5 and 175, respectively. If the ratio of the two numbers is 5:7, the larger of the two numbers is
(a) 35 (b) 25 (c) 45 (d) 75

130. The product of two numbers is 726 and their HCF is 11, then their LCM is
(a) 58 (b) 68 (c) 66 (d) 76

131. If a truck moves at a constant speed of 30 km/h for 1 km and 45 km/h for the next 1 km. What is the average speed of the truck?
(a) 32 km/h (b) 36 km/h
(c) 38 km/h (d) 34 km/h

132. *P*, *Q* and *R*, when working individually, can complete a job in, 36 days, 48 days and 144 days respectively. *P*, *Q* and *R* start working together. *P* leaves the job 12 days before completion and *Q* leaves the job 8 days before completion. *R* works from the beginning till the end of the job. Determine the total number of days taken to complete the job.
(a) 24 (b) 27 (c) 30 (d) 25

133. If $a+b=10$ and $ab=6$, then the value of a^3+b^3 is
(a) 800 (b) 820 (c) 860 (d) 840

134. If $\cos\theta-\sin\theta=\sqrt{2}\sin\theta$, then $(\cos\theta+\sin\theta)$ is
(a) $-\sqrt{2}\cos\theta$ (b) $\sqrt{2}\cos\theta$
(c) $\sqrt{2}\tan\theta$ (d) $-\sqrt{2}\sin\theta$

135. The sides of a triangle are in the ratio 5 : 12 : 13 and its perimeter is 90 cm. Find its area (in cm^2).
(a)150 (b) 270 (c) 30 (d) 60

136. The given pie-chart shows the distribution of the marks scored by Ram in five different subjects (in percentage).

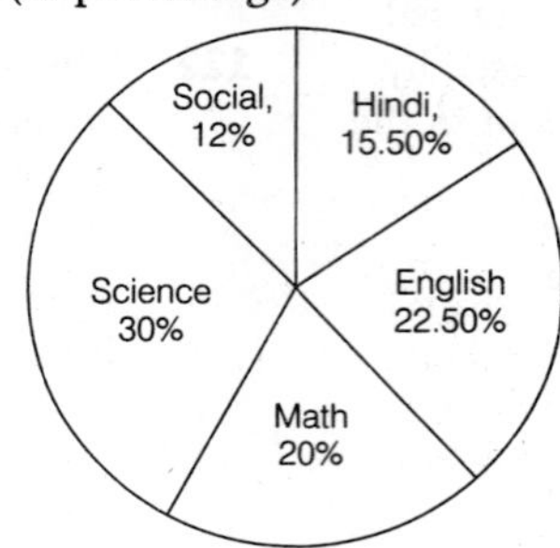

What is the ratio of the central angle of Maths to the central angle of Science?
(a) 5 : 2 (b) 2 : 3
(c) 4 : 3 (d) 3 : 5

137. Study the given data and answer the question that follows.
The tables shows the number of candidates (in lakh) appearing in an entrance exam from four different cities and the ratio of candidates passing and failing in the same.

City	A	B	C	D
Number of candidates	2.15	1.14	1.56	2.35

Ratio of candidates passing and failing within the city.

City	Passing	Failing
A	4	2
B	5	3
C	6	4
D	4	6

What is the number of failed candidates (in lakh) in city D ?
(a) 1.70 (b) 1.25
(c) 1.85 (d) 1.41

138. Two circles of radius 13 cm and 15 cm intersect each other at points *A* and *B*. If the length of the common chord is 12 cm, then what is the distance between their centres?
(a) $\sqrt{145}+\sqrt{184}$
(b) $\sqrt{131}+\sqrt{181}$
(c) $\sqrt{145}+\sqrt{169}$
(d) $\sqrt{133}+\sqrt{189}$

139. Study the given bar-graph and answer the question that follows.
The bar-graph shows the higher secondary students of a school for the years 2008,2009 and 2010.

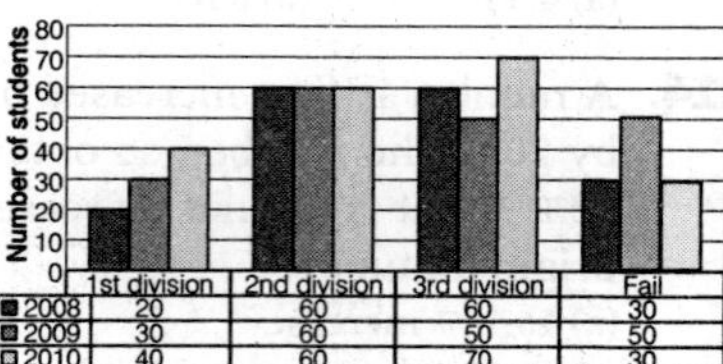

	1st division	2nd division	3rd division	Fail
2008	20	60	60	30
2009	30	60	50	50
2010	40	60	70	30

The percentage of students who passed in the second division in the year 2010 was
(a) 25% (b) 28%
(c) 30% (d) 32%

140. Two numbers are in the ratio 5:3 and the difference between these two numbers is 34. Find the smaller of the two numbers.
(a) 51 (b) 85 (c) 68 (d) 34

141. The radii of the ends of a frustum of a solid right-circular cone 45 cm high are 28 cm and 7 cm. If this frustum is melted and reconstructed into a solid right circular cylinder whose radius of base and height are in the ratio 3 : 5, then find the curved surface area (in cm^2) of this cylinder. [use $\pi = \frac{22}{7}$]
(a) 4580 (b) 4610
(c) 4640 (d) 4620

142. A man runs for 40 km. The time taken by him in the first 10 km is twice the time taken by him in the second 10 km. The time taken in the third 10 km is half of the time taken in the fourth 10 km, and the time taken in the fourth 10 km is equal to the time taken in the first 10 km. If his speed in the first 10 km is 40 km/h, then what is the average speed for 40 km?
(a) 50 km/h (b) $\frac{70}{3}$ km/h
(c) $\frac{160}{3}$ km/h (d) 40 km/h

143. Find the value of $(\tan^2\theta + \tan^4\theta)$.
(a) $\cot^2\theta - \tan^2\theta$ (b) $\sec^4\theta - \sec^2\theta$
(c) $\sec^2\theta - \sec^4\theta$ (d) $\sec^4\theta + \sec^2\theta$

144. If the hypotenuse of a right-angled triangle is 29 cm and the sum of the other two sides is 41 cm, then the difference between the other two sides is
(a) 5 cm (b) 1 cm
(c) 2 cm (d) 10 cm

145. Two numbers are in the ratio 3 : 4. The product of their HCF and LCM is 2700. The sum of the numbers is
(a) 60 (b) 105 (c) 15 (d) 45

146. Rajesh invested ₹ 10000 by dividing it into two different investment schemes, *A* and *B*, at simple interest rates of 8% and 10%, respectively. If the total interest earned in 2 yr is ₹ 1680, the amount invested in scheme *A* is
(a) ₹ 8000 (b) ₹ 2000
(c) ₹ 6000 (d) ₹ 4000

147. If 42, 36 and 35 are the first three terms of a proportion, then the fourth term is
(a) 27 (b) 28
(c) 30 (d) 32

148. If the price of am item is increased by 70% and then allows a scheme discount of 5% and 20% on this marked price. If price is paid in cash and additional discount of 20% is allowed, then what is his gain percentage?
(a) 2.25% (b) 4.36%
(c) 3.25% (d) 3.36%

149. Jonathan had borrowed a sum of money 3 yr ago at 10% interest per annum compounded annually for a 5yr period, with the amount to be paid at the end of the period being ₹161051. However, there is no pre-payment penalty and Jonathan has received some bonus payment now, with which he has decided to clear his debt. How much does Jonathan have to pay now to clear his debt?
(a) ₹ 133000 (b) ₹ 132900
(c) ₹ 133100 (d) ₹ 133200

150. What is the area of a triangle whose sides are of lengths 12 cm, 13 cm and 5 cm?
(a) 30 cm^2 (b) 15 cm^2
(c) 40 cm^2 (d) 70 cm^2

Part IV

English Comprehension

151. Select the incorrectly spelt word.
(a) Interrogate (b) Alienate
(c) Deserve (d) Assasinate

152. Select the most appropriate meaning of the given idiom.
Bend over backwards
(a) Working hard to try to impress
(b) Working slowly and lazily
(c) Going backward
(d) Using wrongful means

153. Select the incorrectly spelt word from the underlined words in the following sentence.
This was a <u>blatent disregard</u> to the <u>advisory.</u> By the host against it and in <u>violation</u> of norms of the meeting.
(a) advisory (b) blatent
(c) disregard (d) violation

154. Parts of the following sentence have been given as options. Select the option that contains an error.
The dancers swayed dainty on the stage last night.
(a) last night (b) on the stage
(c) The dancers (d) swayed dainty

155. Select the most appropriate one-word substitution of the given group of words.
A notice of the death of a person, often with a biographical sketch, as in a newspaper.
(a) Obituary (b) Oblivion
(c) Elegy (d) Advertisement

156. Select the incorrectly spelt word.
(a) Adjacent (b) Accomplish
(c) Agregate (d) Allure

157. Select the most appropriate idiomatic expression that can substitute the underlined segment in the given sentence.
Both Nitin and Uday are <u>of the same interests.</u>
(a) under the weather
(b) birds of the same feather
(c) blowing smoke without fire
(d) different kettles of fish

158. Select the most appropriate Antonym of the word 'moving' in the given sentence and choose the correct option.
The old grandfather clock chimed loudly, marking the passage of time with its steady tick-tock.
(a) Steady (b) Marking
(c) Chimed (d) Passage

159. Select the most appropriate option that can substitute the underlined segment in the given sentence. If there is no need to substitute it, select 'No substitution required'.
Her paintings are way better <u>then</u> her sketches.
(a) off (b) than (c) more
(d) No substitution required

160. Select the most appropriate meaning of the underlined idiom in the given sentence.
I hate to <u>get off on the wrong foot.</u>
(a) To start something with positive factors
(b) To start something with neutral factors
(c) To start a relationship or activity badly
(d) To start something with an injury on the wrong foot

161. Select the most appropriate phrasal verb to fill in the blank.
Arunima .... a lot during her vacation time.
(a) gets on (b) gets after
(c) gets about (d) gets along

162. Select the most appropriate meaning of the given idiom.
The best of both worlds
(a) Good things come after bad things
(b) An ideal situation
(c) Better to show than tell
(d) Make people comfortable

163. Select the option that can be used as a one-word substitute for the underlined group of words.
How did you become interested in learning <u>the art of producing beautiful handwriting?</u>
(a) Lexicography (b) Demography
(c) Calligraphy (d) Graphology

164. Select the most appropriate synonym of the given word.
Haphazard
(a) Random (b) Sociable
(c) Aggressive (d) Confident

165. Parts of the following sentence have been given as options. One of them may contain an error. Select the part that contains the error from the given options. If you don't find any error, mark 'No error' as your answer.
We feed the horse oats for a week because it had eaten all the hay.
(a) No error
(b) it had eaten all the hay
(c) We feed the horse oats
(d) for a week because

166. The following sentence has been split into four segments. Identify the segment that contains a grammatical error.
They will not attend / the event / as they're going / away at end of April.
(a) away at end of April.
(b) as they're going
(c) the event
(d) They will not attend

167. Select the option that can be used as a one-word substitute for the underlined group of words.
Ms. Scarlet was <u>indifferent to pain and pleasure,</u> she never complained.
(a) Hypocrite (b) Stoic
(c) Versatile (d) Amateur

168. You are preparing a speech for the upcoming function. Select a synonym for the highlighted word to make it better.
Despite the advancement in technology, many Rural areas in developing countries still lack access to basic necessities.
(a) Desist (b) Disguise
(c) Avenue (d) Apathy

169. Select the most appropriate meaning of the underlined idiom.
Students often <u>burn the midnight oil</u> to qualify for competitive examinations.
(a) put the things on fire at night
(b) want to be at a place full of light
(c) work until late at night
(d) sleep well

170. Select the most appropriate meaning of the underlined idiom.
More people in Turkey are <u>on the breadline</u> now than thirty years ago.
(a) Be very poor
(b) Are well educated
(c) Be very expensive
(d) Earn a lot of money

171. Select the most appropriate synonym of the given word.
Justifiable
(a) Indefensible (b) Neutral
(c) Maintainable (d) Reasonable

172. Select the most appropriate meaning of the given idiom.
Left out in the cold
(a) To serve stale and cold food
(b) To leave in hurry
(c) To bear extreme weather condition
(d) To be ignored

173. Select the option that can be used as a one-word substitute for the given group of words.
Fear of water
(a) Hydrophobia (b) Bibliophobia
(c) Microphobia (d) Botanophobia

174. Select the option that can substitute the bracketed word segment correctly and complete the following sentence meaningfully.
Lots of kids (was visualised) crossing the road when the bus arrived.
(a) were seen (b) have been seen
(c) are seen (d) was seen

175. Select the most appropriate synonym of the given word.
Dreadful
(a) Feeble (b) Terrible
(c) Auspicious (d) Propitious

176. Select the most appropriate meaning of the underlined idiom.
We <u>dodged a bullet</u> when we didn't fall for the agents' words.
(a) To give something a try
(b) To narrowly avoid situation
(c) To be out of your comfort zone
(d) To start performing better

177. Select the word which means the same as the group of words underlined in the given sentence.
The pandemic deeply affected small business owners, as <u>they have no means of livelihood left.</u>
(a) Pauper (b) Worker
(c) Unemployed (d) Mason

178. Select the option that will improve the underlined part of the given sentence.
<u>The use of chemicals, insecticides and pesticides</u> began after the Green Revolution.
(a) A practice of chemicals, insecticides and pesticides
(b) The custom of chemicals, insecticides and pesticides
(c) Consumption of chemicals, insecticides and pesticides
(d) The usage of chemicals, insecticides and pesticides

179. Select the most appropriate antonym of the given word.
Catastrophic
(a) Calamity (b) Fortuitous
(c) Fiasco (d) Sabotage

180. Select the most appropriate meaning of the given idiom.
An arm and a leg
(a) To ask for too much
(b) A large amount of money
(c) Everything is ready
(d) To be lost and bewildered

181. The following sentence has been split into four segments. Identify the segment that contains a spelling error.
He wrote his dairy / in code / so, that nobody / could understand it.
(a) so, that nobody
(b) could understand it
(c) in code
(d) He wrote his dairy

182. Select the most appropriate antonym for the highlighted word.
The **negligent** attitude of the cops was criticised.
(a) attentive (b) reluctant
(c) amplify (d) bored

183. Select the most appropriate one-word substitution of the given group of words.
A person engaged in or trained for spaceflight.
(a) Astute (b) Astronomer
(c) Astronaut (d) Atrocious

184. Select the most appropriate synonym of the given word.
Site
(a) Lap (b) Location
(c) Globe (d) Pull

185. Select the incorrectly spelt word.
(a) Serene (b) Triumph
(c) Comparsion (d) Unveil

186. The following sentence has been split into four segments. Identify the segment that contains a grammatical error.
She will have participate / in the dance competition / by the time her father / returns from the tour.
(a) in the dance competition
(b) She will have participate
(c) by the time her father
(d) returns from the tour

187. Select the option that can be used as a one-word substitute for the given group of words.
Working or operating quickly and effectively in an organised way.
(a) Efficient (b) Extensive
(c) Excellent (d) Effusive

188. Select the most appropriate synonym of the given word.
Abandon
(a) Perish (b) Desert
(c) Prolong (d) Retain

189. Select the most appropriate antonym of the given word.
Damp
(a) Misty (b) Arid
(c) Tropical (d) Soaked

190. Select the most appropriate meaning of the given idiom.
A leopard can't change his spots
(a) Someone who is cherished above all others
(b) A visual presentation is far more descriptive than words
(c) Something good that isn't recognised at first
(d) You cannot change who you are

Directions (Q. Nos. 191-195) *In the following passage, some words have been deleted. Read the passage carefully and select the most appropriate option for each blank.*

The Amazon rainforest is an awe-inspiring natural wonder that ...(1)... across several South American countries, including Brazil, Peru, Colombia, and Ecuador. Covering an ...(2)...area of 5.5 million square kilometres, it is the largest tropical rainforest on Earth. The Amazon jungle is ...(3)... for its remarkable biodiversity, harbouring an astonishing array of plant and animal species that are still being discovered and studied. The dense vegetation of the jungle creates a ...(4)... and complex ecosystem, supporting countless species and providing crucial ecosystem services such as carbon sequestration and climate regulation. It is also home to ...(5)... communities that have thrived within its rich confines for centuries, preserving their traditions and deep connection to the land.

191. Select the most appropriate option to fill in blank number 1.
(a) reaches (b) lengths
(c) amounts (d) spans

192. Select the most appropriate option to fill in blank number 2.
(a) gauged (b) rated
(c) estimated (d) evaluated

193. Select the most appropriate option to fill in blank number 3.
(a) great (b) acclaimed
(c) renowned (d) pre-eminent

194. Select the most appropriate option to fill in blank number 4.
(a) vigour (b) spirited
(c) vibrant (d) lavish

195. Select the most appropriate option to fill in blank number 5.
(a) late (b) ancient
(c) indigenous (d) organic

Directions (Q. Nos. 196-200) *Read the given passage and answer the question that follows.*

We started our research into organisational and personal excellence by studying a slightly different topic. We figured that if we could learn why certain people were more effective than others, then we could learn exactly what they did, clone it and pass it on to others. We asked people to identify who they thought were their most effective colleagues. In fact, over the past twenty-five years, we have asked over twenty thousand people to identify the individuals in their organisations who could really get things done. We wanted to find those who were not just influential but who were far more influential than the rest.

196. Which real life situation can be the most appropriate to be inferred from the passage?
(a) Inflation has direct influence on the morals and ethics of an individual.
(b) If we do something wrong to decent people, the same comes to haunt us even after many years.
(c) People nowadays do not have patience and want quick success and does not matter what path they choose to obtain their targets.
(d) Jassie is an efficient employee whose work ethics can be a case study to learn more about organisational and personal excellence.

197. Select the most suitable structure for the above passage.
(a) Chronological
(b) Cause and effect
(c) Pragmatic
(d) Compare and contrast

198. Select the most appropriate antonym of the given word.
Effective
(a) Deniable (b) Harmonious
(c) Fruitless (d) Courteous

199. Select the most appropriate title to the given passage.
(a) Research Grants in Organisations
(b) Learn, Clone and Pass
(c) The Most Effective Colleagues
(d) Different Topics

200. Select the statement that most appropriately sums up the passage given.
(a) Some people cannot be identified due to their most effective ways in 25 years.
(b) Research grants in an organisation should be increased for personal excellence.
(c) It takes 25 years of research to make people more effective and influential.
(d) Some people are more effective and more influential than others to get things done.

Know Correct Answers

1. (d)	2. (c)	3. (d)	4. (c)	5. (a)	6. (c)	7. (a)	8. (c)	9. (d)	10. (c)
11. (a)	12. (b)	13. (c)	14. (b)	15. (a)	16. (a)	17. (d)	18. (c)	19. (c)	20. (b)
21. (c)	22. (c)	23. (a)	24. (b)	25. (d)	26. (a)	27. (b)	28. (d)	29. (b)	30. (a)
31. (d)	32. (a)	33. (c)	34. (c)	35. (b)	36. (a)	37. (d)	38. (a)	39. (d)	40. (d)
41. (d)	42. (b)	43. (d)	44. (c)	45. (d)	46. (a)	47. (b)	48. (c)	49. (c)	50. (b)
51. (a)	52. (a)	53. (b)	54. (c)	55. (b)	56. (a)	57. (c)	58. (c)	59. (d)	60. (a)
61. (d)	62. (b)	63. (b)	64. (b)	65. (c)	66. (c)	67. (d)	68. (c)	69. (a)	70. (a)
71. (d)	72. (a)	73. (a)	74. (a)	75. (b)	76. (b)	77. (b)	78. (a)	79. (d)	80. (a)
81. (b)	82. (b)	83. (d)	84. (a)	85. (c)	86. (a)	87. (a)	88. (c)	89. (a)	90. (b)
91. (a)	92. (a)	93. (b)	94. (a)	95. (b)	96. (b)	97. (a)	98. (a)	99. (b)	100. (b)
101. (d)	102. (b)	103. (a)	104. (c)	105. (d)	106. (d)	107. (b)	108. (a)	109. (c)	110. (d)
111. (b)	112. (c)	113. (d)	114. (a)	115. (b)	116. (d)	117. (b)	118. (b)	119. (c)	120. (c)
121. (c)	122. (c)	123. (d)	124. (d)	125. (a)	126. (b)	127 (c)	128. (c)	129. (a)	130. (c)
131. (b)	132. (b)	133. (b)	134. (b)	135. (b)	136. (b)	137 (d)	138. (d)	139. (c)	140. (a)
141. (d)	142. (c)	143. (b)	144. (b)	145. (b)	146. (a)	147. (c)	148. (d)	149. (c)	150. (a)
151. (d)	152. (a)	153. (b)	154. (d)	155. (a)	156. (c)	157. (b)	158. (a)	159. (b)	160. (c)
161. (c)	162. (b)	163. (c)	164. (a)	165. (c)	166. (a)	167. (b)	168. (c)	169. (c)	170. (a)
171. (d)	172. (d)	173. (a)	174. (a)	175. (b)	176. (b)	177. (a)	178. (d)	179. (b)	180. (b)
181. (d)	182. (a)	183. (c)	184. (b)	185. (c)	186. (b)	187. (a)	188. (b)	189. (b)	190. (d)
191. (d)	192. (c)	193. (c)	194. (c)	195 (c)	196 (d)	197. (c)	198. (c)	199. (c)	200. (d)

Answer & Solutions

1. (d) The given figure is embedded in option figure (d).

2. (c) Pattern of the series is as follows,

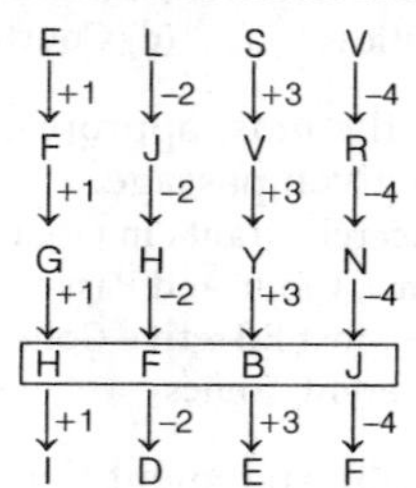

3. (d) As,

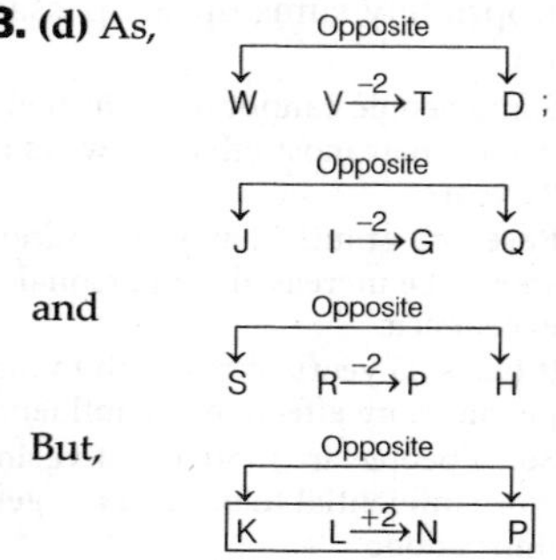

4. (c) According to the question,

(Left) (Right)

A D G E F B C

∴ C sits at the extreme right.

5. (a) According to the question,

G A M E = 8 4 2 6

M U S T = 7 8 5 3

So, code of M = 8

6. (c) As per the given statements,

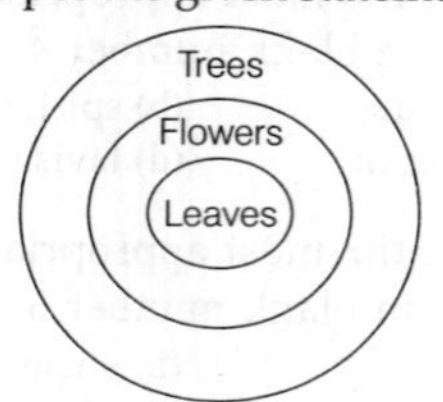

Conclusions

I. (✗) II. (✓)

Hence, only Conclusion II follows.

7. (a) From the positions of the dice, it is clear that numbers '6', '5', '2' and '4' are on adjacent faces of the face showing number '1'.

Hence, number '3' will be on the opposite face of the face showing 1.

8. (c) Figure shown in option (c) is the correct mirror image of the question figure.

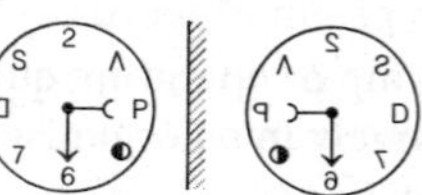

9. (d) Given equation,

$137 \div 56 \times 7 - 6 + 31 = ?$

According to the question,

After interchanging the signs,

+ → −	× → ÷
− → ×	÷ → +

$= 137 + 56 \div 7 \times 6 - 31$

$= 137 + 8 \times 6 - 31$

$= 137 + 48 - 31 = 185 - 31 = \boxed{154}$

10. (c) The correct order as per the English dictionary,

Logician → Loincloth → Lollipop →
(4) (2) (1)

Lonely → Longways
(5) (3)

⇒ 4, 2, 1, 5, 3

11. (a) Pattern of the series is as follows,

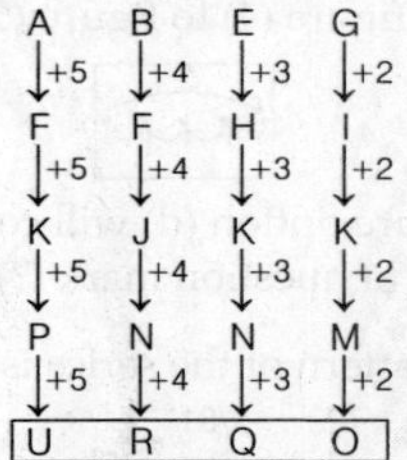

12. (b) According to the question,

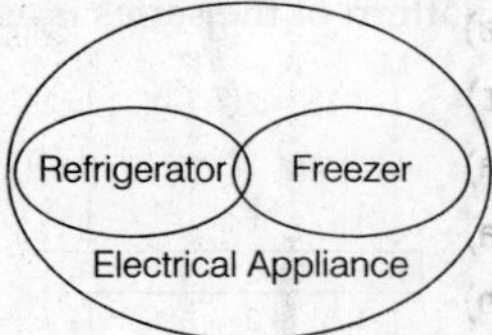

Freezer is a part of refrigerator and both are electrical appliance.

13. (c) As, (7, 35, 42)

$7 \times 5 = 35, 7 \times 6 = 42$

and (4, 20, 24)

$4 \times 5 = 20, 4 \times 6 = 24$

Similarly, (9, 45, 54)

$9 \times 5 = 45, 9 \times 6 = 54$

14. (b) According to the question,

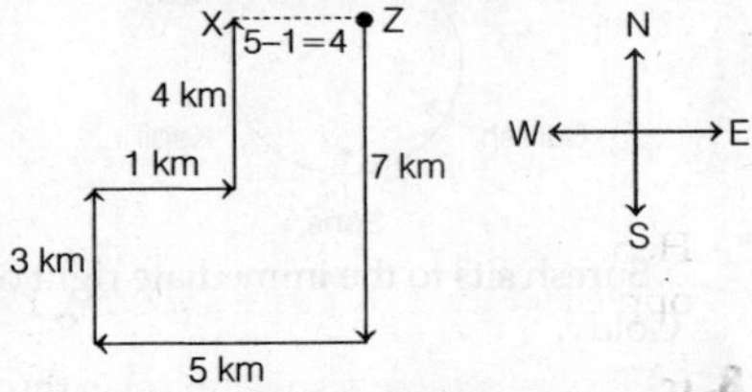

So, he needs to move 4 km towards East to reach Point Z.

15. (a) In the given figure series with each step circles move to the next corners in anti-clockwise direction and the right small rectangle of the middle figure gets shaded and unshaded in alternate figures. Hence, figure given in option (a) will replace the question mark (?).

16. (a) In both the dice, number 5 and 4 are common.

	5	4	1	
Common	↕	↕	↕	Opposite
	5	4	6	

So, 1 is opposite to 6.

17. (d) According to the statements,

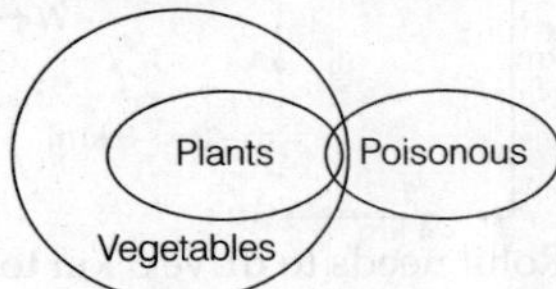

Conclusions

I. (✗) II. (✓)

Hence, only Conclusion II follows.

18. (c) Arranging the words as per the English dictionary, we get

Descend → Desire → Desolate →
(3) (1) (5)

Desperate → Destination → Destructive
(6) (2) (4)

⇒ 3, 1, 5, 6, 2, 4

19. (c) In the given series, the figure is rotating 90° in clockwise direction with each step.

Hence, figure (c) will come at the place of question mark (?)

20. (b) In position of dice I and dice III number 1 and 5 are common.

1	5	2	
↕	↕	↕	Opposite
1	5	4	

So, number 2 is opposite face of 4.

21. (c) As, (264, 462) ⇒ 264 → 462 (+198)

and (132, 330) ⇒ 132 → 330 (+198)

Similarly, (386, 584) ⇒ 386 → 584 (+198)

22. (c) Given equation,

2 B ? D 2 = 4 B 32 D 8

After replacing the signs,

A	B	C	D
+	×	–	÷

$2 \times ? \div 2 = 4 \times 32 \div 8$

$\Rightarrow \quad 2 \times \frac{?}{2} = 4 \times \frac{32}{8}$

$\Rightarrow \quad 2 \times \frac{?}{2} = 4 \times 4$

$? = \boxed{16}$

23. (a) Given equation,

$250 - 10 + 10 \times 5 \div 2 = ?$

After replacing the signs,

+ → ×	× → –
– → ÷	÷ → +

$\Rightarrow 250 \div 10 \times 10 - 5 + 2 = ?$

$\Rightarrow 25 \times 10 - 5 + 2 = 250 - 5 + 2$

$\Rightarrow 252 - 5 = \boxed{247}$

24. (b) As, $W \xrightarrow{+2} Y \xrightarrow{-7} R \xrightarrow{+1} S$;

$P \xrightarrow{+2} R \xrightarrow{-7} K \xrightarrow{+1} L$

and $F \xrightarrow{+2} H \xrightarrow{-7} A \xrightarrow{+1} B$

But, $\boxed{P \xrightarrow{+3} S \xrightarrow{-9} J \xrightarrow{+1} K}$

25. (d) As,

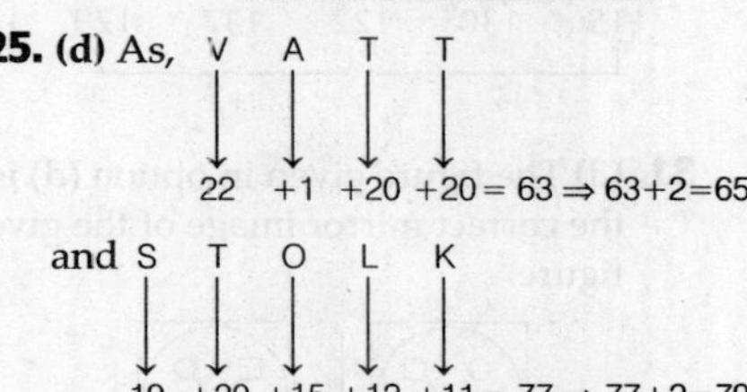

Similarly,

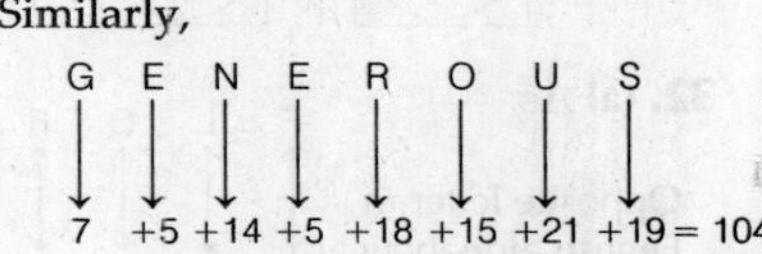

26. (a) Option figure (a) is embedded in question figure.

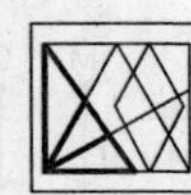

27. (b) Given expression,

$[\{(14 \times 6) - (4 \div 3)\} + (6 - 4)] \div 3$

After interchanging the signs,

+ → ÷	– → +
× → –	÷ → ×

$[\{(14 - 6) + (4 \times 3)\} \div (6 + 4)] \times 3$

$= [\{8 + 12\} \div 10] \times 3$

$= [20 \div 10] \times 3 = 2 \times 3 = \boxed{6}$

28. (d) As,

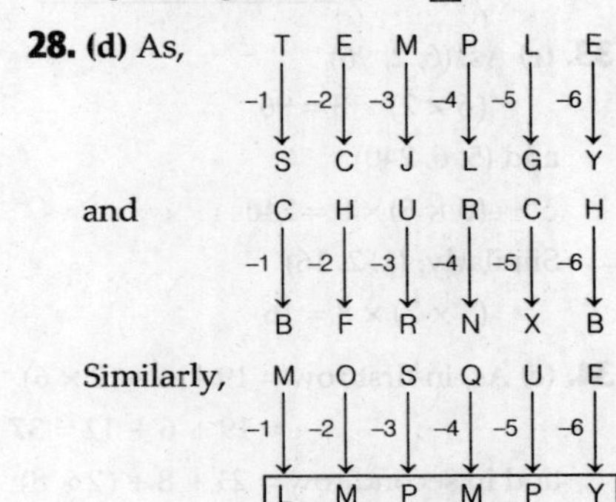

29. (b) As,

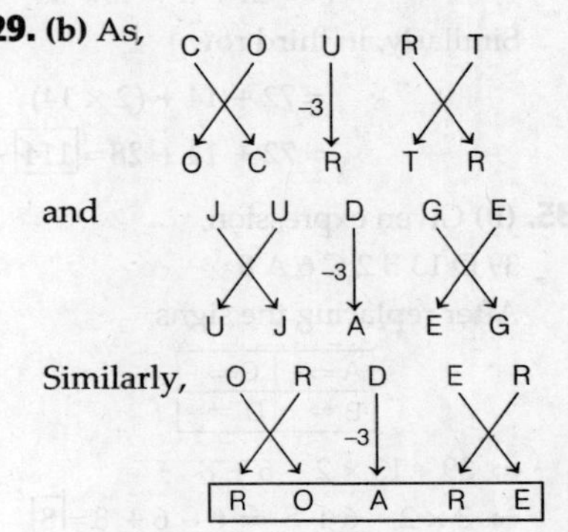

30. (a) Pattern of the series is as follows,

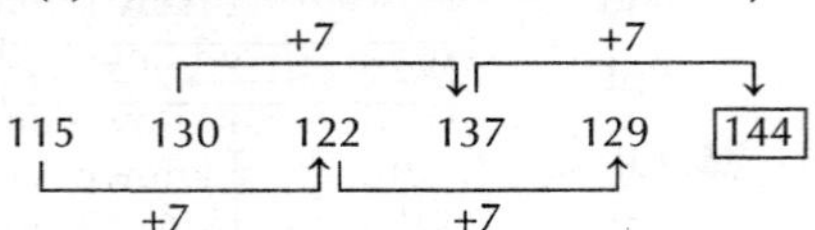

31. (d) The figure given in option (d) is the correct mirror image of the given figure.

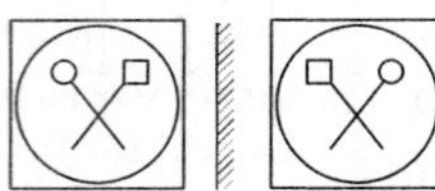

32. (a) As,

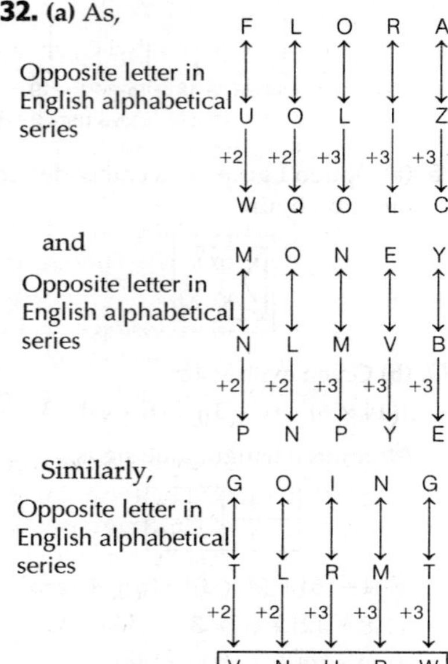

33. (c) As, (6, 2, 96)

$(6 \times 2) \times 8 = 96$

and (5, 6, 240)

$(5 \times 6) \times 8 = 240$

Similarly, (1, 2, 16)

$(1 \times 2) \times 8 = 16$

34. (c) As, in first row $= 19 + 6 + (2 \times 6)$

$= 19 + 6 + 12 = 37$

and in second row $= 21 + 8 + (2 \times 8)$

$= 21 + 8 + 16 = 45$

Similarly, in third row

$= 72 + 14 + (2 \times 14)$

$= 72 + 14 + 28 = \boxed{114}$

35. (b) Given expression,

39 D 13 B 2 C 6 A 8

After replacing the signs,

A ⇒ +	C ⇒ −
B ⇒ ×	D ⇒ ÷

$\Rightarrow 39 \div 13 \times 2 - 6 + 8$

$\Rightarrow 3 \times 2 - 6 + 8 \Rightarrow 6 - 6 + 8 = \boxed{8}$

36. (a) As, (7, 91, 98)

$7 \times \boxed{13} = 91 + 7 = 98$

and (4, 52, 56)

$4 \times \boxed{13} = 52 + 4 = 56$

Similarly, (12, 156, 168)

$12 \times \boxed{13} = 156 + 12 = 168$

37. (d) Given equation,

96 D 3 B 8 C 25 A 14 = ?

After replacing the signs,

A = +	C = −
B = ×	D = ÷

$\Rightarrow 96 \div 3 \times 8 - 25 + 14$

$\Rightarrow 32 \times 8 - 25 + 14$

$\Rightarrow 256 - 25 + 14$

$\Rightarrow 270 - 25 = \boxed{245}$

38. (a) Given equation,

7 A 3 B 24 D 2 = 20 B ? A 3

After replacing the signs,

A = +	C = −
B = ×	D = ÷

$\Rightarrow 7 + 3 \times 24 \div 2 = 20 \times ? + 3$

$\Rightarrow 7 + 3 \times 12 = 20 \times ? + 3$

$\Rightarrow 7 + 36 = 20 \times ? + 3$

$\Rightarrow 43 = 20 \times ? + 3$

$\Rightarrow 40 = 20 \times ?$

$\therefore ? = \boxed{2}$

39. (d) Pattern of the series is as follows,

35 [41] 40 47 45 53 (+6, −1, +7, −2, +8)

40. (d) According to the question,

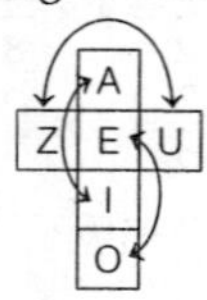

A is opposite to I.

E is opposite to O.

Z is opposite to U.

Hence, only figure (3) is possible.

41. (d) The series is following the two alternate patterns which are given below.

(i) From figure (1) to figure (2) and from figure (3) to figure (4),

N=New letter

(ii) From figure (2) to figure (3) and from figure (4) to figure (5),

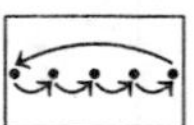

∴ Figure option (d) will come at the place of question mark (?).

42. (b) Pattern of the series is as follows,

−1/729 −1/81 −1/9 [−1] (×9, ×9, ×9)

43. (d) Pattern of the series is as follows,

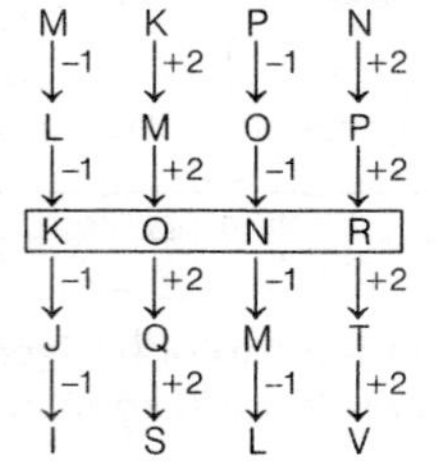

44. (c) As, butterfly is the transformation stage of a caterpillar.

Similarly, a larva is a stage in the life cycle of many insects.

45. (d) According to the question,

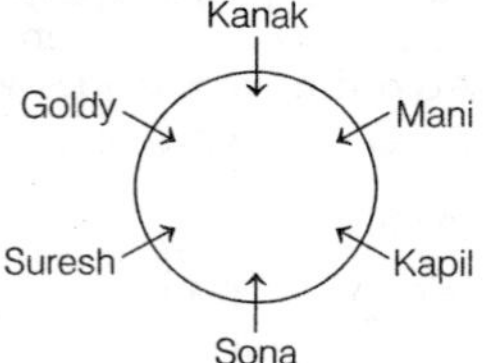

∴ Suresh sits to the immediate right of Goldy.

46. (a) According to the question,

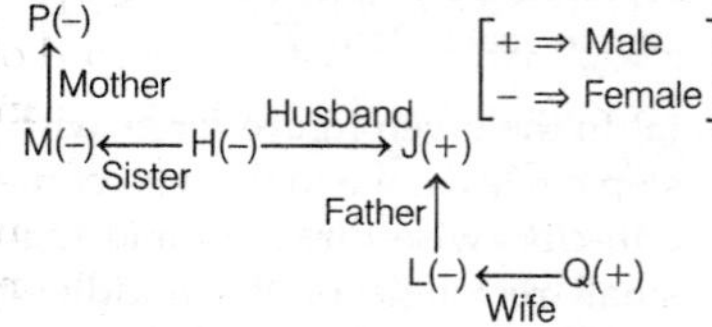

Hence, P is mother's mother of L.

47. (b) According to the question,

C(−) ←Sister— J(−); C —Son→ M(+); Z —Mother→ J

[+ ⇒ Male, − ⇒ Female]

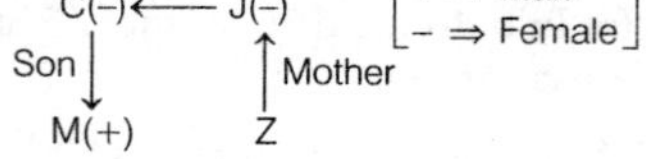

Hence, J is M's mother's sister.

48. (c) According to the question,

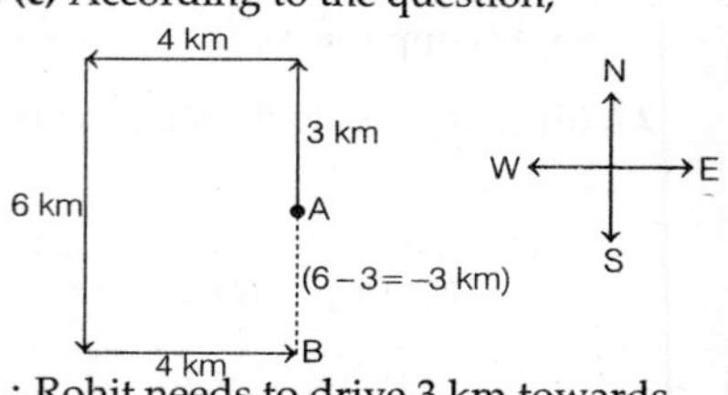

∴ Rohit needs to drive 3 km towards North to reach point A.

49. (c) As,

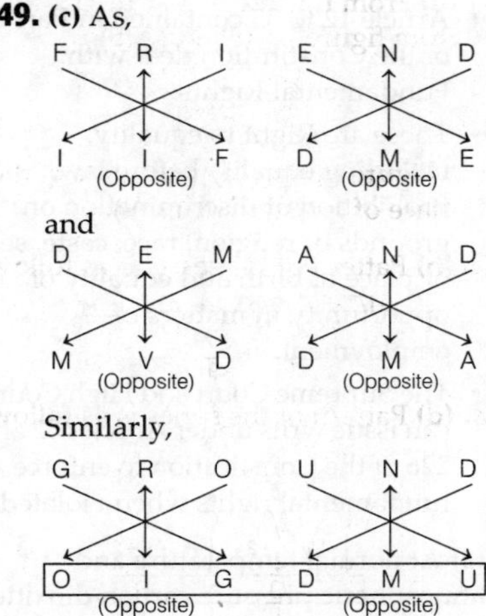

50. (b) According to the venn diagram,

Pencil Eraser Sharpener

∴ Pencil, eraser and sharpener all are different from one another.

51. (a) Ammonia does not belong to the family of organic compounds.

- Ammonia is an inorganic chemical compound of nitrogen and hydrogen with the formula NH_3.
- Furan is an organic compound with the formula C_4H_4O.
- Decane is an alkane with the formula $C_{10}H_{22}$.
- Nonane is an alkane, which is a type of hydrocarbon that has only single bonds between its carbon atoms.

52. (a) In November 2020, Lydian Nadhaswaram has set a record of becoming the worlds fastest piano player ever.

- Lydian Nadhaswaram is an Indian musician prodigy from Chennai, Tamil Nadu.
- He gained international recognition at the young age of 14, when he won the first season of the CBS television show 'The World's Best' in 2019.

53. (b) Kharif crops needs annual precipitation of atleast 100 cm.

- India's Northern and Northern-Eastern plains, coastal regions and deltaic areas are all where rice is farmed.
- Kharif crops also known as monsoon crops are sown in June or July and harvested in September.
- These crops are rice, maize, millet, sugarcane, ragi, pulses, soybean, groundnut, etc.

54. (c) Bhutia dance is performed in Sikkim.

- It is an integral part of Bhutia culture, traditionally performed during festivals, celebrations and community gatherings.
- The Bhutia tribe, widely known for its traditional grandeur, art and cuisine.
- The popular Bhutia folk dances are Denzong-Neh-Na, Ta-Shi-Yang-Ku, Tashi Shabdo, Guru Chinlap, Singhi Chham and Yak Chham.
- On 16th May 1975, Sikkim become the 22nd state of Indian Union, and the monarchy was abolished.

55. (b) The Farakka Treaty was signed between Bangladesh and India on 12th December, 1996 for a period of 30 yr.

- The main goal of the Farakka Barrage Project Complex is to divert an adequate amount of Ganga waters to the Bhagirathi Hoogly river system through a 38.38 km long feeder canal.
- This will help to preserve and maintain Kolkata Port.

56. (a) Ajayaraja was the great ruler of Chauhan dynasty.

- He established the city of **Ajmer** which was originally known as **Ajyameru** in 1113 AD.
- He made it the capital of his kingdom.
- Prithviraj was a ruler of the Chahamana dynasty who ruled from 1177 to 1192 CE.
- Arnoraj was a ruler of the Chahamana dynasty who ruled from 1135 to 1150 CE.

57. (c) 13 Members of Parliament were elected from Punjab to the 17th Lok Sabha.

- There are total 20 members of Parliament from Punjab, 13 in Lok Sabha and 7 in Rajya Sabha.
- The Lok Sabha, constitutionally the House of the People, is the lower house of India's bicameral Parliament, with the upper house being the Rajya Sabha.

58. (c) Private sector was not allowed in all industries, and was not in existence to enforce regulation of the industrial sector.

59. (d) My Story is an autobiographical book written by Indian author and poet Kamala Das (also known as Kamala Surayya or Madhavikutty).

- The book was originally published in Malayalam, titled Ente Katha.
- Suzanna Arundhati Roy is an Indian author best known for her novel 'The God of Small Things (1997)', she won the Booker Prize for Fiction in 1997.

60. (a) Methyl ethyl ketone is an organic compound which is also known as 2-butanone or methylacetone.

- Propanone is also known as acetone.
- It is a colourless, flammable liquid with a sharp. Methyl pentanone is also known as 4-methyl-2-pentanone.
- 2-butanol is also known as sec-butyl alcohol. It is a colourless, flammable liquid with a mild, musty odour.

61. (d) Fundamental Duties in Indian Constitution are made Non-justiciable in nature.

- The constitution does not provide for their direct enforcement by the courts, there is not legal sanction against their violation.
- These Fundamental Duties were mainly inspired by the body of the former Soviet Union there are total 11 fundamental duties in India.
- Article-51 'A' embodied in Part IV of the Constitution deals with Fundamental Duties.

62. (b) KC Neogy was the first Chairman of Finance Commission of India.

- The First Finance Commission was constituted Vice-Presidential Order dated 22nd November, 195,1 under the chairmanship of Shri KC Neogy on 6th April, 1952.
- The Commission decides the basis for sharing the divisible taxes by the centre and the states and principles that govern the grants-in-aid to the states every five years.

63. (b) The 1st Commonwealth Games were held in 1930 at Hamilton, Canada.

- The Commonwealth Games is the second-largest sports festival in the world after the Olympics.
- The Games are held once in four years but only in the middle of the Olympic years.
- India participated for the first time in the second Commonwealth Games held in London in 1934.
- The 2026 Common wealth Games will be held at Glasgow.

64. (b) Continental Shelf which is the shallowest part of the ocean has an average gradient of 1° or even less.

- A continental shelf is the edge of a continent that lies under the ocean.
- A continental shelf extends from the coastline of a continent to a drop-off point called the shelf break.

65. (c) Dhruvasena II was a ruler of the Maitraka dynasty which ruled in western India.

- The Maitraka dynasty was founded by Bhatarka.
- The capital of the dynasty was in Vallabhi, Dhruvasena II ruled the dynasty from 627-641 CE and became a vassal after his defeat to Harshavardhana.

66. (c) The National Commission for Women established under the National Commission for Women Act, 1990.

- The National Commission for Women (NCW) is a statutory body of the Government of India, generally concerned with advising the government on all policy matters affecting women.
- It was established on 31st January, 1992, under the provisions of the Indian Constitution.
- The first head of the commission was Jayanti Patnaik.
- In 2024, Smt. Vijaya Kishore Rahatkar was appointed as Chairman of this commission.

67. (d) Stomata are found on the surface of leaves, on flower petals, on stems and on roots.

- Stomata is one of the essential parts that is involved in gaseous exchange. There are thousands of stomata on the surface of the leaves.
- Most of these are found on the lower side of the leaves.
- They play a crucial role in regulating the exchange of gases between the plant and its environment.

68. (c) The Constitution confers extraordinary powers on the President to deal with the following three types of emergencies

- National Emergency (Article 352)
- President's Rule (Article 356 and 365)
- Financial Emergency (Article 360)

69. (a) In India, all loans that are below ₹ 1 lakh can be considered as micro loans.

- Micro loans are small loans that are typically provided to low income individuals or entrepreneurs who do not have access to traditional banking services.
- Micro loans in India are provided by a variety of organisations, including banks, Non-Bank Financial Institutions (NBFCs) and Micro Finance Institutions (MFIs).

70. (a) Both Statements A and B are correct because, in *p*-block elements, the last electron enters the outermost *p*-orbital and the non-metals and metalloids exist only in the p-block of the periodic table.

- The *p*-block elements have their outermost electrons in the p-orbital and the filling of these orbitals determines their position in the periodic table.
- The p-block of the periodic table is a region that includes elements from groups 13 to 18.

71. (d) Vallabhbhai Patel and Indulal Yajnik helped Gandhi in **Kheda** by organising his tour of the villages and urging the peasants to stand firm against the government.

- The Kheda movement was regulated by Mahatma Gandhi for the Peasant-Patidar Community of Kheda.
- The Peasant-Patidar Community of Kheda had refused to pay the high tax, i.e., 23% tax, even after ruining the whole crop due to the plague and cholera.

72. (a) The deliberations of the representatives at the Third Round Table Conference was held during the later months of 1932.

- The First Round Table Conference was held in London in three sessions between November 1930 and January 1931.
- The conference was attended by representatives of the British Government, Indian princes and various political parties, but the Indian National Congress (INC) did not participate.

73. (a) Part III of the Indian Constitution deals with fundamental rights.

- Article 12 to 35 contained in Part III of the Constitution deal with Fundamental Rights.
- These are Right to equality, including equality before law, prohibition of discrimination on grounds of religion, race, caste, sex or place of birth and equality of opportunity in matters of employment.
- The Supreme Court and High Courts can issue writs under Articles 32 and 226 of the Constitution to enforce fundamental rights when violated.

74. (a) At normal temperature and atmospheric pressure carbon dioxide has a density of 1.87 kg/m^3, which is 1.5 times heavier than air and exists as a liquid below the critical temperature of 31°C.

75. (b) The Sao Joao festival is celebrated in Goa to pay tribute to St. John the Baptist.

- During the Sao Joao festivities, Goans present fruits to each other.
- Sao Joao is an annual Catholic religious festival celebrated on 24th June in Goa.
- Assam is a state in North-Eastern India, known for its lush green landscapes, one-horned rhinoceroses and rich cultural heritage.

76. (b) Based on the Global Hunger Index (GHI) 2022, Afghanistan is the only neighbouring country ranked behind India with a rank of 109 out of 121 countries.

- India's GHI ranking is 107, indicating a 'serious' level of hunger.
- GHI is a tool designed to comprehensively measure and track hunger at the global, regional and country levels.
- According to Global Hunger Index 2024, India ranks 105th out of 127 countries.

77. (b) Satyashodhak Samaj, a social reform society, was founded on 24th September, 1873 by Jyotirao Phule in Maharashtra.

- Its purpose was to liberate the less privileged in society from exploitation and oppression.
- It was established with the ideals of human well-being, unity, equality and easy religious principles and rituals.

78. **(a)** Satish Kumar is the first Indian to participate in a Super Heavy weight Boxing event in the Olympic Games 2020.
- Amit Panghal is an Indian Army Junior Commissioned Officer (JCO) and an amateur boxer.
- He won a silver medal at the 2019 AIBA World Boxing Championships.
- He also won a gold medal at the 2018 Asian Games. He was awarded the Arjuna Award in 2022.

79. **(d)** 'Prithviraj Raso' was written by **Chand Bardai**, in Hindi.
- It was written in Braj Bhasha. An epic poem, it demonstrates the life and contributions of the 12th century king, Prithviraj Chauhan.
- Banabhatta was a Sanskrit poet who lived in the 7th century CE.
- He was the court poet of King Harshavardhana of the Vardhana dynasty.

80. **(a)** Nebular hypothesis is the most widely accepted model to explain the formation and evaluation of the solar system.
- The basic idea behind the nebular hypothesis is that a large cloud of dust and gas (a nebula) collapsed under its own gravity.
- As the nebula collapsed, it spun faster and flattened out into a disk shape.
- This theory was proposed by the German philosopher Immanuel Kant in 1755.

81. **(b)** Six major controls are there globally that influence the climate of a particular zone.
- They are latitude, altitude, pressure and wind system, distance from the sea (continentality), ocean currents and relief features.
- Climate is the long-term pattern of weather in a particular area.

82. **(b)** Moatsu Festival is a post-harvest festival celebrated by the Ao Naga people of Nagaland, India.
- This festival is celebrated after seeds have been sown in the fields.
- Men and women of the tribe gather around large outdoor fires and performing traditional dances.
- The Aos are a major Naga ethnic group native to Mokokchung District of Nagaland.

83. **(d)** Steady increase in the GDP is considered as a good indicator of economic growth.
- GDP growth can be defined as the net increase in the market value of all goods and services produced in an economy.
- Gross Domestic Product (GDP) is the standard measure of the value added created through the production of goods and services in a country during a certain period.

84. **(a)** The full form of PPLO is Pleuro Pneumonia like Organisms.
- It belongs to the genus Bacteria.
- The PPLO are also termed Mycoplasma.
- The reason behind naming mycoplasmas as PPLO is because they are free-living organisms and simple prokaryotes.
- It was first discovered by Louis Pasteur in 1930 when he was dealing with pleuropneumonia in cattle.

85. **(c)** **Laminaria** algae is also called kelp and found in the deep sea.
- Laminaria is a genus of brown seaweed in the order Laminariales (keep) comprising 31 species native to the North Atlantic and Northen pacific oceans.

86. **(a)** Atal Tunnel connected Manali and Lahaul-Spiti valley.
- Atal Tunnel was dedicated to the Nation by the Prime Minister Shri Narendra Modi on 3rd October, 2020.
- The 9.02 km long, strategically significant, Atal Tunnel, that runs under the 'Rohtang Pass' is constructed on the Manali - Leh Highway.
- Atal Tunnel has officially been certified by World Book of Records, as the 'World's Longest Highway Tunnel above 10,000 Feet'.

87. **(a)** The priorities of the government in the fiscal area and its related policies and deviations are mentioned in the Fiscal Policy Strategy Statement section of the budget document.
- This section outlines the government's strategic priorities for the ensuing financial year, including its plans for taxation, expenditure, lending and investments, administered pricing, borrowings and guarantees.
- It also discusses any deviations from previous fiscal measures and provides justification for these deviations.

88. **(c)** The structure that produces and holds sperm cells in bryophytes (non-vascular plants) and ferns is called an antheridium.
- Bryophytes are called 'amphibians of the plant kingdom' because they are terrestrial plants, but require water to complete their life cycle at the time of sexual reproduction.

89. **(a)** Shore temple of Mamallapuram was built by Pallavas.
- The Shore Temple of Mahabalipuram was built in the 8th century CE by Narasimhavarman II, also known as Rajasimha.
- Narasimhavarman II reigned over the Pallava kingdom throughout the early 8th century and was a great patron of the arts.

90. **(b)** Dr. Teejan Bai, awarded Padma Shri, Padma Bhushan and Padma Vibhushan, globally recognised for her contribution to Pandavani traditional performing art form, from Chhattisgarh.
- Pandavani form of folk theatre is popular in the Central Indian state of Chhattisgarh and in the neighbouring areas of Madhya Pradesh, Odisha and Andhra Pradesh.

91. **(a)** There were two phases to the Green Revolution.
- In the first phase (the mid-60s to mid-70s), the use of HYV seeds was restricted to a more affluent state like Punjab, Andhra Pradesh and Tamil Nadu etc.
- Further, the use of HYV seeds primarily benefitted the wheat growing regions only.
- In the second phase (the mid-70s to mid-80s), the HYV technology spread to a larger number of states and benefitted more variety of crops.

92. **(a)** Only Statement B is correct because Himalayas act as a natural barrier, preventing the cold winds from Central Asia from blowing directly into the Indian sub-continent.
- This helps to moderate the climate of the sub-continent. statement A is

incorrect because—The climate of North India varies significantly throughout the year.

- In the winter, the temperatures can drop to below freezing, while in the summer, the temperatures can reach up to 40 °C.

93. (b) In a volleyball game, each team comprise six players.

- It has been a part of the official Olympic programme since 1964.
- The game is played on a rectangular court divided into two equal-sized squares by a net.
- Hockey is considered India's national game because it is one of the oldest games.
- It was approved by the Indian Hockey Federation in 1925.

94. (a) Kalbaisakhi is Pre-monsoon showers and thunderstorms.

- It is also known as Bordoi Sila in Assam.
- It is a localised rainfall and thunderstorm event that occurs in Bangladesh and Eastern India, particularly in the states of Bihar, Jharkhand, Odisha, Tripura, Assam and West Bengal, during the pre-monsoon season, typically from April to May.

95. (b) My Life is an autobiography of the former American President Bill Clinton.

- Becoming is the memoir by former First Lady of the United States Michelle Obama, published on 13th November, 2018.
- Long Walk to Freedom is an autobiography by South Africa's first democratically elected President Nelson Mandela.
- 'My Country My Life' is an autobiography of Lal Krishna Adwani.

96. (b) Tansen, the famous musician sangin the court of Akbar.

- Tansen was a legendary Indian musician who is considered one of the greatest exponents of Hindustani classical music.
- The real name of Tansen was Rama Tanu Pandey.
- Tansen is still revered in India today and his tomb in Gwalior is a popular pilgrimage site.

97. (a) Rukmini Devi Arundale founded the Kalakshetra Foundation in Chennai that is an important centre for the study and performance of fine arts.

- Yamini Krishnamurthy is an Indian dancer of Bharatanatyam and Kuchipudi styles of dancing.

98. (a) Lothar Meyer German chemist was the first to show a graphical representation of the periodicity of an atomic volume plotted against atomic weight.

- John Newlands put forward his law of octaves in 1864 in which he arranged all the elements known at the time into a table in order of relative atomic mass.

99. (b) Sprint is not an Equestrian discipline.

- Equestrian discipline is a broad term that encompasses all activities involving horses, including riding, driving, and vaulting.
- There are many different equestrian disciplines, each with its own unique rules, equipment and goals.

100. (b) The Guru Kelucharan Mohapatra Yuva Pratibha Samman, 2021 was presented to Arushi Mudgal for Odissi dance.

- She is a disciple of Guru Ratikant Mohapatra and has won several awards for her dance, including the National Dance Award.
- Guru Kelucharan Mohapatra recieved Padma Vibhushan in 2000.
- He was the first one to recieve this award from Odisha.

101. (d) Given, ratio of radius of cylinders

$$r_1 : r_2 = 4 : 5$$

And ratio of heights of cylinders

$$h_1 : h_2 = 5 : 2$$

Then, ratio of volume of cylinders

$$= \frac{\pi r_1^2 h_1}{\pi r_2^2 h_2}$$

$$= \frac{(4)^2 \times 5}{(5)^2 \times 2} = \frac{8}{5}$$

Hence, ratio = 8 : 5

102. (b) Given distance = 900 m

And time = 6 min

Then, speed $= \frac{\text{distance}}{\text{time}} = \frac{900}{6}$ m/min

$$= \frac{900}{6} \times \frac{60}{1000} \text{ km/h}$$

$$= 9 \text{ km/h}$$

103. (a) According to the question,

3 goats = 5 sheeps

∴ 6 goats = 10 sheeps

6 goats and 8 sheeps

= 10 + 8 = 18 sheeps.

Time taken by 5 sheeps to graze the field = 54 days.

∴ Time taken by 18 sheeps to graze the field $= \frac{54}{18} \times 5 = 15$ days.

∴ 6 goats and 18 sheeps will graze the field in 15 days.

104. (c) Given, MP = ₹ 3800

and SP = ₹ 3496

Then, discount% = y%

$$= \frac{\text{MP} - \text{SP}}{\text{MP}} \times 100$$

$$= \frac{3800 - 3496}{3800} \times 100$$

$$= \frac{304}{3800} \times 100$$

Then, $y = 8\%$

105. (d) Let total weight = 1000 gm

But, it uses 35% lighter weight then

$$= 1000 - 1000 \times \frac{35}{100} = 650 \text{ gm}$$

Let cost of 1000 gm = ₹ 100

But, he sells it 22% less than SP

$$= 100 - 100 \times \frac{22}{100}$$

SP of article = ₹ 78

Then, cost of 650 gm

$$= 650 \times \frac{100}{1000} = ₹\ 65$$

Then, profit% $= \frac{78 - 65}{65} \times 100 = 20\%$

106. (d) Total number of children in areas P and Q = 20% of 10000 + 30% of 20000

= 2000 + 6000 = 8000

107. (b) Given, $\sin\theta + \operatorname{cosec}\theta = 2$

Then, $\sin\theta + \frac{1}{\sin\theta} = 2$

$\Rightarrow \quad \sin^2\theta - 2\sin\theta + 1 = 0$

$\Rightarrow \quad (\sin\theta - 1)(\sin\theta - 1) = 0$

$\Rightarrow \quad \sin\theta - 1 = 0$

$\Rightarrow \quad \sin\theta = 1$

Now, $\sin^5\theta + \operatorname{cosec}^5\theta = \sin^5\theta + \frac{1}{\sin^5\theta}$

$= (1)^5 + \frac{1}{(1)^5} = 2$

108. **(a)** Total amount spent on expenditures

$= 5425 + 5250 + 6125 + 7525 + 4200 + 6475$

$= 35000$

Expenditure spent on education = 5425

Then, central angle $= \frac{5425}{35000} \times 360°$

$= 55.8°$

109. **(c)** Given, $\frac{0.04}{0.05}$ of $\frac{\left(3\frac{1}{3} - 2\frac{1}{2}\right) \div \frac{1}{2} \text{ of } 1\frac{1}{4}}{\frac{1}{3} + \frac{1}{5} \text{ of } \frac{1}{9}}$

$= \frac{4}{5} \times \frac{\left(\frac{10}{3} - \frac{5}{2}\right) \div \frac{1}{2} \times \frac{5}{4}}{\frac{1}{3} + \frac{1}{5} \times \frac{1}{9}}$

$= \frac{4}{5} \times \frac{\left(\frac{20-15}{6}\right) \div \frac{5}{8}}{\frac{1}{3} + \frac{1}{45}}$

$= \frac{4}{5} \times \frac{\frac{5}{6} \times \frac{8}{5}}{\frac{15+1}{45}} = \frac{4}{5} \times \frac{5}{6} \times \frac{8}{5} \times \frac{45}{16} = 3$

110. **(d)** Given, $\tan A = \frac{4}{3}$

We know, $\tan\theta = \frac{\text{Height}}{\text{Base}}$

By Pythagoras theorem,

$(\text{Hypotenuse})^2 = (\text{Height})^2 + (\text{Base})^2$

$(\text{Hypotenuse})^2 = (4)^2 + (3)^2$

$= 16 + 9 = 25$

Hypotenuse $= \sqrt{25} = 5$

Then, $\sin A = \frac{\text{Height}}{\text{Hypotenuse}} = \frac{4}{5}$

111. **(b)** Factor of $15 = 3 \times 5$

$24 = 2 \times 2 \times 2 \times 3$

$35 = 5 \times 7$

$54 = 2 \times 3 \times 3 \times 3$

Then, LCM

$= 2 \times 3 \times 5 \times 2 \times 2 \times 7 \times 3 \times 3$

$= 7560$

112. **(c)** Total number of graduates who appeared for both CS ad ES together in the year 2022 =(80% of 120 + 78% of 135) in thousand

=(96 + 105.3) in thousands

= 201300

113. **(d)** Given, speed of the boat in still water $(x) = 17$ km/h

And speed of the stream $(y) = 5$ km/h

We know, Time $= \frac{\text{Distance}}{\text{Speed}} = \frac{d}{x+y}$

Then, time taken by the boat to go 110 km downstream

$= \frac{110}{17+5} = \frac{110}{22} = 5\text{ h}$

114. **(a)** Let original number = 100

Then, according to the question,

New number $= 100 \times \frac{110}{100} \times \frac{120}{100} \times \frac{88}{100}$

$= 116.16$

Net increase per cent

$= \frac{116.16 - 100}{100} \times 100$

$= 16.16\%$ (Increase)

115. **(b)** Percentage increase in export

In 2003 $= \frac{6.5 - 5.2}{5.2} \times 100 = 25\%$

In 2005 $= \frac{9.9 - 7.8}{7.8} \times 100 = 26.92\%$

In 2006 $= \frac{10.8 - 9.9}{9.9} \times 100 = 9.09\%$

In 2008 $= \frac{114 - 9.5}{9.5} \times 100 = 20\%$

Hence, maximum increase in parentage of export is in the year 2005.

116. **(d)** The percentage increase during 2020-2021 over 2018-19 in education

outlay $= \frac{8200 - 8000}{8000} \times 100$

$= \frac{200}{8000} \times 100 = 2.5\%$

117. **(b)** Let the CP of first shirt = ₹x

then CP of second shirt = ₹y

According to the question,

SP of first shirt = ₹2 × SP of second shirt

$x \times \frac{108}{100} = y \times \frac{97}{100} \times 2$

$\frac{x}{y} = \frac{97 \times 2}{108} = \frac{97}{54}$

Now Let $x = 97a$ and $y = 54a$

∴ Net percentage profit

$= \frac{97a \times \frac{8}{100} - 54a \times \frac{3}{100}}{97a + 54a} \times 100$

$= \frac{776 - 162}{151} = \frac{614}{151}$

$= 4.0662 \approx 4.07\%$

118. **(b)** Given, ratio of areas of the two triangles $= \frac{4}{3}$

Ratio of their height $= \frac{6}{5} = \frac{h_1}{h_2}$

We know,

Area of triangle $= \frac{1}{2} \times \text{Base} \times \text{Height}$

According to the question,

$\frac{\text{Area of triangles}_1}{\text{Area of triangle}_2} = \frac{\frac{1}{2} \times b_1 \times h_1}{\frac{1}{2} \times b_2 \times h_2}$

$\Rightarrow \quad \frac{4}{3} = \frac{b_1 \times 6}{b_2 \times 5}$

$\Rightarrow \quad \frac{b_1}{b_2} = \frac{20}{18} = \frac{10}{9}$

Hence, ratio of their bases = 10 : 9.

119. **(c)** Largest number of 4 digits = 9999

LCM (17, 36) = 612

∵ When 9999 is divided by 612 then, we get 207 as remainder.

Then, the largest number of 4 digits divisible by 17 and 36

$= 9999 - 207 = 9792$

120. **(c)** According to the question,

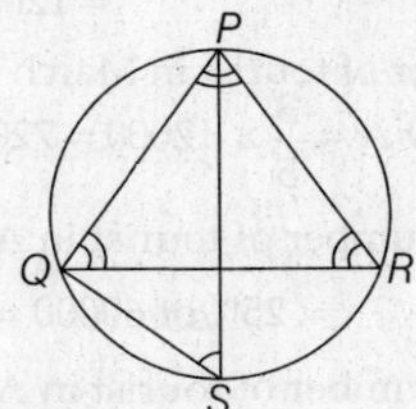

We know,

In equilateral triangle all angles are 60°.

Then, $\angle PSQ = \angle PRQ = 60°$ (angle in the same segment)

So, $\frac{1}{2}\angle PSQ = \frac{60°}{2} = 30°$

121. **(c)** Given, $x + y = 2$ ...(i)

and $\frac{x}{y} + \frac{y}{x} = 1$

$x^2 + y^2 = xy$ ...(ii)

Now, $x^3 + y^3 = (x + y)(x^2 + y^2 - xy)$

$= 2(xy - xy)$ [$\because$ from Eq. (ii)]

$= 2 \times 0$

Hence, $x^3 + y^3 = 0$

122. **(c)** Given, height of a cone $(h) = 7$ cm

And diameter of the base = 12 cm

Then, radius $(r) = \frac{12}{2} = 6$ cm

Volume of a cone $= \frac{1}{3}\pi r^2 h$

$= \frac{1}{3} \times \frac{22}{7} \times 6 \times 6 \times 7$

$= 264\ \text{cm}^3$

123. **(d)** $A \longrightarrow 20\text{d}$ — 3; $B \longrightarrow 30\text{d}$ — 2; $C \longrightarrow 60\text{d}$ — 1; 60 (Total work)

Let A works in 1 day = 3 unit

B works in 1 day = 2 unit

C works in 1 day = 1 unit

A works daily and third day B and C also work with A, then work completed in 3 days

$= 3 + 3 + (2 + 1 + 3)$

$= 6 + 6 = 12$ unit

If total work = 60 unit

And 12 unit work done in 3 days.

Then, 60 unit work done in

$= \frac{3}{12} \times 60 = 15$ days

124. **(d)** Total number of tourist in March from country A and B = 20% of 60000

= 12000

Number of tourist in March from country A $= \frac{3}{5} \times 12000 = 7200$

Total number of tourist in April

= 25% of 60000 = 15000

Then number of tourist in April from country A $= \frac{8}{15} \times 15000 = 8000$

$\therefore$ Required ratio $= \frac{7200}{8000} = 9 : 10$

125. **(a)** Given, $11 \times 11 + 11 \div 11 - 11 \times 11 + 11 + 11 \times 11 - 11 - 11 \times 11$

By using BODMAS,

$= 11 \times 11 + 1 - 11 \times 11 + 11 + 11 \times 11 - 11 - 11 \times 11$

$= 121 + 1 - 121 + 11 + 121 - 11 - 121$

$= 1$

126. **(b)** Let his monthly salary = ₹ x per month

According to the question,

$x - 72\%$ of $x = 5740$

$\frac{28}{100}x = 5740$

$x = \frac{5740 \times 100}{28} =$ ₹ 20500

Then, his annual salary

$= 20500 \times 12 = 246000$

Hence, 10% of his annual salary

= 10% of 246000 = ₹ 24600

127. **(c)** Before 2 yr ago population of city was

$= 352314 \times \frac{100}{115} \times \frac{100}{115}$

$= 266400$

128. **(c)** Given, average speed to going (x) = 36 km/h

Average speed to return (y) = 60 km/h

Then, average speed for the entire journey $= \frac{2xy}{x + y}$

$= \frac{2 \times 36 \times 60}{36 + 60} = 45$ km/h

129. **(a)** Let numbers be $5x$ and $7x$.

Then, we know that,

Product of two numbers

= HCF × LCM

$\Rightarrow \quad 5x \times 7x = 5 \times 175$

$\Rightarrow \quad x^2 = \frac{5 \times 175}{5 \times 7}$

$\Rightarrow \quad x^2 = 25$

$\therefore \quad x = 5$

Then, larger number $= 7x = 7 \times 5 = 35$

130. **(c)** We know, product of two numbers.

= HCF × LCM

$\Rightarrow \quad 726 = 11 \times \text{LCM}$

$\therefore \quad \text{LCM} = \frac{726}{11} = 66$

131. **(b)** If distance is same the average

speed $= \frac{2xy}{x + y}$

(Here, x = 30km/h, y = 45km/h)

$= \frac{2 \times 30 \times 45}{30 + 45}$

= 36 km/h

132. **(b)** P ⟶ 36d — 4; Q ⟶ 48d — 3; R ⟶ 144d — 1; 144 (Total unit)

If P, Q and R work together, then work of 1 day = 4 + 3 + 1 = 8 unit

If P works 12 days then work completed = 4 × 12 = 48 units

And Q works 8 days then work competed = 3 × 8 = 24 units

Then, total work will be

= 144 + 48 + 24 = 216 unit

Hence, time will be taken to do complete work $= \frac{216}{4 + 3 + 1}$ days

= 27 days

133. **(b)** Given,

$a + b = 10$ ...(i)

and $ab = 6$ ...(ii)

On squaring both sides of Eq. (i),

$(a + b)^2 = (10)^2$

$a^2 + b^2 + 2ab = 100$

$a^2 + b^2 = 100 - 2 \times 6 = 88$ ...(iii)

Now, $a^3 + b^3 = (a + b)(a^2 + b^2 - ab)$

From Eqs. (i), (ii) and (iii), we get

$a^3 + b^3 = 10 \times (88 - 6)$

$= 10 \times 82 = 820$

134. **(b)** Given, $\cos\theta - \sin\theta = \sqrt{2}\sin\theta$ ...(i)

On squaring on both sides,

$(\cos\theta - \sin\theta)^2 = (\sqrt{2}\sin\theta)^2$

$\cos^2\theta + \sin^2\theta - 2\sin\theta\cos\theta = 2\sin^2\theta$

$1 - 2\sin^2\theta = 2\cos\theta\sin\theta$ ...(ii)

Now, on squaring,

$(\cos\theta + \sin\theta)^2 = \cos^2\theta + \sin^2\theta + 2\sin\theta\cos\theta$

$(\cos\theta + \sin\theta)^2 = 1 + (1 - 2\sin^2\theta)$ [from Eq. (ii)]

$(\cos\theta + \sin\theta)^2 = 2 - 2\sin^2\theta = 2(1 - \sin^2\theta)$

$\cos\theta + \sin\theta = \sqrt{2\cos^2\theta}$

Hence, $\cos\theta + \sin\theta = \sqrt{2}\cos\theta$

135. **(b)** Let sides of triangle be $5x$,cm $12x$ and $13x$ cm, respectively.

Then, perimeter

$\Rightarrow \quad 5x + 12x + 13x = 90$

$\Rightarrow \quad 30x = 90$

$\Rightarrow \quad x = 3$ cm

Now, sides are 15, 36 and 39 cm.

Then, $s = \frac{a+b+c}{2} = \frac{15+36+39}{2}$

$= \frac{90}{2} = 45$ cm

Hence, Area $= \sqrt{s(s-a)(s-b)(s-c)}$

$= \sqrt{45(45-15)(45-36)(45-39)}$

$= \sqrt{45 \times 30 \times 9 \times 6}$

$= \sqrt{5 \times 9 \times 5 \times 6 \times 9 \times 6}$

$= 9 \times 5 \times 6 = 270 \text{ cm}^2$

136. (b) According to the question,

Central angle of central angles of Maths

$= 20\%$ of $360°$

$= \frac{20}{100} \times 360° = 72°$

And central angle of science

$= 30\%$ of $360° = 108°$

Now, ratio of central angles of Maths and science $= \frac{72°}{108°} = 2:3$

137. (d) Total number of candidates in city D = 2.35 lakhs

Number of candidates failed in city D

$= \frac{6}{10} \times 2.35 = 1.41$ lakhs

138. (d) Given, $AB = 12$ cm, $AO_1 = 15$ cm and $AO_2 = 13$ cm

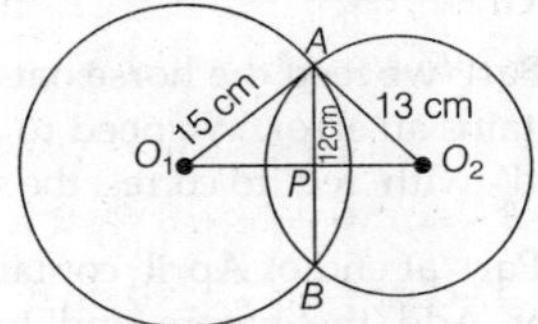

Then, $AP = \frac{1}{2} AB = \frac{12}{2} = 6$ cm

In ΔAO_1P by Pythagoras theorem,

$(AO_1)^2 = (O_1P)^2 + (AP)^2$

$(O_1P)^2 = (15)^2 - (6)^2$

$= \sqrt{225-36} = \sqrt{189}$

Similarly,

In ΔAO_2P

$(PO_2)^2 = (AO_2)^2 - (AP)^2$

$(PO_2) = \sqrt{(13)^2 - (6)^2}$

$= \sqrt{169-36} = \sqrt{133}$

Hence, distance between two centres O_1O_2

$= O_1P + O_2P = \sqrt{189} + \sqrt{133}$ cm

139. (c) Total students passed in 2010

$= 40 + 60 + 70 + 30 = 200$

Now, percentage of students who passed in the second division in the year 2010 was

$= \frac{60}{200} \times 100 = 30\%$

140. (a) Let the numbers be $5x$ and $3x$ respectively.

According to the question,

$5x - 3x = 34$

$\Rightarrow \quad 2x = 34$

$\Rightarrow \quad x = 17$

Now, smaller number

$= 3x = 3 \times 17 = 51$

141. (d) Given, radius of frustum $r_2 = 28$ cm, $r_1 = 7$ cm and height = 45 cm

Let radius of cylinder $= 3x$

and height of cylinder $= 5x$

Now, volume of frustum

= Volume of cylinder

$\frac{1}{3}\pi(r_1^2 + r_2^2 + r_1 \times r_2) \times h = \pi r^2 h$

$\frac{1}{3}\{(7)^2 + (28)^2 + 7 \times 28\} \times 45$

$= 9x^2 \times 5x$

$\Rightarrow \quad \frac{1}{3}(49 + 784 + 196) = \frac{45x^3}{45}$

$\Rightarrow \quad \frac{1}{3} \times 1029 = x^3$

$\Rightarrow \quad x^3 = 343$

$\therefore \quad x = 7$

Radius of cylinder $(R) = 3x = 3 \times 7$

$= 21$ cm

Height of cylinder

$(H) = 5x = 5 \times 7 = 35$ cm

Now, curved surface area of cylinder

$= 2\pi RH$

$= 2 \times \frac{22}{7} \times 21 \times 35 = 4620 \text{ cm}^2$

142. (c) Given total distance = 40 km

And for first 10 km his speed

= 40 km/h

Then, Time $= \frac{\text{Distance}}{\text{Speed}} = \frac{10}{40} = \frac{1}{4}$ h

Let for second 10 km he takes time $= xh$

According to the question,

He takes time in Ist 10 km $= 2xh$

and For IInd 10 km $= xh$

For IIIrd 10 km $= xh$

For IVth 10 km $= 2xh$

Now, $2x = \frac{1}{4}$, then $x = \frac{1}{8}h$

Total time $= 2x + x + x + 2x$

$= 6x = 6 \times \frac{1}{8} = \frac{6}{8}h$

Then, average speed $= \frac{\text{Total distance}}{\text{Total time}}$

$= \frac{40}{\frac{6}{8}} = \frac{160}{3}$ km/h

143. (b) Given, $\tan^2\theta + \tan^4\theta$

$= \tan^2\theta(1 + \tan^2\theta)$

$\therefore \quad = (\sec^2\theta - 1)[\sec^2\theta]$

$[\because \sec^2\theta - \tan^2\theta = 1]$

$= \sec^4\theta - \sec^2\theta$

144. (b)

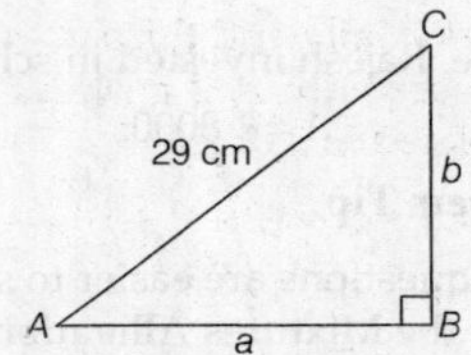

Given, $AC = 29$ cm

and let $AB = a$ cm and $BC = b$ cm

Then, according to questions,

$a + b = 41$ cm ...(i)

And by Pythagoras theorem,

$a^2 + b^2 = (29)^2 = 841$ ...(ii)

Squaring on both sides Eq. (i),

$(a+b)^2 = (41)^2$

$a^2 + b^2 + 2ab = 1681$

$841 + 2ab = 1681$ [$\because$ From Eq. (i)]

$2ab = 1681 - 841 = 840$

$ab = 420$ ...(iii)

Now, $(a-b)^2 = a^2 + b^2 - 2ab$

$= 841 - 2 \times 420$

$= 841 - 840$

$(a-b)^2 = 1$

$\therefore \quad a - b = 1$

145. (b) Let the numbers be $= 3x$ and $4x$

We know that,

Product of two numbers = HCF × LCM

$$3x \times 4x = 2700 \Rightarrow x^2 = \frac{2700}{12}$$

$$\Rightarrow \quad x^2 = 225$$

$$\therefore \quad x = 15$$

Now, sum of the numbers $= 3x + 4x$

$$= 7x = 7 \times 15 = 105$$

146. (a) Let amount invested in scheme

$A = ₹\, x$

and amount invested in scheme

$B = ₹\, 10000 - x$

Then, we know, $SI = \frac{P \times R \times T}{100}$

According to the question,

$$1680 = \frac{x \times 8 \times 2}{100} + \frac{(10000 - x) \times 10 \times 2}{100}$$

$$\Rightarrow 1680 \times 100 = 16x + 200000 - 20x$$

$$\Rightarrow \quad 4x = 200000 - 168000$$

$$\Rightarrow \quad 4x = 32000$$

$$\therefore \quad x = 8000$$

Hence, Rajesh invested in scheme

$A = ₹\, 8000.$

Toppers Tip

Such questions are easier to solve using the Mixtures Alligation Method rather than relying on the traditional approach.

147. (c) Given, $42 : 36 :: 35 : d$

Let fourth term is d.

Then, $\frac{42}{36} = \frac{35}{d}$

$$\therefore \quad d = \frac{35 \times 36}{42} = 30$$

148. (d) Let CP of article = ₹ 100

Then, CP of after 70% increase

$$= 100 + 100 \times \frac{70}{100} = ₹\, 170$$

After 5% of 20% discount on MP

Net discount $= x + y - \frac{xy}{100}$

$$= 20 + 5 - \frac{20 \times 5}{100} = 24\%$$

and again 20% additional discount on cash payment then net discount

$$= 24 + 20 - \frac{24 \times 20}{100}$$

$$= 44 - 4.8 = 39.2\%$$

Now, SP of article $= 170 \times \left(\frac{100 - 39.2}{100}\right)$

$$= ₹\, 103.36$$

Then, profit $= \frac{103.36 - 100}{100} \times 100$

$$= 3.36\%$$

149. (c) Let the amount borrowed be ₹ P.

Then, $A = P\left(1 + \frac{r}{100}\right)^t$

$$\Rightarrow \quad P\left(1 + \frac{10}{100}\right)^5 = 161051$$

$$\Rightarrow \quad P\left(1 + \frac{10}{100}\right)^3 \times \left(\frac{11}{10}\right)^2 = 161051$$

$\therefore$ Amount paid after 3 years,

$$P\left(1 + \frac{10}{100}\right)^3$$

$$= \frac{161051 \times 100}{121} = ₹133100$$

150. (a) We know that,

Area of triangle $= \frac{1}{2} \times B \times H$

Since, 12, 13 and 5 are forming pythagorean triplets.

Therefore, the triangle would be right angled.

Area $= \frac{1}{2} \times 12 \times 5 = 30\ \text{cm}^2$

151. (d) The incorrectly spelt word is 'assasinate'. The correct spelling is 'assassinate'.

152. (a) The idiom 'bend over backwards' means to make every effort to achieve something, especially to be fair or helpful.

153. (b) The incorrectly spelt word is 'blatent'. The correct spelling is 'blatant'.

154. (d) Part 'swayed dainty' contains the error. The verb is followed by an adjective. Hence, we need to replace it by an adverb- 'swayed gracefully' to correct the sentence.

155. (a) An obituary is an piece of writing, often published in newspapers, that gives the news of someone's death.

156. (c) The incorrectly spelt word is 'agregate'. The correct spelling is 'aggregate'.

157. (b) The idiom 'birds of the same feather' means beings (typically humans) of similar type, interest, personality, character, or other distinctive attributes that tend to mutually associate. It fits the situation as the boys have similar interests.

158. (a) The word 'steady' meaning stable is the antonym of 'moving'.

159. (b) The word 'then' is contextually incorrect in the given sentence. Replace it with 'than' to correct the sentence.

160. (c) The underlined idiom 'to get off on the wrong foot' means to make a bad start at something, especially a task or relationship.

161. (c) The correct filler for the given blank is 'gets about'. It means to be socially active .

162. (b) The idiom 'the best of both worlds' means a situation that is ideal from all sides.

163. (c) Calligraphy is the art of producing beautiful handwriting.

164. (a) The word 'haphazard' means lacking any obvious principle of organisation. Its antonym is 'random' which means made, done, or happening without method or conscious decision.

165. (c) Part 'we feed the horse oats' contains an error. We need to replace 'feed' with 'fed' to correct the sentence.

166. (a) Part 'at end of April' contains an error. Add 'the' before 'end' to correct the sentence.

167. (b) The word 'stoic' means an apparent indifference to pleasure or especially to pain often as a matter of principle or self-discipline.

168. (c) 'Avenue' is the synonym of 'Despite'.

169. (c) The underlined idiom 'burn the midnight oil' means 'to work till late'.

170. (a) The underlined idiom 'on the breadline' means 'to be very poor'.

171. (d) The word 'justifiable' means 'that which can be explain with reason or logic'.

172. **(d)** The idiom 'left out in the cold' means to be excluded and ignored.

173. **(a)** Hydrophobia is the fear of water.

174. **(a)** The bracketed part of the sentence is contextually incorrect. Replace it with were 'seen' to correct the sentence.

175. **(b)** The word 'dreadful' refers to something that is horrible and terrible.

176. **(b)** The underlined idiom 'dodged a bullet' means 'to have escaped a bad situation'.

177. **(a)** A pauper is a person who has no proper means of livelihood or earning money.

178. **(d)** The underlined part of the sentence is grammatically correct. Both the words 'use' and 'usage' is correct for the sentence.

179. **(b)** The word 'catastrophic' means 'involving or causing sudden great damage or suffering.' Hence, its antonym is 'fortuitous' which means happening by a lucky chance; fortunate.

180. **(b)** The underlined word 'an arm and leg' means 'very expensive'.

181. **(d)** Part 'He wrote his dairy' contains the error of tense. As the sentence presents a general statement, simple present tense, 'writes', should be used.

182. **(a)** The highlighted word 'negligent' means 'uncaring or ignoring'. Hence, its antonym is 'attentive'.

183. **(c)** An astronaut is a person engaged or trained for spaceflight.

184. **(b)** The word 'site' means 'location'.

185. **(c)** The incorrectly spelt word is 'comparsion'. The correctly spelt word is 'comparison'.

186. **(b)** Part 'she will have participate' contains the error of form of verb. We use 'past participle' form of the verb with 'has/have'.
Hence, use 'participated' to correct the sentence.

187. **(a)** The word 'efficient' means working and operating quickly and effectively in an organised way.

188. **(b)** The word 'abandon' means 'to leave someone behind or desert someone'.

189. **(b)** The word 'damp' means 'wet'. Hence, its antonym is 'arid' which means 'dry'.

190. **(d)** The phrase 'a leopard can't change his spots' means a person cannot change who he/she is.

191. **(d)** The correct filler for the given blank is 'spans'.

192. **(c)** The correct filler for the given blank is 'estimated'.

193. **(c)** The correct filler for the given blank is 'renowned'.

194. **(c)** The correct filler for the given blank is 'vibrant'.

195. **(c)** The correct filler for the given blank is 'indigenous'.

196. **(d)** As the author of the passage states that they want people who work efficiently, from the given options, Jassie can be their case study.This is because she is an efficient employee with a great work ethics.

197. **(c)** The approach of the author of the given passage is practical and pragmatic.

198. **(c)** The antonym of the word 'effective' which means 'fruitful' is 'fruitless'.

199. **(c)** As the given passage talks about a case study conducted by the organisation to find the most effective employee, the most appropriate title of the passage would be 'the Most Effective Colleagues'.

200. **(d)** The given passage states that some people are more effective than the others while getting things done.

CPO SI P-2 SP 20

PAPER-2

SSC CPO SI SOLVED PAPER

8 January 2024 (Shift I)

Instructions

1. This paper contains **200** questions.
2. This paper is based on **English Language and Comprehension.**
3. Each question carries **1 marks.**
4. There will be a negative marking of **0.25 marks** for each wrong answer.

MM : 200 **Time : 2 hr**

1. Sentences of a paragraph are given below. While the first (1) and the last (6) sentences are in the correct order, the sentences in between (A-D) are jumbled up. Arrange the sentences in the correct order to form a meaningful and coherent paragraph.

1. During the colonial rule in India, Robert Bruce was the first who noticed tea plants growing near Rangpur in 1823.

A. The species was found to be similar to that grown in Chinese tea gardens.

B. By 1862, the Assam tea industry comprised around 160 gardens.

C. The leaves of the plants were examined and the consequence was something fruitful.

D. Mr. Maniram Dewan was the first Indian tea planter who established the commercial plantation that we know today as the Assam tea.

6. Today the region has grown to become one of the world's largest tea-producing belts.

(a) DCBA (b) BDAC
(c) CADB (d) ADCB

2. Select the correct direct form of the given sentence.
The ticket collector asked the passenger why he had not purchased a full ticket for his daughter.
(a) The ticket collector said to the passenger, "Why haven't you purchase a full ticket for your daughter?"
(b) The ticket collector said to the passenger, "Why didn't you purchase a full ticket for your daughter?"
(c) The ticket collector said to the passenger, "Why he had not purchased a full ticket for his daughter?"
(d) The ticket collector said to the passenger, "Why haven't you purchased a full ticket for his daughter?"

3. Select the correct active form of the given sentence.
I am often invited by them to join their club.
(a) I often invite them to join the club.
(b) The club often invites me to join them.
(c) They often invite me to join their club.
(d) They have often invited me to join their club.

4. Select the correct indirect form of the given sentence.
You said, "Priya kept watching television till her mother exploded at her."
(a) You said that Priya kept watching television till her mother exploded at her.
(b) You said that Priya had kept watching television till her mother exploded at her.
(c) You said that Priya kept watching television till her mother had exploded at her.
(d) You said that Priya had kept watching television till her mother had exploded at her.

5. Select the antonym of the given word.
Deplore
(a) Mourn
(b) Praise
(c) Dislike
(d) Hate

6. Identify the segment in the sentence which contains a grammatical error.
Two elderly gentlemen told the rather improbable story to mislead the police personnel.
(a) Two elderly gentlemen
(b) story to mislead
(c) told the rather improbable
(d) the police personnel

7. Select the correct passive form of the given sentence.
Why didn't your father accompany you?
(a) Why didn't you be accompanied by your father?
(b) Why were you not accompanied by your father?
(c) Why wasn't your father accompanied by you?
(d) Why have you not been accompanied by your father?

8. Given below are six sentences of a paragraph.
Sentence A is the beginning whereas sentence F is the last sentence of the para. The middle four sentences are jumbled up. Select the option that gives their correct order forming a meaningful and coherent paragraph.

A. It was midday.

B. Voldyrev, a tall country gentleman with a cropped head and prominent eyes, took off his overcoat, mopped his brow with his handkerchief and went into the government office.

C. "Where can I make an inquiry here?" he said, addressing a porter who was bringing a trayful of glasses from the furthest recesses of the office.

D. Voldyrev coughed and went towards the window.

E. "To that one sitting near the window!" said the porter, indicating with the tray the furthest window.

F. There, at a green table spotted like typhus, was sitting a young man with his hair standing up in four tufts on his head, with a long pimply nose, and a long faded uniform.

(a) BCED (b) BDEC
(c) ECDB (d) CBED

9. Select the most appropriate synonym of the given word.
Mundane
(a) Abnormal (b) Ordinary
(c) Wonderful (d) Exciting

10. Select the antonym of the given word.
Taciturn
(a) Laconic
(b) Reticent
(c) Withdrawn
(d) Loquacious

11. Given below are four jumbled sentences. Select the option that gives their correct order forming a meaningful and coherent paragraph.

A. "Your cauldron gave birth," replied the Hodja.

B. "What's this?" asked the neighbour, pointing to the pot.

C. One day Nasreddin Hodja borrowed a cauldron from his neighbour.

D. A few days later, when he had finished with it, he sent it back with a pot inside it.

(a) ACBD (b) BDAC
(c) CBAD (d) CDBA

12. Given below are four sentences. Pick the option that gives the correct order.

A. The Egyptians believed that the body and soul were important to human existence, in life and in death.

B. This ensured the soul's return to the body so that the deceased would live happily ever after.

C. Their funerary practices, such as mummification and burial in tombs, were designed to assist the deceased find their way in the after world.

D. The tombs were thus, filled with food, tools, domestic wares, treasures- all the necessities of life.

(a) ADCB (b) ABCD
(c) ACDB (d) ABDC

13. Given below are four jumbled sentences. Select the option that gives their correct order forming a meaningful and coherent paragraph.

A. A fine carriage with rubber tyres, a fat coachman and velvet on the seats, rolled up to the house of a landowner called Gryabov.

B. A drowsy footman met him in the hall.

C. "Are the family at home?" asked the Marshal.

D. Fyodor Andreitch Otsov, the district Marshal, jumped out of the carriage.

(a) ADBC (b) DBAC
(c) ACBD (d) CBAD

14. Select the most appropriate option to fill in the blank.
Gautam .... all the documents by the time his senior advocate reached the court.
(a) will be examining
(b) examines
(c) had examined
(d) is examining

15. Parts of the given sentence have been given as options. One of them may contain a grammatical error. Select the option that has the error. If there is no error, select 'No error'.
Your mother prepares delicious food, did she?
(a) prepares delicious food
(b) No error
(c) Your mother
(d) did she?

16. Identify the segment in the sentence which contains a grammatical error.
She decided to marry him in spite his habit of spending recklessly.
(a) to marry him
(b) in spite his habit
(c) She decided
(d) of spending recklessly

17. Given below are four jumbled sentences. Select the option that gives their correct order forming a meaningful and coherent paragraph.

A. I have seen a great many houses in my time, little and big, new and old, built of stone and of wood, but of one house I have kept a very vivid memory.

B. It was, properly speaking, rather a cottage than a house - a tiny cottage of one story, with three windows, looking extraordinarily like a little old hunchback woman with a cap on.

C. The cottage was lost to sight among the mulberry-trees, acacias and poplars planted by the grandfathers and great-grandfathers of its present occupants.

D. It had white stucco walls, tiled roof and a dilapidated chimney.

(a) BDAC (b) ACBD
(c) ABDC (d) CDBA

18. Parts of the given sentence have been given as options. One of them may contain a grammatical error. Select the option that has the error. If there is no error, select 'No error'.
I will definitely accept the responsibility while the time comes.
(a) I will definitely accept
(b) while the time comes
(c) the responsibility
(d) No error

19. Select the most appropriate option that can substitute the underlined segment in the given sentence to improve it. If no improvement is required, select 'No improvement required'.

She has given a brilliant dance performance last week.

(a) had been given
(b) was giving
(c) No improvement required
(d) gave

20. Sentences of a paragraph are given below. While the first (1) and the last (6) sentences are in the correct order, the sentences in between (A-D) are jumbled up. Arrange the sentences in the correct order to form a meaningful and coherent paragraph.

1. A vacation is looked forward to as a time to relax.
A. But, destiny had other plans for me.
B. I was very excited to go on a vacation to Goa.
C. My bags were packed and I decided to retire early for the night.
D. It is a welcome break from the daily routine which is often monotonous.
6. I fell off the bed and fractured my foot!

(a) DBCA (b) ABDC
(c) BCDA (d) CBAD

21. Select the most appropriate option to improve the underlined segment in the given sentence. If there is no improvement required, select 'No improvement'.

Passengers travelling by air are prohibited to carry sharp objects in cabin baggage.

(a) No improvement
(b) are prohibit to be carrying
(c) are prohibit for carrying
(d) are prohibited from carrying

22. Select the correct indirect form of the given sentence.

Ankit said to Ashna, "Do you know that the annual meeting has been postponed?"

(a) Ankit asked Ashna that do you know that the annual meeting has been postponed.
(b) Ankit asked Ashna if she had known that the annual meeting was postponed.
(c) Ankit asked Ashna if she knew that the annual meeting had been postponed.
(d) Ankit asked Ashna if she would be knowing that the annual meeting had been postponed.

23. Select the meaning of the given idiom.

Bring to book

(a) Support someone
(b) Punish someone
(c) Calm someone
(d) Teach someone

24. Select the correct active form of the given sentence.

The workers will not be satisfied with empty promises.

(a) Empty promises cannot satisfy the workers.
(b) Empty promises do not satisfy the workers.
(c) Empty promises will not satisfy the workers.
(d) Empty promises would not satisfy the workers.

25. Select the correct indirect form of the given sentence.

She said, "If only I could relive my past!"

(a) She said that she could relive her past.
(b) She wished that if she could relive her past.
(c) She wished that she could relive her past.
(d) She wished if she could relive my past.

26. Fill in the blank with the most appropriate option.

He gazed around the room ...... lay hidden a treasure chest.

(a) whereof (b) whereas
(c) whereby (d) wherein

27. Select the correct active form of the given sentence.

The test flight of Gaganyaan was successfully carried out by the scientists of ISRO.

(a) The test flight of Gaganyaan successfully carried out the scientists of ISRO.
(b) The scientists of ISRO successfully carried out the test flight of Gaganyaan.
(c) The scientists of ISRO will successfully carry out the test flight of Gaganyaan.
(d) The scientists of ISRO are successfully carrying out the test flight of Gaganyaan.

28. Fill in the blank with the most appropriate option.

Each one of the participants in the annual function .... an applause.

(a) is deserving (b) have deserved
(c) deserve (d) deserves

29. Select the correct passive form of the given sentence.

The Election Commission announced the election dates for different states.

(a) The election dates for different states have been announced by the Election Commission.
(b) The Election Commission has been announced the election dates by the different states.
(c) The election dates for different states were announced by the Election Commission.
(d) The election dates for different states will be announced by the Election Commission.

30. Given below are six sentences of a paragraph. Sentence A is the beginning whereas sentence F is the last sentence of the para. The middle four sentences are jumbled up. Select the option that gives their correct order forming a meaningful and coherent paragraph.

A. When I studied Engineering thirty-five years back, I was the only girl in the course.
B. People often ask me how I managed.
C. I could only see boys and more boys everywhere.
D. But when I look back I feel it was not very difficult.
E. Having a girl in the class was unusual for the boys, and initially I was the target for a lot of teasing.
F. But over a period of time they became my best friends.

(a) ECDB
(b) CBDE
(c) BDEC
(d) CBED

31. Select the correct direct form of the given sentence.

The old man prayed to God to help him in his hour of sorrow.

(a) The old man said, "O God, help me in my hour of sorrow."
(b) The old man said, "God must help him in his hour of sorrow."
(c) The old man said, "O God, help him in my hour of sorrow."
(d) The old man said, "O God, help me in his hour of sorrow."

32. Select the correct active form of the given sentence.
May you be blessed with good health.
(a) You should be blessed with good health.
(b) May good health bless you.
(c) May God bless you with good health.
(d) God should bless you with good health.

33. Select the meaning of the given idiom.
Lose your marbles
(a) Lose respect
(b) Miss an opportunity
(c) Be nervous
(d) Go insane

34. Select the correct direct form of the given sentence.
She exclaimed with regret that she had acted very foolishly.
(a) "Ah! Have I acted foolishly?" she said.
(b) "I have acted foolishly," she said.
(c) "Alas! How foolishly I have acted," she said.
(d) "Oh! I regret having acted foolishly," she said.

35. Select the most appropriate option to improve the underlined segment in the given sentence. If there is no improvement required, select 'No improvement'.
Sherpas have prospered and <u>come along the way</u> from being just porters to becoming mountaineers.
(a) come all along
(b) are coming along
(c) No improvement
(d) come a long way

36. Parts of the given sentence have been given as options. One of them contains a grammatical error. Select the option that has the error.
The captain along with all the sailors were warmly welcomed back home by the town people.
(a) by the town people.
(b) along with all the sailors were
(c) warmly welcomed back home
(d) The captain

37. Select the most appropriate option to fill in the blank.
If I go to Bangalore, I ...... with my nephew.
(a) have stayed (b) will stay
(c) stay (d) stayed

38. Identify the segment in the sentence which contains a grammatical error.
The two buses moving side by side gave the illusion of been stationary.
(a) moving side by side
(b) gave the illusion
(c) The two buses
(d) of been stationary

39. Select the correct active form of the given sentence.
By whom have these facts been verified?
(a) Who has verified these facts?
(b) Who is verifying these facts?
(c) Who had verified these facts?
(d) Who have verified these facts?

40. Select the correct direct form of the given sentence.
Looking at his watch Barin Babu observed that they were running more or less on time.
(a) Looking at his watch Barin Babu said, "They had been running more or less on time."
(b) Looking at his watch Barin Babu said, "They were running more or less on time."
(c) Looking at his watch Barin Babu said, "We are running more or less on time."
(d) Looking at his watch Barin Babu said, "We have been running more or less on time."

41. Given below are six sentences of a paragraph.
Sentence A is the beginning whereas sentence F is the last sentence of the para. The middle four sentences are jumbled up. Select the option that gives their correct order forming a meaningful and coherent paragraph.
A. We soon ran into a nomad's tent, where we were well received and allowed to graze our yak to his heart's content.
B. She quickly made us cups of butter tea, and for the first time I drank this brew with relish.
C. This time our hostess was a young woman.
D. Only then did we notice what a picturesque figure our young hostess made.
E. The warmth ran through our frozen bodies and brought us to life again.
F. She wore a sheepskin cloak reaching down to the ground and in her long black pigtail she wore mussel shells, silver coins and various cheap ornaments imported from abroad.
(a) CBED (b) CBDE
(c) BDEC (d) ECDB

42. Select the most appropriate option to fill in the blank.
She was so busy .... writing that when the maid came .... she didn't hear her.
(a) with, by (b) to, in
(c) in, in (d) at, up

43. Select the meaning of the given idiom.
Bad blood
(a) Poor blood circulation
(b) Family of ill-repute
(c) Felling of brotherhood
(d) Hostility between people

44. Select the correct passive form of the given sentence.
His mother accompanies him wherever he goes.
(a) He has accompanied his mother wherever she has gone.
(b) He was accompanied by his mother wherever he went.
(c) He is accompanied by his mother wherever he goes.
(d) He accompanies his mother wherever she goes.

45. Identify the segment in the sentence which contains a grammatical error.
Mona took a little time for thought before she gave her consent to the proposal.
(a) before she gave her consent
(b) Mona took a little
(c) time for thought
(d) to the proposal

46. Select the most appropriate meaning of the given idiom.
A mare's nest
(a) A new situation
(b) A confused situation
(c) A familiar situation
(d) A refreshing situation

47. Select the misspelt word.
(a) Immense (b) Incence
(c) Enhance (d) Elegance

48. Select the correct indirect form of the given sentence.

The airhostess said to the passengers, "This is our inaugural flight starting today."

(a) The airhostess informed the passengers that it was their inaugural flight starting today.
(b) The airhostess told to the passengers that it was their inaugural flight starting that day.
(c) The airhostess said to the passengers that this is our inaugural flight starting today.
(d) The airhostess informed the passengers that it was their inaugural flight starting that day.

49. Select the correct direct form of the given sentence.

He told her that he could not marry her then but he would surely do so the following year.

(a) He said to her, "He cannot marry you now but he will surely do so next year."
(b) He said to her, "I cannot marry you now but I will surely do so next year."
(c) He said to her, "I could not marry you then but I will surely do so next year."
(d) He said to her, "I cannot marry her then but I will surely do so next year."

50. Select the most appropriate antonym of the given word.

Fastidious

(a) Difficult
(b) Fussy
(c) Critical
(d) Indifferent

51. Select the most appropriate option that can substitute the underlined segment in the given sentence to improve it. If no improvement is required, select 'No improvement required'.

You have a lot of coconut trees in your village, <u>do you</u>?

(a) have you?
(b) don't you?
(c) No improvement required
(d) don't they?

52. Select the correct active form of the given sentence.

It was decided by Salim Ali to devote his life to the preservation of Indian birds.

(a) Salim Ali decided to devote his life to the preservation of Indian birds.
(b) Salim devoted his life to the preservation of Indian birds.
(c) Salim Ali has decided to devote his life to the preservation of Indian birds.
(d) Salim Ali had decided to devote his life to the preservation of Indian birds.

53. Select the most appropriate option to substitute the given group of words.

A person who has excessive admiration of themselves

(a) Egotist (b) Egocentric
(c) Narcissist (d) Fanatic

54. Select the most appropriate option that can substitute the underlined segment in the given sentence to improve it. If no improvement is required, select 'No improvement required'.

The pollution level <u>ought to keep</u> under control.

(a) ought to be kept
(b) ought to have kept
(c) No improvement required
(d) ought to be keeping

55. Select the correct option to substitute the given set of words.

One who cannot be corrected

(a) Vulnerable
(b) Versatile
(c) Indefatigable
(d) Incorrigible

56. Select the correct indirect form of the given sentence.

Umesh said to his father, "Can you give me more money?"

(a) Umesh asked his father if he can give him more money.
(b) Umesh asked his father that if he could give him more money.
(c) Umesh asked his father could he give him more money.
(d) Umesh asked his father if he could give him more money.

57. Select the correct indirect form of the given sentence.

He said to his friend, "Let us leave for the trek tomorrow."

(a) He suggested to his friend to leave for the trek the next day.
(b) He told his friend to leave for the trek the next day.
(c) He suggested his friend that let us leave for the trek tomorrow.
(d) He suggested to his friend that they should leave for the trek the next day.

58. Select the correct direct form of the given sentence.

He says that he will clear all his dues by the following month.

(a) He said, "I will clear all my dues by next month."
(b) He said, "I would clear all my dues by next month."
(c) He says, "I will clear all my dues by next month."
(d) He says, "I will clear all his dues by next month."

59. Select the incorrectly spelt word.

(a) Particularly (b) Betrayal
(c) Dilligence (d) Vacation

60. Select the most appropriate option to improve the underlined segment in the given sentence. If there is no improvement required, select 'No improvement'.

Some students think that if they cram a few chapters, they can <u>pass in the exam</u>.

(a) pass the exam
(b) No improvement
(c) be passed in the exam
(d) pass in an exam

61. Select the correct indirect form of the given sentence.

The teacher said to Kavya, "You need a new notebook for English."

(a) The teacher told to Kavya that she needs a new notebook for English.
(b) The teacher told Kavya that she needed a new notebook for English.
(c) The teacher told Kavya that you needed a new notebook for English.
(d) The teacher said to Kavya that you need a new notebook for English.

62. Select the meaning of the given idiom.

Cut from the same cloth

(a) Belong to the same family
(b) To be of a similar nature
(c) To come from the same source
(d) To share resources

63. Select the most appropriate option to improve the underlined segment in the given sentence. If there is no improvement required, select 'No improvement'.

My sister <u>resembles</u> to my mother a lot in looks and in temperament.

(a) No improvement
(b) resembles
(c) has resemblance to
(d) is resembling to

64. Select the most appropriate option to improve the underlined segment in the given sentence. If there is no improvement required, select 'No improvement'.
When he was falsely accused of embezzlement, he was beside himself in anger.
(a) No improvement
(b) he were beside himself
(c) he was besides himself
(d) he went beside himself

65. Select the most appropriate option that can substitute the underlined segment in the given sentence to improve it. If no improvement is required, select 'No improvement required'.
As bombs keep falling on Gaza, hundreds of thousands of children have been order to flee their homes.
(a) has been ordered to flee
(b) have been ordered to flee
(c) have been ordered fleeing
(d) No improvement required

66. Select the correct passive form of the given sentence.
We had repaired the roads before the monsoon set in.
(a) The roads were repaired before the monsoon set in.
(b) The roads had been repaired before the monsoon set in.
(c) The roads have been repaired before the monsoon set in.
(d) The roads are repaired before the monsoon set in.

67. Select the synonym of the given word.
Vitiate
(a) Annihilate (b) Facilitate
(c) Validate (d) Propagate

68. Select the correct indirect form of the given sentence.
He said to me, "I have done my duty."
(a) He told me that I had done my duty.
(b) He told me that he had done his duty.
(c) He told me that he have done his duty.
(d) He told me that he did his duty.

69. Given below are six sentences of a paragraph.
Sentence A is the beginning whereas sentence F is the last sentence of the para. The middle four sentences are jumbled up.
Select the option that gives their correct order forming a meaningful and coherent paragraph.
A. When Tarun failed in his terminal examinations, his father was very angry with him.
B. It was a day he wanted to erase from his life and so he took to running.
C. His friends too made fun of him.
D. The Sun beat down to check his rage but nothing could stop Tarun.
E. He ran all around the park.
F. After about an hour, he was fully exhausted and his fury having subsided, he threw himself on a bench and started to pant.
(a) BDEC (b) CEBD
(c) CBED (d) ECDB

70. Given below are four sentences. Pick the option that gives the correct order.
A. The invention of the airplane was no exception.
B. However, the idea of flying an aircraft was quite repulsive to some people.
C. Many great inventions are initially greeted with ridicule and disbelief.
D. Most people who heard about the first powered flight on 17th December, 1903 were excited and impressed.
(a) DABC (b) DBCA
(c) CDAB (d) CADB

71. Identify the segment in the sentence which contains a grammatical error.
The innocent clerk was accused with misappropriating funds of the company.
(a) misappropriating funds
(b) was accused with
(c) of the company
(d) The innocent clerk

72. Select the most appropriate option to substitute the given group of words.
A wooden frame for holding an artist's work while it is being painted or drawn
(a) Easel
(b) Lectern
(c) Platform
(d) Podium

73. Select the most appropriate option to improve the underlined segment in the given sentence. If there is no improvement required, select 'No improvement'.
He felt like a fish out of water as he was not accustomed for living in a large city.
(a) accustom for
(b) accustomed by
(c) accustomed to
(d) No improvement

74. Select the correct passive form of the given sentence.
Everybody wants others to respect them.
(a) Everybody wanted to be respected by others.
(b) Everybody wants to be respected by others.
(c) They want others to be respected by everybody.
(d) Everybody wants to respect others.

75. Select the most appropriate option that can substitute the underlined segment in the given sentence to improve it. If no improvement is required, select 'No improvement required'
I would love fly a fighter jet one day.
(a) No improvement required
(b) would love to flying
(c) would to love fly
(d) would love to fly

76. Select the correct passive form of the given sentence.
Take these two pills with warm water.
(a) You may take these two pills with warm water.
(b) You are ordered to take these two pills with warm water.
(c) These two pills should be taken with warm water.
(d) Warm water should be taken with these two pills.

77. Select the correct active form of the given sentence.
A party was organised by Rayan on his 40th Birthday.
(a) Rayan organised a party on his 40th Birthday.
(b) A party organised Rayan on his 40th Birthday
(c) Rayan will be organising a party on his 40th Birthday.
(d) Rayan has organised a party on his 40th Birthday.

78. Select the most appropriate option to substitute the given group of words.
One who is skilled and eloquent in public speaking
(a) Lecturer
(b) Orator
(c) Spokesperson
(d) Actor

79. Select the correct option to substitute the given set of words.
A statement open to more than one interpretation
(a) Explicit (b) Palpable
(c) Tangible (d) Ambiguous

80. Select the most appropriate option to substitute the given group of words. The husks of corn or other grains separated by winnowing or threshing.
(a) Chaff (b) Peel
(c) Hay (d) Fodder

81. Select the correct passive form of the given sentence.
Pay that bill today.
(a) That bill will be paid today.
(b) That bill is going to be paid today.
(c) That bill should be paid today.
(d) Let that bill to be paid today.

82. Fill in the blank with the most appropriate option.
I trust him completely. His conduct is .... suspicion.
(a) over (b) under
(c) below (d) above

83. Parts of the given sentence have been given as options. One of them may contain a grammatical error. Select the option that has the error. If there is no error, select 'No error'.
Are you yet afraid of going out in the dark?
(a) No error
(b) afraid of going out
(c) in the dark
(d) Are you yet

84. Given below are six sentences of a paragraph.
Sentence A is the beginning whereas sentence F is the last sentence of the para. The middle four sentences are jumbled up. Select the option that gives their correct order forming a meaningful and coherent paragraph.
A. In the course of my education at MIT, three teachers shaped my thinking.
B. Their combined contributions formed the foundation on which I later built my professional career.
C. Prof. Sponder taught me technical aerodynamics.
D. These three teachers were Prof. Sponder, Prof. KAV Pandalai and Prof. Narasingha Rao.
E. Each one of them had very distinct personalities, but they shared a common impulse—the capacity to feed their students' intellectual hunger by sheer brilliance and untiring zeal.
F. He was an Austrian with rich practical experience in aeronautical engineering.
(a) CBED (b) BCED
(c) BDEC (d) ECDB

85. Select the correct indirect form of the given sentence.
You said to me, "I shall reach in time for the concert."
(a) You told me that I should reach in time for the concert.
(b) You told me that you shall reach in time for the concert.
(c) You told me that you would reach in time for the concert.
(d) You told me that I would reach in time for the concert.

86. Parts of the given sentence have been given as options. One of them may contain a grammatical error. Select the option that has the error. If there is no error, select 'No error'.
Specialists say that this method speeds up language learning tremendously.
(a) No error
(b) language learning tremendously
(c) this method speeds up
(d) Specialists say that

87. Select the most appropriate option that can substitute the underlined segment in the given sentence to improve it. If no improvement is required, select 'No improvement required'.
Tomorrow, they <u>will be take a flight</u> to their dream vacation destination.
(a) be taking a flight
(b) will be taking a flight
(c) will taking a flight
(d) No improvement required

88. Select the correct passive form of the given sentence.
She held the child's hand firmly.
(a) The child's hand is held firmly.
(b) The child's hand has been held firmly.
(c) The child's hand held firmly.
(d) The child's hand was held firmly.

89. Select the most appropriate option that can substitute the underlined segment in the given sentence to improve it. If no improvement is required, select 'No improvement required'.
It seems that these walls <u>have not been painted since years.</u>
(a) have not been paint since years.
(b) have not being painted for years.
(c) have not been painted for years.
(d) No improvement required

90. Select the most appropriate option to improve the underlined segment in the given sentence. If there is no improvement required, select 'No improvement'.
The captain as well as the entire crew <u>have reached</u> the harbour safely.
(a) has reached
(b) have been reaching
(c) are reaching
(d) No improvement

91. Select the correct passive form of the given sentence.
Why do we have to accept these conditions?
(a) Why do these conditions have to be accepted?
(b) Why should these conditions be accepted?
(c) These conditions do not have to be accepted.
(d) Why are these conditions needed to be accepted?

92. Identify the segment in the sentence which contains a grammatical error.
My sister and me have a keen interest in learning classical music.
(a) classical music
(b) have a keen interest
(c) My sister and me
(d) in learning

93. Select the correct option to substitute the given set of words.
To skip about playfully
(a) Scramble (b) Amble
(c) Gambol (d) Trundle

94. Select the synonym of the given word.
Entice
(a) Dissuade (b) Beguile
(c) Repulse (d) Entreat

95. Select the most appropriate option that can substitute the underlined segment in the given sentence to improve it. If no improvement is required, select 'No improvement required'.
I will definitely <u>return your notes at</u> Saturday evening.
(a) return your notes by
(b) returned your notes on
(c) returning your notes at
(d) No improvement required

96. Identify the segment in the sentence which contains a grammatical error.
Hold my hand lest you should not get lost in the huge crowd at the fair.
(a) crowd at the fair
(b) lest you should not
(c) get lost in the huge
(d) Hold my hand

97. Select the correct passive form of the given sentence.
One can achieve nothing without hard work.
(a) Nothing is achieved without hard work.
(b) Nothing will be achieved without hard work.
(c) Nothing has been achieved without hard work.
(d) Nothing can be achieved without hard work.

98. Identify the segment in the sentence which contains a grammatical error.
None than you deserve credit for the success of this project.
(a) for the success (b) deserve credit
(c) of this project (d) None than you

99. Identify the segment in the sentence which contains a grammatical error.
She use to learn fabric painting when she was in middle school.
(a) in middle school
(b) She use to
(c) learn fabric painting
(d) when she was

100. Select the most appropriate option to improve the underlined segment in the given sentence. If there is no improvement required, select 'No improvement'.
The shopping mall is <u>more farther</u> from my house than from my office.
(a) farther (b) more far
(c) far (d) No improvement

101. Select the meaning of the given idiom.
Split one's sides
(a) Be extremely amused
(b) Meet with an accident
(c) Scream in pain
(d) Undergo a surgery

102. Fill in the blank with the most appropriate option.
Hurry up ! There's still .... work left to do.
(a) many (b) much (c) whole (d) lot

103. Select the correct passive form of the given sentence.
Bhavna saw him carrying your suitcase.
(a) Your suitcase carried by him was seen by Bhavna.
(b) He was seen by Bhavna carrying your suitcase.
(c) He had been seen by Bhavna carrying your suitcase.
(d) Your suitcase was seen by Bhavna carrying him.

104. Parts of the given sentence have been given as options. One of them may contain a grammatical error. Select the option that has the error. If there is no error, select 'No error'.
Rohit Sharma's century was very acclaimed in the media.
(a) No error
(b) in the media
(c) very acclaimed
(d) Rohit Sharma's century

105. Select the correct direct form of the given sentence.
Praveen told his mother that he had completed his homework.
(a) Praveen said to his mother, "I have been completing my homework."
(b) Praveen said to his mother, "I have completed my homework."
(c) Praveen said to his mother, "I am completing my homework."
(d) Praveen said to his mother, "He had completed my homework."

106. Parts of the given sentence have been given as options. One of them may contain a grammatical error. Select the option that has the error. If there is no error, select 'No error'.
The food was not as delicious as we had expected.
(a) we had expected
(b) No error
(c) The food was not
(d) as delicious as

107. Select the most appropriate option to improve the underlined segment in the given sentence. If there is no improvement required, select 'No improvement'.
She <u>is married with</u> a rich businessman and has enough money to splurge on luxuries.
(a) No improvement.
(b) is married to
(c) has marriage with
(d) has married with

108. Select the meaning of the given idiom.
Forty winks
(a) A deep sleep (b) A secret signal
(c) A long leave (d) A short sleep

109. Select the most appropriate option to fill in the blank.
The air quality is so bad .... it becomes difficult to breathe.
(a) when (b) that
(c) as (d) since

110. Given below are six sentences of a paragraph.
Sentence A is the beginning whereas sentence F is the last sentence of the para. The middle four sentences are jumbled up. Select the option that gives their correct order forming a meaningful and coherent paragraph.
A. The first hour passed off quietly.
B. In the second, they had Arithmetic.
C. Swaminathan was terribly bored.
D. Vedanayagam went out and returned in a few minutes in the role of an Arithmetic teacher.
E. He droned on monotonously.
F. His teacher's voice was beginning to get on his nerves.
(a) BCDE (b) ECDB
(c) BDEC (d) CBED

111. Given below are four sentences. Pick the option that gives the correct order.

A. She was a busy person and had no time to visit her mother.

B. It was Mothers' Day.

C. She thought her mother would be pleased to receive the flowers.

D. A woman stopped at a flower shop to order some flowers to be sent to her mother.

(a) BCDA (b) BDAC
(c) DABC (d) CADB

112. Select the correct passive form of the given sentence.

Humayun built a city named Dinpanah in 1533 in Delhi.

(a) A city named Dinpanah was built by Humayun in 1533 in Delhi.
(b) A city named Dinpanah had been built by Humayun in 1533 in Delhi.
(c) A city named Humayun was built by Dinpanah in 1533 in Delhi.
(d) A city named Dinpanah was being built by Humayun in 1533 in Delhi.

113. Select the most appropriate option to substitute the given group of words.

Natural talent for something

(a) Flair (b) Feeling
(c) Favour (d) Flavour

114. Select the most appropriate meaning of the given idiom.

Have your heart in your mouth

(a) To be extremely jealous
(b) To behave in a foolish manner
(c) To get worse and worse
(d) To be extremely frightened

115. Select the most appropriate option to substitute the given group of words.

Irrational fear of water

(a) Cacophobia (b) Claustrophobia
(c) Hydrophobia (d) Acrophobia

116. Select the correct active form of the given sentence.

Let the fire be kept burning at night.

(a) You must burn the fire at night.
(b) Let the fire burning at night.
(c) The fire should be burnt at night.
(d) Keep the fire burning at night.

117. Select the most appropriate meaning of the given idiom.

Rock the boat

(a) Pester and irritate someone
(b) Overcome a difficult situation
(c) Divert someone's attention
(d) Disturb a stable situation

118. Select the correct direct form of the given sentence.

I asked my friend how one could be merry when everything was so messed up.

(a) I said to my friend, "How can one be merry when everything is so messed up?"
(b) I asked to my friend, "How can one be merry when everything was so messed up?"
(c) I said to my friend, "How one could be merry when everything was so messed up?"
(d) I said to my friend, "Could one be merry when everything is so messed up?"

119. Select the correct indirect form of the given sentence.

I said to him, "Please stay here tonight."

(a) I requested him to please stay there tonight.
(b) I asked him if he would stay there that night.
(c) I asked him to please stay here that night.
(d) I requested him to stay there that night.

120. Select the correct direct form of the given sentence.

He asked me if anybody had been rude to me.

(a) He said to me, "Anybody has been rude to you?"
(b) He said to me, "Has anybody been rude to you?"
(c) He said to me, "Had has been rude to me?"
(d) He said to me, "Anybody has been rude to me?"

121. Identify the segment in the sentence which contains a grammatical error.

Let us work out the details of our endeavour, shouldn't we?

(a) shouldn't we (b) Let us work out
(c) our endeavour (d) the details of

122. Select the misspelt word.

(a) Iminent (b) Temperament
(c) Reticent (d) Pertinent

123. Select the correct direct form of the given sentence.

Amanda asked Mohit how she had offended his friend.

(a) Amanda said to Mohit, "How did I offended his friend?"
(b) Amanda said to Mohit, "How have I offended your friend?"
(c) Amanda said to Mohit, "How she had offended his friend?"
(d) Amanda said to Mohit, "How have I offend your friend?"

124. Select the correct active form of the given sentence.

A party is being given by her on the occasion of her sixteenth birthday.

(a) She will give a party on the occasion of her sixteenth birthday.
(b) She is giving a party on the occasion of her sixteenth birthday.
(c) She was giving a party on the occasion of her sixteenth birthday.
(d) She has given a party on the occasion of her sixteenth birthday.

125. Parts of the given sentence have been given as options. One of them contains a grammatical error. Select the option that has the error.

You can take a horse to the water but you cannot make it to drink.

(a) to the water (b) make it to drink.
(c) You can take a horse
(d) but you cannot

126. Identify the segment in the sentence which contains a grammatical error.

It is time someone takes concrete steps to alleviate the problem of unemployment in the country.

(a) concrete steps to alleviate
(b) the problem of unemployment
(c) in the country
(d) It is time someone takes

127. Select the most appropriate option to improve the underlined segment in the given sentence. If there is no improvement required, select 'No improvement'.

He refrained from visiting his friend as he <u>had the urgent</u> assignment to complete.

(a) has urgent (b) No improvement
(c) had an urgent (d) had a urgent

128. Select the most appropriate option that can substitute the underlined segment in the given sentence to improve it. If no improvement is required, select 'No improvement required'.

We have received no information <u>so far to</u> the main island.

(a) so farther from
(b) No improvement required
(c) such far from
(d) so far from

129. Select the most appropriate option to complete the given idiom.
Cool as ....
(a) air (b) ice
(c) a cucumber (d) a river

130. Fill in the blank with the most appropriate option.
The small coffee shop at the end of the road is ....
(a) their (b) mine
(c) my (d) our

131. Identify the incorrectly spelt word in the given sentence and select the option that rectifies the spelling error.
It is difficult to describe the pandemonium kicked up by various animals when they spot or suspectt a panther around.
(a) Suspect (b) Dificuult
(c) Panthar (d) Kickd

132. Select the most appropriate option that rectifies the error(s) in the following sentence.
One must do his/her duty proparly.
(a) One must do once duty proparly.
(b) One must do ones duty properly.
(c) One must do one's duti proprly.
(d) One must do one's duty properly.

133. Select the correct direct form of the given sentence.
Isha told Shivani that they didn't need to buy tickets for the match as she had been given free passes for two.
(a) Isha said to Shivani, "They didn't need to buy tickets for the match as I am given free passes for two."
(b) Isha said to Shivani, "They didn't need to buy tickets for the match as she was given free passes for two."
(c) Isha said to Shivani, "We don't need to buy tickets for the match as I have been given free passes for two."
(d) Isha said to Shivani, "We didn't need to buy tickets for the match as I am given free passes for two."

134. Given below are six sentences of a paragraph.
Sentence A is the beginning whereas sentence F is the last sentence of the para. The middle four sentences are jumbled up. Select the option that gives their correct order forming a meaningful and coherent paragraph.
A. The month was January.
B. On the first morning of the festival the mejhi would be set alight invoking the blessings of Agni, the god of fire.
C. There would be much feasting and merriment during the festival.
D. Each household would build a mejhi - a pile of firewood stacked neatly together in their backyard.
E. The Bihu festival was fast approaching.
F. "Let's build a champion mejhi this year." Ricky suggested a few days before the festival.
(a) CBDE (b) CBED
(c) ECDB (d) EDBC

135. Sentences of a paragraph are given below. While the first (1) and the last (6) sentences are in the correct order, the sentences in between(A-D) are jumbled up. Arrange the sentences in the correct order to form a meaningful and coherent paragraph.
1. Nicholas Chorier is not a usual photographer.
A. He uses a kite to hoist his camera into the skies and clicks photographs while the camera dangles mid–air.
B. He is a kite aerial photographer.
C. Fascinated, he literally tied his two hobbies ,kite flying and photography ,together for a living.
D. During a trip to India to make a photo report on kite making, he learnt about this unique style of photography.
6. Today he is one of the most well–known kite aerial photographers in the world.
(a) BADC (b) BCDA
(c) ACDB (d) DABC

136. Select the correct direct form of the given sentence.
I suggested to my brother that we should go to the hills for a change.
(a) I said to my brother, "Shall we go to the hills for a change?"
(b) I said to my brother, " We shall go to the hills for a change."
(c) I said to my brother, " Let us go to the hills for a change."
(d) I requested to my brother, " We should go to the hills for a change."

137. Select the correct active form of the given sentence.
It is said that Einstein was a genius.
(a) People are saying that Einstein was a genius.
(b) People have said that Einstein was a genius.
(c) People say that Einstein was a genius.
(d) People said that Einstein was a genius.

138. Select the correct indirect form of the given sentence.
He said to me, " I am going to France next week."
(a) He said to me that he will go to France next week.
(b) He told me that I am going to France the following week.
(c) He said to me that he were going to France next week.
(d) He told me that he was going to France the following week.

139. Parts of the given sentence have been given as options. One of them may contain a grammatical error. Select the option that has the error. If there is no error, select 'No error'.
We cannot postpone discussion on this issue although it is urgent.
(a) We cannot postpone
(b) No error
(c) discussion on this issue
(d) although it is urgent.

140. Given below are four jumbled sentences. Select the option that gives their correct order forming a meaningful and coherent paragraph.
A. My mother, Vimala Kulkarni, told me similar words when I got married.
B. They were usually like: 'You must adjust to your new house and in-laws, try to learn how they eat and cook their food, go out of your way to be friendly and helpful to everybody,' etc.
C. When I was young, before a girl got married, her mother would give her some words of advice.
D. But along with this, she said something which helped me immensely in later life.
(a) BDAC (b) CBAD
(c) CDBA (d) ACBD

141. Select the misspelt word.
(a) Facetious (b) Exhilerated
(c) Officious (d) Conspicuous

142. Select the most appropriate option to improve the underlined segment in the given sentence. If there is no improvement required, select 'No improvement'.
Scarcely he see his opponent than he went numb with fear.
(a) No improvement
(b) As soon as
(c) Hardly did
(d) No sooner did

143. Select the correct active form of the given sentence.
The meal will have been made ready by the cook by the time you reach the guest house.
(a) The cook will have made the meal ready by the time you reach the guest house.
(b) The cook will be making the meal ready by the time you reach the guest house.
(c) The cook will make the meal ready by the time you reach the guest house.
(d) The cook have made the meal ready by the time you reach the guest house.

144. Select the correct passive form of the given sentence.
Grow more trees.
(a) Let more trees be grown.
(b) You should grow more trees.
(c) More trees should be growing.
(d) More trees should grow.

145. Select the most appropriate option that can substitute the underlined segment in the given sentence to improve it. If no improvement is required, select 'No improvement required'.
By next summer, I will have completed my internship and will have returned to school.
(a) No improvement required
(b) returned to school
(c) will return to school
(d) have returned to school

146. Select the correct passive form of the given sentence.
Our rivals must have spread this rumour.
(a) This rumour must have been spread by our rivals.
(b) This rumour must be spread by our rivals.
(c) This rumour may have been spread by our rivals.
(d) This rumour has been spread by our rivals.

147. Select the most appropriate option to substitute the given group of words.
A legal document authorising the police or another body to make an arrest or search premises
(a) Permit (b) Licence
(c) Decree (d) Warrant

148. Select the correct indirect form of the given sentence.
Rani said to her boss, "I am going to visit Kashmir and Ladakh next month."
(a) Rani informed her boss that she was going to visit Kashmir and Ladakh the following month.
(b) Rani told her boss that I am going to visit Kashmir and Ladakh next month.
(c) Rani informs her boss that she is going to visit Kashmir and Ladakh the next month.
(d) Rani asked her boss that she wanted to visit Kashmir and Ladakh the following month.

149. Select the most appropriate option that can substitute the underlined segment in the given sentence to improve it. If no improvement is required, select 'No improvement required'.
Effective communication is a skill that can significant enhance your personal and professional life.
(a) which can significant enhanced
(b) which can significantly enhancing
(c) No improvement required
(d) which can significantly enhance

150. Select the correct indirect form of the given sentence.
I said to Prachi, "I visited Maldives last week ."
(a) I told Prachi that I had visited Maldives last week.
(b) I told Prachi that I have visited Maldives the previous week.
(c) I told Prachi that I had visited Maldives the previous week.
(d) I told Prachi that I visited Maldives last week.

Directions (Q. Nos. 151-160) *In the following passage, some words have been deleted. Fill in the blanks with the help of the alternatives given. Select the most appropriate option for each number.*

Days after Prime Minister Narendra Modi inaugurated the Ghaziabad priority ...(1).... of the Delhi-Meerut Rapid Rail Transit System (RRTS), the ...(2) of high-rise societies in the National Capital Region called for direct ...(3)... to the public transport service points. The residents in ...(4)... areas of Noida and Ghaziabad said they would be forced to continue ...(5) .... on private vehicles without proper connectivity to the RRTS and ...(6)...public transport modes. "The RRTS is a great development; we want ...(7)... connectivity to key points like Metro stations, railway stations, Delhi, and the RRTS. ...(8)... any proper public transport, many residents are forced to opt ...(9) a personal car," the President of the New Era Flat Owners Welfare Association, Abhishek Kumar, ...(10) .... The 17-km priority section of the Delhi-Ghaziabad-Meerut RRTS corridor was inaugurated by PM Modi on 7th October and it started commercial operations on the next day.

151. Select the most appropriate option to fill in the blank no. 1.
(a) piece (b) fragment
(c) system (d) section

152. Select the most appropriate option to fill in the blank no. 2.
(a) tenants (b) people
(c) residents (d) landlords

153. Select the most appropriate option to fill in the blank no. 3.
(a) connecting (b) connected
(c) connect (d) connectivity

154. Select the most appropriate option to fill in the blank no. 4.
(a) lot (b) very (c) much (d) many

155. Select the most appropriate option to fill in the blank no. 5.
(a) depended (b) depend
(c) depending (d) depends

156. Select the most appropriate option to fill in the blank no. 6.
(a) further (b) other
(c) extra (d) another

157. Select the most appropriate option to fill in the blank no. 7.
(a) successive (b) upright
(c) consecutive (d) direct

158. Select the most appropriate option to fill in the blank no. 8.
(a) In spite of (b) Without
(c) With (d) Despite

159. Select the most appropriate option to fill in the blank no. 9.
(a) for (b) of
(c) to (d) on

160. Select the most appropriate option to fill in the blank no. 10.
(a) said (b) professed
(c) assumed (d) replied

Directions *(Q. Nos. 161-170) In the following passage, some words have been deleted. Fill in the blanks with the help of the alternatives given. Select the most appropriate option for each blank.*

The door behind them was ...(1)... . There was no escape. A strange light was ...(2)... from a corner, one that did not ...(3)... the room but made darkness visible. ...(4).... alien voice was heard which sounded like jargon, ...(5)... to the hapless friends. They went down ...(6)... their knees sobbing, pleading for their lives but the ...(7)... sounds continued. Slowly, a form seemed to ...(8)... right before their eyes which ...(9)... their blood and chilled their ...(10)... It was formless mass with no face!

161. Select the most appropriate word to fill in blank no. 1.
(a) unbolted (b) sealed
(c) vacant (d) ajar

162. Select the most appropriate word to fill in blank no. 2.
(a) emanating (b) commencing
(c) preceding (d) reclining

163. Select the most appropriate word to fill in blank no. 3.
(a) ignite (b) extinguish
(c) kindle (d) illuminate

164. Select the most appropriate word to fill in blank no. 4.
(a) A (b) An (c) Any (d) The

165. Select the most appropriate word to fill in blank no. 5.
(a) invincible (b) indelible
(c) incomprehensible
(d) incorrigible

166. Select the most appropriate word to fill in blank no. 6.
(a) at (b) in (c) on (d) by

167. Select the most appropriate word to fill in blank no. 7.
(a) bizarre (b) familiar
(c) customary (d) regular

168. Select the most appropriate word to fill in blank no. 8.
(a) assume (b) derive
(c) extract (d) emerge

169. Select the most appropriate word to fill in blank no. 9.
(a) curdled (b) spilled
(c) locked (d) flowed

170. Select the most appropriate word to fill in blank no. 10.
(a) bones (b) eyes
(c) head (d) skin

Directions *(Q. Nos. 171-180) Read the passage and answer the questions that follow.*

My path to the house was by no means an easy one. After confused wanderings through tangled hedges, struggling with obstacles that looked strange to me in the surrounding gloom, I arrived in front of a long, low building. There, to my astonishment, I found doors and windows open to the pervading mist, except for one square window through which a light shone from a row of candles on a long mahogany table.

The quiet and apparent emptiness of this odd and picturesque building made me pause. I am not much affected by the appearance of things, but this silent place, with its sinister atmosphere, made me feel uneasy. I was about to reconsider and go back to the road, when a second look at the comfortable interior I was leaving, convinced me that I was being foolish and sent me straight back to the door which stood open so invitingly. But half-way up the path, my progress was halted by the sight of a man coming out of the house that I had wrongly assumed to be empty. He seemed to be in a hurry and, at the moment when I first saw him, was busy putting his watch back in his pocket. He did not shut the door behind him, which I thought odd, especially as he had been looking behind him. He seemed to take in all the details of the place he was so hurriedly leaving.

As we met, he raised his hat. This also struck me as unusual, for he displayed more respect than that usually shown to strangers. I was further puzzled that he showed little surprise at bumping into another person in these remote, misty surroundings. Indeed, he was so little impressed by my being there that he nearly passed me without a word or any other hint of greeting, except the raising of his hat. But this did not satisfy me. I was hungry, cold and eager for creature comforts and the house before me offered not only warmth, but gave out an inviting smell of food being cooked which was difficult to ignore.

171. Which of these can be inferred about the narrator?
(a) He was thankful.
(b) He was foolish.
(c) He was a coward.
(d) He was observant.

172. Why was the narrator shocked when he reached the building?
(a) The house was gloomy and seemed haunted.
(b) The narrator was welcomed by a stranger.
(c) The doors and windows were open in the misty weather.
(d) The interiors were inviting despite the ominous atmosphere.

173. The given extract is
(a) a travelogue (b) a report
(c) a narrative (d) a biography

174. Select the most appropriate meaning of the word 'pervading' as used in the passage.
(a) Spreading (b) Receding
(c) Eerie (d) Immortal

175. Which of these statements is not true?
(a) The narrator first contemplated going back to the road.
(b) The stranger was in a hurry to leave the building.
(c) The narrator was seeking food and shelter.
(d) The stranger leaving the house was its owner.

176. Select the correct meaning of 'implement' as used in the passage.
(a) Inculcate (b) Coordinate
(c) Enforce (d) Commence

177. The new education system has shifted focus on
(a) social and aesthetic development
(b) intellectual development
(c) academic development
(d) spiritual development

178. What is the passage mainly about?
(a) Preparing students for survival in the real world.
(b) Importance of teaching soft skills to students.
(c) The need to change the education system in 21st century.
(d) Participation of students in extra-curricular activities.

179. What has hindered the development of students?
(a) Expanding academics to the outside world.
(b) Getting out into the field.
(c) Not gaining practical experience.
(d) Indulging in co-curricular activities.

180. Which of these does not provide industry exposure to students of business schools?
(a) Text books (b) Conferences
(c) Industrial visits (d) Guest lectures

Directions (Q.Nos. 181-190) *Read the following passage and answer the questions given after it.*

In the pre-dawn tranquillity of the Andaman Sea, a seismic tremor struck, momentarily agitating the ocean's placid surface. The Andaman and Nicobar Islands, an archipelago in the Bay of Bengal, felt the Earth beneath them shudder at 5:50 a.m. on Friday. According to the National Centre for Seismology (NCS), a 4.2 magnitude earthquake occurred at a depth of 10 km, its epicentre originating from a seismically active region beneath the sea. No casualties or damages have been reported.

Earthquakes, like the one experienced in the Andaman Sea, are stark reminders of the Earth's ever-shifting tectonic plates. These seismic events result from the sudden release of energy in the Earth's crust, creating seismic waves that cause the ground to shake. The intensity and impact of an earthquake depends on various factors, including its magnitude, depth and proximity to populated areas. The Andaman and Nicobar Islands are located in a region where several tectonic plates converge, including the Indian Plate, the Burma Plate and the Sunda Plate. The interaction of these plates leads to frequent earthquakes and volcanic activity. With its 4.2 magnitude, the recent earthquake is considered moderate, but its occurrence in this seismically active region serves as a reminder of the unpredictable and potentially devastating nature of such events.

The NCS, the nodal agency of the Government of India, is responsible for monitoring earthquake activity in the country. Using a network of seismographs, the NCS collects and analyses data from seismic events to provide accurate information to the public and relevant authorities.

This data helps scientists understand patterns and trends, leading to a better understanding of earthquake behaviour and potential risks. Earlier this week, Maharashtra's Satara district was also shaken by a 3.3 magnitude earthquake. While these events seem isolated, they form part of a broader pattern of seismic activity across the region. The Andaman and Nicobar Islands have experienced several significant earthquakes in the past, including a 5.8 magnitude earthquake in 2021. The potential consequences of earthquakes can be devastating, causing loss of life and extensive damage to infrastructure. It is therefore vital to have effective early warning systems and disaster management strategies in place.

While the 2.2 magnitude earthquake in the Andaman Sea did not result in any casualties or damages, it underscores the importance of continued investment in earthquake preparedness and resilience measures, particularly in seismically active regions like the Andaman and Nicobar Islands.

181. Which of the following is not one of the themes of the above passage?
(a) Loss of life in Andaman and Nicobar
(b) Unannounced tremors and tangible risks
(c) Seismic tremors in Andaman Sea
(d) Tracking seismic activity

182. "It underscores the importance of continued investment in earthquake preparedness" Here 'underscores' means
(a) emphasises (b) mitigates
(c) undermines (d) extenuate

183. When were the tremors felt in the Andaman and Nicobar Islands?
(a) Before the sunrise
(b) In the afternoon
(c) At night
(d) After the sunset

184. Which of the following is an odd-man out regarding the tectonic plates in Andaman region?
(a) Burma Plate (b) Satara Plates
(c) Sunda Plates (d) India Plates

185. Which of the following is a necessity in Andaman and Nicobar region?
(a) To make the people aware of the tectonic plates and their impact.
(b) To evacuate people from the islands.
(c) To collect and analyse data from seismic events.
(d) To install early warning systems and have disaster management strategies in place.

186. What did the early Roman historians use to fill up details in the historical accounts of events?
(a) Roman and Greek folklore
(b) Texts of laws and treaties
(c) Religious records
(d) List of annual magistrates

187. The passage is mainly about
(a) the ancient documentation of Roman history
(b) the ancient Roman and Greek histories
(c) Rome's first native historian
(d) the use of myths and folklore in ancient Roman history

188. "extant are also Books 21 to 45" here the word 'extant' means
(a) partially lost (b) lost forever
(c) still existing (d) enlarged

189. After reading the passage, it can be inferred that it is an extract from
(a) a news report
(b) an encyclopaedic entry on ancient Rome
(c) a report on Roman conquests
(d) a book on archaeology

190. Which period in ancient Roan history is most poorly documented?
(a) 27 BC- AD 14 (b) 218 BC to 167 BC
(c) 218–201 BC (d) 509–280 BC

Directions (Q. Nos. 191-195) *Read the passage and answer the questions that follow.*

A fact that draws our attention is that, according to his position in life, an extravagant man is either admired or loathed. A successful business man does nothing to increase his popularity by being prudent with his money. A person who is wealthy is expected to lead a luxurious life and to be lavish with his hospitality. If he is not so, he is considered mean, and his reputation in business may even suffer in consequence. The paradox remains that he had not been careful with his money in the first place; he would never have achieved his present wealth. Among the low income group, a different set of values exists. The young clerk, who makes his wife a present of a new dress when he has not paid his house rent, is condemned as extravagant. Carefulness with money to the point of meanness is applauded as a virtue. Nothing in his life is considered more worthy than paying his bills. The ideal wife for such a man separates her housekeeping money into joyless little piles – so much for rent, for food, for the children's shoes, she is able to face the milkman with equanimity every month, satisfied with her economising ways and never knows the guilt of buying something she can't really afford.

As for myself, I fall neither of these categories. If I have money to spare I can be extravagant, but when, as is usually the case, I am hard up and then I am the meanest man imaginable.

191. Select the antonym of 'loathed' as used in the passage.
(a) cursed (b) shunned
(c) adored (d) despised

192. Which of these is not true?
(a) People who lead a luxurious life are expected to entertain lavishly.
(b) A low-income person is considered worthy if he pays bills on time.
(c) The author is at liberty to be extravagant at all times.
(d) The rich amass wealth by spending money economically.

193. The word 'equanimity' in the passage means
(a) tranquillity (b) frustration
(c) anxiety (d) agitation

194. If a successful businessman is judicious with his money
(a) his business flourishes
(b) his reputation suffers
(c) his popularity rises
(d) his prestige improves

195. Which of these can be inferred from the passage?
(a) Extravagance is applauded in some and condemned in others.
(b) Wealthy people are stingy as far as philanthropy is concerned.
(c) For the wealthy, prudence with money is considered a virtue.
(d) People who have a meagre income are expected to be spendthrifts.

Directions (Q.Nos. 196-200) *In the following passage, some words have been deleted. Fill in the blanks with the help of the alternatives given. Select the most appropriate option for each number.*

The Statue of Unity, a towering tribute to India's Iron Man, Sardar Vallabhbhai Patel, 1. ....on the banks of the majestic Sardar Sarovar Dam in Gujarat's Kevadia, has 2. ....a remarkable surge in its annual footfall. In less than five years 3. ....its inauguration, this colossal monument has welcomed nearly 16 crore 4. .... In the first two months after the monument's inauguration in 2028, the world's 5. ....statue witnessed a whopping 4,53,020 visitors followed by over 2.7 crore visitors in 2019. Even in 2020, the year tourism sector was battered by a once-in-a-century pandemic and subsequent movement restrictions, nearly 1.3 crore tourists flocked to the Statue of Unity. While the country was still recovering from the Covid-19 pandemic, the Statue of Unity saw a footfall of over 3.4 crores.

196. Select the most appropriate option to fill in blank no. 1.
(a) situated (b) appeared
(c) found (d) established

197. Select the most appropriate option to fill in blank no. 2.
(a) witnessing (b) witness
(c) witnesses (d) witnessed

198. Select the most appropriate option to fill in blank no. 3.
(a) before (b) since
(c) when (d) on

199. Select the most appropriate option to fill in blank no. 4.
(a) guests (b) visitors
(c) invitees (d) callers

200. Select the most appropriate option to fill in blank no. 5.
(a) tall (b) tallest
(c) most tallest (d) taller

Know Correct Answers

1. (c)	2. (b)	3. (c)	4. (a)	5. (b)	6. (c)	7. (b)	8. (a)	9. (b)	10. (d)
11. (d)	12. (c)	13. (a)	14. (c)	15. (d)	16. (b)	17. (c)	18. (b)	19. (d)	20. (a)
21. (d)	22. (c)	23. (b)	24. (c)	25. (c)	26. (d)	27. (b)	28. (d)	29. (c)	30. (b)
31. (a)	32. (c)	33. (d)	34. (c)	35. (d)	36. (b)	37. (b)	38. (d)	39. (a)	40. (c)
41. (a)	42. (c)	43. (d)	44. (c)	45. (c)	46. (b)	47. (b)	48. (d)	49. (b)	50. (d)
51. (b)	52. (a)	53. (c)	54. (a)	55. (d)	56. (d)	57. (d)	58. (c)	59. (c)	60. (a)
61. (b)	62. (b)	63. (b)	64. (c)	65. (b)	66. (b)	67. (a)	68. (b)	69. (c)	70. (d)
71. (b)	72. (a)	73. (c)	74. (b)	75. (d)	76. (c)	77. (a)	78. (b)	79. (d)	80. (a)
81. (c)	82. (d)	83. (d)	84. (c)	85. (c)	86. (a)	87. (b)	88. (b)	89. (c)	90. (a)
91. (a)	92. (c)	93. (c)	94. (b)	95. (a)	96. (b)	97. (d)	98. (d)	99. (b)	100. (a)
101. (a)	102. (b)	103. (b)	104. (c)	105. (b)	106. (b)	107. (b)	108. (d)	109. (b)	110. (c)
111. (b)	112. (a)	113. (a)	114. (d)	115. (c)	116. (d)	117. (d)	118. (a)	119. (d)	120. (b)
121. (a)	122. (a)	123. (b)	124. (b)	125. (b)	126. (d)	127 (c)	128. (d)	129. (c)	130. (b)
131. (a)	132. (d)	133. (c)	134. (c)	135. (a)	136. (c)	137 (c)	138. (d)	139. (d)	140. (b)
141. (b)	142. (d)	143. (a)	144. (a)	145. (b)	146. (a)	147. (d)	148. (a)	149. (d)	150. (c)
151. (d)	152. (c)	153. (d)	154. (d)	155. (c)	156. (b)	157. (d)	158. (b)	159. (a)	160. (a)
161. (b)	162. (a)	163. (d)	164. (b)	165. (c)	166. (c)	167. (a)	168. (d)	169. (a)	170. (a)
171. (d)	172. (c)	173. (c)	174. (a)	175. (d)	176. (c)	177. (a)	178. (a)	179. (c)	180. (a)
181. (a)	182. (a)	183. (a)	184. (b)	185. (d)	186. (a)	187. (a)	188. (c)	189. (b)	190. (d)
191. (c)	192. (c)	193. (a)	194. (b)	195. (a)	196. (a)	197. (d)	198. (b)	199. (b)	200. (b)

Answer & Solutions

1. (c) The sentences should follow a historical timeline that builds upon the previous sentence. Understanding cause-effect relationships (discovery → examination → establishment → growth) is key to arranging the sentences properly and CADB follows this.

2. (b) To convert the indirect speech into direct speech, follow these steps

(i) **Identify the reporting verb** In indirect speech, 'asked' is the reporting verb. In direct speech, we use quotation marks and the question mark at the end.

(ii) **Tense change** The past perfect tense (had not purchased) in indirect speech changes to the simple past tense ('didn't purchase') in direct speech.

(iii) **Pronoun change** The pronoun 'he' (referring to the passenger) in indirect speech changes to 'you' in direct speech because the ticket collector is speaking directly to the passenger.

(iv) **Correct word order** Maintain the question word (why) and ensure the structure is in the form of a question.

3. (c) In the given sentence, the structure is in Passive Voice:

'I am often invited by them to join their club'.

Active Voice In Active Voice, the subject of the sentence performs the action of the verb. The focus is on the subject performing the action.

- **Passive Voice** 'I am invited by them'
- **Active Voice** 'they invite me'.

When converting passive voice to active voice

- Identify the subject (in passive voice, this is the object of the sentence).
- Swap the subject and object positions.
- Adjust the verb tense if needed, while ensuring subject-verb agreement.

Correct Active Voice 'they often invite me to join their club'.

4. (a) Direct Speech involves quoting the exact words of a speaker, while Indirect Speech involves reporting what someone said without using the exact words, usually with some changes in tense, pronouns and structure.

Key Rules for Conversion to Indirect Speech

(i) **Tense Change**

- Present Simple → Past Simple
- Present Continuous → Past Continuous
- Present Perfect → Past Perfect
- Future Tense → Conditional

(ii) **Pronoun Changes** Pronouns in direct speech change based on the reporting subject.

- 'I' changes to 'she' in the indirect speech and so on.

(iii) **Punctuation** The quotation marks are removed and 'that' is added after the reporting verb.

Direct 'Priya kept watching television till her mother exploded at her'.
Indirect 'You said that Priya kept watching television till her mother exploded at her'.

Tense change from 'had kept' (Past Perfect) to 'kept' (Past Simple) because 'said' is in the past tense.

5. (b) 'Deplore' means to express strong disapproval or regret, especially about something negative. The opposite of 'deplore' is 'praise,' which means to express admiration or approval, usually for something good.

6. (c) The error lies in the use of the article 'the' before the adjective 'improbable'.

- **Correct Usage** We usually don't use the article 'the' before an adjective that is used to describe a noun in general terms unless we're referring to a specific instance. The phrase should be 'told rather improbable story' without 'the'.

Concept Article Usage

- Definite Article 'the' is used to refer to specific, identified nouns.
- Indefinite Articles 'a' or 'an' are used when referring to something general or not yet specified.

7. (b) To convert a question in Active Voice into Passive Voice

(i) Identify the subject and object in the active sentence.

(ii) Swap the subject and object.

(iii) Change the verb to its appropriate form in the passive (using the verb 'to be' + past participle).

Active Voice 'Why didn't your father accompany you?'

Passive Voice 'Why were you not accompanied by your father?'

- The subject 'you' becomes the subject in the passive.
- 'Accompany' becomes 'accompanied,' which is the past participle form.

8. (a) The correct and logical sequence will be BCED.

9. (b) Ordinary (Vocabulary)

- Mundane means something that is dull, ordinary or lacks excitement or interest.
- Ordinary is the correct synonym as it refers to something that is typical or unremarkable, aligning with the meaning of 'mundane'.

10. (d) Taciturn refers to a person who is reserved or quiet, typically someone who speaks very little.

- Loquacious is the correct antonym, meaning talkative or chatty.

11. (d) The correct and logical sequence will be CDBA.

12. (c) The correct and logical sequence will be ACDB.

13. (a) The correct and logical sequence will be ADBC.

14. (c) 'Had examined' The sentence requires the past perfect tense. When an action is completed before another action in the past, the past perfect tense is used. The phrase 'by the time' indicates that one action was completed before another action happened. Therefore, 'had examined' is the correct form.

Grammar Concept: Past Perfect Tense

- The past perfect tense is used to describe an action that was completed before another action in the past.
- Structure: had + past participle (e.g., had examined, had gone, had written).
- **Example** 'By the time the train arrived, I had already left'.

15. **(d)** 'Did she?' The sentence has an error in the use of the tag question. The tag question must agree with the subject and verb in the main sentence. Since the main sentence is positive ('Your mother prepares delicious food'), the tag question should be negative ('doesn't she?'). Therefore, 'did she?' is incorrect here.

Grammar Concept: Tag Questions

- A tag question is a short question added at the end of a statement.
- If the statement is positive, the tag is negative and if the statement is negative, the tag is positive.
- **Example** 'She is coming, isn't she?' (positive statement, negative tag)
- 'She isn't coming, is she?' (negative statement, positive tag)

16. **(b)** The correct phrase should be 'in spite of his habit'. The preposition 'of' is necessary to make the phrase grammatically correct. 'In spite' must be followed by 'of'.

Grammar Concept: Prepositions in Phrasal Expressions

- Some phrasal expressions require specific prepositions for grammatical accuracy.
- 'In spite of' means 'despite' and it is used to introduce a contrast.

Example 'In spite of the rain, they continued their journey'.

17. **(c)** The correct and logical sequence will be ABDC.

18. **(b)** The sentence has a grammatical issue in the phrase 'while the time comes'. The correct expression would be 'when the time comes' instead of 'while the time comes'. The word 'while' is incorrect in this context because 'while' indicates a duration, whereas 'when' refers to a specific point in time, which is what the sentence is trying to convey.

19. **(d)** The sentence 'She has given a brilliant dance performance last week' contains a tense mismatch. The phrase 'last week' indicates that the action took place in the past and is completed, so the correct tense to use here is the simple past tense. 'Gave' is the correct past tense form to indicate an action that happened at a specific time in the past.

20. **(a)** The correct and logical sequence will be DBCA.

21. **(d)** The phrase 'prohibited from' is the correct structure used to indicate something that is not allowed. When we use 'prohibited', we need to follow it with 'from' and the gerund form of the verb (i.e., the verb ending in -ing) to indicate the action that is prohibited. Here, 'carrying' is used as the gerund form of the verb, making the sentence grammatically correct. **Example** 'Passengers are prohibited from smoking'.

This structure is fixed and should not be altered.

22. **(c)** In indirect speech, we report what someone said but change the sentence structure. Key changes are

- **Change in the question form** The direct question 'Do you know?' becomes an indirect question, so we use 'if' or 'whether' instead of the direct 'Do' at the start of the question.
- **Tense changes** The present tense 'has been' changes to the past perfect tense 'had been' because the reporting verb (said) is in the past tense. We also change the pronouns accordingly (from 'you' to 'she').
- **Correct sequence** 'Do you know' → 'if she knew' and 'has been' → 'had been'.
- Example in Indirect Speech
  - **Direct** She said, 'I will go to the market'.
  - **Indirect** She said that she would go to the market.

23. **(b)** The idiom 'bring to book' means to punish or hold someone accountable for their actions. It is often used in legal or disciplinary contexts where someone is held responsible for wrongdoing or misconduct.

Example The corrupt official was finally brought to book for his actions.

24. **(c)** In the active voice, the subject performs the action. The sentence is rewritten by focusing on the empty promises (the subject), which will now not satisfy the workers (the object). This construction keeps the meaning of the sentence intact but changes the structure. The future tense 'will not satisfy' is used here to indicate a future event or outcome.

- Active Voice Example
  - **Passive** The ball was kicked by the player.
  - **Active** The player kicked the ball.

25. **(c)** ' When converting direct speech to indirect speech, we need to follow these steps:

- 'If only' expresses a wish in the past, so it becomes 'wished that' in the indirect speech.
- The modal verb 'could' is retained because it expresses a hypothetical situation.
- The subject pronoun 'I' changes to 'she'.

The correct transformation of a sentence expressing a wish:

- **Direct Speech** 'I wish I could fly'.
- **Indirect Speech** She wished that she could fly.

26. **(d)** The word 'wherein' means 'in which' and is used to refer to the place or location where something is found. It is commonly used in more formal English. In this sentence, it connects the action (gazing) with the location (the room) where the treasure chest is hidden.

- Example with 'wherein'
  - The box wherein I kept my money is missing.

27. **(b)** 'The scientists of ISRO successfully carried out the test flight of Gaganyan'.

This sentence is rewritten in active voice, where the subject (scientists) comes before the verb and the object (test flight) follows. In the active voice, the doer of the action is emphasised more than in the passive voice.

- **Active Voice** The scientist conducts the experiment.
- **Passive Voice** The experiment is conducted by the scientist.

28. **(d)** The phrase 'each one' is singular, which means it requires a singular verb form. Therefore, 'deserves' is the correct form to maintain subject-verb agreement.

Example Each of the students deserves a reward.

29. **(c)** 'The election dates for different states were announced by the Election Commission'.

In passive voice, the object (election dates) becomes the subject of the sentence and the doer (Election Commission) comes at the end with 'by'. The verb 'announced' remains in the past tense but is modified to fit the passive voice construction.

- **Active Voice** The teacher explained the lesson.
- **Passive Voice** The lesson was explained by the teacher.

30. **(b)** The correct and logical sequence will be CBDE.

31. **(a)** 'the old man said, ' O God, help me in my hour of sorrow'.

In direct speech, we report the exact words spoken by the person, using quotation marks. Here, the old man's prayer is being quoted exactly, with the expression 'O God' reflecting direct address. In this case, 'help me' is the imperative request and the tense is preserved as it was spoken in the moment.

- In direct speech, we also preserve the punctuation like exclamations, commas and question marks.

So, the correct direct form is 'O God, help me in my hour of sorrow'.

32. **(c)** 'This sentence is originally in passive voice (May you be blessed with good health). To convert it to active voice, we need to make the subject (God) perform the action. In the active voice, 'God' is the subject and the verb becomes 'bless' in the base form.

- The correct active sentence is 'May God bless you with good health'.

The active voice makes the sentence clearer by focusing on the agent performing the action (God).

33. **(d)** The idiom 'lose your marbles' is used to describe someone losing their mental stability or becoming mentally unstable. It is an informal figurative way of saying someone is losing their mind or going crazy.

- 'Go insane' is the closest meaning to the idiom.

The other options are unrelated:

- 'Lose respect' refers to a loss of admiration.
- 'Miss an opportunity' means to lose a chance to do something.
- 'Be nervous' refers to anxiety, not mental instability.

34. **(c)** In direct speech, the speaker's exact words are quoted. When expressing regret, the interjection 'Alas!' is commonly used. The sentence 'How foolishly I have acted' is in the present perfect tense to show that the action was completed in the past but still affects the present.

'Alas!' is an exclamation of regret, commonly used in direct speech. Thus, the direct form of the sentence is: 'Alas! How foolishly I have acted,' she said.

35. **(d)** The phrase 'come a long way' means to make significant progress or improvement. It's an idiomatic expression used to convey development over time.

36. **(b)** The phrase 'along with' does not affect the number of the subject. In this sentence, 'the captain' is the main subject and it is singular. Therefore, the verb should agree with the singular subject.

- 'The captain was warmly welcomed' is the correct form.
- The error is in the subject-verb agreement. After 'along with,' the verb should still agree with the singular subject (The captain). So, 'was' should be used instead of 'were'.

37. **(b)** This sentence is a first conditional sentence, which is used to talk about real or possible situations in the future. The structure for the first conditional is

- If + present simple, then will + base verb.

The sentence 'If I go to Bangalore' uses present simple in the if-clause, so in the main clause, the verb should be in the future simple tense, which is 'will stay'.

38. **(d)** The phrase 'of been stationary' is incorrect because the preposition 'of' is followed by the gerund form of the verb, which is 'being' (not been).

- The correct form is 'of being stationary'.

This is a common error where 'been' is mistakenly used instead of 'being' after the preposition 'of'.

39. **(a)** 'The sentence is in passive voice. To change it to active voice, we need to make the subject (who) the doer of the action. The verb 'has verified' should be in the present perfect tense.

- The correct active form is 'Who has verified these facts?' This keeps the structure of the sentence in the present perfect while making 'who' the subject.

40. **(c)** In direct speech, the exact words spoken are quoted. The sentence expresses the present continuous action of running on time. Since Barin Babu is referring to the current situation, the correct direct form is 'We are running more or less on time'.

41. **(a)** The correct and logical sequence will be CBED.

42. **(c)** The correct prepositions for this sentence are 'in' and 'in'

- 'Busy in' is the correct expression for being occupied or involved in an activity.
- 'Came in' indicates arrival or entering a place.

43. **(d)** 'The idiom 'bad blood' refers to hostility or animosity between people. It means a situation where there is ill-feeling, resentment or conflict.

44. **(c)** In passive voice, the object of the action (in this case, 'he') becomes the subject of the sentence. The structure of passive voice uses the verb 'is accompanied' and 'by' the agent performing the action (the mother).

Thus, the correct passive form is 'He is accompanied by his mother wherever he goes'.

45. **(c)** The phrase 'time for thought' is incorrect. The correct phrase is 'time to think', which indicates time for reflection or contemplation.

- 'Time to think' is the correct idiomatic expression, meaning an opportunity to reflect.

46. **(b)** The idiom 'a mare's nest' refers to a confused or misunderstood situation.

- It is not related to the other options, which do not convey the figurative meaning of a confused situation.

47. **(b)** The correct spelling of the word is 'incense', which refers to a substance burned for its fragrant aroma.

- 'Incence' is the misspelled word.

48. **(d)** In indirect speech, we change the tense and adjust pronouns. The phrase 'today' changes to 'that day,' and the verb 'is' changes to 'was' in indirect speech.

Thus, the indirect form is 'the airhostess informed the passengers that it was their inaugural flight starting that day'.

49. (b) In direct speech, the exact words spoken by the person are quoted. The tense changes and the pronouns are adjusted accordingly.

- 'I cannot marry you now' reflects the present tense and 'I will surely do so next year' is the future plan.

50. (d) The word 'fastidious' refers to someone who is very particular or hard to please, while 'indifferent' means someone who shows no interest or concern, which is the opposite of being fastidious.

51. (b) 'The sentence is a tag question that follows the statement 'You have a lot of coconut trees in your village'. In tag questions, if the main sentence is in the affirmative (positive), the tag question should be negative and *vice-versa*.

- The statement 'You have a lot of coconut trees in your village' is affirmative, so the tag question should be negative: 'don't you?'

Thus, the correct sentence is 'You have a lot of coconut trees in your village, don't you?'

52. (a) The sentence is in the passive voice and the question asks for the active form. In the passive voice, the subject Salim Ali is receiving the action, whereas in the active voice, Salim Ali is performing the action.

In the passive voice, the sentence is 'It was decided by Salim Ali to devote his life…'

To convert it into the active voice, we change the focus to Salim Ali doing the action. The active voice sentence would be 'Salim Ali decided to devote his life to the preservation of Indian birds'.

53. (c) The word 'narcissist' refers to someone who has an excessive admiration or self-love. It comes from the Greek myth of Narcissus, who fell in love with his own reflection.

54. (a) The phrase 'ought to' is used to express obligation or duty and it is followed by 'be + past participle' in passive voice constructions.

The sentence 'the pollution level ought to keep under control' is incorrect because 'keep' should be changed to the past participle form 'kept' to maintain passive voice. The correct form is 'the pollution level ought to be kept under control'.

55. (d) The word 'incorrigible' refers to a person who cannot be corrected or reformed. It perfectly fits the description of someone who cannot be corrected.

56. (d) This is a direct to indirect speech conversion. The direct speech is a yes/no question, so we use 'if' or 'whether' in the indirect speech. The verb 'could' is used in indirect speech because it is a past request.

57. (d) In indirect speech, 'let us' is reported as 'suggested that we should' (or 'suggested to [someone] that [they] should'). The phrase 'Let us leave' becomes 'suggested that they should leave' in indirect speech.

58. (c) The sentence is in the direct speech form and expresses a future action, so the verb 'says' is used in the present tense and the future tense 'will clear' is retained.

59. (c) The word 'Dilligence' is incorrectly spelled. The correct spelling is 'Diligence', which refers to careful and persistent work or effort.

60. (a) The phrase 'pass the exam' is the correct and idiomatic expression. The word 'in' should be omitted because 'pass the exam' is the standard construction used.

61. (b) In the indirect form, we change the direct speech into reported speech. The pronoun 'you' changes to 'she' to maintain consistency with the subject of the reporting verb (the teacher). The verb 'need' is in the present tense in direct speech, but when reporting it in the past, it should be changed to the past tense 'needed'.

62. (b) The idiom 'cut from the same cloth' means to be very similar in nature or character. It's used when two people or things share similar qualities.

63. (b) The phrase 'resembles to' is grammatically incorrect. The verb 'resemble' is not followed by 'to'. The correct construction is 'resembles'.

Example 'My sister resembles my mother' is the correct form.

64. (c) The expression 'beside oneself' means to be in a state of extreme emotion (such as anger, grief, etc.). The use of 'besides himself' is incorrect because the correct phrase is 'beside oneself'.

65. (b) The correct passive construction is 'have been ordered to flee,' which maintains the correct tense and meaning of the sentence.

- 'Have been ordered' is the appropriate passive form when referring to a past action with current relevance.

66. (b) In passive voice, the verb 'had repaired' changes to 'had been repaired' to reflect the past perfect tense. The action of repairing the roads was completed before the monsoon, hence the use of the past perfect tense in passive voice is correct.

67. (a) The word 'vitiate' means to spoil, impair or make ineffective, which is most closely related to 'annihilate', meaning to destroy or render something completely ineffective. Both words convey the sense of damaging or ruining something.

68. (b) In reported speech, the tense of the verb changes. The sentence 'I have done my duty' (present perfect) becomes 'he had done his duty' (past perfect) when reporting the statement in indirect speech.

69. (c) The correct and logical sequence will be CBED.

70. (d) The correct and logical sequence will be CADB.

71. (b) The correct phrase should be 'accused of' instead of 'accused with'. The verb 'accuse' is always followed by 'of' when referring to the crime or action someone is being accused of. The structure should be

- 'The innocent clerk was accused of misappropriating funds of the company'.

So, the error lies in the use of 'with,' and the correct preposition to use here is 'of'.

72. (a) An easel is a wooden frame used by artists to hold their canvas while painting or drawing, which matches the description in the sentence.

73. (c) The correct phrase is 'accustomed to,' which means being familiar or used to something.

74. (b) The passive voice of the sentence is formed by changing 'wants' into 'is wanted' and making the object of the verb (others) the subject of the sentence.

The correct passive form is

- 'Everybody wants to be respected by others'.

This is the correct way to express the sentence in the passive voice, as the subject 'everybody' is still the doer, but the focus is on the action they want to happen to them.

75. (d) The correct phrase is 'would love to fly,' where 'to' is necessary after 'would love' in this infinitive form.

76. (c) To convert the imperative sentence into passive voice, we need to focus on the object of the sentence (two pills) and place it at the beginning. The correct passive form is

- ' These two pills should be taken with warm water'.

This structure emphasises the action of taking the pills rather than the person who is supposed to take them.

77. (a) Rayan organised a party on his 40th Birthday.

The active form of the sentence is created by shifting the focus from the object (the party) to the subject (Rayan). The correct active form is:

- 'Rayan organised a party on his 40th Birthday'.

This version eliminates the use of 'was organised' and makes it a simple active sentence.

78. (b) An orator is a person who is skilled and eloquent in public speaking, which fits the given definition.

79. (d) The word ambiguous refers to something that is open to more than one interpretation.

80. (a) Chaff refers to the husks of corn or other grains separated by winnowing or threshing. It is the part of the grain that is discarded.

81. (c) The original sentence 'Pay that bill today' is in the imperative mood, which is used to give orders, commands or instructions. In active voice, imperative sentences typically have a subject that is implied (the listener or reader) but is not explicitly stated.

To convert an imperative sentence into the passive voice, we generally follow these rules

(i) The object of the active sentence becomes the subject in the passive sentence.

(ii) The verb 'pay' is changed to 'be paid,' and the auxiliary verb 'should' is added to indicate the requirement or suggestion.

(iii) The original sentence's subject (the implied 'you') is omitted in passive constructions.

(iv) The structure becomes 'Subject + auxiliary verb + past participle'.

82. (d) The correct idiomatic phrase is 'His conduct is above suspicion,' which means that his conduct is beyond doubt or free from suspicion.

83. (d) The sentence 'Are you yet afraid of going out in the dark?' is grammatically incorrect because the phrase 'Are you yet' is not commonly used in questions. The correct way to phrase it is

- 'Are you afraid of going out in the dark yet?'

This structure is more natural and correct for asking if someone is afraid.

84. (c) The correct and logical sequence will be BDEC.

85. (c) When reporting a sentence with 'shall' in the future tense, 'would' is used in indirect speech.

- **Direct speech** 'I shall reach in time for the concert'.
- **Indirect speech** You told me that you would reach in time for the concert.

86. (a) The given sentence is

'Specialists say that this method speeds up language learning tremendously'.

This sentence is grammatically correct. Here's why

- 'Specialists say' is a simple present tense phrase where 'say' is the verb.
- 'This method speeds up language learning' uses the verb 'speeds up' to describe the action performed by the subject 'this method'.
- 'Tremendously' is an adverb modifying the verb 'speeds up,' correctly placed after the verb.

87. (b) The phrase 'will be taking a flight' correctly uses the future continuous tense, which expresses an ongoing action that will happen in the future.

'Tomorrow, they will be taking a flight to their dream vacation destination'.

This tense structure is appropriate here, indicating an action in progress in the future.

88. (b) The original sentence is

'She held the child's hand firmly'.

This sentence is in the past tense, where 'held' is the past form of the verb 'hold'. Now, to change this sentence to passive voice, we follow these steps

(i) The object of the sentence ('the child's hand') becomes the subject in the passive voice.

(ii) The verb 'held' becomes the passive form 'has been held' to reflect the present perfect tense (indicating an action that occurred in the past, but has relevance to the present).

(iii) The adverb 'firmly' remains in place to describe how the action was performed.

89. (c) The phrase 'have not been painted for years' is the correct usage because the word 'for' is used to indicate the duration of time.

- 'Since' is used to refer to the starting point of time and 'for' is used to refer to the length of time.

The correct sentence is 'It seems that these walls have not been painted for years'.

90. (a) The subject of the sentence is 'the captain as well as the entire crew,' which is considered singular. Therefore, the correct verb should agree with the singular subject and be in the singular form.

- The correct sentence would be 'The captain as well as the entire crew has reached the harbour safely'.

91. (a) The sentence 'Why do we have to accept these conditions?' is in the active voice, with 'we' as the subject.

- To convert this into the passive voice, the subject 'we' is replaced by the object 'these conditions'. The verb 'have to accept' becomes 'have to be accepted'.
- The correct passive form is 'Why do these conditions have to be accepted?'

92. (c) The error is in 'My sister and me'.

- The correct form should be 'My sister and I,' because 'I' is the subject form, and when the subject is compound (i.e., involving 'my sister and I'), 'I' is grammatically correct instead of 'me'.

93. **(c)** 'Gambol' means to skip or jump about playfully, which is the most appropriate fit for the given definition.

94. **(b)** 'Entice' means to attract or tempt someone to do something, often by offering something desirable.

95. **(a)** The correct phrase is 'return your notes by Saturday evening'. The preposition 'by' is used to indicate the latest time something will happen.

- 'At Saturday evening' is incorrect because 'at' is used for specific times, not for indicating a deadline.

96. **(b)** lest you should not

- The phrase 'lest you should not' is incorrect. The correct structure should be 'lest you get lost,' which expresses a negative consequence in conditional sentences.
- 'Lest' is used with subjunctive forms, and the verb 'should' is unnecessary in this context.

97. **(d)** The original sentence 'One can achieve nothing without hard work' is in the active voice with 'one' as the subject.

- To convert it into the passive voice, the subject 'one' becomes the object, and 'nothing' becomes the subject.
- The correct passive voice form is 'Nothing can be achieved without hard work'.
- 'Can be achieved' reflects the passive construction appropriately, indicating that 'nothing' is the subject being acted upon.

98. **(d)** The error lies in the phrase 'None than you'. The correct phrase should be 'None but you,' which means only you deserve credit.

- 'None than you' is not grammatically correct in this context.

99. **(b)** The error lies in the phrase 'She use to'. The correct form should be 'She used to'.

- 'Used to' is the correct phrase to indicate a past habit or action that no longer happens.

100. **(a)** The phrase 'more farther' is incorrect because 'farther' is already in its comparative form.

- The correct sentence should be 'the shopping mall is farther from my house than from my office'.
- 'Farther' already expresses the comparison, so no need for 'more'. The correct comparative form is simply 'farther'.

101. **(a)** The idiom 'split one's sides' means to laugh uncontrollably or be extremely amused.

It is often used to describe a situation where something is so funny that it causes one to laugh so hard that it feels like your sides might split.

This is the most fitting option, as 'be extremely amused' directly conveys the meaning of the idiom.

102. **(b)** In this sentence the correct word is 'much'. 'Much' is used for uncountable nouns and since 'work' is uncountable, 'much' is the right choice. On the other hand, 'many' is used for countable nouns.

Thus, the correct form is 'much work' rather than 'many work'.

103. **(b)** To form the passive voice, the object of the action becomes the subject of the sentence and the verb is modified accordingly. In the sentence 'Bhavna saw him carrying your suitcase,' the passive form would be 'He was seen by Bhavna carrying your suitcase'. This keeps the meaning intact and changes the sentence to passive voice.

104. **(c)** The error in this sentence lies in the use of 'very acclaimed'. The word 'acclaimed' already conveys the idea of praise or admiration, so it does not require an intensifier like 'very'. The sentence should be 'Rohit Sharma's century was highly acclaimed in the media' or just 'Rohit Sharma's century was acclaimed in the media'.

105. **(b)** The sentence 'Praveen told his mother that he had completed his homework' is in indirect speech. The correct direct speech for this would be 'I have completed my homework,' as the action of completing the homework is in the present perfect tense.

106. **(b)** The sentence 'the food was not as delicious as we had expected' is grammatically correct. The structure 'as...as' is used for comparisons. The verb 'had expected' is in the past perfect tense, which correctly conveys that the expectation was formed prior to the situation described in the sentence. This makes the sentence accurate and there is no error in it.

107. **(b)** The correct expression is 'married to' when referring to the person someone is married to. The incorrect phrase is 'married with,' which is not used in this context. So, the correct sentence would be 'She is married to a rich businessman'.

108. **(d)** The idiom 'forty winks' refers to a short nap or a brief period of sleep, often during the day. It's commonly used to describe a quick, refreshing sleep, typically lasting around 20-30 minutes. Therefore, 'a short sleep' is the correct meaning of this idiom.

109. **(b)** In this sentence, 'that' is used to introduce a result clause. The phrase 'so bad that it becomes difficult to breathe' shows cause and effect: the bad air quality makes it difficult to breathe. The word 'that' properly connects the cause (the air quality) with the effect (difficulty breathing), so 'that' is the correct choice.

110. **(c)** The correct and logical sequence will be BDEC.

111. **(b)** The correct and logical sequence will be BDAC.

112. **(a)** A city named Dinpanah was built by Humayun in 1533 in Delhi.

The given sentence is in active voice and the task is to convert it into the passive voice.

- In the passive voice, the object of the action becomes the subject.
- The sentence 'Humayun built a city' becomes 'A city was built by Humayun'.
- **Passive form** 'A city named Dinpanah was built by Humayun in 1533 in Delhi'.
- The correct passive form uses 'was built' (past tense) to maintain the correct tense.

113. **(a)** The phrase 'Natural talent for something' is best described by the word flair, which refers to a special ability or talent, especially one that is natural or instinctive.

- Flair perfectly fits this context because it refers to an innate ability or gift for something, such as art or music.

114. **(d)** The idiom 'have your heart in your mouth' means to feel extreme fear or anxiety. It refers to a feeling of panic or fear where the person feels that their heart is racing.

115. **(c)** Hydrophobia is an irrational fear of water. The word is made up of hydro (water) and phobia (fear).

116. **(d)** This is a command that needs to be converted from a passive voice construction into an active one. In active voice, the subject directly performs the action.

- The passive construction 'Let the fire be kept burning' is incorrect because it's a request. In the active voice, the construction is 'Keep the fire burning at night'.

117. **(d)** The idiom 'rock the boat' means to disturb a stable situation or cause trouble where there was previously peace or balance.

118. **(a)** In direct speech, the sentence should directly quote what was said without changing the tense or structure.

- The original sentence uses a question structure, so the direct speech should maintain that.
- The indirect form involves a reporting verb (I asked) and in direct speech, it retains the interrogative structure.

119. **(d)** The indirect form of a sentence like 'Please stay here tonight' is I requested because it conveys a polite request. The sentence must use requested instead of asked in this context.

- 'Please' becomes part of the indirect reporting and the sentence follows a polite tone.

120. **(b)**In direct speech, we retain the question form as it was originally stated.

- The indirect form modifies 'had' to the present perfect 'Has' in the direct speech to make the question grammatically correct.

121. **(a)** The error here lies in the use of 'shouldn't we' at the end of the sentence. In English, when making a suggestion or a statement followed by a question tag like 'shouldn't we?', the subject should be 'we' in this case, but the verb 'should' should also be consistent in its form. The correct form here is 'Let us work out the details of our endeavour, shall we?' because the use of 'shall' is more appropriate when the speaker is suggesting an action. 'Should' is typically used for expressing obligation or advice, whereas 'shall' is used for suggestions, making it the right choice in this context.

Concept Question tags are used to confirm or verify something and they need to follow a specific structure. For example

- If the main sentence is positive, the question tag will be negative 'You are coming, aren't you?'
- If the main sentence is negative, the question tag will be positive 'You aren't coming, are you?'

The use of 'shall we' after a suggestion is grammatically correct in this case.

122. **(a)** The word 'iminent' is a misspelling of the word 'imminent', which means something about to happen soon. The correct spelling is 'imminent'.

123. **(b)** Amanda said to Mohit, 'How have I offended your friend?'

In the original sentence, we have an indirect speech in the form 'Amanda asked Mohit how she had offended his friend'. The reported speech needs to be converted into the direct speech format.

To convert it

- The direct speech of a question is usually framed in the form of a direct query, starting with the subject (Amanda), followed by the verb (asked) and then the reported speech.
- In indirect speech, the past perfect tense 'had offended' is used. To convert it to direct speech, the tense changes to the present perfect ('have offended') to indicate that the action is being questioned in the present.

124. **(b)** The sentence is in passive voice, and we need to convert it to active voice. In active voice, the subject (she) performs the action and the verb needs to be in the present continuous tense:

- 'She is giving a party' fits the context, indicating the ongoing nature of the action.

125. **(b)** The correct idiom is 'You can lead a horse to water, but you can't make it drink,' meaning you can offer opportunities, but you can't force someone to take them. The error in this sentence is the incorrect usage of 'make it to drink'. The correct phrasing is 'make it drink'.

126. **(d)** The phrase 'It is time' is followed by the subjunctive mood. The correct structure requires the verb to be in the base form, so 'someone takes' should be 'someone take'. This follows the rule for sentences beginning with 'It is time,' where the subjunctive form is used to indicate something that should happen in the present or future.

127. **(c)** The phrase 'had an urgent assignment' is correct because 'assignment' is a countable noun and 'an' is needed before it. The phrase 'the urgent assignment' was incorrect because the article should be indefinite, not definite.

128. **(d)** The correct phrase is 'so far from,' which is used to show the extent or degree of something.

129. **(c)** The idiomatic expression is 'cool as a cucumber,' meaning calm, especially in stressful situations.

130. **(b)** The correct possessive pronoun here is 'mine,' which indicates that the coffee shop belongs to the speaker.

131. **(a)** Suspect The correct word is 'suspect' (to suspect, meaning to doubt or consider something likely) rather than 'suspectt,' which is a misspelling.

132. **(d)** The sentence contains errors in both the possessive pronoun and the spelling. The correct form is 'one's duty properly' with the possessive pronoun 'one's' and the correct spelling 'properly'.

133. **(c)** The correct direct speech form would be

- 'We don't need to buy tickets for the match as I have been given free passes for two'.
- The direct speech keeps the verb 'have' for present tense.

134. **(c)** The correct and logical sequence will be ECDB.

135. **(a)** The correct and logical sequence will be BADC.

136. **(c)** 'Let us go to the hills for a change'.

- The sentence 'I suggested to my brother that we should go to the hills for a change' is in indirect speech. When converting it to direct speech, the suggestion in indirect speech (we should go) becomes a direct offer or suggestion in the form of 'Let us' for more immediacy.
- **Direct Speech** 'Let us go to the hills for a change'.

137. **(c)** The sentence 'It is said that Einstein was a genius' is in passive voice, and to convert it into the active voice, we change the subject of the sentence ('People') and use 'say' as the verb.

- **Active Voice** 'People say that Einstein was a genius'.
- **Concept** In passive voice, the subject receives the action, whereas in active voice, the subject performs the action.

138. **(d)** The direct speech 'I am going to France next week' changes to indirect speech by shifting the present continuous tense (am going) to past continuous (was going) and changing 'next week' to 'the following week'.

- **Indirect Speech** 'He told me that he was going to France the following week'.
- **Concept** When converting from direct to indirect speech, we change the tense and time expressions.

139. **(d)** The error lies in the phrase 'although it is urgent'. The correct usage would be 'though it is urgent' or 'because it is urgent,' as 'although' is unnecessary and too formal here.

- **Correct Sentence** 'We cannot postpone discussion on this issue, though it is urgent'.
- **Concept** 'Although' is a conjunction used to show contrast, but here 'though' or 'because' is more appropriate.

140. **(b)** The correct and logical sequence will be CBAD.

141. **(b)** The correct spelling of the word is 'exhilarated', not 'exhilerated'.

Exhilarated means feeling very happy, thrilled or energised and is commonly used, when referring to an intense feeling of joy or excitement.

142. **(d)** The error is in the phrase 'Scarcely he see'. The correct construction would use inversion with phrases like 'No sooner' or 'Hardly'.

The correct sentence is 'No sooner did he see his opponent than he went numb with fear'.

Concept When using 'scarcely,' 'hardly,' or 'no sooner' at the beginning of a sentence, inversion is required (subject and auxiliary verb swap places).

143. **(a)** The original sentence is in passive voice (the meal will have been made ready). To convert it into active voice, we need to bring the subject (the cook) to the front and keep the future perfect tense ('will have made').

- **Active Voice** 'the cook will have made the meal ready by the time you reach the guest house'.
- **Concept** Converting from passive to active voice often requires shifting focus from the receiver of the action (the meal) to the doer (the cook).

144. **(a)** The sentence 'Grow more trees' is an imperative sentence. In passive voice, we use 'Let' with the verb in the base form (be grown) to convey the same meaning in a passive construction.

- **Passive Voice** 'Let more trees be grown'.
- **Concept** In imperative sentences, passive voice is often formed with the verb 'let'.

145. **(b)** The sentence given is 'By next summer, I will have completed my internship and will have returned to school'.

- The phrase 'will have returned' is correct because it uses future perfect tense (will have returned), which refers to an action that will be completed by a certain time in the future (next summer).
- The error lies in the phrase 'will return to school'. This should be changed to 'will have returned' to match the future perfect tense used in the first part of the sentence.
- **Correct sentence** 'By next summer, I will have completed my internship and will have returned to school'.
- **Concept** The future perfect tense (will have + past participle) is used to express actions that will be completed before a certain point in the future.

146. **(a)** The sentence 'Our rivals must have spread this rumour' is in active voice. To convert it into passive voice, we switch the object (this rumour) to the subject and adjust the auxiliary verb accordingly.

- **Passive Voice** 'This rumour must have been spread by our rivals'.
- **Concept** In passive voice, the focus shifts from the subject performing the action to the object receiving the action.

147. **(d)** The given description refers to a legal document that authorises the police or another body to make an arrest or search premises. This description corresponds to the word 'warrant'.

- Warrant is a legal term for a document that gives someone the authority to perform a specific action (such as an arrest or search).
- **Concept** Knowing specific legal terms is important to identify correct synonyms. Other terms like 'permit' and 'licence' are related to permissions, but they don't apply to the specific legal context of arrest or search.

148. **(a)** The direct speech is 'I am going to visit Kashmir and Ladakh next month'.

- In indirect speech, the present continuous (am going) becomes past continuous (was going) and 'next month' changes to 'the following month'.
- **Indirect Speech** 'Rani informed her boss that she was going to visit Kashmir and Ladakh the following month'.
- **Concept** In indirect speech, we adjust tenses and time expressions according to reporting rules.

149. **(d)** The phrase 'significant enhance' is grammatically incorrect because the adjective 'significant' cannot be used in this context. The correct form would be the adverb 'significantly' to modify the verb 'enhance'.

- **Correct Sentence** 'Effective communication is a skill that can significantly enhance your personal and professional life'.
- **Concept** Adjectives and adverbs must be used correctly depending on whether they modify nouns (adjectives) or verbs (adverbs).

150. **(c)** The direct speech 'I visited Maldives last week'. changes in indirect speech by shifting the tense from simple past (visited) to past perfect (had visited) and 'last week' is changed to 'the previous week' in indirect speech.

- **Indirect Speech** 'I told Prachi that I had visited Maldives the previous week'.
- **Concept** In indirect speech, we follow the rules of tense backshift, where simple past becomes past perfect and time expressions like 'last week' change to 'the previous week'.

151. **(d)** The term 'section' refers to a distinct part or subdivision of something, making it the most appropriate word for the blank. The passage talks about a '17-km priority section' of the RRTS corridor.

152. **(c)** The term 'residents' refers to the people who live in a particular place, in this case, the high-rise societies of the National Capital Region. It fits logically with the context, which talks about the people who are calling for improvements in transport connectivity.

153. **(d)** 'Connectivity' refers to the quality or state of being connected, and in this case, it refers to how easily people can access transportation points. This word best completes the idea of calling for direct connectivity to transport service points.

154. **(d)** 'Many' is used to describe a large number of countable items, in this case, the residents in Noida and Ghaziabad who are being referred to. The phrase 'many residents' makes the most sense in this context.

155. **(c)** 'Depending' is the correct choice here. The phrase 'continue depending' refers to an ongoing reliance on private vehicles because of the lack of proper connectivity. In this context, the verb 'continue' requires the present participle (gerund) form of the verb, which is 'depending'.

156. **(b)** 'Other' fits best in this context, referring to additional forms of public transport modes beyond the ones already mentioned. It conveys the idea of additional modes that people might need.

157. **(d)** 'Direct' is the correct adjective here, describing the type of connectivity the residents are requesting. They are asking for direct connectivity, meaning the ability to travel straight to important locations like Metro stations, without unnecessary detours or complexity.

158. **(b)** The phrase 'Without any proper public transport' makes sense, implying that, in the absence of proper public transport, residents are forced to rely on personal cars.

159. **(a)** The phrase 'opt for a personal car' is a standard collocation in English. 'Opt for' means to choose or decide on something, which fits perfectly in this context.

160. **(a)** 'Said' is the correct verb to use in reported speech when referring to someone expressing an opinion or statement. In this case, Abhishek Kumar is quoted as saying something, so 'said' fits appropriately.

161. **(b)** The phrase 'the door behind them was sealed' indicates that the door was shut tightly, leaving no way of escaping. The word 'sealed' implies that the door is not just closed but is securely fastened, making it impossible to open.

162. **(a)** 'Emanating' means something that is emitting or flowing out from a source. In this context, a strange light coming from a corner suggests that the light is emanating from there.

163. **(d)** 'Illuminate' means to light up or make something visible, which fits the context of the strange light making darkness visible.

164. **(b)** 'An' is the correct article to use before the vowel sound in 'alien'. When the following word begins with a vowel sound, we use 'an' instead of 'a'.

165. **(c)** 'Incomprehensible' means something that is difficult or impossible to understand, which fits the context of the voice sounding like jargon, making it hard to understand.

166. **(c)** 'On' is the correct preposition in this case. The phrase 'go down on their knees' is a common expression used to describe someone kneeling down.

167. **(a)** 'Bizarre' means something strange or out of the ordinary, which fits the description of unusual and disturbing sounds.

168. **(d)** 'Emerge' means to come into view or appear, which fits the context of a form seemingly appearing right before their eyes.

169. **(a)** 'Curdled' fits in this context as it refers to something that coagulates or turns thick, especially in the context of fear, implying a reaction where the blood congeals in response to terror or dread. It creates a vivid image of the chilling effect fear can have on someone.

170. **(a)** 'Bones' is the correct choice here, as the chilling effect described in the passage would most likely affect someone's bones, evoking a deep, physical fear.

171. **(d)** From the passage, it is evident that the narrator is keenly observing his surroundings. He takes notice of the details, such as the man raising his hat, the open door, and the peculiar atmosphere. The narrator's attention to these subtleties shows that he is observant rather than being overly emotional or fearful. His observations also help him understand the strange situation around him.

172. **(c)** The narrator was shocked because despite the misty and eerie surroundings, the doors and windows of the building were wide open. This unusual sight in the midst of such gloomy weather added to the mysterious and unsettling atmosphere of the place, which left him feeling uneasy.

173. **(c)** The passage is written as a personal narrative, describing the narrator's journey and experience in reaching a mysterious house. The narrative recounts the events and observations of the narrator, making it a narrative rather than a report, biography or travelogue.

174. **(a)** The word 'pervading' means spreading throughout or filling an area. In the passage, it is used to describe the mist that filled the environment around the building. The mist 'pervades' or spreads through, the area, creating a sense of eerie atmosphere.

175. **(d)** The passage does not provide any clear indication that the stranger leaving the house was its owner. While the narrator notices that the man did not shut the door behind him and was in a hurry, there is no mention of the man being the owner. This statement is not supported by the text, making it the false statement.

176. **(c)** In this context, 'implement' means to put into action or enforce. The passage talks about co-curricular activities providing opportunities to 'implement' what is learned in the classroom. It refers to students using their classroom knowledge in real-life scenarios, thereby applying what they've learned.

177. **(a)** The passage highlights the shift in education towards the overall development of students, including social and aesthetic growth, which encompasses skills such as team-building and character-building. This development is seen as essential alongside intellectual development, moving away from purely academic education.

178. **(a)** The passage is centered around the shift in the education system, especially in the 21st century. It talks about moving away from a purely academic focus to a more holistic approach that emphasises overall student development. This change aims to provide students with practical experience, soft skills and exposure to real-world scenarios, alongside academic learning.

179. **(c)** The passage points out that the traditional focus on academic learning alone has hindered students' development. The lack of practical experience, such as fieldwork and real-life exposure, prevented students from developing fully. The new education system now recognises the importance of practical experience in overall student development.

180. **(a)** Textbooks are used in the classroom to provide theoretical knowledge, but they do not offer industry exposure. In contrast, conferences, industrial visits, and guest lectures provide practical exposure and insights into how industries work, helping students gain real-world experience and apply their classroom knowledge.

181. **(a)** The theme of 'loss of life in Andaman and Nicobar' is not part of the passage. The themes of seismic tremors, tracking seismic activity and earthquake preparedness are addressed in the passage.

182. **(a)** In this context, the word 'underscores' means to highlight or emphasise something. It indicates that the importance of continued investment in earthquake preparedness is being emphasised in the passage.

183. **(a)** The tremors were felt at 5:50 a.m., which is before sunrise. This is mentioned in the passage in the phrase 'In the pre-dawn tranquillity of the Andaman Sea,' which directly refers to the time before the sun rose.

184. **(b)** The passage mentions the Indian Plate, Burma Plate and Sunda Plate as the tectonic plates involved in the seismic activity in the Andaman region. 'Satara Plates' is not mentioned in the passage, making it the odd option out.

185. **(d)** The passage emphasises the importance of earthquake preparedness and resilience measures in seismically active regions like the Andaman and Nicobar Islands. This includes installing early warning systems and having disaster management strategies in place to mitigate the potential consequences of earthquakes.

186. **(a)** The passage states that early Roman historians used native and Greek folklore to fill in the gaps in their historical accounts. This was done because the factual records available at the time were meagre and the folklore helped to flesh out these accounts.

187. **(a)** The passage discusses the challenges early Roman historians faced in documenting the history of early Rome, particularly focusing on the use of folklore and the scarce factual records. It is about the historical documentation of ancient Rome, making this the most appropriate theme.

188. **(c)** In this context, the word 'extant' means still existing or surviving. The passage refers to the first 10 books of Livy and also mentions that Books 21 to 45 are extant, meaning they have survived or are still available.

189. **(b)** The passage provides a detailed and factual account of early Roman history, discussing the challenges faced by historians in documenting events and the use of folklore. This style is consistent with that of an encyclopaedic entry, which is typically informative and objective.

190. **(d)** The passage specifically states that the regal period (753-509 BC) and the early republic (509-280 BC) are the most poorly documented periods of Roman history due to the lack of written historical accounts during those times. Therefore, the correct answer is 509-280 BC.

191. **(c)** In the passage, 'loathed' refers to being intensely disliked or hated. The opposite, or antonym, of loathed would be 'adored,' meaning to be greatly loved or admired.

192. **(c)** The passage explains that the author can be extravagant when money allows, but it also mentions that the author is typically 'hard up,' meaning he often doesn't have the financial freedom to be extravagant.

193. **(a)** 'Equanimity' refers to mental calmness, composure and evenness of temper, especially in difficult situations. In the passage, the wife is described as facing the milkman with equanimity, indicating she remains calm and untroubled, which is best captured by the word 'tranquillity'.

194. **(b)** The passage clearly states that if a wealthy person, such as a businessman, is too prudent or careful with his money, he risks being seen as 'mean' and his reputation in business may suffer.

195. **(a)** The passage draws a contrast between the expectations for extravagance based on one's income group. While a wealthy person is expected to be extravagant, a low-income individual is expected to be careful with money.

196. **(a)** The Statue of Unity is described as being placed or located on the banks of the Sardar Sarovar Dam, which makes 'situated' the most appropriate choice for this context.

197. **(d)** The correct verb tense in this sentence is the past tense to describe an event that has already happened. 'Witnessed' fits the context of an event that occurred, specifically the surge in footfall.

198. **(b)** 'Since' indicates the time elapsed from a particular point. In this case, it refers to the period after the monument's inauguration, making it the appropriate choice.

199. **(b)** The word 'visitors' is the most suitable here, referring to people who come to see the Statue of Unity. 'Guests' would imply a more formal invitation, which doesn't fit the context of the passage.

200. **(b)** The phrase 'the world's tallest statue' refers to the Statue of Unity being the tallest in comparison to all other statues globally. The superlative 'tallest' is the correct form here, indicating that it holds the position of the highest statue in the world.